D1502198

WORLD

COLLECTORS

ANNUARY

Published by:
WORLD COLLECTORS PUBLISHERS BV

Printed in The Netherlands by
KRIPS REPRO MEPPEL

ISBN 90-73165-08-3
ISSN NE 0084-1498

WORLD
COLLECTORS
ANNUARY

checklist of paintings, watercolours,
gouaches, pastels and drawings
sold at auction
1 July 1995-30 June 1996

VOLUME XLVI

Editor

Drs M.J. VAN LAAKE

LIST OF AUCTION HOUSES

AUSTRIA	**Dorotheum**	Dorotheergasse 11, 1010 Vienna
	Sotheby's	Palais Breuner, Singerstr. 16, 1010 Vienna
	Wiener Kunstauktionen GMBH	Kärtnerring 2-5, 2. Stock, 1010 Vienna
DENMARK	**Bukowski's Danmark**	Kongens Nytorv 20-22, 1050 København K
FRANCE	**Antoine Ader**	5, rue de Montholon, 75009 Paris
	Remi Ader	14, Rue Favart, 75002 Paris
	Étude Tajan	37, Rue des Mathurins, 75008 Paris
	Libert et Castor	3, Rue Rossini, 75009 Paris
	Martin et Chausselat	3, Impasse des Chevau-Légers, Versailles
GERMANY	**Hauswedell & Nolte**	Pöseldorferweg 1, 2000 Hamburg 13
	Kunsthaus Lempertz	Neumarkt 3, 5000 Cologne I
	Karl & Faber	Amiraplatz 3/IV, 8000 Munich 2
	Wolfgang Ketterer	Brienner Strasse 25, 8000 Munich 2
	Sotheby's Munich/Berlin	Odeonsplatz 16, 8000 Munich 22
GREAT BRITAIN	**Christie Manson & Woods**	8, King Street St James's London, WIY 6QT
	Christie's South Kensington	85, Old Brompton Road, London SW7 3LD
	Phillips, Son & Neale	7, Blenheim/Nw Bond Str. London WIY OAS
	Sotheby's London	34-35, New Bond Street, London WIA 2AA
	Sotheby's Scotland	112, George Street, Edinburgh EH2 4LH
HONG KONG	**Christie's Swire**	2804-6 Alexandra House, 16-20 Chater Road
ISRAEL	**Sotheby's**	38, Gordon Street, 63414 Tel Aviv
	Christie's	4, Weizmann Street, 64239 Tel Aviv
ITALY	**Finarte Rome**	54, Via Margutta, 00187 Rome
	Milan Finarte	4, Piazzetta Bossi, 20121 Milan
	Christie's Rome	114, Piazza Navona, 00186 Rome
	Christie's Milan	1, Piazza Santa Maria delle Grazie 20123 Milan
	Sotheby's Italy	Via Broggi, 19, 20129 Milan
MONACO	**Christie's**	Park Palace, 98000 Monte Carlo
	Sotheby's	2804-6 Alexandra House, 16-20 Chater Road
NETHERLANDS	**Christie's**	Cornelis Schuytstraat 57, 1071 JG Amsterdam
	A. Mak BV	P.O. Box 483, 3000 AL Dordrecht
	Sotheby Mak van Waay	Rokin 102, 1012 KZ Amsterdam
SPAIN	**Sotheby's**	Plaza de la Independencia 8, 28001 Madrid
SWEDEN	**Bukowskis**	8, Wahrendorffgatan, 11147 Stockholm
	Goteborgs Auktionsverk	7-9, Tredje Langgatan, 41303 Goteborg
SWITZERLAND	**Sotheby's Zurich**	Bleicherweg 20, 8022 Zurich
	Christie's Geneva	8, Place de la Taconnerie, 1204 Geneva
UNITED STATES OF AMERICA	**Christie Manson & Woods**	502 Park Avenue /59th Str. 10022 New York
	Christie's East	219 East 67th Street, 10021 New York, N.Y.
	Sotheby's New York	1334 York Avenue, 10021 New York, N.Y.

INTRODUCTION

After seven years of hard work and dedication, Drs. H. van der Lande decided to end her career as editor/publisher of World Collectors Annuary. Keeping in mind that she, being both the "executive president" and the actual "engineer" of the W.C.A. at one time, I must conclude that she did a great job. I would like to thank Miss van der Lande and her husband Mr. A.A. Quaedvlieg for all their support and patience during the negotiations and the initial W.C.A.-rites.

The concept of the book has, so far, never been changed. For someone like me, who cherishes tradition, this seemed an inviting starting point for the new volumes of the W.C.A.. However, I sincerely doubt if their is any future without innovation. Why not alter within the concept?
We will have to use the new media like CD-ROM and, maybe, even provide information through internet. As for the book which we all are familiar with, I would like to investigate the possibility of dividing the volume in three separate ones: Old Masters, 19th Century and Modern/Contemporary, in order to serve our clients better. In this way we can enlarge our number of impression and as a result, lower the costs.

The making of the W.C.A. has always been the work of *Einzelgänger*, making nocturnal hours in their study. For a change, World Collectors Publishers BV, is now trying to build a small, young team, where tasks can be divided and every person can do what they are best at!
I would like to introduce and thank Prof. M.V.M. van Leeuwe, who as I presume, entered surprisingly the publication business, at a very respectable age; Mr. M.A.E. Sweelssen, the young and eager financial man in our team; and finally, Miss L. Sauer who, as a non-schooled professional Desk Top Publisher, composed this Volume XLVI without any interest or reserve. To her all my gratitude and love...

A final word of thanks goes out to everyone who helped W.C.P. BV during its initial moments, all the Auctioneers around the world who keep sending their catalogues faithfully; the Notary, Mr. M. Seeghers; my friends and family for their advice; and especially Miss Danielle Angenent, Sicco Brakema and Haico Leenders, for all their typing hours, they have been "on the force" more than anyone else.

After summing up all these people, one might wonder about my task. It would be nice to have a small plate on my desk that says: *the Great Intermediator*, however this would be to much honour! For the near future, I would like to answer our readers remarks, their suggestions or their gentle complaints. I hope this new W.C.A. volume, of which we are proud, will be useful to our reader...

Drs. M.J. van Laake
Publisher

LIST OF ABBREVIATIONS

att.	attributed
b.	born
ca.	circa
d	dated
d.	died
doc.	documented
EXH.	exhibited, exhibition
exh.cat.	exhibition catalogue
ex cat.	not in catalogue
fl.	flourished
indist.	indistinctly
inscr.	inscribed, inscription
(L)	Lugt (see below)
LIT.	literature
numb.	numbered
PROV.	provenance
reprod.	reproduced
rev.	reverse
rev. ed.	revised edition
sd	signed and dated
s mono	signed with monogram
s ini.	signed with initial(s)
lc	lower centre
ll	lower left
lr	lower right
ms	manuscript
n.d.	no date
n.n.	no number
uc	upper centre
ul	upper left
ur	upper right
*	reproduced in black and white in the auction catalogue
**	reproduced in colour in the auction catalogue
***	reproduced on the cover of the auction catalogue

DESCRIPTION
Dimensions are given height before width.
If a painting is unframed, this is usually mentioned in the text.

AUTHORSHIP
Bears signature or *with signature*, and/or *bears inscr.* or *with inscr.* and/or *bears date* or *with date*: not by the hand of the artist, according to the auction catalogue.

AVERAGE ANNUAL RATES OF EXCHANGE OF CURRENCY TO US $ (1995-1996)
PLEASE NOTICE: WCA USES MONTHLY AVERAGES

(1 US$ equals:)

GBP	0.6353
DEM	1.4660
FRF	5.0439
CHF	1.2059
ITL	1,577.8555
ESP	125.3817
ATS	10.3137
SEK	6.8865
NLG	1.6425

BUYER'S PREMIUM

All prices for the auctions monitored in this book, are the price results issued by the auction houses concerned. Some include Buyer's Premium and in some exceptional cases Value Added Tax.

For *Christie's* and *Sotheby's* the price shown is the purchase price being the aggregate of the final bid and the premium of 10% (11% in Monte Carlo and Berlin, 14% in Brussels, 15% in the Netherlands and Italy). The stated price also includes Buyer's Premium for *Sotheby's Madrid* (15%) and *Karl & Faber* (15%).

For most French auctioneers the given price includes Buyer's Premium (12.674% to FRF 15,000; 8.226% from FRF 15.001 to FRF 40,000; 6.151% from FRF 40.001 to FRF 300,000; and 4.965% above FRF 300,000).
The prices given in this book for France's *Libert & Castor* and for *Remi Ader* and *Antoine Ader* and for all other auction houses the prices shown are the hammer price.

ABBATE Nicolò dell' (Modena 1509 or 1512-1571 Fontainebleau or Paris) Italian
A CARTOON: THE HEAD AND SHOULDERS OF A BISHOP, HIS HANDS JOINED IN
PRAYER point of the brush and two shades of brown wash over black chalk, 71.8 x 40.8cm.
      Sotheby's London, 3 July 1995 (99*) GBP 11,270   US$ 17,977

ABSOLON Kurt (Vienna 1925-1958 Wulkaprodersdorf) Austrian
LANDSCHAFT MIT GELBEN HAUS oil on canvas, 35 x 49cm. sdll and sdlr 'Kurt 56'
PROV.: Galerie Maier, Innsbruck; Private collection, Vienna.
      Dorotheum Vienna, 21 May 1996 (176**) ATS 250,000   US$ 24,006

ACCONCI Vito (1940 b.) American?
FACE OF THE EARTH (VIDEOTAPE 20 MIN.1974) coloured chalks, coloured crayons and black
and white photographs on paper mounted on board, 40 x 53½in. (101.6 x 135.8cm.) sd and titled lr
''FACE OF THE EARTH' VIDEOTAPE; 20 MIN.1974) Vito Acconci' (1974)
PROV.: The Mayor Gallery, London; Gilman Paper Company, New York.
EXH.: New York, Union Carbide Corporation Gallery, *Art from Corporate Collections*, May 1979.
      Christie's New York, 22 February 1996 (94**) US$ 9,200   US$ 9,200

ACHENBACH Oswald (Düsseldorf 1827-1905 Düsseldorf) German
BLICK AUF DEN GOLF VON NEAPEL MIT DEM PALAZZO DONN'ANNA oil on canvas, 100 x
148cm. slr 'Osw. Achenbach'
EXH.: *Oswald Achenbach*, Kunsthaus Lempertz Cologne, autumn 1995.
      Lempertz Cologne, 18 May 1996 (1493**) DEM 75,000   US$ 48,895

Blick auf den Golf von Neapel mit dem Pallazo Donn'Anna

BLICK AUF DEN FRIEDHOF SANTA CLARA IN NEAPEL oil on canvas, 100 x 144cm. slr 'Osw.
Achenbach'
      Lempertz Cologne, 18 May 1996 (1492**) DEM 40,000   US$ 26,077

ACKERMANN Max (Berlin 1887-1975 Unterlegenhardt (Schwarzwald)) German
BLAUE KOMPOSITION oil on jute, 65 x 50cm. sd on the reverse on label 'Max Ackermann 27. II.
1964' (1927)
      Lempertz Cologne, 29 November 1995 (1**) DEM 32,000   US$ 22,586

ADAMI Valerio (Bologna 1935 b.) Italian
LA MACCHINA PER IL GOLF acrylic on canvas, 73 x 91.5cm. sd titled '68' on the reverse
PROV.: Galleria Alfieri, Venezia; Galleria d'Arte Sianesi, Milan.
      Sotheby's Milan, 28 May 1996 (153**) ITL 29,900,000   US$ 19,204

CULTURA FISICA acrylic on canvas, 89 x 116cm. dlc '1937'; sd '29.4.72-7.5.72' and titled on the
reverse
PROV.: Galleria d'Arte Sianesi, Milan; Galleria La Bertesca, Genoa.
        Sotheby's Milan, 28 May 1996 (223**) ITL 26,450,000   US$ 16,988

FINLANDE acrylic on canvas, 76 6/8 x 102 3/8in. (195 x 260cm.) s ini 'V.A.' (1987)
PROV.: Galleri GKM, Malmö.
EXH.: Helsinki, Galleri Kaj Forsblom, *Collector's choice*, September-October 1988, no. 14.
LIT.: Edition GKM, *Adami*, Malmö 1989 p. 80 (illustrated in colour).
        Christie's London, 23 May 1996 (133**) GBP 13,800   US$ 20,896

ADLER Edmund (Vienna 1876-1965 Mannersdorf) Austrian
A MOTHER'S TOUCH oil on canvas, 21 x 26in. (53 x 66.1cm.) s 'Edmund Adler'
        Christie's New York, 2 November 1995 (68**) US$ 16,100   US$ 16,100

ADLER Jankel (Tuszyn 1895-1949 Aldbourne near London) British (Polish)
STILL LIFE WITH PEARS oil on board, 38.2 x 55.8cm. (15 1/16 x 22in.) sul 'Adler', also s and
inscr. 'III' on the reverse
PROV.: Private collection, London.
        Phillips London, 24 June 1996 (10**) GBP 6,500   US$ 10,023

ADOLFS Gerard Pieter (Semarang (Dutch Indies) 1897-1968 's-Hertogenbosch) Dutch
A TEAPICKER oil on canvas, 73.5 x 60cm. slr
        Sotheby's Amsterdam, 23 April 1996 (86**) NLG 29,500   US$ 17,529

AN ANGLER ON A QUAY oil on panel, 50 x 60cm. sdlr '36'
        Sotheby's Amsterdam, 23 April 1996 (74*) NLG 47,200   US$ 28,047

ADRIAN NILSSON Gösta (Gan) (1884-1965) Swedish
GATUTUNNELN oil on canvas, 71 x 51cm. sll 'G.A-N' (1919)
EXH.: Liljevalch, Liljevalchs Konsthall, *GAN retrospektivt*, 1958, cat. no. 59; Malmö, Konsthall
GAN 1984; Liljevalch, Liljevalchs Konsthall, *GAN 1984*, cat no. 111.
        Bukowskis Stockholm, 26-27 October 1995 (1**) SEK 370,000   US$ 54,187

ELDSVÅDA oil on cardboard, 52 x 55cm. slr 'GAN' (1917)
        Bukowskis Stockholm, 24-25 April 1996 (1**) SEK 200,000   US$ 30,300

INSPIRATION oil on canvas, 80 x 50cm. slr 'GAN' (1928)
EXH.: Göteborg, Konsthall 1928.
LIT.: Niels Lindgren, *Gösta Adrian-Nilsson*, p. 152 (illustrated p. 151).
        Bukowskis Stockholm, 24-25 April 1996 (2**) SEK 295,000   US$ 44,692

TVÅ FRANSKA MATROSER oil on canvas, 81 x 55cm. s with anchormonogram and dedicated lr
'Till Arvid Källström, Paris 1921' (1919)
EXH.: Liljevalch, Konsthall, *GAN retrospektivt*, 1958, cat. no. 59; Malmö, Konsthall *GAN 1984*;
Liljevalch, Konsthall, *GAN 1984*, cat no. 111.
LIT.: Jan-Torsten Ahlstrand, *Gösta Adrian-Nilsson*.
        Bukowskis Stockholm, 26-27 October 1995 (2**) SEK 220,000   US$ 32,219

AELST Willem van (Delft 1627-1683 c. Amsterdam) Dutch
PINK ROSES, A CARNATION AND A POT MARIGOLDS ON A MARBLE LEDGE, WITH A
DRAGONFLY, A SNAIL AND A SINEBAR MOTH, A PAINTED LADY AND RED ADMIRAL
BUTTERFLIES oil on canvas, 15 7/8 x 12½in. (40.5 x 31.5cm.) (late 1670s)
PROV.: With Galerie Sankt Lucas, Vienna 1969, as Rachel Ruys, where purchased by the present
owner.
        Christie's London, 7 July 1995 (201**) GBP 12,075   US$ 19,261

STILL LIFE OF ROSES, VARIEGATED TULIPS, PANSIES, CARNATIONS AND OTHER
FLOWERS IN A GLASS VASE, A WATCH IN A ROCK CRYSTAL CASE TIED WITH A BLUE
RIBBON, AND BUTTERFLIES AND A DRAGONFLY, ALL ON A MARBLE LEDGE. oil on
canvas, 22 ¾ x 18in. (57.8 x 45.7cm.) slr
      Sotheby's New York, 11 January 1996 (31**) US$ 772,500   US$ 772,500

AENVANCK Theodor (Antwerp 1633-1671) Flemish
FRUIT STILL-LIFE oil on canvas, 91 x 114cm. sd 'Theodoer aenvanck. f. 1656'
      Bukowskis Stockholm, 29-31 May 1996 (280a**) SEK 120,000   US$ 17,649

AERTSEN Pieter (Amsterdam 1508-1575 Amsterdam) Dutch
THE LAST SUPPER oil on panel, 89.8 x 124cm.
PROV.: Anon. sale, Mak van Waay Amsterdam, 25 July 1944, lot 1, as School of Pieter Aertsen.
      Christie's Amsterdam, 13 November 1995 (3*) NLG 12,650   US$ 7,973

PEASANTS DANCING AND MAKING MERRY IN AN INTERIOR oil on panel, 42 ¾ x 63¼in.
(108.6 x 160.7cm.)
PROV.: Joseph Satinover, New York, 1916; John del Drago, New York before 1954, by whom given
to; The Carnegie Institute, Pittsburgh, Pennsylvania; Nielsen Gallery, Boston, Massachusetts.
EXH.: Pittsburgh, Pennsylvania, The Carnegie Institute, *Pictures of everyday Life*: *1,500-1900*,
October-December, 1954, illus., pl. 7.
LIT.: *The New York Sun*, December 24, 1916; *Spur Magazine*, January 15, 1917; R. Genaille, 'A
propos d'un tableau retrouvé de Pieter Aertsen, l'Intérieur Paysan avec Danseurs,' *Jaarboek 1983:
Koninklijk Museum Voor Schone Kunsten-Antwerpen*, 1983, pp. 105, passim (illustrated p. 119, fig. 6
(as by Aertsen)).
      Sotheby's New York, 11 January 1996 (69**) US$ 43,125   US$ 43,125

AERTSEN Pieter (circle of) (Amsterdam 1508-1575 Amsterdam) Dutch
THE APOSTLES PETER AND PAUL WITH THE FOUR EVANGELISTS oil on panel, 138 x
114cm.
      Dorotheum Vienna, 6 March 1996 (,300**) ATS 100,000   US$ 9,619

AERTVELT Andries van (1590-1652) Dutch
KRIEGSSCHIFFE AUF AUFGEWÜHLTER SEE IN KÜSTENNÄHE oil on panel, 59.5 x 116cm.
PROV.: Privatsammlung, Paris.
      Lempertz Cologne, 18 May 1996 (1040**) DEM 50,000   US$ 32,597

AFRO {or} Afro Basaldella (Udine 1912-1976 Zurich) Italian
LA PERSIANA III mixed media on canvas, 80 x 100cm. sdlr 'Afro
64'
LIT.: Cesare Brandi, *Afro*, Roma, 1976, p. 196, no. 217 (illustrated).
      Christie's Milan, 20 November 1995 (167**)
ITL 96,637,000   US$ 60,664

COMPOSIZIONE tempera on paper, 57 x 38cm sd 'Afro 1948'
LIT.: *Oeuvre catalogue* in archives Afro under supervision of M.
Graziani, Roma.
      Finearte Rome, 14 November 1995 (108**)
ITL 19,550,000   US$ 12,272

VASO DI FIORI oil on paper, 50 x 35cm. sll 'Afro'
      Finearte Milan, 18 June 1996 (130*) ITL 16,675,000   US$ 10,813

Composizione

LA FABRICA DI SAN PIETRO oil and collage on canvas, 150 x 200cm. sdlr 'afro 60'
PROV.: Catherine Viviano Gallery, New York; Elizabeth Ann Castle, New London, Connecticut.

LIT.: Cesare Brandi, *Afro*, Rome 1977, p. 186, no. 144 (illustrated).

Sotheby's Milan, 28 May 1996 (230***) ITL 283,800,000   US$ 182,274

BOZZETTO PER SILVER DOLLAR CLUB oil on canvas, 37 x 68cm. sdlr 'afro. 56'
LIT.: Cesare Brandi, *Afro*, Rome 1977, p. 180, no. 93 (illustrated).

Sotheby's Milan, 28 May 1996 (187**) ITL 91,700,000   US$ 58,895

AGASSE Jacques Laurent (Geneva 1767-1849 London) Swiss
GEORGE IRVING WITH HIS BLACK HUNTER BENEATH A BLASTED OAK, HOUNDS
BEING PUT INTO COVERT BEYOND oil on canvas, 34 ¾ x 44¼in. (88.5 x 112.5cm.)
PROV.: By descent to Mrs Murray-Usher; her sale, Christie's Edinburgh, 11 May 1984, lot 494.
LIT.: Probably the picture listed in the *artist's account book* under 1803.

Sotheby's London, 12 July 1995 (166**) GBP 155,500   US$ 248,046

AGRICOLA Eduard (Stuttgart 1800 b.) German
POZZUOLI LOOKING TOWARDS ISCHIA oil on canvas, 13½ x 20¼in. (34.3 x 51.5cm.) sd
'E.Agricola/1863'

Christie's South Kensington, 12 October 1995 (233**) GBP 6,187   US$ 9,765

AGUÉLI Ivan (Sala (Dalécarlie) 1869-1917 Barcelona) Swedish
SOMMARKVÄLL oil on canvas, 31 x 38cm. s
EXH.: Göteborgs Konstmuseum, *Ivan Aguéli-utställningen 1957*; Valby Kunstforenning, *Aguéli-utställningen*.

Bukowskis Stockholm, 29 November-1 December 1995 (3**) SEK 230,000   US$ 34,794

AHL Henry Hammond (1869-1953) American
LANDSCAPE WITH IRISES oil on canvas, 25¼ x 30¼in. (64.1 x 76.8cm.) slr 'Ahl'
PROV.: Grand Central Art Galleries, New York; *The Sterling Regal Collection*; Sale: New York,
Sotheby's, May 25, 1988, lot 5.
EXH.: Columbus, Georgia, The Columbus Museum of Art, *Masterworks of American Impressionism
from the Pfeil Collection*, February 1992, pp. 40-42, no. 1, illus.; this exhibition travelled extensively.

Christie's New York, 13 September 1995 (69**) US$ 13,800   US$ 13,800

AIVAZOVSKII Ivan Constantinovich (Feodosia 1817-1900 Feodosia) Russian
A VIEW OF CONSTANTINOPLE BY MOONLIGHT oil on canvas, 22 7/8 x 31 5/8in. (58 x
80.3cm.) s

Phillips London, 12 March 1996 (21**) GBP 65,000   US$ 99,267

Sonnenuntergang an der Küste

SONNENUNTERGANG AN DER KÜSTE oil on
canvas, 39 x 57cm. slc (on boat) 'Aivazovski'
PROV.: Russian nobility.

Lempertz Cologne, 18 May 1996
(1,500**) DEM 30,000   US$ 19,558

A COASTAL LANDSCAPE WITH FIGURES
RESTING ON A BEACH, A TWO-MASTER
BEYOND oil on canvas, 38.5 x 47.5cm. s in
Cyrillic d '1891'

Christie's Amsterdam, 26 October 1995
(220**) NLG 34,500   US$ 21,753

AIZPIRI Paul (1919 b.) French
ST. TROPEZ, VU DU CHAMP CARNAVAL oil on canvas, 28 ¾ x 39¼in. (73 x 99.7cm.) slr
'Aizpiri'
PROV.: Galerie Romanet, Paris.

Christie's East, 7 November 1995 (163**) US$ 23,000   US$ 2,3000

PIERROT oil on canvas, 25½ x 19 5/8in. (64.8 x 50cm.) sll 'Aizpiri'
PROV.: Galerie des Chaudronniers, Geneva.
      Christie's East, 30 April 1996 (208*) US$ 9,200   US$ 9,200

AKKERINGA Johannes Evert Hendrik, Snr (Banka (Blinjoe) 1861-1942 Amersfoort) Dutch
SNOWBERRIES IN A VASE oil on canvas, 36.5 x 47.5 cm s 'J. Akkeringa'
      Christie's Amsterdam, 25 April 1996 (141*) NLG 17,250   US$ 10,250

THE NET-MENDER oil on canvas, 82 x 70cm. s 'J Akkeringa'
PROV.: Kunsthandel P.J. Zürcher, The Hague; Haags Gemeentemuseum, The Hague, inv. no. 21-k-1959 (on loan).
      Christie's Amsterdam, 25 April 1996 (199*) NLG 16,100   US$ 9,567

A QUIET AFTERNOON oil on panel, 27.5 x 27.5cm. slr 'J Akkeringa'
PROV.: Kunsthandel E.J. van Wisselingh and Co., Amsterdam; Anon. Sale, Mak van Waay, Amsterdam, 15 October 1940, lot 75 (sold to the present owner).
      Christie's Amsterdam, 26 October 1995 (333**) NLG 36,800   US$ 23,203

ALBANI Francesco (Bologna 1578-1660 Bologna) Italian
DANCING AMORINI IN A LANDSCAPE WITH VENUS (OR PSYCHE) AND CUPID ON A CLOUD, AND PLUTO ABDUCTING PROSERPINA oil on copper (oval) , 45 x 36½in. (114.3 x 92.7cm.) incised on the verso of the copper 'P.I.C.L.' (ca. 1630)
PROV.: Frederick Augustus, King of Saxony, by whom given to Prince Henry Lubomirski in 1845, kept in the Lubomirski family in Przeworsk Castle, Crakow, Poland until the 1930s, thence by direct descent to the present owner.
LIT.: Possibly C.C. Malvasia, *Felsina Pittrice. Vita de'pittori bolognesi*, 1678 (edition of 1841-42) , vol. II, pp. 183-85 (the letter from Albani to Girolao Bonini on October 24, 1659) ; 197 Possibly A. Bolognini Amorini, *Vite de' pittori ed artefici bolognesi*, 1843, vol. IV, p. 144.
      Sotheby's New York, 16 May 1996 (55**) US$ 266,500   US$ 266,500

ALBERS Josef (Bottrop 1888-1976 New Haven) American (German)
HARBOURED oil on masonite, 17 x 24 ¾in. (43 x 63cm.) s with monogram and d '47-52'; sd '47-52' and titled on the reverse
PROV.: Sidney Janis Gallery, New York; Don Page, New York; H. Prinzen, Kaarst.
EXH.: Raleigh, The North Carolina Museum of Art, *Joseph Albers Retrospective Exhibition*, 1962; New York, The Solomon R. Guggenheim Museum; Baden-Baden, Staatliche Kunsthalle; Berlin, Bauhaus Archiv, *Josef Albers: A Retrospective*, 1988, no. 182 (illustrated).
      Sotheby's London, 27 June 1996 (173**) GBP 13,800   US$ 21,280

STUDY FOR HOMAGE TO THE SQUARE: POTENT oil on masonite, 40 x 40in. (101.6 x 101.6cm.) s with mono. and dlr 'A 68'; sd and titled 'Study for Homage to the Square: 'Potent' Albers 1968' on the reverse
PROV.: Acquired directly from the artist.
EXH.: New York, The Metropolitan Museum of Art, *Josef Albers at The Metropolitan Museum of Art*; Nov. 1971-Jan. 1972, no. 84 (illustrated); New York, The Solomon R. Guggenheim Museum and Baden-Baden, Staatliche Kunsthalle, *Josef Albers: A Retrospective*, Mar.-July 1988, p. 263, no. 220 (illustrated); Munich, Villa Stuck and Bottrop, Josef Albers Museum, *Anni und Josef Albers Eine Retrospektiv*, Dec. 1989-June 1990, p. 13, no. 104 (illustrated).
      Christie's New York, 7 May 1996 (4**) US$ 145,500   US$ 145,500

HOMMAGE TO THE SQUARE: LAST YEAR oil on masonite, 40 x 40in. (101.6 x 101.6cm.) sd ini '64' sd titled '1964' on the reverse
PROV.: Sidney Janis Gallery, New York; Galerie Agnes Lefort, Montreal.
      Christie's London, 23 May 1996 (110**) GBP 51,000   US$ 77,226

HOMMAGE TO THE SQUARE oil on masonite, 16 x 16in. (40.6 x 40.6cm.) sd ini '69'
PROV.: Jackson Pollock Gallery, Toronto.
Christie's London, 23 May 1996 (84**) GBP 19,550   US$ 29,603

HOMAGE TO THE SQUARE oil on masonite, 40 x 40in. (101.6 x 101.6cm) slr with ini. and d '55
EXH.: Munich, Villa Stuck; Bottrop, Josef Albers Museum, *Anni und Josef Albers: Eine
Retrospective*, December 1989-June 1990.
Christie's London, 27 June 1996 (61**) GBP 60,,900   US$ 93,909

UNTITLED gouache on paper, 16 ¾ x 22¼in. (42.5 x56.5cm.) sd ini lr 'A77'
Christie's East, 14 November 1995 (91*) US$ 10,925   US$ 10,925

HOMAGE TO THE SQUARE oil on masonite, 32 x 32in. (81.3 x 81.3cm.) sd mono. 'JA '54'
PROV.: Galerie Hans Strelow, Dusseldorf; Acquired from the above by the present owner.
Christie's London, 26 October 1995 (89**) GBP 28,750   US$ 45,376

ALBERTI Antonio Barbalonga (Messina 1600-1649) Italian
PORTRAIT OF A PRELATE, SAID TO BE CARDINAL JEAN DE BONSI oil on canvas, 56¼ x
44in. (143 x 11.5cm.)
PROV.: By descent in the Bonsi family to the Vicomtesse de Beaumont, née Noailles; Alexis de
Noailles, The Comtesse la Croiz Laval, Chateau de Noailles, Corrèze, from whom acquired ca. 1970
by the present owner.
Sotheby's London, 5 July 1995 (171**) GBP 10,350   US$ 16,510

ALBOTTO Francesco (attr.) (Venice 1722-1757) Italian
THE GRAND CANAL, VENICE, LOOKING SOUTHWEST FROM THE CHIESA DEGLI
SCALZI TO THE FONDAMENTA DELLA CROCE, WITH SAN SIMEONE PICCOLO oil on
canvas, 23 ¾ x 37½in. (60.3 x 95.3cm.)
Sotheby's New York, 6 October 1996 (232*) US$ 18,400   US$ 18,400

ALECHINSKY Pierre (Brussels 1927 b.) Belgian
UNTITLED black crayon and brush and black ink on paper mounted on canvas, 38¾ x 26¼in. (98.4
x 66.6cm.) sdlr 'Alechinsky 1968'
PROV.: Galerie de France, Paris.
Christie's New York, 15 November 1995 (129**) US$ 13,225   US$ 13,225

COTÉ JARDIN oil on canvas, 51 x 38in. (130 x 97cm.) s 'Alechinsky', d 'VIII 59' on the reverse
Christie's London, 30 November 1995 (12A**) GBP 65,300   US$ 102,143

INTERNATIONAL PARK acrylic on paper mounted on canvas; ink on paper, mounted on wood
panel, central canvas: 47¼ x 73in. (120 x 185.5cm.) overall: 67½ x 93¼in. (171.5 x 236.8cm.)
signed, titled and dated '1969' on the reverse; sd '1970' on the reverse of frame
PROV.: Lefèbre Gallery, New York.
Christie's London, 26 October 1995 (44***) GBP 221,500   US$ 349,590

CHEVELURE oil on canvas, 45 x 37cm. slc 'Alechinsky', and sd again and inscr. with title
'Alechinsky 1960-8F' on the reverse
PROV.: Galerie Christel, Helsinki.
Christie's Amsterdam, 5 June 1996 (327**) NLG 25,300   US$ 14,782

GRAPPE DE CELIBATAIRES oil on canvas, 54 x 64½in. (137 x 164cm.) s 'Alechinsky', sd and
titled '1966' on the reverse
PROV.: Hendrickx-van den Bossche, St. Genesius-Rode; Acquired from the above by the present
owner in the 1970's.
EXH.: Brussels, Palais des Beaux-Arts; Humlebaek, Louisiana Museum of Modern Art; Düsseldorf,
Kunstverein; Bremen, Kunsthalle, *Alechinsky Werke 1958-1968*, January-July 1969, no. 26

(illustrated in colour in the catalogue) ; Ostend, Provinciaal Museum voor Moderne Kunst, *CoBrA - Post CoBrA*, July-October 1991 (illustrated in colour p. 66).
LIT.: Jacques Putman, *Alechinsky*, Paris 1967, p. 193 no. 193 (illustrated in colour).
      Christie's London, 30 November 1995 (17a**) GBP 102,700   US$ 160,644

WHALE OF A GOOD TIME oil on canvas, 50 x 88 3/8in. (127 x 224.5cm.) sll 'Alechinsky'; sd 'XI 1961 N.Y.' and titled on the stretcher
PROV.: Gallery Lefèbre, New York; Mr and Mrs Frank Titelman, Pennsylvania (acquired from the above in 1962) ; Thence by descent to the present owner.
      Christie's London, 27 June 1996 (18**) GBP 188,500   US$ 290,671

LA PERCÉE DE BERBERING acrylics and aquatint on Japan laid down on canvas, 67 x 100cm. sdlr 'Alechinsky 1990' sd on the reverse
      Christie's Amsterdam, 6 December 1995 (263B**) NLG 16,100   US$ 9,976

CONTRE COURANT acrylic on paper laid down on board, 58 x 111in. (147.3 x 281.9cm.) s 'Alechinsky' (1965)
PROV.: Lefèbre Gallery, New York; acquired from the above by the previous owner in 1967.
LIT.: Jacques Putman, *Alechinsky*, Milan 1967, p. 174 (illustrated in colour).
      Christie's London, 23 May 1996 (23**) GBP 76,300   US$ 115,536

COMPOSITION acrylic and ink on paper laid down on canvas, 51 1/8 x 37 ¾in. (130 x 96cm.) slr 'Alechinsky' (ca. 1960)
PROV.: Collection Micheline and Charlie Szwajcer, Antwerp.
      Sotheby's London, 21 March 1996 (35**) GBP 16,100   US$ 24,588

RETOUR AUX SOURCES acrylic on paper laid down on canvas, 98 7/16 x 1743 11/16in. (,250 x 365cm.) slr; d 'Bodrum, Turkey et New York 1973' on the reverse
PROV.: Commissioned by the present owner.
EXH.: Darmstadt, Mathildenhöhe, *Pierre Alechinsky*, June-July 1974, no. 58; Rotterdam, Museum Boymans-van Beuningen; Paris, Musée d'Art Moderne de la Ville de Paris, *Alechinsky*, November 1974-April 1975; Brussels, Banque Bruxelles Lambert, *Regard sur la Femme d'Ensor à Combas*, November-December 1994 (illustrated in colour in the catalogue pp. 56-57).
      Christie's London, 27 June 1996 (29**) GBP 287,500   US$ 443,331

ARBRITUDE acrylic on paper laid down on canvas, 44 x 59½in. (112 x 151cm.) sd 'Alechinsky' and '72' on the reverse
EXH.: Darmstadt, Mathildenhohe; Rotterdam Museum Boymans- van Beuningen; Zurich, Kunsthaus *Pierre Alechinsky*, June 1974-June 1975, no. 46 (illustrated in colour).
      Christie's London, 26 October 1995 (38**) GBP 47,700   US$ 75,284

VIEUX THEME oil on canvas, 13 x 16in. (33 x 40.5cm.) sd and titled '1958' on the reverse
PROV.: Galerie Jacques Bénador, Geneva; Acquired directly from the above by the present owner.
      Sotheby's London, 27 June 1996 (147**) GBP 10,350   US$ 15,960

MAJUSCULE acrylic on paper laid down on canvas, 26 x 20½in. (66 x 52cm.) slr 'Alechinsky' sd titled '1978-1979' on the reverse
PROV.: Yves Rivièfe, Paris (the Artist's publisher).
      Sotheby's London, 21 March 1996 (18**) GBP 9,775   US$ 14,928

MISS DELFT oil and Indian ink on paper laid down on canvas, 39 3/8 x 39 3/8in. (,100 x 100cm.) s 'Alechinsky' sd titled '1986-1987' on the reverse
PROV.: Gallery Lelong, New York; acquired directly from the above by the present owner in 1987.
EXH.: New York, Gallery Lelong, *Pierre Alechinsky*, 1987.
      Sotheby's London, 27 June 1996 (254**) GBP 29,900   US$ 46,106

ALEXANDER John (1945 b.)
FIRES OF XANADU oil on canvas, 77 x 83in. (195.6 x 210.8cm.) sd and titled 'John Alexander
'Fires of Xanadu' 819.12.91' on the reverse
PROV.: Marlborough Gallery, New York.
Christie's New York, 15 November 1995 (373**) US$ 17,250   US$ 17,250

ALEXANDER John White (Alleghany City, Pennsylvania 1856-1915) American
THE GREEN GOWN oil on canvas, 40¼ x 22½in. (102.2 x 54.6cm.) sll ini. 'JWA'
PROV.: Estate of the artist; James Graham & Sons, Inc., New York.
EXH.: New Haven, Connecticut, New Haven Paint and Clay Club, *Fourth Annual Exhibition*, 1904;
New York, Arden Gallery, *Exhibition of Selected Works by the Late John White Alexander*,
November-December 1915, no. 23 ;
Pittsburgh, Pennsylvania, Department of Fine Arts, Carnegie Institute, *John White Alexander
Memorial Exhibition*, March 1916, no. 49; Detroit, Michigan, Detroit Institute of Arts, *Memorial
Exhibition of Paintings by the Late John White Alexander*, November 1916, no. 25; Milwaukee,
Wisconsin, Milwaukee Art Institute, *John White Alexander Memorial Exhibition*, February 1917, no.
56 Colorado Springs, Colorado, The Colorado Springs Art Society, *Memorial Exhibition of Paintings
by John White Alexander*, May 1917, no. 22; Rochester, New York, The Memorial Art Gallery, *The
John White Alexander Memorial Exhibition*, October 1917, no. 20.
LIT.: J.C. Van Dyke, *American Painting and Its Tradition*, New York, 1919, p. 229, 231.
Christie's New York, 23 May 1996 (77**) US$ 51,750   US$ 51,750

ALETHEA oil on canvas, 63½ x 52½in. (61.3 x 33.4cm.) sdll 'JW Alexander 95'; inscr. with title on
the stretcher
PROV.: Estate of the artist; James Graham & Sons, Inc., New York; Stuart Pivar, New York; Berry-
Hill Galleries, New York; Irving H. Picard, Receiver for David Peter Bloom, New York; Sale: New
York, Sotheby's, May 25, 1988, lot 165.
EXH.: Paris, Salon du Champ-de-Mars, *Exposition Nationale des Beaux-Arts*, 1895, no. 16;
Pittsburgh, Pennsylvania, The Art Society, *214th Reception, Exhibition of Paintings and
Compositions by John White Alexander*, 1895, no. 6; Philadelphia, Pennsylvania Academy of the
Fine Arts, *Sixty-fifth Annual Exhibition*, 1895-96, no. 10; Munich, 1896; New York, James Graham
& Sons Inc., *John White Alexander 1856- 1915: Fin-de-Siècle American*, 1980, no. 11 (illustrated).
LIT.: 'Review of the Paris Salon', *New York Sun*, 21 April 1895; A.F. Miller, *American Painters at
the Paris Salon*, unidentified periodical, 1895;
'Review of the Paris Salon', *Art Interchange*, New York, July 1895;
M. Guyon, 'Review of the Paris Salon', *Journal des Artistes*, Paris, 5 July, 1895; *Kansas City Star*, 8
November 1903 (illustrated);
Catalogue of the John White Alexander Memorial Exhibition, Pittsburgh, 1916, p. 57; S. Leff,
'Master of Sensuous Line', *American Heritage*, October 1985, p. 82 (illustrated); Berry-Hill Galleries,
American Paintings IV, 1986, p. 52 (illustrated).
Christie's New York, 30 November 1995 (23**) US$ 530,500   US$ 530,500

ONTEORA oil on canvas, 80 x 43in. (203 x 109cm.) sll 'John W. Alexander'
PROV.: Estate of the artist; James Graham & Sons Inc., New York.
EXH.: New York, James Graham & Sons Inc., *John White Alexander: Correspondences*, Oct.-Dec.
1985, p. 14, no. 17 (illustrated); Washington D.C., Marriner S. Eccles Federal Reserve Board
Building, *Out of the Kitchen, Into the Parlor: The Art of Still Life by John White Alexander*, June-
Sept. 1995, no. 24.
Christie's New York, 30 November 1995 (29**) US$ 310,500   US$ 310,500

ALKEN Samuel Henry (Henry Jnr) (1810-1894) British
BEADSMAN, A BROWN COLT, WITH JOHN (TINY) WELLS UP, AT EPSOM oil on canvas, 16
x 20in. (40.6 x 50.8cm.) slr 'H.Alken'
PROV.: With Richard Green, London.
Christie's London, 30 November 1995 (65**) GBP 17,250   US$ 26,983

ALLEBÉ August (Amsterdam 1838-1927 Amsterdam) Dutch
A PEASANT GIRL AND CHILD BY A WELL IN A FARMYARD oil on panel, 48 x 36.5cm. sd
'A. Allebé 69'
LIT.: W. Loos, C. van Tuyll van Serooskerken *Waarde Heer Allebé. Leven en Werk van August Allebé (1838-1927)* , Zwolle 1988, p. 129 (illustrated).
        Christie's Amsterdam, 25 April 1996 (193**) NLG 32,200   US$ 19,134

ALLEGRINI Francesco I, {called} da Gubbio (Gubbio 1587-1663 Rome) Italian
SCENES FROM CLASSICAL MILITARY HISTORY oil on panel (a pair), each: 27½ x 22in. (70 x 56cm.)
        Sotheby's London, 5 July 1995 (285**) GBP 17,250   US$ 27,516

A CAVALRY ENGAGEMENT oil on copper, 11½ x 15 ¾in. (29.5 x 40cm.)
        Sotheby's London, 5 July 1995 (202**) GBP 7,820   US$ 12,474

ALLINGHAM Helen, R.W.S. (1848-1926) British
A COTTAGE NEAR WITLEY, SURREY watercolour with scratching out, 11 3/8 x 8¼in. (29 x 23.5cm.) s 'H. Allingham'
PROV.: With M. Newman, 1954; *The Marley Collection of Watercolours by Helen Allingham*; Christie's 19 September 1991, lot 12.
EXH.: London, *Royal Society of Painters in Watercolours*, 1909, no. 69; Guildford, Guilford House, London, RIBA, and Birmingham, Museum and Art Gallery, *Cottages of Yesteryear*, 1988-90, no. 35.
        Christie's London, 7 June 1996 (514**) GBP 19,550   US$ 30,146

AT SCHOOL GREEN, ISLE OF WIGHT pencil and watercolour with scratching out, 17 x 14 1/8in. (43.1 X 35.9cm.) s 'H. Allingham' (1890)
EXH.: London, The Fine Art Society, 1898, no. 31.
LIT.: I. Taylor, *Hellen Allingham's England*, 1990, p. 82.
        Christie's London, 6 November 1995 (9**) GBP 13,225   US$ 20,687

ALMA TADEMA Laura Theresa, Lady (1852-1909) British
THE BIBLE LESSON oil on canvas, 25½ x 20in. (65 x 51cm.) s and inscr. uc 'op.LVIII'
        Phillips London, 18 June 1996 (82**) GBP 11,500   US$ 17,733

WINTER oil on canvas, 36 x 28¼in. (91.4 x 71.7cm.) sd ' Laura/T.A.T./op XLIX'
EXH.: London, Royal Academy, 1881, no.594.
LIT.: Henry Blackburn (ed.) , *Royal Academy Notes*, 1881, repr. p.62 *Athenaeum*, 2796, 28 May 1881, p.726; Alice Meynell, 'Laura Alma Tadema', *Art Journal*, 1883, p.346, repr.
        Christie's London, 6 November 1995 (211**) GBP 23,000   US$ 35,977

ALMA TADEMA Sir Laurens, O.M., R.A. (Dronrijp 1836-1912 Wiesbaden) British
A ROMAN ARTIST pencil and watercolour with scratching out, 11½ x 11½in. (29.2 x 29.2cm.) s inscr. 'L. Alma Tadema OP CXXX' (before 1882)
PROV.: HJ. Carr by 1882 and thence by descent to his wife by 24 May 1889; T.W. Wright, 1892-1923; Sir Edward Sharp, Bt., Maidstone, 1949; Sir Francis Cook; Lady Cook; Anon. sale, Sotheby's Belgravia, 6 October 1980, lot 48.
EXH.: London, Royal Society of Painters in Watercolours, *70th Summer Exhibition*, 1874, no.268; London, Grosvenor Gallery, *The Works of L. Alma-Tadema*, Winter 1882-3, no.267.
LIT.: *Athenaeum*, 2426, 25 April 1874, p.566; Carel Vosmaer, *Alma-Tadema Catalogue*, 1885, no.153; Portfolio, 1892; Rudolph Dircks, 'The Later Works of Sir Lawrence Alma Tadema', *Art Journal, Christmas Supplement*, 1910, p.28.
        Christie's London, 7 June 1996 (558**) GBP 11,270   US$ 17,379

THE LETTER FROM AN ABSENT ONE black lead, pen and black ink, watercolour on white paper, 15 3/8 x 10 3/8in. (39 x 26.4cm.) sd 'L Alma Tadema 71' with numbers '411' and '41' (1875)
PROV.: Ernest Gambart, London; James Barrot, Liverpool, by 1886; Anon. sale, Liverpool,

Exchange Gallery, May 17, 1918, lot 169 (£200 at proof stage); Anon. sale, Sotheby's, London, May 31, 1961, lot 20, (£38 to Charles Jerdein); Tames Coates, New York.
EXH.: Liverpool, Walker Art Gallery, *Grant Loan Exhibition of Pictures*, 1886, no. 850 (as Reading to a Lady); Manchester, *Royal Jubilee Exhibition*, 1887, no. 1475, as *La Lecture*; New York, Robert Isaacson Gallery, April-May, 1962, no. 2; Palm Beach, The Society of the Four Arts, *English Paintings of the Victorian Era*, February 5-27, 1966, no. 3.
LIT.: C.Vosmaer, L. Alma-Tadema, C.Vosmaer, *Alma-Tadema Catalogue Raisonné,* unpublished manuscript, circa 1885, no. 103 (as From an absent One); R. Dircks, 'The Later Works of Sir Lawrence Alma-Tadema', *Art Journal*, London, Christmas Supplement, 1910, p. 27, listed as being burned (opus 83 was burned, the oil counterpart); D. Hine, *An Exhibition to Commemorate the 50th Anniversary of the Death of Sir Lawrence Alma-Tadema*, New York, 1962, p.5; V. Swanson, *Porfolio: Alma-Tadema, 19th Century*, New York, 1977, p. 66 (illustrated).

Christie's New York, 22 May 1996 (75**) US$ 74,000	US$	74,000

ALT Franz, {called} Altamura (Vienna 1821-1914) Austrian
DIE CA D`ORO IN VENEDIG oil on canvas, laid down on cardboard, 21.7 x 29.4cm. sdlr 'Franz Alt 1858' on the reverse s 'Franz Alt'

Wiener Kunst Auktionen, 26 September 1995 (117**) ATS 90,000	US$	8,748

ALT Jacob (1789-1872) German
SEGELSCHIFF IM HAFEN oil on panel, 31.6 x 39.5cm. sdlr 'J. Alt 1848'

Wiener Kunst Auktionen, 26 March 1996 (71**) ATS 400,000	US$	38,476

ALT Rudolf von (Vienna 1812-1904 Vienna) Austrian
INNSBRUCK watercolour on paper, 44 x 32cm. sll 'R.Alt'

Wiener Kunst Auktionen, 26 September 1995 (88**) ATS 450,000	US$	43,742

BLICK AUF PERSENBEUG watercolour on paper, 10 x 15.6cm. sll 'R. Alt'

Dorotheum Vienna, 6 November 1995 (90**) ATS 250,000	US$	25,078

THE ENTRANCE OF A CHURCH black chalk and watercolour on paper, 11 x 11cm. (28 x 28cm.) s 'R. Alt' d inscr. 'Gastein 25 Aug. 88' (1888)

Christie's New York, 22 May 1996 (68**) US$ 18,400	US$	18,400

REPARATURARBEITEN AN DER NIKOLAUSKIRCHE IN GASTEIN watercolour on paper laid down on cardboard, 45.5 x 27cm. sd inscr. lr 'R Alt Gastein 891'
EXH.: Miethke, Wien 1906, no. 156.
LIT.: Walter Koschatzky, *Rudolf von Alt. 1812-1905*; Residenz Verlag, Salzburg 1975, p. 293, Wkv.-nr. 91/09; Ausstellungskatalog, *Rudolf von Alt. 1812-1905*; *Graphische Sammlung Albertina*, Wien 29-2-29.4 1984, p. 156, cat.-no. 246 (ill.).

Wiener Kunst Auktionen, 26 September 1995 (121**) ATS 280,000	US$	27,217

VIEW OF THE INTERIOR OF THE 'STEPHANSDOM' IN VIENNA watercolour on paper, 37.5 x 28.5cm. sd 'R. Alt 1845'
LIT.: Walter Kochatzky, *Rudolf von Alt*, Residenzverlag 1975, no. 45/47.

Dorotheum Vienna, 25 October 1995 (175**) ATS 110,000	US$	11,034

BURG EGER watercolour on paper, heightened with white, 26.5 x 37.5cm. slr 'R. Alt' dll and titled 'Eger 10. Sept (1) 876'

Wiener Kunst Auktionen, 26 September 1995 (84**) ATS 120,000	US$	11,664

INNENANSICHT EINES SALONS DES SCHLOSSES OBERWALTDORF watercolour on paper, 9 7/8 x 14 1/8in. (25 x 36cm.) sd 'R Alt 1842'
PROV.: Commissioned by Johan Fürst Trautmannsdorf and thence by descent to the present owner.

Christie's London, 11 October 1995 (36**) GBP 19,550	US$	30,855

STILL-LIFE WITH ELDERS, PINKS, VEGETABLES AND FISH watercolour, heightened with
white on paper, 14 x 19cm. sdll 'R. Alt(1) 893.'
        Wiener Kunst Auktionen, 26 September 1995 (51**) ATS 120,000   US$ 11,664

ALTENBOURG Gerhard (Rödichen 1926-1989 Meißen) Geman
ÜLDIGUNG FÜR QUIRINUS KÜHLMANN watercolour and different kinds of ink, 52 x 37.3cm.
sd mono. and titled on the reverse (1963)
        Hauswedell & Nolte Cologne, 6 June 1996 (6**) DEM 17,000   US$ 11,045

ALTINK Jan (Groningen 1885-1976) Dutch
A COUNTRY ROAD, GRONINGEN oil on canvas, 90 x 74cm. slr 'J.Altink' (ca. 1928)
        Christie's Amsterdam, 6 December 1995 (168**) NLG 21,850   US$ 13,539

FARM IN A LANDSCAPE oil on canvas, 55 x 65cm. sdlr 'J Altink 24'
PROV.: Kunsthandel Fijnaut B.V., Amsterdam.
        Sotheby's Amsterdam, 7 December 1995 (186**) NLG 27,140   US$ 16,817

ALTOMONTE Martino (Napels 1659-1745 Vienna) Italian
THE RESSURECTION OF THE CROSS BY EMPERESS HELENA oil on canvas, 36 x 80cm.
PROV.: Former Collection Austrian immigrants in the USA.
        Dorotheum Vienna, 17 October 1995 (174**) ATS 150,000   US$ 15,046

ALTSON Abbey (1894 - 1917 fl.) British
STEPPING ABOARD 'L'HIRONDELLE' oil on canvas, 39½ x 52¼in. (100.3 x 132.7cm.) sdll
'ABBEY 1902'
        Sotheby's Arcade Auctions New York, 20 July 1995 (135**) US$ 11,500   US$ 11,500

AMBERGER Christoph (1505 c.-1562 Augsburg) German
A PORTRAIT OF A LADY, PROBABLY URSULA HARRACH, GRÄFIN FUGGER, TURNED
TO THE RIGHT AND HOLDING A PAIR OF GLOVES oil on pine wood panel, 19 ¾ x 16½in. (50
x 42cm.) dur '1541'
PROV.: Perhaps Jacob Fugger, and by descent; Prince Fugger-Babbenhausen, Augsburg, by 1907
and until after 1925; With M. Perls, Berlin, 1928; Baron Heinrich Thyssen-Bornemizsa, by 1930.
EXH.: Munich 1930, no. 5, pl. 22; Paris 1970, no. 1, pl. 2; Dusseldorf 1970-1, no. 1; Lausanne etc.,
1986-7, no. 13.
LIT.: M.J. Friedländer, in F. Thieme, U. Becker, *Allgemeines Lexikon der bildenden Künstler.*, vol. I,
1907, p. 388, as one of several works of the highest quality from the artist's best period; K Scheffler,
Bildnisse aus drei Jahrhunderten, 1925, p. 33, no. 39; R.A. Peltzer, *Joachim von Sandrarts
Academie der Bau-, Bild- und Mahlerei-Künste von 1675.*,1925, p. 332, under footnote 1507; K.
Feuchtmayr, 'Christoph Amberger und Jorg Hermann', *Münchner Jahrbuch der bildenden Kunst*,
1938-9, p. 84, under footnote 30; R. Heinemann 1937, vol. I, no. 5, vol. V, pl. 45.
        Sotheby's London, 6 December 1995 (63**) GBP 56,500   US$ 86,950

AMBROS Raphael von (19th Century) Austrian
THE FRUIT SELLER oil on panel, 19 1/8 x 24in. (48.7 x 61cm.) sdlr inscr. 'R. Ambros, Paris 90.'
        Phillips London, 12 March 1996 (19**) GBP 9,000   US$ 13,745

AMELIN Albin (1902-1975) Swedish
BLOMSTERSTILLEBEN oil on canvas, 92 x 74cm. sdlr 'Amelin 40'
        Bukowskis Stockholm, 24-25 April 1996 (4**) SEK 48,000   US$ 7,272

AMERLING Friedrich Ritter von (Vienna 1803-1887 Vienna) Austrian
MÄDCHEN MIT FRÜCHTENKORB oil on canvas, 74 x 60cm.
        Dorotheum Vienna, 6 November 1995 (86**) ATS 320,000   US$ 32,100

AMIGONI Jacopo (Venice 1675-1752 Madrid) Italian
PUTTI AS APELLES AND CAMPASPE oil on canvas, 47 ¾ x 60 5/8in. (121.5 x 154cm.)
    Christie's London, 20 October 1995 (42**) GBP 8,625   US$ 13,613

AMIGONI Jacopo (attr.) (Venice 1675-1752 Madrid) Italian
ALEXANDER PRESENTING CAMPASPE TO APELLES oil on canvas, 62¼ x 48in. (158 x 122cm.)
    Sotheby's London, 6 December 1995 (175**) GBP 27,600   US$ 42,475

AMOROSI Antonio Mercurio (Comunanza 1660-1738 Comunanza) Italian
A BOY AND A GIRL EMBRACING IN A PALATIAL INTERIOR; AND A CHILD
COMFORTED BY A GIRL, AS A MONKEY HELD BY A BLACK PAGE-BOY PLUCKS
FEATHERS FROM A HEN oil on panel (a pair) , 50½ x 37 1/8in. (128.3 x 94.3cm.)
    Christie's London, 7 July 1995 (360**) GBP 24,150   US$ 38,523

ANASTASI Auguste Paul Charles (1820-1889) French
SUNSET LANDSCAPE oil on canvas, 53½ x 73in. (135 x 185.4cm.) slr 'A. Anastasi'
    Christie's New York, 22 May 1996 (169**) US$ 55,200   US$ 55,200

ANDERSON Sophie (1823-1903) British (French)
THE FAIRY QUEEN oil on canvas, 21 x 17in. (53.3 x 43cm.)
    Christie's London, 6 November 1995 (190**) GBP 26,450   US$ 41,373

ANDERSON William (1757-1837) Scottish
EVENING, SHIPPING IN A STIFF BREEZE, COAST OF ENGLAND; EVENING, A CALM,
COAST OF HOLLAND oil on panel (a pair) , each: 11½ x 15¼in. (29.5 x 38.5cm) on eslr on a spar
    Phillips London, 12 December 1995 (27**) GBP 10,000   US$ 15,389

ANDERSSON Mårten (1934 b.) Swedish
KAFFEDRICKARNA oil on canvas, 197 x 205cm. sd 'Mårten 1964'; inscr. 'En av mina viktigaste
målningar, Mårten A'
LIT.: Teddy Gummerus, *Mårten Andersson*, p. 36 (illustrated p. 37).
    Bukowskis Stockholm, 26-27 October 1995 (6**) SEK 150,000   US$ 21,968

ANDRÉ Albert (Lyon 1869-1954 Laudun, Gard) French
SUR LA PLAGE oil on cardboard, 15 x 18in. (38.1 x 45.7cm.) slr 'Alb. André'
PROV.: Galerie Durand-Ruel, Paris.
    Sotheby's New York, 2 May 1996 (163**) US$ 16,100   US$ 16,100

ANDREA Lippo d' (1377-after 1427) Italian
VIRGIN AND CHILD WITH SAINTS JOHN THE BAPTIST AND ANOTHER SAINTS AND
TWO ANGELS gold ground, oil on panel, with shaped top, 46 x 23¼in. (116.8 x 59.1cm.)
    Sotheby's New York, 16 May 1996 (218**) US$ 28,750   US$ 28,750

ANDREA DEL SARTO Andrea d' Agnolo di Francesco, {called} (studio of) (Florence 1486-1530 Florence) Italian
THE BORGHERINI HOLY FAMILY oil on panel, 57 x 43¼in. (144.5 x 110cm.)
EXH.: Nottingham, 1982, no. 54, as after del Sarto.
LIT.: Waagen, 1857, p. 497, as by *Andrea del Sarto*, 'a delicate picture by the master'; Richter, 1901,
no. 54, as *studio of del Sarto;* J. Shearman, *Andrea del Sarto*, vol. II, 1965, pp. 276-77, no. 90 .
    Sotheby's London, 6 December 1995 (22**) GBP 40,000   US$ 61,557

ANDREA DI BARTOLO (Siena 1389-1428 active) Italian
THE MADONNA AND CHILD tempera on panel, gold ground, 21 x 15 ¾in. (53.2 x 40cm.)
    Sotheby's London, 17 April 1996 (79**) GBP 17,250   US$ 26,156

THE MADONNA OF HUMILITY tempera on gold ground panel, shaped top, 28 ¾ x 19 5/8in. (73 x 50cm.) including frame
EXH.: Groningen, Museum voor Stad en Land, 28 March-28 April 1969, Aartsbisschoppelijk Museum, 2 May-9 June 1969, *Sienese Paintings in Holland*, no. 1 (catalogue by H. van Os).
        Christie's London, 7 July 1995 (113**) GBP 44,400   US$ 70,825

ANDREAS Martin (late 17th century) Belgian
DORFSTRASSE MIT EINER KUTSCHE oil on panel, 30 x 48.5cm. slr 'Martin'
        Lempertz Cologne, 15 November 1995 (1312**) DEM 19,000   US$ 13,411

ANDREOTTI Federico (1847-1930) Italian
MISIC HATH CHARMS oil on canvas, 17 ¾ x 14in. (45.1 x 35.6cm.) slr 'F Andreotti'
        Christie's New York, 2 November 1995 (140**) US$ 18,400   US$ 18,400

ANDRIESSEN Jurriaan (Amsterdam 1742-1819 Amsterdam) Dutch
CAPRICES ARCHITECTURAUX DANS LA CAMPAGNE ROMAINE ANIMÉS DE PERSONNAGES oil on canvas (a quartet) , two: 180 x 116cm.; the other two: 180 x 100cm.
PROV.: Collection Sir Edward Mountain; His sale, Christie's, 10 June 1938, lot 127 (Hubert Robert); Collection Mrs. M.R.M. Ogilvy Spence; Her sale, Christie's, 8 December 1961, lot 102 (Hubert Robert).
        Étude Tajan Paris, 12 December 1995 (89**) FRF 170,000   US$ 34,242

ITALIANATE LANDSCAPE oil on canvas, a set of six canvases, different monumental sizes (around 1805)
        Christie's London, 7 July 1995 (43**) GBP 89,500   US$ 142,766

ANESI Paolo (1700-1761 Rome) Italian
THE ROMAN FORUM (CAMPO VACCINO) AND THE PANTHEON oil on canvas (a pair of paintings) , each: 24¼ x 30in. (61.6 x 76.2cm.)
        Sotheby's New York, 16 May 1996 (92**) US$ 107,000   US$ 107,000

ANGERMAYER Johann Adalbert (Bilin (Bohemia) 1674-1740 c. Prague) Czech
FOXES BANDAGING A HOUND ON A ROCK BY A TREE IN A LANDSCAPE oil on copper, 17.5 x 28.2cm. scl 'I.A.20/Angermey'
        Christie's Amsterdam, 13 November 1995 (11*) NLG 27600   US$ 17,395

ANGUISSOLA Sofonisba (Cremona 1531/1532-1625 Palermo) Italian
PORTRAIT OF A LADY THREE-QUARTER LENGHT oil on canvas, 116 x 82cm.
        Christie's Rome, 21 November 1995 (225**) ITL 20,000,000   US$ 12,555

ANGUISSOLA Sofonisba (attr.) (Cremona 1531/1532-1625 Palermo) Italian
PORTRAIT OF AN OLD WOMAN SEATED IN A CHAIR AND HOLDING A BOOK, SAID TO BE A PORTRAIT OF THE ARTIST oil on canvas, 44 x 37in. (111.8 x 94cm.)
PROV.: Sale: Dorotheum Vienna, 17 March 1970, lot 4 (illustrated); where acquired by the present owner.
        Sotheby's New York, 16 May 1996 (154**) US$ 23,000   US$ 23,000

ANNIGONI Pietro (Milan 1900/1910 b.) Italian
NELLO STUDIO oil on canvas, 47.5 x 69cm. slr with the pseudonym of the artist (ca 1935)
EXH.: Milan, 'Casa d'Artisti', 1936.
LIT.: *Annigoni*, Gonelli, Firenze, 1945, no.29; U. Longo, *Pietà e amore nell'arte di Pietro Annigoni*, ediz. galleria d'arte Cortina, Milan, 1968, (illustrated)
        Finearte Rome, 12 June 1996 (215**) ITL 41,400,000   US$ 27,148

ANQUETIN Louis (Etrépagny (Eure) 1861-1932 Paris) French
SCENE DE CIRQUE pastel on card, 18¼ x 24 3/8in. (46.5 x 62cm.) sdll 'L Anquetin 87'

PROV.: Collection of Mr.Borderie, Neuilly (France); Collection of Elizabeth and Bernard French, Kidderminster; Private collection.

     Phillips London, 27 November 1995 (10***) GBP 75,000   US$ 117,316

ANSINGH Lizzi (Maria Elisabeth Georgina) (Utrecht 1875-1959 Amsterdam) Dutch
STILL LIFE WITH A WAYANG-PUPPET AND A CHINESE DOLL oil on canvas, 109.5 x 80 cm
sd 'L. Ansingh 1918'

     Christie's Amsterdam, 25 April 1996 (48*) NLG 9,200   US$ 5,467

ANTES Horst (Heppenheim 1936 b.) German
KNIELENDE FIGUR UND HAUS aquatec with saw-dust on three-ply wood, 180 x 200cm. sd and titled on the reverse (1987)
EXH.: Berlin, *Horst Antes - die Berliner Bildergalerie*, Galerie Stuttgart 1989, cat. 7 (illustrated in colour).
LIT.: 'Horst Antes' in *Künstler, Kritisches Lexikon der Gegenwartskunst*, Vol. 10, Bruckmann, Munich 1990, p. 12 (illustrated in colour no. 15).

     Hauswedell & Nolte Cologne, 2 December 1995 (4**) DEM 86,000   US$ 59,668

ANTHONISSEN Hendrick van (Amsterdam 1606-1654/60 Amsterdam) Flemish
A FISHING BOAT IN ROUGH SEAS WITH OTHER LARGER SAILING VESSELS oil on panel, 12 ¾ x 20¼in. (32.7 x 51.5cm.) sdlr '(16) 33/H.V. ANTON'
PROV.: Anon. sale, London Christie's, 11 May 1923, lot 84, to Silvano Lodi, Munich, before 1973.
LIT.: K.J. Müllenmeister, *Meer und Land im Licht des 17. Jahrhunderts*, vol. I, 1973, p. 48 (illustrated).

     Sotheby's London, 5 July 1995 (182**) GBP 9,775   US$ 15,593

ANUSKIEWICZ Richard (1930 b.) American
SUNGAME acrylic on canvas, 60 x 60in. (152.4 x 152.4cm.) sd 'RICHARD ANUSKIEWICZ 1970' on the reverse

     Christie's East, 7 May 1996 (71*) US$ 9,775   US$ 9,775

TRANSLUCENT acrylic and paper collage mounted on panel, 21 x 16in. (53.4 x 40.7cm.) sd and titled 'RICHARD ANUSKIEWICZ 1971 TRANSLUCENT' on the reverse

     Christie's East, 7 May 1996 (70*) US$ 7,475   US$ 7,475

ANZINGER Siegfried (Weyer/Enns 1953 b.) German
VORDERRHEIN tempera on canvas, 120 x 90cm. sd 'Anzinger 1988' on the reverse
LIT.: *Bilderstreit, Widerspruch, Einheit und Fragment in der Kunst seit 1960*, DuMont Buchverlag, Cologne 1989, p. 504, no. 19.

     Dorotheum Vienna, 21 May 1996 (146**) ATS 220,000   US$ 21,125

UNTITLED dispersion on molino, fixed on molino, 155 x 148cm.(painting) 164 x 159cm. (entirely)

     Wiener Kunst Auktionen, 27 September 1995 (582**) ATS 110,000   US$ 10,692

UNTITLED acrylic on canvas, 189.5 x 159.5cm. s twice and dlr 'Anzinger 81'

     Wiener Kunst Auktionen, 26 March 1996 (469**) ATS 120,000   US$ 11,543

APOL Louis (Lodewijk Franciscus Hendrik) (The Hague 1850-1936 The Hague) Dutch
HORSE-DRAWN CARTS AND FAGGOT GATHERERS IN THE SNOW oil on canvas, 41 x51cm. sll 'Louis Apol f'

     Christie's Amsterdam, 7 September 1995 (285***) NLG 17,250   US$ 10,529

A SNOWY WOODED LANDSCAPE WITH A FROZEN CREEK oil on canvas, 80.5 x 101cm. sll 'Louis Apol'

     Christie's Amsterdam, 26 October 1995 (113*) NLG 29,900   US$ 18,852

A WOODED WINTER LANDSCAPE oil on canvas, 48 x 79 cm s 'Louis Apol'
    Christie's Amsterdam, 25 April 1996 (144*) NLG 34,500   US$ 20,500

APPEL Karel (Amsterdam 1921 b.) Dutch
PAYSAGE VOLANTE oil on canvas, 51¼ x 77in. (130 x 195cm.) sdll 'APPEL '59'
PROV.: Martha Jackson Gallery, New York.
    Christie's London, 26 October 1995 (30**) GBP 18,750   US$ 29,593

A SCREAMING FIGURE coloured crayons and gouache on paper laid down on paper, 51 x 40cm.
sdlr 'Ck. Appel`50'
PROV.: H. Plomper, Bergen (N-H).
    Christie's Amsterdam, 6 December 1995 (335**) NLG 48,300   US$ 29,929

KIND EN BAL waxed crayons on cardboard paper, unframed, 62.5 x 45.5cm. sdlr 'C.K. Appel 51',
and inscr. with title on the reverse
    Christie's Amsterdam, 5 June 1996 (397**) NLG 63,250   US$ 36,956

FURIOUS RED PERSONNAGE mixed media on paper, 21 x 30in. (55 x 76cm.) sdll 'appel 1960'
PROV.: Cobra Gallery, Eindhoven.
    Christie's Tel Aviv, 14 April 1996 (94**) US$ 12,650   US$ 12,650

PERSONNAGE DANS LA TEMPETE oil on canvas, 51¼ x 76 ¾in. (130 x 195cm.) sd 'Appel 62'
PROV.: Galerie Maeght, Paris; Galleria Michaud, Florence; Acquired from the above by the present
owner in the 1960s.
EXH.: Florence, Galleria Michaud, *Mostra del CoBrA*, March 1968, no. 23.
LIT.: Peter Bellow, *Karel Appel*, Milan 1968, no. 165 (illustrated in colour).
    Christie's London, 26 October 1995 (43**) GBP 54,300   US$ 85,701

UNTITLED ACRYLIC ON CANVAS, 63 ¾ x 51in. (1626 x 130cm.) sdlr 'appel 1973'
PROV.: Galerie Ile de France, Paris; Galerie Chaistec, Helsinki.
    Christie's Tel Aviv, 12 October 1995 (88**) US$ 34,500   US$ 34,500

Femme, Enfants, Animaux

FEMME, ENFANTS, ANIMAUX oil on canvas, 67 x 110¼in. (170 x 280cm.) sd 'K.Appel '51'
PROV.: Acquired directly from the artist by the father of the present owner.
EXH.: Ostend, Provincial Museum voor Moderne Kunst, *CoBrA Post CoBrA*, July-Oct. 1991
(illustrated on the cover of the catalogue).
LIT.: Michel Ragon, *Karel Appel. Peinture 1937-1957*, Paris 1988, p. 22-23, no. 30 (illustrated in
colour).
    Christie's London, 30 November 1995 (14**) GBP 386,500   US$ 604,567

FIGURE WITH BIRD oil on canvas, 120 x 90cm. slr 'Appel'
    Bukowskis Stockholm, 24-25 April 1996 (154**) SEK 72,000   US$ 10,908
DEUX PERSONNAGES oil on canvas, 63 x 55in. (160 x 139.7cm.) sdlr 'Appel '58'
PROV.: Galerie Stadler, Paris.
EXH.: The Dallas Museum for Contemporary Arts, *Texas Collects 20th Century Art*, May 1963.
    Christie's New York, 8 May 1996 (227**) US$ 85,000   US$ 85,000

KISSING oil on canvas, 60 x 81cm. slr 'Appel' and inscr. with title on the stretcherand inscr. again and d on a label on the stretcher '1964'
PROV.: American Art Gallery; Court Gallery, Copenhagen.
EXH.: Helsinki Didrichsenin Taidemuseo Didrichsens Konstmuseum,*Cobra*, 29 September - 21 October 1979, no. 6.
    Christie's Amsterdam, 6 December 1995 (280**) NLG 46,000   US$ 28,504

DON QUICHOTTE oil on canvas, 60.5 x 45.5cm. sll 'appel' (1988)
    Bukowskis Stockholm, 26-27 October 1995 (144**) SEK 70,000   US$ 10,252

A BIRD oil on canvas, 79 x 114cm. sdll 'C.K. Appel `54'
PROV.: Galerie Nova Spectra, The Hague; Galerie Beyler, Geneva; Galerie Cats, Brussels.
    Christie's Amsterdam, 6 December 1995 (284**) NLG 97,750   US$ 60,571

PERSON WITH BUTTERFLY oil on canvas, 80 x 64in. (203.2 x 162cm.) slr 'Appel' (1982)
PROV.: Fabian Carlsson, Gothenburg; acquired from the above by the present owner.
    Christie's London, 19 March 1996 (80**) GBP 14,950   US$ 22,831

QUATRE PERSONNAGES gouache on paper, 19¼ x 24 3/8in. (49 x 62cm.) sd lower centre '51
    Christie's London, 23 May 1996 (19**) GBP 18,400   US$ 27,862

ETUDE POUR UN MOULIN oil and coloured oilsticks on canvas-unframed, 76 ¾ x 74 ¾in. (195 x 189.8cm.) slr 'Appel'; titled and d '1984 Etude pour un moulin' on the stretcher
PROV.: Galerie Beyeler, Basel.
    Christie's East, 7 May 1996 (141**) US$ 8,625   US$ 8,625

A RECLINING FIGURE gouache on paper laid down on canvas, 55 x 75cm. sdll 'CK Appel `56'
    Christie's Amsterdam, 6 December 1995 (332**) NLG 12,650   US$ 7,839

THE HAPPY BIRDDAY acrylics on canvas, 203.5 x 203.5cm. sdll 'Appel 75', and inscr. with title on the stretcher
    Christie's Amsterdam, 5 June 1996 (378**) NLG 46,000   US$ 26,877

STILLEVEN IN LANDSCHAP oil on canvas, 195 x 130cm. slr 'Appel' and d and inscr. with title on the stretcher '1985'
    Christie's Amsterdam, 6 December 1995 (340**) NLG 55,200   US$ 34,205

ABSTRACT COMPOSITION crayon and watercolour on paper laid down on board, 35¼ x 47 1/8in. (89 x 119.7cm.) sd 'Appel 61'
PROV.: Au Petit Musée, Bruges.
    Christie's London, 19 March 1996 (4**) GBP 20,125   US$ 30,735

PERSONNAGIO oil on canvas, 115 x 89cm. slr 'Appel' (ca. 1954)
    Christie's Amsterdam, 5 June 1996 (389**) NLG 55,200   US$ 32,252

A BIRD black ink and coloured crayons on paper, 31.5 x 48.5cm. sdlr 'CK Appel 51'
    Christie's Amsterdam, 5 June 1996 (350**) NLG 29,900   US$ 17,470

PERSONNAGE oil on canvas, 44 x 29¼in. (112 x 74cm.) sdll '51
PROV.: Niveau Gallery, New York.
    Christie's London, 27 June 1996 (17**) GBP 194,000   US$ 299,152

CAT oil on canvas, 40.5 x 51cm. slc 'Appel' (1981)
PROV.: Jaski Art Gallery, Amsterdam.
    Sotheby's Amsterdam, 7 December 1995 (256**) NLG 21,830   US$ 13,527

UNTITLED gouache, watercolour and wax crayon on paper, 26 ¾ x 18 7/8in. (68 x 48cm.) sdlc 'K. Appel 53'
PROV.: Property from the Estate of Margaret F. Levee since the 1950's.
    Sotheby's London, 27 June 1996 (133**) GBP 25,300   US$ 39,013

DOUBLE HEAD OF A CAT gouache and crayon on paper, 25 x 19 5/8in. (63.5 x 49.8cm.) sd center of left edge '53
PROV.: Martha Jackson Gallery, New York.
EXH.: New York, Martha Jackson Gallery, *Karel Appel: The Early Fifties, Paintings, Gouaches, Drawings, Ceramics 1950-56*, Sept.-Oct. 1973 (illustarted in the catalogue).
LIT.: Marshall McLuhan, *Karel Appel: Works on Paper*, New York 1980, p. 170, no. 145 (illustrated in colour, titled 'Cat Standing on my Head'); Eleanor Flomenhaft, *The Roots and Development of Cobra Art*, New York 1985, p. 81 (illustrated).
    Christie's London, 23 May 1996 (18**) GBP 18,400   US$ 27,862

OISEAUX gouache on paper, 19¼ x 24 3/8in. (49 x 62cm.) sd 'Appel 53'
    Christie's London, 19 March 1996 (10**) GBP 14,950   US$ 22,831

SAUT DANS L'ESPACE oil on canvas, 56 x 43½in. (142 x 110cm.) sd 'K. Appel '53'
PROV.: James Goodman Gallery, New York.
LIT.: Michel Ragon, *Karel Appel Peinture 1937-1957*, Paris 1988, pp. 425-426, no. 727 (illustrated in colour) ; Peter Bellew, *Karel Appel*, Milan 1968, no. 80 (illustrated).
    Christie's London, 30 November 1995 (17**) GBP 166,500   US$ 260,441

DIER oil on canvas, 25½ x 17¼cm. (65 x 44cm.) sdll 'K. Appel '48' and s on the reverse
    Christie's London, 19 March 1996 (17**) GBP 38,900   US$ 59,407

FEMME TOURMENTÉE oil on canvas, 51 x 38in. (129.5 x 96.5cm.) sdlr '58
PROV.: Galerie Stéphane Janssen, Brussels; Acquired from the above by the brother of the present owner in 1974.
EXH.: Brussels, Palais des Beaux Arts, *Karel Appel*, 1958, no. 30; Knokke, Casino, *4ème Foire d'Art Actuel*, May-June 1974.
    Christie's London, 27 June 1996 (28**) GBP 34,500   US$ 53,200

TWO BIRDS waxed crayons and oil on paper, 50 x 64cm. sdlr 'CK Appel 53'
    Christie's Amsterdam, 5 June 1996 (303**) NLG 25,300   US$ 14,782

SWIRLING HEADS gouache and waxed crayons on paper, 56 x 75cm. sdll 'Appel '60'
PROV.: Esther Robels Gallery, Los Angeles.
    Sotheby's Amsterdam, 7 December 1995 (214**) NLG 27,140   US$ 16,817

THE TORCH BEARERS NO.3 oil on canvas, 31½ x 45½in. (80 x 116cm.) s 'Appel' (1988)
PROV.: Zaar Johansson Fine Art, Helsingborg.
    Christie's London, 23 May 1996 (187**) GBP 16,100   US$ 24,379

BIRDS gouache and coloured crayon on paper, 53 x 75cm. sdlr 'Appel 57'
    Christie's Amsterdam, 5 June 1996 (301**) NLG 18,400   US$ 10,751

ANNE oil on canvas, 194.5 x 130.5cm. sdlr 'Appel 62', and inscr. with title on the stretcher (1962)
PROV.: Gimpel, Hannover; Dr.R.E.Blum, Zumikon; Gimpel Fils Gallery, London; Mr and Mrs Charles Lowe.
LIT.: Peter Below, *Le grand monografie d'Appel*, 1968, no. 164.
    Christie's Amsterdam, 5 June 1996 (325**) NLG 74,750   US$ 43,675

TWO oil on canvas, 31 7/8 x 21 5/8in. (81 x 55cm.) sdll 'Appel 69'
    Sotheby's London, 27 June 1996 (165**) GBP 21,275   US$ 32,806

A BEAST Gouache on paper, 26 x 37cm. sd and dedicated ll 'van Karel Appel en Tony voor mevr. Thommesen 1 dec. 1948'

    Christie's Amsterdam, 5 June 1996 (305**) NLG 16,100   US$ 9,407

APPIANI Andrea (Milan 1754-1817 Milan) Italian
VENUS HOLDING AN AMPHORA AND CUPID WEEPING oil on canvas, 29 x 23in. (73.7 x 58.4cm.) (ca. 1790)

    Sotheby's New York, 16 May 1996 (107**) US$ 33,350   US$ 33,350

APSHOVEN Thomas van (Antwerp 1622-1664) Flemish
A FLEMISH VILLAGE WITH FARMERS AT WORK oil on panel, 29.5 x 44cm.
PROV.: Collection Count Czernin, Vienna; Catalogue K. Wilczek, 1936, p. 87, no. 180.
EXH.: London, Brod Gallery, 1962.

    Dorotheum Vienna, 6 March 1996 (4**) ATS 160,000   US$ 15,391

SKITTLING FARMERS ON A TOWN-SQUARE oil on canvas, 24 x 35cm. (framed)

    Dorotheum Vienna, 17 October 1995 (153**) ATS 180,000   US$ 18,055

ARDON Mordecai (Max Bronstein) (Tuchow (Poland) 1896-1992) Polish
KIDRON VALLEY oil on canvas, 45 x 57 5/8in. (114.3 x 148.4cm.) sdll 'M. Ardon-Bronstein 39'
PROV.: Prof. and Mrs. Zvi Scharfstein, New York, given to the Metropolitan Museum of Art in 1971.
EXH.: New York, The Jewish Museum, *M. Ardon-Bronstein*, Jan.-March 1948, no. 9; New York, The Jewish Museum, *Artists of Israel: 1920-1980*, 1981, no. 4; Tel Aviv, Museum of Art, *Ardon: Retrospective*, May-Oct. 1985, no. 17.
LIT.: M. Vishny, *Mordecai Ardon*, New York, 1973, no. 4 (illustrated).

    Christie's Tel Aviv, 12 October 1995 (74**) US$ 244,500   US$ 244,500

ARELLANO Juan de (Santorca(z) 1614-1676 Madrid) Spanish
IRISES, PARROT TULIPS, WHITE ROSES, GERANIUMS, A DAFFODIL AND OTHER FLOWERS IN A BASKET ON A STONE LEDGE oil on canvas, 22 x 27½in. (56.2 x 70cm.) s 'Luan de Are / llano'

    Christie's London, 7 July 1995 (90**) GBP 133,500   US$ 212,953

AN IRIS, A POPPY, PARROT TULIPS, ROSES, CARNATIONS AND OTHER FLOWERS IN A BASKET ON A STONE PEDESTAL oil on canvas, 22 x 27½in. (56.2 x 70cm.) s 'Juan deAre / llano' (on the ledge)

    Christie's London, 7 July 1995 (91**) GBP 133,500   US$ 212,953

ARENTSZ Arent, {called} Cabel (Amsterdam 1585/1586-1635 Amsterdam) Dutch
AN INLET WITH FISHERMEN oil on panel, unframed, 8 1/8 x 11½in. (20.6 x 29.2cm.)

    Sotheby's New York, 11 January 1996 (29**) US$ 57,500   US$ 57,500

ARGONAUT MASTER The Argonaut Master (act. in Florence, second half of the 15th Century) Italian
THE MADONNA ADORING THE INFANT CHRIST tempera on panel, gold ground, 26 x 19¼in. (66 x 49cm.)
EXH.: Nottingham, 1968, no. 8, plate VII (as Tuscan School), late 15th Century; Nottingham, 1982, no. 42, as Master of the Via Romana Lunette, recording Everett Fahy's connection of the panel with the *Madonna and Child* in the Museum of Fine Arts in Boston,then attributed to the Master of the Via Romana Lunette; Sheffield, Graves Art Gallery, on loan, 1992 - 1994.
LIT.: Richter, 1901, no. 23, as *anonymous Tuscan working in the manner of Baldovinetti*; Nicolson, 1968, p. 163, 'combining Florentine and Sienese elements in the late Quattrocento'; E. Fahy, 'The Argonaut Master', in: *Gazette des Beaux-Arts*, vol. CXIV, December 1989, pp. 295, 299, note 49.

    Sotheby's London, 6 December 1995 (16**) GBP 45,500   US$ 70,022

ARIKHA Avigdor (Bukovina (Roumania) 1929 b.) Israelian
POMEGRANATES oil on canvas, 8 5/8 x 13 ¾in. (22 x 35cm.) sdlc 'Arikha 74'; titled and s again on the stretcher '17.x.74'
PROV.: Marlborough-Gerson Gallery Inc., New York.
EXH.: Washington D.C., The Corcoran Gallery of Art, *Avigdor Arikha Twenty-Two Paintings 1974-1978*, June-Aug. 1979, no. 4 (illustrated).
    Christie's Tel Aviv, 12 October 1995 (110**) US$ 36,800   US$ 36,800

COMPOSITION oil on canvas, 28½ x 45½in. (72.4 x 115.5cm.) sll 'Arikha'; s again in Hebrew and numbered on the reverse '343'
    Christie's Tel Aviv, 12 October 1995 (96**) US$ 9,200   US$ 9,200

COMPOSITION oil on canvas, 57½ x 44 ¾in. (146 x 113.7cm.) slr 'Arikha', s in Hebrew (ca. 1965)
    Christie's Tel Aviv, 14 April 1996 (90**) US$ 12,650   US$ 12,650

ARMAN Fernandez Pierre, {called} (Nice 1928 b.) American (French)
ACCUMULAZIONE wristwatch-gears on plexiglass, 37 x 30.4cm. sd 'Arman 69'
LIT.: This work is recorded in the Archives Denyse Durand-Ruel, under no. A3179, and will be included in the forthcoming *Arman catalogue raisonné*.
    Sotheby's Milan, 28 May 1996 (154**) ITL 15,525,000   US$ 9,532

GORGONE accumulation on paint tubes on painted canvas, 58 x 45 ¾in. (147.3 x 116cm) sll 'Arman' (1986)
LIT.: This work is registered at Archives Denyse Durand-Ruel under no. DDR 5623 and will be included in the forthcoming *Arman Catalogue Raisonné* being prepared by Denyse Durand Ruel.
    Christie's London, 19 March 1996 (58**) GBP 10,925   US$ 16,684

ARNTZENIUS Floris (Pieter Florentius Nicolaas Jacobus) (Soerabaja (Dutch Indies) 1864-1925 The Hague) Dutch
LANGE VOORHOUT IN DEN HAAG, IN WINTER oil on canvas, 51 x 78cm. sd 'fl. Arntzenius '07'
    Christie's Amsterdam, 25 April 1996 (185**) NLG 80,500   US$ 47,834

AROCH Arie (1908-1974)
THE RAILWAY'S CAP oil stick and pencil on paper mounted at the corners on board, 7¼ x 10in. (18.4 x 25.4cm.) sll in Hebrew, dll '68'
PROV.: Acquired directly from the Artist by the present owner ca. 1970.
    Christie's Tel Aviv, 14 April 1996 (93**) US$ 12,650   US$ 12,650

AROSENIUS Ivar Axel Henrick (Göteborg 1878-1909 Alvängen, Bohuslän) Swedish
EVA, KONSTNÅRENS HUSTRU oil on canvas laid down on board, 52 x 42cm. s 'IA'
PROV.: Skriftställaren Hasse Z.
    Bukowskis Stockholm, 29-31 May 1996 (5**) SEK 90,000   US$ 13,236

ARP Jean (Hans) (Strasburg 1887-1966 Basle (Switzerland)) French
APPARITION FORESTIERE pencil on paper, 51 x 38cm s 'Arp' (1961)
    Finearte Milan, 12 December 1995 (73*) ITL 11,241,000   US$ 7,052

CONSTELLATION collage on paper laid down by the artist on board, 13 x 15 ¾in. (33 x 40cm.) sd and titled on the artist's label affixed to the reverse 'Arp Constellation 1956'
PROV.: Galerie d'Art Moderne, Basel; Martha Jackson Gallery, New York; David Anderson Gallery, New York; The Pace Gallery, New York.
    Christie's East, 7 November 1995 (216*) US$ 7,475   US$ 7,475

ARTHOIS Jacques d' (1613-1686) Flemish
LANDSCAPE WITH HUNTING-SCENE oil on canvas, 125 x 156cm.
      Bukowskis Stockholm, 29 November-1 December 1995 (214**) SEK 100,000   US$ 15,128

ARTINGSTALL W. British
MOROCCAN FRUIT SELLERS oil on canvas, 30 x 40in. (76.3 x 101.6cm.) sdll 'WArtinstall/1884'
      Christie's East, 20 May 1996 (194*) US$ 12,650   US$ 12,650

ARTSCHWAGER Richard (1924 b.) American
U.R.H. RAIN FOREST acrylic on celotex, in painted artist's frame, 32 x 57 x 2½in. (81.3 x 144.8 x
6.4cm.) sd and titled 'U.R.H. RAIN FOREST ARTSCHWAGER '87' on the reverse of the wooden
frame
PROV.: Leo Castelli Gallery, New York; Private collection, New York.
      Christie's New York, 8 May 1996 (352**) US$ 32,200   US$ 32,200

UNTITLED liquitex on celotex in artist's frame, 53½ x 79½in. (135.8 x 202cm.) sd 'Richard
Artschwager 1974' on the masonite backing
PROV.: Acquired directly from the artist.
      Christie's New York, 14 November 1995 (31**) US$ 88,300   US$ 88,300

DESK Liquitex on celotex in the artist`s frame, 30 x 35 1/8 x 3¼in. (76.2 x 89.2 x 8cm.) s titled d
'Richard Artschwager 1965 Desk' on the reverse (1965)
PROV.: Acquired directly from the artist.
      Christie's New York, 15 November 1995 (238**) US$ 25,300   US$ 25,300

ARTZ Constant David Ludovic ('Constant') (Paris 1870-1951 Soest) Dutch
DUCKS ALONG A DITCH oil on canvas, 50 x 72 cm s 'Constant Artz'
      Christie's Amsterdam, 7 February 1996 (216*) NLG 10,925   US$ 6,653

DUCKS ON A RIVERBANK oil on canvas, 40 x 50 cm s 'Constant Artz'
      Christie's Amsterdam, 7 February 1996 (222*) NLG 9,200   US$ 5,603

ASCH Pieter Jansz. van (Delft 1603-1678) Dutch
FLUSSLANDSCHAFT MIT FISCHERBOOTEN oil on panel, 59 x 92cm. sslr mono 'SVR' (linked
Salomon van Ruysdael)
PROV.: 442. Lempertz-Auktion, Köln, 4-05-1955, Lot 1; Rheinische Privatsammlung.
      Lempertz Cologne, 18 May 1996 (1001*) DEM 14,000   US$ 9,127

ASCIONE Aniello (active Napels 17th Century end of/doc.1680 - 1708) Italian
POMEGRANATES, PEACHES, PLUMS, A VASE OF FLOWERS AND A BOWL OF FRUIT ON
A PLATFORM WITH A STONE BUST ENTWINED WITH MORNING GLORY ON A PLINTH,
IN A ROCKY LANDSCAPE oil on canvas, 38 ¾ x 52¼in. (98.5 x 132.7cm.)
      Christie's London, 19 April 1996 (230**) GBP 20,700   US$ 31,387

ASPERTINI Amico (Bologna 1474/75-1552 Bologna) Italian
PORTRAIT OF A MAN, BUST LENGTH, IN BLACK COSTUME AND A BLACK HAT, A
LANDSCAPE BEYOND oil on panel, 18 x 14 1/8in. (45.7 x 36.2cm.)
LIT.: A hitherto unrecorded version of the picture in the Städelische Kunstinstitut, Frankfurt (B.
Berenson, *Italian Pictures of the Renaissance: Central and North Italian Schools*, London, 1968, I,
p.21, and III, pl. 1725).
      Christie's London, 8 December 1995 (69**) GBP 48,800   US$ 75,100

ASSCHE Henri van (Brussels 1774-1841 Brussels) Belgian
AN ITALIANATE RIVER LANDSCAPE WITH PEASANTS DRIVING CATTLE NEAR A
CLASSICAL FOUNTAIN oil on panel, 44 x 63.5cm. s 'Hrij. Van Assche'
      Christie's Amsterdam, 25 April 1996 (222*) NLG 10,925   US$ 6,492

ASSELINEAU Antoinette (Hambourg 1811) German
L'INTÉRIEUR D'UNE CLASSE DE JEUNES FILLES oil on canvas, 74.5 x 100cm. sdll 'Ant
Asselineau 1839'
PROV.: Anonymous sale, Paris, Palais Galliera, (Maîtres Loudmer -Poulain) , 6 December 1975, no.
41, where purchased by the present owner.
Étude Tajan Paris, 25 June 1996 (74**) FRF 120,000   US$ 23,172

AST Balthasar van der (Middelburg 1593/94-1657 Delft) Dutch
FRUIT ON A DISH, FLOWERS IN A *WANLI KRAAK PORCELEIN* VASE, SPRIGS OF
CHERRIES AND REDCURRANTS, SEASHELLS, A ROSE, A TULIP, A PINK, A LIZARD, A
SNAIL AND A RED ADMIRAL ON A STONE LEDGE, DRAGONFLIES ABOVE oil on panel,
18¼ x 33¼in. (46.5 x 84.5cm.) sd '.B.vander.ast.fe.1626.'
PROV.: In the possession of the present owner's great-grandfather in Westphalia.
Christie's London, 8 December 1995 (38**) GBP 210,500   US$ 323,946

BEARDED IRISES, A PINK AND WHITE
ROSE, LILY OF THE VALLEY IN A GLASS
PITCHER WITH A PARROT TULIP AND A
QUEEN OF SPAIN FRITILLARY IN A
NICHE oil on panel, 12 1/8 x 7 ¾in. (30.8 x
19.7cm) sdlc 'B. van der. Ast fe 1621.'
PROV.: J.H.J. Mellaart, London, 1925; with the
Brod Gallery, London (*Old Master Paintings*,
1976-7, no. 5).
EXH.: Amsterdam, Kunsthandel D.A.
Hoogendijk, *Zeldzame Meesters uit de
Zeventiende Eeuw*, 1932, no. 3; Amsterdam,
Kunsthandel P. de Boer, *De Helsche en de
Fluweelen Brueghel*, 10 Feb.-26 March 1934,
no. 236.
LIT.: L.J. Bol, *The Bosschaert Dynasty*, Leigh-
on-Sea, 1960, p. 69, no.1; S. Segal, *Balthasar
van der Ast*, in the catalogue of the exhibition,
Masters of Middelburg, Kunsthandel K. & V.
Waterman, Amsterdam, March 1984, pp. 50 and
61, note 8.
Christie's London, 7 July 1995
(21**) GBP 309,500   US$ 493,699

*Bearded Irises, a pink and white Rose, Lily
of the Valley in a glass Pitcher with a
Parrot Tulip and a Queen of Spain
Fritillary in a Niche*

SHELLS, A BOTTLE AND QUINCES ON A DRAPED TABLE oil on panel, 66.8 x 104.4cm.
Christie's Amsterdam, 7 May 1996 (64**) NLG 80,500   US$ 46,939

A BASKET OF FRUIT WITH FLOWERS, SEA-SHELLS AND INSECTS ARRANGED ON A
LEDGE oil on panel, 34.5 x 56.5cm. sdlr 'B. vander ast fe.: 1626'
PROV.: Dr. J. Exalto, The Hague, 1930.
EXH.: Utrecht, Centraal Museum, *Lustral exhibition taken from the art collections of alumni of the
Utrecht Student Corps*, 1956, no. 1.
LIT.: L.J. Bol, *The Bosschaert Dynasty*, 1960, p. 78, no. 69.
Sotheby's Amsterdam, 6 May 1996 (5**) NLG 56,640   US$ 33,026

ATLAN Jean-Michel (Constantine 1913-1960 Paris) French
COMPOSITION oil on canvas, 39 3/8 x 25½in. (,100 x 65cm.) sll 'Atlan' (1957)
PROV.: Acquired directly from the artist by the present owner.

EXH.: Mannheim, Städtische Kunsthalle, *Nouvelle Ecole de Paris*, 1958-59.
LIT.: In *Manheimmer Morgen*, 14 December 1958 (illustrated) ; Denise and Camille Atlan, Jacques Polieri and Editions Gallimard, *Jean-Michel Atlan Catalogue Raisonné*, Paris 1996, pp. 290-91, no. 440 (illustrated).
Sotheby's London, 27 June 1996 (150**) GBP 20,700   US$ 31,920

COMPOSITION oil on canvas, 31¼ x 20¼in. (79.2 x 52cm.) sdlr 'Atlan 59'
PROV.: Galerie Zaira Miss, Brussels Acquired directly from the above by the present owner.
LIT.: To be included in the forthcoming *Jean Michel Atlan Catalogue Raisonné* being prepared by Denise and Camille Atlan, Jacques Polieri and Editions Gallimard, Paris.
Sotheby's London, 21 March 1996 (19**) GBP 21,850   US$ 33,369

COMPOSITION oil on burlap, 56 ¾ x 34in. (144 x 86.5cm.) sd 'Atlan 59'
PROV.: Gallery The Contemporaries, New York; Madame de Winter, New York.
EXH.: New York, Gallery The Contemporaries, *Atlan*, April 1960; Paris, Musée National d'Art Moderne, *Jean Atlan*, 1959, no. 106bis.
LIT.: To be included in the *Atlan Catalogue Raisonné*, being prepared by Denise and Camille Atlan.
Christie's London, 30 November 1995 (15**) GBP 40,000   US$ 62,568

ATTERSEE Christian Ludwig (Vienna 1941 b.) Austrian
TORTE MIT SPEISEKUGELN UND SPEISEBLAU acrylic on primed canvas, 105 x 105cm. s 'ATTERSEE' (1967)
LIT.: *Attersee, Katalog, Biennale di Venezia 1984*, p. 110 (background at 'Der Siegbild', 1967) ; *Attersee. Bilder 1975 bis 1985*, Catalogue of the Kestner Gesellschaft, Hannover, 1 Nov.-8 Dec. 1985, p. 26 (at 'Der Siegbild') ; Exhibition catalogue, *Attersee. Die gemalte Reise*, Künstlerhaus Wien, Sept.-Oct. 1990, p. 49 (illustrated no. 21) ; *Attersee. Werkverzeichnis, 1963-1994*, Residenz Verlag, Salzburg-Vienna 1994, p. 177, no. 90.
Wiener Kunst Auktionen, 26 March 1996 (398***) ATS 340,000   US$ 32,705

SO LIEB ICH DICH, EI UND ZIEGEL Acrylic and Lacquer on canvas in artist's frame, 105 x 80cm. (1981)
Lempertz Cologne, 28 November 1995 (516**) DEM 17,500   US$ 12,352

WETTERHAHN acrylic and varnish on canvas, 121 x 96cm. sd and titled ll 'ATTERSEE 91'
LIT.: *Catalogue raisonné Attersee 1963-1994*, Residenz Verlag, Salzburg-Vienna, 1994, no. 3390, p. 295 (illustrated no. 68, p. 100).
Wiener Kunst Auktionen, 27 September 1995 (501**) ATS 180,000   US$ 17,497

GROSSES SUPPENSCHÖPFERBILD acrylic and varnish on primed canvas, 105 x 105cm. sdlr 'ATTERSEE 68'
LIT.: Exhibition catalogue, *Attersee. Österreichischer Sonnenschein*, Galerie Bischofsberger, Zürich; Galerie Bernard, *Solothurn*, 1968 (illustrated); *Attersee. Werkverzeichnis 1963-1994*, Residenz Verlag, Salzburg 1994, p. 179, no. 138.
Wiener Kunst Auktionen, 27 September 1995 (488**) ATS 550,000   US$ 53,462

AUBLET Albert (1851-1938) French
THE NEW DOLL oil on canvas, 54½ x 31in. (138.5 x 79cm.) sd 'Albert Aublet 1887'
Christie's London, 15 March 1996 (27**) GBP 17,250   US$ 26,344

AUDUBON John James Laforest (Santo Domingo 1785-1851 New York) American
CANADA GOOSE watercolour, graphite, gouache and charcoal on paper laid down on board, 39¼ x 26½in. (99.7 x 67.3cm.) sd and inscr. lr 'John J. Audubon of Louisiana, Boston July 1833'
PROV.: Acquired directly from the artist; Robert Gould Shaw, Boston; Francis George Shaw, his son; Sarah Blake Sturgis, his wife; Robert Shaw Barlow, her grandson; Louisa Barlow Jay, his sister; Ellen Jay Garrison, her daughter; by descent in the family to the present owners.
Christie's New York, 30 November 1995 (3**) US$ 222,500   US$ 222,500

AUERBACH Frank (1931 b.) British (German)
HEAD OF J.Y.M. III oil on canvas, 16¼ x 20¼in. (41.3 x 51.4cm.) (1982)
PROV.: Marlborough Fine Art Ltd., London; Acquired directly from the above by the present owner in 1983.
EXH.: London, Marlborough Fine Art, *Frank Auerbach: Recent Work*, 1983, p. 11, no. 17 (illus.).
      Sotheby's London, 21 March 1996 (72**) GBP 29,900   US$ 45,663

CARRERAS FACTORY, MORNINGTON CRESCENT oil on panel, 36¼ x 48in. (92.1 x 121.9cm.) (1961)
PROV.: Beaux Arts, London where purchased by a private American collector in 1965.
      Christie's London, 22 May 1996 (51**) GBP 188,500   US$ 285,433

AVED Jacques (Douai 1702-1766 Paris) French
PORTRAIT OF A LADY IN THE ROPE OF CLEOPATRA oil on canvas, 119 x 95cm sd 'AVED 1734'
      Finearte Milan, 25 November 1995 (58*) ITL 27,600,000   US$ 17,326

AVERY Milton (Altmar (N.Y.) 1893-1965 New York) American
UNDER THE BROOKLYN BRIDGE oil on canvas, 25 x 30½in. (63.6 x 77.5cm.) sll 'Milton Avery'
PROV.: Alfredo Valente Gallery, New York; Sale: New York, Sotheby's, 29 May 1986, lot 264.
      Christie's New York, 13 September 1995 (105**) US$ 16,100   US$ 16,100

GERANIUM oil on board, 20 x 15 7/8in. (50.8 x 40.4cm.) sdll 'Milton Avery 1955'
PROV.: Mrs. Sally Avery, New York.
LIT.: This painting will be included in Dr. Marla Price's forthcoming *catalogue raisonné of the paintings of Milton Avery.*
      Christie's New York, 13 March 1996 (129**) US$ 39,100   US$ 39,100

HORSE GRAZING oil on canvas, 28 x 40in. (71.2 x 101.6cm.) sdll 'Milton Avery 1961'; sd and inscr. with title on the reverse
PROV.: Estate of the artist; Sale: Sotheby's New York, 30 Nov. 1989, lot 295; Yares Gallery, Scottsdale, Arizona.
      Christie's New York, 30 November 1995 (77**) US$ 59,700   US$ 59,700

Horse Grazing

BACARISAS Gustavo (1873-1971) Spanish
BARRIO DE GRANADA oil on canvas, 80 x 100cm.
    Sotheby's Madrid, 23 November 1995 (61**) ESP 1,410,000   US$ 11,590

LA FERIA oil on canvas, 80 x 70cm.
    Sotheby's Madrid, 23 November 1995 (63**) ESP 1,292,500   US$ 10,624

BACCANI Attilio (19th century) Italian
SIGHT oil on canvas, 50 1/8 x 19 1/8in. (127.2 x 48.5cm.) sdlr (1882)
    Phillips London, 12 March 1996 (44**) GBP 13,000   US$ 19,853

BACKHUYZEN Ludolf (Emden 1631-1708 Amsterdam) Dutch
A GALJOOT, A STATES YACHT AND OTHER SMALL DUTCH MERCHANT VESSELS,
WITH A MAN-O'-WAR BEYOND, IN A SHORT CHOP ON AN ESTUARY oil on canvas, 17 ¾ x
23in. (45 x 58cm.) s ini. 'LB'
PROV.: Probably Edward Parker-Jervis, Aston hall, Sutton Coldfeld, Staffordshire; Anon. sale,
London, Christie's, 3 Feb. 1976, lot 119, as Ludolf Backhuysen the younger, 1,700gns. to Richard
Green; with Richard Green, London, from whom acquired by the father of the present owner.
    Sotheby's London, 5 July 1995 (21**) GBP 34,500   US$ 55,033

SHIPPING IN A STORM OFF A ROCKY MEDITERRANEAN COAST oil on canvas, 38½ x 50
5/8in. (97.8 x 128.5cm.) sd ini. 'LB 1702'
PROV.: King Stanislaus III Augustus Poniatowski of Poland (1732-1798), Lazienski Palace,
Warsaw; his heir, Prince Josef Poniatowski; Sold on 7 October 1815 to Count Kazirnierz Rzewuski,
and by inheritance, by 1923, to the Counts Lanckoronski, Vienna.
LIT.: C. Hofstede de Groot, *A Catalogue Raisonné*, etc., VII, London, 1923, pp. 280-1, no. 287; T.
Mankowski, 'La Galerie de Stanislas Auguste', in *Galerja Stanislawa Augusta*, Lwów, 1932, p. 393,
no. 1761, illustrated.
    Christie's London, 19 April 1996 (236**) GBP 67,500   US$ 102,350

BACON Francis (Dublin 1909-1992 Madrid) Irish
WATERCOLOUR 1929 watercolour and bodycolour, 8¼ x 5½in. (21 x 14cm.) sdlr 'F. Bacon 29'
PROV.: Eric Alden, London; Roy de Maitre, London; Mayor Gallery, London.
LIT.: J. Rothenstein (intro) and R. Alley, *Francis Bacon*, London, 1964, no. 1; H.M. Davies, *Francis
Bacon, the early and middle years*, New York and London, 1978, pl. 4.
    Christie's London, 22 May 1996 (6**) GBP 17,250   US$ 26,121

HEAD OF A WOMAN oil on canvas, 31.7 x 21.7in. (90 x 70cm.) (1960)
PROV.: Marlborough Fine Art Ltd., London; Mrs. Elizabeth Blake, Dallas; Mrs. Lewis H. Lapham,
New York.
EXH.: London, Marlborough Fine Art Ltd., *Francis Bacon: Paintings 1959-60*, March-April 1960,
no. 19 (illustrated in the catalogue); Mannheim, Kunsthalle; Turin, Galleria Civica d'Arte Moderna;
Zurich, Kunsthaus; Amsterdam, Stedelijk Museum, *Francis Bacon*, July 1962-February 1963, no.
67; Paris, Galeries Nationales du Grand Palais; Düsseldorf, Kunsthalle, *Francis Bacon*, October
1971-May 1972, pp. 47 and 112, no. 33 (illustrated in the catalogue); Washington, Smithsonian
Institution, Hirshhorn Museum and Sculpture Garden; Los Angeles, The County Museum of Art;
New York, The Museum of Modern Art, *Francis Bacon*, October 1989-August 1990, no. 22
(illustrated in colour in the catalogue).
LIT.: John Rothenstein and Ronald Alley, *Francis Bacon*, London 1964, p. 129, no. 161 (illustrated);
Lorenza Trucchi, *Francis Bacon*, New York 1975, no. 62 (illustrated).
This work is featured in the film *Francis Bacon Paintings 1944-62*, by the Arts Council of Great
Britain and Marlborough Fine Art, London, 1962-63.
    Christie's London, 27 June 1996 (20*) GBP 540,500   US$ 833,462

BACON Henry (1839-1912) American
BEACH AT ETRETAT oil on canvas, 18 x 21 3/4in. (45.7 x 55.2cm.) sdll 'Henry Bacon 1881' inscr.
'Etretat'
   Christie's New York, 23 May 1996 (53**) US$ 63,000   US$ 63,000

THE TEARFUL SCHOOLBOY oil on panel, 12 ¾ x 9½in. (32.5 x 24cm.) sdlr 'Henry Bacon 1867'
   Christie's East, 28 November 1995 (91*) US$ 9,775   US$ 9,775

BAEN Jan de (1633-1702) Dutch
PORTRAIT OF JOHANN MORITZ VON NASSAU WITH A LETTER WITH HIS NAME oil on
canvas, 139 x 116.5cm.
   Dorotheum Vienna, 11 June 1996 (277**) ATS 500,000   US$ 46,410

BAERTLING Olle (Halmstad 1911-1981) Swedish
ARDI oil on canvas, 180 x 92cm. sd 'Baertling 1963' on the reverse
   Bukowskis Stockholm, 24-25 April 1996 (10**) SEK 75,000   US$ 11,362

YOYAM oil on canvas, 81 x 130cm. sd 'Baertling 1970' on the reverse
   Bukowskis Stockholm, 26-27 October 1995 (9**) SEK 80,000   US$ 11,716

BAES Firmin (Sint-Joost-ten-Node 1874-1945 Brussels) Belgian
THE CENTER OF ATTENTION pastel on paper laid down on canvas, 55 x 79in. (139.7 x 200.7cm.)
sdll 'Firmin Baes-/1913.'
   Christie's New York, 2 November 1995 (91**) US$ 79,500   US$ 79,500

BAETS Marc (1700 c. active) Flemish
RIVER LANDSCAPE WITH PROMENADING PEOPLE oil on panel (a pair), each: 15 x 19cm. sll
mono. 'M.B.'
   Étude Tajan Paris, 26 March 1996 (13**) FRF 42,000   US$ 8,302

BAJ Enrico (Milan 1924 b.) Italian
FEMME NUE RENVERSÉE acrylic, collage, wadding and trimming on canvas, 80 x 80cm. sur 'Baj'
LIT.: E. Crispolti, *Catalogo generale Bolaffi dell'opera di Enrico Baj*, ed. Giulio Bolaffi, Turin 1973,
p.205, no.1484.
   Finearte Milan, 19 March 1996 (25**) ITL 16,100,000   US$ 10,301

A MAGIC mixed media and mirror glass, 60 x 59cm. sd '60'
PROV.: Galleria del Naviglio, Milan; Studio Santandrea, Milan; Ercole Grisani, Milan.
LIT.: Enrico Crispolti, *Catalogo Generale Bolaffi dell' Opera di Enrico Baj*, Turin 1973, pag. 103,
no. 643 (illustrated).
   Sotheby's Milan, 28 May 1996 (149**) ITL 10,350,000   US$ 6,647

BAK Samuel (1933 b.)
STILL LIFE oil on canvas, 39 3/8 x 32in. (,100 x 81cm.) sll 'BAK'
   Christie's Tel Aviv, 14 April 1996 (38**) US$ 19,550   US$ 19,550

BIRDS oil on canvas, 15 ¾ x 12 ¾in. (40.3 x 32.5cm.) sll 'BAK'
   Christie's Tel Aviv, 14 April 1996 (40**) US$ 8,050   US$ 8,050

BALDESSARI John (1931 b.) American
CUTTING RIBBON, MAN IN WHEELCHAIR, PAINTING acrylic on black and white photograph,
75 5/8 x 35 5/8in. (192.1 x 90.5cm.) (1988)
PROV.: Sonnabend Gallery, New York.
   Christie's New York, 22 February 1996 (96**) US$ 13,800   US$ 13,800

BALEN Hendrik I van with Jan Brueghel the Younger (1601-1678) (Antwerp 1575-1632 Antwerp) Flemish
DIANA AND HER NYMPHS RESTING IN A WOODLAND GLADE WITH THE SPOILS OF THE CHASE, ACTAEON WITH HIS HOUNDS IN A LANDSCAPE BEYOND oil on panel, 21 x 37in. (53.5 x 93.5cm.) the reverse of the panel bears the brand of the Antwerp Panel Makers' Guild and the makers' mark 'MV' (Michiel Vriendt)

Sotheby's London, 6 December 1995 (156**) GBP 23,000	US$	35,396

BALEN Jan van (1611-1654) Flemish
THE ADORATION OF THE SHEPHERDS oil on transferred panel, 84.3 x 62.1cm.-in a Louis XV-style carved, and gilt frame s (strengthened) and d lr 'I.V Balen/1650'

Christie's Amsterdam, 7 May 1996 (141*) NLG 12,650	US$	7,376

BALESTRA Antonio (attr.) (Verona 1666-1740 Verona) Italian
THE ARTIST IN HIS STUDIO oil on canvas, 151.5 x 222cm.

Christie's Rome, 4 June 1996 (595**) ITL 76,000,000	US$	49,287

BALLA Giacomo (Turin 1871-1958 Rome) Italian
RITMO + RUMORE + VELOCITA D'AUTOMOBILE varnish on paper laid down on canvas, 64.5 x 72.5cm. slc 'Futurballa, Ritmo + rumore + velocitá d' automobile' (1913-14)
EXH.: Turin, Galleria Civica d'Arte Moderna, *Giacomo Balla*, 1963, no. 76, p. 31; Venezia, *XXXIV Esposizione Internazionale d'Arte, 'Quattro maestri del futurismo italiano'*, 1968, no. 18, cat. p. XLIX; Roma, Galleria Nazionale d'Arte Moderne, *Giacomo Balla*, Dec. 1971-Feb 1972, no. 43, p. 165; Paris, Musée d'Art Moderne, *Balla*, May-July 1972, no. 13, pp. 74, 75; Tokyo, *,100 Years of modern Italian Art 1880-1980*, 1980 no. 37; Rome, *Arte Astratta in Italia 1909-1959*, 1980, p. 27 ed. De Luca; Venezia, Palazzo Grassi, *Futurismo & Futurismi*, 1986, p. 83 of the catalogue, ed. Bompiani; Mantova, Palazzo del Té, *L'Auto dipinti*, Sept.-Nov. 1992, p.70, no.11.
LIT.: M. Drudi Gambillo and T. Fiori, *Archivi del Futurismo*, ed. De Luca, Roma 1962, no. 76, pp. 84 and 156; E. Crispolti, preface, in Werner Hofmann, *La Pittura del XX secolo*, ed. Capelli, Bologna 1963; Giovanni Lista, *Giacomo Balla*, ed. Fonte d'Abisso, Modena 1982, no. 323, p. 201; Maurizio Fagiolo dell'Arco, *Balla The Futurist*, ed. Rizzoli, New York 1988, p. 92; *La riabilitazione cognitiva assista da computer*, ed Marrapese, Roma 1989 (illustrated); M. Fagiolo dell'Arco, *Futur-Balla, la vita e le opere*, ed. Electa, Milan, 1992, p. 107.

Finearte Milan, 12 December 1995 (294***) ITL 546,250,000	US$	342,691

COMPENETRAZIONE IRIDESCENTE watercolour on cardboard laid down on canvas, 30.5 x 42cm s 'Balla' (ca.1914)

Finearte Rome, 14 November 1995 (227**) ITL 51,750,000	US$	32,486

AUTOSMORFIA oil on canvas, 55 x 35.5cm (1900)
LIT.: G.Lista, *Balla*, Fonte d`Abisso, Modena, 1982, p.105, no.21.

Finearte Rome, 14 November 1995 (229**) ITL 47,150,000	US$	29,598

FORZE SPAZIALI tempera on board, 18 x 20.5cm. sul 'Balla' (1918)
LIT.: M. Drudi Gambillo-T. Fiori, *Archivi del futurismo*, ed. De Luca, Rome 1962, vol.II, no.373, p.144.

Finearte Milan, 19 March 1996 (70**) ITL 31,050,000	US$	19,866

LINEA DI VELOCITA PIU RUMORE tempera on cardboard, 21 x 26.5cm. slc 'Balla' (1919)

Christie's Milan, 20 November 1995 (130**) ITL 16,499,000	US$	10,357

TRASFORMAZIONI FORME E SPIRITI pencil on 'Fabriano' paper, 48 x 62cm. sdll 'Balla 1918'
PROV.: Sylvia and Joseph Slifka, New York.
EXH.: Madison, Mead Hall-Drew University, *Sixteen Works of Giacomo Balla*, spring 1957.
LIT.: This work will be included in the forthcoming *catalogue raisonné Giacomo Balla*.

Christie's Milan, 20 November 1995 (132**) ITL 55,389,000	US$	34,770

VELOCITA ASTRATTA - AUTO IN CORSA oil on canvas, 20 x 25 ¾in. (50.5 x 65.6cm.) sll
'BALLA' sd and titled on the reverse 'VELOCITA ASTRATTA - auto in corsa - 1913 - BALLA'
PROV.: The Artist; Galleria 'Ongine', Rome, 1951; Dr W. Loeffler, Zurich, by whom purchased from
the above in 1951 and thence by descent; Galerie Bischoffsberger, Zurich, by whom bought from the
above in 1976; Purchased by the present owner circa 1977.
EXH.: Rome, *Galleria 'Origine', Omaggio a Giacomo Balla Futurista*, 1951, no. 7; Winterthur,
Kunstmuseum Winterthur, *il Futurismo*, Oct.-Nov. 1959, no. 3; New York, Sidney Janis Gallery;
Gstaad, Hotel Palace Gstaad, *Les Classiques du XXeme siècle*, 1977, no. 2; Paris, Artcurial, *Giacomo
Balla - Un Art de Vivre*, May-July 1995.
Christie's London, 25 June 1996 (20**) GBP 749,500

	US$	1,155,744

PALPA ink on paper, 32 x 21.5cm. sdll 'Futurballa 1916' (1916)
PROV.: famiglia Balla.
Finearte Milan, 26 October 1995 (168**) ITL 20,700,000

	US$	12,897

COMPENETRAZIONE IRIDESCENTE, STUDIO watercolour and pencil on paper, 12.5 x 19cm.
(ca 1913)
EXH.: Basilea, *Balla e i futuristi*, 1989, under supervision of M. Fagiolo dell'Arco, p.22.
LIT.: M. Fagiolo dell;Arco, *Futurballa, la vita e le opere*, ed. Electa, Milan 1992, p.100; *Balla, The
Futurist*, ed. Rizzoli, New York 1987, p.69.
Finearte Milan, 26 October 1995 (169**) ITL 20,125,000

	US$	12,539

PAESAGGIO FUTURISTA tempera on cardboard, 43.5 x 61.5cm. slc 'FUTUR BALLA' (1920/23)
PROV.: Private collection, Zürich.
EXH.: Paris, Musée d'Art Moderne, 1972; Roma, Galleria 'Il Collezionista'; Roma, Galleria d'arte
San Marco; Napoli, Il Centro, galleria d'arte contemporanea.
LIT.: Exhibition catalogue, *Balla*, Musée d'Art Moderne, Paris 1972, p. 142; Giovanni Lista,
Giacomo Balla. Futuriste, L'Age d'Homme, p. 219, no. 1203 (illustrated p. 18).
Wiener Kunst Auktionen, 27 September 1995 (409**) ATS 300,000

	US$	29,161

BALLABENE Rudolf Raimund (Zurndorf 1890-1968 Vienna) Austrian
TONSCHÖPFUNG oil on canvas, ,100 x 90cm. s with monogram and dlr 'R R B 52'
Wiener Kunst Auktionen, 27 September 1995 (439**) ATS 70,000

	US$	6,804

BALLAVOINE Jules Frédéric (1855-1901) French
A QUIET SPOT oil on panel, 22 ¾ x 14in. (57.8 x 35.5cm.) sll 'J. Ballavoine'
Christie's East, 20 May 1996 (235*) US$ 18,400

	US$	18,400

BALLESIO Federico (19th Century) Italian
THE CARPET SELLER watercolour on paper laid down on paperboard, 21¼ x 29 ¾in. (54 x
75.6cm.) sll inscr. 'Ballesio./Roma. Tivoli'
Christie's New York, 10 January 1996 (40**) US$ 40,250

	US$	40,250

BALTEN Pieter (Antwerp 1525-1598) Flemish
LANDSCAPE WITH HERDSMAN DEFENDING HIS SHEEP oil on panel, 50 x 72cm.
Dorotheum Vienna, 6 March 1996 (90**) ATS 500,000

	US$	48,095

BALTHUS Balthazar Klossowski de Rola, {called} (Paris 1908 b.) French
PORTRAIT DE MADAME HEDWIG MÜLLER oil on canvas, 31 7/8 x 25 5/8in. (81 x 65cm.) sll
'Balthus'; s again d and titled on the reverse 'Balthus Hedwig Müller peint à Zurich en 1924'
LIT.: ed. D. Bozo, *Balthus*, Paris 1983 (Centre Georges Pompidou exhibition catalogue) no. 16
(illustrated, p. 342); J. Leymarie, *Balthus*, Geneva 1990, p. 123.
Christie's New York, 1 May 1996 (172**) US$ 34,500

	US$	34,500

JEUNE FILLE ENDORMIE pencil on paper, 22 x 16 ¾in. (56 x 42.5cm.) (1956-1957)
PROV.: E.V Thaw & Co., New York; B.C Holland Gallery, Chicago.

EXH.: Chicago, The Museum of Contemporary Art, *Balthus in Chicago*, Aug.-Nov., 1980, no.29 (illustrated, p.8); Chicago, The Art Institute, *Chicago Collects; Selections from the Collection of Dr. Eugene A. Solow*, May-Aug.,1988, no.4.
LIT.: Virginie Minnier will include this drawing in the *Balthus catalogue raisonné* to be published by Editions Gallimard, Paris.
Christie's New York, 1 May 1996 (251**) US$ 85,000 — US$ 85,000

JEUNE FILLE LISANT pencil on paper, 14 ¾ x 11in. (37.5 x 27.9cm.) slr 'Balthus'
PROV.: Mlle. Frédérique Tison (acquired from the artist); Acquired from the above by the present owner on 3 December 1972.
EXH.: Neuchâtel, Galerie Arts Anciens, 1975.
Sotheby's New York, 2 May 1996 (287**) US$ 32,200 — US$ 32,200

LE JARDIN DU LUXEMBOURG oil on canvas, 25 ¾ x 19½in. (65.4 x 49.5cm.) sll 'Balthus' (ca 1927)
LIT.: This work is to be included in the forthcoming *Balthus catalogue raisonné* currently being prepared by Virginie Monnier under the direction of Gérard Réguier.
Christie's London, 26 June 1996 (300**) GBP 29,900 — US$ 46,106

BALZE Raymond (Rome 1818-1909) Italian (French)
ODE TO RAPHAEL oil on canvas, 86.5 x 114.5cm. sdlr 'R. BALZE P FLORENCE 1861'
Étude Tajan Paris, 12 December 1995 (119**) FRF 90,000 — US$ 18,128

BARANOFF-ROSSINÉ Vladimir (1888-1942) French (Russian)
ADAM ET EVE oil on canvas, 61 x 86½in. (154.9 x 219cm.) sd ini. '1912'
PROV.: Family of the artist, Paris.
EXH.: London, Rutland Gallery, *Vladimir Baranoff-Rossiné*, 1970, no. 57, illustrated; Paris, Galerie Verneuil Saints Peres, *Baranoff-Rossiné, 1888-1944*, 1984, no. 23, illustrated p. 25.
LIT.: P. Breuillard-Limondin and M.J. Mausset, *Baranoff-Rossiné*, University of Paris VIII, 1979-80, no. 236, illustrated p. 88.
Sotheby's New York, 2 May 1996 (195**) US$ 96,000 — US$ 96,000

BARATTI Filippo (19th Century, late) British
GUNSMITHS AT THE PALACE OF ALHAMBRA, GRANADA oil on panel, 23 5/8 x 32in. (60.1 x 81.3cm.) sdll. 'F. Baratti 1878'; and inscr. 'Una Scetta d' nella Sala dell' Alhambra/Granada/Dipinti da Fillippo Baratti/par/Il Sig. Mr. F; Nathan/Londra/1878' on the reverse
PROV.: F. Nathan, London, 1878.
Christie's New York, 2 November 1995 (47**) US$ 129,000 — US$ 129,000

BARBARINI Emil (Vienna 1855-1930 Vienna) Austrian
BLUMENSTANDELN AM NASCHMARKT oil on panel, 20.8 x 31.5cm. slr 'E.Barbarini'
Wiener Kunst Auktionen, 29 November 1995 (585**) ATS 130,000 — US$ 13,041

BARBELLI Giangiacomo (Crema 1590-1656) Italian
THE INFANCY OF CHRIST oil on canvas, in a painted arched top, 122 x 59in. (310 x 150cm.)
Christie's London, 20 October 1995 (27**) GBP 10,925 — US$ 17,243

BARBIERI Giovanni Francesco {called} Guercino (Bologna 1591-1666) Italian
SASANNAH AND HER ELDERS red chalk, laid down, 30.5 x 33.2cm.
Phillips London, 5 July 1995 (149***) GBP 140,000 — US$ 223,321

BARBIERI Giovanni Francesco {called} Guercino (and studio) (Cento 1591-1666 Bologna) Italian
THE SYBIL HELLESPONTICA oil on canvas, 38½ x 33in. (98 x 84cm.) inscr. 'ILLE DEI LEGEM COMPLE:/BIT. NON VIOLABIT/SIBILLA/HELLESPONTICA'
PROV.: Frederick, 1st Marquess of Bristol.

LIT.: 1st Marquess, 1837, no. 1, as 'Sibyl by Guercino' and as hanging in the library; Gage, 1838, pp. 303-9, as in the library; *The Antique Collector*, 1961, p.219; *Inventory*, 1910, p. 9.; Farrer, 1913, no. 49, as Landscape with figures, 'a copy of a picture by Claude Gellée, called Claude Lorrain'; *Inventory*, 1952, p. 10, as *after Claude Lorraine*; Figgis, 1992, p. 40.

Sotheby's London, 11-12 June 1996 (478**) GBP 65,300	US$	100,694

BARCELO Miguel (1957 b.) Spanish
BODEGON PERILLOS mixed media on canvas, 76 ¾ x 90½in. (195 x 230cm.) sd '1984' on the reverse
PROV.: Galerie Bischofberger, Zurich.
EXH.: Bordeaux, Musée d'Art Contemporain; Madrid, Palacio de Velasquez; Boston, Institute of Contemporary Art, *Miguel Barcelo:Paintings from 1983-1985*, May 1985-April 1986 (illustrated in colour in the catalogue p.73).

Christie's London, 19 March 1996 (66**) GBP 54,300	US$	82,926

QUELQUES OBJETS DANS LE FLEUVE oil on canvas, 102 3/8 x 118 1/8in. (260 x 300cm.) sd and titled 'Paris I. 85' on the reverse
PROV.: Jan Eric Loewenadler, New York; acquired from the above by the present owner.
EXH.: Bordeaux, Musée d'Art Contemporain; Madrid, Palacio de Velasquez; Boston, Institute of Contemporary Art, *Miguel Barcelo:Paintings from 1983-1985*, May 1985-April 1986 (illustrated in colour in the catalogue p.84).

Christie's London, 19 March 1996 (70**) GBP 23,000	US$	35,125

BARDELLINO Pietro (Naples 1731 c.-1806 Naples) Italian
MARTIRIO DI SANT'ORSOLA oil on canvas, 51 x 31.5cm.

Finearte Rome, 22 November 1995 (158**) ITL 18,400,000	US$	11,551

A MAN PLAYING THE LUTE / A CONCERT oil on canvas (a pair), 36½ x 37 ¾in. (93 x 96cm.) (ca. 1770)
PROV.: With Thos Agnew and Sons, london, 1966, from whom acquired by the present owner.
EXH.: London, Thos. Agnew and Sons, *Baroque and Rococo in Italy*, nos. 23 and 25, as by Francesco de Mura.
LIT.: N. Spinosa, *Pittura napoletana del Settecento dal Rococo al Classicismo*, 1987, p. 121. no. 158.

Sotheby's London, 6 December 1995 (199**) GBP 34,500	US$	53,093

BARGUE Charles (1825 ca-1883) French
L'ALMÉE (TOGETHER WITH PENCIL STUDY OF L'ALMÉE) oil on panel (pencil on paper), 16 3/8 x 9 5/8in. (41.6 x 24.5cm.) / 11 x 7in. (28 x 17.9cm.) sdlr 'BARGUE-79-'
PROV.: With Goupil & Co., Paris, June 1879, commissioned from the artist, (bt. Samuel P. Avery for William H. Vanderbilt, New York for 35,000 gold francs); Thence by descent to William H. Vanderbilt; Thence by descent to brigadier General Cornelius Vanderbilt; William H. Vanderbilt Collection; sale Parke-Bernet, New York, April 18 and 19, 1945, p. 79, no. 110 (illustrated) (sold by the order of Mrs. Cornelius Vanderbilt); Private Collection, New York (until 1986).
EXH.: New York, The Metropolitan Museum of Art, 1902-1919 (lent by George W. Vanderbilt).
LIT.: J.D. Champlin, Jr., *Cyclopedia of Paintings*, New York, 1900, I, p. 100; E. Strahan (E. Shinn), *Mr. Vanderbilt's House and Collection*, Boston, 1883, III, p. 12 (and illustrated in detail) Thieme-Becker, *Künstler-Lexikon*, Leipzig, 1908, vol. II, p. 496.

Christie's New York, 2 November 1995 (46**) US$ 96,000	US$	96,000

BARKER Wright, R.B.A. (1880 c.-1941 d.) British
HIS RESERVED SEAT oil on canvas, 36½ x 28¼in. (92.7 x 71.8cm.) sdll 'Wright Barker/1895'

Christie's New York, 2 November 1995 (214**) US$ 14,950	US$	14,950

BARLACH Ernst (Wedel 1870-1938 Güstrow) German
LEGENDE 1 charcoal on paper, 24.2 x 19.9cm. sll 'E Barlach' (1923/24)

Hauswedell & Nolte Cologne, 1 December 1995 (26**) DEM 22,000	US$	15,264

DREI HEXEN ink over pencil on paper, 32.5 x 31.5cm. slr 'Ebarlach'
LIT.: Ed. Carl Einstein, *Neue Blätter*, vol. I, script 4, Berlin 1912, p. 25.

Hauswedell & Nolte Cologne, 5/6 June 1996 (25*) DEM 32,000	US$	20,791

BARNES Robert, A.R.W.S. (19th Century) British
A MERRY-GO ROUND ON THE ICE pencil and watercolour with gum arabic and scratching out, 13 5/8 x 22½in. (34.6 x 57.2cm.) sd 'R. Barnes 1888' on the sledge
EXH.: London, *Royal Society of Painters in Watercolours*, 1888. no.309.

Christie's London, 29 March 1996 (43**) GBP 20,125	US$	30,735

BARNOIN Henri-Alphonse (20th Century) French
MARKET DAY, CONCARNEAU oil on canvas, 23 ¾ x 28 ¾in. (60.5 x 73cm.) sll 'H. Barnoin'

Phillips London, 14 November 1995 (63**) GBP 4,200	US$	6,570

BARON Henri-Charles-Antoine (1816-1885) French
DANS LE JARDIN oil on panel, 21 7/8 x 18 1/8in. (55.6 x 46cm.) s 'H Baron'

Christie's London, 14 June 1996 (54**) GBP 29,900	US$	46,106

BARONZIO Giovanni (Rimini active 1343-1345-) Italian
JESUS CLIMBING THE CAVALRY ROAD tempera on panel, 15.5 x 17cm.

Finearte Milan, 3 April 1996 (128**) ITL 62,100,000	US$	39,681

BARRA Didier {called} Monsu Desiderio (II) (attr.) (Metz 1590-1647, after Naples) Italian (Lorraine)
THE TORTURE OF ST. GENNARO oil on canvas, 63 x 101.5cm.
PROV.: Sale, Milan, Finearte, 20 November 1985.
LIT.: M.R. Napp, *François de Nomè e Didier Barra, l'enigma Monsù Desiderio*, Rome, 1991, D62, pp. 395-306 and C20, p. 243.

Christie's Rome, 4 June 1996 (598**) ITL 32,000,000	US$	20,752

BARRAUD Henry (1811-1874)
STUDY OF A BAY HUNTER AND A CHESTNUT HUNTER IN A WOODED RIVER LANDSCAPE oil on canvas, 31 5/8 x 48¼in. (81.5 x 122.5cm.) indistinctly sdlr

Phillips London, 18 June 1996 (53**) GBP 14,500	US$	22,359

BARRET George, Senior, R.A. (1728/32-1784) British
A WOODED RIVER LANDSCAPE WITH ANGLERS AND RUINED MILL oil on canvas, 39½ x 49in. (100.3 x 124.5cm.) sll 'G. Barret' (before 1762)
PROV.: H. Russell, Canterbury; Mrs. Marshall Russell, Aiken, South Carolina, by 1938; M. Knoedler & Co., New York; from whom purchased by Ralph Beaver Strassburger, Gwynedd Valley, Pennsylvania, October, 1940; thence by descent to J.A. Peter Strassburger, Normandy Farms, Blue Bell, Pennsylvania, and by descent in the family.
EXH.: Dallas, Joseph Sartor Galleries, *Famous Paintings*, April 9-23, 1939, no., 6; New Haven, Yale University, Gallery of Fine Arts, *Exhibition of Eighteenth-Century Italian Landscape Painting and its Influence in England*, January 18-February 25, 1940, no. 36, (illustrated).

Sotheby's New York, 11 January 1996 (103**) US$ 57,500	US$	57,500

FIGURES AND A DONKEY ON PATH IN A WOODED RIVER LANDSCAPE oil on canvas, 38½ x 50 ¾in. (98 x 129cm.)

Phillips London, 12 December 1995 (49**) GBP 12,000	US$	18,467

BARTLETT Jennifer (1941 b.) American
9 PLATE SERIES baked enamel and silkscreen ink on nine steel plates, each: 12 x 12in. (30.5 x 30.5cm.) each titled and numbered consecutively '9 plate series (1-9)' on the reverse (1972)

PROV.: Acquired directly from the artist.
      Christie's New York, 15 November 1995 (363**) US$ 13,800   US$ 13,800

BARZAGHI Cattaneo Antonio (1834-1922) Italian
LADY JANE GREY oil on canvas, 76 ¾ x 26 3/8in. (195 x 67cm.) s mono 'CB'
EXH.: Roma, *Esposizione di Belle Arti*, no. 1, as 'Giovanna Grey'.
      Phillips London, 11th June 1996 (69**) GBP 7,500   US$ 11,565

BASELITZ Georg (Deutschbaselitz/Oberlauslitz 1938 b.) German
WEINSTOCK dispersion on canvas, 63 ¾ x 51 3/16in. (162 x 130cm.) slr with ini. and dlr '69
PROV.: Galerie Franz Dahlem, Darmstadt.
EXH.: Berlin, Nationalgalerie Altes Museum, *Georg Baselitz: Bilder aus Berliner Privatbesitz*,
April-June 1990, no. 12 (illus. in colour in cat. p. 41); Milan, Galleria del Credito Valtellinese,
Refettorio delle Stelline, *Georg Baselitz*, April 1990-July 1991, no. 9 (illus. in colour in cat. p.73).
      Christie's London, 27 June 1996 (70**) GBP 84,000   US$ 129,530

UNTITLED oil and pastel on paper laid down on canvas, 105 x 59¼in. (266.7 x 150.5cm.) sdlr ini.
'16.IV.87'
PROV.: Galerie Meyer-Hohmeister, Karlsruhe; Pierre Nahon, Paris.
EXH.: Karlsruhe, Galerie Meyer-Hohmeister, *Georg Baselitz, Fünf farbige Arbeiten auf Canson*,
October 1987 (illustrated in the catalogue p. 5); Basel Kunstmuseum, *Georg Baselitz: Der Vorhang
'Anna Selbdritt' von 1987 und die dazugehörigen Zeichnungen*, June-August 1993, no. 2 (illustrated
in the catalogue p. 13, pl. 4).
      Christie's London, 27 June 1996 (74**) GBP 100,500   US$ 154,973

PEITSCHENFRAU watercolour and pencil on paper, 23 3/8 x 19 1/8in. (62 x 48.5cm.) slc 'G.
Baselitz' (1964)
      Sotheby's London, 27 June 1996 (216**) GBP 29,900   US$ 46,106

DIE FRAU IN DER TUR oil and tempera on canvas, 130 x 98½in. (330 x 250cm.) sd 'GB 79'
PROV.: The Saatchi Collection, London; acquired from the above by the present owner.
LIT.: Ex. Cat. *Georg Baselitz*, Kunstverein, Braunschweig 1981 (illustrated p. 116, incorrectely
titled); Rudi Fuchs, Hilton Kramer, Peter Schjeldahl, *Art of our Time, The Saatchi Collection:
Baselitz, Guston, Kiefer, Morley, Polke, Schnabel*, London, no. 12 (illustrated in the catalogue).
      Christie's London, 30 November 1995 (46**) GBP 139,000   US$ 217,425

ADLER oil on canvas-unframed, 98½ x 78 3/4in. (,250 x 200cm.) sdlr '1977 G. Baselitz'; sd and
titled 'G. Baselitz Adler Mai/Juni 1977' on the reverse
PROV.: Galerie Heiner Friedrich, Cologne.
EXH.: Kunsthalle Düsseldorf, *Georg Baselitz, Gerhard Richter*, May-July 1981, n.n. (illustrated);
London, Whitechapel Art Gallery; Amsterdam, Stedelijk Museum and Basel, Kunsthalle, *Georg
Baselitz: Paintings 1960-1983*, July 1983-April 1984, p. 94, no. 24.
      Christie's New York, 14 November 1995 (49**) US$ 189,500   US$ 189,500

BLAUER ELKEKOPF oil on canvas, 78 3/4 x 63½in. (,200 x 161.3cm.) sdlr 'Baselitz 80' (1980)
PROV.: Acquired directly from the artist; Galerie Fred Jahn, München.
LIT.: A. Haase, *Gespräche mit Künstlern*, Cologne, 1982, p. 21 (illustrated).
      Christie's New York, 7 May 1996 (37**) US$ 178,500   US$ 178,500

BASOEKI ABDULLAH R. (1915-1993) Indonesian (?)
A BEAUTY WITH A PURPLE SHAWL oil on canvas, 90 x 60cm. Sdll '54'
PROV.: Acquired direcly from the Artist by the present owner.
      Sotheby's Amsterdam, 23 April 1996 (67*) NLG 30680   US$ 18,230

IMPRESSION OF CAIRO',- A BEARDED MAN WITH A CHILD oil on canvas, ,100 x 75cm. slr
PROV.: Acquired directly from the Artist by the present owner.
       Sotheby's Amsterdam, 23 April 1996 (69*) NLG 25,960   US$ 15,426

BASQUIAT Jean Michel (1960-1988) American
AIR POWER oil on canvas, 66 x 60in. (167.6 x 152.4cm.) sd and titled '1984' on the reverse
PROV.: Mary Boone Gallery, New York, Galerie Bruno Bischofberger, Zurich; Warsh Rankin-Reid
Fine Art Ltd., New York.
       Christie's London, 30 November 1995 (51**) GBP 78,500   US$ 122,791

UNTITLED coloured crayons on paper, 20½ x 14½in. (52.1 x 36.8cm.) (ca. 1983)
PROV.: Acquired directly from the artist.
       Christie's East, 7 May 1996 (144**) US$ 16,100   US$ 16,100

HENRY GELDZAHLER graphite, oil and paper collage on panel, 23 7/8 x 10in. (60.6 x 75.4cm.)
(ca.1982)
PROV.: Acquired directly from the artist.
       Christie's New York, 8 May 1996 (108**) US$ 40,250   US$ 40,250

ZING acrylic and coloured oilsticks on canvas, unframed, 60 x 40in. (152.3 x 101.6cm.) sd and titled
"ZING' 1984 Jean Michel Basquiat' on the reverse
PROV.: Mary Boone Gallery, New York; Galerie Michael Werner, Cologne.
       Christie's New York, 8 May 1996 (413**) US$ 10,700   US$ 10,700

SAMO acrylic, coloured crayons and coloured felt-tip pens on canvas, 39 x 50 3/4in. (99 x 129cm.)
titled and d 'SAMO NEW YORK 1981' on the reverse
PROV.: Private collection, New York.
       Christie's New York, 15 November 1995 (322**) US$ 51,750   US$ 51,750

BASSANO Gerolamo da Ponte (Bassano 1566-1621 Venice) Italian
CHRIST WITH MARTHA AND MARY oil on canvas, 89.5 x 148cm.
       Étude Tajan Paris, 28 June 1996 (40*) FRF 46,000   US$ 8,883

BASSANO Jacopo da Ponte, {called} (Bassano del Grappa 1510 c.-1592 Bassano del Grappa) Italian
ANNUNCIATION TO THE SHEPHERDS oil on canvas, 43¼ x 35 5/8in. (109.9 x 90.5cm.) (late 1550's)
PROV.: John Deacon, Mabledon, Tondbridge, Kent, by 1830 (and hanging in the chapel of that house); Sale, Lawrence's, Bletchingley, Surrey, 5-7 September 1989, lot 1512; where purchased by the present owner.
       Sotheby's New York, 16 May 1996 (26**) US$ 68,500   US$ 68,500

SPRING oil on canvas, 31¼ x 40½in. (79.3 x 102.9cm.)
       Christie's South Kensington, 18 April 1996 (118*) GBP 5,750   US$ 8,719

Annunciation to the Shepherds

PORTRAIT OF A BEARDED MAN oil on paper laid down on panel, 10¼ x 7 3/8in. (26 x 18.7cm.)
       Sotheby's New York, 11 January 1996 (195**) US$ 34,500   US$ 34,500

BASSEN Bartholomeus van (Antwerp 1590 c.-1652 The Hague) Flemish
A CATHEDRAL INTERIOR WITH FIGURES oil on canvas, 52 x 58½in. (132 x 148in.) sll 'B. van
Bassen f/1642'
        Sotheby's London, 17 April 1996 (58**) GBP 18,400   US$ 27,900

A CAPRICCIO OF A CLASSICAL CHURCH INTERIOR, WITH A WOMAN WITH A CHILD IN
FRONT OF AN ALTAR oil on panel, 19 ¾ x 26½in. (59 x 67.5cm.) dur 'ANNO. 1635'
PROV.: Anon. sale, Amsterdam, Sotheby's Mak van Waay, 26 April 1977, lot 4 where bought by the
present owner.
        Sotheby's London, 17 April 1996 (655**) GBP 10,350   US$ 15,694

BATONI Pompeo Girolamo (Follower of) (Lucca 1708-1787 Rome) Italian
THE MADONNA AND CHILD WITH THE INFANT SAINT JOHN THE BAPTIST oil on copper
(oval), 16 x 13in. (40.8 x 33cm.) s '.onca'
        Christie's South Kensington, 6 November 1995 (2**) GBP 18,000   US$ 28,156

BATTAGLIOLI Francesco (Modena 1722 ca. b.) Italian
A CAPRICCIO OF AN AVENUE ON THE OUTSKIRTS OF A TOWN WITH ELEGANT
COUPLES AND TOWNFOLK PROMENADING oil on canvas, 19 3/8 x 28 3/8in. (49.3 x 72cm.)
        Christie's London, 7 July 1995 (399**) GBP 27,600   US$ 44,026

BAUCHANT André (Chateau-Renault 1873-1958 Montoire) French
PAYSAGE BUCOLIQUE oil on panel, 13 x 15 ¾in. (33 x 40cm.) sdlm '1936 A Bouchard'
PROV.: Charles Laughton, esq.; Private collection London.
EXH.: Rhode Island School of Design; Museum of Art, *Providence*, R.I., 1943.
        Phillips London, 26 June 1995 (26**) GBP 8,000   US$ 12,765

OISEAUX DANS LES ARBRES oil on canvas, 21¼ x 25 5/8in. (54 x 65cm) sdlr 'A Bauchant 1930'
        Christie's London, 26 June 1996 (331**) GBP 14,950   US$ 23,053

PERSONNAGES AU BORD DE LA MER oil on canvas, 30¼ x 38¼in. (77 x 97.8cm.) sdlc 'A.
Bauchant 1928'
PROV.: Galerie Kriegel, Paris; Galerie Shapiro, Paris.
EXH.: Munich, Haus der Kunst, *Die Kunst der Naiven* 1974, no. 199; Amsterdam,. Stedelijk
Museum, *De Grote Naieven: Rousseau, Seraphine, Bauchant, Bombois, Vinvin*, 1975. The exhibition
traveled to Galerie Kriegel, Paris, 1976.
        Christie's East, 30 April 1996 (107**) US$ 9,200   US$ 9,200

BAUDESSON Nicolas (Troyes 1611-1680 Paris) French
FLOWERS IN A VASE oil on linen, 41x 32cm.
        Dorotheum Vienna, 17 October 1995 (155**) ATS 220,000   US$ 22,067

BAUER Johann Gottlieb (Frankfurt am Main 1822-1882) German
KAISER FRANZ JOSEPH I. VON ÖSTERREICH, IN DER GALAUNIFORM EINES
FELDMARCHALLS MIT DEM ORDEN VOM GOLDENEN VLIES, MIT DEN
GROßKREUZSTERNEN DES MILITÄR-MARIA-THERESIN, -DES ST. STEPHANS, -DES
LEOPOLDS, -DES EISERNE-KRONE-ORDENS, SOWIE DEM RUSSISCHEN ST. GEORGS-
KREUZ VI. KLASSE / KAISERIN ELISABETH IM EFEUSCHMUCK oil on canvas (an oval pair),
73 x 58cm. both sd 'J.G. Bauer Junior 1857'
        Dorotheum Vienna, 6 November 1995 (5**) ATS 160,000   US$ 16,050

BAUER Mari Alexander Jacques (Marius) (Den Haag 1867-1932 Amsterdam) Dutch
FIGURES BY A MOSQUE, CAIRO oil on canvas, 55 x 35cm. slr titled 'M Bauer'
PROV.: Kunsthandel E.J. van Wisselingh and Co., Amsterdam, inv.no.1722.
        Christie's Amsterdam, 26 October 1995 (33**) NLG 12,650   US$ 7,976

COURTYARD OF AN ORIENTAL PALACE oil on canvas, 54 x 74cm. s 'M Bauer'
PROV.: Kunsthandel E.J. van Wisselingh and Co., Amsterdam,inv.no.3420.
EXH.: The Hague, Panorama Mesdag, year unknown; Amsterdam, Kunsthandel E.J. van Wisselingh
and Co., Oct.-Nov. 1917, no.14 (?).

Christie's Amsterdam, 26 October 1995 (34*) NLG 12,650	US$	7,976

BAUER Rudolph (Lindenwald Silezia 1889-1953 Deal/New Jersey) German
TEMPO oil on board, 29 x 41in. (73.8 x 104.1cm.) sll 'Rudolf Bauer' (1918)
PROV.: The Solomon R. Guggenheim Museum, New York (deaccessioned in 1979); Donald
Karshan, Southhampton, New York (acquired by the present owner, 1983).
LIT.: *Art of Tomorrow: Fifth Catalogue of The Solomon R. Guggenheim Collection of Non-Objective
Paintings*, New York, 1939, pl. 18 (illustrated).

Christie's East, 7 November 1995 (204**) US$ 20,700	US$	20,700

BAUERFEIND Gustav (1848-1904) German
DAVIDSTRASSE, JERUSALEM oil on canvas, 50 7/8 x 35½in. (129.2 x 90.2cm.) sdlr
'G.Bauerfeind (sic) 1887/Jerusalem'

Christie's Tel Aviv, 14 April 1996 (6**) US$ 158,700	US$	158,700

STREET SCENE IN JERUSALEM oil on panel, 10½ x 8in. (26.5 x 20.3cm.) s and inscr. ll 'G.
Bauernfeind Jerusalem'
PROV.: M.E. Lorentin, 1908.

Christie's Tel Aviv, 12 October 1995 (5**) US$ 90,500	US$	90,500

AN ARAB STREET SCENE oil on panel, 20½ x 29½in. (52.1 x 74.9cm.) s 'G Bauernfeind'
PROV.: W.S. Hoare Esq.; Christie's, 17 Feb 1912, lot 161 (sold for 33gns.).

Christie's London, 15 March 1996 (128**) GBP 45,500	US$	69,487

BAUGNIET Charles (Brussels 1814-1886 Sèvres) Belgian
THE BRIDE oil on panel, 22¼ x 17 1/8in. (56.5 x 43.5cm.) sll 'C. Baugniet'

Christie's New York, 14 February 1996 (98**) US$ 20,700	US$	20,700

BAUM Paul (1859-1932) German
KOPFWEIDENREIHE AN SONNIGEN FRÜHLINGSWIESEN MIT SCHILFGRAS DURCH
WACHSENEM BACH oil on canvas framed, 60 x 50cm. sll 'Paul Baum' (1906)

Lempertz, Cologne, 29 November 1995 (22**) DEM 65,000	US$	45,878

BAUMEISTER Willi (Stuttgart 1889-1955 Stuttgart) German
LINIENKOMPOSITION MIT MUSCHELFORM crayon, coloured crayon and charcoal on paper,
39.3 x 36.9cm. sdlr 'Baumeister 32/ 161'

Hauswedell & Nolte Cologne, 1 December 1995 (34*) DEM 19,000	US$	13,183

FARBIGE ZONEN II. oil on paper, 47 x 56cm. sdul '. 4.46' (1946)

Hauswedell & Nolte Cologne, 5/06 June 1996 (39**) DEM 115,000	US$	74,719

FARBIGE BEWEGUNG oil on board, 65 x 81cm. sdlr 'Baumeister 3 51', sd again and titled with
pencil '3, 1951 Farbige Bewegung I. Fass. 81 x 65 cm Baumeister' on the reverse
PROV.: Collection Alexander v.Wölffel, Essen.

Lempertz Cologne, 1 June 1996 (571**) DEM 180,000	US$	116,951

FIGUREN-MAUER watercolour and goache on paper, 12 x 18½in. (30.5 x 47cm.) sdlr 'Baumeister
47'
PROV.: Marlborough Fine Art Ltd., London; Galerie Roman Norbert Ketterer, Campione; Galerie
Evelyn Hagenbeck, Hamburg; Petteplace Gallery, Hamilton, Ontario.
EXH.: London, Marlborough Fine Art Ltd., *Expressionism, Bauhaus, Dada: Drawings,
Waterercolours,Collages*, 1966, no. 5, illustrated.

LIT.: Felicitas Karg-Baumeister, *Willi Baumeister, Werkverzeichnis der Zeichnungen, Gouachen und Collagen*, Cologne 1988, p. 313, no. 1809, illustrated.

Sotheby's London, 21 March 1996 (1**) GBP 11,500   US$ 17,563

GEISTER MIT ROT (PART OF HIS SERIES 'AFRIKANISCHE GEISTER') oil on hardboard, 11 5/8 x 15 5/8in. (29 x 39.8cm.) sdlr 'Baumeister 59'

Sotheby's London, 21 March 1996 (15**) GBP 17,250   US$ 26,344

REIHE 1944 oil on canvas, 19½ x 47¼in. (49.7 x 120cm.) sd and titled 'W. Baumeister Komposition W. Baumeister 1944 Reihe' on the reverse (1944)
LIT.: W. Grohmann, *Willi Baumeister, Life and Work*, London and Cologne, 1963, no. 725, p. 296.

Christie's London, 26 June 1996 (255**) GBP 18,400   US$ 28,373

TENNISSPIELER MIT ZUSCHAUERN charcoal and pencil on cardboard, 18½ x 14½in. (47 x 37cm.) sdlr 'Baumeister 35' and numbered '319a'
PROV.: Petteplace Gallery, Hamilton, Ontario.
LIT.: Dietmar J. Ponert, *Willi Baumeister, Werksverzeichnis der Zeichnungen, Gouachen und Collagen*, Cologne 1988, p. 223, no. 570 (illustrated).

Sotheby's London, 27 June 1996 (137**) GBP 12,075   US$ 18,620

KEGELSPIEL IN METAPHYSISCHER LANDSCHAFT I oil on canvas, 31½ x 25¼in. (80 x 64cm.) sdlr 'Baumeister 10.46'
PROV.: Purchased from the Artist by the father of the present owner in 1947.
EXH.: Strasbourg, Chateau des Rohand, *La Grande Aventure de l'Art du XXième Siècle*, Jan.-Sept. 1963, no. 12.
LIT.: W. Grohmann, *Willi Baumeister: Life and Work*, Cologne, no. 1083, p. 312 (the dimensions inverted).

Christie's London, 28 November 1995 (48**) GBP 183,000   US$ 286,251

BAUMGARTNER Peter (1834-1911) German
FIGURES IN AN INTERIOR oil on panel, 9 ¾ x 12¼in. (24.8 x 31.2cm.) slr 'P Baumgartner.'

Christie's New York, 14 February 1996 (81**) US$ 18,400   US$ 18,400

BAZIOTES William (Pittsburgh (Pennsylvania) 1912-1963 New York) American
WATER REFLECTIONS coloured chalks and charcoal on paper mounted on panel, 38¼ x 25in. (95.6 x 63.5cm.) slr 'Baziotes' (1953)
PROV.: Kootz Gallery, New York.
EXH.: New York, Whitney Museum of American Art, *Annual Exhibition*, Nov. 1955-Jan. 1953no. 83.

Christie's New York, 15 November 1995 (145**) US$ 34,500   US$ 34,500

BEARDEN Romare (1914-1988) American
CALL TO THE LOA watercolour and paper collage on paper, 30 x 22¼in. (76.2 x 56.5cm.) slc 'Romare Bearden'; titled 'Call to the Loa' on the reverse

Christie's East, 7 May 1996 (90*) US$ 8,625   US$ 8,625

BEAUBRUN Charles (et Henri Beaubrun 1603-1677) (Amboise 1602 ca.-1660 Paris) French
LA GRANDE MADEMOISELLE EN ATHÉNA oil on canvas, 75.5 x 63cm.

Étude Tajan Paris, 26 March 1996 (74**) FRF 72,000   US$ 14,232

BECCAFUMI Domenico Mecarino, {called} (Valdibiana 1486 c.-1551 Siena) Italian
VIEW OF PISA: DESIGN FOR THE STAGE pen and brown ink, brown and pink wash, pricked for the compass, 7¼ x 15¼in. (18.3 x 38.5cm.) inscr. 'perino del vaga' numb. '85' (1536-1540)
PROV.: J. Pope-Hennesy.
EXH.: London, The Courtauld Institute, *Exhibition of Architectural and Decorative Drawings*, 1941, no. 41; Munich, Haus der Kunst, *Das Aquarell, 1400-1950*, 1972-1973, pp. 54-55, no. 59, illustrated;

Florence, *Il potere e lo spazio. La scena del Principe*,1980, pp. 337-8, no. 3.2; Siena, Pinacoteca
Nazionale di Siena, *Domenico Beccafumi e il suo tempo*, 1990, no. 139, illustrated.
LIT.: J. Pope-Hennessy, *Some Aspects of the Cinquecento in Siena*, Art in America, 1943, XXXI, pp.
69-70, fig. 3; D. Sanminiatelli, *Domenico Beccafumi*, Milan, 1967, p. 153, no. 73; C. Monbeig-
Goguel, *Il manierismo fiorentino*, Milan, 1971, p. 82, plate X.; C. Eisler, *The Seeing Hand*, New
York, 1975, p. 53, illustrated; L. Zorzi, *Il teatro e la cittá. Saggi sulla scena italiana*, Turin, 1977, p.
54, note 72 and pp. 194-5, note 99; B.P. Gordley, *The Drawings of Beccafumi*, Ann Arbor, 1989, no.
74, fig. 162; J. Pope-Hennessy, *Learning to Look*, New York and London, 1991 p. 314; M.
Maccherini, *Domenico Beccafumi e 'L'Amore Costante' di Alessandro Piccolomini*, Prospettiva,
1992, no. 65, fig. 1.

Christie's New York, 10 January 1996 (14**) US$ 68,500	US$	68,500

BECHI Luigi (Florence 1830-1919) Italian
BLOWING BUBBLES oil on canvas, 20½ x 26½in. (52 x 67.3cm.) slr 'L. Becchi'

Christie's South Kensington, 14 March 1996 (129***) GBP 17,250	US$	26,344

IL PRIMO RIMPROVERO oil on canvas, 30¼ x 39½in. (76.8 x 100.3cm.) s 'L. Bechi'

Christie's London, 15 March 1996 (151**) GBP 23,000	US$	35,125

BOY PLAYING A CLARINET oil on canvas, 47 1/8 x 33¼in. (119.7 x 84.5cm.) sll 'L. Bechi.'

Christie's New York, 22 May 1996 (256**) US$ 25,300	US$	25,300

BECK Jacob Samuel (Erfurt 1715-1778) German
STILL-LIFE OF CABBAGES, ARTICHOKES, MELONS, CUCUMBERS AND PEAS oil on
canvas laid down on panel, 19½ x 32¼in. (49.5 x 82cm.) slr 'J.S. Beck***'

Sotheby's London, 5 July 1995 (133**) GBP 15,525	US$	24,765

BECKER Carl Ludwig Friedrich (1820-1900) German
IN THE LOOKING GLASS oil on panel, 21 x 15in. (53.5 x 38cm.) slr 'C.Becker'

Christie's East, 13 February 1996 (151**) US$ 7,475	US$	7,475

BECKMAN Ford (1952 b.) American
UNTITLED 14 acrylic, wax and varnish on canvas mounted on plywood-unframed, 88 x 68 x 4½in.
(223.5 x 172.7 x 10.8cm.) sd titled and numbered 'UNTITLED 14 BLACK WALL PAINTING 87
FORD BECKMAN' on the reverse

Christie's East, 7 May 1996 (175*) US$ 13,800	US$	13,800

BECKMANN Max (Leipzig 1884-1950 New York) German
SITZENDER WEIBLICHER AKT crayon on paper, 27.5 x 13.3cm. slr 'Beckmann'
PROV.: Collection Reinhard Piper, Munich (according to a label on the reverse); With Karl & Faber,
Munich, 1981, under no. 77 (exhibited).
EXH.: Bremen, *Max Beckmann in der Sammlung Piper*, Kunsthalle 1974, cat. no. 2; Munich, *180
Zeichnungen und Aquarelle aus den Sammlungen R.P.München* , Galerie Frank 1975, cat. no. 2;
Bielefeld, *Max Beckmann*, Kunsthalle 1977, cat. no. 32 (illustrated).

Hauswedell & Nolte Cologne, 1 December 1995 (41*) DEM 23,000	US$	15,958

BECKMANN Wilhelm Christiaan Constant (1853-1942) Dutch (?)
THE OX-CART oil on canvas, 80 x 116cm. sll
LIT.: L. Haks & G. Maris, *Lexicon on Foreign Artists who Visualized Indonesia (1600-1950)*,
Utrecht 1995 (illustrated in colour p. 456, no. C 154).

Sotheby's Amsterdam, 23 April 1996 (72**) NLG 17,700	US$	10,518

BÉCQUER Joaquín Domínguez (1811-1879) Spanish
RETRATO ROMANTICO EN UN INTERIOR, CON PATIO SEVILLANO AL FONDO oil on
canvas, 124 x 95.5cm. sd 'Sevilla 1843' and dedicated 'A mi querido amigo D. Manuel Williams'

Sotheby's Madrid, 23 November 1995 (36**) ESP 3,642,500	US$	29,941

BEECHEY Sir William, R.A. (Burford (Oxfordshire) 1753-1839 London) British
PORTRAIT OF QUEEN CHARLOTTE, THREE-QUARTER-LENGHT, IN A WHITE DRESS, A
YELLOW SHAWL AND BLACK MANTILLA, HOLDING A MALTESE DOG, IN THE
GROUNDS OF FROGMORE HOUSE oil on canvas, 51½ x 41in. (130.8 x 104.2cm.)
PROV.: Perhaps the' half-lenght copy', painted for Prince Edward, Duke of Kent (1767-1820); W.L.
Elkins, Philadephia, 1907; Private collection, U.S.A.
LIT.: W. Roberts, *Sir William Beechey R.A.* London and New York, 1907, (illustrated opp. p. 62; O.
Millar, *Later Georgean Pictures in the Royal Collection*, 1969, London, 1969, London and New
York, I, p. 6, under no. 659.
   Christie's London, 10 November 1995 (25**) GBP 8,050   US$ 12,592

BEELT Cornelis (1659-1702 before) Dutch
LE RETOUR A LA PECHE oil on canvas, 87 x 128cm. sll 'JK beelt'
   Étude Tajan Paris, 28 June 1996 (70**) FRF 100,000   US$ 19,310

BEERSTRAATEN Abraham (act. c. 1643-1665) Dutch
A WINTER LANDSCAPE WITH A CITY GATE AND A BRIDGE OVER A FROZEN
WATERWAY, ELEGANT FIGURES AND SKATERS oil on canvas, 35½ x 50in. (90 x 127cm.) s
'A Beerstraaten'
   Christie's London, 8 December 1995 (15**) GBP 23,000   US$ 35,396

SKATERS BY THE SCHREIERSTOREN BEFORE THE GELDERSEKADE IN AMSTERDAM
oil on canvas, 79 x 108.5cm. slr 'A. Beerstraeten'
PROV.: Arthur E. Guinness, his sale, London, Christie's, 10 July 1953, lot 32; Lt. Col. Pinto, his sale,
London, Christie's, 3 June 1955, lot 2.
   Sotheby's Amsterdam, 14 November 1995 (23***) NLG 80,240   US$ 50,570

BEERSTRAATEN Anthonie (active in Amsterdam between 1639 and 1665) Dutch
A VIEW OF THE CHEESE MARKET, DE WAAG, ALKMAAR oil on canvas, 30 ¾ x 25in. (78 x
63.5cm.) sd 'ABEER.ST. /RAATEN / 1663'
   Christie's South Kensington, 7 December 1995 (144**) GBP 7,875 US$ 12,119

PATINEURS PRES DE LA RIVE D'UNE RIVIERE GELÉE oil on oakpanel, 66 x 107cm.
   Étude Tajan Paris, 12 December 1995 (73**) FRF 205,000   US$ 41,292

BEERSTRAETEN Jan Abrahamsz. (1622-1666) Dutch
AN AMSTERDAM MAN-'O-WAR AND OTHER DUTCH SHIPPING ON A RIVER BY A
CASTLE oil on canvas, 41 5/8 x 56 ¾in. (105.7 x 144cm.) sll ini. 'J.B'
PROV.: Marks Collection; Anon. sale, Christie's, 30 Nov. 1979, lot 130 (GBP 11,000).
   Christie's London, 8 December 1995 (14**) GBP 62,000   US$ 95,414

BEERT Osias I (1580 c.-1624) Flemish
STILL-LIFE WITH OYSTERS ON A PEWTER PLATE, A 'WAN-LI' BOWL OF FRAISES DE
BOIS, A 'WAN-LI' PLATE OF PEACHES AND PEARS, PEWTER PLATES OF WALNUTS AND
HAZELNUTS AND MULBERRIES, FAÇON DE VENISE GLASSES, BOXES AND A SILVER
CUP, A ROLL AND A KNIVE oil on panel, 21½ x 30in. (54.6 x 76.2cm.)
PROV.: Purchased by the grandfather of the present owner ca. 1940 and thence by descent to the
present owner.
   Sotheby's New York, 16 May 1996 (27**) US$ 233,500   US$ 233,500

A DUCK ON A PEWTER PLATE, HAZELNUTS, ALMONDS AND RAISINS IN 'WANLI
KRAAK PORCELEIN' BOWLS A ROEMER AND A KNIFE ON A PEWTER PLATE, A WINE
GLASS, A BREAD ROLL, AND AN ORANGE ON A CANDLE-LIT PLATE, OLIVES AND
GOOSEBERRIES IN PEWTER DISHES, ALMONDS AND RAISINS IN A 'WANLI KRAAK
PORCELEIN' BOWL, SWEETMEALS ON A TAZZA, A JUG, BREAD AND A KNIFE ON A
TABLE oil on panel (a pair), 20 1/8 x26 5/8in. (51 x 67.6 cm) and 19 7/8 x 25 3/8in. (50.6 x 64.4cm)

the first panel s mono. 'OBF' (just before 1610)
LIT.: E. Greindl, *Les Peintres Flamands de Nature Morte au XVII Siècle*, Sterrebeek 1983, pp. 182
and 336, nos. 23 and 24, pls. 16 and 17, without reference to the monogram.
<table><tr><td>Christie's London, 7 July 1995 (14**) GBP 441,500</td><td>US$</td><td>704,259</td></tr></table>

BELL Cecil C. (1906-1970) American
WASHINGTON SQUARE POOL oil on masonite, 29 x 34in. (73.6 x 86.4cm.) sdur 'Cecil C. Bell
'51'
<table><tr><td>Christie's East, 21 May 1996 (193**) US$ 13,800</td><td>US$</td><td>13,800</td></tr></table>

BELLA Stefano della (1610-1664) Italian
A GROUP OF DWARFS WATCHING A PUPPET SHOW, WITH A CARRIAGE IN THE
BACKGROUND black chalk, pen and brown ink, gray wash., 7 x 10 ¾in. (17.8 x 27.4cm.)
numbered '65'; with inscription on a seperate label laid down on the mount 'Bambocciate/Di Stefano
della Bella, fatte per il divertimento del/Principe Ferdinando di Toscane di lui Scolare'
PROV.: Probably Ferdinand de Medici, Grand Duke of Tuscany; By descent to the Marquess of
Cholmondeley; Sotheby's, London, 19 February 1930, part of lot 83; with Hans Calmann.
LIT.: F. Viatte, 'Allegorical and Burlesque Subjects by Stefano della Bella', *Master Drawings*, 1977,
XV, p. 355, note 46, pl. 10; J. Pope-Hennessy, *Learning to Look*, New York & London 1991, p. 314.
<table><tr><td>Christie's New York, 10 January 1996 (24**) US$ 27,600</td><td>US$</td><td>27,600</td></tr></table>

BELLEI Gaetano (1857-1922) Italian
THE GYPSY SINGER oil on canvas, 39½ x 34½in. (100.3 x 87.6cm.) sduc 'Bellei G./Modena 1921'
<table><tr><td>Christie's East, 30 October 1995 (238*) US$ 18,400</td><td>US$</td><td>18,400</td></tr></table>

BELLOTTO Bernardo (studio of) (Venice 1721-1780 Warsaw) Italian
PIAZZA DEL CAMPIDOGLIO, SANTA MARIA D'ARACOELE, AND THE CORDONATA,
ROME oil on canvas, 34 ¾ x 57½in. (88.3 x 146.1cm.)
<table><tr><td>Sotheby's New York, 11 January 1996 (138**) US$ 85,000</td><td>US$</td><td>85,000</td></tr></table>

BELLOWS George Wesley, N.A. (Columbus (Ohio) 1882-1924 New York) American
KITTLE BRIDGE, WOODSTOCK oil on board, 18 x 22in. (46 x 56cm.) suc 'Geo. Bellows'; inscr.
'Little Bridge' on the reverse
PROV.: Estate of Emma S. Bellow; H.V. Allison & Co., Inc., New York.
EXH.: New York, The Gallery of Modern Art, *The Alfredo Valente Collection*, n.d.
<table><tr><td>Christie's East, 28 November 1995 (20**) US$ 46,000</td><td>US$</td><td>46,000</td></tr></table>

BENARD Jean-Baptiste (Paris 1720 c.-1789 before) French
A SHEPHERDESS RESTING BY THE WATER WATCHING A PAIR OF SWANS oil on canvas,
23½ x 28 ¾in. (59.7 x 73cm.)
<table><tr><td>Sotheby's New York, 6 October 1996 (156**) US$ 8,050</td><td>US$</td><td>8,050</td></tr></table>

BENJAMIN-KENNINGTON Thomas (1856-1916) British
FORBIDDEN FRUIT oil on canvas, 25 x 30in. (63.5 x 76cm.)
EXH.: London, Royal Institute of Painters in Oil, 1895-96, no. 162.
<table><tr><td>Christie's New York, 22 May 1996 (98**) US$ 112,500</td><td>US$</td><td>112,500</td></tr></table>

BENLLIURE José (Benlliure y Gil) (Valencia 1855-1937 Valencia) Spanish
CARD PLAYERS IN A BODEGA oil on panel, 14½ x 20½in. (37 x 52cm.) sll
PROV.: Rayner MacConnal, London.
<table><tr><td>Sotheby's London, 13 March 1996 (112**) GBP 33,350</td><td>US$</td><td>50,932</td></tr></table>

BENNER Gerrit (Leeuwarden 1897-1981) Dutch
A LANDSCAPE oil on canvas, ,100 x 130cm. s on the reverse 'BNR'
PROV.: Acquired directly from the artist by the father of the present owner.
<table><tr><td>Christie's Amsterdam, 5 June 1996 (297**) NLG 51,750</td><td>US$</td><td>30,237</td></tr></table>

BOSRAND oil on paper laid down on board, 57 x 77cm. slr with monogram; s on the reverse
PROV.: Acquired from the artist by the family of the present owner.
EXH.: Indonesia, Travelling Exhibition, *Hollandse Schilders*, 1953.
    Sotheby's Amsterdam, 7 December 1995 (211**) NLG 23,600   US$ 14,624

PAARDJES oil on card, 65.5 x 45.5cm. slr with monogram
PROV.: Acquired from the artist by the family of the present owner.
    Sotheby's Amsterdam, 7 December 1995 (215**) NLG 20,060   US$ 12,430

LANDSCHAP oil on canvas, 80 x 100cm. s on the reverse (1970)
PROV.: Acquired from the artist by the present owner.
    Sotheby's Amsterdam, 7 December 1995 (220***) NLG 47,200   US$ 29,248

WATER EN LUCHT oil on canvas, 120 x 90cm. s on the reverse (1961)
PROV.: Acquired from the artist by the present owner.
LIT.: Hans Redeker, *Gerrit Benner*, Amsterdam 1967, no. 10 (illustrated).
    Sotheby's Amsterdam, 7 December 1995 (233**) NLG 47,200   US$ 29,248

LANDSCAPE gouache on card, 40 x 47cm. slr with monogram (ca. 1972)
PROV.: Acquired from the artist by the present owner.
    Sotheby's Amsterdam, 7 December 1995 (244**) NLG 16,520   US$ 10,237

VROUW IN EEN PARK gouache on paper, 33.5 x 50cm. slr with monogram (ca. 1945)
PROV.: Acquired from the artist by the present owner.
    Sotheby's Amsterdam, 7 December 1995 (246**) NLG 11,210   US$ 6,946

BENNETT Frank Moss (1874-1953) British
THE END OF THE RUBBER oil on canvas, 23 x 33in. (58.4 x 83.7cm.) sd 'F.M. Bennett 1934'
    Christie's London, 6 November 1995 (222**) GBP 31,050   US$ 48,569

THE HUNTSMAN'S TALE oil on canvas, 16 x 20in. (40.1 x 51cm.) sdlr 'FMBennet 38'
    Phillips London, 18 June 1996 (59**) GBP 4,000   US$ 6,168

AFTER THE SHOOT oil on canvas, 15 x 20in. (38.1 x 50.8cm.) sdll 'F M Bennett 1930'
    Christie's East, 30 October 1995 (207*) US$ 20,700   US$ 20,700

THE SPORTMAN'S RETURN oil on canvas, 22 x 30in. (55.9 x 76.3cm.) sdll 'F.M Bennett 1924'
    Christie's East, 30 October 1995 (209*) US$ 10,925   US$ 10,925

THE BROTHERS oil on canvas, 14¼ x 20in. (36.2 x 50.7cm.) sdll 'FM Bennett/1921'
    Christie's East, 30 October 1995 (214*) US$ 14,375   US$ 14,375

A BOWL OF PUNCH oil on canvas, 15 x 20in. (38.1 x 20.8cm.) sdll 'F M Bennett 1934'
    Christie's East, 30 October 1995 (221*) US$ 14,550   US$ 14,550

THE LETTER oil on panel, 10 x 17¼in. (25.4 x 36.2cm.) sdll 'F M Bennett 1916'
    Christie's East, 30 October 1995 (223*) US$ 13,800   US$ 13,800

BENSON Ambrosius (Lombardy 1495-1550 Brughes) Flemish (Italian)
THE IMMACULATE CONCEPTION oil on panel, painted shaped top, 33½ x 23 ¾in. (85 x 60.5cm.) extensively inscribed
    Christie's London, 8 December 1995 (11**) GBP 210,500   US$ 323,946

BENSON Frank Weston, N.A. (1862-1951) American
SUNSHINE AND SHADOW oil on canvas, 30¼ x 25¼in. (77 x 64cm.) slr 'F.W. Benson'
PROV.: The artist; Mr. W.J. Johnson, Uniontown, Pennsylvania; By descent in the family to the

present owner.
   Christie's New York, 30 November 1995 (20**) US$ 354,500   US$ 354,500

BENTON Thomas Hart, N.A. (Neosho (Missouri) 1889-1975 Kansas City) American
STILL LIFE WITH VASE oil and tempera on masonite, 25 x 16 1/8in. (63.5 x 41cm.) sdlr 'Benton
67'
PROV.: Mr. And Mrs. E.L. Combest, Overland Park, Kansas; private collection, St. Louis, Missouri;
Midtown Payson Galleries, New York.
EXH.: St. Joseph, Missouri, The Albrecht-Kemper Museum of Art, March 1970.
LIT.: M. Baigell, *Thomas Hart Benton*, New York, 1974, no. 209, illus.
   Christie's New York, 23 May 1996 (149**) US$ 101,500   US$ 101,500

BENVENUTI Giovanni Battista, {called} Ortolano (Ferrara 1487 c.-1527) Italian
THE MADONNA AND CHILD SAINTS SEBASTIAN JAMES THE GREATER oil on panel, 16 ¾
x 23½in. (42.5 x 59.7cm.)
   Christie's London, 8 December 1995 (71**) GBP 43,300   US$ 66,636

BÉRARD Christian (Paris 1903-1949 Paris) French
VISAGE watercolour and gouache on joined pink paper, 40 1/8 x 29½in. (102 x 75cm.) (1935)
PROV.: Mme. La Comtesse de Beaumont, Paris.
   Sotheby's London, 20 March 1996 (236**) GBP 8,970   US$ 13,699

BÉRAUD Jean (Saint Petersburg 1849-1936 Paris) French
LE PONT DE L`EUROPE oil on canvas, 19 x 28 ¾in. (48.3 x 73.1cm.) slr 'Jean Béraud'
PROV.: Henry Hilton; sale, American Art Galleries, New York, feb 13, 1900, lot 77 (as *La Place de
l'europe, Paris*); Henry seligman; Robert Lebel, Paris (by 1943); Hirschl & Adler Galleries, New
York; Private Collection , U.S.A.
EXH.: New York, *Coordinating Council of French Relief Societies*, Paris, 1943-44, no.18.
LIT.: 'Paris Reconstructed in Relief Show,' *Art Digest*, January 1, 1944, p.11 (illustrated); E. Bénézit,
Dictionaire des Peintres, Sculpteurs, Dessinateurs et Graveurs, Paris, 1976, I, p. 641 (as *La place de
l'Europe à Paris*); *Gustave Caillebotte, Urban impressionist*, (exh. cat.), Chicago, 1995, p. 102
(illustrated); This painting will be included in the forthcoming *Béraud catalogue raisonné* being
prepared by Patrick Offenstadt with the help of the fondation Wildenstein.
   Christie's New York, 2 November 1995 (19**) US$ 420,000   US$ 420,000

BERCHEM Nicolaes Pietersz (Haarlem 1620-1683 Amsterdam) Dutch
PEASANTS IN A ROCKY LANDSCAPE oil on canvas, 43½ x 38 3/8in. (110.5 x 97.5cm.) sdlr 'N.
Berchem F. 1670 10/23
   Sotheby's New York, 16 May 1996 (81**) US$ 85,000   US$ 85,000

SAINT PETER oil on panel, 24¼ x 19¼in. (61.6 x 48.9cm.) sdcl 'CBerchem/1644'
PROV.: John C. Stillwell, New York, by whom purchased in the 1890's in Vienna (Sale: The
Anderson Galleries, New York, Dec. 1, 1927, lot 235, illus.); Henry Blank, Glen Ridge, NJ. (His
Sale: Parke-Bernet Galleries, Inc., New York, Nov. 16, 1949, lot 29) there purchased by Lock
Galleries; Baron Cassel van Doorn, Englewood, NJ. (His Sale: Parke-Bernet Galleries, Inc., New
York, December 9,1955, lot 46); there purchased by the present owner.
LIT.: G. F. Muller, 'Two portrait heads by Claesz Pieters Berchem,' *Art in America*, Feb. 1919, pp.
79-84, illus. fig. I; C. Hofstede de Groot, *Beschreibendes und kritisches Verzeichnis der Werke der
hervorragendsten Holländischen Maler des VII. Jahrhunderts*, vol. 9, 1926, p.59, no. 31 and p. 279
(with incorrect dimensions and a slightly different description).
   Sotheby's New York, 11 January 1996 (99**) US$ 360,000   US$ 360,000

Saint Peter

BERCHERE Narcisse (1819-1891) French
ARAB TRAVELLERS RESTING BY RUINS oil on canvas, 28½ x 43¼in. (72.5 x 109.8cm.) sd 'Berchère 1869'
PROV.: With Mathaf Gallery.
LIT.: L. Thornton, *The Orientalists Painter-Travellers*, Paris, 1994, p. 31.

Christie's London, 15 March 1996 (94**) GBP 12650 US$ 19,319

BERCKHEYDE Gerrit Adriaensz. (Haarlem 1638-1698 Haarlem) Dutch
TRAVELLERS HALTED BY A FOUNTAIN ON A MOUNTAIN PASS IN AN ITALIANATE LANDSCAPE oil on canvas, 53 x 62.5cm. slc 'Gerrit Berk.hey(de?)'

Christie's Amsterdam, 7 May 1996 (82*) NLG 13,800 US$ 8,047

TRAVELLERS HALTED BY A FOUNTAIN ON A MOUNTAIN PASS IN ITALIANATE LANDSCAPE oil on canvas, 53 x 62.5cm. s centre l 'Gerrit Berk.heyde'

Christie's Amsterdam, 13 November 1995 (55*) NLG 25,300 US$ 15,945

SCHAUSTELLER VOR DER STADT oil on canvas, 47.6 x 55.8cm.
PROV.: Slg. Freiherr Speck von Sternburg, Luetschena (1831); Slg. Karl Bergsten, Stockholm (1923); Galerie Pallamar, Wien; Österreichische Privatsammlung.

Lempertz Cologne, 18 May 1996 (1007**) DEM 17,000 US$ 11,083

BERCKHEYDE Job Adriaensz. (Haarlem 1630-1693 Haarlem) Dutch
DISTINGUISHED GENTLEMEN PLAYING CARDS IN A DUTCH HOUSE oil on canvas, 50 x 41.5cm.

Dorotheum Vienna, 6 March 1996 (10**) ATS 110,000 US$ 10,581

BERG Else (Ratibor (Silesia) 1877-1942 Oswizcim, near) Dutch
A STILL-LIFE WITH FLOWERS oil on canvas, 83.5 x 70cm. slr 'E. Berg'

Christie's Amsterdam, 5 June 1996 (18**) NLG 8,625 US$ 5,039

BERLEBORCH Gerard (Active Amsterdam 1649-1655) Dutch
A PEELED LEMON IN A ROEMER ON A STONE LEDGE oil on canvas laid down on panel, 40.5 x 35.1cm.
PROV.: With S. Nijstad, The Hague, 972, as *Jan Jansz. van de Velde III*, from whom purchased by the present owner.

Christie's Amsterdam, 7 May 1996 (75*) NLG 29,900 US$ 17,434

A STILL LIFE OF FRUIT IN A *WANLI* PORCELAIN DISH, A PARTLY PEELED LEMON IN A ROEMER ON A SILVER PLATTER, GRAPES, POMEGRANATES AND OTHER OBJECTS ON A TABLE PARTLY DRAPED WITH A CLOTH TRIMMED WITH GOLD BRAID oil on oak panel, 21 ¾ x 29in. (55 x 73.5cm.) sdll 'G v Berleborch f 1655'
PROV.: With Benedict, Paris, 1957; With Brian Koetser, London, 1966; Anon. sale, Lucerne, Galerie Fischer, November 1974, lot 2181; With Galerie Edel, Cologne, from whom bought by Dr. Jellissen.
EXH.: London, Brian Koetser, Spring 1966, no. 11.
LIT.: B.J.A. Renckens, in *Oud Holland*, 1967, pp. 236, 238, reproduced p. 238, fig. 2; N.R.A. Vroom, *A Modest Message.*, 1980, vol. ll, p. 10, reproduced; E. Gemar-Koeltzsch, *Holländische Stillebenmaler im 17. Jahrhundert*, 1995, vol. 2, p. 88, no. 26/3, reproduced.

Sotheby's London, 6 December 1995 (183**) GBP 21,850 US$ 33,626

BERNARD Émile (Lille 1868-1941 Paris) French
LE ROUET oil on canvas, 17 7/8 x 21 ¾in. (45.4 x 55.3cm.) sdlr 'Emile Bernard 87'
PROV.: Family of the artist; Hirschl & Adler Galleries Inc., New York (acquired by Richard Smart,

1973).
EXH.: New York, Hirschl & Adler Galleries Inc., *Emile Bernard, Paintings of the Pont-Aven Period*, Feb.-March 1963, no. 10; London, Tate Gallery, *Gauguin and the Pont-Aven Group*, Jan.-Feb. 1966, no. 77.
LIT.: J.-J. Luthi, *Emile Bernard, Catalogue raisonné de l'oeuvre peint*, Paris 1982, no. 70 (illustrated p.15).

Christie's New York, 1 May 1996 (150**) US$ 43,000	US$	45,500

AUTOPORTRAIT A LA PALETTE oil on canvas, 78.5 x 84.5cm. sd '1912'

Étude Tajan Paris, 28 March 1996 (2*) FRF 38,000	US$	7,511

BERNHARDT Sarah (France 1844-1923) French
SELF-PORTRAIT AS PIERROT oil on canvas, 22¼ x 16 ¾in. (56.5 x 42.5cm.)
EXH.: New York, Shepherd Gallery, *French 19th Century Paintings*, March-April 1977, no. 2.

Christie's New York, 2 November 1995 (184**) US$ 17,250	US$	17,250

BERNINGER Edmund (1843-1914 after) German
A VIEW OF CONSTANTINOPLE oil on canvas, 39½ x 86½in. (100.4 x 209.7cm.) slr inscr. 'E. BERNINGER/München.'
PROV.: Schlossleine, Hanover.

Christie's New York, 2 November 1995 (45**) US$ 200,500	US$	200,500

BERTEAUX H. (19ᵗʰ Century) French
A BACCHANALIAN PROCESSION oil on canvas, 47¼ x 67½in. (120 x 171.5cm.) sd 'HBerteaux 1869'

Christie's South Kensington, 13 June 1996 (219**) GBP 20,700	US$	31,920

BERTRY Nicolas-Henry Jeaurat de (attributed) (1728-1796) French
STILL-LIFE WITH A SILVER CHOCOLATE POT, A BLUE AND WHITE PORCELAIN CUP AND SAUCER, A BREAD ROLL AND OTHER OBJECTS ON A TRAY. oil on panel, 11¼ x 17 7/8in. (28.6 x 45.4cm)

Sotheby's New York, 11 January 1996 (158**) US$ 16,100	US$	16,100

BERUETE Aureliano (1845-1912) Spanish
PUERTO DE BRETAÑA oil on panel, 15 x 24cm. slr 'A de Beruete'

Sotheby's Madrid, 23 November 1995 (72**) ESP 2,350,000	US$	19,317

BESCHEY Balthasar (Antwerp 1708-1776 Antwerp) Flemish
THE PRODIGAL SON; THE GOOD SAMARITAN oil on panel (a pair), each: 43 x 32.5cm. one slr 'B. Beschey'

Sotheby's Amsterdam, 6 May 1996 (61*) NLG 12,980	US$	7,569

BESCHEY Balthasar (attr.) (Antwerp 1708-1776 Antwerp) Flemish
CAVALIERS WITH AN OSTLER BY A TAVERN; FIGURES CROSSING A RIVER WITH A VILLAGE BEYOND oil on coper (a pair), each: 18.5 c 23cm.

Sotheby's Amsterdam, 6 May 1996 (3**) NLG 20,060	US$	11,697

BESCHEY Carel (Antwerp 1706 b.-1770 c.) Flemish
WIDE FLEMISH LANDSCAPE WITH TRAVELLERS oil on copper, 26.5 x 35.5cm.

Dorotheum Vienna, 6 March 1996 (88**) ATS 450,000	US$	43,286

ELEGANT COMPANY AT A LAKE oil on panel, 7 1/8 x 8 1/8in. (18 x 20.6cm.)

Christie's London, 8 December 1995 (267**) GBP 12,075	US$	18,583

VILLAGE NEAR A RIVER WITH BOATS oil on panel, 30 x 55.5cm. slc 'F.C. Beschey'

Dorotheum Vienna, 11 June 1996 (198**) ATS 280,000	US$	25,989

RIVERLANDSCAPE WITH FARMHOUSES, BOATS AND TRAVELLERS oil on panel, 17 x 22cm. (framed)
>Dorotheum Vienna, 17 October 1995 (154**) ATS 150,000 — US$ 15,046

BESKOW Elsa (1874-1953) Swedish
MORS LILLA OLLE watercolour on paper, 30.5 x 25cm. sdlr 'EB -09'
>Bukowskis Stockholm, 29 November-1 December 1995 (14**) SEK 111,000 — US$ 16,792

BESNARD Paul Albert (1849-1934) French
LADY WITH PARROT oil on canvas, 24¼ x 19 ¾in. (61.6 x 50.2cm.) s
PROV.: Bernheim Jeune & Cie, Paris; The Stoney-Edwards Collection; Robert Schoelkopf Gallery, New York; Sale: Sotheby Parke-Bernet, New York, 2 February 1972, lot 137.
EXH.: Buenos-AIres, *Exposition Internationale de Centenaire*, 1910, cat. no. 50; New York, Brooklyn Museum, 2 February 1922.
>Sotheby's Arcade Auctions New York, 17 January 1996 (399*) US$ 8,625 — US$ 8,625

BEUCKELAER Joachim de (Antwerp 1533 c.-1576 c. Antwerp) Flemish
THE POOL AT BETHESDA oil on oak panel, 32½ x 57½in. (82.5 x 146.1cm.) inscr. lr 'IOHA.5/CAP'
PROV.: Hoftrat Harse, Luisenpark, no. 1, *Jungbrunnen*, according to a label affixed to the panel; Hoftrat Marx, his sale, Berlin, Lange, 14-15 June 1938, lot 3; Anon. sale, London, Christie's, 19 July 1974, lot 235; With Julius Weitzner, London, 1976.
EXH.: On loan, Duncaster Museum and Art Gallery, 1977-1993.
>Sotheby's London, 5 July 1995 (47**) GBP 56,500 — US$ 90,126

BEUYS Joseph (Krefeld 1921-1986) German
WORDS WICH CAN HEAR each: ink and pencil on paper in Artist's frames in six parts, one: 25.5 x 33.4cm. (10 x 13 1/8in.) One: 96.7 x 62.5cm. (38 x 24 5/8in.) four: 96.7 x 49cm. (38 x 191¼in.) ink and pencil on paper in artist's frames in six parts (1977 during Dokumenta VI, Kassel)
PROV.: Lucrezia de Domizio Durini, Bolognano, Pescara (acquired directly from the artist in 1977).
EXH.: London, Anthony d'Offay Ltd., *Joseph Beuys*, 1983 Bolognano, Pescara, Palazzo Durini, *Defense of Nature*, 1984.
LIT.: *Interview Joseph Beuys & Jean Pierre Van Tieghem: 21.5.1975*, Galerie Isy Brachot, Paris 1989, p. 122, illustrated Lucrezia de Domizio, Buby Durini & Italo Tamassoni, *Incontro con Beuys*, Pescara 1984, p. 110, illustrated Achille Bonito Oliva, *Verba*, Rome 1990, illustrated in colour.
>Sotheby's London, 21 March 1996 (73**) GBP 58,700 — US$ 89,646

CONSIDER THE THOUGHT pencil and watercolour on paper, 8½ x 11in. (21.5 x 28cm.) (1978)
PROV.: Anthony d'Offay Gallery, New York.
LIT.: Germano Celant, *Beuys Tracce in Italia*, Naples 1978, illustrated.
>Sotheby's London, 27 June 1996 (213**) GBP 9,200 — US$ 14,187

OHNE TITEL gouache, watercolour, and crayons on paper, 20 x 24.5cm. s mono 'JB.' sd mono on the reverse 'JB. 1943' adn sd 'Joseph Beuys 1941 (?)'
>Lempertz Cologne, 31 May 1996 (48**) DEM 80,000 — US$ 52,155

FEUERSPEIENDER BERG watercolour and pencil on Van Gelder-Bütten, 25 x33cm. s mono 'JB.' sd titled 'Joseph Beuys 1947 Feuerspeiender Berg'
LIT.: Düsseldorf, catalogue *Joseph Beuys, Natur Materie Form, Kunstsammlung Nordrhein-Westfalen*, 1991-1992, cat. no. 3.
>Lempertz Cologne, 31 May 1996 (49**) DEM 35,000 — US$ 22,818

BEYEREN Abraham Hendricksz. van (The Hague 1620/21-1690 Overschie or (Alkmaar)) Dutch
A DEAD HARE, ORANGES, GRAPES AND A MELON ON A PEWTER PLATE, WITH A GLOBE AND A SILVER-GILT CUP AND COVER ON A PARTIALLY DRAPED LEDGE oil on

canvas, 42 x 34¼in. (106.8 x 87cm.)
        Christie's South Kensington, 18 april 1996 (272**) GBP 8,280   US$ 12,555

A STILL WITH A LOBSTER ON A SILVER *PLOOI* PLATTER, A NAUTILUS SHELL, GRAPES, A GILT GOBLET AND A SALT ON A TABLE DRAPED WITH A VELVET CLOTH, A *ROEMER* CONTAINING WHITE WINE AND GIRDLED WITH A VINE SPRAY, SET IN A GOTHIC STONE NICHE BEHIND, SURMOUNTED BY A SWAG OF FLOWERS HANGING ABOVE oil on oak panel, 35¼ x 45½in. (89.3 x 115.5cm.)
PROV.: Fridt; Oskar Huldschinski, his sale, Berlin, Cassirer & Helbing, 10-11 May 1928, lot 1; F.J.E. Horstmann, Chateau Oud Clingendaal, his sale, Amsterdam, Fk. Muller, 19-21, November 1929, lot 3; With Goudstikker, Amsterdam 1930-33; With Kleinberger, Paris; Baron Heinrich Thyssen-Bornemisza, after 1933 and by 1941.
EXH.: Berlin, Kaiser Friedrich Museumsverein, 1906, no. 12; Amsterdam, Goudstikker, 1930; Amsterdam, Goudstikker, *Het Stilleven*, 1933, no. 12; Bern 1960; Düsseldorf 1970-1, no. 3; Lausanne etc., 1986-7, no. 47.
LIT.: H.E. van Gelder, *W.C. Heda, A. van Beyeren, W. Kalf*; 1941(?), p. 34, reproduced p. 31, (as signed); H. Gerson, *Van Geertgen tot Frans Hals*, 1951, reproduced plate 181; C. Clemm, *in Stilleben in Europa*, exhibition catalogue, 1979, p. 186, reproduced; S. Segal, *A Prosperous Past*, exhibition catalogue, 1988, p. 172, reproduced p. 173, fig. 9.2, (as dated 1651).
        Sotheby's London, 6 December 1995 (111**) GBP 95,000   US$ 146,199

BIAGIO Vincenzo di {called Catena} (ca. 1470-1531) Italian
PORTRAIT OF A GENTLEMAN, SAID TO BE GONZALVO FERNANDEZ DE CORDOBA oil on panel, 35½ x 18½in. (90.2 x 47cm.)
PROV.: Cardinal Fesch, Rome, by whose heirs sold to Marchesa Marianna Dionigi, Rome, 1875; thence by descent to Count Phillipo Frediani-Dionigi, Rome, until 1931.
EXH.: New York, Acquavella Galleries, *Renaissance Portraits*, 6 November- 6 December 1939, no. 1 (as Mariotto Albertinelli), illustrated.
        Sotheby's New York, 2 April 1996 (112*) US$ 40,250   US$ 40,250

BIANCHI Mosé (Milan/Monza 1840-1904) Italian
UN MOMENT DI RACCOGLIMENTO oil on board, 27 x 18 ¾in. (68.8 x 47.8cm.) s 'M Bianchi'
PROV.: The Bernasconi Collection.
        Christie's London, 15 March 1996 (183**) GBP 11,500   US$ 17,563

GIOVINETTA oil on board, 27 x 19½in. (68.6 x 49.5cm.) s mono inscr. 'Verona' s ini numb 'MB 178 on the reverse'
PROV.: The Bernasconi Collection.
        Christie's London, 15 March 1996 (184**) GBP 12,075   US$ 18,441

BIARD Auguste (Lyon 1798-1882 Fontainebleau, near) French
THE SMUGGLER (SOLDIERS AND PEASANTS CHECKING OUT THE INVENTORY OF THE SMUGGLER IN AN INN) oil on canvas, 99 x 131cm. slr 'Biard'
        A. Mak B.V. Dordrecht, 21 June 1996 (30***) NLG 30,000   US$ 17,528

BICCI DI LORENZO (Florence 1373-1452 Arezzo) Italian
THE NATIVITY AND THE ADORATION OF THE SHEPHERDS tempera on panel, gold ground, 10 x 24in. (25.5 x 62in.) (ca 1435)
PROV.: Harold J. Pratt, New York; With Wildenstein, until 1976.
EXH.: New York, Wildenstein, *Italian Paintings*, 1947, no. 7; Hartford, Wadsworth Atheneum, *Life of Christ*, March-April 1948, no. 13; London, Wildenstein, *Paintings by Rembrandt, Boucher, Cezanne, Hals, Guardi, Gauguin and others,* June-Aug. 1959, no. 11; London, Wildenstein, *Religious Themes in Painting from the 14th Century*, March-May 1962, repr. no. 4; On loan, the Bowes Museum, Barnard Castle, County Durham, 1977-1995.
LIT.: B. Berenson, *Italian Pictures of the Renaissance*, 1932, p. 85; B. Berenson, *Italian Pictures of the Renaissance: Florentine School*, vol I, 1963, p. 30; T. Crombie, 'Sacred and Profane in Italian

Art; The Early Italians at Wildenstein', in *Apollo*, April 1962, p. 146.

Sotheby's London, 5 July 1995 (49**) GBP 133,500	US$	212,953

BIDAULD Jean Joseph Xavier (Carpentras 1758-1846 Montmorency) French
LANDSCAPE WITH A VIEW OF THE BRIDGE AT SORA oil on canvas, 18½ x 25in. (47 x 63.5cm.) sdlr 'Jph. Bidauld/ 1815.'
PROV.: Duc de Berry (bought at the Salon of 1812 for ,900 francs); Duchesse de Berry; Château de Rosny (Her Sale: Paris, February 22, 1836, lot 8); Galerie Jean-François et Philippe Heim, Paris; Colnaghi, New York from whom acquired by the present collector.
EXH.: Paris, Salon of 1814, no. 94 ('Vue d'un pont de l'Isola di Sora, au royaume de Naples'); Paris, Galerie Jean-François et Philippe Heim, *Peintures, Aquarelles, Dessins 1755-1891*; New York, Colnaghi New York, *Claude to Corot; The Development of Landscape Painting in France*, ed. by A. Wintermute, Nov.-Dec. 1990, pp. 271-73, illus. in colour.
LIT.: Le Chevalier Bonnemaison, *Galerie de Son Altesse Royal;e Madame la Duchesse de Berry, Ecole française de peintures modernes*, 1822, Vol. II, (illus.); *Jean-Joseph-Xavier Bidauld*, exhibition catalogue, Caprentas, 1978, catalogue nos. 29 and 52 and p. 2 (entries by S. Gutwirth).

Sotheby's New York, 11 January 1996 (152A**) US$ 90,500	US$	90,500

BIERSTADT Albert, N.A. (1830-1902) American (German)
WESTERN LAKE SCENE oil on paper laid down on masonite, 12½ x 9 ¾in. (31.5 x 25cm.) sll 'A. Bierstadt; with initials conjoined

Christie's East, 28 November 1995 (136*) US$ 8,050	US$	8,050

KING'S RIVER CANYON, CALIFORNIA oil on canvas stretched over panel, 20 x 28½in. (50.8 x 72.4cm.) slr 'ABierstadt' s and titled on the reverse (ca. 1873-74)
PROV.: Private collection, London, since 1890; by descent in the family.

Christie's New York, 23 May 1996 (28**) US$ 156,500	US$	156,500

SAILBOATS ON THE HUDSON AT IRVINGTON oil on canvas, 15 x 21in. (38.1 x 53.3cm.) slr 'A Bierstadt' (late 1860's)

Christie's New York, 23 May 1996 (32**) US$ 85,000	US$	85,000

STREET IN NASSAU oil on canvas, 13 x 19in. (35.5 x 48.3cm.) sll 'ABierstadt'

Christie's New York, 23 May 1996 (41**) US$ 90,500	US$	90,500

STUDY FOR YOSEMITE VALLEY, GLACIER POINT TRAIL oil on board, 10 x 14in. (25.5 x 35.6cm.) sll twice with conjoined ini. 'AB'; s 'A. Bierstadt' and inscr. 'Yosemite' on the reverse

Christie's New York, 30 November 1995 (37**) US$ 145,500	US$	145,500

BIEVRE Marie de (Brussels 1865 b.) Belgian
ROSES ON A FOUNTAIN oil on canvas, 91 x 72cm. s 'Bievre'

Dorotheum Vienna, 28 February 1996 (578**) ATS 100,000	US$	9,698

BIGOT Trophime (Arles 1579-1650 Arles) French
THE DENIAL OF SAINT PETER oil on canvas, 29 x 36in. (73.7 x 92.7cm.)
PROV.: Private collection, Paris in the early 1950's.
LIT.: B. Nicolson, 'Un Caravaggiste Aixois - Le Maitre à la Chandelle', *Art de France*, 1964, illustrated pl. 33; B, Nicholson 'the Rehabilitation of Trophime Bigot', *Art and Literature*, IV, 1965, p. 26 (English translation); B. Nicholson, *The International Caravaggesque Movement*, 1979, p.22; B. Nicholson *Caravaggism in Europe*, 1990 vol.I, p. 62; vol. II, ilustrated. 844.

Sotheby's New York, 16 May 1996 (43**) US$ 51,750	US$	51,750

BILL Max (Winterthür 1908-1994) Swiss
GELBES NEUNTEL oil on canvas, 15 ¾ x 15 ¾in. (40 x 40cm.) sd '1959-1969' on the stretcher
PROV.: Galleria Internazionale, Milan.

Sotheby's London, 21 March 1996 (53**) GBP 24,150	US$	36,881

1 - 4 AROUND WHITE oil on canvas, 31 3/8 x 31 3/8in. (79.7 x 79.7cm.) sd '69' on the reverse
PROV.: Acquired directly from the artist by the present owner.
        Christie's London, 23 May 1996 (82**) GBP 31,050   US$ 47,017

UNTITLED oil on canvas, 15 ¾ x 15 ¾in. (40 x 40cm.) sd '1972-73' on the reverse
PROV.: Galleria d'Arte Sianesi, Milan; Galleri Ressle, Stockholm.
        Sotheby's London, 27 June 1996 (182**) GBP 11,500   US$ 17,733

BILLET Etienne (1821 b.) French
ARABS IN THE DESERT oil on canvas, 32 x 51in. (81.2 x 129.5cm.) slc 'E. Billet'
        Christie's New York, 22 May 1996 (259**) US$ 47,150   US$ 47,150

BIRCH Thomas (1779-1851) American
THE BATTERY AND HARBOR oil on canvas, 28 3/4 x 40 3/4in. (73 x 103.5cm.) s "Tho' Birch'
inscr. 'New York'
PROV.: Russell W. Thorpe, New York; Mr. and Mrs. Wayne W. Johnson, New York; Alexander
Gallery, New York.
EXH.: New York, C. W. Lyon, Inc., *Benefit Exhibition for Bundles for Britain*, March-April, p. 14.
LIT.: R. Gilder, *The Battery*, 1936, p. 123.
        Christie's New York, 23 May 1996 (5**) US$ 211,500   US$ 211,500

BIRD Harrington (1846 b.) British
ARABIANS IN AN EXOTIC LANDSCAPE watercolour over traces of pencil on paperboard, 15 x
21¼in. (38.1 x 54cm.) sdll 'Harrington Bird/1905'
        Christie's New York, 28 November 1995 (88**) US$ 36,800   US$ 36,800

ARABIANS IN THE DESERT watercolour over traces of pencil on paper, 15½ x 22in. (39.4 x
55.9cm.) sdlr 'Harrington Bird/1905'
        Christie's New York, 28 November 1995 (89**) US$ 36,800   US$ 36,800

BIROLLI Renato (Verona 1906-1959 Milan) Italian
INCENDIO DELLE CINQUE TERRE oil on canvas, 114.5 x 143cm. slr 'Birolli 957' and signed on
the reverse 'Renato Birolli, Anversa 1957 (1957)
EXH.: Bruxelles, *Expo 58-50 ans d'art moderne*, Palais International des Beaux-Arts, 1958; Rome,
VIII Quadriennale Nazionale d'Art di Roma, giovane pittura romana 1930/1945, Palazzo delle
Esposizione, sala personale, 1959-'60; Venice, *XXX Biennale Internazionale d'Arte*, sala personale,
1960, no.54.
LIT.: Z. Birolli, *Birolli*, ed. Feltrinelli, Milan, 1978, no.1957/67 (793).
        Finearte Rome, 2 April 1996 (216***) ITL 124,200,000   US$ 79,361

GIOVANE CONTADINO oil on canvas, 72 x 50,5cm. sd '1946' on the reverse
PROV.: Galleria dell'Annunciata, Milan; Galleria Nord Sud 4, Lugano.
LIT.: Zeno Biroll, *Birolli*, Milan 1978, p. 236, no. 1945.8(311) (illustrated).
        Sotheby's Milan, 28 May 1996 (94**) ITL 12,650,000   US$ 8,125

BISCHOFFSHAUSEN Hans (Feld am See 1927-1987 Villach) Austrian
SCHRIFT oil, PVC on wood, ,100 x 122cm. sd and titled 'BISCHOFFSHAUSEN 1958 TARVIS' on
the reverse
        Wiener Kunst Auktionen, 26 March 1996 (350**) ATS 120,000   US$ 11,543

BISHOP Walter Follen (1856-1936) British
IN THE HEART OF THE FORREST pencil and watercolour with scratching out, 28 ¾ x 49in. (73 x
124.5cm.) sll 'W. Follen Bishop' and s and inscr 'In the heart of the forest/W. Follen Bishop/41 South
Hill Road/Liverpool' on an old label on the reverse
PROV.: George M. Brander by 1 Mach 1954.
EXH.: London, Royal Academy, 1888, no.1329; Liverpool, Walker Art Gallery, 1888, no.918, priced

at GBP75.

Christie's London, 29 March 1996 (17**) GBP 17,825 US$ 27,222

BISSCHOP Christoffel (1828-1904) Austrian
THE LOOKING GLASS oil on panel, 20 x 15¼in. (51 x 38.8cm.) s 'C. Bisschop'
Christie's London, 17 November 1995 (32**) GBP 13,225 US$ 20,687

BISSIER Julius (Freiburg im Breisgau 1893-1965 Ancona) German
KOMPOSITION tempera and gold on canvas, 19.2 x 21.5cm. sdlc 'Julius Bessier/H 26. Aug. 62 Be'
Hauswedell & Nolte Cologne, 2 December 1995 (33**) DEM 25,000 US$ 17,345

KOMPOSITION tempera on canvas, 14.5 x 22.6cm. sd 'Julius Bissier 16 XI. 56'
Hauswedell & Nolte Cologne, 6 June 1996 (37**) DEM 25,000 US$ 16,243

MONDINE watercolour on paper, 6 x 9½in. (15 x 24cm.) sd '7. Januar '62'
PROV.: Acquired directly from the Artist by the present owner in the late 1960s.
Christie's London, 26 October 1995 (4**) GBP 8,050 US$ 12,705

BISSIERE Roger (Villeréal (Lot-et-Garonne) 1886-1964 Boissiérette (Lot)) French
VERT PAYSAGE oil on paper laid down on board, 13 1/8 x 16 1/8in. (33.2 x 41cm.) sdlr 'Bissière 58'
PROV.: Galerie Jeanne Bucher, Paris; Albert Skira, Geneva; Acquired directly from the above by the present owner.
EXH.: Paris, Musée Nation d'Art Moderne, *Roger Bissière - Exhibition of Paintings, Gouaches, Pastels*, 1959.
Sotheby's London, 27 June 1996 (128**) GBP 16,100 US$ 24,827

BLAAS Eugen de (von) (1843-1932) Austrian
ON THE TERRACE oil on canvas, 26 x 18¼in. 966 x 46.5cm.) sd 'Eugene de Blaas 1885'
Christie's London, 15 March 1996 (22**) GBP 28,750 US$ 43,907

THE COURTSHIP oil on canvas, 42 x 27½in. (107 x 70cm.) sd 'E. de Blaas 1887'
Christie's London, 15 March 1996 (28**) GBP 54,300 US$ 82,926

LA BELLA VENEZIANA oil on canvas, 28 ¾ x 22¼in. (73 x 56.5cm.) sd 'Eg. Blaas 1875'
Christie's London, 17 November 1995 (30**) GBP 10,350 US$ 16,190

LE BOUQUET DE DIMANCHE oil on panel, 49 3/8 x 31¼in. (125.4 x 79.4cm.) sdlr 'Eugène de Blaas. 1893.'
Christie's New York, 2 November 1995 (162**) US$ 233,500 US$ 233,500

BLACKLOCK William Kay (1872-1930 c.) British
SUNLIGHT AND SHADOW oil on canvas, 36¼ x 30½in. (92.2 x 77.5in.) s inscr.'Sunlight and Shadow/W.Kay Blacklock/166 Gunter Grove/London.S.W.' on the reverse
EXH.: Bradford, 1912.
Christie's London, 7 June 1996 (631**) GBP 95,000 US$ 146,492

BLANCHET Louis-Gabriel (Paris 1705-1772 Rome) French
PORTRAIT OF THE ARTIST GIOVANNI PAOLO PANINI oil on canvas, 38 x 30in. (96.5 x 76cm.) indistinctly sdll 'L G Blanchet .it/ 1736'; inscr. 'Paolo Panini, peintre d'Architecture peint par G. Blanchet à Rome' on the reverse
PROV.: With A. Tooth Gallery, London; Anon. sale, Sotheby's London, 28 March 1979, lot 69, as *Carle van Loo*.
EXH.: On loan, Marble Hill House, Twickenham, 1985-1995.
LIT.: F. Arisi, *Gian Paolo Panini e i fasti della Roma del 700*, 1986 (illustrated in colour as frontipiece, as by *Charles André van Loo, Ritratto di Gian Paolo Panini*); M. Kiene, *Panini*.

Exposition dossier, Musée du Louvre, 1993, p. 21 as by *Carle van Loo*.
      Sotheby's London, 5 July 1995 (54**) GBP 188,500   US$ 300,686

JEUNE FEMME JOUANT AVEC SON CHAT / LA LETTRE DE RUPTURE oil on copper (a pair),
27 x 39cm. / 26.5 x 38.5cm. sdr 'L. Gab Blanchet inv et pinxit Romæ 1759' sdul 'L. Blanchet pinxit
Romæ 1759'
      Étude Tajan Paris, 12 December 1995 (99**) FRF 105,000   US$ 21,150

PORTRAIT OF A GENTLEMAN IN A RED COAT oil on canvas, 38 x 28½in. (96.5 x 72.4cm.) sd
'Rome ce 27 7bre (for septembre) 1755 Blanchet'
PROV.: De la Pappe, Paris; (Sale: Parke-Bernet Galleries, New York, 14 October 1948, lot 42);
there purchased by F.J. Cuthbertsch.
EXH.: Lyon, Musée des Beaux-Arts, before 1948.
      Sotheby's New York, 16 May 1996 (221**) US$ 19550   US$ 19,550

BLANCHET Thomas (Paris 1614-1689 Lyon) French
AN ITALIANATE LANDSCAPE WITH FIGURES RESTING NEAR A FOUNTAIN oil on canvas,
28 ¾ x 36 ¾in. (73 x 93.5cm.)
PROV.: Pietro Paolo Avila, Rome.
LIT.: *Inventario delle robbe.del sigr Pietro Poalo Avila.*Rome, Archivio di Stato, Not. Trib dell'A.C.
Pollius Bernardus, vol. 3873, folios 619-621; L. Galactéros-de-Boissier, *Thomas Blanchet*, 1991, p.
373, nos. P174-177, under lost paintings, and as part of a set of four.
      Sotheby's London, 6 December 1995 (260**) GBP 10,350   US$ 15,928

BLANCO Antonio Maria (b. 1927)
A SELF PORTRAIT oil on canvas, 28.5 x 24.5cm. sul and s again on the reverse
PROV.: Collection Kullicke, New York, no. 5174.
      Sotheby's Amsterdam, 23 April 1996 (27**) NLG 30680   US$ 18,230

BLANKENBURG Adolf (19th Century) German
THE SWIMMING PARTY oil on canvas, 24 ¾ x 29in. (62.8 x 73.7cm.) sdlr 'ABlankenburg'
      Christie's East, 13 February 1996 (185**) US$ 9,200   US$ 9,200

BLARENBERGHE Louis-Nicolas van (Lille 1716/1719-1794 Fontainebleau) French
TRAVELLERS WITH A COVERED WAGON oil on panel, 9 x 13cm. slr 'van Blarenberghe'
      Dorotheum Vienna, 6 March 1996 (115**) ATS 200,000   US$ 19,238

BLAU Tina <née> Lang (Vienna 1845-1937 Vienna) Austrian
SANDGRUBE MIT BLICK AUF PÖTZLEINSDORF oil on panel, 23 x 34cm. s on the reverse
      Dorotheum Vienna, 6 November 1995 (20**) ATS 200,000   US$ 20,063

ST. VEIT BEI WIEN (ON THE REVERSE AN OLD DRAWING: NR. 48 ST. VEIT BEI WIEN,
TINA BLAU) oil on panel, 12.5 x 21cm. slr 'T. Blau, Wien'
      Dorotheum Vienna, 6 November 1995 (85**) ATS 140,000   US$ 14,044

WIENER PRATER oilstudy on panel, 23.5 x 31cm. s 'Tina Blau' sd titled on the reverse 'Tina Blau
Wiener Prater 1883'
      Dorotheum Vienna, 17 April 1996 (417**) ATS 300,000   US$ 28,346

SOMMER IM PRATER oil on panel, 20.7 x 26.9cm. sll 'Tina Blau'
PROV.: C.J. Wawra, Vienna.
      Wiener Kunst Auktionen, 26 March 1996 (166**) ATS 280,000   US$ 26,933

WEISSENKIRCHEN IN DER WACHAU oil on cardboard, 39.5 x 50cm. slr 'Tina Blau'; sd and
titled 'Tina Blau Lang Weissenkirchen i.d. Wachau 1910 Wien 1915'
      Wiener Kunst Auktionen, 26 September 1995 (141**) ATS 380,000   US$ 36,937

BLECHEN Carl (Kottbus 1798-1840 Berlin) German
FIGURES IN A WOODED LANDSCAPE oil on board, 5 1/8 x 6½in. (13 x 16.5cm.) / 4 5/8 x 6½in. (!2.5 x 16.5cm.) s
        Phillips London, 12 March 1996 (12a (a pair)**) GBP 6,000   US$ 9,163

BLECKNER Ross (1949 b.) American
UNTITLED oil and encaustic on canvas-unframed, 26 x 26in. (66 x 66cm.) (1981)
PROV.: Mary Boone Gallery, New York; Portica, Philadelphia.
EXH.: Philadelphia Art Alliance, *Keys to a Special World Collection of Helen Herrick and Milton Brutten*, May-June 1987, no. 9 (illustrated).
        Christie's East, 7 May 1996 (178**) US$ 8,050   US$ 8,050

PIECES OF MONTHS oil on canvas mounted on panel, 13½ x 13½in. (34.3 x 34.3cm.) sd titled ans numbered 'Ross Bleckner 1985-1987 12 'pieces of months" on the reverse
PROV.: Mary Boone Gallery, New York; Fredrik Roos, Malmö.
        Christie's East, 7 May 1996 (194*) US$ 7,475   US$ 7,475

DOME oil and wax on canvas, 26 x 26in. (66 x 66cm.) sd titled 'Ross Bleckner 1993 DOME'
PROV.: Acquired directly from the artist.
        Christie's New York, 15 November 1995 (281**) US$ 23,000   US$ 23,000

SECOND GOLD COUNT oil on canvas unframed, 96 x 72in. (243.8 x 182.8cm.) sd titled 'Ross Bleckner 1990 SECOND GOLD COUNT' on the reverse
PROV.: Mary Boone Gallery, New York.
        Christie's New York, 15 November 1995 (307**) US$ 92,700   US$ 92,700

BOTANICAL STUDY oil, powdered pigment, oil-based resin and wax on canvas-unframed, 60 x 60in. (152.4 x 152.4cm) sd and titled 'Ross Bleckner 1993 'BOTANICAL STUDY" on the rverse
PROV.: Acquired directly from the artist.
EXH.: New York, The Solomon R.Guggenheim Museum, *Ross Bleckner Retrospective*, March-May 1995, no.53 (illustrated).
        Christie's New York, 8 May 1996 (368**) US$ 55,200   US$ 55,200

BLES David Joseph (The Hague 1821-1899 The Hague) Dutch
LA SURPRISE oil on panel, 32 x 41cm. s 'DBles ft'
PROV.: Possibly collection William II, King of the Netherlands 1840-1849; His Sale, The Hague, 12 Aug. 1850, part I, cat. no. 5(to de Vries Dfl. 500,-)cf.
LIT.: E. Bénézit, *Dictionaire peintres, sculpteurs etc.*, Paris 1976, Vol II, p. 80.
        Christie's Amsterdam, 26 October 1995 (104**) NLG 14,950   US$ 9,426

BLIECK Daniel de (1673 d. Middelburg) Dutch
THE INTERIOR OF A CHURCH oil on panel, 16½ x 11 5/8in. (41.9 x 29.5cm.) sd ' D B B / 1654'
PROV.: Sir Ralph Lawson; Christie's, 21 June 1968, lot 104, (504 to Chandler).
        Christie's South Kensington, 7 December 1995 (143**) GBP 7,312   US$ 11,253

BLINKS Thomas (1860-1912) British
LA CAZA DEL ZORRO oil on canvas, 92 x 142.5cm. sdlr '97' (1897)
        Sotheby's Madrid, 23 November 1995 (29**) ESP 3,407,500   US$ 28,010

BLOEMAERT Abraham (after) (Gorinchem 1564-1651 Utrecht) Dutch
THE DREAM OF JACOB oil on canvas-unframed, 45 ¾ x 37 ¾in. (116.3 x 96cm.)
        Christie's South Kensington, 7 December 1995 (81**) GBP 19,125   US$ 29,432

BLOEMEN Jan Frans van {called} Orizzonte (Antwerp 1662-1749 Rome) Flemish
SHEPHERDS BY TORRENT, A FORTIFIED MANSION ON A HILLTOP AND A BRIDGE BEYOND oil on canvas, 98.6 x 61.3cm.

Christie's Amsterdam, 7 May 1996 (80A**) NLG 34,500   US$ 20,117

CLASSICAL LANDSCAPES WITH FIGURES oil on canvas (a pair), each: 18 x 29in. (46 x 74cm.)
PROV.: The Lanfranchi Collection, Pisa, according to an old label on the reverse; In the Drury-Lowe Collection by 1868.
EXH.: Leeds, *National Exhibition of Works of Art*, 1868, no. 5; Nottingham, 1968, nos. 26 & 27.
LIT.: Richter 1901, nos. 206 & 207, as by *Orizzonte*.

Sotheby's London, 6 December 1995 (35**) GBP 40,000   US$ 61,557

BLOEMEN Pieter van, {called} Standard (Antwerp 1657-1720 Antwerp) Flemish
FIGURES BY A FARRIER'S SHOP oil on panel, 41 x 30.5cm.

Sotheby's Amsterdam, 14 November 1995 (25**) NLG 20,060   US$ 12,643

A RIDING SCHOOL BY A CLASSICAL RUIN oil on canvas, 24 x 33 5/8in. (61 x 85.5cm.) sd ini.
'P.V.B. 1713'

Christie's London, 19 April 1996 (212**) GBP 16,675   US$ 25,284

BLOEMERS Arnoldus (1786-1844) Dutch
ELABORATE FLOWER STILL-LIFES IN TERRACOTTA URNS RESTING IN MARBLE
LEDGES oil on canvas (a pair), each: 18¼ x 15in. (46.4 x 38.1cm.) s ini. ll 'AB'

Sotheby's New York, 16 May 1996 (111**) US$ 140,000   US$ 140,000

A STILL LIFE WITH ROSES, RHODODENDRONS, PEONIES, DAHLIA, A MORNING-
GLORY, CORNFLOWER AND A NASTURTIUM IN A VASE ON A LEDGE oil on canvas, 49.5
x 39cm. sll mono.

Christie's Amsterdam, 26 October 1995 (194**) NLG 48,300   US$ 30,454

BLOMMAERT Abraham (ca. 1626-after 1675) Dutch
EXTENSIVE LANDSCAPE WITH A SHEPHERD AND HIS DOG oil on canvas, 33 x 48in. (83.8 x
121.9cm.) inscr.ll 'Both'

Sotheby's New York, 11 January 1996 (91**) US$ 9,200   US$ 9,200

BLOMMERS Bernardus Johannes (The Hague 1845-1914 The Hague) Dutch
CHILDREN ON A SEASHORE oil on canvas, 20 1/8 x 26 ¾in. (51 x 68cm.) slr 'Blommers'

Phillips London, 14 November 1995 (7**) GBP 21,000   US$ 32,848

WAITING FOR THE FISHING-FLEET pencil, pen and brush and black ink and watercolour
heightened with white on paper, 37 x 55 cm s 'Blommers'
PROV.: The Cooling Galleries Ltd., London; Collection James Sanderson Esq.

Christie's Amsterdam, 25 April 1996 (73**) NLG 34,500   US$ 20,500

BLOOS Richard (1878-1956) French (?)
JARDIN DES TUILERIES oil on canvas, 19 ¾ x 25½in. (50 x 65cm.) sdlr 'R Bloos, Paris 11', s
again and titled on the stretcher 'Jardin des Tuileries'

Christie's South Kensington, 24 June 1996 (163***) GBP 11,500   US$ 17,733

BLOOT Pieter de (Rotterdam 1602-1658 Rotterdam) Dutch
SUMMERMORNING IN HOLLAND oil on panel, 39 x 58cm. Slc 'P. de Bloot'
PROV.: Sale, Dorotheum, Vienna, 12 March 1974, lot 13, illustration nos. 8 and VIII (colour);
Private collection, Italy.
LIT.: *Die Presse*, Vienna, 13 March 1974.

Dorotheum Vienna, 6 March 1996 (103**) ATS 300,000   US$ 28,857

BLUHM Oscar (1867-1912) German
IN THE PARK bodycolour on paper, 14½ x 21 5/8in. (37 x 55cm.) sd 'Oscar Bluhm/Meissen 8'

Christie's London, 15 March 1996 (15A**) GBP 23,000   US$ 35,125

BLUM Ludwig (1891-1975)
VIEW OF JERUSALEM oil on canvas, 23 ¾ x 30½in. (60.4 x 100.4cm.) sdll 'L. Blum 1944'; s in Hebrew and dlr
PROV.: A.C. Barnes, London.
      Christie's Tel Aviv, 14 April 1996 (3**) US$ 14,950

	US$	14,950

BOCCHI Faustino (Brescia 1659-1742 c. Brescia) Italian
SCENE GROTESQUE oil on canvas, 82.5 x 72cm.
      Finearte Milan, 3 April 1996 (83*) ITL 11,500,000

	US$	7,348

AUTUMN ALLEGORY oil on canvas, ,100 x 150cm.
      Finearte Milan, 3 April 1996 (115**) ITL 185,000,000

	US$	118,211

BOCH Anna (La Louvière 1848-1933 Brussels) Belgian
AN INTERIOR oil on canvas, 70 x 60cm. sdal 'A.Boch 6'
      Christie's Amsterdam, 5 June 1996 (233*) NLG 13,800

	US$	8,063

BÖCKSTIEGEL Peter August (1889-1951) German
MEIN VATER oil on canvas, 66 x 57cm. sdlr 'P.A. Böckstiegel / Arrode 26'; d and titled on the frame
      Hauswedell & Nolte Cologne, 1 December 1995 (47**) DEM 45,000

	US$	31,222

BODDINGTON Henry John (1811-1865) British
ANGLERS BY A STREAM WITH A WATERMILL oil on canvas, 36¼ x 54in. (92.1 x 137.2cm.) sdll 'H J Boddington'
      Christie's East, 13 February 1996 (55**) US$ 12,650

	US$	12,650

BODENMÜLLER Alphons (Munich 1847-1886 Munich) German
DER ERSTE SCHÄFFLERTANZ oil on canvas, 43½ x 37 ¾in. (110.5 x 95.9cm.) sd & inscr.'Alphons Bodenmüller/München' and sd. & inscr.'Alphons Bodenmüller/München Barrerstr./37./Erster-Schäfflertanz im Pestjahre 1517/preis 6500 reichsmarks' on an old label on the reverse
EXH.: Munich, Glaspalast, 1876; Düsseldorf, *4. Allgemeine Deutsche Kunstausstellung*, 1880; Nürnberg, *Bayrische Landesausstellung*, 1882.
LIT.: H.C. Ebertshäuser, *Malerei im 19. Jahrhundert, Münchner Schule*, Munich 1979, p. 170; F. V. Boetticher, *Malerwerke des Neunzehnten Jahrhunderts*, Hofheim am Taunus 1974, vol. I, i, p. 119 no. 3.
      Christie's London, 11 October 1995 (58**) GBP 17,250

	US$	27,225

BODMER Karl (1809-1893) Swiss
FOREST WITH DUCKS AND FROGS oil on canvas, 32 x 39¼in. (81.3 x 99.6cm.) sll 'K. Bodmer'
      Christie's New York, 23 May 1996 (105**) US$ 29,900

	US$	29,900

BOECKHORST Johann (the earlier) (Münster 1605-1668 Antwerp) Flemish (German)
A PERSONIFICATION OF RHETORIC oil on canvas, 55½ x 63in. (141 x 159.8cm.)
PROV.: Dr. F. Lieben, Vienna.
EXH.: Vienna, Secession, *Drei Jahrhunderte Flämische Kunst*, 11 Jan- 2 March 1930, no. 166.
      Christie's London, 8 December 1995 (250**) GBP 11,500

	US$	17,698

BOECKL Herbert (Klagenfurt 1894-1966 Vienna) Austrian
LANDSCHAFT BEI ST. KATHREIN watercolour on paper, 34.5 x 49.5cm. inscr. by the artist's wife 'Herbert Boeckl 1950, Landschaft bei St. Kathrein' on the reverse (1950)
      Dorotheum Vienna, 21 May 1996 (128**) ATS 200,000

	US$	19,205

BOETTCHER Christian Eduard (Imgenbroich near Aachen 1818-1889 Düsseldorf) German
DIE HEIMKEHR VOM FELDE oil on canvas, 51 x 67cm. sdlr 'C. E. Boettcher pxt. 1872'

PROV.: Hessische Privatsammlung.
EXH.: Bismeyer & Kraus, Düsseldorf 1873; Kunstverein Wiesbaden.
LIT.: Boetticher, *Malerwerke des 19. Jahrhunderds*, I/1, p. 123, no. 28.
      Lempertz Cologne, 15 November 1995 (1717**) DEM 19,000   US$ 13,411

BOETTCHER Christian Eduard (Imgenbroich near Aachen 1818-1889 Düsseldorf) German
DIE ERSTEN SCHRITTE oil on canvas, 83 x 104cm. sdlr C.E. Boettcher pxt. 1866'
      Lempertz Cologne, 18 May 1996 (1507**) DEM 44,000   US$ 28,685

BOGDANI Jacob (Eperjes-Presov 1660-1724 London) Hungarian
STILL-LIFES OF VARIEGATED TULIPS, ROSES, HYACINTH, MORNING GLORY AND
POPPIES IN AN ELABORATE METAL URN ON A LEDGE, AND PEACHES, APPLES,
GRAPES, CURRANTS AND OTHER FRUIT, NUTS AND A BUTTERFLY, ALL ON A
MARBLE LEDGE oil on canvas (a pair), each: 29¼ x 24¼in. (74.3 x 61.6cm.) s 'J. Bogdani'
PROV.: Viscount Midleton; purchased by the present collector in the 1950's.
      Sotheby's New York, 11 January 1996 (130**) US$ 299,500   US$ 299,500

FLORAL STILL-LIFE IN A WOODED LANDSCAPE oil on canvas, 45½ x 35½in. (115.6 x
90.2cm.)
      Sotheby's New York, 16 May 1996 (62**) US$ 46,000   US$ 46,000

DOMESTIC FOWL IN A GARDEN, PEACOCKS BY A CLASSICAL FOUNTAIN IN A
COURTYARD BEYOND oil on canvas, 57¼ x 81½in. (145.4 x 207cm.) s 'J. Bogdani' (on the wall,
by the turkey) (after 1696)
PROV.: With J. Leger, London, 1930.
      Christie's London, 19 April 1996 (232**) GBP 111,500   US$ 169,067

A PAPILLLON DOG IN A LANDSCAPE WITH A SQUIRREL, A BLUE-TIT, PLUMS,
PEACHES AND AN ORNAMENTAL FOUNTAIN BEYOND oil on canvas, 24¼ x 30in. (61.6 x
76.3cm.) s ini. 'J.B.'
PROV.: With Carlton Hobbs, London; Count Alarico Palmieri, Geneva.
LIT.: Clarice Waud and Mark Hutchings, *The Papillon 'Butterfly' Dog*, 1985, pl. 3 repr.
      Christie's London, 28 March 1996 (23**) GBP 27,600   US$ 42,150

TULIPS, IRISES, HOLLYHOCKS, APPLEBLOSSOM, HONEYSUCKLE AND OTHER
FLOWERS IN A BRONZE URN, A BASKET OF STRAWBERRIES, FIGS, PLUMS, APPLES,
REDCURRANTS, GRAPES AND A PARROT ON A LEDGE oil on canvas, 27 ¾ x 48½ in. (70.5 x
123.2cm)
PROV.: with Richard Green. A similar piece by Bogdani was sold By Christie's London, 27 April
1995, lot 114.
      Christie's London, 7 July 1995 (3**) GBP 54,300   US$ 86,617

BOGDANI Jacob (attributed to) (Eperjes-Presov 1660-1724 London) Hungarian
PEONIES, ROSES, MORNING GLORY AND TULIPS IN AN URN ON A STONE LEDGE oil on
canvas, 18½ x 39in. (47 x 99.1cm.)
      Christie's South Kensington, 14 February 1996 (291**) GBP 15,750   US$ 24,197

BOGGS Frank Myers (Springfield (Ohio) 1855-1926 Meudon) French (American)
CANAL EN HOLLANDE oil on canvas, 54 x 65cm. sll
      Étude Tajan Paris, 1 February 1996 (79) FRF 30,000   US$ 6,139

BOHATSCH Erwin (1951 b.) German
UNTITLED oil on canvas, 240 x 140.5cm. sd on reverse 'Bohatsch Okt.88'
LIT.: Christian Krawagna, *Erwin Bohatsch*, Residenz Verlag, Salzburg-Wien 1992, p. 11, ill. p.65.
      Wiener Kunst Auktionen, 27 September 1995 (565**) ATS 130,000   US$ 12,636

BOHEMEN Kees (Cornelis Bernardus) van (The Hague 1928-1986) Dutch
TOMORROW IT'S MY TURN oil on canvas, 150 x 150cm. sdlr 'K.v.Bohemen 78', and inscr. with
title and d again on the stretcher
        Christie's Amsterdam, 5 June 1996 (329**) NLG 40,250   US$ 23,517

GIRL WITH HAT oil on canvas, 80 x 80cm. sdlr 'v.Bohemen 78'
        Christie's Amsterdam, 5 June 1996 (356**) NLG 33,350   US$ 19,486

GIRLS LEAVING THE FACTORY oil on canvas, 140 x 140cm. sdlr 'K.v.Bohemen 75'
        Christie's Amsterdam, 6 December 1995 (305**) NLG 41,400   US$ 25,654

BÖHLER Hans (Vienna 1884-1961 Vienna) Austrian
DIE GARTNERSFRAU oil on canvas, 58 x 70cm.
PROV.: Private collection, Vienna.
        Dorotheum Vienna, 21 May 1996 (81**) ATS 200,000   US$ 19,205

BÖHM Pal (Grosswardein 1839-1905 Munich) Hungarian
DIE PILZSAMMLER oil on panel, 30 x 39in. (76.2 x 99cm.) s & inscr. 'Fest. Böhm P München'
EXH.: possibly Düsseldorf, *4. Allgemeine Kunstausstellung*, 1880.
LIT.: possibly F. von Boetticher, *Malerwerke des Neunzehnten Jahrhunderts*, Hofheim am Taunus,
1974, vol.I, i, p. 121, no. 13.
        Christie's London, 11 October 1995 (79**) GBP 14,375   US$ 22,688

BOILLY Louis-Léopold (La Bassée (Nord) 1761-1845 Paris) French
PORTRAIT OF ARNOULT-JOVITE-POLYCARPE BOILLY, FATHER OF THE ARTIST black
lead, black and white chalk heightened with white chalk, on a tablet with the label of the paper
supplier 'Coiffier, rue du coq-honoré on the *verso*, 9 x 7½in. (22.8 x 19cm.) s 'L. Boilly del' (in the
margin) and with inscription '59' and '103' *verso*
LIT.: The present drawing will be included in the forthcoming *Louis Léopold Boilly catalogue
raisonné* being prepared by Etienne Breton and Paul Zuber.
        Christie's New York, 22 May 1996 (17**) US$ 48,300   US$ 48,300

BOISSELIER Antoine-Félix (1790-1857) French
AN ARTIST SITTING IN A TREE, SKETCHING black chalk, brush and brown ink, brown wash on
wove paper, 5 7/8 x 4 1/8in. (15 x 10.7cm.) with inscription 'Par Boisselier' twice on the mount
PROV.: From an album assembled by Madame Jacques-Félix Duban (1797-1871) born Debret, to
her nephew, Paul Duvivier de Streel, and thence to the present owner.
        Christie's New York, 22 May 1996 (34**) US$ 13,800   US$ 13,800

BOLDINI Giovanni (Ferrara 1842-1931 Paris) Italian
PORTRAIT OF THE LUISA CASATI, WITH A GREYHOUND oil on canvas, 99 ¾ x 55¼in.
(253.4 x 140.4cm.) sd 'Boldini/1908'
PROV.: Sold by the artist by Baron Maurice de Rothschild.
EXH.: Paris, Salon, 1909, no. 119.
LIT.: *Femina*, December 1909, (illustrated); *L'illustration*, 1931, p. 33; E. Cardona, *Vie de Jean
Boldini*, Choisy-Le-Roi, 1931, p. 99; E. Cardona, *Boldini Parisien d'Italie*, Milan, 1952, p. 47; D.
Cecchi, *Boldini*, Turin, 1962, pp. 207-209; C. Ragghianti and E. Camesasca, *L'opera completa di
Boldini*, Milan, 1970, p. 123, no. 445 (illustrated); P. Moneli, *La Belle Epoque*, New York, 1978, p.
58; E. Piceni, *Boldini L'uomo e l'opera,* Turin, 1981, pp. 16, 18; V. Doria, *Boldini Unpublished work*,
bologna, 1982, pp. 36, 104; G. Reynolds, *Giovanni Boldini and Society Portraiture* 1880-1920, New
York, 1984, p. 48; D. Cecchi, *Coré*, Bologna, 1986, p. 11, (illustrated pl. XII); D. Wistow, *Augustus
John*, (exh. cat.), Toronto, 1987, pp. 4-5 (illustrated); P. Mauriès, *Boldini*, Milan, 1987 pp. 72-75
(illustrated); G. Marcenaro, *Giovanni Boldini*, Genoa, 1987, p. 138; G. Piazza, *Boldini*, Milan, 1989,
p. 306.
        Christie's New York, 1 November 1995 (6***) US$ 1,542,500   US$ 1,542,500

THE BLACK SASH Oil on canvas, 83 x 39½in. (210.8 x 100.3cm.) sll 'Boldini' (1890)
PROV.: Sold by the Artist to Baron de Rothschild.
LIT.: P. Mauriès, *Boldini*, Italy 1987, p. 60 (illustrated p. 61).
    Christie's New York, 1 November 1995 (9**) US$ 365,500   US$ 365,500

PORTRAIT OF MADAME HUGO, AND HER SON oil on canvas, 83 x 47½in. (210.8 x 120.6cm.)
sd 'Boldini/1898'
PROV.: Sold by the Artist to Baron de Rothschild.
EXH.: New York, Wildenstein & Co.,*Loan Exhibition Paintings by Boldini* 1845-1931, March 20-
April 8 1933, no. 18.
LIT.: C. Ragghianti ans E. Camesasca, *l'Opera Completa di Boldini*, Milan ,1970, p. 113, no. 297
(iluustrated);P. Mauriès, *Boldini*, Italy 1987, p. 60 (illustrated p. 61).
    Christie's New York, 1 November 1995 (14**) US$ 437,000   US$ 437,000

The Black Sash

PORTRAIT OF GIOVINETT ERRAZURIZ Oil on canvas, 79 ¼ x 39 ¾in. (201.3 x 101cm.) sdll 'Boldini /1892'
PROV.: Sold by the artist to Baron Maurice de Rothschild.
EXH.: Paris, *Exposition Nationale des Beaux-Arts*, May 1892, no. 138 (as'Mlle. E.'); Venice, Biennale, 1897, no. 37; New York, Wildenstein and Co., *Loan Exhibition Paintings by Boldini* 1845 - 1931, March 20-April 8,1933, no 14.
LIT.: E. Cardona, *Boldini Parisien d'Italie*, Milan, 1952, p. 104; New York Evening Post, 27 March 1933(illustrated); D. Cecchi, *Boldini*, Turin, 1962, p. 134;C. Ragghianti ans E. Camesasca, *l'Opera Completa di Boldini*, Milan ,1970, p. 108, no. 232 (illustrated); G. Piazza, *Boldini*, Milan, 1989, p.298.
    Christie's New York, 1 November 1995 (15**) US$ 382,000   US$ 382,000

BOMBERG David (Birmingham 1890-1957 London) British
A CONVERSATION pen, brush, black ink, watercolour and bodycolour, 13½ x 10½in. (33.4 x 26.7cm.) sdlc 'Bomberg 1920'
PROV.: James Kirkman, London.
    Christie's London, 21 March 1996 (22**)
GBP 8,625   US$ 13,172

BOMBOIS Camille (Vénarey-lès-Laumes 1883-1970 Paris) French
LA CUEILLETTE oil on canvas, 23 5/8 x 28 ¾in. (60 x 73cm.) s (1925)
PROV.: Perls Galleries, New York; Dina Vierny, Paris.
    Sotheby's New York, 2 May 1996 (363**) US$ 57,500   US$ 57,500

LES PUITS DU VILLAGE oil on canvas, 25 ¾ x 36½in. (65.4 x 92.7cm.) slr 'Bombois' (ca. 1926)
PROV.: Perls Galleries, New York.
    Sotheby's New York, 2 May 1996 (382**) US$ 40,250   US$ 40,250

LE CLOWN oil on canvas, 21½ x 18¼in. (54.5 x 46.3cm.) slr 'Bombois.Clle'
PROV.: Gallery Moos Ltd., Toronto.
    Christie's East, 7 November 1995 (161**) US$ 48,300   US$ 48,300

LE VIEUX DONJON oil on canvas, 23 5/8 x 31 7/8in. (60 x 81cm.) sll 'Bombois.C.lle' (1928)
PROV.: Dr. Franz Meyer-Mahler, Zurich; Perls Galleries, New York.
EXH.: Salzburg, Residenz Galerie, *Die Welt der naiven Malerei*, July-Sept., 1964, no number.
Christie's New York, 8 November 1995 (333**) US$ 46,000

| | | US$ | 46,000 |

LE PECHEUR AUX GRANDS ARBRES oil on canvas, 25 5/8 x 36¼in. (65 x 92cm.) sbr
'Bombois.C.lle'
PROV.: Dr. Franz Meyer-Mahler, Zurich; Perls Galleries, New York.
EXH.: Basel, Kunsthalle, *Bauchant, Bombois, Séraphine, Vivin*, June-Aug., 1956, no. 62.
Christie's New York, 8 November 1995 (346**) US$ 40,250

| | | US$ | 40,250 |

BOMPIANI Roberto (1821-1908) Italian
THE SONGBIRD oil on canvas, laid down on board, 27 ¾ x 19 ¾in. (70. 5 x 50cm.) sdlr 'R.
Bompiani. 1874'
Phillips London, 12 March 1996 (43**) GBP 6,000

| | | US$ | 9,163 |

BONHEUR Auguste (1824-1884) French
THE PATH HOME oil on canvas, 25 5/8 x 39¼in. (65.1 x 99.7cm.) slr 'Auguste Bonheur'
Christie's New York, 22 May 1996 (177**) US$ 14,950

| | | US$ | 14,950 |

**BONHEUR Rosa (Marie-Rosalie) (Bordeaux 1822-1899 By, Seine-et-Marne (or Mellun))
French**
TENDING THE FLOCK oil on canvas, 19 ¾ x 25½in. (50.2 x 64.8cm.) sdlr 'R Bonheur' and bears
signature and date 'R Bonheur /Roma 1854'
Christie's New York, 2 November 1995 (96**) US$ 21,850

| | | US$ | 21,850 |

BONITO Giuseppe (Castellamare di Stabia (Campania) 1707-1789) Italian
CONCERTINO oil on canvas, 76 x 102cm. (ca. 1740)
PROV.: Collection Zagari, Milan 1938.
EXH.: Naples, 1938, *Mostra della pittura napoletana del '600, ',700 e '800*.
Christie's Rome, 4 June 1996 (575**) ITL 40,000,000

| | | US$ | 25,940 |

BONNARD Pierre (Fontenay-aux-Roses 1867-1947 Le Cannet) French
THE PROMENADE oil on cardboard, 15 x 12¼in. (38 x 31cm.) slr 'Bonnard' (ca. 1900)
PROV.: Bought from Hessel in 1919 by Bernheim-Jeune, sold to Mr. Thomas Justice; Former
collection of Henry-Jean Laroche.
EXH.: Maison de la Pensée Française, *Pierre Bonnard*, summer 1955, exh. no. 2 (dated circa 1898).
LIT.: François Joachim Beer, *Pierre Bonnard*, Editions Françaises d'art, 1947, reproduced on p. 54,
plate 34 under the title Jeunes femmes; Jean and Henry Dauberville, *Bonnard, catalogue raisonné de
l'oeuvre peint, 1888-1905*, Paris, Editions Bernheim-Jeune, 1965, described and reproduced p. 246,
volume I, under the no. 243 (errors in measurement); Michel Terrasse, *Pierre Bonnard - Du dessin
au tableau*, Imprimerie Nationale.
Étude Tajan Paris, 13 December 1995 (7***) FRF 2,100,000

| | | US$ | 422,995 |

BOULEVARD DES BATIGNOLLES (LA PLUIE) oil on canvas, 24 3/4 x 25 5/8in. (63 x 65cm.) slr
'Bonnard' (ca. 1926)
PROV.: Galerie Bernheim-Jeune, Paris (acquired from the artist in 1931); Katia Granoff, Paris; Sir
Kenneth Clark, London; Roland, Browse & Delbanco, London; The Lefevre Gallery, London; Mrs.
John Armstrong, London; Drs. Fritz and Peter Nathan, Zurich; Acquired from the above by the late
owner circa 1957.
EXH.: Melbourne, *Herald Exhibition of French and British Contemporary Art*, 1939, no. 8. The
exhibition traveled to Adelaide; London, Roland, Browse & Delbanco, *Between Monet and
Bonnard*, June-July, 1949, no. 8; London, Roland, Browse & Delbanco, *Bonnard*, June, 1950, no. 31;
London, Marlborough Fine Art Ltd., *Roussel, Bonnard, Vuillard*, May-June, 1954, p. 44, no. 39;
London, The Lefevre Gallery, *XlXe and XXe Century French Paintings*, Sept.-Oct., 1956, p. 3, no. 2
(illustrated, p. 5); Paris, Petit Palais, *De Gericault à Matisse, Chèfs-d'oeuvre français des collections*

suisses, March-May, 1959, no. 5; (illustrated, pl. 45); London, Royal Academy of Arts, *Pierre Bonnard, 1867- 1947*,Jan.-March, 1966, p. 55, no. 159; Hamburg, Kunstverein, *Pierre Bonnard: Gemälde, Aquarelle, Zeichnungen und Druckgraphik*, Feb.-April, 1970, no. 27 (illustrated, pl. 30). LIT.: A. Morance, 'Pierre Bonnard,' *L'Art d'aujourd'hui*, autumn, 1927, no. 15 (illustrated, pl. 53); *Art News Annual*, vol. XXVI, 1957 (illustrated, p. 18); F. Nathan, *Dr. Fritz Nathan und Dr. Peter Nathan, 25Jahre, 1936-1961*, Zurich, 1961, p. 60 (illustrated); J. and H. Dauberville, *Bonnard, Catalogue raisonné de l'oeuvre peint*, Paris, 1973, vol. III (1920-1939), p. 285, no. 1351(illustrated, p. 286).

Christie's New York, 7 November 1995 (3**) US$ 442,500	US$	442,500

LANDSCAPE WITH PALM oil on canvas, 22 x 30 ¾in. (56 x 53cm.) sll 'Bonnard' (1923)
PROV.: Purchased from Bonnard in 1923 by Bernheim-Jeune and sold to Henry-Jean Laroche.
LIT.: Jean and Henry Dauberville, *Bonnard, catalogue raisonné de l'oeuvre peint, 1920-1939*, Paris, Editions Bernheim-Jeune, 1965, described and reproduced p. 148, volume III, under the no. 1165.

Étude Tajan Paris, 13 December 1995 (8***) FRF 800,000	US$	161,141

ENVIRONS OF CANNES oil on canvas, 22 x 18in. (56 x 46cm.) sll 'Bonnard' (ca. 1923)
PROV.: Druet Gallery, Paris (number 9966, under the title: 'le parc à Arcachon'; former collection of Mr. Henry-Jean Laroche.
LIT.: Jean and Henry Dauberville, *Bonnard, catalogue raisonné de l'oeuvre peint, 1920-1939*, Paris, Editions Bernheim-Jeune, 1965, described and reproduced p. 150, volume III, under the no. 1168.

Étude Tajan Paris, 13 December 1995 (9***) FRF 500,000	US$	100,713

BOUQUET DES CHAMPS oil on canvas, 16 x 13 1/8in. (40.6 x 33.3cm.) s (ca. 1888)
PROV.: Galerie Beyeler, Basel; The Lefevre Gallery (Alex Reid & Lefevre Ltd.), London; Sale: Sotheby's, London, June 27, 1989, lot 25; Acquired by the present owner at the above sale.
EXH.: New York, Acquavella Galleries, *Bonnard*, 1977, no. 1; Basel, Galerie Beyeler, *Bonnard*, 1977, no. I; London, The Lefevre Gallery, *An Exhibition of Works by Pierre Bonnard*, 1978, no. I; London, Royal Academy of Arts; Washington D.C., National Gallery of Art, *Post-Impressionism*, 1979-80, no. 27.
LIT.: Jean and Henry Dauberville, *Bonnard, Catalogue raisonné de l'oeuvre peint, 1888-1905*, vol. 1, Paris, 1965, no. 4, illustrated p. 83.

Sotheby's New York, 2 May 1996 (147**) US$ 79,500	US$	79,500

LE CANNET, LA ROUTE ROSE oil on canvas, 21 5/8 x 25 1/8in. (55 x 64cm.) slr 'bonnard' (ca. 1935)
PROV.: Estate of the artist; Mrs Henry C. Woods, Chicago.
EXH.: Paris, Galerie Bernheim-Jeune, *Exposition rétrospective Bonnard*, 1950, no. 59.
LIT.: Jean and Henry Dauberville, *Bonnard, Catalogue raisonné de l'oeuvre peint, 1920-1939*, Paris 1973, vol. III, p. 417, no. 1533 (illustrated).

Sotheby's London, 24 June 1996 (60**) GBP 287,500	US$	443,331

LE PETIT DEJEUNER. HOMME ET FEMME oil on card laid down on cradled panel, 10 7/7 x 13in. (27.5 x 33cm.) sd 'Bonnard 94' (1894)
PROV.: The Artist's estate.
LIT.: J. and H. Dauberville, *Bonnard catalogue raisonné de l'oeuvre peint*, supplement 1887-1939, Vol. IV, Paris, 1965, no. 1757 (illustrated p. 155).

Christie's London, 26 June 1996 (138**) GBP 73,000	US$	112,567

LE BOULEVARD EXTERIEUR: BOULEVARD DE CLICHY ET ANGLE DE LA RUE DE DOUAI oil on canvas, 38 5/8 x 29 7/8in. (98 x 76cm.) sll 'Bonnard' (ca 1904)
PROV.: Bernheim Jeune, Paris, from whom aquired by the father of the present owner in 1918.
EXH.: F. Fosca, *Bonnard*, Geneva, 1919, p. 24 (illustrated pl. V111); C. Terasse, *Bonnard*, Paris, 1927 (illustrated p. 77); J. and H. Dauberville, *Bonnard, catalogue raisonné de l'oeuvre peint*, 1888-1905, vol. 1, Paris, 1965, no. 309 (illustrated p. 284).

Christie's London, 28 November 1995 (9**) GBP 914,500	US$	1,430,471

BOULEVARD DES BATIGNOLLES oil on board, 13 7/8 x 10 5/8in. (35.2 x 27cm.) sd and dedicated ll 'à Ronaï P. Bonnard 95' (1895)
PROV.: Josef Rippl Ronaï, Budapest; The Lefèvre Gallery, London (46/58), from whom bought by the previous owner and thence by descent to the present owner.
EXH.: London, The Lefèvre Gallery, *A Group of XIX and XXth Century French Paintings*, Nov.-Dec. 1958, no. 1; London, The Tate Gallery, *Private Views, Works from the Collection of twenty Friends of the Tate Gallery*, Apr-May 1963, no. 74; London, Royal Academy of Arts, *Bonnard*, 1966, no. 9.
LIT.: J. & H. Dauberville, *Bonnard 1888-1905*, Paris, 1965, vol.I, no. 114 (illustrated p. 160); N. Watkins, *Bonnard*, London, 1994, p.40 (illustrated fig.28 p.41).
Christie's London, 29 November 1995 (108**) GBP 112,000   US$ 175,192

BOULEVARD DES BATIGNOLLES (LA PLUIE) oil on canvas, 24 ¾ x 25 5/8in. (63 x 65cm.) slr 'Bonnard' (1926)
PROV.: Galerie Bernheim-Jeune, Paris (acquired from the artist in 1931); Katia Granoff, Paris; Sir Kenneth Clark, London; Roland, Browse & Delbanco, London; The Lefevre Gallery, London; Mrs. John Armstrong, London; Drs. Fritz and Peter Nathan, Zurich; Acquired from the above by the late owner *circa* 1957.
EXH.: Melbourne, *Herald Exhibition of French and British Contemporary Art*, 1939, no. 8. The exhibition traveled to Adelaide; London, Roland, Browse & Delbanco, *Between Monet and Bonnard*,June-July, 1949, no. 8; London, Roland, Browse & Delbanco, *Bonnard*,June, 1950, no. 31; London, Marlborough Fine Art Ltd., *Roussel, Bonnard, Vuillard*, May-June, 1954, p. 44, no. 39; London, The Lefevre Gallery, *XIXe and XXe Century French Paintings*, Sept.-Oct., 1956, p. 3, no. 2 (illustrated, p. 5); Paris, Petit Palais, *De Géricault à Matisse, Chefs-d'oeuvre francais des collections suisses*, March-May, 1959, no. 5 (illustrated, pl. 45); London, Royal Academy of Arts, *Pierre Bonnard, 1867- 1947*,Jan.-March, 1966, p. 55, no. 159; Hamburg, Kunstverein, *Pierre Bonnard: Gemälde, Aquarelle Zeichnungen und Druckgraphik*, Feb.-April, 1970, no. 27 (illustrated, pl. 30).
LIT.: A. Morancé, 'Pierre Bonnard,' *L'Art d'Aujourd'hui*, autumn, 1927, no. 15 (illustrated, pl. 53); *Art News Annual*, vol. XXVI, 1957 (illustrated, p. 18); F. Nathan, *Dr. Fritz Nathan und Dr. Peter Nathan, 25 Jahre, 1936-1961*, Zurich, 1961, p. 60 (illustrated). J. and H. Dauberville, *Bonnard, Catalogue raisonné de l'oeuvre peint*, Paris, 1973, vol. III (1920-1939), p. 285, no. 1351 (illustrated, p. 286).
Christie's New York, 8 November 1995 (3**) US$ 442,500   US$ 442,500

FEMME ALLONGÉE oil on cradled panel, 20 ½ x 18in. (52 x 45.7cm.) ll 'Bonnard 99' (1899)
Christie's New York, 8 November 1995 (167**) US$ 63,000   US$ 63,000

PETIT COMPOTIER D' ORANGES oil on canvas, 15 ¾ x 12 ¼in. (40 x 31cm.) sur 'Bonnard' (1924)
PROV.: Galerie Bernheim-Jeune, Paris (acquired from the artist, 1924); Charles Pacquement, Paris; sale, Galerie Georges Petit, Paris, Dec. 12, 1932, lot 11; Dr. Albert Charpentier, Paris (acquired from the above).
LIT.: J. and H. Dauberville, *Bonnard, Catalogue raisonné de l'oeuvre peint*, Paris, 1974, vol. III (1920-1930), no. 1,250 (illustrated, p. 209).
Christie's New York, 8 November 1995 (191**) US$ 365,500   US$ 365,500

BONNET Rudolf (Johan Rudolf) (Amsterdam 1895-1978) Dutch
NI SUSUAN pastel, 68 x 45.5cm. sur; d and inscr. ul 'ni gusti aju/Bali 1950'
LIT.: Dr. H. Roever-Bonnet, *Rudolf Bonnet. Een zondagskind*, Wijk en Alburg 1993, (illustrated p. 118).
Sotheby's Amsterdam, 23 April 1996 (9**) NLG 40120   US$ 23,840

NI NYOMAN SAMA AND NI KETUT pastel, 110 x 65.5cm. sdur 'Bali 1975' and inscr. with title ul
Sotheby's Amsterdam, 23 April 1996 (29**) NLG 153,400   US$ 91,152

WIDYANA pastel, 90 x 61cm. sdur 'R. BONNET/BALI 1977'; inscr. ul 'WIDYANA/MASULING'
EXH.: Amsterdam, Galerie Inart, *Rudolf Bonnet*, 16 September-8 October 1977.
        Sotheby's Amsterdam, 23 April 1996 (53**) NLG 34,220   US$ 20,334

A PORTRAIT OF SI AJOE black chalk heightened with white, 44 x 32.5cm. sur 'R. BONNET';
inscr. and dul 'Si Ajoe/Bali '48'
        Sotheby's Amsterdam, 23 April 1996 (99**) NLG 25,960   US$ 15,426

BONNIER Alice (France) French
A GAME OF SOLITAIRE oil on canvas, 38 x 38in. (96.5 x 96.5cm.) sdlc 'ABonnier./98'
        Christie's New York, 2 November 1995 (191**) US$ 12,650   US$ 12,650

BONVIN François (Vaugirard 1817-1887 Saint-Germain-en-Laye) French
L'ECOLIER EN RETENUE oil on panel, 9¼ x 7 3/8in. (23.5 x 18.8cm.) sdll 'F. Bonvin. 1873.'
PROV.: Collection of J. Seure; sale, Paris, 1888.
EXH.: Paris, Galerie D. Rothschild, *Exposition de Tableaux et Dessins par F. Bonvin*, 1886, no. 46.
        Christie's New York, 14 February 1996 (106**) US$ 25,300   US$ 25,300

BOQUET Pierre-Jean (1751-1817) French
EXTENSIVE RIVER LANDSCAPE WITH A SHEPHERD AND HIS FLOCK oil on canvas, 17 ¾ x
20in. (45.1 x 50.8cm.) slr 'Boquet'
        Sotheby's New York, 16 May 1996 (264**) US$ 13,800   US$ 13,800

BORES Francisco (Madrid 1898-1972 Paris) Spanish
GIRL READING A BOOK IN AN INTERIOR oil on canvas, 81 x 65cm. sdlr 'Bores 67'
        Christie's Amsterdam, 5 June 1996 (156*) NLG 29,900   US$ 17,470

LUMIERE DU JOUR oil on canvas, 65 x 81cm. sdlr 'Bores '39'
PROV.: Galerie Simon, Paris; Private collection, Estocolmo; Private collection, Madrid.
        Sotheby's Madrid, 23 November 1995 (76**) ESP 2,820,000   US$ 23,180

INTERIEURE oil on canvas, 50 x 61cm. sdlr 'Bores '35'
PROV.: Galería Bética, Madrid (1979); Private collection, Madrid.
EXH.: Madrid, Galería Bética, *Bores. 1926-1942*, 1978.
        Sotheby's Madrid, 23 November 1995 (79**) ESP 1,645,000   US$ 13,522

FEMMES A TABLE oil on canvas, 36¼ x 28½in. (92 x 72.5cm.) sdlr 'Bores '71'
        Christie's South Kensington, 24 June 1996 (133**) GBP 10,350   US$ 15,960

BORSELEN Jan Willem van (Gouda 1825-1892 The Hague) Dutch
A RIVER LANDSCAPE WITH ANGLERS AND AN ARTIST SKETCHING IN A ROWING
BOAT, WINDMILLS BEYOND oil on panel, 22 x 35 cm s 'JW van Borselen. ft'
        Christie's Amsterdam, 25 April 1996 (145**) NLG 51,750   US$ 30,750

BOSBOOM Johannes (The Hague 1817-1891 The Hague) Dutch
A CHURCH INTERIOR WITH SEVERAL BELIEVERS oil on panel, 21.5 x 27.5 slr 'J. Bosboom'
        Christie's Amsterdam, 26 October 1995 (37*) NLG 19,550   US$ 12,327

BOSCH Ernst (Krefeld 1834-1917 Duesseldorf) German
BUEFFELHIRTEN IN DER TOSKANA oil on canvas, 77 x 102cm. sdll 'E. Bosch Df. 1859'
LIT.: Siegfried Weiß, *Ernst Bosch - Leben und Werk*, Muenchen 1992, p. 18, WVZ-no. 26.
        Lempertz Cologne, 18 May 1996 (1510**) DEM 30,000   US$ 19,558

BOSCH Hieronymus (circle of) ('s-Hertogenbosch 1453 (?)-1516 's-Hertogenbosch) Dutch
MADONNA oil on panel, 9 x 6¼in. (22.9 x 15.9cm.)
        Sotheby's New York, 6 October 1996 (182*) US$ 6,900   US$ 6,00

BOSCH Paulus van der (unknown-) Dutch
A SILVER-GILT CUP AND COVER, AN UPTURNED ROEMER, WITH BREAD AND
RADISHES ON A PEWTER PLATE ON A DRAPED TABLE oil on canvas, 22 x 19½in. (55.8 x
49.5cm.) sd 'P.v Bosch.f.1653'
PROV.: with P. de Boer, Amsterdam; with Alan Jacobs, London, (Winter Exhibition of Dutch
Masters of the 17th century, 1971-72, no.13).
EXH.: Dordrecht, Dordrechts Museum, *Nederlands Stillevens uit vier eeuwen*, Jul-Sept. 1954, no.22.
Christie's South Kensington, 19 October 1995 (405**) GBP 7,875   US$ 12,429

BOSSCHAERT Jan Baptist (1667 c.-1746) Flemish
CARNATIONS, TULIPS, IRISES, NARCISSI, ANEMONES, ROSES, SNOWBALLS, LOBELIA,
MORNING GLORY AND OTHER FLOWERS ADORNING AN URN WITH PEACHES AND
SHELLS ON A LEDGE, A LANDSCAPE BEYOND oil on canvas, 47¼ x 42 5/8in. (126 x
108.3cm.)
Christie's London, 19 April 1996 (119**) GBP 14,950   US$ 22,669

PARROT-TULIPS, PEONIES, ANEMONES, YELLOW ROSES AND OTHER FLOWERS IN A
SCULPTED GILT URN ON A LEDGE oil on canvas, 30 x 25in. (76.3 x 63.5cm.)
Christie's South Kensington, 19 October 1995 (406***) GBP 9,562   US$ 15,092

BOSSCHAERT Johannes (1613-1628 after) Flemish
TULIPS, ROSES, AN IRIS FRITILARY AND OTHER FLOWERS IN A BASKET, WITH
SHELLS, A BUNCH OF GRAPES AND SPRIGS OF APRICOTS AND REDCURRANTS ON A
STONE LEDGE oil on inset panel, 14 3/8 x 21½in. (36.5 x 54.6cm.) sd ini. '.I.B.1624'
PROV.: Anon. Sale, Lempertz, Cologne, Nov. 1968, as. 'Monogrammist J.B.1624' (DM 110,000).
LIT.: P. Mitchell, *European Flower Painters*, London, 1973, pp. 60 and 68, fig. 88 (colour).
Christie's London, 8 December 1995 (35**) GBP 375,500   US$ 577,870

A BASKET WITH FRUIT, GRAPES, PEACHES ETC AND FLOWERS ON A WOODEN TABLE
oil on panel, 51.5 x 83.4cm. s 'I Bosschart f'
Christie's Monaco, 14 June 1996 (11**) FRF 393,300   US$ 75,946

BOSSOLI Carlo (1815-1884) Italian
FIGURES BEFORE A EUROPEAN CITY gouache on paper, laid down on canvas, 30 ¼ x 54 ¾in.
(77 x 139cm.) sll 'C. Bossoli'
Phillips London, 14 November 1995 (85**) GBP 6,500   US$ 10,167

SMYRNA FROM THE CITADEL ON MOUNT PAGUS, THE CESME PENINSULA, AND THE
GARDENS OF BORNORA WITH THE COAST OF PHOCAEA tempera on paper laid down on
canvas, 44¼ x 77 7/8in. (112.4 x 197.8cm.) s 'C. Bossoli' (1839)
PROV.: A Peyrot, Carlo Bossoli, Turin, 1974, pp. 67-8, no. 40.
Christie's London, 17 November 1995 (139**) GBP 32,200   US$ 50,368

PLACE DE LA CONCORDE, PARIS pen and ink, watercolour and bodycolour on paper, 38 1/8 x
51in. (84.2 x 129.5cm.) sdlr 'C. Bossoli. 1853'
Christie's New York, 2 November 1995 (20**) US$ 189,500   US$ 189,500

BOSSUET François Antoine (Ieper 1798-1889 Sint-Joost-ten-Node) Belgian
A VIEW OF SEVILLE FROM THE RIVER oil on canvas, 36 x 58½in. (91.5 x 148.6cm.) slr
'F.Bossuet'
Christie's East, 30 October 1995 (250**) US$ 18,400   US$ 18,400

BOTERO Fernando (Medellin 1932 b.) Colombian
SAN ESTEBAN oil on canvas, 78 x 78cm. sdll 'BOTERO - 65'
Hauswedell & Nolte Cologne, 2 December 1995 (34**) DEM 52,000   US$ 36,079

BOTH Jan Dirksz. (Utrecht 1618 (1615 c.)-1652 Utrecht) Dutch
AN ITALIAN LANDSCAPE WITH MULETEERS ON A PATH BY A WATERFALL oil on
canvas, 133.3 x 110.4cm.
PROV.: with P. de Boer, Amsterdam, as *Jan Both*.
      Christie's Amsterdam, 7 May 1996 (53**) NLG 34,500   US$ 20,117

BEWALDETE BERGLANDSCHAFT oil on linen, 93.5 x 120cm. slr 'JBoth ft.'
PROV.: 464. Lempertz-Auktion, Köln, 26-04-1961, lot 16; private collection, Westfalen.
      Lempertz Cologne, 15 November 1995 (1208**) DEM 42,000   US$ 29,644

BÖTTGER Herbert (1898-1954) German
STILL LIFE OF FLOWERS IN A LANDSCAPE oil on canvas, 17½ x 15 3/8in. (44.5 x 39cm.) s
with monogram and dlr '42'
      Phillips London, 27 November 1995 (34**) GBP 4,400   US$ 6,883

BOUCHARD Paul Louis (1853-1937) French
THE DEATH OF CLEOPATRA oil on canvas, 108 x 144in. (274.3 x 365.5cm.) sdll 'Paul
Bouchard/1887'
PROV.: Caelt Gallery, London (until 1972); Malcolm Forbes Collection, Morocco.
      Christie's New York, 10 January 1996 (44**) US$ 23,000   US$ 23,000

BOUCHER François (Paris 1703-1770 Paris) French
A LANDSCAPE WITH DISTANT BUILDINGS AND A HERDSWOMAN WITH CATTLE AND
SHEEP CROSSING A RIVER oil on canvas, 33 ¾ x 26 ¾in. (85 x 67.9cm.) (after 1731)
PROV.: Possibly M. de Montulle (Sale: Lebrun, Paris, December 22, 1783, lot 166, ,400 livres to Le
Brun); Baron Henry de Rothschild, Paris, until 1946; Baron Philippe de Rothschild, Paris; Sale:
Paris, April 6, 1954, lot 65; Pardo Gallery, Paris 1954-9; Private collection, Rome, until 1960.
EXH.: Paris, Musée Carnavalet, *Chefs-d'oeuvres des collections parisiennes*, 1950, no. 4, reproduced
on the cover and as plate XVI (described as having a companion in a private collection, Paris);
Geneva, Musée de l'Art et de l'Histoire, *De Watteau à Cézanne*, 1951, no. 2 (as 'L'abrevoire'); Rome,
Il Settecento a Roma, 1959, no. 96.
LIT.: H. Voss, 'Francois Boucher's Early Development,' *The Burlington Magazine*, March, 1953, p.
85, (illustrated); plate 43 (as in the James de Rothschild collection); *The Connoisseur*, June, 1959; A.
Ananoff, *François Boucher*, 1976, vol. I, p. 188, no. 52, illus., and vol. II, p. 322, under 'Ventes du
dix-huitieme Siècle, Tableaux de François Boucher restant à authentifier'; I. Nemilova, *The
Hermitage: Catalogue of Western European Painting, French Painting, Eighteenth Century*, 1986, p.
59, under no. 18 (where it is noted that the Hermitage picture was once joined as one long picture
with another painting in the collection).
      Sotheby's New York, 11 January 1996 (182**) US$ 398,500   US$ 398,500

LE JOUEUR DE FLAGEOLET oil on canvas (an oval), 21 ¾ x 27¼in. (55.5 x 44.1cm.) sdll
'f.Boucher/1766'
PROV.: Pierre-Jacques-Onesyme Bergeret, his (deceased) sale, Paris, Folliot et al., 24 April 1786, lot
50,300 livres to Quenet; Robert de Saint-Victor, Conseiller au Parlement et President de la Chambre
des Comptes de Rouen, his (deceased) sale, Paris, Roux, 26 November 1822, lot 614 for 41 francs;
Anon. sale, Paris, Febvre,30 March 1854, lot 8; H. F. Broadwood, Lyne Capel, Surrey, his (deceased)
sale *et al.*, London, Christie's, 25 March 1899, lot 49, GBP1102.10s. toAgnews; Sold by the above to
Charles Sedelmeyer, Paris, 1899; Sold by the above to 'S. de Gange', 1899; De Yonge, New York;
With the Reinhardt Gallery, New York; Mrs. E.S. Bayer, later Comtesse Sala, Paris and New York;
Baron Heinrich Thyssen-Bornemisza, by 1930.
EXH.: London, Royal Academy of Arts, *France in the Eighteenth Century*, 1968, no. 66; Paris 1970,
no. 43; Düsseldorf 1970-1, no. 6; Lausanne etc., 1986-7, no. 50.
LIT.: *The 6th One Hundred of Paintings by Old Masters belonging to the Sedelmeyer Gallery*, Paris,
1900, no. 69; P. de Nohlac, 'Les Quatre Saisons, *Les Arts*, March 1905, pp.2-7, reproduced p. 152; L.
Soullié and C. Masson, in A. Michel, *François Boucher*, 1906, pp.82, no. 1484, and 83, no. 1491; P.
de Nohlac, *François Boucher*, 1907, p.152 and 157; H. Macfall, *Boucher*, 1908, p.148, reproduced

fig. 128;

R. Heinemann 1937, vol. I, no. 47, vol. II, plate 263; G. Wildenstein, 'Un amateur de Boucher et de Fragonard, Jacques-Onesyme Bergeret (1715-1785), *Gazette des Beaux-Arts*, LVII, July-August, 1961, p.69, no. 68, reproduced p. 71, fig. 26; A. Ananoff, *François Boucher*, 1976, vol. II, pp. 264-5, no. 633, fig. 1664; A. Ananoff & D. Wildenstein, *L'opera completa di Boucher*, 1980, p. 138, no. 669.

Sotheby's London, 6 December 1995 (78**) GBP 825,500	US$	1,270,391

BOUCLE Peter van (Antwerp ca. 1610-1673 Paris) Flemish
STILL-LIFE WITH CARP, ONIONS AND VEGETABLE ON A LEDGE oil on oak panel, 46 x 71.5cm. sll mono 'BC'
PROV.: Collection B. Bordeaux in 1974.
EXH.: *Nature morte de Brueghel à Soutine*, Galerie des Beaux-Arts, Bordeaux, 1978, no. 19 (illustrated).
LIT.: M.Faré, *Le grand siècle de la nature morte en France, le XVIIe siècle*, Fribourg 1974, p. ,100 (illustrated).

Étude Tajan Paris, 12 December 1995 (95**) FRF 80,000	US$	16,114

STILL-LIFE WITH FRUIT AND A PERROQUET oil on canvas, 95 x 122.5cm.

Étude Tajan Paris, 26 March 1996 (45**) FRF 210,000	US$	41,510

BOUDEWYNS Adriaen Frans I (Brussels 1644-1711 Brussels) Flemish
PEASANTS LOADING WAGGONS IN A HARBOUR oil on canvas, 26.4 x 36.5cm.
PROV.: this painting was made in co-operation with Pieter Bout (1658-1719).

Christie's Amsterdam, 7 May 1996 (91**) NLG 16,100	US$	9,388

PEASANTS LOADING PACKAGES ONTO WAGGONS IN A HARBOUR oil on canvas, 26.4 x 36.5cm.
PROV.: see Pieter Bout co-painter.

Christie's Amsterdam, 13 November 1995 (39**) NLG 19,550	US$	12,321

FEASTING PAESANTS IN A VILLAGE oil on panel, 24 x 32cm.

Dorotheum Vienna, 17 October 1995 (164**) ATS 130,000	US$	13,040

BOUDIN Eugène Louis (Honfleur 1824-1898 Deauville) French
LA PLAGE DE TROUVILLE watercolour over pencil on paper mounted at the edges on board, 6½ x 10¼in. (16.5 x 26cm.) stamped with ini. lr 'E.B.' (1865-1866)
PROV.: A. Devilder, Roubaix; Spengler, Mulhouse; Galerie Schmit, Paris; Thomas Agnew & Sons Ltd., London; The Lefevre Gallery (Alex. Reid & Lefevre Ltd.), London.
EXH.: Mulhouse, Maison d'Art Alsacienne, *Boudin, Jongkind, Pissarro, 49 Peintures, dessins et pastels*, 1931; Washington, D.C., National Gallery of Art (on loan).

Christie's New York, 1 May 1996 (101**) US$ 25,300	US$	25,300

LAVEUSES oil on panel, 9¼ x 13 7/8in. (23.5 x 35.3cm.) sdll 'E. Boudin 82'
EXH.: Washington D.C., National Gallery of Art (on loan).

Christie's New York, 1 May 1996 (126**) US$ 173,000	US$	173,000

ROUEN, VUE PRISE DU COURS DE LA REINE oil on canvas, 18 1/8 x 25 5/8in. (46 x 65cm.) sdll 'E Boudin Rouen 95'
PROV.: M. Michaud, Rheims; Anon. sale, Hôtel Drouot, Paris, 22 June 1910, lot 9 ; Van Houten, Paris; sale, Hôtel Drouot, Paris, 12 June 1953, lot 5 (illustrated); The Estate of Norman B. Woolworth, Monmouth, Maine; sale, Parke-Bernet Galleries, Inc., New York, 31 Oct. 1962, lot 16; Mr. and Mrs. Arnold S. Askin, Katonah, New York; Stephan Hahn Gallery, New York (1976); M. Knoedler & Co., New York; Wally Findlay Galleries, Inc., Beverly Hills (acquired by Richard Smart, 1977).
EXH.: Paris, Ecole Nationale des Beaux-Arts, *Exposition des oeuvres d'Eugène Boudin*, Jan. 1899,

no. 314; New York, E. V. Thaw & Co., *Eugene Boudin*, Dec. 1962, no. 18 (illustrated); New York, Paul Rosenberg & Co., *Cross Currents in Modern Art*, 1966, no. 27 (illustrated).
LIT.: R. Schmit, *Eugène Boudin*, Paris, 1973, vol. III, no. 3465 (illustrated, p. 324).
  Christie's New York, 1 May 1996 (148**) US$ 200,500

US$ 200,500

DEAUVILLE, LE BASSIN oil on panel, 10½ x 8 ¾in. (26.5 x 22.4cm.) sll 'E.Boudin' (ca. 1888-1895)
PROV.: James Connell & Sons, Glasgow; Christie's London, 20 May 1960, lot 46, sold for 1.,500 gns.; Gooden & Fox, London; Mrs.C.K.Prestige, London; Sotheby's London, 24 April 1968, lot 80, sold for GBP4,800.
LIT.: R.Schmidt, *Eugène Boudin, 1824-1898*, vol.II, Paris, 1973, no.2310 (ill. p.378).
  Christie's South Kensington, 18 March 1996 (7**) GBP 20,700

US$ 31,613

ANVERS, BATEAUX SUR L'ESCAULT oil on canvas, 15 ¾ x 25 5/8in. (40 x 65.1cm.) slr (ca. 1871-74)
PROV.: Hurault, Paris (sold: Paris, Hotel Drouôt, *vente Hurault*, February 6, 1874); Henri Pasauier' Paris (sold: Paris, Galerie Georges Petit, *vente H. Pasquier*, May 2, 1905, no. 10); Sale: Paris, Palais Galliéra,June 12, 1964; Sale: Sotheby's, London, 27 June 1977, lot 75; Edgardo Acosta, Beverly Hills; Acquired from the above by the present owner.
EXH.: Paris, Galerie Alfred Daber, *Exposition Paysages*, 1965, no. 27.
LIT.: Robert Schmit, *Eugène Boudin*, vol. 1, Paris, 1973, no. 758, illustrated p. 270.
  Sotheby's New York, 2 May 1996 (113**) US$ 200,500

US$ 200,500

FECAMP. LE PORT oil on cradled panel, 13 x 16 1/8in. (33 x 41cm.) sd '92' and inscr. 'Fecamp'
PROV.: Galerue Durand-Ruel, Paris (acquired from the artist 2 March 1893).
EXH.: Paris, Ecole Nationale des Beaux-Arts, *Exposition des oeuvres d'Eugène Boudin*, 1899, no. 243; London, Grafton Gallery, *Sisley and Boudin*, 1905, no. 29.
LIT.: Robert Schmit, *Eugène Boudin*, vol. III, Paris, 1973, no. 2919, (illustrated p. 130).
  Sotheby's New York, 2 May 1996 (123**) US$ 79,500

US$ 79,500

TROUVILLE - LE PORT oil on panel, 10½ x 8¼in. (27 x 21cm.) sdll 'E. Boudin 90'
PROV.: Gustave Cahen, Paris (vente, Paris, Hotel Drouot, *2ème Vente Gustave Cahen*, 5th June 1929, lot 139).
EXH.: Paris, Ecole Nationale des Beaux-Arts, *Exposition des oeuvres d Eugène Boudin*, 1899, no. 286.
LIT.: Ruth L. Benjamin, *Eugène Boudin*, New York, 1937, p. 181, illustrated; Robert Schmit, *Eugène Boudin*, Paris, 1973, vol. III, p. 45, no. 2674, illustrated.
  Sotheby's London, 20 March 1996 (27**) GBP 45,500

US$ 69,487

LAVEUSE AU BORD DE LA TOUCQUES oil on panel, 7 x 10 ¾in. (18 x 27cm.) sll 'Boudin' (ca. 1885-90)
LIT.: Robert Schmit, *Eugene Boudin, 1824-1898*, Paris, 1973, vol. II, p. 294, no. 2072, illustrated.
  Sotheby's London, 24 June 1996 (4**) GBP 67,500

US$ 104,086

VENISE: LE CAMPANILE, LE PALIAS DUCAL ET LA PIAZETTA VUE PRISE DE SAN GIORGIO oil on canvas, 14 ¾ x 22in. (37.5 x 56cm.) sd inscr. 'Venise E. Boudin, 19 juin' (1895)
PROV.: Arnold & Tripp, Paris; Acquired by the family of the present owner circa 1930.
EXH.: London, Marlborough Fine Art, *Eugene Boudin, 1824-1898*, 1958, no. 75.
LIT.: Robert Schmit, *Eugène Boudin*, Paris, 1973, vol. III, p. 308, no. 3447 (illustrated).
  Sotheby's London, 24 June 1996 (17**) GBP 265,500

US$ 409,406

BERCK. LA PLAGE, MARÉE BASSE oil on canvas, 18 5/16 x 26in. (46.5 x 66cm.) sdlr inscr. 'E. Boudin 81' 'Vinton' dedicated 'à Mr. F. Vinton'
PROV.: Frederick Porter Vinton, Boston; Jess Houghton Metcalf, Boston; Rhode Island School of design, Providence, R.I., Silberman, New York; Sam Salz, New York (until 1945); Private collection New York.

EXH.: 1911-1913, Boston Museum of Fine Arts.
LIT.: R.L. Benjamin, *Eugène Boudin*, New; York: Raymond & Raymond, 1937; pp. 194-195; Robert Schmitt, *Eugène Boudin. 1824-1898*, vol. II, Paris: Robert Schmitt, cat. no. 1508, p. 90 (ill.).
Phillips London, 26 June 1995 (31**) GBP 44,000

US$ 70,209

VACHES AU CHAMP oil on canvas, 21¼ x 29 ¾in. (54 x 75cm.) sd 'Boudin 31 juillet' (ca 1892-96)
PROV.: M. Gérard, Paris; M. Baker, Paris.
LIT.: R. Schmitt, *Eugène Boudin 1834-1898*, vol. III, Paris, 1973, no. 3065 (illustrated p. 180).
Christie's London, 26 June 1996 (131**) GBP 17,250

US$ 26,600

SORTIE DE MESSE EN BRETAGNE oil on panel, 27 x 22cm. slr dedicated 'à M. Fredinand Martin, E. Boudin' (ca. 1865-70)
PROV.: Collection F. Martin, Le Havre; Collection Muller, Paris.
LIT.: R. Schmit, *Eugène Boudin 1824-1898*, Paris, 1973, I, p. 137, no. 373.
Étude Tajan Paris, 27 October 1995 (13**) FRF 60,000

US$ 12,136

TROUVILLE, LE PORT, MARÉE BASSE oil on canvas, 14¼ x 23in. (36 x 58.4cm.) sdll '97. E. Boudin'
PROV.: A. A. Healy, New York, Associated American Artists, New York, 15 Feb. 1907, lot 65 ($550, Galerie Georges Petit, Paris Continental Galleries, Montreal.
LIT.: R. Schmit, *Eugene Boudin 1824-1898*, vol. 111, Paris, 1973, no. 3648 (illustrated p. 392).
Christie's London, 28 November 1995 (1**) GBP 84,000

US$ 131,394

TROUVILLE, LE PORT oil on panel, 12 ¾ x 18 1/8in. (32.5 x 46cm.) sd inscr. ll 'Trouville E. Boudin 94' (1894)
PROV.: Raphaël Gérard, Paris; Hôtel Drouot, Paris, 8 July 1931, lot 4.
LIT.: R. Schmit, *Eugène Boudin, 1824-1898*, vol.II, Paris, 1973 no. 3314 (illustrated p. 271).
Christie's London, 29 November 1995 (101**) GBP 35,000

US$ 54,747

ENVIRONS DE TROUVILLE oil on panel, 9½ x 13in. (24 x 33cm.) sll 'Boudin' (ca. 1880-85)
PROV.: Anon. sale, Paris, Hôtel Drouot, 4-5 June 1901, lot 24 (FF610); Anon. sale, Paris, Hôtel Drouot, 27 Feb. 1909, lot 5 (FF410); Anon. sale, Paris, Hôtel Drouot, 23 June 1960, lot 70
LIT.: R. Schmit, *Eugène Boudin, 1824-1898*, vol.II, Paris, 1973 no. 1375 (illustrated p. 47).
Christie's London, 29 November 1995 (106**) GBP 45,000

US$ 70,389

VENISE, LE QUAI DE LA GIUDECCA oil on canvas, 18½ x 25 ¾in. (47 x 65.5cm.) sdlr 'E.Boudin Venise 95' d again lc 'Juin 95' (June 1895)
PROV.: Galerie Raphael Gerard, Paris; Andrew T. Reid, Perthshire; sale, Christie's, London, March 27, 1942, lot 75 (illustrated); Maxwell Galleries, San Francisco (acquired at the above sale); Arthur Tooth & Sons Ltd., London; Acquired from the above by the present owner.
LIT.: R. Schmit, *Eugene Boudin, Paris, 1973*, vol. III, p. 311, no. 3429 (illustrated).
Christie's New York, 30 April 1996 (1**) US$ 310,500

US$ 310,500

BATEAUX ECHOUES ET PECHEURS oil on canvas, 18 3/8 x 25 ¾in. (46.6 x 65.5cm.) sdll 'E. Boudin 80.' (1880)
PROV.: Beugniet et Bonjean, Paris; Samuel P. Avery, New York; Meyer H. Lehman, New York (acquired from the above, 1902); Harriet Lehman and Bertha Rosenheim; Elsie Rose Weil and Dr. Henry Lehman Weil (by descent to George L. Weil, 1952).
EXH.: New York, Hirschl & Adler Galleries, Inc., *Eugène Boudin Retrospective Exhibition*, Nov., 1966, no. 38 (illustrated).
LIT.: R. Schmit, *Eugène Boudin*, Paris, 1973, vol. II, no. 1288 (illustrated, p.20).
Christie's New York, 8 November 1995 (113**) US$ 70,700

US$ 70,700

BRETAGNE, COUCHER DE SOLEIL SUR LA MER. oil on cradled panel, 25 7/8 x 41in. (65.7 x 104.1cm.) sdll 'E. Boudin 69' (1869)
PROV.: M. Gondouin, Paris; Galeries Durand-Ruel, Paris (acquired from the above, 1891); Hammer

Galleries, New York.
EXH.: Paris, Ecole National des Beaux-Arts, *Exposition des oeuvres d'Eugène Boudin*, Jan., 1899,
no. ,200 (titled *Clair de lune*; incorrectly dated 1865).
LIT.: C. Roger-Marx, *Eugène Boudin*, Paris, 1927, pl. 6 (illustrated) R. Schmit, *Eugène Boudin*,
Paris, 1973, vol. I, no. 476 (illustrated, p. 176).

Christie's New York, 8 November 1995 (123**) US$ 74,000	US$	74,000

LE HAVRE, LE BASSIN CASIMIR DELAVIGNE oil on panel, 13 x 16 1/8in. (33 x 41cm.) sdll 'E.
Boudin. 92 le Havre' (1892)
PROV.: Galerie Georges Petit, Paris; Dr. Delineau, Paris; sale, Hôtel Drouot, Paris, Feb. 1, 1901, lot
19; David B. Findlay Galleries, New York (acquired by the present owner, 1967).
EXH.: Paris, Ecole National des Beaux-Arts, *Exposition des oeuvres d'Eugène Boudin*, Jan., 1899,
no. 19; Paris, Galerie Alfred Daber, *Jongkind, Boudin*, Feb.-March, 1951, no. 27; San Diego, Fine
Arts Gallery, *20th Century Tempo*, June-Aug., 1968, no number.
LIT.: R. Schmit, *Eugène Boudin*, Paris, 1973, vol. III, no. 2960 (illustrated, p. 143).

Christie's New York, 8 November 1995 (130**) US$ 101,500	US$	101,500

BOUGH Samuel, R.S.A. (1822-1878) Scottish
THE POOL OF LONDON oil on canvas, 14 x 18½in. (35.6 x 47cm.) sd 'Sam Bough/1856'
PROV.: Lawrence Robertson.
EXH.: Edinburgh, Royal Scottisch Academy, 1857, no. 265; Possibly Glasgow, 1901, no. 342 (as the
Port of London, lent by D. Brodie MacLeod).
LIT.: Sidney Gilpin, *Sam Bough, R.S.A., Some account of his life and works*, 1905, p.135.

Christie's London, 6 November 1995 (143**) GBP 17,250	US$	26,983

GOING THROUGH THE LOCK oil on canvas, 25½ x 41½in. (65 x 105.5cm.) sdlr '1852'

Phillips London, 18 June 1996 (73**) GBP 16,000	US$	24,672

BOUGUEREAU William Adolphe (La Rochelle 1825-1905 La Rochelle) French
FRERE ET SOEUR (FILLE PORTANT UN ENFANT) oil on canvas, 71 x 32in. (180.5 x 81.2cm.)
sd 'W. Bouguereau 1887'
LIT.: M.S. Walker, *W. Bouguereau: l'Art Pompier* New York, 1991, p. 72.

Christie's New York, 2 November 1995 (30**) US$ 178,500	US$	178,500

LA GUERRE oil on canvas, 33 x 41½in. (83.9 x 105.5cm.) sd 'W. Bouguereau/1864'
PROV.: Comte Daupais, Lisbon; Comte Daupais Collection; Sale Paris,Galerie George Petit, 16-17
May 1892, no. 81 (illustrated).
LIT.: L. Baschet *Catalogue illustré des oeuvres de W. Bouguereau*, Paris, 1885, p. 20 (illustrated by
an engraving) 1860; M. Vachon, *W. Bouguereau*, Paris, 1,900 p. 147, 1860; M.S. Walker, *W.
Bouguereau: l'Art Pompier'* New York, 1991, p. 72.

Christie's New York, 2 November 1995 (31**) US$ 195,000	US$	195,000

L'AMOUR AU REPOS oil on canvas, 18 x 9¼in. (45.8 x 23.5cm.) sdll 'W-BOUGUEREAU-1891'
(1891)

Christie's New York, 2 November 1995 (98**) US$ 85,000	US$	85,000

REFLECTION oil on canvas, 39½ x 27¼in. (100.3 x 69.3cm.) sdur 'W-BOUGUEREAU-1898'

Christie's New York, 2 November 1995 (99**) US$ 74,000	US$	74,000

BOURDILLON Frank Wright (active 1881-1892-) British
ACROSS THE BEACH oil on canvas, 8 ¾ x 10 ¾in. (22.3 x 27.3cm.) sdlr 'F. Bourdillion.1887.'

Christie's East, 13 February 1996 (221**) US$ 8,050	US$	8,050

BOURGEOIS DE MERCEY Frédéric (1805-1860) French
VIEW ON THE PORT OF BASTIA oil on canvas, 46.5 x 74cm. sd 'F.Mercey 1839'

Christie's Monaco, 14 June 1996 (55**) FRF 58,500	US$	11,296

BOUT Pieter (Brussels 1658-1719 Brussels) Flemish
PEASANTS LOADING WAGGONS IN A HARBOUR oil on canvas, 26.4 x 36.5cm.
PROV.: this painting was made in co-operation withAdriaen Fransz. Boudewijns (1644-1711).
      Christie's Amsterdam, 7 May 1996 (91**) NLG 16,100   US$ 9,388

A VIEW OF THE SEINE, FROM THE POINT DE LA CITÉ oil on canvas, 46½ x 77¼in. (118 x 196cm.) (before 1654)
      Christie's London, 8 December 1995 (361**) GBP 65,300   US$ 100,492

PEASANTS LOADING PACKAGES ONTO WAGGONS IN A HARBOUR oil on canvas, 26.4 x 36.5
PROV.: see Adriaen Fransz. Boudewijns co-painter.
      Christie's Amsterdam, 13 November 1995 (39**) NLG 19,550   US$ 12,321

BOUTS Albrecht (Albert) (1452/1454-1549 Leuven) Dutch
THE MEETING OF ABRAHAM AND MELCHISEDEK oil on panel, 19 ¾ x 12½in. (50 x 32in.) (after 1500)
PROV.: Hommel Collection, Zurich; With Steinmeyer, Lucerne, in 1920; Possibly with Haberstock, Berlin; With F. Kleinberger, Paris, before 1930 (according to the Friedländer archive in the RKD, The Hague);
Baron Heinrich Thyssen-Bornemisza, by 1930.
EXH.: Munich 1930, no. 36; Paris 1970, no. 3; Düsseldorf 1970-71, no. 7; Lausanne etc., 1986-7, no. 2.
LIT.: M.J. Friedländer, *Die Altniederländische Malerei*, III, 1934, p. 114, no. 43; W. Schone, *Dieric Bouts und seine Schule*, 1938, p. 190, no. 82; R. Heinemann, 1937, vol. l, no. 48; M.J. Friedländer, *Early Netherlandish Painting*, 1968, vol. III, p. 65, no. 43, reproduced plate 59.
      Sotheby's London, 6 December 1995 (68**) GBP 54,300   US$ 83,564

BOUVARD Antoine (1956 d.) French
FIGURE IN A GONDOLA BEFORE A BRIDGE ON A VENETIAN CANAL oil on canvas, 19 ¾ x 25 5/8in. (50.2 x 65cm.) slr 'Bouvard'
      Phillips London, 12th March 1996 (26**) GBP 5,800   US$ 8,858

A VENETIAN BLACKWATER oil on canvas, 9½ x 13in. (24.2 x 33cm.) slr 'Bouvard'
      Christie's East, 13 February 1996 (211**) US$ 6,900   US$ 6,900

VENICE, THE GRAND CANAL oil on canvas, 25½ x 35¼in. (64.5 x 92cm.) sll
      Sotheby's London, 13 March 1996 (114**) GBP 24150   US$ 36,881

SAILING VESSELS AND GONDOLAS AT THE ENTRANCE TO A VENETIAN CANAL oil on canvas, 21 3/8 x 32in. (54.2 x 81.3cm.) s
      Phillips London, 14 November 1995 (71**) GBP 7,000   US$ 10,949

GONDOLAS ON A VENETIAN CANAL oil on canvas, 19 ¾ x 26 ¾in. (50.2 x 68cm.) s 'Bouvard'
      Christie's South Kensington, 16 November 1995 (206**) GBP 9,225   US$ 14,430

BOUYS André (Eoubes (Toulon) 1656-1740) French
A SITTING LADY COUNTING HER MONEY ON A KITCHENTABLE WITH GROCERIES, BREAD AND A FISH oil on panel, 97 x 130cm. (1737)
PROV.: Mr. Cailleux, 1930.
EXH.: Paris, Salon of 1737, together with the pendant titled, *'Deux Servantes revenant du marché*; Paris Société Nationale des Beaux-Arts, Grand Palais, *Exposition du Salon de 1737*, May-June, 1930, no. 17.
LIT.: M. and F. Faré, *La Vie Silencieuse en France, La Nature morte au XVIIè Siècle*, Fribourg 1976, p. 47, note 52.
      Christie's Monaco, 14 June 1996 (21**) FRF 257,400   US$ 49,704

BRACKMAN Robert (1898-1980) American
STILL LIFE WITH POTTED GERANIUM, WHITE PITCHER AND FRUIT oil on canvas, 30 x 36in. (76.2 x 91.5cm.) s 'Robert Brackman' inscr. 'Still Life 102' and 'Noank Conn' on the reverse
    Christie's East, 28 November 1995 (233*) US$ 7,130   US$ 7,130

BRADFORD William, A.N.A. (1823/30-1892) American
CRUSHED IN THE ICE oil on canvas, 28 x 44¼in. (71.1 x 112.4cm.)
    Christie's New York, 13 March 1996 (23**) US$ 134,500   US$ 134,500

BRADLEY Helen (1900-1979) British
LOOK AT OUR WILLIE'S NEW CLOTHES oil on canvas laid down on board, 13 x 16in. (33 x 40.6cm.) slr with a fly; sd and inscr. 'Look at Willie's new Clothes cried that dreadful Annie Murgatroyd when we met on our afternoon walk through the cemetery. Mrs Murgatroyd and Annie were also in new clothes, and since their uncle had come to live with them their mother no longer went out cleaning. When George and I caught up with their Mother, Grandma, Miss Carter (who whore pink) and the other Aunts they were all talking about Willie's Uncle and although they talked and talked about him for days, they could not remember an Uncle of the name of Edward in the family. Still he took them all to Blackpool for Lees Wakes and the year was 1907. Helen Layfield Bradley, 1971' (on a label attached to the reverse)
PROV.: Mercury Gallery, London, Oct. 1971, where purchased by the present owner.
    Christie's London, 20 June 1996 (123**) GBP 6,900   US$ 10,640

MONDAY oil on board, 11 x 14in. (28 x 36cm.) slc with a fly 'Helen Bradley' (1907)
PROV.: The Artist Family.
    Christie's London, 21 November 1995 (250**) GBP 10,350   US$ 16,190

SUNDAY oil on board, 11 x 14in. (28 x 36cm.) slc with a fly 'Helen Bradley' (1907)
PROV.: The Artist Family.
    Christie's London, 21 November 1995 (255**) GBP 15,525   US$ 24,284

BRAEKELEER Ferdinand the Younger de (Antwerp 1828-1857 Antwerp) Belgian
THE DISPUTE AND RECONCILIATION oil on canvas (a pair), each: 38 x 46cm.
    A. Mak B.V. Dordrecht, 12 December 1995 (36*) NLG 16,000   US$ 9,914

BRAKENBURGH Richard (Haarlem 1605-1702 Haarlem) Dutch
THE TWINS oil on canvas, 46.5 x 54.5cm. sll 'R. Brakenburg'
    Étude Tajan Paris, 12 December 1995 (47**) FRF 75,000   US$ 15,107

BRAMER Leonaert (Delft 1596-1674 Delft) Dutch
THE DISCOVERY OF PYRAMUS AND THISBE oil on panel, 15 x 21in. (38.1 x 53.3cm.) slr mono. 'L.B.'
PROV.: King of Poland, by whom given to Prince Radziwill (acc. to an old label on the reverse; private Dutch collection, 1944.
LIT.: J. Foucart, 'Le Pyrame et Thysbé de Leonart Bramer', *Revue du Louvre et des Musées de France*, 40, 1990 (illustrated fig. 40); *Leonaert Bramer: Ingenious Painter and Draughtsman in Rome and Delft*, exhibition catalogue, 1994, p. 299, cat. no. S223.1 (as by Bramer).
    Sotheby's New York, 16 May 1996 (148**) US$ 31,050   US$ 31,050

BRAND Johann Christian (Vienna 1722-1795 Vienna) Austrian
WOODED LANDSCAPE WITH A STREAM AND A BRIDGE oil on canvas, 164 x 117cm.
    Dorotheum Vienna, 17 October 1995 (177**) ATS 240,000   US$ 24,073

DISTINGUISHED HUNTING COMPANY; EVENING VISITORS ON A FARM oil on copper (a pair) 29.2 x 40.5cm. / 29.5 x 41cm
    Wiener Kunst Auktionen, 26 September 1995 (5 (a pair)**) ATS 90,000   US$ 8,748

BRANDL Herbert (Graz 1959 b.) Austrian
UNTITLED oil on canvas, ,100 x 100cm. sd ' H Brandl 90' on the reverse
    Dorotheum Vienna, 21 May 1996 (153**) ATS 100,000

	US$	9,602

UNTITLED Acrylic on canvas, 278 x 275cm. sd on the reverse 'H. Brandl 1988'
    Wiener Kunst Auktionen, 27 September 1995 (579**) ATS 150,000

	US$	14,581

BRANDS Eugène (Eugenius Antonius Maria) (Amsterdam 1913 b.) Dutch
MEISJE MET MAAN oil on paper, 41 x 48cm. sdll 'Brands 5.54'
LIT.: Ed Wingen, *Eugène Brands*, The Hague 1988, p. 97(ill.).
    Christie's Amsterdam, 5 June 1996 (286*) NLG 9,775

	US$	5,711

LENTE MAAN acrylics on paper laid down on canvas, 130 x 140cm. sll with initials 'E.B.' and s
again and d 1985 on the reverse
    Christie's Amsterdam, 5 June 1996 (299**) NLG 12,650

	US$	7,391

VICTORY BORFIMAH II oil on canvas, 69 x 110cm. sdlc 'Brands 10/49', and numbered 'no. 2' on
the reverse
PROV.: Steef de Vries, Schiedam.
EXH.: Schiedam, Stedelijk Museum, *40 jaar verzamelen in het Stedelijk Museum Schiedam:
Hoogtepunten uit de schilderijen en beeldenverzameling 1945-1980*, 1985, no. 17.
    Christie's Amsterdam, 5 June 1996 (326**) NLG 34,500

	US$	20,158

SUNNY ROOM oil on canvas, ,100 x 125cm. sd and inscr. with title and numbered 'Brands 1972 17'
on the reverse
    Christie's Amsterdam, 6 December 1995 (314**) NLG 18,400

	US$	11,402

BRANDT Josef (Szczebrzesyn 1841-1915) Polish
LANDSCHAFT MIT BERITTENEN KOSAKEN oil on canvas, 70 x 111cm. slr 'Jósef Brandt
z'Warsawy Monachium'
    Lempertz Cologne, 18 May 1996 (1512**) DEM 55,000

	US$	35,856

BRANGWYN Sir Frank, R.A. (Brughes 1864-1956 Ditching (Sussex)) British (Belgian)
SUSANNAH AND THE ELDERS oil on canvas, 47 x 64in. (119.5 x 162.5cm.) (ca 1908)
PROV.: The Carpenter Collection, U.S.A, by whom purchased at the 1925 exhibition; Desmoines
Art Center, Iowa; Salender-O'Reilly Galleries, Inc., New York.
EXH.: London, Barbizon House, Queen's Gate, *Retrospective Exhibition of Works by Frank
Brangwyn*, R.A., May-June 1924, no.50; Boston, Vose Galleries, *Frank Brangwyn, R.A.*, March
1925; Venice, 1925 (not traced).
LIT.: W. Shaw-Sparrow, *Frank Brangwyn and his Work*,Edinburgh, 1915, p.235; R. Brangwyn,
Brangwyn, London, 1978, pp.222, 224.
    Christie's London, 21 March 1996 (10**) GBP 12,650

	US$	19,319

BRAQUE Georges (Argenteuil-sur-Seine 1882-1963 Paris) French
BAIGNEUSE oil on canvas, 7 7/8 x 14½in. (20 x 36.8cm.) sdlr indistinctly (ca. 1929)
PROV.: Marlborough Fine Art, London; Sale: Christie's, London, 1 December 1980, lot 37.
EXH.: London, Marlborough Fine Art, *A Tribute to Paul Maze, The Painter and His Time*, May-June
1967, no. 51.
LIT.: Maeght Editeur, *Catalogue de l'oeuvre de Braque, Peintures 1928-1935*, Paris 1962 (illustrated
p. 21 (dated 1929)).
    Sotheby's New York, 2 May 1996 (216**) US$ 101,500

	US$	101,500

BARQUE ET FALAISE oil on canvas, 13 x 18in. (33 x 45.7cm.)
PROV.: Galerie Louise Leiris, Paris; Galerie Theo, Barcelona; Galerie Theo, Madrid.
    Sotheby's New York, 2 May 1996 (217**) US$ 96,000

	US$	96,000

BOUTEILLE ET CLARINETTE oil on canvas, 25½ x 19 ¾in. (65 x 50cm.) s 'Braque' on the reverse
(1910-11)
PROV.: D.-H. Kahnweiler, Galerie Kahnweiler, Paris; Galerie Simon, Paris (6852, as La Clarinette);
Private European collector, by whom probably purchased directly from Galerie Simon in the late
1920s.
EXH.: Basle, Kunsthalle, 1966 (on loan); Zurich, Kunsthaus (on loan, as Die Klarinette).
LIT.: G. Isarlov, Georges Braque, Paris, 1932, no. 107; G. Apollinaire, in 'Georges Braque', Cahiers
d' Art, Paris,1933 (illustrated p. 18); C. Einstein, 'Georges Braque', XXe Siecle, Paris, 1934
(illustrated pl. XI - titled Le Flageolet and dated 1911); N. Worms de Romilly and J. Laude, Braque,
Le Cubisme, Catalogue de l'oeuvre, 1907-14, Paris, 1982, no. 94 (illustrated p. 135).
Christie's London, 25 June 1996 (22***) GBP 3,521,500   US$ 5,430,224

NATURE MORTE AU COUTEAU oil on canvas, 13¼ x 24 ¾in. (33.5 x 63cm.) sll 'G. Braque'
(1943)
PROV.: Galerie Louise Leiris, Paris; Arthur Tooth & Sons, London (5950); G.R. Kennerly, London,
by whom purchased from the above.
LIT.: N. Mangin (Maeght ed.), Catalogue de l'Oeuvre de Georges Braque, Peintures 1942-1947,
paris, 1960 (illustrated p. 42); Labyrinthe, no. 4, 15 Jan 1945 (illustrated p. 2, showing a photograph
of Georges Braque's studio in 1943).
Christie's London, 26 June 1996 (250**) GBP 139,000   US$ 214,341

NATURE MORTE A LA FAUCILLE oil on canvas, 23 x 18½in. (58.4 x 47cm.) slr 'G. Braque' and s
on the reverse (1944)
PROV.: Galerie Maeght, Paris; Galerie Rosengart, Lucerne from whom purchased by the previous
owner on 31 Aug. 1950.
EXH.: Paris, Salon d'Automne, 1944; Amsterdam, Stedelijk Museum, Braque, Oct.-Nov. 1945, no.
7.; London, British Council - Tate Gallery, Braque-Rouault, 1946, no. 19.; Brussels, Musée des
Beaux-Arts, George Braque, 1946.; Zurich, Kunsthaus, Braque, Kandinsky, Picasso, Sept.-Oct.
1946, no. 26.; Paris, Galerie Maeght, Braque, June 1947, no. 5.
LIT.: Cahiers d'Art, 1940-1944, 1944 (illustrated p. 110 as La Faucille); S. Fumet, Braque, Paris,
1948, no. 54 (illustrated pl.22); P. Reverdy, Une Aventure Méthodique, Paris, 1949, p. 79 (illustrated
pl. 3 as Le pot et la faucille); M. Gieure, Georges Braque, Paris, 1956, (illustrated pl. 120); N.
Mangin, Maeght (ed.), Catalogue de l'Oeuvre de Georges Braque, Peintures 1942-1947, Paris, 1960,
(illustrated p. 72).
Christie's London, 26 June 1996 (280**) GBP 78,500   US$ 121,049

VERRE ET RAISINS oil on canvas laid down on masonite, 9 5/8 x 13 1/8in. (24.4 x 33.3cm.) slr 'G
Braque 30' (1930)
PROV.: Galerie Paul Rosenberg, Paris; Theodore Schemmp & Co., New York (acquired by the late
owner, 1945).
EXH.: Paris, Galerie Paul Rosenberg, Braque, 1938; New York, Paul Rosenberg & Co., Georges
Braque-An American Tribute: The Thirties, April-May, 1964, no. 7 (illustrated).
LIT.: 'Georges Braque,' Cahiers d'Art, 1933, vols. 1-2, p. 66 (illustrated); ed. Maeght, Catalogue de
l'oeuvre de Georges Braque, Paris, 1962 (Peintures 1928-1935), p. 52 (illustrated).
Christie's New York, 8 November 1995 (249**) US$ 140,000   US$ 140,000

BRASILIER André (1929 b.) French
FETE HIPPIQUE EN ROSE oil on canvas, 44 7/8 x 57½in. (114 x 146cm.) slr 'André Brasilier'; sd
and titled on the reverse 'A. Brasilier 1975 Fête hippique en rose à Fère en Tardenois-AISNE'
PROV.: David B. Findlay Galleries, New York.
Christie's East, 30 April 1996 (198**) US$ 13,800   US$ 13,800

BRAUER Arik (Erich) (Vienna 1929 b.-) Austrian
DATTELPALME IM SACK mixed techique on paper, 1 x 41.5cm. slr 'BRAUER'; titled on the
reverse
Dorotheum Vienna, 21 May 1996 (139**) ATS 160,000   US$ 15,364

SPEIL MIT DEM ATOMKERN oil on panel, 93 x 111cm. sll 'BRAUER'; titled, s and numbered 'Nr. 137 1970' on a label on the reverse
PROV.: Paul Facchetti Gallery, Paris; Marlborough Gallery, Zürich.
Wiener Kunst Auktionen, 26 March 1996 (366**) ATS 300,000　　　　US$　　28,857

BRAUN Maurice (1877-1941) American
EUCALYPTUS oil on canvas, 20 x 24in. (50.8 x 61cm.) sll 'Maurice Braun' and inscr. with title on the reverse
PROV.: Mrs. William E. Mee, Sr., Colorado Springs; Mrs. William Mee, Jr., Oklahoma City; By descent in the family to the present owner.
Christie's New York, 23 May 1996 (98**) US$ 13,800　　　　US$　　13,800

BRAUNER Victor (Pietra Naemtz 1903-1966 Paris) Roumenian
COUPE DES CENT-VINGTS DISPOSITIONS ÉROTOMAGIQUES oil and wax on board, 26 x 20½in. (66 x 52.1cm.) sd and titled '10.I.1946'; s and titled on the reverse
PROV.: Mme. Stassar, Paris.
Sotheby's New York, 2 May 1996 (305**) US$ 123,500　　　　US$　　123,500

AUTOENROULEMENT oil on canvas, 31 7/8 x 25½in. (81 x 65cm.) sd titled lr 'Victor Brauner IV 1961'
PROV.: H Jeppe, South Africa (sale Sotheby's London, 4th July 1973, lot 107); Sale Sotheby's London, 26th June 1990, lot 61 (purchased by the present owner at GBP132,000).
Sotheby's London, 20 March 1996 (63**) GBP 78,700　　　　US$　　120,189

OUTIL SPIRITUEL II wax, oil and collage on canvas laid down on board, 25 7/8 x 32in. (66 x 81cm.) sd ini. 'V.B. XI 1958'
PROV.: Richard L. Feigen, Chicago; Galleria Cavalino, Venice.
Christie's London, 29 November 1995 (168**) GBP 41,000　　　　US$　　64,133

BRAVO Claudio (Valparaiso 1936 b.-l) Chilean
HECTOR pastel an coloured crayon on paper, 45.5 x 61.5cm. sdlr 'Claudio Bravo/MCMLXIII'
PROV.: Acquired directly from the by Héctor Marabini; private collection, Madrid.
Sotheby's Madrid, 23 November 1995 (117**) ESP 1,527,500　　　　US$　　12,556

BRAYER Yves (1907-1990) French
CHASSEURS DANS LES ALPILLES oil on canvas, 29 x 36in. (74 x 91.5cm.) sll 'Yves Brayer', titled and d '1973' on the reverse
Christie's South Kensington, 18 March 1996 (110**) GBP 13,225　　　　US$　　20,197

LES BAUX DE PROVENCE oil on canvas, 35 7/8 x 46in. (91 x 117cm.) slr 'Yves Brayer'inscr. and d on the reverse 'les Baux de Provence 1967'
Christie's South Kensington, 24 June 1996 (149**) GBP 10,350　　　　US$　　15,960

PRINTEMPS AUX BAUX , 25½ x 21¼in. (65 x 54cm.) slr 'Yves Brayer', bears inscr. with title on the reverse
PROV.: Private collection, U.K.
Phillips London, 27 November 1995 (40**) GBP 10,500　　　　US$　　16,424

BREANSKI Alfred Snr, de (1852-1928) British
THE RIVER TEITH; AND LOCH KATRINE oil on canvas (a pair), 8 x 12in. (20.3 x 30.5cm.) s 'Alfred de Breanski'
Christie's London, 6 November 1995 (160**) GBP 8,625　　　　US$　　13,491

STRONACHLACHER, N.B. oil on canvas, 24 x 36in. (61 x 91.5cm. sll; s and inscr. on the reverse
Phillips London, 12 December 1995 (56**) GBP 20,000　　　　US$　　30,779

NEAR IVERGARRY, EVENING oil on canvas, 20 x 30in. (51 x 76cm.) s s inscr. with title on the reverse

Phillips London, 23 April 1996 (91) GBP 5,600	US$	8,491

BEN NEVIS, N.B. oil on canvas, 44 x 64in. (112 x 162.5cm.) s 'A. de Breanski' s titled and inscr. on the reverse

Sotheby's London, 29 August 1995 (701**) GBP 34,500   US$ 55,843

A WELSH MOUNTAIN RIVER SCENE oil on canvas, 30 x 50in. (76.2 x 127cm.) slr 'Alfred de Breanski'

Christie's East, 30 October 1995 (36*) US$ 20,700   US$ 20,700

A SALMON RIVER IN SCOTLAND oil on canvas, 30 x 50in. (76.2 x 127cm.) s 'Alfred de Breanski' s inscr.'(A Salmon River in Scotland)/Alfred de Breanski/ Copyright/Reserved/A.de B.' on the reverse

Christie's London, 7 June 1996 (609**) GBP 36,700   US$ 56,592

BREDAEL Jan Frans I (Antwerp 1686-1,750 Antwerp) Flemish
A RIVERLANDSCAPE WITH A WINDMILL AND BOATS oil on panel, 15 x 19cm.

Dorotheum Vienna, 11 June 1996 (255**) ATS 110,000   US$ 10,210

BREDAEL Jan Peter I van (Antwerp 1654-1745 Antwerp) Flemish
CELEBRATING FARMERS IN FRONT OF A VILLAGE IN A RIVERLANDSCAPE. oil on canvas, 29 x 36cm.(framed)

Dorotheum Vienna, 17 October 1995 (119**) ATS 200,000   US$ 20,061

BREDAEL Joseph van (Antwerp 1688-1739 Paris) Flemish
RIVER LANDSCAPE WITH VILLAGE BUILDINGS INCLUDING A CHURCH ON THE HORIZON AND A WINDMILL ON THE RIGHT BANK, NUMEROUS FIGURES AND SEVERAL FERRIES AND OTHER BOAT CROSSING THE RIVER oil on canvas, 29 ¾ x 44½in. (75.5 x 113cm.) (ca. 1720)

Sotheby's London, 5 July 1995 (4**) GBP 51,000   US$ 81,353

THE TEMPTATION OF THE HOLY ANTONIUS oil on copper, 25 x 32cm.

Dorotheum Vienna, 6 March 1996 (107**) ATS 220,000   US$ 21,162

AN EXTENSIVE WOODED LANDSCAPE WITH PEASANTS IN A WAGON FORDING A STREAM oil on copper, 11 1/8 x 14½in. (28.2 x 38.9cm.)
PROV.: Anon. sale, Christie's 30 March 1979, lot 48, as *Jan Brueghel II* (GBP26,000).

Christie's London, 8 December 1995 (3**) GBP 45,500   US$ 70,022

BREDAEL Peeter van (Antwerp 1629-1719 Antwerp) Flemish
ITALIANATE MARKET SCENES oil on canvas laid on board (a pair), 26 7/8 x 32½in. (68.1 x 82.4cm.) both sll 'Pieter van Bredael'

Christie's London, 20 October 1995 (67**) GBP 12,650   US$ 19,965

BREEN Adam van (1612 - 1646 act. Amsterdam-) Dutch
A WINTER SCENE WITH SKATERS AND MASKED FIGURES ON A FROZEN RIVER oil on canvas, 27½ x 36 ¾in. (70 x 93.5cm.)

Sotheby's London, 6 December 1995 (259**) GBP 20,700   US$ 31,856

BREENBERGH Bartholomeus (Deventer 1598/1600-1657 Amsterdam) Dutch
A PORTRAIT OF A GENTLEMAN oil on oak panel, 17 x 13½in. (43.5 x 34.5cm.) sll 'BBreenberg fecit'; inscr. and dur 'Ætatis sua. 57.A°1641'
PROV.: Presumed to have been in the family of the present owner since at least the last quarter of the 19th century.

LIT.: M. Roethlisberger, *Bartholomeus Breenbergh - The Paintings*, 1981, pp. 79-80, no. 202 a, reproduced.

       Sotheby's London, 6 December 1995 (46**) GBP 67,500   US$ 103,878

BREITNER Georg Hendrik (Rotterdam 1857-1923 Amsterdam) Dutch
PORTRAIT OF THE VAN DER WEELE CHILDREN oil on canvas, 101 x 77.5cm. (ca. 1895-98)
PROV.: Hermanus Johannes van der Weele, thence by descent to the present owner.

       Christie's Amsterdam, 25 April 1996 (191**) NLG 40,250   US$ 23,917

BREKELENKAM Quiringh Gerritsz. van (Zwammerdam, near Leyden 1620 (c.)-1667/68 Leiden) Dutch
LADY WITH CAVALIER; 'THE MUSIC-HOUR' oil on panel, 42 x 33.5cm. s with mono. and dlr 'Q.B. 1666'

       Dorotheum Vienna, 6 March 1996 (9**) ATS 120,000   US$ 11,543

THE DRUNKARD ASLEEP oil on oak panel, 23.5 x 21cm. slr mono 'QGB'
PROV.: Anon. sale, Paris Hôtel Drouot, 28 June 1957, no. 142 (70,000 FFR).

       Étude Tajan Paris, 12 December 1995 (50**) FRF 40,000   US$ 8,057

KITCHENMAID CLEANING FISH oil on panel, 28 x 32cm. sd (on the table) 'Quierijn 1664'

       Dorotheum Vienna, 17 October 1995 (126**) ATS 150,000   US$ 15,046

,
A CONNLER IN HIS WORKSHOP oil on panel, 46 x 62cm. s with monogram cr 'QVB'
PROV.: The Duchess Françoise Melzi d'Eril da Lodi, her sale, Brussels, Le Roy, 29 April 1929; Anon. sale, Brussels, Fievez, 26 May 1930, lot 18, where bought by the ancestors of the present owner.

       Sotheby's Amsterdam, 6 May 1996 (8**) NLG 21,240   US$ 12,385

TWO ELEGANT COUPLES IN AN INTERIOR oil on oak panel, 15 x 20in. (38 x 51cm.) s with a monogram on the back of the chair 'Q v B' (ca. 1655)
PROV.: With Kleinberger, Paris; Baron Heinrich Thyssen-Bornemisza, by 1930.
EXH.: Munich 1930, no. 38; Bern 1960, no. 15; Düsseldorf 1970-71, no. 8; Paris 1970, no. 16, plate 7; Lausanne etc. 1986-87, no. 29.
LIT.: R. Heinmann 1937, vol. I, no. 51, as *Brekelenkam*; A. Lasius, *Quiringh van Brekelenkam*, 1992, pp. 156-157, no. B44, under 'Uncertain Attributions'.

       Sotheby's London, 6 December 1995 (99**) GBP 16,100   US$ 24,777

BRENNAN Michael George (1839-1874)
THE ACOLYTE oil on canvas, 26 ¾ x 35 ¾in. (68 x 90.8cm.) sdll and inscr. 'M G Brennan Roma 1870'; s and inscr. 'No.1 The Acolyte M G Brennan Cafe del Greco Rome' and ' No 1 An Acolyte M G Brennan' on the reverse

       Christie's London, 9 May 1996 (17**) GBP 11,500   US$ 17,414

BRETON Jules Adolphe Aimé Louis (Courrières (Pas-de-Calais) 1827-1906 Paris) French
LA FEMME A L'OMBRELLE; BAIE DE DOUARNEZ oil on canvas, 25½ x 35 3/4in. (65 x 91cm.) sdlr 'Jules Breton/1871'
PROV.: The Artist's Collection (until 1894); Possibly with Goupil et Cie., Paris; Pellerano Collection, Buenos Aires (by 1900); Thence by descent; Anon. sale; Sotheby's New York, 22 February 1989, lot 169.
EXH.: *Nondissenters: One hundred and seventy French Nineteenth Century Drawings, Pastels, and Watercolors*, Shepherd Gallery, New York, no. 30; *Jules Breton and the French Realist Tradition*, Joslyn Art Museum, Omaha, Nebraska; Dixon Gallery and Gardens, Memphis, Tennessee; Sterling and Francine Clark Institute, Williamstown, Massachusets, 1983, pp.92-3, no. 37.
LIT.: This painting will be included in the forthcoming *Breton catalogue raisonné* being prepared by Annette Bourrut Lacouture.

       Christie's New York, 22 May 1996 (90**) US$ 607,500   US$ 607,500

BRETT John Edward, A.R.A. (Bletchingley (Sussex) 1830-1902 London) British
A WINDY DAY; SUNSET, LOW TIDE oil on board a pair (2), 7 x 14in. (18 x 35.5cm.) a pair, one
dul 'Sep 26 '71', the other d 'Oct 21 '71'
         Phillips London, 18 June 1996 (70**) GBP 6,500   US$ 10,023

BREYDEL Karel (Charles) (called le Chevalier) (Antwerp 1677-1733 Antwerp) Flemish
MERCHANTS AND TRAVELLERS NEAR A COASTAL INLET oil on canvas, 29.6 x 41.7cm.
sdlc 'Karl Breydel 1720'
         Christie's Amsterdam, 7 May 1996 (90**) NLG 25,300   US$ 14,752

MERCHANTS AND TRAVELLERS NEAR A COASTAL INLET oil on canvas, 29.6 x 41.7cm. sd
cl 'Karl Breydel 1720'
         Christie's Amsterdam, 13 November 1995 (38**) NLG 19,550   US$ 12,321

A CAVALRY SKIRMISH BY A LAKE, A TOWN BEYOND oil on copper, 19 x 24.2cm. slr 'c.
breijdel'
         Christie's Amsterdam, 13 November 1995 (88*) NLG 11,500   US$ 7,248

BRIANCHON Maurice (Fresnay-sur-Sarthe 1899-1979) French
MARÉE BASSE oil on canvas, 28 7/8 x 36¼in. (73.5 x 92cm.) slr 'Brianchon'
PROV.: Findlay Galleries, New York (Acquired by the late owner).
         Christie's East, 30 April 1996 (112**) US$ 13,800   US$ 13,800

NU ASSIS DANS INTERIEUR oil on canvas, 28 ¾ x 19 ¾in. (73 x 50cm.) sll 'Brianchon'
PROV.: Wally Findlay Galleries, New York (acquired by the late owner).
         Christie's East, 30 April 1996 (174**) US$ 12,650   US$ 12,650

SCENE DU THEATRE oil on canvas, 15 x 24in. (38.1 x 60.9cm.) sll 'Brianchon'
PROV.: Galerie Alfred Daber, Paris (acquired by Mildred S. Hilson, 1956).
         Christie's New York, 8 November 1995 (344**) US$ 17,250   US$ 17,250

BRICHER Alfred Thompson, A.N.A. (1837-1908) American
PICNIC BY THE MERRIMAC RIVER AT NEWSBURYPORT, MASSACHUSETTS oil on
canvas, 30 x 40in. (76 x 102cm.) sdkr 'A.T. Bricher 59'
         Christie's East, 21 May 1996 (11**) US$ 10,350   US$ 10,350

AUTUMN LANDSCAPE oil on board, 10 x 19 1/8in. (25.4 x 48.6cm.) sdlc 'A T Bricher 1870'
PROV.: John Duncan Preston.
LIT.: J.D. Preston, 'Alfred Thompson Bricher, 1837-1908', *The Art Quarterly*, summer 1962, pp.
148-157, p. 152 (illustrated).
         Christie's New York, 23 May 1996 (17**) US$ 27l,600   US$ 27,600

BRICKDALE Eleanor Fortescue (1871-1945) British
SPRING AND AUTUMN pencil and watercolour with bodycolour on paper laid down on canvas,
circular, 24 ¾in. (63cm.) diameter s ini. 'EFB'
         Christie's London, 6 November 1995 (49**) GBP 10,120   US$ 15,830

BRIDGMAN Frederick Arthur (1847-1928) French/American
AT THE FOUNTAIN, ALGIERS oil on canvas, 15 x 18¼in. (38.1 x 46.4cm.) slr 'F.A. Bridgman'
         Christie's East, 13 February 1996 (208**) US$ 16,100   US$ 16,100

LES VOISINES, TERRASSES D`ALGER oil on canvas, 34 3/4 x 25 7/8(88.3 x 65.7cm.) sdlr 'F.A.
Bridgman 1887'
PROV.: Private collection, Canada.
LIT.: F.A. Bridgman, *Winters in Algeria*, New York, 1890, (illustrated by engraving).
         Christie's New York, 14 February 1996 (34**) US$ 217,000   US$ 217,000

EVENING OVER ALGIERS oil on canvas, 21½ x 39 3/4in. (64.7 x 101cm.) slr 'F.A. Bridgman
PROV.: Madamne d'Alexandry, Paris; Mrs. Pope, England.
     Christie's New York, 22 May 1996 (11**) US$ 217,000

    US$ 217,000

AN ARAB WATERING HIS HORSE oil on canvas, 29 x38½in. (73.7 x 97.7cm.) s 'F.A. Bridgman'
(1890-1900)
PROV.: T. Stebbins, Jr. (as Horse at Biskra).
LIT.: To be included in Ilene Susan Forth's forthcoming *catalogue raisonné on Bridgman*.
     Christie's London, 17 November 1995 (126A**) GBP 20,700

    US$ 32,379

ALGIERS oil on canvas, 19 x 25½in. (48.3 x 64.8cm.) sdll 'F A Bridgman/Alger 1886/(Feb)'
     Christie's New York, 2 November 1995 (249**) US$ 28,750

    US$ 28,750

TEMPLE D'ABOO SIMBEL, LA FETE DU PHAROAN oil on canvas, 23 ¾ x 33 ¾in. (63 x
85.3cm.) slr 'F.A. Bridgman'
PROV.: F.A. Bridgman Studio; sale, Hotel Druout, Paris, November 25-26, 1929, no. 91 (illustrated).
     Christie's New York, 2 November 1995 (260**) US$ 17,250

    US$ 17,250

BRIL Paulus (attr.) (Antwerp 1554-1626 Rome) Flemish
RIVER LANDSCAPE WITH MOORED BOATS AND FIGURES oil on panel, 35.5 x 52cm. sll
with initials '.PB.'
PROV.: Said to be from the Royal House of Savoy, Turin.
LIT.: *The Burlington Magazine*, June 1977, pl. XIII.
     Sotheby's Amsterdam, 6 May 1996 (38**) NLG 17,700

    US$ 10,321

BRIL Paulus (attributed) (Antwerp 1554-1626 Rome) Flemish
WOODED LANDSCAPE WITH BIRDS oil on copper, 22.5 x 17cm.
     Dorotheum Vienna, 11 June 1996 (244**) ATS 140,000

    US$ 12,995

BROECK Elias van den (Amsterdam 1650-1708 Amsterdam) Dutch
NATURE MORTE DE SOUS-BOIS AVEC SAUTERELLES, SCARABÉE AU CLAIR DE LUNE
oil on canvas, 60 x 51cm. sll 'E van den Broeck'
LIT.: C.G. Marcus, 'Otto Marseus van Schrieck et les peintres de reptiles, insectes et sous bois', *Art et
Curiosité*, September 1974, p. 89 (illustrated fig. XV).
     Étude Tajan Paris, 12 December 1995 (27***) FRF 280,000

    US$ 56,399

BROODTHAERS Marcel (Brussels 1924-1976 London) Belgian
HEURE gouache and crayon on canvas, 39 x 95cm. s with initials and dlr 'M.B.74'
PROV.: Galerie Isy Brachot, Brussels.
     Christie's Amsterdam, 6 December 1995 (379**) NLG 11,500

    US$ 7,126

LEVERKUSEN PROPOSAL three handwritten letters in one frame, 27.5 x 21cm. each sd 'Marcel
Broodthaers 25 août 1969 Brussels'
PROV.: Galerie Isy Brochot, Brussels, no. B291.
     Christie's Amsterdam, 6 December 1995 (382**) NLG 25,300

    US$ 15,677

LA PESTE acrylic and ink on canvas, 56 ¾ 44 1/8in. (144 x 112cm.) (1974-75)
PROV.: Marian Goodman Gallery, New York.
EXH.: New York, Marian Goodman Gallery, *Marcel Broodthaers, Multiples*, September-October
1982; New York, Marian Goodman Gallery, *Marcel Broodthaers*, November 1984, no. 13
(illustrated in colour in the catalogue); New York, Tony Shafrazi Gallery, *Words*, January-
February1989; Minneapolis, Walker Art Center; Los Angeles, Museum of Contemporary Art;
Pittsburgh, Carnegie Museum of Arts; Brussels, Palais des Beaux Arts, *Marcel Broodthaers*, April
1989-June 1990; Paris, Galerie Nationale du Jeu de Paume; Madrid, Centro de Arte Reina Sofia,
Marcel Broodthaers, December 1991-June 1992 (illustrated in colour in the catalogue p. 287).
LIT.: Wilfried Dickhoff (ed.) *Marcel Broodthaers: Le poids d'un oeuvre d'art*, Cologne 1994, p. 171

(illustrated in colour).
Christie's London, 26 October 1995 (82**) GBP 21,850

US$ 34,485

UNTITLED paintrollers, paintbrushes, plastic sphere and plaster on sponges mounted on wood panel, 24 3/8 x 37 ¾in. (61.8 x 96cm.) (ca 1963-64)
PROV.: Galerie Saint Laurent, Brussels; Acquired from the above by the present owner.
Christie's London, 30 November 1995 (29**) GBP 24,150

US$ 37,776

BROOKING Charles (1723-1759) British
A KETCH-RIGGED ROYAL YACHT IN A FRESH BREEZE OFF DOVER oil on canvas, 47½ x 71½in. (120 x 182cm.) sdlc on sail 'C. Brooking' and dlr on spit '1754'
PROV.: D. Stirling.
EXH.: Bristol City Art Gallery, *Charles Brooking 1723-1759*, 1966, p. 20. no. 63 (illustrated p. 29).
Sotheby's London, 12 July 1995 (2**) GBP 56,500

US$ 90,126

BROOKS James (1906-1992) American
T-1953 oil on muslin mounted on linen, 46 x 54¼in. (116.8 x 137.8cm.) sll 'J. Brooks' (1953)
PROV.: Kootz Gallery, New York; Private collection, New York.
Christie's New York, 15 November 1995 (169**) US$ 17,250

US$ 17,250

BROSAMER Hans (Fulda (?) 1,500 c.-1554 c. Erfurt) German
PORTRAIT OF JOCHUM WIRMAN oil on panel, 19¼ x 13¼in. (49 x 34cm.) sdur with monogram '1521/HB'; inscr. at the top 'IN DIESER GESTALT WARD JOCHVM WIRMAN 24 JAR ALT'
PROV.: Anon. sale, Lucerne, Galerie Fischer, 16-22 June 1969, lot 2194, when accompanied by a certificate of Prof. Alfred Stange.
LIT.: I. Kühnel-Kunze, 'Hans Brosamer und der Meister HB mit dem GReifenkopf', in *Zeitschrift für Kunstwissenschaft*, 1960, pp. 78-9 (illustrated pl. 21).
Sotheby's London, 5 July 1995 (162**) GBP 20,700

US$ 33,020

BROTO José Manuel (1949 b.-) Spanish
UNTITLED oil on canvas, 190 x 250cm. sd '27,4,82' on the reverse
PROV.: Galería Maeght, Barcelona; Private collection, Madrid.
EXH.: Zaragoza, *Preliminar*, I Bienal Nacional de Artes Plásticas, 1983.
Sotheby's Madrid, 23 November 1995 (113**) ESP 2115,000

US$ 17,385

BROUWER Adriaen (Oudenaerde 1605 c.-1638 Antwerp) Dutch (Flemish)
THE SENSE OF A HEARING: A BOOR SINGING TO THE SOUND OF A VIOLIN, PLAYED BY ANOTHER IN A BARN oil on panel, 24.2 x 17.4cm. slr 'AB' (linked)
PROV.: Lippman von Lissingen; Sale, Paris, 18 March 1876, lot 9; Baron de Beurnonville; Sale, Paris, 9 May 1881, lot 224; M. Flersheim, Paris; J. Krueger, Stockholm; Sale, 14 September 1932, lot 37; with P. de Boer, Amsterdam, 1935.
EXH.: Vienna, 1873, no. 161.
LIT.: C. Hofstede de Groot, *A Catalogue Raissonné etc.*, III, 1910, no. 83.
Christie's Amsterdam, 13 November 1995 (123**) NLG 51,750

US$ 32,615

BROWN George Loring (Boston 1814-1889 Malden (Mass.)) American
VIEW OF MYSTIC POND GROUNDS, WEST MEDFORD, MASSACHUSETTS oil on canvas, 10 5/8 x 14 ¾in. (27 x 37.5cm.) sdlr 'Geo. L. Brown 1863'
Christie's New York, 13 September 1995 (10*) US$ 9,775

US$ 9,775

BROWN John George (1831-1913) American
THE BOYS' NEW TORK oil on canvas, 24 x 16in. (61 x 40.6cm.) sdll 'J. G. Brown N.A. 1886'
Christie's New York, 13 September 1995 (48*) US$ 10,350

US$ 10,350

BROWN James (1951 b.) American
STABAT MATER (BROWN I) lead, oil and nails on panel, 51 x 35½in. (129.6 x 90.2cm.) s twice, d

and titled 'James Brown 'stabat mater brown I' paris 1988-9'
PROV.: Acquired directly from the artist.
EXH.: New York. Leo Castelli Gallery, *James Brown*, April 1989; Madrid, Galeria de Art Solidad
Lorenzo, *James Brown*, Dec. 1989.
Christie's New York, 22 February 1996 (148**) US$ 10,350

US$ 10,350

BROWN William Mason (1828-1898) American
WINTER LANDSCAPE oil on canvas, 12 x 18in. (30.5 x 45.7cm.) slr 'Wm M Brown'
Christie's East, 21 May 1996 (7**) US$ 8,625

US$ 8,625

AUTUMN SCENE ON THE CONNECTICUT oil on canvas, 12¼ x 18in. (30.5 x 45.7cm.) slr 'WM
Brown' titled on the reverse'
Christie's New York, 23 May 1996 (45**) US$ 16,100

US$ 16,100

BRUCK Lajos (Papa 1846-1910 Budapest) Hungarian
DIE GRATULANTEN oil on canvas, 80 x 100cm. slr 'Bruck Lajos'
Dorotheum Vienna, 6 November 1995 (24**) ATS 250,000

US$ 25,078

BRUCKMAN Willem Leendert (1866-) Dutch
A VIEW OF MAASTRICHT WITH THE BRIDGE OF ST. SERVAAS AND THE ONZE LIEVE
VROUWE CHURCH BEYOND oil on canvas, 28 x 36¼in. (71 x 92cm.) s 'W.L. Bruckman
PROV.: With the Rowley Gallery, London.
EXH.: Glasgow, The Rowley Gallery and Co., 1913, no. 1371.
Christie's London, 17 November 1995 (2**) GBP 8,050

US$ 12,592

BRUEGHEL Abraham (Antwerp 1631-1697 Naples) Flemish
A BOUQUET OF FLOWERS HELD BY A MAIDEN, IN A LANDSCAPE SETTING oil on
canvas, 38½ x 29in. (97 x 73.5cm.) slc 'ABrueghel. F. Roma'
Sotheby's London, 5 July 1995 (60**) GBP 32,200

US$ 51,364

MELONS, PEACHES, PLUMS, PEARS AND A VASE OF FLOWERS ON A BANK oil on canvas
laid down on board, 24 7/8 x 34in. s 'ABrueghel.fect'
Christie's London, 8 December 1995 (87**) GBP 51,000

US$ 78,486

BRUEGHEL Jan I, {called} de Velours (Brussels 1568-1625 Antwerp) Flemish
A VIEW OF A TOWN BY A RIVER WITH MOORED SAILING VESSELS BY A QUAY AND A
FISHMARKET BY A LANDING STAGE IN THE FOREGROUND oil on panel, 17.2 x 26.8cm.
Christie's Amsterdam, 13 November 1995 (128**) NLG 97,750

US$ 61,606

**BRUEGHEL Jan I, {called} de Velours (and studio P.P. Rubens) (Brussels 1568-1625 Antwerp)
Flemish**
THE VIRGIN AND CHILD IN A LANDSCAPE oil on panel, 150 x 130cm. (ca. 1623-24)
Christie's Monaco, 14 June 1996 (12**) FRF 538,900

US$ 104,061

BRUEGHEL Jan II (1601-1678) Flemish
STUDIES OF AN ARTICHOKE, ASPARAGUS, SPRIGS OF OAK WITH ACORNS, APPLES,
AND A SPRIG OF APPLES BLOSSOM, MEDLAR, PLUMS AND A SPRIG OF BLACKBERRY
oil on panel, 20 ¾ x 27in. (52.4 x 68.4cm.) (1620's)
PROV.: Lord Bateman, Kelmarsh Hall, Northamptonshire, his sale, London, Christie's, 11 April
1896, lot 137, as Snyders, 15 gns to Christie; Anon. sale, London, Christie's, 18 May 1917, lot 85, as
F. Snyders, 10 gns; Mr and Mrs Hanns Schaffer, New York; Dr. Ludwig Burchard, London; With P.
& D. Colnaghi, London, 1974.
EXH.: Brussels, Palais des Beaux Arts, date unknown, no. 22, lent by Ludwig Burchard; London, P.
& D. Colnaghi, *Old Master Paintings*, 1974, no. 42, as Jan Brueghel the Elder.
LIT.: H. Gerson, *Art and Architecture in Belgium, 1600-1800*, 1960, reproduced plate 44b, as Jan
Brueghel the Elder; J. Foucart, in *Le siècle de Rubens dans les collections publiques françaises*,

exhibition catalogue, 1978, p. 54, under no. 18; K. Ertz, *Jan Brueghel the Younger*, 1984, pp. 503-4, no. 334, colour plate 65.

Sotheby's London, 5 July 1995 (12**) GBP 100,500		US$	160,313

THE ADORATION OF THE MAGI oil on panel, 15½ x 22¼in. (39.2 x.56.8cm.) (1560's)
PROV.: H. Gerson, *Art and Architecture in Belgium, 1600-1800*, 1960, reproduced plate 44b, as Jan Brueghel the Elder; J. Foucart, in *Le siècle de Rubens dans les collections publiques françaises*, exhibition catalogue, 1978, p. 54, under no. 18; K. Ertz, *Jan Brueghel the Younger*, 1984, pp. 503-4, no. 334, colour plate 65.

Sotheby's London, 5 July 1995 (18**) GBP 155,500		US$	248,046

VILLAGE NEAR A RIVER WITH ROWERS, A CITY BEYOND oil on copper, 16.5 x 25.5cm.

Dorotheum Vienna, 6 March 1996 (150**) ATS 750,000		US$	72,143

A VILLAGE BY A RIVER WITH PEASANTS ON A TRACK oil on copper, 4 x 6 5/8in. (10.2 x 16.8cm.)
PROV.: With Pieter de Boer, Amsterdam; Anon. Sale, Christie's 7 July 1978, lot 234, as Jan Brueghel I (GBP24,000).

Christie's London, 8 December 1995 (2**) GBP 19,550		US$	30,086

FARMERHOUSE NEAR A BROOK oil on copper, 18.5 x 26cm.

Dorotheum Vienna, 11 June 1996 (289**) ATS 860,000		US$	79,825

ADAM AT WORK AFTER THE FALL OF MAN oil on copper, 76.3 x 96.2cm. slr 'I.BRE.GHEL F'
PROV.: Anon. Sale, Leo Spik Berlin, 2 May 1957, lot 84, as *Jan Brueghel I and H. van Balen*.
LIT.: K. Ertz, *Jan Brueghel the younger (1601-1678)*, 1984, p.54, p.294, no 117 with ill.

Christie's Amsterdam, 13 November 1995 (129**) NLG 74,750		US$	47,110

FOREST LANDSCAPE, WITH REST ON THE FLEE TO EGYPT oil on panel, 38.5 x 61cm.(framed)

Dorotheum Vienna, 17 October 1995 (125**) ATS 600,000		US$	60,184

AFFORESTED LANDSCAPE WITH WOODCUTTERS oil on panel, 24 x 36cm. (framed)
PROV.: Wiener Privatsammlung.

Dorotheum Vienna, 17 October 1995 (145**) ATS 350,000		US$	35,107

RIVER LANDSCAPE WITH BIRDS OR AN ALLEGORY ON AIR oil on canvas, 120 x 171cm. slr 'J Brueghel' (ca 1640)
PROV.: Ehemals, London, Christie's 30 May 1980, no. 46.
LIT.: Klaus Ertz, *Jan Brueghel the Younger, 1601-1678, the paintings with oeuvre catalogue*, Freren, 1984, pp. 53 and 78, cat no. 327 (illustrated).

Étude Tajan Paris, 28 June 1996 (59**) FRF 160,000		US$	30,896

BRUEGHEL Jan II (with Sir Peter Paul Rubens 1577-1640) (Antwerp 1601-1678) Flemish
LANDSCAPE WITH PAN AND SYRINX oil on oakpanel, 23 x 37¼in. (58 x 94.5cm.)
PROV.: Graf Schonborn, Schloss Pommersfelden; Graf A.M. Schonborn, his sale, Paris, Drouot, 17-18 May 1867, lot 210, 7,000 francs; Salomon Goldschmidt, his (anonymous) sale, Paris, Georges Petit, 14-17 March 1898, lot 95, 9,200 francs to Max; Baron Rothschild, Vienna; Kunstsalon Franke, Leipzig, 1933; With Rosenberg & Stiebel, New York, circa 1960; Brian Jenks, Astbury Hall, Shropshire (according to Jaffé, see Literature); With Edward Speelman, London, 1979-80.
EXH.: On loan, London, National Gallery, 1980-1988; London, Agnew's, *Thirty-five Paintings from the Collection of the British Rail Pension Fund*, 8 November-14 December 1984, no. 3, reproduced in the catalogue; On loan, Leeds Castle, 1988-1995; Boston, Museum of Fine Art, Toledo, Museum of Art, *The Age of Rubens*, September 1993 - April 1994, no. 17.
LIT.: G. Campori, *Riccolta di catal. Ed. invent. ined.*, 1870, p. 191 (according to Sutton op. cit.); Possibly J. Denuce, 'Brieven en Documenten betreffend Jan Brueghel I en II', in *Bronnen voor de*

geschiedenis van de Vlaamsche kunst, vol. III, 1934, p. 142; A. Pigler, *Barockthemen*, 1956, p. 191; M. Jaffé, 'Rubens and Raphael', in *Studies in Renaissance and Baroque Art presented to Anthony Blunt*, 1967, p. 100, reproduced fig. 3; M. Jaffé, *Rubens and Italy*, 1977, p. 23, note 50; K Ertz, *Jan Brueghel derAltere*, 1979, pp. 417, 420, 622-3, no. 384a, reproduced p. 419, fig. 504 (as by Rubens and Jan Brueghel the Elder, datable circa 1623); *The Burlington Magazine*, September 1980, p. 664, reproduced p. 646, fig. 63; K Ertz, *Jan Brueghel the Younger*, 1984, pp. 70, 81, 417-8, no. 256, reproduced p. 417 (as by *Rubens and Studio and Jan Brueghel the Younger*, datable to the late 1620s); M. Jaffé, *Rubens, Catalogo Completo*, 1989, p. 231, no. 442, reproduced, (as by Rubens and Jan Brueghel the Elder, painted circa 1617); P.C. Sutton, *The Age of Rubens*, catalogue of the Boston-Toledo exhibition, 1993, pp. 260-263, no. 17, reproduced in colour, (as by *Rubens and Jan Brueghel the Elder*).

Sotheby's London, 5 July 1995 (42**) GBP 749,500

	US$	1.195.565

BRUEGHEL Jan II with Hendrick van Balen (1575-1632)(attr.) (Antwerp 1601-1678) Flemish
DIANA AND HER NYMPHS RESTING IN A WOODLAND GLADE WITH THE SPOILS OF THE CHASE, ACTAEON WITH HIS HOUNDS IN A LANDSCAPE BEYOND oil on panel, 21 x 37in. (53.5 x 93.5cm.) the reverse of the panel bears the brand of the Antwerp Panel Makers' Guild and the makers' mark 'MV' (Michiel Vriendt)

Sotheby's London, 6 December 1995 (156**) GBP 23,000

	US$	35.396

BRUEGHEL Jan Pieter (Antwerp 1628-1662 Italy) Flemish
STILL-LIFE WITH FLOWERS oil on panel, 40 x 31cm. slc

Hauswedell & Nolte Cologne, 6 June 1996 (15**) DEM 22,000

	US$	14,294

BRUEGHEL Pieter III (1589 b.-) Flemish
PEASANTS PAYING TITHES oil on panel, 28½ x 42½in. (72.4 x 107.3cm.)

Christie's London, 7 July 1995 (31A**) GBP 73,000

	US$	116,446

BRUEGHEL Pieter the Younger {called} Brueghel d'Enfer (Brussels 1564 <circa>-1637/38 Antwerp) Flemish
A PEASANT KERMESSE oil on panel, 30½ x 67in. (77.5 x 170.5cm.)
PROV.: Sold, New York, Sotheby's, 9 June 1983, lot 66.

Sotheby's London, 5 July 1995 (278**) GBP 73,000

	US$	116,446

PEASANTS PAYING TITHES oil on panel, 29½ x 49¼in. (75 x 125cm.) s '.P BREVGHEL.'
PROV.: Maurice Plessis, Paris.

Christie's London, 8 December 1995 (7**) GBP 111,500

	US$	171,591

SPRING : GARDENERS, SHEEP SHEARERS AND PEASANTS MEERY-MAKING oil on panel, 16 7/8 x 22 ¾in, (42.8 x 57.8 cm.) s 'P.BrEVGHEL.' (ca 1565)
PROV.: Mrs. A. Eecen-van Setten, Harlingersingel 7, Leeuwarden; with Alfred Brod, London,1969.
EXH.: Amsterdam, Kunsthandel P. de Boer, *De Helsche en de Fluweelen Brueghel*, 10 Feb. - 26 March 1934, no. 20. pl. 4; Amsterdam, Kunsthandel P. de Boer, and Vienna, Galerie Sanct Lucas, *Die jungeren Brueghel und ihr Kreis*,1935, no. 56; Ghent and Breda, De Beyerd Cultureel Centrum, *Landschap in de Nederlanden*, 1960-1, no. 20, illustrated; Laren. Singer Memorial Foundation, *Modernen van toen*, 1963, no. 55; Haarlem, Frans Halsmuseum, *De Landman en zijn Muze*, 14June - 29 Aug. 1965, no.7.
LIT.: G. Marlier, *Pierre Breughel le Jeune*, Brussels, 1969, pp. 222-3, no. 3, fig. 132 (detail).

Christie's London, 8 December 1995 (8**) GBP 518,500

	US$	797,938

A WINTER LANDSCAPE WITH SKATERS AND A BIRD TRAP oil on panel, 15 3/8 x 22¼in. (39.1 x 56.8cm.)
PROV.: Dr. B. Lohse, Switzerland, by 1943.
LIT.: G. Marlier, Pierre Breughel le Jeune, Brussels, 1969, p. 244, no. 18.

Christie's London, 8 December 1995 (9**) GBP 243,500

	US$	374,731

THE WEDDING DANCE oil on oak panel, 16 x 22¼in. (40.6 x 56.7cm.) sdll 'P.BREUGHEL.1623'
PROV.: Samuel Francis Barlow (1748-1800); Thence by Barlow family at Hampton Manor House,
Hampton Court, Middlesex and Middlethorpe Hall, York to Cecilia Arabella Barlow, Lady
Wendleydale of Amptill Park, Bedfordshire; Thence to her grandson, George Howard (1843-1911),
later 9th Earl of Carlisle, Thence by descent at Castle Howard, Yorkshire.
LIT.: Lord Hawkesbury, *Catalogue of the Portraits, Miniatures, etc, at Castle Howard*, Yorkshire,
and Naworth Castle, Cumberland, *The Transactions of the East Riding Antiquarian Society*, vol. XI,
1903, p. 79, no. 125.

Sotheby's London, 6 December 1995 (7**) GBP 375,500	US$	577,870

A WEDDING FEAST oil on oak panel, 16 ¾ x 28 ¾in. (42.8 x 72.7cm.) slr 'P.BREVGHEL'
PROV.: Prince Serge Koudacheff, St. Petersburg, his ('Prince Tartarsky') sale, Amsterdam, Fk.
Muller, 1905, lot 7; Anon. sale, Berlin, Lepke, 11 February 1913; With P. de Boer, Amsterdam,
1946; Anon. sale, (The Property of a Lady), London, Christie's, 20 March 1964, lot 47, (when sold
with the certificate of Max J. Friedländer), 16,000 gns to Leadbeater; With the Hallsborough Gallery,
1965; Anon. sale, (Property of a German Collector), London, Christie's, 27 June 1969, lot 104,
24,000 gns to Peters; The Bernissart Family, Flanders, their wax seal affixed to the reverse.
EXH.: Manchester, City Art Gallery, *Between Renaissance and Baroque: European Art 1520-1600*,
March-April 1965, p. 23, no. 54.
LIT.: *The Connoisseur*, May 1965, p. xxi, reproduced; G. Marlier, *Pierre Brueghel le Jeune*, 1969, p.
379, no. 2, details reproduced figs. 232, 233.

Sotheby's London, 6 December 1995 (61**) GBP 496,500	US$	764,081

PEASANTS MERRY-MAKING oil on panel, circular, 9 5/8in. (24.5cm.) diam. s 'P. Brevghel' lower
centre
PROV.: Salmon Collection, Paris (according to a label on the reverse); Anon. sale, Galerie
Charpentier, Paris, 16 Dec. 1958, lot 34; with Eugene Slatter, London; with Robert Finck, Brussels.
EXH.: Vienna, Galerie Sankt Lucas, *Die jüngeren Brueghel*, April, 1935, fig. 253.
LIT.: G. Marlier, *Pierre Brueghel le Jeune*, Paris, 1969, p. 405.

Christie's London, 7 July 1995 (31**) GBP 150,000	US$	239,273

THE VISIT TO THE FARM oil on panel, 16 1/8 x 22½in. (41 x57.2cm.)
PROV.: Marcq Collection, Brussels, 1969.
LIT.: G. Marlier, Pierre Brueghel le jeune, Brussels, 1969, p.261, no.18.

Christie's London, 7 July 1995 (32**) GBP 78,500	US$	125,219

BRUNERY François (19th Century) Italian
LA CHASSE A LA SOURIS oil on panel, 18 x 21½in. (45.7 x 54.5cm) s F. Brunery'
PROV.: Mrs. Kingston, 1965.

Christie's London, 17 November 1995 (48C**) GBP 21,850	US$	34,178

IL SALTARELLO oil on canvas, 43¼ x 37½in. (109.9 x 95.3cm.) slr 'F. Brunery'

Christie's New York, 2 November 1995 (133**) US$ 63,000	US$	63,000

BRUNERY Marcel (19/20th Century) French
THE CARDINAL'S FEAST oil on canvas, 32 x 39¼in. (81.5 x 100cm.) slr

Sotheby's London, 13 March 1996 (74**) GBP 41,100	US$	62,767

A BIRTHDAY TOAST oil on canvas, 23 5/8 x 28 7/8in. (60 x 73.3cm.) s 'M. Brunery'

Christie's London, 14 June 1996 (47**) GBP 26,450	US$	40,786

THE NEW ACQUISITIONS oil on canvas, 24 1/8 x 30 3/8in. (61.3 x 77.2cm.) s 'M. Brunery'

Christie's London, 14 June 1996 (48**) GBP 27,600	US$	42,560

BRÜNING Peter (Düsseldorf 1929-1970 Düsseldorf) German
KOMPOSITIOM NR. 10 oil on canvas, 60 x 80cm. sd on the reverse '10' (1960)
Hauswedell & Nolte Cologne, 6 June 1996 (49**) DEM 47,000   US$ 30,537

LEGENDS -3/65 oil on canvas, 38 1/8 x 51 1/8in. (97 x 130cm.) sd '65'; titled ad numbered 'N° 3/65'
on the reverse; sd '65' on the stretcher
PROV.: Acquired directly from the artist by the present owner ca. 1965.
EXH.: Paris, Galerie Creuze & Galerie Europe, *La figuration Narrative dans l'Art Contemporain*,
Paris 1965, no. 5.
LIT.: Marie-Louise Otten, *Peter Brüning: Studien zu Entwicklung und Werk, Werkverzeichnis*,
Cologne 1987, p. 400, no. 577 (illustrated).
Sotheby's London, 21 March 1996 (57**) GBP 8,050   US$ 12,294

KOMPOSITION 1/V, 57 oil on canvas, 38 x 51in. (96.5 x 129.6cm.) sdlr '57'; sd and titled 'I/V'57' on
the stretcher
PROV.: Private Collection, Germany.
EXH.: Düsseldorf, Kunsthalle, *Düsseldorfer Kunst im Jan Wellem Jahr*, 1958 (illustrated in the
catalogue p. 9); Hagen, Karl-Ernst Osthaus Museum, Westdeutscher Künstlerbund: *8. Ausstellung*,
1958, no. 22; Mannheim, Kunsthalle; Hagen, Karl-Emst-Osthaus Museum, *Peter Brüning*, May-July
1962, no. 11; Saarbrücken, Moderne Galerie des Saarland-Museums; Dortmund, Museum am
Ostwall, *Peter Brüning - Retrospektive seines Werkes*, June-October 1988, no. 23 (illustrated in
colour in the catalogue).
LIT.: In: 'Cimaise', vol. 7, no. 49, Pierre Restany, Peter Brüning (on de l'espace gothique chez un
peintre du geste), Paris, July-August-September 1960, pp. 40-51 (illustrated p. 44); Marie-Luise
Otten, Peter Brüning, Cologne 1988, p. 347, no. 179 (illustrated and illustrated again in colour pl.
15).
Christie's London, 27 June 1996 (40**) GBP 25,300   US$ 39,013

KOMPOSITION crayon and ink on paper laid down on cardboard, 59.5 x 77.5cm slr 'Bruening 60.'
(1960)
Lempertz Cologne, 28 November 1995 (581*) DEM 18,000   US$ 12,705

BRUNNER Ferdinand (Vienna 1870-1945) Austrian
FISCHERHAUSER AN DER DONAU oil on canvas, 29 x 40cm. sll 'F. Brunner'; sd and titled on a
label on the reverse (1937)
EXH.: Vienna, Künstlerhaus, 1937/2026.
Dorotheum Vienna, 21 May 1996 (87**) ATS 160,000   US$ 15,364

WALDVERTIER BAUERNHOF oil on canvas, 98 x 119.4cm. sdll '1919 FERDINAND BRUNNER'
Wiener Kunst Auktionen, 29 November 1995 (610**) ATS 520,000   US$ 52,163

BRUS Günter (Ardning 1938 b.-) Austrian
DIE 12 MONATE 12 pictures in mixed technique on panel, 40 x 30.5cm. each each sd and numbered
'Brus 81' on the reverse
Wiener Kunst Auktionen, 27 September 1995 (484**) ATS 200,000   US$ 19,441

BRUSCO Cornelio (with François de Nomé) (act. first half of the 18th Century-) Italian
THE CONVERSION OF ST. PAUL oil on canvas, 76 x 101cm.
LIT.: M.R. Nappi *François De Nomé e Didier Barra, l'enigma Monsu Desiderio*, Rome, 1991 A, pp.
51-52 (illustrated).
Christie's Rome, 4 June 1996 (568**) ITL 56,000,000   US$ 36,316

BRUSSELMANS Jean (Brussels 1884-1953 Dilbeek) Belgian
LA BARQUE DE PECHE NOIRE - ZWARTE VISSERSBOOT oil on canvas, 81 x 99cm. sdll 'Jean
Brusselmans 1930'
PROV.: G. van Geluwe, Brussels.

EXH.: Brussels, Palais des Beaux Arts, *Marineschilders*, 5-20 March 1955, no. 15; Charleroi, Salle de la Bourse, Cercle Royal Artistique et Littéraire, 29e salon ., *Retrospective Jean Brusselmans*, 12-31 March 1955, no. 55; Venice, 29e Biennale Belgisch Paviljoen, June-September 1958, no. 2; Eindhoven, Stedelijk Van Abbemuseum, *Brusselmans*, 2 April-9 May 1960, no. 17; Amsterdam, Stedelijk Museum, *Brusselmans*, 14 May-2 June 1960, no. 17; Breda, Cultuurcentrum 'de Beyerd', *Brusselmans*, 1-31 July 1960, no. 17.
LIT.: Robert-L. Delevoy, *Jean Brusselmans*, Brussels 1972, no. 301, ill. no.36 and p.349 (ill.).

Christie's Amsterdam, 5 June 1996 (240**) NLG 55,200	US$	32,252

La Barque de peche noire

BUCKLAND Arthur Herbert (1870 b.)
SPRINGTIME oil on canvas, 72 x 42in. (182.9 x 106.7cm.) sdll 'ATHUR. H BUCKLAND./London. 1896.'
EXH.: London, The Royal Academy, 1896, no. 963.

Christie's New York, 2 November 1995 (224**) US$ 43,700	US$	43,700

BUENO Antonio (Berlin 1918-1984 Florence) Italian
CONCERTINO oil on canvas, 45 x 55cm s 'A.Bueno' (1979)
LIT.: *Oeuvre catalogue* in the archives of Bueno on the no. AByR no.26-F.

Finearte Rome, 14 November 1995 (137**) ITL 31,050,000	US$	19,492

PROFILE FEMMINILE SU FONDO ROSSO oil on canvas, 40 x 30cm s 'A.Bueno' (1965)
LIT.: *Oeuvre catalogue* in the archives of Bueno no.647/G.

Finearte Rome, 14 November 1995 (187*) ITL 13,800,000	US$	8,663

BUENO Xavier (Vera da Vidasoa 1915-1979 Fiesole) Italian
STILLIFE WITH VASE oil on board, 45 x 35cm. sd in the composition (1946)

Finearte Milan, 18 June 1996 (65*) ITL 28,750,000	US$	18,645

RAGAZZA E BAMBINA oil and sand on canvas, 60 x 73cm. sul 'Xavier Bueno' (1977)
LIT.: This work is recorded at 'Archivio Fotografico Generale delle Opere di Xavier Bueno', no. 66 s.

Christie's Milan, 20 November 1995 (150**) ITL 27,105,000	US$	16,642

RAGAZZA oil on canvas, 70 x 50cm. sul 'Xavier Bueno' (1968-69)
PROV.: Galleria d'Arte L'Incontro, Arezzo.
LIT.: This work is registrated in the 'l'Archivio Fotografico Generale delle Opere di Xavier Bueno' under no. 522/G.

Sotheby's Milan, 28 May 1996 (93**) ITL 20,000,700	US$	12,846

BUFFET Bernard (Paris 1928 b.) French
MELUN (SEINE ET MARNE), L'ÉCLUSE oil on canvas, 35 x 51in. (89 x 130cm.) suc 'Bernard Buffet' dur '1974' titled and numbered 'AH 19' on the reverse

Étude Tajan Paris, 10 June 1996 (50**) FRF 200,000	US$	38,620

BOUQUET DE FLEURS oil on canvas, 74 x 60cm. slr 'Bernard Buffet'; dll '1981'

Bukowskis Stockholm, 24-25 April 1996 (161**) SEK 210,000	US$	31,815

ENVIRONS DE VICHY, LE VILLAGE DE MONTLORE oil on canvas, 35 5/8 x 51½in. (89.8 x 130.8cm.) sd 'Bernard Buffet 1974' and titled 'Environs de Vichy Allier' on the back (1974)
PROV.: Maurice Garnier, Paris; Everard Read Gallery, Johannesburg; Pieter Wenning,

Johannesburg.
> Christie's London, 26 June 1996 (312**) GBP 20,700

US$ 31,920

NATURE MORTE AUX CÉRISES oil on canvas, 65.5 x 100.5cm. sdur 'Bernard Buffet 62'
PROV.: Galerie Maurice Garnier, Paris; Inheritance Jean Gabin.
> Wiener Kunst Auktionen, 27 September 1995 (407**) ATS 500,000

US$ 48,602

FLEURS JAUNE DANS UN BROC DE PORCELAINE oil on isorel, 36 x 27.5cm. sll 'B.Buffet'
inscr 'Pour Lucie, Annabel et Bernard. Noël 92' (1992)
> Étude Tajan Paris, 28 March 1996 (52**) FRF 85,000

US$ 16,802

BUKOVAC Vlaho (agram 1855-1922 Prague) Hungarian
SOMMER oil on panel, 30.5 x 25cm. s 'Bukovac'
> Dorotheum Vienna, 6 November 1995 (72**) ATS 110,000

US$ 11,035

BULGARINI Bartolomeo di Messer (ca. 1300/10-1378) Italian
CRUCIFIXION WITH THE MOURNING VIRGIN AND SAINT JOHN THE EVANGELIST gold
ground, tempera on panel, 11 x 7½in. (27.9 x 19.1cm.)
EXH.: San Francisco, California Palace of the Legion of Honor, after 1973.
> Sotheby's New York, 16 May 1996 (9**) US$ 63,000

US$ 63,000

BUNEL Jacob (1588-1614) French
PORTRAIT OF HENRY IV IN FULL ARMOUR oil on canvas, 198 x 138cm.
PROV.: Sale Tribunal de Grande Instance de Paris, 29 April 1994.
> Étude Tajan Paris, 18 December 1995 (145**) FRF 60,000

US$ 12,086

BUNOL Laureano Barrau Y (1863-1957) Spanish
IMMIGRANT WORKERS ON A TRAIN oil on canvas, 52 x 69 ¾in. (132 x 177cm.) s
> Phillips London, 11 June 1996 (70**) GBP 6,500

US$ 10,023

BUONVISI Pittore di Paolo (act. in Lucca (Italy) 1482-1498) Italian
SAN GIOVANNI EVANGELISTA E SAN GIUSTINO; MADONNA COL BABINO IN TRONO E
DUE ANGELI; SAN GIULIANO E SANTA CATERINA (A TRIPTYCH) oil on panel, 160 x 70cm;
160 x 80cm; 160 x 220cm
PROV.: Collection W.Fuller-Maitland, London, first of 1870; Collection Lady H.Somerset, Eastnor
Castle, circa 1870-1917; Alte Pinakothek, Monaco di Baviera.
LIT.: *J.A. Crowe - G.B.Cavalcaselle, Geschichte der Italienischen Malerei*, Lipsia 1870, vol.III,
p.216 (as Raffaellino del Garbo). J.A.Crowe - G.B.Cavalcaselle, *History of Painting in Italy*, London
1903-1914, vol.IV, p.306 (as Raffaellino del Garbo). M.Natale, *Maestri del quattrocento lucchese*, in
'La Provincia di Lucca', XI, 1971, p.105, fig.4, (as Maestro dell`Immacolata Concezione). M.Ferretti,
Percorso lucchese, in 'Annali della Scuola Normale superiore di Pisa. Classe di Lettere e Filosofia',
serie III, vol.V, 1975, pp.1044-1045, (as Maestro dell`Immacolata Concezione). E.Fahy, *Some
Followers of Domenico Ghirlandaio*, New York 1976, p.178 (as Maestro dell`Immacolata
Concezione). M.Natale, *Note sulla pittura lucchese alla fine del Quattrocento*, 'The J.Paul Getty
Museum journal', vol.VIII, 1980, p.54, fig.32 (as Pittore di Paolo Buonvisi).
> Finearte Milan, 25 November 1995 (108 bis**) ITL 966,000,000

US$ 606,403

BURCHFIELD Charles Ephraim (Ashtabula (Ohio) 1893-1967 Gardenville) American
BARBER SHOP watercolour, gouache and pencil on paper, 9 x 12in. (23 x 30.5cm.) sdll 'Chas
Burchfield 1918'
LIT.: J.S. Trovato, *Charles Burchfield: A Catalogue of Paintings in Public and Private Collections*,
Utica, New York, p. 82, no. 498.
> Christie's New York, 23 May 1996 (146**) US$ 8,050

US$ 8,050

MIDMORNING watercolour and pencil on paper, 12 x 9in. (30.5 x 23cm.) sdlr 'Chas Burchfield
1916'; inscr. with title and d 'June 1916' on the reverse

PROV.: Sale: New York, Christie's, 9 Dec. 1983, lot 288.
EXH.: New York, Owen Gallery, *Modernism: An American View*, May-June 1994.
LIT.: J.S. Trovato, *Charles Burchfield: A Catalogue of Paintings in Public and Private Collections*,
Utica, New York, p. 82, no. 498.

	US$	20,700

Christie's New York, 23 May 1996 (147**) US$ 20,700

VILLAGE CHURCH IN AUGUST watercolour on paper laid down on board, 44 3/4 x 31 3/4in.
(113.6 x 80.6cm.) sdlr ini. 'CEB 1962-63'
PROV.: Frank K. M. Rehn Gallery, New York.
LIT.: J. S. Trovato, *Charles Burchfield: Catalogue of paintings in Public and Private Collections*,
Munson-Williams-Proctor Institute, Utica, 1970, p. 300, no. 1284.

Christie's New York, 30 November 1995 (69**) US$ 74,000 — US$ 74,000

BURGERS Hein (1834-1899) Dutch
LES AMANTS oil on canvas, 55 x 70 cm s 'Hein J. Burgers f'
Christie's Amsterdam, 25 April 1996 (140*) NLG 18,400 — US$ 10,934

PICKING FLOWERS oil on canvas, 46 x 32 cm s 'H.J Burgers'
Christie's Amsterdam, 25 April 1996 (142*) NLG 28,750 — US$ 17,084

BURGH Hendrick van der (Honselersdijk 1627-1669) Dutch
A LADY SEWING IN AN INTERIOR oil on oak panel, 9¼ x 8in. (23.5 x 20cm.)
PROV.: With Steinmeyer, Lucerne; With Paul Cassirer, Amsterdam, before 1930; Baron Heinrich
Thyssen-Bornemisza, by 1930.
EXH.: Munich 1930, no. 57; Paris 1970, no. 19, plate 10; Düsseldorf 1970-1, no. 11; Lausanne etc.,
1986-7, no. 31.
LIT.: R. Heinemann, vol. I, no. 68; W. Valentiner, *Pieter de Hooch*, 1929, p.215, reproduced; W.
Bernt, *The Netherlandish Painters of the Seventeenth Century*, 1969, vol. I, reproduced plate 210; P.
Sutton, 'Hendrick van der Burch', *Burlington Magazine*, May 1980, p.323, reproduced figure 51.
Sotheby's London, 6 December 1995 (95**) GBP 12,650 — US$ 19,468

BÜRKEL Heinrich (Pirmasens 1802-1869 Munich) German
A VIEW OF ROME WITH THE COLISEUM oil on canvas, 17 x 24in. (43 x 61cm.)
PROV.: Galerie del Vecchio, Leipzig.
LIT.: G. Buchheit, *Heinrich Bürkel, ein Pfälzer Landschafts - und Genre Maler*, Kaiserslautern,
1929, p. 15, no. 50 (illustrated); L von Bürkel, *Heinrich Bürkel, Ein Maler-Leben Der
Biedermeierzeit*, Munich, 1940, p. 43, no. 91 (illustrated); W. Weber in *2,000 Jahre Stadt Pirmasens*,
"Der Maler Heinrich Bürkel", Pirmasens, July 1963, p. 149; H.P. Bühler and A. Krückl, *Heinrich
Bürckel*, Munich, 1989, p. 291, no. 562 (illustrated).
Christie's London, 17 November 1995 (13**) GBP 8,970 — US$ 14,031

BURNE-JONES Sir Edward Coley, Bt., A.R.A. (Birmingham 1833-1898 London) British
A STUDY FOR 'KING COPHETUA AND THE BEGGAR MAID' black chalk heightened with
white on grey paper, 13 ¾ x 10in. (35 x 25.4cm.) sd ini. 'E.B.J./1882/to/J.C.C.'
LIT.: Eve Adam (ed.), *Mrs J. Comyns carr's Reminiscenses (1925)*, p. 62.
Christie's London, 6 November 1995 (69**) GBP 9,430 — US$ 14,751

THE MASQUE OF CUPID watercolour over pencil heightened, 21 ¾ x 52½in. (55 x 133.5cm.) (ca.
1872)
PROV.: The artist's studio sale, 16th & 18th july, 1898, lot 45, bt. Thomas Agnew & Sons (235gns.);
R.H. Benson, (a friend of the artist), Buckhurst Park, Withy, Sussex; His executors sale Christie's,
1921, lot 82, bt, Joubert; By descent in the Benson family.
EXH.: London, Burlington Fine Arts Club, *Exhibition of Drawings and Studies by Edward Burne-
Jones, Bart*, 1899, no. 1899, no. 7; London, Tate Gallery, *Centenary of Paintings and Drawings by
Sir Edward Burne-Jones, Bart. (1833-1898)*, 1933, no. 34; London Hayward Gallery, Birmingham,
City Museum and art Gallery, *Burne-Jones*, 1975-76, no. 207.

LIT.: George Burne-Jones, *Memorials of Edward Burne-Jones*, 1904, Vol. II, p. 306; Fortunée de L'Isle, *Burne-Jones*, 1904, p. 189.

        Sotheby's London, 10 July 1995 (93**) GBP 31,050

US$ 49,529

BURRA Edward (1905-1976) British
FORTUNE TELLERS watercolour and bodycolour, 22 x 30½in. (55.8 x 76.3cm.) s 'E J Burra' (1929)
PROV.: Purchased directly from the Artist circa 1947.
EXH.: Cape Town, South African National, *Master Works on Paper*, Oct. 1984, no. 3.
LIT.: J. Rothenstein, *Edward Burra*, London, 1945, p. 17, pl. 1.; A. Causey, *Edward Burra*, Oxford, 1985, no. 82, p. 114 (illustrated).

        Christie's London, 20 June 1996 (94**) GBP 43,300

US$ 66,769

BURRI Alberto (Citta di Castello 1915-1995) Italian
COMPOSIZIONE acryl, sugar and material on cardboard, 17.8 x 44.2cm sd on the reverse 'Burri N.Y.55'

        Finearte Rome, 14 November 1995 (208**) ITL 132,250,000

US$ 83,019

SACCO (SC 2) jute, oil, gold and mixed media on canvas, ,100 x 86cm. sd on the reverse 'Burri Roma 53' (1953)
EXH.: Siena, Palazzo Pubblico, Magazzini del Sale, *L'immagine dell'arte, Omaggio a Cesare Brandi, 21 July-1 Oct. 1989, p.122 illustrated.*
LIT.: *Cesare Brandi-Vittorio Rubiu*, Burri, Contributo al catalogo generale, Editalia, Rome 1963, no.199; *Burri, Contributi al catalogo generale*, Petruzzi editore, Città di Castello 1990, no.255 .

        Finearte Milan, 19 March 1996 (69**) ITL 609,500,000

US$ 389,955

CRETTO burned paper on worked board, 26 x 19cm. sd ded. 'Burri, Casenove, 3 ottobre 63' on the reverse

        Finearte Milan, 26 October 1995 (209**) ITL 47,150,000

US$ 29,377

COMBUSTIONE T card, cardboard, acrylic, vinavil and combustion on paper laid down on canvas, 22½ x 17 ¾in. (57 x 45cm.) sd '60' on the reverse
PROV.: Galerie Blu, Milan.
LIT.: Enrico Crispolti, *Burri, un Saggio e Tre Note*, Milan 1961, no. VIII (illustrated); Cesare Brandi & Vittorio Rubiu, *Burri Contributo al Catalogo Generale*, Rome 1963, no. 318 (illustrated); Fondazione Palazzo Albizzini, *Burri Contributi al Catalogo Sistematico*, Città di Castello 1990, p. 442, no. 1905 (illustrated).

        Sotheby's London, 27 June 1996 (207**) GBP 45,500

US$ 70,162

BUSH Jack (1909 b.) Canadian
PARIS 4 oil on canvas, 38¼ x 57¼in. (97.2 x 145.4cm.) sdlr 'Jack Bush '62'; sd and titled 'Jack Bush 1962, Paris 4' on the reverse
PROV.: Corcoran Gallery of Art, Washington D.C.; The Edmonton Art Gallery, Edmonton.

        Christie's East, 14 November 1995 (181**) US$ 7,475

US$ 7,475

LIGHT GREY acrylic on canvas, 89 x 69in. (226 x 172cm.) sd and titled 'Light Grey Jack Bush Toronto July 1968' on the reverse
PROV.: Waddington Galleries, London; Louis Cabot, Boston; André Emmerich Gallery, New York.
LIT.: P. Rajagopal and J.Mason, *Discreet Mathematics for Computer Science*, Toronto 1992 (illustrated on the cover).

        Christie's New York, 8 May 1996 (273**) US$ 18,400

US$ 18,400

BUTLER Howard Russel (1856-1934) American
GONDOLAS IN VENICE oil on canvas, 21½ x 32¼in. (54.6 x 81.1cm.) sll 'Howard Russel Butler'

        Christie's East, 21 May 1996 (120**) US$ 9,775

US$ 9,775

BUTTERSWORTH James Edward (1817-1894) American
TWO AMERICAN NAVAL VESSELS ENTERING HARBOR oil on panel, 8 1/8 x 12in. (20.6 x 30.5cm.) slr 'J E Buttersworth'
        Christie's New York, 13 September 1995 (8**) US$ 11,500 | US$ | 11,500

IN FULL SAIL, NEW YORK HARBOR oil on board, 8 x 12in. (20.4 x 30.5cm.) slr 'J E Buttersworth'
        Christie's New York, 13 September 1995 (9**) US$ 18,400 | US$ | 18,400

THE APPROACHING STORM oil on board, 9 1/8 x 12 1/8in. (23.1 x 30.8cm.) slr 'J E Buttersworth'
        Christie's New York, 13 September 1995 (17**) US$ 13,800 | US$ | 13,800

THE SLOOP GALATEA oil on canvas, 20¼ x 30in. (50.4 76.2cm.) slr 'JE Buttersworth'
        Christie's New York, 23 May 1996 (13**) US$ 59,700 | US$ | 59,700

'GRACIE,' 'VISION,' AND 'CORNELIA' ROUNDING SANDY HOOK IN THE NEW YORK YACHT CLUB REGATTA OF TUNE 11, 1874 oil on canvas, 26 x 35 3/4in. (66 x 90.7cm.) slr 'J.E. Buttersworth'
PROV.: William Henry Jenkins, New York, by 1891; By descent in the family to the present owner.
EXH.: New York, South Street Seaport Museum, *Ship, Sea & Sky: The Marine Art of James Edward Buttersworth*, April-September 1994, no. 33.
LIT.: R.B. Grassby, *Ship, Sea & Sky: The Marine Art of James Edward Buttersworth*, New York 1994, p. 101, illus.
        Christie's New York, 23 May 1996 (15**) US$ 244,500 | US$ | 244,500

YACHTS ROUNDING THE NORE LIGHT SHIP IN THE ENGLISH CHANNEL oil on board, 8 x 12in. (20.4 x 30.5cm.) slr 'J E Buttersworth'
        Christie's New York, 13 September 1995 (26**) US$ 15,525 | US$ | 15,525

BYLERT Jan van (Utrecht 1598-1671 Utrecht) Dutch
A YOUNG MAN IN A FEATHERED CAP HOLDING A PEWTER FLAGON oil on canvas, 30¼ x 25¼in. (77 x 64cm.) (between 1625-30)
PROV.: Anon. sale ('The Property of a Lady of Title'), London, Christie's, 1 November 1968, lot 58, as *Terbrugghen*, 300gns. to Strecher.
        Sotheby's London, 5 July 1995 (212**) GBP 11,500 | US$ | 18,344

A young Man in a feathered Cap holding a pewter Flagon

VENUS CHASTISING AMORETTI oil on canvas, 49 5/8 x 57 5/8in. (126 x 146.5cm.) s 'J. bijlert fe'

PROV.: Anon. Sale, Sotheby's, 9May 1951, lot 154.

LIT.: G.J. Hoogewerff, (Jan van Bijlert, schilder van Utrecht (1598-1671)), *Oud Holland*, 80, 1965, no. 36.

      Christie's London, 8 December 1995 (31**) GBP 34,500   US$ 53,093

MOTHER WITH CHILDREN oil on canvas, 97 x 80cm.

      Wiener Kunst Auktionen, 26 March 1996 (18**) ATS 110,000   US$ 10,581

CACCIANIGA Francisco (1700-1781) Italian
AN ALLEGORY OF PAINTING BEING SCORNED BY IGNORANCE oil on canvas, 49¼ x 67in.
(125.1 x 170.2cm.)
PROV.: Borghese Collection, Rome; Othon Goetz, Esq., Nairobi, Kenya and Switzerland, by 1959,
from whom acquired by the present owner in 1964.
EXH.: Nairobi. Kenya, The Kenya Arts and Crafts Society, *Exhibition of the Works by Great
Masters*, 13 July-30 July 1959, exhibition catatalogue no. 16 (illustrated as by Jacob Jordaens) .
LIT.: 'Caccianiga, Francesco,' *Dizianario biografico degli italiani*, vol. 16, 1973, entry by Anthony
Clark, p. 3; David Cast, *The Calumay of Apelles: A Study in the Humanist Tradition*, 1980, p. 192-
193, illustrated, fig. 61; *La Pittura in Italia: Il Settecento*, 1989, vol. II, pp. 642-643; Giancarlo
Sestieri, *Repertorio della Pittura Romana della Fine del Seicento e del Settecento*, 1993, vol. I, p. 38.
Sotheby's New York, 6 October 1996 (94**) US$ 49,450   US$ 49,450

CADELL Francis Campbell Boileau, R.S.A., R.S.W. (1883-1937) Scottish
IONA oil on board, 14¼ x 17in. (36 x 43.5cm.) slr 'F.C.B.Cadell' (ca. 1935)
PROV.: Purchased from the Artist in 1935 by miss Simpson of Edinburgh and thence by descent to
the present owner.
Sotheby's London, 29 August 1995 (1008**) GBP 20,700   US$ 33,506

BEN MORE FROM IONA oil on canvas, 25 x 30in. (63.5 x 76cm.) slr 'F.C.B. Cadell'
PROV.: George Service; The Fine Art Society, 1986.
EXH.: Edinburgh, Society of Eight, 1922, no. 13; Edinburgh, National Gallery of Scotland, *Cadell
Memorial Exhibition*, 1942, no. 137; London, Edinburgh & Glasgow, The Fine Art Society, *F.C.B.
Cadell*, 1983, no. 43.
Sotheby's London, 29 August 1995 (1010**) GBP 23,000   US$ 37,229

CAILLE Léon (1836-1907) French
THE CENTRE OF ATTENTION oil on panel, 17¾ x 21 7/8in. (45 x 55.6cm.) sd 'Léon Caille/1878'
Christie's London, 14 June 1996 (53**) GBP 35,050   US$ 54,048

CAILLEBOTTE Gustave (1848-1894) French
LE PEINTRE MOROT DANS SON ATELIER oil on canvas, 18 x 21¾in. (45.7 x 55.2cm.) s and
dedicated 'à l'ami Morot' (ca. 1874)
PROV.: Sale: Christie's, London, December 2, 1966, lot 92; Mrs. L. Phillips, Montreal; Luis E.
Monsanto; M. Knoedler & Co., New York; Mr. Samuel Josefowitz, Lausanne (sale: Sotheby Parke
Bernet, New York, April 3, 1968, lot 61); Hammer Galleries, New York; Sale: Sotheby's, Los
Angeles, November 29, 1973, lot 18; Estate of Pauline K. Cave (sale: Sotheby's, New York,
November 16, 1984, lot 15); Acquired by the present owner at the above sale.
EXH.: Marie Berhaut, *Caillebotte: Sa Vie et son Oeuvre*, Paris, 1978, no. 12, illustrated p. 79; Pierre
Wittmer, *Caillebotte and His Garden at Yerres*, New York, 1990, p. 276; Marie Berhaut, *Gustave
Caillebotte: Catalogue Raisonné des Peintures et Pastels*, Paris, 1994, no. l7 (illustrated p.66) .
Sotheby's New York, 2 May 1996 (107**) US$ 74,000   US$ 74,000

CALANDRUCCI Giacinto (attr.) (1646-1707) Italian
THE RAPE OF PROSERPINA oil on canvas, 120 x 170cm.
Christie's Rome, 21 November 1995 (247**) ITL 64,000,000   US$ 40,176

CALDER Alexander (1898-1976) American
UNTITLED gouache on paper, 22½ x 42 3/8in. (57.2 x 107.7cm.) sdlr 'Calder 66'; inscr. 'M' on the
reverse
PROV.: Galerie Maeght, Paris; The Redfern Gallery, London.
Christie's East, 14 November 1995 (23*) US$ 6,900   US$ 6,900

UNTITLED coloured crayons and pen and black ink on paper, 18 7/8 x 25in. (48 x 63.5cm.) slr
'Calder' (ca. 1928)
PROV.: Katherine Kuh, Chicago.

Christie's New York, 15 November 1995 (164**) US$ 9,775

| | US$ | 9,775 |

UNTITLED oil on canvas, unframed, 26 x 30in. (66 x 76.6cm.) sdlr 'CALDER 58'
PROV.: Acquired directly from the artist.
Christie's New York, 22 February 1996 (3**) US$ 40,250

| | US$ | 40,250 |

TWO MEN, TWO PYRAMIDS oil on canvas, 42 x 24in. (106.7 x 60.9cm.) sdlr 'CALDER 56'
PROV.: Perls Galleries, New York.
Christie's New York, 22 February 1996 (14**) US$ 66,300

| | US$ | 66,300 |

BEACH PEOPLE gouache on paper, 23 x 29in. (58.4 x 73.7cm.) sdlr 'Calder 56'
PROV.: Perls Galleries, New York.
Christie's East, 7 May 1996 (23*) US$ 12,650

| | US$ | 12,650 |

CALDERON Philip Hermogenes (1833-1898) Spanish
'FAREWELL!' oil on canvas, 53 x 31¼in. (134.6 x 72.3cm.) sd 'P.H. Calderon 1892'
PROV.: Sir R.P. Cooper, and by descent to the present owner.
EXH.: London, Royal Academy, 1892, no. 323.
LIT.: Henry Blackburn (ed.) , *Royal Academy Notes*, 1892, p.13, repr. p.81.
Christie's London, 6 November 1995 (203**) GBP 24,150

| | US$ | 37,776 |

THE BLACK HAT oil on panel, 19¼ x 15 5/8in. (48.9 x 39.7cm.) s with mono. and dll '1892'
PROV.: With Gooden & Fox, London.
Christie's New York, 14 February 1996 (96**) US$ 19,550

| | US$ | 19,550 |

CALIARI Paolo {called} Paolo Veronese (Verona 1528-1588 Venice) Italian
VENUS WITH A SATYR AND CUPID IN A LANDSCAPE oil on canvas, 62 1/8 x 50 3/8in. (157.8 x 128cm.)
PROV.: possibly Giuseppe Caliari, the nephew of the artist; David M. Koetser Gallery, Zurich, by 1976, there purchased by the present collector.
LIT.: C. Ridolfi, *Le Maraviglie dell'arte.*, 1648, I, p. 344 (Ed. Von Hadeln, 1914-24); M. Boschini, *La Carta del navegar pitoresco.* 1660, p. 665 (Ed. A. Pallucchini, 1966); D. von Hadeln, 'Pictures left by Veronese in his Studio, *the Burlington Magazine*, LIIII, July, 1928, pp. 3-4; L. Becherucci, ' Recensione a: Hadeln, D. von, 'Pictures left by Veronese in his studio.', *L'Arte*, 1929, pp. 41-42; G. Fiocco, *Paolo Veronese*, 1934, p. 113; R. Marini, *Tutta la pittura di Paolo Veronese*, P. 133, mo. 333; Terisio Pignatti, *Veronese*, 1976, Vol. I, P. 126, No. 139, illus. Vol. II, fig. 396.
Sotheby's New York, 11 January 1996 (56**) US$ 156,500

| | US$ | 156,500 |

CALVAERT Denys (Dionys) (Antwerp 1540-1619 Bologna) Flemish
THE ADORATION OF THE MAGI oil on copper, 19½ x 15¼cm. (49.5 x 38.5cm.) (1590's)
PROV.: Acquired by The Hon. Mrs. Shiell in the 1830's; Thence by descent to the present owner.
Sotheby's London, 5 July 1995 (1**) GBP 34,500

| | US$ | 55,033 |

THE AGONY IN THE GARDEN oil on metal, 21 x 16in. (54.3 x 41.5cm.)
PROV.: Possibly Frederick, 1st Marquess of Bristol; Certainly Frederick, 4th Marquess of Bristol.
LIT.: Farrer, 1913, no. 16, as *Correggio*; *Inventory*, 1952, p. 43, as *Carracci*; *The Antique Collector*, 1961, p.221.
Sotheby's London, 11-12 June 1996 (480**) GBP 27,600

| | US$ | 42,560 |

CAMOIN Charles (1879-1965) French
FENETRE OUVERTE SUR LE GLACIS DU PORT DE SAINT-TROPEZ oil on panel, 25 5/8 x 21in. (65 x 53.4cm.) slr 'Ch. Camoin' (1928-1932)
PROV.: Mme Charles Camoin, Paris; Campanile Galleries Inc., Chicago (acquired by Richard Smart, 1972) .
Christie's New York, 1 May 1996 (157**) US$ 79,500

| | US$ | 79,500 |

PORT DE CASSIS oil on canvas, 31¼ x 39½in. (79.4 x 110.3cm.) sll 'Charles Camoin' (1901)
 Sotheby's New York, 2 May 1996 (171**) US$ 85,000   US$ 85,000

BOUQUET DE FLEURS oil on canvas-board, 16½ x 13in. (41 x 33cm.) slr 'Ch Camoin'
 Christie's London, 26 June 1996 (325**) GBP 10,925   US$ 16,847

VASE WITH ROSES oil on canvas, 46 x 38cm. slr 'Ch. Camoin
 Étude Tajan Paris, 27 October 1995 (16***) FRF 50,000   US$ 10,114

VILLAGE DE PECHEURS EN CORSE oil on canvas, 19¾ x 24in. (50 x 61cm.) sll 'CH Camoin' (1906)
 Christie's London, 29 November 1995 (122**) GBP 25,000   US$ 39,105

CAMPENDONCK Heinrich (Krefeld 1889-1957) German
MÄDCHEN MIT SCHWAN oil on canvas, 27¼ x 39in. (69 x 99cm.) sdlr 'C 1919'
PROV.: Alfred Flechtheim, Düsseldorf; Werner Jaegers, Cologne.
EXH.: Düsseldorf, Galerie Flechtheim, *Heinrich Campendonck-Josef Eberz*, 1920, no. 32.
LIT.: A. Firmenich, *Heinrich Campendonck 1889-1957: Leben und expressionistisches Werk*,
Recklinghausen, 1989, no. 768 (not illustrated) .
 Christie's London, 11 October 1995 (158**) GBP 67,500   US$ 106,534

DIE BADENDEN-BADENDE FRAUEN MIT FISCH oil on canvas, 93.5 x 58.5cm. (ca. 1920)
PROV.: Collection Paul van Ostaven; Collection P.G.van Hecke, Bruxelles (1923); Galerie Le
Centaure, Bruxelles; Stedelijk Museum, Amsterdam, (on loan from the family) .
EXH.: salzburg 1957, *Expressionistische Malerei in Österreich, Deutschland, Schweiz*, p. 24; Ixelles
(Brussels) , 1958, cat. no. 46; Münster, 1959, cat. no. 9; Krefeld, 1960, Museum Haus Lange,
Heinrich Campendonk, cat. no. 56 (illustrated) .
LIT.: Mathias T. Engels *Heinrich Campendonk* (Monographien zur Rheinisch-Westphälischen Kunst
der Gegenwart VIII) , Recklinghausen, 1958, p. 29; Paul van Ostayen/Berend Hendriks, 'Heinrich
Campendonk, een hommage', in *Een schrift gewijd aan nieuwe en oude kunst, op steiger, no. 1*,
Amsterdam 1961, p. 7.
 Lempertz Cologne, 1 June 1996 (599**) DEM 185,000   US$ 120,200

CAMPIGLI Massimo (1895-1971 Saint Tropez) Italian
RITRATTO FEMMINILE CON COLLANA oil on canvas, 41 x 32cm sd 'Campigli 69'
LIT.: *Oeuvre catalogue* in the archives of Campigli no.5875733.
 Finearte Rome, 14 November 1995 (217**) ITL 63,250,000   US$ 39,705

LE MONDINE oil on canvas, 46.5 x 56cm. sdlr 'Campigli 33'
 Finearte Milan, 18 June 1996 (227bis**) ITL 281,750,000   US$ 182,717

FIGURE oil on canvas, 48 x 58cm. sdll 'Campigli 47' and lr 'Campigli 48' (1947-1948)
 Finearte Milan, 19 March 1996 (48**) ITL 253,000,000   US$ 161,868

FIGURE NELLE NICCHIE oil on canvas, 49 x 42.4cm. sdlr 'Campigli 58'
PROV.: Galleria dell'Annunciata, Milano.
 Christie's Milan, 20 November 1995 (156**) ITL 58,925,000   US$ 36,990

COMPOSITION WITH FIGURE oil on canvas, 39 x 54cm. sdlr 'Campigli 65' (1965)
 Finearte Milan, 26 October 1995 (177**) ITL 73,600,000   US$ 45,857

DUE ATTRICI oil on canvas, 72 x 92cm. sdlr 'Campigli 45-46'
PROV.: Acquired directly by the aunt of the present owner in 1949.
LIT.: AA. VV., *Omaggio a Campigli*, Rome 1969, p. 295 (illustrated) .
 Sotheby's Milan, 28 May 1996 (192**) ITL 334,650,000   US$ 214,933

DUE FIGURE oil on canvas laid down on masonite, 65 x 58cm. sdlr 'Campigli 48'
PROV.: Galleria del Naviglio, Milan; Galleria Marescalchi, Bologna; Acquired by the present owner ca. 1976.
EXH.: Venice, *XXVI Biennale Internazionale d'Arte*, 1948.
      Sotheby's Milan, 28 May 1996 (212**) ITL 249,900,000

US$ 160,501

PALLA A VOLO oil on canvas, 18 1/8 x 21¾in. (46 x 55.2cm.) sdlr 'M. CAMPIGLI 1931' (1931)
      Christie's New York, 8 November 1995 (294**) US$ 140,000

US$ 140,000

CAMPO Federico del (1881 - 1889 active) Peruvian

THE CA D'ORO, VENICE oil on canvas, 20½ x 34½in. (52 x 87.5cm.) sd 'F. del Campo/Venezia 1888'
PROV.: With MacConnal-Mason & Son.
      Christie's London, 15 March 1996 (155**) GBP 91,700

US$ 140,043

PALAZZO CAVALLI-FRANCHETTI AND THE PALAZZO BARBARO FROM THE ACCADEMIA BRIDGE oil on canvas, 14 ¼ x 23¼in. (36.2 x 59cm.) s 'F. del Campo'
PROV.: With MacConnel-Mason & Son.
      Christie's London, 15 March 1996 (156**) GBP 27,600

US$ 42,150

PONTE DELLA CALCINA, DORSODURO, VENICE oil on canvas, 13½ x 22in. (34.3 x 56cm.) sd 'F. del Campo/Venezia. 1888'
PROV.: With Frost & Reed; with MacConnal-Mason & Son.
      Christie's London, 15 March 1996 (158**) GBP 23,000

US$ 35,125

CAMPRIANI Alceste (Terni 1848-1933 Napels) Italian

MATINO ESTIVO oil on canvas, 37 x 61½in. (94 x 156.2cm.) s and s on the reverse
EXH.: Venice, *IX Esposizione Internazionale d'Arte della Citta di Venezia*, 1914, Sala 23, p. 83, no. 3.
      Sotheby's Arcade Auctions New York, 17 January 1996 (609*) US$ 17,250

US$ 17,250

THE ROAD TO MARKET oil on canvas, 21 x 32in. (53.7 x 81.3cm.) slr 'A. Campriani.'
      Christie's New York, 2 November 1995 (239**) US$ 48,300

US$ 48,300

CANAL Giovanni Antonio {called} Canaletto (1697-1768) Italian

THE PIAZZA SAN MARCO, VENICE, LOOKING EAST ALONG THE CENTRAL LINE oil on canvas, 23 7/8 x 36½in. (60.7 x 92.8cm.) (1720's)
PROV.: Wadham Knatchbull (1794-1876) , Sherbonne, Dorset; Christie's, 24 June 1876, lot 118; unsold at 210gns. and sent to Captain Knatchbull, Babington, Bath; with Edward Speelman, London, from whom purchased in 1947 by Sir Henry Philip Price, 1st and last Bt. (d. 1963) , Wakehurst Place, Ardingly, Sussex; with Frank Partridge, London, from whom purchased by Sir Michael Sobell (1892-1993) on 17 May 1962 (with the following lot: GBP 35,000) .
LIT.: W.G. Constable, *Canaletto*, Oxford, 1962, and subsequent editions, 11, under no. 3; L. Puppi, *L'opera completa del Canaletto*, Milan, 1968, no. 243B; J.G. Links, *Canaletto. The Complete Paintings*, London, 1981, p. 64, under no. 201.
      Christie's London, 8 December 1995 (74**) GBP 1,046,500

US$ 1,610,496

A CAPRICCIO OF A RUINED RENAISSANCE ARCADE AND PAVILLION BY A WATERWAY CROSSED BY A WOODEN FOOTBRIDGE, AN ORIENTAL IN AN EXOTICALLY DECORATED BOAT IN THE FOREGROUND oil on canvas, 39¾ x 33¾ (101.2 x 86cm.) (mid 1750's)
PROV.: Acquired by Warburton Davies (1790-1870) of Woodgate, Sussex, who was collecting in the 1820s, and by inheritance at Elmley Castle, Worcestershire to Colonel Francis Thomas Davies; with Agnew's, London, from whom purchased by Sir Michael Sobell (1892-1993) on 23 April 1959 for £14,000.
LIT.: W.G. Constable, *Canaletto*, Oxford, 1962, and subsequent editions, 1, pl. 93; 11, no. 511,

under no. 511(c) and under no. 823; L. Puppi, *L'opera completa del Canaletto*, Milan, 1968, no. 314C, illustrated; S. Kozakiewicz, *Bernardo Bellotto*, London, 1972, 1, p. 240, fig. C 121; 11, p. 488, under no. Z398.; W.L. Barcham in *Italian Paintings XIV-XVIII Centuries from the collection of the Baltimore Museum of Art*, ed. G. Rosenthal, Baltimore, 1981, p. 252; A. Corboz, Canaletto. Una Venezia immaginaria, Milan, 1985, 11, p. 725, no. P 438, illustrated; Catalogue of the exhibition, *Venetian Eighteenth-Century Painting*, Thos. Agnew & Sons Ltd., London, 5June-19July 1985, p. 16; P. Stein in P.C. Sutton, catalogue of the exhibition, *Prized Possessions: European Paintings from Private Collections of Friends of the Museum of Fine Arts*, Boston, Museum of Fine Arts, Boston,17 June-16 Aug. 1992, p. 130, under no. 17.

Christie's London, 8 December 1995 (76**) GBP 419,500   US$ 645,583

THE GRAND CANAL, VENICE, LOOKING SOUTH WEST FROM THE SCALZI CHURCH TOWARDS SAN SIMEONE -PICCOLO AND THE FONDAMENTA DELLA CROCE oil on canvas, 18¾ x 31in. (47.6 x 78.7cm.)

Christie's South Kensington, 18 april 1996 (292**) GBP 19,550   US$ 29,644

CANAL Giovanni Antonio {called} Canaletto (studio of) (Venice 1697-1768) Italian
VENICE, THE MOLO FROM THE BACINO DI SAN MARCO oil on canvas, 24½ x 38in. (62 x 97cm.)
PROV.: Italian private collection; Baron Heinrich Thyssen-Bornemisza, by 1930.
EXH.: Munich 1930, no. 63, plate 99, as *Bernardo Belotto*; Amsterdam, Stedelijk Museum, 1934, no. 35, as *Bernardo Belotto*; Paris 1970, no. 44, plate 18; Düsseldorf 1970-1, no. 14, as *Canaletto*; Lausanne etc. 1986-87, no. 55, as *Canaletto*.
LIT.: R. Heinemann, 1937, vol. I, p. 26, no. 73, vol. II, plate 225, as *Canaletto*; W.G. Constable and J.G. Links, *Canaletto*, 1989, vol. II, p. 239, no. 109 (c) , as *'a school piece'*.

Sotheby's London, 6 December 1995 (83**) GBP 73,000   US$ 112,342

CANELLA Giuseppe (attr.) (Verona 1788-1847 Florence) Italian
ON THE PIAZZA SAN MARCO, VENICE gouache, 22 x 31cm. (8¾ x 12¼in.)

Sotheby's London, 10 July 1995 (29**) GBP 12,650   US$ 20,179

CANTATORE Domenico (Ruvo di Puglia 1906 b.-) Italian
ODALISCA oil on canvas, 35 x 50cm. sdul 'Cantatore 69'
PROV.: Galleria Molino, Roma.

Christie's Milan, 20 November 1995 (151**) ITL 14,142,000   US$ 8,878

CAPELLE Jan van de (Amsterdam 1626-1679) Dutch
A VILLAGE BY A RIVER IN WINTER, WITH SKATERS AND HORSE-DRAWN SLEDGES ON THE ICE, A TRAVELLER ON A BRIDGE BEYOND oil on panel, 72 x 87.2cm. indistinctly slr 'Jvespef'
PROV.: E.M. Sherry; Sale, Christie's, 28 January 1944, lot 28, as Molenaer (28 gns. to Katz) .

Christie's Amsterdam, 13 November 1995 (83*) NLG 20,700   US$ 13,046

SHIPPING IN A CALM oil on oak panel, 23¼ x 17¼in. (59 x 43.5cm.) sdlr 'J.V. Capelle/ 1661'
PROV.: English Private Collection; Baron Heinrich Thyssen-Bornemisza, by 1930.
EXH.: Munich 1930, no. 64, plate 61; Bielefeld, Kunsthalle, *Landschaften aus vier Jahrhunderten aus dem Kunstmuseum Düsseldorf*, 1973, no. 10; Lausanne etc., 1986-87. no. 45.
LIT.: R. Heinemann 1937, vol. I, no. 75, vol. II, plate 165; M. Russell, *Jan van de Capelle*, 1975, pp. 27, 89, no. 4, reproduced plate 16.

Sotheby's London, 6 December 1995 (116**) GBP 54,300   US$ 83,564

CAPOGROSSI Giuseppe (Rome 1900-1972) Italian
SUPERFICIE CP/37 tempera on paper, 34.5 x 50cm. (1957-59)
LIT.: *Capogrossi: Gouaches, Collages, Disegni*, Milano 1981, pag. 317, no. 309. (illustrated) .

Sotheby's Milan, 28 May 1996 (111**) ITL 12,650,000   US$ 8,125

SUPERFICIE 481 oil on canvas, 120 x 80cm. sd '1963' and titled on the reverse
PROV.: Tokyo Gallery, Tokyo.
LIT.: Giulio Carlo Argan, *Capogrossi*, Rome 1967, p. 197, no. 518 (illustrated) .
      Sotheby's Milan, 28 May 1996 (210**) ITL 65,550,000   US$ 42,100

SUPERFICIE 350 oil on canvas, 50 x 75cm. slr; sd '1956' and titled on the reverse
PROV.: Galleria del Naviglio, Milan; Galleria Seno, Milan.
LIT.: Giulio Carlo Argan, *Capogrossi*, Rome 1967, p. 167, no. 260 (illustrated incorrectly no. 261) .
      Sotheby's Milan, 28 May 1996 (226**) ITL 56,350,000   US$ 36,191

CARABAIN Jacques François (Amsterdam 1832-1892) Belgian (Dutch)
COCHERM ON THE MOSELLE oil on canvas, 31½ x 43½in. (79.3 x 110.5cm.) s 'Js. Carabain' sd
authenticated 'Bruxelles 16 Mars 1868'
PROV.: Painted for W.E. Atler, Philadelphia; Anon. sale Christie's 16 Nov. 1982, lot 249.
      Christie's London, 14 June 1996 (3**) GBP 36,700   US$ 56,592

A VILLAGE SQUARE oil on canvas, 30½ x 22¼in. (77.5 x 56.5cm.) s 'J.Carabain'
      Christie's East, 20 May 1996 (51**) US$ 13,800   US$ 13,800

MARKET DAY, LANDSHUT, BAVARIA Oil on panel, unframed, 61.5 x 84 cm s 'J. Carabain'
      Christie's Amsterdam, 26 October 1995 (68**) NLG 48,300   US$ 30,454

CARELLI Consalvo (Naples 1818-1900 Naples) Italian
AN EXTENSIVE VIEW OF SORRENTO oil on panel, 14¼ x 9¼in. (36.2 x 23.5cm.) s inscr. 'C.
Carelli/Sorrento'
      Christie's London, 15 March 1996 (164**) GBP 10,120   US$ 15,455

CARELLI Giuseppe (Napels 1858-1921 Portici) Italian
NEAPOLITAN FISHERMEN WITH CAPRI IN THE DISTANCE oil on canvas, 24 x 39in. (61 x
99.1cm.) s and inscr. lr 'NAPOLI'
      Sotheby's Arcade Auctions New York, 17 January 1996 (608*) US$ 12,650   US$ 12,650

CARLEVARIJS Luca (1663-1730) Italian
CAPRICIO VIEW OF A HARBOUR WITH HORSEMEN PASSING BENEATH AN ARCH;
CAPRICCIO VIEW OF A SEAPORT WITH FIGURES UNLOADING BOATS ON THE
QUAYSIDE BESIDE A TRIUMPHAL ARCH oil on canvas (a pair) , each: 35¼ x 50¾in. (89.5 x
129cm.)
PROV.: With G.C. Baroni, Florence.
EXH.: On loan, Doncaster Museum and Art Gallery, 1977-1993.
      Sotheby's London, 5 July 1995 (51**) GBP 106,000   US$ 169,086

VENICE VIEW OF THE GRAND CANAL WITH SANTA MARIA DELLA SALUTE oil on
canvas, 26 x 51½in. (66 x 131cm.)
PROV.: Sir Richard Waldie-Griffith, Bt.; His Sale, Christie's, 6 April 1945, lot 101, as Cimaroli.
      Sotheby's London, 17 April 1996 (190**) GBP 161,000   US$ 244,124

A CAPRICCIO OF A MEDITERRANEAN SEAPORT WITH AUSTRIAN SHIPPING,
MERCHANTS AND SAILORS ON QUAYS IN THE FOREGROUND, A COMPANY OF
MILITIA NEAR THE ARCH OF CONSTANTINE AND CASTEL SANT'ANGELO BEYOND oil
on canvas, 51¾ x 113¾in. (131.5 x 289cm.) s ini. 'L.C.' (ca 1705)
PROV.: Conte Giovanni Benedetto Giovanelli (1652-1732) and his brother Conte Giovanni Paolo
Giovanelli (1658-1734) , Villa Giovanelli, Noventa Padovana (Inventory of 10January 1735: 'Due
Quadri grandi con soazze dipinte di porfido con Filli d'oro di Lucca Carlevari alti q.te 7½ crescenti
larghi q.te 17 rappresentano, uno Porto di Mare, altro Battaglia navale', see F. Montecuccoli Degli
Erri, 'Commitenze artistiche di una famiglia patrizia emergente: i Giovanelli di Venezia', Atti
dell'Istituto Veneto di Scienze, *Lettere ed Arti*, n.s., XV, 1993, p. 774); Acquired by the grandmother

of the present owner in Milan before the Second World War, when said to come from Caserta.
LIT.: Dr. Dario Succi intends to publish the paintings in *his catalogue raisonné of the work of Luca Carlevarijs*, due to be published this autumn.
　　　　　Christie's London, 19 April 1996 (253***) GBP 1,651,500　　　　US$　　2,504,170

A SEA BATTLE WITH SARDINIAN AND VENETIAN WARSHIPS AND SARDINIAN AND EGYPTIAN(?) GALLEYS IN THE FOREGROUND oil on canvas, 51¾ x 115 1/8 (131.5 x 292.5cm.) (ca 1705)
PROV.: Conte Giovanni Benedetto Giovanelli (1652-1732) and his brother Conte Giovanni Paolo Giovanelli (1658-1734) , Villa Giovanelli, Noventa Padovana (Inventory of 10January 1735: 'Due Quadri grandi con soazze dipinte di porfido con Filli d'oro di Lucca Carlevari alti q.te 7½ crescenti larghi q.te 17 rappresentano, uno Porto di Mare, altro Battaglia navale', see F. Montecuccoli Degli Erri, 'Commitenze artistiche di una famiglia patrizia emergente: i Giovanelli di Venezia', Atti dell'Istituto Veneto di Scienze, *Lettere ed Arti*, n.s., XV, 1993, p. 774); Acquired by the grandmother of the present owner in Milan before the Second World War, when said to come from Caserta.
LIT.: Dr. Dario Succi intends to publish the paintings in *his catalogue raisonné of the work of Luca Carlevarijs*, due to be published this autumn.
　　　　　Christie's London, 19 April 1996 (254**) GBP 1,541,500　　　　US$　　2,337,377

CARLSEN Dines (1901-1966) American
STILL LIFE WITH CANTON BOWL oil on canvas stretched over board, 25 x 30in. (63.5 x 76.2cm.) sdlr 'Dines Carlsen 1935'
　　　　　Christie's New York, 13 September 1995 (72**) US$ 20,700　　　　US$　　20,700

THE WHITE JUG oil on masonite, 26 x 23 1/8in. (66 x 58.7cm.) sll 'Dines Carlsen'; s inscr. with title and 'Falls Village, Conn.' on the reverse
PROV.: Grand Central Art Galleries, New York.
　　　　　Christie's New York, 13 September 1995 (82**) US$ 12,650　　　　US$　　12,650

CARLSEN Sören Emil (1853-1932) American (Danish)
THE SKY AND THE OCEAN oil on canvas, 50 x 70in. (127 x 178cm.) slr 'Emil Carlsen'; sd '1913' and inscr. with the title on a board affixed to the stretcher
　　　　　Christie's New York, 23 May 1996 (118**) US$ 32,200　　　　US$　　32,200

CARLSON John Fabian (1875-1945) Swedish
WINTER, WOODSTOCK oil on canvas, 18 x 24in. (46 x 61cm.) slr 'John F. Carlson'
　　　　　Christie's East, 28 November 1995 (7**) US$ 23,000　　　　US$　　23,000

CARLSUND Otto G. (1897-1948) Swedish
MEGAFONMANNEN II oil on panel, 124 x 57.5cm. sdlr 'O.C.26'
　　　　　Bukowskis Stockholm, 24-25 April 1996 (17**) SEK 325,000　　　　US$　　49,237

DEKORATIV KOMPOSITION oil on canvas, 55 x 33cm. sdll 'OTTO G.CARLSUND 33.'
　　　　　Bukowskis Stockholm, 24-25 April 1996 (18**) SEK 115,000　　　　US$　　17,422

CARMICHAEL John Wilson (1800-1868) British
THE INSPECTION OF THE FLEET oil on canvas, 40 x 66 1/8in. (101.5 x 168cm.) sdlr 'J.W.Carmicheal 1852'
　　　　　Phillips London, 18 June 1996 (32**) GBP 24,000　　　　US$　　37,008

CARO Baldassare de (Naples 1689-1750) Italian
LANDSCAPE WITH HOUNDS BY DEAD GAME, A HUNTING BAG AND A GUN oil on canvas, 59¾ x 79¾in. (152 x 203cm.) s 'BDCaro/p'
　　　　　Sotheby's London, 17 April 1996 (166**) GBP 12,650　　　　US$　　19,181

CARO-DELVAILLE Henri (1876 b.) French
THE LETTER oil on canvas, 25¾ x 31 7/8in. (65.5 x 81cm.) sdll 'H. Caro. Delvaille/1910.11'
    Christie's New York, 2 November 1995 (192**) US$ 16,100

US$	16,1(

CARPENTIER Evariste (Kuurne 1845-1922 Liege) Belgian
A SHEPHERDESS RESTING BY A TREE oil on panel, 26 x 21½in. (66 x 54.6cm.) slr
'E.Carpentier' and s and inscr. 'Evte Carpentier/Paris' on reverse
    Christie's New York, 14 February 1996 (77**) US$ 9,200

US$	9,2(

CARPIONI Giulio (Venice 1613-1679 Vicenza) Italian
ALLEGORY ON THE WINTER oil on canvas, 38 x 38cm
    Finearte Milan, 25 November 1995 (31*) ITL 16,100,000

US$	10,10(

ALLEGORY ON FEELING oil on canvas, 118 x 140cm
    Finearte Milan, 25 November 1995 (71**) ITL 80,500,000

US$	50,53

THE FLAYING OF MARSYAS oil on canvas, 34 x 46in. (86.3 x 117cm.)
    Sotheby's London, 6 December 1995 (154**) GBP 29,900

US$	46,01

CARRA Carlo (Quargnento 1881-1966 Milan) Italian
REMY DE GOURMONT ink on paper, 30 x 19cm sd 'C.Carra`914' (1914)
LIT.: F.Russoli-M. Carra *Carlo Carra Disegni*, ed. Graphis, Bologna 1977, no.111.
    Finearte Milan, 12 December 1995 (79*) ITL 20,700,000

US$	12,98(

MOTHER AND DAUGHTER ink on paper, 23 x 20cm sd 'C.Carra` 919' (1919)
LIT.: F.Russoli-M. Carra, *Carlo Carra Disegni*, ed. Graphis, Bologna 1977, no.338.
    Finearte Milan, 12 December 1995 (81*) ITL 21,850,000

US$	13,708

PAESAGGIO oil on canvassed board, 40 x 50cm. sdll 'C. Carra 943' (1943)
PROV.: Galleria Farsetti, Prato, no. 8943.
EXH.: Milan, Palazzo Reale, *Carra' mostra antologica*, April-June 1987; this exhibition later
traveled to Baden Baden, October-December 1987, no. 112.
    Finearte Milan, 12 December 1995 (281**) ITL 82,800,000

US$	51,945

DONNA SULLA SCALA pencil on paper, 26.5 x 14.5cm sd 'C.Carrà 911' titled inscr. (1911)
EXH.: Macerata, *Le 'Muse irrequiete' di Leonardo Sinisgalli*, Palazzo Ricci, July-October 1988,
cat.n.20.
LIT.: F. Russoli/M.Carrà, *Carrà, disegni*, Bologna 1977, n.44.
    Finearte Rome, 14 November 1995 (99*) ITL 18,975,000

US$	11,911

MADRE E FIGLIO gouache, watercolour and wash on paper laid down on canvas, 26¾ x 18¼in. (68
x 46.5cm.) sdll 'C. Carrà 917' (1917)
PROV.: Renato Cardazzo, Milan (purchased from the artist); Galleria d'arte del Naviglio, Milan;
Purchased by the present owner from the above in 1978.
EXH.: Venice, Galleria del Cavallino and Milan, Galleria d'arte del Naviglio, *Omaggio alla
Metafisica con opere di Giorgio de Chirico e Carlo Carrà*, 1952; Winterthur, Kunstmuseum
(travelling exhibition) *Rot konstruiert und Super Table, Eine Schweizer Sammlung moderner Kunst*,
1980, n.n., illustrated in colour in the catalogue.
    Sotheby's London, 24 June 1996 (68**) GBP 73,000

US$	112,567

CARRE Hendrick (1656-1721)
A GENTLEMAN OFFERING AN ORANGE TO A LADY, SEATED AT A TABLE IN AN
INTERIOR oil on canvas, 48 x 39cm. skk 'H Caree.f'
    Christie's Amsterdam, 7 May 1996 (127*) NLG 10,350

US$	6,035

CARRIER-BELL Pierre (1851-1932/33) French
PORTRAIT OF THE ARTIST'S MODEL oil on cnavas, 69 x 33¼in. (175.3 x 84.5cm.) sd '1904'
      Sotheby's Arcade Auctions New York, 20 July 1995 (278*) US$ 13,800   US$ 13,800

CARRIÉRE Eugène Gabriel (1849-1906) French
MOTHERHOOD oil on canvas, 24½ x 19 7/8in. (62.2 x 50.5cm.) sll 'Eugene Carriere'
PROV.: Charles Merrill; James Merill; Thence by descent to the present owner.
      Christie's New York, 10 January 1996 (105**) US$ 8,050   US$ 8,050

CARRINGTON Dora (1893-1932) l
TULIPS IN A TWO-HANDLED JUG oil on canvas, 20 x 16 in. (50.8 x 40.6cm.)
PROV.: R.J. Buckingham, thence by descent.
EXH.: London, Barbican Art Gallery, *Carrington - The Exhibition*, Sept.-Dec. 1995, no. 1995.
      Christie's London, 21 March 1996 (31**) GBP 12,650   US$ 19,319

CARTER Samuel John (1835-1892) British
PORTRAIT OF JOHN MUSTER, FULL LENGHT oil on canvas, 96½ x 80¼in. (245 x 204cm.) sd
'Sam Carter 1877'
      Christie's London, 7 June 1996 (655**) GBP 21,850   US$ 33,693

CARUCCI Jacopo Carucci, {called} Pontormo (Pontormo 1494-1556/57 Florence) Italian
SELF-PORTRAIT tempera and oil on roofing-tile, 50.5 x 36cm
EXH.: Palazzo Strozzi, *Mostra del Cinquecento toscane*, Firenze 1940, sala V, no.4; Palazzo Strozzi,
Mostar del Pontormo o del primo manierismo fiorentino, Firenze 1956, no.81.
LIT.: L.Berti, *Mostra del Pontormo*, catalogo della mostra, Firenze 1956, p.52; D.Sanminiatelli, 'The
Pontormo Exhibition in Florence', in *The Burlington Magazine*, XCVIII, 1956, p.242; L.Berti,
'Sembianze del Pontormo', in *Quaderni Pontormeschi*, 2, Firenze 1956/57, B.Berenson, *Italian
Pictures of the Renaissance. Florentine School*, London 1963, p.180; L.Berti, *Pontormo*, Firenze
1964, p.101; J.Cox-Rearick, *The Drawings of Pontormo. A Catalogue Raisonné with Notes on the
Paintings*, Cambridge 1964, pp. 112 e 281 pp.12-13; L.Berti, *precisazione sul Pontormo*, in
'Bollettino d`Arte', LI, 1966, p.54; L.Berti, *L`opera completa del Pontormo*, Milano 1973, pp.84 e
105; L.Berti, 'Un ritrovamento: il ritratto di Francesca Capponi del Pontormo', in *Critica d`Arte*, LV,
2-3, 1990, p.31; L.Bellosi, 'Per il giovane Mirabello Cavalori', in *Prospettiva* 66, 1992, p.90;
P.Costamagna, *Pontormo*, ed. Electa, Milano 1994, no.A47, p.290-291.
      Finearte Milan, 25 November 1995 (130**) ITL 402,500,000   US$ 252,668

CASALI Andrea (Civitavecchia 1,700 c.-1784 Rome) Italian
ANGELICA AND MEDORO oil on canvas, 18 x 14½in. (45.7 x 36.8cm.)
      Sotheby's New York, 11 January 1996 (208**) US$ 20,700   US$ 20,700

CASCELLA Michele (Ortona a Mare 1892-1989 Milan) Italian
BRINE IN TUSCANY oil on canvas, 40 x 60cm. sll 'Michele Cascella' (1982-84)
LIT.: Giuseppe Bonini, *Catalogo Ragionato dei dipinti di Michele Cascella*, ed. G. Mondadori e ass.,
Milano 1988, no. 80-88/183, p. 447.
      Finearte Milan, 12 December 1995 (243*) ITL 10,925,000   US$ 6,854

S. ANGELO (ISCHIA) oil on canvas, 50 x 65cm. sd 'Michele Cascella 1955'
      Finearte Milan, 12 December 1995 (262**) ITL 13,800,000   US$ 8,657

VICOLO DI GADAMES, 1934 watercolour on cardboard, 67 x 92cm sd 'Gadames febb. 1934
Michelle Cascella'
      Finearte Rome, 14 November 1995 (47*) ITL 20,125,000   US$ 12,633

PORTOFINO coloured pastel on carton, 81 x 100cm. sdll 'Michele Cascella 1979' (1979)
EXH.: Milan, Palazzo Reale, *Mostra di Michele Cascella*, April-May 1981, no.102.
      Finearte Milan, 19 March 1996 (31**) ITL 20,700,000   US$ 13,244

VASO DI FIORI coloured pastel on cardboard, 102 x 77cm. sdll 'Michele Cascella 1981' (1981)
LIT.: G. Bonini, *Catalogo generale dei dipinti di Michele Cascella*, ed. Giorgio Mondadori, Milan 1988, no.81/42, p.372.
Finearte Milan, 19 March 1996 (85**) ITL 17,250,000

US$ 11,0:

COLLE VAL D'ELSA oil on canvas, 76 x 127cm. sdll 'Michele Cascella'
PROV.: Gallery Juarez, Los Angeles.
Christie's Milan, 20 November 1995 (178**) ITL 32,160,000

US$ 20,18

PARIGI oil on canvas, 50 x 70cm. sdlr 'Paris 53'
PROV.: This work is recorded at the 'Archivio Michele Cascella' under supervision of Galleria Torcular, Milano under no. 53/7.96.
Sotheby's Milan, 28 May 1996 (164**) ITL 19,550,000

US$ 12,55

FIORI DI SETTEMBRE oil on canvas, 100 x 70cm. sd 'Portofino 1951'
LIT.: Giuseppe Bonini, *Catalogo Ragionato Generale dei Dipinti di Michele Cascella*, Milano 1988, p. 215, no. 51/1 (illustrated) .
Sotheby's Milan, 28 May 1996 (181**) ITL 28,750,000

US$ 18,46!

I TUILLERIES IN AUTUNNO oil on canvas, 32 x 39 1/8in. (81.3 x 99.5cm.) sll 'Michele Cascella'
PROV.: Galerie Juarez, Inc., Los Angeles (acquired by the father from the present owner) .
Christie's East, 30 April 1996 (25**) US$ 14,950

US$ 14,95C

NOTRE DAME oil on canvas, 24 x 36in. (61 x 91.5cm.) sdll 'Michele Cascella Paris 1960'
PROV.: Galerei Juarez, Inc., Los angeles (acquired by the father of the present owner) .
Christie's East, 30 April 1996 (95*) US$ 8,625

US$ 8,625

CASORATI Felice (Novara 1883-1963 Turin) Italian
NUDO SU FONDO BLU tempera on cardboard, 50 x 60cm. slr 'F. Casorati' (1954)
Finearte Milan, 12 December 1995 (278**) ITL 34,500,000

US$ 21,644

NATURA MORTA CON LE UOVA oil on board, 61x 43cm. slc 'F. Casorati' (1951)
PROV.: with collection Bassani, Triest.
EXH.: Turin, Galleria Civica d'Arte Moderna, *Casorati*, April-June 1964, no. 227.
LIT.: Luigi Carlucci, *Casorati*, ed. Teca, Turin 196, no. 165, pp. 140 and 373.
Finearte Milan, 18 June 1996 (226**) ITL 132,250,000

US$ 85,765

NUDO DI RAGAZZA NEI CAMPI oil on canvas, 69.5 x 59cm. slr 'F. Casorati' (ca 1958)
Finearte Milan, 19 March 1996 (55**) ITL 147,200,000

US$ 94,178

CLELIA oil on canvas, 110 x 63cm. slr 'F. Casorati' (1937)
PROV.: Collection Galleria Le Immagini, Turin and Galleria Cocorocchia, Milan.
Finearte Milan, 26 October 1995 (188**) ITL 356,500,000

US$ 222,118

NATURA MORTA CON RAPE E RAVANELLI oil on panel, 44 x 36cm. slr 'F. Casorati' (1927)
LIT.: Giorgina Bertolino-Francesco Poli, *Catalogo Generale delle Opere di Felice Casorati. Il Dipinti (1904-14963)* , Turin 1995, vol. II, no. 315 (illustrated) .
Sotheby's Milan, 28 May 1996 (196**) ITL 80,400,000

US$ 51,638

CASSANA Giovanni Agostino (Venice 1658 ca.-1720 Genova) Italian
A BOAR ATTACKED BY A BOAR-HOUND ON A HILLSIDE oil on canvas, 57 1/8 x 72 7/8in. (147 x 185cm.)
PROV.: With Count Alarico Palmieri, Geneva.
Christie's London, 28 March 1996 (81**) GBP 11,500

US$ 17,563

CASSATT Mary Stevenson (1845-1926) American
IN THE BOX oil on canvas, 17¼ x 24½in. (43.8 x 62.2cm.) (1870's)
PROV.: Durand-Ruel, Paris, France (Probably acquired from M. Doucet, April 1881); Mrs. Thomas
A. Scott, Philadelphia 1883; By descent in the family to the present owner.
EXH.: Paris, France, *Fourth Impressionist Exhibition*, 1879; London, England, Durand-Ruel, 1882;
London, England, Dowdeswell and Dowdeswells', *Paintings, Drawings and Pastels by Members of
'La Société des Impressionistes,'* 1883, no. 37 as *Au Balcon*; New York, Durand-Ruel, *Exposition of
Paintings, Pastels and Etchings by Miss Mary Cassatt*, 1895, no. 32 as *Au Theatre*; Philadelphia,
Pennsylvania, Pennsylvania Academy of the Fine Arts, *Exhibition of Paintings and Drawings by
Representative Modern Artists*, 1920, no. 10 as *In the Theater*; Philadelphia, Pennsylvania,
Pennsylvania Museum of Art, *Cassatt Memorial Exhibition*, 1927; Brooklyn, New York, The
Brooklyn Museum, *Leaders of American Impressionism: Mary Cassatt, Childe Hassam, J.H.
Twachtman and J. Alden Weir*, 1937, no. 20 as *Au Balcon*; Haverford, Pennsylvania, Haverford
College, *Mary Cassatt, 1845-1926*, 1939, no. 7, illus. as *Au Balcon*; Pittsburgh, Pennsylvania,
Carnegie Institute, *Survey of American Painting*, 1940, no. 200 as *Au Balcon*; Chicago, Illinois, Art
Institute of Chicago, *Sargent, Whistler and Mary Cassatt*, 1954, no. 6, illus., and travelling;
Philadelphia, Pennsylvania, Pennsylvania Academy of the Fine Arts, *150th Anniversary Exhibition*,
1955, no. 177, illus. Philadelphia, Pennsylvania, Philadelphia Museum of Art, *Mary Cassatt*, 1960;
Philadelphia, Pennsylvania, Peale House Galleries, Pennsylvania Acadamy of the Fine Arts, *Mary
Cassatt*, 1965, no. 10; New York, M. Knoedler & Co., *Mary Cassatt*, 1966, no. 7, illus.; Washington,
DC, National Gallery of Art, *Mary Cassatt*, 1970, no. 13, illus.; New York, Wildenstein, *A Loan
Exhibition 'One Hundred Years of Impressionism'*, 1970, no. 45, illus. *as Dans la Loge*; Philadelphia,
Pennsylvania, Philadelphia Museum of Art, *Mary Cassatt and Philadelphia*, 1985, no. 4, illus.
LIT.: 'Miss Mary Cassatt,' *Art Amateur*, vol. 32, no. 6, May 1895, no. 158 as *Au Theatre*;
'Philadelphia Honors Works of Mary Cassatt,' *Art News*, vol. 25, no. 31, May 7, 1927, no. 2; F.
Watson, 'Philadelphia Pays Tribute to Mary Cassatt,' *The Arts*, vol. 11, no. 6, June 1927, p. 289, illus.;
F. A. Sweet, *Miss Mary Cassatt: Impressionist from Philadelphia*, Norman, Oklahoma, 1966, no. 86,
plate 9; K. Flint, *The Impressionists in England: The Critical Reception*, London, 1984, p. 45; N. M.
Mathews, *Cassatt and Her Circle: Selected Letters*, New York, 1984, pp. 163-165, 166-167, 174-
176; *Mary Cassatt*, New York, 1987, nos. 40, 48, p. 40, illus.; This painting will be included in The
Cassatt's Committee's revision of Adelyn Dohme Breeskin's *catalogue raisonné Mary Cassatt*.
Christie's New York, 23 May 1996 (70**) US$ 4,072,500   US$ 4,072,500

HEAD OF A CHILD pencil on paper, 3 5/8 x 6 3/8in. (9.2 x 16.2cm.)
Christie's New York, 23 May 1996 (71*) US$ 13,800   US$ 13,800

LYDIA SEATED ON A PORCH, CROCHETING oil and tempera on canvas, 15 x 24¼in. (38.1 x
61.5cm.) sll 'Mary Cassatt' (ca. 1881)
PROV.: Galerie Durand-Ruel, Paris, France; Mrs. Montgomery Sears, Boston, Massachusetts; Mrs.
Cornelius J. Sullivan, New York; Sale: New York, Sotheby's, December 6, 1939, lot 169; Durand-
Ruel Galleries, New York; Mrs. E.N. Graham (Elizabeth Arden), New York; M. Knoedler & Co.,
Inc., New York; Mr. and Mrs. Lansing W. Thoms, St. Louis, Missouri; Sale: London, England,
Christie's, 6 April 1976, lot 17 as *La Serre*.
EXH.: Paris, France, Galerie Durand-Ruel, *Exposition de tableaux et pastels pour Mary Cassatt*,
March 1924, no. 31; Springfield, Massachusetts, Museum of Fine Arts, *The Opening Exhibition in
Honor of James Philip and Julia Emma Gray*, October-November 1933, no. 100; Palm Beach,
Florida, Society of the Four Arts, *The French Impressionists*, February-March 1946, no. 4; St. Louis,
Missouri, City Art Museum, *A Galaxy of Treasures Jiom St. Louis Collections*, January-February
196; New York, M. Knoedler & Co., Inc. *The Paintings of Mary Cassatt*, February 1966, no. 9, illus.
St. Louis, Missouri, City Art Museum, *American Art in St. Louis*, October-November 1969.
LIT.: *Arts*, June 1927, vol. II, p. 296, no. 6; *City Art Museum of St. Louis Bulletin*, 1961, vol. 44, p.
33, no. 4, illus.; A.D. Breeskin, *Mary Cassatt, A Catalogue Raisonné of the Oils, Pastels,
Watercolors and Drawings*, Washington, DC, 1970, p. 64, no. 102, illus.; this painting will be
included in the Cassatt Committee's revision of Adelyn Dohme Breeskin's *catalogue raisonné* of the
works of Mary Cassatt.
Christie's New York, 23 May 1996 (75**) US$ 860,500   US$ 860,500

MOTHER, SARA AND THE BABY pastel on paper laid down on panel, 36 x 29½in. (91.5 x 75cm.)
slr 'Mary Cassatt' (ca 1901)
PROV.: Galerie Ambroise Vollard, Paris , Acquired from the Artist in 1908; Dalzell Hatfield
Galleries, Los Angeles, Hal B. Wallis, Los Angeles.
EXH.: Paris, Galerie Durand-Ruel, *Tableaux et Pastels par Mary Cassatt*, Nov. 1908, no. 39.; Los
Angeles, County Museum of Art, Jan. 1987-Feb. 1989 (on loan) .
LIT.: A.D. Breeskin, *Mary Cassatt: A Catalogue Raisonné of the Oils, Pastels, Watercolours and
Drawings,* Washington D.C., 1970, p. 158, no. 381 (illustrated) .
      Christie's New York, 30 April 1996 (33**) US$ 1,432,500   US$ 1,432,500

CASSIGNEUL Jean Pierre (1935 b.) French
NATURE MORTE AUX FRUITS oil on canvas, 21¼ x 25 5/8in. (54 x 65cm.) sdlc 'CASSIGNEUL
60'
PROV.: The Railings Gallery, London.
      Christie's East, 30 April 1996 (111**) US$ 10,350   US$ 10,350

SOIR D'ETE oil on canvas, 31 7/8 x 25 5/8in. (81 x 65cm.) sll 'CASSIGNEUL.'
PROV.: Wally Findlay Galleries, Beverly Hills (acquired by the present owner, 1978) .
      Christie's East, 30 April 1996 (172**) US$ 39,100   US$ 39,100

LE MANTEAU DE FOURVURE oil on canvas, 24 x 19½in. (61 x 49.5cm.) str 'CASSIGNEUL'; s
on the reverse 'Cassigneul'
PROV.: Wally Findlay Galleries, Palm Beach (acquired by the present owner) .
      Christie's East, 7 November 1995 (92**) US$ 32,200   US$ 32,200

CASSINARI Bruno (Piacenza 1912-1992 Milan) Italian
SERA NELL'ATELIER oil on canvas, 130 x 160 cm. sdlr 'Cassinari 60'
      Finearte Milan, 18 June 1996 (214**) ITL 29,900,000   US$ 19,390

FIORI oil on canvas, 70 x 98cm. sdlr 'Cassinari 60' sd and titled on the reverse (1960)
      Finearte Milan, 26 October 1995 (158**) ITL 26,450,000   US$ 16,480

CASTEELS Peter III (the Younger) (Antwerp 1684-1749 Richmond) Flemish
ROSES, HYDRANGEAS, CARNATIONS, BLOSSOM, MORNING GLORY AND OTHER
FLOWERS IN A SCULPTED URN ON A LEDGE oil on canvas, 49¾ x 40in. (126.4 x 101.6cm.) sd
'PCasteels.F./1715.'
      Christie's London, 20 October 1995 (44**) GBP 20,700   US$ 32,670

A PEACOCK, DUCKS, A PHEASANT, A PIGEON, A COCKEREL, A HEN AND CHICKS BY A
PLINTH oil on canvas, 56 7/8 x 78 5/8in. (114.4 x 199.7cm)
      Christie's London, 7 July 1995 (8**) GBP 54,300   US$ 86,617

CASTEL Moshe (1909-1991)
PASSOCER SEDER oil on canvas, 24 x 35in. (61 x 89cm.) sdlr 'Castel 1949' and s in Hebrew
      Christie's Tel Aviv, 12 October 1995 (19**) US$ 13,800   US$ 13,800

SABBATH DINNER oil on canvas, 21 5/8 x 18 1/8in. (54.9 x 46cm.) sll 'Castel' and s again in
Hebrew (late 1930's)
PROV.: Safrai Gallery, Jerusalem.
      Christie's Tel Aviv, 12 October 1995 (75**) US$ 29,900   US$ 29,900

SAFED VIEW oil on canvas, 21 7/8 x 18¼in. (55.6 x 46.5cm.) sll in Hebrew (ca. 1940)
      Christie's Tel Aviv, 12 October 1995 (76**) US$ 51,750   US$ 51,750

SONG OF SONGS oil on canvas, 36 3/8 x 25 5/8in. (92.4 x 65.2cm.) sll in Hebrew 'à Fred Man en
toute amitié Kisling'; dlr 'Philadelphia Novembre 1943'

PROV.: The Artist's Estate.

    Christie's Tel Aviv, 12 October 1995 (92**) US$ 29,900   US$ 29,900

TO THE WELL watercolour, goauche, wax crayons and pen and ink on paper laid down on card,
19¼ x 12¾in. (49 x 32cm.) slr 'Castel', s again Hebrew (1930's)
PROV.: Goldman Gallery, Haifa.

    Christie's Tel Aviv, 14 April 1996 (42**) US$ 9,200   US$ 9,200

BASALT ground lava stone and pigment on canvas, 29¾ x 21¼in. (72.8 x 54cm.) slr 'Castel', s again
on the reverse

    Christie's Tel Aviv, 14 April 1996 (50**) US$ 13,800   US$ 13,800

CASTELFRANCO Giorgio da Castelfranco, called Giorgione (circle of) (1477/78-before 1510) Italian

A LANDSCAPE WITH A PAIR OF LOVERS oil on paper laid down on canvas, 12¾ x 21¾in. (32.4
x 55.2cm.)
PROV.: Richard Cosway, 1791, according to a label on the reverse; Miss Rogers, London, by 1844
(as Giorgione, see Jameson literature); Samuel Rogers (Sale: Christie's London, April 28- May 10,
1856); Sir John Ramsden, Bt., by 1868 (Sale: Christie's London, July 7, 1930, lot 34, as Giogione,
unsold); Christie's London, May 27, 1932, lot 73 (as
Giorgione) there purchased by Frank T. Sabin, London; Galerie Cramer, The Hague, by 1969 (as
School of Giorgione, according to the Supplement to *The Burlington Magazine,* vol. CXI, June 1969)
Sale: Sotheby's London, July 13, 1977, lot 86 (as Follower of Giorgione, accompanied by a
certificate by Antonio Morassi, 1969, as an early work by *Titian*, circa 1508-1510, unsold) thence by
descent to the present owner.
EXH.: Leeds, *National Exhibition of Works of Art*, 1868, no. 210 (as *Giorgione*) .
LIT.: Mrs. A.Jameson, *Companion to the most celebrated Private Collections of Art in London*,
1844, p.412 (as *Giorgione*); G.F. Waagen, *Treasures of Art in Great Britain*, vol. II, 1854, p. 267 (as
Giorgione); J.A. Crowe and G.B. Cavalcaselle, 1912 edition, vol. III, p. 55 (as Bolognese School); T.
Borenius, 'A Landscape by Titian', *Burlington Magazine*, vol. LXXII, April 938, pp. 153-4, illus. (as
Titian); B. Berenson, *Italian Pictures of the Renaissance: Venetian School*, 1957, vol. I, p. 86 (as
Giorgionesque furniture painting); *Supplement to The Burlington Magazine*, vol. CXI, June 1969, pl.
xix, illus. (as School of Giorgione) .

    Sotheby's New York, 11 January 1996 (185**) US$ 28,750   US$ 28,750

CASTELLANI Enrico (Castelmassa 1930 b.) Italian

SUPERFICIE SAGOMATA mixed media in frame, 50 x 70cm. sd '1962' on the reverse
EXH.: Bologna; Galleria d'Arte moderna, *Europa -America*, May-June 1976; Milan, Padiglione
d'Arte Contemporanea, *Azimuth-Azimuth*, June-July 1984.

    Finearte Milan, 12 December 1995 (285**) ITL 36,225,000   US$ 22,726

SUPERFICIE BLU oil on canvas, 120 x 100cm (1972)
PROV.: Collezione Janlet, Bruxelles; Galleria dell`Ariete, Milano, no.2143.

    Finearte Rome, 14 November 1995 (175**) ITL 24150,000   US$ 15,160

SUPERFICIE BIANCA NO. 2 tempera and nails on canvas, 39 3/8 x 39 3/8in. (100 x 100cm.) sd
titled '1967' on the stretcher
PROV.: Galleria dell'Ariete, Milan.

    Christie's London, 23 May 1996 (88**) GBP 8,050   US$ 12,190

SUPERFICIE BIANCA painted and worked canvas, 101 x 150cm. s on the reverse (ca. 1975)
PROV.: Galleria La Polena, Genova; Galleria Peccola, Livorno.
EXH.: Genova, Galleria La Polena, *Castellani*, 1976.

    Sotheby's Milan, 28 May 1996 (175**) ITL 37,950,000   US$ 24,374

CASTELLI Giovanni Paolo, {called} Spadino (Florence 1659-1730 c.) Italian
STILL-LIFE WITH FRUIT IN A GLASS BOWL, PUMPKINS AND POMEGRANATE oil on canvas, 96 x 70cm.

    Bukowskis Stockholm, 29 November-1 December 1995 (217**) SEK 200,000   US$ 30,256

CASTELLO Valerio (Genua 1625-1659) Italian
MADONNA WITH CHILD AND S. GIOVANNINO oil on canvas, 72 x 53cm. (oval)

    Finearte Rome, 24 October 1995 (512**) ITL 29,325,000   US$ 18,271

CASTIGLIONE Giovanni Benedetto, {called} il Grechetto (a follower of) (Genua 1610-1665 Mantua) Italian
A MOUNTAINOUS LANDSCAPE WITH TRAVELLERS AND HERSDSMEN OF A PATH oil on canvas, 24 x 39in. (61 x 99cm.) s 'Gio. Bene'po / Castiglione / Genouese'

    Christie's South Kensington, 7 December 1995 (104*) GBP 66,750   US$ 102,724

CATHELIN Bernard (1919 b.) French
PREMIERE NIEGE DANS LA VALÉE DU MORIN oil on canvas, 38¼ x 63¾in. (97 x 162cm.) sdlr 'Cathelin 65'; sd titled on the reverse 'Catheline Février 1965 'Première neige dans la valée du Morin''
PROV.: Findlay Galleries, New York (acquired by the late owner) .

    Christie's East, 30 April 1996 (85**) US$ 12,650   US$ 12,650

MARCHÉ MEXICAIN oil on canvas, 36¼ x 23 5/8in. (92 x 60cm.) sdlr 'Cathelin 74'; sd and titled on the reverse 'Cathelin 1974 'Marché mexicain''

    Christie's East, 7 November 1995 (250*) US$ 7,475   US$ 7,475

CAUCHOIS Eugène Henri (1850-1911) French
STILL LIFE WITH CHRYSANTHEMUMS IN A PORCELAIN BOWL oil on canvas, 19¾ x 24in. (50.2 x 61cm.) slr

    Phillips London, 12th March 1996 (31***) GBP 6,200   US$ 9,469

CAULLERY Louis de (Cambrai 1582 before-1621/22 Antwerp) Flemish
AN INTERIOR SCENE WITH ELEGANT COMPANY DANCING AND PLAYING MUSIC oil on panel, 19¼ x 28¼in. (49 x 71.8cm.)
PROV.: Anonymous sale in these Rooms, 4 July 1990, lot 101. (GBP 15,000) .

    Sotheby's London, 5 July 1995 (111**) GBP 11,500   US$ 18,344

THE CRUCIFIXION oil on panel, 21 x 29¾in. (53.5 x 75.5cm.) sdlc 'Cauleri in fecit 1619'

    Sotheby's London, 5 July 1995 (223**) GBP 27,600   US$ 44,026

LES PRÉPARATIFS DU BAL DANS UN INTÉRIEUR DE PALAIS oil on oakpanel, 56.5 x 100cm.

    Étude Tajan Paris, 12 December 1995 (66**) FRF 350,000   US$ 70,499

CRUCIFIXION oil on panel, 86.5 x 62.5cm.
PROV.: Private collection.
EXH.: Brussels, Musées Royaux des Beaux-Arts de Belgique, *Maitres flamands du dix-septieme siècle du Prado et des collections privées espagnoles*, May-June 1975, cat. no. 6, p. 36.
LIT.: M. Díaz Padrón, M. Royo-Villanova, 'Una crucifixion de Louis de Caulery en el Museo del Prado', *Boletí del Museo del Prado*, Tomo XIV, no. 32, p. 47, fig. 9.

    Sotheby's Madrid, 23 November 1995 (6**) ESP 3,290,000   US$ 27,044

CAUWER Emile Pierre Joseph de (1828-1873) Belgian
FIGURES IN A CHURCH INTERIOR oil on canvas, 31¾ x 25 3/8in.(80.5 x 64.5cm.) slr

    Phillips London, 11th June 1996 (11**) GBP 12,000   US$ 18,504

CAVALLINO Bernardo (1616-1656) Italian
THE HEALING OF BLIND TOBIT oil on canvas, 29¾ x 39¾in. (75.6 x 101cm.)

PROV.: Olivetti, Rome; Corsi, Florence; Durlacher Bros., New York by June 1951; Gift to the present owner by the Seattle Art Museum; Guild (Acc. no. 51.124) .
EXH.: San Francisco, California Palace of Legion of Honor, 1950; Vancouver, Art Gallery, *Baroque Paintings*, 1952; Tacoma, Washington, The Broadway Gallery, *Old Master Paintings*, 1958.
LIT.: E. Sestieri, 'Ricerche su Cavallino,' *Dedalo*, II, I, 1921, pp. 181-182, fig. 182 (as by Cavallino); S. Ortolani, *Cavalliniana* (10 Dicembre 1622-10 Dicembre 1922) , *L'Arte*, 25, 1922, pp. 190-99 (as by Cavallino); S. Ortolani, *la mostra della pittura napoletana dei secoli XVII-XVIII-XIX, exhibition catalogue,* Naples 1938, p. 65 (as *by Cavallino Seattle Art Museum: Annual Report*, 1951, p. 37 (as by Cavallino); A. Percy, *Bernardino Cavallino*, Master's thesis, Pennsylvania State University, 1965, p. 63, no. 76 (as a copy); R. Causa, *La pittura del Seicento a Napoli dal naturalismo al barocco*, in 5 vol., plate 2 of *Storia di Napoli*, 1972, p. 982, no. 110 (as a copy); Burton B. Fredericksen and Federico Zeri, *Census of Pre-Nineteenth Century Italian Paintings in North American Public Collections*, 1972, pp. 50, 638 (as a copy); *Bernard Cavallino of Naples 1616-1656*, 1984, cat. by A. T. Lurie and A. Percy, P. 229, no. 4, illus. p. 99, fig. 24f (as a copy) .
    Sotheby's New York, 11 January 1996 (22**) US$ 26,450   US$ 26,450

CAVALLUCCI Antonio (1752-1795) Italian
ST BONA RECEIVES THE CONVENT DRESS oil on canvas, 74 x 74cm. (ca. 1791)
    Christie's Rome, 21 November 1995 (243**) ITL 55,000,000   US$ 34,526

CECCARELLI Naddo (Siena 14th Century, active mid) Italian
CHRIST THE MAN OF SORROWS tempera on gold ground panel (triangular) , 8¼ x 7¾in. (21 x 19.7cm.) (ca. 1320)
    Christie's London, 8 December 1995 (65**) GBP 25,300   US$ 38,935

CERQUOZZI Michelangelo (1602-1660) Italian
A MEDITERRANEAN COAST WITH BOATS AND A COMPANY MAKING MUSIC IN THE FOREGROUND oil on canvas, 87 x 116cm.
    Christie's Rome, 21 November 1995 (117**) ITL 17,000,000   US$ 10,672

A STILL-LIFE WITH A BASKET FILLED WITH APPLES AND GRAPES, SURROUNDED BY PLUMBS, PEACHES AND FIGS oil on canvas, 114 x 80cm.
    Bukowskis Stockholm, 29 November-1 December 1995 (219**) SEK 290,000   US$ 43,871

CESARI Giuseppe, {called} Cavalier d'Arpino (Arpino or Rome 1568-1640 Rome) Italian
THE ASSUMPTION OF THE VIRGIN oil on copper, 17¼ x 13½in. (44 x 34.5cm.)
EXH.: Leeds, 1868, no. 242, as by *Arpino*.
LIT.: Waagen. 1857, p. 497, as *Giuseppe d' Arpino*; Richter, 1901, no. 48, as *Cavalier d' Arpino*.
    Sotheby's London, 6 December 1995 (12**) GBP 8,050   US$ 12,388

CESETTI Giuseppe (Tuscany 1902-1990) Italian
CAVALLI oil on canvas, 89 x 116cm. sll 'Cesetti'
    Finearte Milan, 18 June 1996 (222**) ITL 20,700,000   US$ 13,424

RITRATTO MASCHILE oil on canvas, 93 x 56cm. slr 'Cesetti' (1930)
LIT.: *Catalogo Generale dei dipinti di Giuseppe Cesetti*, ed. Giorgio Mondadori, Milan 1989, vol.I, no.30/12.
    Finearte Milan, 19 March 1996 (77**) ITL 28,750,000   US$ 18,394

CÉZANNE Paul (Aix en Provence 1839-1906) French
PAYSAGE oil on paper laid down on board, 7 7/8 8 1/4in (20 x 21cm.) (ca. 1865)
PROV.: Paul Cézanne *fils*, Paris; Anonymous sale, Galerie Charpentier, Paris, 1 June 1949, lot 6 (illustrated) .
LIT.: This painting will appear as no. 51 in the late John Rewald's forthcoming *catalogue* raisonné *of Cézanne's paintings* being prepared in collaboration with Walter Feilchenfeldt and Jayne Warman.
    Christie's New York, 1 May 1996 (111**) US$ 123,500   US$ 123,500

GRANDS ARBRES AU JAS DE BOUFFAN oil on canvas, 28¾ x 23¼in. (73 x 59cm.) (ca. 1890)
PROV.: Ambroise Vollard, Paris; Ralph C. Coe, Cleveland; M. Knoedler & Co., New York; Mrs.
John Wintersteen, Chestnut Hill, Pennsylvania; Paul Rosenberg, Paris; Private collection, Paris; E.V.
Thaw, New York.
EXH.: Toledo, Museum of Art, 1936, no. 35; San Francisco, San Francisco Museum of Art, *Paul
Cézanne: Exhibition of Paintings, Water-Colors, Drawings and Prints*, 1937, no. 25, illustrated in the
catalogue Paris, Galerie Paul Rosenberg, *Cézanne (1839-1906) organisée à l'occasion de son
centenaire*, 1939, no. 12, illustrated in the catalogue.
LIT.: Lionello Venturi, *Cézanne, son art - son oeuvre*, Paris, 1936, no. 474, illustrated Fritz Novotny,
Cezanne und das Ende der wissenschaftlichen Perspektive, Vienna, 1938, p. 200, no 57; Maurice
Raynal, *Cézanne*, London, 1939, illustrated; Alfonso Gatto and Sandra Orienti, *L 'Opera completa di
Cézanne*, Milan, 1970, p. 104, no. 396, illustrated John Rewald, *Cézanne*, New York, 1986, p. 149,
illustrated in colour; John Rewald, *Cézanne*, New York 1986, p. 149 illustrated in colour; This
painting will appear as no. 546 in the late John Rewald's forthcoming *Cézanne Catalogue raisonné*
being prepared in collaboration with Walter Feilchenfeldt and Jayne Warman.
Sotheby's London, 24 June 1996 (24**) GBP 5,171,500   US$ 7,974,557

PORTRAIT DE L'ARTISTE oil on canvas, 13 3/8 x 9½in. (34 x 24cm.) (ca. 1885)
PROV.: Galerie Bernheim-Jeune, Paris; Baron C. E. Janssen, Brussels; sale, Sotheby & Co., London,
May 6, 1959, lot 26 (illustrated in colour on the frontispiece) Drs. Fritz and Peter Nathan, Zurich
(acquired at the above sale); Acquired from the above by the late owner circa 1959.
EXH.: Brussels, Palais des Beaux-Arts, *Panorama de L'Art Contemporain dans les musées et
collections Belges,* May-June, 1953, no. 8; Schaffhausen, Switzerland, Museum zu Allerheiligen, *Die
Welt des Impressionismus*, June-Sept., 1963, p. 17, no. 8 (illustrated in colour) .
LIT.: J. Meier-Grafe, *Cezanne*, London, 1927, pl. XXII (illustrated); *L'Art Vivant*, Feb. 1, 1929, p.
129 (illustrated); G. Rivière, *Cezanne, le peintre solitaire*, Paris, 1933 (illustrated on the
frontispiece); J. Rewald, 'Iconographie de Cézanne, vu par lui-meme,' *Amour de l'Art*, May, 1936,
fig. 3 (illustrated); L. Venturi, *Cézanne son art - son oeuvre*, Paris 1936, vol. I, p. 176, no. 518
(illustrated, vol. II, pl. 159); G.Jedlicka, *Cezanne*, Bern, 1948, fig. 27 (illustrated); R. Gaffe,
Introduction d la peinture française (de Manet à Picasso), Paris 1954, p. 77 (illustrated); F. Nathan,
Dr. Fritz und Dr. Peter Nathan, 25Jahre, 1936-1961, Zurich 1961, p. 45 (illustrated in colour); C.
Ikegami, *Cézanne*, Tokyo 1969, fig. 18; S. Orienti, *The Complete Paintings of Cezanne*, New York
1972, p. 110, no. 510 (illustrated); M. Gasser, 'Bilder aus einer Privatsammlung', *Du*, Dec. 1974, p.
18 (illustrated); This painting will appear as no. 586 in the late John Rewald's forthcoming *catalogue
raisonné of Cézanne's paintings* being prepared in collaboration with Walter Feilchenfeldt and Jayne
Warman.
Christie's New York, 7 November 1995 (7**) US$ 1,542,500   US$ 1,542,500

CHABAS Maurice (1862-1947) French
FIGURES BY THE RIVER WITH CLASSICAL RUINS oil on canvas, 44½ x 76¾in. (113 x
195cm.) slr 'Maurice Chabas'
Christie's New York, 2 November 1995 (102**) US$ 19,550   US$ 19,550

CHABOT Hendrik (1894-1949) Dutch
AARDAPPELSCHILLENDE VROUW EN DOCHTER oil on canvas, 154 x 113cm. sdll 'H.Chabot
46', and inscr. with title on a label on the stretcher
PROV.: Acquired directly from the artist by the family of the present owner.
EXH.: Eindhoven, Stedelijk Van Abbemuseum, *Overzichtstentoonstelling Hendrik Chabot*, 10
November-10 December 1951, no.32.
Christie's Amsterdam, 6 December 1995 (187A**) NLG 34,500   US$ 21,378

CHAGALL Marc (Vitebsk 1887-1985) French (Russian)
L'ANCIEN TESTAMENT RACONTÉ PAR ESOPE gouache on tan paper mounted at the edges on
the board, 20 1/8 x 16¾in. (51 x 41.5cm.) sll 'Chagall' (1926-27)
PROV.: Galerie Louis Manteau, Brussels (acquired from the artist; acquired by the family of the
present owner in 1927) .

EXH.: Paris, Galerie Bernheim-Jeune, *La Fontaine par Chagall*, Feb 1930, no. 16; Galerie Le Centaure, March, 1930 and Berlin, Galerien Flechtheim, April 1930.

Christie's New York, 1 May 1996 (214**) US$ 134,500	US$	134,500

LES AMOUREUX gouache, watercolour, brush and black ink on Japan paper, 38 5/8 x 23 5/8in. (98 x 60cm.) sdlr 'Marc Chagall 1956'
EXH.: Nagoya, City Art Museum, *Chagall*, Jan.-March 1990, no. 104. (illustrated) .

Christie's New York, 1 May 1996 (338**) US$ 184,000	US$	184,000

L'ALOUETTE ET SES PETITS AVEC LE MAITRE D'UN CHAMP gouache on buff paper mounted at the edges on board, 18½ x 15 5/8in. (47 x 40cm.) slr 'Chagall' (ca. 1927)
PROV.: Ambroise Vollard, Paris; Galerie Bernheim-Jeune, Paris.
EXH.: Paris, Galerie Bernheim-Jeune, *La Fontaine par Chagall*, Feb., 1930, no. 9. The exhibition traveled to Brussels, Galerie Le Centaure, March, 1930 and Bedin, Galerien Flechtheim, April, 1930.

Christie's New York, 1 May 1996 (346**) US$ 99,300	US$	99,300

COUPLE AU CIEL BLUE gouache, 18½ x 12¾in. (46.5 x 32.5cm.) sll 'M. Chagall' (ca. 1946-47)

Étude Tajan Paris, 10 June 1996 (37**) FRF 400,000	US$	77,239

LES AMOUREUX AUX BOUQUETS pastel, gouache and watercolour on paper, 19¾ x 24¾in. (50 x 63cm.) slr 'Marc Chagall'
PROV.: Waddington Galleries, London.

Christie's Tel Aviv, 12 October 1995 (16**) US$ 222,500	US$	222,500

OISEAU ROUGE, CHEVAL BLEU oil on canvas, 13¾ x 10¾in. (35 x 27.3cm.) sll 'Chagall' (ca. 1970)
PROV.: The Artist's Estate.

Christie's Tel Aviv, 12 October 1995 (59**) US$ 112,500	US$	112,500

FLEUR DE LA VIE gouache and watercolour on paper, 29 x 22 1/8in. (73.7 x 56cm.) sdlr 'Marc Chagall, 1952-6'
PROV.: Galerie Alex Maguy, Paris (no.1163) .

Christie's Tel Aviv, 14 April 1996 (26**) US$ 178,500	US$	178,500

SCENE BIBLIQUE gouache, watercolour, pastel and collage on paper, 13 x 10in. (33 x 25.4cm.)

Christie's Tel Aviv, 14 April 1996 (43**) US$ 32,200	US$	32,200

LE CERF ET LA VIGNE gouache on paper, 20 1/8 x 16½in. (51.1 x 41.9cm.) s
PROV.: Galerie Bernheim, Paris; Galerie Bouchon, Paris.
EXH.: *Marc Chagall, Les Fables de La Fontaine*, Ceret, Musée d'art Moderne and Nice, Musée National *Message Biblique Marc Chagall*, 1995-1996, illustrated p. 129.

Sotheby's New York, 2 May 1996 (353A**) US$ 79,500	US$	79,500

LE SALUT gouache on paper, 24¾ x 19 1/8in. (62.9 x 48.6cm.) sll 'Marc Chagall' (ca. 1927)
PROV.: Galerie Y.M. Bernard, Paris; Madame Adler, Paris.
LIT.: Franz Meyer, *Marc Chagall, Life and Work*, New York, 1963, no. CC482, illustrated.

Sotheby's New York, 2 May 1996 (169**) US$ 211,500	US$	211,500

LES AMOUREUX oil on board, 27 7/8 x 19 1/8in. (70.7 x 50cm.) sd dedicated in cyrillic '916 for my wife' (1916)
PROV.: Private collection Berlin (acquired in the 1920s); Emma Norton, London (purchased in the late 1940s); Thence by descent to the present owner.
LIT.: Franz Meyer, *Marc Chagall, Life and Work*, New York, 1963, p. 244 discussed; p. 749, no. 247 illustrated (centimetre size incorrectly recorded as inches) .

Sotheby's London, 24 June 1996 (37**) GBP 2,751,500	US$	4,242,868

LA MANSARDE goache on paper, 18 1/8 x 15½in. (46 x 49.5cm.) sd in cyrillic 'Chagall 1916'
PROV.: Nadezhda Yevseevna Dobitchina, St. Petersburg; Mme Pujurovskaya, St. Petersburg;
Acquired from a descendant of the above.
Sotheby's London, 24 June 1996 (38**) GBP 133,500 US$ 20,5860

NOCE ET MUSIQUE oil on canvas, 24 x 15in. (61 x 38cm.) sll 'Marc Chagall' (ca. 1939)
PROV.: Svensk-Franska Konstgalleriet, Stockholm (acquired from the artist in 1939); Perls
Galleries, New York; Sale, London, Christie's, 2 December 1975, lot 80.
EXH.: Stockholm, Liljevalchs Konsthall, *Fran Cézanne till Picasso*, 1954, no. 78; Copenhagen,
Charlottenborg, *Chagall-Kokoschka Udstillingen*, 1960.
Sotheby's London, 24 June 1996 (66**) GBP 287,500 US$ 443,331

FEMME AU TRAPEZE gouache on paper, 25¾ x 19¾in. (65.5 x 50in.) slr 'Chagall' (1927)
PROV.: Bernheim-Jeune, Paris; Svensk-Franska Konstgalleriet, Stockholm (1937); anon. sale,
Sotheby's, London, 7 Dec. 1977, lot 132 (illustrated) where purchased by the present owners.
EXH.: Stockholm, Svensk-Franska Konstgalleriet, *Franske konst*, September 1937, no. 29;
Stockholm, Svensk-Franska Konstgalleriet, *Franske konst*, November 1939, no. 36; Stockholm,
Liljevalchs Konsthall, Moderna Museets Vanner, *Fran Cezanne till Picasso*, September 1954, no. 82.
LIT.: R. Escholier, *La Peinture Francaise au XXeme Siècle*, Paris, 1937, p. 137 (illustrated) .
Christie's London, 25 June 1996 (31**) GBP 144,500 US$ 222,822

LES PAYSANS DE VENCE oil on canvas, 43¾ x 32¼in. (111 x 82cm.) slr 'Marc Chagall' s and
titled on the reverse 'Marc Chagall Les Paysans de Vence' (1967)
EXH.: Saint Paul de Vence, Fondation Maeght, *Hommage à Marc Chagall*, 1967; Munich
Kunsthalle der Hypo-Kulturstiftung, *Marc Chagall* 1991, no. 96 (illustrated in colour); Andros,
Greece, Musée d'Art Moderne, Fondation Basil et Elise Goulandris, summer 1994.
Christie's London, 25 June 1996 (47**) GBP 551,500 US$ 850,424

LE VILLAGE BLEU oil on canvas, 30¾ x 28in. (78 x 71cm.) sd 'Marc 1955-59' and 'Chagall' s
again on the reverse
PROV.: Mr and Mrs Leigh Block, Chicago; Acquavella Galleries, New York; anon. sale, Sotheby's,
London, 26 March 1980, lot 34 (illustrated in colour) , where purchased by the present owners.
EXH.: Santa Barbara, Santa Barbara Museum of Art, California (on loan from Mr and Mrs Leigh
Block); Zurich, Kunsthaus, *Chagall*, May-July 1967, no. 157; Saint-Paul de Vence, Fondation
Maeght, Hommage d Marc Chagall, 1967, no. 50.
LIT.: F. Meyer, *Marc Chagall Leben und Werk*, Cologne, 1961, no. 978 (illustrated); G. Arpino,
Marc Chagall, Milan, 1978, (illustrated in colour p. 88) .
Christie's London, 25 June 1996 (51**) GBP 804,500 US$ 1,240,555

LE PEINTRE pencil, pastel, watercolour and gouache on paper, 15 x 22¼in. (38.1 x 56.5cm.) sd
'Marc Chagall 941-942' (America, 1941-42)
LIT.: F. Meyer *Marc Chagall*, London, 1964, p. 4356, no. 689 (illustrated) .
Christie's London, 26 June 1996 (181**) GBP 71,900 US$ 110,871

LE MUSICIEN AMOUREUX brush and black ink on paper, 37¾ x 26½in. (96 x 67.3cm.) s 'Marc
Chagall' (1964)
PROV.: Galerie Maeght, Paris.
Christie's London, 26 June 1996 (197**) GBP 54,300 US$ 83,732

LES PAYSANS RUSSES gouache, watercolour and pencil on cream paper, 25½ x 19¾in. (65.3 x
65.2cm.) slr 'Chagall Marc' (ca. 1925)
PROV.: Galerie 'Le Centaure', Brussels; their sale 17 Oct. 1932, lot 114 (BF 1900) , to Zollinger for
P. A. Regnault; P. A. Regnault, Laren (NH); his sale, Amsterdam, Paul Brandt, 22-23 October 1958,
lot 14 (illustrated in colour); Colonel C. Michael Paul, Palm Beach; Galerie Beyeler, Basel (no.
10867) .
EXH.: Eindhoven, Stedelijk van Abbe Museum, *Moderne Meesters*, Dec. 1947-Feb. 1948, no. 117;

Delft, Stedelijk Museum, Reizend Buitenland (Chagall e.a.) , May 1948; Eindhoven, Stedelijk van Abbe Museum, *Marc Chagall en Massimo Campigli uit de collectie P. A. Regnault*, 1950, no. 14, p. 20 (illustrated p. 18 as *Russische Boer*); Hannover, Kestner Gesellschaft, *Marc Chagall*, 1955, no. 64 (as *Knabe mit Schaufel*); Zurich, Kunsthaus, *Marc Chagall, Retrospective der Arbeiten auf Papier*, 1985.
LIT.: C. Roodenburg-Schadd, *Goed Modern Werk, De Collectie Regnault in Het Stedelijk*, Zwolle, 1995, p. 145.

Christie's London, 28 November 1995 (21**) GBP 331,500	US$	518,536

LA MARIÉE DE NOTRE-DAME oil on canvas, 28¾ x 23 5/8in. (73 x 60cm.) sll 'Marc Chagall' (ca 1970)
PROV.: The Artist's Estate, from whom purchased by the present owner.

Christie's London, 28 November 1995 (42**) GBP 419,500	US$	656,186

ST PAUL DE VENCE, PEINTRE ET BOUQUET DE FLEURS oil on canvas, 25 5/8 x 19 5/8in. (65 x 50cm.) sll 'Chagall' s again on the reverse 'Marc Chagall' (ca 1978)
PROV.: Galerie Maeght, Paris (16754); Marcel Bernheim, Paris, from whom bought by the previous owner.

Christie's London, 28 November 1995 (49**) GBP 287,500	US$	449,711

LE TEMPS QUI VOLE pastel and gouache on paper, 15 x 11in. (38 x 29cm.) slr 'Marc Chagall'
PROV.: Jean Tiroche Gallery, New York; Galleria Internazionale, Milan.
EXH.: Turin, Galleria Gissi, *Maestri Italiani*.

Christie's London, 29 November 1995 (152**) GBP 70,000	US$	109,495

PERSECUTION pastel, gouache and watercolour on paper, 22 x 14 7/8in. (55.9 x 37.8cm.) slr 'Chagall' (ca 1941)
PROV.: Mrs James McClane, Los Angeles;.
LIT.: F. Meyer, *Marc Chagall: Life and Work*, London 1964, no. 699 (illustrated p. 757); J. Cassou, *Chagall*, London, 1965, no. 183 (illustrated p. 259, as *Blue Crucifixion*) .

Christie's London, 29 November 1995 (208**) GBP 90,000	US$	140,779

JACOB ET L'ANGE ink and pastel on paper, 11¾ x 9½in. (30 x 24cm.) slr 'Marc Chagall'

Christie's East, 30 April 1996 (130*) US$ 17,250	US$	17,250

LE SATYRE coloured wax crayons, pen and India and brown ink on paper, 9¼ x 5 7/8in. (23.5 x 15cm.) slr 'Marc Chagall' (1942-1943)
PROV.: Wally F Galleries, New York (acquired by the present owner, 1971) .

Christie's East, 30 April 1996 (135*) US$ 8,625	US$	8,625

LES MARIÉS AU BOUQUET DE FLEURS oil on canvas, 28 x 20 ½in. (71.1 x 52cm.) Slc 'Marc Chagall' (1975)
PROV.: Estate of the artist; Acquired from the above by the previous owner in 1986.

Christie's New York, 7 November 1995 (61**) US$ 827,500	US$	827,500

MERE ET ENFANT pen, India ink and coloured wax crayons on paper, 7 5/8 x 3½in. (19.4 x 8.9cm.) sul 'Marc Chagall'
PROV.: Anon. sale; Sotheby's, London, 18 Oct. 1985, lot 61 (acquired by the present owner) .

Christie's East, 7 November 1995 (174*) US$ 16,100	US$	16,100

L'HOMME A LA FAUX gouache on brown paper laid down on board, 18 5/8 x 12 1/4in. (47.4 x 31cm.) lr 'Marc Chagall' (1911)
EXH.: Tokyo, Musée National d'Art Occidental, *Marc Chagall*, Oct.-Nov., no. 122 (illustrated) . The exhibition traveled to Kyoto, Musée Municipal, Nov.-Dec., 1963. Philadelphia, Museum of Art, 1967 (on loan) .

Christie's New York, 8 November 1995 (197**) US$ 85,000	US$	85,000

LE MARIAGE oil on canvas, 18 1/4 x 10 5/8in, (46.4 x 27cm.) ll 'Chagall 1932' (1932)
PROV.: Galerie Moderne, Paris; James Vigeveno Galleries, Los Angeles (acquired by the late owner, 1955) .
EXH.: Basel, Kunsthalle, *Marc Chagall*, Nov.-Dec., 1933, no. 102 (titled *Les fiancés);* Chicago, The William Findlay Gallery, *Chagall, Utrillo, Vlaminck, Important Loan Exhibition to benifit the Scolarship Fund*, School of The Art Institute of Chicago, Oct., 1961, no. 4.

Christie's New York, 8 November 1995 (217**) US$ 497,500	US$	497,500

L'ACROBAT ET LE MUSICIEN gouache on paper, 25 x 19 1/4in. (63.5 x 48.9cm.) l center 'Marc Chagall'

Christie's New York, 8 November 1995 (243**) US$ 200,500	US$	200,500

LA FIANCÉE REVANT oil on canvas, 22 x 20 1/2in. (56 x 52cm.) lr 'Marc Chagall' (1952)
PROV.: Galerie Rosengart, Lucerne; Galerie Beyeler, Basel.
LIT.: F.Meyer, *Marc Chagall*, New York, 1963, no. 880 (illustrated) .

Christie's New York, 8 November 1995 (291**) US$ 431,500	US$	431,500

CHAMPAIGNE Philippe de (1602-1674) Flemish
CEPHALUS AND PROCRIS oil on canvas, 40¾ x 67 1/8in. (103.5 x 170.5cm.) (1620s - 1640's)

Christie's London, 19 April 1996 (250**) GBP 36,700	US$	55,648

LE SACRIFICE D'ISAAC oil on canvas, 179.5 x 149.5cm.
PROV.: Probably anonymous sale, Paris, 20 March 1780, no 168 (without dimensions); Couvent des Jésuites de la rue saint Antoine in 1790; Dépot des Grands Augustins, Paris, before 1795; Sale Th. Jos van Dooren, Tilburg, 31 May 1837 (Maltre Sala) , no 25; Private collection, Central Europe; Collection Madame Cheremitchieff, Paris, 1976.
LIT.: Anonymous, *Inventaire de l'ex couvent des ci-devant Jésuites de la rue saint Antoine*, Paris, 24 September 1790 (dans la chambre du prieur sept tableaux (dons) l'un représente le sacrifice d'Abraham par Philippe de Champaigne); A. Lenoir, *Catalogue historique et chronologique des peintures et tableaux réunis au dépot national des monuments français*, adressé au Comité d'Instruction Publique le 11 vendémiaire an III par Alexandre Lenoir.', *Revue Universelle des Arts*, XXI, 1865, p. 81, no. 126; H. Stein, *Nouvelles Archives de l'Histoire de l'Art Français*, Paris 1890, p. 122; B. Dorival, *L'information d'Histoire de l'Art*, Paris 1973, p. 56, no 2 (illustrated); B. Dorival, *Philippe de Champaigne*, Paris 1976, vol. II, pp. 12- 13, no 11 (illustrated p. 399, pl. 11) .

Étude Tajan Paris, 25 June 1996 (41**) FRF 500,000	US$	96,549

THE VISTATION oil on canvas, 31 x 40in. (77 x 99cm.)
PROV.: (Possibly) Collection of the artist, his inventaire post mortem, no.61; Cardinal de Berins, Bordeaux and Paris, and by descent; Houdot Collection; sale, Nantes, 26 Nov. 1856, lot 127; Malherbe Collection; sale, Valenciennes, 17-18 Oct. 1883, lot 13. Private collection, Eastbourne; with Newhouse Galleries, New York; Moody Collection, Texas.
LIT.: (Possibly) *Nouvelles Archives de l'Art Français*, 1892, p. 185, no. 61; B. Dorival, *Philippe de Champaigne 1602-1674*, Paris, 1976, II, p. 208, no. 473; B. Dorival, *Supplément au catalogue raisonné de l'oeuvre de Philippe de Champaigne*, Paris, 1992, pp. 19-20, no. 10, fig. 10.

Christie's London, 7 July 1995 (71A**) GBP 56,500	US$	90,126

CHAPLIN Charles (1825-1891) French
A YOUNG LADY HOLDING A BIRD'S NEST oil on canvas, 18 1/8 x 11in. (46 x 28cm.) sll 'CH Chaplin'

Christie's New York, 2 November 1995 (171**) US$ 12,650	US$	12,650

CHARCHOUNE Serge (1888-1975) Russian
UNTITLED (VIOLON RUSTIQUE) oil on canvas, 22 x 15in. (56 x 38cm.) slr; s on the reverse (1946)

Christie's London, 23 May 1996 (14**) GBP 7,820	US$	11,841

CHARRETON Victor Leon Jean Pierre (1864-1936/37) French
HIVER, CLERMONT FERRAND oil on canvas, 23 5/8 x 28½in. (60 x 72.4cm.) sll 'Victor
Charreton'
PROV.: Dudensing Galleries, New York.
      Christie's East, 30 April 1996 (22**) US$ 11,500   US$ 11,500

LE PRINTEMPS oil on board laid down on masonite, 24 x 28in. (61 x 71.1cm.) lr 'Victor Charreton'
      Christie's New York, 8 November 1995 (162**) US$ 12,650   US$ 12,650

CHASSÉRIAU Théodore (1819-1856) French
UNE CHARITÉ oil on panel, 8½ x 6¼in. (21.5 x 16cm.) 'vente Théodore Chassériau' on an old label
on the back
LIT.: Marc Sandoz, *Théodore Chassériau, catalogue raisonné des peintures et estampes*, Arts et
Métiers Graphiques Editeur, Paris, 1974 (probably mentioned as no. 69, p. 168, being number 20 at
the 'Chassériau Sale') .
      Étude Tajan Paris, 13 December 1995 (20**) FRF 45,000   US$ 9,064

CHATELET Claude Louis (1753-1794) French
VIEW OF THE PARC ST. CLOUD, PARIS oil on canvas, 23½ x 28½in. (59.7 x 72.4cm.)
      Sotheby's New York, 16 May 1996 (95**) US$ 20,700   US$ 20,700

CHECA Y SANZ Ulpiano (1860-1916) Spanish
FANTASIA oil on canvas, 11¾ x 18¼in. (29.8 x 46.3cm.) sll 'U. Checa'
      Christie's New York, 2 November 1995 (252**) US$ 12,650   US$ 12,650

CHELMINSKY Jan van (1851-1925) Polish
NAPOLEON RETREATING FROM MOSCOW oil on canvas, 28 48in. (70 x 120cm.) s 'Jan V.
Chelminsky'
      Christie's New York, 14 February 1996 (119**) US$ 20,700   US$ 20,700

CHELMONSKY Josef (1850-1914) Polish
BORDERS OF POLAND oil on canvas, 39½ x 73¼in. (110.4 x 186.1cm.) sdll inscr. 'JOSEF
CHELMONSKY? Paris 1877/ Souvenir d'un voyage en Ukraine'
PROV.: Henry C. Gibson Collection (until 1892).
EXH.: Paris, Salon of 1878.
      Christie's New York, 14 February 1996 (118**) US$ 37,950   US$ 37,950

CHIA Sandro (1946 b.) Italian
POMERIGGIO oil on canvas, 73 x 92cm. sdlr 'Chia 90'
PROV.: Galleria Mazzoli, Modena.
      Finearte Milan, 12 December 1995 (268**) ITL 27,600,000   US$ 17,315

L' HOMME ASTRAL oil on canvas, 64 1/8 x 60¾in. (162.8 x 154.3cm.) slr 'S. Chia' titled on the
reverse (1990)
PROV.: Galerie Thaddaeus Ropac, Salzburg; acquired from the above by the present owner.
EXH.: Milan, La Fondazione Mudima, *Sandro Chia*, May-June 1990; Berlin, Nationalgalerie,
Sandro Chia, September-November 1992. (illustrated in colour in the catalogue p. 185) .
      Christie's London, 19 March 1996 (76**) GBP 21,850   US$ 33,369

BRUTES AS PROTAGONISTS OF A MONKEY'S EROTIC FANTASY oil on canvas-unframed,
80 x 111¼in. (203 x 282.8cm.) sd 'Sandro Chia 79' lower right
PROV.: Sperone Westwater Fischer Gallery, New York.
      Christie's New York, 22 February 1996 (113**) US$ 26,450   US$ 26,450

L'INDUSTRIEL VIOLET oil on canvas, 68 7/8 x 53 3/8in. (175 x 135.5cm.) slr 'S Chia' titled on the
reverse (1990)

PROV.: Galerie Thaddaeus Ropac, Salzburg & Paris; Galerie Daniel Templon. Paris.
EXH.: Berlin, Nationalgalerie, 1992, p. 175, illustrated Palm Springs, The Palm Springs Desert
Museum, *Sandro Chia*, 1993, p. 175, illustrated in colour Paris, Galerie Thaddaeus Ropac, *Sandro Chia*, 1993.

Sotheby's London, 27 June 1996 (280**) GBP 16,100

US$ 24,82?

UNTITLED oil and colored oilsticks on paper, 53½ x 47½in. (135.9 x 120.7cm.) s and dedicated
"TO HENRY WITH LOVE' SANDRO CHIA' LOWER RIGHT (1987)
PROV.: Acquired directly from the artist.

Christie's New York, 8 May 1996 (120**) US$ 20,700

US$ 20,70?

THE FLIGHT OF THE BUMBLEBEES oil printed paper collage, graphite, coloured pencils and
black felt-tip pen on canvas, 82½ x 52¼in. (209.5 x 132.7cm.) sd 'Sandro Chia 1976' on the reverse
PROV.: Gian Enzo Sperone, Rome; Albert Baronian Gallery, Antwerp.

Christie's New York, 8 May 1996 (390**) US$ 34,500

US$ 34,500

CHIGHINE Alfredo (Milan 1914-1974 Pisa (Paris?)) Italian
FOGLOIE SU FONDO BRUNO oil on canvas, 92 x 73cm. sd titled '1968' on the reverse
EXH.: Milano, Galleria delle Ore, 11-24 October 1969 (illustrated) .

Christie's Milan, 20 November 1995 (86) ITL 10,017,000

US$ 6,288

FORMA ROSSO GIALLA oil on canvas, 100 x 73cm. sdlr 'A Chighine 54' sd titled on the reverse
'Giugno 54'

Sotheby's Milan, 28 May 1996 (150**) ITL 16,100,000

US$ 10,340

CHINNERY George, R.H.A. (1774-1852) British
THE GROTTO OF CAMOES oil on canvas, 13½ x 16½in. (34 x 42cm.)
LIT.: Patrick Connor, *George Chinnery*, 1993, p. 186 (illustrated pl. 65) .

Sotheby's London, 12 July 1995 (112**) GBP 62,000

US$ 98,899

THE INNER HARBOUR MAGAU, SEEN FROM THE CASA GARDENS oil on canvas, 17¼ x
13½in. (44 x 34cm.)
LIT.: Patrick Connor, *George Chinnery*, 1993, p. 187 (illustrated pl. 66) .

Sotheby's London, 12 July 1995 (113**) GBP 98,300

US$ 156,803

CHINTREUIL Antoine (1816-1873) French
LE BOIS ENSOLEILLÉE AU PARC DE MILLEMONT oil on canvas, 84 x 54in. (210 x 135cm.) s
'Chintreuil' (ca 1868)
PROV.: Commissioned by M. Maurice Richard, then Minister of Culture; M. de Coster; Clement;
Victor Doisteau; Albert Esnault-Pelterie, Paris; Bernard Lorenceau, Paris; Walter P. Chrysler Jr.,
New York; H. D. G.; sale, Paris, 5 March 1912, lot 31 (to M. Lair-Dubreuil?) .
EXH.: Paris, Palais des Champs-Elysées, *Salon de 1869*, May 1869 no. 484; Dayton, The Dayton Art
Institute, *French Paintings 1788-1929 from the Collection of Walter P. ChryslerJr.*, 25 March 22
May 1960, no. 41.
LIT.: A. de la Fizeliere, *La Vie et L'Oeuvre de Chintreuil*, Paris, 874, no. 364 (p. XXXVI); G.
I'illement, *Les Pre-Impressionistes*, Zoug, 1974, pp. 132 and 137.

Christie's London, 14 June 1996 (74**) GBP 62,000

US$ 95,605

CHIRICO Giorgio de (Volo 1888-1978 Rome) Italian
GLADIATEUR ET PHILOSOPHE oil on canvas, 18 x 13 1/8in. (45.7 x 33.4cm.) sul 'G. de Chirico'
(1927-28)
PROV.: Galleria del Millione, Milan; Mr. Tosi Milan (acquired from the above, 1946) .
LIT.: M. Fagiolo dell'Arco and P. Baldacci, *Giorgio de Chirico, Parigi 1924-1929, Dalla Nascita del
Surrealismo al Crollo di Wall Street*, Milan, 1982, no. 213 (illustrated p. 540) .

Christie's New York, 1 May 1996 (230**) US$ 90,500

US$ 90,500

VENEZIA (ISOLA SAN GIORGIO) oil on canvas, 29 7/8 x 45 5/8in. (78 x 116cm.) slr 'G. de
Chirico'; s again, titled and inscr. on the reverse 'Quesa 'Venezia' (Isola S. Giorgio) à opera autentica
da me eseguita e firmata Giorgio de Chirico' (1957)
PROV.: Galleria Santo Stefano, Venice (1958) .
EXH.: Venice, Galleria Santo Stefano, *Giorgio de Chirico*, 1958.
      Christie's New York, 1 May 1996 (406**) US$ 178,500   US$ 178,500

IL SOLE IN POLTRONA oil on canvas, 80 x 60cm. sll 'G. de Chirico' (1971)
PROV.: Turin, Galleria La Bussola.
LIT.: C. Bruni Sakraischik, *Giorgio De Chirico, Catalogo generale*, ed. Electa, Milan, vol.II, no.310.
      Finearte Milan, 19 March 1996 (49**) ITL 241,500,000   US$ 154,511

LE MUSE INQUIETANTI oil on canvas, 39¼ x 26in. (99.7 x 66cm.) s and titled on the reverse;
titled on the stretcher (1960)
LIT.: Claudio Bruni, *Catalogo Generale Giogio de Chirico: opere dal 1951 al 1971*, vol. 3, Venice,
n.d., no. 390.
      Sotheby's New York, 2 May 1996 (330**) US$ 321,500   US$ 321,500

CASTORE DOMATORE DI CAVALLI oil on canvas, 17¾ x 23 3/8in. (45.1 x 59.4cm.) slr 'G. de
Chirico' (ca. 1930)
PROV.: Nicholas M. Acquavella Galleries, New York.
      Sotheby's New York, 2 May 1996 (348**) US$ 107,000   US$ 107,000

PIAZZA D'ITALIA oil on canvas, 40 x 50cm. sll 'G. de Chirico' (1960's)
      Christie's Milan, 20 November 1995 (181**) ITL 129,635,000   US$ 81,378

DUE CAVALLI oil on canvas, 31 x 39 3/8in. (80 x 100cm.) sdll 'G. de Chirico 1927'; s and titled on
the reverse
PROV.: Galerie L'Effort Moderne (Leonce Rosenberg) , Paris; Ettore Russo, Rome; Galleria la
Barcaccia, Rome.
EXH.: Mexico City, Museo de Arte Moderno (travelling exhibition) , *Arte Italiano de 1920 a hoy*,
1966-67, no. 14.
LIT.: *Bulletin de l'Effort Moderne*, Paris, 1927, no. 35 (titled *Chevaux devant la mer*); Claudio Bruni
Sakraischik, *Catalogo generale Giorgio de Chirico, volume terzo, opere dal 1908 al 1930*, Milan,
1973, no. 228, illustrated (catalogued with the incorrect measurements and titled *Cavalli sulla
spiaggia*); Maurizio Fagiolo dell'Arco and Paolo Baldacci, *Giorgio de Chirico, Parigi 1924-1929*,
Milan, 1982, p. 519, no. 139, illustrated.
      Sotheby's London, 24 June 1996 (67**) GBP 199,500   US$ 307,633

APRES LE COMBAT oil on canvas, 18¼ x 24in. (46.5 x 61cm.) slr 'G. de Chirico' (ca 1929)
PROV.: Kunsthandel G.J. Nieuwenhuizen Segaar, The Hague, from whom purchased by the father of
the present owner circa 1960.
      Christie's London, 26 June 1996 (216**) GBP 67,500   US$ 104,086

DUE ARCHEOLOGI IN UN INTERNO oil on canvas, 80 x 60cm. sur 'G. Chirico' (1925-26)
PROV.: Collection Raffaele Carrieri, Milan; collection Riccardo Jucker, Milan.
EXH.: Como, Galleria Borromini, *Mostra di pittura contemporanea*, April-May 1944; Lausanne,
Museum Cantonale, *Quarante Ans d'Art Italien*, 1947; Salsomaggiore, *Cinquant'anni di pittura
italiana*, 1949 (catalogue under supervision of Ettore Gian Ferrari); Milan, Palazzo Reale, *Giorgio de
Chirico*, 1970, no. 71. (illustrated in the catalogue) .
      Finearte Milan, 26 October 1995 (196***) ITL 1,265,000,000   US$ 788,162

FRUTTA CON LA CUPOLA DI S PIETRO oil on canvas, 40 x 49.8cm. slr 'G de Chirico' (1940's)
PROV.: Galleria R. Rotta, Genova.
LIT.: Isabella Far, *Giorgio De Chirico*, Roma 1953 (illustrated) .
      Sotheby's Milan, 28 May 1996 (176**) ITL 84,920,000   US$ 54,541

CAVALIERI oil on canvas, 40.3 x 50cm. sll 'G de Chirico'
PROV.: Galleria Gian Ferrari, Milan.
      Sotheby's Milan, 28 May 1996 (211**) ITL 86,050,000   US$ 55,267

COMBATTIMENTO DI PURITANI oil on canvas, 40.5 x 60.5cm. slr 'G. de Chirico'; s and titled on the reverse
      Sotheby's Milan, 28 May 1996 (227**) ITL 142,550,000   US$ 915,54

CHRISTO Javacheff (Grabova 1935 b.) Bulgarian
SURROUNDED ISLANDS, PROJECT FOR BISCAYNE BAY, GREATER MIAMI, FLORIDA collage with coloured crayon, pencil, pastel, charcoal and map on card (2x) , 15 x 96in. (38 x 244 cm.) & 42 x 96in. (106.6 x 244cm.) sd and titled (1981)
PROV.: Acquired directly from the Artist by the present owner in 1981.
LIT.: To be in included in the forthcoming *Christo Catalogue Raisonné* being prepared by Daniel Varenne, Geneva.
      Christie's London, 26 October 1995 (92**) GBP 43,300   US$ 68,340

RUNNING FENCE (PROJECT FOR MARIN AND SONOMA COUNTIES, STATE OF CALIFORNIA) (a pair) a) coloured crayon on carton laid down on cardboard; b) pastel and coloured crayon on paper laid down on cardboard, a) 40 x 245cm.; b) 108 x 245cm. sd 'Christo 1975'
      Bukowskis Stockholm, 26-27 October 1995 (154**) SEK 340,000   US$ 49,794

THE PONT NEUF WRAPPED charcoal, pastel, pencil and printed architectural diagram on paper, i)15 x 95 5/8in. (38 x 243cm.) ii) 41 6/8 x 95 5/8in. (106 x 243cm.); overall: 56 11/16 x 95 5/8in. (144 x 243cm.) sdlr 1985 and titled
PROV.: Daniel Varenne, Geneva.
      Christie's London, 27 June 1996 (68**) GBP 45,500   US$ 70,162

RUNING FENCE (PROJECT FOR SONOMA AND MARIN COUNTIES, CALIFORNIA) pastel, charcoal, pencil, tape, technical data and topographical map on card, sd and titled '1976'/titled 15 x 96in. (38 x 244cm.) and 42 x 96in. (106.6 x 244cm.)
PROV.: Acquired directly from the Artist by the present owner in 1978.
      Christie's London, 30 November 1995 (36**) GBP 45,500   US$ 71,172

THE UMBRELLAS (JOINT PROJECT FOR JAPAN AND USA) enamel, coloured crayons, graphite, ball-point pen and black and white photograph on board mounted on panel, 14 x 11in. (35.5 x 28cm.) sdlr 'Christo 1991'; titled 'The Umbrellas (Joint project For Japan and USA) lower edge
PROV.: Acquired directly from the artist.
      Christie's East, 7 May 1996 (180***) US$ 12,650   US$ 12,650

RUNNING FENCE charcoal, coloured chalks, graphite, tape, map and technical data in two parts, top panel: 15 x 96in. (38.3 x 243.8cm.) , bottom panel: 42 x 96in. (106.7 x 243.8cm.) , overall: 57 x 96in. (144.9 x 243.8cm.) sd and titled l edge 'Christo 1976 Running Fence/Project for Sonoma County and Marin County, State of California/Pacific Ocean, Town of Valley Ford, State Highway, Petaluma Valley Ford Road, Freeway 101, Meacham Hill.
PROV.: Acquired directly from the artist.
EXH.: Lincoln, De Cordova Museum and Sculpture Park, *Christo Lecture Series*, Sept.-Nov. 1993.
      Christie's New York, 8 May 1996 (298**) US$ 57,500   US$ 57,500

STORE FRONT PROJECT YELLOW FROM MERTKLIN PAINT CO., INC. N.Y. oil, graphite and black crayon on board, fabric, paper, cut-out cardboard, acetate film and metal collage mounted on masonite-unframed, 22 x 28in. (55.8 x 71cm.) sdll 'Christo 65' and titled 'STORE FRONT (PROJECT YELLOW from MERKLIN PAINT CO. INC. N.Y.)' ur
      Christie's New York, 15 November 1995 (119**) US$ 40,250   US$ 40,250

CHRISTUS Petrus (Probably born in Baerle recorded Bruges 1444-1475/76) Flemish
THE VIRGIN AND CHILD oil on oak panel, image: 23 x 15¾in. (58.5 x 39.8cm.) , overall: 28 x
20½in. (71 x 52cm.) sd inscr. on the original frame 'AVE REGINA CELORV MATER REGIS
ANGELORV O MA FLOS VIRGINV VEVD ROSA VEL LILIV FVNDE RECES AD FILIV PRO
SALVTE FEDELIVM + PETRVS XPI ME FECIT Ao DI 1449'
PROV.: Count Matuschka-Greiffenklau Collection, Schloss Vollrads, Rheingau; Baron Heinrich
Thyssen-Bornemisza, by 1930.
EXH.: Munich 1930, no. 91; Paris 1970, no. 5; Dusseldorf 1970-1, no. l5; Lausanne etc., 1986-7, no.
1.
LIT.: W. Cohen, 'Ein neuaufgefundenes Werk von Petrus Christus', *Zeitschrift fur christliche Kunst*,
vol. XXI, 1908, pp. 225-30, reproduced fig. 8; A. Wauters, 'Un nouveau tableau signé et daté de
Pierre Christus', *Bulletin de l'Academie Royale de Belgique*, 1909, pp. 393ff; W.H J. Weale, 'Notes et
documents: Les Christus', *Annales de la Société d'Emulation de Bruges*, 1090, vol. 59, pp. 363-4; W.
Cohen, 'Die Austellung alter Gemälde aus Wiesbadener Privatbesitz', *Der Cicerone*, 19l0, vol. II, p.
221, reproduced; E. Durand-Greville, 'Les deux Christus', in *Revue de l 'art ancien et moderne*, vol.
XXX, 1911, pp. 44, 141, reproduced fig. 13, 199-200, 202-4; F.T. Klingelschmitt, *Mainzer
Goldgulden auf dem Eligiusbild*, 1918; M. Conway, The Van Eycks and their followers, 1921, p.
110; O. Pächt, 'Die Datierung des Brussler Beweinung des Petrus Christus', *Belvédère*, 1926, vol. IX,
p. 165; F. Dulberg, *Niederländische Malerei der Spätgotik und Renaissance*, 1929, p. 32; W.R.
Deusch, 'Sammlung Schloss Rohoncz zur Ausstellung in den neuen Pinakothek', *Die Kunstauktion*,
no. 28, July 1930, p. 152; A. L. Mayer, ' Die Ausstellung der Sammlung Schloss Rohoncz in der
neuen Pinakothek, Munich', *Pantheon*, vol. Vl, 1930, pp. 303, 308, reproduced; M.J. Friedländer, *Die
Altniederländische Malerei*, I, 1934, pp. 147-8, reproduced plate LII; J. Marix, *Les Musiciens de la
Cour de Bourgogne au XVe siècle*, 1937, pp. 189-90; R. Heinemann 1937, vol. I, no. 111, vol. II,
plate 65; W. Schone, *Dieric Bouts und Seine Schule*, 1938, p. 56, no. 10; L. van Puyvelde, *The
Flemish Primitives*, 1948, p. 27; L. Baldaß, *Jan van Eyck*, 1952, p. 62, n3; E. Panofsky, *Early
Netherlandish Painting*, 1953, p. 313, n297(1); J. Bruyn, *Van Eyck Problemen*, 1957, p. 102; J. Folie,
'Les oeuvres authentifiées des primitifs flamands', *Institut Royal du Patrimoine Artistique Bulletin*,
vol. Vl, 1963, p. 205, fig. 15; M.J. Friedländer, *Early Netherlandish Painting*, 1967, vol. I, p. 83, no.
43, reproduced plate 75; L. Gellman, *Petrus Christus*, Ph.D. Thesis, 1970, pp. 81-2, 383-5; D. de
Vos, 'De Madonna en Kindtypologie bij Rogier van der Weyden en enkele minder gekende
flemalleske voorlopers', *Jahrbuch der Berliner Museen*, vol. XIII, 1971, pp. 145-6, reproduced fig.
78; P.H. Schabacker, *Petrus Christus*, 1974, pp. 92-93, no. 7, fig. 7; J.M. Upton, *Petrus Christus -
His Place in Fifteenth Century Flemish Painting*, 1990, pp. 45, 52-55, fig. 50; M. W. Ainsworth, 'The
Art of Petrus Christus', in the exhibition catalogue *Petrus Christus - Renaissance Master of Bruges*,
New York, Metropolitan Museum, 1994, pp. 30, 38, 41-42, 61, 81, reproduced p. 28, fig. 12, p. 42,
fig. 44.

Sotheby's London, 6 December 1995 (66**) GBP 133,500　　　　US$　　　205,448

CHURCHILL Sir Winston Spencer, O.M. Hon., R.A. (1874-1965) British
GARDEN SCENE oil on canvas, 29 x 24in. (73.6 x 61cm.) s ini 'WSC' (ca 1924)
PROV.: Lady Lytton, thence by descent.
LIT.: D. Coombs, *Churchill, his Paintings*, London, 1967, p. 116, no. 67 (illustrated) .

Christie's London, 20 June 1996 (67**) GBP 25,875　　　　US$　　　39,900

THE WATER GARDEN AT CHARTWELL oil on canvas, 20 x 14in. (50.8 x 35cm.) s ini. 'WSC'
(ca 1925)
PROV.: Sarah, Lady Audley; The Studio, Chartwell.
EXH.: London, Wylma Wayne Fine Art, *Sir Winston Churchill*, June-July 1982, no. 17, pl. 14.
LIT.: D. Coombs, *Churchill, his Paintings*, London, 1967, no. 123, p. 130 (illustrated) .

Christie's London, 20 June 1996 (68**) GBP 18,400　　　　US$　　　28,373

CIARDI Emma (1879-1933) Italian
GONDOLAS ON THE GRAND CANAL, VENICE oil on panel, 14¾ x 20in. (37.5 x 50.7cm.) slr
PROV.: With the Fine Art Society, 1945.

Phillips London, 12 March 1996 (59**) GBP 9,000　　　　US$　　　13,745

CIARDI Guglielmo (Venice 1842-1917) Italian
A VIEW OF THE VENETIAN LAGOON oil on board, 24½ x 40in. (62 x 102cm.) slr
    Sotheby's London, 13 March 1996 (107***) GBP 126,900   US$ 193,800

CIFRONDI Antonio (1656-1730) Italian
A YOUNG LADY MILKING A COW oil on canvas, 122 x 82cm. (ca. 1712-15)
EXH.: P. Dal Pogetto, *Antonio Cifrondi*, Bergamo 1982, no. 500/129, p. 500, fig. 4, p. 589.
    Christie's Rome, 4 June 1996 (588**) ITL 19,000,000   US$ 12,322

**CIPPER Giacomo Francesco, {called} il Todeschini ((Bergamo and Brescia active) 1670-1738)
Italian**
GIOCATORI DI CARTE oil on canvas, 147 x 116cm
    Finearte Milan, 25 November 1995 (83**) ITL 34,500,000   US$ 21,657

CAMP CONCERT oil on canvas, 147 x 116cm
    Finearte Milan, 25 November 1995 (84**) ITL 34,500,000   US$ 21,657

CIRCLE OF THE MASTER OF FRANKFURT (CIRCA 1460-?) German
THE HOLY FAMILY ENTHRONED, ANGELS AND A LANDSCAPE BEYOND oil on panel,
72.6 x 53cm.
    Christie's Amsterdam, 13 November 1995 (66a*) NLG 25,300   US$ 15,945

CIVERCHIO Vincenzo (1470-1544) Italian
SAINT PETER, IN A FEIGNED ARCHITECTURAL NICHE oil on panel, 8¼ x 7½in. (20.9 x
19.1cm.)
PROV.: Anon, sale, Christie's, New York, June 12, 1981, lot 126 (one of a group of four) as
attributed to Carlo Crivelli ($16,000) .
    Christie's New York, 10 January 1996 (91**) US$ 27,600   US$ 27,600

SAINT JOHN THE EVANGELIST, IN A FEIGNED ARCHITECTURAL NICHE oil on panel, 8
1/16 x 7¼in. (20.5 x 18.4cm.)
PROV.: Sale: Christie's New York, 12 June 1981, lot 124 (sold as one of a group of four predella
panels, with other parts of the predella, with the suggestion that the group formed the predella of
Crivelli's altarpiece in the church of Porto San Giorgio); there acquired by the present owner.
    Sotheby's New York, 16 May 1996 (5**) US$ 10,350   US$ 10,350

**CLAESSENS Jacob {called Jacob van Utrecht} (Antwerp (?) 1506-1530 after Lübeck) German
(Dutch)**
THE ANNUNCIATION oil on panel, 57¾ x 39¼in. (146.5 x 100cm.)
PROV.: Gustav Nebehay, Berlin, by whom given to his brother-in-law, Carl Sonntag, Berlin (died
1930); By inheritance to his wife Laura, son and two daughters, at Grossdeuben, near Leipzig;
Enforced sale, Leipzig, Hans Klemm, 18-20 August 1941, without lot no., pre-empted on behalf of
the Museum der bildenden Kunste, Leipzig; Leipzig, Museum der bildenden Kunste, inv. no. 1343,
1942-1994, where labelled *Barent van Orley* ?, but in their 1979 catalogue as by *Jacob van Utrecht*;
Returned to the daughters of Carl Sonntag in 1994.
EXH.: Leipzig, Museum der bildenden Kunste, *Alte Meister aus mitteldeutschen Besitz, exhibition to
celebrate the centenary of the Kunstverein Leipzig*, May-August 1937, no. 57, as Barent van Orley,
lent by the family of Carl Sonntag.
LIT.: J.J. de Mesquita, 'Nog meer nieuw Werk van Jacob van Utrecht', in *Oud Holland*, vol. LVIII,
1941, pp. 73-4, reproduced p. 71, fig. 7; S. Heiland (ed.) , *Museum der bildenden Kunste Leipzig,
Katalog der Gemälde*. 1979. p. 100, no.1343, reproduced p. 279, as by *Jacob Claesz., called Jacob
van Utrecht*.
    Sotheby's London, 5 July 1995 (71**) GBP 117,000   US$ 186,633

CLAESZ Aert, {called} Aertgen van Leyden (1498-1564) Dutch
THE ADORATION OF THE SHEPHERDS brush and brown ink and brown wash over black chalk;

the top right corner made up; laid down, 28.8 x 20.1cm.
PROV.: Lord Broweslow; Gallery Kekko, April 1971, as *Pieter Aertsen*.
    Phillips London, 17 April 1996 (117*) GBP 6,000   US$ 9,098

CLAESZ Pieter (Burgsteinfurt 1597-1660 Haarlem (Spaarne)) Dutch (German)
AN 'ONTBIJTJE', A STILL-LIFE OF A CRAB ON A LARGE PEWTER PLATE, A BREAD ROLL
AN A PEELED LEMON ON TWO SMALLER PEWTER PLATES, ALL RESTING ON A WHITE
CLOTH, FLANKED BY A 'ROEMER' AND ENCIRCLED BY A VINE SPRAY, ALL ON A
LEDGE oil on oak panel, 30¼ x 43in. (77 x 109cm.) sdlr in monogram and on the blade of the knife
'Pc 1644.'
PROV.: Franz von Lenbach, Munich; Thence by descent until sold London, Sotheby's, 4 April 1984,
lot 82.
    Sotheby's London, 6 December 1995 (6**) GBP 84,000   US$ 129271

CLAUS Emile (Vive-Saint-Eloi 1849-1924 Astène) Belgian
BY THE RIVERSIDE oil on canvas, 45½ x 33in. (115.6 x 83.9cm.) slr 'Emile Claus'
    Christie's New York, 2 November 1995 (93**) US$ 156,500   US$ 156,500

SUNSET OVER WATERLOO BRIDGE oil on canvas, 30 x 25in. (76.2 x 63.6cm.) sd inscr. 'Emil
Claus London 16'
PROV.: Robert Younger, Baron Blanesburgh, London; The Royal Caledonian Schools; sale,
Christie's, London, 12 Dec. 1969, lot 203 (360 gns. to Pierpont Gallery); Pierpont Gallery, London,
where purchased by the previous owner.
    Christie's London, 26 June 1996 (201**) GBP 34,500   US$ 53,200

CLAVÉ Antoni (1913 b.) Spanish
LA FEMME AU COQ oil on canvas laid down on board, 32 x 23 5/8in. (81.4 x 60cm.) slr 'Clavé'
and titled on the reverse (1947)
LIT.: This work is registered at the *Archives Antoni Clavé* under no. 47 HTPN 3.
    Christie's London, 19 March 1996 (33**) GBP 19,550   US$ 29,856

LA REINE oil on paper laid down on canvas, 39 3/8 x 28¾in. (100 x 73cm.) s 'Clavé' titled on the
stretcher (1957)
PROV.: Galerie Beyeler, Basel; Dr. Bernard Zelter, Montreal.
EXH.: Basl, Galerie Beyeler, *Antoni Clavé*, April-May 1957, no. 27.
LIT.: Pierre Cabanne, *Clavé*, Paris 1979, p. 34, no. 14 (illustrated) .
    Christie's London, 30 November 1995 (26**) GBP 43,300   US$ 67,730

COQ A LA CHAISE oil on canvas, 39 1/4 x 29 1/4in. (100 x 74.3cm.) lr 'Clavé' on the reverse 'Coq
à la chaise' (1943)
PROV.: Acquired from the artist by the present owner *circa* 1951.
LIT.: J.Cassou, *Antoni Clavé*, Barcelona, 1960, pl. 25 (illustrated, p. 42); P.Seghers, *Clavé*,
Barcelona, 1972, no. 327 (illustrated, p. 321) .
    Christie's New York, 8 November 1995 (216**) US$ 33,350   US$ 33,350

ARLEQUIN oil on canvas, 31 7/8 x 25 1/2in. (81 x 64.8cm.) lr 'Clavé', on the stretcher 'CLAVÉ' and
on the reverse 'Arlequin' (1948)
PROV.: Galerie Galanis-Hentschel, Paris.
    Christie's New York, 8 November 1995 (275**) US$ 75,100   US$ 75,100

CLAYS Paul Jean Charles (Brughes 1819-1900 Brussels) Belgian
A VIEW OF THE PORT OF DUNQUERQUE WITH A THREE-MASTER SETTING OUT, A
PADDLE STEAMER IN THE DISTANCE AND A SAILING-VESSEL TACKING IN THE
FOREGROUND oil on canvas, 116 x 166cm. sd 'P.J. Clays 1841'
    Christie's Amsterdam, 26 October 1995 (66*) NLG 14,950   US$ 9,426

CLAYTON Harold (1896-1979)
SUMMER SPLENDOUR oil on canvas, 20 x 24in. (51 x 61cm.) sll 'Harold Clayton'
PROV.: Stacy Marks, Polegate, East Sussex, stock no.11.04.83 C1274.
    Christie's South Kensington, 26 October 1995 (70**) GBP 7,312   US$ 11,540

CLEMENTE Francesco (1952 b.) Italian
INTO THE CLOUD pastel and charcoal on paper, 26 3/8 x 40in. (67 x 101.5cm.) (1989)
PROV.: Anthony d'Offay Ltd., London; Edward Totah Gallery Ltd., London.
    Sotheby's London, 21 March 1996 (84**) GBP 10,350   US$ 15,806

DISCIPLINE oil on linen, 44 x 36in. (111.8 x 91.5cm.) sd and titled 'discipline Francesco Clemente 1977'
PROV.: Galerie Bruno Bischofsberger, St. Moritz.
    Christie's New York, 15 November 1995 (313**) US$ 34,500   US$ 34,500

BIRTH OF THE WIND watercolour on paper, 22 x 30 1/8in. (55.9 x 76.3cm.) sd and titled "BIRTH OF WIND' Francesco Clemente PARIS September 1990' on the reverse
PROV.: Acquired directly from the artist.
    Christie's New York, 8 May 1996 (136**) US$ 29,900   US$ 29,900

UNTITLED watercolour on paper, 23 7/8 x 18in. (59.6 x 45.7cm) sd 'Francesco Clemente 1990' on the reverse
PROV.: Galerie Beyeler, Basel.
    Christie's New York, 8 May 1996 (388**) US$ 65,200   US$ 65,200

CLEMENTSCHITSCH Arnold (Villach 1887-1970 Villach) Austiran
VOR DEM HAUS oil on canvas, 60 x 68cm. sd 'Clementschitsch 1937'
    Dorotheum Vienna, 6 December 1995 (544**) ATS 130,000   US$ 12,820

CLERICI Fabrizio (1913-1993) Italian
COUP DEUIL oil on canvas, 111 x 140cm. slr 'F. Clerici' (ca 1971)
PROV.: Rome, collection F. Fellini.
    Finearte Rome, 2 April 1996 (199**) ITL 32,200,000   US$ 20,575

LO SPECCHIO oil on panel, 41.5 x 60cm. sll 'Clerici'
    Christie's Milan, 20 November 1995 (192**) ITL 10,607,000   US$ 6,659

CLEVE Hendrick van (Antwerp 1525-1589) Flemish
NIMROD UNDERING THE CONSTRUCTION OF THE TOWER OF BABEL oil on copper, 19 3/8 x 26in. (49.2 x 66cm.) the copper support is stamped with Pieter Staes's maker's mark, the coat-of-arms of the city of Antwerp and dated 1609
    Christie's London, 20 October 1995 (28**) GBP 19,550   US$ 30,855

CLEVE Joos van (attr.) (Cleve (?) 1485 c.-1540/41 Antwerp) Flemish
VIRGIN WITH CHRIST STANDING ON A PILLOW oil on panel, 14 x 10¾in (35.6 x 27.3cm.) inscr.ul ':IHS:' inscr.ur ':Maria:'
    Sotheby's New York, 16 May 1996 (2**) US$ 233,500   US$ 233,500

A PORTRAIT OF A MAN WITH A GLOVE oil on panel, 24¼ x 18½in. (61.8 x 46.7cm.) (around 1520)
PROV.: Baron Heinrich Thyssen-Bornemizsa, by 1937.
EXH.: Düsseldorf 1970-71, no. 16; Lausanne etc. 1986-87, no. 5.
LIT.: R. Heinemann 1937, vol. I, no. 85, vol. II, plate 92; J.O. Hand, *Joos van Cleve*, PhD. Thesis, Princeton, 1978.
    Sotheby's London, 6 December 1995 (71**) GBP 36,700   US$ 56,479

CLEVE Marten I van (Circle of) (1527-1581) Flemish
LA CUISINE DES TETES oil on panel, 39 x 55.5cm.
LIT.: A. Wijsman, *De Legende van de bakker van Eeclo*, Oud Holland, LIV, 1937, pp. 173/74; K.
Hazelzet, *Heethoofden, misbaksels en halve garen*, 1988, pp. 49,51 and 58, fig. 48.
        Christie's Amsterdam, 7 May 1996 (128**) NLG 32,200   US$ 18,776

CLEVELEY SEN. John ((fl. 1726-1777) British
DEPTFORD SHIPYARD oil on canvas, 42¾ x 71in. (108.5 x 180cm.) sdll 'I Cleveley. Pinxit 1754'
        Sotheby's London, 12 July 1995 (7**) GBP 199,500   US$ 318,233

THE LANDING OF PRINCESS CHARLOTTE AT HARWICH IN 1761 oil on canvas, 34½ x 67in.
(87 x 170in.) sd 'Cleveley Pinx. 1762' inscr. 'The Landing of /Her Majesty/ Queen Charlotte/ at
Harwich/in 1762/ painted for Queen/Charlotte' (on an old label)
PROV.: Presented to the Albert Institute, May 1881, by M.S. Campbell, J.P. of the High Street,
Windsor (according to an old label) .
        Christie's London, 18 April 1996 (29**) GBP 43,300   US$ 65,656

A SHIP-RIGGED NAVAL SLOOP IN THREE POSITIONS oil on canvas, 35 x 53in. (89 x134cm.)
sdll 'I. Cleveley Pinx:/1761'
        Christie's London, 10 November 1995 (49**) GBP 43,300   US$ 67,730

CLOAR Carroll (1913 b.) American
ABANDONED RAILROAD STATION tempera on masonite, 20 x 26in. (50.8 x 66cm.) sll 'Carroll
Cloar'
PROV.: The Downtown Gallery, New York.
        Christie's East, 28 November 1995 (254*) US$ 16,100   US$ 16,100

CLOSE Chuck (1940 b.-) American
PHIL finger prints and black ink on paper, 15½ x 11in. (39.4 x 27.9cm.) sd 'Chuck Close 1980' on
the reverse
PROV.: The Pace Gallery, New York; Jeffrey Hoffeld, New York.
EXH.: New York, Isidore Ducasse Fine Arts, *Photorealism:The Early Years*, Sept.-Dec. 1991, p.18
(ill.); Palm Beach, Jack Wright Gallery, *Really, Real, Realism Show*, Jan. 1993; Philadelphia,
University of Pennsylvania, Institute of Contemporary Art, Omaha, Joselyn Art Museum, and
Greensboro, Wheatherspoon Art Gallery, *Face Off: The Portrait in Recent Art Exhibition Itinerary*,
Sept. 1994-May 1995.
LIT.: L.Lyons and R.Storr, *Chuck Close*, New York 1987, p.98 (ill.); L.Meisel, *Photorealism Since
1980*, New York 1993, p.99 (ill.) .
        Christie's New York, 8 May 1996 (321**) US$ 29,900   US$ 29,900

CLOUGH Prunella (1919 b.) British
NETS AND ANCHOR oil on canvasboard, 27¾ x 1903/4in. (70.5 x 50cm.) slr 'Clough'
PROV.: David Carr, thence by descent.
EXH.: London, Leger Gallery, *Recent Paintings by Prunella Clough*, March-April 1947, no. 9.
        Christie's London, 22 May 1996 (9**) GBP 8,625   US$ 13,060

CLYMER John Ford (1907-1989) American
THE LEDGE oil on masonite, 20 x 24in. (51 x 61.5cm.) slr 'John Clymer'; inscr. with title and
'Mountain Goat' on the reverse
PROV.: Grand Central Art Galleries, Inc., New York.
        Christie's East, 28 November 1995 (142*) US$ 10,925   US$ 10,925

COCCORANTE Leonardo (Napels 1680-1750) Italian
ARCHITECTURE WITH FIGURES oil on canvas, diameter 51cm.
        Finearte Milan, 11 June 1996 (5**) ITL 34,500,000   US$ 22,374

COCK César (Ghent 1823-1904) Belgian
A BROOK IN A FOREST oil on canvas, 70 x 51.5cm. sdlr 'Cesar de Cock 1880'
    Christie's Amsterdam, 26 October 1995 (69**) NLG 20,700   US$ 13,052

ANGLERS BY A RIVER oil on canvas, 19¼ x 27½in. (48.9 x 69.8cm.) sd 'Cesar de Cock/1873'
    Christie's South Kensington, 14 March 1996 (75**) GBP 12,650   US$ 19,319

COCK Jan Wellens de (Leyden 1480 c.-1526 c. Antwerp) Dutch
HELL oil on panel, 9½ x 12½in. (24.1 x 31.8cm.)
PROV.: A.J. Pani, Paris (Sale: Kende Galleries, New York, 17 December 1942, lot 42); Sale:
Sotheby's New York, 19 January 1984, lot 105; Sale; Sotheby's New York, 11 January 1990, lot 37
($ 65,000) where acquired by the present owner.
LIT.: M. J. Friedländer, *Early Netherlandisch Painting*, 1974, XI, p. 79, no. 121, plate 98.
    Sotheby's New York, 11 January 1996 (187**) US$ 43,700   US$ 43,700

COCK Jan Wellens de (attr.) (Leyden 1480 c.-1526 c. Antwerp) Dutch
CALVARY oil on panel, 67¾ x 47½in. (172 x 120.5cm.) inscr. 'L.C.A.(?) '
PROV.: Hugh Robert Hughes (1827-1911) , Kinmel Park, Clwyd; With R.W. de Vries, Amsterdam;
Private Collection, Paris, 1927; Achillio Chiesa, Milan, his sale, Milan, April 1928; With L. Bellini,
Florence, from whom purchased by the grandparents of the present owner in 1933.
EXH.: Possibly London, Royal Academy, 1887, no. 200, as 'German School - The Day of
Crucifixion', lent by H.R. Hughes; Bruges, *Exposition des Primitifs Flamands et d 'Art Ancien*, 1902,
no. 354, as artist unknown; Reputedly London, Burlington Fine Arts Club, 1911, according to an
inscription on a label affixed to the reverse.
LIT.: G. Hulin de Loo, *Catalogue Critique*, 1902, pp. 99,115, no. 354, as Dutch School;
F. Dulberg, 'Frühholländer in der Schweiz', in *Anzeiger fur Alterkamskunde*, 1902-3, p. 160-7, as
studio of *Cornelis Engelbrechtsz*; MJ. Friedländer, 'Die Antwerpener Manieristen von 1520', in
Jahrbuch der Preussischen Kunstammlungen, xxxvi, 1915, pp. 65-70, as attributed to Jan de Beer; F.
Winkler, *Die Altniederländische Malerei*, 1924, p. 214, as Jan de Cock; P. Wescher, 'Um Jan de
Cock', in *Zeitschrift fur bildende Kunst*, 1925-6, vol. LIX, pp. 147-54, as by or after Jan de Cock; F.
Winkler, 'Durerstudien', in *Jahrbuch der Preussischen Kunstammlungen*, 50, 1929, p.l64, as Jan de
Cock; MJ. Friedländer, *Die Altniederländische Malerei*, 1934, vol. Xl, p. 126, no. 107, as by Jan de
Cock; N. Beets, 'Zestiende-eeuwsche Kunstenaars iv. Lucas Corneliszoon de Kock. 3. *De*
schilderijen van Lucas Cornelisz de Kock en van Cornelis Cornelisz. Kunst. Ex. cat 'Jan Wellens de
Cock', in Oud Holland, LIII, 1936, pp. 71-2, reproduced fig. 62, as attributed to *Cornelis Cornelisz.*
Kunst or his brother Lucas Cornelisz de Kock; F. Winkler, *Die Zeichnungen Albrecht Durer*s, 1937,
vol. II, p. 43, note 6; CJ. Hoogewerff, De Noord-Nederlandsche Schilderkunst, 1939, vol. III, p. 340,
reproduced fig. 180, as *workshop of Cornelis Engelbrechtsz*; M. J. Friedländer, 'Jan de Cock oder
Lucas Kock', in *Miscellanea*; Leo van Puyvelde, 1949, pp. 84-8, re-confirming the earlier attribution
to Jan de Cock; W.R. Valentiner, 'Notes on the so-called Jan de Cock', in *The Art Quarterly*, vol.
XIII, 1950, pp. 60-64; N. Beets, 'Nog eens 'Jan Wellens de Cock' en de zonen van Cornelis
Engelbrechtsz: Peter Cornelis Kunst, Cornelis Cornelisz Kunst, Lucas Cornelisz de Kock', in *Oud*
Holland, LXVII, 1952, pp. 15-17, reproduced fig. 10, as attributed to Cornelis Cornelisz.; B. Lossky,
'Peintures inspirées du Grand Calvaire d'Albert Durer, in *La Revue des Arts*, IX, 1959, no. 4; M. J.
Friedländer, ed. H. Pauwels, *Early Netherlandish Painting: The Antwerp Mannerists and Adriaen*
Isenbrandt, 1974, vol. XI, p. 78, no. 107, reproduced plate 91, fig. 107, as by *Jan de Cock*; K Ertz,
Jan Brueghel de Altere, 1979, pp. 436-9, reproduced p. 437, fig. 526, as *Jan de Cock*.
    Sotheby's London, 5 July 1995 (24**) GBP 210,500   US$ 335,779

CODAZZI Viviano (Bergamo 1604-1670 Rome) Italian
ARCHITECTURAL CAPRICCIO WITH THE 'ARSENALE DI CIVITAVECCHIO' oil on canvas,
70 x 102cm.
    Christie's Rome, 21 November 1995 (252**) ITL 30,000,000   US$ 18,832

CHRIST EXPELSES THE MERCHANTS FROM THE TEMPLE oil on canvas, 125 x 175cm.
    Christie's Rome, 21 November 1995 (254**) ITL 32,000,000   US$ 20,088

BANDITS IN A ROMAN RUIN AND BATHING SCENE WITH ELEGANTLY DRESSED
FIGURES STROLLING IN AN ARCHITECTURAL SETTING oil on canvas (a pair) , each: 29½ x
57½in. (74.9 x 146.1cm.)

<blockquote>Sotheby's New York, 16 May 1996 (261**) US$ 34,500</blockquote>

	US$	34,500

CODAZZI Viviano (with Artemisia Gentileschi (1593-ca. 1652) and Domenico Gargiulo (1612-1675)) (Bergamo 1604-1670 Rome) Italian

SUSANNAH AND THE ELDERS oil on canvas, 104 x 82¾in. (265 x 210cm.)
PROV.: Probably Luigi Romeo, Barone di San Luigi, Naples, before 1642.
EXH.: Bernardo de Dominici, *Vite de'pittori, scultori, ed architetti napoletani*, vol. III, 1742, pp.
198-9; 'Notable Works of Art now on the Market', *Burlington Magazine*, vol. CV, June 1963,
supplement; E. Brunetti, L. Trezzani and L. Laureati, 'Viviano Cocazzi', in *I Pittori Bergamaschi dal
XIII al XIX secolo, Il Seicento*, I, 1983, p. 706, no. 161, under missing works; N. Spinosa, *La pittura
napoletana del '600*, 1984, reproduced plate 424 and colour plate VII; M.D. Garrard, *Artemisia
Centileschi*, 1989, pp. 121-2,516 n.212, as untraced; R. Contini, in the exhibition catalogue,
Artemisia, Florence, Casa Buonarotti, 1991, pp. 113, 179; D. Ryley Marshall, *Viviano and Niccolo
Codazzi and the Baroque Architectural Fantasy*, 1993, pp. 153-55, no. VC56.

<blockquote>Sotheby's London, 6 December 1995 (53**) GBP 194,000</blockquote>

	US$	298,553

CODDE Pieter Jacobsz. (Amsterdam 1599-1678 Amsterdam) Dutch

GROUPPORTRAIT OF THREE CHILDREN DRESSED UP AS HUNTERS IN A LANDSCAPE
oil on copper, 28.7 x 35.7cm. (ca. 1650)

<blockquote>Hauswedell & Nolte Cologne, 6 June 1996 (27*) DEM 10,000</blockquote>

	US$	6,497

MUSIKALISCHE SZENE oil on panel, 38.5 x 32cm.

<blockquote>Lempertz Cologne, 15 November 1995 (1220**) DEM 20,000</blockquote>

	US$	14,116

A MUSICAL PARTY SEATED AROUND A TABLE IN AN INTERIOR oil on oak panel, 14¾ x
21in. (37.5 x 53cm.) sd mono. 'PC. 1639'
PROV.: With D. Hoogendijk, Amsterdam; With Galerie Heinemann-Fleischmann, Munich, 1929, by
whom presumably sold to Baron Heinrich Thyssen-Bornemisza, by 1930.
EXH.: Munich 1930, no. 76; On Loan to the Kunstmuseum, Basel, 1975-1985; Paris 1970, no. 22,
plate 6; Düsseldorf 1970-71, no. 17; Lausanne etc., 1986-87, no. 26.
LIT.: R. Heinemann 1937, vol. I, no. 88.

<blockquote>Sotheby's London, 6 December 1995 (109**) GBP 54,300</blockquote>

	US$	83,564

ELEGANT COMPANY MAKING MUSIC oil on panel, 12¼ x 16 1/8in. (31.4 x 41cm) s mono. 'PC'
(on the score) (around 1630)
PROV.: P. Smidt van Gelder, Amsterdam; sale Moos, Geneva, 7 April 1933, lot 6; Anon sale,
Christie's 11 Dec. 1984, lot 105; with Johnny van Haeften, London, 1985; with Robert Noortman,
Maastricht and London.

<blockquote>Christie's London, 7 July 1995 (54**) GBP 45,500</blockquote>

	US$	72,579

COECKE VAN AELST Pieter (Aelst 1502-1550 Brussels) Flemish

MADONNA AND CHILD ENTHRONED WITH SAINT JOSEPH READING shaped top, oil on
panel, 34 x 22in. (86.4 x 55.9cm.)

<blockquote>Sotheby's New York, 11 January 1996 (64**) US$ 57,500</blockquote>

	US$	57,500

SUSANNAH AND ELDERS oil on panel, 107.5 x 87.5cm

<blockquote>Finearte Milan, 25 November 1995 (72*) ITL 21,850,000</blockquote>

	US$	13,716

COELENBIER Jan (Courtrai 1,600 c.-1677 Haarlem) Dutch

VILLAGE NEAR A RIVER oil on panel (an oval) , 40 x 53cm. s 'Jan Coelenbier'
LIT.: Hans-Ulrich Beck, *Künstler um Jan van Goyen*, 1991, p. 108, no. 110.

<blockquote>Dorotheum Vienna, 6 March 1996 (292**) ATS 160,000</blockquote>

	US$	15,391

COFFERMANS Marcellus (1549 - after 1575, active-) Flemish
THE ANNUNCIATION AND THE VISITATION (A PAIR) oil on panel, wings of an altarpiece, 22 3/8 x 7 1/8in. (56.8 x 18.1cm.)
PROV.: The Hon. Mrs. V. Charteris, by whom bequeated to the present owner.
           Christie's London, 7 July 1995 (258**) GBP 21,850   US$ 34,854

COLE George Vicat, R.A. (1833-1893) British
CORNFELD oil on canvas, 19 x 32in. (48.2 x 81.3cm.) sd mono. 'GVC 1890'
PROV.: Bought from the Artist by Arthur Tooth for GBP 250.
           Christie's London, 29 March 1996 (150**) GBP 17,825   US$ 27,222

COLEMAN William Stephen (1829/30-1904) British
THE TOY BOAT oil no canvas, 24 x 36in. (74 x 92cm.) sdll 'W.S. Coleman/1903'
           Christie's New York, 14 February 1996 (15**) US$ 11,500   US$ 11,500

COLLE Raffaellino del (attr.) (1,500 c.-1566 Sansepolcro) Italian
THE HOLY FAMILY WITH SAINT ANNE AND THE INFANT SAINT JOHN THE BAPTIST oil on panel, 49.½ x 41¼in. (126 x 105cm.)
           Sotheby's London, 6 December 1995 (164**) GBP 20,700   US$ 31,856

COLLIER Evert (or Edward) (Breda 1640 c.-1706 Leyden) Dutch
STILL-LIFE WITH GLOBE, VIOLIN AND MUSIC BOOK oil on canvas, 35 x 29cm. sdlr 'E. Collier f 1688'
           Dorotheum Vienna, 6 March 1996 (20**) ATS 110,000   US$ 10,581

STILL-LIFE oil on canvas, 70 x 91cm.
           Dorotheum Vienna, 6 March 1996 (294**) ATS 80,000   US$ 7,695

A TROMPE L'OEIL OF LETTERS, PAMPHLETS, A QUILL, SEALING WAXES, A MINIATURE OF CHARLES I AND OTHER OBJECTS oil on canvas, 32¾ x 19in. (83.5 x 48.5cm.) scr 'E.Collier'
           Phillips London, 18 June 1996 (35**) GBP 15,000   US$ 23,130

TROMPE L'OEIL OF A PRINT SHOWING AN ALLEGORY OF SIGHT AFFIXED TO PINE PANELLING oil on canvas, 17 x 13¼in. (43.2 x 34cm.) sd on the feigned print 'Edward Collier.fecit/Leyden 1706.'
PROV.: Anon. sale, Stockholm, Bukowski, 26 April 1983, lot 744.
           Sotheby's London, 18 October 1995 (91**) GBP 8,050   US$ 12,705

COLLINS Charles (c. 1680-1744 d.) British
ORNAMENTAL BIRDS IN A LANDSCAPE oil on canvas (a set of three paintings) , each: 18 x 13in. (46 x 35½cm.) one slr 'Chars Collins. 1736'
PROV.: The Gilbey family.
           Sotheby's London, 12 July 1995 (125**) GBP 54,300   US$ 86,617

COLMAN Samuel (1832-1920) American
TORRE DEL VINO, ALHAMBRA oil on canvas, 15 5/8 x 12½in. (39.8 x 31.9cm.) slr 'S. Colman'
           Christie's New York, 13 September 1995 (32*) US$ 7,475   US$ 7,475

COMERRE Léon François (1850-1916) French
LOUISE THEO IN THE ROLE OF LA JOLIE PARFUMEUSE oil on canvas, 78¾ x 39¾in. (,200 x 101cm.) sd '1886'
EXH.: Paris, *Salon de 1886*, no. 566.
LIT.: George Comerre & Denise Lion-Comerre, *Leon Comerre*, Paris 1980, p. 61 (illus. p. 68); Louis Enault, *Paris-Salon 1886*, Paris 1886 (illus. p. 45); *Salon de 1886 Catalogue Illustré*, Paris 1886.
           Sotheby's Arcade Auctions New York, 17 January 1996 (416*) US$ 8,050   US$ 8,050

COMPTON Edward Theodor (London 1849-1921) British
VIEW ON CORTINA D'AMPEZZO oil on canvas, 72 x 122cm. sd 'E.T. Compton 1918'
Dorotheum Vienna, 17 April 1996 (499**) ATS 350,000   US$ 33,070

CONCA Sebastiano (Gaeta 1680-1764) Italian
RACHEL AT THE WELL oil on canvas, 28 x 38¼in. (71.1 x 97.2cm.)
Sotheby's New York, 11 January 1996 (127**) US$ 32,200   US$ 32,200

JOSEPH'S DREAM oil on canvas, 31¼ x 24½in. (79.5 x 62.2cm.) sdlr 'Sebast°.Conca f. Anno.
1727.'
Sotheby's London, 18 October 1995 (6**) GBP 9,775   US$ 15,428

I TRE MAGI SI CONGEDANO DA ERODE oil on canvas, 77 x 145.5cm.
Finearte Rome, 22 November 1995 (159**) ITL 575,00,000   US$ 36,095

CONCA Sebastiano (attr.) (1680-1764) Italian
THE APPARITION OF FAITH APPEARING TO SAINT BENEDICT oil on canvas, arched top,
24½ x 14 3/8in. (62.2 x 36.5cm.)
Sotheby's New York, 16 May 1996 (188**) US$ 18,750   US$ 18,750

CONINCK David de (Antwerp 1643/46-1699 Brussels) Flemish
A DOG SNARLING AT A CAT AND A DOG WITH DEAD GAME oil on canvas, 29 5/8 x 39in.
(75.2 x 99.1cm.) a pair
PROV.: Dunraven Limerick Estates Company, 1965, on loan to the Dunraven Arms Hotel, according
to a label on the reverse.
Christie's South Kensington, 18 april 1996 (273**) GBP 9,200   US$ 13,950

A HUNTING STILL LIFE WITH A DEAD HARE, BIRDS AND SPANIELS oil on canvas, 22 x
27in. (55.9 x 68.6cm.)
PROV.: Dr. Robertson (acc. to an inscription on the stretcher) , when attributed to Jan Feyt; Mrs,
Saunders, Seaforth, Edinburgh.
Christie's London, 7 July 1995 (209**) GBP 17,825   US$ 28,434

CONINCXLOO Gillis III van (Antwerp 1544-1607 Amsterdam) Flemish
WOODED LANDSCAPE WITH GAMEHUNTERS oil on panel, 74 x 107cm.
Dorotheum Vienna, 6 March 1996 (316**) ATS 350,000   US$ 33,667

A WOODED LANDSCAPE WITH MEN HUNTING oil on panel, 13½ x 19¾in. (34.5 x 50.5cm.)
(between 1599-1603)
LIT.: Prof. H.G. Franz, in the exhibition catalogue, Erkenbert Museum, Frankenthal, *Frankenthal um
1600*, 1995, p. 104 (illustrated); This painting will be included in the forthcoming *catalogue on
Coninxloo*, currently being prepared by Dr. Jan Briels.
Sotheby's London, 17 April 1996 (57**) GBP 28,750   US$ 43,594

THE HOLY FAMILY WITH SAINT ANNE oil on panel, 29¼ x 25¾in. (74 x 65.3cm.)
Sotheby's London, 5 July 1995 (228**) GBP 26,450   US$ 42,192

CONOR William, R.H.A., P.R.U.A. (1884-1968) British
RETURNING FROM THE FAIR oil on canvas, 16 x 20in. (41 x 51cm.) sll 'Conor'
PROV.: James Gorry, 1981.
Christie's London, 9 May 1996 (64**) GBP 11,500   US$ 17,414

CONSTABLE John, R.A. (East Bergholt, Suffolk 1776-1837 London) British
A DELL black chalk on buff laid paper, 13¾ x 19½in. (35 x 49.5cm.) (ca 1805)
PROV.: John Dunthorne (?); H.W. Underdown, 1921; The Rev. Gerald S. Davies, Master of
Charterhouse, d. 1927.

EXH.: London, Tate Gallery, *Constable*, June-Sept. 1991, no. 227, repr.
LIT.: Sir Charles Holmes, *Constable, Gainsborough and Lucas*, 1921; L. Parris and I. Fleming-Williams, *Constable, exhibition catalogue*, Tate Gallery, 1991, pp. 394-6, repr.
        Christie's London, 11 July 1995 (38**) GBP 34,500

       US$ 55,033

CLOUD STUDY oil on paper laid on panel, 9½ x 11¾in. (24 x 30cm.) (1822)
PROV.: Hugh Constable, grandson of the artist, from whom bought by Leggatt Brothers and sold to Frederick Anthony White, November 1899.
EXH.: Leggatt Brothers, *Exhibition of Works by John Constable*, 1899, no. 85.
        Sotheby's London, 12 July 1995 (106**) GBP 17,250

       US$ 27,516

CONSTANT Constant Anton Nieuwenhuis (Amsterdam 1920 b.-l) Dutch
MENSEN coloured crayons and watercolour on paper, 45 x 61cm. sdlr 'Constant 82'
PROV.: Collection d'Art, Amsterdam.
        Christie's Amsterdam, 5 June 1996 (358*) NLG 21,850

       US$ 12,767

COOK Howard Norton (1901-1980) American
THE BATTERY, NEW YORK oil on canvas, 16 x 20in. (40.5 x 51cm.) slr 'Howard Cook'
PROV.: Estate of Joseph Blumenthal, New York.
        Christie's East, 21 May 1996 (240**) US$ 9,775

       US$ 9,775

COOKE Edward William, R.A. (1811-1880) British
DUTCH PINKS OFF KATWIJK oil on canvas, 21¾ x 37in. (55.1 x 94cm.) sd 'E.W. Cooke/1853' and sd inscr. 'Dutch pincks off Katwijk/E.W. Cooke A.R.A.1853' on the reverse
EXH.: London, British Museum, 1853, no.136.
        Christie's London, 6 November 1995 (150A**) GBP 40,000

       US$ 62,568

A CALM DAY ON THE SCHELDT oil on canvas, 38¼ x 55½in. (97.2 x 141cm.) sd 'E.W. Cooke RA.,FRS 1870'
PROV.: Lord Brassey.
EXH.: London, Royal Academy, 1870, no. 189; Whitechapel Art Gallery, 1890.
LIT.: *Art Journal*, 1870, p.166.
        Christie's London, 7 June 1996 (588**) GBP 73,000

       US$ 112,567

COOMANS Pierre Olivier Joseph (1816-1889) Belgian
THE LAST HOUR OF POMPEI - THE HOUSE OF THE POET oil on canvas, 39¾ x 62¼in. (101 x 158.1cm.) sd 'Joseph Coomans 1869'
PROV.: Mrs. C. H. Hughes; Christie's, 5 May 1919, lot 120 (56gns. To Mitchell) .
        Christie's London, 17 November 1995 (44**) GBP 82,900

       US$ 129,673

COOPER Thomas Sidney, R.A. (1803-1902) British
ON THE KENTISH COAST BY FOLKESTONE oil on canvas, 30¼ x 49in. (77 x 124.5cm.) sdlr '1865'
EXH.: Probably at the Royal Academy, London, 1865, no. 496.
        Phillips London, 12 December 1995 (86**) GBP 10,000

       US$ 15,389

SHEEP RESTING ON THE BANKS OF A RIVER oil on panel, 9 x 12in. (22.8 x 30.5cm.) sdlr 'T. Sidney Cooper RA/1869'
PROV.: Richard Green, London.
        Christie's East, 13 February 1996 (41**) US$ 8,280

       US$ 8,280

SHEEP ON THE KENT COAST oil on canvas, 30 43in. (76.2 x 109.1cm.) s 'T. Sidney Cooper'
        Christie's London, 7 June 1996 (663**) GBP 34,500

       US$ 53,200

COOPSE Pieter (1660 - 1680 active) Dutch
NAVIRES HOLLANDAIS SUR UNE MER AGITÉE oil on oakpanel, 27.5 x 46cm. slr with mono.

'P.C'
       Étude Tajan Paris, 12 December 1995 (76**) FRF 70,000   US$ 14,100

COOSEMANS Alexander (1627-1689) Flemish
DECORATIVE STILL-LIFE WITH FRUIT, A SILVER BOWL AND A GOLDEN CUP oil on
canvas, 92 x 116cm. sll 'J. D. De Heem'
PROV.: Since 60 years in a private collection, Vienna.
       Dorotheum Vienna, 6 March 1996 (119**) ATS 650,000   US$ 62,524

A SILVER EWER ON A SILVER EIGHT-POINTED DISH, MUSICAL INSTRUMENTS AND
SCORES, FRUIT IN A 'WANLI KRAAK PORCELEIN' BOWL, A WINEGLASS, A FAÇON DE
VENISE WINEGLASS, GRAPES, LEMONS, FIGS AND HAZELNUTS ON A DRAPED TABLE,
A LANDSCAPE TROUGH A CASEMENT BEYOND oil on canvas, 27 x 39¾in. (86.6 x 101cm.) s
'A. Coosemans'
       Christie's London, 19 April 1996 (127**) GBP 67,500   US$ 102,350

FRUIT STILL-LIFE WITH GRAPES, PEACHES AND CORN oil on canvas, 59 x 80cm. s on the
stone 'Alex Coosemans f'
       Bukowskis Stockholm, 29-31 May 1996 (258**) SEK 185,000   US$ 27,208

COPLEY William (New York 1919-1996 New York) American
THINK BIG acrylic on canvas, 44¾ x 44¾in. (113.7 x 113.7cm.)
PROV.: Georges Pompidou Center, Paris.
       Christie's East, 14 November 1995 (56*) US$ 11,500   US$ 11,500

UNTITLED oil on canvas, 53 x 73cm. sdlr 'Cyply 60'
       Lempertz Cologne, 31 May 1996 (126*) DEM 16,000   US$ 10,431

**CORBUSIER Charles Edouard Jeanneret-Gris, {called} Le (La Chaux-de-Fonds 1887-1965
Roquebrune-Cap-Martin) Swiss/French**
WOMAN WITH CANDLE AND TWO FIGURES oil and pastel on paper, 18¾ x 23 7/8in. (47.6 x
60.6cm.) (ca. 1946)
PROV.: Acquired directly form the artist; By descent to the present owner.
       Sotheby's New York, 2 May 1996 (336**) US$ 23,000   US$ 23,000

CORCOS Vittorio Matteo (1859-1933) Italian
PLAYMATES oil on canvas, 36 x 28in. (91.5 x 71cm.) sur 'V. Corcos'
       Christie's New York, 22 May 1996 (241**) US$ 74,000   US$ 74,000

CORDUA Joannes (-ca. 1698/1702) unknown
AN OLD WOMAN FACING HER MIRROR, ALLEGORY ON VANITY oil on canvas, 47.5 x
39.5cm.
       Dorotheum Vienna, 11 June 1996 (143**) ATS 140,000   US$ 12,995

CORREA Benito Rebolledo (1880-1964) Chilean
A WOMAN ON A BEACH oil on canvas, 43 3/8 x 27½in. (110 x 70cm.) sdll '1938/Benito
Rebolledo'
       Christie's New York, 22 May 1996 (115**) US$ 77,300   US$ 77,300

COTTON William Henry (1880-1958) American
MOTHER AND CHILD oil on canvas, 30 x 25in. (76.2 x 63.5cm.) sdll 'William Cotton 1911'
PROV.: Estate of the artist; Mildred Cotton, Pennsylvania (the artist's wife); sale: New York,
Sotheby's, 30 April- 1 May 1980, lot 365A.
       Christie's New York, 23 May 1996 (140**) US$ 29,900   US$ 29,900

CORINTH Lovis (Tapiau 1858-1925 Zandvoort) German
DIE ROSE - PORTRAIT OF LUCIE MAINZER oil on canvas, 60 x 43cm. sdlr ' Lovis Corinth 1914'
and al 'Aetatis suae XV'
PROV.: Dr. F. Mainzer, Berlin; Private Collection Berlin.
EXH.: Berlin nationalgalerie, *Werke aus Privatbesitz*, 1923, nr 85; Berlin Nationalgalerie,
Gedächtnisausstellung Lovis Corinth, 1926, nr. 252.

Christie's Amsterdam, 5 June 1996 (248**) NLG 86,250	US$	50,394

CORNEILLE Cornelis Willem van Beverlo, {called} (Luik (Belgium) 1923 b.) Dutch
AN ABSTRACT COMPOSITION watercolour and bodycolour on paper, 46 x 61cm. sdll 'Corneille
'62'

Christie's Amsterdam, 5 June 1996 (348**) NLG 21,850	US$	12,767

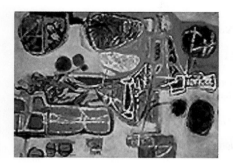

L'Ile verte et heureuse

FEMME, FLEURS ET OISEAUX PARTOUT
oil on canvas, 21¾ x 26 3/8in. (55 x 66cm.) sdul
'Corneille 50', sd and inscr. with title on the
reverse (1950)

Christie's Tel Aviv, 14 April 1996 (85**) US$ 36,800	US$	36,800

L'ILE VERTE ET HEUREUSE oil on canvas,
29 1/8 x 39 1/8in. (74 x 100cm.) sd 'Corneille
'54'
PROV.: Galerie Craven, Paris.

Christie's London, 26 October 1995 (39**) GBP 28,750	US$	45,376

JOURNÉE VÉGÉTALE oil on canvas, 32 x 39 ¼in. (81 x 100cm.) sdlr "68 Corneille'; sd and titled
on the reverse

Christie's London, 26 October 1995 (42**) GBP 9,200	US$	14,520

COMPOSITION watercolour on paper, 17½ x 22½in. (44.5 x 57cm.) sdur 'Corneille 60'
PROV.: Galerie Motta, Geneva; Acquired directly from the above by the present owner in 1966.

Sotheby's London, 27 June 1996 (100**) GBP 3,680	US$	5,675

UNTITLED gouache on paper, 50.5 x 65cm. sdlr 'Corneille. 80'

Wiener Kunst Auktionen, 27 September 1995 (406**) ATS 150,000	US$	14,581

L'OISEAU DE FETE oil on canvas, 60 x 60cm. sdul 'Corneille '79'; sd and titled on the reverse

Sotheby's Amsterdam, 7 December 1995 (241**) NLG 21,240	US$	13,161

UNTITLED gouache on paper, 40 x 49cm. sdlr 'Corneille '50'
PROV.: On loan to the Stedelijk Museum, Schiedam.

Sotheby's Amsterdam, 7 December 1995 (245**) NLG 21,240	US$	13,161

CORNELISZ Cornelis van Haarlem (Haarlem 1562-1638) Dutch
PORTRAIT OF A WOMAN oil on panel, 24.5 x 20cm. s in monogram and dul 'CH 1622'
PROV.: Prince Paul Galitzin, 1st secretary of the Russian legation, his sale, Brussels, 17-20 January
1870, lot 62.

Sotheby's Amsterdam, 6 May 1996 (21**) NLG 18290	US$	10,665

CORNELL Joseph (1904-1972) American
DESERTED PERCH mixed media box construction, 16 3/8 x 13 x 4in. (41.5 x 33 x 10.2cm.) s titled
on the reverse (1949)
PROV.: Jeanne Reynal, New York.
EXH.: New York, Egan Gallery, *Aviary by Joseph Cornell*, 1949-50, no. 17; New York, The

Solomon R. Guggenheim Museum, *Joseph Cornell*, 1967, p. 373, illustrated; Palm Springs, Palm Springs Desert Museum, *The Return of the Narrative* 1984, no. 30, illustrated; Tokyo, Gatodo Gallery, *The Crystal Cage (Portrait of Berenice)* , 1987, no. 2, illustrated; Kamakura, The Museum of Modern Art; Shiga, The Museum of Modern Art; Ohara, Museum of Art, Kawamura, The Memorial Museum of Art, *Joseph Cornell*, 1992-93, no. 14, illustrated.
LIT.: Dore Ashton, *A Joseph Cornell Album*, New York 1974 pp. 95 & 100, illustrated; Diane Waidman, *Joseph Cornell*, New York 1977, no. 78, illustrated; Sandra Leonard Starr, *Box Constructions & Collages by Joseph Cornell*, Tokyo 1987, p. 14, illustrated.
Sotheby's London, 21 March 1996 (23**) GBP 76,300   US$ 116,524

CHAMBRES INTIMES VASTE HALL paper collage, watercolour and coloured chalks on paper in artist's frame, 14¾ x 11¾in. (37.5 x 29.8cm.) s and titled "CHAMBRES INTIMES VASTE HALL' Joseph Cornell' on the reverse (ca. 1960)
PROV.: Acquired directly from the artist.
EXH.: New York, Barbara Mathes Gallery, *Joseph Cornell*, Feb. 1989; New York, Lennon Weinberg Gallery, *Joseph Cornell*, Feb.-March 1993.
Christie's New York, 22 February 1996 (9**) US$ 25,300   US$ 25,300

UNTITLED (MEDICI VARIANT) oil, printed paper mounted on board, plaster, wood, glass and painted wooden ball-box construction, 15½ x 10¾ x 4½in. (39.4 x 27.4 x 11.4cm.) s 'Joseph Cornell', on a label affixed to the reverse (ca. 1955)
PROV.: The Joseph and Robert Cornell Memorial Foundation; Richard Gray Gallery, Chicago; Private Collection, Paris.
LIT.: F.Camard, 'Collections-Claude Berri', *Galeries Magazine*, Oct.-Nov. 1990, p.188 (ill.) .
Christie's New York, 8 May 1996 (225**) US$ 96,000   US$ 96,000

COROT Camille Jean-Baptiste (1796-1875) French
LES VACHERES A LA FONTAINE oil on canvas, 22 5/8 x 32¾in. (57.5 x 83.2cm.) slr 'COROT'
PROV.: Charles François Daubigny (a gift from Corot); With Goupil & Cie., Paris (no. 13433); With Durand-Ruel, Paris (1878); Richard F. Haseltine, Washington (circa 1890); With McClees Galleries, Ardmore, Pennsylvania.
EXH.: Paris, l'École des Beaux-Arts, *Exposition de 1' Oeuvre de Corot*, 1875, no. 4 (lent by Daubigny); Paris, Durand-Ruel, *Exposition Rétrospective de Tableaux et Dessins par Maîtres Modernes* 1878, no. 88 (lent by Daubigny); Chicago, The Art Institute of Chicago, *Corot Exhibition* 1960, exhibition cattalogue.no. 138.
LIT.: A. Robaut, *l'Oeuvre de Corot*, Paris, 1965, III, no. 2415 (illustrated) .
Christie's New York, 14 February 1996 (57**) US$ 761,500   US$ 761,500

LE CHEMIN AUX POMMIERS oil on canvas, 15 x 24½in. (38.1 x 62.2cm.) slr 'COROT'
PROV.: Théodore Duret (1866-1880); Lataste Collection, Paris; Possibly Durand Ruel, Paris; Blakeslee & Co.; sale, Fifth Avenue Art Galleries, New York; August 4-5, 1893, no. 124 (illustrated); With Knoedler & Co., New York; Samuel P. Avery, Jr. (until February 14, 1902); Meyer H. Lehman (by 1902); Mrs. Harriet Lehman Weil and Mrs. Bertha Lehman; Roenheim Mrs. Elsie Rosenheim Weil and Dr. Henry Lehman Weil; George L. Weil. Washington, D.C. (by 1952).
LIT.: A. Robaut, *l`Oeuvre de Corot*, II, Paris, 1965, no. 813; (illustrated).
Christie's New York, 22 May 1996 (136**) US$ 332,500   US$ 332,500

VACHERE SUR UN COTEAU BOISE oil on panel, 8½ x 6in. (21.6 x 15.3cm.) sll 'COROT'
PROV.: With Hollander et Cremetti, London (circa 1880); Robert Pattison, Edinburgh; With William Scott & Sons, Edinburgh; Hon. Frederick Nichols With Laing Galleries, Toronto.
LIT.: This painting will be included in the fifth supplement of the *catalogue raisonné Corot* by Martin; Dieterle and André Pacitti.
Christie's New York, 22 May 1996 (138**) US$ 43,700   US$ 43,700

BATELIER A LA POINT DE L'ILE oil on canvas, 19½ x 29¼in. (49.5 x 74cm.) slr 'COROT'
PROV.: With Tedesco, Paris (1872).

	US$	321,500

Christie's New York, 22 May 1996 (139**) US$ 321,500

COUPE DES BOIS DANS LES FOSSES DES REMPARTS D`ARRAS oil on canvas, 13 x 18¼in. (33 x 46.3cm.) sll 'COROT'
PROV.: Cléophas, Paris (1871); De Villars, Paris (1872); Diot, Paris (1886).
LIT.: A. Robaut, *l'Oeuvre de Corot*, III, Paris, 1965, no. 2404 (not illustrated)This painting has been examined and authenticated by; Martin Dieterle, and will be included in *the fifth supplement of the catalogue raisonné Corot* by Martin Dieterle and André Pacitti.

	US$	123,500

Christie's New York, 22 May 1996 (140**) US$ 123,500

L'ILE HEUREUSE oil on canvas, 28 5/8 x 21 1/8in. (72.7 x 53.7cm.) sll 'COROT'
PROV.: Chtchoukine Collection, Russia (possibly purchased directly from Corot); Sears Collection; with Knoedler & Co., New York (from 1942); R.K.O. Theatres, 1958; With Hirschl & Adler, New York.
EXH.: New York, Wildenstein, *The serene world of Corot*, 11 November-12 December 1942, no. 51.
LIT.: *The Connoisseur*, vol. 171, no. 689 (July 1969); M. Pantazzi, V. Pomarede and G. Tinterow, *Corot* exh. cat. Paris, 1996, p. 368; This painting will be included in the forthcoming *fifth supplement of the Corot catalogue raisonné*, by Martin Dieterle and André Pacitti.

	US$	189,500

Christie's New York, 22 May 1996 (142**) US$ 189,500

PAYSAGE AU BORD DU LAC oil on canvas, 15¾ x 21 3/8in. (40 x 54.3cm.) slr 'COROT' (ca. 1865-70)
PROV.: G. Feuiller, Arras (ca. 1880); Possibly with max Kleber, Paris (until 1888); Possibly with Boussod, Valadon & Cie, Paris (by 5 Sept. 1888); Possibly with Knoedler & Co, New York (by 5 or 24 Sept.1888) or Goupil, New York; Mr. and Mrs Harry O. Havemeyer, New York (by 6 Dec. 1888, until 1929); Mr. and Mrs Harry O. Havemeyer Sale, New York, American Art Association, New York 10 April 1930, lot 70; O.B. Carrot, Thence by descent.
LIT.: G. World, *Splendid Legacy: The Havemeyer Collection*, exh. cat., New York 1993, pp. 310-311, no. 122 (illustrated); This painting will be included in the forthcoming fifth supplement of the *Corot catalogue raisonné*, by Martin Dieterle and André Pacitti.

	US$	55,200

Christie's New York, 22 May 1996 (143**) US$ 55,200

PAYSAGE charcoal on paper, 12¼ x 18¼in. (32 x 47.5cm.) slr 'COROT'

	US$	31,050

Christie's New York, 22 May 1996 (144**) US$ 31,050

DEUX JEUNES VACHERES DANS LA PRAIRIE AU BORD DE L'EAU oil on canvas, 16¼ x 18½in. (41.5 x 47cm.) s 'Corot' (ca 1850-55)
PROV.: Everard sale, 31 March 1881, no. 17 (6,,000 fr.); with Galerie Bernheim-Jeune, Paris; with M. Knoedler & Co., New York; with Galerie Artco-France, Paris.
EXH.: G. Bazin, *Corot*, Paris, 1942, no. 95 (illustrated); A. Robaut, *L'Oeuvre de Corot*, Paris, 1965, vol. 11, p. 314, no. 1023 (illustrated) .

	US$	205,860

Christie's London, 14 June 1996 (65**) GBP 133,500

ROUTE EN NORMANDIE oil on canvas, 7 7/8 x 12in. (20 x 30.5cm.) s 'Corot' and with inscr. 'M Corot 58. fran.' on the reverse, and inscr. '17/Corot/Route en Normandie/.7 inv.' on an old label on the reverse
LIT.: A. Robaut, *L'Oeuvre de Corot*, Paris, 1965, vol. 111, p. 124, no. 1595 (illus.) .

	US$	79,775

Christie's London, 17 November 1995 (84**) GBP 51,000

ANGLER AN EINEM BEWACHSENEM UFER oil on canvas, 38.2 x 46.3cm. slr 'Corot'
PROV.: Surville, Paris (1877); Allard et Noël, Paris (ca. 1890); Galerie Abels, Köln (um 1935); Slg. Baldus.
LIT.: A. Robaut, *L'Oeuvre de Corot*, BD. III, Paris 1965, p. 236 f., WVZ-no. 1989.

	US$	169,503

Lempertz Cologne, 18 May 1996 (1523***) DEM 260,000

LA LISEUSE (PAYSAGE) oil on canvas, 16 x 10¾in. (40.7 x 27.4cm.) slr 'COROT' (ca. 1870-1872)
PROV.: Dr. Chambaz, France (1874); Bernheim Jeune, Paris (1892); J.P. Robson, London (1907);
With Wildenstein and Co.
LIT.: A. Robaut, *L'Oeuvre de Corot*, III, Paris, 1965, no. 2390 (illustrated) .
    Christie's New York, 2 November 1995 (110**) US$ 68,500   US$ 68,500

Le Chemin aux Pommiers

VACHES SOUS DE GRANDS ARBRES oil on canvas, 9½ x 12 7/8in. (24.2 x 32.7cm.) slr
'COROT' (ca. 1873-74)
PROV.: Desavary, Arras (1874); with Galerie Georges Petit, Paris, (1881); Paulme (1917); M. Stein;
with Arthur Tooth & Sons, Ltd., London (until September 4, 1964; purchased by Richard J.;
Robertson, Connecticut) .
LIT.: A. Schoeller and J. Dieterle, *l'Oeuvre de Corot*, 2nd supplement, Paris, 1956, no.66 (illustrated)
    Christie's New York, 2 November 1995 (111**) US$ 46,000   US$ 46,000

ENVIRON DE ROTTERDAM - PETITES MAISONS AU BORD D'UN CANAL oil on canvas,
11½ x 18in. (29 x 46cm.) (1854)
PROV.: Monsieur de Borderieux, Paris (a friend of the artist, acquired circa 1855); Allard et Noel,
Paris (circa 1878); Leonard Benatov, Paris (1941); Delagrange, Paris (1947).
EXH.: Paris, Ecole des Beaux-Arts, *L 'Oeuvre de Corot*, 1875, no. 48 (titled *Canal de Harlem*);
Paris, Galerie Schmit, *Corot*, 1971, no. 29, illustrated in the catalogue.
LIT.: Alfred Robaut, *L 'Oeuvre de Corot: Catalogue raisonné et illustré*, Paris, 1905, vol.II, no. 745.
    Sotheby's London, 24 June 1996 (3**) GBP 144,500   US$ 222,822

BORD DE MER oil on canvas, (ca. 1850-55)
PROV.: Galerie Georges Petit, Paris; Darras Estate, Tours (1955); Jean Offenstadt, London (Sale:
13th July 1960, lot 124); Vente: Versailles, 20 November 1960, lot 67; Vente: Paris, Hôtel Drouot,
8th May 1967, lot 82.
LIT.: Jean Dieterle, *Corot, Troisième Supplément à l'Oeuvre de Corot* par A. Robaut et Moreau-
Nélaton, 1974, no. 17, illustrated.
    Sotheby's London, 24 June 1996 (7**) GBP 40,000   US$ 61,681

CORT Hendrik Frans de (Antwerp 1742-1810 London) Belgian
VIEW FROM THE NORTH WEST OF CASTLE HOWARD, YORKSHIRE, AND THE
MAUSOLEUM, OVER THE GREAT LIME AVENUE, WITH FIGURES AND DEER IN THE
FOREGROUND oil on panel, 41½ x 60 7/8in. (105.5 x 154.5cm.) bears mostly erased inscr. in china
white on the reverse '.sis 1800'
PROV.: Probably painted for Frederick Howard, 5th Earl of Carlisle; The painting subsequently left
the Howard family at a time unknown; Purchased late 1940's by the present owner's husband.
    Phillips London, 18 June 1996 (42**) GBP 70,000   US$ 107,941

CORTES Edouard Léon (1882-1969) French
CHILDREN IN A GARDEN oil on canvas, 13 x 18in. (33 x 45.7cm.) slr 'Edouard Cortes.'
      Phillips London, 11 June 1996 (56**) GBP 8,500   US$ 13,107

LES GRANDES BOULEVARDS, LA MADELEINE, PARIS oil on canvas, 18 x 22in. (45.8 x
55.8cm.) slr 'Edouard Cortes'
      Christie's East, 13 February 1996 (224**) US$ 16,100   US$ 16,100

PARIS, BOULEVARD ABENDSTIMMUNG oil on canvas, 22 x 15in. (55 x 38cm.) slr 'E. Cortès'
PROV.: Dobiaschofsky, Bern, 5 May 1977, lot 158.
      Sotheby's London, 17 April 1996 (748**) GBP 12,075   US$ 18,309

NOTRE DAME AND BOOKSTALLS oil on canvas, 13 x 18in. (33 x 45.7cm.) sll 'Edouard Cortes'
      Sotheby's Arcade Auctions New York, 17 January 1996 (445*) US$ 10,925   US$ 10,925

BY THE HARBOR oil on canvas, 25 1/8 x 36in. (63.8 x 91.4cm.) sll 'Edouard Cortes'
PROV.: Wally Findlay Galleries, Chicago.
      Sotheby's Arcade Auctions New York, 17 January 1996 (451*) US$ 10,925   US$ 10,925

PORTE ST. DENIS oil on canvas, 15 x 18in. (38.1 x 45.7cm.) slr 'Edouard Cortes' (1966)
      Sotheby's Arcade Auctions New York, 20 July 1995 (413*) US$ 16,100   US$ 16,100

PLACE DE LA BASTILLE oil on canvas, 18 1/8 x 21 5/8in. (46 x 54.9cm.) sll 'Edouard Cortes'; s
titled on the stretcher (ca. 1955)
      Sotheby's Arcade Auctions New York, 20 July 1995 (414*) US$ 16,100   US$ 16,100

PLACE ST. MICHEL, NOTRE DAME oil on canvas, 19½ x 25½in. (49.5 x 64.8cm) sll 'Edouard
Cortes.'
      Christie's East, 20 May 1996 (268**) US$ 13,800   US$ 13,800

PORT ST. DENIS oil on canvas, 19½ x 25½in. (49.5 x 64.8cm) sll 'Edouard Cortes'
      Christie's East, 20 May 1996 (269**) US$ 16,675   US$ 16,675

THE PORTE ST MARTIN AND THE PORTE ST. DENIS, PARIS oil on canvas, 46 x 60cm. s
'Edouard Cortes'
      Christie's Amsterdam, 25 April 1996 (177**) NLG 18,400   US$ 10,934

TROLLEYS BY THE PLACE DE LA REPUBLIQUE oil on canvas, 13 x 18¼in (33 x 4.3cm.) slr
'Edouard Cortes'
      Christie's East, 30 October 1995 (340**) US$ 16,100   US$ 16,100

FLOWER STALLS BY THE MADELEINE oil on canvas, 13 x 18in. (33 x 45.8cm.) slr "Edouard
Cortes'
      Christie's East, 30 October 1995 (341**) US$ 19,550   US$ 19,550

PORT ST. MARTIN IN WINTER oil on canvas, 18 x 22in. (45.7 x 55.8cm.) slr 'Edouard Cortes'
      Christie's East, 30 October 1995 (343**) US$ 17,250   US$ 17,250

COSSIERS Jan (1600-1671) Flemish
LE CONTEUR DE BONNE AVENTURE oil on copper, 34.5 x 48cm.
      Étude Tajan Paris, 25 June 1996 (33**) FRF 110,000   US$ 21,241

COSTA Oreste (Italy 1851) Italian
A BOUNTIFUL HARVEST OF GRAPES oil on canvas, 42½ x 31in. (108 x 78.8cm.) slr inscr
'O.Costa Firenze'
      Christie's New York, 2 November 1995 (200**) US$ 18,400   US$ 18,400

COSTANTINI Giuseppe (1850 c. born-) Italian
PICKING FLOWERS ALONG A WALLED COUNTRY PATH oil on canvas, 34 x 23¼in. (86.3 x
59cm.) slr 'Constantini'
    Christie's East, 30 October 1995 (248**) US$ 7,475   US$ 7,475

COSTANZI Placido (Rome 1690-1759) Italian
THE ANGEL APPEARING TO HAGAR AND ISHMAEL oil on canvas, 52¾ x 38in. (134 x
96.5cm.)
PROV.: Walter P. Chrysler, Jr., His Sale, New York, Sotheby's 1 June 1989, lot 63.
EXH.: Norfolk, Virginia, The Chrysler Museum, on loan, February 1977.
    Sotheby's London, 6 December 1995 (264**) GBP 9,200   US$ 14,158

COSTER Adam de (1586 c.-1643) Dutch
A BOY SINGING BY CANDLELIGHT oil on canvas, 26¾ x 20¾in. (67.9 x 52.7cm.) (ca. 1640)
    Sotheby's New York, 16 May 1996 (225**) US$ 28,750   US$ 28,750

A YOUNG BOY HOLDING A CANDLE WITH A MAN LEANING OVER HIS SHOULDER TO
LIGHT HIS PIPE oil on canvas, 36½ x 27¼in. (92.7 x 69.2cm.)
    Sotheby's Arcade Auctions New York, 17 January 1996 (145*) US$ 9,200   US$ 9,200

COTES Francis, R.A. (1725/26-1770) British
PORTRAIT OF CHARLES HOWARD, 10TH DUKE OF NORFOLK (1720-1786) THREE-
QUARTER-LENGHT, SEATED IN A BROWN SUIT TRIMMED WITH GOLD BRAID, WHITE
SHIRT AND STOCK, A PEN IN HIS RIGHT HAND, HIS LEFT ARM PLACED ON A DESK
WITH PAPERS AND BOOKS, A COLLUMN BEHIND oil on canvas, 50¼ x 40 1/8in. (127.6 x
102cm.) sd 'FCotes pxt. 1768'
PROV.: By descent in the family of the sitter to Bernard, 16th Duke of Norfolk: Christie's 11
February 1938, lot 76 (40gns. to Spiller) .
LIT.: E.M. Johnson, Francis Cotes, Oxford, 1976, no. 261.
    Christie's London, 18 April 1996 (12**) GBP 29,900   US$ 45,337

COURBET Gustave (Ornans 1819-1877 La Tour de Peilz (Switzerland)) French
APPLES, PEARS AND GRAPES ON A TABLE oil on canvas, 14¼ x 26 1/8in. (36 x 66.4cm.) s 'G.
Courbet' (ca 1871-77)
EXH.: Sydney, Queensland Art Gallery, 1959, 22.
LIT.: To be included in forthcoming *Courbet catalogue raisonné* supplement currently being
prepared by Jean-Jacques Fernier.
    Christie's London, 14 June 1996 (66**) GBP 78,500   US$ 121,049

POMMIERS A ORNANS oil on canvas, 15 x 18¼in. (38.2 x 46.4cm.) bears signature ll 'G Courbet'
PROV.: With C.W. Kraushaar, New York; Mrs. Oliver B. James.
    Christie's New York, 14 February 1996 (56**) US$ 64,100   US$ 64,100

A MILL oil on canvas, 23½ x 29in. (59.7 x 73.7cm.) bears signature and date 'G. Courbet/.73' (1873)
    Christie's New York, 22 May 1996 (167**) US$ 18,400   US$ 18,400

COURTIN Jacques François (Sens 1672-1752 Paris) French
LA PARTIE DE TRICTRAC oil on canvas, 64 x 80cm.
    Étude Tajan Paris, 12 December 1995 (98***) FRF 210,000   US$ 42,299

**COURTOIS Jacques, {called} Giacomo Cortese, Borgognone (Saint-Hippolyte 1621-1676
Rome) French**
A CAVALRY SKIRMISH BY A FORTIFICATION oil on canvas, 45.9 x 59.8cm.
    Christie's Amsterdam, 13 November 1995 (90a*) NLG 18,400   US$ 11,596

CAVALRY SKIRMISHES oil on canvas, 15½ x 29¾in. (39.4 x 60.3cm.) a pair (2)
Christie's South Kensington, 18 april 1996 (190**) GBP 6,900   US$ 10,462

COUSE Eanger Irving (1866-1936) American
SMOKE PURIFICATION oil on canvas, 46 x 35in. (106.8 x 88.8cm.) slr 'c E I Couse NA'
PROV.: The artist; Cornelia Mershon Wickes, Saginaw, Michigan; State Representative John P.
Schuch, Saginaw, Michigan; Jim Fowler, Period Gallery West, Scottsdale, Arizona; Fenn Galleries,
Ltd., Santa Fe, New Mexico; Private collection, Georgia.
EXH.: New York, Architectural League, 1912; Saginaw, Michigan, *Paintings from The Saginaw
Collection*, April 1949; Scottsdale, Arizona, Period Gallery West, *Reflections of the Old West*, 1976;
Santa Fe, New Mexico, Santa Fe Festival of the Arts, *Santa Fe Salutes*, October 1977.
LIT.: N. Woloshuk, *E. Irving Couse*, Santa Fe, New Mexico, 1976, pp. 12, 15.
Christie's New York, 23 May 1996 (111**) US$ 107,000   US$ 107,000

COWPER Frank Cadogan, R.A. (1877-1958) British
THE PATIENT GRISELDA pencil and watercolour heightened with bodycolour, 16 10in. (40.7 x
25.4cm.) signed and inscribed 'GRISELDA la pazienta/Marchesa di Saluzzo /delineata da
F.C.Cowper' and signed and inscribed 'The Patient Griselda/(see Boccaccio) /Frank Cadogan
Cowper/38 Barrow Hill Road/St. Johns Wood/N.W./No.1' on an old label on the reverse
PROV.: Sidney Morse, Campden Hill, 1906; Mrs. J.M. Morse; Christie's, 19 March 1937, lot 85 (3
gns. to Wallman) .
EXH.: London, Royal Society of Painters in Watercolours, *Summer exhibition,* 1906, no.126.
LIT.: *Studio*, XLI, 1907, p.61, (illustrated).
Christie's London, 6 November 1995 (113**) GBP 35,600   US$ 55,686

COZENS John Robert (1752-1797) British
LONDON FROM GREENWICH HILL pencil and watercolour, 20¾ x 14½in. 52.8 x 36.8cm.) sd 'Jn
Cozens 1792'
PROV.: With Agnew's, 1957.
EXH.: London, Agnew's, *Annual Exhibition of Watercolour and drawings*, 1957, no.32.
LIT.: F. Hawcroft, *Watercolours by John Robert Cozens*, exh. cat., Manchester, Whitworth Art
Gallery, and London, Victoria and Albert Museum, March-May 1971, p.34, under no.94;A. Wilton,
The Art of Alexander and John Robert Cozens, exhibition catalogue, New Haven, Yale; Centre for
British Art, September-November 1980, p.51, under no.137.
Christie's London, 30 November 1995 (10**) GBP 34,500   US$ 53,965

COZZARELLI Guidoccio di Giovanni (Siena 1450-l1516/17) Italian
THE FLIGHT INTO EGYPT tempera on panel, 11¼ x 22½in. (28.6 x 57.2cm.)
PROV.: Probably Conte Giuseppe Placidi, Siena Palmieri Nuti Palace, Siena;
Onnes van Nijenrode, Nijenrode Castle, Holland (Sale: Mensing, Amsterdam,July 4, 1933, lot 2,
illus.); Munich, private collection, before 1937; H.L. Larsen, New York (Sale: Parke-Bernet
Galleries, Inc., November 6, 1947, lot 24, illus.) , purchased by Kurt Stern.
LIT.: U. Thieme and F. Becker, *Allgemeines Lexikon der bildenden Künstler*, vol. VIII, 1913, p. 38;
Bernard Berenson, 'Quadri senza case, Il quattrocento Sienese' I, *Dedalo*, vol. XI, March, 1931, p.
642 (illustrated); *Collection Onnes de Nijenrode, du Chateau de Nijenrode*, July 4-7, 1933, p. 1, cat.
no. 2 (illustrated); Raimond van Marle, *The Development of the Italian Schools of Painting*, vol.
XVI, 1937, pp.376-378 (illustrated p. 376, fig. 215); Probably Bernard Berenson, *Italian Paintings of
the Renaissance: Central and North Italian Schools*, 1968, vol. I, p. 100 (as ex-Conte Giuseppe
Placidi); Bernard Berenson, *Homeless Paintings of the Renaissance*, 1969, pp. 56-57 (illustrated fig.
81) .
Sotheby's New York, 6 October 1996 (73*) US$ 79,500   US$ 79,500

CRABETH Wouter Pietersz. (Gouda, active 1595 c.-1644) Dutch
CHRIST AND HIS APOSTLES IN PRAYER oil on canvas, unframed, 155.6 x 197cm.
PROV.: Conrad Hinrich Donner (1774-1854), Altona; thence by descent to the present owner.
Christie's Amsterdam, 13 November 1995 (5**) NLG 25,300   US$ 15,945

CRADOCK Marmaduke (Ilchester 1660 c.-1717 London) British
A CONCERT OF EXOTIC BIRDS IN A PARK LANDSCAPE oil on canvas, 33½ x 44½in. (85 x 113cm.)
    Phillips London, 18 June 1996 (45**) GBP 12,000   US$ 18,504

CRAEN Laurens (1655 - 1664 active-) Dutch
STILL-LIFE WITH RAISINS, PEARS AND LEMONS ON A LEDGE oil on panel, 49 x 63cm.
    Étude Tajan Paris, 18 December 1995 (115**) FRF 82,000   US$ 16,517

CRAGG Tony (1948 b.-) British
KNIVE, FORK AND SPOON painted wood, plastic paper and wood, overall: 72 x 72in. (183 x 183in.) (1981)
PROV.: Lisson Gallery, London; Frederik Roos, Malmö.
    Sotheby's London, 27 June 1996 (277**) GBP 12,650   US$ 19,507

CRALI Tullio (Igalo 1910 b.) Italian
TRIESTE 3 NOVEMBRE 1918 oil on panel, 45.5 x 35.7cm s studio stamp 'Crali, Gorizia' on the reverse (ca. 1932)
EXH.: Roma, *Mostra del Bersagliere nell`Arte*, 1932 a.X.
    Finearte Rome, 14 November 1995 (119**) ITL 12,650,000   US$ 7,941

CRAMER Konrad (1888-1963) German
ZINNIAS 3 oil on board, 24 x 20in. (61 x 51cm.) sdlr 'Konrad Cramer 28'
    Christie's East, 28 November 1995 (19**) US$ 16,100   US$ 16,100

CRANACH Lucas I (1472-1553) German
DIE MADONNA MIT DEN ERDBEEREN oil on panel, 49 x 34cm.
PROV.: Slg. Pfarr-Resignat J.B. Schmitter Hug, Bad Ragaz (Cat. Ragaz 1864 no. 16); Slg. Geheimrat J. Stumpf, Berlin (sold at Lepke Berlin, May 1918, lot 49); German private collection; 500. Lempertz-Auktion, Köln; 29-11-1968, Lot 13; Private collection, Köln.
LIT.: *Velhagen und Klasings Monatshefte*, Jg. 1910/11, Bd. 1, s. 154 ff.; M.J. Friedländer and J. Rosenberg, *The paintings of Lucas Cranach*, London 1978, p. 148; Nr. 391e (likely to have been painted by Lucas Cranach the younger); D. Koeplin. T. Falk, *Lukas Cranach - Gemälde, Zeichnungen, Druckgraphik*, vol II, Basel 1974, p. 536.
    Lempertz Cologne, 15 November 1995 (1224**) DEM 300,000   US$ 211,745

LUCRETIA oil on panel, 29 7/8 x 21 5/8in. (76 x 55cm.) s with the serpent device (after 1537)
    Christie's London, 19 April 1996 (239**) GBP 89,500   US$ 135,709

CRANACH Lucas I (attr.) (1472-1553) German
VIRGIN AND CHILD WITH THE INFANT SINT JOHN THE BAPTIST AND TWO PUTTI oil on panel, 19¾ x 14¼in. (50.2 x 36.2cm.) (ca. 1538)
PROV.: Dr. Benedict & Co., Berlin; Van Diemen Galleries, New York; Mr. and Mrs. William Timken, bequeathed by Mrs. Timken in 1959 to The Metropolitan Museum of Art, New York; (Sale Sotheby's New York, 1 June 1990, lot 3, illustrated); there purchased by the present owner.
LIT.: Katherine Baetjer, *European Paintings in the Metropolitan Museum Of Art*, New York, 1980, vol I, p. 37, vol. II, (illustrated p. 297) .
    Sotheby's New York, 16 May 1996 (21**) US$ 63,000   US$ 63,000

CRAPELET Louis Amable (1822-1867) French
FIGURES WITH CAMEL ON THE BANKS OF THE NILE oil on canvas, 26 x 37¾in. (66 x 96cm.) sdlr 'Nubie'; s inscr. 'Marseille' d '1859' on the reverse (1859)
    Phillips London, 14 November 1995 (57**) GBP 5,800   US$ 9,072

CRAWFORD William, ARSA (1825-1869) British (?)
ELIZA ANNE LOCHART (NANA) (B.23.8.1848) , WILLIAM FREDERICK (BILL) (B.1.6.1855)

MIDDLETON, PLAYING CROQUET IN A GARDEN BEFORE A CORNFIELD oil on canvas,
arched top, 56 x 43½in. (142 x 110cm.)
Phillips London, 18 June 1996 (71**) GBP 9,000   US$ 13,878

PORTRAIT OF JESSIE CAROLINE (COLLA) (B.5.2.1851) , ALFRED HAROLD (B.25.3.1857)
AND ALICE EDITH (B.4.5.1861) MIDDLETON oil on canvas, arched top, 56 x 43½in. (142 x
110cm.) sdlr '1864'
Phillips London, 18 June 1996 (72**) GBP 9,000   US$ 13,878

CREMER Jan (Enschede 1940 b.) Dutch
HIROSJIMA oil and mixed media on canvas, 42 x 116.5cm sdll 'Cremer 58' sd again on the reverse
and inscr. with title on a label on the stretcher
Christie's Amsterdam, 5 June 1996 (109*) NLG 9,200   US$ 5,375

CREMONINI Leonardo (1925 b.) Italian
LE VOYAGE oil on paper laid down on canvas, 19 x 26½in. (48.2 x 67.8cm.) s with ini. and dul
'L.C. 67.69', sd again and inscr. on the reverse
PROV.: Il Gabbiano, Rome.
Christie's South Kensington, 24 June 1996 (218**) GBP 10,925   US$ 16,847

CREPIN Louis-Philippe (1772-1851) French
THE BATTLE OF MONTE-SANTO (MONT ATHOS) THE TURKISH VESSEL AND TWO
FRIGATES ARE ON FIRE; THE VESSEL SEDD-AL-BAKR IS UNSEAWORTHY, AND ITS
COMMANDER, CAPTAIN BEY CORNES ALONGSIDE THE RUSSIAN ADMIRAL'S oil on
canvas, 52½ x 78¼in. (133.4 x 198.7cm.) sdlr 'Crepin Ft/Paris 1827'
EXH.: Paris, The Salon 1827, no. 242.
Christie's New York, 22 May 1996 (104**) US$ 244,500   US$ 244,500

THE BATTLE OF MONTE-SANTO (MONT-ATHOS), 1807 BETWEEN THE RUSSIAN FLEET
UNDER THE COMMAND OF ADMIRAL SENIAVIN, AND THE TURKISH FLOTILLA,
COMMANDED BY CAPTAIN PASHA SEYDI-ALI 'THE ALGERIAN' 19 JUNE 1807 oil on
canvas, 52½ x 78¼in. (133.4 x 198.8cm.) sdlr 'Crepin Ft/Paris 1827'
EXH.: Paris, The Salon 1827, no. 243.
Christie's New York, 22 May 1996 (105**) US$ 222,500   US$ 222,500

CRESPI Giuseppe Maria {called} Spagnolo (Bologna 1665-1747) Italian
JUPITER AMONG THE CORYBANTES oil on canvas, 42 x 37in. (106.8 94cm.) (around 1728-29)
Christie's London, 7 July 1995 (104**) GBP 40,000   US$ 63,806

CRESTI Domenico, {called} Passignano (Florence 1560-1636 Florence) Italian
THE EXPULSION OF ADAM AND EVE FROM THE GARDEN oil on canvas, 72 x 60in. (182.9 x
152.4cm.)
LIT.: Compare L. Laureati, 'Brevi aggiunte al catalogo di Domenico Cresti detto il Passignano',
Scritti in onore di Guliano Briganti, 1990, p. 150, fig 3 (illustrated) .
Sotheby's New York, 11 January 1996 (112**) US$ 68,500   US$ 68,500

CRIPPA Roberto (Milan 1921-1972 Bresso) Italian
ROTAZIONE oil on canvas, 78 x 98cm. sd on the reverse (1952-53)
PROV.: Collection G. Giani, Turin.
LIT.: This painting is recorded in the *Archives R. Crippa* under number A.D.N. 269.
Finearte Milan, 12 December 1995 (235*) ITL 11,500,000   US$ 7,215

GIOCOLIERI oil on masonite, 129 x 93cm. (1955)
PROV.: Collection Gianpiero Giani.
LIT.: G. Giani, *Spazialismo*, ed. della Conchiglia, Milano 1956, no. 29.
Finearte Milan, 12 December 1995 (266**) ITL 25,300,000   US$ 15,872

CROOS Anthony Jansz. van der (The Hague 1606-1662) Dutch
DUTCH RIVERLANDSCAPE WITH FISHERMEN oil on panel, 24 x 20.5cm. (framed) slm (on driftwood) 'A.V. Croos'
Dorotheum Vienna, 17 October 1995 (79**) ATS 220,000   US$ 22,067

DUTCH RIVERLANDSCAPE WITH FISHERMEN oil on panel, 24 x 20.5cm. (framed)
LIT.: Hans-Ulbrich Beck, *Künstler um Jan van Goyen*, 1991, p. 75, ill. 144 (drawing) .
Dorotheum Vienna, 17 October 1995 (80**) ATS 200,000   US$ 20,061

A VIEW OF RHENEN FROM THE SOUTH BANK OF THE NEDERRIJN oil on canvas, 32 3/8 x 39in. (82.3 x 99cm.) sd '.S.F.1652'
PROV.: Anon. Sale, Christie's, 21 April 1989, lot 43.
Christie's London, 20 October 1995 (77**) GBP 12,650   US$ 19,965

CROOS Jacob van der (17th Century, active 2nd half) Dutch
PANORAMIC LANDSCAPE WITH A TOWN DIVIDED BY A RIVER, SAID TO BE THE CITY OF FRANKFURT oil on panel, 27 x 35in. (68.6 x 88.9cm.) inscribed ll IC and possibly d 165 (4 or 5)
PROV.: S. Nystad, The Hague by 1951, there purchased by the family of the present collector.
LIT.: H.-U. Beck, *Künstler um Jan van Goyen; Maler und Zeichner*, p. 110, cat. no. 278 (B 21) , illus. (as attributed to Anthony van der Croos) .
Sotheby's New York, 11 January 1996 (34**) US$ 63,000   US$ 63,000

CROPSEY Jasper Francis (1823-1900) American
AUTUMN LANDSCAPE oil on canvas, 12 x 20in. (30.5 x 51cm.) sdll 'J.F. Cropsey 1875'
Christie's New York, 13 September 1995 (20**) US$ 68,500   US$ 68,500

AUTUMN LANDSCAPE-SAUGERTIES, NEW YORK oil on canvas, 12 x 20in. (30.5 x 50.8cm.) sdlr 'J.F. Cropsey 1886'
PROV.: William Furman Hobbie, Plainfield, New Jersey; By descent in the family to the present owner.
Christie's New York, 13 March 1996 (39**) US$ 46,000   US$ 46,000

ON THE RAMAPO RIVER oil on canvas, 24 x 20in. (61 x 50.8cm.) sdll 'J.F. Cropsey/1888'
PROV.: Mrs. William Hawes, Warwick, New York.
LIT.: This painting will be included in the forthcoming *catalogue raisonné* of the artist's work being prepared by the Newington-Cropsey Foundation, Hastings-on-Hudson.
Christie's New York, 23 May 1996 (23**) US$ 51,750   US$ 51,750

CONVERSATION AT THE FENCE oil on canvas, 8 1/8 x 14 1/8in. (20.6 x 35.8cm.) sdll 'J.F. Cropsey 1873'
PROV.: Kenneth Lux Galleries, New York Private Collection, New York.
LIT.: This painting will be included in the forthcoming *catalogue raisonné* of the artist's work, which is being prepared by the Newington-Cropsey Foundation, Hastings-on-Hudson.
Christie's New York, 23 May 1996 (35**) US$ 25,300   US$ 25,300

AUTUMN ON THE LAKE watercolour and pencil on paper, 12½ x 11in. (32 x 28cm.) sdlr 'JF Cropsey 1892'
LIT.: This watercolour will be included in the forthcoming *catalogue raisonné* of the artist's work, which is being prepared by the Newington-Cropsey Foundation, Hastings-on-Hudson.
Christie's East, 28 November 1995 (68*) US$ 9,200   US$ 9,200

CROSATO Giovanni Batista (Venice 1686-1758) Italian
DIANA KIDNAPPING IPHIGENIE FROM ALTAR oil on panel, 84 x 96cm.
Dorotheum Vienna, 17 October 1995 (44**) ATS 140,000   US$ 14,043

CRUYS Cornelis (active ca. 1644-1660-) Dutch
A 'ROEMER', A BREAD ROLL AND PEPPER WITH AN OVERTURNED CONICAL 'ROEMER'
AND OYSTERS ON A PEWTER PLATE ON A DRAPED TABLE oil on panel, 42.8 x 35cm.
    Christie's Amsterdam, 7 May 1996 (46**) NLG 161,000   US$ 93,878

CUCUEL Edward (San Francisco 1875-1951 Los Angeles) American
QUIET WATERS oil on canvas, 20 x 23½in. (51 x 60cm.) sll 'Cucuel'; s and titled again on the
reverse with the artist's card bearing the artist's address at the Art Student's League
    Christie's New York, 13 September 1995 (93**) US$ 85,000   US$ 85,000

IM VERSTECK: THE SECRET LANDING PLACE oil on canvas, 80 x 80cm. s 'Cucuel' s titled on
the stretcher
    Christie's Amsterdam, 25 April 1996 (295***) NLG 230,000   US$ 136,669

CURRAN Charles Courtney (1861-1942) American
HIGH COUNTRY oil on canvas, 30¼ x 30¼in. (76.8 x 76.8cm.) sdll 'Charles C. Curran 1917'
PROV.: Lagakos-Turak Gallery, Philadelphia, Pennsylvania.
EXH.: Portland, Maine, Portland Musuem of Art, *Impressionism and Post Impressionism: The
Collector's Passion*, July-October 1991, no. 60, p. 101 (illustrated); Orlando, Florida, Orlando
Museum of Art, *Hidden Treasures: American Paintings from Florida Private Collections*, January-
February 1992, fig. 52, (illustrated) n.p.; Orlando, Florida, Orlando Museum of Art, *Idyllic Visions in
American Art*, March-June 1993.
    Christie's New York, 23 May 1996 (128**) US$ 46,000   US$ 46,000

CUYP Albert (Dordrecht 1620-1691 after) Dutch
GENTLEMEN AND A LADY ON A TRACK AT THE EDGE OF A WOOD WITH THE ARTIST
SKETCHING IN THE FOREGROUND oil on canvas, 39¾ x 55 1/8in. (101 x 140cm.) s 'A.cuyp.)
(1643)
PROV.: Mrs M.G. Young, Faringdon; Anon. Sale, Sotheby's, 27 March 1968, lot 49 (£7,,200 to
Agnew's); Anon. Sale, Sotheby's, 13July 1977, lot15 (£10,000) .
LIT.: 'The Chronology of Aelbert Cuyp', *The Burlington Magazine*, LXXXI, no. 475, Oct. 1942, p.
259, pp. 258-9, fig.; A.S. Reiss, *Aelbert Cuyp*, London, 1975, p. 104, no. 69, illustrated 'on the fring'
of the early Cuyp school and possibly a collaboration between two artists.
    Christie's London, 8 December 1995 (20**) GBP 144,500   US$ 222,376

FLOODED RIVER LANDSCAPE WITH TWO SHEPHERDS AND THEIR FLOCK OF SHEEP
AND GOATS oil on panel, 19 x 29in. (48.3 x 73.7cm.) slr 'A. cuyp' (1646-47)
PROV.: Possibly Baron Antrobus, Amesbury, Wiltshire; Duits and Co., London by 1967; from
whom acquired by Christian Humann, thence by descent to the present owner.
EXH.: New York, Metropolitan Museum of Art, 1968-1974.
LIT.: Possibly C. Hofstede de Groot, *A Catalogue Raisonné.*, 1909, Vol. II, no. 301; 'A Landscape by
Aelbert Cuyp,' *Duits Quarterly*, no. 12, 1968, pp. 3-7, illus. in colour (dated to about 1647); S. Reiss,
Aelbert Cuyp, 1975, p. 88, cat. no. 53, illus., as possibly Aelbert Cuyp, circa 1646; C. van Hasselt,
*Rembrandt and His Century; Dutch Drawings of the Seventeenth Century from the Collection of
Frits Lugt*, Institut Neerlandais, Paris, 1977-78, p. 43, under cat. no. 27 (he dates the painting to circa
1647); Dordrechts Museum, Dordrecht, *Aelbert Cuyp en zijn familie, schilders te Dordrecht*, 1977-
78, p. 150; Yapou, 1981, p. 160.
    Sotheby's New York, 16 May 1996 (31**) US$ 167,500   US$ 167,500

BARGES CLOSE-HAULED IN LIGHT AIRS ON A RIVER oil on panel, 12 1/8 x 16 7/8in. (30.8 x
42.9cm.) s 'A. Cuijp.' (early 1650s)
PROV.: David P. Sellar; S. Sellar, London; sale, Petit, Paris, 6 June1889, lot 11; with Galerie
Sedelmeyer, Paris (acc. to a seal on the reverse); Prince Liechtenstein, Vienna, by 1909, inv. no. 899
(acc. to a label on the reverse transferred to Vaduz at the end of the second world War.
EXH.: London, Royal academy, *Winter exhibition*, 1885, no. 114; Lucerne, Kunstmuseum,
Meisterwerke aus den Sammlungen des Fürsten von Liechtenstein, 1948, no. 155.

LIT.: C. Hofstede de Groot, *A Catalogue Raisonné*, etc., II, London, 1909 p. 193, no. 648, and p.201,
no. 671.; In 1889 did Deville an engraving after this painting.

      Christie's London, 7 July 1995 (38**) GBP 265,500   US$ 423,513

CUYP Benjamin Gerritsz. (1612-1652 after) Dutch
THE ADORATION OF THE MAGI oil on panel, 39.2x 55.8cm.

      Christie's Amsterdam, 7 May 1996 (110*) NLG 10,350   US$ 6,035

PEASANTS CAROUSING IN A TAVERN oil on panel, 41 x 54.5cm. slr 'Cuyp'

      Sotheby's Amsterdam, 14 November 1995 (18**) NLG 17,110   US$ 10,783

DA FERRARA Antonio Alberti (act. 1420-1442-) Italian
THE MADONNA OF HUMILITY tempera on gold ground panel, 14 x 13½in. (35.5 x 34.3cm.)
PROV.: With Agnew's as *Jacobello de' Fiori.*
     Christie's London, 8 December 1995 (64**) GBP 47,700   US$ 73,407

DA GAVARDO Martino (Gavardo (Brescia) doc. from 1510 until 1530 -) Italian
ENTHRONED MADONNA WITH THE CHILD oil on panel, 122 x 67cm. sd on the base of the
throne 'Opus Martini de Garvardo die 28 mtij 1510'
     Finearte Rome, 21 May 1996 (71**) ITL 41,400,000   US$ 26,590

DAEL Jan Frans van (Antwerp 1764-1840 Paris) Flemish
STILL-LIFE OF ROSES IN A BASKET RESTING ON A STONE LEDGE oil on panel, 26 7/8 x 21
5/8in. (68.3 x 54.9) sll 'Vandael'
PROV.: David Rockefeller.
     Sotheby's New York, 16 May 1996 (125**) US$ 134,500   US$ 134,500

DAHL Hans Andreas (Hardanger 1849-1937) Norwegian
ÜBER SONNIGEN WELLEN oil on canvas, 113 x 186cm. sll 'Hans Dahl/Berlin'
     Bukowskis Stockholm, 29 November-1 December 1995 (191**) SEK 125,000   US$ 18,910

LE PASSEUR oil on canvas, 86 x 136cm. sdll 'Hans Dahl 1878 Df.'
     Bukowskis Stockholm, 29-31 May 1996 (327**) SEK 115,000   US$ 16,913

Der Ausbruch der Vesuv

DAHL Johan Christian Clausen (1788-1857) Norwegian
DER AUSBRUCH DER VESUV oil on canvas, 37 x 55¼in. (94 x 140cm.) sd 'J Dahl/1824'
PROV.: purchased by Prince Christian Frederik (Christian VIII) from the artist in 1824-25.; Grevinde
Danner; sale, Copenhagen, 1874, lot 5 Private Collection and thence by descent to the present owner.
EXH.: Dresden, Academy, 1824; Copenhagen Academy 1825 no.44; Copenhagen, Exhibition at the
Academy on the occasion of the coronation of King Christian VIII and Queen Sophie Amalie, 1840,
no.22; Copenhagen, Exhibition at the academy arranged by Kunstforeningen in aid of the restoration
of Frederiksborg Castle, 1860, no.37; Copenhagen Academy 1869, no.44; Copenhagen, *Den
Nordiske Industriog Kunstudstilling*, 1872, no.810; Oslo Nasjonalgalleriet, *Dahls Dresden*, 1980,
no.69 Copenhagen, Thorvaldsens Museum, *J.C. Dahl i Italien 1820-1821*, 1987; Oslo
Nasjonalgalleriet, *Jubileumutstilling 1988*, no.81.
LIT.: C. Reitzel, *Fortegnelseover Dasnke Kunstneres arbeider paa de ved det Kgl. akademi for de*

Skjönne Kunster i Aarene 1807-1882 afholdte Charlottenborg-Udstillinger, Copenhagen, 1883, pag. 106; F. von Boetticher, *Malerwerke des 19 Jahrhunderts, Dresden, 1891-1901*, no. 10; A. Aubert, *Maleren Johan Christian Dahl*, Oslo, 1920 pp.134 and 442; P. Helsted, *Christian VIII: an Intelligent Amateur*, Apollo, 1984, p.421, (illus. fig. 2); M.L. Bang, *Johan Christian Dahl 1788-1857; Life and Works*, Oslo 1987, vol.2, p.157, no.451 (illus.pl.182).
Christie's London, 11 October 1995 (29**) GBP 309,500   US$ 488,479

DAHL Peter (1934 b.) Swedish
FÖREVIGAT oil on canvas, ,150 x 200cm. sd 'Peter Dahl 1986'
Bukowskis Stockholm, 26-27 October 1995 (20**) SEK 200,000   US$ 29,290

DALENS Dirk III (Amsterdam 1688-1753) Dutch
A FROZEN RIVER LANDSCAPE WITH SKATERS AND HORSEDRAWN SLEDGES ON THE ICE AND BUILDINGS BEYOND oil on copper, 7¼ x 10in. (18.5 x 25cm.) sll 'D.DALENS'
PROV.: Mrs. Felten, The Hague, 1965; Wolfgang Stechow, 1974; With Leonard Koetser; Anonymous Sale, London, Christie's 18 April 1980, lot 31, where bought by the present owner.
Sotheby's London, 17 April 1996 (661**) GBP 17,250   US$ 26156

DALI Salvador (Figueras 1904-1989) Spanish
PAYAGE FANTASTIQUE; MIDI HÉROIQUE oil on canvas, 20 x 18in. (50.7 x 45.7cm.) slc 'GALA S DALI' (1943)
PROV.: Carstair Gallery, New York (acquired by the present owner, ca. 1954).
EXH.: Montreal, Museum of Fine Arts, *Dali*, April-July 1990, no. 61 (illustrated in colour).
Christie's New York, 1 May 1996 (231**) US$ 365,500   US$ 365,500

LA TRES SAINTE TRINITÉ ADORÉ PAR TROIS ARCHEVEQUES gouache, watercolour, brush and grey wash on board laid down on masonite, 37¾ x 49in. (96 x 124.5cm.) sdul titled 'Dalí 1960'
PROV.: Anon. sale Parke-Bernet Galleries, Inc. New York 26 April 1961, lot 88 (US$ 9,500).
Christie's New York, 1 May 1996 (236**) US$ 101,500   US$ 101,500

LE CHEVALIER watercolour and ballpoint pen on paper, 23 x 29in. (58.4 x 73.7cm.) sdll 'Dali 1954'
Sotheby's New York, 2 May 1996 (296**) US$ 55,200   US$ 55,200

LE VOYAGEUR watercolour and soft pencil on paper, 13¾ x 18¾in. (35 x 47.5cm.) sd 'Dali 1967'
PROV.: Madame Jean Krebs, Brussels.
Christie's London, 26 June 1996 (232**) GBP 28,750   US$ 44,333

LES JUGES pen and indian ink on wove paper, 19¾ x 23 3/8in (50.2 x 59.4cm.) (ca 1933)
PROV.: Julian Green, Paris, by whom bought directly to the Artist.
LIT.: R. Descharnes, *Salvador Dali, The Work, The Man*, New York 1984 (illustrated p. 142); R. Descharnes and G. Néret *Salvador Dali 1904-1989*, Vol I, 1904-1946, Cologne, 1994 (illustrated p. 238); The drawing is recorded in the Descharnes Archives under no. D-660/570.
Christie's London, 29 November 1995 (175**) GBP 28,000   US$ 43,798

COUPLE ET TROIS HOMMES black ink transfer and pencil on paper, 23 x 19¾in. (58.4 x 50.2cm.) sdlc 'Dali 1963'
PROV.: M. Knoedler & Co., Inc., New York; Mr. William W. Brenn, Briello, New Jersey (acquired from the above, 1965).
EXH.: New York, M. Knoedler & Co., Inc., *George Keller presents Dali*, Nov.-Dec., 1963 (not listed in the catalogue).
LIT.: S. Longstreet, *The Drawings of Dali*, Alhambra, California, 1964, n.p.
Christie's East, 30 April 1996 (176*) US$ 13,,800   US$ 13,800

LE CORRIDOR DE PALLADIO AVEC SURPRISE DRAMATIQUE oil on canvas, 28¾ x 41in. (73 x 104.1cm.) sdlr 'Salvador Dali 1938'

PROV.: Mr. and Mrs. R. Kirk Askew, Jr., New York; Lily Dache, New York; Galleria Gissi, Turin; B. Valla, Turin; Segialan Anstalt, Vaduz; James Goodman Gallery, Inc., New York.
EXH.: New York, Museum of Modern Art, *Salvador Dali, Paintings, Drawings, Prints*, Nov., 1941-Jan., 1942, pp. 22 and 27, no. 40 (illustrated in color, p. 67); New York, Gallery of Modern Art, *Salvador Dali, 1910-1965*, Dec., 1965-Feb., 1966; Turin, Galleria Gissi, Temi *Cavallereschi e Religiosi nell'ultimo Salvador Dali e dipinti del Surrealismo*, 1970, no. 3 (illustrated in color); Rotterdam, Boymans-van Beuningen Museum, Dali, Nov.,1970-Jan., 1971, no. 60 (illustrated); Paris, Centre Georges Pompidou, Musée National d'Art Moderne, *Salvador Dali, retrospective 1920-1980*, Dec., 1979-April, 1980, p. 313, no. 255 (illustrated in colour); London, Tate Gallery, Salvador Dali, May-July, 1980, p. 28, no. 163; Paris, *Artcurial, Les noces catalanes: Barcelone-Paris*, 1870-1970, May-July, 1985, p. 104, no. 42; New York, Sidney Janis Gallery, *20th Century European Masters*, Dec., 1985Jan., 1986.
LIT.: R. Morse, *Dali, A Study of His Life and Work*, New York, 1958, p. 55; S. Dali, *Dali de Draeger*, New York, 1968, no. 146 (illustrated); I. Gomez de Liano, *Dali* Barcelona, 1983, no. 82 (illustrated); R. Descharnes, *Salvador Dali, The Work, The Man*, New York, 1984, p. 234 (illustrated in color); R. Descharnes, *Salvador Dali*, New York, 1985, p. 88, no. 68 (illustrated); R. Descharnes and G. Neret, *Salvador Dali, 1904-1989*, Cologne, 1994, vol. I (*The Paintings 1904-1946*), p. 300, no. 669 (illustrated in colour).
   Christie's New York, 7 November 1995 (46**) US$ 695,500   US$ 695,500

PORTRAIT DE MON FRERE MORT OIL ON CANVAS, 69 x 69in. (175.3 x 175.3cm.) sll 'Dali' (1963)
PROV.: Gala Dali, Cadaques.
EXH.: Tokyo, Hotel Prince Gallery, Salvador Dali, Sept.-Oct. 1964, pp. 118 and 132, no. 66 (illus.). The exhibition traveled to Nagoya, Prefectural Museum of Art, Oct. 1964 and Kyoto, Municipal Art Gallery, Nov. 1964; New York, Gallery of Modern Art, *Salvador Dali 1910-1965*, Dec. 1965-Feb. 1966, p. 156, no. 167 (illustrated p. 138); Stockholm, Moderna Museet, *Salvador Dali*, Dec. 1973-Feb. 1974, p. 27, no. 22; Frankfurt, Städelsches Kunstinstitut, *Salvador Dali*, March-May 1974, p. 16, no. 18; Paris, Centre Georges Pompidou, Musée National d'art Moderne, *Salvador Dali, retrospective 1920-1980*, Dec. 1979-April 1980, p. 273, no: 207 (illustrated in colour); London, Tate Gallery, *Salvador Dali*, May-July 1980, p. 30, no. 218 (illustrated in colour); Stuttgart, Staatsgalerie, *Salvador Dali 1904-1989*, May-July 1989, p. 360, no. 272 (illustrated in colour, p. 361). The exhibition traveled to Zurich, Kunsthaus, Aug.-Oct. 1989; Montreal, Museum of Fine Arts, *Salvador Dali*, April-July 1990, p. 160, no. 95 (illustrated in colour, p. 161).
LIT.: S. Dali, *Dali de Draeger*, New York 1968, no. 132 (illustrated in colour); R. Descharnes, *Salvador Dali,The Work,The Man*, New York 1984, p. 361 (illustrated in colour); R. Descharnes and G. Neret, *Salvador Dali, 1907-1989*, Cologne 1994, vol. II (*The Paintings 1946-1989*), p. 552, no 1229 (illustrated in colour).
   Christie's New York, 7 November 1995 (64**) US$ 882,500   US$ 882,500

DALLINGER VON DALLING Johann Baptis d.j. (Vienna 1782-1868 Vienna) Austrian
LANDSCAPE WITH COVERED WAGGON AND A CHURCH BEYOND oil on panel, 62 x 73.5cm. sdll 'Joh. v. Dallinger f. 1833.' inscr. d and titled on old label 'Dallinger Joh. 1833.'
PROV.: According to a label on reverse: bought by S. Durchlaucht (from Jozef Lenz); by descent on 8 June 1897.
   Wiener Kunst Auktionen, 26 September 1995 (57**) ATS 80,000   US$ 7,776

DANCE Nathaniel, R.A. (1735-1811) British
PORTRAIT OF ADMIRAL SAMUEL PITCHFORD CORNISH (1739-1816), HALF-LENGHT, IN NAVAL UNIFORM, A BATON IN HIS RIGHT HAND oil on canvas, 36 x 28in. (91.4 x 71.7cm.)
   Christie's London, 10 November 1995 (18**) GBP 6,900   US$ 10,793

DANDINI Pier (Florence 1646-1712) Italian
BACCHANAL oil on canvas, 23 x 53¼ion. (58.6 x 135.4cm.)
   Sotheby's London, 18 October 1995 (82**) GBP 13,,800   US$ 21,780

CLEOPATRA oil on canvas, 34¼ x 28¾in. (87 x 73cm.)
    Christie's London, 7 July 1995 (363**) GBP 13,225   US$ 21,096

DANDRILLON Pierre Charles (Paris 1757-1812 Paris) French
LANDSCAPE WITH AN OBELISK AND FOUNTAIN, LANDSCAPE WITH CLASSICAL
BUILDINGS ON A MOUNTAIN SIDE oil on canvas (a pair), 74¾ x 40¾in. (189.9 x 103.5cm.) sd
'dandrillon 1791'
PROV.: Possibly Mr. Roques, Dandrillon's Patron.
    Sotheby's New York, 11 January 1996 (148**) US$ 107,000   US$ 107,000

DANEDI Stefano {called il Montalto} (1608-1689) Italian
SALOMÉ oil on canvas, 94.5 x 142cm.
    Christie's Rome, 21 November 1995 (216**) ITL 9,000,000   US$ 5,650

DANIELS Andries (attributed) (1580 b.-)
A BOUQUET OF FLOWERS IN A VASE oil on panel, 64 x 51.5cm.
PROV.: Over 60 years in a private collection, Vienna.
    Dorotheum Vienna, 6 March 1996 (121**) ATS 600,000   US$ 57,715

DANTAN Edouard Joseph (1848-1897) French
UN MOULAGE SUR NATURE oil on canvas, 51½ x 40½in. (130.8 x 102.9cm.) sdll 'E.
Dantan/1887'
LIT.: A photograph of the painting is recorded in the *Photograph Archives of the Clark Art Institute*,
Williamstown, Massachusetts.
    Christie's New York, 2 November 1995 (18**) US$ 239,000   US$ 239,000

DAPHNIS Nassos (1914 b.)
35 acrylic on paper mounted on board, 11 x14in. (27.9 x 35.6cm.) sd and titled '58 Nassos Daphnis'
on the reverse
PROV.: Leo Castelli Gallery, New York.
EXH.: Wadsworth Atheneum, Hartford.
    Christie's East, 14 November 1995 (41*) US$ 7,820   US$ 7,820

DARGELAS André Henri (1828-1906) French
BLIND MAN'S BUFF oil on panel, 7 x 10¼in. (17.8 x 26cm.) s 'Dargelas'
    Christie's South Kensington, 12 October 1995 (176**) GBP 6,525   US$ 10,298

DARNAUT Hugo (Dessau 1851-1937 Vienna) Austrian
MOTIV AUS MÄHREN oil on board, 43 x 56cm. sll 'H. Darnaut' (ca. 1910)
    Dorotheum Vienna, 13 September 1995 (678**) ATS 120,000   US$ 11,664

OBSTBLÜTE BEI PLANKENBERG oil on panel, 32 x 47cm. slr 'H. Darnaut'
    Wiener Kunst Auktionen, 29 November 1995 (597**) ATS 210,000   US$ 21,066

DAUBIGNY Charles François (1817-1878) French
ON THE BANKS OF THE OISE oil on canvas, 29 x 43½in. (73.7 x 110.5cm.) sdlr 'Daubigny 1865'
PROV.: With Durand-Ruel, Paris; Sigismund Ojserkis; Anon., sale; Parke Bernet, New York, 24
May 1940, lot 26.
LIT.: R. Hellebranth, *Charles François Daubigny*, Morges, 1976, p. 98, no. 283 (illustrated).
    Christie's New York, 2 November 1995 (109**) US$ 51,750   US$ 51,750

DAUMIER Honoré (1808-1879) French
LE SAUVETAGE (THE RESCUE) oil on canvas, 6¼ x 9 7/8in. (15.8 x 25.3cm.) s ini. lr 'HD' (ca.
1870)
PROV.: Galerie Tanner, Zurich; Galerie Bernheim-Jeune, Paris; J. Bomford; sale, Christie's, London,
July 25, 1952, lot 42; Acquired at the above sale by Mr. Joseph H. Hazen.

EXH.: Berlin, Galerie Matthiesen, *Honoré Daumier: Ausstellung*, Feb.-March, 1926, p. 40, no. 46; London, The Tate Gallery, *Daumier: Paintings and Drawings*, June-July, 1961, p. 30, no. 17, pl. 22h (illustrated);
Cambridge, Massachusetts, Fogg Art Museum, *Paintings from the Collection of Joseph H. Hazen*, Oct.-Dec., 1966, no. 10.
LIT.: E. Fuchs, *Der Maler Daumier*, Munich, 1927, p. 48, no. 64a (illustrated); K.E. Maison, *Honoré Daumier, Catalogue Raisonné of the Paintings, Watercolours and Drawings*, Greenwich, England, 1968, vol. I, p. 177, no. 1-228b, pl. 34 (illustrated).

Christie's New York, 30 April 1996 (12**) US$ 178,500	US$	178,500

DAVID Gerard Jansz. (1460/65-1523) Flemish
TEHE LAMENTATION oil on panel, 22¾ x 19¼in. (57.8 x 48cm.)
PROV.: With Julius Böhler, munich, by 1924; with Tomas Harris, London, 1935.
LIT.: M.J. Friedländer, *Die Altniederländische Malerei*, VI, Leyden, p. 150, no. 193, pl. XC; M.J. Friedländer, *Early Netherlandish Painting*, VI, ed. N. Veronée-Verhaegen, Leyden and Brussels, 1971, part II, p. 104, no. 193, pl. 200.

Christie's London, 8 December 1995 (12**) GBP 111,500	US$	171,591

DAVID Jacques-Louis (Paris 1748-1825 Bruxelles) French
CARACALLA KILLS HIS BROTHER GETA IN THE ARMS OF HIS MOTHER pen and black ink, grey wash heightened with white, 22.3 x 29.2cm. sdll 'L. David inv 1782' numbered 'no. 233' titled in latin 'Caracalla fratrem Getam trucidat, in gremio Julia Matris'
PROV.: Bears collection stamp Flury-Herard (n° 233) (cf.: Lugt n° 1015); Sale Flury-Herard, 13-15 May 1861, n° 106; Bears stamp 'ARD' (cf.: Lugt 172).
EXH.: Paris, Louvre, *Louis David*, October 1989 - February 1990, no. 46 (illustrated in the catalogue).

Étude Tajan Paris, 12 December 1995 (116**) FRF 860,000	US$	173,226

DAVIS Gene (1920-1985) American
CITRUS oil on canvas, 57 x 72in. (144.8 x 182.8cm.) titled 'Citrus' on the stretcher
PROV.: Acquired directly from the artist.

Christie's East, 14 November 1995 (88**) US$ 7,475	US$	7,475

DAVIS Stuart (1894-1964) American
ABSTRACTION IN HIGH KEY gouache on paper, 11½ x 9¼in. (29.3 x 23.5cm.) sll 'Stuart Davis' inscr. '31' on the reverse (ca. 1936)
PROV.: Estate of the artist; The Downtown Gallery, New York.

Christie's New York, 30 November 1995 (67**) US$ 54,050	US$	54,050

DAWSON Henry (1811-1878) British
HARVEST oil on canvas, 42 x 59½in. (106.7 x 151.1cm.) sd 'H. Dawson 1860-1'
PROV.: James Hayllar, R.B.A. (1829-1920); With Frost & Reed, London; Thomas Agnew & Sons; Christie's, 8 June 1901, lot 71 (unsold at 130 gns.).
EXH.: London, British Institution, 1861, no.73 (200 gns.).
LIT.: Alfred Dawson, *The Life of Henry Dawson*, 1891, p.79.

Christie's London, 6 November 1995 (152**) GBP 33,350	US$	52,166

DAWSON Montague, R.S.M.A., F.R.S.A. (1895-1973) British
THE CLIPPER 'NICOYA' UNDER FULL SAIL oil on canvas, 20 x 30in. (48.3 x 76.2cm.) sll 'Montague Dawson'
PROV.: Christie's London, 6 November 1981, lot 266.

Sotheby's London, 17 April 1996 (740**) GBP 11,500	US$	17,437

STEEPS SEAS; THE WALMER CASTLE oil on canvas, 24 x 36in. (61 x 91.5cm.) sll 'Montague Dawson' inscr. 'Steep seas/ the Walmer Castle a blackwall Frigate of 1.064 tons.. in 1855 at Sunderland'

PROV.: With the Cooling Galleries Ltd., London.
    Christie's New York, 22 May 1996 (286**) US$ 57,500   US$ 57,500

OVER THE CREST: THE LIGHTNING oil on canvas, 40 x 50in. (101.6 x 127cm.) sll 'Montague. Dawson'
PROV.: With Frost & Reed, London.
    Christie's New York, 28 November 1995 (144**) US$ 90,500   US$ 90,500

DE MEIJIER A.A. (1806-1867) Dutch
FISHING AND MERCHANTSHIPS ON CALM SEA oil on panel, 55 x 74cm. sd '1854'
    A. Mak B.V. Dordrecht, 21 June 1996 (228*) NLG 23,000   US$ 13,439

DEBRÉ Olivier (b. 1920-) French
LE BAC oil on canvas, 31½ x 39in. (80 x 99cm.) slr; s ant titled on the reverse (1954-55)
    Christie's London, 23 May 1996 (4**) GBP 6,900   US$ 10448

,
DECKER Cornelis Gerritsz. (place unknown 1623 (before 1643)-1678 Haarlem) Dutch
A RIVER LANDSCAPE WITH AN ANGLER NEAR A COTTAGE oil on canvas, 31 1/8 x 39¾cm. (79 x 101cm.) sd 'C. Decker / 1656'
PROV.: With Richard Green, April-May 1970; Anon. Sale, Christie's, 2 Dec. 1983, lot 63.
    Christie's London, 8 December 1995 (263**) GBP 14,950   US$ 23,007

DEDREUX Alfred (Paris 1810-1860 Paris) French
THE RUNAWAY HORSE watercolour, 9 5/8 x 13 1/8in. (24.5 x 33.3cm.) s
    Phillips London, 11 June 1996 (47**) GBP 4,000   US$ 6,168

TWO JOCKEYS BEFORE THE START oil on canvas, 29 x 36in. (74 x 91.5cm.) slr 'Alfred De Dreux'
    Christie's New York, 28 November 1995 (51***) US$ 217,000   US$ 217,000

DEFRANCE Léonard (Liège 1735-1805) Belgian
L'HEURE DU THÉ oil on canvas, 90 x 145cm.
LIT.: J. Philippe, *Meuble, styles et Décors entre Meuse et Rhin*, Liège, 1977, p. 343, no. 428; F. Dehousse, M. Pacco, M. Pauchen, *Léonard Defrance, l'Oeuvre Peint*, Liège, 1985, p. 108, no. 70. (illustrated).
    Étude Tajan Paris, 26 March 1996 (49*) FRF 55,000   US$ 10,872

DEFREGGER Franz von (Stronach 1835-1921 Munich) German
BAUERNDIRNDL oil on panel, 18 x 14cm. sul 'Defregger'
    Dorotheum Vienna, 6 November 1995 (7**) ATS 140,000   US$ 14,044

WEIBLICHER AKT oil on canvas, 50 x 65cm. slr 'Defregger'
PROV.: Ancient Kölner private collection.
    Lempertz Cologne, 18 May 1996 (1527*) DEM 26,000   US$ 16,950

DEGAS Edgar (1834-1917) French
PERSONNAGES D'OPÉRA watercolour heightened with pastel on silk laid down on paper, 12¼ x 25½in. (31 x 64.8cm.) sll 'Degas' (ca. 1880)
EXH.: Philadelphia, Museum of Art, *Edgar Degas in Philadelphia Collections*, Feb.-April 1985, no. 45.
LIT.: P.A. Lemoisne, *Degas et son oeuvre*, Paris 1946, vol. II, no. 594 (illustrated p. 335).
    Christie's New York, 1 May 1996 (131**) US$ 79,500   US$ 79,500

FEMME NUE ASSISE, SE COIFFANT charcoal and green chalk on paper laid down by the artist on board, 43¼ x 38 1/8in. (109.8 x 97cm.) stamped with signature ll 'Degas'; stamped on the blackboard 'ATELIER ED. DEGAS'

PROV.: Atelier Degas, Third Sale, Galerie Georges Petit, Paris, 7-9 April 1919, lot 314 (illustrated p. 226); Galerien Flechtheim, Berlin and Düsseldorf; Lefevre Gallery (Alex. Reid & Lefevre Ltd.), London (acquired by Otto Preminger, 1959).

> Christie's New York, 1 May 1996 (143**) US$ 200,500   US$ 200,500

FILLETE PORTANT DES FLEURS DANS SON TABLIER oil on canvas, 28¾ x 22in. (73 x 56cm.) s stamped (ca. 1860-62)
PROV.: Atelier Edgar Degas (Vente: Galerie Georges Petit, Paris, lere Vente, 6th May 1918, no. 94); Max Dearly, Paris.
EXH.: Paris, Galerie Schmit, *Degas*, 1975, p. 9, no. 4, illustrated in colour in the catalogue.
LIT.: Paul-André Lemoisne, *Degas et son Oeuvre*, Paris, 1946, vol. II, p. 42, no. 81, illustrated; *Jacques Lassaigne and Fiorella Minervino, Degas*, Paris, 1990, p. 88, no. 52, illustrated.

> Sotheby's London, 24 June 1996 (1**) GBP 331,500   US$ 511,180

SCENE DE BALLET pastel on silk laid down on board, 11 5/8 x 23¼in. (29.5 x 59cm.) s 'Degas' (ca. 1885)
PROV.: Paul Paulin, Paris; Wildenstein Inc., New York.
EXH.: New York, Wildenstein Inc., *French Pastels*, 1979, no. 14; Northampton, Smith College Museum of Art, *Degas and Dance*, 1979, no. 14, illustrated in the catalogue; Tubingen, Kunsthalle and Berlin, Nationalgalerie, *Edgar Degas, Pastelle, Ölskizzen Zeichnungen*, 1984, no.157, illustrated on a double page in the catalogue.
LIT.: Paul Lafond, *Degas*, Paris, 1919, vol. II, p. 34, illustrated; Paul-André Lemoisne, *Degas et son oeuvre*, Paris, 1946, vol. II, p. 334, no. 595, illustrated (dated circa 1880); H. R. Hoetink, *Franse Tekeningen uit de 19e Eeuw. Catalogus van de Verzameling in het Museum Boymans-van Beuningen*, Rotterdam, 1968, no. 74; Franco Russoli and Fiorella Minervino, *Degas*, Milan, 1970, no. 553, illustrated; Antoine Terrasse, *Edgar Degas*, Munich, 1973, p. 42, illustrated; Theodore Reff, *The Notebooks of Edgar Degas. A Catalogue of the Thirty-Eight Notebooks in the Bibliotheque Nationale and other Collections*, Oxford, 1976, Notebook no. 36, pp. 17,19, 21-24, 30 & 46-49, discussed; Marc Gerstein, 'Degas's Fans', in *The Art Bulletin*, no. LXIV, New York, 1st March 1982, p. 110, catalogued; p.117, illustrated; Götz Adriani, *Edgar Degas, Pastelle, Ölskizzen, Zeichnungen*, Kunsthalle, Tubingen, 1984, no. 157, illustrated; Jean Sutherland Boggs, *Degas*, Grand Palais, Paris, 1988, p. 382, fig. 188, illustrated (as dating from 1885 and titled *Eventail: Scene de ballet de l 'opera 'Sigurd ')*.

> Sotheby's London, 24 June 1996 (21**) GBP 133,500   US$ 205,860

FEMME AU TUB pastel on paper, 30 x 34in. (76.2 x 86.4cm.) sll stamped (Lugt 568) 'Degas' (1884)
PROV.: Atelier Degas; First Sale, Galerie Georges Petit, Paris, May 6-8, 1918, lot 268 (illustrated, p. 142); Galerie Ambroise Vollard, Paris (acquired at the above sale); Arthur Tooth & Sons, Ltd. and Pinakos, Inc., London; M. Knoedler & Co., Inc., New York (acquired from the above, Feb., 1956); Acquired from the above by Mr. Joseph H. Hazen on May 3, 1956.
EXH.: New York, Wildenstein & Co., Inc., *Degas*, April-May, 1960, no. 40 (illustrated); Los Angeles, University of California, The Art Galleries, *Paintings from the Collection of Joseph H. Hazen*, Jan.-Feb., 1967, no. 6.
LIT.: P.A. Lemoisne, *Degas et son oeuvre*, Paris, 1946, vol. III, p. 434, no. 766 (illustrated, p. 435); J. Rewald, *The History of Impressionism*, New York, 1961, p. 527 (illustrated in colour); J. Lassaigne and F. Minervino, *Tout l'oeuvre peint de Degas*, Paris, 1974, p. 126, no. 907 (illustrated, p. 127); R. Gordon and A. Forge, *Degas*, New York, 1988, p. 242 (illustrated in colour).

> Christie's New York, 30 April 1996 (13**) US$ 5,447,500   US$ 5,447,500

CAVALIERS SUR UN ROUTE oil on cradled panel, 18½ x 23½in. (47 x 59.8cm.) stamped with signature lr 'Degas' (L 658) (1864-1868)
PROV.: Atelier Degas; First Sale, Galerie Georges Petit, Paris, May 6-8, 1918, lot 80 (illustrated); Mr. Gumaelius, Paris (acquired at the above sale); sale, 1922, lot 7; Galerie Ambroise Vollard, Paris; Galerie Mouradian-Vallotton, Paris; Acquired by Mr. Nathan Cummings before 1965.
EXH.: London, Adams Gallery, *Degas*, Nov.-Dec., 1937, no. 7 (illustrated); Paris, Galerie Mouradian-Vallotton, *Degas*, March, 1938, no 9; Minneapolis, Institute of Arts, *Paintings from the*

Cummings Collection, Jan.-March, 1965; New London, Lyman Allyn Museum, *Paintings and Sculpture from the Collection of Mr. and Mrs. Nathan Cummings*, Jan.-Feb. 1968; Washington, D.C., National Gallery of Art, *Selections from the Nathan Cummings Collection*, June-Sept. 1970, p. 18, no. 6 (illustrated). The exhibition traveled to New York, Metropolitan Museum of Art, July-Sept., 1971; Chicago, Art Institute, *Major Works from the Collection of Nathan Cummings*, Oct.-Dec. 1973, p. 15, no. 6 (illustrated).
LIT.: P.A. Lemoisne, *Degas et son oeuvre*, Paris, 1946, vol. 11, p. 60, no. 121 (illustrated, p. 61).

Christie's New York, 30 April 1996 (19**) US$ 244,500	US$	244,500

ESQUISSE POUR UN PORTRAIT (M. ET MME. LOUIS ROUART) charcoal and pastel on paper, 43¼ x 27½in. (110 x 70cm.) stamped signature (1904)
PROV.: 3eme Vente Degas, Paris, 1919, no. 365; Collection Veillet, Paris
(possibly) Galerie Grange, Paris Arcade Gallery, London; Miss D.V. Watson (purchased from the above in 1944 in celebration of the Normandy invasion).
EXH.: Paul-Andre Lemoisne, *Degas et son oeuvre*, Paris, 1946, vol. III, no. 1443, illustrated.

Sotheby's London, 24 June 1996 (34**) GBP 111,500	US$	171,935

APRES LE BAIN, FEMME S'ESSUYANT charcoal with traces ored chalk on buff paper laid down on board, 22 1/8 x 25¾in. (56.2 x 65.4cm.) s stamped 'Degas' (1890's)
PROV.: The Artist's studio, Troisième Vente, Galerie Georges Petit, Paris, 7-9 April 1919, lot 183; Galerie Drouant-David, Paris.

Christie's London, 26 June 1996 (116**) GBP 91,700	US$	141,403

LE PETIT DEJEUNER APRES LE BAIN (LE BAIN) pastel on paper laid down board, 32 5/8 x 31½in. (83 x 80cm.) studio stamp ll 'Degas' (1895-1898)
PROV.: The Artist's Studio, Premiere Vente, Galerie Georges Petit, Paris, 6 May 1918, lot 303 (illustrated p. 160); Ambroise Vollard, Paris; Durand-Ruel, Paris, 1918; Durand-Ruel, New York, 1920.
EXH.: New York, Durand-Ruel, *Exhibition of Pastels and Drawings by Degas*, March 1923, no. 3; New York, Durand-Ruel, *Exhibition of Pastels and Gouaches by Edgar Degas and Camille Pissarro*, Jan. 1932, no. 6; New York, Durand-Ruel, *Pastels of Degas*, March 1943, no. 10; New York, Durand-Ruel, *Degas*, Nov. 1947, no. 22; Paris, Durand-Ruel, *Degas* ,June-Oct. 1960 New York, Museum of Modern Art (on loan).
LIT.: P. A. Lemoisne, *Degas et son Oeuvre*, vol. III, Paris, 1947, no. 1206, with incorrect measurements (illustrated).

Christie's London, 28 November 1995 (11**) GBP 903,500	US$	1,413,265

FEMME NUE ASSISE, SE COIFFANT pastel and charcoal on joined sheets of buff paper laid down on board, 27½ x 21in. (70 x 53.5cm.) studio stamp lr 'Degas' (L.658) (ca 1887-90)
PROV.: The Artist's Studio, Deuxième Vente, Galerie Georges Petit, Paris, 11-13 Dec. 1918, lot 107 (illustrated p. 59); Henri Fèvre, Monte Carlo; his sale, Paris, 22 June 1925, lot 53; Marczell de Nemès, Budapest; his sale, Munich, 15 June 1931, lot 98; Dalzell Hatfield Gallery, Los Angeles.
EXH.: Los Angeles, County Museum of Art, *Degas*, March-April 1958.
LIT.: P.A. Lemoisne: *Degas et son Oeuvre*, vol. III, Paris, 1946, no. 931 (illustrated p. 543).

Christie's London, 28 November 1995 (18**) GBP 216,000	US$	337,870

LOGE D'ACTRICES pastel over etching on paper, 6½ x 9in. (16.5 x 23cm.) str 'Degas' (ca. 1885)
PROV.: James Inglis; sale, American Art Galleries, New York, March 11-12, 1909, lot 18 (illustrated); Hugo Reisinger, New York; sale, American Art Galleries; New York, Jan. 18-20, 1916, lot 44 (illustrated); M. Knoedler & Co., Inc., New York; Irene Mayer Selznick, New York.
EXH.: Boston, Museum of Fine Arts, *Edgar Degas: The Painter as Printmaker*, 1984, p. 167, no. 50A (illustrated in colour).
LIT.: P. Brame and T. Reff, *Degas et son oeuvre, a Supplement*, New York, 1984, p. 106, no. 97 (illustrated, p. 107).

Christie's New York, 30 April 1996 (34**) US$ 640,500	US$	640,500

Apres le Bain (Femme nue couchee)

APRES LE BAIN (FEMME NUE COUCHÉE) pastel on paper mounted on the edges by the Artist on board, 19 x 32¼in. (48.3 x 82.3cm.) s stamped 'Degas' (ca 1885)
PROV.: Atelier Degas; First Sale, Galerie Georges Petit, Paris, May 6-8, 1918, lot 152 (illustrated); Galerie Ambroise Vollard, Paris (acquired at the above sale); Galerie Durand-Ruel, Paris; Beatrice Stein Steegmuller, New York; Francis Steegmuller, New York; E.V. Thaw & Co., Inc., New York; Mr. and Mrs. Arnold Askin, New York (acquired from the above in 1963); Coe Kerr Gallery, New York.
EXH.: New York, Durand-Ruel Galleries, *Degas*, Nov., 1947, no. 5; New York, Acquavella Galleries, Inc., *Edgar Degas*, Nov.-Dec., 1978, no. 35 (illustrated in colour); New York, Coe Kerr Gallery, *The Askin Collection*, April-May, 1989 (illustrated in color).
LIT.: P.A. Lemoisne, *Degas et son oeuvre*, Paris, 1946, vol. III, p. 496, no. 855 (illustrated, p. 497); R. Gordon and A. Forge, *Degas*, New York, 1988, p. 265 (illustrated in color); G. Tinterow, 'The 1880s: Synthesis and Change,' Degas, New York, 1988 (exh. cat., The Metropolitan Museum of Art), p. 454 (illustrated, fig. 252); J.S. Boggs and A. Maheux, *Degas Pastels*, New York, 1992, p. 138, no. 50 (illustrated in color, p. 139).
Christie's New York, 7 November 1995 (10**) US\$ 2,367,500   US\$ 2,367,500

LE SORTIE DU BAIN (FEMME S'ESSUYANT) pastel over monotype on paper, 17¼ x 9½in. (44 x 24cm.) sbr 'Degas' (1885)
PROV.: Tadamasa Hayashi, New York; sale, American Art Galleries, New York, Jan. 8-9, 1913, lot 66 (illustrated; titled *Femme d'eshabillée*); Galeries Durand-Ruel, Paris; M. Pridonoff, Paris; sale, Galerie Georges Petit, Paris, May 27, 1932, lot 6; M. Schoeller, Paris; Mme Gillou, Pans; sale, Galerie Charpentier, Paris, March 24, 1952, lot 6 (illustrated); Anon. sale, Hôtel Drouot, Paris,June 24, 1988, lot 10; Anon. sale, Habsburg Feldman, New York, Nov. 12, 1989, lot 11 (acquired by the present owner).
EXH.: Boston, Fogg Art Museum, *Degas Monotypes*, April-June, 1968, no. 128 (illustrated).
LIT.: P. A. Lemoisne, *Degas et son oeuvre*, Paris, 1946, vol. III, no. 836 (illustrated, p. 485); E. P. Janis, 'The Role of the Monotype in the Working Method of Degas,'Burlington Magazine, vol. LIX, part II, Feb., 1967, p. 26, fig. 45 (illustrated, p. 78); G. Tinterow, 'The 1880s: Synthesis and Change', *Degas*, New York, 1988 (Metropolitan Museum of Art exhibition catalogue), p. 414 (illustrated, fig. 225).
Christie's New York, 8 November 1995 (114**) US\$ 503,000   US\$ 503,000

TROIS DANSEUSES EN MAILLOT, LES BRAS LEVÉS charcoal on joined tracing paper laid down by the artist on board, 30 5/8 x 20in. (77.8 x 50.8cm.) stamped with signature ll 'Degas' (Lugt

658); stamped on the reverse 'ATELIER ED. DEGAS' (Lugt 657)
PROV.: The artist's studio; second sale, Galerie Georges Petit, Paris, March 6-8, 1918, lot 259
(illustrated, p. 152); Galerie Jean-Claude Bellier, Paris; Gallery Felicie, New York (acquired by the
present owner, 1983).

Christie's New York, 8 November 1995 (128**) US$ 90,500	US$	90,500

DEKKERS Ad (1938-1974) Dutch
RELIEF MET DRIE CIRKELS white polyester, 180 cm. diam. sd and inscr. with title on the reverse
'Ad Dekker 1967'
PROV.: Acquired directly from the artist by the present owner.
LIT.: C. Blotkamp, *Ad Dekkers*, The Hague 1981, no. 95.

Christie's Amsterdam, 6 December 1995 (358**) NLG 16,100	US$	9,976

DELACROIX Eugène (Ferdinand Victor Eugène) (1798-1863) French
FEMME JUIVE D'ALGER watercolour, 8¾ x 5¾in. (22 x 14.5cm.) slr with the studio stamp
PROV.: Edgar Degas Collection; bought at the Degas sale by Mr. Gaston Bernheim; thence by
descent.
EXH.: *Eugène Delacroix*, Paris, Musée du Louvre, June-July 1930, no. 320, (illustrated in the
catalogue of the exhibtion, p. 38, no. 318).

Sotheby's London, 10 July 1995 (100**) GBP 67,500	US$	107,673

DELAUNAY Robert (1885-1941) French
VERSEUSE peinture à la colle and wax on paper laid down on canvas, 37 x 50 3/8in. (94 x 128cm.)
(1915-16)
PROV.: Galerie Bing, Paris; Jorge de Brito, Lisbon; Sale: Sotheby's, London, 1 December 1982, lot
49.
LIT.: Guy Habasque, *Robert Delaunay , du Cubisme à l'art abstrait, documents inédits suivus d'un
catalogue de l'oeuvre de R. Delaunay*, Paris, 1957, no. 168 (illustrated p. 277).

Sotheby's New York, 2 May 1996 (196**) US$ 134,500	US$	134,500

LA VERSEUSE PORTUGAISE pastel on paper laid down on canvas, 29 7/8 x 41¼in. (76 x 105cm.)
s 'Delaunay' (1916)
PROV.: Louis Carré & Cie., Paris.
EXH.: Basle, Galerie Beyeler.

Christie's London, 26 June 1996 (282**) GBP 106,000	US$	163,454

TRIOMPHE DE PARIS oil on canvas, 23 5/8 x 31 7/8in. (60 x 81cm.) slc 'R. Delaunay' (Paris, 1928
-1929)
PROV.: M. Gorse, Paris (acquired from the Artist in 1932).
LIT.: G. Hasbasque, *Robert Delaunay: Du Cubisme à l'Art Abstrait*, Paris, 1957, p. 398, no. 23.

Christie's New York, 30 April 1996 (60**) US$ 200,500	US$	200,500

DELAUNAY Sonia (1885-1979) French
NATURE MORTE PORTUGAISE oil on wax on paper laid down on ccnavas, 26 x 36¼in. (66 x
92.1cm.) s indistinctly; s on the stretcher and numbered '564' (1916)
PROV.: Kunsaustellung der Sturm (Herwarth Walden), Berlin (acquired from the artist); Sale:
Sotheby's, London, 5 Decmber 1973, lot 72.
EXH.: Paris, Musée d'art et histoire, *Sonia Delaunay*, 1964, no. 67.

Sotheby's New York, 2 May 1996 (197**) US$ 85,000	US$	85,000

DELAVALLÉE Henri (1862-1943) French
LE PUITS EN HIVER oil on canvas, 15 x 18in. (38 x 46cm.) sdlr 'H Delavalee 87 (1887)

Étude Tajan Paris, 13 December 1995 (24**) FRF 300,000	US$	60,428

DELOBRE Emile (1873-1956) French
PAYSAGE ITALIEN oil on panel, 13 1/8 x 16in. (33.2 x 40.7cm.) s on the reverse 'Mecredi 6 Aôut

1950'
PROV.: Estate of the Artist.
        Christie's East, 7 November 1995 (32*) US$ 7,475   US$ 7,475

VASE DE FLEURS oil on panel, 16 x 13 5/8in. (40.7 x 34.5cm.) s on the reverse 'Samedi 3 Juin 44'
PROV.: Estate of the Artist.
        Christie's East, 7 November 1995 (37*) US$ 6,900   US$ 6,900

DELORT Charles Edouard (1841-1895) French
AFTER CHURCH oil on canvas, 32 x 46¾in. (81.3 x 118.7cm.) sll 'C.DeLort'
        Christie's New York, 2 November 1995 (160**) US$ 27,600   US$ 27,600

DELPY Hippolyte Camille (1842-1910) French
WASHERWOMEN ON A RIVERBANK oil on panel, 16 x 28in. (40.5 x 71cm.) sd 'H.C. Delpy
1902'
LIT.: To be included in Michèle Lannoy's forthcoming *catalogue raisonné* on Delpy.
        Christie's London, 15 March 1996 (39**) GBP 17,825   US$ 27,222

WASHERWOMEN AND FISHERMEN ON A RIVERBANK oil on panel, 16 x 26¼in. (40.6 x
66.6cm.) sd 'H.C. Delpy 1903'
PROV.: With the Edward Brandus Gallery, New York, no. 5012.
LIT.: To be included in Michèle Lannoy-Duputel's forthcoming *catalogue raisonné* on Delpy.
        Christie's London, 17 November 1995 (82**) GBP 9,775   US$ 15,290

WASHERWOMEN ALONG THE RIVERBANK oil on panel, 13 x 23 5/8in. (33 x 60cm.) slr 'H.C.
Delpy' and incised with ini. 'H.C.D.' on the reverse
LIT.: This painting will be included in the forthcoming *catalogue raisonné* on Delpy by Michele
Lannoy-Duputel.
        Christie's New York, 22 May 1996 (150**) US$ 11,500   US$ 11,500

DELVAUX Paul (Antheyt (Liège) 1898-1994) Belgian
LES TROIS LAMPES oil on canvas, 43¼ x 55in. (109.9 x 139.7cm.) sd 'Paul Delvaux I-64'
PROV.: Staempfli Gallery, New York; Acquired from the above by the Benjamin family in 1964.
EXH.: New York, M. Knoedler & Co., *Lawyers Collect*, 1965, no. 16; New York, Staempfli Gallery,
1965, no. 14; New Haven, Yale University Art Gallery, *The Helen and Robert M. Benjamin
Collection*, 1967, no. 36
New York, Staempfli Gallery, 1969, no. 13.
LIT.: P.A. de Bock, *Paul Delvaux*, Brussels, 1967, no. 157, illustrated p. 300; Michel Butor, Jean
Clair and Suzanne Houbart Wilkin, *Delvaux:Catalogue de l'oeuvre peint*, Lausanne Paris, 1975, no.
286, illustrated p. 284.
        Sotheby's New York, 2 May 1996 (267***) US$ 635,000   US$ 635,000

LE VIADUC oil on canvas, 39½ x 51½in. (100.3 x 130.8cm.) sdlr 'Paul Delvaux 3-63'
PROV.: Staempfli Gallery, New York; Acquired from the above by the Benjamin family in 1963.
EXH.: New York, Staempfli Gallery, 1963; New York, Finch College Museum of Art, *Art from
Belgium*, 1965, no. 9 New Haven, Yale University Art Gallery, *The Helen and Robert M. Benjamin
Collection*, 1967, no.35
New York, Staempfli Gallery, *Paul Delvaux - Paul Wunderlich*, 1971, no. 5; Tokyo, Isetan Museum
of Art; travelling exhibition: Hiroshima, Yokohama, Yamanashi, Asakihawa and Osaka, Surrealism,
1983, no. 64.
LIT.: P.A. de Bock, Paul Delvaux, Brussels, 1967, no. 151, illustrated p. 300;
J.-CI. Guilbert, *Le réalisme fentestique, 10 peintres européens de l'imaginaire*, Paris, 1973,
illustrated p. 41; Michel Butor, Jean Clair and Suzanne Houbart Wilkin, *Delvaux: Catalogue de
l'oeuvre peint*, Lausanne Paris, 1975, no. 276, illustrated p. 259; K. Nakayama, Y. Tono and S. Ooka
(eds.), 'Paul Delvaux' in *Art Gallery, vol. 19*, Tokyo, 1986, no. 13, illustrated p. 19.
        Sotheby's New York, 2 May 1996 (269**) US$ 376,500   US$ 376,500

VUE DE PONT D'ANSEREMME watercolour and pen and brush and ink, 21½ x 28 3/8in. (54.5 x 72cm.) sd '4.28' (1928)
PROV.: Galerie Lou Cosyn, Brussels; Monsieur G. Van Extergem, Brussels; Purchased by the parents of the present owner in the 1960's.
          Sotheby's London, 20 March 1996 (280**) GBP 12,075   US$ 18,441

FEMME DRAPÉE A L'ANTIQUE oil on panel, 77½ x 38 3/8in. (197 x 97.5cm.) sd inscr. 'J'atteste que cette peinture provenant de la peinture murale de la maison de Gilbert Périer est peinte de ma main, le 22 octobre 1968, Paul Delvaux (on the reverse) (ca 1954-56)
PROV.: Gilbert Périer, Brussels; Probably Margareth Krebs, Brussels.
EXH.: Osaka, Musée d'art de Daimaru, Umeda, Paul Delvaux, Nov. 1989, no. 29 (illustrated in colour p. 29). This exhibition later travelled to Kyoto, Musée d'art de Daimaru,Jan. 1990; Tokyo, Musee d'art d'Isetan, Feb. 1990; Himeji, Musée d'art Municipal, March-April 1990 and Yokohama, Musée des Beaux-Arts, April-May 1990.
LIT.: Brussels, Les Beaux-Arts, 8 June 1956, no. 763 (illustrated p. 1); Brussels, La Lanterne, 9 Sept. 1959; London, Sphere, 21 Nov. 1959; R. Benayoun, Erotique du Surrealisme, Paris, 1965, p. 226; P.-A. de Bock, Paul Delvaux, l'homme, le peintre, psychologie d'un art, Brussels, 1967 (illustrated p. 252); J. Dypreau, Le Surréalisme en Belgique, Brussels; Paris, Connaissance des Arts, August 1970, no. 222, pp. 84-85; A. Terrasse and J. Saucet, Paul Delvaux, Berlin, 1972, p. 12; Brussels, Het Laatste Nieuws, 18 April 1973; M. Butor, J. Clair and S. Houbart-Wilkin, Delvaux, catalogue de l'oeuvre peint, Lausanne-Paris, 1975 no. 332 (illustrated p. 279).
          Christie's London, 25 June 1996 (43**) GBP 216,000   US$ 333,076

FEMME AU CHAPEAU DANS UN PAYSAGE CLASSIQUE - VROUW MET HOED IN EEN KLASSIEK LANDSCHAP pen and ink on paper, 11½ x 9in. (29 x 22.7cm.) sdlr 'P. Delvaux 4-37' (april 1937)
PROV.: Paul van Laethem, Brussels.
          Christie's London, 26 June 1996 (213**) GBP 13,800   US$ 21,280

FEMME ASSISE SUR LA PLAGE - VROUW OP HET STRAND watercolour, lavis, pen and indian on paper, 23 5/8 x 16½in. (60 x 42in.) sd inscr. 'P. Delvaux Westende7-30' (July 1930)
EXH.: Ghent, Banque Degroof, Paul Delvaux, Nov. 1992.
          Christie's London, 26 June 1996 (270**) GBP 23,000   US$ 35,466

COMPOSITION AVEC TROIS PERSONNAGES watercolour with pen and black ink on paper, 28 3/8 x 21¼in. (72 x 54cm.) sdlr '8.83 P.Delvaux' (august 1983)
PROV.: Galerie Guy Pieters, Knokke.
          Christie's London, 29 November 1995 (160**) GBP 30,000   US$ 46,926

DEMARNE Jean Louis {called} Demanette (Brussels 1754-1829 Paris) Belgian/French
FOUR SCENES OF THE HISTORY OF RUTH AND BOOZ oil on walnutwood (4 panels), each: 17.5 x 23cm.
          Étude Tajan Paris, 18 December 1995 (213**) FRF 140,000   US$ 28,200

COMMENT UN MILITAIRE PAIE LE PRIX D'UN BAISER oil on panel, 25 x 29.5cm.
PROV.: Sale Chevalier de S. (Sitivan), Paris, rue de Clery, (Maître Lacoste) 19 - 20 April 1830, n° 11 (1300 francs); Sale Forestier, Paris, Hotel Drouot, (Maitre Perrot) 11 - 15 December 1871, n° 76 (680 Francs).
EXH.: J. Watelin, Le peintre J.L. De Marne, Paris et Lausanne, 1962, n° 856.
          Étude Tajan Paris, 25 June 1996 (72**) FRF 80,000   US$ 15,448

LA FAMILLE DU MARÉCHAL-FERRANT oil on panel, 28 x 38.5cm.
PROV.: Anon. Sale, 5 March 1840 (according to Watelin); Anonymous Sale, Paris, Hotel Drouot, 27 October 1936, no. 69, (illustrated).
LIT.: Probably J. Watelin, Le peintre J.L. De Marne, Paris et Lausanne, 1962, no. 741.
          Étude Tajan Paris, 25 June 1996 (73**) FRF 78,000   US$ 15,062

DENIS Maurice (1870-1943) French
BEATRICE SULLA TERRAZZA CON I CIPRESSI oil on canvas, 28 x 47.5cm. sll 'M.D' (1904)
    Finearte Milan, 19 March 1996 (64**) ITL 36,800,000   US$ 23,544

LES PREMIERS PAS DE NOELE oil on board, 18 1/8 x 24in. (46 x 61cm.) sd mono '97' (1997)
PROV.: Estate of the Artist.
    Sotheby's New York, 2 May 1996 (158**) US$ 79,500   US$ 79,500

MARTHE DENIS ET SES ENFANTS AU BALCON, LE SOIR oil on board, 14½ x 10¼in. (37 x 26cm.) slr witn ini. 'MAV'
PROV.: J.F. Denis, Aleçon.
    Christie's London, 26 June 1996 (323**) GBP 11,500   US$ 17,733

DENIS Simon J.A.C. (Antwerp 1755-1813 Napels) Flemish
ITALIAN MOUNTAIN LANDSCAPE WITH FIGURES oil on panel, 48 x 61cm. sd 'S. Denis. f. Romae 1790'
    Bukowskis Stockholm, 29-31 May 1996 (323**) SEK 110,000   US$ 16,178

DEPERO Fortunato (Fondo 1892-1960 Rovereto) Italian
DANZANTI watercolour on paper, 39 x 49cm. s 'Fortunato Depero' (1916)
EXH.: Galleria Goethe, *Fortunato Depero, opere dal 1914 al 1952*, Bolzano 1991, nr. 5 of the exhibition catalogue conceived by Bruno Passamani.
    Finearte Milan, 12 December 1995 (96*) ITL 13,225,000   US$ 8,297

PROSPETTIVE ALPESTRI (FALCIATORI E ABBEVERATA) tempera on cardboard-paper, 77 x 93cm. (1930)
EXH.: Bolzano, Galleria Goethe, *Fortunato Depero, opere dal 1914 al 1952*, 1991, no. 37 in the exhibition catalogue, conceived by Bruno Passamani.
    Finearte Milan, 12 December 1995 (286**) ITL 44,850,000   US$ 28,137

DERAIN André (1880-1954) French
NATURE MORTE oil on canvas, 22 x 23¾in (55.9 x 60.3cm.) slr (ca. 1920)
PROV.: Hirschl & Adler Galleries, New York; Sir Chester Beatty, London.
    Sotheby's New York, 2 May 1996 (321**) US$ 48,875   US$ 48,875

BAIGNEUSES watercolour on paper, 17¼ x 21in.(44 x53cm.) s 'a. Derain' (1905)
    Christie's London, 26 June 1996 (188**) GBP 14,950   US$ 23,053

LES DEUX PICHETS oil on canvas, 24½ x 29½in. (62 x 75cm.) slr 'a. Derain'
EXH.: Paris, Galerie Schmidt, *Derain*, 12 May-20 June 1976, no.60.
    Christie's London, 26 June 1996 (335**) GBP 27,600   US$ 42,560

NATURE MORTE oil on board laid down on canvas-board, 4¾ x 11in. (12 x 28cm.)
PROV.: Alice Derain, Paris; Germaine Patat, Paris (gift from the above, 1949).
    Christie's East, 7 November 1995 (11*) US$ 9,200   US$ 9,200

ROSES SUR UNE TABLE oil on canvas, 10 5/8 x 8¾in. (27 x 22.2cm.) slr 'A. Derain'
PROV.: Mrs. Oliver B. James (bequest to the Phoenix Art Museum, 1970).
    Christie's East, 7 November 1995 (12*) US$ 9,775   US$ 9,775

LE REPOS oil on canvas laid down on board, 5 1/8 x 15in. (13 x 38cm.) stamped and numbered on the reverse'Atelier Derain 433'
    Christie's East, 7 November 1995 (28**) US$ 9,200   US$ 9,200

FEMME AU CHEVEUX ROUGE oil on canvas, 16 171 x 13 171in. (42 x 34.3cm.) slr 'A Derain'
PROV.: Paul Guillaume, Paris; Detroit Institute of Arts (acquired from the above, 1928).

EXH.: Regina, Sasketchewan, Norman Mackenzie Art Gallery, *André Derain in North american Collections*, Oct-Dec. 1982, no. 32 (illustrated); the exhibition later traveled to Berkeley, University of California Art Museum, Jan.-Mar., 1983.
LIT.: W.R. Valentier, 'André Derain,' *Bulletin of the Detroit Institute of Arts*, vol. X, no. 2, 1928-1929, p. 25 (illustrated); *Bulletin of the Detroit Institute of Arts*, vol. X, no. 5, 1929, p. 65 (illustrated).

Christie's East, 7 November 1995 (29**) US$ 23,000	US$	23,000

ARLEQUIN A LA GUITARE oil on canvas, 17 3/8 x 12 5/8in. (44.3 x 32.1cm.) lr 'A Derain' (1936-1938)
PROV.: Mrs. H. C.Hanszen, Houston (by descent to the present owner).

Christie's New York, 8 November 1995 (228**) US$ 23,000	US$	23,000

DESCH Auguste Théodore (1877 b.) French
AU SOLEIL oil on canvas, 31¾ x 25½in. (80.6 x 64.8cm.) sdll '1904'
EXH.: Paris, Salon D'Automne, 1905.

Sotheby's Arcade Auctions New York, 20 July 1995 (195*) US$ 10,350	US$	10,350

DESGOFFE Blaise-Alexandre (1830-1901 Paris) French
LE BUREAU DE LOUIS XV PAR LES ÉBÉNISTES OEBEN ET RIESENER, DANS UN INTÉRIER ARCHITECTURÉ AVEC UNE AIGUIERE EN CRISTAL ET BRONZE SUR UNE SOIE BRODÉE oil on canvas, 110 x 135cm. sll 'B. Desgoffe'

Étude Tajan Paris, 27 October 1995 (11**) FRF 41,000	US$	8,293

DESHAYS Jean-Baptiste Henri, {called} de Colleville (1729-1756) French
A BEGGAR LEANING ON A STAFF black chalk heightened with white on light brown paper, 47.7 x 40.9cm.
LIT.: Recorded in the 1779 catalogue of M. Vassal de Saint-Hubert, no. 156, *Un homme tenant son bonnet et appuyé sur un baton*.

Phillips London, 6 December 1995 (223**) GBP 8,000	US$	12,311

DESPORTES Alexandre François (Champigneulle 1661-1743 Paris) French
HOUNDS WITH GAME IN A LANDSCAPE, A HOOPOE FLYING OVERHEAD AND A HUNTING PARTY BEYOND oil on canvas, 37¾ x 51¼in. (96 x 130cm.) (ca. 1716)
PROV.: Possibly commissioned by Charlotte de Valois, Duchess of Modena (1700-1761); Acquired by the uncle of the present owner in Italy in 1969.

Sotheby's London, 5 July 1995 (82**) GBP 298,500	US$	476,152

DESPORTES Claude François (Paris 1695-1774) French
LES PRÉPARATIFS DU REPAS DEVANT LA CHEMINÉE oil on canvas, 147.5 x 114cm.
LIT.: M. et F. Faré, *La vie silencieuse en France, la nature morte au XVIII siècle*, 1976, p. 64, no. 88, (illustrated).

Étude Tajan Paris, 25 June 1996 (57**) FRF 130,000	US$	25,103

DETTI Cesare-Auguste (1847-1914) Italian
THE ENCAMPMENT oil on canvas, 26 x 49¼in. (66.1 x 125.1cm.) sdll 'C. Detti. 78/Roma'

Christie's New York, 2 November 1995 (138**) US$ 23,000	US$	23,000

A YOUNG GIRL HOLDING A CHALICE oil on panel, 16¼ x 12 7/8in. (41.3 x 32.7cm.) sll 'C. Detti'

Christie's New York, 2 November 1995 (158**) US$ 13,800	US$	13,800

DI COCCO Francesco (Roma 1900-1989 Roma) Italian
FISHERMEN oil on panel, 43 x 72cm (ca. 1931)
EXH.: Roma, *Francesco di Cocco*, Galleria Arco Farnese, 1991, cat.no.47.

Finearte Rome, 14 November 1995 (153**) ITL 14,950,000	US$	9,385

DI SEGNA Niccolo (act. 1st half of the 14th century-) Italian
KING DAVID tempera on gold ground panel, an arched top, 10 7/8 x 7in. (27.5 x 17.8cm.)
      Christie's London, 8 December 1995 (327**) GBP 33,350   US$ 51,323

DI TOMME Luca (act. 1356-1395-) Italian
VIRGIN AND CHILD WITH A BIRD tempera and gold on panel, shaped top, 37 3/8 x 18½in. (94.9 x 47cm.)
PROV.: Sale: Ader Picard Tajan, Paris, December 12, 1988, lot 31, there purchased for FFr 800,000 by Colnaghi, London and New York, from whom acquired by the present collector.
EXH.: New York, Colnaghi, *Master Paintings* 1350-1800, winter 1989-90, pp. 9-14, illus. p. 11 in color (entry by Gaudenz Freuler).
      Sotheby's New York, 11 January 1996 (47**) US$ 442,500   US$ 442,500

DIAZ DE LA PEÑA Narçisse Virgile (1807-1876) French
ON THE ROAD TO MORLAIX oil on panel, 20 1/8 x 28¾in. (51.1 x 73cm.) slr 'N. Diaz.'
      Christie's New York, 2 November 1995 (105**) US$ 25300   US$ 25,300

THREE GYPSY GIRLS oil on panel, 11½ x 9in. (29.3 x 22.9cm.) sdlr 'N.Diaz-/59.'
      Christie's New York, 22 May 1996 (128**) US$ 14,950   US$ 14,950

DICKSEE Margareth Isabel (1858-1903) British
MISS ANGEL (ANGELICA KAUFFMANN, INTRODUCED BY LADY WENTWORTH, VISITS MR. REYNOLDS' STUDIO oil on canvas, 44 x 34in. (112 x 86.5cm.) sd 'Margareth Isabel Dicksee/1892'
PROV.: A.W. Holliday; Christie's, 2 February 1951, lot 80 (42 gns. to Sabin).
EXH.: London, Royal Academy 1892, no. 71.
LIT.: Henry Blackburn (ed.), *Royal Academy Notes*, 1892, pp. 6, 38 (repr.); Frances Gerard, 'Angelica Kauffmann and Joshua Reynolds. By Miss Margareth Dicksee', *Art Journal* article 1897.
      Christie's London, 29 March 1996 (116**) GBP 25,300   US$ 38,638

DIEBENKORN Richard (1922-1993) American
OCEAN PARK # 26 oil on canvas, 88¾ x 81in. (225.4 x 205.5cm.) sdlr ini. 'R.D. 70' sd titled on the reverse 'R. DIEBENKORN 1970 OCEAN PARK #26'
PROV.: Marlborough-Gerson Gallery, New York.
EXH.: San Francisco Museum of Modern Art, *Resource/Response: Richard Diebenkorn Paintings 1948-1983*, May-July 1983, no. 22.
      Christie's New York, 14 November 1995 (11**) US$ 607,500   US$ 607,500

UNTITLED brush and black ink, gouache and black chalk on paper, 14 x 11½in.(35.6 x 29.2cm.) initialed and dlr 'RD 56'
PROV.: Pointdexter Gallery, New York; Salander- O'Reilly Galleries, Beverly Hills.
EXH.: Beverly Hills, Salander- O'Reilly Galleries, *Figurative Paintings*, March-April 1991, no. 20.
      Christie's New York, 15 November 1995 (170**) US$ 23,000   US$ 23,000

DIEMER Michael Zeno (1867-1939) German
SHIPPING OFF CONSTANTINOPLE oil on canvas, 39 x 56¾in. (99.1 x 144.2cm.) slr 'M. Zeno Diemer'
      Christie's New York, 2 November 1995 (264**) US$ 83,900   US$ 83,900

DIEST Adriaen van (1655-1704 London) Dutch
WOODED RIVER LANDSCAPE, WITH A CHURCH BEYOND; HILLY COASTAL LANDSCAPE WITH FIGURES ON A PATH oil on canvas (a pair), each: 57 x 44½in. (145 x 113cm.)
      Sotheby's London, 18 October 1995 (99**) GBP 7,475   US$ 11,798

DIEST Jeronimus (The Hague 1631 (?)-1673) Dutch
A DUTCH MAN-O'-WAR, BEARING THE ARMS OF AMSTERDAM, A GALJOOT AND
OTHER SHIPPING IN CHOPPY SEA oil on canvas, 37 7/8 x 50¼in. (96.2 x 127.7cm.) s ini. 'IVD'
(on the ballast of the galjoot)
Christie's London, 7 July 1995 (255**) GBP 18,400   US$ 29,351

DIEST Willem Hermansz. van (1610 c. (before)-1663 c.) Dutch
WIJDSCHIPS SAILING CLOSE-HAULED ON A RIVER WITH SHIPPING BEYOND, IN A
STIFF BREEZE oil on panel, 43.1 x 49.7cm. indistinctly sll 'W.D(?)'
Christie's Amsterdam, 7 May 1996 (14**) NLG 11,500   US$ 6,706

MARINE DEVANT LA VILLE DE DORDRECHT oil on oakpanel, 40.5 x 67.5cm.
Étude Tajan Paris, 12 December 1995 (34**) FRF 130,000   US$ 26,185

DIETRICH Adelheid (1827 b.-) German
STILL LIFE OF FLOWERS oil on canvas, 26½ x 22in. (67.4 x 55.8cm.) sdlr 'gemt. Adelheid
Dietrich. 1878.'
PROV.: General William R. Smedberg, San Francisco, Califonia by descent in the family to the
present owner.
Christie's New York, 13 September 1995 (14**) US$ 29,900   US$ 29,900

DIETRICH Christian Wilhelm Ernst (1712-1774) German
PORTRAIT OF AN OLD MAN WITH A BEARD oil on panel, 56 x 40cm.
Sotheby's Amsterdam, 6 May 1996 (22**) NLG 9,440   US$ 5,504

DIEZ Johann Gottlieb (active in the 18th century -) German (?)
A SCHOLAR SEATED AT A TABLE WITH A YOUNG BOY oil on canvas, 67¼ x 55½in. (170.5
x 141cm.)
Sotheby's London, 6 December 1995 (177**) GBP 6,900   US$ 10,619

DILLENS Hendrick-Joseph (1812-1872) Belgian (?)
A BITE FOR MY BEST FRIEND oil on panel, 25 x 20in. (63.5 x 50.9cm.) sll 'A A Dillens.'
Christie's East, 13 February 1996 (173***) US$ 9,200   US$ 9,200

DILLON Gerard, R.H.A., R.U.A. (1916-1971) Irish
SELF-PORTRAIT (RECTO); FIGURES AND COTTAGES IN A CONNEMARA LANDSCAPE
(VERSO) oil on canvas, 28 x 21¼in. (71.1 x 54cm.) sll 'Gerard Dillon'
PROV.: The Artist's Family, thence by descent.
Christie's London, 9 May 1996 (131**) GBP 18,400   US$ 27,862

DINE Jim (Cincinnati 1935 b.l) American
SELF PORTRAIT IN A SCOTTISH COAT black and white chalks and graphite on paper, 36 1/8 x
31¼in. (91.7 x 79.4cm.) sdlc 'Jim Dine 1979', titled 'Self Portrait in a Scottish Coat' on the reverse
PROV.: Odyssia Gallery, New York.
Christie's New York, 8 May 1996 (322**) US$ 21,850   US$ 21,850

DIXON Arthur Percy (1884-1917) Scottisch
AN EDINBURGH FLOWER MARKET oil on canvas, 39¾ x 59¾in. (101 x 151.7cm.) sd
'A..Dixon/18.'
PROV.: William Newton, Leith.
EXH.: Edinburgh, Royal Scottisch Academy, 1899, no. 49.
Christie's London, 6 November 1995 (201**) GBP 16,100   US$ 25,184

DIXON Maynard (1875-1946) American
THE NAVAJO oil on canvas, 20 1/8 x 30 1/8in. (51 x 76.5cm.) sd and inscr with the artist's device
'Mynard Dixon 1914' ll

PROV.: Dennis G. Madsen Estate, Salt Lake City, Utah; Private Collection, California; Private Collection, New Mexico.
EXH.: San Francisco, California, Vickery, Atkins and Torrey Provo, Utah, Brigham Young University, *Retrospective Exhibition*, January 1973; Santa Fe, New Mexico, Museum of Fine Arts, *Desert Dreams: The Art of Maynard Dixon*, Aprill-September 1993, and travelling.
LIT.: W. M. Burnside, *Maynard Dixon: Artist of the West,* Provo, Utah, 1974, p. 155; D. J. Hagerty, *Desert Dreams, The Art and Life of Maynard Dixon*, Layton, Utah, p. 77, no. 56.

Christie's New York, 23 May 1996 (110**) US$ 140,000	US$	140,000

DIZIANI Antonio (1737-1797) Italian
AN AMBUSH IN AN WOODED LANDSCAPE oil on canvas, 27 1/8 x 40 1/8in. (68.9 x 102cm.)
PROV.: Sir Eardly Wilmot; sale, 18 Nov. 1921, as Salvator Rosa (30gns. to Taplin) (label on the reverse).

Christie's London, 8 December 1995 (357**) GBP 16,100	US$	24,777

PAESAGGIO FLUVIALE oil on canvas, 63 x 113cm.

Finearte Rome, 22 November 1995 (152**) ITL 71,300,000	US$	44,758

DIZIANI Gaspare (Belluno 1689-1767 Venice) Italian
CHRIST HEALING THE PARALYTIC; AND CHRIST AND THE CENTURION oil on canvas (a pair of ovals), 38 3/8 x 30½in. (97.5 x 77.5cm.)

Christie's London, 7 July 1995 (103**) GBP 45,500	US$	72,579

DOBROWSKY Josef (Karlsbad 1889-1964 Mauerbach near Vienna) Austrian
HAUSER AM BERG oil on canvas, 39.5 x 49.5cm. sdlr 'J. Dobrowsky 3.'
PROV.: Private collection, Vienna.

Dorotheum Vienna, 21 May 1996 (95**) ATS 180,000	US$	17,284

VÖLS AM SCHLERN IN SÜDTIROL oil on cardboard, 48 x 61.4cm. sll with monogram 'J. D'

Wiener Kunst Auktionen, 26 September 1995 (283**) ATS 150,000	US$	14,581

DOLCI Carlo (Florence 1616-1686) Italian
ST. MARK oil on canvas, octagonal, 40 x 32 5/8in. (101.5 x 83cm.) (ca 1640)
PROV.: Painted for the artist's confessor (probably Domenico Carpanti), Florence (according to Baldinucci, see below); Giovanni Battista Galli (b. 1642), who purchased the set (possibly from the above) for 120 scudi before 1677, Palazzo Galli,Via Pandolfini, Florence; Marchese Cosimo Riccardi (1671-1751), Palazzo Medici-Riccardi, and by descent until 1810; Acquired by Lucien Bonaparte from the Riccardi family in 1810; sale, Stanley's, London, 16 May 1816, lot 154, incorrect, identified as Saint Luke; Acquired by Nieuwenhuys on 8 July 1826 for 20,000 francs; King Willem II of the Netherlands (1792-1849), by 1843; sale, The Hague, 12-20 Aug. 1850, lot 153, erroneously described as Saint Luke, unsold at 5,900 guilders, but subsequently sold 14 Oct. 1850 for Dfl. 8,000 to Friedrich zu Wied, Prince of the Netherlands, and by inheritance in 1883 to Marie, Fürsten zu Wied, Princess of the Netherlands, Schloss
Neuwied, Germany; Sotheby's, 5 July 1967, lot 18, es 'C. Dolci' (GBP420).
EXH.: Florence, Cloister of Santissima Annunziata, 1729; (Possibly) Florence, Cloister of Santissima Annunziata, 1767.
LIT.: G. Cinelli and F. Bocchi, *Le bellezze della cittá di Firenze*, Florence, 1677, p. 370; F. Baldinucci, *Notizie de'professori del disegno da Cimabue in qua*, Florence, 1681-1728, ed. 1845-7, V, 1846, p. 341; C.N. Cochin, *Voyage d'ltalie*, Paris, 1758, II, p. 76. Elogi de Carlo Dolci, etc., Florence, 1775, p. 33; M. Lastri, *L'Etruria Pittrice orvero storia della pittura toscana dedotta dai suoi monument) che si esibiscono in stampa dal secolo X fino al presente, II*, Florence, 1795, pl. CX.; L. Lanzi, Storia pittorica della Ralia dal risorgimento delle Belle Arte fin presso la fine del XVIII secolo, Bassano, 1795-6, I, p. 178; W. Buchanan, *Catalogue of the Collections of Pictures of Lucien Bonaparte, Prince of Canino*, London, 1815, no. 57; W. Buchanan, Memoirs of Painting, London, 1824, II, pp. 272-3, no. 52, and p. 287, 'The character of the head, the drawing of the hands, the cast of the draperies, and the general colouring of the whole are excellent'. C.J. Nieuwenhuys,

Description de la Collection des Tableaux qui ornent le Palais de S.A.R.M. le Prince d'Orange, à Bruxelles, Brussel, 1837, pp. 65-6, no. 33, 'Jamais peintre ne prit plus de vein pour amener ses ouvrages a la perfection, que Carlo Dolci, et quoique l'exécution y soit portée a un fini extraordinaire, sa manière de peindre est toujours largement concu, les couleurs y sont fondues avec un molleux et une transparence qui forment un des traits caracteristiques du beau talent de cet artist célèbre dont les ouvrages vent de la plus grand rareté: celui-ci est du nombre de ses meilleures productions.'; CJ. Nieuwenhuys, Description de la Galerie des Tableaux de S.M. Le Roi des Pays-bas, Paris, 1843, no. 125; K. Busse, *Carlo Dolci*, in U. Thieme - F. Becker, *Allgemeines Lexikon der bildenden Künstler*, XI, Leipzig, 1913, p. 387; F. Borroni *Salvadori, Le esposizioni d'arte a Firenze dal 1674 al 1767, Mitteilungen des Kunsthistorischen Institutes in Florenz*, XVI11, 1, 1914, pp. 29 and 80;B.B. Fredericksen, The Four Evangelists by Carlo Dolci, *The J. Paul Getty Museum Journal,* III, 1976, pp. 67-73; G. de Julius, Appunti su una quadreriaforentina: la collezione dei marches) Riccardi, *Paragone*, 357, 1981, pp. 88-9, note 64 and p. 91, note 81; G. Cantelli, *Repertorio della pittura fiorentina del seicento*, Fiesole, 1983, p. 74; C. McCorquodale, in the catalogue of the exhibition Il Seicento *Fiorentino.* Arte a Firenze da Ferdinando I a Cosimo IIL Florence, 1986, 111, p. 82.; M.J. Minicucci, Parabola di un museo, Rivista d'arte, XXXIX, III, 1987, p. 381; F Baldassari in La pittura in Italia. Il Seicento, Milan, 1989, II, p. 726; E. Hinterding and F. Horsch, 'A small but choice collection': the art gallery of King Willem II of the Netherlands (1792-1849); *Simiolus*, XIX, 1989, p. 103, no. 154, with an illustrated reconstruction of the painting; M.B. Guerrien Borsoi, Carlo Dolci, in *Dizionario Biografico degli Italiani*, Rome, 1991, no. 40, p. 421; B. Edelein-Badie, La collection de tableux de Lucien Bonaparte, Prince de Canino, doctoral dissertation, Université Paul Valéry Montpellier, III, 1992, II, pp. 280 -1, no. 62; The Index of Paintings Sold in the British Isles during the Nineteenth Century, ed. B.B. Fredencksen, III, Santa Barbara and Oxford1993, p. 337; F.Baldassari, Carlo Dolci, Turin, 1995, pp. 21-2 and pp. 66-7, no. 32, illustrated, and colour pl. XI; Luciano Bonaparte, le sue collezioni d'arte le sue residenze a Roma, nel Lazio, in Ralia (1804-1840), ed. M. Natoli, Rome, 1995, p. 4, no. 11.

    Christie's London, 8 December 1995 (103***) GBP 287,500   US$ 442,444

DOLL Anton (Munich 1826-1887) German
A WINTER VILLAGE oil on canvas, 22½ x 29 1/8in. (57.2 x 74cm.) sll and inscr. 'A Doll. München'
    Christie's East, 13 February 1996 (63**) US$ 16,100   US$ 16,100

VILLAGERS IN AN ALPINE LANDSCAPE oil on canvas, 25½ x 33¾in. (64.8 x 85.5cm.) s inscr. 'A Doll München'
    Christie's London, 15 March 1996 (11A**) GBP 12,075   US$ 18,441

DOLPH John Henry (1835-1903) American
HOUNDS AT REST oil on canvas, 18 x 24in. (45.8 x 61cm.) sll 'JHDolph'
    Christie's East, 21 May 1996 (86**) US$ 7,475   US$ 7,475

DOMERGUE Jean Gabriel (1889-1962) French
BÉRANGERE oil on isorel, 55 x 46cm. sll
    Étude Tajan Paris, 1 February 1996 (194) FRF 29,000   US$ 5,934

DOMINGUEZ Oscar (Tenerife 1906-1958) Spanish
PERSONNAGES DANS UNE VILLE oil on board, 19½ x 26in. (49.5 x 66cm.) sll 'Dominguez'
    Christie's London, 26 June 1996 (329**) GBP 14,950   US$ 23,053

LE STUDIO oil on canvas, 31 7/8 x 39¼in. (80.7 x 99.8cm.) sdlr 'Dominguez 50'
PROV.: Galerie Apollo, Brussels; Brook Street Gallery, London, from whom bought by the present owner in 1950.
EXH.: Tel Aviv, The Tel Aviv Museum, *Exhibition of Abstract and Surrealist Paintings*, Jan-March 1965.
    Christie's London, 29 November 1995 (234**) GBP 28,000   US$ 43,798

DOMMELSHUIZEN Cornelis Christiaan (Utrecht 1842-1928 The Hague) Dutch
A VIEW IN THE JEWISH QUARTERS, AMSTERDAM oil on canvas, 54 x 64cm. sd 'Chr.
Dommelshuizen 1890'
   Christie's Amsterdam, 25 April 1996 (259**) NLG 51,750   US$ 30,750

DOMMERSEN Pieter Cornelis (P. Christiaan) (Dommershuizen) (Utrecht 1834-1908 England) Dutch
SAILING SHIPS AT THE JETTY oil on canvas, s
   A. Mak B.V. Dordrecht, 12 December 1995 (60*) NLG 9,000   US$ 5,577

ON THE SPAARN, NEAR HAARLEM oil on panel, 11¾ x 16in. (30 x 40.5cm.) sdlr 'P.C.
Dommersen (indistinctly) 1899' also inscr. with title and artist`s seal on the reverse
   Phillips London, 12th March 1996 (1**) GBP 5200   US$ 7941

FIGURES IN AN AMSTERDAM STREET oil on canvas, 30¼ x 24½in. (76.8 x 62.2cm.) slr 'Chr.
Dommersen
PROV.: Christie's 20 Feb. 1976, lot 11.
   Christie's South Kensington, 13 June 1996 (202**) GBP 32200   US$ 49653

DOMOTO Hisao (1928 b.) Japanese
RENDEZ-VOUS oil on canvas, diptych framed, 38 3/8 x 29 3/8in. (,100 x 74.5cm.) sll 'Domoto';
roman script, on the reverse 'Domoto', t 'Rendez-Vous' d 'Paris. 1962 (Juillet)' also signed in Japanese
'Domoto Hisao'
   Christie's New York, 31 October 1995 (487**) US$ 10,350   US$ 10,350

DONDUCCI Giovanni Andrea {called Mastellatta} (Bologna 1575-1655 Bologna) Italian
LANDSCAPE WITH FEAST AT A RIVER / LANDSCAPE WITH A BANQUET SCENE oil on
canvas (a pair), 97 xc 120cm.
   Finearte Rome, 21 May 1996 (144**) ITL 155,250,000   US$ 99,711

THE GATHERING OF MANNA oil on canvas, 64 x 74¾in (162 X 189.9cm.)
   Sotheby's London, 17 April 1996 (46**) GBP 28,750   US$ 43,594

DONGEN Kees (Cornelis Theodorus Maria) van (Delfshaven 1877-1968 Monte Carlo (Monaco)) Dutch
PORTRAIT DE JEAN-MARIE VAN DONGEN oil on canvas, 25 5/8 x 19 7/8in. (65 x 50.5cm.) sur
'van Dongen'
LIT.: The Wildenstein Institute will include this painting in their forthcoming *van Dongen catalogue raisonné*.
   Christie's New York, 1 May 1996 (400**) US$ 464,500   US$ 464,500

LES TRICOTEUSES watercolour and gouache, 26 x 21½in. (66 x 55cm.) sll mono 'V.D.'
EXH.: Paris, Galerie Charpentier, *Van Dongen, cinquante ans de peinture*, 1942.
   Étude Tajan Paris, 10 June 1996 (22**) FRF 60,000   US$ 11,586

CARROUSEL, PLACE PIGALLE oil on canvas, 21¾ x 18 1/8in (55.2 x 46cm.) sll 'Van Dongen' ssd
titled on the stretcher and teh reverse '1904'
EXH.: Paris, Galerie Charpentier, *Van Dongen*, 1949.
LIT.: Louis Chaumeil, *Van Dongen, L'homme et L'artiste - La vie et l'oeuvre*, Geneva, 1967, no. 38,
illustrated p. 317.
   Sotheby's New York, 2 May 1996 (165**) US$ 233,500   US$ 233,500

FEMME NUE BLONDE oil on canvas, 45¼ x 57½in. (114.9 x 146.1cm.) slr 'Van Dongen' (ca.
1906)
PROV.: Private Collection, Paris; Perls Galleries, New York.
EXH.: Bernheim-Jeune, Paris, *Le Nu à Travers les Ages*, 1954; Musée de l'Athenée, Geneva, *Van*

Dongen, 1976, no. 18.
LIT.: This work will be included in the forthcoming *catalogue raisonné* being prepared by the
Wildenstein Institute.

Sotheby's New York, 2 May 1996 (166**) US$ 250,000	US$	250,000

MAUD ET RAYMONDE oil on canvas, 51¼ x 38¼in. (130 x 97cm.) s 'van Dongen' s inscr. 'van
Dongen, 29 Villa Said XVI' on the stretcher (1921)
PROV.: Commissioned from the Artist by the family of the present owners.
EXH.: Paris, Galerie Charpentier, *Exposition van Dongen, cinquante ans de Peinture*, 1942, no. 67;
Paris, Musée National d'art Moderne, *Van Dongen*, 1967, no. 112 (illustrated); Rotterdam, Museum
Boymans-van Beuningen, *Van Dongen*, 1968, no. 112 (illustrated); Arizona, The University of
Arizona Museum of Modern Art, *Cornelis Theodorus Marie Van Dongen 1877-1968*, 1971, no. 87
(illustrated p. 57).
LIT.: H. Floury, Van Dongen, Paris, 1925, no. 91 (illustrated in colour). *Van Dongen*, Exh. cat.,
Musée National d'art Moderne, Paris, 1967, no. 112 (illustrated*); Cornelis Theodorus Marie Van
Dongen 1877-1968*, Exh. cat., The University of Arizona Musuem of Art, Arizona, 1971 (illustrated
p. 57); J.M. Kyriazi, *Van Dongen après le fauvisme*, Lausanne, 1976, no. 87, p. 107 (illustrated in
colour).

Christie's London, 25 June 1996 (49**) GBP 221,500	US$	341,557

SCENE DE PLAGE - DEAUVILLE oil on canvas, 15 x 21¾in. (38 x 55.2cm.) s 'van Dongen' (ca
1925)
PROV.: Galerie Paul Pétridès, Paris; anon. sale, Sotheby's London, 1980, lot 58 (GBP 26,000).
LIT.: To be included in the forthcomming *Van Dongen catalogue raisonné* currently being prepared
by madame Christine Tolofroger of the Wildenstein Institute.

Christie's London, 26 June 1996 (167**) GBP 100,500	US$	154,973

JEUNE FEMME AU VILLAGE (LA GARÇONNE) oil on canvas, 21¾ x 18¼in. (55.3 x 46.3cm.) s
twice 'van Dongen' (ca 1920)
PROV.: Albert lespinasse, Paris, his sale, Hotel Drouot, Paris 23 June 1986, lot 40.
EXH.: Paris, Musée Galliera, *Femme d'hier et d'aujourd'hui*, October 1960, no. 102.

Christie's London, 26 June 1996 (168**) GBP 150,000	US$	231,303

MERE ET ENFANT watercolour on paper, 24 x 19¼in. (61 x 49cm.) s inscr. 'Van Dongen.
Deauville' (1925)
LIT.: The Wildenstein Institute will include this watercolour in their forthcoming *Van Dongen
catalogue raisonné.*

Christie's London, 26 June 1996 (191**) GBP 16,100	US$	24,827

NU DANS UN PAYSAGE oil on board, 25½ x 19¾in. (64.8 x 50.2cm.) slr 'van Dongen' (1920)
PROV.: Bernheim-Jeune, Paris; anon sale Sotheby's London, 26 March 1980, lot 36 (GBP 26,000),
where purchased by the present owners.

Christie's London, 26 June 1996 (198**) GBP 122,500	US$	188,897

VASE DE CHRYSANTHEMES oil on canvas, 51 3/8 x 35¼in. (130.5 x 89.4cm) sll 'van Dongen'
(1918)
PROV.: Galerie Charpentier, Paris; Galerie Paul Pétridès, Paris; O'Hana Gallery, London; Nathan A.
Bernstein Co., New York.
EXH.: Paris, Galerie Charpentier, *L'Automne*, 1943; Tucson, Arizona, The University of Arizona
Museum of Art and Kansas City, The Nelson Atkins Museum of Art, *Kees van Dongen, The First
American Retrospective*, Feb.-March 1971, no. 10 (illustrated in colour).
LIT.: To be included in the forthcoming *van Dongen catalogue raisonné* currently being prepared by
the Wildenstein Institute.

Christie's London, 26 June 1996 (281**) GBP 104,900	US$	161,758

LE PAYS DE JONGKIND, MOULIN oil on canvas, 46.5 x 55.5cm. sll 'van Dongen'
PROV.: Bernheim-Jeune & Cie, Paris.
LIT.: This painting will be included in the forthcoming *catalogue raisonné Kees van Dongen*,
currently being prepared by the Wildenstein Institute.

Étude Tajan Paris, 28 March 1996 (47**) FRF 80,000	US$	15,813

L'OULED NAIL oil on canvas, 25¾ x 18in. (65.5 x 45.7 cm.) sur 'van Dongen'
PROV.: André Romanet, Paris (acquired by the present owner, 1955).

Christie's New York, 8 November 1995 (174**) US$ 222,500	US$	222,500

DOOMER Lambert (1624-1,700) Dutch
A TOWN BY A RIVER oil on canvas, 91.5 x 117.7cm.

Christie's Amsterdam, 13 November 1995 (159**) NLG 74,750	US$	47110

DOOYEWAARD Willem (Amsterdam 1892-1980) Dutch
FEEDING THE BABY black chalk and pastel, 61.5 x 50cm. scr

Sotheby's Amsterdam, 23 April 1996 (54**) NLG 20,60	US$	11,920

CAN CAN DANSERES oil on canvas, ,100 x 72.5cm. s 'W. Dooijewaard' s titled on the stretcher

Christie's Amsterdam, 25 April 1996 (189**) NLG 17,250	US$	10,250

DORAZIO Piero (Rome 1927) Italian
STOP oil on canvas, 70 x 35cm. sd titled on the reverse 'Stop 1972-75'
LIT.: Giorgio Crisafi, *Dorazio*, ed. Alfieri, Venezia 1977, no. 1275.

Finearte Milan, 12 December 1995 (237*) ITL 12,075,000	US$	7,575

SUK I oil on canvas, 70 x 90cm sd on the reverse 'Piero Dorazio 1978 'Suk I"
PROV.: Galleria Editalia, Roma.
LIT.: *Oeuvre catalogue* in the archives of Dorazio no.957.

Finearte Rome, 14 November 1995 (176**) ITL 21,850,000	US$	13,716

SOSPENSIONE BLEU oil on canvas, 51 x 113.8cm. s, d and titled '1946' on the reverse
LIT.: This work is registered at studio Piero Dorazio, Todi, 26-03-1996.

Sotheby's Milan, 28 May 1996 (144**) ITL 44,850,000	US$	28,805

SENZA TITOLO oil on canvas, 35.3 x 25.2cm. sd '58' on the reverse
LIT.: This work is registered in 'Studio Piero Dorazio', Todi, 26-03-1996.

Sotheby's Milan, 28 May 1996 (152**) ITL 12,075,000	US$	7,755

DORÉ Paul-Gustave-Louis-Christophe (1832-1883) French
ANDROMEDA oil on canvas, 100½ x 67½in. (255.2 x 171.5cm.) sd 'Gve Doré/1869'
PROV.: With The Doré Gallery, London, 1870-92; U.S. Art Import Company, 1899-1927; Anon.
sale; Manhattan Storage & Warehouse Co., New York, September 9, 1947, lot 22; Eugene Leone,
New York.
EXH.: The Doré Gallery, London, 1870-92; Carnegie Music Hall, *The Doré Collection*, New York,
1892, pp. 43-44; The Art Institute of Chicago, *Illustrative Catalogue of the Doré Gallery*, Chicago,
circa 1894, pp. 25-26.
LIT.: F.R. Conder, *Descriptive Catalogue of the Pitcures by M. Gustave Doré on View at 35, New
Bond Street*, London, London, 1883, pp. 59-60, no. 27; B. Jerrold, *Life of Gustave Doré ,London,
1891, pp. 261, 408; L. Dèze,* Gustave Doré: Bibliographie et Catalogue Complet de l'Oeuvre, Paris,
1930, p. 123; H. Leblanc, *Catalogue de l'Oeurre Complet de Gustave Doré*, Paris, 1931, p. 54; S.
Lieber, *New York Herald Tribune Sunday Magazine*, 18 May 1947 (illustrated); *Gustave Dore 1832-
1883*, Musée d'art Moderne, Strasbourg, 1983, p. 52.

Christie's New York, 22 May 1996 (83**) US$ 46,000	US$	46,000

DOU Gerard (1613-1675) Dutch
PORTRAIT OF THE ARTIST, HALF LENGTH, IN HIS STUDIO oil on panel, arched, 4 7/8 x
31/4in. (12.4 x 8.3cm.) s mono. 'GDou' upper left on the curtain (ca 1645)
PROV.: This painting may be identified with the one listed by Hofstede de Groot as having belonged
to Count Fraula, Brussels, and sold 21 July 1738, lot 123 for 105 florins (C. Hofstede de Groot, *A
Catalogue Raisonné*, etc., I, London, 1908, p. 437, no. 279b, with the Fraula sale lot number
erroneously listed as lot 122; G. Hoet, Catalogus of naamlyst van schilderyen, etc., The Hague, 1752,
no. 122, where the size given 'hoog 5 duym breet 3 duym en half corresponds with the measurements
of the present picture), or is either a variant of, or identical to, a picture that has been identified as
either a 'Portrait of Rembrandt?' (ibid., no. 310) or a possible self-portrait by Gerard Dou (W. Martin,
Gerard Dou, des Meisters Gemälde, Stuttgart and Berlin, 1913, p. 21, illustrated on the left) which
was formerly in the E. Warneck Collection, Paris, and exhibited at F. Muller and Co., Amsterdam,
1908, no. 33. Since Martin (ibid., p. 180) found it 'impossible to certify' [the Warneck painting's]
originality', it may have been only a copy of the present picture, perhaps in a different state. The
Warneck picture is larger and rectangular in format, including the finial of the sitter's chair, the
capital of the column and the back right, and more of the curtain hanging overhead and to the left.
The present painting is on a panel which is bevelled on all sides and appears complete; thus the
Warneck painting may only be a copy enlarging its design. The sitter's identification is supported by
comparison with Dou's self-portraits in the Residenzgalerie, Salzburg; ibid., illustrated p. 18 left) and
the Herzog Anton Ulrich-Museum, Brunswick, no. 30; (ibid., illustrated p. 18 right). The sitter's pose
is derived from Rembrandt's Sef-Portrait of 1640, in the National Gallery, London, no. 672, which
also inspired many other Dutch painters' portrait. The studio props (the shield, globe and tall parasol)
which appear at the back beside the easel recur in several other paintings of artist's studios by Dou.
The painting on the easel appears to depict the Rest on the Flight into Egypt, a subject which was
treated by several Leiden artists in the circle of Dou and of Rembrandt (see, for example, Stichting
Foundation Rembrandt Research project *A Corpus of Rembrandt Paintings*, 1, 1625-1631, 1982, no.
C6).
Christie's London, 8 December 1995 (33A**) GBP 177,500

| | US$ | 273,161 |

AN ARTIST IN HIS STUDIO oil on panel, 23¼ x 17in. (59.1 x 43.2cm.) (ca. 1630-32)
PROV.: Charles Sedelmeyer, Paris by 1894; John Wanamaker, Philadelphia; Wanamaker's, New
York from whom purchased by G. F. Plympton, Hackensack, New Jersey.
LIT.: *Catalogue of ,100 Paintings of Old Masters*, Charles Sedelmeyer Gallery, 1894, no. 8, illus.;
W. Martin, *Het leven en de werken van Gerrit Dou*, 1901, p. 114; *Collection Catalogue of John
Wanamaker*, 1904, p. 43, no.73; C. Hofstede de Groot, *A Catalogue Raisonné of the Works of the
Most Eminent Dutch Painters of the Seventeenth Century*, 1908, Vol. I, pp. 443-44, no. 311; W.
Martin, *Gerard Dou*, 1911, p. 203, no. 235 (as a lost but certain work of Dou); W. Martin, *Gerard
Dou*, 1913, plate 12; H.-J. Raupp, *Untersuchung zu Kunstlerbildniss und Kunstlerdarstellung in den
Niederlanden im 17. Jahrhundert*, 1984, pp. 276-277; R. Baer, *Gerrit Dou*, PhD. Diss., Institute of
Fine Arts, New York University, 1990, cat. no. 6; W. Sumowski, *Gemälde der Rembrandt-Schuler,
Vol. VI* 1994, pp. 3525, 3534, illus. p. 3564, in color; The painting will be included in Ronnie Baer's
forthcoming *catalogue raisonne of Gerrit Dou* as cat. no. 6.1, datable circa 1630-32.
Sotheby's New York, 11 January 1996 (206**) US$ 107,000

| | US$ | 107,000 |

DOUCET Jacques (1924 b.) French
L'ATELIER DU PORTIER oil on canvas, ,150 x 150cm. sll 'doucet'; d '1989' on the reverse
Bukowskis Stockholm, 24-25 April 1996 (163**) SEK 65,000

| | US$ | 9,847 |

ZONE BOGOMILE oil on canvas, 44 7/8 x 63¾in. (114 x 162cm.) sd and titled on the reverse (ca
mid 1950s)
PROV.: Court Gallery, Copenhagen; Galerie Christel, Helsinki; Acquired from the above by the
present owner in the 1970's.
Christie's London, 26 October 1995 (48**) GBP 13,800

| | US$ | 21,780 |

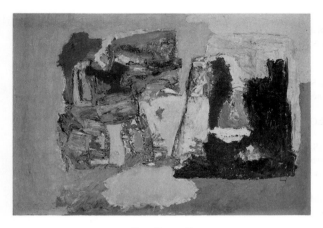

Zone Bogomile

DOVA Gianni (Rome 1925-1991 Pisa) Italian
RITRATTO DELLA MADRE mixed media on cardboard laid down on canvas, 80 x 60cm sd 'Dova
46' (1946)
PROV.: Galleria Schettini, Milano, no.3752.
LIT.: F. Russoli, *Gianni Dova*, edit. Prearo, Milano, 1975.
    Finearte Rome, 14 November 1995 (107**) ITL 13,225,000   US$ 8,302

APPARIZIONE NOTTURNA DI FIORI E UCCELLI, BRETAGNA oil on canvas, 115 x 155cm. s
and titled on the reverse (1969)
PROV.: Galleria Arte Borgogna, Milan, no. 117.
    Finearte Milan, 18 June 1996 (224**) ITL 23,000,000   US$ 14,916

FIGURE IN MOVIMENTO oil on canvas, ,100 x 140cm. slc, titled on the reverse (1966)
PROV.: Galleria Borgogna, Milano.
EXH.: Milano, Palazzo Reale - Sala delle Cariatidi, *Gianni Dova*, Dicembre 1971 Gennaio 1972,
pag. 60, n. 44, illustrated in colour; Paris, Musée Galliera, *Gianni Dova*, 1972, illustrated in colour;
Viareggio, Palazzo Paolina; Cesena, Galleria Comunale d'Arte; Mantova, Casa del Mantegna, *Gianni
Dova - Mostra antologica*, 1991, pag.27, n.13, illustrated in colour.
LIT.: Franco Russoli, *Gianni Dova*, Milano 1975, illustrated in colour.
    Sotheby's Milan, 28 May 1996 (146**) ITL 29,900,000   US$ 19,204

DOVASTON Margaret (1884 b.) British
THE NEW MODEL oil on canvas, 20½ x 27¼in. (52 x 69.2cm.) sll 'M.Dovaston'
    Christie's East, 30 October 1995 (208*) US$ 12,650   US$ 12,650

HIS STRADIVARIUS oil on canvas, 20 x 27in. (50.8 x 68.6cm.) sdll 'M.Dovaston/1950'
    Christie's East, 30 October 1995 (213*) US$ 14,375   US$ 14,375

DOVE Arthur Garfield (1880-1946) American
GAS TANK 2 watercolour and pencl and blaack ink on paper, 5½ x 9in. (14 x 23cm.) slc 'Dove'
(1937)
PROV.: Alfred Stieglitz Collection, New York; The Down Town Gallery, New York; Terry
Dintenfass, Inc., New York.
    Christie's East, 28 November 1995 (246*) US$ 8,625   US$ 8,625
DRAPER Herbert James (1864-1920) Brsitish
'IN THE STUDIO' oil on canvas, 14½ x 22in. (36.8 x 55.9cm.) s with ini. 'H.J.D'
    Christie's South Kensington, 7 March 1996 (172*) GBP 42,000   US$ 64,142

DRECHSLER Johan-Baptist (1756-1811) Austrian
FLORAL STILL-LIFE oil on panel, 28¾ x 23in. (73x 58.4cm.)
      Sotheby's New York, 16 May 1996 (118**) US$ 40,250   US$ 40,250

DROOCHSLOOT Cornelis (1630-1673) Dutch
BEGGARS ACCOSTING PEASANTS IN A VILLAGE STREET, OTHER PEASANTS
DRINKING OUTSIDE TAVERNS BEYOND oil on panel, 60.4 x 84.8cm. indistinctly slc 'c.'
(strengthened) 'd' (strengthened) 'rooghsloot'
      Christie's Amsterdam, 7 May 1996 (48**) NLG 51,750   US$ 30,175

VILLAGE STREETS WITH TRAVELLERS AND PEASANTS oil on panel (a pair), 48.4 x 64.8cm.
/ 48.3 x 64.3cm.-in 17th century ebonised frames slc 'c.droochsloot; indistinctly sll 'c.droochsloot'
      Christie's Amsterdam, 7 May 1996 (99*) NLG 32,200   US$ 18,776

DROOCHSLOOT Joost Cornelis (1586-1666 Utrecht) Dutch
A VILLAGE SCENE WITH AN APOTHECARY oil on canvas, 32½ x 45¼in. (82.5 x 114.5cm.) s
and indistinctly dlc 'JC (in ligature). DS (in ligature): 16.3'
PROV.: D.W. Martin, The Hague.
      Sotheby's London, 5 July 1995 (256**) GBP 31,050   US$ 49,529

A VILLAGELANDSCAPE WITH CHEERFULL COMPANY HAVING A DRINK oil on panel, 36
x 55cm.
      Dorotheum Vienna, 6 March 1996 (82**) ATS 250,000   US$ 24,048

TRAVELLERS AMBUSHED ON A ROAD BY CLASSICAL RUINS oil on canvas, 102 x
135.2cm. sdll 'Jcd' (linked) 'rooch sloot 1641'
      Christie's Amsterdam, 7 May 1996 (49**) NLG 23,000   US$ 13,411

FAIR IN DUTCH VILLAGE oil on panel,
      Dorotheum Vienna, 11 June 1996 (245**) ATS 220,000   US$ 20,420

BEGGARS ACCOSTING A GENTLEMAN IN A VILLAGE oil on panel, 52 x 73.8cm sll 'JDf'
      Christie's Amsterdam, 13 November 1995 (122**) NLG 46,000   US$ 28,991

VILLAGE SCENE oil on canvas, 29½ x 42½in. (74.9 x 108cm.) sdll mono. 'JCDS 1647'
PROV.: Lidvall, St. Petersburg, Russia, by 1898; then Stockholm, Sweden by 1916; and thence to the
present owner.
      Sotheby's New York, 16 May 1996 (260**) US$ 31,050   US$ 31,050

MERRY SCORE oil on canvas, 52.6 x 62.6cm. slm mono 'JS DS f'
      Wiener Kunst Auktionen, 26 September 1995 (1**) ATS 140,000   US$ 13,608

DROST Willem (1678 d.) Dutch
PORTRAIT OF A FLUTE PLAYER oil on canvas, 29½ x 24½in. (74.9 x 62.2cm.)
PROV.: Possibly Petronella de la Court (Sale: Amsterdam, October 19, 1707, lot 112, 'Een
Fluitspeeler van den Drost'); French & Co., New York, 1951.
LIT.: A. Sumowski, 'Beiträge zu Willem Drost,' *Pantheon*, XXVII, 1969, pp. 378 and 382; A.
Sumowski, - *Gemälde der Rembrandt Schüler*, vol. I, 1983, pp. 608-609 and p. 615, cat. no. 325,
illus.
      Sotheby's New York, 11 January 1996 (35**) US$ 46,000   US$ 46,000

DROUAIS François Hubert (Paris 1727-1775) French
PORTRAIT DE JEUNE FEMME AU MANTEAU ORNE DE ROSES oil on canvas (an oval), 73 x
60.5cm. sdcl Drouais le fils / 175(?)
      Étude Tajan Paris, 25 June 1996 (54**) FRF 130,000   US$ 25,103

DROUAIS Jean-Germain (1763-1788) French
MARIUS AT MINTURNES black chalk, pen and brown ink,grey wash on paper, 7 1/8 x 9 7/8in.
(18.2 x 25.2cm.)
        Christie's New York, 22 May 1996 (4**) US$ 42,550   US$ 42,550

DRULMAN Marinus Johannes (Amsterdam 1912 b.-1978|) Dutch
A PASSENGER-SHIP OF THE HOLLAND-AMERIKA LIJN ON THE MAAS, ROTTERDAM oil
on canvas, 60 x ,100 cm s 'M. de Jongere'
        Christie's Amsterdam, 7 February 1996 (350*) NLG 9,775   US$ 5,953

DRUMMOND Arthur (1871-1951) British
AN ALLEGORY OF THE BRITISH EMPIRE oil on canvas, 137 x 81in. (305 x 208.7cm.) sd
'Arthur Drummunod 1901'
        Christie's London, 29 March 1996 (238**) GBP 26,450   US$ 40,394

DUBOIS Guillam (attr.) (1610 c.-1680) Dutch
A DUNE LANDSCAPE AND A SMALL VILLAGE WITH HUNTERS BEYOND oil on canvas,
52.3 x 66.7cm. bears signature lr 'Koninck'
PROV.: With Goudstikker, Amsterdam, no. 1554; with Alfred Brod, London, 1960; J.A. Holt Esq.,
Wales, 1960.
EXH.: Manchester, City Art Gallery, *Exhibition if Works of Art from Private Collections in the North
West and North Wales*, 21 September-30 October 1960, no. 93.
        Sotheby's Amsterdam, 6 May 1996 (39**) NLG 27,140   US$ 15,825

DUBREUIL Victor (act. 1888-1900-) American
MONEY TO BURN oil on canvas, 24 x 32in. (61 x 81.3cm.) sdlr 'V. Dubreuil NY 1893'
PROV.: Kennedy Galleries, New York.
EXH.: Milwaukee, Wisconsin, Milwaukee Art Museum, *Pop Art & the American Tradition*, April-
May 1965; New York, Berry-Hill Galleries, *Old Money: American Trompe L'Oeil Images of
Currency*, November-December 1988, no. 24; New York, Berry-Hill Galleries, *Virtual Reality:
American Trompe L'Oeil Paintings*, May-June 1994.
LIT.: *Kennedy Quarterly*, New York, January 1965, no. 81.
        Christie's New York, 23 May 1996 (59**) US$ 288,500   US$ 288,500

DUBUFE Edouard Louis (1820-1883) French
PORTRAIT OF THE MARQUESS D'AOUST NÉE DE SAVEYE, SITTING ON A COACH oil on
canvas, 130 x 97.5cm. sd 'Edouard - Dubufe./1857'
PROV.: In the collection of the d'Aoust family.
        Christie's Monaco, 14 June 1996 (57**) FRF 114,660   US$ 22,141

DUBUFFET Jean (1901-1985) French
CORPS DE DAME pen and india ink on paper, 10 5/8 x 8¼in. (27 x 21cm.) sdll 'Jean Dubuffet Paris
dimanche 15 Octobre 1950'
PROV.: B.C. Holland Gallery, Chicago.
EXH.: Chicago University, David and Alfred Smart Gallery, *Jean Dubuffet: Forty Years of His Art*,
Oct.-Dec. 1984, no. 24 (illustrated p. 52); Chicago, The Art Institute, *Chicago Collects: Sellections
from the Collection of Dr. Eugene A. Solow*, May-Aug. 1988, no. 13.
LIT.: ed. M. Loreau, *Catalogue des travaux de Jean Dubuffet (Fascilule VI: Corps de dame)*,
Lausanne, 1965, no. 136 (illustrated p. 93).
        Christie's New York, 1 May 1996 (263**) US$ 189,500   US$ 189,500

SITE ALEATOIRE AVEC CINQ PERSONNAGES acrylic and paper collage laid down on canvas,
26 3/8 x 39 3/8in. (67 x 100cm.) s ini. 'J.D.' (1982)
PROV.: Mademoiselle Dubuffet, Paris.
LIT.: *Catalogue Intégral des Travaux de Jean Dubuffet, fasc. XXXV: Sites Aléatoires*, Paris, 1986, p.
44, no. 71 (illustrated).

Christie's London, 19 March 1996 (16**) GBP 71,900	US$	109,805

DONNÉE acrylic on paper laid down on canvas, 26½ x 39in. (67.3 x 100cm.) slr ini. 'J.D. '84'
PROV.: Galerie Beyeler, Basel; James Goodman Gallery, New York.
LIT.: *Catalogue Intégral des Travaux de Jean Dubuffet*, fasc. *XXXVII: Non-Lieux*, Paris 1989, p. 27, no. 53 (illustrated).

Christie's London, 19 March 1996 (36**) GBP 32,200	US$	49,175

PROPOS GALANTS oil on Isorel, 25½ x 32in. (64.8 x 81.3cm.) sd '51'; sd and titled 'Août 51' on the reverse
PROV.: Pierre Matisse Gallery, New York; Acquired from the above by the family of the present owner in 1959.
LIT.: Max Loreau, *Catalogue des Travaux de Jean Dubuffet*, fasciclue VII, Lausanne 1967, no. 81 (illustrated p. 58).

Sotheby's New York, 2 May 1996 (334**) US$ 288,500	US$	2885,00

TABLE DE FORME INDÉCISE oil ond plaster on board, 28¾ x 36¼in. (73 x 92cm.) sll 'J.Dubuffet' (August 1951)
PROV.: Roland Penrose, London; Richard L. Feigen Gallery, Chicago & New York; Galerie Beyeler, Basel; Viktor and Marianne Langen, Dusseldorf; Galerie Baudoin Lebon, Paris.
EXH.: Paris, CercleVolney,*Jean Dubuffet*, 1954, no. 105; Paris, Musée des Arts Décoratifs, *Jean Dubuffet*, 1960, p. 297, pl. 38, illustrated; New York, Museum of Modern Art, Chicago, The Art Institute of Chicago; Los Angeles; Los Angeles County Museum, *The Work of Jean Dubuffet*, 1962, p. 58, illustrated; Kassel, *Dokumenta III*, 1964, p. 134, no. 2, illustrated; London, Arts Council of Great Britain at the Tate Gallery, *Jean Dubuffet*, 1966, p. 33, no. 45, illustrated; Amsterdam, Stedelijk Museum, *Jean Dubuffet*, 1966, p. 18, no. 36, illustrated New York, Richard L. Feigen Gallery, *Dubuffet and the Anticulture*, 1970, no. 15, illustrated; Washington, Hirshhorn Museum and Sculpture Garden, Smithsonian Institution, *Jean Dubuffet 1943 - 1963: Paintings, Sculptures and Assemblages*, 1993, p. 80, no. 36, illustrated.
LIT.: Peter Selz, *The Work of Jean Dubuffet*, New York 1962, p. 58, illustrated; Goëtam Picon, *Le Travail de Jean Dubuffet*, Geneva 1973, p. 71, illustrated; *Catalogue Integral des Travaux de Jean Dubuffet: Tables Paysages, Paysages du Mental, Pierres Philosophiques*, fasc. VII, Paris 1979, p. 47, no. 64, illustrated.

Sotheby's London, 21 March 1996 (21**) GBP 131,300	US$	200,519

PORTRAIT DE FEMME oil and paper collage on paper, 26 1/8 x 19½in. (66.2 x 49.2cm.) sd 'J. Dubuffet Oct. 57'
PROV.: Galerie Baudoin Lebon, Paris.
LIT.: *Catalogue Intégral des Travaux de Jean Dubuffet: Célébration du Sol I, Lieux Cursifs, Texturologies, Topographies, fasc. XIII*, Lausanne 1969, p. 70, no. 93, illustrated.

Sotheby's London, 21 March 1996 (43**) GBP 108,200	US$	165,241

CONCOMITANCES acrylic and paper collage mounted on canvas, backed composition board, 30 x 21in. (76.2 x 53.2cm.) ini. and dll 'J.D.79'
PROV.: Waddington Gallery, London; Hokin Gallery, Palm Beach.
LIT.: ed. M.Loreau, *Catalogue des travaux de Jean Dubuffet-Théâtres de Memoire*, fascicule XXXII, Paris 1982, p.176, no.405 (ill.).

Christie's New York, 22 February 1996 (15**) US$ 110,300	US$	110,300

BUSTE black ink and paper collage on paper, 26 3/8 x 18 3/8in. (67 x 46.7cm.) sd '55'
PROV.: Marlborough Gallery, Rome. Hirschl & Adler Galleries Inc. New York.
LIT.: *Catalogue Intégral des Travaux de Jean Dubuffett, fasc. XI: Charettes, Jardins, Personnages, Monolithes*, Paris 1969, p. 34, no. 27 (illustrated).

Christie's London, 23 May 1996 (22**) GBP 35,600	US$	53,907

SITE AVEC 4 PERSONNAGES acrylic on paper laid down on canvas, 19¾ x 26¾in. (50.2 x 68cm.) sd ini 'J.D. 82'
PROV.: Waddington Galleries, London.
LIT.: *Catalogue Intégral des Travaux de Jean Dubuffet, fasc. XXXIV: Psycho-sites*, Paris 1984, p. 129, no. 487 (illustrated).
   Christie's London, 23 May 1996 (49**) GBP 33,350   US$ 50,500

BARBES DES SONGES FUMEUX india ink and collage on paper laid down on board, 26 3/8 x 19 5/8 in. (67 x 50cm.) sdlr '59; sd Août '59 and titled on the reverse
PROV.: Galerie Daniel Cordier, Paris.
EXH.: Bari, Pinacoteca Provinciale, *Mostra Internazionale: Aspetti dell'Informale*, January-February 1971.
LIT.: *Catalogue Intégral des Travaux de Jean Dubuffet, fasc. XV: As-Tu, cueilli la Fleur de Barbe*, Paris 1964, p. 49, no. 60 (illustrated).
   Christie's London, 27 June 1996 (19**) GBP 131,300   US$ 202,467

LIEU FREQUENTE acrylic and paper collage on paper laid down on canvas, 26½ x 39½in. (67 x 100cm.) sll with ini. and d '82
PROV.: Private Collection, France.
LIT.: *Catalogue Intégral des Travaux de Jean Dubuffet, fasc. XXXV: Sites Aléatoires*, Paris 1984, p. 64, no. 120 (illustrated in colour).
   Christie's London, 27 June 1996 (51**) GBP 56,500   US$ 87,124

FABULATION DU LAVABO (LAVABO II) vinyl on paper laid down on canvas, 39 3/8 x 31 7/8in. (,100 x 81cm.) sd 'J Dubuffet 65'sd and titled on the reverse 'février 65'
PROV.: Lawrence Alloway, New York (acquired directly from the artist).
EXH.: New York, The Solomon R. Guggenheim Museum, *Jean Dubuffet 1962-66*, October 1966-February 1967, no. 60 (illustrated in the catalogue).
LIT.: *Catalogue Intégral des Travaux de Jean Dubuffet, fasc. XXI: L'Hourloupe II*, Lausanne 1968, p. 48, no. 76 (illustrated).
   Christie's London, 30 November 1995 (34**) GBP 100,500   US$ 157,203

TABLE AUX PIECES D'HISTOIRE NATURELLE oil and modeling paste on canvas, 57½ x 45in. (146 x 114.3cm.) sduc 'J Dubuffet 51'
PROV.: Pierre Matisse Gallery, New York.
EXH.: New York, Pierre Matisse Gallery, *Landscaped Tables, Landscapes of the Mind, Stones of Philosophy*, Exhibition of Paintings executed in 1,950 and 1951 by Jean Dubuffet, Feb.- March 1952, no. 7 (illustrated); New York, M. Knoedler & Co., Inc., *The Colin Collection*, April-May 1960, no. 94 (illustrated); New York, The Museum of Modem Art; The Art Institute of Chicago, and Los Angeles County Museum of Art, *The Work of Jean Dubuffet*, Feb.-Aug. 1962, p. 65, no. 73 (illustrated); New York, The Solomon R. Guggenheim Museum, and Paris, Grand Palais, *Jean Dubuffet: A Retrospective*, April-Dec.1973, p. 88, no. 49 (illustrated). Bedin, Akademie der Kunst; Vienna, Museum Moderner Kunst, and Cologne, Josef-Haubrich-Kunsthalle, *Dubuffet Retrospective*, Sept. 1980-March 1981, p. 101, no. 94 (illustrated).
LIT.: G. Limbour, *Tableau Bon Levaina Vous de Cuire la Pate-L'Art Brut de Jean Dubuffet*, Paris 1953, p. 87 (illus.); ed. M. Loreau, *Catalogue des travaux de Jean Dubuffet-Tables Paysagées, paysages du mental, pierres philosphiques*, fascicule VII, Paris 1979, p. 21, no. 12 (illus.in colour).
   Christie's New York, 14 November 1995 (6**) US$ 387,500   US$ 387,500

AFFAIRES ET DÉMARCHES oil on canvas, 64 7/8 x 78½in. (164.8 x 199.2cm.) sdlr 'J. Dubuffet 61'; sd and titled 'J. Dubuffet décembre 61 Affaires et démarches' on the reverse
PROV.: Galerie Daniel Cordier, Paris; Pierre Matisse Gallery, New York.
EXH.: Paris, Galerie Daniel Cordier, *Dubuffet, Paris Circus*, June 1962, no. 20 (illustrated).
LIT.: ed. M. Loreau, *Catalogue des travaux de Jean Dubuffet-Paris Circus*, fascicule XIX, Lausanne 1965, p. 125, no. 239 (illustrated).
   Christie's New York, 14 November 1995 (14**) US$ 662,500   US$ 662,500

DUCK Jacob (1600-1667 (after 1660)) Dutch
A MAN AND A WOMAN PLAYING BACKGAMMON BY AN OPEN WINDOW; A WOMAN
SMOKING A PIPE BEHIND oil on panel, 13¼ x 11½in. (33.7 x 29.2cm.) slr JA (in ligature) Duck
PROV.: Achillito Chiesa, Milan; Sale: American Art Gallery, New York, November 27, 1925, lot 10,
there acquired by Lionel Perry, by descent in the family.

Sotheby's New York, 11 January 1996 (32**) US$ 63,000	US$	63,000

DÜCKER Eugen Gustav (1841-1916) German
WATCHING THE BOATS oil on canvas, 26 x 40in. (66.1 x 101.7cm.) sdll 'E.Ducker 1900'

Christie's South Kensington, 13 June 1996 (95**) GBP 6,670	US$	10,285

DUCROS Louis (1748-1810) French
VIEW OF THE CASCADE AT TIVOLI watercolour, 68 x 105cm. (ca. 1784)

Sotheby's London, 3 July 1995 (200**) GBP 20,700	US$	33,020

DUDREVILLE Leonardo (Venice 1885-1976 Ghiffa) Italian
GLI STORMI oil on panel, 40 x 39cm. sdll 'L. Dudreville 1926'
EXH.: Venezia, *XV Biennale Internazionale d'arte*, 1926.

Finearte Milan, 12 December 1995 (241**) ITL 13,800,000	US$	8,657

DUFFIELD William L. (1816-1863) British
STILL LIFE WITH FRUIT AND A DUCK ON A TABLE oil on canvas, 20 x 32¼in. sd (1861)

Phillips London, 23 April 1996 (52) GBP 4,200	US$	6,368

DUFRESNE Charles Georges (1876-1938) French
FEMME DANS UN INTÉRIEUR (ARLEQUIN) oil on paper laid down on canvas, 65 x 54cm. s
stamped (ca. 1920)

Étude Tajan Paris, 28 March 1996 (8*) FRF 25,000	US$	4,942

DUFY Jean (1888-1964) French
LA PLACE DE LA CONCORDE-VUE SUR LA TOUR EIFFEL oil on canvas, 13 x 18½in. (33 x
47cm.) slr 'Jean Dufy'
PROV.: L. Linas, Paris.

Christie's Tel Aviv, 12 October 1995 (29**) US$ 16,100	US$	16,100

PARIS, LES PONTS SUR LA SEINE, VUE SUR LA TOUR EIFFEL oil on canvas, 18 x 24in. (46 x
61cm.) slr 'Jean Dufy'

Christie's London, 26 June 1996 (318**) GBP 24,150	US$	37,240

PLACE DE LA CONCORDE oil on canvas, 19¾ x 24in. (50 x 61cm.) slc 'Jean Dufy'

Christie's London, 29 November 1995 (158**) GBP 15,000	US$	23,463

SCENE DU PORT oil on canvas, 19¾ x 25½in. (50.2 x 64.8cm.) slr 'Jean Dufy'
PROV.: Frederick Muellet Fine Paintings, Miami Beach.

Christie's East, 30 April 1996 (197**) US$ 14,950	US$	14,950

DANS LE PARC oil on canvas, 15 1/8 x 18 3/8in. (38.5 x 46.8cm.) slr 'Jean Dufy'
PROV.: Frederick Muellet Fine Paintings, Miami Beach.

Christie's East, 30 April 1996 (201**) US$ 13,800	US$	13,800

LA MAISON AU JARDIN oil on canvas, 22 x 13¼in. (55.8 x 33.6cm.) sll 'Jean Dufy'
PROV.: Wally Findlay Gallery, Palm Beach (acquired by the present owner).

Christie's East, 7 November 1995 (181*) US$ 7,475	US$	7,475

LA DANSE oilon canvas, 15 x 18¼in. (38.1 x 46.3cm.) slc 'Jean Duffy'
PROV.: Wally Findlay Galleries, Chicago (acquired by the father of the present owner ca. 1960).

Christie's East, 7 November 1995 (202**) US$ 15,525	US$	15,525

DUFY Raoul (Le Havre 1877-1953 Forqualquier, Basses-Alpes) French
PADDOCK A NICE watercolour and gouache over pencil on paper, 19¾ x 25 5/8in. (50 x 65cm.) slr
'Raoul Dufy' (1927)
PROV.: Paris, Galerie Jean-Claude et Jacques Bellier, *D'Ingres à nos jours, aquarelles, pastel et dessins* 1960, no. 25 (illustrated).
LIT.: F. Guillon-Lafaille, *Raoul Dufy, Catalogue raisonné des aquarelles, gouaches et pastels*, Paris, 1981, vol. I no. 890 (illustrated p. 325).

Christie's New York, 1 May 1996 (222**) US$ 107,000	US$	107,000

NATURE MORTE oil on canvas, 28 5/8 x 36in. (72.7 x 91.4cm.) slr 'Raoul Dufy' (1920)
PROV.: Galerie Bernheim-Jeune, Paris; Le Portique, Paris; Otto M. Gerson, New York; Acquired from the above by Mr. Joseph H. Hazen on Jan. 5, 1952.
EXH.: Jerusalem, Israel Museum, *Paintings from the Collection of Joseph H. Hazen*, summer, 1966, no. 7 (illustrated); The exhibition traveled to Cambridge, Massachusetts, Fogg Art Museum, Oct.-Dec., 1966; Los Angeles, University of California, The Art Galleries, Jan.-Feb., 1967; Berkeley, University of California, Art Museum, Feb.-March, 1967; Houston, Museum of Fine Arts, April-May, 1967, and Honolulu, Academy of Arts, June-Aug., 1967.
LIT.: C. Zervos, *Raoul Dufy*, Paris, 1928, no. 27 (illustrated) J. Cassou, *Raoul Dufy: Poète et Artisan, Paris, 1946, no. 4 (illustrated in colour); M. Raynal, Dufy: Masterpieces of French Painting*, Geneva, 1953, no. 3 (illustrated); J. Lassaigne, *Dufy*, Lausanne, 1954, p. 37 (illustrated); M. Laffaille, *Raoul Dufy, Catalogue raisonné de l'oeuvre peint*, Geneva, 1977, vol. III, p. 332, no. 1332 (illustrated).

Christie's New York, 30 April 1996 (7**) US$ 244,500	US$	244,500

SAINT-ADRESSE oil on canvas, 18 1/8 x 21 5/8in. (46 x 55cm.) slr 'Raoul Dufy' (1924-25)
PROV.: Anon. sale, Palais Galliéra, Paris. 6 December 1966, lot 108.
LIT.: M. Lafaille, *Raoul Dufy, Catalogue raisonné de l'oeuvre peint*, Geneva, 1973, vol. II, no. 715 (illustrated p. 242).

Christie's New York, 1 May 1996 (337**) US$ 134,500	US$	134,500

LA RÉGATE A HENLEY oil on canvas, 25 3/8 x 31 7/8in. (64.6 x 81cm.) sll 'Raoul Dufy' (1930-35)
PROV.: Estate of the artist; Galerie André Weil, Paris (acquired by the present owner).
LIT.: This painting will be included in the second supplement Lafaille's *Dufy catalogue raisonné*.

Christie's New York, 1 May 1996 (359**) US$ 255,500	US$	255,500

VENCE oil on canvas, 25½ x 32in. (65 x 81cm.) sll 'Raoul Dufy'
LIT.: Maurice Lafaille, *Raoul Dufy*, catalogue raisonné III, Editions Motte, Genève, 1973, p. 116, no. 548.

Étude Tajan Paris, 10 June 1996 (46**) FRF 300,000	US$	57,930

LA NAISSANCE DE VENUS oil on panel, 9½ x 16¼in. (24.1 x 41.3cm.) s on the reverse
PROV.: Sale: Geneva, Galerie Motte, September 27, 1958, no. 244 Alex, Reid & Lefevre, Ltd., London; Galerie Roman, Paris.
LIT.: Maurice Laffaille, *Raoul Dufy: Catalogue Raisonné de l'oeuvre Peint*, vol. 4, Geneva, 1977, no. 1611, illustrated p. l71.

Sotheby's New York, 2 May 1996 (167**) US$ 79,500	US$	79,500

GRAND NU DE FACE SUR FOND BLUE oil on canvas, 36 1/8 x 28¾in. (92 x 73cm.) slr 'Raoul Dufy'
EXH.: Bièvres, Moulin de Vauboyen, *Raoul Dufy*, 1968-69, no. 17; Lausanne, Galerie Paul Vallotton, *Exposition Anniversaire, A l'occasion du 60ième anniversaire de sa fondation*, 1973, no. 24, illustrated in the catalogue.
LIT.: Maurice Laffaille, *Raoul Dufy, Catalogue raisonné de l'ocuvre peint*, Geneva, 1976, vol. III, p.

159, no. 1125, illustrated.
      Sotheby's London, 20 March 1996 (82**) GBP 56,500   US\$ 86,286

LE BASSIN oil on canvas, 51¼ x 63¾in. (130 x 162cm.) sll 'Raoul Dufy' (1929)
PROV.: Galerie Bernheim-Jeune, Paris.
EXH.: London, Hayward Gallery, *Raoul Dufy*, November 1983-February 1984, no. 81 (illustrated in colour).
LIT.: Berr de Turique, *Raoul Dufy, catalogue raisonné de l'oeuvre peint*, vol. II, Geneva 1973, no. 816 (illustrated p. 322).
      Christie's London, 25 June 1996 (50**) GBP 463,500   US\$ 714,726

INTERIEUR, VERNET LES BAINS oil on canvas, 23¾ x 28¾in. 960.3 x 73cm.) slr Raoul Dufy' (1943)
PROV.: Galerie Drouant-David, Paris; Schoneman Galleries Inc., New York; Mrs Patrick Butler, St. Paul, Minnesota; Anon sale, Christie's London, 6 April 1976, lot 45 (GBP 19,000), where purchased by the present owners.
EXH.: New York, Hirschl & Adler Gallery, *Raoul Dufy*, Nov.-Dec. 1965, no. 23.
LIT.: M. Lafaille, *Raoul Dufy, Catalogue Raisonné de l'Oeuvre Peint*, vol. III Geneva, 1977, no. 1252 (illustrated p. 271).
      Christie's London, 26 June 1996 (178**) GBP 98,300   US\$ 151,581

BATEAUX AU PORT oil on canvas, 18 x 21½in. (46 x 54.7cm.) slr 'Raoul Dufy' (ca 1930)
PROV.: Galerie Europe, Paris.
LIT.: M. Lafaille, *Raoul Dufy, Catalogue Raisonné de l'Oeuvre Peint*, vol. II Geneva, 1977, no. 820 (illustrated p. 342).
      Christie's London, 26 June 1996 (179**) GBP 76,300   US\$ 117,656

LES EQUILIBRISTES gouache on paper, 25 x 19½in. (63.5 x 49.5cm.) slr 'Raoul Dufy' (1923)
PROV.: Collection Hageman, Newport, Rhode Island; anon. sale, Sotheby's, London, 23 June 1965, lot 84 (illustrated); anon. sale, Maître Blache, Versailles, 3 June 1981, lot 158.
LIT.: F. Guillon-Laffaille, *Raoul Dufy, catalogue raisonné des aquarelles, gouaches et pastels*, Vol.II, Paris, 1982, no.1697 (illustrated p.229); P. Courthion, *Chroniques du Jour*, Paris, 1929, pl.5.
      Christie's London, 26 June 1996 (192**) GBP 24,150   US\$ 37,240

TROIS BAIGNEUSES oil on canvas, 25¾ x 21¼in. (65.5 x 54cm.) s 'Raoul Dufy' (1939)
PROV.: Anon. sale, Hotel Rameau, Versailles, May 13, 1964, lot 41; Galerie Paul Pétridès, Paris; anon. sale, Hotel George V, Paris, 13 March 1974 lot 16; anon. sale, Christie's, New York, 18 May 1983, lot 393 (illustrated) where purchased by the present owners.
LIT.: M. Laffaille, *Raoul Dufy, Catalogue raisonné de l'Oeuvre peint*,Vol. IV, Geneva, 1977, no.1537 (illustrated p.111).
      Christie's London, 26 June 1996 (200**) GBP 73,000   US\$ 112,567

LA PLAGE DE SAINTE-ADRESS oil on canvas, 23 5/8 x 28¾in. (60 x 73cm.) slr 'Raoul Dufy' (ca 1905)
PROV.: Galerie Amanthe, Paris, from whom bought by the father of the present owner (ca 1950).
      Christie's London, 28 November 1995 (19**) GBP 276,500   US\$ 432,504

ASCOT oil on canvas, 15 x 18 1/8in. (38 x 46cm.) sll 'Raoul Dufy' (1930)
LIT.: To be included in the forthcoming *supplement to the Raoul Dufy Catalogue Raisonné*, currently being prepared by Fanny Guilon-Laffaille.
      Christie's London, 29 November 1995 (223**) GBP 80,000   US\$ 125,137

LE GRAND CIRQUE oil on canvas, 35 x 45 5/8in. (89 x 116cm.) slr 'Raoul Dufy' (ca 1935)
PROV.: Marlborough Fine Art, Ltd., London.
EXH.: Bordeaux, Galerie des Beaux-Arts, *Raoul Dufy 1877-1953*, May-Sept., 1970, p. 16, no. 92 (illustrated in colour as the frontispiece); Paris, Galerie Schmit, *Tableaux des Maîtres français 1900-*

1955, May-June, 1973, no. 25 (illustrated in colour).
LIT.: M. Lafaille, *Raoul Dufy, Catalogue raisonné de l'oeuvre peint*, Geneva, 1977, vol. IV, p. 151, no. 1587 (illustrated in colour).

Christie's New York, 30 April 1996 (61**) US$ 596,500	US$	596,500

LA PROCESSION GRECQUE gouache on paper, 39½ x 30¾in. (,100 x 78cm.) stamped lr 'RD Bianchini Férier'

Christie's East, 30 April 1996 (202**) US$ 11,500	US$	11,500

LA PLAGE DE SAINTE-ADRESSE oil on canvas, 21 1/4 x 25 1/2in. (54 x 65cm.) slr 'Raoul Dufy' (1901)
PROV.: Galerie Hervé, Paris.
LIT.: M. Laffaille, *Raoul Dufy, Catalogue raisonné de l'oeuvre peint*, Paris, 1972, vol. I, no. 55 (illustrated, p. 53).

Christie's New York, 8 November 1995 (136**) US$ 156,500	US$	156,500

REGATES CANS LE PORT DE TROUVILLE-DEAUVILLE oil on canvas, 18 1/4 x 43 3/8in. (46.4 x 110.2cm.) lr 'Raoul Dufy' (ca 1938)

Christie's New York, 8 November 1995 (235**) US$ 294,000	US$	294,000

DUGHET Gaspard, {called} Gaspar Poussin (Rome 1615-1675) French
ITALIANATE LANDSCAPE SCENE WITH TWO FIGURES NEAR A STREAM, A MAN RESTING BY THE ROADSIDE AND A SHEPHERD BEYOND oil on canvas, 29¼ x 38in. (74 x 96.4cm.)
PROV.: Property of Fürst zu Löwenstein, removed from Schloss Kleinheubach.

Sotheby's London, 5 July 1995 (186**) GBP 28,750	US$	45,861

FIGURES IN CLASSICAL LANDSCAPES WITH MOUNTAINS AND HILL TOP TOWNS oil on canvas (a pair), each: 27 x 19¾in. (68.5 x 50cm.)
PROV.: Possibly John, Lord Hervey, circa 1740.
EXH.: Inventory, 1952, p. 22, as Gaspar Poussin, a pair; The Antique Collector, 1961, p.223.

Sotheby's London, 11-12 June 1996 (485**) GBP 18,400	US$	28,373

DULLAERT Heyman (Rotterdam 1636-1684) Dutch
A ROAST GUINEA-FOWL, AN ORANGE, AND A PEELED LEMON IN A SILVER CHAFING DISH, A PLATE WITH A LEG OF FOWL,A FLUTE, A GLASS OF BEER, A KNIFE AND A BREAD ROLL ON A PARTIALLY DRAPED TABLE oil on canvas, 21½ x 28¾cm. (54.6 x 73cm.)
PROV.: With Douwes, Amsterdam; with Hoogsteder, The Hague, 1977, as Simon Luttichuys.
LIT.: N.R.A. Vroom, *A Modest Message as intimated by the painters of the 'Monochrome Banketje'*, Schiedam 1980, I, p. 192, fig. 262, colour; II, p.93, no. 461.

Christie's London, 8 December 1995 (44**) GBP 40,000	US$	61,557

DUNHAM Carroll (1949 b.) American?
HORIZON PROBLEM casein, dry pigment, flashe, graphite and charcoal on oak, walnut and maple veneer-unframed, 65 x 45in. (165.2 x 114.2cm.) sd titled "HORIZON PROBLEM' Caroll Dunham 1984' on the reverse
PROV.: Daniel Weinberg Gallery, Los Angeles.; Gagosian Gallery, New York.

Christie's New York, 15 November 1995 (282**) US$ 23,000	US$	23,000

DUNOYER DE SEGONZAC André de (1884-1974) French
GARDEN SCENE, BOUQUET AND WIDE-BRIMMED HAT ON A TABLE oil on canvas, 21¼ x 32in. (54 x 81cm.) sul 'A.D. de Segonzac' (1927)
PROV.: Former Collection of Henry-Jean Laroche.
LIT.: Paul Jamot, *Dunoyer de Segonzac*, Paris, Librairie Floury, 1941, illustrated (without signature) on p. 67.

Étude Tajan Paris, 13 December 1995 (15***) FRF 200,000	US$	40,285

LES LYS ROUGES watercolour and ink on paper, 22 x 32¼in. (56 x 81cm.) s 'a. Dunoyer de Segonzac
PROV.: Aquavella Galleries, New York.

        Christie's London, 26 June 1996 (307**) GBP 20,700   US$ 31,920

LA TABLE EN PROVENCE watercolour and pen and black ink on paper, 19 25¾in. (48.5 x 65.5cm.) sll 'A. Dunoyer de Segonzac'

        Christie's London, 29 November 1995 (127**) GBP 14,000   US$ 21,899

DUNTZE Johannes Bartholomaus (Rablinghausen 1823-1895) German
SKATERS ON A FROZEN RIVER BEFORE A WINDMILL oil on canvas, 16 ½ x 26 1/8in. (42 x 66.5cm) sd (1889)

        Phillips London, 14 November 1995 (27**) GBP 4,500   US$ 7,039

DUPLESSIS Joseph Siffrede (Carpentras 1725-1802 Versailles) French
PORTAIT OF COUNTESS D'ESTAVAYE oil on canvas, 31 x 25cm. (an oval)
PROV.: Galerie Renée Drouin.
EXH.: Paris, Galerie Charpentier, *Portraits français*, 1945.

        Étude Tajan Paris, 18 December 1995 (185***) FRF 40,000   US$ 8,057

DUPRÉ Jules (Nantes 1811-1889 L'Isle-Adam) French
A COTTAGE IN A LANDSCAPE oil on canvas, 15 x 21¾in. (38.1 x 55.2cm.)

        Christie's East, 13 February 1996 (79**) US$ 12,650   US$ 12,650

A LANDSCAPE WITH A WINDMILL oil on canvas, 12¾ x 16in. (32.4 x 40.7cm.) sll 'J.Dupré' (ca.1850-1855)
EXH.: New York, The Shepherd Gallery, *The forest of Fontainebleau: Refuge of reality, French Landscape* 1800-1870, April 22-June 10, 1972, no. 34.

        Christie's New York, 2 November 1995 (106**) US$ 23,000   US$ 23,000

CREPUSCULE oil on canvas, 28¾ x 23½in. (73.1 x 59.7cm.) slr 'J. Dupré'
PROV.: Alexandre Dumas Collection; H. Beeche, sale; Galerie George Petit, Paris, May 9, 1904; Rosenberg, Paris, for Ralston, New York, (bt. $5,500); With Vose Gallery, *Boston Annuary*, 1944), purchased by W.B.P. Weeks; With Brodney Galleries, Boston (until April 1, 1953), purchased by Wilmon and Katherine More Brewer, Great Hills.
LIT.: *The Connoisseur*, June 30, 1904, vol. IV, no. 31; M. M. Aubrun, *Jules Dupré*, Paris, 1974, no. 690, p. 247 and 257 (illustrated).

        Christie's New York, 2 November 1995 (115**) US$ 25,300   US$ 25,300

COWS WATERING AT A POND oil on panel, 12¾ x 16¼in. (32.4 x 41.2cm.) slr 'J. Dupré'

        Christie's New York, 22 May 1996 (131**) US$ 17,250   US$ 17,250

STACKING HAY oil on canvas, 21 ¼ x 25¾in. (54 x 65.4cm.) sll 'JULIEN DUPRE.'

        Christie's New York, 22 May 1996 (172**) US$ 107,000   US$ 107,000

THE COW PASTURE oil on canvas, 18 x 21 5/8in. (45.7 x 55cm.) sll 'JULIEN DUPRE'

        Christie's New York, 22 May 1996 (173**) US$ 23,000   US$ 23,000

DUPUIS Pierre (1610-1682) French
STILLEBEN oil on canvas, 74 x 100cm.
EXH.: Copenhagen, *Kunstforeningens udstilling af hollandske og flamske sileben fra 1600 talet.*, 1965, No. 59.

        Lempertz Cologne, 18 May 1996 (1039**) DEM 42,000   US$ 27,381

DUPUY Paul Michel (1869-1949) French
ENFANTS AU JARDIN DES TUILERIES, PARIS oil on canvas, 10¾ x 15¾in. (27.3 x 40cm.) sdlr

'P.M. Dupuy 1901'
  Sotheby's Arcade Auctions New York, 20 July 1995 (196***) US$ 10,350   US$ 10,350

DURRIE George Henry (1820-1863) American
WINTER LANDSCAPE oil on canvas, 14 x 24in. (35.6 x 61cm.) s insdist. lr 'Durrie'
  Christie's New York, 23 May 1996 (16**) US$ 38,100   US$ 38,100

DUVIEUX Henri (France -) French
IL BACINO, VENICE oil on canvas, 19¾ x 36¼in. (50.2 x 92.1cm.) slr 'Duvieux-'
  Christie's New York, 2 November 1995 (230**) US$ 13,800   US$ 13,800

DUYFHUIJSEN Pieter Jacobsz. (called Colinchovius) (Rotterdam 1608-1677) Dutch
TEH LACEMAKER oil on oak panel, 13½ x 10¼in. (34 x 26cm.) slr 'PDuyfhuisen'
EXH.: On loan, Doncaster Museum and Art Gallery, 1978-1993; Leeds, City Art Gallery, *Dutch 17th Century Paintings from Yorkshire Public Collections*, 27 November 1983-29 January 1984, no. 19; Birmingham, City Museum and Art Gallery, *Images of a golden Age; Dutch Seventeenth Century Paintings*, 1989, no. 90.
LIT.: W.L. van de Watering, 'Pieter Duyfhuysen (1608-1677): een reconstructie van het oeuvre van een vergeten Roterdamse schilder van boereninterieurs', (extract from: *Holländiche Genremalerei im 17. Jahrhundert*, Acts of the symposium Berlin 1984), *Jahrbuch Preussischer Kulturbesitz*, Sondernband 4, 1987, p. 360, reproduced p. 382, fig. 20.
  Sotheby's London, 5 July 1995 (31**) GBP 69,700   US$ 111,182

DUYSTER Willem Cornelisz. (1599-1635) Dutch
A PAIR MAKING MUSIC oil on panel, 26 x 35cm.
  Dorotheum Vienna, 11 June 1996 (279**) ATS 250,000   US$ 23,205

DYCK Abraham van (Amsterdam 1635-1672) Dutch
A YOUNG GIRL AT A BALLUSTRADE oil on canvas, 46¼ x 32¼in. (117.5 x 81.5cm.)
PROV.: Murray Backer Collection, Amsterdam; With J. Goudstikker, Amsterdam, 1927 (his exhibition of that year no. 5); Baron Heinrich Thyssen-Bornemisza, by 1930.
EXH.: Munich 1930, no. 29, as Bol; Lausanne etc., 1986-87, no. 28, as Bol.
LIT.: R. Heinemann, 1937, vol. I, no. 37, vol. II, reproduced plate 130, as Bol; A. Blankert, *Ferdinand Bol*, 1982, no. R216, under rejected attributions.
  Sotheby's London, 6 December 1995 (96**) GBP 8,050   US$ 12,388

DYCK Floris van (Haarlem 1575-1651) Dutch
AN 'UITGESTALD' STILL LIFE OF FRUIT AND OLIVES IN VARIOUS BLUE AND WHITE CHINESE EXPORT PORCELAIN BOWLLS , A SIEGBURG STONEWARE 'SCHNABELKANNE', A 'BEKERSCHROEF' SILVER-GILT RUMMER MOUNT CONTAINING A 'BERKEMEYER' CONICAL RUMMER, A ROEMER, AN UPTURNED 'FAÇON-DE-VENISE' BEAKER WITH LION MASK PRUNTS, A STEMMED FLUTE, OLD AND YOUNG CHEESE ON A SILVER PLATE, A KNIFE AND VARIOUS SCATTERED FRUITS AND NUTS, ALL ARRANGED UPON A WHITE DAMASQUE CLOTH LAID OVER A ROSE DAMASQUE CLOTH COVERING A LEDGE oil on oak panel, 29¼ x 44¾in. (74.5 x 114cm.)
PROV.: Anonymous sale, Cologne, Lempertz, 8 May 1937, lot 68, where bought by the father of the present owner.
LIT.: F.G. Meijer, in *Dawn of the Golden Age..*, exhibition catalogue, 1993, pp. 604-5, under footnote 2. Sotheby's London, 6 December 1995 (58**) GBP 320,500   US$ 493,229

DYCK Sir Anthony van (Antwerp 1599-1641 London) Flemish
A PORTRAIT OF A LADY oil on canvas, 29¼ x 23¼in. (74.5 x 59cm.) (1625-26)
PROV.: Mc. Cornick Collection, Chicago; Rattier Collection; Von Mumm Collection, Berlin (possibly the 'North German private collection' mentioned in the 1930 exhibition catalogue); Baron Heinrich Thyssen-Bornemisza, by 1930.
EXH.: Munich 1930, no. 104; Munich 1931, Paris 1970, no. 23, plate 16; Düsseldorf 1970-1, no. 19;

Lausanne etc., 1986-7, no. 19.
LIT.: G. Gluck, *Van Dyck*, 1931, p. 176; R. Heinemann 1937, vol.II, no. 129, vol. II, plate 109; E.
Larsen, *L 'Opera completa di Anthony van Dyck*, 1980, vol. I, p. 119, no. 465, reproduced, as painted
circa 1625-6; E. Larsen, *The Paintings of Anthony an Dyck*, 1988, vol. II, p. 160, no. 392,
reproduced, as painted *circa* 1625.
Sotheby's London, 6 December 1995 (90**) GBP 62,000 US$ 95,414

DYCK Sir Anthony van (and his Studio) (Antwerp 1599-1641 London) Flemish
PORTAIT OF PHILIP HERBERT, 4TH EARL OF PEMBROKE AND 1ST EARL OF
MONTGOMERY oil on canvas, 30 x 24¾in. (76 x 63cm.) inscr. lr with the identitty of the sitter
PROV.: Sir William Feilding, 1ˢᵗ Earl of Denbigh (1582-1643).
LIT.: G. Gluck, *Van Dyck*, 1931, p. 444; Erik Larsen, *L'Opera Completa di van Dyck 1626-1641*,
1980, p. 116, no. 844; Erik Larsen, *The Paintings of Anthony van Dyck*, vol. II, 1988, p. 367, no. 939.
Sotheby's London, 12 July 1995 (14**) GBP 20,700 US$ 33,020

DYCK Sir Anthony van (attr.) (Antwerp 1599-1641 London) Flemish
PORTRAIT, SAID TO BE THE MARCHESA BALBI oil on paper, laid on canvas, laid on panel,
12½ x 10¾in. (33 x 27cm.) inscr. ul in a later hand '..Balbi (?)/..' (ca. 1623)
PROV.: Frederick, 1st Marquess of Bristol.
LIT.: Seguier, 1819, possibly no. 76, (valued at GBP5), as by Rubens; Farrer, 1913, no. 207; Farrer,
Additional Ickworth List,1913,no.207, as Lady; Inventory, 1952, p. 47, as Van Dyck; Dr Susan
Barnes, who has inspected the painting in the original, supports the attribution to Van Dyck and will
include the picture in the forthcoming *catalogue raisonné*, currently in preparation by Dr Barnes, Sir
Oliver Millar, Horst Vey and Nora de Poorter.
Sotheby's London, 11-12 June 1996 (484**) GBP 133,500 US$ 205,860

DYCK Sir Anthony van (studio of) (Antwerp 1599-1641 London) Flemish
SELF PORTAIT OF THE ARTIST WITH A SUNFLOWER oil on canvas, 23 x 28½in. (58.5 x
72.5cm.) inscr. ul 'A. Van Dyck/by Van Dike (ca. 1635-36)
PROV.: Frederick, 1st Marquess of Bristol.
EXH.: Grosvenor Gallery, *Exhibition of the Works of Sir Anthony van Dyck, 1887*, no.1.
LIT.: Segiuer, 1819, no.27 (valued at GBP80); Sir Lionel Cust, *Anthony van Dyck*, 1900, p.285,
no.208B; Willoughby, 1906, part III, p.87, illustrated p.90; Catalogue, 1907 The Antique Collector,
1961; E. Larsen, *The Paintings of van Dyck*, two volumes, 1988, p.510, no. A299/2; The Antique
Collector, 1991, p.110, illustrated p.lll.
Sotheby's London, 11-12 June 1996 (433**) GBP 210,500 US$ 324,595

DYKSTRA Johan (Groningen 1896-1978) Dutch
GEZICHT OP DE SPILSLUIZEN VANAF DE EBBINGERBRUG, GRONINGEN oil on canvas, 51
x 64.5cm. sll
PROV.: Collection F. Kleinhof, Twello.
LIT.: Adriaan Venema, *De Ploeg 1918-1930*, Baarn 1978, p. 112A (illustrated in colour).
Sotheby's Amsterdam, 7 December 1995 (185**) NLG 47,200 US$ 29,248

DZUBAS Friedel (1915 b.) American
BUILT UP magna on canvas, 47 x 108in. (119.4 x 274.3cm.) sd and titled 'Dzubas 'BUILT UP' 1981'
on the reverse
PROV.: M.Knoedler & Co., Inc., New York.
Christie's New York, 22 February 1996 (40**) US$ 23,000 US$ 23,000

EARDLEY Joan Kathleen Harding, R.S.A. (1921-1963) Scottish
SNOW 1 oil on canvas, 24 x 27¼in. (61 x 69cm.) slr 'EARDLEY'
EXH.: Edinburgh, Aitkin Dott and Son, *Joan Eardley Exhibtion*, 1961, no. 21; Edinburgh, The Arts
Council of Great Britain-Scottish Committee, *Joan Eardley Memorial*, 1964, no. 83.
    Sotheby's London, 29 August 1995 (1000**) GBP 7,820   US$ 12,658

EARLE Eyvind (1916 b.) American
BIG SUR oil on masonite, 22 x 28in. (71.2 x 55.9cm.) slr 'Eyvind Earle'; dll '1972'
    Christie's East, 7 May 1996 (159*) US$ 8,050   US$ 8,050

SHADOW PATTERNS oil on masonite, 30 x 20in. (76.2 x 50.8cm.) sdlr 'Eyvind Earle 2-8-77'
    Christie's East, 7 May 1996 (160*) US$ 8,050   US$ 8,050

EARL Maud (1943 d.) British
COMEDIAN HOWLING AT THE MOON oil on canvas, 24 x 20in. (61 x 50.8cm.) slr 'Maud Earl'
PROV.: With the St. James's Gallery, New York.
    Christie's New York, 14 February 1996 (143**) US$ 6,900   US$ 6,900

EARL Ralph (1785-1838) American
PORTRAIT OF JOHN PHELPS oil on canvas, 77 x 49in. (195 x 124.5cm.) sdll 'R. Earl Phelps'
    Christie's New York, 23 May 1996 (3**) US$ 233,500   US$ 233,500

EDZARD Dietz (Bremen 1893-1963 Paris) German
AU BALCON oil on canvas, 28¾ x 23 5/8in. (73 x 60cm.) sll 'D. Edzard'
    Christie's East, 30 April 1996 (116*) US$ 7,475   US$ 7,475

EERELMAN Otto (Groningen 1839-1926 Groningen) Dutch
SPORTSMEN AT THE GATE oil on canvas, 80 x 65.5cm. s 'O.Eerelman'
    Christie's Amsterdam, 25 April 1996 (200**) NLG 17,250   US$ 10,250

HET OPTREKKEN DER PINKEN, SCHEVENINGEN oil on canvas, 39 x 73cm. s 'O. Eerelman' s
titled on a label on the stretcher
EXH.: Maastricht, *Tentoonstelling Momus*, afd. Beeldende Kunsten, 1906.
    Christie's Amsterdam, 25 April 1996 (201**) NLG 149,500   US$ 88,835

YOUNG ST. BERNHARDS: A FASCINATING ENCOUNTER oil on canvas, 49.5 x 62cm. sl 'O.
Eerelman' s again inscr. with title on a label on the stretcher, oil on canvas
    Christie's Amsterdam, 26 October 1995 (304**) NLG 78,200   US$ 49,306

EGGER-LIENZ Albin (Striebach 1868-1926 Zwolfmalgreien) Swiss
HAUSSTUDIE oil on canvas, 58.5 x 49cm. slr 'Egger-Lienz' (ca. 1902)
PROV.: from the Artist's Estate, Vienna.
LIT.: Heinrich Hammer, *Albin Egger-Lienz*, Tyrolia Verlag, Innsbruck 1930, p. 268 (size as 56 x
46cm.); Wilfried Kirschl, *Albin Egger-Lienz. 1868-1926. Das Gesammtwerk*, Edition Tusch, Vienna
1977, no. M179.
    Wiener Kunst Auktionen, 26 March 1996 (174**) ATS 400,000   US$ 38,476

SÄMANN UND TEUFEL watercolour and gouache on paper laid down on cardboard, 73 x 81.2cm.
sll 'Egger Lienz' (ca. 1920)
    Wiener Kunst Auktionen, 29 November 1995 (632**) ATS 750,000   US$ 75,235

VORPOSTEN gouache on paper, 59 x 43cm. s 'Egger-Lienz'
    Dorotheum Vienna, 6 December 1995 (472**) ATS 150,000   US$ 14,792

EGMONT Pieter Cornelisz. van (1615-1663 c.) Dutch
PORTRAIT OF THE PAINTER IN HIS STUDIO oil on oak panel, 74 x 62cm. sll 'PVC Egmonsz'

PROV.: Galerie Leegenhoek, Paris, 1968 (as Jacob van Spreeuwen).
LIT.: F.J. Meijer, 'Pieter Cornelisz van Egmont, een Kennismaking', *Oud Holland*, pp 262, 263,
illustrated pl. 7 (location unknown); W. Sumowski, *Gemälde der Rembrandt Schüler*, Landau, 1983,
VI, no. 2273, illustrated p. 3861.

Étude Tajan Paris, 12 December 1995 (44**) FRF 75,000	US$	15,107

EGNER Marie (Radkersburg 1850-1940 Vienna) Austrian
LANDSCHAFT MIT BLÜHENDER WIESE oil on cardboard, 23.8 x 34.5cm. sll 'M. Egner'

Wiener Kunst Auktionen, 26 March 1996 (170**) ATS 100,000	US$	9,619

ALMATRIEB BEI GMÜND oil on canvas, 30 x 45cm. s 'Gmünd' stamped 'Aus dem Nachlaß Prof.
Marie Egner' (ca. 1885)
LIT.: Martin Suppan/Erich Tromayer, *Marie Egner*, 1981, p. 133, pl. 38.

Dorotheum Vienna, 6 December 1995 (401**) ATS 65,000	US$	6,410

SCHWERTLILIEN oil on canvas, 43.5 x 54.5cm. s 'M. Egner'

Dorotheum Vienna, 6 December 1995 (482**) ATS 600,000	US$	59,168

EHRENBERG Willem van (Antwerp 1630-1676 Antwerp) Flemish
THREE LADIES AND DOG ON A TERRACE OF A RENAISSANCE PALACE oil on canvas,
40.5 x 46.5cm. sd 'Ehrenberg fc. 1668'

Dorotheum Vienna, 17 October 1995 (287**) ATS 160,000	US$	16,049

EISENHUT Ferencz-Franz (1857-1903) Hungarian
AN ARAB SLAVE MARKET oil on canvas, 53 ¼ x 87 5/8in. sdll inscr. 'Muenchen' (1888)
EXH.: Munich, Jubiläums-Ausstellung, 1888.
LIT.: Friedrich von Boettiger, *Malerwerke des Neunzehnten Jahrhunderts*, Vol I, in Hofheim am
Taunus, 1969, p. 275, no. 6.; Philip Hook and Mark Poltimore, *Popular 19th Century Painting,*
Woodbridge, 1986, p.33 (illustrated).

Phillips London, 14 November 1995 (49**) GBP 44,000	US$	68,825

EISMAN Johan Anton (attr.) (ca. 1689 (act.)) German (Italian)
A MEDITERRANEAN COAST WITH A FORTIFIED TOWER AND A DUTCH MAN-O'-WAR
IN THE BAY oil on canvas, 70 x 102cm. sd (indistinctly) 'Giovan Battista Lam. fece in Venezia
l'anno 16.'

Christie's Rome, 4 June 1996 (515**) ITL 32,000,000	US$	20,752

VIEW ON THE RIVER SALZACH, THE CITY OF SALZBURG BEYOND oil on canvas, 100.5 x
150.5cm.
PROV.: Private Collection, Prague.

Dorotheum Vienna, 6 March 1996 (190**) ATS 140,000	US$	13,467

EKSTRÖM Per (Segerstad (Öland) 1844-1935 Mörbylånga) Swedish
SOLDNEGÅNG ÖVER ÖLÄNSK GÅRD oil on canvas, 80 x 116cm. sll 'P. Ekström'

Bukowskis Stockholm, 29-31 May 1996 (22**) SEK 74,000	US$	10,883

STOCKHOLM IN WINTER oil on canvas, 28½ x 52in. (72.4 x 132.1cm.) slr 'P.EKSTRÖM'
EXH.: Philadelphia, Pennsylvania Academy of Fine Arts, *Representative Works of Contemporary
Swedish Artists*, 1896 exh. cat no. 17.

Christie's New York, 14 February 1996 (140**) US$ 6,900	US$	6,900

ELLIGER Ottmar I (1633-1679) Swedish
IRISES, TULIPS, ANEMONES, ROSES, CARNATIONS, FORGET-ME-NOTS, A DAFFODIL,
SNOWDROPS, MARIGOLDS AND OTHER FLOWERS IN A GLASS VASE WITH ORANGES
ON A TWIG ON A MARBLE LEDGE oil on canvas, 73.4 x 60.3cm

Christie's Amsterdam, 13 November 1995 (138**) NLG 69,000	US$	43,486

ELLIGER Ottmar II (Hamburg 1666-1735 St Petersburg) German
ACHILLE DÉCOUVERT PARMI LES FILLES DE LYCOMEDE; SALOMÉ DANSANT
DEVANT HÉRODE oil on canvas (a pair), each: 55 x 68cm.
PROV.: Anonymous sale, Phillips, London, 6 December 1988, lot 75 (illustrated).
       Étude Tajan Paris, 12 December 1995 (86**) FRF 120,000   US$ 24,171

ELSEVIER Louwys Aernout (Leyden 1617-1675) Dutch
DUCKS BY A DECOY IN A RIVER LANDSCAPE oil on panel, 57 x 82cm.
       Sotheby's Amsterdam, 14 November 1995 (22**) NLG 21,240   US$ 13,386

ENGSTRÖM Leander (1886-1927) Swedish
PATIENS , 100 x 80cm. sdlr 'Leander Engström 11'
       Bukowskis Stockholm, 24-25 April 1996 (21**) SEK 140,000   US$ 21,210

HAMNEN I VIAREGGIO oil on canvas, 92 x 105cm. sd 'Leander Engström 1922'
EXH.: Pittsburgh, Carnegie Institute, reg. no. 49, cat, no. 424.
LIT.: Nils Palmgren, *Leander Engström* (illustrated p. 103).
       Bukowskis Stockholm, 26-27 October 1995 (28**) SEK 410,000   US$ 60,045

ENJOLRAS Delphin (1857-1945) French
UNE SOIRÉE SUR LA TERRASSE oil on canvas, 23¾ x 28¾in. (60.3 x 73cm.) sll 'D Enjolras'
       Christie's New York, 2 November 1995 (189**) US$ 18,400   US$ 18,400

ENNEKING John Joseph (1841-1916) American
BERRYING AT THE SEASHORE oil on canvas laid down on masonite, 15½ x 23½in. (39.4 x
59.7cm.) sdlr 'Enneking 79'
       Christie's New York, 13 September 1995 (51**) US$ 17,250   US$ 17,250

EARLY AUTUMN oil on canvas, 20¼ x 24in. (51.5 x 61cm.) slr 'Enneking.'
       Christie's New York, 13 September 1995 (57**) US$ 9,200   US$ 9,200

ENSOR James, baron (Oostende 1860-1949) Belgian (British)
CROQUIS POUR 'ECHEC' coloured pencil on paper, 7 5/8 x 10 5/8in. (19.4 x 27cm.) s and inscr.
'Croquis pour échec, Reine, une tour et un pion'; also s and inscr. in the artist's address on the verso
PROV.: Galerie Motte, Geneva; Acquired from the above by the present owner on 29 June 1969.
EXH.: Zurich, Galerie M. Knoedler; New York, M. Knoedler & Co., *Gustav Klimt, Egon Schiele,
James Ensor, Alfred Kubin: Künstler der Jahrhundertwende*, 1983-84, p.222.
       Sotheby's New York, 2 May 1996 (144**) US$ 21,850   US$ 21,850

COQUILLAGES ET PLANTES MARINES oil on canvas, 19 7/8 x 24in. (50.5 x 61cm.) slr 'J. Ensor'
(1932)
PROV.: Augusta Boogaerts, Brussels; Claes-Boogaerts, Brussels; Vente, Brussels, Galerie Giroux,
28th March 1952, lot 139; Sale Sotheby's, London, 3 December 1981, lot 627 (purchased by the
present owner at GBP 14,850).
EXH.: London, Leicester Galleries, *Paintings, Drawings and Etchings by James Ensor*, 1936, no. 72;
Paris, Galerie de l'Elysée, *James Ensor*, 1937; Leuven, Galerie Fonteyn, *Salon* 1938; *James Ensor*,
1938, no. 1.
LIT.: Xavier Tricot, James Ensor, *Catalogue raisonné of the Paintings*, Antwerp, 1992, vol. II, p.
564, no. 606, illustrated.
       Sotheby's London, 20 March 1996 (32**) GBP 51,000   US$ 77,886

LE MONTÉE AU CALVAIRE - THE ROAD TO CALVARY oil on canvas, 31½ x 39 3/8in. (80 x
100cm.) sdlr 'Ensor 1914'
PROV.: L. Fierens, Antwerp; A. Crespin, Brussels; A. Pisart, Brussels; Ph. Bogaerts, Brussels;
Monsieur François, Brussels; Private collection, Belgium.
EXH.: 1936, Paris, Galerie de l`Elysée, 'Sainte; Veronique'; 1945, (13 October-4 November),;

Brussels, Galerie Georges Giroux,; *Hommage à Ensor*, no. 113.; Catalogued as 'Portement de Croix'; and stated as being from 1920.; Brussels, Beaux-Arts, 'Sainte Véronique'.
LIT.: *Sélection*, IV, no. 2, 11-1924, p. 158; (ill.); A. De Ridder, *James Ensor*, Paris, 1930, pl. 44 (ill.), as dated 1922.; J. E. Payro, *James Ensor*, Buenos Aires, 143, n.n. (ill.); Gisèle Ollinger-Zinque, *Ensor par Lui; même*, Brussels, 1976, no. 90, p.135 (ill.); Xavier Tricot, *James Ensor. Catalogue Raisonné; of the paintings*, vol. II, London: Philip Wilson, 1992, no. 512,; p. 497 (ill.). Catalogued as *La montée au Calvaire*, 1924.

Phillips London, 26 June 1995 (38**) GBP 87,000   US$ 138,822

The Road to Cavalry

LE CALVAIRE-DE CALVARIEBERG oil on canvas, 23 5/8 x 29½in. (60 x 75cm.) slr 'Ensor' s titled again on the reverse (March 1940)
LIT.: G. Ollinger-Zinque, *Ensor een zelfportret*, Brussels 1977, no.27 p. 104; X. Tricot, *Ensoriana*, Ostend, 1985, p. 34, no. 20B; X. Tricot, *James Ensor Catalogue Raisonné of the paintings, vol II*, London, 1992 no. 822 (illustrated p. 680).

Christie's London, 26 June 1996 (227**) GBP 29,900   US$ 46,106

ERNST Max (Brühl 1891-1976 Paris) American (German)
PAYSAGE AU SOLEIL oil on canvas, 59.7 x 48.9cm. slr 'MAX ERNST' (1926)
PROV.: Richard Feigen Gallery, Chicago; Collection Claire B. Zeisler, Chicago.
EXH.: Chicago, *Dada and Surrealism Chicago collections,*, Museum of Contemporary Art, 1984-85.
LIT.: *In the Mind's Eye: Dada and Surrealism*, catalogue of the exhibition in the Museum of Contemporary Art. Chicago 1984-85, p. 143.

Hauswedell & Nolte Cologne, 1 December 1995 (245**) DEM 218,000   US$ 151,252

L'OISEAU DE NUIT oil on panel, 14 x 17.5cm. slr 'MAX ERNST' (1954)
PROV.: Aram D. Mouradian, Paris; Jordan Guttermann, Houston, Texas.

Hauswedell & Nolte Cologne, 1 December 1995 (246**) DEM 90,000   US$ 62,444

MARIE-BERTHE AURENCHE oil and gouache on canvas, 54.2 x 65cm. slr 'max ernst', titled 'portrait de Marie-Berthe' on the reverse (1928)
PROV.: Galerie Michael Hertz, Bremen; Bayrische Staatsgemäldesammlungen München; Galerie Beyeler, Basel.
EXH.: Mechelen 1971, Staatsarchief *De menselijke figuur in de kunst*, 1910-1960, no.41; Basel 1974, *Max Ernst*, Galerie Beyeler no.21 (Ausstellungsaufkleber); Essen 1987, *Deutsche Kunst im 20.Jahrhundert*, Galerie Neher; London 1988/1989, *Max Ernst, Paintings, Sculptures, Works on Papier.*
LIT.: Cat. Neue Pinakothek/Neue Staatsgalerie München, *Französische Meister des 20.Jahrhunderts, Augestellte Werke I*, Munich 1996, S.38, ill.S.164 (Inv.-No.12800 mit dem Vermerk 'Ankauf 1958'); Edward Quinn, *Max Ernst*, Paris 1976, no.161, ill.138.

Lempertz Cologne, 1 June 1996 (674**) DEM 190,000	US$	123,449

PORTRAIT OF ANDRÉ BRETON black crayon on paper, 14¼ x 10¼in. (36 x 26cm.) sdlr 'Max Ernst 1926'
PROV.: Former collection Valentine Hugo.

Étude Tajan Paris, 13 December 1995 (32*) FRF 100,000	US$	20,143

LA FUITE oil on canvas, 37 x 28¾in. (94 x 73cm.) slr Max Ernst'
PROV.: Private collection, Paris.
EXH.: Paris, Centre Georges Pompidou, *Paris - New York*, September 1977, no. 467, p. 601.
LIT.: Werner Spies, Sigrid and Günter Metken, *Max Ernst, Oeuvre-Katalog: Werke 1939-1953*, Cologne 1987, p. 28, no. 2356 (illustrated).

Sotheby's New York, 2 May 1996 (285**) US$ 453,500	US$	453,500

THE LOOK oil on canvas, 10 x 8in. (25.5 x 20.5cm.) slr 'Max Ernst'; sd '48' and titled on the reverse
PROV.: Pierre Matisse Gallery, New York La Boetie Gallery (Helen Serger) New York; Sale, London, Christie's, 11 December 1980, lot 48 (purchased by the present owner).
EXH.: London, The Surrealist Art Centre, *Surrealist Masters*, 1974, no. 26 (illustrated in the catalogue).
LIT.: Werner Spies, *Max Ernst, Oeuvre-Katalog, Werke 1939-53*, Cologne 1987, vol. 4, p. 160, no. 2604 (illustrated).

Sotheby's London, 20 March 1996 (57**) GBP 56,500	US$	86,286

LE CIMETIERE DES OISEAUX oil on canvas, 39 3/8 x 31 7/8in. (100 x 81cm.) slr 'Max Ernst' (1927)
PROV.: Galerie Guillaume Campo, Antwerp; Roman Norbert Ketterer, Campione di Lugano Alexander Iolas Gallery, New York; Catherine Schlumberger Jones, USA (purchased from the above in December 1968. Sale: Sotheby's, New York, 13 November 1990, lot 55) Purchased by the present owner at the above sale.
EXH.: Campione di Lugano, Roman Norbert Ketterer, *Katalog V*, 1968, no. 16, illustrated in colour in the catalogue.
LIT.: Werner Spies, *Max Ernst Oeuvre-Katalog: Werke 1925-1929*, Cologne, 1976, p. 201, no. 1181, illustrated.

Sotheby's London, 24 June 1996 (71**) GBP 364,500	US$	562,066

VENUS VOIT DE LA TERRE oil on canvas, 18 x 37.5in. (45.8 x 37.5cm.) lr 'Max Ernst' (1962)
PROV.: The New Arts, Houston; Alexander Iolas Gallery, New York (acquired by the present owner *circa* 1963).
EXH.: Chicago, Museum of Contemporary Art, *Dada and Surrealism in Chicago Collections*, Dec., 1984-Jan., 1985.

Christie's New York, 8 November 1995 (261**) US$ 112,500	US$	112,500

ERNST Rudolph (1854-1932) Austrian
A SCHOLARLY BOOK oil on canvas, 24 x 20 1/8in. 61 x 51cm. bears signature

Phillips London, 14 November 1995 (39**) GBP 5,200	US$	8,134

THE NARGHILE SMOKER oil on panel, 21¾ x 18in. (55.2 x 45.7cm.) s 'R. Ernst'
Christie's London, 15 March 1996 (134**) GBP 80,700   US$ 123,244

ES Jacob van (1596?-1666) Flemish
STILL-LIFE WITH GRAPES AND MISPELS oil on canvas, 45 x 66cm.
PROV.: Private collection, Vienna.
Dorotheum Vienna, 17 October 1995 (103**) ATS 180,000   US$ 18,055

ESPAGNAT Georges d' (1870-1950) French
PORTRAIT DE JEUNE FEMME oil on canvas, 25 3/8 x 32in. (64 x 81.4cm.) sur ini 'GdE'
PROV.: Durand-Ruel, Paris; Sale, Brussels, Palais des Beaux-Arts, 11 May 1966, lot 107; Robert
Bijou, San Francisco.
Sotheby's London, 20 March 1996 (288**) GBP 6,900   US$ 10,538

NU ASSIS SUR UN SOFA oil on canvas, 131 x 163cm. sll mono 'G d E'
Christie's Milan, 20 November 1995 (147**) ITL 28,284,000   US$ 17366

LE MODELE oil on canvas, 24¼ x 20in. (61.5 x 50.8cm.) slr with ini. 'GdE'
PROV.: Durand Ruel & Cie, Paris (1944); Anon. sale; Parke-Bernet Galleries Inc., New York, 29-31
Oct. 1952, lot 154; Anon. sale, Sotheby' Parke Bernet Inc., New York, 12 June 1981, lot 82
(illustrated; acquired by the present owner).
Christie's East, 7 November 1995 (47*) US$ 12,650   US$ 12,650

ESSELENS Jacob (1626-1687) Dutch
A BEACH WITH BOATS AND FISHERMEN oil on canvas, 100.5 x 128cm.
Christie's Monaco, 14 June 1996 (8**) FRF 198,900   US$ 38,407

WEITE LANDSCHAFT oil on linen, 70.5 x 55.5cm. slm 'J Esselens'
Lempertz Cologne, 15 November 1995 (1246**) DEM 12,500   US$ 8,823

ESSEN Cornelis van (Amsterdam 1,700 c. active) Dutch
A RESTING HORSEMAN IN FRONT OF A TAVERN oil on panel, 31 x 40cm. slr mono
Dorotheum Vienna, 6 March 1996 (85**) ATS 180,000   US$ 17,314

RESTING HORSEMEN IN FRONT OF A TAVERN oil on panel, 31 x 40cm. sll mono 'CVE'
Dorotheum Vienna, 17 October 1995 (159**) ATS 180,000   US$ 18,055

ESTES Richard (1936 b.) American
GENERAL MACHINISTS oil on masonite, 48 x 60in. (122 x 152.2cm.) sc 'RICHARD ESTES' (ca.
1969)
PROV.: Allan Stone Gallery, New York; Mr. and Mrs. Monroe Meyerson, New York.
EXH.: Milwaukee Art Center, and Houston, Contemporary Arts Museum, *Directions 2: Aspects of a
New Realism,* June-Aug. 1969; Washington D.C., Corcoran Gallery of Art, *32nd Biennial Exhibition,*
Feb.-April 1971, no. 3.
LIT.: L. Meisel, *Photorealism,* New York 1980, P. 228, no. 475 (illustrated); L. Meisel, *Richard
Estes: The Complete Paintings 1966-1985,* New York 1986, P. 84, no. 95 (illustrated).
Christie's New York, 14 November 1995 (58**) US$ 167,500   US$ 167,500

ESTEVE Maurice (1904 b.) French
TROUVERE - PAYSAGE oil on canvas, 46 x 32in. (116 x 81cm.) sdll 'Estève 54' sd titled on the
reverse (1954)
PROV.: Galerie Galanis, Paris; Collection Moltzau, Oslo; Private collection, Suisse; Galeries Albert
Loeb et Krugier (according to an old label on the reverse).
EXH.: Expositions: Paris, *Estève, Peintures recentes,* galerie Galanis,1955; Geneva, *Pérennité de
l'Art francais,* Museum of Athens,1957, reproduced; Oslo, *Collection Moltzau,* Kunstindustrimuseet,
1961; Paris, *Rencontre* 1970, Galerie Framond,1970; Ulm, *Maurice Estève,* Ulmer Museum, 1973;

Bremen, *Maurice Estève*, Kunsthalle, 1974; Paris, *Estève (Oeuvres 1919-1985)*, RMN, Galeries rationales du Grand Palais,1986, reproduced page 41; Heovikodden (Norvege), *Estève (oeuvres 1919-1985)*, RMN, Fondation Sonja Henie-Niels Onstad,1987; Tubingen (Germany), *Estève, (oeuvres 1919-1985)*, RMN, Kunsthalle.
LIT.: Robert Maillard, *Estève, catalogue raisonné de l'oeuvre peint*, Editions Ides et Calandes, Neuchâtel, 1995, reproduced in colour p. 318, no. 447.

        Étude Tajan Paris, 13 December 1995 (69**) FRF 630,000   US$ 126,898

General Machinists

VINDON oil on canvas, 24½ x 20in. (61 x 50cm.) sdll 'Estève 66' sd titled on the reverse (1966)
PROV.: Neue Galerie Zurich; Private collection, Switzerland.
EXH.: Zurich, Neue galerie, *Maurice Estève*, 1967 (illustrated).
LIT.: Robert Maillard, *Estève, catalogue raisonné de l'oeuvre peint*, Editions Ides et Calandes, Neuchâtel, 1995, reproduced in colour p. 375, no. 584.

        Étude Tajan Paris, 13 December 1995 (70**) FRF 280,000   US$ 56,399

LES SCAPHANDRIERS oil on canvas, 19¾ x 25½in. (50.2 x 64.7cm.) sdll 'Estève 47' and sd and titled on the reverse
PROV.: Galerie Louis Carré, Paris.

        Christie's London, 19 March 1996 (12**) GBP 23,000   US$ 35,125

AQUARELLE NO. 1031 watercolour and pencil on paper, 27¼ x 20½in. (69 x 52cm.) sdll 'Esteve 70'
PROV.: Neue Galerie, Zurich.
EXH.: Zurich, Neue Galerie, *Estève Aquarelle*, 1973, p. 39, no. 29, illustrated in colour).

        Sotheby's London, 21 March 1996 (17**) GBP 17,825   US$ 27,222

LA BUANDERIE oil on canvas, 36 3/8 x 25¾in. (92.6 x 65.3cm.) sdlr 'Estève 47' sd titled on the reverse
PROV.: Galerie Louis Carré, Paris; Svensk-Franska Konstgalleriet; Stockholm Galerie Artel, Geneva.
EXH.: Brussels, Musée des Beaux Arts d'Ixelles, *Maurice Estève*, 1977-78, no. 24.
LIT.: *Hommage à Estève, Numéro Spécial de XXème Siècle*, Paris 1975, p. 51, illustrated.

        Sotheby's London, 21 March 1996 (26**) GBP 35,600   US$ 54,368

RIFOULET oil on canvas, 13 x 18½in. (33 x 46cm.) sd 'Esteve 62' sd and titled '62' on the reverse'
PROV.: Neue Galerie, Zurich.
EXH.: Zurich, Neue Galerie, *Maurice Estève*, December 1967-February 1968, no. 8.
LIT.: Robert Maillard and Monique Prudhomme-Estève, *Estève: Catalogue Raisonné de L'Oeuvre Peint*, Neuchâtel 1995, p. 366, no. 558 (illustrated).
       Christie's London, 23 May 1996 (26**) GBP 32,200   US$ 48,758

L'ARBRE AU RIVAGE oil on canvas, 25½ x 36in. (65 x 91.5cm) sd 'Estève 49'
PROV.: Mr. and Mrs. Charles Zadok, New York.
EXH.: Chicago, The Arts Club of Chicago, *The School of Paris at Mid-Century. A Selection of Modern Paintings from the Collection of Mr and Mrs Charles Zadok*, May-June1962.
LIT.: Pierre Francastel, *Estève*, Paris 1956, p. 87 (illustrated in colour); "Hommage a Estève", *XXième Siècle*, Paris 1975, p. 54 (illustrated).
       Christie's London, 30 November 1995 (3**) GBP 40,000   US$ 62,568

EVERGOOD Philip Howard Francis (1901-1973) American
ELECTION DAY oil on canvas, 20 x 12in. (51 x 31.7cm.) sll 'Philip Evergood'; slr '1953'
       Christie's East, 28 November 1995 (44**) US$ 10,350   US$ 10,350

EVERSEN Adrianus (Amsterdam 1818-1897 Delft) Dutch
FIGURES IN A WINTER STREET BEFORE A CANAL oil on board, 6 ½ x 8 1/8in. (16.5 x 20.5cm.) s
       Phillips London, 14 November 1995 (16**) GBP 4,500   US$ 7,039

FIGURES IN A DUTCH STREET oil on panel, 22 ½ x 29 1/8in. (57 x 74cm.) sll
       Phillips London, 14 November 1995 (24**) GBP 32,000   US$ 50,055

TOWNFOLK STROLLING IN A WINTERSTREET oil on panel, 44 x 36cm. s 'A. Eversen'; s again on an old label on the reverse
       Christie's Amsterdam, 25 April 1996 (246**) NLG 97,750   US$ 58,084

A VIEW IN HAARLEM IN WINTER oil on canvas, 56 x 46.5cm. s 'A. Eversen'
PROV.: MacConnal-Mason & Son Ltd. Fine Paintings, London.
       Christie's Amsterdam, 25 April 1996 (255**) NLG 74,750   US$ 44,417

EYBL Franz (Vienna 1806-1880 Vienna) Austrian
THE INN-KEEPER FROM KROTHENSEE oil on canvas (30.5 x 34.6cm. sd 'F.Eibl 1834'
       Dorotheum Vienna, 28 February 1996 (568**) ATS 140,000   US$ 13,577

EYCK Jan van (studio of) (Maaseik ca. 1390-1441 Brugge) Flemish
CHRIST AS SALVATOR MUNDI oil on panel, 16¾ x 11½in. (42.5 x 29.2cm.) (ca. 1470)
PROV.: Newhouse Galleries, New York, 1949; Mrs. Moody, San Antonio, Texas, from whom purchased by the present owner.
       Sotheby's New York, 16 May 1996 (181**) US$ 65,750   US$ 65,750

175

FABBI Fabio (1861-1946) Italian
THE SLAVE MARKET oil on canvas, 39½ x 21¾in. (100.4 x 55.3cm.) sll 'F. Fabbi'
PROV.: With Frost & Reed, London.
        Christie's New York, 10 January 1996 (36**) US$ 23,000   US$ 23,000

FABRIS Pietro (1754 -1778 active) Italian
A VIEW OF NAPLES FROM THE WEST WITH PEASANTS GAMING AND MERRYMAKING
IN THE FOREGROUND oil on canvas, 28¼ x 39in. (71.4 x 98.9cm.) inscr. on the reverse 'Fabris P.'
(ca. 1765)
        Sotheby's London, 17 April 1996 (154**) GBP 80,700   US$ 122,365

FAED Thomas, R.A., H.R.S.A. (1826-1900) British
HOME AND THE HOMELESS oil on panel, 14 x 20in. (35.6 x 50.8cm.) s 'Faed', with inscr. 'Home
and the Homeless/by/Thomas Faed R.A.'
PROV.: Edward Barclay, Esq.
EXH.: Scottish National Exhibition, Glasgow, 1911.
        Christie's South Kensington, 7 March 1996 (161**) GBP 10,000   US$ 15,272

FAHRINGER Carl (Wiener Neustadt 1874-1952 Vienna) Austrian
HOLLÄNDISCHER MARKT oil on canvas, 79.5 x 62.3cm. slr 'C. Fahringer'
        Wiener Kunst Auktionen, 29 November 1995 (677**) ATS 270,000   US$ 27,085

FAIRMAN James (1826-1904) American
JAFFA oil on canvas, 32 1/8 x 45 1/8in. (81.6 x 114.5cm.) sd 'J. Fairman 74'
        Christie's London, 14 June 1996 (89**) GBP 21,850   US$ 33,693

FAISTAUER Anton (St Martin bei Lofer/Sbg 1887-1930 Vienna) Austrian
APFELSTILLLEBEN AUF ROSA STUHL oil on canvas, 70 x 57cm. sdll 'A. Faistauer 26'; inscr.
'Nachlaß Faistauer, apfelstilleben auf rosa Stuhl' on the reverse
PROV.: With Inge Asenbaum, Vienna.
        Dorotheum Vienna, 21 May 1996 (48**) ATS 350,000   US$ 33,609

FALCIATORE Filippo (1718 by-1768) Italian
THE ANNUNCIATION oil on copper, 34 x 27cm.
        Christie's Rome, 21 November 1995 (242**) ITL 21,000,000   US$ 13,183

FALCONET Pierre Étienne (Paris 1741-1791) French
PORTRAIT DE MISS NANETTE THELLUSON, SOEUR DU PREMIER LORD RENDLESHAM
oil on canvas (an oval), 71 x 66cm. sdlc 'P. Falconet F / 1768'
PROV.: Anon. Sale, Paris, Palais Galliera, 26 March 1974, no. 11 (illustrated).
        Étude Tajan Paris, 25 June 1996 (62**) FRF 200,000   US$ 38,620

FALENS Carel van (Antwerp 1683-1733 Paris) Dutch
THE DEPARTURE oil on canvas, 19½ x 25½in. (50 x 60cm.) inscr. ll 'J C vanfalens'
        Sotheby's London, 11-12 June 1996 (520**) GBP 13,800   US$ 21,280

HUNTSMEN'S RETURN oil on canvas, 20 7/8 x 24¾in. (53 x 62.9cm.) sll 'c. van falens'
PROV.: J.W.G. Dawis , Esq., London (acc. to an old label on the reverse); Sale: Hotel Drouot, Paris,
25 february 1869, lot 25.
        Sotheby's New York, 16 May 1996 (79**) US$ 25,300   US$ 25,300

FANFANI Enrico (19th century) Italian
BY THE SEA oil on canvas, 45¼ x 33in. (115 x 83.9cm.) slr 'E. Fanfani'
        Christie's East, 13 February 1996 (117**) US$ 10,350   US$ 10,350

FANTIN-LATOUR Ignace Henri Jean Théodore (1836-1904) French
ANDROMEDE oil on canvas, 61 x 52cm. slr 'Fantin-Latour' (1902)
PROV.: Sale Loriot-Lecaudey, June 1904.
EXH.: Grenoble, Musée-Bibliothèque, *Centenaire de Henri Fantin-Latour*, 1936, no. 78.
LIT.: Madame Fantin-Latour, *Catalogue de l'Oeuvre complet (1849-1904) de Fantin-Latour*, Floury éditeur, Paris, 1911, no. 1909.

Étude Tajan Paris, 27 October 1995 (14**) FRF 130,000

US$ 26,296

ROSES TRÉMIERES oil on canvas, 29 x 23¾in. (73.8 x 60.5cm.) sd 'Fantin 89'
PROV.: Mrs Edwin Edwards, London; John Wheeldon Burns; his sale, Christie's, London, 11 June 1909, lot 220 (410 guineas); F. and J. Tempelaere, Paris; Galerie Bernheim Jeune, Paris; Stephen Mitchell of Boquhan, Kippen, Stirlingshire; his sale, Christie's, London, 24 November 1939, lot 97; Sir Bernard Eckstein, London; Anon. sale, Christie's, London, 8 December 1948, lot 35 (4,,200 guineas). M. Newman & Co., London; Anon. sale, Sotheby's, London, 18 October 1959, lot 90 (GBP2,600); Alex Reid & Lefevre, London (0103,9018); Albert D. Lasker, New York, June 1951; Marlborough Fine Art and Alex Reid & Lefevre, London, 1976-77.
EXH.: London, Royal Academy, *121st Exhibition*, 1890, no. 35; Dallas, Museum of Fine Arts, *An Exhibition of 69 Paintings from the Collection of Mrs Albert D. Lasker for the benefit of the American Cancer Society in memory of Albert D. Lasker*, 6-29 March 1953, no. 32; San Francisco, Califomia Palace of the Legion of Honour, *67 Paintings from the collection of Mrs Albert D. Lasker for the benefit of the American Cancer Society in memory of Albert D. Lasker*, 7 March-4 April 1954, no. 31; New York, Acquavella Galleries, *Flowers by Fantin-Latour*, 3 Nov.-3 Dec. 1966, no. 17; Paris, Galerie Nationale du Grand Palais, *Fantin-Latour*, Nov. 1982; Ottawa, National Gallery of Canada, *Fantin-Latour*, 17 March-22 March 1983, no. 103.
LIT.: Mme Fantin-Latour, *Catalogue de l'oeuvre complet de Fantin-Latour*, Paris, 1911, no. 1375; The Albert D. Lasker Collection, *Renoir to Matisse*, New York, 1958 (illustrated p. 21).

Christie's London, 25 June 1996 (4**) GBP 804,500

US$ 1,240,555

DAHLIAS oil canvas, 23¼ x 29 1/9in. (59 x 74cm.) sd 'Fantin '96'
PROV.: Mrs Edwin Edwards, London, by whom acquired directly from the Artist; F. & J. Tempelaere, Paris; M. Bonjean, Paris; M. Dubosc, Sainte-Adresse; Galerie Brame & Lorenceau, Paris.
EXH.: Paris, Palais de l'Ecole Nationale des Beaux-Arts, *Exposition de l'oeuvre de Fantin-Latour*, 1906, no. 81; Grenoble, Musée-Bibliotheque, *Centenaire de Henri Fantin-Latour*, 1936, no. 183 (illustrated); Paris, Grand Palais, *Fantin-Latour*, 1983, no. 146 (illustrated); this exhibition later travelled to Ottawa, National Gallery of Canada and San Francisco, California Palace of the Legion of Honour.
LIT.: Madame Fantin-Latour, *Catalogue de l'Oeuvre complèt de Fantin-Latour*, Paris, 1911, no. 1414 (incorrectly dated 1890); To be included in the forthcoming *Fantin-Latour catalogue raisonné* being prepared by Philippe Brame and Bernard Lorenceau.

Christie's London, 28 November 1995 (7**) GBP 881,500

US$ 1,378,852

FLEURS, GROS BOUQUET AVEC TROIS PIVOINES oil on canvas, 16 3/8 x 13¼in. (41.6 x 33.5cm.) sdul 'Fantin-79' (1879)
PROV.: Mrs. Edwin Edwards, London; Montgomery Sears, Boston; Mrs. J.D. Cameron Bradley, Boston; E.V. Thaw & Co. Inc., New York; I.A. Davidson (1950); M. Knoedler & Co. Inc., New York (1950-1954); Sydney M. Schoenberg, St. Louis (acquired from the above); Acquavella Galleries Inc., New York.

Christie's New York, 1 May 1996 (108**) US$ 266,500

US$ 266,500

VASE DE FLEURS oil on canvas, 14 1/8 x 11in. (35.9 x 27.9cm.) sd '68'
PROV.: Mme. de La Chapelle, Paris; Sale: Sotheby's, New York, May 11, 1987, lot 21; Acquired by the present owner at the above sale.
EXH.: Charlotte, North Carolina, Mint Museum of Art, 1956; San Francisco, California Palace of the Legion of Honor, 1959; San Francisco, California Palace of the Legion of Honor, 1971 .
LIT.: Michel Hoog, 'A propos de l'Exposition Fantin-Latour, les Fleurs et les Poètes' in *L'Oeil*,

December 1982, illustrated p. 58.

   Sotheby's New York, 2 May 1996 (116**) US$ 90,500   US$ 90,500

AURORA oil on canvas, 16½ x 13¼in. (42 x 33.7cm.) s 'Fantin'
PROV.: George T. Fulford.
LIT.: Madame Fantin-Latour, *Catalogue de l'Oeuvre de Henri Fantin-Latour*, Paris, 1911, no. 1104.

   Christie's London, 17 November 1995 (99**) GBP 13,225   US$ 20,687

STILL-LIFE WITH FLOWERS oil on canvas, 18¼ x 15¼in. (46.4 x 38.7cm.) sd '1862'
PROV.: Whitford and Hughes, London.

   Sotheby's New York, 2 May 1996 (110**) US$ 244,500   US$ 244,500

LA TOILETTE oil on canvas, 21¼ x 25 5/8in. (54 x 65.1cm.) sll 'Fantin'
PROV.: G. Tempelaere, Paris; Sevadjian; Germain; anon, sale, Hôtel Drouot, Paris, May 31, 1967,
no. 41.
LIT.: Mme. Fantin Latour, *catalogue de l'Oeuvre Complet de Henri Fantin-Latour*, Paris, 1911, p.
226, no. 2144.

   Christie's New York, 2 November 1995 (103**) US$ 34,500   US$ 34,500

FANTIN-LATOUR Victoria, {née} Dubourg (1840-1926) French
A STILL-LIFE WITH ASSORTED FLOWERS oil on canvas, 9 7/8 x 12¼in. (25.1 x 31.2cm.)
unframed slr with initials ' V D'

   Christie's New York, 2 November 1995 (203**) US$ 13,800   US$ 13,800

A STILL-LIFE OF CARNATIONS oil on canvas, 8¼ x 10 7/8in. (21 x 27.7cm.) unframed slr with
initials 'V D'

   Christie's New York, 2 November 1995 (204**) US$ 13,800   US$ 13,800

FARNY Henry F. (1847-1916) American
PAINTING POTS gouache on paper, 13¾ x 21 1/8in. (34.9 x 51.1cm.) sdlr 'H.F. Farny 1880'

   Christie's New York, 23 May 1996 (109**) US$ 123,500   US$ 123,500

FARQUHARSON Joseph, R.A. (1846-1935) Scottish
BENEATH THE SNOW-ENCUMBERED BRANCHES oil on canvas, 44¼ x 34¼in. (112.4 x
87cm.) sdlr 'J.Farquharson 1901.'
EXH.: London, The Royal Academy 1901, no. 390.

   Christie's New York, 2 November 1995 (212**) US$ 55,200   US$ 55,200

WHEN THE MIST WITH EVENING GLOWS oil on canvas, 39½ x 54in. (100.3 x 137.1cm.) sll 'J.
Farquharson'
PROV.: Sir Jeremiah Colman, Bt., Gatton Park, Reigate, Surrey; Christie's 18 September 1942, lot 71
(52gns. to De Caserz); with E. Stacy Marks, Eastborne.
EXH.: London, Royal Academy, 1900, no. 256.
LIT.: Henry Blackburn (ed.), *Academy Notes*, 1900, p.17.

   Christie's London, 29 March 1996 (146**) GBP 109,300   US$ 166,921

THE FROSTY CLOSE OF DAY oil on canvas, 20 x 30in. (51 x 76cm.) sll 'J Farquharson'

   Sotheby's London, 29 August 1995 (761**) GBP 45,500   US$ 73,648

FATTORI Giovanni (Livorno 1825-1908 Florence) Italian
IN PERLUSTRAZIONE oil on panel, 6½ x 10in. (16.5 x 25.3cm.) s 'Giov. Fattori'

   Christie's London, 14 June 1996 (150**) GBP 35,600   US$ 54,896

FAUTRIER Jean (Paris 1898-1964 Chatenay Malabry) French
LA BOBINE oil on canvas, 10 x 13 3/8in. (25.5 x 34cm.) sd ini. 'F 56'
PROV.: Sidney Janis Gallery, New York; acquired directly from the above by the parents of the

present owner in 1957.
LIT.: Palma Bucarelli, *Jean Fautrier*, Milan 1960, p. 333, no. 241 (illustrated).
      Christie's London, 30 November 1995 (11**) GBP 78,500   US$ 122,791

PAYSAGE gouache and pastel on paper, 6¾ x 8in. (17.3 x 20.1cm.) s 'Fautrier' (1937)
      Christie's London, 19 March 1996 (1**) GBP 10,350   US$ 15,806

MORT DU SANGLIER oil on canvas, 63¾ x 51 3/8in. (162 x 130.5cm.) sul (1927)
PROV.: Florence Gould, Cannes.
EXH.: Paris, Galeries Nationaux du Grand Palais, *Jean Fautrier*, February-April 1974, no. 549.
LIT.: Palma Bucarelli, *Jean Fautrier*, Milan 1960, p. 296, no. 68 (illustrated).
      Christie's London, 27 June 1996 (5**) GBP 298,500   US$ 460,293

LE BOUQUET EN BLANC ET BLEU oil on canvas, 38 9/16 x 24 5/8in. (98 x 62.5cm.) sdll '1929'
PROV.: Paul Guillaume, Paris; Galerie Jeanne Castel, Paris.
LIT.: Palma Bucarelli, *Jean Fautrier,Pittura e Materia*, Milan 1960, p. 306, no. 105 (illustrated).
      Christie's London, 23 May 1996 (21**) GBP 41,100   US$ 62,235

FAYUM (fayum region second century (AD)) Egyptian
PORTRAIT OF AN EGYPTIAN/GREEKIAN/ROMAN GENTLEMAN WITH EVEN, CLEAR,
FRESH, PINK, FEATURES WITH YELLOW/BROWN HUES, BLACK CURLING HAIR,
CURLING BAIRD, SMALL MOUSTACHE, TRACES OF A GOLDEN LAURELWREATH IN
HIS HAIR, AND A WHITE ATTIRE. encaustic on panel, 38.5 x 20cm.
PROV.: Ca. 1890, collection Theodor Graf, Vienna.
      Dorotheum Vienna, 17 October 1995 (75**) ATS 350,000   US$ 35,107

FEARNLEY Thomas (1802-1842 Munich) Norwegian
VADSTENA CASTLE ON LAKE VÄTTERN, SWEDEN oil on canvas, 19 3/8 x 27½in. (49.2 x
79.8cm.) sd 'Th. Fearnley px/1831'
EXH.: Modum, Stiftelsen Modums Blaafarvevaerk, *Thomas Fearnley 1802-1842*, 24-30 May 1986,
no. 22 (illustrated in colour p. 31).
      Christie's London, 14 June 1996 (109**) GBP 23,000   US$ 35,466

FEININGER Lyonel (New York 1871-1956 New York) American
THE RED ENSIGN ink- and pencildrawing and watercolour on paper, 18.3 x 26.5cm. monogram
and sll 'Feininger / L.F.'; dlr 'i o 4i'; titled on the reverse (1941)
      Hauswedell & Nolte Cologne, 05/06 June 1996 (198**) DEM 17,000   US$ 11,045

BLUE SAILS watercolour with pen-drawing over ink-drawing, 48.2 x 66.4cm. sdll 'FEININGER
1940'
PROV.: Dr. Sidney Tamarin, New York.
      Hauswedell & Nolte Cologne, 1 December 1995 (259***) DEM 115,000   US$ 79,789

ABEND AM STRANDE watercolour and pen and ink on paper, 11¾ x 15¼in. (29.8 x 38.7cm.) sd
titled 'Feininger 15 xii 26'
PROV.: Willard Gallery, New York; Acquired from the above in 1965.
EXH.: Boston, Boston University, 1961 New York, Museum of Modern Art, *The Intimate World of
LionelFeininger*, 1963.
      Sotheby's New York, 2 May 1996 (253**) US$ 34,500   US$ 34,500

OHNE TITLE (SEGELBOOTTE) watercolour, pen and black ink on paper, 7 5/8 x 11in. (19.4 x
28cm.) sll 'Feininger'; dlr '1944'
PROV.: Mr. and Mrs. H. Gates Lloyd, Haverford, Pennsylvania (by descent to the present owner).
      Christie's New York, 1 May 1996 (198**) US$ 43,700   US$ 43,700

DAS SIGNALSCHIFF watercolour, pen and black ink on paper, 9 3/8 x 12 1/8in. (23.8 x 30.8cm.)
across the bottom 'Feininger Das Signallschiff 1920' (1920)
PROV.: La Boetie, Inc., (Helen Serger), New York.
        Christie's New York, 8 November 1995 (247**) US$ 43,700   US$ 43,700

SKETCH FOR MURAL:'MARINE TRANSPORTATION' watercolours and ink on paper, 24 x
62.8cm. sd 'Sketch for Mural 'Marine Transportation'' in pencil (1938)
        Lempertz Cologne, 1 June 1996 (686**) DEM 42,000   US$ 27,289

THE HOUSES ON THE BORD OF THE RIVER oil on canvas, 19¾ x 30in. (50.5 x 76cm.) slr 'L
Feininger' sd '1948-1949' on the stretcher
PROV.: Galerie Curt Valentin; New York; private collection, U.S.A.; private collection, Paris.
EXH.: Pittsburgh, Carnegie Institute, *Retrospective exhibition of Paintings of previous
International's 1958-1959*, reproduced under no. 89; Cleveland, Cleveland Museum of Art, *Lyonel
Feininger memorial exhibition*, 1959-1961; York, The City Art Gallery, afterwards London, The Art
Council Gallery, *Lyonel Feininger Memorial Exhibition*,1960, no. 31.
LIT.: H. Hess, *Lyonel Feininger*, New York, 1949, p. 295, no. 482, reproduced p. 233, pl. 61.
        Étude Tajan Paris, 13 December 1995 (68**) FRF 635,000   US$ 127,906

LEUTE AUF EIN SEE-STEG II watercolour and pen and ink on paper, 9 3/8 x 13in. (23.8 x 33cm.)
sd titled 'Feininger 1949' inscr. 'for Christopher, with a 'Merry Christmas' 1949 on the reverse
PROV.: Ulfert Wilke (a gift from the artist); Kraushaar Galleries, New York; Acquired from the
above in 1963.
EXH.: New Haven, Yale University Art Gallery, *The Helen and Rohert M. Benjamin Collection*,
1967, no. 57.
        Sotheby's New York, 2 May 1996 (252**) US$ 37,950   US$ 37,950

TWO FIGURES ON THE BEACH, A SAILING-BOAT BEYOND pen-drawing and watercolour
over a pencil-drawing, 19.5 x 28.5cm. sll 'FEININGER'; dlr '4. ix. '52.'
        Hauswedell & Nolte Cologne, 1 December 1995 (258**) DEM 22,000   US$ 15,264

FEITELSON Lorser (1898-1978) American
MAGICAL SPACE FORMS oil on canvas, 60 x 52in. (152.4 x 132cm.) sd and titled twice 'Lorser
Feitelson 'Magical Space Forms' Feb 1962' on the reverse, sd again 'Lorser Feitelson Feb 1962'
PROV.: Acquired directly from the artist.
EXH.: San Fransisco Museum of Modern Art, and Los Angeles, University of California, The
Frederick S.Wight Art Gallery, *Lorser Feitelson and Helen Lundeberg: A Retrospective Exhibition*,
Oct. 1980-May 1981, no. 49.
        Christie's New York, 8 May 1996 (278**) US$ 18,400   US$ 18,400

FEITO Luis (Madrid 1929 b.) Spanish
PEINTURE 153 oil and sand on canvas, 35 x 45 5/8in. (89 x 116cm.) sll sd titled '1959' on the
reverse
PROV.: Galerie Arnaud, Paris.
        Christie's London, 23 May 1996 (65**) GBP 14,950   US$ 22,638

FERNANDEZ J. (active ca. 1650 in Haarlem)
STILL-LIFE WITH HERING, BREAD, WINE, RUMMER AND A LIGHTENED CANDLE oil on
panel, 662 x 51cm.
        Dorotheum Vienna, 06 March 1996 (120**) ATS 220,000   US$ 21,162

FERNANDEZ Juan {called El Labrador} (documented Madrid (1629-1636)) Spanish
A STILL-LIFE OF GRAPES, ACORNS, HAZELNUTS, WALNUTS, APPLES, A *BOTIJO* AND A
WINE GLASS, ALL ON A TABLE oil on canvas, 25 x 19in. (64 x 48cm.)
        Sotheby's London, 6 December 1995 (9**) GBP 166,500   US$ 256,233

FERNELEY John E. Snr (1782-1860) British
PHILIP, A BAY RACEHORSE, THE PROPERTY OF LORD ELCHO, WITH JOCKEY UP oil on
canvas, 34 x 42in. (86.5 x 106.7cm.) sd 'Melton Mowbray/1838'
PROV.: Newhouse Galleries Inc. New York; Sold Sotheby's New York 7 June, 1991, lot 58 for $
(SA) 140,000.
        Sotheby's London, 12 July 1995 (153**) GBP 67,500   US$ 107,673

FERNHOUT Edgar Richard Johannes (Bergen (N.-Holland) 1912-1974) Dutch
VRUCHTEN oil on canvas, 30 x 30cm. s with ini. and dlr 'F 37', and sd again and inscr. with title
'Edgar Fernhout Alassio aug. 1937' on the reverse
        Christie's Amsterdam, 6 December 1995 (178*) NLG 10,350   US$ 6,413

FERON William (1858-1894) Swedish
ELEGANT FIGURES ON THE BEACH oil on canvas, 23 5/8 x 31¾cm. (60 x 80.7cm.) sdll
'William Feron '86'
        Phillips London, 14 November 1995 (46**) GBP 4,500   US$ 7,039

FERRARI Gaudenzio (Valduggia ca 1475-Milan 1546) Italian
SANTA CATERINA D'ALESSANDRIA AND SANTA APOLLONIA oil on board, 88.5 x 61.3cm.
PROV.: London, collection J.C. Preston.
LIT.: 'Arte Antica e Moderna', Jan.-March 1962, pag. XVIII; B. Berenson, *Italian Pictures of the
Renaissance, Central Italian and North Italian Schools*, I, London 1968, pag.160; G. Romano,
Casalesi del Cinquecento, Turin 1970, fig.40.
        Finearte Milan, 11 June 1996 (58***) ITL 782,000,000   US$ 507,134

FERRIS Jean Léon Gérôme (1863-1930) American
THE ALHAMBRA oil on canvas, 35 1/8 x 19½in. (89.3 x 49.6cm.) sdll 'GFERRIS '87'
        Christie's New York, 14 February 1996 (29**) US$ 32,200   US$ 32,200

FETTING Rainer (1949 b.) German
RAINER, LUCIANO - INDIAN MEAL dispersion on canvas, 210 x 270cm. sd, titled on the reverse
'Fetting 82 Rainer, Luciano - indian meal'
EXH.: Aachen, Suermondt-Ludwig Museum und Museumsverein, *Junge und expressive Kunst in
Italien und Deutschland*, 1983 (illustrated in colour in the catalogue p. 4).
        Lempertz Cologne, 28 November 1995 (650**) DEM 22,000   US$ 15,528

BRUSH HEADS paint tubes and brushes mounted on canvas-unframed, 72¼ x 90in. (183.5 x
228.6cm.) sd titled 'Fetting 84 brush heads' on the reverse
PROV.: Raab Galerie, Berlin.
EXH.: Berlin, Raab Galerie, *Rainer Fetting* 1973-1984, Nov. 1985, (illustrated).
        Christie's New York, 15 November 1995 (258**) US$ 11,500   US$ 11,500

FIDANI Orazio (Florence 1606-1656) Italian
THE FISH SELLER oil on canvas, 40 x 54½in. (101.5 x 138.4cm.)
PROV.: Florence, Palazzo Strozzi, *70 Pitture e Sculture del ',600 e ',700 Fiorentino*, October 1965,
no. 17 (illustrated).
LIT.: R. Longhi, 'Sui Margini della Mostra del 1922', in *Scritti Giovanili*, 1961, p. 497.
        Sotheby's London, 6 December 1995 (225**) GBP 21,850   US$ 33,626

FILLA Emil (1882-1953) Czech
FIGURES AT A WINDOW oil on canvas, 163 x 130cm. sdlr 'Emil Filla 37'
        Bukowskis Stockholm, 24-25 April 1996 (164**) SEK 230,000   US$ 34,845

STILL-LIFE WITH BIRD AND GUITAR oil on canvas, 146 x 88.6cm. sdlr 'Emil Filla 26'
        Wiener Kunst Auktionen, 27 September 1995 (404**) ATS 650,000   US$ 63,182

181

FINI Leonor (1908-1996) Italian
L'EGARÉE DE STAGLIENO oil on canvas, 36¼ x 35½in. (92 x 65cm.) slr 'Leonor Fini' (1974)
PROV.: Sale London, Christie's, 28th June 1977, lot 76 (purchased by the present owner at GBP7,000).
EXH.: Paris, Galerie Altmann-Carpentier, *Leonor Fini*, 1974, n.n.
LIT.: José Alvares, *Das Grosse Bilderbuch*, Munich, 1975, p. 82, illustrated; Jean-Claude Dedieu, *Leonor Fini*, Paris, 1978, p. 75, illustrated.

Sotheby's London, 20 March 1996 (61**) GBP 28,750	US$	43,907

FISCHER Paul (1860-1934) Danish
THE ARTIST'S FAMILY ON THE VERANDA OF SOFIEVEY 23, HELLERUP oil on canvas, 18½ x 15¾in. (47 x 40cm.) sd 'Paul Fischer 1914'
PROV.: With Henser Kunsthandel, Copenhagen.
LIT.: Possibly S. Linvald, *Paul Fischer Kobenhavbernes Maler*, Copenhagen, 1984, p. 125.

Christie's London, 15 March 1996 (51**) GBP 20,700	US$	31613

LOOKING OUT TO SEA oil on canvas, 15 x 21¼in. (38.1 x 54cm.) sdll 'PAUL/FISCHER/1910'

Christie's New York, 22 May 1996 (232**) US$ 48,300	US$	48,300

A QUIET MOMENT oil on panel, 16¾ x 24 3/8in. 941.6 x 61.9cm.) s 'Paul Fischer'

Christie's London, 15 March 1996 (62**) GBP 10,350	US$	15,806

ROW IN FRONT OF A THEATERCAFE, COPENHAGEN oil on canvas, 58 x 75cm. sll 'Paul Fischer'

Bukowskis Stockholm, 29-31 May 1996 (217**) SEK 175,000	US$	25,738

FISCHETTI Fidele (1732-1792) Italian
ALLEGORY ON VALOR oil on canvas, 130 x 133cm. (before 1680)

Christie's Rome, 4 June 1996 (493**) ITL 50,000,000	US$	32,425

FISCHL Eric (1948 b.) American
BATHROOM I oil and adhesive labels on four sheets of glassine mounted on board, 73½ x 76 3/8in. (186.7 x 194cm.) (1980)
PROV.: Mary Boone Gallery, New York; private collection, New York.
EXH.: Miami, Bass Museum of Art; Madison Art Center; Saskatchewan, Norman MacKenzie Art Gallery; Anchorage Historical and Fine Arts Museum, and Santa Barbara Museum of Art, *Large Drawings*, Jan. 1985-May, no. 7 (illustrated).

Christie's New York, 22 February 1996 (120**) US$ 28,750	US$	28,750

UNTITLED oil on paper, 35 x 46in. (89 x 117cm.) (1985)
EXH.: New York, Mary Boone Gallery, *Eric Fischl*, Jan. 1987.

Christie's New York, 22 February 1996 (122**) US$ 32,200	US$	32,200

FISH Janet (20th Century) American
UNTITLED oil on canvas, 40 x 48in. (101.6 x 121.9cm.) (ca.1967)
PROV.: Acquired directly from the artist.

Christie's New York, 22 February 1996 (83**) US$ 11,500	US$	11,500

FIUME Salvatore (Comiso 1915 b.) Italian
SILO DI PIETRA oil on chipboard, 50 x 77cm. slr 'Fiume'

Finearte Milan, 18 June 1996 (166*) ITL 172500,000	US$	111,868

ISOLE DI PIETRA oil on masonite, 49 x 69cm. sll 'Fiume' (1915)

Finearte Milan, 18 June 1996 (124*) ITL 16,100,000	US$	10,441

PITTORE E MODELLA oil on board, 74 x 102cm. sll 'Fiume'

Finearte Milan, 12 December 1995 (274**) ITL 24,150,000	US$	15,151

ODALISCA CON VELO oil on masonite, 35.5 x 53.5cm. slr 'Fiume'

Finearte Milan, 19 March 1996 (11*) ITL 13,800,000	US$	8,829

FLAMENCO oil on masonite, 35 x 53cm s 'Fiume'

Finearte Rome, 14 November 1995 (140**) ITL 13,800,000	US$	8,663

Still-life with Vase of Flowers, Glass of Wine, Citrons and a fried Pheasant

FLEGEL Georg (Olmütz 1566-1638 Frankfurt-am-Main) German (Moravian)
STILL-LIFE WITH VASE OF FLOWERS, GLASS OF WINE, CITRONS AND A FRIED PHEASANT oil on beech-wood, 34.5 x 26cm. (late 1620's)
PROV.: An Austrian noblefamily.
LIT.: Dr. Ketelsen-Volkhardt will include this painting in her *catalogue raisonné* on Georg Flegel; Jacob Hoefnagel, *Archetypa Studiaque..*, Frankfurt, 1592, Ed. Vingau, München 1995 Pars 1,9.

Dorotheum Vienna, 17 October 1995 (195**) ATS 1,700,000	US$	170,520

FLEISCHMANN Adolf Richard (1892-1968) German
KOMPOSITION gouache, 62.5 x 47cm. slr (ca. 1955)

Hauswedell & Nolte Cologne, 2 December 1995 (76**) DEM 30,000	US$	20,815

UNTITLED gouche on paper, 25½ x 19¾in. (65 x 50.2cm.) slr
PROV.: Rose Fried Gallery, New York.

Christie's London, 23 May 1996 (83**) GBP 8,625	US$	13,060

OPUS 1 oil on canvas, 75 x 63cm. s 'fleischmann' (1954)
EXH.: Münster, Westphälisches Museum für Kunst und Kulturgeschichte, *Richard Fleischmann, Retrospektive*, 1973.

Hauswedell & Nolte Cologne, 6 June 1996 (100**) DEM 66,000	US$	42,882

FLINCK Govaert (1615-1660) Dutch
PORTRAIT OF A YOUNG MAN HOLDING AN OTTOMAN SHORT SWORD IN AN ELABORATE SCABBARD oil on canvas, 39½ x 34in. (100.3 x 86.4cm.) d inscr. 'Rembrandt f. 1644' (1640-50)
PROV.: Henry Isaacs, Esq., London by 1765; E. G. van Tindinghorste, Amsterdam by 1777; R Locquet, Amsterdam by 1783; Lord Southesk; from whom purchased in 1855 by Robert Stayner Holford, Esq., Westonbirt, Gloucestershire and by descent to Sir George Lindsay Holford; from whom purchased in 1928 by M. Knoedler & Co., Inc., London; from whom purchased by Sir Harry Oakes and by descent in the family (Sale: Sotheby's New York, January 12, 1989, lot 42 where acquired by the present collector at US$ 407,000).
EXH.: London, Royal Academy, *Winter Exhibition*, 1893, cat. no. 108; Amsterdam, Rijksmuseum, *Rembrandt Tentoonstelling*, 1898, cat. no. 61; Paris, *Exposition Hollandaise*, 1921, cat. no. 43; London, Burlington Fine Arts Club, *Exhibition of the Hoyord Collection*, 1921-22, cat. no. 91; London, Royal Academy, *Exhibition of Dutch Art*, 1929, cat. no. 118; Providence, Rhode Island, Rhode Island School of Design, March 1932; New York, M. Knoedler & Co., Inc., April 1933; Brunswick, Maine, Bowdoin College Museum of Art, 1938-73; Los Angeles, Los Angeles County Museum of History, Science and Art, November 1947; Raleigh, North Carolina, North Carolina

Museum of Art, *Rembrandt and his Pupils*, November-December 1956; Raleigh, North Carolina,
North Carolina Museum of Art, *Dr.Valentiner Memorial Exhibition*, April 1959; Mexico City,
Instituto Anglo-Mexicana de Cultura, *Pittura Britanica en Mexico: Siglos XVI a XIX*, December
1963.
LIT.: J. Smith, *Catalogue Raisonné of the Works of the Dutch, Flemish and French Painters*, Vol.
VII, 1836, cat. no. 458 (as by Rembrandt); G. Waagen, *Treasures of Art in Great Britain*, 1854, Vol.
II, p. 200 (as by Rembrandt); C. Vosmaer, *Rembrandt*, 1877, pp. 367, 564 (as by Rembrandt); E.
Dutuit, *Tableaux et Dessins de Rembrandt*, 1885, pp. 45, 58, 63, cat. no. 343 (as by Rembrandt); A.
von Wurzbach, *Rembrandt Galerie*, 1886, cat. no. 491 (as by Rembrandt); E. Michel, *Rembrandt*,
1894, Vol. II, p. 236 (as by Rembrandt); M. Bell, *Rembrandt van Rijn and his Work*, 1899, p. 147 (as
by Rembrandt); W. Bode, *The Complete Works of Rembrandt*, 1900, Vol. I, p.24; Vol. IV cat. no.
259 (as by Rembrandt); A. Rosenberg and W. R. Valentiner, *Rembrandt, Klassiker der Kunst*, Vol.
II, 1909, pp. 274, 558, cat. no. 274, illus. (as by Rembrandt); C. Hofstede de Groot, *Catalogue of the
Works of the Most Eminent Dutch Painters*, 1916, Vol. VI, cat. no 746 (as by Rembrandt); R.
Benson, *The Holford Collection*, 1924, illus. pl. lxxx (as by Rembrandt); S. de Ricci, 'La Collection
Holford,' *Gazette des Beaux-Arts*, January; 1925, p. 40 (as by Rembrandt); W. Gibson, ' The Holford
Collection,' *Apollo*, May 1928, pp. 201-02, illus. p. „200 (as by Rembrandt); M. Chamot, 'The Last of
a Great Collection,' *County Life*, May 5, 1928, pp. 637-38, illus. p. 636 (as by Rembrandt);
Frankfurter Fine Arts Magazine, May 1933, illus. (as by Rembrandt); O. Benesch, *Rembrandt, Werk
und Forschung*, 1935, p. 33 (as by Rembrandt, probably a self portrait); A. Bredius, *ThePaintings of
Rembrandt*, 1937, p.13, cat. no. 235 and illus. p. 235 (as by Rembrandt); J. Rosenberg, *Rembrandt*,
1948, p. 245 (as by Rembrandt); W.R.Valentiner, *Rembrandt and his Pupils*, 1956, cat. no. 16, illus.
(as by Rembrandt, a self portrait); K. Bauch, *Rembrandt Gemälde*, 1966, eat. no. 184 (as by
Rembrandt, probably a self portrait); H. Gerson, *Rembrandt Paintings*, 1968, cat. no. C 113 (as by an
artist in Rembrandt's circle); A. Bredius (revised by H. Gerson), *Rembrandt, Complete Edition of the
Paintings*, 1969, p. 567 (eat. no. 235), illus. p. 187; W. Sumowski, *Die Gemälde die Rembrandt-
schüler*, vol. VI, 1994, p. 3695, cat. no. 2207, illus. in colour, p. 3791, fig. 2207.
Sotheby's New York, 11 January 1996 (145**) US$ 360,000 | US$ | 360,000

PORTRAIT OF A LADY HOLDING A ROSE, PERHAPS AS THE GODDESS FLORA oil on
canvas, 27 x 21½in. (68.6 x 54.6cm.) sll 'G. Flinck' inscr with an inventory number '333' (ca 1658)
Sotheby's New York, 11 January 1996 (124**) US$ 68,500 | US$ | 68,500

FLINT Sir William Russell, R.A., P.R.W.S. (1880-1969) Scottish
MADELINA tempera, 12¾ x 21½in. (32.4 x 54.6cm.) sll 'W. Russell Flint' s inscr. on the reverse
'Madelina (tempera) W. Russell Flint'
PROV.: Closson Gallery, Cincinatti.
Christie's London, 21 November 1995 (326**) GBP 20,125 | US$ | 31,480

THE FLOATING PLANK watercolour on paper, 20 1/8 x 27in. (51.1 x 68.6cm.) slr 'W.RUSSEL
FLINT' sd inscr. on the reverse 'WRussel Flint./1935-37'
Christie's New York, 22 May 1996 (283**) US$ 25,300 | US$ | 25,300

THE POOL OF THE VANITIES watercolour and bodycolour, 19¼in x 26¼in. (49 x 66.7cm.) slr
'W.Russell Flint' sd inscr. on the reverse 'The Pool of the Vanities W Russell Flint 1948-1957 Started
at Compiegne June 1948 Completed Oct. 1957'
Christie's London, 21 November 1995 (347**) GBP 23,000 | US$ | 35,977

FLOCH Josef (Vienna 1894-1977 New York) Austrian
THREE ROADS oil on canvas, 36 x 51.5cm. slr 'Floch'
LIT.: Will be included in the forthcoming *catalogue raisonné*.
Wiener Kunst Auktionen, 26 March 1996 (254**) ATS 75,000 | US$ | 7,214

READY TO LEAVE oil on canvas, 81.5 x 53cm. sdlr 'Floch 1955'
Wiener Kunst Auktionen, 29 November 1995 (690**) ATS 150,000 | US$ | 15,047

STILLEBEN MIT FLASCHE oil on canvas, 51 x 48cm. slr 'Floch'
        Dorotheum Vienna, 21 May 1996 (101**) ATS 150,000   US$ 14,404

BLAUE OBSTSCHALE oil on board, 60.5 x 50cm. sll 'Floch'
        Dorotheum Vienna, 21 May 1996 (92**) ATS 140,000   US$ 13,443

AM FENSTER oil on canvas, 61 x 40.8cm. slr 'Floch'
LIT.: Will be included in the forthcoming *catalogue raisonné*.
        Wiener Kunst Auktionen, 26 March 1996 (253**) ATS 90,000   US$ 8,657

FLORIS Frans {called} Frans I de Vrient (Antwerp 1516-1570) Flemish
ALLEGORY OF PIECE oil on panel, 38 x 44¼in. (96.5 x 112.4cm.) inscr. ll with a coat of arm
PROV.: Galerie Schedelmeyer, Paris (from a red wax seal on the reverse); Robert Hoe, New York;
His sale: American Art Association, New York, 17 Febraury 1911, lot 118 (illustrated).
        Sotheby's New York, 16 May 1996 (267**) US$ 90,500   US$ 90,500

THE DEATH OF ABELE oil on canvas, 163 x 210cm.
        Finearte Rome, 18 October 1995 (405**) ITL 55,200,000   US$ 34,393

THE FAMILY OF ADAM AND EVE oil on board, 163 x 210cm.
        Finearte Rome, 18 October 1995 (404**) ITL 69,000,000   US$ 42,991

FONTANA Lucio (Rosario di Santa Fé 1899-1968 Varese) Italian
CONCETTO SPAZIALE waterpaint on canvas and laquered wood frame, 4½ x 47¼ x 2½in. (110.6
x 120 x 6.3cm.) sd and titled '1965' on the reverse
PROV.: Alexander Iolas Gallery, New York.
LIT.: Enrico Crispolti, *Lucio Fontana Catalogue Raisonné*, Brussels 1974, vol. II, p. 172, no. 65 TE
63 (ill.); Enrico Crispolti, *Fontana Catalogo Generale*, Milan 1986, vol. II, p. 605, no.65 TE 63 (ill.).
        Christie's London, 23 May 1996 (78**) GBP 43,300   US$ 65,566

CONCETTO SPAZIALE, LA FINE DI DIO oil on canvas, 70 x 48¼in. (178 x 123cm.) s and s on
the reverse (1963)
PROV.: Acquired directly from the Artis by the father of the present owner in the 1960's.
EXH.: London, The Tate Gallery, *Painting and Sculpture of a Decade '54-'64*, April-June 1964, no.
43a (illustrated in the catalogue, p. 82).
LIT.: Enrico Crispolti, *Lucio Fontana Catalogue Raisonné*, Brussels 1974, vol.II, p. 136, no. 63 FD 7
(illustrated); Enrico Crispolti, *Fontana Catalogo Generale*, Milan 1986, vol.II, p. 463, no. 63 FD 7
(illustrated).
        Christie's London, 30 November 1995 (19**) GBP 342,500   US$ 535,742

CONCETTO SPAZIALE, TEATRINO waterpaint on canvas and lacquered wood, 69 x 69in. (175 x
175cm.) st on the reverse (1966)
PROV.: Paul Haim & Co., Paris; Marlborough Gallery, New York/Rome; Enrico Baj, Vergiate;
Acquired from the above by the present owner in the 1970's.
EXH.: Humblebaek, Louisiana Museum, *Fontana*, January-February 1967, no. 57; Amsterdam,
Stedelijk Museum; Eindhoven, Stedelijk van Abbemuseum, *Lucio Fontana Concetti Spaziali*,
March-June 1967, no. 63; Stockholm, Moderna Museet, *Fontana: Idéer om rymden*, August-October
1967, no. 57; Hanover, Kestner-Gesellschaft, *Lucio Fontana*, Jan.-Feb. 1968, no 57 (illustrated in the
catalogue); Florence, Palazzo Pitti, Fontana, April-June 1980, no. 53 (illustrated in the catalogue).
LIT.: In: *AL2*, 'Vinicio Saniantoni, Arte, Cultura, Atualitá Rome', June 1972, p.3 (illustrated); Enrico
Crispolti, *Lucio Fontana: Catalogue Raisonné*, Brussels, 1974, Vol. II, p. 174, no. 65-66 TE 16
(illustrated); In: *Corriere della Sera*, Sebastiano Grasso, 'Fontana Rivisitato: Un Centinaio di Opere
dal 1931 al 1968 nelle Sale d'Arte Contemporanea del Comune di Rimini', Milan July 1982, no. 88
(illustrated); Enrico Crispolti, *Fontana: Catalogo Generale*, Milan 1988, Vol. II, p. 616, no. 65-66
TE 16 (illustrated).
        Christie's London, 26 October 1995 (45**) GBP 60,900   US$ 96,117

CONCETTO SPAZIALE, ATTESE waterpaint on canvas, 28¾ x 36¼in. (73 x 92cm.) s inscr. and titled 'Sette per nove quarantanove giusto!' on the reverse (1965-66)
PROV.: Gallerie Pierre, Stockholm.
LIT.: This work is registered at the Archivio Lucio Fontana under no. 2661/2.
      Christie's London, 30 November 1995 (22**) GBP 144,500   US$ 226,028

CONCETTO SPAZIALE, FORMA ink, pencil, glue and hessian collage on hessian, 65 x 47¼in. (165 x 120cm.) slr and sd titled and inscr. '58' on the reverse
PROV.: Acquired directly from the Artist by the father of the present owner.
EXH.: Venice, *XXIX Biennale Internazionale d'Arte*, June-October 1958. D. 22; London, The Institute of Contemporary Art, *Paintings from the Damiano Collection: Fontana, Dova, Crippa, Clemente*, January 1959, p. 7.
LIT.: Giampiero Giani, *Lucio Fontana*, Venice 1958, pl. 6 (illustrated); In: *Evento*, 'Toni Toniato, L'Invenzione Poetica di Fontana', Venice April- July 1958, pp. 35-38 (illustrated p. 39); In: *La Biennale di Venezia*, 'Nello Ponente, Continuita di Fontana', Venice December 1966, p. 17, no. 15 (illustrated); Enrico Crispolti, *Lucio Fontana Catalogue Raisonné*, Brussels 1974, vol. II, p. 60, no. 58 I 2 (illustrated); Enrico Crispolti, *Fontana Catalogo Generale*, Milan 1986, vol. I, p. 210, no. 58 I 2 (illustrated).
      Christie's London, 19 March 1996 (38**) GBP 78,500   US$ 119,884

CONCETTO SPAZIALE, ATTESE waterpaint on canvas, 36¼ x 28¾in. (92 x 73cm.) s titled and inscr. 'Vorrei Addormentarmi su il Piu Bel Prato Verde' on the reverse (1964)
PROV.: Galerie Burén, Stockholm; Acquired from the above by the present owner in 1966.
LIT.: Enrico Crispolti, *Fontana: Catalogue Raisonné*, Brussels 1974, vol. II, p. 152, no. 64 T 31 (illustrated p. 153); Enrico Crispolti, *Fontana: Catalogo Generale*, Milan 1986, vol. II, p. 520, no. 64 T 31 (illustrated).
      Christie's London, 27 June 1996 (52**) GBP 111,500   US$ 171,935

CONCETTO SPAZIALE oil on canvas, 78¾ x 78¾in. (,,200 x 200cm.) s and titled on the reverse (1959-60)
PROV.: Galerie Denise Rene-Hans Mayer, Dusseldorf; Private Collection, Milan; Galerie Neuendorf, Frankfurt.
EXH.: Krefeld, Galerie Merian Edition, *Lucio Fontana 1899-1968*, September-October 1973 (illustrated in the catalogue); Milan, Galleria Medea, *L'aventura spaziale di Lucio Fontana*, October-November 1974, no. 11 (illustrated in the catalogue and on the front cover); Milan, Galleria Medea, *Lucio Fontana*, April-May 1976, no. 18; Cologne, Galerie Karsten Greve, *Cy Twombly, Jannis Kounellis, Hans Brosch, Piero Manzoni; Cologne, Dia Art Foundation, Lucio Fontana 1926-1968*, March-May 1981; Frankfurt, Galerie Neuendorf, *Lucio Fontana*, December 1987-January 1988, no. 41 (illustrated in colour in the catalogue).
LIT.: Enrico Crispolti, *Lucio Fontana: Catalogue Raisonné*, Brussels 1974, vol. II, p. 66, no. 59 60 B5 (illustrated on p. 67); Enrico Crispolti, Fontana: *Catalogo Generale*, Milan 1986, vol. 1, p. 233, no. 59 60 B5 (illustrated and illustrated again in colour on p. 234).
      Christie's London, 27 June 1996 (55**) GBP 452,500   US$ 697,764

CONCETTO SPAZIALE oil, pencil and carving on canvas, 130 x 97cm. s, s titled on the reverse (1966-67)
PROV.: Enrico Crispolti, *Lucio Fontana Catalogue Raisonné*, Brussels 1974, Vol. II, pag. 142; Enrico Crispolti, *Lucio Fontana Catalogo Generale*, Milano 1986, Vol. II, pag. 493, n. 66-67 O 2, illustrated.
      Sotheby's Milan, 28 May 1996 (170**) ITL 131,250,000   US$ 84,297

CONCETTO SPAZIALE, ATTESE waterpaint on canvas, 49¼ x 39¼in. (125 x 100cm.) s inscr. 'Attese/1+1-73A/Mi piacerebbe una cravatta cosi rossa' on the reverse (1960)
PROV.: Acquired directly from the artist by the father of the present owner in the 1960's.
LIT.: Enrico Crispolti, *Lucio Fontana Catalogue Raisonné*, Brussels 1974, vol. II, p. 90, no. 60 T 8 (illustrated p. 91); Enrico Crispolti, *Lucio Fontana Catalogue Raisonné*, Milan 1986, vol. I, p. 314,

no. 60 T 8 (illustrated).

      Christie's London, 30 November 1995 (24**) GBP 122,500   US$ 191,616

CONCETTO SPAZIALE ATTESA waterpaint on canvas, 100 x 81cm. sd '1960' and inscr. 'Atessa I + 1 - 3310' on the reverse

      Sotheby's Milan, 28 May 1996 (186**) ITL 136,900,000   US$ 87,925

CONCETTO SPAZIALE, ATTESE waterpaint on canvas, 24 x 19¼in. (61 x 49.5cm.) s, titled and inscr. 'Che schifo schiacciare un verme' on the reverse (1963)
PROV.: Galeria Theo, Madrid.

      Sotheby's London, 27 June 1996 (198**) GBP 45,500   US$ 70,162

CONCETTO SPAZIALE oil, graffiti and carvings on canvas, 91 x 65cm. sd and inscr. 'all'amico incosciente Cap. Donato, 1 + 1-7A7E' on the reverse
PROV.: Galleria Gastaldelli, Milan.
LIT.: Michel Tapié, *Devenir de Fontana*, Turib 1961 (illustrated); *The Geijutsu Shincho*, no. 12, Tokyo 1962, p. 2 (illustrated); Enrico Crispolti, *Fontana Catalogue Raisonné*, Brussels 1974, vol. II, p. 108 (illustrated); enrico Crispolti, *Fontana - Catalogo Generale*, Milan 1986, vol. I, p. 364, no. 61 O 18 (illustrated).

      Sotheby's Milan, 28 May 1996 (199**) ITL 103,000,000   US$ 66,153

FONTANA Prospero (1512 c.-1597) Italian
THE MADONNA AND CHILD WITH THE INFANT SAINT JOHN THE BAPTIST oil on canvas, 11 x 9¾on. (27.9 x 24.8cm.)
PROV.: Newhouse Galleries, New York, circa 1963.

      Sotheby's New York, 11 January 1996 (52**) US$ 60,250   US$ 60,250

FONTEBASSO Francesco Salvator (attr.) (Venice 1709-1769) Italian
THE JUDGEMENT OF SALOMON / WORSHIP OF SALOMON oil on canvas (a pair), each: 114 x 97cm.

      Étude Tajan Paris, 28 June 1996 (12**) FRF 170,000   US$ 32,827

FORAIN Jean Louis (1852-1931) French
A STANDING NUDE pastel, 28 x 23in. (71 x 58cm.) slr

      Sotheby's London, 13 March 1996 (50**) GBP 6,325   US$ 9,659

DANSEUSE AU DECOR oil on canvas, 25¾ x 32 3/8in. (65.4 x 82.2cm.) sdlr 'Forain 1905'
PROV.: Arthur Tooth & Sons Ltd., London; Anon. sale; Sotheby's & Co., London, Feb. 25, 1987, lot 65 (acquired by the present owner).

      Christie's East, 7 November 1995 (24**) US$ 13,800   US$ 13,800

FORBES Elizabeth Adela Stanhope (1859-1912) Canadian
THE CHRISTMAS TREE black crayon, watercolour and bodycolour, 17¾ x 14in. (45 x 35.5cm.) sll 'EAS Forbes'
PROV.: Colonel Edward Penrose, thence by descent to the present owner.

      Christie's London, 21 November 1995 (82**) GBP 8,625   US$ 13,491

FORBES Stanhope Alexander, R.A. (1857-1947) British
CHILDREN ON THE BEACH oil on canvas, 18 x 13in. (45.7 x 33cm.) (ca 1891)
PROV.: Private Collection, Brittany, from whom purchased by the present owner.

      Christie's London, 21 November 1995 (99**) GBP 54,300   US$ 84,937

THE VILLAGE STREAM oil on canvas, 20¼ x 25¼in. (51.5 x 64.2cm.) slr 'Stanhope A Forbes'
PROV.: m. Newman Ltd., London.

      Christie's London, 21 November 1995 (86**) GBP 17,250   US$ 26,983

FORNENBURG Jan Baptist van (Delft 1600-1649 's-Gravenhage) Dutch
STILL-LIFE WITH FLOWERS IN A GLASS VASE WITHIN A STONE NICHE, INSECTS,
REPTILES AND FLOWER PETALS ON THE FLOOR OF THE NICHE oil on panel, 42¼ x 30in.
(107.3 x 76.2cm.) sdlr 'Jan bat. v. F. [162?]6'
PROV.: Acquired by an ancestor of the present owner, ca. 1850, and thence by descent in the family.
      Sotheby's New York, 16 May 1996 (39**) US$ 519,500   US$ 519,500

APPLES, A QUINCE AND A WALNUT ON A STONE LEDGE, A BUTTERFLY NEARBY oil on
panel, 24.3 x 40.5cm sd 'JBVF'
PROV.: Anon. sale Robinson & Fischer London, 12 April 1923, lot 46, as A. Bosschaert; Anon.
Sale, Christie's London 31 Oct. 1975, lot 127, with ill.; with J. Kraus, Paris (catalogue 1976, no. 25,
with ill.); with K. Müllenmeister, Solingen, from whom acquired by the present owner in 1977.
      Christie's Amsterdam, 13 November 1995 (154**) NLG 34,500   US$ 21,743

FORREST Captain James Haughton (19th Century)
PADDLE STEAMER OFF A ROCKY COASTLINE oil on canvas, 17 7/8 x 24¼in. (45.5 x 61.5cm.)
sdll '1856'
      Phillips London, 18 June 1996 (34**) GBP 4,200   US$ 6,476

FORTE Luca (Napoli 1,600 c.-1670 c.) Italian
STILL-LIFE WITH FRUIT oil on canvas, 92 x 78cm.
      Finearte Rome, 21 May 1996 (146**) ITL 57,500,000   US$ 36,930

FORTI Ettore (Rome 19th Century) Italian
UNA DISTRAZIONE PERICOLOSA oil on canvas, 23¾ x 39½in. (60.4 x 100.3cm.) s inscr. 'E
Forti/Roma'
      Christie's London, 14 June 1996 (133**) GBP 14,950   US$ 23,053

FORTT Frederick (19th century) British
THE FORTUNETELLER oil on canvas, 50 x 40in. (127 x 101.6cm.) sd '1884'
      Sotheby's Arcade Auctions New York, 20 July 1995 (165*) US$ 6,900   US$ 6,900

FOSCHI Pier Francesco (Ancona 19th Century-1805 d. Rome) Italian
WINTERLANDSCAPE WITH A WATERFALL AND PEOPLE oil on canvas, 71 x 99cm.
PROV.: Anon. Sale, Christie's Monaco, 2 December 1989, no. 41, reproduced in colour (as Jean
Pillement); Anon. sale, Paris, Hotel George V, 29 March 1994, no. 60 reproduced in colour;
Acquired by the current proprietor at Galerie Bob Haboldt, Paris.
EXH.: *Paysage d'eau douce*, Paris, Galerie Charpentier, 27 April 1945, no. 105 (as Jean Pillement).
      Étude Tajan Paris, 12 December 1995 (106**) FRF 230,000   US$ 46,328

WINTER CAPRICCIO WITH A COUNTRY HOUSE AND A VESTAL TEMPLE BEYOND oil on
canvas, 74 x 98cm.
      Christie's Rome, 21 November 1995 (116**) ITL 24,000,000   US$ 15,066

FOSTER Walter (fl. 1861-1888) British
OTTER HUNTING oil on canvas, 36 x 56½in. (91.5 x 43.5cm.) s
PROV.: See also John Sargent Noble (51) co-painter.
      Phillips London, 10 October 1995 (51*) GBP 6,000   US$ 9,470

FOUBERT Emile Louis (1840-1910) French
LES BORDS DE LA SEINE A VETHEUIL oil on panel, 9½ x 12¾in. (24.1 x 32.4cm) sdlr 'E.
FOUBERT/1907.'
      Christie's New York, 22 May 1996 (186**) US$ 7,820   US$ 7,820

FOUJITA Tsugharu Léonard (Tsuguji) (1886-1968) French (Japanese)
RENDEZ-VOUS DE BICYCLIST oil on canvas, 14 x 18cm. s twice, d and inscr. with title ll 'Foujita

1939 Paris' and sd again and inscr. 'Paysage de Paris Squai Carpeaux' on the stretcher
    Christie's Amsterdam, 5 June 1996 (241**) NLG 59,800   US$ 34,940

PORTRAIT D'ENFANT oil on canvas, 7 1/8 x 5 1/2in. (18 x 14cm.) bottom center 'Foujita'
PROV.: Galerie Paul Pétridès, Paris.
    Christie's New York, 8 November 1995 (257**) US$ 46,000   US$ 46,000

LE VENT oil on canvas, 16¼ x 9 5/8in. (41.3 x 24.4cm.) slr 'Foujita'
PROV.: Paul Pétridès, Paris.
    Sotheby's New York, 2 May 1996 (358A**) US$ 189,500   US$ 189,500

FEMME AU PETIT CHAT oil on canvas, 23 5/8 x 28¾in. (60 x 73cm.) sd 'Foujita 1939 Paris' sd
again on the stretcher
PROV.: Purchased directly from the Artist by the previous owner, presumebly for 120FFR -as
marked on the stretcher (probably by Foujita).
    Christie's London, 25 June 1996 (48**) GBP 177,500   US$ 273,709

MERE ET ENFANT pen, brush and indian ink, 8 7/8 x 5 7/8in. (22.5 x 15cm.) sd 'Foujita Paris 1950'
    Christie's London, 26 June 1996 (194**) GBP 14,950   US$ 23,053

JEUNE FILLE AU CHAT BLANC oil on canvas, 16¼ x 10¾in. (41.3 x 27.3cm.) sdlr 'Foujita 1957'   US$
    Sotheby's New York, 2 May 1996 (414**) US$ 266,500   266,500

LA PETITE CUISINIERE oil on canvas, 7¼ x 5¾in. (18.5 x 14.6cm.) slr 'Foujita' s titled and inscr.
on the reverse
PROV.: Kimiyo Foujita, Paris, by whom given to Mrs. Max Stern Montreal.
    Christie's London, 26 June 1996 (206**) GBP 43,300   US$ 66,769

NU ALLONGE pen and ink with watercolour, gouache and charcoal, 15¾ x 19¼in. (40 x 49cm.) sdll
'Foujita 1932'
    Phillips London, 27 November 1995 (23**) GBP 17,000   US$ 26,592

FOUQUIER Jacques (Antwerp 1585 c.-1659 Paris) Flemish
WOODED RIVERLANDSCAPE WITH TRAVELLERS oil on copper, 15 x 19cm.
    Dorotheum Vienna, 06 March 1996 (136**) ATS 180,000   US$ 17,314

FRAGONARD Jean Honoré (Grasse 1732-1806 Paris) French
DEUX FEMMES SUR UN LIT JOUANT AVEC UN PETIT CHIEN: LE LEVER oil on canvas, 74
x 59cm. (1770's)
PROV.: Collection Comte de Reilhac, 1889; Collection Eugene Kraemer before 1913; His Sale,
Paris, Galerie Georges Petit, 28-29 April 1913, (Maîtres Lair, Dubreuil, Baudoin), no 20, reproduced;
Collection S. Grencer, before1933; His sale, Paris, Galerie Charpentier, 27 March 1933 (Maître
Beaudoin), no 23, reproduced; Anon. sale, Paris, Palais d'Orsay, 28 March 1979, no 164, reproduced
en colour (1 ,700 ,000 FF).
EXH.: *Chardin et Fragonard*, Paris, Galerie Georges Petit, 1907.
LIT.: R. Portalis, *L'oeuvre de Fragonard*, Paris, 1889, p. 282, reproduced p. 126; P. de Nolhac, *Jean
Honoré Fragonard*, Paris, 1906, p. 121 (82 x 54 cm); A. Dayot et L. Vaillat, *L'oeuvre de Jean
Baptiste Siméon Chardin et de Jean Honoré Fragonard*, Paris, 1907, no. 112, reproduced; G.
Wildenstein, *The paintings of Fragonard*, Bath, 1960, no. 291 or 292; D. Wildenstein, *L'opera
completa di Fragonard*, Milan, 1972, no 309, reproduced; Jean-Pierre Cuzin, *Fragonard, vie et
oeuvre*, Paris, 1982, p. 298, no 202, reproduced; P. Rosenberg, *Tout l'oeuvre peint de Fragonard*,
Paris, 1989, no 259, reproduced.
    Étude Tajan Paris, 12 December 1995 (101**) FRF 8,200,000   US$ 1,651,694

PORTAIT OF A CHILD oil on oak panel, 20 x 16.5cm.
    Étude Tajan Paris, 18 December 1995 (170*) FRF 120,000   US$ 24,171

MANDRICARDO DISMISSES DORALICE'S ESCORT AND ABDUCTS HER (ARIOSTO, 'ORLANDO FURIOSO', XIV, 62). black chalk and brown wash, 39,6 x 27.5cm. (1780's)
PROV.: Hippolyte Walferdin, who probably purchased the complete Aristo set from the Fragonard family, his sale, Paris, Hotel Drouot, 12-16 April 1880, lot 228; Louis Roederer, Reims; Roederer heirs until 1923; Dr. A.S.W. Rosenbach, Philadelphia.
EXH.: Baron R. de Portalis, *Les Dessinateurs d 'illustration au dix-huitième siecle*, Paris 1877, pp.222ff; idem., *Fragonard, Sa vie et son oeuvre*, Paris 1889, p. 311; H. Cohen and S. de Ricci, *Guide de l'amateur de livres à gravures du XVIII siècle*, Paris 1912, p.97; S. de Ricci, *The Roederer Library of French Books*, Philadelphia 1923, n.p.; Elizabeth Mongan, Philip Hofer and Jean Seznec, *Fragonard Drawings for Ariosto*, London 1945, pp.48, 75, pl.. 103; Thomas Agnew & Sons Ltd., *Fragonard Drawings for Orlando Furioso*, London 1978, n.p. (in list of locations of all the drawings as no. 103) .
Sotheby's London, 3 July 1995 (155**) GBP 17,250   US$ 27,516

FRANCAIS François-Louis (1814-1897) French
LES VAUX DE CERNAY oil on canvas, 15 x 18in. (38 x 45.8cm.) slr 'Francais'
Christie's New York, 22 May 1996 (181**) US$ 9,775   US$ 9,775

FRANCESCHINI Marcantonio (Bologna 1648-1729) Italian
THE LAST COMMUNION OF SAINT MARY OF EGYPT FROM THE HERMIT ZOSIMUS oil on copper, 16¾ x 21 3/8in. (42.6 x 54.3cm.)
PROV.: The Bolognese Senate, by whom given to Pope Clement XI, *circa* 1709;
Henry Willet; Cannon Robert Wadman, St Joseph's Presbytery, Bridgewater;(+) sale, Puttick & Simpson, London, Oct. 16, 1914, from whom purchased by; Lionell Grace, 114 Queen Victoria Street, London; with Thos. Agnew and Sons, London.
LIT.: G.P. Zanotti, *Storia dell'Accademia Clementina di Bologna*, I, 1739, pp. 223-4; D.C. Miller, *Two early Paintings by Marcantonio Franceschini and a Gift of the Bolognese Senate to Pope Clement XI*, The Burlington Magazine, CXII,June, 1970, pp. 373-8, fig. 39; A. Ottani Cavani and R. Roli, *Commentario a G. P. Zanotti, Storia dell'Accademia Clementina di Bologna*, in Atti e Memorie dell'Accademia Clementina di Bologna, XII, 1977, pp. 66, 259, 261; R. Roli, *Pittura Bolognese 1650-1800, Dal Cignani ai Gandolfi*, 1977, pp. 23, 101, 261; D. Biagi in the catalogue of the exhibition, *La Raccolta Molinari Pradelli*, Bologna, Palazzo del Podestà, May 26-Aug. 29, 1984, p. 104, under no. 62; J. Pope-Hennessy, *Learning to Look*, 1991, p. 317.
Christie's New York, 10 January 1996 (103**) US$ 112,500   US$ 112,500

FRANCESCHINI Marcantonio (Bologna 1648-1729) Italian
BIBLE SCENE / JACOB AND RACHEL oil on canvas (a pair), 152 x 115cm.
Finearte Milan, 03 April 1996 (127**) ITL 92,000,000   US$ 58,786

TARQUIN AND LUCRETIA oil on canvas, 72¾ x 72¾in. (184.5 x 184.5cm.) (ca. 1706)
PROV.: Commissioned from the artist in May 1706 by Prince Johann Adam Andreas for the Garden Palace at Rossau, Vienna; Thence by descent in the Liechtenstein collection (1872 catalogue no. 388) until sale, Paris, Charles Pillet, 4-5 March 1881, lot 92.
LIT.: D.C. Miller, *Marcantonio Franceschini and the Liechtensteins*, 1991, pp. 54, 104-105, 262-263, 266, 269-270, 272, no. 40.
Sotheby's London, 6 December 1995 (52**) GBP 78,500   US$ 120,806

FRANCESE Franco (Milan 1920 b.) Italian
AGNELLI DO KRONSTADT oil on canvas, 115 x 155cm. sd and titled '20.5.1963/4.9.1969' on the reverse
PROV.: Galleria del Girasole, Udine, no. 2040; Galerie d'Eendt, Amsterdam.
Finearte Milan, 18 June 1996 (204**) ITL 19,550,000   US$ 12,678

FRANCHI Antonio {called Il Lucchese} (Villa Basilica (Lucca) 1634-1709 Florence) Italian
THE IDOLATRY OF SOLOMON oil on canvas, 102½ x 126½in. (260 x 321cm.) (ca 1680-81)
PROV.: Commissioned from the artist by Marchese Carlo Andrea Rinuccini, Palazzo Rinuccini,

Fondaccio di S. Spirito, Florence; Probably given by the above to Lucrezia Rinuccini on the occasion of her marriage in 1681 to Marchese Filippo Corsini (1647-1703), Thence by descent in the Corsini family, Palazzo Corsini, Florence; Private Collection, Switzerland.
EXH.: Florence, Palazzo Pitti, *Mostra della Pittura italiana del Seicento e del Settecento*, 2nd edit. 1922, no. 757A, as Pietro da Cortona.
LIT.: F.S. Baldinucci, 'Vita del Pittore Antonio Franchi', in ed. A. Matteoli, F.S. Baldinucci, *Vite di Artisti dei secoli XVII-XVIII*, in *Raccolta di Fonti per la storia dell'arte.*, 2nd series, vol. III, 1975, p. 44; S.B. Bartolozzi, *Vita di Antonio Franchi Lucchese*, 1754, pp. XVII-XVIII, as belonging to Falco (sic) Rinuccini; R. Longhi, *Scitti Giovanili - 1912-22*, 1961, p. 587, as possibly by Ciro Ferri; H. Voss, *Die Malerei des barock in Rom*, 1924, pl. 265, as 'Richtung des Pietro da Cortona'; M. Gregori, 'Ricerche per Antonio Franchi', in *Paradigma*, 1977, vol. l, pp. 73-75.
Sotheby's London, 5 July 1995 (76**) GBP 309,500   US$ 493,699

TEMPLE OF VENUS oil on canvas, 102½ x 126½in. (260 x 321cm.) (ca. 1680-81)
PROV.: Commissioned from the artist by Marchese Carlo Andrea Rinuccini, Palazzo Rinuccini, Fondaccio di S. Spirito, Florence; Probably given by the above to Lucrezia Rinuccini on the occasion of her marriage in 1681 to Marchese Filippo Corsini (1647-1703), Thence by descent in the Corsini family, Palazzo Corsini, Florence; Private Collection, Switzerland.
EXH.: Florence, Palazzo Pitti, *Mostra della Pittura italiana del Seicento e del Settecento*, 2nd edit. 1922, no. 757A, p. 144.
LIT.: F.S. Baldinucci, 'Vita del Pittore Antonio Franchi', in ed. A. Matteoli, F.S. Baldinucci, *Vite di Artisti dei secoli XVII-XVIII*, in *Raccolta di Fonti per la storia dell'arte.*, 2nd series, vol. III, 1975, p. 44; S.B. Bartolozzi, *Vita di Antonio Franchi Lucchese*, 1754, pp. XVII-XVIII, as belonging to Falco (sic) Rinuccini; M. Gregori, 'Ricerche per Antonio Franchi', in *Paradigma*, 1977, vol. l, pp. 73-75.
Sotheby's London, 5 July 1995 (76**) GBP 1,156,500   US$ 1,844,792

FRANCHI Rossello di Jacopo (1377 c.-1456) Italian
SAINT FRANCIS RECEIVING THE STIGMATA oil on panel, 26 3/ x 7 7/8in. (68 x 20cm.)
PROV.: H.M. Sinclair, Dalky Lodge, Dalky, Dublin; Christie's 8 June 1928, lot 81 as Mater of the Bambino Vispo (280gns. To P. de Boer).
Christie's London, 19 April 1996 (244**) GBP 36,700   US$ 55,648

FRANCIS Sam (San Mateo 1923 b.-1994) American
UNTITLED acrylic and watercolour on paper, 36 2/8 x 71 5/8in. (92 x 182cm.) sd '1974' s ini and numb '74-700' on the reverse
PROV.: Galerie Jean Fournier, Paris; acquired from the above by the present owner.
LIT.: This work is registered with The Sam Francis Estate/The Sam Francis Art Foundation under no. 74-700.
Christie's London, 23 May 1996 (46**) GBP 54,300   US$ 82,223

VERTICAL BLUE AND YELLOW oil on canvas, 32½ x 15¾in. (82.4 x 40cm.) sd 'Sam Francis 1959' on the reverse
PROV.: The Waddington Galleries, London.
Christie's New York, 14 November 1995 (17**) US$ 167,500   US$ 167,500

UNTITLED acrylic on paper, 29½ x 49¼in. (75 x 125cm.) initialed, numbered and d 'SF 78.400' on the reverse
PROV.: Smith Anderson Gallery, Palo Alto.
Christie's New York, 15 November 1995 (161**) US$ 46,000   US$ 46,000

EVERGREEN LICKS acrylic on canvas, 60 x 72in. (152 x 183cm.) sd 'Sam Francis 1987' on the reverse
PROV.: André Emmerich Gallery, New York.
Christie's New York, 15 November 1995 (199**) US$ 100,400   US$ 100,400

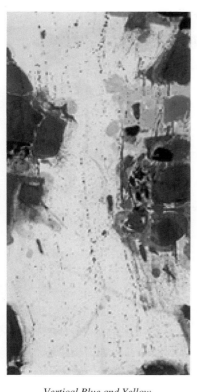

Vertical Blue and Yellow

UNTITLED acrylic on shaped canvas, diameter: 63in. (160cm.) sd 'SAM FRANCIS 1987' on the reverse
PROV.: Galerie Jean Fournier, Paris; Galerie Beyeler, Basel.
    Christie's New York, 22 February 1996 (16**) US$ 85,000   US$ 85,000

E IV acrylic on canvas, 72¾ x 42in. (184.8 x 106.7cm. sd 'Sam Francis 1970' on the reverse
PROV.: André Emmerich Gallery, New York.
    Christie's New York, 22 February 1996 (49**) US$ 74,000   US$ 74,000

UNTITLED acrylic on canvas, 42 x 42in. (106.8 x 106.8cm.) s 'Sam Francis' on the reverse (1985)
PROV.: André Emmerich Gallery, New York; Adams-Middleton Gallery, Dallas.
EXH.: Dallas, Adams-Middleton Gallery, *Recent Abstract Paintings*, Sept.-Oct. 1985.
    Christie's New York, 8 May 1996 (444**) US$ 88,300   US$ 88,300

RED, YELLOW AND BLUE gouache on paper, 13 x 9½in. (33 x 24cm.) sd 'Sam Francis 1963 Tokyo' (on the reverse)
    Christie's Tel Aviv, 14 April 1996 (95**) US$ 24,150   US$ 24,150

FRANCKEN Frans I (and studio) (Herenthals 1542-1616) Flemish
JOSEPH AND HIS BROTHERS oil on canvas, 139 x 188cm.
    Étude Tajan Paris, 28 June 1996 (38**) FRF 135,000   US$ 26,068

FRANCKEN Frans II (Antwerp 1581-1642 Antwerp) Flemish
ELEGANT FIGURES DANCING IN AN INN oil on copper, 19¾ x 29in. (50.2 x 73.7cm.) s inscr. ll 'Do ffranck in et f'
PROV.: Possibly sale: Christie's London, November 23, 1965, lot 89, illus.; Possibly sale: Palais Galliera, Paris, March 26, 1977, lot 25, (illustrated).
LIT.: Possibly Ursula Harting, *Frans Francken II*, 1989, p.366, cat. no. 433, illus. 85 (as possibly by Frans III).
    Sotheby's New York, 11 January 1996 (192**) US$ 37,950   US$ 37,950

LE REPAS CHEZ SIMON oil on panel, 30 x 66cm.
    Étude Tajan Paris, 12 December 1995 (2**) FRF 60,000   US$ 12,086

JUDEAN MARKETSCENE WITH TREASURES FROM EGYPT oil on copper, 70 x 87cm.
    Bukowskis Stockholm, 29-31 May 1996 (267**) SEK 125,000   US$ 18,384

FRANCKEN Frans III (1607-1667) Flemish
THE ADORATION OF THE MAGI oil on copper, 41 x 32cm.
    Bukowskis Stockholm, 29-31 May 1996 (259**) SEK 80,000   US$ 11,766

FRANCKEN Frans the Younger & Paul Vredeman de Vries (1567-1630) (Antwerp 1578-1628) Flemish
SALOMÉ PRESENTING THE HEAD OF ST JOHN THE BAPTIST TO KING HEROD oil on panel, 24¼ x 35¼in. (61.5 x 89.8cm.) (ca. 1610-1615)
LIT.: G. Glück, *Die Sammlung Tritsch*, pp. 19-41 (illustrated); U. Härting, *Frans Francken der Jüngere*, 1989, p. 259, no. 98 (illustrated).
Sotheby's London, 17 April 1996 (59**) GBP 28,750 US$ 43,594

FRANCKEN Hieronymus III (Brugge 1611) Belgium
THE WORKS OF CHARITY oil on canvas, 55 x 81.5cm.
Dorotheum Vienna, 11 June 1996 (215**) ATS 120,000 US$ 11,138

FRANCKEN (ATTR.) Hieronymus II (1578-1623 (1628?)) Flemish
COGNOSCENTI IN A ROOM HUNG WITH PICTURES oil on panel, 37 ¼ x49in. (94.6 x 124.5cm.)
PROV.: Sir William Eden, Windlestone Hall, Co, Durham, and by descent to the present owner.
Christie's London, 7 July 1995 (48**) GBP 155,500 US$ 248,046

FRANGIPANE Niccolo (act. 1563-1597) Italian
CHRIST CARRYING THE CROSS oil on panel, 21 x 17¾in. (53.3 x 45.1cm.) sd or inscr. '1574 Nicolaus Frangi./ Pons. Eni. Titano'
Sotheby's New York, 16 May 1996 (207**) US$ 14,950 US$ 14,950

FRANGIPANE Niccolo (attr.) (act. 1563-1597) Italian
A YOUNG BEARDED MAN WITH A FLUTE oil on canvas, 26 x 21¼in. (65.8 x 53.4cm.)
Sotheby's London, 17 April 1996 (1**) GBP 11,500 US$ 17,437

FRANK Friedrich (Frankenmarkt 1871-1945 Werfenweng) Austrian
DIE RINGSTRAßE MIT DEM PARLAMENT watercolour and white on paper, 32.5 x 49cm. s and inscr. lr 'PARLAMENT WIEN - FRIEDRICH FRANK -'
Wiener Kunst Auktionen, 29 November 1995 (582**) ATS 100,000 US$ 10,031

FRANKENTHALER Helen (1928 b.) American
TRAVELOGUE II acrylic on canvas, 26½ x 28½in. (67.2 x 72.4cm.) sll 'Frankenthaler', s twice and d three times 'frankenthaler 1981' on the reverse
PROV.: André Emmerich Gallery, New York.
Christie's New York, 8 May 1996 (275**) US$ 27,600 US$ 27,600

APPROACH oil on canvas, 82 x 77¾in. (208.3 x 197.5cm.) (1962)
PROV.: André Emmerich Gallery, New York; The Abrams Family Collection, New York.
EXH.: Los Angeles County Museum of Art, Minneapolis, Walker Art Center, and Toronto, The Art Gallery of Ontario, *Post Painterly Abstraction*, June-Sept. 1966.
LIT.: B.Rose, *Frankenthaler*, New York 1970, no. 107 (ill.); J. Elderfield, *Frankenthaler*, New York 1989, pp.154-155 (ill.).
Christie's New York, 8 May 1996 (270**) US$ 112,500 US$ 112,500

FRANKL Gerhart (Vienna 1901-1965 Vienna) Austrian
GIEßHÜBL oil on canvas, 50.8 x 77cm. sdlr 'Gerh Frankl 1924'; titled on a label on the reverse
Wiener Kunst Auktionen, 26 September 1995 (258**) ATS 600,000 US$ 58,322

FREIST Greta (Weikersdorf 1904-1993 Paris) Austrian
LA DANSEUSE oil on canvas, 99 x 71.5cm. sdur 'Freist 38'
Dorotheum Vienna, 21 May 1996 (93**) ATS 320,000 US$ 30,728

FRENCH SCHOOL 19TH CENTURY
PORTRAIT OF A GIRL IN THE GUISE OF PEACE oil on canvas, 19 5/8 x 15¾in. (50 x 40cm.)

indistinctly s

Phillips London, 14 November 1995 (56**) GBP 7,000 — US\$ — 10,949

FRERE Edouard (1819-1886) French
THE GOURMAND oil on panel, 10 x 7¾in. (25.4 x 19.8cm.) sdlr 'Ed.Frere.8'
PROV.: Elizabeth C. Anketell.

Christie's East, 20 May 1996 (172*) US\$ 11,500 — US\$ — 11,500

THE HOUR OF PRAYER oil on panel, 14¾ x 11 5/8in. (37.5 x 29.5cm.) sdll '1878'
PROV.: Leggatt Brothers.

Sotheby's Arcade Auctions New York, 17 January 1996 (417*) US\$ 8,625 — US\$ — 8,625
,
FREUD Lucian, O.M. (1922 b.) British
HEAD OF A GIRL black and white white chalk on coloured paper, 7¼ x 5¼in. (18.4 x 13.3cm.) s ini
'LF' again under the mount

Christie's London, 22 May 1996 (59**) GBP 12,650 — US\$ — 19,155

FREUNDLICH Otto (Stolp 1878-1943 Lublin) German
KOMPOSITION pastel on paper, 32 x 24cm. slr mono

Hauswedell & Nolte Cologne, 5-6 June 1996 (205**) DEM 18,500 — US\$ — 12,020

FREY Johann Jakob (1813-1865) Swiss
AN EXTENSIVE VIEW OF SORRENTO oil on canvas, 39 3/8 x 53 7/8in. (110 x 137cm.) sdll 'J. J.
Frey 1847'

Phillips London, 11th June 1996 (32**) GBP 24,000 — US\$ — 37,008

FIGURES IN AN ANDALUSIAN LANDSCAPE oil on canvas, 39 x 54in. (99 x 137cm.) sdlr '1854';
inscr. 'Andalusia'; inscr. 'Auf der strasse von Alcalic.al Real nach Granada bei Illora in Andalusien'
on the stretcher on the reverse

Sotheby's London, 13 March 1996 (16**) GBP 15,525 — US\$ — 237,10

FREYMUTH Alphons (Haarlem 1940 b.) Dutch
THREE FIGURES oil on canvas, 140 x 80cm. s on the reverse 'Freymuth'

Christie's Amsterdam, 5 June 1996 (373*) NLG 6,900 — US\$ — 4,032

FRIEDRICH Caspar David (Greifswald 1774-1840 Dresden) German
TREE STUDY pencil on paper, 31.6 x 26cm. d '1806' sd on the reverse '1.89 Caspar David Friedrich
f.'
PROV.: Private collection, Dresden.

Dorotheum Vienna, 17 October 1995 (224**) ATS 430,000 — US\$ — 43,132

STUDIE EINSES WIESENBACHES (RECTO) / FELSEN ZWISCHEN BAUMSTAMMEN
(VERSO) watercolour and pen on paper, 35.7 x 25.8cm. (recto) sdll 'Caspar David Friedrich. f. / +
zu Dresden d. 7 Mai 1840'

Hauswedell & Nolte Cologne, 6 June 1996 (148**) DEM 122,000 — US\$ — 79,267

FRIESE Richard Bernhard Louis (1854-1918) German
A POLAR BEAR AND CUBS IN AN ARCTIC LANDSCAPE oil on canvas, 37 x 50½in. (94 x
128.3cm.) slr 'Rich. Friese.'
EXH.: Munich, *Jahres Ausstellung*, 1903, no. 1072.

Christie's New York, 28 November 1995 (164**) US\$ 112,500 — US\$ — 112,500

FRIESEKE Frederick Carl, N.A. (1874-1939) American
WOMAN AT A DRESSING TABLE oil on canvas, 31 7/8 x 26in. (81 x 66cm.) sll 'F.C. Frieseke'

Christie's New York, 23 May 1996 (78**) US\$ 112,500 — US\$ — 112,500

WOMAN AND GOAT oil on canvas, 25 x 31 7/8in. (63.5 x 81cm.) slr 'F C Frieseke'
PROV.: Hirschl & Adler Galleries, New York; Estate of Stephen Richard Currier and Audrey
Currier; Sale: New York, Christie's, June 1, 1984, lot 168.
LIT.: This painting will be included in the forthcoming *catalogue raisonné* of Frieseke's work being
compiled by Nicholas Kilmer, the artist's grandson.

Christie's New York, 23 May 1996 (83**) US$ 101,500	US$	101,500

FRIESZ Achile Émile-Othon (1879-1949) French
LE BASSIS DU HAVRE oil on canvas, 24¾ x 32in. (63 x 81cm.) sd 'Othon Friesz 06' (1906)
PROV.: Former collection Léon Pédron.
EXH.: Galerie Druet, Paris, 1912.
LIT.: *Cahiers d'Art*, 1929; *M. Gauthier*, 1957; Robert Martin and Odile Aittouarès, *Emile Othon
Friesz, l'oeuvre peint*, Edition Aittouarès, Paris, 1995, no. 13 p. 54.

Étude Tajan Paris, 13 December 1995 (40**) FRF 650,000	US$	130,927

PAYSAGE A CASSIS oil on canvas, 12½ x 15 3/8in. (31 x 39cm.) sll 'Othon Friesz' (ca. 1909)
PROV.: The Independant Gallery, London; Paul Maze and thence by descent through the family to
the step grand-daughter (the present owner).
EXH.: Edinburgh, The Scottish Arts Council, *Colour, Rhythm and Dance*, no. 66.

Christie's South Kensington, 24 June 1996 (42**) GBP 7,475	US$	11,527

FEMME NUE ENDORMIE oil on canvas, 38½ x 51¼in. (97.8 x 130.2cm.) sdll 'E. Othon Friesz
1921'
PROV.: Mrs. Sadie May, Baltimore; Himan Brown, New York (gift to The Metropolitan Museum of
Art, 1978).
EXH.: Paris, Musée d'Art Moderne de la Ville de Paris, *L'Exposition d'Art Francais Contemporaire*,
1937. The exhibition traveled to Lettaye, Musée de la Ville, 1937 and Amsterdam, Société Arti et
Amicitie, 1937; Baltimore Museum of Art (on loan); Pittsburgh, The Carnegie Institute (on loan);
New York, The Metropolitan Museum of Art, *Recent Acquisitions*, Oct.-Dec. 1970.

Christie's East, 7 November 1995 (63**) US$ 6,900	US$	6,900

BAIGNEUSES SUR LA RANCE oil on canvas, 21¼ x 25 5/8in. (54.1 x 65cm.) slr 'E. Othon Friesz',
d and titled 'Baigneuses sur la Rance, aôut 35' on the reverse (1935)

Christie's London, 26 June 1996 (321**) GBP 26,450	US$	40,786

LA GRANDE ROUE oil on canvas, 25½ x 32in. (65 x 81cm.) sll 'Othon-Friesz'
PROV.: Vente, Paris, Enghien, 29 March 1981.

Sotheby's London, 20 March 1996 (41**) GBP 67,500	US$	103,085

FRITH Sir William Powell, R.A. (1819-1909) British
A LONDON FLOWER GIRL oil on canvas, 30 x 20½in. (76.2 x 52.1cm.) sd 'W.P.Frith, 1884'
EXH.: The Royal Academy, no. 431 in 1884.

Christie's South Kensington, 7 March 1996 (178***) GBP 17,000	US$	25,962

FROHNER Adolf (Groß-Inzerdorf/Weinviertel 1934 b.) Austrian
GROßES FAMILIENBILD mixed technique, material, plaster on three-ply wood, 170 x 130 x 20cm.
PROV.: Sao Paulo, *Biennale*, 1969; Osnabrück, 17 Feb.-31 March 1991.

Wiener Kunst Auktionen, 27 September 1995 (470**) ATS 160,000	US$	15553

FROMENTIN Eugene (La Rochelle 1820-1876) French
OASIS AT LAGROUNT oil on canvas, 56 x 39 ¼in. (142.3 x 99.7cm.)
LIT.: J. Thompson and B. Wright, *La Vie et l'oeuvre d'Eugène Fromentin*, Paris, 1987, pp. 255-256
(illustrated).

Christie's New York, 2 November 1995 (49**) US$ 112,500	US$	112,500

AU BORD DU NIL oil on panel, 19¾ x 26¼in. (50.2 x 66.7cm.) slr 'Eug.-Fromentin'; dll '-1875.-'
PROV.: Brice Collection; sale Parke-Bernet, New York, 1 Jan. 1948, lot 85; Raymond Abrams
Collection; sale, Sotheby's, New York, 15 June 1979, lot 400.
LIT.: J. Thompson and B. Wright, *Les Orientalistes: Eugène Fromentin*, Paris 1987, p. 279
(illustrated).

Christie's New York, 14 February 1996 (27**) US$ 26,450	US$	26,450

FUCHS Ernst (Vienna 1930 b.) Austrian
BILDNIS mixed technique on vellum, 23 x 17.3cm. sdul 'E. Fuchs 1953'

Dorotheum Vienna, 21 May 1996 (170**) ATS 160,000	US$	15,364

FUJISHIMA Takeji (1865-1943) Japanese
PROFILE OF A WOMAN oil on panel, 17 7/8 x 15in. (45.5 x 38cm.) sll 'T. Fujishima' (1926-27)
EXH.: Tokyo, Metropolitan Museum of Art, *Fujishima Takeji isaku tenrankai (Fujishima Takeji
Posthumous Exhibition)*, Nov.-Dec., 1943, no. 67 (illustrated, pl. 38); Tokyo, Bridgestone Museum
of Art, *Seitan hyakunen kinen Fujishima Takeji ten (Fujishima Takeji 100th Year Memorial
Exhibition)*, April-May, 1967, no. 83 (illustrated).
LIT.: K. Kumamoto, *Fujishima Takeji*, Tokyo, 1967 (illustrated, pl. 81); S. Takashima, J. Rimer and
G. Bolas, *Paris in Japan: The Japanese Encounter with European Painting*, St. Louis, 1987, pp. 98-
99 and 128-137.

Christie's New York, 30 April 1996 (59**) US$ 684,500	US$	684,500

FUNI Achille (Ferrara 1890-1972 Appiano Gentile) Italian
SCENA DI SACRIFICIO charcoal and coloured pastels on paper, 200 x 160cm.

Finearte Milan, 18 June 1996 (262**) ITL 32,200,000	US$	20,882

ALLEGORIA: GIOVE E GIUNONE coloured pastels, chalk, chaorcoal on stretched paper, 170 x
151,5 cm. sdlr 'A. Fumni 1936'

Finearte Milan, 18 June 1996 (213**) ITL 17,250,000	US$	11,187

FURINI Francesco (Circle of) (1603-1646) Italian
SAINT AGATHA oil on canvas, 25 x 20 172in. (63.5 x 51.5cm.)

Christie's South Kensington, 7 December 1995 (22*) GBP 8,437	US$	12,984

FUSSMANN Klaus (Velbert/Rheinland 1938 b.) German
AKT VOR SPIEGEL oil on canvas, 126 x 141cm. sd '24.VI.1977 Fußmann Berlin'

Lempertz Cologne, 31 May 1996 (176*) DEM 22,000	US$	14,343

STILLEBEN oil on canvas', 100 x 116cm. sdur 'Fußmann Berlin 27.2.79' (1979)

Lempertz Cologne, 28 November 1995 (659**) DEM 20,000	US$	14,116

FYT Jan (Antwerp 1611-1661) Flemish
GREYHOUND WATCHING THE CAPTURED HARES oil on canvas, 172.5 x 130cm. s in the
collar of the dog ll 'Joannes Fyt'
PROV.: Private collection, Vienna.

Dorotheum Vienna, 6 March 1996 (97**) ATS 300,000	US$	28,857

GABRINI Pietro (1865-1926) Italian
THE INVENTOR'S LABORATORY oil on canvas, 38 1/8 x 28 ¾in. (96.9 x 73cm.) slr 'P. Gabrini'
     Christie's New York, 2 November 1995 (134**) US$ 16,100   US$ 16,100

GABRON Willem (or Guillaum) (Antwerp 1619-1678) Flemish
STILL-LIFE WITH A PEWTER FLAGON AND A GLASS ON A GREEN CLOTH-DRAPED
TABLE , 20½ x 27in. (52.1 x 68.6cm.) s middle left *Guil Gabron/fe*
     Sotheby's New York, 11 January 1996 (39**) US$ 54,625   US$ 54,625

STILL-LIFE WITH FRUIT, GOLD AND SILVER VESSELS AND A SQUIRREL, ALL ON A
TABLE COVERED BY TURKEY RUG oil on canvas, 61¼ x 47½in. (155.6 x 120.7cm.) slr 'Guil
Gabron/f' (ca. 1652)
PROV.: Sale: Sotheby Parke Berney Inc. New York, 20 November 1980, lot 82, illustrated, where
bought by the present owner.
     Sotheby's New York, 16 May 1996 (88**) US$ 85,000   US$ 85,000

GADDI Agnolo (1333-1396 Florence) Italian
A PORTABLE TRIPTYCH WITH THE MADONNA ENTHRONED, WITH ANGELS AND GOD
THE FATHER IN A ROUNDEL; ON THE WINGS SAINTS ANTHONY ABBOT, JOHN THE
BAPTIST, MARY MAGDALEN AND OTHER SAINTS, AND THE CRUCIFIXION, WITH THE
ANNUNCIATION ABOVE tempera on gold ground panel in an integral frame, overall (open) 28
7/8 x 23 ¾in. (73.4 x 60.3cm.)
PROV.: Howell Wills; Christie's, 17 Feb. 1894, lot 58, as Bernardo Daddi (14 gns. to H. Quilter);
Harry Quilter, 42 Queens Gata Gardens, London; Christie's, 7 April 1906, lot 89, as 'Andrea di
Niccolo' corrected to Paolo di Giovanni (22 gns. to Wagner); Henry Wagner, and by inheritance.
     Christie's London, 7 July 1995 (111**) GBP 122,500   US$ 195,406

GAEL Barent (Haarlem 1635 c.-1685 after Amsterdam) Dutch
CHEERFULL COMPANY IN FRONT OF A FARMHOUSE oil on canvas, 38.5 x 44cm. slr 'B.
Gael'
     Dorotheum Vienna, 6 March 1996 (86**) ATS 250,000   US$ 24,048

GAGNERAUX Bénigne (Dijon 1756-1795 Florence) French
L'ÉDUCATION D'ACHILLE oil on canvas, 96 x 125.5cm. sdll 'B. Gagneraux fecit 1785'
PROV.: Collection Cardinal de Bernis, 1785; Anon. Sale, Versailles, Palais des Congrès, 30 April
1972 (Maître Paul Martin), no. 117 (2,800 FF).
LIT.: *Memorie per le Belle Arti*, Rome, December 1785, pp. CXC-CXCI;
'per il Casaletti', *Giornale delle Belle Arti e della incisione, antiquario, musica e poesiaper l'anno..,*
Rome, II, 17 December 1785, p. 384; Probably G.K. Nagler, *Neues allgemeines Künstler lexikon..,*
Munich, 1837, V, p. 239; H. Baudot, *Eloge historique de Bénigne Gagneraux peintre d'histoire de
S.M. Ie Roi de Suede, Membre de l'Academie de 'Forti', à Rome, Membre et professeur des Beaux-
Arts à Florence*, Dijon, 1889, p. 40, no. 4; L. Vicchi, *Les Français pendant la Convention 1792-
1795, Rome, Paris, Londres, 1892, p. 146; C. Sutter, 'Gagneraux Benigne',* Allgemeines Lexikon der
bildenden Künstler von der Antike bis zur Gegenwart, Leipzig, 1920, Vol. XIII, pp. 66-68; S.
Laveissiere, *Dictionnaire des artistes et ouvriers d'art de Bourgogne*, Paris, 1980, t. I, pp. 223; B.
Sandstrom, *Bénigne Gagneraux, 1756-1795. Education, inspiration, ceuvre*, Stockolm, 1981, pp.
128-129; S. Laveissiere, *Bénigne Gagneraux (1756-1795) un peintre bourguignon dans la Rome
neo-classique*, Rome, Dijon, June-September 1983, pp. 104-105.
     Étude Tajan Paris, 25 June 1996 (58**) FRF 450,000   US$ 86,894

GAHO Hashimoto (1835-1908) Japanese
MT. HORAI Hanging scroll, ink and colour on silk, 143 x 70cm. s 'Gaho ga' sealed, mounted on
brocade in inscr. wood box by the artist
     Christie's New York, 31 October 1995 (453**) US$ 29,900   US$ 29,900

GAINSBOROUGH Thomas, R.A. (1727-1788) British
THREE HORSES AND A DROVER ON A COUNTRYROAD pencil, brown and grey wash
heightened with white and reddish-brown bodycolour, 18 x 16¼in. (45.8 x41.9cm.) s ini. 'TH' (ca
1763)
PROV.: Myron T. Herrick, US ambassador in Paris, 1912-14 and 1920-29; George Herrick Esq.;
Christie's, 20 November 1984, lot 83 (GBP 21,600).

Christie's London, 11 July 1995 (5**) GBP 27,600	US$	44,026

PORTRAIT OF MRS. MARY GAINSBOROUGH, THE ARTIST'S DAUGHTER, LATER MRS.
FISCHER oil on canvas, 25¼ x 19in. (64 x 48cm.)

Sotheby's London, 12 July 1995 (49**) GBP 21,850	US$	34,854

GAISSER Jakob Emanuel (1825-1899) German
GRACE oil on canvas, 37 x 46¼in. (94 x 117cm.) s 'J.E. Gaisser'

Christie's London, 17 November 1995 (29**) GBP 17,250	US$	26,983

GALIEN-LALOUE Eugène (1854-1941) French
POMMIERS ET FLEURS oil on canvas, 35¼ x 45½in. (89.6 x 115.6cm.) slr 'E Galien-Laloue'

Christie's New York, 14 February 1996 (60**) US$ 14,950	US$	14,950

PLACE DE LA CONCORDE gouache, 7 1/8 x 12in. (18cm. x 30.5cm.) sll E. 'Galien-Laloue'

Phillips London, 11 June 1996 (54**) GBP 7,000	US$	10,794

THE PLACE DU CHATELET UNDER SNOW, PARIS oil on canvas, 25¼ x 36¼in. (64 x 92cm.)
sll

Sotheby's London, 13 March 1996 (56**) GBP 54,300	US$	82,926

FIGURES ON A RIVERBANK oil on canvas, 13 x 18in. (33.1 x 45.8cm.) sll 'E. Galien-Laloue'

Christie's New York, 2 November 1995 (126**) US$ 17,250	US$	17,250

CHATELET gouache on paper laid down on board, 7½ x 12 ¾in. (19.1 x 32.4cm.) sll 'E. Galien-
Laloue'

Christie's New York, 2 November 1995 (180**) US$ 16,100	US$	16,100

QUAI VOLTAIRE watercolour and gouache over traces of pencil on paper, 10¼ x 13½in. (26 x
34.3cm.) sll 'E.Galien-Laloue'

Christie's East, 30 October 1995 (339**) US$ 16,100	US$	16,100

GALLÉ Hieronymus I (Antwerp 1625-1682 Brussels) Flemish?
SNOWBALLS, ANEMONES, PEONIES, POPPIES, CARNATIONS, A TULIP, MORNING LORY
AND OTHER FLOWERS IN A VASE ON A STONE LEDGE oil on canvas, 62.5 x 77.8cm.

Christie's Amsterdam, 7 May 1996 (25**) NLG 86,250	US$	50,292

FLOWERS IN A VASE POSED ON A MARBLE LEDGE oil on canvas, 41 x 32cm. (ca. 1650)

Christie's Monaco, 14 June 1996 (24**) FRF 58,500	US$	11,296

STILL-LIFE OF PEONIES, TULIPS, POPPIES, NARCISSI, STEPHANOSIS AND OTHER
FLOWERS IN AN URN POSITIONED ON A STONE LEDGE oil on canvas, 26 ¾ x 18¼in. (68 x
46cm.) sll 'Giero. Gallee f./Anno.1667'

Sotheby's London, 18 October 1995 (25**) GBP 16,100	US$	25,410

GANDARA Antonio de la (1862-1917) French
PORTRAIT OF A FAMILY WITH THEIR COLLIE oil on canvas, 79½ x 46in. (201.9 x 116.8cm.)
slr 'A de La Gandara'

Christie's New York, 2 November 1995 (21**) US$ 85,000	US$	85,000

GANDOLFI Gaetano (San Matteo della Decima 1734-1802 Bologna) Italian
AN ALLEGORY OF THE SACRAMENT OF BAPTISM oil on canvas, 12 x 9¼in. (30.5 x 23.5cm.)
(ca. 1800)
LIT.: Prisco Bagni, *I Gandolfi, Affreschi Dipinti Bozzetti Disegni*, 1992, p. 367, no. 345.
Sotheby's New York, 16 May 1996 (259**) US$ 17,250   US$ 17,250

A SHEET OF STUDIES OF HEADS WITH ELABORATE HAIR STYLES pen and brown ink, 29 x
20.3cm. s ini. 'G.G.' (1770's)
Sotheby's London, 3 July 1995 (130**) GBP 24,150   US$ 38,523

GANDOLFI Mauro (Bologna 1764-1834 Bologna) Italian
AN ALLEGORY OF PAINTING AND ARCHITECTURE pen and grey ink with wash heightened
with red chalk on vellum, (oval) 29.4 x 22.9cm. s 'M Gandolfi f.'
Phillips London, 5 July 1995 (165**) GBP 10,000   US$ 15,952

GAREMYN Jan Anton (Bruges 1712-1799) Flemish
FISHERMEN SELLING THEIR WARES OUTSIDE A HOUSE BY THE SEASHORE oil on
canvas, 97 x 135cm.
Sotheby's Amsterdam, 6 May 1996 (2**) NLG 20,060   US$ 11,697

GARF Salomon (1879-1943) Dutch
A SUNNY DAY AT THE BEACH oil on canvas, 29 x 39 cm s 'S. Garf'
Christie's Amsterdam, 7 February 1996 (382***) NLG 16,100   US$ 9,805

GARGIULO Domenico {called} Micco Spadaro (Naples 1612-1675 Naples) Italian
THE SACRIFICE OF NOAH oil on canvas, 41½ x 54 1/8in. (105.4 x 137.5cm.)
PROV.: Purchased by the present owner's father in Leipzig in the 1930's.
Christie's London, 19 April 1996 (187**) GBP 14,950   US$ 22,669

**GARGIULO Domenico {called} Micco Spadaro (with Artemisia Gentileschi (1593-ca. 1652)
and Viviano Codazzi (1604-1670)) (Naples 1612-1675 Naples) Italian**
SUSANNAH AND THE ELDERS oil on canvas, 104 x 82 ¾in. (265 x 210cm.)
PROV.: Probably Luigi Romeo, Barone di San Luigi, Naples, before 1642.
EXH.: Bernardo de Dominici, *Vite de'pittori, scultori, ed architetti napoletani*, vol. III, 1742, pp.
198-9; 'Notable Works of Art now on the Market', *Burlington Magazine*, vol. CV, June 1963,
supplement; E. Brunetti, L. Trezzani and L. Laureati, 'Viviano Cocazzi', in *I Pittori Bergamaschi dal
XIII al XIX secolo, Il Seicento*, I, 1983, p. 706, no. 161, under missing works; N. Spinosa, *La pittura
napoletana del '600*, 1984, reproduced plate 424 and colour plate VII; M.D. Garrard, *Artemisia
Centileschi*, 1989, pp. 121-2,516 n.212, as untraced; R. Contini, in the exhibition catalogue,
Artemisia, Florence, Casa Buonarotti, 1991, pp. 113, 179; D. Ryley Marshall, *Viviano and Niccolo
Codazzi and the Baroque Architectural Fantasy*, 1993, pp. 153-55, no. VC56.
Sotheby's London, 6 December 1995 (53**) GBP 194,000   US$ 298,553

GARNIER François (attr.) (1672) Flemish
FRUIT STILL-LIFE WITH CHERRIES, STRAWBERRIES, PEACHES ETC. oil on canvas, 45 x
66cm.
PROV.: Private Collection, Wien.
Dorotheum Vienna, 17 October 1995 (161**) ATS 250,000   US$ 25,076

GARNIER Michel (Saint Cloud 1793 c.-1819) French
JEUNE FEMME TERMINANT SA TOILETTE oil on canvas, 46.5 x 38cm. sdll 'M. Garnier / 1796'
Étude Tajan Paris, 12 December 1995 (100**) FRF 280,000   US$ 56,399

GAROUSTE Gérard (1946 b.)
UNTITLED oil on canvas, 78 ¾ x 70 ¾in. (200 x 180cm.) (1986-87)
PROV.: Bought directly from the artist in his studio by the current owner.

EXH.: Paris, Musée National d'Art Moderne, *Gérard Garouste*, 1988, illustrated in colour, p. 55.
Étude Tajan Paris, 13 December 1995 (81**) FRF 150,000 — US$ — 30,214

GARRIDO Eduardo Léon (Madrid 1856-1949 (1906?) Caen) Spanish
LA FARANDOLE oil on panel, 36¼ x 28¼in. (92.1 x 71.8cm.) sll 'E.L. Gariddo.'
Christie's New York, 22 May 1996 (238**) US$ 68,500 — US$ — 68,500

GARZI Luigi (1638-1721) Italian
REBECCA AT THE WELL oil on canvas, 29 x 39 ¾in. (73.7 x 101cm.)
Sotheby's New York, 11 January 1996 (181**) US$ 21,850 — US$ — 21,850

GASCARS Henri (1635 c.-1701) British?
PORTAIT OF BARBARA, COUNTESS OF CASTLEMAINE AND DUCHESS OF CLEVELAND
AND HER DAUGHTER LADY CHARLOTTE FITZROY, COUNTESS OF LICHFIELD oil on
canvas, 38 ¾ x 46 ¾in. (98.5 x 119cm.)
PROV.: Viscount Dillon, Ditchley.
Sotheby's London, 12 July 1995 (19**) GBP 7,475 — US$ — 11,924

GASSEL Lucas (1480-1570) Flemish
THE PARABLE OF THE GOOD AND THE BAD SHEPHERDS, WITH CHRIST BLESSING THE
PHARISEES, CHRIST AS THE GOOD SHEPHERD LEADING HIS FLOCK AND CHRIST
HEALING THE BLIND MAN IN AN EXTENSIVE RIVER LANDSCAPE oil on panel, 21½ x 32
7/8in. (54.6 x 83.5cm.)
PROV.: Sir Bruce Ingram, and by inheritance to the present owner.
Christie's London, 8 December 1995 (1**) GBP 47,700 — US$ — 73,407

THE MEETING OF ABRAHAM AND MELCHIZEDEK oil on panel, 77 x 106.5cm.
Sotheby's Amsterdam, 6 May 1996 (24**) NLG 112,100 — US$ — 65,364

GASSEL Lucas (circle of) (1480-1570) flemish
ST HIERONYMUS DOING PENITENCE oil on panel, 34 x 46.3cm. inscr. on the reverse 'no.
464/Jean/Van Eyck'
Christie's Monaco, 14 June 1996 (3**) FRF 11,660 — US$ — 22,141

GATTA Xavier della (1777-1811) Italian
THE BAY OF NAPLES FROM MERGELLINA bodycolour, watermark Strasbourg lily, 335 x
550mm. sd 'Xav. Gatta. P./1785'
Christie's South Kensington, 19 April 1996 (146***) GBP 19,550 — US$ — 29,644

GAUERMANN Friedrich (1807-1862) Austrian
RÜCKKEHR VON DER JAGD oil on panel, 17½ x 14in. (44.5 x 35.5cm.) s 'F.Gauermann'
PROV.: Julius Resch; sale, Dorotheum, Vienna, 17-19 Oct. 1923, lot 110; Anon. sale, C.J. Wawra,
29 Feb. 1928, lot. 134.
Christie's London, 11 October 1995 (55**) GBP 12,650 — US$ — 19,965

GAUGUIN Paul (1848-1903) French
NATURE MORTE oil on canvas, 12 3/8 x 15 5/8in. (31.4 x 39.7cm.) dedicated ul 'Ripipont à Marie
Souvenir'; dur 'Pouldu 89'
PROV.: Marie Henry, Pont Aven; Arthur B. Davies, New York; Chester Dale, New York; sale,
Parke-Bernet Galleries, Inc., New York, March 6, 1944, lot 71; William Schab Gallery, New York
(acquired at the above sale); Dr. Albert W. Blum, Short Hills, New Jersey; Margaret and Sydney
Lowy.
EXH.: New York, Feragil Gallery, 1926, no. 19; New York, Wildenstein & Co., Inc., *Modern French
Artfrom the Chester Dale Collection*, 1928, no. 13; New York, Wildenstein & Co., inc., *Still Life
from Chardin to the Abstract*, 1930, no 9; San Francisco, Museum of Modern Art, Gauguin, 1936,
no. 9; Toledo, Museum of Art, *Cézanne-Gauguin*, 1936, no. 9 .

LIT.: C. Chasse, *Gauguin et le group de Pont-Aven*, Paris 1921, p. 39; J. Rewald, *Post-Impressionism, From Van Gogh to Gauguin*, New York 1956, p. 298 (illustrated); G. Wildenstein, *Gauguin*, Paris 1964, no. 376 (illustrated p. 143).

Christie's New York, 1 May 1996 (117**) US$ 398,500	US$	398,500

PAYSAGE D'AUTOMNE oil on canvas, 25½ x 39 5/8in. (64.8 x 100.5cm.) sdll 'P. Gauguin 1877'
PROV.: Mette-Sophie Gauguin, Copenhagen (wife of the artist); Mme Benny Dessau, Copenhagen; A. M. Einar Dessau, Copenhagen.
EXH.: Copenhagen, Ny Carlsberg Glyptotek, *Paul Gauguin*, June, 1948, no. 1; Edinburgh, Royal Scottish Academy, *Gauguin*, 1955, no. 1. The exhibition traveled to London, The Tate Gallery, Sept.-Oct., 1955; Paris, Galerie Charpentier,*Cent oeuvres de Gauguin*, 1960, no. 5 (illustrated); Munich, Haus der Kunst, *Gauguin*, April-May, 1960, no. 8 (illustrated).
LIT.: G. Wildenstein, *Gauguin*, Paris, 1964, vol. I, no. 1 (illustrated, p. 2; dated 1871); M. Bodelson, 'The Wildenstein-Cogniat Gauguin Catalogue,' *Burlington Magazine*, vol. CVIII, no. 754, Jan., 1966, p. 34 (dated 1877); G. M. Sugana, *L'Opera completa di Gauguin*, Milan, 1972, no. 1 (illustrated, p. 87; dated 1871).

Christie's New York, 8 November 1995 (109**) US$ 354,500	US$	354,500

GAULLI Giovanni Battista, {called} Baciccio (Genoa 1639-1709 Rome) Italian
THE VIRGIN IN GLORY BLESSING A CROWD OF PENITENTS pen and brown ink and wash heightened with white over traces of black chalk, 22.8 x 16.7cm.
PROV.: Benjamin West (L.419).

Sotheby's London, 3 July 1995 (134**) GBP 5,520	US$	8,805

GEERARDS Jaspar (ca 1620-ca 1654) dutch
A BOWL OF PEACHES AND GRAPES, A ROEMER, LEMONS AND A PEELED LEMON ON A PEWTER PLATE ON A DRAPED TABLE oil on panel, 29 1/8 x 22 ¾in. (74 x 57.8cm.) sd 'Jasper .geerardi./ fecit 1648'
PROV.: Baron Gudin; sale, Frankfurt, 10 Dec. 1913, lot 8; Anon. Sale, Cologne, 10 May 1916, lot 49.
LIT.: F.G. Meijer, A Fragment of a Pronkstilleven by Jasper Geerards in the Bredius Museum, Mercury, no. 4,1986, p. 44, fig.6.

Christie's London, 8 December 1995 (219**) GBP 36,700	US$	56,479

GEETS Willem (Mechelen 1838-1919 Mechelen) Belgian
SHOWING THE JEWELS oil on canvas, 44 x 68in. (112 x 172cm.) sdlr 'W. Geets 30 Xbre 7' (1907)

Sotheby's London, 17 April 1996 (749**) GBP 12650	US$	19,181

GEIGER Rupprecht (Munich 1908 b.) German
UNTITLED gouache, 69 x 86.5cm. sd on the reverse (1962)

Hauswedell & Nolte Cologne, 2 December 1995 (91**) DEM 15,000	US$	10,407

GELDORP Gortzius (attr.) (Louvain 1553-1619 c. Cologne) Flemish
PORTRAIT OF A GENTLEMAN, HALF-LENGHT oil on panel, 66 x 49.5cm.

Christie's Rome, 21 November 1995 (165A**) ITL 10,000,000	US$	6,277

GELIBERT Jules-Bertrand (1834-1916) Belgian
A PACK OF GUNDOGS ATTACKING A RED DEER oil on canvas, 44 x 60cm. sd 'Jules Gelibert 1880'

Christie's Amsterdam, 25 April 1996 (162*) NLG 51,750	US$	30,750

GELLÉE Claude {called} Claude Lorrain (1600-1682) French
THE COASTLINE OF SANTA MARINELLA (RECTO) A CHALK SKETCH OF A HARBOUR, POSSIBLY CIVITAVECCHIA pen and brown ink and brown, grey and red washes, with touches of white heightening in the sky, 21.8 x 32.3cm. bears inscription on the old mount: 'C.L. Tasa 2 Rs.' (ca. 1638)

EXH.: London, Thomas Agnew & Sons, *Master Drawings and Prints*, 1975, cat. 10 (illustrated).
LIT.: Marcel Roethlisberger, 'Dessins Inédits de Claude Lorrain', *L'Oeil*, no. 226, May 1974, p. 34, no. 6 (illustrated).

Sotheby's London, 3 July 1995 (138**) GBP 52,100	US$	83,107

A WOODED LANDSCAPE WITH PEASANTS FORDING A STREAM oil on canvas, 28 x 37½in. (71 x 95.2cm.) (1635-37)
PROV.: Anon. sale (The Property of an Institution), Christie's, 13 July 1979, lot 142, as Herman van Swanevelt.
EXH.: Munich, Haus der Kunst, *Im Licht von Claude Lorrain*, 12 March-29 May 1983, pp. 65-6, no. 2, illustrated in colour (catalogue by M. Roethlisberger); Kobe, Prefectural Museum of Modern Art, 2-27 Nov. 1983; Nagoya, Prefectural Museum of Modern Art, 2-25 Dec. 1983; Tokyo, Seibu Museum of Arts, 5-29Jan. 1984; Hiroshima, Prefectural Museum, Feb. 1984; Kitakiushu, Prefectural Museum, 2-25 March 1984, *The Rediscovery of Nature: An Anthology of Nineteenth-Century Landscape Painting in the West*, no. T1.
LIT.: M. Roethlisberger, *Around a Landscape by Claude Lorrain*, The Register of the Spencer Museum of Art, V, no. 10, Spring 1982, pp. 18 and 27, note 14, fig. 10; G. Jansen in the catalogue of the exhibition, *Franse schilderkunst uit Nederlands bezit1600-1800*, Musée des Beaux-Arts, Dijon, Institut Néerlandais, Paris, and Museum Boymans-van Beuningen, Rotterdam, 1992-3, pp. 147-8.

Christie's London, 7 July 1995 (72**) GBP 102,700	US$	163,822

GELLER Johann Nepomuk (Vienna 1860-1954 Weißenkirchen) Austrian
MARKTPLATZ oil on board, 29 x 40cm. sll 'Joh. Nep. Geller'

Dorotheum Vienna, 6 November 1995 (88**) ATS 120,000	US$	12,038

GESCHIRRMARKT IN KREMS oil on canvas laid down on board, 40 x 57cm. sll 'Joh. Nep. Geller'

Dorotheum Vienna, 6 November 1995 (128**) ATS 180,000	US$	18,057

SONNTAG IM PRATER oil on canvas, 57.5 x 88.3cm. sll 'Joh Nep Geller' (ca. 1908)
LIT.: Exhibition catalogue, Kunsthandel Giese & Schweiger, Vienna 1981, cat. no. 10 (illustrated).

Wiener Kunst Auktionen, 26 March 1996 (98**) ATS 220,000	US$	21,162

GENNARI Benedetto the Younger (1633-1715) Italian
PORTRAIT OF HORTENSE MANCINI, DUCHESS OF MAZARIN (1646-1699), AS DIANA oil on canvas, 90 x 70in. (228.5 x 178cm.)
PROV.: Commisioned by the sitter.
LIT.: Prisco Bagni, *Benedetto Gennari e la Bottega del Guernico*, 1986, p. 156, no. 91 (listed amongst the pictures executed in London between 1674-1688).

Sotheby's London, 12 July 1995 (23**) GBP 172,000	US$	274,366

GENPAUL Eugène Paul, {called} (1895-1975) French
LE MANEGE oil on canvas, 60 x 73.5cm. slr 'GenPaul'

Étude Tajan Paris, 1 February 1996 (136**) FRF 55,000	US$	11,255

GABY LE JONGLEUR oil on canvas, 101 x 65.5cm. sdlr 'GenPaul' sd titled on the reverse (1942)

Étude Tajan Paris, 1 February 1996 (138**) FRF 38,000	US$	7,776

GENTILESCHI Artemisia (with Viviano Codazzi (1604-1670) and Domenico Gargiulo (1612-1675)) (Rome 1593-1652/53) Italian
SUSANNAH AND THE ELDERS oil on canvas, 104 x 82 ¾in. (265 x 210cm.)
PROV.: Probably Luigi Romeo, Barone di San Luigi, Naples, before 1642.
EXH.: Bernardo de Dominici, *Vite de'pittori, scultori, ed architetti napoletani*, vol. III, 1742, pp. 198-9; 'Notable Works of Art now on the Market', *Burlington Magazine*, vol. CV, June 1963, supplement; E. Brunetti, L. Trezzani and L. Laureati, 'Viviano Cocazzi', in *I Pittori Bergamaschi dal XIII al XIX secolo, Il Seicento*, I, 1983, p. 706, no. 161, under missing works; N. Spinosa, *La pittura napoletana del '600*, 1984, reproduced plate 424 and colour plate VII; M.D. Garrard, *Artemisia*

Centileschi, 1989, pp. 121-2,516 n.212, as untraced; R. Contini, in the exhibition catalogue, *Artemisia*, Florence, Casa Buonarotti, 1991, pp. 113, 179; D. Ryley Marshall, *Viviano and Niccolo Codazzi and the Baroque Architectural Fantasy*, 1993, pp. 153-55, no. VC56.

      Sotheby's London, 6 December 1995 (53**) GBP 194,000   US$ 298,553

GENTILESCHI Orazio (1562/63-1639/47) Italian
JUDITH AND HER MAIDSERVANT WITH THE HEAD OF HOLOFERNES oil on canvas, 51½ x 39 ¾in. (131 x 101cm.) sd with inscription 'B Capranica IN 68'; with inscription on the 18th Century relining canvas 'Hora.Gentileschi A 1612.Pizzo / GM R ' (now covered by a recent relining canvas but illustrated by Pepp, see under literature below)
PROV.: (Possibly) Natale Rondanini (1540-1627), Rome; Felice Zacchia Rondanini (active 1662-1710), Rome; and by descent to Giuseppe, Marchese Rondanini (1725-1801; his initials 'G M R ' on the relining canvas, see above), Rome; by whom bequeathed to Don Bartolomeo Capranica, by 1806 until 1841 when the palace (and presumably its contents) was sold; with Colnaghi, New York (Ralian, Dutch and Flemish Baroque Paintings, 4 April - 5 May 1984, no. 11).
EXH.: Rome, *Cloister of San Salvatore in Lauro*, 10-13 Dec. 1694 (as 'Ginditta del Gentileschi'); Rome, *Cloister of San Salvatore in Lauro*, 10-13 Dec. 1710 (as 'Giaditta con la testa d'Oloferne del Gentileschi'); Florence, Casa Buonarroti, *Artemisia*, 18 June - 4 Nov. 1991, no. 2, as Orazio Gentileschi (entry by Gianni Papi).
LIT.: Inventory of the collection of Felice Rondanini, 1662, as 'UnaJuditta che ho [sic] tagliata la testa ad Holoferne, tela da Imperatore [= 6 palmi = 132cm.] dices) di mano di Orazio Gentileschi con cornice dorata nelle stanze del Cardinale' (see L. Salerno, Palazzo Rondanini, 1966, pp. 279 and 284); G. Ghezzi, Quadri delle Case de'Prencipe in Roma, Ms., Palazzo Braschi, Rome, 1700, fols. 40 and 159 (where the two San Salvatore in Lauro exhibitions are cited); R. Ward Bissell, Orazio Gentileschi and the Poetic Tradition in Caravaggesque Painting, University Park (Pennsylvania) and London, 1981, pp. 154, under no. 26, 156, under no. 27, and 218, no. L-31, as lost; S. Pepper, Baroque painting at Colnaghi's (Exhibition Review), *The Burlington Magazine*, CXXVI, no. 974, May 1984, p. 3 and p. 314, figs. 39 and 40 (detail of the inscription on the verve of the canvas); Catalogue of the exhibition, Around 1610: *The Onset of the Baroque*, Matthiesen Fine Art Ltd., London, 14 June - 16 Aug.1985, p. 48; M. Garrard, *Artemisia Gentileschi*, Princeton, 1989, p. 498, note 56 (as probably not by Orazio Gentileschi).

      Christie's London, 8 December 1995 (97**) GBP 58,700   US$ 90,335

THE FINDING OF MOSES oil on canvas, 101¼ x 118½in. (257 x 301cm.)
PROV.: Possibly commissioned by Charles I; In the Royal Collection by 1649, when it was recorded at Greenwich; Acquired on 23 October 1651 by Lord Latham and his Fourth Dividend of the King's creditors; Probably sent to Spain by Don Luis de Haro; Philip IV of Spain; Probably Spanish Royal Collection: possibly given to Philippe I d'Orléans by Charles II of Spain; Orléans Collection by 1701, as Diego Velázquez; Acquired collectively by the Earl of Carlisle, the Earl of Bridgewater and the Earl of Gower after the first Orléans sale, 1792; Reserved by the Earl of Carlisle for Castle Howard before the Orléans sale, London, 1798; Thence by descent at Castle Howard.
EXH.: London, Royal Academy of Arts, *Seventeenth Century Art in Europe*, 1938, no. 285; Rome, Villa Medici, Roma 1630, Il Trionfo del Penello, 1994-5, pp. 204-211.
LIT.: L. F. Du Bois de Saint-Gelais, *Description des tableaux du Palais Royal*, 1727, pp. 116-1; G. Vertue, 'Notebooks 1713 - 1756', in the *Walpole Society*, vol. IV, 1935-36, p.131; J. Couché, *Galerie du Palais Royal*, vol. II, 1808, plate 86; W. Buchanan, *Memoirs of Painting with a Chronological History of the Importation of Pictures by the Great Masters into England since the French Revolution*, 1824, vol. I, pp. 11-12, 14, 17-19, 146; Dr. Waagen, *Treasures of Art in Great Bratain*, 1854, vol. Il, p. 319, as by Gerard van Honthorst; C .Justi, *Diego Velázquez and His Times*, 1889, pp. 380-81; C. Stryienski, *La galerie du Régent, duc d'Orléans*, 1913, no. 330, pp. 9-11, 176; G.H. Chettle,The Queen's House, Greenwich, 1937, p. 104 (the bill of 16334 for the frame); G. Howard, *Castle Howard*, 1958; C. Sterling, 'Gentileschi in France', in the *Burlington Magazine*, 1958, no. 37, p. 118; O. Millar in A. Van der Doort, 'Catalogue of the Collections of Charles I', *Walpole Society*, vol. XXXVII, 1958-60, pp. XVI ff.; W.L.F. Nuttall, 'King Charles I's Pictures and the Commonwealth Sale', *Apollo*, vol. LXXXII, 1965, pp. 302, 304, 308; A.E. Pérez Sanchéz, *Pintura italiana del siglo XVII en España*, 1965, p. 502; E. Harris, 'Orazio Gentileschi's Finding of Moses in

Madrid', in the *Burlington Magazine*, vol. CIX, 1967, pp. 86-7,&no.5,p.89; A.E. Pérez Sanchéz, Cason del Buen Retiro, 1970, p. 282; O. Millar (ed.), 'Pictures, Statues Plate and Effects of King Charles I: 'The Inventories and Valuations of the King's Goods 1649-1651', in *The Walpole Society*, vol XLII, 1970-72, no. 1, p. 137; R. Ward-Bissell, *Orazio Gentileschi and the Poetic Tradition in Caravaggesque Painting*, 1981, no. 66, pp. 52, 56, 58, 60, 189, 191-192, fig. 124.; O. Bonfait, in the catalogue of the exhibition, Roma 1630, 1994, pp.204-11.

Sotheby's London, 6 December 1995 (61A**) GBP 5,061,500	US$	7,789,320

GENTILINI Franco (Faenza 1909-1981 Rome) Italian
CHIOGGIA oil on canvas, 48 x 60cm. sdur 'Gentilini 1943'

Finearte Milan, 12 December 1995 (272**) ITL 31,050,000	US$	19,479

CATTEDRALE tempera on cardboard paper, 71 x 55cm. sdul 'Gentilini 56'
PROV.: Galleria La Barcaccia, Roma, no. 979.

Finearte Milan, 12 December 1995 (296**) ITL 20,700,000	US$	12,986

BETSABEA oil on canvas, 40 x 40cm. slr 'Gentilini' (1967)
PROV.: Galleria del Naviglio, Milan, no. 3148.

Finearte Milan, 12 December 1995 (304**) ITL 42,550,000	US$	26,694

MODELLE NELLO STUDIO oil on canvas, 140 x 100cm sd 'Gentilini 1937'
EXH.: Pittsburgh, Carnegie Institute, *Personal*, 1937; Firenze, *Arte Moderna in Italia, 1915-1935*, Palazzo Strozzi, November 1966-Februari 19676, cat.no.1865, pag.262.

Finearte Rome, 14 November 1995 (215**) ITL 115,000,000	US$	72,191

CATHEDRAL OF SAN ZENO oil on canvas, 95.5 x 130cm. sdlr 'Gentilini 59' (1959)

Finearte Milan, 26 October 1995 (183**) ITL 124,200,000	US$	77,383

GEOFFROY Henry Jules Jean (1853-1924) French
LUNCHTIME oil on canvas, 19 5.8 x 14½in. (50 x 37cm.) sdlr (1884)

Phillips London, 14 November 1995 (62**) GBP 6,500	US$	10,167

LE PETIT COMMISSAIRE INFIDELE oil on canvas, 22 x 15¼in. (55.8 x 38.7cm.) s 'Geo' s inscr. 'le petit commissaire infidèle/ par Jean Geoffroy'

Christie's London, 17 November 1995 (51**) GBP 18,400	US$	28,781

GÉRARD Marguerite (1761-1837) French
A GENTLEMAN CONSOLING A LADY AFTER READING A LETTER oil on panel, 10 1/8 x 7 7/8in. (25.7 x 20cm.)

Christie's South Kensington, 18 april 1996 (224*) GBP 6,670	US$	10,114

GERICAULT Jean Louis André Théodore (Rouen 1791-1824) French
TWO HORSES AND A SLEEPING GROOM black lead, pen and brown ink, brown and gray wash on paper, 11¾ x 15¼in. (30 x 38.8cm.)
PROV.: A.M. Legetil-Marcotte.
LIT.: C. Clément, *Géricault*, Paris 1879, no. 147.

Christie's New York, 22 May 1996 (26**) US$ 145,500	US$	145,500

GERINI Nicolo di Pietro (1368 - 1415 active Florence) Italian
CROWNED SAINT (ST. SIGISMOND?) oil on panel, on gold ground, 41 x 26.5cm. (ca. 1390)
PROV.: Anon. Sale, Paris, Palais d'Orsay, 15 June 1978, ascribed to Niccolo di Pietro Gerini.

Étude Tajan Paris, 25 June 1996 (1**) FRF 180,000	US$	34,758

GÉROME Jean Léon (1824-1904) French
POLYPHEMUS oil on canvas, 24 x 39 3/8in. (61 x 100cm.) sll 'J.L. GEROME'
PROV.: Aimé Morot, the artist's son-in-law; Anon. sale, Hôtel Drouot, Paris, 25 Nov. 1974, no. 21.

LIT.: *L'Art en marge des grands Mouvements: Salon orientalisted de 1850 á 1930*, no. 15 (illustrated); *Jean-Léon Gérôme: 1824-1804* (exh. cat.), Musée Garret, Vesoul 1981, p. 91 (illustrated); G.A. Ackerman, *The Life and Work of Jean Léon Gérôme*, London 1986, no. 471 (illustrated).

Christie's New York, 14 February 1996 (12**) US$ 57,500	US$	57,500

GÉROME AND TANAGRA oil on canvas, 6 7/8 x 6 7/8in. (17.6 x 17.6cm.) sul 'J.L. GEROME.'

Christie's New York, 14 February 1996 (13**) US$ 90,500	US$	90,500

LES PIGEONS oil on canvas, 23 5/8 x 31 7/8in. (60 x 81cm.) sll 'J.L. GEROME'
PROV.: The Duke of Choiseuil, France; With Knoedler's, New York; With H. Schickman Gallery, New York; Private Collection, Florida; The Sordini Family Collection, Wilkes-Barre, Pennsylvania; Mr. and Mrs. Joseph Tanenbaum, Toronto; With Joan Michaelmann Ltd., New York; Private Collection, England; With Galerie d'Orsay, Paris.
EXH.: New York, Schickman Gallery, *The Neglected 19th Century*, 1970.
LIT.: R. Ettinghausen, *Jean-Léon Gérôme (1824-1904)*, (exh. cat.), 1972, p. 24, no. 14; L. Thornton, *Women as portrayed in Orientalist Painting*, Paris, 1985, p. 61; G. Ackerman, *Jean-Léon Gérôme*, 1986, London, p. 171, cat. no. 486.

Christie's New York, 14 February 1996 (24**) US$ 552,500	US$	552,500

LA MOSQUÉE BLEUE oil on canvas, 28½ x 41in. (72.4 x 104.1cm.) slr 'J.L. GEROME'
PROV.: Boussod Valadon, Paris 1878; with Knoedler's, New York 1879; Well; sale: American Art Association, New York, 12-13 Nov. 1936, no. 47; Eli Whitney Debevoise; With Galerie d'Orsay, Paris.
LIT.: G.M. Ackerman, *The Life and Work of Jean-Léon Gérôme*, London 1986, pp. 242-43, no. 268 (illustrated).

Christie's New York, 14 February 1996 (30**) US$ 662,500	US$	662,500

LE RETOUR DE LA CHASSE oil on canvas, 29 x 23½ in. (73.7 x 59.7cm.) slc 'J.L. GEROME'
PROV.: Private Collection, New York; With Kurt E. Schon, Ltd., New Orleans Private Collection Houston; Coral Petroleum; sale, Sotheby`s, New York, May 23, 1985, lot 23 (bt. $280,000); With Galérie d`Orsay, Paris.
EXH.: Paris, *Exposition Universelle*, 1878, no. 365; Washington, D. C., The National Gallery, *The Orientalists: Delacroix to Matisse*, 1984, p. 75, exh. cat. no. 35 (illustrated).
LIT.: E. Strahan (E. Shinn), *Gérome, A Collection of the Works of J. L. Gérome in One Hundred Photogravures*, New York 1881-83, vol. II, pl. LXVII (illustrated); F. F. Herring, *Gerome, His Life and Works*, New York, 1892, pl. 193 (illustrated); Paris Photographs:*Gérome Oeuvres*, Paris, Bibliothèque, Cabinet des Estampes, *28 volumes of mounted photographs of Gérome's paintings and sculptures, the gift of his widow*, vol. XIV
M. A. Stevens, *The Orientalists: Delacroix to Matisse (European Painters in North Africa and the Near East)*, London, 1984, pp. 144-145.

Christie's New York, 14 February 1996 (35**) US$ 442,500	US$	442,500

FEMME DE CONSTANTINOPLE, DÉBOUT oil on canvas, 16 x 12¾in. (40.5 x 32.5cm.) sur 'J.L. GEROME' (ca. 1876)
PROV.: Mr. and Mrs. Joseph M. Tanenbaum, Toronto; With Galerie d'Orsay, Paris.
EXH.: New York, Shickman Gallery, *The Neglected Nineteenth Century*, 1971, no. 2.
LIT.: L. Thornton, *Women as Portrayed in Orientalist Painting*, Paris, 1985, p. ,200 (illustrated) G. Ackermann, *The Life and Work of Jean-Léon Gerome*, London, 1986, pp. 240-1, no. 256 (illustrated); F. F. Herring, *Gerome: His Life and Works*, New York, 1892, p.242.

Christie's New York, 14 February 1996 (39**) US$ 200,500	US$	200,500

SKETCH FOR 'WHOEVER YOU ARE HERE IS YOUR MASTER' (LOVE THE CONQUEROR) oil on canvas, 8 7/8 x 12¼in. (22.5 x 31cm.)
PROV.: The family of the artist; Thence by descent to the present owner.

Christie's New York, 14 February 1996 (51**) US$ 35,650	US$	35,650

PRAYER AT THE SULTAN'S TOMB (LE TOMBEAU DE KALIFES A BROUSSE) oil on canvas, 23 5/8 x 33¼in. (59.6 x 84.5cm.) sll 'J.L.GEROME'
PROV.: Eugene Glenzer, New York Tomkins; sale, American Art Association, New York, May 5, 1915, ($379 to L. C. Hooker); Helen Cranford Thibaut and Margaret Cranford (Alumnae of the Packer Collegiate Institute, 1908 and 1909, respectively, who donated this painting to the school in 1958).
LIT.: Probably Paris Catalogue, 1883, p. 59; G. M. Ackerman, *The Life and Works of Jean Léon Gerome*, New York, 1986, p. 242, no. 266 (illustrated).
    Christie's New York, 22 May 1996 (113**) US$ 121,300   US$ 121,300

LA DANSE PYRHIQUE oil on canvas, 25 5/8 x 32in. 965 x 81.2cm.) s 'J.L. Gérôme (1885)
PROV.: Budge Collection, Hamburg; Hans w. Lang, Berlin, 6-7 Dec. 1937, lot 54 (illustrated no. 13) where purchased by the parents of the present owner.
LIT.: Paris Photographs: *Gérôme, Oeuvres,* Cabinet des estampes, Bibliothèque Nationale, Paris, vol. XVI, p. 9; F.F. Hering *The Life and Works f J.L. Gérôme*, New York, 1986, p. 256, no. 335 (illustrated) as location unknown.
    Christie's London, 14 June 1996 (78***) GBP 804,500   US$ 1,240,555

WHOEVER YOU ARE HERE IS YOUR MASTER (LOVE, THE CONQUEROR) oil on canvas, 39 ¼ x 63in. (99.7 x 160cm.) s. 'J.L. GEROME.'
PROV.: The Harding Museum, Chicago.
EXH.: Paris, *Salon*, 1889, no. 1152.
LIT.: F.F. Hering, *The Life and Works of J.L. Gérôme*, New York, 1982, p. 272; G.M. Ackerman, *The Life and Works of Jean Léon Gérôme*, New York, 1986, pp. 130, 262-263, no. 361 (illustrated in colour and black and white); J.P. Brown, 'The Return of the Salon: Jean-Léon Gérôme in the Art Institute', *The Art Institute of Chicago: Museum Studies*, vol. 15, no. 2, 1989, pp. 165-168 (illustrated).
    Christie's New York, 2 November 1995 (33***) US$ 662,500   US$ 662,500

GEROME FERRIS Jean L éon (1863-1930) American
THE ALHAMBRA oil on canvas, 35 1/8 x 19½in. (89.3 x 49.6cm.) sdll 'GFerris '87'
    Christie's New York, 14January 1996 (29**) US$ 32,200   US$ 32,200

GERTLER Mark (1891-1939) British
BATHERS AT GARSINGTON oil on canvas, 23 ¾ x 26 ¾in. (60.3 x 68cm.) sd 'M. Gertler Sept. 1919'
PROV.: Siegfried Sassoon, Warminster.
LIT.: N. Carrington, Mark Gertler Selected Letters, London, 1965, pp. 176-77.
    Christie's London, 20 June 1996 (79**) GBP 28,750   US$ 44,333

STILL LIFE WITH FRUIT oil on canvas, 11 x 15in. (28 x 38cm.) sdlr 'Mark Gertler 1917'
PROV.: Edgar Astaire; Campbell & Franks Fine Arts, London, where purchased by the present owner.
    Christie's London, 21 March 1996 (21**) GBP 4,600   US$ 7,025

THE JAPANESE VIOLIN oil on canvas, 31 x32in. (78.2 x 81.3cm.) sdul 'Mark Gertler 1926'
    Christie's London, 21 November 1995 (232***) GBP 60,900   US$ 95,260

BLACK AND WHITE COTTAGE oil on canvas, 20¼ x14in. (51.5 x 35.5cm.) sdll 'Mark Gertler 1914'
PROV.: The Mayor Gallery, London; Leicester Galleries, London; Lady Hamilton, by whom given to Violet Asquith (1887-1969) on her mariage to Sir Maurice Bonham Carter in December 1915.
EXH.: London, N.E.A.C., *Winter Exhibition*, Nov. 1914, no ; London, Whitechapel Art Gallery, *Mark Gertler Memorial Exhibition*, June-July 1949, no.21; Colchester, The Minories, *Mark Gertler*, 1971, no.12: this exhibition travelled to London, Morley College; Oxford, Ashmolean Museum; and Sheffield, Graves Art Gallery.

LIT.: N. Carrington (ed.) *Selected Letters*, London, 1965, pp.73, 107, pl.5; J. Woodeson, *Mark Gertler*, London, 1972, pp.5, 169, 204, 342, 364, pl.24; J. Lomax (foreword), *Mark Gertler Paintings and Drawings, Camden Arts Centre Exhibition Catalogue*, London, 1992, p.79,. pl.73.

Christie's London, 21 November 1995 (233**) GBP 38,900	US$	60,848

GESTEL Leo (Leendert) (Woerden 1881-1941 Hilversum) Dutch
KOEDIJK watercolour on paper, 67 x 103cm. sdlr 'Leo gestel 19'

Christie's Amsterdam, 5 June 1996 (251*) NLG 8625	US$	5,039

COWS IN THE BEEMSTER watercolour on paper, 54 x 71cm. sdlr 'Leo Gestel beemster '22'

Christie's Amsterdam, 5 June 1996 (253*) NLG 13,800	US$	8,063

BOATS IN THE AMSTEL oil on panel, 18.5 x 24cm. sdll 'Leo Gestel 08'

Christie's Amsterdam, 5 June 1996 (264**) NLG 21850	US$	12,767

A FARM BEHIND TREES BEEMSTER oil on canvas, 35 x 49cm. sll 'Leo Gestel' and s again and d 20 on the reverse
PROV.: W.F. Selderbeek, Amsterdam.
EXH.: Amsterdam, Vondelkerk, *Bergense School*, 1992; Laren, Singer Museum, *Leo Gestel*, 28 November 1993-30 january 1994, no. 99.

Christie's Amsterdam, 5 June 1996 (271*) NLG 14,950	US$	8,735

A FARM AMONG TREES oil in canvas, 65 x 50cm. sdlr 'Leo Gestel 1922'

Christie's Amsterdam, 6 December 1995 (172*) NLG 21,850	US$	13,539

The dead Christ supported by het Virgin, Saint John the Evangelist and Joseph of Arimathea

GHIRLANDAIO Davide (Florence 1452-1525) Italian
THE DEAD CHRIST SUPPORTED BY THE VIRGIN, SAINT JOHN THE EVANGELIST AND JOSEPH OF ARIMATHEA tempera on panel, 33½ x 27 ¾in. (85 x 70.5cm.)
PROV.: Rev. Robert I. Nevin (rector of the American church in Rome); His sale, Galleria Sangiorgi, Rome, 26 April 1907, lot 418 as scuola del Ghirlandaio; Marcel von Nemes, Budapest; His sale, Paris, Galerie Manzi,Joyant, 17June 1913, lot 8, as by Mainardi; Kaunas, Lithuania, Museum of Religious Art, by 1938 (note on photograph at the Villa I Tatti, Florence).
EXH.: Düsseldorf, Stadt. Kunsthalle, *Sammlung des Rates Marczell von Nemes ...*, 1912, no. 4 as by Mainardi.
LIT.: G. von Térey, *Katalog der Gemälde aus der Sammlung des Kgl. Rates Marczell von Nemes*, Budapest, exhibition catalogue, Düsseldorf, 1912, no. 4, reproduced; G. Biermann, 'Die Sammlung Marczell de Nemes', in *Der Cicerone*, vol. V, 1913, p. 374; G. de Francovich, 'Sebastiano Mainardi' in *Cronache d'arte*, vol. IV, 1927, p. 269; R. van Marle, *The Development of the Italian Schools of Painting*, 1931, vol. XIII, pp. 142-3; G. de Francovich, 'Davide Ghirlandaio II', in *Dedalo*, XI, 1930, p. 146; B. Berenson, *Italian Pictures of the Renaissance, Florentine School*, 1963, vol. I, p. 127 as by Mainardi.

Sotheby's London, 5 July 1995 (68**) GBP 89,500	US$	142,766

GHISOLFI Giovanni (1623-1683) Italian
LANDSCAPE WITH RUINS AND FIGURES oil on canvas, 172 x 128cm.

Bukowskis Stockholm, 29 November-1 December 1995 (225**) SEK 200,000	US$	30,256

GIACOMETTI Alberto (Stampa 1901-1966 Coira) Swiss
PAYSAGE A MALOJA oil on canvas, 18 x 21 5/8in. (45.7 x 55cm.) sdlr 'Alberto Giacometti 1953'

PROV.: Galerie Maeght, Paris; Galerie Beyeler, Basel (acquired from the above in 1956); World House Galleries, New York (acquired from the above in 1959); Acquired from the above by Mr. Joseph H. Hazen on Nov. 26, 1960.
EXH.: New York, World House Galleries, *Giacometti*, Jan.-Feb. 1960, no. 19 (illustrated); Jerusalem, Israel Museum, *Paintings from the Collection of Joseph H. Hazen*, summer, 1966, no. 9 (illustrated). The exhibition traveled to Cambridge, Massachusetts, Fogg Art Museum, Oct.-Dec., 1966; Los Angeles, University of California, The Art Galleries, Jan.-Feb., 1967; Berkeley, University of California, Art Museum, Feb.-March, 1967; Houston, Museum of Fine Arts, April-May, 1967, and Honolulu, Academy of Arts, June-Aug., 1967.

Christie's New York, 30 April 1996 (9**) US$ 508,500	US$	508,500

DIEGO ASSIS DANS L'ATELIER oil on canvas, 28½ x 23½in. (72.2 x 59.7cm.) sd on the reverse 'Alberto Giacometti 1950'
PROV.: Hannover Gallery, London; Sir Edward and Lady Hulton, London; Marlborough Galleries, New York; Acquired by Mrs. Joanne Toor Cummings *circa 1980*.
EXH.: London, Tate Gallery, *A Selection of Pictures, Drawings and Sculpture from the Collections of Sir Edward and Lady Hulton*, Aug.-Sept., 1957, no. 14; Wuppertal, Kunst-und Museumsverein, *Sammlung Sir Edward and Lady Hulton*, 1964, no. 18 (illustrated). The exhibition traveled to Rotterdam, Museum Boymans-van Beuningen, Nov. 1964-Jan. 1965; Frankfurt, Kunstverein Steinemes Haus, Feb.-March 1965; Munich, Staatliche Galerie im Lenbachhaus, April-May 1965, and Dortmund, Museum am Ostwall, June-Aug. 1965; Stockholm, Moderna Museet, *Hulton-Samlingen*, July-Aug. 1966, no. 14 Saint-Paul de Vence, Fondation Maeght, *Alberto Giacometti*, July-Sept. 1978, p. 125, no. 135 (illustrated in colour) London, Lefevre Gallery, *Important 19th and 20th Century Paintings*, June-July, 1981, no. 12 (illustrated in colour).

Christie's New York, 30 April 1996 (17**) US$ 1,872,500	US$	1,872,500

BUSTE DE DIEGO oil on canvas, 39¼ x 25½in. (,100 x 65cm.) sdlr 'Alberto Giacometi 1957'
PROV.: Marguerite and Aime Maeght, Paris; Galerie Jan Krugier, Geneva; Acquired by Mrs. Joanne Toor Cummings *circa 1983*.
EXH.: Rome, Villa Medici, *Alberto Giacometti*, Oct.-Dec., 1970, p. 17 (illustrated); Saint-Paul de Vence, Fondation Maeght, *Alberto Giacometti*, July-Sept. 1978, p. 135, no. 160 (illustrated); Saint-Paul de Vence, Fondation Maeght, *L'univers d'Aime et Marguerite Maeght*, 1982, no. 69.
LIT.: Y. Bonnefoy, *Giacometti*, Paris, 1991, p. 428, no. 410 (illustrated).

Christie's New York, 30 April 1996 (24**) US$ 717,500	US$	717,500

ETUDES ball point on an envelope, 6¼ x 4 7/8in. (15.9 x 12.4cm.) slc 'Alberto Giacometti' (1954)
PROV.: James Lord (acquired from he Artist); Robert Elkon Gallery, New York; acquired by the Benjamin family from the above in 1967.

Sotheby's New York, 2 May 1996 (256**) US$ 17,250	US$	17,250

PORTRAIT DE PIERRE REVERDY black ballpoint pen on paper, 11½ x 8in. (29 x 20.5cm.) (1962)
PROV.: Galerie Jean Krugier, Geneva (JK4793).
LIT.: To be included in the forthcomming catalogue raisonné of Alberto Giacometti's work, currently being prepared by Mary Lisa Palmer and the Association Alberto and Annette Giacometti.

Christie's London, 26 June 1996 (248**) GBP 12,650	US$	19,507

NU DEBOUT pencil on paper, 20 x 14 5/8in. (50.8 x 37.2cm.) slr 'Alberto Giacometti'
PROV.: Galerie Jan Krugier, Geneva.

Christie's New York, 8 November 1995 (305A*) US$ 27,600	US$	27,600

FIGURINE oil on canvas, 10 ¾ x 8 ¾in. (27.4 x 22.2cm.) sdlr 'Alberto Giacometti 1953' (1953)
PROV.: Saidenberg Gallery Inc., New york (acquired by the present owner, 1955).
LIT.: J. Dupin, *Alberto Giacometti*, Paris, 1962, p. 117 (illustrated).

Christie's New York, 8 November 1995 (325**) US$ 211,500	US$	211,500

GIANLISI Antonio (Rizzolo di San Giorgio 1677-1727 Cremona) Italian
STILLIFE WITH FLOWERS AND FRUIT ON A CARPET oil on canvas, 95 x 122cm.
 Finearte Rome, 24 October 1995 (551**) ITL 35,650,000 US$ 22,212

GIANNI Gian (19th Century) Italian
A VIEW OF MARSAMXETT HARBOUR BY MOONLIGHT WITH MANOEL ISLAND AND
VALLETTA IN THE BACKGROUND oil on board, 7¼ x 14 1/8in. (18.5 x 36cm.) sd (1878)
PROV.: The companion, VIEW OF THE GRAND HARBOUR WITH FORT ST ANGELO AND
SENGLEA IN THE BACKGROUND, ALSO SIGNED.
 Phillips London, 12th March 1996 (53 (a pair)**) GBP 5,500 US$ 8,400

GIAQUINTO Corrado (Mo(l)fetta 1703-1765 Napels) Italian
MERCURY AND ARGUS oil on canvas, 12½ x 16½in. (32.2 x 41.8cm.) (mid 1730's)
 Sotheby's London, 6 December 1995 (198**) GBP 23,000 US$ 35,396

GIBSON David Cooke (1827-1856) British
THE LITTLE STRANGER oil on canvas, 26½ x 36in. (66.6 x 91.5cm.) sd 'D C Gibson 1855'
PROV.: With Thomas Agnew and Sons, London; with Frost and Reed, London; The Rev. S.
Calverwell.
EXH.: London, Royal Academy, 1855, no. 153.
LIT.: Art Journal, 1855, p. 172; Christopher Wood, Victorian Painters, 1995, p. 192.
 Christie's London, 6 November 1995 (191**) GBP 21,275 US$ 33,279

GIFFORD Sanford Robinson, N.A. (1823-1880) American
TWILIGHT oil on canvas, 10¾ x 20 1/8in. (27.3 x 51.2cm.) sdlr 'SR Giffard 1867'
EXH.: New York, Berry-Hill Galleries, Inc. *Hudson River School Days*, November 1992-January
1993.
 Christie's New York, 23 May 1996 (9**) US$ 68,500 US$ 68,500

ON THE HUDSON oil on paper laid down on canvas, 7½ x 10½in. (19 x 26.6cm.) sll 'SR Gifford'
 Christie's New York, 23 May 1996 (36**) US$ 25,300 US$ 25,300

GIGANTE Giacinto (Napels 1806-1876) Italian
LANDSCAPE WITH DECORATIVE FIGURE oil on board, 42 x 55.5cm. sd 'G. Gigante 1853'
 Dorotheum Vienna, 13 September 1995 (610**) ATS 100,000 US$ 9,720

GILBERT Stephen (20th Century)
PAPILLON oil on canvas, 29 x 23cm. s and inscr. with title on the stretcher,'Stephen Gilbert'
 Christie's Amsterdam, 5 June 1996 (328*) NLG 9,200 US$ 5,375

GILBERT Victor (1847-1933) French
THE CHAMPS ELYSEE, PARIS oil on panel, 10 5/8 x 13 ¾in. (27 x 34.9cm.) slr 'Victor Gilbert'
 Christie's New York, 2 November 1995 (178**) US$ 18,400 US$ 18,400

THE FRUIT SELLER oil on canvas, 25½ x 21¼in (64.8 x 54cm.) sll 'Victor Gilbert.'
 Christie's New York, 22 May 1996 (219**) US$ 13,800 US$ 13,800

THE BALL oil on canvas, 25 ¾ x 36¼in. (65.4 x 92.1cm.) slr 'Victor Gilbert'
PROV.: Anon., sale; Christie's, New York, February 25, 1987, lot 12.
 Christie's New York, 2 November 1995 (182**) US$ 28,750 US$ 28,750

GARDENING oil on canvas, 22¼ x 18 ¾in. (56.5 x 47.6cm.) sal 'Victor Gilbert'
 Christie's New York, 2 November 1995 (185**) US$ 34,500 US$ 34,500

GILBERT AND GEORGE (1934 b. and 1942 b.) British
GOLD WORLD postcards mounted on board, 96 x 70in. (243.8 x 177.8cm.) s titled d 'GOLD

WORLD Gilbert + George' on a paper label l center
PROV.: Robert Miller Gallery, New York.
EXH.: New York, Robert Miller Gallery, *Twenty Five Worlds by Gilbert and George,* May-June
1990, n.n. (illustrated).
LIT.: R. Rosenblum*, Worlds and Windows by Gilbert and George,*; New York 1990, 1990 n.n.
(illustrated).

Christie's New York, 15 November 1995 (269**) US$ 8,050	US$	8,050

GILL Edmund (1820-1894) British
FALL ON THE CLYDE, CORA LINN, LANARK oil on canvas, 44 x 34in. (110.8 x 86.4cm.) sdll
'E.Gill 1862'

Christie's East, 30 October 1995 (32*) US$ 9,200	US$	9,200

GILLES Werner (1894-1961) German
FISCHERBOOTE AUF ISCHIA oil on canvas, 60.5 x 72cm. slr 'WGilles'

Lempertz Cologne, 29 November 1995 (163**) DEM 12,000	US$	8,470

GIMIGNANI Giacinto (1611-1681) Italian
LANDSCAPE WITH MERCURY PRESENTING THE GOLDEN APPLE TO PARIS AND
LANDSCAPE WITH THE JUDGEMENT OF PARIS oil on canvas (a pair), each: 86½ x 51½in.
(219.7 x 130.8cm.) sdlr 'Hy Gimignanus Pisto BAS. 1675'

Sotheby's New York, 16 May 1996 (48**) US$ 211,500	US$	211,500

SAINT CATHERINE OF SIENA RECEIVING THE ROSARY FROM THE VIRGIN MARY,
ATTENDED BY SAINT CATHERINE OF ALEXANDRIA oil on canvas, 37 5/8 x 52 5/8in. (95.6 x
133.7cm.)

Sotheby's New York, 16 May 1996 (180**) US$ 34,500	US$	34,500

GIORDANO Luca (Naples 1634-1705) Italian
THE CRUCIFIXION oil on canvas, 39 ¾ x 29¼in. (101.3 x 74.3cm.)

Sotheby's London, 18 October 1995 (83**) GBP 16,100	US$	25,410

PAN AND SIRINGA oil on canvas, 210 x 234.5cm.

Finearte Rome, 21 May 1996 (153***) ITL 155,250,000	US$	99,711

GIOVANE Joseph Heinz, il Giovane (attr) (Augsburg ca 1600-ca 1678) German
A) B) C) TURKISH SCENES oil on canvas, 75 x 118cm.

Finearte Rome, 18 October 1995 (385**) ITL 143,750,000	US$	89,564

GIOVANE Paolo da Caylina Il (Brescia 1485 c.-1554 c.) Italian
PRAYER IN THE GARDEN oil on board, 48 x 36.5cm.

Finearte Milan, 3 April 1996 (88**) ITL 20,700,000	US$	13,227

GIOVANNI DEL BIONDO (documented Florence (1356-1392) -) Italian
THE CORONATION OF THE VIRGIN ADORING ANGELS SAINT BARTOLOMEW AND
ONUPHRIUS AND IN THE LUNETTE ABOVE, A HALF FIGURE OF CHRIST IN
BENEDICTION tempera on panel, gold ground, arched top, overall: 35¼ x 18 ¾in. (89.5 x 48cm.),
main panel: 18 x 16½in. (46 x 42.5cm.), lunette: 10 x 14 ¾in. (25.5 x 37.5cm.)
EXH.: London, 1884, no. 227, as Andrea Orcagna; Birmingham, 1953, no. 166; Nottingham, 1968,
no. 6, plate V, as Giovanni del Biondo; Nottingham, 1982, no. 7, as ascribed to Giovanni del Biondo,
and recording that the attribution had been questioned (private communication) by Millard Meiss;
Nottingham, 1986, no. 6, as attributed to Giovanni del Biondo; Sheffield, Graves Art Gallery, on
loan, 1992 - 1994.
LIT.: Richter, 1901, no. 28, as Florentine School, 14th Century, perhaps by Orcagna; Cornforth,
1968, pp. 404-5, fig. 4, as Giovanni del Biondo; Nicolson, 1968, p. 163, as by or from the circle of
del Biondo; Smart, 1968, p. 206, as by Giovanni del Biondo; Vertova, 1968, p. 26, as not by Biondo;

Calvocoressi, 1976, fig. 8, as attributed to Giovanni del Biondo.
Sotheby's London, 6 December 1995 (15**) GBP 100,500   US$ 154,663

**GIOVANNI DI SER GIOVANNI {called} Lo Scheggia (San Giovanni Valdarno 1406-1486
Florence) Italian**
A TRIUMPHAL SCENE tempera on panel, gold ground, 17¼ x 33½in. (44 x 85cm.)
PROV.: Baron Marochetti, and thence by descent in the family Count Trotti, Paris; Achillito Chiesa,
his sale, New York, American Art Galleries, 16 April 1926, lot 29, as in the manner of Masaccio;
Purchased by Kleinberger, New York, for William Randolph Hearst; By whom given, in 1946, to the
Los Angeles County Museum of Art, inv. no. A.5141-292; By whom sold for acquisition funds, New
York, Sotheby's, 17 January 1986, lot 23, for $41,000.
LIT.: P. Schubring, 'New Cassone Panels', in *Apollo*, March 1927, vol. V, pp. 108 - 109, as by the
Anghiari Master, reproduced; B. Berenson, 'Quadri senza case. Il Quattrocento fiorentino, I', in
Dedalo, vol. XII, 1932, pp. 537-539; B. Berenson, 'Quadri senza Casa', in *Dedalo*, vol. XVII, 1937,
p. 7, as attributed to Francesco di Antonio; R. van Marle, *The Development of the Italian Schools of
Painting*, 1937, vol. XVI, pp. 195, 196, note 1, as not by the Master of Fucecchio; *Bulletin of the Art
Division of the Los Angeles County Museum*, Spring 1948, vol. 1, nos. 3 and 4, p.3, reproduced;
Bulletin of the Art Division, Los Angeles County Museum, Summer 1950, vol. 3, no. 2, p. 18, no.8, as
Workshop of Paolo Uccello, Florentine, c. 1440; B. Berenson, *Italian Pictures of the Renaissance,
Florentine School*, 1963, vol. I, p. 63, as by Francesco di Antonio; B. Berenson, *Homeless Paintings
of the Renaissance*, 1969, p. 166, as by Francesco di Antonio; B. Fredericksen and F. Zeri, *Census of
Pre-Nineteenth Century Paintings in North American Public Collections*, 1972, pp. 129,591, as
Studio of the Master of Fucecchio; E. Callmann, *Apollonio di Giovanni*, 1974, p. 86, as not by
Apollonio di Giovanni; R. Fremantle, *Florentine Gothic Painters*, 1975, p. 549, reproduced, as by
the Master of Fucecchio.
Sotheby's London, 5 July 1995 (66**) GBP 51,000   US$ 81,353

GIOVANNINI Vincenzo (1816-1868) Italian
THE PAPAL CARRIAGE AND ESCORT BEFORE AN EXTENSIVE LANDSCAPE OF ROME
oil on canvas, 18 1/8 x 37¼in.(46 x 94.5 cm.) sdlr inscr. 'Roma' (1865)
Phillips London, 12th March 1996 (64**) GBP 9,000   US$ 13,745

GIRARDET Eugène Alexis (1853-1907) French
THE SACRED FIRE OF JERUSALEM oil on canvas, 78 ¾ x 51 ¼in. (,200 x 130.2cm.)
Christie's New York, 2 November 1995 (48**) US$ 354,500   US$ 354,500

GLACKENS William James (1870-1938) American
CAP NOIR-ST PIERRE oil on canvas, 25 x 30in. (63.5 x 76.2cm.) slr 'W. Glackens' sd 'on the
reverse '1902'
Christie's New York, 23 May 1996 (89**) US$ 299,500   US$ 299,500

THE GREEN BEACH COTTAGE, BELLPORT, LONG ISLAND oil on canvas, 25 x 30in. (63.5 x
76.2cm.) slr 'W.Glackens'
PROV.: Estate of the artist; John H. Surovek Gallery, Palm Beach, Florida.
Christie's New York, 23 May 1996 (94**) US$ 266,500   US$ 266,500

TOWN PIER - BLUE POINT, LONG ISLAND oil on canvas, 26 x 32in. (66 x 81.3cm.) slr 'W.
Glackens' inscr. with the title
PROV.: Kraushaar Galleries, New York.
EXH.: (Probably) New York, Whitney Museum of American Art, *William Glackens Memorial
Exhibition*, December, 1938- January, 1939, no. 19, as *Beach Scene_Great South Bay*.
LIT.: I. Glackens, *William Glackens and The Eight: The Artists Who Freed American Art*, New York,
1983, pp. 170-77; R.J. Wattenmaker, 'William Glackens's Beach Scenes at Bellport' *Smithsonian
Studies in American Art*, vol.II, no. 2, Spring 1988, pp. 74-94.
Christie's New York, 30 November 1995 (57**) US$ 1,047,500   US$ 1,047,500

GLARNER Fritz (Zurich 1899-1972) Swiss
RELATIONAL PAINTING TONDO NO. 61 oil on masinite applied to a heavy circular wooden
board, 49¼in. (125.1cm.) diameter sd and titled on the reverse 'Fritz Glaner Relational Painting
Tondo 61 1964'
PROV.: Mr and Mrs Armand Bartos, New York.
EXH.: New York, Whitney Museum of American Art, *1965 Annual Exhibition of Contemporary
American Painting*, Dec. 1965-Jan. 1965; Chicago Museum of Contemporary Art, *Fritz Glarner* (?),
1965; San Fransisco, San Fransisco Museum of Art, *Fritz Glarner - Retrospective*, Nov. 1970-April
1971; Bern, Kunsthalle, *Fritz Glarner*, 1972, no. 49.

	Christie's London, 28 November 1995 (47**) GBP 298,500	US$	466,917

GLAUBER Johannes, {called} Polidoro (Utrecht 1646-1726 Schoonhoven) Dutch
CLASSICAL RUINS IN A WOODED LANDSCAPE, WITH WASHERWOMEN AT A
FOUNTAIN BY A TOMB AND A SHEPHERD RESTING ON A PLINTH oil on canvas, 23 1/8 x
33½in. (58.8 x 85cm)

	Christie's London, 8 December 1995 (258**) GBP 9,430	US$	14,512

GLEHN Oswald von (1858) German (British)
BOREAS AND ORITHYIA oil on canvas, 24 2/4 x 63in. (63 x 142cm.) slr with mono.
PROV.: Morris D. Solow; Sotheby Parke Bernet, Los Angeles, 22 May 1972, lot 29; Forbes
Magazine Collection.
EXH.: London, Royal Academy, 1879, no.151; Minneapolis, Minnesota, University Art Gallery, *The
Art and Mind of Victorian England: Paintings from the Forbes Magazine Collection*, 1974, no.15.
LIT.: Henry Blackburn (ed.), *Academy Notes*, 1879, p.21; *The Times*, 6 June1879, p.4; *Art Journal*,
1879, p.128.

	Christie's London, 29 March 1996 (80**) GBP 17,250	US$	26,344

GLENAVY, R.H.A. Lady Beatrice (1883-1968)
THE INTRUDER oil on canvas, 28 x 38in. (71.1 x 96.5cm.) skr with mono.; inscr. 'The Intruder
Beatrice Elvery (Lady Glenavy) Clonard Kimmage Road Terenure Dublin', on a label on the reverse
PROV.: Professor Fearon, by whom acquired direct from the artist, thence by family descent.
EXH.: Dublin, *Aonach Tailteann Exhibition of Irish Art*, 1932, no.l33; Dublin, Royal Hibernian
Academy, 1932, no.37; London, Royal Academy, 1933, no.l2; Dublin, Waddington Gallery, 1955;
Dublin, National Gallery of Ireland, *Irish Women Artists From the Eighteenth Century to the Present
Day*, 1987, no.ll2, p.l33 (illustrated): this exhibition travelled to Trinity College, Douglas Hyde
Gallery; and Hugh Lane Municipal Gallery of Modern Art.
LIT.: Lady Glenavy, *Today we will only gossip*, London, 1964.

	Christie's London, 9 May 1996 (84**) GBP 27,600	US$	41,793

GLENDENING Alfred Augustus (1861-1907) British
NEAR GODALMING, SURREY oil on canvas, 24 x 36in. (61 x 91.5cm.) s with ini. and d 'A.A.G.
73' (1873)

	Christie's South Kensington, 6 June 1996 (96*) GBP 5,520	US$	8,512

HERDING SHEEP IN A SUNSWEPT VALLEY oil on canvas, 20 x 32¼in. (51 x 82cm.) sdlr 'A A
GLENDENING '89'

	Phillips London, 12 December 1995 (119*) GBP 6,000	US$	9,234

GLIKSBERG Chaim (Pinsk 1904-1970) Israelian
THE FIRST PARADE IN TEL AVIV oil on canvas, 21 7/8 x 18 3/8in. (55.5 x 46.5cm.) slr in
Hebrew (1950)
EXH.: Tel Aviv, Museum of Art, *Chaim Gliksberg - Portraits, Interiors, Landscape, Still Lives and
Flowers*, April 1976, no. 27; Tel Aviv, Rubin Museum, *Tel Aviv at 80*, June 1989.

	Christie's Tel Aviv, 12 October 1995 (71**) US$ 17,250	US$	17,250

GLINDONI Henry Gillard, A.R.W.S. (1852-1913) British
THE FLOWER-GIRL oil on canvas, 30 x 25in. (76.5 x 63.5cm.) s 'H. Glindoni'
      Christie's London, 6 November 1995 (200**) GBP 13,225   US$ 20,687

GLISENTI ACHILLE (1906) Italian
THE ARTIST'S STUDIO oil on panel, 25 x 35 ¾in. (63.5 x 90.8cm.) sll 'A.Glisenti.'
      Christie's New York, 14 February 1996 (111**) US$ 23,000   US$ 23,000

GLOAG Isobel Lilian (1865-1917) British
THE CHOICE oil on canvas, 54 x54in. (137 x 137cm.)
PROV.: Richard Green, London.
EXH.: London, Royal Academy, 1913, no. 3.
LIT.: *Royal Academy Pictures*, London, 1913, p. 3.
      Christie's London, 21 November 1995 (231**) GBP 17,250   US$ 26,983

GNOLI Domenico (1933-1970) Italian
DONNE PERUVIANE ink and watercolour on paper, 45 x 35cm. (1960)
PROV.: Acquired directly from the artist.
EXH.: Verona, Galleria d'Arte Moderna e Contemporanea, Palazzo Forti, *Domenico Gnoli*,
November 1982 - January 1983; Spoleto, Festival dei due mondi, *Domenico Gnoli*, 25 June - 14 July
1985, cat. p. 109, n.S3 (illustrated); Roma, Galleria Nazionale d'Arte Moderna, *Mostra antologica
Domenico Gnoli*, 21 February-12 April 1987, cat. n. 132 (illustrated).
LIT.: A. de Garron, *L'Opera grafca di Domenico Gnoli*, Milano 1985, p. 158 (illustrated).
      Christie's Milan, 20 November 1995 (94*) ITL 10,607,000   US$ 6,659

GODWARD John William (Wimbledon 1858/61-1922) British
PORTRAIT OF LILY PETTIGREW oil on canvas, 14½ x 12in. (36.4 x 30.5cm.) insc. 'Lily' (ca
1900)
PROV.: Possibly Rose Pettigrew (Mrs. Waldo Warner), the sitter's younger sister.
LIT.: Possibly Bruce Laughton, Philip Wilson Steer, 1971, p. 116.
      Christie's London, 29 March 1996 (82**) GBP 38,900   US$ 59,407

SABINELLA oil on canvas, 19¾ x 15 3/8in. (50.1 x 39cm.) sd 'J.W. Godward./1912' s inscr. titled
on the reverse 'J.W. GODWARD/ROME' (last half 1911)
PROV.: Countess Clara de Courten, purchased directly from the Artist; her sale Simpson's Houston
January 1981, no. 280; purchased by the present owner.
LIT.: This painting will be included in the forthcoming *catalogue raisonné* being prepared by Dr.
Vern G. Swanson.
      Christie's New York, 22 May 1996 (88**) US$ 74,000   US$ 74,000

GOEDAERT Johannes (Middelburg 1620-1668 Middelburg) Dutch
A DUNE LANDSCAPE IN THE ENVIRONS OF MIDDELBURG WITH A PEASANT WOMAN
RESTING BY A TRACK, COTTAGES BEYOND oil on copper, 8 x 10in. (20.3 x 25.4cm.) s
'Joh.goedae.'
PROV.: Mrs. R.R. Douglas; Christie's 28 January 1921, lot 89, as Elsheimer.
      Christie's London, 19 April 1996 (104**) GBP 133,500   US$ 202,426

GOENEUTTE Norbert (1854-1894) French
NATHALIE GOENEUTTE, THE ARTIST'S SISTER ON A RIVER BANK oil on canvas, 21½ x 17
¾in. (55 x 45cm.) s and dedicated ll 'à mon ami Sortais'; titled in French on a label on the stretcher
(ca. 1879)
      Sotheby's London, 13 March 1996 (101**) GBP 24,150   US$ 36,881

GOETZ K.O. French
BYAS mixed media on canvas, 39 5/8 x 47¼in. (100.5 x 120cm.) s 'K.O. Goetz' sd titled '62' on the
reverse

PROV.: L'Attico Galleria d'Arte, Rome.
      Christie's London, 23 May 1996 (59**) GBP 16,100   US$ 24,379

GOGH Vincent van (Groot Zundert (N.-Brabant) 1853-1890 Auvers sur Oise) Dutch
POLLARD BIRCHES oil on canvas laid down on panel, 17 x 22 5/8in. (43 x 58cm.) (Nuenen, May 1884)
PROV.: Oldenzeel Art Gallery, Rotterdam (1903); J. A. Fruin, Rotterdam (1927-28); W. Moll, The Hague; W. Brinkman, Schipluiden.
EXH.: Rotterdam, Oldenzeel Art Gallery, *Vincent van Gogh*, 1903, no. 47; Rotterdam, Kunsthandel Unger en van Mens, *Vincent van Gogh*, 1927-28, no. 21.
LIT.: J. B. de la Faille, *L 'Oeuvre de Vincent van Gogh, Paris and Brussels*, 1928, *vol. I*, p. 20, no. 31, catalogued; vol. II, pl. VI, no. 31, illustrated; W. Van Beselaere, *Der Hollandsche periode (1880-85) in het Werk van Vincent van Gogh*, Amsterdam, 1937, pp. 282 and 414; J. B. de la Faille, *The Works of Vincent van Gogh, his Paintings and Drawings*, Amsterdam, 1970, no. F. 31, illustrated; Paolo Lecaldano, *Tout l'Oeuvre peint de van Gogh*, Paris, 1971, vol. I, p. 95, no. 41, illustrated; Jan Hulsker, *The Complete van Gogh. Paintings. Drawings. Sketches*, Oxford, 1980, p. 112, no. 477, illustrated; Ingo F. Walther & Rainer Metzger, *Vincent van Gogh, L 'Oeuvre Complète Peintures*, Oldenberg, 1990, vol. I, p. 40, illustrated.
      Sotheby's London, 24 June 1996 (12**) GBP 496,500   US$ 765,613

WATERMILL AT GENNEP oil on canvas, 33½ x 59 3/8in. (85 x 151cm.) (Nuenen, November 1884)
PROV.: C. Mouwen Jr., Breda (Sale: Amsterdam, May 3rd 1904, no. 5); Oldenzeel Art Gallery, Rotterdam (Sale: Rotterdam, December 10th 1918, no. 42); F. J. P. Van der Eerden Art Gallery, Rotterdam; C. Staib, Rotterdam (1927-28); RegnaultJr., Laren; E. Regnault, Laren (1947); E. J. Van Wisselingh, Amsterdam .
EXH.: Rotterdam, Oldenzeel Art Gallery, *Vincent van Gogh*, 1903, no. 48; Rotterdam, Oldenzeel Art Gallery, *Vincent van Gogh*, 1904, no. 45; Rotterdam, Kunsthandel Unger en van Mens, 1927-28, no. 18.
LIT.: J. B. de la Faille, *L'Oeuvre de Vincent van Gogh*, Paris and Brussels, 1928, vol. I, p. 44, no. 125; vol. II, pl. XXXII, no. 125, illustrated; W. Van Beselaere, *Der Hollandsche periode (1880-85) in het Werk van Vincent van Gogh*, Amsterdam, 1937, pp. 283 and 415; J. B. de la Faille, *The Works of Vincent van Gogh, his Paintings and Drawings*, Amsterdam, 1970, no. F. 125, illustrated; Paolo Lecaldano, *Tout l'oeuvre peint de Van Gogh*, Paris, 1971, vol. I, p. 96, no. 62, illustrated; Jan Hulsker, *The Complete van Gogh. Paintings. Drawings. Sketches*. Oxford, 1980, no. H 525, p. 123, illustrated; Ingo F. Walther and Rainer Metzger, *Vincent van Gogh. L'Oeuvre Complète Peintures*, Oldenberg, 1990, vol. I, p. 54, illustrated .
      Sotheby's London, 24 June 1996 (14**) GBP 551,500   US$ 850,424

NATURE MORTE, VASE AVEC OEILLETS oil on canvas, 16¼ x 12½in. (41 x 32cm.) (Auvers, June 1890)
PROV.: Johanna van Gogh-Bonger, Amsterdam, by whom sold in May 1905 to Paul Cassirer, Berlin by whom sold in May 1905 to Georg Schwarz, Berlin; Barbazanges Galerie, Paris; Alphonse Kann, St. Germain-en-Laye; Paul Rosenberg, New York; Millicent A. Rogers, New York; Arturo Peralta-Ramos, New York; sale, Sotheby Parke-Bennet, New York, 26 April 1972, lot 21.
EXH.: Berlin, Paul Cassirer, *VII Ausstellung*, April 1905, no. 17 (sold). Zurich, Zuricher Kunsthaus, *Französische Kunst des XIX und XX Jahrhunderts*, 1917, no. 573; Paris, Galerie Bemheim-Jeune, *Retrospective Van Gogh*, 1927; Toledo, Ohio, Museum of Art, *Flower Paintings*, 1930; Cleveland, Museum of Art, *Van Gogh*, 1948, no. 17 (illus. pl. XVI).
LIT.: A. Bonger, *Catalogue des Oeuvres de Vincent van Gogh*, Paris, 1891, no. .300 (as 'Verre rempli de fleurs', unpublished handwritten inventory list); J.-B. de la Faille, Paris, *L'Epoque de van Gogh*, London, 1927, p. 119; J.-B. de la Faille, Paris and Brussels, *L'Oeuvre de Vincent van Gogh*, London, 1928, vol. I, no. 598, p. 168 (illustrated Vol. II, pl. CLXII - as painted in Arles in 1889); W. Scherjon and W. Jos. de Gruyter, *Vincent van Gogh's Great Period*, 1937, no. 191 (illustrated p. 195); J.-B. de la Faille, *Vincent van Gogh*, Paris, 1939, no. F598 (illustrated p. 414); J.-B. de la Faille, *The Works of Vincent van Gogh: His Paintings and Drawings*, Amsterdam, 1970, no. F598

(illustrated p. 31 - as painted in Auvers); J.Hulsker, *The Complete Van Gogh: Paintings, Drawings, and Sketches*, Oxford, 1977, no. 2043 (illustrated p. 468 - as painted in Auvers); P. Lecaldano, *L'Opera Pittorica Completa di Van Gogh, vol. II, Da Arles a Auvers*, Milan, 1977, no. 828 (illustrated p. 228 - as painted in Auvers); A. Mothe, *Vincent Van Gogh à Auvers-sur-Oise*, Paris, 1987, no. F598 (illustrated p. 173) (as painted in Auvers); W. Feilchenfeldt, *Vincent van Gogh and Paul* Cassirer, Berlin, the Reception of van Gogh in Germany from 1901 to 1914, Zwolle, 1990, p. 19 (illustrated p. 106 as F.598).

Christie's London, 25 June 1996 (8**) GBP 3,081,500	US$	4,751,735

INTERIEUR D'UN RESTAURANT oil on canvas, 21¼ x 25¼in. (51.1 x 65.4cm.) (1887-1888)
PROV.: Galerie Ambroise Vollard, Paris; Mrs. Esther S. Sutro, London (1896); Alfred Sutro, London (1929); Mrs. van Gruisen; Alex. Reid & Lefevre, London; Marcel Gieure; Carroll Carstairs Gallery, New York; Acquired by the family of the present owner in 1935.
EXH.: London, New Gallery, *Impressionist Painters*, 1909; London, Leicester Galleries, *Vincent van Gogh*, Dec., 1923, p. 22, no. 37; London, Tate Gallery, *Opening Exhibition of the Modern Foreign Gallery*,June-Oct., 1926, p. 7; London, Royal Academy of Arts, *Dutch Art 1450-1900*, Jan.-March, 1929, no. 463; Amsterdam, Stedelijk Museum, *Vincent van Gogh en zijn tijdgenooten*, Sept.-Nov., 193O, p. 15, no. 68; Manchester, City Art Gallery, *Vincent van Gogh*, Oct.-Nov., 1932; New York, Bignou Gallery, *A Nineteenth Century Selection of French Paintings*, March, 1935, no. 5; New York, The Museum of Modern Art, *Vincent van Gogh*, Dec., 1935-Jan., 1936, no. 45 (illustrated). The exhibition traveled to Philadelphia, Museum of Art,Jan.-Feb., 1936; Boston, Museum of Fine Arts, Feb.-March, 1936; Cleveland, Museum of Art, March-April, 1936; San Francisco, California Palace of the Legion of Honor, April-May, 1936; Kansas City, The William Rockhill Nelson Gallery of Art, June-July, 1936; Minneapolis, Institute of Arts, July-Aug., 1936; Chicago, The Art Institute, Aug.-Sept., 1936, and Detroit, Museum of Art, Oct., 1936; Boston, Museum of Fine Arts, *Paintings, Drawings and Prints from Private Collections in New England*, June-Sept., 1939, pp. 42-43, no. 55 (illustrated, pl. XXXIX); New York, Wildenstein & Co., Inc., *The Art and Life of Vincent van Gogh*, Oct.-Nov., 1943, p. 80, no. 39 (illustrated); Hartford, Wadsworth Atheneum, Harvest of Plenty, Oct.-Dec., 1963, p. 8, no. 17 (illustrated, pl. III); Toronto, Art Gallery of Ontario, *Vincent van Gogh and the Birth of Cloisonism*, Jan. March, 1981, p. 134, no. 23 (illustrated, p. 135). The exhibition traveled to Amsterdam, Rijksmuseum Vincent van Gogh, April-June, 1981; Providence, Rhode Island School of Design, Museum of Art, May, 1987-March, 1996 (on periodic loan); Amsterdam, Rijksmuseum Vincent van Gogh, *Vincent van Gogh*, March-July, 1990, p. 80, no. 25 (illustrated in colour, p. 82).
LIT.: 'Van Gogh in 1929: Europe and America,' *International Studio*, New York, June, 1929, p. 41 (illustrated); L. Eglington, 'Bignou Holds Fine Display in Beautiful New Gallery,' *Art News*, New York, March 9, 1935, pp. 1 and 4 (illustrated, p. 4); E.A. Jewell, *Vincent van Gogh*, New York, 1946, p. 50 (illustrated); J.-B. de la Faille, *The Works of Vincent van Gogh: His Paintings and Drawings*, Amsterdam, 1970, p. 232, no. 549 (illustrated); J. Hulsker, *The Complete van Gogh: Paintings, Drawings, Sketches*, Amsterdam, 1977, p. 360, no. 1572 (illustrated); I.F. Walther and R. Metzger, *Vincent van Gogh: The Complete Paintings*, Cologne, 1990, vol. II, p. 406 (illustrated in colour).

Christie's New York, 30 April 1996 (31**) US$ 10,342,500	US$	10,342,500

GOLDSCHMIDT Hilde (Leipzig 1897-1980 Kitzbühel) German
VERBUNDENES ZUSAMMEN oil on canvas, 70 x 90cm. sd mono. 'HG 68'

Dorotheum Vienna, 6 December 1995 (610**) ATS 120,000	US$	11,834

GOLTZIUS Hendrick (Mühlbracht, near Venlo 1558-1617 Haarlem) Dutch
THE ILL-MATCHED COUPLE: AN OLD MAN OFFERING GOLD TO A YOUNG WOMAN oil on canvas, 27 x 23in. (68.5 x 58.5cm.) sdur mono. 'HG/1615'
PROV.: Probably Anon. sale: Zurich, Uto, 25 November 1985, lot 1429, as by Christiaen van Couwenburgh.
Sotheby's London, 5 July 1995 (19**)

GBP 47,700	US$	76,089

The Ill-Matched Couple

A VANITAS: A PUTTO STEPPING ON A SKULL, BLOWING BUBBLES, A LANDSCAPE BEYOND, FLOWERS IN A VASE AND A SMOKING URN ON A LEDGE IN THE FOREGROUND oil on panel, 52.6 x 35.3cm. inscr. and d 'QVIS EVADET 1603'
PROV.: Peltzer, Cologne; sale, Amsterdam, 26 May 1914, lot 31.
LIT.: Th. von Frimmel, *Geschichte der Wiener Gemälde Sammlungen*, 1899, III, fig. XXVIII; O. Hirschmann, *Hendrick Goltzius als Maler 1600-1617*, IX, 1916, p.95; W.L. Strauss, *The illustrated Bartsch, III-Commentary*, 1982, p. 346.
　　　　　Christie's Amsterdam, 13 November 1995 (28*)
NLG 12,650　　　　　　　　　　　　　　　　　US$　　　　7,973

GOLUB Leon Albert (1922 b.) American
HEAD VI oil on canvas-unframed, 47 ¾ x 40½in. (121.2 x 102.8cm.) slr 'GOLUB'; sd and titled 'GOLUB 'HEAD' (VI)' on the reverse
PROV.: Allan Frumkin Gallery, Chicago.
　　　　　Christie's East, 7 May 1996 (45*) US$ 18,400　　US$　　　18,400

GONZALES Eva (Mrs Henri Guérard) (1849-1883) French
LE CHIGNON oil on canvas laid down on board, 20 x 15 ¾in. (51 x 40cm.) stamped with the signature (between 1865-70)
PROV.: Jean-Raymond Guerard, Paris (vente, Paris, Hotel Drouot, 2 April 1981, no. 31); Vente, Paris Hotel Drouot, 7 July 1982, no. 77 (acquired by the present owner).
EXH.: Tokyo, Takashimaya Art Gallery and travelling, *Six femmes peintres*, 1983, no. 36, illustrated in the catalogue; Tokyo, Isetan Art Museum and travelling, *Les Femmes Impressionnistes: Morisot, Cassatt, Gonzales*, 1995, no. 83, illustrated in colour in the catalogue.
LIT.: Marie-Caroline Sainsaulieu and Jacques de Mons, *Eva Gonzales, 1849-1883, Etude critique et catalogue raisonné*, Paris, 1990, p. 72, no. 14, p. 73, illustrated in colour.
　　　　　Sotheby's London, 20 March 1996 (16**) GBP 43,300　　US$　　66,127

GONZALEZ Juan (act. Santiago de Compostella 16th century) Spanish
EPISODE DE LA VIE DE SAINT JACQUES oil on canvas laid down on panel, 62 x 80cm. sdlr 'Juan Gonzalez 16(?)9'
　　　　　Étude Tajan Paris, 28 June 1996 (20**) FRF 16,000　　US$　　3,090

GONZALEZ Julio (Barcelona 1876-1942) Spanish
ETUDE POUR SCULPTURE pen and black ink on yellow paper, 10 x 6 3/8in. (25.3 x 16.2cm.) s with ini. and dll 'J.G.1937,7-1' (1937)
PROV.: David Grob, London, from whom purchased by the present owner's father.
　　　　　Christie's South Kensington, 18 March 1996 (47**) GBP 8,050　　US$　　12,294

CONSTRUCTION III india ink and gray wash on paper, 11 ¾ x 9½in. (29.8 x 24.1cm.) s with ini. and d '7-12-39'
PROV.: Kleemann Galleries, New York.
EXH.: New York, Kleemann Galleries, *Julio González*, 1956, no. 20.
　　　　　Sotheby's New York, 2 May 1996 (289**) US$ 11,500　　US$　　11,500

PERSONNAGE ABSTRAIT DANSANT gouache and pen with black ink on grey paper, 12 ¾ x 9½in. (32.5 x 24.2cm.) sdlr ini. '28-1-40 15-2-39 J.G.'
PROV.: Jeffrey Hoffeld, New York (525); Mary-Anne Martin Fine Arte, New York (CIN/BO2); Royal S. Marks Gallery, New York (855).
LIT.: A. Cerni, *Julio Gonzalez*, Rome, 1962 (illustrated p. 19, pl.VII); J. Gibert, *Julio Gonzalez:*

Catalogue raisonné des Dessins - 'Projets pour Sculpture: Personnages', Paris, 1973, (illustrated p. 89).

        Christie's London, 29 November 1995 (231**) GBP 8,500   US$ 13,296

ETUDE POUR 'L'HOMME CACTUS' (RECTO); 'L'HOMME' (VERSO) colored wax crayons, pen, black ink and pencil(recto); pencil(verso) on paper, 12 5/8 x 9 ½in. (32 x 24.2cm.) lr on the *recto* 'J.G. 7-11', right center '11-11-38', and again on the *verso* 'j.g. 1937 21-8' (1937-1938)
PROV.: Estate of the artist; Galerie the France, Paris; Galerie Marwan Hoss, Paris; Julia Lublin, Buenos Aires.

        Christie's New York, 8 November 1995 (264**) US$ 10,925   US$ 10,925

GOODWIN Philip Russell (1882-1935) American
THE PRIZE CATCH oil on canvas, 38 x 24½in. (96.5 x 62.3cm.) sll 'Philip R. Goodwin.'

        Christie's New York, 13 September 1995 (99*) US$ 9,775   US$ 9,775

GORBATOV Konstantin Ivanovich (1876-1928) Russian?
DER GRAVE TAG oil on canvas, 31½ x 25in. (80 x 63.5cm.) sll 'C. Gorbatoff' and inscr. on the back of the canvas 'C. Gorbatoff, Der Grave Tag.1933'

        Christie's New York, 18 April 1996 (29**) US$ 11,500   US$ 11,500

GORE Spencer Frederick (1878-1914) British
A MUSIC-HALL TURN, THE ALHAMBRA pastel on blue paper, 14 x 7¼in. (35.5 x 18.4cm.) (1909)
PROV.: The Artist's Estate; purchased by the present owner at the 1987 exhibition.
EXH.: New York, Hirschl & Adler Galleries, *British Modernist Art 1905-1930*, Nov.1987-Jan. 1988, no. 20 (illustrated).

        Christie's London, 20 June 1996 (31**) GBP 12,075   US$ 18,620

GORKY Arshile (1904-1948) American (Armenian)
UNTITLED pen and black ink and graphite on paper, 12½ x 22¼in. (31.7 x 56.5cm.) (1936)
PROV.: Hans Burckhardt, Los Angeles.

        Christie's New York, 15 November 1995 (157**) US$ 18,400   US$ 18,400

GOROKHOFF Ivan Lavrentievitch (1863 b.-) Russian
ZHITEL'NITSA (THE VILLAGE GIRL) oil on canvas, 52 x 28in. (133 x 71cm.) sdlr in Cyrillic 'I. Gorohkoff, 1902'
PROV.: Presented to the Syrian Prime Miniser Khaled El-Azm by President Nikita Krushchev.

        Christie's New York, 18 April 1996 (28**) US$ 14,950   US$ 14,950

GOSSAERT Jan (1475/78-1532) Flemish
THE MADONNA AND CHILD, THE FLIGHT INTO EGYPT IN A WOODED VALLEY BEYOND oil on panel, 121.5 x 103.2cm.
PROV.: with J. van der Kellen, Rotterdam (label on the reverse).

        Christie's Amsterdam, 7 May 1996 (23**) NLG 46,000   US$ 26,822

GOTSCH Friedrich Karl (Pries bei Kiel 1900-1984 Schleswig) German
INTERIEUR oil on canvas, 101 x 114cm. s with mono. 'FKG'; s and titled on the reverse (1934-60)

        Hauswedell & Nolte Cologne, 1 December 1995 (284**) DEM 15,000   US$ 10,407

IN DER PROVENCE oil on canvas, 68 x 84cm. s with mono. lr 'F K G'; inscr. 'Häuser in Sanary sur Mer, 1929' on the reverse (1955)
LIT.: H. Th. Flemming, *Freidrich Karl Gotsch*, Hamburg 1963, section 132, (illustrated in colour no. 16).

        Hauswedell & Nolte Cologne, 5-6 June 1996 (232**) DEM 48,000   US$ 31,187

GOTCH Thomas Cooper, R.W.A. (1854-1931) British
A PORTRAIT OF MISS WINNIFRED GRACE HEGAN KENNARD oil on canvas, 64 x 45in.
(162.5 x 114cm.) sdll 'T.C. Gotch/1893'
EXH.: London, Royal Academy, 1893, no. 220.
                Christie's New York, 22 May 1996 (272**) US$ 34,500   US$ 34,500

GOTTLIEB Adolph (1903-1974) American
EXTREMES oil on canvas, 48 x 72in. (121.8 x 182.8cm.) sd, titled and numbered '6613 Adolph
Gottlieb 'EXTREMES' 1966' on the reverse
PROV.: Marlborough Galleria d'Arte, Rome.
EXH.: London, MArlborough Fine Art, and Zurich, Marlborough Galerie AG, *Adolphe Gottlieb:
Paintings 1959-1971*, Nov. 1971-March 1972, p. 26, no. 8 (illustrated).
LIT.: B. Denvir, 'London Letter', *Art International*, Jan. 1972, p. 48 (illustrated).
                Christie's New York, 14 November 1995 (26**) US$ 129,000   US$ 129,000

WHITE HALO oil on paper, 24 19in. (60.6 x 48cm.) sd numbered ll 'Adolph Gottlieb 1970' stamped
'Adolph en Esther Gottlieb Foundation, inc.' on the reverse
PROV.: Adolph & Esther Gottlieb Foundation, inc., New York.; Manny Silvermann Gallery, Los
Angeles.
EXH.: Allentown, Muhlenberg College, Center for the Arts, *Adolph Gottlieb: Works on Paper*,
March-April 1984.
                Christie's New York, 15 November 1995 (160**) US$ 36,800   US$ 36,800

DAWN oil on canvas, 90 x 72in. (228.6 x 182.9cm.) sd and titled 'Adolph Gottlieb 'DAWN' 1960' on
the reverse
PROV.: Sidney Janis Gallery, New York.
EXH.: New York, Sidney Janis Gallery, *Gottlieb: New Paintings*, Nov.-Dec. 1960.
                Christie's New York, 7 May 1996 (7**) US$ 266,500   US$ 266,500

GOUBAU Antoni (1616-1698) Flemish
A ROMAN FAIR oil on canvas, 125 x 250cm. (framed)
                Dorotheum Vienna, 17 October 1995 (61**) ATS 450,000   US$ 45,138

GOUBIE Jean Richard (1842-1899) French
SETTING OUT oil on canvas, 15 x 22¼in. (38.1 x 56.5cm.) sdll 'R. Goubie/1885'
PROV.: With Goupil & Cie., Paris.
                Christie's New York, 22 May 1996 (223**) US$ 17,250   US$ 17,50

GOUWE Adriaan Herman (Alkmaar 1875-1965 Papeete (Tahiti)) Dutch
THE REAPER oil on canvas, 53 x 77cm. s 'A.H. Gouwe'
                Christie's Amsterdam, 18 June 1996 (364**) NLG 9,775   US$ 5,711

GOVAERTS Abraham (Antwerp 1589-1626) Flemish (In co-operation with Frans Franken II)
THE FLIGHT INTO EGYPT WITH THE MIRACLE OF THE STATUE, AND BABIES
MASSACRED BY HERODS SOLDIERS oil on panel, 15 1/8 x 16 3/8in. (38.2 x 41.7) s init. 'FFF.'
(on the plinth)
PROV.: With Acquavella, New York.
                Christie's London, 7 July 1995 (29**) GBP 20,700   US$ 33,020

GOW R.A. Andrew Carrick (1848-1920) British
THE RELIEF OF LEYDEN oil on canvas, 48 x 73½in. (121.9 x 186.7cm.) sd '1876'; s, titled and
inscr. '35 Fitzroy Square/ W' on the reverse
EXH.: London, National Art Gallery of N.S.W., n.d., no. 919.
                Sotheby's Arcade Auctions New York, 17 January 1996 (240*) US$ 14,950   US$ 14,950

GOYA Y LUCIENTES Francisco José de (1746-1828) Spanish
SORTING THE BULLS oil on tin plate, 16 ¾ x 12½in. (42.6 x 32cm.) inscr. '5 and 9' on the reverse
Sotheby's London, 5 July 1995 (84***) GBP 1,816,500 — US$ 2,897,591

GOYEN Jan Josefsz. van (Leyden 1596-1656 The Hague) Dutch
A ROWING BOAT WITH SAILING BOATS IN AN ESTUARY WITH A FRESH BREEZE oil on panel, 14 x 12 ¾in. (35.5 x 32.5cm.) s mono. 'VG'
PROV.: With Ch. Sedelmeyer, Paris, 1873; E. Kums, his sale, Antwerp,17 May 1898, lot 101, 2,,700 B.Frs to the Le Roy brothers; With D.A. Hoogendijk, Amsterdam, circa 1930; Albert K Schneider, his sale, New York, 14 October 1953, lot 53, $950; With Arthur Tooth & Sons, London, where bought by the grandfather of the present owner.
EXH.: Vienna, 1873, no. 67; London, Arthur Tooth and Sons, *Catalogue IX,* 1954, no. 24.
LIT.: C. Hofstede de Groot, *A Catalogue Raisonné..*, 1990, p. 51, no. 164 (as a View of the Moerdijk), and pp. 272-3, no. 1087; *Illustrated London News*, 13 November 1954, p. 853, reproduced; H.-U. Beck, *Jan van Goyen*, 1973, vol II, p. 98, no.205, reproduced.
Sotheby's London, 5 July 1995 (3**) GBP 177,500 — US$ 283,139

A) A PEASANT WOMAN MILKING CATTLE ON A RIVERBANK, WITH PEASANT IN A ROWING BOAT BEARING A MILK CHURN TIED UP NEARBY; B) PEASANTS LOADING A CART WITH PRODUCE IN A LANDSCAPE oil on panel (a pair), each: diameter 10 ¾in. (27.5cm.) painting a) sd on the boat 'VG 1631'
PROV.: W. Baillie, 1796 (not 1776 as Beck states); John, 2nd Marquess of Bute and 7th Earl of Dumfries, Luton Park, Bedfordshire, his sale, London, Christie's, 7 June 1822, lot 39, 16 gns to Mortimer; Richard Mortimer, his (deceased sale), London, Foster, 28 April 1829, lot 24, GBP16.5-6 to Eckford; John Cowper, Carleton Hall, Penrith, Cumberland, his (deceased sale), London, Foster, 16-17 June 1897, lot 56 (A) GBP28.7.0, lot 56 (B) GBP23.2.0, both to Colnaghi; With P. & .D. Colnaghi, London, until at least 1903; With F.A.C. Prestel, Frankfurt-am-Main, 1905-6; Max von Grunelius, bears his label on the reverse of each, with inventory number: V, 150; His son, Ernst-Max von Grunelius.
EXH.: Amsterdam, 1903, no.l4; Frankfurt-am-Main, Summer 1925, nos. 88, 89 (nos. 89 and 90 in the small exhibition catalogue).
LIT.: C. Hofstede de Groot, *A Catalogue Raisonné*, vol III, 1927, p. 117, no. 445 (B), p. 183, no. 708 (A); H. U. Beck, *Jan van Goyen 1596-1656*, 1973, vol. II, *Gemälde*, pp. 60-61, no. 118, reproduced (A), p. 67, no. 134 (B).
Sotheby's London, 5 July 1995 (28**) GBP 69,700 — US$ 111,182

A WOODED RIVER LANDSCAPE WITH A WASHERWOMAN KNEELING ON THE BANK oil on panel, 21 ¾ x 18¼in. (55.5 x 46.5cm.) sdlr 'VG 1633'
PROV.: With Douwes, Amsterdam; Lambertus de Vries, Berlin; P. Rosenthal, Berlin, 1928; Bought by the grandfather of the present owner probably in the 1950s.
LIT.: H.-U. Beck, *Jan van Goyen*, vol. II, *Katalog der Gemälde*, 1973, p. 79, no. 164 (illustrated).
Sotheby's London, 5 July 1995 (93**) GBP 36,700 — US$ 58,542

A VILLAGE ON THE BANKS OF A RIVER WITH FERRY BOATS oil on panel, 15 ¾ x 21 ¾in. (40 x 55.5cm.) sdlr 'VG 1646'
Sotheby's London, 5 July 1995 (94**) GBP 98,300 — US$ 156,803

PEASANTS RESTING ON A SANDY TRACK BY FARM BUILDINGS oil on panel, 15 1/8 x 21in. (38.4 x 53.4cm.) sd mono. 'VG 1631'
PROV.: Anon. sale, Kende, Vienna, 30 March 1925, lot 52; Herman Reif: Christie's 28 June 1935, lot 151.
Christie's London, 8 December 1995 (23**) GBP 34,500 — US$ 53,093

THE CHURCH OF SAINT MARTINUS AT EMMERICH ON THE RHINE oil on panel, 36.5 x 44.5cm. s with monogram and dlc 'VG 1638'
PROV.: Anon. sale, Berlin, 24 May 1927, lot 146; With Pieter de Boer, Amsterdam, in 1927; With

Galerie Sanct Lucas, Vienna, in 1930; With Galerie Internationale, The Hague; Jonkheer C.Th.F.
Thurkow, The Hague, 1941; Sold, London, Christie's, 14 December 1990, lot 93, where purchased
by the present owner.
LIT.: H-U. Beck, *Jan van Goyen*, vol. II, 1973; pp. 330-331, no. 730, (illustrated).
Sotheby's Amsterdam, 14 November 1995 (37**) NLG 70,800   US$ 44,621

VIEW OF A FARMHOUSE ACROSS A FROZEN CANAL WITH VARIOUS FIGURES
CHOPPING WOOD AND SKATING oil on panel, 8¼ x 16½in. (21 x 41.9cm.) slr mono. 'VG' (ca.
1628)
PROV.: A. Eigner, Augsburg;Dr. H. M. Schletterer, Augsburg (Sale: Frankfurt am Main, March 4,
1895, lot 51); F. Vormbaum, Frankfurt/Main (Sale: Frankfurt am Main, November 18, 1921, lot 41);
P. de Boer, Amsterdam by 1925; H. Maas, The Hague by 1927;Van Diemen & Co,
Amsterdam/Berlin; Sale: Berlin, April 26, 1935, lot 33; Ewald Schwartz, Cologne by 1973.
EXH.: C. Hofstede de Groot, *A Catalogue Raisonné..*, vol. VIII, 1929, cat. nos. 1207 and 1208, see
also no. 115; H.-U. Beck, *Jan van Goyen*, vol. II, 1973, cat. no. 9 illus.; vol. III, 1987, p. 148.
Sotheby's New York, 16 May 1996 (29**) US$ 118,000   US$ 118,000

FARM ON THE RIVERSIDE WITH FARMERS AND A HAYWAGON oil on panel, 33 x 53.5cm
slr mono 'VG'
PROV.: G.W. Lundens van Schalcken, sold in Amsterdam, Roos, 18 Nov. 1913, lot 13, ill.; R.
Peltzer, sold in Amsterdam, Frederik Mueller, May 26 1914, lot 315, fl 450.; Kunsthandel
Goudstikker, Amsterdam; J. Dolman; sold in Amsterdam Frederik Mueller; 19 Oct. 1943, lot 33, ill.;
sold at Pongs Dusseldorf, 17 Oct. 1953, lot 24, DEM 8000; Kunsthandlung Abels Cologne, 1954; Dr.
H.A. Wetzlar, Amsterdam, who sold in London, Sotheby`s, 8 Dec. 1965, sold to Mrs. A. Quinn;
Kunsthandel P. de Boer, Amsterdam 1956; Charles Spaen, Brussels, who sold in Paris, 20 June 1966,
lot 32 (illustrated).
LIT.: C. Hofstede de Groot, *A Catalogue Raissonné.*; 1918, Bd. VIII, p. 118 and p. 122, no. 481 and
483/501.; *Die Weltkunst*, 1 April 1954 (illustrated); Hans Ulrich Beck, *Jan van Goyen*, 1973, Bd. II,
p. 516,; no. 1187 (illustrated)
Dorotheum Vienna, 17 October 1995 (135**) ATS 600,000   US$ 60,184

A LANDSCAPE WITH PEASANTS ON A TRACK, A FARM AND INN BEYOND oil on panel,
14 1/8 x 22 5/8in. (35.9 x 57.5cm.) sd 'V GOYEN 1633'
PROV.: Mme Calmon, Hamburg; Lepke, Berlin, 9 Oct. 1894, lot 31; anon. sale, Lepke Berlin 5 April
1898, lot 48; with Heinenmann, Munich, 1928; with P. de Boer, Amsterdam ca. 1930.
LIT.: H.-U. Beck, *Jan van Goyen*, vol. II, Amsterdam 1973, p. 455, no. 1013; vol. III, Doornspijk,
1987, illustrated, p. 260.
Christie's London, 19 April 1996 (131**) GBP 25,300   US$ 38,362

A RIVER LANDSCAPE WITH FISHERMEN oil on canvas, 44 x 69 ¾in. (112 x 177cm.) sdlc 'I
VGoyen. 1632
PROV.: Maria Magdalena Sluypwijk, Countess von Moens, her deceased sale, Amsterdam, van der
Schley *et al*, 20-21 April 1803, lot 29, 280 florins to Josi; Anon. (?Terburg family) sale, Amsterdam,
16 July 1819, lot 63, ,100 florins to De Vries; The Hon. W.F.B. Massey-Mainwaring, 1903, his sale,
London, Christie's, 23 May 1903, lot, 70, GBP 399 to Wertheimer; The Marquess of Zetland,
London, his sale, London, Christie's, 27 April 1934, lot 116, GBP892 to Speelman; With D. Katz,
Dieren; A. Holle, Paris, 1950, his sale, Paris, Drouot, 23June 1950, lot 4, for 950,,000 francs; With
D. Katz, Dieren, 1952/3; Anon. sale, Lucerne, Galerie Fischer, 12 June 1956, lot 1878; J.G.
Wurfbain, Gelderse Toren Castle, Spankeren near Dieren, 1958; Anon. sale, London, Sotheby's, 23
March 1960, lot 112, GBP2,,200 to Gordon Schaeffer; Anon. sale, Amsterdam, Paul Brandt, 6 June
1961, lot 32, for 33,,000 florins; Anon. sale, London, Christie's, 2 July 1965, lot 135, for GBP5,040;
Anon. sale, Zurich, Koller, 3 November 1965, lot 1235A, for 70,,000 sfr.; Metzemaker collection,
Best, Holland, circa 1970; Anon. sale (Property of a Gentleman), London, Sotheby's, 9 July 1975, lot
61.
EXH.: London, Thos. Agnew & Sons, 1922, no. 17; The Hague, Kleykamp, 1934, no. 76.
LIT.: C. Hofstede de Groot, *A Catalogue Raisonné of the Works of the most Eminent Dutch Painters*

of the Seventeenth Century, vol. VIII, 1927, p. 183, no. 711; A. Dobrzycka, *Jan van Goyen*, 1966, p. 94, no. 58; H-U. Beck, *Jan van Goyen*, vol. II, 1973, pp. 216-17, no. 447, reproduced; H-U. Beck, *Jan van Goyen - Ergänzungsband*, vol. III, 1987, p. 195, no. 447.

Sotheby's London, 6 December 1995 (42**) GBP 89,500	US$	137,735

RIVER LANDSCAPE WITH FIGURES IN BOATS NEAR A PIER oil on panel, 14 x 22in. (36 x 56cm.) sdll 'VG 1636'
PROV.: John Templeman Coolidge, Boston, Massachussetts, ca. 1900; Thence by descent until sold, Boston, Massachussetts, Skinner, 15 May 1980, lot 78; With Richard Green, London, 1980; With Jacques van Rijn, Maastricht, 1981; English private collection.
LIT.: Advertised in *Tableau*, vol. 6, 1981, p. 697, reproduced; H-U. Beck, *Jan van Goyen 1696-1656*, 1987, vol. III, p. 197, no. 461A, reproduced.

Sotheby's London, 6 December 1995 (135**) GBP 41,100	US$	63,250

AN ESTUARY SCENE WITH TWO SMALL VESSELS oil on oak panel, 19 ¾ x 28¼in. (50 x 72cm.) This picture is traditionally described as signed and dated 1643 or 4
PROV.: J.B. Puthon, Vienna, 1840 (according to Hofstede de Groot); Josef Dintl, his sale, Vienna, (Miethke), 28 April 1873, lot 43, for 1,700 florins; Anton Fischer, Ritter von Ankern, his deceased sale, Vienna (Wawra), 16 March 1903, lot 41, K770 to Wawra; With D. Domter, Amsterdam, 1921; With G. Arnot, London, 1926; Kiefer-Hablitzel collection, by whom given in 1951 to the Kunstmuseum, Lucern, inv. no. 422x, 1983 catalogue pp. 32-3, reproduced in colour; De-accessioned after 1983; Acquired by the late owner from Klaus Edel.
LIT.: C. Hofstede de Groot, *A Catalogue Raisonné..*, vol. VIII, 1927, p. 233, no. 941; *Beeld. Kunst*, vol. VIII, 1921, no. 36, reproduced; H.-U. Beck, *Jan van Goyen 1596-1656*, vol. II, *Gemälde*, 1973, p. 414, no. 921; H.-U. Beck, *Jan van Goyen 1596-1656*, vol. II, *Ergänzungen*, 1987, p. 251, no. 921, reproduced.

Sotheby's London, 6 December 1995 (239**) GBP 49,900	US$	76,793

GRAAT Barend (1628-1709) Dutch
A FAMILY PORTRAIT OF A LADY AND A GENTLEMAN WITH THEIR SON PLAYING WITH A SPANIEL IN A SOUTHERN LANDSCAPE oil on canvas, 23¼ x 27 ¾in. (59.3 x 70.5cm.) sdll 'BG.f. 1677.'
PROV.: Max von Grunlius, bears his label on the reverse of the frame, with inventory number: V, 160.

Sotheby's London, 5 July 1995 (304**) GBP 25,300	US$	40,357

TWO SHEPHERDESSES PREPARING FOR A BATH oil on canvas, 18 x 16¼in. (45.7 x 41.3cm.)

Sotheby's New York, 16 May 1996 (172**) US$ 14,950	US$	14,950

GRACHT Gommaert van der (Lier ca. 1590-1639 Malines) Flemish
LANDSCAPE WITH TRAVELERS HALTED NEAR A BRIDGE oil on panel, 13½ x 21in. (34.5 x 53.5cm.) when it was sold in 1974 this picture was signed in monogram and dated 1624
PROV.: Anon. sale, Wichtracht, Auction Heininger, Autumn 1974.
EXH.: J. de Maer & M. Wabbes, *Illustrated Dictionary of 17th Century Flemish Painters*, 1994, pl. 496.

Sotheby's London, 6 December 1995 (230**) GBP 9,775	US$	15,043

GRAMATTE Walter (Berlin 1897-1929 Hamburg) German
SINNENDES MÄDCHEN II watercolour and ink on pencilsketch on heavy paper, 48.5 x 37cm. sdl 'Gramatté 1920' sd inscr. reverse 'Sinnendes Mädchen II. Walter Gramatté 20 Berlin. (1920)
EXH.: Winnipeg 1981. *Walter Gramatté. Bilder und aquarelle*.

Lempertz Cologne, 29 November 1995 (171**) DEM 15,000	US$	10,587

GRAMMATICA Antiveduto (Tuscany 1570 c.-1626 Rome) Italian
SANTA BARBARA oil on canvas, 106 x 86cm.
PROV.: General director Leo Edler von Mannheimer Wien; Dr. Rudolf Eugen Dreiling, Wien;

German private collection.
>   Dorotheum Vienna, 11 June 1996 (35**) ATS 120,000   US$ 11,138

GRAUBNER Gotthard (1930 b.) German
UNTITLED (KISSENBILD) acrylic on foam filled canvas, 88 x 60¼ x 6in. (203 x 153 x 15.2cm.) sd
'89/90' on the reverse
PROV.: Galerie Karsten Greve, Cologne/Paris.
>   Christie's London, 23 May 1996 (140**) GBP 41,100   US$ 62,235

GRAVES Abbott Fuller (1859-1936) American
POND LILIES oil on canvas, 30 x 40in. (76.2 x 101.6cm.) sll 'Abbott Graves'
PROV.: Acquired directly from the artist, 1915; By descent in the family to the present owner.
LIT.: *Boston Sunday Post*, 4 May 1913 (illustrated).
>   Christie's New York, 30 November 1995 (24**) US$ 200,500   US$ 200,500

GRAVES Morris (1910 b.) American
WOODPECKER gouache on paper, 27¼ x 20¼in. (69 x 51.5cm.) sbc 'MGraves'
PROV.: Frank Crowninshield, New York.
EXH.: Northampton, Massachusetts, Smith College Museum of Art, *Some Paintings from Alumnae
Collections*, June, 1948; Cedarburg, Wisconsin, Meta Mold Aluminum Company, *Contemporary Art
Collected by American Business*, Apnl, 1953, no. 17; New York, The Downtown Gallery, *Art Our
Children Live With*, December, 1957, no. 17; New York, M. Knoedler & Co., Inc., *The Colin
Collection*, April-May, 1960, no. 103, illus.
>   Christie's New York, 13 September 1995 (115*) US$ 9,200   US$ 9,200

**GRAZIANI Francesco, {called} Ciccio Napoletano (active Napels 17th Century, 2nd half of)
Italian**
BATTLE SCENE oil on canvas, 22 x 30cm.
>   Finearte Rome, 24 October 1995 (107*) ITL 12,075,000   US$ 7,523

GREBBER Pieter Fransz de (1600-1653) Dutch
THE FOUR EVANGELISTS oil on canvas, 52 x 74½in. (132.1 x 189.2cm.) (mid 1630's)
>   Sotheby's New York, 11 January 1996 (228**) US$ 24,150   US$ 24,150

GRECO Domenikos Theotokopoulos, {called} El (and school) (1541-1614) Spanish (Greek)
THE ESPOLIO oil on panel, 28 1/8 x 18in. (71.4 x 45.7cm.)
PROV.: Manfrin, Venice, until 1874; Carl Justi, Bonn (1874-1912); Ludwig Justi, Potsdam, until
circa 1930; Mrs. Hugo Moser, New York, before 1962; acquired by the present owners in the early
1970's.
EXH.: Boston, Museum of Fine Arts (lent by Mrs. Moser).
LIT.: *Catalogo dei quadri esistenti nella galleria Manfrin in Venezia, 1856, cat. no. 303 (as by
Barocci); Justi,* Miscellaneen, 1908, vol. II, p. 233 (reproduces the present lot mistakenly as the
prime version of the composition in the Toledo cathedral); M. B. Cossio, *El Greco*, 1908, pp. 36,
170-173, 188, illus., fig. 28 (as a replica); A.L. Mayer, *El Greco*, 1926, cat. no. 72a; Legendre and
Hartmann, *El Greco*, 1937, illus., p. 204 (as El Greco); J. Camon Aznar, *Domenico Greco*, 1950, cat.
nos. 147 and 149, illus., fig. 81 (as El Greco); M. B. Cossio, *Domencio Theotocopuli, El Greco*,
1955, p. 36; H. Wethey, *El Greco and His School*, 1962, vol. I, illus., fig. 58, vol. II, pp. 55-56, cat.
no. 82 (as a workshop replica); J. Gudiol, *The Complete Paintings of El Greco*, 1983, p. 343, cat. no.
54 (as El Greco, circa 1580-1585).
>   Sotheby's New York, 16 May 1996 (17**) US$ 508,500   US$ 508,500

GRECO Gennaro {called} Mascacotta (Naples 1663-1714) Italian
NYMPHS BATHING BENEATH THE RUINS OF A CLASSICAL PALACE oil on canvas, 51¼ x
36 ¾in. (130 x 93.4cm.)
>   Sotheby's London, 5 July 1995 (289**) GBP 12,650   US$ 20,179

A CAPRICCIO OF CLASSICAL RUINS OVERLOOKING A MEDITERRANEAN HARBOUR oil on canvas, 17 x 24in. (43.2 x 61cm.)

Christie's South Kensington, 7 December 1995 (151**) GBP 8,100	US$	12,465

ITALIANATE LANDSCAPES WITH RESTING BY CLASSICAL RUINS AND FOUNTAINS oil on canvas (a pair), 14¼ x 23 1/8in. (36.2 x 58 .7cm.)

Christie's London, 19 April 1996 (226**) GBP 27,600	US$	41,850

GREEN Charles (1840-1898) British
THE CONSULTATION oil on canvas, 29 x 39½in. (73.7 x 100.3cm.) slr 'C Green/1879' and inscr. 'The Consultation..Charlecote Hampstead Hill Gardens' on the stretcher
EXH.: London, The Royal Academy, 1879, no. 377; Liverpool, The Walker Art Gallery, *Grand Loan Exhibition of Pictures*, 1886, no. 14.
LIT.: *Art Journal*, 1879, p. 151.

Christie's New York, 14 February 1996 (2**) US$ 25,300	US$	25,300

GRENIER DE LA CROIX Charles François, {called} Lacroix de Marseille (Paris 1729 c.-1782 c. Berlin) French
SUNRISE: SAILORS BEARING AMMUNITION ONTO A BOAT, IN THE FOREGROUND TWO ORIENTAL MERCHANTS / SUNSET: FISHERMEN TAKING IN THE NETS, A FORTIFIED TOWER IN THE FOREGROUND oil on copper (a pair), 24 x 32.8cm. / 23.5 x 32.2cm. the former sd 'De/Lacr/oix/Rom/1761' the latter sd 'La/Croi/Rom/1760'
EXH.: Paris, Galerie Charpentier, *Marines*, 1944, nos. 91-92.

Christie's Monaco, 14 June 1996 (39**) FRF 527,700	US$	101,898

GREUZE Jean-Baptiste (Tournus 1725-1805 Paris) French
PORTRAIT DE JEUNE FEMME AU NOEUD DE SATIN BLANC oil on canvas (an oval), 63.5 x 53cm.
PROV.: Collection Vicomte de Curel before 1918; His sale, paris, Galerie Georges Petit (Maîtres Lair-Dubreuil) 25 November 1918, no. 40; Collection Madame André Saint before 1935; His Sale, Paris, Galerie Charpentier, 20 May 1935, no. 38, (illustrated pl. IV).

Étude Tajan Paris, 25 June 1996 (61**) FRF 370,000	US$	71,447

STUDY OF THE HEAD OF A DOG black and red chalk with beige wash, 26.9 x 32.5cm.

Sotheby's London, 3 July 1995 (132**) GBP 18,400	US$	29,351

LE DEPART POUR LA CHASSE black chalk and grey wash, 27 x 31.4cm. (ca. 1800)

Sotheby's London, 3 July 1995 (201**) GBP 43,300	US$	69,070

GREVENBROECK Alessandro (1717 c.-1724 act.) Italian
MEDITERRANEAN HARBOUR SCENES oil on canvas (a pair), each: 37 ¾ x 51in. (95.5 x 129.5cm.)

Sotheby's London, 5 July 1995 (175**) GBP 20,700	US$	33,020

MEDITERRANEAN HARBOUR SCENES oil on canvas (a pair), each: 37 ¾ x 51in. (95.5 x 129.5cm.)

Sotheby's London, 5 July 1995 (176**) GBP 14,950	US$	23,848

GREVENBROECK Charles-Léopold (1730 after -1759 active) Dutch
A CAPRICCIO VIEW OF A MEDITERRANEAN HARBOUR oil on copper, 11 x 16¼in. (28 x41.1cm.)

Sotheby's London, 6 December 1995 (137**) GBP 16,100	US$	24,777

GREVENBROECK Orazio (1670 - 1730 active Paris) Dutch
MEDITERRANEAN HARBOUR VIEWS oil on panel (a pair), each: 8¼ x 32½in. (21.4 x 87.6cm.)

Sotheby's London, 17 April 1996 (171**) GBP 13,800	US$	20,925

GRIFFIER Jan the Elder (Amsterdam 1645-1718 London) Dutch
TWO ITALIANATE LANDSCAPES WITH RUINS AND FIGURES (WITH ANTIPODE) oil on
canvas, both 76 x 63cm. slc 'John Griffier' / sll 'GRIFF.'
Dorotheum Vienna, 6 March 1996 (40**) ATS 380,000   US$ 36,553

AN EXTENSIVE MOSAN CAPRICCIO RIVER LANDSCAPE, WITH MOORED BOATS AND
GROUPS OF FIGURES oil on copper, 20¼ x 23¼in. (51.2 x 58.8cm.) slr 'J. GRiFFieR' (ca. 1700)
PROV.: Anon. sale, Lempertz Cologne, 1-2 Febr. 1940, lot 39, where bought by the father of the
present owner.
Sotheby's London, 6 December 1995 (3**) GBP 95,000   US$ 146,199

GRIGORIEV Boris (Moscow 1886-1939 Paris) Russian
PORTRAIT EINER DAME oil on canvas, 59.5 x 59.5cm. s
Hauswedell & Nolte Cologne, 5/6 June 1996 (261*) DEM 36,000   US$ 23,390

GRIMMER Jacob (Antwerp 1525 c.-1590 Antwerp) Flemish
SKATERS ON A FROZEN RIVER BY A VILLAGE / A RIVER LANDSCAPE WITH HUNTERS
oil on panel (a pair), each: 10¼ x 15 ¾in. (26.1 x 40.4cm.)
PROV.: With Edward Speelman, London, circa 1970; private Collection, Brussels; Anon. sale
Sotheby's London, 8 April 1981 (GBP 28,000), where bought by the present owner.
LIT.: R. de Bertier de Sauvigny, *Jacob et Abel Grimmer*, 1991, pp. 106-7, no. 8 (illustrated pp. 111
and 171, colour pl. 38, fig. 54).
Sotheby's London, 17 April 1996 (659**) GBP 49,900   US$ 75,663

GRIMOU Alexis (Romont 1680-1733 or 1740 Paris) French
PORTRAIT D'HOMME AU BONNET oil on canvas, 113.5 x 86cm.
Étude Tajan Paris, 28 June 1996 (95*) FRF 40,000   US$ 7,724

GRIMSHAW John Atkinson (1836-1893) British
THE CUSTOM HOUSE, LIVERPOOL oil on canvas, 12 x 18in. (.30.5 x 45.7cm.) sll 'Atkinson
Grimshaw'; inscr. and s 'Liverpool/Custom House/Atkinson Grimshaw' on the reverse
PROV.: Thought to have been purchased from the Artist by the grandfather of the present owner.
Christie's South Kensington, 6 June 1996 (176***) GBP 32,200   US$ 49653

GREENOCK HARBOUR oil on canvas laid down on board, 12 x 18in. (30.5 x 46cm.) sd 'Atkinson
Grimshaw S93/+'
Christie's London, 6 November 1995 (136**) GBP 28,750   US$ 44,971

ENDYMION ON MOUNT LATMOS oil on canvas, 32½ x 48in. (82.5 x 122cm.) sdll 'Atkinson
Grimshaw/1/8/9/+'; inscr. and d 'Painted by Atkinson Grimshaw/Knostrop Old Hall/Leeds/Atkinson
Grimshaw/February 1879/80/Endymminis somnum dormira'
PROV.: Christie's London, 26 march 1982, lot 93.
EXH.: London, Royal Academy. 1880, no. 325; Agnew, *Springs Exhibition*.
LIT.: D. Bromfield, *The Art of Atkinson Grimshaw*, exhibition catalogue, Leeds, Southampton,
Liverpool, 1979-80, pp. 18, 19, 39 & 43; Philip Hook and Mark Poltimore, *Popular 19th Century
Painting: A Dictionary of European Genre Painters*, Antique Collector's Club, Woodbridge, 1986,
illus. p. 344; A. Robertson, *Atkinson Grimshaw*, Phaidon, Oxford, 1988, p. 59.
Sotheby's London, 17 April 1996 (720**) GBP 67,500   US$ 102,350

AN ODE TO SUMMER oil on board, 11 ¾ x 25¼in. (30 x 64.5cm.) sdlr 'Atkinson Grimshaw 1879+'
PROV.: Sotheby's London, 10 November 1981, lot 54.
LIT.: A. Robertson, *Atkinson Grimshaw*, Phaidon, Oxford, 1988, p. 58.
Sotheby's London, 17 April 1996 (722**) GBP 20,700   US$ 31,387

GREENOCK HARBOUR AT NIGHT oil on canvas, 12 x 18in. (30.5 x 45.7cm.) sd 'John Atkinson
Grimshaw 93'

Christie's London, 29 March 1996 (204**) GBP 29,900	US$	45,663

GLASGOW oil on canvas, 12 x 18in. (30.4 x 45.8cm.) s 'Atkinson Grimshaw' and bears inscr.
'Glasgow/Atkinson Grimshaw' on the relining

Christie's South Kensington, 7 March 1996 (204**) GBP 48,000	US$	73,305

GRIS Juan (José Victoriano Gonzales) (1887-1927) Spanish
LE MOULIN A CAFE oil on canvas, 23 5/8 x 31 7/8in. 60 x 81cm. sd 4-20
PROV.: Galerie L'Effort Moderne (Leonce Rosenberg), Paris; Raoul La Roche, Paris; Jos. Hessel,
Paris; Galerie Pierre, Paris;Andre Lefèvre, Paris (vente: Paris, Palais Galliéra, 25th November 1965,
lot 41); Pierre Bérès, Paris; Mme Maus, Geneva.
EXH.: London, Royal Academy of Arts, *L'Ecole de Paris*, 1951, no. 11; Paris, Galerie Charpentier,
Le pain et le vin, 1954, no. 88; Paris, Musée National d'Art Moderne, *Collection André Lefevre*,
1964, no. 104;
Paris, Orangerie des Tuileries, *Chefs-d'Oeuvres des Collections Suisses de Manet à Picasso*, 1967,
no. 231, illustrated in the catalogue.
LIT.: *Cahiers d 'art*, Paris, 1933, nos. 5-6, illustrated; Daniel-Henry Kahnweiler, *Juan Gris, his Life
and Work*, London, 1947, pl. 61, illustrated; Douglas Cooper,*Juan Gris*, Berggruen éditeur, Paris,
1977, vol. II, p. 132, no. 553, illustrated.

Sotheby's London, 24 June 1996 (53**) GBP 469,000	US$	723,207

LE JACQUET (BACKGAMMON) oil on canvas, 31½ x 21in. (80 x 53.5cm.) (Dec. 1913-Jan. 1914)
PROV.: Galerie Kahnweiler, Paris; Second Sale, Hotel Drouot, Paris, Nov. 17-18, 1921, lot 145;
Galerie Simon, Paris; Galerie Louise Leiris, Paris; Acquired by Mr. Joseph H. Hazen circa 1955.
EXH.: Paris, Musée National d'art Moderne, *Le Cubisme: 1907*, 1914,Jan.-April, 1953, no. 126; New
York, Metropolitan Museum of Art, *Modern European Paintings from New York Private Collections*,
June-Sept., 1956; New York, Metropolitan Museum of Art, *Impressionist and Modern Paintings
from Private Collections*, July-Sept., 1957 Jerusalem, Israel Museum, *Paintings from the Collection
of Joseph H. Hazen*, summer, 1966, no. 10 (illustrated); The exhibition traveled to Cambridge,
Massachusetts, Fogg Art Museum, Oct.-Dec., 1966; Los Angeles, University of California, The Art
Galleries, Jan.-Feb., 1967; Berkeley, University of California, Art Museum, Feb.-March, 1967;
Houston, Museum of Fine Arts, April-May, 1967, and Honolulu, Academy of Arts, June-Aug., 1967.
LIT.: D.-H. Kahnweiler, *Juan Gris: His Life and Work*, Paris, 1946, p. 256 (illustrated); J. Lassaigne,
Spanish Painting from Velasquez to Picasso, Geneva, 1952, p. 126 (illustrated in colour); J.A. Gaya-
Nuno, *Juan Gris*, London, 1975, p. 216, no. 289 (illustrated); D. Cooper, *Juan Gris, Catalogue
raisonné de l'oeuvre peint*, Paris, 1977, vol. I, p. 120, no. 71 (illustrated, p. 121).

Christie's New York, 30 April 1996 (10***) US$ 3,412,500	US$	3,412,500

LE VIOLON gouache and pencil on board, 12 1/8 x 10¼in (30.5 x 26cm.) image, 18¼ x 11 ¾in.
(46.3 x 29.8cm) sheet (ca 1915-16)
PROV.: The Artist's Estate, Josette Gris and George Gonzalez Gris, until 1955; Saidenberg Gallery,
New York, 1956; Mr and Mrs Isadore Levin, Detroit, c. 1956-85, by whom purchased from the
above; Stephen Mazoh and Co., New York; Donald Morris Gallery, Inc., Birmingham, Michigan.
EXH.: New York, Saidenberg Gallery, *Gris-Laurens*, April-May 1956; New York, Museum of
Modern Art, *Juan Gris*, April-June 1958, p. 56 (illustrated); This exhibition later travelled to
Minneapolis, Minneapolis Institute of Arts,June-July 1958; San Francisco, San Francisco Museum of
Art, Aug.-Sept.1958; Los Angeles, Los Angeles County Museum of Art, Sept.-Oct. 1958.
LIT.: P. Reverdy, *Au Soleil du Plafond*, Paris, 1955; J. Thrall Soby, *Juan Gris*, Museum of Modern
Art, New York, 1958 (illustrated p. 56); G. Tinterow, *Juan Gris*, Ministerie de Cultura y Banco de
Bilbao, 1985, p. 341 (illustrated in colour).

Christie's London, 28 November 1995 (25**) GBP 265,500	US$	415,298

NATURE MORTE AVEC GUITARE black Conté crayon heightened with white gouache on paper,
7 ½ x 11 ¼in. (19 x 28.6cm.) ll 'Juan Gris' (1923-1924)
PROV.: Marie Harriman Gallery, New York; Anon. sale, Sotheby's, London, Dec. 7, 1966, lot 115;
Anon. sale, Sotheby's, New York, Nov. 19, 1986, lot 66 (acquired by the present owner).

EXH.: Spain, Centro Cultural Consolidado, *Juan Gris*, Aug.-Sept., 1992.
> Christie's New York, 8 November 1995 (180**) US$ 34,500   US$ 34,500

GROEBER Hermann (1865-1935) German
A MOTHER WITH HER CHILD oil on canvas, 34 3/8 x 28in. (87.3 x 71.1cm.) sll 'H. Groeber'
> Christie's East, 13 February 1996 (122**) US$ 14,950   US$ 14,950

GROMAIRE Marcel (1892-1971) French
VILLAGE BRUN ET BLEU oil on panel, 12 ¾ x 16 1/8in. (32.4 x 41cm.) sdlr 'Gromaire 1934'; sd
and s with ini. on the reverse 'GROMAIRE 1934 VILLAGE BRUN ET BLEU mg'
LIT.: F. Chibret-Plaussu and F. Gromaire, *Marcel Gromaire: la vie et l'oeuvre: catalogue raisonné
des peintures*, Paris, 1993, p. 168, no. 427 (illustrated).
> Christie's East, 30 April 1996 (183*) US$ 9,200   US$ 9,200

GROSZ George (Berlin 1893-1959 Berlin) American (German)
SITTING NUDE gouache on paper, 58.3 x 39.5cm. sll (stamped signature) 'Grosz' (executed *circa*
1942)
PROV.: Estate of the artist, no. 1-A12-7.
> Christie's Amsterdam, 5 June 1996 (246**) NLG 17,250   US$ 10,079

STUDY FOR PAINTING BALLROOM pen and black ink on paper, 54.5 x 42.5cm. sdlr 'Grosz '26'
PROV.: Richard A. Cohn, new York.
> Christie's Amsterdam, 5 June 1996 (247**) NLG 20,700   US$ 12,095

THE VOICE OF THE CITY watercolour on paper, 62.5 x 42.5cm. with signaturestamp (1933/34)
> Hauswedell & Nolte Cologne, 5/06 June 1996 (268*) DEM 15,000   US$ 9,746

KRIEGSZENE coloured wax crayons, pen and black ink on paper mounted, 9 7/8 x 7 7/8in. (25.2 x
20cm.) sdll 'Grosz 15'
PROV.: B.C.Holland Gallery, Chicago (acquired by Dr.Eugene A.Solow, 1966).
EXH.: Chicago, The Art Institute, *Chicago Collects: Selections from the Collection of Dr.Eugene
A.Solow*, May-Aug., 1988, no.20.
> Christie's New York, 1 May 1996 (279**) US$ 21,850   US$ 21,850

STRASSEN SZENE gouache, watercolour and pen and ink, 22 ¾ x 17¼in. (58 x 44cm.) s inscr. and
numbered 'No. 11' on the reverse, stamped with the 'nachlass mark' (ca. 1929-30)
PROV.: Sale, New York, Christie's 5 November 1981, lot 410 (purchased by the present owner).
> Sotheby's London, 20 March 1996 (79**) GBP 17,250   US$ 26,344

NUDE oil on board, 57 x 45.5cm. slr 'Grosz' stamped with the 'Grosz nachlass' stamp
> Christie's Milan, 20 November 1995 (148**) ITL 17,678,000   US$ 11,097

NUDE oil on board, 40 x 51cm. s; stamped with the *Geoge Grosz Nachlass* mark and numbered 1
A6 4 on the reverse (1942)
EXH.: Saint-Vincent, Casino de la Vallee, *George Grosz, opere inedite*, 1982, no. 59 (ill. in colour).
LIT.: Giorgui Mondadori, 'Grosz, I nudi di New York' in *Arte*, no. 135, 1983, pp. 60-61 (ill. in
colour).
> Sotheby's Amsterdam, 7 December 1995 (198**) NLG 47,200   US$ 29,248

GRUBACS Carlo (1829-1919) German
FESTA DI CARNEVALE NELLA PIAZZETTA SAN MARCO oil on canvas, 91 x 113cm.
> Finearte Rome, 22 November 1995 (112**) ITL 27,025,000   US$ 16,965

GRUBER Francis (1912-1948) French
LANDSCAPE oil on canvas, 55 x 46cm. sll 'F. Gruber' dur '1943'
> Étude Tajan Paris, 1 February 1996 (143) FRF 30,000   US$ 6,139

GRÜNEWALD Isaac (1889-1946) Swedish
FRÅN STADSGÅRDEN oil on canvas, ,100 x 81cm. slr 'Isaac Grünewald' (ca. 1915)
PROV.: Viggo Madsen.
LIT.: J.P. Hodin, *Isaac Grünewald*, catalogus no. 102.
Bukowskis Stockholm, 24-25 April 1996 (32**) SEK 230,000   US$ 34,845

STADSGÅRDEN OCH KATARINAVÄGEN oil on panel, 62 x 49.5cm. slr Grünewald'
Bukowskis Stockholm, 24-25 April 1996 (35**) SEK 125,000   US$ 18,937

BLOMMORNA VATTNAS oil on canvas, 108 x 198cm. slr 'Grünewald'
Bukowskis Stockholm, 26-27 October 1995 (38**) SEK 350,000   US$ 51,258

GRÜTZNER Eduard von (1846-1925) German
VOR DER VESPER oil on canvas, 13½ x 10¼in. (34.2 x 26cm.) sd & inscr.'E.Grützner./1909'
PROV.: With Helbing, Munich, March 1911.
LIT.: L. Balogh, *Eduard von Grützner 1846-1925*, Mainburg, 1991, p. 194, no. 283 (illus.).
Christie's London, 11 October 1995 (59**) GBP 11,270   US$ 17,787

VESPERZEIT oil on canvas, 19 x 14¼in. (48.2 x 36.2cm.) sd 'Ed. Grützner/1900'
Christie's London, 11 October 1995 (60**) GBP 9,200   US$ 14,520

FALSTAFF IN SEINER KNEIPE oil on canvas, 66 x 53cm. sdll 'Eduard Grützner/1868'
EXH.: München, Kunst Vereinz, 1868; Vienna, *Dritten algemeinen Kunst Ausstellung*, 1868.
LIT.: Friedrich von Boetticher, *Malerwerke des neunzehnten Jahrhunders*, Frankfurt 1969, Vol. I, p. 446, no. 2.
Christie's Amsterdam, 26 October 1995 (398**) NLG 69,000   US$ 43,506

GRUYTER Willem Jr. (1817-1880) Dutch
SHIPPING ON THE IJ, AMSTERDAM oil on panel, 22 x 34cm. slr with ini. 'W.G.jr.'
PROV.: Kunsthandel P.A. Scheen, The Hague, 1956.
LIT.: Pieter A. Scheen, *lexicon Nederlandse Beeldende Kunstenaars*, The Hague 1969, Vol.I, illus.no. 349.
Christie's Amsterdam, 26 October 1995 (186*) NLG 16,100   US$ 10,151

GRYFF Adriaen de (Antwerp 1670-1715 Brussels) Flemish
A DOG AND A CAT QUARRELING ABOUT A BONED OX, A BOYING RUSHING UP TRYING TO STOP THEM, ON THE RIGHT A WOMAN FEEDING A DONKEY oil on canvas, 162 x 227cm. sll on the edge 'JA (linked)'
PROV.: Collection from Count Attems, Graz; Private collection, Graz; Private collection, Vienna.
Dorotheum Vienna, 11 June 1996 (204**) ATS 160,000   US$ 14,851

GUARDI Francesco (1712-1793) Italian
A CAPRICCIO OF A RUINED ARCH WITH CORINTHIAN CORINTIAN COLUMNS AND FIGURES ADMIRING THE VENETIAN LAGOON oil on panel, 7 5/8 x 5 7/8in. (19.5 x 14.8cm.) (1785)
PROV.: Anon. sale, Sotheby's 1 Nov.1978, lot 61 (with another: GBP 36,000).
Christie's London, 8 December 1995 (77**) GBP 27,600   US$ 42,475

A CAPRICCIO OF FIGURES BENEATH AN ARCH AND BY THE STEPS OF A CANAL pen and brown ink with wash, 18.3 x 13cm.
PROV.: Fischer, Lucerne, 2 July 1973, lot 1294.
Phillips London, 17 April 1996 (105**) GBP 8,500   US$ 12,889

A VIEW IN THE VENETIAN LAGOON oil on canvas, 12 ¾ x 21in. (32.8 x 53.6cm.) (1760's)
PROV.: Dr.James Simon, Berlin; With Julius Bohler, Munich; Baron Heinrich Thyssen-Bornemisza, by 1930.

EXH.: Munich 1930, no. 140; Dusseldorf 1970-1, no. 20; Dusseldorf, Kunstmuseum, *Landschaften aus vier Jahrhunderten*, 1973, no. 25; Lausanne etc., 1986-7, no. 57.
LIT.: R. Heinemann 1937, vol. I, no. 174; A. Morassi, 'Circa gli esordi del vedutismo di Francesco Guardi con qualche cenno sul Marieschi', in *Studies in art history dedicated to William E. Suida*, 1959, p. 348, fig. 15, as Francesco Guardi; H. Voss, in *Pantheon*, March - April 1966, p. 103, fig. 5, as Francesco Tironi; A. Morassi, *Guardi*, 1973, vol. I, pp. 224, 432, no. 657, vol. II, fig. 612, as 'Squisita opera giovanile, di timbro azzurro-argenteo e di alto afflato poetico'; L.R. Bortolatto, *L'opera completa di Francesco Guardi*, 1974, pp. 119, 121, no. 533, reproduced.

       Sotheby's London, 6 December 1995 (84**) GBP 155,500   US$ 239,304

LANDSCAPE CAPRICCIO WITH A PALM TREE AND A HORSEMAN AND CHAPEL ON THE DISTANCE AND A LANDSCAPE CAPRICCIO WITH A FISHERMAN oil on canvas (a pair), each: 14 x 10in. (35.6 x 25.4cm.)
PROV.: Fanto collection, ca. 1932; Nagler collection, Vienna; Acquired before 1936 by Dr. Gustav Arens, father of Ann Unger.
LIT.: Antonio Morassi, *Guardi: I dipinti*, 1973, vol. I, p. 476, cat. 896 (illustrated vol. II, fig. 806, (Landscape Capriccio with a Palm Tree only)); Luigina Rossi Bortolatto, *L'Opera Completa di Francesco Guardi*, 1975, p. 111, cat. 373 (illustrated p. 110 (Landscape Capriccio with a Palm Tree only)); Antonio Morassi, *Guardi: I Dipinti*, 1984, vol. I, p. 4756, cat. 896 (illustrated vol. II, fig. 806 (Landscape Capriccio with a Palm Tree only)).

       Sotheby's New York, 6 October 1996 (185**) US$ 156,500   US$ 156,500

GUARDI Giacomo (Venice 1764-1835) Italian
THE RIVA DEGLI SCHIAVONI WITH THE PIETA CHURCH oil on, 28 x 47cm.
PROV.: International private collection.

       Dorotheum Vienna, 6 March 1996 (41**) ATS 800,000   US$ 76,953

GUARDI Giovanni Antonio (1698 (1699)-1760) Italian
A SULTAN RECEIVING TRIBUTE; AND TURKS AT PRAYER IN A MOSQUE oil on canvas (a pair), 18 x 24 ¾ (45.8 x 62.8cm.) (1742-43)
PROV.: Two of the 43 quadri Turchi painted in 1742-3 for Field Marshal CountJohann Matthias von der Schulenburg (1661-1747), Palazzo Loredan a San Trovaso, Venice; Bequeathed to his nephew Christian Gunther von der Schulenburg, Berlin; Anon. sale, Christie's, 2 Dec. 1977, lot 11 (the first only); Anon. sale, Christie's, 7 July 1978, lot 139 (GBP 15,000).
LIT.: *Inventario Generale della Galleria di S.E. Maresciallo Co: di Schulemburg....*, Venice, 30 June 1741, addendum: *Tableaux achétés après le sudit Cattalogue*, 1746 (Hannover, Niedersächsisches Staatsarchiv, Depositum 82, Abt. 111, no. 37), 'Guardi - 43 Tabl rappt: les Coutumes des Turcs' (A. Binion, La Galleria scomparsa del maresciallo von der Schulenburg, Milan,1990, p. 245); *Quadri e Ritratti Essistenti nelle differenti Camere del Palazzo del Defonto Eccellentissimo Maresciallo*, Venice, August 1747 (Hannover, Niedersächsisches Staatsarchiv, Depositum 82, Abt. 111, no. 33), 'Guardi - Quaranta tre quadri rapresentano costumi dei Turchi' (in the 'Camera del Sigr Ten.t Col.o Arcoleo' in Palazzo Loredan a San Trovaso, see Binion, op. cit., p. 259); D. Succi, Tre vedute inedite di Francesco Guardi e due nuove 'sceneturche', in the catalogue of the exhibition, *Guardi. Metamorfosi dell'immagine, Castello di Gorizia*,June-Sept. 1987, pp. 112-13, fig. 101 (the first only); D. Succi, Vedute e capricci veneziani del settecento nella galleria di Johann Matthias von der Schulenburg, in the catalogue of the exhibition, Capricci Veneziani del Settecento, Castello di Gorizia, June-Oct. 1988, pp. 85 and 88, fig. 3; M. Beal, An Ambassador's Reception at the Sublime Porte; *Rediscovered Paintings by Antonio Guardi and his Studio*, Apollo, CXXVII, no. 313, March 1988, pp. 176 and 179, note 15, fig. 5 (the first only); F. Pedrocco and F. Montecuccoli degli Erri, *Antonio Guardi*, Milan, 1992, pp. 131-2, no. 78, and p. 214, fig. 96 (the first only); A. Bettagno in the catalogue of the exhibition, *Guardi. Quadriturcheschi, Galleria di Palazzo Cini*, Venice, 28 Aug.-21 Nov. 1993, pp. 100-3, nos. 36-7, both illustrated (as whereabouts unknown).

       Christie's London, 8 December 1995 (81**) GBP 210,500   US$ 323,946

GUARDI Nicolo' (Venice 1715-1786 Venice) Italian
VENICE, RIALTO BRIDGE FROM THE SOUTH oil on canvas, 58 x 81.5cm.
      Finearte Milan, 3 April 1996 (107**) ITL 138,000,000   US$ 88,179

GUCCIONE Piero (Scicli 1935 b.-l) Italian
GLI AEREI PASSANO IN ALTO oil on canvas, 70 x 50cm. slr 'Guccione 66.' (1966)
      Finearte Rome, 2 April 1996 (162**) ITL 20,700,000   US$ 13,227

GUDE Hans Fredrik (1825-1903) Norwegian
AFTER THE STORM oil on canvas, 34 x 66in. (86.5 x 167cm.) sdlr '1894'
      Sotheby's London, 13 March 1996 (92**) GBP 24,725   US$ 37,760

SKEPP I STILTJE oil on canvas, 79 x 108cm. sdlr 'HF Gude 1855'
      Bukowskis Stockholm, 29-31 May 1996 (219**) SEK 190,000   US$ 27,944

GUDIN Jean Antoine Théodore (1802-1880) French
A NAVAL ENGAGEMENT WITH GREEK SAILORS oil on canvas, 31½ x 43in. (80 x 109.2cm.) s
'T.Gudin'
      Christie's South Kensington, 14 March 1996 (41**) GBP 12,650   US$ 19,319

GUÉRARD-GONZALES Jeanne (1868-1908) French
BOUQUET DE ROSES DE JUIN oil on canvas, 24 x 19 7/8in. (61 x 50.5cm.) slr 'Jeanne Gonzales'
PROV.: Jean-Raymond Guerard, Paris.
EXH.: Paris, *Salon*, 1878, no. 1048; Tokyo, Isetan Art Museum and travelling, *Les Femmes Impressionnistes: Morisot, Cassatt, Gonzales*, 1995, no. 96,
illustrated in colour in the catalogue.
LIT.: Marie-Caroline Sainsaulieu and Jacques de Mons, *Eva Gonzales, 1849-1885, Étude critique et catalogue raisonné*, Paris, 1990, p. 35, illustrated in colour.
      Sotheby's London, 20 March 1996 (15**) GBP 13,800   US$ 21,075

GUERRIERI Giovanni Francesco (1589-1657) Italian
SUSANNA AND THE ELDER oil on canvas, 47¼ x 70in. (120 x 177.8cm.)
      Sotheby's New York, 16 May 1996 (42**) US$ 46,000   US$ 46,000

GUERY Armand (1850-1912) French
COUCHER DE SOLEIL AU CHAMPAGNE oil on panel, 25¼ x 36¼in. (64.1 x 92.1cm.) sdll
'Armand Gúery-1902-'
      Christie's New York, 22 May 1996 (184**) US$ 12,650   US$ 12,650

GUIDI Virgilio (1892-1984) Italian
FIGURE NELLO SPAZIO oil on canvas, 90 x 120cm. slr 'Guidi' sd and titled on the reverse (1956)
EXH.: *XXVII Premio Internazionale F.P. Michetti*, Francavilla al Mare, July-August 1963; Parco del Valentino, *Guidi*, Turin, 23 Oct.-23 Nov. 1965.
LIT.: S. Branzi, *Virgilio Guidi*, ed. Bucciarelli, Bologna 1965, no.75.
      Finearte Milan, 19 March 1996 (29**) ITL 21,850,000   US$ 13,980

FIGURA DI DONNA oil on canvas, 92 x 72cm. sd on the reverse (1952)
      Finearte Milan, 26 October 1995 (191**) ITL 39,100,000   US$ 24,361

GUIETTE René (1893-1976) Belgian
LA BARQUE oil on canvas, 81 x 100cm slr 'René Guiette' (ca. 1935)
PROV.: E.L.T. Mesens and by descent to the present owner.
LIT.: M. de Kerckhove D`Ousselghem, *René Guiette*, Antwerp 1991, no. 225 (ill. in colour p. 61).
      Christie's Amsterdam, 5 June 1996 (296**) NLG 17,250   US$ 10,079

PAYSAGE oil and mixed media on canvas, 114 x 146cm. slr 'René Guiette' (ca. 1956)

LIT.: Manuela de Kerckhove d'Ousselghem, *René Guiette*, Antwerp 1991, no. 879.
    Christie's Amsterdam, 5 June 1996 (307**) NLG 8,050   US$ 4,703

OU, 7.8-1958 oil on canvas, 80 x 250cm. slr 'Renné Guiette' (ca. 1955)
EXH.: Paris, Galerie Internationale d'Art Contemporaine, *René Guiette*, 24 October -24 November
1958; Paris, Musée d'Art Moderne de la Ville de Paris, *XVe Salon de Mai*, 9; May- 31 May 1965, no.
65; Beirut, Centrum voor Hedendaagse Kunst, *René Guiette*, May 1961,; no. 125.
LIT.: Manuela de Kerckhove d'Ousselghem, *René Guiette*, Antwerp 1991, no. 1088.
    Christie's Amsterdam, 5 June 1996 (311**) NLG 11,500   US$ 6,719

GUIGOU Paul Camille (1834-1871) French
A HUNTER IN A LANDSCAPE oil on canvas, 8½ x 10 7/8in. (21.6 x 27.6cm.) sdll 'Paul Guigou'
    Christie's New York, 2 November 1995 (117**) US$ 32,200   US$ 32,200

GUILLAUMIN Jean Baptiste Armand (Paris 1841-1927 Orly, Val-de-Marne) French
CROZANR, MATINÉE DE NOVEMBRE oil on canvas, 26 x 36 5/8in. (66 x 93cm.) slr
'Guillaumin'; titled and d on the stretcher 'Crozanr.1897-Matinée de Novembre'
PROV.: Wally Findlay Galleries, New York; Alexander Kahn Fine Arts Ltd., New York; Anon. sale,
Chistie's New York, 13 May 1987, lot 272.
LIT.: G. Serret and D. Fabiani, *Armand Guillaumin, Catalogue raisonné de l'oeuvre peint*, Paris
1971, no. 378 (illustrated).
    Christie's New York, 1 May 1996 (136**) US$ 40,250   US$ 40,250

LES FORGES A IVRY oil on canvas, 23½ x 39½in. (59.7 x 100.3cm.) sll, also dll '73' possibly in
another hand
PROV.: Galerie Durand-Ruel, Paris; Edgardo Acosta, Beverly Hills; Acquired from the above by the
present owner.
LIT.: Georges Serret and Dominique Fabiani, *Armand Guillaumin, Catalogue raisonné de l'Oeuvre
Peint*, Paris, 1971, no. 17 (illustrated).
    Sotheby's New York, 2 May 1996 (120**) US$ 68,500   US$ 68,500

CROZANT, LE PUY BARRIOU oil on canvas, 19 ¾ x 28 ¾in. (50 x 73cm.) sll 'Guillaumin' (1898)
PROV.: Galerie J. Le Chapelin, Paris; Michael David, london.
LIT.: To be included in the forthcoming *Guillaumin catalogue Raisonné* currently being prepared by
Georges Serret and Dominique Fabiani.
    Christie's London, 26 June 1996 (134**) GBP 16,100   US$ 24,827

PAYSAGE DU MIDI oil on canvas, 60 x 73cm. sll 'Guillaumin' (1910)
PROV.: Former collection E. Blot, Paris.
LIT.: G. Serret and D. Fabiani, *Armand Guillaumin 1841-1927, catalogue raisonné de l'oeuvre peint*,
édition Mayer, Paris, no. 755; Will be included in the *catalogue raisonné Armand Guillaumin*,
currently being prepared by Miss Jacqueline Derbanne and Mr. André Pacitti.
    Étude Tajan Paris, 27 October 1995 (26**) FRF 180,000   US$ 36,409

BORDS DE L'ISERE A PONTCHARRA oil on canvas, 24 x 28 ¾in. (61 x 73cm.) slr 'Bords de Isère
à Pontcharra sept 1091'
LIT.: G. Serret and d. Fabiani, *Armand Guillaumin, Catalogue raisonné de l'oeuvre peint*, Paris1971,
no. 548 (illustrated).
    Christie's New York, 8 November 1995 (104**) US$ 32,200   US$ 32,200

PAYSAGE A PONTGIBAUD oil on canvas, 25 1/8 x 32in. (63.8 x 81.3cm.) sll 'Guillaumin'; titled
on the stretcher 'Pontgibaud' (ca. 1893)
PROV.: Lucien Chaffois, Geneva; Hammer Galleries, New York; Bronson-Rollins & Associates
Inc., Los Angeles (acquired by the present owner, 1988).
EXH.: Paris, Galerie Serret-Fauveau, *Exposition A. Guillaumin*, May-June, 1957, no. 17 (titled
Auvergne Pontgibaud; incorrectly dated 1895).

LIT.: G. Serret and D. Fabiani, *Armand Guillaumin, Catalogue raisonné de l'oeuvre peint*, Paris, 1971, no. 254 (illustrated).
    Christie's New York, 8 November 1995 (121**) US$ 46,000   US$ 46,000

GUSTON Philip (1913-1980) Canadian
PINK LIGHT gouache on paper, 30 1/8 x 40in. (76.5 x 101.6cm.) slr 'Philip Guston' s again, titled and d 'PHILIP GUSTON'PINK LIGHT' 1963' on the reverse
PROV.: Acquired directly from the artist; Gertrude Kasle, Detroit.
EXH.: Rochester, Michigan, Oakland University, Meadow Brook Art Gallery, *Creative Encouters-Gertrude Kasle Collection of Contemporary Art*, Oct.-Nov. 1976, no.10.
    Christie's New York, 22 February 1996 (32**) US$ 36,800   US$ 36,800

GUTMAN Nachum (1898-1980) Israelian
YOUNG GIRL WITH FIGS oil on canvas, 25 3/8 x 19½in. (64.5 x 49.5cm.) sdkk 'N. Gutman 36'; s again in Hebrew, s again on the stretcher
PROV.: The Artist's Estate.
EXH.: Venice, *XXIV Expositione Internazionale D'Arte*, Palestine Pavillion, 1948, no. 8; Jerusalem, Grapics Gallery, *A Tribute to Nachum Gutman*, 1988.
LIT.: G. Ofrat, *On the Ground Early Eretz Israeli Art*, vol. II, Israel, 1993, pp. 683-703.
    Christie's Tel Aviv, 12 October 1995 (66**) US$ 57,500   US$ 57,500

FISHERMEN oil on paper laid down on canvas, 16 3/8 x 22½in. (41.5 x 57cm.) sll in Hebrew and d '58'
    Christie's Tel Aviv, 14 April 1996 (68**) US$ 10,350   US$ 10,350

NEVEH TSEDEK, TEL AVIV oil on canvas, 32 1/8 x 23 ¾in. (81.5 x 60.2cm.) sll in Hebrew, dll '69'
PROV.: Purchased directly from the Artist by the present owner.
    Christie's Tel Aviv, 14 April 1996 (78**) US$ 26,450   US$ 26,450

GUTTUSO Renato (Bagheria 1912-1987 Rome) Italian
FIGURA DI DONNA oil on canvas, 150.5 x 52.5cm. slc 'Guttuso'
    Finearte Milan, 12 December 1995 (273**) ITL 24,150,000   US$ 15,151

LA FINESTRA DELLO STUDIO DI VELATE oil on canvas, 64 x 50cm. slr 'Guttuso' d '1960' on the reverse
    Finearte Milan, 12 December 1995 (288**) ITL 21,275,000   US$ 13,347

SEATED GIRL, FROM THE BACK gouache on stretched paper, 126 x 104cm. sc 'Guttuso' (1967)
LIT.: Enrico Crispolti, *Cataloguo ragionato generale dei dipinti di R. Guttuso*, vol. 5 (addendum), nos. 67/125, p. 195.
    Finearte Milan, 18 June 1996 (167*) ITL 13,225,000   US$ 8,577

OMAGGIO A MORANDI oil on canvas, 89 x 82cm. sdlc 'Guttuso 66'; sd on the reverse
EXH.: Milano, Galleria del Milione, *Da Morandi, 12 dipinti, 35 desegni e guazzi di Renato Guttuso*, 1966; Roma, Galleria La Nuova Pesa, *Renato Guttuso: da Morandi*, 1966.
LIT.: Enrico Crispolti, *Catalogo ragionato generale dei dipinti di R. Guttuso*, ed. G. Mondadori e Ass., Milan 1985, no. 66/3, p. 6.
    Finearte Milan, 18 June 1996 (215**) ITL 21,850,000   US$ 14,170

OMMAGIO A MORANDI oil on canvas, 86 x 86cm. sdlr 'Guttuso 66'
EXH.: Milan, Galleria del Milione, *Da Morandi, 12 dipinti, 35 desegni guazzi di renato Guttuso*, 1966; Rome, Galleria La Nuova Pease, *Renato Guttuso: da Morandi*, 1966.
LIT.: Enrico Crispolti, *Catalogo ragionato geerale dei dipinti di R. Guttuso*, ed. G. Mondadori e Ass., Milan, 1985, no. 66/1, p. 6.
    Finearte Milan, 18 June 1996 (247**) ITL 37,950,000   US$ 24,611

231

PAOLETTA oil on canvas, 81 x 75cm. sll 'Guttuso' (1965)
    Finearte Milan, 19 March 1996 (88**) ITL 26,450,000   US$ 16,923

MENDICANTE oil on canvas, 45 x 35cm. sdlr 'Guttuso 45'
PROV.: Jan Greenlees, Firenze Lino Mezzacane, Rome.
EXH.: London, Redfern Gallery, *Exhibition of Contemporary Italian Painting*, p. 16, no. 39
(illustrated); Moscow, Gosudarstvenyi Musei Isobrasitelnih Iskussti Imeni A.S. Puskina, *Renato
Cuttuso*, 1961, p. 20 (This exhibition later travelled to Leningrad and Novosibirsk); Berlin,
Nationalgalerie - Altes Museum, *Renato Guttuso*, 18 Feb.- 2 April 1967 (This exhibition later
travelled to Lipia, Darmstadt and Recklinghausen) cat. no. 8 (illustrated); Verona, Palazzo Forti,
Guttuso - 50 anni di pittura, June-Sept. 1987.
LIT.: L. Venturi, *La Peinture Contemporaine*, Milan 1949, pl. 209; Lothar Lang, *Renato Guttuso*,
Berlin 1975, p. 14.
    Christie's Milan, 20 November 1995 (122*) ITL 17,,678,000   US$ 11,097

QUATTRO CANI oil on canvas, 37.5 x 105cm. slr 'Guttuso' (1959)
PROV.: Galleria Chiurazzi, Roma; McRobert and Tonnard Ltd. London.
    Christie's Milan, 20 November 1995 (182**) ITL 35,355,000   US$ 22,194

COMPOSIZIONE CON FIASCO E BOTTIGLIA oil on board, 38.5 x 79.4cm. sll (1955-56)
    Sotheby's Milan, 28 May 1996 (178**) ITL 71,300,000   US$ 45,793

SENZA TITOLO collage and mixed media on cardboard, 67 x 50cm. slr (ca. 1960)
    Sotheby's Milan, 28 May 1996 (205**) ITL 20,125,000   US$ 12,925

ACCIAIERE (TERNI) oil on canvas, 55 x 45cm. sdlr 'Guttuso 49'
PROV.: Galleria del Secolo, Rome; Contemporarte, Arezzo.
LIT.: Enrico Crispolti, *Catalogo Ragionato Generale dei Dipinti di Renato Guttuso*, Milan 1983, vol.
I, p. 192, no. 49/2 (illustrated).
    Sotheby's Milan, 28 May 1996 (216**) ITL 28,750,000   US$ 18,465

GUZZARDI Leonardo (ca. 1799) Italian (?)
PORTRAIT OF ADMIRAL NELSON, STANDING FULL-LENGTH BESIDE A CANNON,
WEARING CHELINGK oil on canvas, 33¼ x 19 ¾in. (84.5 x 50.5cm.)
EXH.: Victoria Art Gallery, Bath, 'The Navy of Nelson's Day', May 1955.
    Phillips London, 18 June 1996 (27**) GBP 5,500   US$ 8,481

GYSELS Pieter (Antwerp 1621-1690) Flemish
A WINTER LANDSCAPE WITH A VILLAGE NEAR A FROZEN RIVER oil on oak panel, 10½ x
14in. (26.5 x 35.4cm.) slc 'P. GYSELS'
PROV.: Anon. sale, Vienna Dorotheum, 13-18 December 1917, lot 878.
    Sotheby's London, 6 December 1995 (2**) GBP 34,500   US$ 53,093

VILLAGERS MUSIC-MAKING BY A POND oil on copper, 6½ x 9¼in. (16.5 x 23.5cm.)
    Christie's London, 7 July 1995 (27**) GBP 29,900   US$ 47,695

A RIVER LANDSCAPE WITH GENTRY AND PEASANTS DANCING ON A QUAY oil on
copper, 6 5/8 x 9 3/8in. (16 x 23.8cm.)
PROV.: Anon sale, Sotheby's, 8 April 1970, lot 69, as Jan Brueghel II (sold with a pendant (Villagers
music-making by a pond).
    Christie's London, 7 July 1995 (27**) GBP 29,900   US$ 47,695

GYSIS Nikolas (1842-1901 Munich) Greek
CAUGHT OUT! oil on canvas, 27 x 15in. (68.5 x 38cm.) sdlr (5.1870)
    Phillips London, 12th March 1996 (20**) GBP 125,000   US$ 190,898

HAAG Carl (Erlangen 1820-1915 Oberwesel-Rein) German
FILIAL LOVE watercolour on paper, 46 x 31in. (117 x 79cm.) sdlr 'Filial Love/Carl Haag/1872'
    Christie's East, 13 February 1996 (205**) US$ 10,350   US$ 10,350

THE ARTIST'S STUDIO, CAIRO (RECTO); AND A PENCIL STUDY OF THE ARTIST'S
STUDIO (VERSO) pencil, watercolour and bodycolour on paper, 19¼ x 13½in. 949 x 34.3cm.) s
inscr. 'Carl Haag/ Our studio in Cairo' sd inscr. 'My painting room in Cairo/in the Chritian (sic)
quater (sic), Sooknaza, No. W N/Espekia/Carl Haag/1859'
    Christie's London, 15 March 1996 (83**) GBP 18,400   US$ 28,100

HAANEN Remigius Adrianus (Oosterhout 1812-1894 Aussee) Dutch
WALDWEG AM BACHUFER oil on panel, 50 x 37cm. s with mono. and d 'RvH 69'
    Dorotheum Vienna, 6 November 1995 (53**) ATS 60,000   US$ 6,019

HAAXMAN Pieter (1854-1937) Dutch
SOLITUDE oil on panel, 17¾ x 29in. (45 x 73.7cm.) s 'P. Haaxman'
PROV.: The Dixon family, Sparreholm Castle, Sormland, Sweden.
    Christie's London, 14 June 1996 (13**) GBP 6,670   US$ 10,285

HACKERT Jacob Philipp (Prenzlau 1737-1807 San Pietro di Careggi (Coreggio), near Florence) German
IDEAL LANDSCAPE WITH DANCING COUPLE AND MANY OTHER FIGURES oil on canvas,
50 x 67cm.
    Dorotheum Vienna, 17 October 1995 (149**) ATS 220,000   US$ 22,067

HACKERT Jacob Philipp (attr.) (Prenzlau 1737-1807 San Pietro di Careggi (Coreggio), near Florence) German
A LANDSCAPE WITH TWO FIGURES DANCING WITH TAMBOURINES (AFTER CLAUDE
LORRAINE) oil on canvas, 58¾ x 78in. (149 x 199cm.) (ca. 1779-80)
PROV.: Presumably Frederick John, 4th Earl of Bristol, 'The Earl Bishop' by 1802.
LIT.: Possibly Rev. G. Vaughan Sampson, *Statistical Survey of the County of Londonderry*, 1802, p.
421, as 'A landscape - by Hackert, a copy of the Altieri Claude'; 1st Marquess, 1837, no. 6, as 'a large
copy of the Aldobrandini Claude - ', and as hanging in the library; Gage, 1838, pp. 303-9, as hanging
in the library, 'a copy of the Mulino of Claude'; Farrer, 1913, no. 49, as *Landscape with fgures*, 'a
copy of a picture by Claude Gellée, called Claude Lorrain'; Inventory, 1952, p. 10, as after Claude le
Lorraine; Figgis, 1992, p. 40.
    Sotheby's London, 11-12 June 1996 (477**) GBP 69,700   US$ 107,479

HAENSBERGEN Jan van (1642-1705) Dutch
PORTAIT OF A NOBLE WOMAN, SEATED SMALL THREE QUARTER LENGHT IN A
LANDSCAPE, WEARING A BLUE SILK DRESS WITH OCHRE WRAP, LACE CHEMISE AND
PEARLS, A HOUND AT HER SIDE oil on canvas, 51.6 x 42cm. sdll 'J.V.H.f/1687' with signature
and the date on the reverse on the relining canvas
PROV.: Probably the Sohier de Vermandois family; by descent to J.E. Baroness van Pallandy,
Neerijen, until 1972.
LIT.: F.G.L.O. Kretschmar, Vreemde Eenden in de bijt; 'Aantekeingen bij enkele portretten op
Kasteel Neerijen' in *Jaarboek van het Centraal Bureau voor Genealogie*, XXXVI, 1972, pp. 38/39
and 41, figs.8 and 9, p. 38.
    Christie's Amsterdam, 7 May 1996 (119**) NLG 48,875   US$ 28,499

PORTAIT OF A NOBLE WAOMAN, SEATED SMALL THREE QUARTER LENGHT BY A
SCULPTED FOOUNTAIN, WEARING A CLASSICAL STYLE RED SILK DRESS, WITH LACE
CHEMISE AND PEARLS, FLOWERS IN A BASKET ON THE BENCH BESIDE HERE, A
LANDSCAPE BEYOND oil on canvas, 51.4 x 42.4cm. sdll 'J.V.H.f/1687' with signature and the
date on the reverse on the relining canvas
PROV.: Probably the Sohier de Vermandois family; By descent to J.E. Baroness van Pallandy,

Neerijen, until 1972.
LIT.: F.G.L.O. Kretschmar, Vreemde Ennden in de bijt; 'Aantekeingen bij enkele portretten op
Kasteel Neerijen' in *Jaarboek van het Centraal Bureau voor Genealogie*, XXXVI, 1972, pp. 38/39
and 41, figs.8 and 9, p. 38.

Christie's Amsterdam, 7 May 1996 (120**) NLG 48,875	US$	28,499

HAGBORG August (1852-1921) Swedish
MUSSELPLOCKNING VID EBB oil on canvas, 82 x 117cm. s 'Hagborg'

Bukowskis Stockholm, 29-31 May 1996 (38**) SEK 66,000	US$	9,707

HAGER R A (19th/20th century) Austrian
AT THE FAIR oil on canvas, 213/4 x 29¼in. (55.3 x 74.3cm.) s and inscr. 'Wien'
PROV.: Hugo Arnot Gemalde-Salon; Vienna.

Phillips London, 11 June 1996 (29**) GBP 7,000	US$	10,794

HAINES William Henry (1812-1884) British
VIEW OF ST MARK'S SQUARE, VENICE oil on canvas, 33 x 50¼in. (76.2 x 127cm.) sdll 'W
Henry 1861'

Christie's East, 30 October 1995 (258*) US$ 13,800	US$	13,800

HALLÉ Noël (1711-1781) French
THE RAPE OF EUROPA;AND DIANA AND ENDYMION oil on canvas, 42 x 51½in. (116.8 x
130.8cm.) a pair

Christie's South Kensington, 18 april 1996 (113**) GBP 10,350	US$	15,694

HALLEY Peter (1953 b.) British or American
GREY TO BLACK three attached panels-Acrylic on canvas, 62¼ x 128in. (158 x 325.2cm.) (1988)
PROV.: Rhona Hoffman Gallery, Chicago; Private collection, Vancouver.
EXH.: Sarasota, The John and Mable Ringling Museum of Art, and Miami Center for Fine Arts,
Abstraction; in Question, Jan.-July 1989.

Christie's New York, 15 November 1995 (284**) US$ 36,800	US$	36,800

HALLSTRÖM Eric (1893-1946) Swedish
UTSIKT FRÅN RÖRSTRANDSKAJEN MOT KUNGSHOLMEN oil on panel, 63.5 x 90cm. sdll
'Eric Hallström 24'

Bukowskis Stockholm, 24-25 April 1996 (36**) SEK 75,000	US$	11,362

HALLSTRÖM Staffan (1914-1976) Swedish
VILANDE HUNDAR oil on canvas, 73 x 133cm. sdll 'SH 64'
LIT.: Stig Johansson, *Staffan Hallström*, p. 126.

Bukowskis Stockholm, 24-25 April 1996 (38**) SEK 60,000	US$	9,090

HALS Dirck (Haarlem 1591-1656 Haarlem) Dutch
LES GENTILSHOMMES A LA MODE oil on oakpanel, 44 x 68.5cm.
PROV.: Collection Kellner, Berlin before 1927; His sale, Berlin, 3 December 1927, lot 8
(illustrated); Collection Singer, Prague; Collection van Es, Wassenaar; Collection Leroux, before
1968; His sale, Paris, Hôtel Drouot, 23 March 1968, lot 55 (illustrated).
EXH.: Paris, Musée de l'Orangerie des Tuileries, *Le Cabinet de l'amateur*, Jan.-Feb. 1956, no. 63
(illustrated pl. XIV).

Étude Tajan Paris, 12 December 1995 (72**) FRF 210,000	US$	42,299

'FRÖHLICHE TISCHGESELSCHAFT' oil on panel, 47 x 56.5cm. sd 'D. Hals 1648'

Lempertz Cologne, 15 November 1995 (1268**) DEM 19,000	US$	134,11

HALS Frans (attr.) (Antwerp 1580-1666 Haarlem) Dutch (Flemish)
A PORTRAIT OF THEODORUS SCHREVELIUS oil on copper (an oval), 6¼ x 4¾in. (15.7 x

11.8cm.) d inscr. on the book 'AET.44/ 1617' and ur 'AETAT SVAE.'
PROV.: E. Warneck, Paris, by whom acquired from a pastor in Holland in 1864 (according to the
Warneck sale catalogue), his sale, Paris, Petit, 27-8 May 1926, lot 46 (300,000 Francs to Cassirer);
Baron Heinrich Thyssen-Bornemisza, by 1930.
EXH.: The Hague, Haagsche Kunstkring, *Tentoonstelling van oude portretten*, 1 July-30 September
1903, no. 35; Paris, Jeu de Paume, *Exposition rétrospective des grands et Petits Maîtres Hollandais*,
April 1911, no. 60; Munich 1930, no. 145, as Hals; Birmingham, Museum and Art Gallery, *Some
Dutch Cabinet Pictures of the 17 th Century,* 1950, no. 23; Amsterdam, Rijksmuseum*, Drie eenwen
portret in Nederland*, 1952, no. 42; Haarlem, Frans Hals Museum, *Frans Hals*, 1962, no. 7, as Hals;
Paris 1970, no. 24, plate 10, as Hals; Düsseldorf 1970-1, no. 21; Lausanne etc., 1986-7, no. 23, as by
Frans Hals; Washington, National Gallery of Art, London, Royal Academy, Haarlem, Frans
Halsmuseum, *Frans Hals*, October 1989 -July 1990, no. 5; Frankfurt, Schirn Kunsthalle, *Leselust*, 24
September 1993-2 January 1994, no. 36, as by Frans Hals (and as lent by the Musée National
d'Histoire et d'Art).
LIT.: W. Bode, *Frans Hals und seine Schule*, 1871, p. 11; W. Bode, *Studien zur Geschichte der
holländischen Malerei*, 1883, pp. 43, 85, no. 79; E.W. Moes, *Iconographia Batava*, 1897-1905, no.
7038, I, and 7130, I, (wrongly as of Petrus Scriverius); C. Hofstede de Groot, *Meisterwerke der
Porträtmalerei.*, 1903, no. 35, reproduced pl. 22; G.S. Davies, *Frans Hals*, 1904, pp. XI, 129; A. von
Würzbach, *Niederländisches Kunstler-Lexikon*, 1906, vol. I, p. 640; E.W. Moes, *Frans Hals, sa vie
et son oeuvre*, 1909, pp. 27,103, no. 69; C. Hofstede de Groot, *A Catalogue Raisonné...*, vol. III,
1910, p. 67, no. 222 (as probably having been in the Bloudoff collection, Brussels, in 1873*);* A.
Dayot, Grands et Petits Maîtres Hollandais, exhibition cat., 1911, p. 136, no. 60, reproduced; W. von
Bode, M.J. Binder, *Frans Hals, sein Leben und seine Werke*, 1914, no. 93, reproduced pl. 46a; W.R.
Valentiner, *Frans Hals des Meisters Gemälde, Klassiker der Kunst*, vol. XXVIII, 1923, p. 13; Ed.
G.J. Hoogewerff, I.Q. van Regteren Altena, Arnoldus Buchelius, *Res Pictoriae*, 1928, p. 66; R.
Heinemann 1937*,* vol. I, no. 181, vol. Il, pl. 116; S. Slive, *Frans Hals,* 1970, vol. I, pp. 8, 28-9, 59,
125, 154, vol. II, plate 23, his earliest painting and his smallest picture, and his earliest small scale work; C. Grimm, *Frans
Hals: Entwicklung Werkanalyse, Gesamtkatalog* 1972, no. A 26, as a copy; C. Grimm, E.C.
Montagini, *L 'Opera Completa di Frans Hals*, 1974, pp. 87-8, under no. 11, as a copy of a presumed
lost original; S. Slive, Frans Hals, vol. III, *Catalogue*, 1974, p. 7, no. 8; R. Andree, *Kunstmuseum
Dusseldorf - Malerei*, 1976, no. 4; B.P.J. Broos, 'A Monument to Hals', review of Slive 1970-74, in
Simiolus, vol. X, 1979, p. 118, as not by Hals; C. Grimm, *Frans Hals, Das Gesamtwerk*, 1989, pp.
32, 53, illustrated p. 54, fig 47a, as a copy, presumably of a lost work; C. Grimm, *Frans Hals, The
Complete Work*, 1990 (English edition of the above), pp. 32, 53, reproduced p. 54, fig. 47a, as a
copy, presumably of a lost work; S. Slive, *Frans Hals, exhibition catalogue*, 1989, pp. 109, 141-3,
no. 5, 185, 189, 246, 383, 400, reproduced p.142; B. Werche, in *Leselust*, exh. Cata., Frankfurt, 1993,
p. 206, no. 36, illustrated in colour on the facing page.

Sotheby's London, 6 December 1995 (93**) GBP 62,000	US$	95,414

HALS Harmen (Haarlem 1611-1669 Haarlem) Dutch
THE SENSE OF HEARING: BOORS MAKING MUSIC IN A TAVERN oil on panel, 36 x 31.9cm.
slr (strengthened) 'HAL'

Christie's Amsterdam, 7 May 1996 (132**) NLG 34,500	US$	20,117

INTERIEUR MIT EINER BAUERNFAMILIE oil on panel, 30 x 37cm.

Lempertz Cologne, 18 May 1996 (1061*) DEM 10,000	US$	6,519

HALSWELLE Keeley, A.R.S.A. (1832-1891) Scottish
SUNNY HOURS oil on canvas, 26½ x 36in. (67.3 x 91.5cm.) sdll and inscr. 'Kelley Halswelle
ARSA/Newhaven 1866'

Christie's East, 30 October 1995 (300*) US$ 10,925	US$	10,925

HAMAGUCHI Yozo (1903 b.) Japanese
BOWL WITH FRUIT watercolour, 9.1 x 12.2cm. sd '1957'
PROV.: Collection Nathan Chaikin, Paris.

Hauswedell & Nolte Cologne, 6 June 1996 (132**) DEM 15,000	US$	9,746

HAMBOURG André (1909 b.) French
A MARÉE BASSE, ÉTÉ 1963 oil on canvas, 46 x 65cm. sll 'A Hambourg' sd titled on the reverse
        Étude Tajan Paris, 28 March 1996 (71*) FRF 53,000   US$ 10,476

FIN DU JOUR A VENISE oil on canvas, 31 7/8 x 39 1/8in. (81 x 100cm.) sll 'A. Hambourg'; titled
and dated on the reverse "Fin du jour' à Venise 59-60'
PROV.: Wally Findlay Galleries, Inc., Beverly Hills (acquired by Richard Smart, 1976).
        Christie's East, 30 April 1996 (55**) US$ 18,400   US$ 18,400

HAMDY-BEY Osman Pacha Zadeh (1842-1910) Turkish
THE TOMB OF MEHMED I, YESIL TÜRBE, BURSA oil on canvas, 24 x 20in. (61 x 50.8cm.) sd
'Hamdy Bey 1881'
        Christie's London, 17 November 1995 (138**) GBP 452,500   US$ 707,805

HAMILTON Letitia Marion, A.R.H.A. (1878-1964) Irish
THE HARBOUR CUP, THE WESTMEATH POINT-TO-POINT oil on canvas, 22 x 26in. (55.9 x
66cm.) sll with ini. 'LMH'
PROV.: The Artist's Family, thence by descent.
        Christie's London, 9 May 1996 (34**) GBP 14,950   US$ 22,638

HANSEN Carl Lodewijk (Amsterdam 1765-1840 Vaassen) Dutch
INTERIOR WITH A WOMAN SPINNING oil on canvas, 54 x 64.5cm. slr 'C.L./Hansen'
        Sotheby's Amsterdam, 14 November 1995 (17**) NLG 14,750   US$ 9,296

HANTAI Simon (1922 b.) French
UNTITLED acrylic on canvas, 84¼ x 69¼in. (214 x 176cm.) sdlr ini. 'S.H. 1973'
PROV.: Galerie Jean Fournier, Paris.
LIT.: Alfred Pacquement, Art en France depuis 1945.
        Christie's London, 19 March 1996 (45**) GBP 51,000   US$ 77,886

BLEU acrylic on canvas, 97 5/8 x 88½in. (248 x 225cm.) sd ini. 'SH 67'
PROV.: Galerie Jean Fournier, Paris.
        Christie's London, 23 May 1996 (44**) GBP 58,700   US$ 88,886

HARDIMÉ Pieter (Antwerp 1677-1758 Antwerp) Flemish
FLOWER STILL-LIFE oil on canvas, 46.5 x 38cm. slr 'P. hardime'
PROV.: Private Collection, New York.
        Dorotheum Vienna, 6 March 1996 (297**) ATS 110,000   US$ 10,581

HARDIMÉ Pieter (attr.) (1677-1758 Antwerp) Flemish
FLOWER STILL-LIFE oil on canvas, 75.5 x 61.5cm.
PROV.: Collection Aubry-Vilette, according to an old label on the reverse.
        Étude Tajan Paris, 26 March 1996 (34*) FRF 68,000   US$ 13,441

HARDY Heywood, A.R.W.S., R.E., R.O.I. (1843-1933) British
HEYWOOD HARDY oil on canvas, 20 x 15in. (50.8 x 38.1cm.) sdll 'Heaywood Hardy 1893'; inscr.
'Mildred Mary Swan my/Grandmother as a young/girl riding on the/Sands in Durham..'
        Christie's South Kensington, 9 November 1995 (172*) GBP 9,000   US$ 14,078

THE PET DOVE oil on canvas, 152 x 90cm. s 'Heywood Hardy'
EXH.: Bristol, Bristol Art Gallery.
        Bukowskis Stockholm, 29-31 May 1996 (221**) SEK 235,000   US$ 34,562

HARING Keith (Kutztown 1958-1990) American
UNTITLED acrylic, enamel and printed paper collage on canvas-unframed, 60½ x 60in. (153.6 x
152.2cm.) sd 'K. Haring NOV. 21 1988' on the overlap

PROV.: Hoskin Gallery, Bal Harbour.
LIT.: ed. G. Celant, *Keith Haring*, New York 1992, no. 171 (illustrated).
      Christie's New York, 15 November 1995 (326**) US$ 46,000   US$ 46,000

HARLAMOFF Alexei Alexeivich (1842 (?)-1915) Russian
A YOUNG GIRL WITH A PEARL NECKLACE oil on canvas, 18 x 15in. (46 x 38cm.) slr
      Sotheby's London, 13 March 1996 (76**) GBP 47,700   US$ 72,847

A YOUNG BEAUTY oil on canvas, 21¼ x 15¾in. (54 x 40cm.) sd 'Harlamoff/1884'
      Christie's London, 14 June 1996 (72**) GBP 67,500   US$ 104,086

A GIRL WITH A WHITE VEIL oil on canvas, 20 x 15½in. (51 x 39.5cm.) s 'A. Harlamoff'
      Christie's London, 17 November 1995 (55**) GBP 73,000   US$ 114,187

HARMS Anton Friedrich (Braunschweig 1695-1745 Kassel) German
NATURE MORTE AU LIEVRE, COUPE DE FRUITS ET PANIER DE PROVISIONS oil on
canvas, 87 x 106cm. indistinctly sdll 'A F Harms 1733'
      Étude Tajan Paris, 12 December 1995 (88**) FRF 140,000   US$ 28,200

FISCHSTILLEBEN OIL ON CANVAS, 92 x 81cm. sdlm 'AF(linked) Harms 1734'
      Lempertz Cologne, 18 May 1996 (1063*) DEM 18,000   US$ 11,735

HARNETT William Michael (1848/51-1892) American
PLUMS IN A PAPER WRAP ON A MARBLE TOPPED TABLE oil on canvas, 11 x 15in. (27.9 x
38.1cm.) sd 'WHM (monogram) ARNETT. / München. / 1881'
      Christie's South Kensington, 14 March 1996 (14**) GBP 13,800   US$ 21,075

HARPIGNIES Henri Joseph (1819-1916) French
SOUVENIR DE LA TRUMELIERE oil on canvas, 32 x 25¾in. (81.3 x 65.4cm.) sdll 'hjharpignies
1907'
PROV.: With Marlborough Fine Art Ltd., London.
      Christie's New York, 22 May 1996 (151**) US$ 18,400   US$ 18,400

SPRING LANDSCAPE oil on canvas, 21¾ x 14¾in. (55.2 x 37.5cm.) sdll 'hjharpignies. 83'
PROV.: With Thomas Mclean, London; With M. Knoedler & Co., New York.
      Christie's New York, 22 May 1996 (152**) US$ 22,425   US$ 22,425

HARRIS Edwin (1855-1906) British
PORTRAIT OF A MOTHER AND DAUGHTER READING oil on canvas, 50 x 40in. (127 x
101.5cm.) sdll 'E. Harris 1903'
      Christie's New York, 22 May 1996 (271**) US$ 27,600   US$ 27,600

HART William M. (1823-1894) American
SUNY AFTERNOON ON THE BANKS OF LAKE GEORGE oil on canvas, 15 x 25¾in. (38 x
65.5cm.) sdll 'Wm Hart Lake George Sep 14 69'
      Christie's East, 28 November 1995 (72*) US$ 8,625   US$ 8,625

HART NIBBRIG Ferdinand (Amsterdam 1866-1915 Laren (N.-Holland)) Dutch
VIEW OF A FARM oil on canvas, 41 x 56.5cm. slr
      Sotheby's Amsterdam, 7 December 1995 (202**) NLG 25,960   US$ 16,086

HARTLEY Marsden, N.A. (1877-1943) American
MOVEMENT NO. 3, PROVINCETOWN oil on board, 20 x 16in. (50.7 x 40.6cm.)
PROV.: Alfred Stieglitz Collection, New York; Hudson D. Walker, Minneapolis, Minnesota.
EXH.: Minneapolis, Minnesota, University of Minnesota, University Gallery, on extended loan, circa
1950-July 1957; Minneapolis, Minnesota, University of Minnesota, University Gallery, *Marsden*

Hartley Retrospective, 1952; New York, Salander-O'Reilly Galleries, Inc., *Marsden Hartley:*
Paintings and drawings, 1985, no. 51, illus.

Christie's New York, 13 September 1995 (103**) US$ 134,500	US$	134,500

ARTICHOKE AND CALLA LILY oil on canvas, 10 7/8 x 18½in. (27.6 x 47cm.) inscr. 'artichoke '
on the stretcher
PROV.: Babcock Galleries, New York.

Christie's New York, 30 November 1995 (66**) US$ 36,800	US$	36,800

HARTUNG Hans Heinrich Ernst (Leipzig 1904-1989 Antibes) French (German)
T 1971 - H48 oil on canvas, 72 x 92cm. sdlr 'Hartung 71'
PROV.: Galleria Gissi, Turin, no. 4941; Galleria Nuovo Sagittario, Milan, no. 1129.

Finearte Milan, 12 December 1995 (297**) ITL 32,200,000	US$	20,201

P1974-G32 acrylic on cardboard, 30¾ x 46½in. (78.2 x 118cm.) sdll dedicated 'A Jean Le Süun très
aimmablement 1-1-75' (6th August 1974)
PROV.: A gift from the Artist to the present owner in 1975.

Sotheby's London, 21 March 1996 (37**) GBP 13,225	US$	20,197

P 1948-19 pastel on paper, 19¼ x 15¾in. (49 x 40cm.) sdll '48
PROV.: Galerie Jacques Benador, Paris.
LIT.: Pierre Daix, Hartung, Paris 1991, p. 176, no. 227 (illustrated in colour).

Christie's London, 23 May 1996 (6**) GBP 17,250	US$	26,121

T1963 - E38 oil on canvas, 39 3/8 x 63 6/8in. (,100 x 162cm.) sdlr '63' s titled on the stretcher
PROV.: Daniel Gervis, Paris; acquired from the above by the present owner.

Christie's London, 23 May 1996 (45**) GBP 38,900	US$	58,904

T 1950-27 oil on panel, 19¾ x 25½in. (50 x 64.8cm) sdll 'Hartung '50'
PROV.: Galerie Louis Carré, Paris.
LIT.: This work is recorded at The archives Hans Hartung in Paris.

Christie's London, 26 October 1995 (17**) GBP 47,700	US$	75,284

T1947-28 oil on canvas, 25 5/8 x 31 7/8in. (65 x 81cm.) sdll '47; s and titled on the stretcher
PROV.: Galerie Daniel Gervis, Paris.
EXH.: Evreux, Musée d'Evreux, Hans Hartung, 1985 (illustrated in colour in the catalogue).
LIT.: Pierre Daix, Hartung, Paris 1991, p. 169, no. 223 (illustrated in colour).

Christie's London, 27 June 1996 (10**) GBP 87,300	US$	134,618

T 1958-4 oil on canvas, 36 x 23½in. (91.5 x 59.7cm.) sdlr '58
PROV.: Galerie Charpentier, Paris; Saidenberg Gallery, New York; Acquired from the above by
Joseph H. Hazen in 1960.
EXH.: Paris, Galerie Charpentier, Ecôle de Paris, 1958.

Christie's London, 27 June 1996 (36**) GBP 43,300	US$	66,769

T1961-H44 acrylic on canvas, 36¼ x 59in. (92 x 150cm.) sdlr '61; sd on the stretcher
PROV.: Galleria La Polena, Genoa.
LIT.: Pierre Daix, *Hartung*, Paris 1991, no. 309 (illustrated in colour).

Christie's London, 27 June 1996 (39**) GBP 56,500	US$	87,124

T 1966 H 3 (N.C. 1508) vinylic on canvas, 40 x 105cm. sdlr 'Hartung 66' titled on the reverse
PROV.: Galleria d'Arte Boccioni, Milano; Galleria Nuovo Sagittario, Milano; Galleria Gianni Emeri,
Milano.

Sotheby's Milan, 28 May 1996 (143**) ITL 33,350,000	US$	21,419

HARVEY Harold C., R.A. (1874-1941) British
WADING ASHORE oil on canvas, 16¼ x 14in. (41.5 x 35.5cm.) sdll 'Harold Harvey 9'
PROV.: devon and Cornwall Galleries, Plymouth; Mrs. Spooner, Plymouth, thence by descent to the
present owner, her great granddaughter.
        Christie's London, 21 November 1995 (92**) GBP 13,800   US$ 21,586

HASELTINE William Stanley, N.A. (1835-1900) American
VALLE DEI MOLINI - AMALFI oil on board, 20¼ x 16½in. (52 x 42cm.) sdll 'W.S. Haseltine New
York 1871'
        Christie's New York, 13 September 1995 (27**) US$ 9,200   US$ 9,200

HASSAM Frederick Childe, N.A. (1859-1935) American
MCSORLEY'S BAR oil on panel, 5 x 5 5/8in. (12.7 x 14.2cm.) s with crescent sd 'Childe Hassam
1916' inscr. 'signed with crescent in lower right hand corner painted 1891'
PROV.: Bernard Danenberg Galleries, New York; Mr. and Mrs. Frank Sinatra.
EXH.: Tuscon, Arizona, University of Arizona Art Museum, *Childe Hassam, 1867-1935*, 5 Feb.-5
March 1972, no. 35, p. 73, (illustrated); This exhibition later traveled to Santa Barbara, California,
Santa Barbara Museum of Art, 26 March-30 April 1972.
LIT.: This painting will be included in Stuart P. Feld's and Kathleen M. Burnside's forthcoming
catalogue raisonné of the artist's work.
        Christie's New York, 1 December 1995 (66**) US$ 108,100   US$ 108,100

A WALK IN THE PARK oil on canvas laid down on panel, 15 x 21¾in. (38.1 x 55.3cm.) sll 'Childe
Hassam'
EXH.: Cambridge, Fogg Art Museum, Harvard University, *The Discerning Eye*, Oct. -Nov. 1974, no.
89.
LIT.: This painting will be included in the forthcoming *Hassam catalogue raisonné*, being prepared
by Stuart P. Feld and Kathleen M. Burnside.
        Christie's New York, 23 May 1996 (69**) US$ 497,500   US$ 497,500

LARKSPURS AND LILIES watercolour and gouache on paper, 19 x 13in. (48.2 x 33cm.) sd 'Childe
Hassam 1893'
LIT.: Celia Thaxter, *An Island Garden*, Boston, Massachusetts, 1894, p. 50, illus.; D.P. Curry, *Childe
Hassam: An Island Revisited*, New York, 1990, pp. 68-69, no. 21, illus.; This watercolour will be
included in Stuart P. Feld's and Kathleen M. Burnside's forthcoming *catalogue raisonné* of the artist's
work.
        Christie's New York, 23 May 1996 (76**) US$ 288,500   US$ 288,500

THE BATHER oil on canvas, 24½ x 20¼in. (61.5 x 51.5cm.) slr 'Childe Hassam' titled on the
reverse (ca. 1905)
PROV.: William Young Marsh, Esq., Williamstown, Massachusetts ;
William Young Marsh, Jr., Montreal, Canada; Walter Klinkhoff Gallery, Montreal, Canada.
LIT.: This painting will be included in Stuart P. Feld's anc Kathleen M. Burnside's forthcoming
catalogue raisonné of the artist's work.
        Christie's New York, 23 May 1996 (79**) US$ 70,700   US$ 70,700

THE FRENCH BREAKFAST oil on canvas, 28¾ x 19¾in. (73 x 50.2cm.) sdlr 'Childe Hassam 1910'
sd ini on the reverse
PROV.: American Academy of Arts and Letters, New York; Dr. and Mrs. Gerard Fountain,
Scarsdale, New York; Meredith Long & Company, Houston, Texas .
EXH.: Washington, DC, The Corcoran Gallery of Art, *Childe Hassam: A Retrospective Exhibition*,
1965, no. 44 and
travelling; New York, Bernard Danenberg Galleries, *Recent Acquisitions by American Artists*,
Spring/Summer 1969, no. 36, illus. on
backcover; Tucson, Arizona, University of Anzona Art Museum, *Childe Hassam: 1859-1935* Feb.-
March 1972, no. 79.

LIT.: U.W. Hiesinger, *Childe Hassam: American Impressionist*, New York, 1994, p. 144, p. 142, illus.

Christie's New York, 23 May 1996 (81**) US$ 266,500	US$	266,500

LOWER FIFTH AVENUE oil on canvas, 25¼ x 21in. (64.1 x 53.3cm.) sd 'Childe Hassam 1890' inscr. 'New York'
PROV.: Mrs. Roland C. Lincoln, Jamaica Plains, Massachusetts. Sale: New York, American Art Association, January 20, 1922, no. 42, as *Fifth Avenue*; William MacBeth, Inc. New York; Private Collection, New York.
EXH.: St. Louis, Missouri, St. Louis Art Museum, January-August 1994 (on extended loan).
LIT.: This painting will be included in Stuart P. Feld's and Kathleen M. Burnside's forthcoming *catalogue raisonné* of the artist's work.

Christie's New York, 23 May 1996 (82**) US$ 1,872,500	US$	1,872,500

STREET SCENE, LA RONDA, SPAIN oil on panel, 25½ x 20½in. (64.6 x 52cm.) sdll 'Childe Hassam 1910'
PROV.: Horatio S. Rubens, New York; Kennedy Galleries, Inc., New York; Bemard Danenberg Gallery, New York.
EXH.: New York, Bernard Danenberg Gallery, *Recent Atquisitions_Important American Paintings*, no. 28, illus.; Tucson, Anzona, University of Arizona Art Museum, *Childe Hassam: 1859-1935*, February-March 1972, no.82.
LIT.: This painting will be included in Stuart P. Feld's and Kathleen M. Burnside's forthcoming *catalogue raisonné* of the artist's work.

Christie's New York, 23 May 1996 (87**) US$ 222,500	US$	222,500

AUTUMN LANDSCAPE oil on board, 5½ x 7¾in. (14 x 19.8cm.) sdll 'Childe Hassam 1903'

Christie's New York, 13 September 1995 (61**) US$ 20,700	US$	20,700

HAUPTMANN Ivo (Erker near Berlin 1886-1937 Hamburg) German
LANDSCHAFT BEI AX oil on canvas, 53.8 x 63.5cm. (ca. 1955)

Hauswedell & Nolte Cologne, 5/06 June 1996 (274*) DEM 11,250	US$	7,309

HAUSLEITHNER Rudolf (Mannswörth 1840-1918 Vienna) Austrian
DIE ERSTEN VEILCHEN oil on panel, 40.5 x 50cm. sdlr 'Rudolf Hausleithner 1876'

Wiener Kunst Auktionen, 26 September 1995 (80**) ATS 110,000	US$	10,692

HAVARD James (1937 b.) American
HOPI MASK acrylic on canvas-unframed, 54 x 60in. (137.2 x 152.4cm.) sd titled and numbered 'NO. 715 HOPI MASK Havard 82' on the overlap
PROV.: Louis K. Meisel Gallery, New York.

Christie's East, 7 May 1996 (93*) US$ 8,050	US$	8,050

KIOWA acrylic on canvas-unfranmed, 46 x 114in. (116.9 x 289.6cm.) sdul 'Havard 77'; sd titled and numbered 'Havard 77 KIOWA NO> 472' on the overlap
PROV.: Louis K. Meisel Gallery, New York; Janus Gallery, Venice.

Christie's East, 7 May 1996 (97*) US$ 8,050	US$	8,050

HAWKINS Louis Welden (1849-1910) French (British)
PERFECT HARMONY oil, watercolour and gold paint on canvas, 21½ x 18in. (54.5 x 46cm.) slc 'LOUIS. WLDEN.HAWKINS'
PROV.: Sotheby's London, 24 November 1976, lot 176.

Sotheby's London, 17 April 1996 (731**) GBP 8,050	US$	12,206

HAYET Louis (1854-1940) French (?)
PAYSAGE D'AIX LES BAINS oil on canvas, 15 x 21¾in. (38 x 55cm.) (1890)

Christie's South Kensington, 24 June 1996 (33**) GBP 14,950	US$	23,053

HECKEL Erich (Döbeln 1883-1970 Radolfzell) German
FRAUENBILDNIS watercolour on paper, 67 x 49.5cm. sdlr 'Erich Heckel 20' (1920)
      Hauswedell & Nolte Cologne, 1 December 1995 (314**) DEM 27,000   US$ 18,733

KARUSSEL watercolour and tempera over crayon, 49.5 x 60.5cm. slr 'Erich Heckel'; titled ll
'Karussel ' (1929)
PROV.: From the Artist's estate.
      Hauswedell & Nolte Cologne, 1 December 1995 (315**) DEM 20,000   US$ 13,876

VORM BAD crayon drawing on paper, 57 x 38.2cm. sdlr 'Erich Heckel 14'
      Hauswedell & Nolte Cologne, 1 December 1995 (317**) DEM 26,000   US$ 18,039

GEBIRGSSTOCK watercolour and chalk on paper, 49 x 61.2cm. sdlr 'Erich Heckel 24'; titled ll
'Gebirgsstock' (1924)
      Hauswedell & Nolte Cologne, 5-6 June 1996 (278*) DEM 15,000   US$ 9,746

INNENRAUM water colour on buetten with watermark framed under glass, 33.6 x 50cm. slr; titled
with pencil 'Heckel 15 innenraum' (1942)
      Lempertz Cologne, 29 November 1995 (190a**) DEM 34,000   US$ 23,998

HECKENDORF Franz (1888-1962 Munich) Berlin
RHEINLANDSCHAFT oil on canvas, 39¼ x 27½in. (99.7 x 70cm.) sdll 'F.Heckendorf 21'
      Christie's South Kensington, 24 June 1996 (60**) GBP 6,900   US$ 10,640

HEDA Gerrit Willemsz. (Haarlem 1620-1702 c. Haarlem) Dutch
STILL-LIFE WITH A GILT BEKERSCHROEF HOLDING A ROEMER AND ANOTHER
OVERTURNE D ROEMER ON A SHAPED SILVER PLATE, OYSTERS, A SILVER SALT
CELLAR, A JUG, A CLOTH AND OTHER OBJECTS ALL ON A DRAPED TABLE oil on panel,
35¾ x 27½in. (90.8 x 69.9cm.) sd 'HEDA. 1647' with added 'WK'
      Sotheby's New York, 16 May 1996 (37**) US$ 354,500   US$ 354,500

HEEL Jan (Johannes Jacobus) van (Rotterdam 1898 b.-) Dutch
ZOMER, SPAANS LANDSCHAP oil on canvas, 100 x 121 cm sd 'janvheel 63'; s on the reverse
EXH.: The Hague, Jacob Marisprijs, 1964; The Hague, Haags Gemeentemuseum, *Jan van Heel*,
1966, no. 36; Budapest, Museum Budapest and Museum Pecs, *Jan van Heel*, 1966, no. 36.
      Christie's Amsterdam, 7 February 1996 (484*) NLG 8,050   US$ 4,903

HEEM Cornelis Davidsz de (Leyden 1631-1695 Antwerp) Dutch
STILL-LIFES OF GRAPES, PEACHES AND PLUMS ON PEWTER PLATTERS: A PAIR OF
PAINTINGS both oil on canvas, 10 x 14in. (25.4 x 35.6 cm.)
      Sotheby's New York, 11 January 1996 (40**) US$ 112,500   US$ 112,500

ORANGES, ROSES, A MARYGOLD, A TIGERLILY AND OTHER FLOWERS HANGING
FROM A BLUE RIBBON ON A NAIL WITH *FRAISES-DE-BOISES* AND GOOSEBERRIES ON
A *WAN-LI* DISH, ROSES, A PEELED LEMON, CHERRIES, A POPPY AND OTHER FRUIT
AND FLOWERS ON A STONE LEDGE BELOW oil on canvas, 66.8 x 54.5 cm slr 'C DE HEEM f'
PROV.: with Ch. Staal, Amsterdam, circa 1950, from whom acquired by the present owner.
      Christie's Amsterdam, 13 November 1995 (164**) NLG 230,000   US$ 144,955

HEEM Jan Davidsz. de (Utrecht 1606-1684 Antwerp) Dutch
BOOKS, MANUSCRIPTS, A GLOBE, AN INKWELL AND A QUILL ON A TABLE oil on panel,
11 1/8 x 13 1/8in. (28 x 33.3cm.) sd 'Johann./ Heem / Anno / 1628' on the central manuscript
PROV.: The Bigland Family, Bigland Hall, Lancashire.
      Christie's London, 8 December 1995 (52**) GBP 27,600   US$ 42,475

Still-Life with Apples, Plums, Grapes, a Lemon, Peaches on a Silver Plate

STILL-LIFE WITH APPLES, PLUMS, GRAPES, A LEMON, PEACHES ON A SILVER PLATE,
AND CRUSTACEANAS. oil on panel (framed), 41.5 x 52cm. sdll 'J.D. Heem F. A. !662'
PROV.: Sold Paris, Charpentier, May 16; 1939, lot 29; collection H. Wetzlar, Amsterdam, Catalogue
1952, no. 42; Mevrouw S. M. Wulf-van Leeuwen Den Haag; Kunsthandel P. de Boer, Amsterdam,
1956, cat. no. 2,; ill.
EXH.: Dordrecht, Dordrechts Museum; *Nederlandse Stillevens uit de 17de eeuw*, 1962, cat.; no. 62;
Jubileumtentoonstelling, Kunsthandel Gebr. Douwes, Amsterdam, 1965, cat. no. 28.
      Dorotheum Vienna, 17 October 1995 (144**) ATS 900,000   US$ 90,275

**HEEMSKERCK Jvr Jacoba Berendina van Heemskerck van Beest (The Hague 1876-1923
Domburg) Dutch**
AN ABSTRACT COMPOSITION oil on canvas, 38 x 38cm. (executed *circa* 1919)
PROV.: Acquired directly from the estate of the artist by the present owner.
      Christie's Amsterdam, 5 June 1996 (243**) NLG 13,800   US$ 8,063

COMPOSITION NO. 3 oil on canvas, 56.5 x 46.5 slr 'Jacoba v. Heemskerck' and inscr. with title on
a label on the reverse
PROV.: Acquired directly from the estate of the artist by the present owner.
      Christie's Amsterdam, 5 June 1996 (244*) NLG 32,200   US$ 18,814

COMPOSITIE NR. 68 oil on canvas, ,100 x 100cm. sll 'Jacoba v Heemskerck' (1917)
EXH.: Leyden, Stedelijk Museum de Lakenhal, *Kunst van Vrienden*, 1967, no. 14 (illustrated).
      Sotheby's Amsterdam, 7 December 1995 (187**) NLG 84,960   US$ 52,646

A COMPOSITION gouache and brown ink on paper laid down on board, 62.5 x 77.5cm. sll 'Jacoba
van heemskerck'
      Christie's Amsterdam, 5 June 1996 (245**) NLG 11,500   US$ 6,719

HEEMSKERK Egbert the Younger van (1634-1704) Dutch
PEASANTS IN A TAVERN oil on canvas, 13¾ x 19¾in. (34.9 x 50.2cm.) dur '1689'

PROV.: Throckmorton sale (acc. to an old label on the reverse of the stretcher).

Sotheby's New York, 11 January 1996 (90**) US$ 9,200   US$ 9,200

THE TEMPTATION OF SAINT ANTHONY oil on canvas, 85.3 x 135.3cm. sl centre 'HK'(linked)

Christie's Amsterdam, 13 November 1995 (12*) NLG 14,950   US$ 9,422

HEEREMANS Thomas (1640-1697) Dutch
FISHERFOLK ON THE BEACH AT SCHEVENINGEN oil on panel, 11 3/8 x 16¼in. (29 x 41.3cm.) sd 'THMANS .1665'
PROV.: Anon. Sale, Christie's, 30 March 1979, lot 81 (GBP12,000).

Christie's London, 8 December 1995 (255**) GBP 11,500   US$ 17,698

IDYLLIC VILLAGESCENE ON THE STREET IN FRONT OF A TAVERN oil on panel, 32 x 39cm. sdlr 'THM MANS 1681'

Wiener Kunst Auktionen, 26 March 1996 (6**) ATS 90,000   US$ 8,657

HEEREMANS Thomas (with Abraham Storck (1635-1709)) (active in Haarlem 1640-1697) Dutch
AMSTERDAM, A VIEW IN WINTER ALONG THE FROZEN OUDE SCHANS, SEEN FROM THE SCHEEPJESBRUG TOWARDS THE Y, WITH THE MONTALBAANSTOREN TO THE LEFT oil on canvas, sdll 'FMANS 1682'
PROV.: Anon. Sale London, Sotheby's 9 July 1975, lot 97, as by Heeremans (GBP 6000).

Sotheby's London, 6 December 1995 (48**) GBP 34,500   US$ 53,093

HEFFNER Karl (Würzburg 1849-1925 Munich) German
RIVER LANDSCAPE WITH COTTAGES oil on canvas, 39¾ x 59¾in. (101 x 151.8cm.) slr 'K. Heffner'

Christie's East, 13 February 1996 (60**) US$ 8625   US$ 8,625

RIVERLANDSCAPE oil on canvas, 82 x 121cm. slr 'K. Heffner'

Dorotheum Vienna, 13 September 1995 (607**) ATS 100,000   US$ 9,720

BOATING ON THE CHIEMSEE oil on canvas, 24 ¼ x 47in. (61.7 x 119.5cm.) slr and inscr. 'Muenchen'

Phillips London, 14 November 1995 (38**) GBP 4,200   US$ 6,570

A SUMMER LAKE LANDSCAPE WITH FIGURES IN A BOAT oil on canvas, 30 ½ x 53 ¼in. (97.8 x 135.3cm.) sdll. 'J. Duntze. 1850.'

Christie's New York, 2 November 1995 (56**) US$ 10,925   US$ 10,925

HEIL Daniel van (1604-1662) Flemish
SKATINGSCENE oil on panel, 24 x 34cm.

Dorotheum Vienna, 6 March 1996 (143**) ATS 250,000   US$ 24,048

HEILBUTH Ferdinand (Hamburg 1826-1889 Paris) French
PORTRAIT OF AN ELEGANT LADY IN HER WINTERGARDEN oil on canvas, 73 x 59.5cm. sdlr 'F. HEILBUTH 1858'

Étude Tajan Paris, 18 December 1995 (131**) FRF 68,000   US$ 13697

HEINTZ Joseph the Elder (Basel 1564-1609 Prague) Swiss
VENUS AND AMOR oil on copper, 13.5 x 9.5cm.
PROV.: Private Collection, Belgium.

Dorotheum Vienna, 17 October 1995 (199**) ATS 200,000   US$ 20,061

FIGURES ADORING A STATUE OF THE 'MAGNA MATER', AFTER POLIDORI pen and brown ink and wash, heightened with (partially oxidised) white, 36.8 x 32.3cm. sd in brown ink on the base

of the statue 'Joseph Heintz noh polidor Rom. 1585'
PROV.: W.A. Freund (L.954, verso) possibly his sale, Amsterdam., de Vries, 20-21 February 1901;
Marquis de Granges de Surgères, his sale Brussels, 14 June 1921, lot 222 (as 'Maturino(?)').
        Sotheby's London, 3 July 1995 (97**) GBP 4,600   US$ 7,338

HEINTZ Joseph the Younger (Augsburg 1,600 c.-1678 Venice) German
A BULLFIGHT IN THE COURTYARD OF THE DOGE'S PALACE, VENICE oil on canvas, ,100
x 116.8cm.
        Christie's Amsterdam, 7 May 1996 (37**) NLG 92,000   US$ 53,644

HEISS Johann (1640-1704) German
VULCAN SURPRISING VENUS AND MARS IN BED BEFORE AN ASSEMBLY OF GODS oil
on canvas, 33 1/8 x 77½in. (134.9 x 196.9cm.) sdlr 'JHeiss 1679'
LIT.: Peter Königfeld, *Der Maler Johan Heiss*, 1982, p. 173, cat. no. 125.
        Sotheby's New York, 11 January 1996 (114**) US$ 96,000   US$ 96,000

HEIZER Michael (1944 b.) American
UNTITLED 9 polivinyl latex on shaped canvas, 89 x 116in. (226 x 294.6cm.) (1974)
PROV.: Fourcade Droll Gallery, New York.; Private collection, Texas; Janie C. Lee Gallery,
Houston.
        Christie's New York, 15 November 1995 (239**) US$ 13,800   US$ 13,800

HÉLION Jean (Couterne 1904-1987) France
COMPOSITION NO. 9 oil on canvas, 32 x 25 5/8in. (81.3 x 65cm.) on the reverse 'Hélion 1933 n.9'
(1933)
PROV.: Theodore Schemmp & Co., New York (acquired from the artist, 1959; acquired by the late
owner, 1960).
EXH.: New York, Gallery of Modern Art, *Jean Hélion*, Nov.-Dec., 1964, no.4.
        Christie's New York, 8 November 1995 (271**) US$ 90,500   US$ 90,500

HELLEU Paul César (1859-1927) French
PORTRAIT OF LUCETTE coloured chalks on canvas, 31 7/8 x 25 3/8in. (81 x 64.5cm.) s 'Helleu'
twice (ca 1913)
PROV.: Madame Luce Poisson; by descent to the present owner.
EXH.: Honfleur, Musée Eugène Boudin, Paul Helleu (1859-1927), 3 July-4 Oct. 1993, no. 82.
        Christie's London, 14 June 1996 (57**) GBP 20,700   US$ 31,920

FEMME ALLONGEE coloured chalks on paper, 20 5/8 x 28¾in. (52.5 x 72cm.) s 'Helleu'
        Christie's London, 14 June 1996 (58**) GBP 23,000   US$ 35,466

MADAME HELLEU black and white chalks on paper, 25 x 19in. (63.5 x 48.2cm.) s 'Helleu' (ca
1900-02)
        Christie's London, 17 November 1995 (60**) GBP 12,075   US$ 18,888

REGATES A COWES oil on canvas, 23½ x 29in. (60 x 73.7cm.) s 'Helleu' (1896)
        Christie's London, 17 November 1995 (64**) GBP 56,500   US$ 88,378

HEM Piet van der (Wirdum (Leeuwarderadeel) 1885-1961 The Hague) Dutch
PORTRAIT OF GEERTJE FROM VOLENDAM oil on canvas, unframed, 120 x 100cm. slr
'PvanderHem'
PROV.: Collection W. Beffi, Amsterdam.
        Christie's Amsterdam, 7 September 1995 (63**) NLG 18,400   US$ 11,230

HEMSLEY William, R.B.A. (1819 b.-l) British
THE WEEKLY NEWSPAPER oil on canvas, 24¼ x 30¼ (61.6 x 76.8cm.) s inscr. 'The Weekly
Newspaper/William Hemsley' on the reverse

PROV.: T. Mclean; Christie's, 16 February 1895, lot 134 (22gns. to Wroz).
EXH.: London, Royal Society of British Artists, 1872, no. 74, priced at GBP120.
Christie's London, 29 March 1996 (235**) GBP 21,850   US$ 33,369

HENDRICKS Dirck, {called} Teodoro d'Errico ((Naples, active) 1544 c.-1618) Dutch??
THE MADONNA OF GRACE AND THE ARCHANGEL MICHAEL AND ST.FRANCIS OF
ASSISI oil on panel, 78.5 x 103.5cm.
Christie's Rome, 4 June 1996 (593**) ITL 30,000,000   US$ 19,455

HENDRIKS Gerardus (19th Century, first half) Dutch
THE FERRY BOAT oil on canvas, 42.5 x 55 cm s 'G. Hendriks'
Christie's Amsterdam, 25 April 1996 (8*) NLG 9,200   US$ 5,467

HENDRIKS Wijbrand (Amsterdam 1744-1831 Haarlem) Dutch
TULIPS, AN OPIUM POPPY, HYACINTHS, ANEMONES,AURICULAE, CONVOLVULI, A
PEONY AND OTHER FLOWERS WITH A BEE, A FLY, A CATERPILLAR, A BUTTERFLY
AND ANTS IN A SCULPTED URN, A BIRDS'S NEST AND A SNAIL ON A STONE LEDGE oil
on panel, 25 5/8 x 19¼in. (60 x 49cm.) sd 'Jan van Os 1782'
PROV.: Lord Boothby; Overstrand Ltd.; Christie's, 10 July 1987, lot 67.
Christie's London, 8 December 1995 (46**) GBP 67,500   US$ 103,878

PREMIER FRITILLARIES, ROSES, AN IRIS, GENTIANS, NARCISSI, PEONIES,
CARNATIONS, MORNING GLORY AND OTHER FLOWERS IN A SCULPTED URN ON A
PEDESTAL; HOLLYHOCKS, COCKSCOMB, CAMPANULA, A PINEAPPLE, MELON,
GRAPES, PEACHES, PLUMS, BLACKBERRIES AND GOOSEBERRIES IN A BLACK
BASKET, GRAPES, MORNING GLORY AND A MOUSE EATING A WALNUT ON A
PEDESTAL oil on panel (2 panels), 23 3/x 18 5/8in. (60.4 x 47.3cm) s 'Wd - Hendriks, / pinx.'
EXH.: The present pictures are close in style to a picture offered at Christie's London, 10 July 1987,
lot nr. 67, and to a signed pair of pictures also sold at Christie's London, 18 June 1937, lot 62. Similar
works by the artist are also in the National Gallery, London and the Fitzwilliam Museum,
Cambridge.
Christie's London, 7 July 1995 (23**) GBP 111,500   US$ 177,859

HENRI Robert, N.A. (1865-1929) American
PORTRAIT OF KATHERINE CECIL STANFORD oil on canvas, 32 x 25½in. (81.2 x 64.6cm.) slc
'Robert Henri'
Christie's New York, 13 March 1996 (113**) US$ 51,750   US$ 51,750

A NEW MEXICO BOY oil on canvas, 23½ x 20in. (59.7 x 50.8cm.) sll 'Robert Henri'; inscr. with
title and '199J' on the reverse
PROV.: The Milch Galleries, New York.
EXH.: New York, The Milch Galleries, 1917-1918; Travelling Exhibition, 1919-1920 (Springfield,
Detroit, Cincinatti, Muskegan, Rochester, Memphis, Buffalo, Columbus, Baltimore and Chicago).
Christie's New York, 30 November 1995 (45**) US$ 167,500   US$ 167,500

HENRY Paul, R.H.A. (1876-1958) Irish?
CONNEMARA LANDSCAPE, NEAR LEENANE oil on canvas-board, 14 x 16in. (35.5 x 40.5cm.)
sll 'Paul Henry'
PROV.: Mr. Sibley, 1960.
Christie's London, 9 May 1996 (37**) GBP 11,500   US$ 17,414

MOUNTAIN LAKE AFTER RAIN oil on panel, 13 x 16in. (33 x 40.6cm.) sdlr 'Paul Henry 1913'
Christie's London, 9 May 1996 (39**) GBP 17,825   US$ 26,991

HEPWORTH Dame Barbara, D.B.E. (1903-1975) British
PROJECT FOR SCULPTURE (MERIDIAN) oil on gesso-prepared board, 21½ x 12in. (54.5 x

30.5cm.) sd 'Barbara Hepworth 1957' sd inscr. 'Barbara Hepworth one of the drawings which led
toward Meridian 1957 'project for sculpture' oil'
PROV.: Scottish Gallery, Edinburgh.
        Christie's London, 22 May 1996 (65**) GBP 9,430   US$ 14,279

HERBERT John Rogers, R.A. (1810-1890) British
RUTH AT MEAL TIME WITH THE REAPERS IN THE FIELD OF BOAZ; COUNTRY NEAR
BETHLEHEM, THE MOUNTAINS OF MOAB ON THE DISTANCE oil on canvas, 39¾ x 77
1/8in. (101 x 196cm.) sll 'J.R. Herbert. RA'
EXH.: London, Royal Academy, 1884, no. 266.
LIT.: Henry Blackburn (ed.); *Academy Notes*, London, 1884, p. 23.
        Christie's Tel Aviv, 14 April 1996 (4**) US$ 35,650   US$ 35,650

HERBIN Auguste (Quievy, Cambresis 1882-1960) French
SAISON NO. 2 gouache on paper, 23 5/8 x 18in. (60 x 45.7cm.) sd titled '1959'
PROV.: Galerie d'Ile de France, Paris.
        Sotheby's New York, 2 May 1996 (374**) US$ 25,300   US$ 25,300

VACHE oil on canvas, 28¾ x 39½in. (73 x 100cm.) sdlr 1947
and titled
PROV.: Canguilhem Collection, France.
LIT.: Geneviève Claisse, *Herbin: Catalogue Raisonné de
L'Oeuvre Peint*, Lausanne 1993, p. 437, no. 887 (illustrated).
        Christie's London, 23 May 1996 (11**) GBP 24,150   US$ 36,569

COMPOSITION oil on canvas, 28¾ x 36¼in. (73 x 92cm.) slr
'herbin' (1929)
PROV.: Galerie Beyeler, Basel.
LIT.: G. Claisse, *Herbin Catalogue Raisonné de l'oeuvre peint*,
Paris 1993, no. 648 (illustrated p. 393).
        Christie's London, 26 June 1996 (286**)
Route en Montagne en Corse   GBP 16,100   US$ 24,827

ROUTE ET MONTAGNES EN CORSE oil on canvas, 21¾ x 18in. (55.3 x 46cm.) slr 'Herbin'
(1907)
PROV.: Galerie Neupert, Zurich; Marlborough Fine Art, Ltd., London;
Galerie des Arts Anciens et Modernes, Schaan, Liechtenstein; Acquired from the above by Mr.
Joseph H. Hazen on 29 Nov. 1957.
EXH.: Cambridge, Massachusetts, Fogg Art Museum, *Paintings from the Collection of Joseph H.
Hazen*, Oct.-Dec. 1966, no. 44; The exhibition travelled to Los Angeles, University of California,
The Art Galleries, Jan.-Feb. 1967; Berkeley, University of California, Art Museum, Feb.-March,
1967; Houston, Museum of Fine Arts, April-May, 1967, and Honolulu, Academy of Arts, June-Aug.,
1967.
LIT.: G. Claisse, *Herbin: Catalogue raisonné de l'oeuvre peint*, Lausanne 1993, p. 298, no. 108
(illustrated).
        Christie's New York, 30 April 1996 (11**) US$ 244,500   US$ 244,500

HERDMAN Robert Inerarity, R.S.A., R.S.W. (-) Scottish
SIGHTING A DEER - PORTRAIT OF T.V. WENTWORTH, ESQ., DALL oil on canvas, 103 x
67in. (261.5 x 170cm.) sd mono. 'RH 66' (1866)
        Sotheby's London, 29 August 1995 (639**) GBP 18,400   US$ 29,783

HERMANS Charles (Brussels 1839-1924 Menton) Belgian
YOUNG LADY IN BLUE oil on canvas, 41¼ x 30in. (105 x 76cm.) slr 'C. Hermans'
PROV.: Beaux Arts, Brussels, 1-4 March 1977, lot 1105.
        Sotheby's London, 17 April 1996 (817**) GBP 20,700   US$ 31,387

HERNANDEZ Daniel (1856-1932) Peruvian
THE FRUIT SELLER oil on panel, 21 x 14¾in. (53.5 x 37.5cm.) sll 'Daniel Hernandez'
    Christie's New York, 14 February 1996 (92**) US$ 23,000   US$ 23,000

HERRI MET DE BLES (CALLED CIVETTA) (Bouvignes, near Dinant 1510 c.-1555) Flemish (Mosane)
SAINT JEROME IN PENINTENCE IN A FANTASTIC PANORAMIC LANDSCAPE; THE
TEMPTATION OF SAINT ANTHONY WITH A BURNING VILLAGE BEYOND oil on oak panel
tranferred to another panel, within painted tondi with gilt surround (a pair), each current size; 5½ x
5½in. (14 x 14cm.); each painted diameter: 4¾in. (12cm.)
PROV.: Anon. sale ('The Property of a Gentleman'), London, Christie's, 4 May 1979, lot 55.
EXH.: On loan to the Geffrye Museum, London, September 1981-1995.
    Sotheby's London, 5 July 1995 (33**) GBP 51,000   US$ 81,353

HERRING John Frederick Jnr (1820-1907) British
A TERRIER; A SETTER; FOX TERRIERS; A GREAT DANE; A LURCHER; A SPRINGER
SPANIEL; A FOXHOUND; A BOSTON BULL TERRIER: A STUDY OF DOGS IN EIGHT
PAINTED ROUNDELS oil on canvas, each of four 3 3/8in. diameter (8.5cm.); the other four 5 1/8in.
diameter (13cm.), overall canvas size 15 7/8 x 15 7/8in. (40.5 x 40.5cm.)
PROV.: Sir W.H.B.Peck, MP (19th Century).
    Phillips London, 18 June 1996 (52**) GBP 16,000   US$ 24,672

JACK SPIGOT' A DARK BAY RACEHORSE, WITH WILLIAM SCOTT UP, A RACECOURSE
BEYOND oil on canvas, 22 x 30in. (55.9 x 76.2cm.) sdll 'J.F. Herring/1823'
PROV.: with Frost & Reed, London.
    Christie's London, 10 November 1995 (63**) GBP 19,500   US$ 30,502

HERZIG Wolfgang (Judenburg 1941 b.) Austrian
MAUER oil on canvas, 125 x 183cm. s with monogram and dlr "HW 66'
    Dorotheum Vienna, 21 May 1996 (209**) ATS 130,000   US$ 12,483

VERLOBTE oil on canvas, 115 x 93cm. sdll mono 'H W 67'
    Wiener Kunst Auktionen, 27 September 1995 (545**) ATS 320,000   US$ 31,105

HERZOG Hermann (1832-1932) American (German)
GEBIRGSBACH MIT MÜHLEN oil on canvas, 52 x 83½in. (132 x 212cm.) sd 'H. Herzog, 1858'
EXH.: Bremen, Kunstverein, no. 623.
    Christie's London, 11 October 1995 (47**) GBP 12,650   US$ 19,965

DEER IN MOONLIT LANDSCAPE oil on canvas, 20 x 29in. (50.8 x 73.6cm.) slr 'H Herzog'
    Christie's New York, 23 May 1996 (101**) US$ 26,450   US$ 26,450

HESSE Alexandre (Paris 1806-1879 Paris) French
PORTRAIT OF A YOUNG LADY oil on canvas, 66 x 51cm. sll 'A. Hesse'
    Libert & Castor Paris, 29 November 1995 (61**) FRF 50,000   US$ 10,232

HEUSCH Jacob de (Utrecht 1657-1701 Amsterdam) Dutch
A) PAESAGGIO CON ROVINE B) PAESAGGIO FLUVIALE (A PAIR) oil on canvas, 57 x 96cm.
    Finearte Rome, 22 November 1995 (141**) ITL 55,200,000   US$ 34,652

HEUSCH Willem (Utrecht 1618 c.-1692) Dutch
AN ITALIANATE RIVER LANDSCAPE WITH SHEPHERDS AND ANGLERS ON A BANK, A
TOWN AND A VOLCANOE BEYOND oil on canvas, 22¾ x 30¾in. (57.8 x 78cm.) sd 'W. de.
Heusch 16.'
    Christie's South Kensington, 7 December 1995 (205**) GBP 15,750   US$ 24,238

HEYDEN Jacques (J.C.J.) van der ('s-Hertogenbosch 1928 b.) Dutch
A TRIPTYCH-RED-YELLOW-BLUE acrylics on canvas, 72 x 103cm. sd on the reverse 'J.C.J van
Heyden 1990'
PROV.: Acquired directly from the artist by the present owner.
Christie's Amsterdam, 5 June 1996 (362**) NLG 11,500   US$ 6,719

RODE STAANDE oil on canvas, 40 x 40cm. s twice on the stretcher 'J.C.J. van der Heyden'
PROV.: Kunsthandel Lambert Tegenbosch, Leusden.
Christie's Amsterdam, 5 June 1996 (363) NLG 7,475   US$ 4,368

HEYDEN Jan van der (Gorkum 1637-1712) Dutch
GARDEN OF THE OLD PALACE IN BRUSSELS oil on panel, 36 x 43cm.
PROV.: Durand Ruel, Paris; Metropolitan Museum of Art, New York.
LIT.: Hofstede de Groot, no. 265a' Helga Wagner, *Jan van der Heyden*, 1971, illustration no. 30;
Metropolitan Museum of Art, New York, Catalogue 1980, *European Paintings*, illustration nos. 66.
62.5, p. 451, vol. III.
Dorotheum Vienna, 6 March 1996 (81**) ATS 200,000   US$ 19,238

VIEW IN THE VALLEY OF THE RHINE oil on panel, 17½ x 21½in. (44.5 x 54.6cm.) slr. 'Vder
Heyden'
PROV.: Sale: Christie's London, 22 december 1937 lot 78; acquired by Douwes, Amesterdam.
LIT.: H. Wagner, *Jan van der Heyden*, 1971, pp. 50, 110, no. ,200 (illustrated).
Sotheby's New York, 16 May 1996 (91**) US$ 43,125   US$ 43,125

HIBBARD Aldro Thompson (1886-1972) American
COUNTRY ROAD IN WINTER oil on canvas, 22 x 30in. (56 x 76.5cm.) slr 'A.T. Hibbard'
Christie's New York, 13 September 1995 (74*) US$ 10,350   US$ 10,350

ASPEN TREES oil on canvas, 36 x 30in. (92 x 76.5cm.) sll and lr 'A.T. Hibbasrd' and inscr. with
title on the stretcher
PROV.: The artist; By descent in the family to the present owner.
Christie's New York, 23 May 1996 (100**) US$ 18,400   US$ 18,400

FLAGS FLYING, PIAZZA ST. MARK'S, VENICE oil on canvas, 25 x 21in. (63.5 x 53.5cm.) slr
'A.T.Hibbard'
PROV.: The Artist; Legendsea Gallery, Rockport, Massachusetts; Inherited by a relative of the
Artist.
Christie's East, 21 May 1996 (154***) US$ 29,900   US$ 29,900

HICKEL Joseph (Leipa 1736-1807 Vienna) Austrian
PORTRAIT OF PIETRO LEOPOLDO, GRANDDUC OF TUSCANY WITH A CROWN oil on
canvas, 128 x 95.5cm. sd 'Richard Hickel 1779'
Dorotheum Vienna, 6 March 1996 (185**) ATS 250,000   US$ 24,048

HICKS George Elgar (1824-1914) British
THE WATER CARRIER oil on canvas, 30 x 25in. (76 x 63.5cm.) sd 'G.E. Hicks/1874'
Christie's London, 6 November 1995 (176**) GBP 12,075   US$ 18,888

HILAIRE Camille (1916-1988) French (?)
L'ETANG EN OCTOBRE oil on canvas, 36 x 29in. (91.5 x 73.5cm.) slr 'Hilaire', s again and titled
on the reverse
Christie's South Kensington, 18 March 1996 (118**) GBP 7,475   US$ 11,416

TETE A TETE AU CAFE DU PARC oil on canvas, 35 x 45¾in. (89 x 116cm. sll 'Hilaire'
Phillips London, 26 June 1995 (59**) GBP 5,800   US$ 9,255

HILL Thomas (1829-1908) American
MOUNTAIN LAKE oil on canvas, 20 x 30in. (50.7 x 76.2cm.) sdll 'T. Hill 1887'
    Christie's New York, 13 September 1995 (23**) US$ 34,500   US$ 34,500

HILLIER Tristram, R.A. (1905-1983) British
CATALAN FISHING CRAFT, ALTEA oil on panel, 29 x 28½in. (73.7 x 71.5cm.) d inscr. 'Catalan
fishing craft altea 1934' on the reverse
PROV.: Mayor Gallery, London.
EXH.: Brussels, Musées Royaux des Beaux-Arts, Exposition Internationale d'Art Moderne, 1935, no.
729.
    Christie's London, 20 June 1996 (49**) GBP 14,950   US$ 23,053

HILVERDINK Johannes Jacobus Antonius (Amsterdam 1837-1884 Amsterdam) Dutch
ARABS RESTING ON A ROCKY OUTCROP, JERUSALEM BEYOND oil on canvas, 31 x 52in.
(78.8 x 132.2cm.) sd 'Johs Hiverdink/1855'
    Christie's South Kensington, 16 November 1995 (236**) GBP 10,125   US$ 15,838

HIRSCHFELD Emil Benediktoff (Odessa 1867-1922) Russian
AN ATTENTIVE AUDIENCE oil on canvas, 55 ¼ x 81½in. (140.5 x 207cm.) slr
    Phillips London, 14 November 1995 (48**) GBP 7,500   US$ 11,732

HIRST Damien (1966 b.) British
ADRENOCHROME SEMICARBAZONE SULFONATE gloss household paint on canvas, 65 x
75in. (165 x 190cm.) inscr. '7 x 8 5 inch spots' (1992)
PROV.: Jay Joplin Fine Art, London; Luis Campana, Cologne.
    Christie's London, 22 May 1996 (133***) GBP 32,200   US$ 48,758

HIRT Heinrich (19th Century-) German
THE PET SQUIRREL oil on canvas, 13 x 10in. (33 x 25.4cm.) slr 'H.Hirt.'
PROV.: With The Cooling Galleries, Toronto.
    Christie's New York, 14 February 1996 (82**) US$ 20,700   US$ 20,700

GRANDMOTHER`S TALES oil on canvas, 25¾ x 21½in. (65.5 x 54.5cm.) sdll inscr. 'H. Hirt
München 1879'
LIT.: E. Benezit *Dictionnaire des Peintres,; Sculpteurs, Dessinateurs et Graveurs'*, Vol 5, Librairie
Grund,; Paris, 1976, p. 55, possibly as *'Les;contes de Grand-mère'*.
    Phillips London, 12th March 1996 (17**) GBP 31,000   US$ 47,343

HITCHENS Ivon (1893-1979) British
STILL LIFE WITH SPRING FLOWERS oil on canvas, 22 x 24in. (56 x 61cm.) slr 'Ivon Hotchens';
S and inscr. 'Ivon Hitchens Greenleaves Lavington Common Pertwoth Sussex 'Flowers'' on a label
attached to the stretcher (ca. 1936)
PROV.: Given to Jack PRitchard, London, by the Artist in 1960, thence by descent.
    Christie's London, 22 May 1996 (17**) GBP 24,150   US$ 36,569

SUMMER ORATORY oil on canvas, 20¼ x 41½in. (51.5 x 105.5cm.) sll 'Hitchens'; s and inscr.
'Summer Oratory by Ivon Hitchens Greenleaves Lavington Common Petworth Sussex England' on a
label attached to the stretcher (ca. 1957)
PROV.: New Art Centre, London.
    Christie's London, 22 May 1996 (23**) GBP 13,800   US$ 2,0896

HJERTÉN Sigrid Grünewald- (1885-1948) Swedish
KUNISERNA oil on board, 28½ x 26in. (72.5 x 66cm.) s 'Hjertén'
EXH.: Sundsval Museum, Sigrid Hjertén Minnesutställning, 1985 no. 11, p. 16.
    Christie's London, 15 March 1996 (65**) GBP 17,825   US$ 27,222

BLONDINEN PÅ TAKTERASSEN oil on canvas, ,100 x 81cm. slr 'Hjertén' (1923)
EXH.: Konstakademin, 1936; Skånska Konstmuseum, 1938; Sundvalls Konstförening, 1958;
Moderna museet, 1964; Liljevalchs KOnsthall, 1995.
LIT.: *Liljevachs exhibitioncatalogue* (illustrated in colour no. 53).
      Bukowskis Stockholm, 24-25 April 1996 (41**) SEK 460,000   US$ 69,690

LES PECHEURS oil on canvas, 81 x 66cm. slr 'Hjertén' (1929)
LIT.: Jämför Liljevalchs Konsthall, *Sigrid Hjertén*, 1995, calatogue no. 62.
      Bukowskis Stockholm, 24-25 April 1996 (42**) SEK 320,000   US$ 48,480

INTERIÖR oil on canvas, 73 x 92.5cm. sll 'Hjertén'
      Bukowskis Stockholm, 26-27 October 1995 (44**) SEK 360,000   US$ 52,723

FLICKA I ROSA HATT oil on canvas, 46 x 55.5cm. slr 'Hjertén' (1916)
EXH.: Liljevalch, Liljevalchs Konsthall, 1918, cat. no. 414.
      Bukowskis Stockholm, 26-27 October 1995 (45**) SEK 320,000   US$ 46,864

HJORTH Bror (1894-1968) Swedish
FLICKAN OCH LEJONET oil on canvas laid down on board, ,100 x 105cm. sll 'Bror Hjorth' (1966)
EXH.: Oslo, Kunstnernes Hus, 1973, catalogue no. 189.
LIT.: Bror Hjorth, *Mitt liv i konsten* (illustrated p. 180); Ulf Linde, *Möte med Bror Hjorth* (illustrated
in colour p. 200).
      Bukowskis Stockholm, 24-25 April 1996 (45**) SEK 725,000   US$ 109,837

HJORTZBERG Olle (1872-1959) Swedish
MIDSOMMARBLOMSTER oil on canvas, 73 x 60cm. sdlr 'Olle Hjortzberg 1941'
      Bukowskis Stockholm, 29 November-1 December 1995 (56**) SEK 110,000   US$ 16,641

HOBBEMA Meindert (attr.) (Amsterdam 1638-1709) Dutch
A CANAL LANDSCAPE WITH BARGES MOORED BY HOUSES oil on canvas, 27¼ x 35in.
(69.7 x 89cm.) bears signature on the foremost vessel in the centre 'M. hobbema' (ca. end of 1650s)
PROV.: Anonmous sale, (Dr. Seymour Maynard, London, et al), Berlin, Lepke, 22 March 1910, lot
87; Marczell von Nemes, Budapest and Munich, by 1911; With Haberstock, Berlin, 1924; Baron
Heinrich Thyssen-Bornemisza, by 1930.
EXH.: Budapest, Szopmuveszeti Museum, *Collection des peintures de la collection Marcel de
Nemes*, 1910-11, no. 33; Said to be Munich, Alte Pinakothek, June-December 1911; Munich 1930,
no. 153; Bern 1960, no. 25; Paris 1970, no. 27, plate 15; Düsseldorf 1970-71, no. 24; Lausanne etc.,
1986-7, no. 43.
LIT.: C. Hofstede de Groot, *A Catalogue Raisonné..*, vol. IV,1912, pp.361-2, no. 27, wrongly as on
panel, an early work; G. von Terey, 'Die Sammlung Marczell von Nemes..', in Kunst und Künstler,
vol. IX, 1910-11, p. 223; R. Heinemann 1937, vol. I, no. 192, vol. II plate 163, as Hobbema; G.
Broulhiet, *Meindert Hobbema*, 1938, p.421, no. 325, reproduced p. 264, as Hobbema, as on panel.
      Sotheby's London, 6 December 1995 (103**) GBP 47,700   US$ 73,407

HÖCH Hannah (Gotha 1889-1978 Berlin) German
GEGEN GRUNEN GRUND watercolour over pencildrawing, 31.2 x 19.1cm. sdlc 'H,Höch / 19,';
titled 'Gegen grünen Grund' ll; slr with mono. (1919)
PROV.: Galerie Nierendorf, Berlin.
      Hauswedell & Nolte Cologne, 5/06 June 1996 (313**) DEM 16,000   US$ 10,396

HOCKNEY David, R.A. Elect (1937 b.-l) British
UNTITLED acrylic on canvas, 23¾ x 29¾in. (60.4 x 75.6cm.) s and dedicated'DEAR HENRY GET
WELL SOON LOVE DAVID' lower center (ca.1986)
PROV.: Acquired directly from the artist.
      Christie's New York, 8 May 1996 (159**) US$ 34,500   US$ 34,500

MARINKA, NUDE colored crayons and colored pencils on paper, 17 x 14in. (43.2 x 35.6cm.) sd ini
'DH. 77' (1977)
PROV.: André Emmerich Gallery, New York.
EXH.: New York, André Emmerich Gallery, *David Hockney: New Paintings, Drawings and Graphics*, Oct.-Nov. 1977 (illustrated).
    Christie's New York, 7 May 1996 (40**) US$ 46,000   US$ 46,000

HODGES Charles Howard (London 1764-1837 Amsterdam) British
PORTRAIT OF JACOBUS CATHARINUS DE JONCHEERE (1801-1858), HALF LENTH,
WEARING BLACK COSTUME, YELLOW WAISTCOAT AND WHITE CHEMISE; AND
PORTRAIT OF HELENA CORNELIA LUBERTA DE JONCHEERE, *NEE* VAN BEUSECHEM,
VROUWE VAN HARMELEN (1807-1886), SEATED HALF LENGTH, WEARING A SILK
BROWN-GREY DRESS, SCARF AND GARNET NECKLACE oil on canvas, 73.4 x 62cm. and
72.8 x 61.8cm. with inscriptions identifying the sitters on the reverse of the relined canvases
LIT.: A.S.A.W. van der Feltz, *Charles Howard Hodges*, 1982, p. 181, nos. 288 and 289, with ill. p.
180, where dated to circa 1830.
    Christie's Amsterdam, 13 November 1995 (86*) NLG 14,950   US$ 9,422

HODGKIN Howard (1932 b.) British
MENSWEAR oil on wood in artist's frame, 32¾ x 42½in. (83 x 108cm.) sd and titled '1980-85' on
the reverse of the frame
PROV.: Waddington Galleries, London; M. Knoedler & Co., New York; Saatchi Collection, London.
EXH.: London, Whitechapel Art Gallery, Howard Hodgkin: Ten Paintings 1979-85, September-
November 1985, no. 2 (illustrated in colour in the catalogue p. 7); Pittsburgh, Museum of Art,
Carnegie Institute, Carnegie International, November 1985-January 1986 (illustrated in the catalogue
p. 141); London, M. Knoedler & Co., Howard Hodgkin: Recent Work, May-June 1986, no. 3
(illustrated in colour in the catalogue p. 7); London, Royal Academy of Arts, British Art in the 20th
Century: The Modern Movement, January-April 1987, no. 291 (illustrated in colour in the
catalogue).
LIT.: Alistair Hicks, New British Art in the Saatchi Collection, London 1989, p. 54, no. 40
(illustrated in colour); Michael Auping, John Elderfield, Susan Sontag, Marla Price, Howard
Hodgkin Paintings, London1995, p. 184 no. 198 (illustrated).
    Christie's London, 30 November 1995 (37**) GBP 117,000   US$ 18,3013

IN THE BAY OF NAPLES oil on panel, 54 x 60in. (137.2 x 152.4cm.) sd and titled 'Howard
Hodgkin In hte Bay of Naples 1980-82' on the reverse
PROV.: M. Knoedler & Co., Inc., New York; Private collection, New York; Washburn Gallery, New
York.
EXH.: New York, M. Knoedler & Co., Inc., *Howard Hodgkin Paintings*, Nov.-Dec. 1982, no. 6;
Venice, *XLI Esposizione Biennale Internazionale d'Arte*, June- Sept. 1984; Washington, D.C., *The
Phillips Collection*; New Haven, Yale Center for British Art; Hannover, Kestner-Gesellschaft and
London, Whitechapel Art Gallery, *Howard Hodgkin: Forty Paintinys 1973-84*, Oct. 1984-Aug. 1985,
pp.68-69 (illustrated); New York, Hirschl & Adler Galleries, *The British Imagination: Twentieth
Century Paintings, Sculpture, and Drawings*, Nov. 1990-Jan. 1991, p. 132, no. 67 (illustrated); New
York, The Metropolitan Museum of Art, *Howard Hodgkn Paintings*, Oct. 1995-Jan. 1996, p. 81, no.
170 (illustrated).
LIT.: A. Graham-Dixon, *Howard Hodgkin*, London and New York 1994, p. 99, no. 101 (illustrated).
    Christie's New York, 7 May 1996 (13**) US$ 486,500   US$ 486,500

CHEZ SWOB oil on panel, unframed, 17½ x 25¼in. (44.4 x 64.2cm.) sd and titled 'Howard Hodgkin
'Chez Swob' 1977-1980' on the reverse
PROV.: M.Knoedler & Co.Inc., New York; Waddington Galleries, London.
EXH.: M.Auping, J.Elderfield and S.Sontag, *Howard Hodgkin Paintings*, London 1995, p.172,
no.151 (ill.).
    Christie's New York, 8 May 1996 (406**) US$ 57,500   US$ 57,500

HODGKINS Frances (1869-1947) Australian
STILL LIFE WITH GOURDS watercolour and bodycolour, 16 x 21in. (40.6 x 53.3cm.) slr 'Frances Hodgkins'
PROV.: Lefevre Gallery, London; Purchased by the present owners' grandmother at the 1941 exhibition.
EXH.: London, Leicester Galleries, Frances Hodgkins, Oct 1941, no. 122.

Christie's London, 21 March 1996 (29**) GBP 8,625	US$	13,172

HOECKE Gaspar van den (1575 c.-1648 c.)
DIVES AND LAZARUS oil on panel, 37.6 x 54.8cm.
PROV.: Sold in these rooms on 21 May 1985, lot 184, with ill. where acquired by the present owner (dfl. 29.640).

Christie's Amsterdam, 13 November 1995 (70*) NLG 23,000	US$	14,495

HOECKE Robert van den (Antwerp 1622-1668) Flemish
A WINTER LANDSCAPE WITH SKATERS ON A FROZEN RIVER BY A MANSION, ELEGANT COMPANY IN A HORSE AND CARRIAGE BEYOND oil on panel, 23.9 x 33.4cm.

Christie's Amsterdam, 7 May 1996 (52**) NLG 40,250	US$	23,469

HOERLE Heinrich (Köln 1895-1936 Köln) German
GRUPPE oil on light cardboard, 45.9 x 28.5cm s with ini. and dlc/r 'h 31' (written with pecil while ink was still wet)d, inscr. and numbered 'h 1931/11' on the reverse

Lempertz Cologne, 1 June 1996 (733**) DEM 50,000	US$	32,487

HOFER Carl (Karlsruhe 1878-1955 Berlin) German
BLUMENWERFENDE MÄDCHEN oil on canvas, 48½ x 38¾in. (123.3 x 98.6cm.) sdll 'CH 34' inscribed with the title on the back of the stretcher (1934)
PROV.: Galerie Nierendorf, Berlin, from whom purchased for the Joseph Winterbotham Collection, Art Institute of Chicago, 1934; Transferred to the General Collection of the Art Institute of Chicago from the above in 1966.
EXH.: Pittsburg, Carnegie Institute, Department of Fine Arts, Karl Hofer, Paintings, Drawings and Prints, Jan. 1939. no. 14; New York, Karl Nierendorf Gallery, 1939; Chicago, The Arts Club of Chicago, Paintings and Drawings by Karl Hofer, Dec. 1939, no. 23; Chicago, The University of Chicago, on loan, May-Sept. 1949 and Dallas, Museum of Fine Arts, Oct. 1949.
LIT.: Winterbotham, Art Institute of Chicago, 1946, p. 24 (illustrated); The Years 1946-1947, the Bulletin of the Art Institute of Chicago, vol. 42, pt. 3, Feb. 1940, p. 11 (illustrated); The Art News, vol. 35, pt. 1, 26 Dec. 1936, p. 25 (illustrated p. 10); Paintings in the Art Institute of Chicago, Netherlands, 1961, p. 217.

Christie's London, 11 October 1995 (163**) GBP 232,500	US$	366,951

PORTRAIT OF FREDA BRAUN oil on canvas, 45 x 31½in. (114.3 x 80cm.) sd ini. '1929'
PROV.: Acquired directly from the Artist by the family of the present owner.

Sotheby's New York, 2 May 1996 (390**) US$ 43,125	US$	43,125

FESTLICHER TAG oil on canvas, 51¼ x 41in. (130 x 104cm.) s mono. 'CH' s titled on the stretcher (ca. 1922)
PROV.: Private collection, Germany (purchased in 1934).
EXH.: *Deutsche Kunst und Dekoration*, no. 53, Munich, 1923-24, p. 9, illustrated (dated 1921); Benno Reifenberg, *Karl Hofer*, Leipzig, 1924, pl. 13, illustrated; Benno Reifenberg, *Der Cicerone*, Berlin, 1924, p. 1051, illustrated; Benno Reifenberg, *Jahrbuch der jungen Kunst*, Leipzig, 1924, vol. 5, p. 363, illustrated; To be included in the *Hofer Werkverzeichnis* being prepared by Karl Bernhard Wohlert.

Sotheby's London, 24 June 1996 (42**) GBP 551,500	US$	850,424

HOFFMEISTER (?)C.L. (active, Vienna ca. 1830 -) German
UHRENBILD MIT EINER ANSICHT VON INNSBRUCK oil on metal, 51 x 68cm. sdlr 'C. L.

Hoffmeister pinx. 1827'
PROV.: Hessische privatsammlung.

    Lempertz Cologne, 15 November 1995 (1786*) DEM 64,000   US$ 45,172

HOFKER Willem Gerard (The Hague 1902-1981 (1980)) Dutch
AN ELEGANT YOUNG BEAUTY pencil, black and red chalks on paper, 52 x 35 cm s twice d and
inscr. 'W.G. Hofker 1953 voor Maria'

    Christie's Amsterdam, 25 April 1996 (50*) NLG 20,700   US$ 12,300

HOFMANN Hans (Weissenburg 1880-1965 New York) American (German)
UNTITLED oil, watercolour and coloured crayons on paper mounted on composition board, 26 x
22in. (66 x 55.8cm.) sdlr 'hans hofmann 4.21.47'
PROV.: André Emmerich Gallery, New York.

    Christie's New York, 22 February 1996 (18**) US$ 21,850   US$ 21,850

FRAGANCE oil on canvas, 48 x 36in (121.8 x 91.4cm.) sdlr 'hans hofmann 62'; sd and titled
'Fragance 1962 hans hofmann' on the reverse
PROV.: Kootz Gallery, New York; André Emmerich Gallery, New York.
EXH.: New York, André Emmerich Gallery, *Hans Hofmann*, Jan. 1968; Philadelphia, Makler
Gallery, *Hans Hofmann*, May-April 1969; Montreal, Galerie Godard Lefort, *Hans Hofmann*, Oct.
1971; New York, André Emmerich Gallery, *Hans Hofmann-Ten Major Works*, Jan. 1973, n.n. (ill.);
New York, André Emmerich Gallery, *Hans Hofmann-Major Paintings 1954-1965*, Jan. 1985.
LIT.: G. Glueck, 'The 20th Century Artists Most Admired by Other Artists', *Art News*, Nov. 1977, p.
94 (ill.).

    Christie's New York, 14 November 1995 (16**) US$ 134,500   US$ 134,500

TERPSICHORE oil on canvas, 60 x 48½in.
(152.4 x 123.2cm.) sdlr 'Hans Hofmann 58'; sd
abd titled 'Terpsichore 1958 hans hofmann' on the
reverse
PROV.: Kootz Gallery, New York.
LIT.: S. Hunter, *Hans Hofmann*, New York 1963,
no. 96 (illustrated).

    Christie's New York, 14 November
1995 (22**) US$ 420,500   US$ 420,500

UNTITLED oil on board mounted on canvas, 31
7/8 x 24in. (81 x 61cm.) stamped with Hans
Hofmann Estate number 'M 537/17' on stretcher.
(1964)
PROV.: André Emmerich Gallery, New York.

    Christie's New York, 15 November
1995 (163**) US$ 77,300   US$ 77,300

Frolic

FROLIC oil on canvas, 60 x 48in. (152.5 x 121.9cm.) sdlr 'hans hofmann'; sd and titled "Frolic' 1959
hans hofmann' on the reverse
PROV.: Acquired directly from the artist.

    Christie's New York, 7 May 1996 (8**) US$ 167,500   US$ 167,500

UNTITLED oil on paperboard, 12 x 11¼in. (30.5 x 25.7cm.) sd and numbered lr 'hans hofmann 62
'29'
PROV.: Michel Tapié, Paris.
EXH.: Turin, International Center of Aesthetic Research, *Hans Hofmann*, May 1963, no.29.

    Christie's New York, 22 February 1996 (20**) US$ 13,800   US$ 13,800

SUCCULENCE oil on masonite, 22½ x 15 1/8in. (57.2 x 38.4cm.) sdlr 'hans hofmann 46', titled 'Succulence' on the reverse
PROV.: Mortimer Brandt Gallery, New York.
EXH.: Roslyn, Nassau County Museum of Art, *The Long Island Collections, A Century of Art: 1880-1980*, Apr.-July 1982, p.75, no.107 (ill.).

Christie's New York, 8 May 1996 (267**) US$ 34,500	US$	34,500

HOFMANN Ludwig von (Darmstadt 1861-1945 Pillnitz) German
AM BRUNNEN oil on canvas, 99 x 85.5cm. s with mono.

Hauswedell & Nolte Cologne, 5/6 June 1996 (324**) DEM 10,000	US$	6,497

HOFSTETTER William Alfred (1884 b-?)
CHILDREN FISHING BY A STREAM oil on canvas, 30¼ x 36in. (76.8 x 91.5cm.) slr 'A.Hofstetter'

Christie's East, 28 November 1995 (117*) US$ 12,650	US$	12,650

HOLBEIN Hans the Elder (Augsburg ca. 1465-1524 Basel) German
THE VIRGIN AND CHILD (THE MADONNA MONTENUOVO) oil on pine panel, 18 x 13½in. (45.5 x 34.5cm.) sur 'iOHANES.HO/.LBAIN.IN.AVG./VSTA. BINGWAT.' inscr. ul '.CARPET. ALIQIS/ CICUS.QVAM./IMITATIBVR.'
PROV.: Freiherr von Wirz von Rudenz, Wil, St. Gallen, Switzerland; PastorJ.B. Schmitter-Hug, Ragaz, Switzerland, 1866-68; Alexander Posonyi, Vienna, 1874; Prince Alfred Montenuovo Collection, Vienna; Baron Heinrich Thyssen-Bornemisza, Villa Favorita, Castagnola, by whom purchased on 16 July 1932, 50,000 Dutch Guilders.
EXH.: Basel, Kunstmuseum, *Die Malerfamilie Holbein in Basel*, 1960, no. 13b; Paris 1970, no. 6; plate 1.; Dusseldorf 1970-1, no. 25; Houston, Museum of Fine Arts, on loan, 1983-1985.
LIT.: A. Woltmann, *Hans Holbein und seine Zeit*, 2nd ea., 1874-6, vol. I, pp. 87ff, 153, 494, vol.11, p. 90, no. 285; W. Suida, in Osterreichische Kunstschätze, vol. I, 1911, reproduced plate 27; P. Ganz, *Hans Holbein d.J., des Meisters Gemälde, Klassiker der Kunst*, vol. XX, 1912, p. XI; W. Suida, in Belvedere, vol. IV, 1923, p. 132; C. Glaser, in F. Thieme, U. Becker, *Allgemeines Lexikon der Bildenden Kunstler*, vol. XVII, 1924, p. 335; E. Buchner, 'Zum Werk Hans Holbeins des Alteren' in *Beitrage zur Geschichte der deutschen Kunst*, vol. II, 1928, pp. 138, 155ff; L. Baldaß, 'Niederlandische Bildgedanken im Werke des alteren Hans Holbein' in *Beitrage zur Geschichte der deutschen Kunst*, vol.II, 1928, pp. 175ff 182, 185, 188; H. Tietze, in *Kunstchronik und Kunstliteratur, Beilage für Bildende Kunst*, vol. IV, 1929, p. 42; A.L. Mayer, in *Pantheon*, vol.III, 1929, p. 158; R. Heinemann 1937, vol. I, no. 194, vol.II, plate 21; *Katalog der Gemäldegalerie Wien*, 2nd ed., 1938, p. 80; A. Stange, *Deutsche Malerei der Gotik*, vol. XVIII, pp. 72, 75; K. Feuchtmayr, in *Festschrift fur Hans Vollmer*, 1957, p. 144; N. Lieb, A. Stange, *Hans Holbein der Ältere*, 1960, no. 35; E. Treu, in *Die Malerfamilie Holbein in Basel*, exhibition cat., 1960, pp. 70-1, no. 13b, reproduced plate 4.

Sotheby's London, 6 December 1995 (64**) GBP 106,000	US$	163,127

HOLLEGHA Wolfgang (1929 b.) Austrian
UNTITLED oil on canvas, 131 x 202cm. (1980)
EXH.: Vienna, Akademie der Bildenden Künste, 1981 (illustrated); Salzburg, Galerie Academia.

Wiener Kunst Auktionen, 27 September 1995 (463**) ATS 220,000	US$	21,385

HOLSOE Carl Vilhelm (1863-1935) Danish
AN INTERIOR WITH A CELLO oil on canvas, 29¾ x 24¼in. (75.5 x 61.8cm.) s 'C. Holsoe'

Christie's London, 14 June 1996 (112**) GBP 10,120	US$	15,605

AN INTERIOR WITH A WOMAN READING oil on panel, 21 1/8 x 18 1/8in. (53.8 x 45.9cm.) s 'C. Holsöe'

Christie's London, 15 March 1996 (52**) GBP 16,100	US$	24,588

MANUAL LABOUR AT THE WINDOW oil on panel, 55 x 43cm. slr 'C. Holsöe'

Bukowskis Stockholm, 29 November-1 December 1995 (193**) SEK 100,000	US$	15,128

HOLST Laurits Bernhard (Bogense 1848 b.) Danish
A ROCKY COASTLINE WITH DISTANT SHIPPING oil on canvas, 33 x 51in. (83.8 x 139.6cm.)
sd 'L.Holst 85'
Christie's South Kensington, 12 October 1995 (127**) GBP 7,650
US$ 12,074

HÖLZEL Adolf (Olmütz 1853-1934 Stuttgart) German
VORALPENLANDSCHAFT oil on canvas, 74.5 x 112.5cm. s with mongram 'AH' and d '1901'
Dorotheum Vienna, 13 September 1995 (754*) ATS 110,000
US$ 10,692

HONDECOETER Gillis Claesz. d' (Antwerp 1575 c.-1638 Amsterdam) Dutch (Flemish)
A RIVER LANDSCAPE WITH CATTLE AND SWANS oil on panel, 13¼ x 10½in. (33.6 x 26.7cm.)
PROV.: Probably acquired in the 1890s by the great-grandmother of the present owner.
Sotheby's London, 6 December 1995 (141**) GBP 14,950
US$ 23,007

HONDECOETER Melchior d' (circle of) (Utrecht 1636-1695 Amsterdam) Dutch
A PEACOCK AND OTHER EXOTIC BIRDS IN AN ELABORATE PARKLAND SETTING oil on canvas, 58¾ x 95¼in. (149.2 x 241.9cm.)
PROV.: Colnaghi, London; T.J. Blakeslee, New York, by 1904; Julia A. Berwind, The Elms, Newport, Rhode Island (sale: Parke-Bernet Galleries, Inc., New York [sold at The Elms], June 27, 28, 1962, lot 503, illus. (as by Melchior de Hondecoeter), where purchased by Schaeffer Galleries, Inc., New York, from whom acquired by the present owner on February 15, 1964 (Acc. no. 64.51).
LIT.: Peter C. Sutton, *A Guide to Dutch Art in America*, 1968, p. 338 (as attributed to or tentatively ascribed to Hondecoeter).
Sotheby's New York, 11 January 1996 (4**) US$ 118,000
US$ 118,000

HONDIUS Abraham Danielsz. (Rotterdam 1625/30-1695 after London) Dutch
A CROWD WATCHING BEAR-BAITING IN A TOWN SQUARE oil on canvas, 30½ x 34¾in. (77.5 x 87.3cm.) s 'Hondius fecit' on the reverse of the unlined canvas with inventory number 403 (1670's)
Christie's London, 8 December 1995 (225**) GBP 52,100
US$ 80,179

HONDIUS Abraham Danielsz. (Rotterdam 1625/30-1695 after London) Dutch
SPORTSMAN OFFERD REFRESHMENT OUTSIDE IN AN ITALIANATE INN WHILE HIS DOGS REST AFTER THE HUNT oil on panel, 34¼ x 42¼in. (87 x 107.3cm.) sd 'A.D.Hont.f. 1651'
PROV.: H.L. Bischoffsheim, Bute House, London (sale: Christie's, 7 May 1926, lot 110, as by J.B. Weenix and A. Hondius, sold with a pendant) there purchased by Parsons.
Sotheby's New York, 16 May 1996 (86**) US$ 162,000
US$ 162,000

LANDSCAPE WITH HUNTSMEN AND HOUNDS oil on canvas, 34½ x 55¾in. (87 x 141.7cm.)
sdll '...ham Hondius 1685'
Sotheby's London, 18 October 1995 (15**) GBP 8,050
US$ 12,705

A SPANIEL ATTACKING A PHEASANT oil on canvas, 39¾ x 50in. (100.9 x 127cm.)
Christie's London, 28 March 1996 (129**) GBP 8,050
US$ 12,294

HOOCH Pieter de (Rotterdam 1629-1684 (?) Amsterdam) Dutch
A SOLDIER AN HIS FAMILY IN AN INTERIOR oil on canvas, 24½ x 30¾in. (62 x 78cm.) slr 'P.d.hoogh' (ca. 1655)
PROV.: Marquis de Salamanca, his sale, Paris, 3-6 march 1867, lot 93, for 380 florins; Serafin Martinez collection; Victor Bachau, his sale, Brussels, de Brauwere, 3 February 1874, lot 34; With Pieter de Boer, Amsterdam; Anon. sale, London, Sotheby's, 9 April 1986, lot 63, withdrawn.
LIT.: H. Harvard, *L'Art et les Artistes Hollandais*, vol. III, 1860, p. 131, no. 2; C. Hofstede de Groot, *A Catalogue Raisonnné..*, vol. I, 1907, p. 548, no. 263; P.C. Sutton, *Pieter de Hooch*, 1980, pp. 14, 77, no. 11 bis, reproduced plate 9b.
Sotheby's London, 6 December 1995 (47**) GBP 80,700
US$ 124,192

HOOG Johan Bernard ('Bernard') de (Amsterdam 1866-1943 The Hague) Dutch
DOMESTIC BLISS oil on canvas, 31¾ x 39¾in. (80.7 x 101cm.) sll 'Bernard. de Hoog.'
Christie's New York, 2 November 1995 (88**) US$ 19,550 — US$ 19,550

A QUIET AFTERNOON SLEEP oil on canvas, 67 x 51cm. s 'Bernard de Hoog'
Christie's Amsterdam, 25 April 1996 (198**) NLG 14,950 — US$ 8,883

HOPPENBROUWERS Johannes Franciscus (The Hague 1819-1866 The Hague) Dutch
SKATERS AND A *KOEK EN ZOPIE* ON A FROZEN WATERWAY ALONG A WINDMILL oil
on panel, 24.5 x 34.5 cm sd 'J.F. Hoppenbrouwers ft. 58'
Christie's Amsterdam, 25 April 1996 (19) NLG 16,100 — US$ 9,567

A RIVER LANDSCAPE WITH FIGURES oil on panel, 24.5 x 31cm. slr 'JF Hoppenbrouwers'
Christie's Amsterdam, 26 October 1995 (11*) NLG 14,950 — US$ 9,426

HOPPER Edward (1882-1967) American
FINAL STUDY FOR NIGHTHAWKS crayon conté, charcoal and white chalk on paper, 11 x 14in.
(27.9 x 38.2cm.) slr 'Edward Hopper' (ca. 1942)
EXH.: New Britain, Connecticut, The New Britain Museum of Amencan Art, *Sound and Silence*,
November-December 1973 (illustrated on the cover); New York, Whitney Museum of Art, *Edward
Hopper: The Art and The Artist*, September 1980-January 1981, no. 387, p. 270, illus., and travelling;
London, England, Hayward Gallery, *Edward Hopper, 1882-1967*, February-March 1981, no. 192, p.
56 (illustrated on the cover); Evanston, Illinois, Terra Museum of American Art, *Twentieth Century
American Drawings-The Figure in Context*, April-June 1984, no. 44, and travelling; Yonkers, New
York, The Hudson River Museum, *Form or Formula: Discourse on Drawing and Drawings*, April-
May 1986; Hartford, Connecticut, Aetna Institute Gallery, *20th Century American Realism*, March-
May 1988 (illustrated); Hartford, Connecticut, Wadsworth Atheneum, *Masterworks from Private
Connecticut Collections*, October 1993-January 1994.
LIT.: J. Canaday, 'The Solo Voyage of Edward Hopper, American Realist,' *Smithsonian*, September
1980, p. 127, illus.; G. Levin, 'Edward Hopper's 'Nighthawks,'' *Arts*, May 1981, p. 159, illus.; 'Artist's
Panel', *Art Joumal*, Summer 1981, p. 153, illus.; M. Holthof, 'Die Hopper-Methode: Vom narrative
zum abstrakten realism,' in *Edward Hopper: 1882-1967*, Frankfurt, Germany, 1992, p. 24, illus.;
Reiner Moritz Associates, *,100 Great Paintings, Masterworks: Art Institute of Chicago*, London,
England, (television program broadcast in Europe); I. Kranzfelder, *Edward Hopper 1882- 1967:
Vision der Wirklichkeit*, 1994, Benedikt Taschen Verlag GmbH, Germany, p. 141, illus.; G. Levin,
Edward Hopper: An Intimate Biography, New York, 1995, p. 349.
Christie's New York, 23 May 1996 (150**) US$ 827,500 — US$ 827,500

HOPPNER John, R.A. (1758-1810) British
PORTRAIT OF EDWARD, VISCOUNT LASCELLES (1764-1814) oil on canvas, 45½ x 38in.
(115.5 x 96.5cm.)
PROV.: By descent to the sitter's sister Lady Frances Lascelles, who married Lord John Douglas;
Thence by descent at Dalmahoy House, to Sholto, 19th Earl of Morton (1844-1935) by whom sold,
Christie's, 8th July 1910, lot 139, bt. Knoedler; Mr and Mrs van Horn Ely, by whom given to the
Phoenix Art Museum.
LIT.: William McKay and W. Roberts, *John Hoppner R.A.*, 1909, p. 337; William McKay and W.
Roberts, *John Hoppner R.A., Supplement*, 1914, p. 31.
Sotheby's London, 12 July 1995 (69**) GBP 23,000 — US$ 36,688

PORTAIT OF THE HON. LEICESTER FITZGERALD CHARLES STANHOPE, LATER 5TH
EARL OF HARRINGTON, AS A CHILD oil on canvas, 54¾ x 44in. (139.1 x 111.8cm.)
PROV.: Charles Stanhope, 3rd Earl of Harrington, father of the sitter; by whom given to Lord Henry
Fitzgerald, Boyle Farm, Thames Ditton godfather of the sitter; Henry, Lord de Ros, Boyle Farm,
Thames Ditton; from whom purchased by Sir Edward Sugden, Lord Chancellor of Ireland, 1834;
H.L. Bischoffsheim, Esq., Bute House, London (Sale: Christie's, London, May 7, 1926, lot 42, illus.);
there purchased by M. Knoedler & Co., Inc., New York; John R. Thompson, Chicago (Sale: Parke-

Bernet Galleries, Inc., New York, January 15, 1944, lot 34 (illustrated); Mrs.John W. Ryan (Eleonore
Thompson, daughter of the above); John W. Ryan, and thence to the present owner.
EXH.: London, Royal Academy, 1791, no. 420; London, Grafton Galleries, *Fair Children
Exhibition*, 1895,no. 112.
LIT.: William MacKay and W. Roberts, *John Hoptner*, R.A.,1914, p. 243;
John Wilson, *The Life and Work of John Hoppner 1758-1810*, PhD dissertation, Courtauld Institute,
1992, pp. 171-72 (illustrated fig. 36 (as location unknown)).

Sotheby's New York, 6 October 1996 (208*) US$ 54,625	US$	54,625

HOREMANS Jan Josef the Elder (Antwerp 1682-1759) Flemish
THE COURTYARD OF AN INN oil on canvas, 26½ x 33½in. (67.3 x 85cm.)

Christie's London, 8 December 1995 (237**) GBP 11,500	US$	17,698

ALLÉGORIE DE L'HIVER oil on canvas, 47 x 65.5cm. slr 'J. Horemans'

Étude Tajan Paris, 12 December 1995 (84**) FRF 220,000	US$	44,314

PEASANTS IN A TAVERN oil on canvas, 15 3/8 x 12 7/8in. (39 x 32.7cm.)

Christie's South Kensington, 18 april 1996 (222**) GBP 5,520	US$	8,370

INTERIOR OF A MERCERS SHOP; A FAMILY AT TEA oil on canvas (a pair), each: 19¼ x
22¾in. (49 x 58cm.) one sdlr 'J.Horemans. 1752'; the other sdll 'J.Horemans/1752'

Sotheby's London, 18 October 1995 (75**) GBP 12,650	US$	19,965

HOREMANS Jan Josef the Younger (1714-1790) Flemish
A COMPANY AT TABLE IN AN INTERIOR oil on canvas, 66.2 x 85.5cm.

Christie's Amsterdam, 13 November 1995 (18*) NLG 11,500	US$	7,248

A SCHOOL MASTER HANDING OUT EGGS oil on panel, 37 x 30.5cm. slr 'JHoremans'
PROV.: With Nystadt Antiquairs NV, Lochem, 1967; Anon. sale, Dordrecht, Mak, 26 November
1968, lot 23; Anon. sale, Amsterdam, Paul Brandt, 23 November 1971, lot 74.

Sotheby's Amsterdam, 14 November 1995 (69*) NLG 29,500	US$	18,592

HOREMANS Peter Jacob (Antwerp 1700-1776 Munich) Flemish
A LADY ABOUT TO GIVE BIRTH, SURROUNDED BY HER FAMILY AND DOCTORS
WITHIN A BEDROOM INTERIOR; A GROUP OF DOCTORS ADMIRING THE BABY AFTER
THE BIRTH WITH OTHER FIGURES PRESENT oil on canvas (a pair), each: 28¼ x 35¼in. (71.5
x 90cm.) sll 'P Horemans./1734'
PROV.: The Counts Sandizell, Schloss Sandizell; thence by descent.
EXH.: Munich, Alte Pinakothek, *Peter Jacob Horemans* 7 May-3 Nov. 1974, nos. 24, 25 (p. 29 in
the catalogue, where illustrated pl. 14).
LIT.: E. Pfeiffer-Belli, 'Der Maler Peter Jacob Horemans' in *Suddeutsche Zeitung*, 20 May 1974.

Sotheby's London, 5 July 1995 (137**) GBP 41,100	US$	65,561

LE RETOUR DE LA CHASSE oil on canvas, 103 x 126cm.
PROV.: Anon. sale, Paris, Drouot Montaigne, 29 June 1989, no. 82 (illustrated in colour); Acquired
by the present owner at Galerie Gismondi.

Étude Tajan Paris, 12 December 1995 (87**) FRF 120,000	US$	24,171

ELGANT FIGURES DINING IN THE GROUNDS OF A PALACE; ELEGANT FIGURES
MAKING MUSIC AND DANCING IN THE GROUNDS OF A PALACE oil on canvas (a pair),
each: 31½ x 40½in. (80 x 103cm.) sdlr 'P. Horemans./1745' sdll 'P. Horemans./1745'

Sotheby's London, 17 April 1996 (30**) GBP 31,050	US$	47,081

HÖRMANN Theodor von (Imst, Tirol 1840-1895 Graz) Austrian
DIE BEGLEITUNG oil on panel, 11 x 11½in. (28 x 29.2cm.) s 'Theod.v.Hörmann' sd.&
inscr.'Theod. v. Hörmann/dei Begleitung/...' on an old label on the reverse

257

Christie's London, 11 October 1995 (45**) GBP 51,000	US$	80,492

HUNGARIAN FISHERMEN REPAIRING THE NETS oil on canvas, 34.5 x 58.5cm. s 'Theod. v. Hörmann'
| Dorotheum Vienna, 17 April 1996 (420**) ATS 350,000 | US$ | 33,070 |

KLOSTERHOF IN 'MILLSTATT' oil on canvas, 37.5 x 55.5cm. dlr and titled ' Millstatt 28. Aug. (1)878
| Wiener Kunst Auktionen, 26 September 1995 (135**) ATS 380,000 | US$ | 36,937 |

HORNEL Edward Atkinson, R.O.I. (1864-1933) Australian (Scottish)
JAPANESE GIRLS oil on canvas laid down on panel, 30 x 13½in. (76 x 34cm.) slc 'E.A. Hornel'
| Sotheby's London, 29 August 1995 (880A**) GBP 19,550 | US$ | 31,645 |

HOROVITZ Leopold (Rozgony near Kaschau 1838-1917 Vienna) Austrian
EMPEROR FRANZ JOSEPH I. oil on canvas, 90.7 x 66.7cm. sdul 'L Horovitz. 1902.'
| Wiener Kunst Auktionen, 26 March 1996 (38**) ATS 160,000 | US$ | 15,391 |

HORTON William Samuel (1865-1936) American
STREET SCENE, PONTARLIER, FRANCE oil on panel, 17 x 21½in. (43.1 x 54.6cm.) sdll 'William S. Horton 1909'
PROV.: Estate of the artist; the artist's son, W. Grey Horton.
| Christie's New York, 13 September 1995 (29*) US$ 3,680 | US$ | 3,680 |

CHILDREN ON THE BEACH oil on panel, 15 x 18in. (38.1 x 45.7cm.) (ca. 1910)
PROV.: Estate of the artist; Galerie Charpentier, Paris.
EXH.: Paris, Galerie R. Creuze, May 1947, no. 5.
| Christie's New York, 23 May 1996 (113**) US$ 32,200 | US$ | 32,200 |

HOSEMANN Theodor (Brandenburg a/d Havel 1807-1875 Berlin) German
DER KLEINE ZIEGENHIRTE oil on canvas, 29.3 x 37cm. sdll 'Th Hosemann 1857' sd again on the reverse
| Wiener Kunst Auktionen, 26 September 1995 (126**) ATS 100,000 | US$ | 9,720 |

HOUCKGEEST Gerrit (The Hague ca. 1600-1661 Bergen op Zoom) Dutch
INTERIOR OF A RENAISSANCE CHURCH oil on oak panel, 41 x 32cm. sdlr 'G. Hougheest 1638'
| Étude Tajan Paris, 12 December 1995 (51**) FRF 115,000 | US$ | 23164 |

HOVE Bartholomeus Johannes van (The Hague 1790-1880 The Hague) Dutch
A DUTCH RIVER TOWN WITH FIGURES IN A PUNT BEFORE A BRIDGE oil on panel, 15½ x 19½in. (39.3 x 49.5cm.) s 'JB (linked) van Hove'
| Christie's South Kensington, 13 June 1996 (206**) GBP 10,350 | US$ | 15960 |

HRDLICKA Alfred (Vienna 1928 b.) Austrian
TODESKUSS tempera, crayon on canvas, 218 x 248cm. sdll 'ALFRED HRDLICKA 1965'
| Wiener Kunst Auktionen, 29 November 1995 (777**) ATS 380,000 | US$ | 38119 |

HUBER Ernst (Vienna 1895-1960) Austrian
FIGURES SKATING IN A VILLAGE BEFORE AN ALPINE LANDSCAPE oil on canvas, 73 x 92cm. (28¾ x 36¼in.) slr 'E. HUBER'
| Phillips London, 24 June 1996 (3**) GBP 19,000 | US$ | 29298 |

HUCHTENBURG Jan van (Haarlem 1647-1733 Amsterdam) Dutch
L'ATTAQUE D'UN CAMPEMENT MILITAIRE PAR LA CAVALERIE TURQUE oil on canvas, 53 x 62cm. slr with mono. 'JHb F'
| Étude Tajan Paris, 12 December 1995 (19**) FRF 90,000 | US$ | 18,128 |

SOLDIERS SACKING A VILLAGE oil on canvas, 28 x 33in. (71 x 83.8cm.) s with monogram 'JHB'
PROV.: With Buttery: Christie's, 17 March 1916, lot 91 (21gns. to Dubyk); H.B.Burney:Christie's, 30 June 1924, lot 29 (14gns. to Farr).

Christie's South Kensington, 18 april 1996 (187**) GBP 8,970	US$	13,601

HUET Christophe (1734 - 1759 active) French
A MASTIFF AND HER PUPPIES IN AN OUTHOUSE oil on canvas, 50 1/8 x 57 5/8in. (127.5 x 146.5cm.) sd 'C. Huet. 1734'

Christie's London, 28 March 1996 (171**) GBP 34,500	US$	52,688

HUET Jean Baptiste Marie the Elder (Paris 1745-1811) French
AN AMOROUS SHEPHERD AND SHEPHERDESS SEATED BY A POOL - IN A FEIGNED PAINTED AND GILDED OCTAGONAL FRAME oil on metal, 7 7/8 x 11 1/8in. (19.5 x 28.3cm.)

Christie's London, 7 July 1995 (324**) GBP 12,075	US$	19,261

HUGGINS William John (1781-1845) British
THE STONES OF CHESTER, OR RUINS OF ST. JOHN'S PRIORY oil on canvas, 36¾ x 31in. (93.4 x 78.8cm.) sdlc 'WHuggins/1874'; indistinctly inscr. 'W. J. Huggins/The Groves'; inscr. as titled on a label on the stretcher
EXH.: Liverpool, Walker Art Gallery, *Autumn Exhibition*, 1874, no. 422.

Christie's New York, 14 February 1996 (68**) US$ 20,700	US$	20,700

HUGHES Edward Robert, R.W.S. (1851-1914) British
SIBLINGS oil on canvas, 49½ x 41¼in. (125.7 x 102.3cm.) oval sdlr 'Edward Hughes/1894'

Christie's East, 30 October 1995 (10*) US$ 16,100	US$	16,100

HUGO Victor Marie (1802-1885) French
LES GRANDS ARBRES ink wash heightened with white on paper, 14.5 x 8.5cm.
PROV.: Former collection Paul Meurice, France.

Étude Tajan Paris, 1 February 1996 (31) FRF 30,000	US$	6,139

HUILLIOT Claude Nicolas (Reims 1632-1702 Paris) French
FLOWERS IN A BRONZE VASE oil on canvas (a pair), each: 96 x 130cm.

Étude Tajan Paris, 26 March 1996 (65*) FRF 65,000	US$	12,848

HULK Abraham, {called} the Elder (London 1813-1897 London) Dutch
AN ESTUARY: SHIPPING IN A CALM, MIDDELBURG IN THE DISTANCE oil on canvas, 42 x 65.5cm. s 'A. Hulk f.'

Christie's Amsterdam, 25 April 1996 (253*) NLG 28,750	US$	17,084

HULK Johan Frederik the Elder (Amsterdam 1829-1911 Haarlem) Dutch
A VIEW IN TOWN WITH NUMEROUS VILLAGERS ON A BRIDGE AND SEVERAL TOWNSFOLK LOADING BOATS ON A QUAY ALONG A CANAL oil on panel, 40.5 x 32cm. sdlr 'F. Hulk'

Christie's Amsterdam, 26 October 1995 (200*) NLG 16,100	US$	10,151

HULK Johan Frederik the Younger (Amsterdam 1855-1913 Vreeland) Dutch
HIS LAST RACE oil on canvas, 243 x 170 cm s 'John. F. Hulk'; s and inscr with title on the reverse

Christie's Amsterdam, 25 April 1996 (41*) NLG 23,000	US$	13,667

HULST Frans de (Haarlem 1610 ca-1661) Dutch
DUNELANDSCAPE WITH AND AN BIZAR, MOSTLY DIED OAKTREE oil on panel, 37.8 x 51cm. (oval)
PROV.: Sotheby's, London 1January 1937, lot 147; E. Burg-Berger, Stockholm, 1938, as van Goyen.

Hauswedell & Nolte Cologne, 6 June 1996 (52*) DEM 12,000	US$	7,797

WALLED CITY NEAR A RIVER, A BASTION BEYOND oil on panel, 34 x 54cm.
    Dorotheum Vienna, 6 March 1996 (293**) ATS 90,000   US$ 8,657

THE VALKHOF, NIJMEGEN, WITH A FERRY ON THE WAAL IN THE FOREGROUND oil on
panel, 30.8 x 49.3cm sll 'F.d. Hulst'
PROV.: Anon. Sale, Sotheby`s London, 9 December 1959, lot 74; with H. Terry-Engell, London
(exhibition catalogue, October/November 1961, no.14, illustrated); Mrs M.T.Warde; Sale, Christie`s,
19 March 1965, lot 73 (sold GBP630) with F. Enneking, Amsterdam, 1965; with Galerie Knoeckel,
Frankfurt (exhibited Munich 1967); from whom purchased by the present owner in 1967.
LIT.: K.J. Müllenmeister, *Meer und Land im Licht des 17. Jahrhunderts*, I, 1973, p.118 (illustrated);
H.U.Beck, *Künstler um Jan van Goyen*, 1991, p.191, no. 518-A17 (illustrated).
    Christie's Amsterdam, 13 November 1995 (153**) NLG 43,700   US$ 27,541

VIEW ON TWO TOWN ON A RIVER IN HOLLAND oil on panel (a pair), each: 35.5 x 58cm. slc
'F. de Hulst, sll 'F. de Hulst'
    Étude Tajan Paris, 26 March 1996 (40*) FRF 150,000   US$ 29,650

HUMBORG Adolf (1847-1913) Austrian
PREPARING FOR THE BANQUET oil on canvas, 22 x 34 7/8in. (56 x 88.5cm.) slr inscr.
'Muenchen'
    Phillips London, 11 June 1996 (17**) GBP 6,800   US$ 10,486

HUNDERTWASSER Friedrich Stowasser (Vienna 1928 b.) Austrian
LA RENCONTRE DANS LA PISCINE DELIGNY mixed media, oil and egg tempera on paper
mounted on hemp, 21¼ x 28¾in. (54 x 73cm.) sdll 'Friedensreich Hundertwasser 4. July 1966
PROV.: Galerie St. Léger, Geneva; Acquired from the above by the present owner in 1973.
EXH.: London, Hanover Gallery; Paris, Karl Flinker Galerie; Geneva, Galerie Moos et Krugier,
Hundertwasser, April-June 1967, no. 628 (illustrated in colour in the catalogue).
    Christie's London, 19 March 1996 (15**) GBP 43,300   US$ 6,6127

APRES LE FIN DU COMMUNISME: UNE DES CONSTRUCTIONS LE THEATRE A
L'ENVERS: UNE EXPLOSION ATOMIQUE egg, oil, acrylic, gold paint, gold leaf, and wrapping
paper on polyvynil and chalk primed burlap, 51 1/8 x 38 1/8in. (130 x 97cm.) s four times and d
three times'60'; sd and titled 'Août 1960 La Picandière' and numbered '444' on a label affixed to the
reverse
PROV.: Galerie Raymond Cordier, Paris; Marquis de Segur, Paris; J.J. Aberbach, New York.
EXH.: Venice, *XXXI Biennale Internazionale dell' Arte*, 1962; Paris, Artcurial, *Hundertwasser:
Peintures Recèntes*, Paris 1982, p. 13, no. 444 (illustrated in colour).
LIT.: *Hundertwasser, Vollständiger Oeuvre-Katalog*, Hannover 1964, p. 205, no. 444 (illustrated;
incorrectly dated 1962).
    Sotheby's London, 21 March 1996 (20**) GBP 67,500   US$ 103,085

CONTRACTFORM MIT 22 DEUTUNGEN watercolour and pencil on paper, 14 x 9 7/8in. (35.4 x
25cm.) sd titled '2.10.54 Rom Ospedale S.Spirito' on the reverse
PROV.: La Medusa, Studio d'Arte Contemporanea, Rome; acquired from the above by the present
owner in 1964.
EXH.: Rome, Studio d'Arte Contemporanea, no. 432.
LIT.: Exhibition catalogue: *Hundertwasser*, Kestner-Gesellschaft, Hanover 1964, p. 128. no. 197
(titled differently).
    Christie's London, 23 May 1996 (58**) GBP 17,250   US$ 26,121

CETTE FLEUR AURA RAISON DES HOMMES eggtempera, watercolour and goldleaf on chalk
primed cardboard, 30¾ x 47½in. (78 by 120.5cm.) sd 'Hunderwasser 1957 Paris' numbered '134' on
the reverse
PROV.: Galerie Hélène Kamer, Paris; Société Baralipton, Paris; Anne Abels, Cologne .
EXH.: Brussels, Musée des Beaux-Arts d'Ixelles *Friedensreich Hundertwasser*, 1977-78, no. 36.

LIT.: *Hundertwasser, Vollständiger Oeuvre-Katalog*, Hannover 1964, p. 157, no. 314.
        Sotheby's London, 27 June 1996 (211**) GBP 36,700   US$ 56,592

TETE-KOPF-HEAD oil on three-ply wood primed with chalk, 54 x 51cm. sdlr 'Hundertwasser 1953
Paris 1977 Hahnsäge'
EXH.: Paris, Studio Paul Facchetti, 1954.
LIT.: *Hundertwasser art agenda 1989 and 1990*, caesar Art International, Stutgart (illustrated);
Hundertwasser Art Jahrbuch, 1991, caesar (illustrated); Hundertwasser art clou, 1991, caesar
(illustrated).
        Wiener Kunst Auktionen, 27 September 1995 (408**) ATS 350,000   US$ 34,021

DIE GLORIEREICHEN SIEBEN watercolour and gold leaf on paper, 14½ x 19¾in. (37 x 50cm.)
signed,taitled and dated 'Venezia 1953'
PROV.: Galleria d'Arte del Naviglio, Milan.
EXH.: Venice, Galleria Sandri; *Hundertwasser*, 1952 (illustrated in the catalogue); Milan, Galleria
Brera, *Hundertwasser*, 1963, pl. 162 (illustrated in the catalogue); Hanover, Kestner-Gesellschaft;
Bern, Kunsthalle; Hagen, Karl-Ernst-Osthaus Museum; Vienna, Museum des 20. Jahrhunderts;
Amsterdam, Stedelijk-Museum; Stockholm, Moderna Museet, *Hundertwasser*, March 1964-February
1965, no. 135 (illustrated in colour in the catalogue p. 50); Geneva, Galerie Georges Moos,
Hundertwasser: Retrospective, May-June 1967 (illustrated in the catalogue); Geneva, Galerie
Krugier & Cie, *Hundertwasser: Peintures récentes*, June-July 1967 (illustrated in the catalogue).
LIT.: Wieland Schmied, *Hundertwasser*, Feldafing 1964, p. 17.
        Christie's London, 26 October 1995 (35**) GBP 60,900   US$ 96,117

HUNT Bryan (1947 b.) American
UNTITLED graphite, wax and oilstick on paper, 93 7/8 x 42in. (238.4 x 106.7cm.) (1987)
PROV.: Blum Helman Gallery, New York; Richard Green Gallery, Los Angeles.
EXH.: Purchase, Neuberger Museum; Toledo Museum of Art; Kansas City, Nelson-Atkins Museum
of Art, *Figuratively Speaking: draings by Seven Artists*, April 1989-Feb. 1990, p. 55, no. 23
(illustrated).
        Christie's East, 7 May 1996 (188*) US$ 7,475   US$ 7,475

HUNT Charles, Jnr (1829-1900) British
MISHAP AT THE CROSSROADS oil on canvas, 40¼ x 59 7/8in. (102.3 x 151.7cm.) sd 'C. Hunt
1880'
PROV.: Probably acquired from the Artist by Sir Andrew Barclay Walker (died 1893), who founded
the Walker Art Gallery, Liverpool, in the 1870's.
        Christie's London, 29 March 1996 (187**) GBP 13,225   US$ 20,197

HUNT Walter (1861-1941) British
CATTLE, DUCKS AND CHICKENS IN A FARMYARD oil on canvas, 30¼ x 45in. (76.8 x
114.3cm.) sd 'W.Hunt/1908'
        Christie's South Kensington, 7 March 1996 (127**) GBP 11,000   US$ 16,799

THE WEANLINGS oil on canvas, 58 x 80in. (147.3 x 203.2cm.) sdll 'W. Hunt.89' (1889)
EXH.: London, Royal Academy, 1889, no. 658.
        Christie's New York, 22 May 1996 (275**) US$ 57,500   US$ 57,500

HURT Louis Bosworth (1856-1929) British
THE HILLS OF SKYE oil on canvas, 31 x39in. (79 x 99cm.) sd 'Louis B. Hurt 1905' and inscr. 'The
Hills of Skye' on the reverse
        Christie's London, 6 November 1995 (164**) GBP 10,350   US$ 16,190

HIGHLAND CATTLE oil on canvas, 24 x 40in. (61 x 101.6cm.) sdlc 'Louis B. Hurt. 1905'
        Christie's New York, 2 November 1995 (216**) US$ 14,375   US$ 14,375

HUSSEM Willem Frans Karel (Rotterdam 1900-1974) Dutch
AN ABSTRACT COMPOSITION oil on canvas, 90 x 110cm. s with initials dll 'W.H. 62' numbered
and d again on the stretcher 'No. 66'
       Christie's Amsterdam, 5 June 1996 (148*) NLG 10,350   US$ 6,047

AN ABSTRACT COMPOSITION oil on canvas, ,100 x 120cm. s with initials and dated ll 'WH57'
PROV.: Galerie Nouvelles Images, The Hague.
       Christie's Amsterdam, 6 December 1995 (362*) NLG 19,550   US$ 1,2114

HUSZAR Vilmos (Boedapest 1884-1960 Harderwijk) Dutch (Hungarian)
A RECLINING LADY oil on board unframed, 68 x 100cm. slr V. Huszar
       Christie's Amsterdam, 5 June 1996 (261*) NLG 8,625   US$ 5,039

HUTTER Wolfgang (Vienna 1928 b.) Austrian
DAS BLUMENSCHIFF oil on three-ply wood, 45 x 50.3cm. sdll 'W. Hutter 64'; titled on the reverse
EXH.: Hannover, Kestner-Gesellschaft, 1965, no. 182.
       Wiener Kunst Auktionen, 27 September 1995 (434**) ATS 380,000   US$ 36,937

DIE BRANDSTIFTERINNEN oil on canvas, 60 x 80cm. sd 'W.Hutter 65'
PROV.: Private collection, Switzerland.
LIT.: Otto Breicha, *Wolfgang Hutter*, Verlag Jugend und Volk, 1969, no. 142, pl. 19.
       Dorotheum Vienna, 8 November 1995 (702**) ATS 250,000   US$ 25,078

HUYSMANS Cornelis (Antwerp 1648-1727 Mechlin) Flemish
WOODED RIVER LANDSCAPE WITH FIGURES ON THE NEAR BANK oil on canvas, 22½ x
25½in. (57.2 x 64.8cm.)
PROV.: A.W. Liddell, April 1847, according to a label on the reverse.
       Sotheby's London, 18 October 1995 (16**) GBP 8,625   US$ 13,613

HUYSMANS Jan Baptist (Antwerp 1654-1716 Antwerp) Flemish
WOODED LANDSCAPE WITH A SHEPHERD oil on canvas, 41 x 44cm.
       Dorotheum Vienna, 17 October 1995 (291**) ATS 60,000   US$ 6,018

PORTRAIT OF CATHERINE OF BRAGANZA oil on canvas, 48½ x 37¾in. (123.2 x 95.9cm.)
       Sotheby's New York, 6 October 1996 (199*) US$ 19,550   US$ 19,550

HUYSUM Justus the Elder, van (Amsterdam 1659-1716 Amsterdam) Dutch
A STILL-LIFE OF LILIES, ROSES, CARNATIONS AND OTHER FLOWERS IN A GLASS
VASE ON A STONE LEDGE WITH A BUTTERFLY oil on canvas, 27 x 21¼in. (64 x 54cm.) slr
'Jan van Huysum' (just before 1716)
PROV.: With Haberstock, Berlin; Baron Heinrich Thyssen-Bornemisza, by 1930.
EXH.: Manchester, City Art Museum, *Exhibition of 17th Century Dutch Flower Painting*, (date and
number unknown), according to a label on the reverse; Munich 1930, no.161; Paris 1970-71, no. 29,
plate 16; Bielefeld 1973, no. 10; Düsseldorf 1970-1, no. 27; Lausanne etc., 1986-87, no. 48.
LIT.: R. Heinemann 1937, vol. I, no. 204.
       Sotheby's London, 6 December 1995 (110**) GBP 40,000   US$ 61,557

IBBETSON Julius Caesar, R.A. (1759-1817) British
THE VALLEY OF THE WYE LOOKING TOWARDS CHEPSTOW AND PIERCEFIELD oil on
canvas, 27¼ x 37in. (69.2 x 94cm.) sd ' J. Ibbeston pt 1815 [6?]
PROV.: W. Curling, 1866; Sir Thomas Devitt; Christie's 16 May 1924, lot no. 105 (22gns. to
Leggatt).
EXH.: Possibly London, Royal Academy, 1815, no. 467, as 'the Junction of the Severn and the Wye'.
Christie's London, 18 April 1996 (36**) GBP 25,300   US$ 38,362

'THE RYDAL VALLEY', FIGURES IN A CART DESCENDING A WOODED VALLEY PATH
oil on canvas, unframed, 19 7/8 x 26in. (50.5 x 66cm.)
Phillips London, 18 June 1996 (44**) GBP 9,500   US$ 14,649

IMMENDORFF Jörg (1945 b.) German
STUKA-FLIEGER BEUYS oil on canvas, 50 x 50cm. sdlc 'Immendorff 93' (1993)
Lempertz Cologne, 28 November 1995 (731*) DEM 13,000   US$ 9,176

INDIANA Robert (1928 b.) American
HOMMAGE A PICASSO oil on canvas, 60 x 50in. (152.4 x 127cm.) stenciled with s and d
'ROBERT INDIANA 2 NEW YORK SPRING 1974' on the reverse
PROV.: Marisa del Re Gallery, New York.
EXH.: C. Weinhardt Jr., *Robert Indiana*, New York 1990, p. 143 (illustrated).
Christie's New York, 22 February 1996 (65**) US$ 49,450   US$ 49,450

AMERICAN LOVE oil on canvas (a linked pair), overall: 12 1/8 x 24¼in. (31 x 61.6cm.) stenciled
with ini. and d 'R.I. ASPEN 1968' on the reverse of the left canvas and dedicated twice 'For Bert
Stern' on the overlap of each canvas
PROV.: Acquired directly from the artist; Bert Stern, New York.
EXH.: C. Weinhardt Jr., *Robert Indiana*, New York 1990, p. 143 (illustrated).
Christie's New York, 22 February 1996 (70**) US$ 29,900   US$ 29,900

RED SAILS acrylic on canvas, 60 x 50in. (153 x 127cm.) titled; sd inscr. and titled with stencil
'ROBERT INDIANA RED SAILS 1963 COUNTIES SLIP USA NEW YORK CITY' on the reverse
PROV.: Stable Gallery, New York.
EXH.: Philedelphia, Institute of Contemporary Art of Pennsylvania; San Antonio, McNay Institute;
Indianapolis, Herron Museum of Art, *Robert Indiana*, April-Sept. 1968, no. 10 (illustration of the
exhibition view in colour p. 4).
Christie's London, 30 November 1995 (35**) GBP 14,950   US$ 23,385

INDUNO Gerolamo (Milan 1827-1890) Italian
THE RETURN OF THE CONSCRIPT oil on canvas, 17½ x 13½in. (44.5 x 34.3cm.) s 'Gir. Induno'
Christie's London, 17 November 1995 (142**) GBP 31,050   US$ 48,569

INGANNATI Pietro degli (Veneto 1490-ca. 1550 Venice) Italian
THE HOLY FAMILY IN A LANDSCAPE oil on panel (in sculpted Italian Renaissance frame), 57 x
97cm.
Dorotheum Vienna, 06 March 1996 (383**) ATS 80,000   US$ 7,695

INGANNI Angelo (1807-1880) Italian
IN THE FOUNDRY oil on canvas, 15¾ x 11 7/8in. (40 x 30.3cm.) sdlcr 'Angelo Inganni/1876'
Christie's New York, 14 February 1996 (9**) US$ 21,850   US$ 21,850

INGRES Jean Auguste Dominique (Montauban 1780-1867 Paris) French
ANDROMEDA CHAINED black crayon, 13.5 x 8.7cm. sll 'Ingres'
Étude Tajan Paris, 24 November 1995 (70*) FRF 78,000   US$ 15,962

263

PORTRAIT OF MADEMOISELLE MARIE REISET, LATER VICOMTESSE ADOLPHE-LOUIS-EDGAR DE SÉGUR-LAMOIGNON black lead on paper, 13 ½ x 9½in. (34.4 x 24.2cm.) s 'Ingres D'
PROV.: Frederic Reiset; By inheritance to his daughter Vicomtesse Adolphe- Louis- Edgar de Ségur-Lamoignon, née Marie Reiset; By inheritance to her daughter Marquise Adolphe-Marie de Moy, née Marie- Eugenie- Hortense- Valentine de Segur- Lamoignon; Georges Bourgarel; Paris, 15-16 June 1922, lot 115, illustrated (3,900 Francs to Henry Lapauze); Henry Lapauze; Paris, 21 June 1929, lot 31, illustrated (141,000 Francs to Knoedler's); With M. Knoedler & Co., 1951; Richard S. Davis; With M. Knoedler & Co., 1956.
EXH.: Paris, Salon des Arts-Unis, *Dessins [d'Ingres] tirés de collections d'amateurs*, 1861, no. 71; Paris, Galeries George Petit, *Ingres*, 1911, no. 161; Cambridge, Fogg Art Museum, *French Drawings and Prints of the Nineteenth Century*, 1934, no. 48; Cincinnati, Cincinnati Art Museum and elsewhere, *The Place of David and Ingres in a Century of French Painting*, 1940 (ex catalogue); Cambridge, Fogg Art Museum, *French Paintings of the XIX and XX Centuries*, 1941 (ex catalogue); Toledo, Toledo Museum of Art, *French Drawings and Watercolors*, 1941, no. 73, illustrated ;New York, American British Art Center, *Drawings of the 19th and 20th Centuries*, 1944, no. 3; Pittsburgh, Carnegie Institute, *French Painting, 1110-1900*, 1951, no. 157, illustrated; Cambridge, Fogg Art Museum, *Ingres Centennial Exhibition*,1967, no. 94, illustrated; New York, Metropolitan Museum of Art, *Classicism and Romanticism, French Drawings and Prints, 1800-1860*, 1970, no. 56.
LIT.: E. Galichon, 'Description des dessins de M. Ingres exposés au Salon des Arts-Unis', *Gazette des Beaux-Arts*, 15 March 1861, p. 361; H. Delaborde, *Ingres*, Paris, 1870, no. 408; P. de Chennevieres, 'Souvenirs d'un directeur des Beaux-Arts', *L'Artiste*, III, Paris, 1886, pp. 91, 94; H. Lapauze, *Les portraits dessinés deJ.-A.-D. Ingres,* Paris, 1903, no. 82, illustrated; H. Lapauze, *Ingres*, Paris, 1911, p. 428, illustrated; Sir Bnnsley Ford, 'Ingres' Portraits of the Reiset Family', The *Burlington Magazine*, November 1953, p. 356; D. Ternois, *Les dessins d'Ingres au Musée de Montauban, les portraits*, *Inventaire général des dessins des Musées de Province*, Paris, 1959, under no. 169; M.B. Cohen, *The Original Format of Ingres' Portrait Drawings*, Montauban, 1969, pp. 23 and 25; H. Naef, *Die Bildniszeichnungen von J.-A.-D. Ingres*, V, Bern, 1980, pp. 330-31, no. 423, illustrated.
Christie's New York, 22 May 1996 (48***) US$ 354,500 | US$ | 354,500

IRAS Roberto Baldessari (Rovereto 1895-1965 Innsbruck) Italian
BANCO DI COCOMERI mixed media and collage on cardboard-paper, 42 x 50cm. sdlr 'R.M.Baldessari 1918'
Finearte Milan, 12 December 1995 (293**) ITL 31,050,000 | US$ | 19,479

ISABEY Louis Gabriel Eugène (Paris 1803-1886) French
LE BAC oil on canvas, 41 x 59cm. sdll 'E. Isabey / 1836'
Étude Tajan Paris, 28 June 1996 (101***) FRF 65,000 | US$ | 12,551

ISABEY Louis Gabriel Eugène (Paris 1803-1886) French
UN PORT EN BRETAGNE oil on canvas, 32½ x 481in. (82.5 x 123.2cm.) sdlr 'E. Isabey.61' (1861)
PROV.: With Noortman &Brod, New York, 1981 (cat. no. 32).
LIT.: P. Miquel, *Eugène Isabey 1803-1886 La Marine au XIX siècle*, Maurs-La-Jolie, 1980 vol II, p. 22, no. 1260 (illustrated).
Christie's New York, 22 May 1996 (103**) US$ 40,250 | US$ | 40,250

ISAKSON Karl Oscar (1878-1922) Swedish
SITTANDE MODELL oil on canvas, 98 x 77cm. (1914-15)
EXH.: Liljevalch, Konsthall, *Liljevalchs jubilerar, Svensk Konstkavalkad*, 1956, catalogue 221, no. 48; Oslo, Göteborg, Odense, Köpenhavn, *Karl Isaksonudstilingen*, catalogue no. 39.
LIT.: Gustaf Engwall, *Karl Isakson* (illustrated p. 160); *Bonniers Lexicon* (ilustrated in colour).
Bukowskis Stockholm, 24-25 April 1996 (48**) SEK 90,000 | US$ | 13,635

ISENBRANDT Adriaen (Bruges 1490 ca. act.-1551 d.) Flemish
THE MAGDALENE READING oil on panel, 30¾ x 25½in. (78 x 64.5cm.)

	US$	22,122
Sotheby's London, 6 December 1995 (130**) GBP 14,375		

SAINT JEROME IN PENTINENCE oil on panel, 10.8 x 7¾in. (27 x 19.7cm.)
PROV.: with Dr. Wendland, Berlin, 1928; with P. de Boer, Amsterdam, 1944.
LIT.: M.J. Friedländer, *Early Netherlandish Painting, XI*, ed. H. Pauwels, Leyden and Brussels, 1974, p.91, no.204, pl.145.

	US$	51,364
Christie's London, 7 July 1995 (23**) GBP 32,200		

ISHIKAWA Kin'Ichiro (1871-1913) Japanese
TEMPLE AT RIVER`S EDGE watercolour on paper, 14½ x 213/4in. (36.8 x 55.7cm.) sll 'Kin-Ishikawa'

	US$	19,550
Christie's New York, 31 October 1995 (450**) US$ 19,550		

ISRAELS Isäac Lazerus (Amsterdam 1865-1934 The Hague) Dutch
IN FRONT OF THE MIRROR oil on canvas, 128 x 78cm. slr 'Isaac Israels' (1917)
PROV.: Kunsthandel Buffa et Fils, The Hague, inv. No. 7693 (Jan. 1918).

	US$	159,521
Christie's Amsterdam, 26 October 1995 (331***) NLG 253,000		

PORTRAIT OF A RED-HAIRED WOMAN oil on canvas, 100 x 70cm. sdlr 'Isaac Israels/1923'

	US$	14,502
Christie's Amsterdam, 26 October 1995 (332*) NLG 23,000		

HALFNAAKT oil on canvas, 36¾ x 28¾in. (93.5 x 73cm.) slr 'Isaäc Israëls'

	US$	24,150
Christie's Tel Aviv, 14 April 1996 (12**) US$ 24,150		

In front of the Mirror

A STREETSCENE, BATAVIA oil on canvas, 65 x 80cm. sll 'Isaäc Israëls' (1922)
PROV.: Sale Amsterdam, studio of the Artist, 2 April 1935, no. 49, illustrated on the cover; Dr. H. van Marken Lichtenbelt, Zeist; Private collection, Zeist.
EXH.: Amsterdam, Stedlijk museum, *Isaäc Israëls*; The Hague, Gemeente Museum;Eindhoven, van Abbemuseum, 1959, no. 49; Zeist, Slot Zeist. *143 x Isaäc Israëls*, 1974, no. 118.
LIT.: Anna Wagner, *Isaäc Israëls*, Venlo 1985, with Ill. no. 179a.

	US$	52,588
Sotheby's Amsterdam, 23 April 1996 (39**) NLG 88,500		

A BALINESE WOMAN SEATED oil on canvas, 65 x 40cm. slr 'Isaäc Israëls'
PROV.: Kunsthandel Buffa & Zonen, Amsterdam; Anon. sale, Paul Brandt, 2 Nov. 1965, lot 193 (illustrated).

	US$	70,117
Sotheby's Amsterdam, 23 April 1996 (71**) NLG 118,000		

A GAMELAN ORCHESTRA oil on canvas, 100 x 80cm. slr 'Isaäc Israëls'
PROV.: Frans Buffa & Fils, Amsterdam, October 1916, no. 7381; Collection J.M.P. Glerum. Amsterdam, inv. no. A92; Sale, Mak van Waay, Collection J..P.M. Glerum., 28 Feb. 1933, lot 73; Collection Hamburg, Utrecht; E.J. van Wisselingh & Co., Amsterdam, inv. no. 276X/1478X.

	US$	143,740
Sotheby's Amsterdam, 23 April 1996 (80**) NLG 241,900		

A PORTRAIT OF A JAVANESE DANCER watercolour, 32.5 x 48cm. slr 'Isaäc Israëls'
PROV.: Kunsthandel Borzo, 's-Hertogenbosch, exhibited Sep. 1976, no. 33 (illustrated in the cat.).

Sotheby's Amsterdam, 23 April 1996 (131**) NLG 25,960	US$	15,426

ACROBAT pencil, black chalk and watercolour on paper, 52.5 x 36.5 cm s on the reverse 'Isaäc
Israëls'

Christie's Amsterdam, 25 April 1996 (53*) NLG 19,550	US$	11,617

VERTIER OP AMSTERDAMSE BRUG pencil and charcoal on paper, 41 x 44 cm s 'Isaäc Israëls'
EXH.: Groningen, Groninger Museum, *Isaäc Israëls*, 1965, no. 65.
LIT.: Anna Wagner, *Beeldende kunst in Nederland*, The Hague 1969.

Christie's Amsterdam, 7 February 1996 (476*) NLG 23,000	US$	14,007

THREE MEN IN A CAFE (RECTO) FIGURES READING IN A CAFE (VERSO) black chalk and
watercolour on paper, 24 x 33 cm s 'Isaäc Israëls' (ca 1905)

Christie's Amsterdam, 7 February 1996 (698**) NLG 10,925	US$	6,653

ISRAELS Josef (Groningen 1824-1911 The Hague) Dutch
WHILE BABY SLEEPS oil on canvas, 41¼ x 55½in. (104.7 x 141cm.) sll 'Josef Israels.'

Christie's New York, 14 February 1996 (73**) US$ 25,300	US$	25,300

VISSERSMEISJE OP HET STRAND oil on panel, 15 x 11½in. (38 x 29cm.) sll 'Josef Israels'
PROV.: Julius Oehme, New York, until 1903; Meyer Lehmann, New York, by 1903, thence by
descent to George L. Weil.

Christie's Tel Aviv, 12 October 1995 (1**) US$ 25,300	US$	25,300

BREIEND VISSERSMEISJE OP EEN HEUVEL oil on cradled panel, 20¾ x 17¾in. (52.7 x
45.1cm.) slr 'Josef Israels'

Christie's Tel Aviv, 12 October 1995 (3**) US$ 23,000	US$	23,000

SPELEVAREN oil on canvas, 7 5/8 x 12in. (19.5 x 30.5cm.) slr 'Josef Israels'

Christie's Tel Aviv, 14 April 1996 (1**) US$ 18,975	US$	18,975

EEN BOERIN IN'T VELD watercolour on paper laid down on cardboard, 11 3/8 x 16 3/8in. (28.3 x
41.7cm.) slr 'Josef Israels'

Christie's Tel Aviv, 14 April 1996 (9**) US$ 13,800	US$	13,800

WOOD GATHERERS charcoal, pen and black ink, watercolour and bodycolour on paper, 26 x 45.5
cm s 'Josef Israels'

Christie's Amsterdam, 25 April 1996 (74*) NLG 10,925	US$	6,492

AARDAPPELROOISTER: POTATO-LIFTER watercolour on paper, 28 x 40cm. slr 'Jozef Israels'

Christie's Amsterdam, 26 October 1995 (249a*) NLG 11,500	US$	7,251

A WOOD-GATHERER IN A LANDSCAPE oil on panel, 19 x 35.5cm. sll 'Jozef Israels'
PROV.: Mrs Aleida Cohen-Tervaert, The Hague.

Christie's Amsterdam, 26 October 1995 (31*) NLG 9,200	US$	5,801

HET ROKERTJE oil on panel, 40 x 30cm. slr 'Jozef Israels'
PROV.: Collection W. Scholtens, Groningen; Anon. Sale, location unkn., 15 May 1917, lot no. 75.
EXH.: The Hague, *Jozef Israels*, 1911-1912, no. 66.

Christie's Amsterdam, 26 October 1995 (114*) NLG 20,700	US$	13,052

IVARSON Ivan (1900-1939) Swedish
VI ROSENTRÄDET oil on canvas, 85 x 99cm. slr 'I. Ivarson'

Bukowskis Stockholm, 24-25 April 1996 (50**) SEK 155,000	US$	23,482

PÅ VERANDAN oil on panel, 61 x 61cm. sll 'I. Ivarson'
    Bukowskis Stockholm, 24-25 April 1996 (51**) SEK 180,000   US$ 27,270

IVARSON Ivan (1900-1939) Swedish
MOR OCH BARN oil on canvas, 80 x 88cm. sll 'Ivan Ivarson'
EXH.: Göteborg, Göteborgs Konstmuseum, 1975, *Sveriges Allmänna Konstförening 1975.*
    Bukowskis Stockholm, 26-27 October 1995 (47**) SEK 280,000   US$ 41,006

JACOMIN Alfred Louis Vigny (1842-1913) French
A RIVER LANDSCAPE WITH ROWERS oil on panel, 13 x 16in. (33 x 40.6cm.) slr 'A.Jacomin'
  Christie's East, 13 February 1996 (90**) US$ 7,475   US$ 7,475

JACQUE Charles Émile (1813-1894) French
DROVER WATERING CATTLE AT A POND oil on canvas, 16¼ x 23½in. (41.3 x 59.7cm.) sll
'Ch. Jacque'
  Christie's New York, 2 November 1995 (114**) US$ 20,700   US$ 20,700

THE SHEPHERDESS pastel on brown paper, 21 1/8 x 37 11/16in. (53.6 x 95.8cm.) slr 'Ch Jaque'
  Christie's New York, 22 May 1996 (162**) US$ 55,200   US$ 55,200

JACQUET Gustave J. (France 1846-1909) French
L'ÉTUDE DE FLEURS oil on panel, 13 x 9¼in. (33 x 23.5cm.) sdll and inscr. with the title on the
reverse 'Jacquet/1890'
  Christie's New York, 2 November 1995 (159**) US$ 27,600   US$ 27,600

JEANNIN Georges (1841-1925) French
SPRING TIME BOUQUET oil on canvas, 51½ x 64 1/8in. (130.8 x 163.2cm.) sdll 'G. Jeannin. 1889'
  Christie's New York, 22 May 1996 (220**) US$ 40,250   US$ 40,250

JAHN Gustav (Vienna 1879-1919 Vienna) Austrian
RUINE HINTERHAUS, IM HINTERGRUND SPITZ A. D. DONAU (WACHAU) oil on canvas, 95
x 59cm. slr 'Gust. Jahn'
  Dorotheum Vienna, 21 May 1996 (28**) ATS 200,000   US$ 19,205

JAMES William (1746/54 - 1771 fl.) British
VIEW 0N THE CANAL GRANDE EASTWARDS FROM THE SAN STAE CHURCH TOWARDS
THE FABBRICHE NUOVO, VENICE oil on canvas, 41 x 62cm. (ca 1765)
  Dorotheum Vienna, 11 June 1996 (29**) ATS 380,000   US$ 35,271

VIEW OF THE GRAND CANAL, VENICE, LOOKING SOUTH EAST TO THE FABRICHE
NUOVO DI RIALTO oil on canvas, 23¼ x 37½in. (59 x 95cm.)
EXH.: Victoria Art Gallery Bath, *Bath Festival*, 1969.
  Sotheby's London, 12 July 1995 (118**) GBP 23,000   US$ 36,688

JANCO Marcel (1895-1984) Romenian
VILLAGE BRULÉ oil on board, unframed, 50 x 70cm. slr 'Janco'
EXH.: Venice, *26th Biennale Internazionale*, 1952.
  Christie's Amsterdam, 5 June 1996 (336*) NLG 18,400   US$ 10,751

MOUTONS ET CHEVRES oil on canvasboard, 19 5/8 x 27 3/8in. (50 x 69.5cm.) slr 'Janco', titled,
numbered and dated on an atelier sticker '195 1950' (on the reverse)
PROV.: The Artist's Estate.
  Christie's Tel Aviv, 14 April 1996 (75**) US$ 16,100   US$ 16,100

JANSEM Jean (1920 b.) French
LE JOUR DU LAVAGE oil on canvas, 50 3/8 x 64½in. (128 x 164cm.) slr 'Jansem'
  Sotheby's London, 20 March 1996 (331*) GBP 11,500   US$ 17,563

LE RETOUR DE LA FAMILLE oil on canvas, 51¼ x 64in. (130.2 x 162.5cm.) sll 'Jansem'
PROV.: Wally F. Galleries, New York (acquired by the present owner).
  Christie's East, 30 April 1996 (84**) US$ 18,400   US$ 18,400

FEMME ASSISE A LA TABLE oil on canvas, 45¾ x 35in. (116 x 89cm.) sll 'Jansem'
PROV.: Galerie Hervé, Paris (acquired by the family of the present owner, 1956).
　　　　Christie's East, 7 November 1995 (97**) US$ 17,250　　　　　　　US$　　17,250

JANSEN Johannes (Janson), the Elder (Ambon (Moluk islands) 1729-1784 Leyden) Dutch
WINTER LANDSCAPE WITH SKATERS oil on panel, 12¼ x 16¼in. (31 x 41.6cm.) sll 'J.Janson ft'
　　　　Sotheby's London, 17 April 1996 (147**) GBP 9,775　　　　　　　US$　　14,822

JANSEN Willem George Frederik (1871-1949) Dutch
A VIEW OF THE HARBOUR OF HARLINGEN oil on canvas, 35 x 50 cm s 'WGF Jansen'
　　　　Christie's Amsterdam, 25 April 1996 (101*) NLG 17,250　　　　　　US$　　10,250

JANSEN Willem George Frederik (1871-1949) Dutch
SHIPPING IN THE HARBOUR OF HARLINGEN oil on canvas, 51 x 65.5cm. slr 'WGF Jansen'
　　　　Christie's Amsterdam, 26 October 1995 (169*) NLG 13,800　　　　　US$　　8,701

JANSSEN Horst (Hamburg 1929-1995 Hamburg) German
VRIEDERICH watercolour and pencil-drawing, 20.6 x 33.3cm. sdlc 'Vriederich 10.10.77'; inscr. lr
'mit Widmung an Frau Clement vom 18.10.1977'
EXH.: Vienna. *Horst Janssen. Zeichnungen. Graph. Sammlungen Albertina*, 1982, cat. no. 124
(illustrated in colour).
　　　　Hauswedell & Nolte Cologne, 2 December 1995 (112**) DEM 15,000　　US$　　10,407

FICK IN MIMICHE coloured crayon, 41.5 x 29cm. sdlr titled '1968'
EXH.: Venice, *XXIV Esposizione Biennale Internazionale d'Arte*, 1968.
LIT.: Catalogue *XXXIV Biennale*, Venice.
　　　　Hauswedell & Nolte Cologne, 6 June 1996 (184**) DEM 23,000　　　US$　　14,944

BLUMENSTRAUß IN VASE crayon and pencil on paper, 17¾ x 11½in. (45 x 29cm.) sd ini. 'H.J.
5.8.75'
PROV.: A gift from The Artist to the present owner.
　　　　Christie's London, 19 March 1996 (25**) GBP 13,800　　　　　　　US$　　21,075

JANSSENS Abraham (1575-1632) Flemish
THE VIRGIN AND CHILD WITH THE INFANT SAINT JOHN THE BAPTIST oil on canvas, 56¾
x 43¼in. (144 x 110cm.)
　　　　Sotheby's London, 5 July 1995 (25**) GBP 45,500　　　　　　　US$　　72,579

JUPITER AND SEMELE oil on canvas, 48½ x 49in. (123.2 x 124.5cm.) (around 1625)
　　　　Christie's London, 7 July 1995 (56**) GBP 17,250　　　　　　　　US$　　27,516

JANSSENS Hieronymus {called Den Danser} (Antwerp 1624-1693 Antwerp) Flemish
CHEERFULL COMPANY IN A HALL oil on canvas, 60 x 75cm. sll 'H. Janssens'
　　　　Dorotheum Vienna, 6 March 1996 (89**) ATS 280,000　　　　　　US$　　26,933

INTERIOR WITH A MUSIC PARTY AND AN ELEGANT COUPLE DANCING oil on panel, 22¼
x 38in. (56.5 x 96.5cm.)
　　　　Sotheby's London, 5 July 1995 (112**) GBP 18,400　　　　　　　US$　　29,351

INTERIOR WITH ELEGANT FIGURES DANCING oil on panel, 24 x 37¾in. (61 x 96cm.)
　　　　Sotheby's London, 5 July 1995 (113**) GBP 9,200　　　　　　　　US$　　14,675

DANCING COMPANY oil on canvas, 114 x 166cm. sd 'H. Janssens fecit A° 1652' on the reverse
PROV.: 1792 Thomas Tottie; Mr Adolf Wohlfahrt; J.N. Pettersson; 1885, Mr Sirénius, Göteborg.
　　　　Bukowskis Stockholm, 29 November-1 December 1995 (234**) SEK 460,000　US$　　69,588

JAUDON Valerie (1945 b.) American
HOMEWOOD oil on canvas-unframed, 48 x 48in. (121.9 x 121.9cm.) sd and titled 'HOMEWOOD
Valerie Jaudin 1976' on the overlap
PROV.: Holly Solomon Gallery, New York.
Christie's East, 7 May 1996 (69*) US$ 8,050   US$ 8,050

JAWLENSKY Alexej von (Torschok 1864-1941 Wiesbaden) Russian
LEID UND LIEBE ENG VERSCHLUNGEN oil on paper laid down on cardboard, 17.5 x 12.5cm. s
with mono. and d (1937)
EXH.: Bonn, *Alexej von Jawlensky - Adolf Hoezler*, Städt. Kunstsammlungen, cat. no. 44; Berlin,
Alexej von Jawlensky, Haus am Waldsee, cat. no. 90; Cologne, *Alexej von Jawlensky*, Galerie Aenne
Abels, cat. no. 65; Munich, *Alexej von Jawlensky*, Lenbachhaus, cat. no. 64; *Alexej von Jawlensky.
Catalogue Raisonné of the Oil Paintings*, vol. III, p. 375 (illustrated in colour).
Hauswedell & Nolte Cologne, 1 December 1995 (340**) DEM 50,000   US$ 34,691

GROSSES STILLEBEN: HORTENSIEN oil on paper
laid down on board, 24.5 x 18.8cm. sll with mono.;
dlr '35' (1935)
Hauswedell & Nolte Cologne, 5-6 June
1996 (333**) DEM 90,000   US$ 58,476

MYSTISCHER KOPF: ASCONESER KOPF oil on
board, 15¾ x 11 5/8in. (40 x 29.7cm.) sdll 'A
Jawlensky', dated on the reverse W.11.1918
LIT.: C. Weiler, *Alexej Jawlensky*, Cologne, 1959, no.
232 (illustrated pl. 244); M. Jawlensky., L. Pieroni-
Jawlensky, A. Jawlensky, *Alexej von Jawlensky,
Catalogue Raisonné of the Oil Paintings, vol. II,
1914-1933*, London, 1992, no. 968 (illustrated p.
254).
Christie's London, 11 October 1995
(151**) GBP 188,500   US$ 297,506

Grosses Stilleben: Hortensien

HEILANDSGESICHT: DORNEN oil on linen-finished paer laid down on board, 14 x 10½in. (35.6 x
26.7cm.) sll (1920)
PROV.: The artist's studio; Galka Scheyer, Hollywood, CA (1928); Acquired by the family of the
present owner in the 1930s, presumably from the above.
EXH.: Dusseldorf, Haus Leonhard Tietz AG, Das Junge Rheinland, *I. Internationale
Kunstausstellung*, 1922, no. 667; New York, Daniel Gallery, *The Blue Four*, 1925, no. 43; Los
Angeles County Museum, *The Blue Four*, 1926, no. 25; Oakland, CA., Oakland Art Gallery, *The
Blue Four*, 1926, no. 7; Portland, OR., Museum of Art; Spokane, WA., Grace Campbell Memorial
Building, *The Blue Four*, 1927, no. 28; Hollywood, CA., Braxton Gallery, 1930, no. 43; San
Francisco, California Palace of the Legion of Honor, *Jawlensky-Paul Klee*, 1931, no. 24; Santa
Barbara, CA., Faulkner Memorial Art Gallery, *The Blue Four*, 1932, no. 18; Chicago, Arts Club, *The
Blue Four*, 1932, no. 57; New York, Nierendorf Gallery, 1941 or 1944.
LIT.: Maria Jawlensky, Lucia Pieroni-Jawlensky and Angelica Jawlensky, *Alexej von Jawlensky,
Catalogue Raisonné of the Oil Paintings*, Volume III, London, 1993, no. 2246, illustrated p. 412.
Sotheby's New York, 2 May 1996 (233**) US$ 167,500   US$ 167,500

MEDITATION oil on painter's cardboard with line structure framed under glass, 17.1 x 13cm. sll
monogram 'A.J.' d r 35' reverse sd inscr. 'A. Jawlensky 1935. VII. N 5.' on frame 'A. Jawlensky 1936.
Mit innigster verehrung A. Jawlensky.' (1935)
EXH.: Frankfurter Kunstverein/Hamburger Kunstverein 1967, cat. no. 56.
Lempertz Cologne, 29 November 1995 (217**) DEM 50,000   US$ 35,291

MEDITATION oil on linencardboard framed under glass, 19 x 12.5cm. sll monogram 'A.J. dr '36' (april 1936)
PROV.: 1962 Galerie Otto Stangl, Muenchen; A. Gessner, Wiesbaden, on loan in Museum Wiesbaden.
EXH.: Frankfurt/Hamburg 1967, Kunstverein, *Alexej von Jawlensky*, Cat. No. 62 ill.; Wiesbaden 1991, Museum, *Alexej von Jawlinsky zum 50. Todesjahr*, Cat. no. 155 with col. ill.; Rotterdam 1994, *Alexej von Jawlinsky*, Geneva 1995, Musée Rath.

Lempertz Cologne, 29 November 1995 (218**) DEM 90,000	US$	63,523

GROSSE VARIATION : STURMTAG oil on linen-finish paper laid down on cardboard, 20¼ x 14in. (53.5 x 35.4cm.) (ca 1916)
PROV.: The Artist's Estate.
EXH.: Geneva, Galerie Krugier, 1963 (no.27).
LIT.: C. Weiler, *Alexej Jawlensky*, Cologne, 1959, no. 644 (illustrated p. 272); M. Jawlensky, L. Pieroni Jawlensky and A. Jawlensky, *Alexej von Jawlensky, catalogue raisonné of the oil paintings, 1914-1933, vol.II*, London, 1992, no. 840 (illustrated p. 166).

Christie's London, 29 November 1995 (219**) GBP 70,000	US$	109,495

ITALIENISCHES MADCHEN oil on board, 15 1/2 x 11 5/8in. (39.4 x 29.5cm.) ll 'A. Jawlensky.' again on the reverse 'A. Jawlensky 1918 Italienisches Mädchen N2.' (1918)
PROV.: Galka Scheyer, Los Angeles; Alfred E. Stendahl, Los Angeles (acquired by the late owner, 1955).
EXH.: San Francisco, Museum of Art, *Jawlensky*, May, 1937.

Christie's New York, 8 November 1995 (245**) US$ 244,500	US$	244,500

INNERES SCHAUEN oil on board, 16 1/2 x 12 1/2in. (42 x 31cm.) ll 'A.J.' again on the reverse 'A. V.Jawlensky 1928 Inneres Schauen' (1928)
PROV.: Evelyn S. Mayer, San Francisco (acquired from the artist); Joseph W. Dammann, Los Angeles (acquired by the late owner, 1956).

Christie's New York, 8 November 1995 (279**) US$ 310,500	US$	310,500

MEDITATION: KLEINER KOPF oil on linen-textured paper laid down by the artist on board, Image size: 7 x 5 3/8in. (17.8 x 13.7cm.). Mount size: 12 3/8 x 9 5/8in. (31.4 x 24.4cm.) ll 'A.J.' ,lr '35', on the mount '1935 II' , on the reverse 'A. Jawlensky 1935 N120 j.' (1935)
PROV.: Galka Scheyer, Los Angeles (1935); Felix Landau Gallery, Los Angeles.
EXH.: Nierendorf Gallery, New York, 1939.

Christie's New York, 8 November 1995 (284**) US$ 33,350	US$	33,350

JENKINS Paul (1923 b.) American
PHENOMENA OVER THE FACE OF THE DIALS acrylic on canvas, 96 x 72in. (243.9 x 182.9cm.) sll 'Paul Jenkins'; sd and titled 'Paul Jenkins 'Phenomena Over The Face of The Dials' 1966' on the overlap and again on the stretcher

Christie's East, 7 May 1996 (32*) US$ 11,500	US$	11,500

JENSEN Johan Laurentz (1800-1856) Danish
PINK, RED, YELLOW AND WHITE ROSES AND HONEYSUCKLE ON A MOSSY BANK oil on canvas, 21 x 25½in. 953 x 65cm.) s 'J.L. Jensen'

Christie's London, 14 June 1996 (104**) GBP 38,900	US$	59,985

LILAC ON A LEDGE oil on canvas, 9 x 12¼in. (23 x 31cm.) sd 'I.L. Jensen 1840'

Christie's London, 15 March 1996 (58**) GBP 9,200	US$	14,050

ROSES, CONVOLVULI AND HONEYSUCKLE oil on canvas, 21¾ x 28½in. (55.2 x 72.5cm.) sd 'J.L. Jensen/1854'

Christie's London, 17 November 1995 (102**) GBP 52,100	US$	81,495

JESPERS Floris (1889-1965) Belgian
STANDING CLOWN oil on glas (verre églomisé), 61.5 x 27.5cm. slr 'Jespers' (executed *circa* 1927)
PROV.: Acquired directly from the artist by the grandmother of the present owner, thence by discent.
  Christie's Amsterdam, 5 June 1996 (234b**) NLG 29,900   US$ 17,470

LE CONGO ROYAL oil on board, 148 x 105cm. sdll 'Jespers' and s again and inscr. with title and
'Kamina' on the reverse
PROV.: Estate of the artist.
  Christie's Amsterdam, 5 June 1996 (239**) NLG 11,500   US$ 6,719

WOMEN FROM THE CONGO oil on canvas, 87 x 105cm. slr 'Jespers'
  Christie's Amsterdam, 6 December 1995 (244**) NLG 10,350   US$ 6,413

JIRLOW Lennart (1936 b.) Swedish
FRUKOST I DET GRÖNA gouache on paper, 48 x 50cm. slr 'L. Jirlow'
  Bukowskis Stockholm, 24-25 April 1996 (54**) SEK 68,000   US$ 10,302

LES HORTICULTEURS oil on canvas, 97 x 129cm. slr 'L. Jirlow'
PROV.: Galerie d'Art Colisée, Paris 1991.
  Bukowskis Stockholm, 24-25 April 1996 (55**) SEK 170,000   US$ 25,755

MÅLAREN I SIN TRÄDGÅRD oil on canvas, 89 x 116cm. sll 'L. Jirlow'
  Bukowskis Stockholm, 26-27 October 1995 (51**) SEK 140,000   US$ 20,503

JOHANSSON Carl (1863-1944) Swedish
MOTIV FRÅN GÅRDSVIK oil on canvas, 80 x 122cm. sdlr 'Carl Johansson 86'
  Bukowskis Stockholm, 29-31 May 1996 (64**) SEK 60,000   US$ 8,824

JOHANSSON Stefan (1876-1955) Swedish
AFTON EFTER REGN watercolour on linnen, 58 x 42cm. sdlr 'Stefan 34'
  Bukowskis Stockholm, 29-31 May 1996 (69**) SEK 115,000   US$ 16,913

JOHN Augustus Edwin, O.M., R.A. (1878-1961) British
DORELIA WEARING A YELLOW AND RED SCARF oil on canvas, 9½ x 14in. (24 x 36cm.) slr
'John' (ca 1910-12)
PROV.: American British Art Gallery, New York.
EXH.: Pennsylvania, Academy of Fine Arts, Peale Galleries, *Augustus John*, Jan.-March 1968, no.
18.
  Christie's London, 21 March 1996 (51**) GBP 18,400   US$ 28,100

DORELIA IN EASTERN DRESS pencil, watercolour and bodycolour, 17¾ x 9¾in. (45 x 25cm.) slc
'John' (ca 1906)
PROV.: Mrs. Archibald Douglas, London; Mrs. Dudley Tooth, London, by whom bequeathed to the
present owners.
EXH.: Newcastle-Upon-Tyne, Palace of Art, *North East Coast Exhibition*, May-Oct. 1929, no.427 as
'Figure Study'; New York, British Council, British Pavilion, New York World's Fair, *Exhibition of
Contemporary British Art*, 1939, no.5 as 'Lady in Eastern Dress with red Trousers'; London, Royal
Academy, *Works by Augustus John*, March-June 1954, no.139; Sheffield, Graves Art Gallery,
Augustus John, 1956, no.86.
LIT.: L. Browse, *Augustus John: Drawings*, London, 1941, p.21, pl.36.
  Christie's London, 21 March 1996 (52***) GBP 26,450   US$ 40,394

PERDITA oil on board, 20 x 15½in. (51 x 40cm.) (ca 1908)
PROV.: Edgar Hesslein, New York; Arthur Tooth & Sons Ltd., London, where purchased by the
present owners.
EXH.: New York, Brooklyn Museum, *Paintings by Contemporary English and French Painters*,

Nov. 1922-Jan. 1923, no.30; New York, *Scott & Fowles, Augustus John in American Collections*, April 1949, no.14; Pennsylvania, Academy of Fine Arts, Peale Galleries, *Augustus John*, Jan.-March 1968, no.22.

Christie's London, 21 March 1996 (53**) GBP 34,500

US$ 52,688

JOHN Gwen (1876-1939) British

A SITTING GIRL WEARING A SPOTTED BLUE DRESS oil on canvas, 14 x 10¾in. (35.5 x 27.5cm.) (ca 1914-15)
PROV.: The Estate of the Artist; P.J.63; Mrs. Cheever Cowdin, New York, 1946, purchased from Matthiesen Ltd., London.
EXH.: possibly, Paris, Salon des Tuileries, 1924 (ex catalogue); London, Matthiesen Ltd., *Gwen John Memorial Exhibition*, Sept.-Oct. 1946, no.23.
LIT.: C. Langdale, *Gwen John*, Yale, 1987, no.29, pl.188.

Christie's London, 21 March 1996 (68**) GBP 43,300

US$ 66,127

YOUNG WOMAN WITH A VIOLIN oil on canvas, 18 x 16in. (46 x 41cm.) (ca 1897-98)
PROV.: Given by the artist to Augustus John, until 1961, thence to Dorelia John, until 1969.
EXH.: London, C.E.M.A., British Institute of Adult Education, *British Paintings 1900-1940*, 1941, no.13; London, Matthiesen Ltd., *Gwen John Memorial Exhibition*, Sept.-Oct. 1946, no.2 as 'Grace Westrey (sic) playing the violin'; London, Arts Council of Great Britain, Tate Gallery, *Ethel Walker, Frances Hodgkins, Gwen John: A Memorial Exhibition*, May-June 1952, no.107 as 'Grace Westrey (sic) playing the Violin'; London, Arts Council of Great Britain, Arts Council Gallery, *Gwen John*, Jan.-March 1968, no.2: this exhibition travelled to Sheffield, Graves Art Gallery, March-April1968; and Cardiff, National Museum of Wales, April-May 1968; New York, Davis & Long Company, *Gwen John A Retrospective Exhibition*, Oct.-Nov. 1975, no.3 (illustrated).
LIT.: M. Holroyd, *Augustus John: A Biography* I, London, 1974, p.59; M. Taubman, *Gwen John*, London, 1986, p.22, pl.8; C. Langdale, *Gwen John*, New Haven, 1987, no.4, p.134, pl.5.

Christie's London, 21 March 1996 (76**) GBP 46,600

US$ 71,167

JOHN Joseph W. (America) American

LIFE'S MORNING AND EVENING oil on canvas, 30 x 40in. (76 x 102cm.) sdlr 'J. John 1872'
EXH.: Cincinnati, Ohio, *Cincinnati Industrial Exposition*, 1875, no. 245.

Christie's New York, 13 September 1995 (21**) US$ 10,925

US$ 10,925

JOLI Antonio (Modena 1,700 c.-1777 Naples) Italian

VIEW OF THE RUINS AT PAESTUM oil on canvas, 27¾ x 38¾in. (70.5 x 98.4cm.)

Sotheby's New York, 11 January 1996 (126**) US$ 85,000

US$ 85,000

VENICE, THE ENTRANCE TO THE GUIDECCA, WITH THE PUNTA DELLA DOGANA TO THE LEFT AND SAN GIORGIO MAGGIORE TO THE RIGHT oil on canvas, 23½ x 39¾in. (59.3 x 101cm.) s on a box on a boat 'Mr. Jolli/Fecit' (ca. 1744)
PROV.: presumably commissioned from the artist by John James heidegger (1666-1749), and probably intended for the latter's house at 4 Maids of Honour Row, Richmond; Mr. Norbert Fischmann, 1943; possibly, Mrs. M.J. Railing, Whitechapel, 1951; Anonymous sale, Sotheby's London, 12 July 1978, lot 38 (GBP 5,800), where bought by the present owner.
LIT.: T. Borenius, 'Heidegger and Joli - another link', in *Burlington Magazine*, LXXII, no. 482, May 1943, p. 124, (illustrated).

Sotheby's London, 17 April 1996 (628**) GBP 69,700

US$ 105,686

A CAPRICCIO OF ROMAN RUINS WITH THE MASSACRE OF THE INNOCENTS oil on canvas, 49¾ x 39¾in. (126.4 x 101cm.)
PROV.: Painted for John Stuart, 3rd Earl of Bute; His sale, London, Christie's 19 March 1796, lot 69, GBP18.18s6d. to van Heygheusen; The hon M.A. Borthwick, 1928 and thence by descent; Sale, London, Christie's 14 April 1978 (as by Panini, for GBP 10,000), where bought by the present owner.

Sotheby's London, 17 April 1996 (629***) GBP 43,300

US$ 65,656

THE PIAZZA NAVONA, ROME oil on canvas, 19 x 25 5/8in. (48.3 x 65.1cm.)
PROV.: Mrs. Edith Cragg; Christie's, 26 June 1925, lot 157, a pair, as Vanvitelli, (9 gns.).
Christie's South Kensington, 18 april 1996 (290**) GBP 5,175   US$ 7,847

ROME, A VIEW OF THE CAMPO VACCINO, WITH THE COLLOSSEUM IN THE DISTANCE
oil on canvas, 46 x 60½in. (117 x 154cm.)
PROV.: Siegfried Sassoon of Heytesbury House, Wiltshire; Thence by inheritance at Heytesbury.
Sotheby's London, 6 December 1995 (50**) GBP 89,500   US$ 137,735

JONES Allen (Southhampton 1937 b.) British
ORANGE SKIRT acrylic on canvas, 183 x 152cm. inscr., titled and d 'Allen Jones 1964' on the
reverse
EXH.: Kassel, *Documenta III*, 1964.
LIT.: Exhibition catalogue, *Documenta III*, Kassel 1964, p. 358, no. 2.
Wiener Kunst Auktionen, 27 September 1995 (418**) ATS 450,000   US$ 43,742

JONES Francis Coates (1857-1932) American
WOMEN IN A ROWBOAT oil on canvas, 21¼ x 31in. (54 x 78.8cm.) slr 'Francis C. Jones'
Christie's New York, 13 September 1995 (63**) US$ 64,100   US$ 64,100

JONES Hugh Bolton (1848-1927) American
MEADOW CROSSING oil on canvas, 30 x 36in. (76.2 x 91.5cm.) slr 'H. Bolton Jones'
PROV.: Marvin Arenson, Florida.
Christie's New York, 23 May 1996 (65**) US$ 32,200   US$ 32,200

JONGKIND Johan Barthold (Lattrop (Ov.) 1819-1891 Côte St.-André near Grenoble) Dutch
ROTTERDAM HARBOUR oil on canvas, 16 5/8 x 22 3/8in. (42 x 56.8cm.) sd 'Jongkind 57'
Christie's London, 14 June 1996 (67**) GBP 87,300   US$ 134,618

A MOONLIT RIVER LANDSCAPE oil on canvas, 16½ x 25½in. (41.9 x 64.8cm.) sdlr 'Jongkind
1870'
PROV.: Oscar Simon Collection, Dinard, France; M. Knoedler & Co., New York (until April 20,
1909); Mayer H. Lehman (by 1909); Mrs. Harriet Lehman Weil and Mrs. Bertha Lehman
Rosenheim; Mrs. Elsie Rosenheim Weil and Dr. Henry Lehman Weil; George L. Weil, Washington,
D.C. (by 1952).
Christie's New York, 2 November 1995 (80**) US$ 46,000   US$ 46,000

LA JETÉE A HONFLEUR oil on canvas, 13 1/8 x 17in. (33.3 x 43.2cm.) sdlr 'Jongkind 1865'
PROV.: Probably Theophile Bascle, Bordeaux; .Anon. sale; Georges Petit, Paris, Apnl 12-14, 1883,
no. 83; Collection M. C. V. Anon. sale; Georges Petit, Paris, 27 May 1920, no.48; C. Vignier, Paris;
With Jacques Dubourg, Paris; With E. J. van Wisselingh and Co., Amsterdam; Anon. sale; Laing
Gallery, Toronto, 1948, to Mrs. T. P. Lownsborough, Toronto ca. 1948-1956; With E.J. van
Wisselingh & Co., Amsterdam 1956 Purchased by present owner, 1957.
EXH.: Toronto, Laing Gallery, 1938 Hartford, Wadsworth Atheneum, *Connecticut Collects*, 1957,
no. 24, pl. III (illustrated) Chicago, The Art Institute of Chicago, *Masterpieces from Private
Collenions in Chicago*, 1969, p. 3, no. 25 Sterling and Francine Clark Art Institute, *Jongkind and The
Pre-lmpressionists*, Dec. 1976-Feb. 1977, no. 10.
LIT.: V. Hefting, *Jongkind, Sa Vie, Son Oeuvre, Son Epoque*, Paris, 1975, no. 339 (illustrated);
C.Cunningham, *Jongkind and the Pre-impressionists: Painters of the École Saint Simeon*, Sterling
and Francine Clark Art Institute, 1977, no. 10 (illustrated).
Christie's New York, 22 May 1996 (101**) US$ 145,500   US$ 145,500

LA LAVADIERE oil on panel, 14 x 12cm. sll 'Jongkind'
Étude Tajan Paris, 27 October 1995 (12) FRF 36,000   US$ 7,282

JONSON Sven (1902-1981) Swedish
PRELUDIUM oil on canvas, 130 x 76cm. sd 'Sven Jonson 48'
    Bukowskis Stockholm, 26-27 October 1995 (56**) SEK 62,000   US$ 9,080

JORDAENS Hans III (Antwerp 1595 c.-1643/44 Antwerp) Flemish
MOUNTAINLANDSCAPE WITH PAULUS' CONVERSION oil on panel, 46 x 74.5cm. Painted in
co-operation with Joost de Momper (Antwerp 1564-1635)
PROV.: Sale, Lempertz, Cologne, 5 November 1925, illustration X; Ph. van Limburg Stirum,
Anregem, Belgium, 1954; Dr. Hans Wetzlar, Amsterdam; Sale, Sotheby's Mak van Way,
Amsterdam, 9 June 1977, lot 57, no. 17.
EXH.: Laren, Singer Museum, *A Selection from the Collection of Dr. H.A. Wetzlar*, 1968/69, no. 17.
LIT.: Dr. Klaus Ertz, *Josse de Momper der Jüngere*, 1986, p. 518, illustration no. 180, dated ca.
1630.
    Dorotheum Vienna, 6 March 1996 (153**) ATS 700,000   US$ 67,334

THE CONVERSATION OF SAINT PAUL oil on panel, 45.8 x 74.6cm.
PROV.: also Joos de Momper (121) co-painter.; Baumeister; Sale, Lempertz Cologne, 29 November
1909, lot 130, with ill.; Wedever; Sale Lempertz Cologne, 25 November 1925, fig. X; Ph. van
Limburg Stirum, Anregem, Belgium, 1954; Dr Hans Wetzlar, Amsterdam (†); Sale, Sotheby Mak
van waay; Amsterdam, 9 june 1977, lot 57, with ill.
EXH.: Laren Singer museum, *A Selection from the Collection of Dr H.A. Wetzlar,*; 14 December
1968-26 January 1969, no. 17.
LIT.: K Ertz, *Josse de Momper de Jüngere*, 1986, p. 518, no. 180, where dated to circa 1630.
    Christie's Amsterdam, 13 November 1995 (121**) NLG 48,300   US$ 30,441

JORDAENS Jacob (Antwerp 1593-1678 Antwerp) Flemish
AN OLD MAN PLAYING THE FLUTE oil on canvas, 80.2 x 62.4cm.
    Christie's Amsterdam, 13 November 1995 (127**) NLG 17,250   US$ 10,872

JORN Asger (1914-1973) Danish
AN ABSTRACT COMPOSITION oil on canvas, 55 x 46cm. sdlr 'Jorn 66'
    Christie's Amsterdam, 5 June 1996 (298**) NLG 29,900   US$ 17,470

UNTITLED oil on masonite, 30.5 x 30cm. sdal 'Jorn 50' d again and inscr. '2 agganakker' on the
reverse
PROV.: Galerie Birch, Copenhagen; Valdemar Rohde, Copenhagen.
LIT.: Guy Atkins, *Jorn in Skandinavia 1930-1953*, London 1968, p.251, no. 637 (ill.).
    Christie's Amsterdam, 5 June 1996 (302**) NLG 29,900   US$ 17,470

UNTITLED oil on paper mounted on panel, 29 x 42cm. sdll 'Jorn '53' (1953)
LIT.: Guy Atkins, *Asger Jorn, Supplement to the oeuvre catalogue of his paintings from 1930-1973*,
London 1986, S.97.
    Christie's Amsterdam, 5 June 1996 (318**) NLG 23,000   US$ 13,439

MODIFICATION oil on canvas, 61.5 x 50cm. (ca. 1962)
EXH.: Köln, Museum Ludwig, *Europa/Amerika*, 1986, no. 76.
LIT.: G. Atkins, *Asger Jorn, Supplement: Paintings 1930-1973*, London 1986, no. 143 (ill.).
    Christie's Amsterdam, 5 June 1996 (380**) NLG 19,550   US$ 11,423

UNTITLED oil on canvas, 72 x 90cm. sdlr 'Asger Jörgensen 37'
PROV.: Dr Hnas Kjaerholm, Aarhus.
LIT.: Guy atkins, *Jorn in Skandinavia 1930-1953*, London 1968, p. 206, no.64, p. 321 (ill.).
    Christie's Amsterdam, 6 December 1995 (263**) NLG 23,000   US$ 14,252

LE REGARD AU DOS oil on canvas, 75 x 49cm. slr 'Jorn' s again and inscr. with title on the reverse
LIT.: Guy Atkins, *Asger Jorn The crucial years* 1954-1964, London 1977, no. 1416(ill.).
Christie's Amsterdam, 6 December 1995 (281**) NLG 92,000   US$ 57,008

OPVAAGNEN - THE AWAKENING I oil on hardboard, 55 x 43.3cm. sll 'Jorn' and s again and
inscr. with title on the reverse (painted in 1952-53 in Silkeborg)
PROV.: A. Sondergaard, Silkeborg.
EXH.: Copenhagen, Galerie Birch, *Asger Jorn*, 19 September - 10 October 1953, no. 56 (the
exhibition travellet to Odense, *Tapet og Kunst*; Gallery, 12-23 October 1953).
LIT.: G. Atkins, *Jorn in Skandinavia* 1930-1953, London 1968, p.403, no. 798 (ill.);.
Christie's Amsterdam, 6 December 1995 (295**) NLG 55,200   US$ 34,205

UNTITLED oil on board, 72 x 62cm. sdar 'Asger Jorn 45' and s again and inscr. with a swedish poem
on the reverse **(illustrated on the cover of this W.C.A.Volume)**
PROV.: André Emmerich, New York.
LIT.: G. Atkins, *Asger Jorn Recent Discoveries (Addenda to the supplement)*, Silkeborg 1986, no.
S.227.
Christie's Amsterdam, 6 December 1995 (316**) NLG 184,000   US$ 114,017

DEN VILDE JAGD oil on canvas, 31½ x 39 3/8in. (80 x 100cm.) slr 'Jorn' sd titled and dedicated
'Gunni Busck Tak' on the reverse
PROV.: A gift from the Artist to the present owner in 1957.
LIT.: Guy Atkins, *Asger Jorn: The Crucial Years: 1954-1964*, London 1977, no. 1166, illustrated.
Sotheby's London, 21 March 1996 (34**) GBP 13,800   US$ 21,075

THE PROPHECY oil on panel, 18¼ x 23¾in.(46.5 x 60cm.) sd 'Jorn '51'
PROV.: Galerie Birch, Copenhagen; Palle Dije, Copenhagen; Lefebre Gallery, New York.
EXH.: Touring exhibition organized by the 'Council of Art Societies Outside Copenhagen', *6 Malere*,
1951-1952, no. 67; Munich, Städtische Galerie im Lenbachhaus, *Asger Jorn*, January-March 1987,
no. 26 (illustrated in the catalogue p.117).
LIT.: Guy Atkins, *Jorn in Scandinavia 1930-1953*, London 1968, no. 698 (illustrated).
Christie's London, 26 October 1995 (36**) GBP 25,300   US$ 39,931

PORTRAIT DE MISTER X oil on canvas, ,100 x 81 titled on the reverse (1956)
LIT.: G. Atkins, *Asger Jorn, Supplement to the oeuvre catalogue*, ed. Lund Humphries, London
1986, no. S.100a.
Finearte Milan, 26 October 1995 (205**) ITL 80,500,000   US$ 50,156

SENZA PIETA oil on canvas, 39 3/8 x 31 7/8in. (,100 x 81cm.) slr; sd 1967 amd titled on the reverse
PROV.: Galleria Gastaldelli, Milan.
EXH.: Paris/New York, Espace Pierre Cardin, *1950- 1980 European Trends in Modern Art*,1980;
Saint Etienne, Musée d'Art et d'Industrie, *Works between 1957-1967*, March-April 1983; Lyon, *Le
Biennale d'Art Contemporain de Lyon*, *Et Tous ils changent le Monde*, September-October 1993
(illustrated in colour in the catalogue p. 69).
LIT.: Guy Atkins, *Asger Jorn: The Final Years 1965-1973*, London 1980, no. 1747 (illustrated).
Christie's London, 27 June 1996 (26**) GBP 102,700   US$ 158,365

REPOSE oil on board, 59½ x 49 3/8in. (151 x 120.3cm.) slr 'Jorn' sd and titled '1953-1959' on the
reverse
PROV.: Galerie Rive Gauche, Paris.
EXH.: Paris, Galerie Rive Gauche, *Trente et Une Peintures de Asger Jorn*, May 1960, no. 23
(illustrated in the catalogue); Recklinghausen, Städtische Kunsthalle; Amsterdam, Stedelijk Museum,
Polarität, June-September 1961, no. D.22 (illustrated in the catalogue); Basel, Kunsthalle, *Asger Jorn
- Eugène Dodeigne*, October-November 1964, no. 70; Amsterdam, Stedelijk Museum, *Jorn*,
December 1964-January 1965, no. 81; Humlebaek, Louisiana Museum of Modern Art, *Jorn*,
February 1965, no. 83; Arnhem, Gemeentemuseum, *Oog in oog met Hans en Alice de Jong,* June-

September 1970, no. 78 (illustrated in colour in the catalogue); Haarlem, Frans Halsmuseum, *Collection Hans and Alice deJong*, June-July 1971.
LIT.: Guy Atkins, *Jorn in Scandinavia: 1930-1953*, London 1968, p. 405, no. 822 (illustrated in colour p. 135).
    Christie's London, 30 November 1995 (13**) GBP 144,500   US$ 226,028

JOSEPHSON Ernst (1851-1906) Swedish
ADAM OCH EVA oil on canvas, 23 x 17.5cm. slr 'Ernst Josephson' (1895)
EXH.: Liljevalchs Konsthall, *Minnesutställningen*, 1951, Riksförbundet för Bildande Konst, *Naiv Tradition*; Stockholm, Nationalmuseum, *Ernst Josephson*, 1972.
LIT.: Erik blomberg, *Ernst Josephson*, p. 662 (illustrated p. 661); Erik Blomberg, *Från Näcken till Gåslisa*, p. 225 (illustrated p. 227), catalogue p. 411.
    Bukowskis Stockholm, 29 November-1 December 1995 (67**) SEK 98,000   US$ 14,825

DEN FLYGANDE HOLLÄNDAREN oil on panel, 14.5 x 24cm. slr 'Ernst Josephson' (1893)
LIT.: Erik Blomberg, *Ernst Josephdon konst. Från Näcken till Gåslisa*, pp. 103-104 (illustrated p. 102).
    Bukowskis Stockholm, 29-31 May 1996 (72**) SEK 325,000   US$ 47,798

JOUDREVILLE Isaäc de (Leyden ca. 1612-ca. 1645 Leyden) Dutch
PORTRAIT OF A YOUNG LADY EN PROFIL oil on oak panel, 40 x 31.5cm.
PROV.: Collection L. Nardus à Suresnes (Rembrandt); Collection Mrs Alfred Seymour, London 1915, Anonymous Sale,The Hague, 3 May 1944 (Van Marle and Bignell), n° 144; anonymous Sale, Paris, Hotel Drouot, 9 February 1954.
LIT.: E.W. Moes, *Iconographia Batava*, Amsterdam, 1897-1905, n° 6686, n°10; C.R.P and Bandzahl, J. Bruyn, B. Haak, S.H. Levie, P.J.J. van Thiel, E. van de Wetering, *A corpus of Rembrandt Paintings*, La Haye, Boston, London, 1986, II, p. 165; C. Hofstede de Groot, *A catalogue raisonné*, London, 1916, p. 332, quoted under n° 698; W. Sumowski, *Gemälde der Rembrandt Schüler*, Landau, 1983, V, n° 2104a, repr. p. 3242.
    Étude Tajan Paris, 12 December 1995 (53**) FRF 230,000   US$ 46,328

JOY Thomas Musgrave (1812-1866) British
GIRL IN A RED HAT WITH A BASKET OF FLOWERS oil on canvas, 36¼ x 24½in. (92 x 62cm.) sd mono (1859)
    Phillips London, 23 April 1996 (49*) GBP 5,500   US$ 8,340

JUNG Georg (Salzburg 1899-1957 Vienna) Austrian
ROSA EINSAM IM ORANGE; MAN KAN ES NICHT ERREICHEN oil on canvas in artist's frame, 60 x 71cm.; 62 x 73cm. with frame slr 'G. JUNG'
    Wiener Kunst Auktionen, 26 March 1996 (363**) ATS 115,000   US$ 11,062

JUNGWIRTH Martha (Vienna 1940-) Austrian
UNTITLED watercolour on paper, 215 x 300cm. sdlr 'M. Jungwirth 82'
    Wiener Kunst Auktionen, 27 September 1995 (553**) ATS 120,000   US$ 11,664

JUTZ Carl (Windschlag 1838-1916 Pfaffendorf near Koblenz) German
FASANE UND REBHÜHNER VOR DEN BÄDISCHEN BERGEN oil on canvas, 90 x 108cm. sll 'Carl Jutz'
    Wiener Kunst Auktionen, 29 November 1995 (537**) ATS 200,000   US$ 20,063

KAEMMERER Frederik Hendrik (The Hague 1839-1902 Paris) Dutch
L'INVITATION AU PATINAGE oil on canvas, 22 x 31½in. (55.9 x 80cm.) sll 'F H KAEMMERER'
      Christie's New York, 2 November 1995 (137**) US$ 43,700   US$ 43,700

LE BAPTEME oil on canvas, 43 x 29½in. (109.3 x 75cm.) sll 'F.H.Kaemmerer.'
      Christie's New York, 2 November 1995 (146**) US$ 55,200   US$ 55,00

KAHN Leo (1894-1983)
STILL LIFE WITH A MANDOLINE oil on canvas, 23 5/8 x 32in. (60 x 81cm.) sll 'L.Kahn' (early 1940's)
      Christie's Tel Aviv, 14 April 1996 (58**) US$ 11,500   US$ 11,500

KALF Willem (1622-1693) Dutch
STILL-LIFE WITH ARMS AND ARMOR, MARTIAL TRUMPETS, AN ELABORATE SILVER GILT SALVER, A NAUTILUS CUP, A SILVER GILT EWER AND OTHER OBJCTS ARRANGED ON A TABLE, A SILVER THREAD TRIMMED VELVET CHAIR AND FLOOR, WITH A SELF PORTRAIT BEYOND oil on canvas, 60¼ x 65¼in. (153 x 165.7cm.) (ca. 1643-44)
PROV.: Speelman Gallery, London.
LIT.: S. Segal, *A Prosperous Past*, 1988, p. 185 (illustrated p. 184, fig. 10.2).
      Sotheby's New York, 16 May 1996 (89**) US$ 129,000   US$ 1290,00

KALLSTENIUS Gottfried Samuel Nikolaus (1861-1943) Swedish
FLICKA PÅR SOMMARÄNG oil on canvas, 98 x 123cm. sdlr 'G. Kallstenius 88' (1888)
      Bukowskis Stockholm, 29-31 May 1996 (77**) SEK 340,000   US$ 50,004

KALTENMOSER Max (1806-1867) German
A GAME OF DICE oil on canvas, 36 x 53½in. (91.5 x 135.8cm.) s 'Max Kaltenmoser/München 1873'
      Christie's New York, 2 November 1995 (66**) US$ 27,600   US$ 27,600

KANDINSKY Wassily (Moscow 1866-1944) Russian
STRAHLEN watercolour, pen and coloured inks on paper laid down by the artist on board, 20 7/8 x 13¼in. (53 x 33.8cm.) s with monogram and dll 'K 29'; titled, d again and numbered on the reverse 'Strahlen 1929 no. 343'
PROV.: J.B. Neumann, New York (1935); Nierendorf Gallery, New York; Galka Scheyer, Los Angeles (until 1945); Milton Wichner, Los Angeles (until 1950; acquired by the present owner).
EXH.: Saarbrücken, Staatliches Museum, *Kollektiv-Ausstellung Wasslly Kandinsky*, Jan.-Feb. 1930, no. 32; London, The Mayor Gallery, *International Exhibition: A Survey of Contemporary Art*, Oct. 1933; New York, New Art Circle (J. B. Neumann), *Vasily Kandinsky*, Feb. 1936, no. 5; Boston, The Institute of Modern Art, *Contemporary German Art*, Nov.-Dec. 1939, no. 23.
LIT.: *The artist's handlist*, IV 1929,343; V. E. Barnett, *Kandinsky Watercolours, Catalogue Raisonné*, Ithaca, New York, 1994, vol. II (1922-1944), no. 934 (illustrated, p. 250).
      Christie's New York, 1 May 1996 (192**) US$ 107,000   US$ 107,000

WASCHSENDE FLECKEN (GROWING SPOTS) watercolour and ink on paper attached to carton, 32.1 x 48.5cm. sdll 'K.32' (1932)
PROV.: Galka E. Scheyer, Los Angeles, 1933-1945; Nina Kandinsky, Paris,end 1972; Galerie Beyeler, Basel, 1972-1981; Galerie Marwan Hoss, Paris 1981.
EXH.: Oakland, Oakland Art Gallery, *Paintings by Wassily Kandinsky, the Old Master of Abstract Art*, January 1935; Paris, Galerie Maeght, *Kandinsky: Aquarelles et gouaches Collection privée de Madame N. Kandinsky, Sept.-Nov.1957, no. 35; Cologne, Wallraf-Richartz-Museum,* Kandinsky, 25 Sept.-30 Nov. 1958, n. 86; Nantes, Musée des Beaux-Arts, *Kandinsky*, 18 April- 18 May 1959, no. 20; New York, Salomon R. Guggenheim Museum, *Vasily Kandinsky*, 25 January-7 April, 1963, no. 23; Stockholm, Muderna Museet, *Kandinsky*, April 1963, no. 89; Saint Paul de Vence, Fondation Maeght, *Kandinsky Centenaire 1866-1944*, 23 June-30 Sept. 1966, no.78;
New York, The Museum of Modern Art, *Kandinsky Watercolors*, 2 April- 11 May 1969, no. 27;

Humlebaek, Louisiana Museum, *Klee-Kandinsky*, 30 Oct.-9 Jan. 1971, no. 62; Basel, Galerie
Beyeler, *Kandinsky: Acquarelle und Zeichnungen*, June-July 1972, no. 53; Vienna, Galerie Ulysses,
Kandinsky-Klee-Kupka Olbilder, Aquarelle, Zeichnungen,15 Feb.-31 March 1977.
LIT.: J. Cassou, 'The Later paintings of Wassily Kandinsky', in *Apollo*, vol. LXXVm, no. 180, (Aug.
1963), p. 118; Tower, *Klee and Kandinsky in Munich and at the Bauhaus*, 1981, p. 200; Vivian
Endicott Barnett, *Kandinsky watercolours*, vol. II, ed. Electa 1994, no. 1063, p. 323.

Finearte Milan, 19 March 1996 (43**) ITL 276,000,000	US$	176,583

MELODISCH watercolour and ink on paper laid down on board, 32 x 23.2cm. sdll 'K. 24' inscr. on
the reverse 'No 121/1924/Melodisch/Coll Kandinsky' (1924)
PROV.: Los Angeles, Galka E. Scheyer, 1928-1945; Paris, Nina Kandinsky, end of 1971; Paris,
Galerie Berggruen, 1971; Turin, Galleria Galatea, 1974.
EXH.: Berlin, *Russische Kunstausstellung,* 1924; Oakland, The Oakland Art Gallery, *Kandinsky*,
1929, no.1; Hollywood, Braxton Gallery, *Kandinsky*, 1-15 March, no.12; Oakland, The Oakland Art
Gallery, *The Bleu Four: Feininger, Jawlensky, Kandinsky, Paul Klee,* August/Sept.1931, 34;
Pasadena, Pasadena Art Museum, Vasily Kandinsky 1866-1944: A Retrospective Exhibition, 15
Jan.-15 Feb. 1963, no.13;Paris, Berggruen, *Kandinsky, aquarelles et dessins*, Oct. 1972, no.19;
London, Lefevre Gallery, *Oil paintings and Watercolours by Wassily Kandinsky, 12 April-19 May,
1973, no.18*.
LIT.: Vivian Endicott Barnett, *Kandinsky watercolours*, vol.II, ed. Electa 1994, no.677, p.98.

Finearte Milan, 19 March 1996 (72**) ITL 437,000,000	US$	279,591

VON EINEM ZUM ANDEREN gouache on black paper, 17 7/8 x 9¼in. (48 x 23.5cm.) sd 'wk 37'
PROV.: Galerie Thannhauser, Paris (1938-40); Noelle Lecoutour, Paris (1944); Frau Ferdinand
Moller, Cologne (by 1958); Emil Georg Buhrle, Zurich; Marlborough Fine Art, London; Sale,
Sotheby's, London, 5 April 1978, lot 131 (purchased by the present owner at GBP11,000).
LIT.: Will Grohmann, *Wassily Kandinsky, Life and Works*, London, 1959, p. 347, catalogued, p. 411,
no. 741, illustrated; Vivian Endicott Barnett, *Kandinsky Watercolours, Catalogue raisonné, 1922-
1944*, London, vol. II, 1994, p. 427, no. 1215, illustrated.

Sotheby's London, 20 March 1996 (58**) GBP 99,400	US$	151,802

ENTWURF ZU 'KOMPOSITION VII (SKETCH FOR 'COMPOSITION VII') s with the monogram,
15½ x 18 1/8in. 39.2 x 46cm. s mono 'WK' (1913)
PROV.: Mr and Mrs Frederick Zimmerman, New York (until 1966); Richard L. Feigen, New York
(circa 1967); Peter Bensinger, Chicago (1967); Richard Gray Gallery, Chicago; Stephen Hahn, New
York, (purchased by the present owner in 1974).
EXH.: Chicago, Museum of Contemporary Art, *20th Century Drawings from Chicago Collections*,
1973; Düsseldorf, Kunstsammlung Nordrhein-Westfalen and Stuttgart, Staatsgalerie, *Kandinsky:
Small Pleasures. Watercolours and Drawings*, 1992, no. 34, illustrated in colour in the catalogue.
LIT.: Vivian Endicott Barnett, *Kandinsky Watercolours, Catalogue Raisonné*, 1900-1921, London,
1992, vol. I, p. 325, no. 363, catalogued and illustrated; p. 331, illustrated in colour.

Sotheby's London, 24 June 1996 (43**) GBP 936,500	US$	1,444,102

GELB ROSA watercolour with pen and black ink on paper laid on board, 16 x 19in. (40.5 x 48.1cm.)
sd mono. 'wk 29'
PROV.: Galerie Maeght, Paris; Galeria D'Arte del Naviglio, Milan; Finarte-Ketterer, Milan (Nov.
1962, no. 107); Finarte, Milan (Dec. 1971, no. 101).
EXH.: Berlin, Galerie Flechtheim, *Deutsche Bau-Ausstellung*, May-Aug. 1931, no. 14; Zurich,
Kunsthaus, *Novemberausstellung*, Nov.-Dec. 1931, no. 71 Stockholm, Gummesons Konsthall,
Kandinsky, Sept. 1932, no. 24; Milan, Galleria del Milone, *Kandinsky*, Apr.-May 1934, no. 365; New
York, Sidney Janis Gallery, *XX Century Painting*, Feb.-March 1949 Lucerne, Galerie Rosengart,
Kandinsky Exhibition: Paintings,Watercolours, Drawings, June-Sept. 1953, no. 9; Milan, Galleria
del Naviglio, *Wassily Kandinsky*, Feb.-March 1960, no. 3.
LIT.: V. Endicott Barnett, *Kandinsky Watercolours, Catalogue Raisonné*, vol. II, 1922-1944,
London, 1994, no. 959 (illustrated p. 271).

Christie's London, 28 November 1995 (30**) GBP 89,500	US$	139,997

LAUNELINIE watercolour, gouache and indian ink on paper, 18 7/8 x 12½in. (48 x 32cm) sd mono. 'WK 27'
PROV.: Alfred Hess, Erfurt; Gutekunst and Klipstein, Bern, 5-7 Dec. 1940, no. 797; Dr. Robert Ammann, Aarau; Anon. Sale, Sotheby's, London, 23 March 1983, lot 138, (illustrated in colour).
LIT.: *The Artist's Handlist*, where it is recorded as xi 1927, 242, *Launelinie*; V. Endicott Barnett, *Kandinsky Watercolours: Catalogue Raisonné, 1922-1944*, Vol. II, London, 1994, no. 809 (illustrated p. 174).

	Christie's London, 28 November 1995 (35**) GBP 183,000	US$	286,251

ZEICHEN MIT BEGLEITUNG oil on canvas, 31 7/8 x 20½in. (81 x 52cm.) sd mono. ll 'WK 27'
PROV.: Nierendorf Gallery, New York; Solomon R. Guggenheim, New York; The Solomon R. Guggenheim Foundation, New York, donated by the above in 1937; sale, Sotheby's, London, 30 June 1964, lot 24 (illustrated in colour; GBP5,,200 to T. W. Hills); T. W. Hills, London, by whom purchased at the above sale; Marlborough Fine Art, London; Galerie d'art Moderne (Marie-Suzanne Feigl), Basle.
EXH.: Berlin, Abstrakt, 1927; New York, The Solomon R. Guggenheim Foundation, *Art of Tomorrow*, June 1939, no. 290 (illustrated); New York, Museum of Non-Objective Paintings, *In Memory of Wassily Kandinsky*, March-May 1945, no. 109; Pittsburgh, Carnegie Institute, *Memorial Exhibition*, 1946, no. 55; U.S.A., Solomon R. Guggenheim Museum extended Loan Programme, 1954-1960 Paris, Galerie Maeght, *Kandinsky: Bauhaus de Dessau*, 1927-1933, 1955, no. I; New York, Marlborough-Gerson Gallery, *Kandinsky and his friends, a centenary exhibition*, Nov.-Dec. 1966, no. 21 (illustrated in colour).
LIT.: W. Grohmann, *Wassily Kandinsky, Life and Work*, London, 1959, p. 336 (pl. 250, illustrated p. 370); P. Overy, *Kandinsky:The Language of the Eye*, New York, 1969 (illustrated pl. 48, p. 139); H. K. Roethel and J. K. Benjamin, *Kandinsky, Catalogue Raisonné of the Oil-Paintings*, vol. II, 1916-1944, London, 1984, no. 825 (illustrated p. 768).

	Christie's London, 28 November 1995 (36**) GBP 441,500	US$	690,599

RECIPROQUE gouache with pen and black ink and pencil on paper, 19 3/4 x 25 3/4in. (50.1 x 65.3cm.) sdll 'WK 35'
PROV.: Nina Kandinsky, Paris, until 1972; Galerie Beyeler, Basle, 1972.
EXH.: Tenerife, Circulo de bellas artes, *Esposicion de arte contemporaneo: Collection 'Gacetade arte'*, June 1936, no. 42.; This exhibition later travelled to Barcelona and Madrid; Paris, Galerie Maeght, *Kandinsky: Aquarelles et gouaches, Collection privée de Madame W. Kandinsky*, 1957, no. 62, New York, Solomon R. Guggenheim Museum, *Wassily Kandinsky, 1866-1944: A Retrospective Exhibition*, Jan-April 1963, no. 25.This exhibition later travelled to Paris, Musée National d'Art Moderne, April-June 1963; The Hague, Gemeente Museum, July-Aug. 1963; Basle, Kunsthalle, Sep.- Nov. 1963; Basle, Galerie Beyeler, *Kandinsky: Aquarelle und Zeichnungen*, June-July 1972, no. 65; Paris, Galerie Karl Flinker, *Kandinsky: peintures, dessins, gravures, éditions, oeuvres inédites*, Oct.-Dec. 1972, no.8; New York, The Pace Gallery, *Kandinsky: Watercolours and Drawings, 1911-1943*, March - April 1973, no. 21 (illustrated on the cover of the catalogue).
LIT.: V. Endicott Barnett, *Kandinsky Watercolours, Catalogue Raisonné, 1922-1944*, vol. II, London, 1994, no. 1189 (illustrated p.413).

	Christie's London, 28 November 1995 (50**) GBP 95,000	US$	148,600

LANDSCHAFT BEI MURNAU MIT STURMISCHEM HIMMEL oil on board, 13 x 16 1/8in. (33 x 41cm.) lr 'Kandinsky 1908' (1908)
PROV.: Arthur Jerome Eddy, Chicago; Stendahl Art Galleries, Los Angeles (acquired by the late owner, 1939).
EXH.: Chicago, Art Institute, *Treasures of Chicago Collectors*, April-May, 1961, no number.
LIT.: H.K.Roethel and J.K.Benjamin, *Kandinsky, Catalogue Raisonné of the Oil-Paintings*, New York, 1982, vol. I (1900-1915), no. 231 (illustrated, p. 225).

	Christie's New York, 8 November 1995 (244**) US$ 310,500	US$	310,500

KANOLDT Alexander (Karlsruhe 1881-1939 Berlin) German
KLOSTERKAPELLE VON SÄBEN oil on canvas, 35 x 29cm. sdlr 'Kanoldt 1920', sd again and

numbered 'Kanoldt 1920 XXI No 137'
PROV.: Collection Franz Friedrich Kästner, Erfurt.
        Lempertz Cologne, 1 June 1996 (754**) DEM 28,000   US$ 18,192

KANTERS Hans (1947 b.-) Dutch
DE FILATELISTEN oil on panel, 34 x 28.5cm. sdar 'Hans kanters 75-76'
PROV.: Galerie Siau, Amsterdam.
        Christie's Amsterdam, 5 June 1996 (280*) NLG 10,350   US$ 6,047

KARSEN Kasparus (Amsterdam 1810-1896 Bieberich) Dutch
A FRUIT AND VEGETABLE MARKET IN A STREET, GERMANY oil on canvas, 67 x 56cm. s
'K. Karsen'
        Christie's Amsterdam, 25 April 1996 (260a*) NLG 12,650   US$ 7,517

KATE Herman Frederik Carel ten (The Hague 1822-1891 The Hague) Dutch
A GAME OF DRAUGHTS oil on panel, 17 7/8 x 28 3/8in. (45.5 x 72cm.) s
        Phillips London, 14 November 1995 (6**) GBP 8,000   US$ 12,514

MEMBERS OF THE CIVIC GUARD IN A COUNCIL ROOM oil on panel, 30 x 41cm. s 'Herman
ten Kate ft'
        Christie's Amsterdam, 25 April 1996 (154*) NLG 16,100   US$ 9,567

A TAVERN INTERIOR WITH A GENTLEMAN AMONGST SEVERAL PEASANTS Watercolour
heightened with white on paper, 35 x 50cm. s 'Herman ten Kate.ft.'
        Christie's Amsterdam, 26 October 1995 (252*) NLG 48,300   US$ 30,454

A KITCHEN INTERIOR WITH A COOK HOLDING A LITTLE BIRD pen and black and brown
ink, 35 x 50cm. s Herman ten Kate.ft.'
        Christie's Amsterdam, 26 October 1995 (252*) NLG 48,300   US$ 30,454

KATE Johan Mari Henri ('Mari') ten (the Elder) (The Hague 1831-1910 Driebergen) Dutch
FIGURES IN AN INTERIOR oil on canvas, 24½ x 38in. (62.2 x 96.5cm.) slr 'Jan Tenkate'
        Christie's New York, 10 January 1996 (75**) US$ 9,200   US$ 9,200

A VIEW OF THE ESTATE P.J.J.A. GEESINK, MERAPI, JAVA oil on canvas, 48 x 71cm. slr
        Sotheby's Amsterdam, 23 April 1996 (18**) NLG 33,040   US$ 19,633

THE PHEASANT oil on panel, 24.5 x 32cm. slr 'Mari ten Kate'
PROV.: A.R Cuneau, his sale, Batavia Indonesia, 23 April 1866   According to a label on the reverse
the present lot was a prize in the lottery of the Society Arti et Amicitiae, Amsterdam, and was won
by Mr. Cuneau.
        Christie's Amsterdam, 26 October 1995 (290**) NLG 12,650   US$ 7,976

AN ARBRITARY DOG oil on panel, 37.5 x 50cm. Slr 'M ten Kate'
        Christie's Amsterdam, 26 October 1995 (291**) NLG 57,500   US$ 36,255

KATZ Alex (1927 b.) American
THE FERRY oil on masonite, 16 x 16¼in. (40.7 x 41.3cm.) sur 'Alex Katz' (ca. 1955)
        Christie's East, 7 May 1996 (54*) US$ 8,050   US$ 8,050

KAUFFMAN Angelica, R.A. (Chur 1741-1807 Rome) Swiss
DAMON AND MUSIDORA oil on metal, 20 x 16cm. (ca 1782)
PROV.: Major-General Kenneth Greg Heuderon, Sale Christie's, 20 December 1902, lot 37 (32 gns.
to Legott); British private collection.
        Dorotheum Vienna, 17 October 1995 (194***) ATS 410,000   US$ 41,125

CLEONE oil on copper, oval, unframed, 12¼ x 10¼in. (31 x 26cm.) slr, bears label on the reverse
'..Cleone..for Mr.Birchall..no.47?..'
      Phillips London, 18 June 1996 (41**) GBP 9,000   US$ 13,878

KAUFMANN Isidor (Arad 1853-1921) Austrian
YESHIVA SCHULER MIT ARBA KANFOT oil on panel, 12 x 9 3/4in. (30.5 x 24.9cm.) sll 'Isodor
Kaufmann'
      Christie's Tel Aviv, 14 April 1996 (5**) US$ 83,900   US$ 83,900

THE BACHELOR'S BIRTHDAY oil on panel, 131 x 11¼in (34.3 x 28.6cm.) slr 'Isidor Kaufmann'
      Christie's New York, 22 May 1996 (244**) US$ 43,700   US$ 43,700

JUNGE FRAU IN DER SYNAGOGE oil on panel, 20¼ x 14 7/8in. (51.5 x 37.8cm.) sll 'Isidor
Kaufmann'
EXH.: Vienna, Jüdisches Museum der Stadt Wien, *Bilder des Wieners Malers Isidor Kaufmann
1853-1921*, 24 Feb.-7 May 1995, p.,200 (ill. p.201).
      Christie's Tel Aviv, 14 April 1996 (7**) US$ 167,500   US$ 167,500

KAULBACH Friedrich August von (Hannover 1850-1920 Murnau) German
PORTRAIT OF LUDWIG I, KING OF BAVARIA oil on canvas laid down on board, 65 x 46½in.
(165.1 x 118.1cm.) slr 'FvKaulbach'
PROV.: Charles R. Hagedorn, until 1869.
      Christie's New York, 14 February 1996 (3**) US$ 9,200   US$ 9,200

KAULBACH Hermann (1846-1909) German
THE DRAWING LESSON oil on panel, 15 x 10 3/4in. 938 x 27.4cm.) s 'Herm. Kaulbach'
      Christie's London, 14 June 1996 (26**) GBP 36,700   US$ 56,592

KAUS Max (Berlin 1891-1977 Berlin) German
FRAU MIT LILIEN oil on canvas, 90 x 75cm. sll (1931)
      Hauswedell & Nolte Cologne, 1 December 1995 (344**) DEM 29,000   US$ 20,121

STILLEBEN MIT SCHLAFENDEM JUNGEN oil on canvas laid down on panel, 30½ x 25 3/8in.
(77.5 x 64.4cm.) (1920s)
      Christie's London, 11 October 1995 (191**) GBP 17,250   US$ 27,225

KAYAMA Matazo (1927 b.-) Japanese
KONCHU mineral pigment on paper mounted on board, framed and glazed, 14 1/8 x 17 3/16in.
(35.9 x 43.7cm.) with artist`s certificate signed 'Kayama Matazo', titled 'Konchu'
      Christie's New York, 31 October 1995 (454**) US$ 57,500   US$ 57,500

KAYE Otis (1885-1974) American
FIVE DOLLAR BILL watercolour, ink, oil and pencil on paper, 3 1/8 x 7 3/8in. (8 x 18.7cm.) sdlr
'Otis Kaye 1955'
PROV.: Acquired directly from the artist by descent in the family to the present owner.
      Christie's New York, 13 September 1995 (37*) US$ 9,200   US$ 9,200

PENNIES MAKE DOLLARS WHICH MAKE A BLUNCH OF MONEY oil on panel, 13 x 15in.
(33 x 38.2cm.) sll 'Kaye'
PROV.: Acquired directly from the artis; By descent in the family to the present owner.
      Christie's New York, 13 March 1996 (61**) US$ 32,200   US$ 32,200

LAND OF THE FREE, HOME OF THE BRAVE oil on panel, 25½ x 36¼in. (64.6 x 92cm.) slr 'Mr.
Otis Kaye' and sll 'O. Kaye'
PROV.: Acquired directly from the artist by descent in the present owner.
      Christie's New York, 13 September 1995 (71***) US$ 156,500   US$ 156,500

TWO SIDES TO EVERYTHING oil on artist's board, 12 x 14in. (30.5 x 35.5cm.) sar 'O. Kaye'
PROV.: Acquired directly from the artist by descent in the family to the present owner.
    Christie's New York, 13 September 1995 (73**) US$ 25,300   US$ 25,300

KEATING Sean, P.R.H.A., H.R.A., H.R.S.A. (1889-1978) Irish
THE PLAYBOY OF THE WESTERN WORLD oil on board, 48 x 48in. (122 x 122cm.) slr 'Keating'
PROV.: J.R. Johnston, Jedburgh, by whom purchased at the 1958 exhibition.
EXH.: Edinburgh, Royal Scottish Academy, 1958, no. 92.
    Christie's London, 9 May 1996 (88**) GBP 15,525   US$ 23,508

KEIL Bernhard (Eberhart), {called} Monsu Bernardo (Elsinore 1624-1687 Rome) Danish
PERSONIFICATION OF THE SENSES OF SIGHT, TASTE, HEARING AND SIGHT oil on panel
(a set of four), diameter of each: 14in. (35.5cm.) (ca. 1650s)
PROV.: Possibly commissioned for Giovanni Carlo Savorgan, Palazzo Savorgan Venice in the
1650s.
    Sotheby's London, 5 July 1995 (97**) GBP 45,500   US$ 72,579

FOUR PEASANTS IN A LANDSCAPE: ALLEGORY OF HEARING AND SIGHT oil on canvas,
39 x 54½in. (99.1 x 138.4cm.)
PROV.: W. Brightman; Sale: Sotheby's London, July 26, 1950, lot 161; William Hallsborough Ltd.,
London; Koetser Gallery, New York by 1956, where acquired by the present owner (56.52).
LIT.: *The Art Quarterly*, XIX, 1956, pp. 304-05; P. B. Wilson, ' A Talent for Portraiture,' *Christian
Science Monitor*, October 5, 1972; B. Fredericksen and F. Zeri, *Census of Pre-Nineteenth-Century
Italian Paintings in North American Collections*, 1972, pp. 102, 502, 638; N. Spinosa, 'La pittura con
scene di genere,' in *Storia dell'arte italiana*, XI, 1982, illus. fig. 76 (with no indication of location);
M. Heimbürger, *Bernardo Keilhau detto Monsu Bernardo*, 1988, p. 227, cat. no. 147 (illus.).
    Sotheby's New York, 11 January 1996 (25**) US$ 101,500   US$ 101,500

KEIRINCX Alexander (Antwerpen 1600-1652 Amsterdam) Flemish
WOODED LANDSCAPE WITH CHRIST HEALING THE BLIND oil on panel, 59 x 84cm.
    Dorotheum Vienna, 17 October 1995 (163**) ATS 130,000   US$ 13,040

KELLER Friederich von (1840-1914) German
GROßMUTTER AM SPINNRAD oil on canvas, 60 x 48cm. sdlr 'Fr. Keller / München 74'
    Dorotheum Vienna, 6 November 1995 (111**) ATS 280,000   US$ 28,088

THE POOL oil on canvas, 42 3/4 x 50in. (108.5 x 127cm.) sd 'Ferdinand Keller.1911'
PROV.: Montreal, Museum of Fine Arts *Lost Paradise: Symbolist Europe*, 8 June-15 October 1995,
no. 187 (illustrated no. 179, p. 155).
    Christie's New York, 22 May 1996 (85**) US$ 48,300   US$ 48,300

KELLY Ellsworth (1923 b.-l) American
RED, YELLOW, BLUE oil on mailed postcard, 5 7/8 x 4in. (14.6 x 10.2cm.) s and dedicated 'My
Dear Henry.. Ells' on the reverse (1964)
PROV.: Acquired directly from the artist.
    Christie's New York, 8 May 1996 (177**) US$ 9,200   US$ 9,200

KELLY Sir Gerald Festus, P.R.A., R.H.A. (1879-1972) British
PORTRAIT OF SAO OHN NYUNT oil on canvas, 43½ x 30in. (110.5 x 76.2cm.) sll 'Kelly' inscr.
on a label attached to the canvas-overlap 'Sao Ohn Nyunt XXIII'
PROV.: E. Stacy-Marks, Eastbourne.
    Christie's London, 21 November 1995 (73**) GBP 24,150   US$ 37,776

KELPE Paul (1902-1985) American
UNTITLED oil on canvas laid down on masonite, 18 3/4 x 15 5/8in. (47.6 x 39.7cm.) sd 'Paul Kelpe
1934' on the reverse

PROV.: Sid Deutsch Gallery, New York.
    Christie's New York, 23 May 1996 (151**) US$ 20,700   US$ 20,700

KEMP-WELCH Lucy Elisabeth (Bournemouth (Hampshire) 1860-1968) British
THE GUARDIAN oil on canvas, 20 x 24in. (61 x 50.8cm.) sll 'L Kemp-Welch', s and inscr. on the stretcher 'The Guardian' original oil painting by Lucy Kemp-Welch'
    Christie's London, 21 March 1996 (104**) GBP 8,625   US$ 13,172

KENNEDY Cecil (1905 b.) British
WHITE FLOWERS: MAGNOLIA, CAMELLIA, WHITE IRIS, MAY BLOSSOM AND SPIRAEA oil on canvas, 30 x 25in. (76.2 x 63.5cm.) s 'Cecil Kennedy'
PROV.: Fine Art Society, London, April 1959.
    Christie's London, 20 June 1996 (75**) GBP 19,550   US$ 30,146

KENSETT John Frederick, N.A. (1818-1872) American
CATSKILL MOUNTAIN SCENERY oil on canvas, 9 x 12 1/8in. (22.8 x 30.8cm.) sdlr (indist.) '1852'
PROV.: G. P. Putnam, 1853; W. W. Olyphant; Judge Henry A. Bunsche; By descent in the family; Babcock Gallenes, New York.
LIT.: G. Putnam, *The Home Book of the Picturesque*, New York, 1852, p. 71, (illus.).
    Christie's New York, 23 May 1996 (8**) US$ 36,800   US$ 36,800

KENT Rockwell (1882-1971) American
DONEGAL oil on canvas, 34 x 44in. (86.4 x 111.8cm.) sdlr 'Rockwell Kent 26-7'
PROV.: Larcada Gallery, New York.
EXH.: Santa Barbara, California, Santa Barbara Museum of Art, *An Enkindled Eye: The Paintings of Rockwell Kent*, June 1985- March 1986, no. 52.
LIT.: R. V. West, 'Rockwell Kent Rediscovered,' *American Art Review*, vol.IV, no. 3, December 1977, pp. 84-93, 130-37, p. 135 (illustrated).
    Christie's New York, 23 May 1996 (165**) US$ 33,350   US$ 33,350

July

KENZO Okada (1902-1982) Japanese
JULY oil on canvas framed, 63 3/4 x 51¼in. (161.9 x 130.2cm.) sll 'Kenzo Okada' (1981)
PROV.: Mrs. Albert D. Lasker; Marisa del Re Gallery Inc., New York.
EXH.: New York, New York, Marisa del Re Gallery Inc., *Kenzo Okada and Nature*, Feb.-March 1986.
LIT.: Marisa del Re Gallery, Inc., *Kenzo Okada and Nature*, New York, 1986.
    Christie's New York, 31 October 1995 (483***) US$ 46,000   US$ 46,000

KERCKHOVEN Jacob van de, {called} Jacopo da Castello (Antwerp 1637 c.-1712 c. Venice) Flemish
A STILL-LIFE OF POULTRY, GAME, ASPARAGUS, ORANGES, AND A BASKET OF OYSTERS oil on canvas, 98 x 119.2cm.
    Sotheby's London, 17 April 1996 (162**) GBP 8,050   US$ 12,206

KESSEL Jan I van (1626-1679) Flemish
THE FOUR ELEMENTS oil on copper (a set of four), each: 5¼ x 7½in. (13.4 x 19.2cm.) on s 'J.v..'
PROV.: Frederick Phillips, ca. 1875, great-grandfather of the present owners.
    Sotheby's London, 5 July 1995 (108**) GBP 95,000   US$ 151,539

SWAGS OF TULIPS, ROSES,LILIES, CARNATIONS, HYACINTHS, CORNFLOWERS, FORGET-ME-NOTS, AND OTHER FLOWERS DECORATING A STONE CARTOUCHES WITH A RELIEF OF THE CHRIST, WITH A DRAGONFLY, MOTHS AND OTHER INSECTS oil on panel, 15 3/4 11in. (40 x 28cm.) s 'J van Kessel' (1670's)
Christie's London, 8 December 1995 (40**) GBP 34,500 · US$ · 53,093

BIRDS ON A RIVERBANK oil on copper (a pair), 5 3/4 x 8in. (14.6 x 20.3cm.) (1st half 1660's)
Christie's London, 8 December 1995 (204**) GBP 44,400 · US$ · 68,329

ASSEMBLY OF BIRDS IN A LANDSCAPE oil on paner, 10 3/4 x 13 5/8in. (27.3 x 34.6cm.)
PROV.: Sale: Sotheby's London, December 8, 1971, lot 126 where probably acquired by Roy Miles Gallery, London, from whom acquired by the present owner in December 1972 (Acc. no.72.74).
LIT.: *Gazette des Beaux Arts* (Supplement), no. 1261, February 1974, p.251 (attributed to Jan van Kessel).
Sotheby's New York, 11 January 1996 (15**) US$ 12,650 · US$ · 12,650

MONKEY MAGISTRATES GATHERING TAXES oil on copper, 13 3/4 x 17in. (34.9 x 43.2cm.) d '1649' on the open book and on the paper on the wall
Sotheby's New York, 16 May 1996 (83**) US$ 54,625 · US$ · 54,625

A STILL-LIFE OF FLOWERS WITH ROSES, TULIPS AND OTHER FLOWERS, ON A STONE LEDGE AGAINST A WALL WITH A FRAMED PAINTING OF A BOWL OF FRUIT AND FLOWERS oil on panel, 17½ x 14in. (44.5 x 37cm.) sdll 'J.V. Kessel. fecit (A) 1653
PROV.: With Thos. Agnew Ltd. London (inv. no. 11501; Anonymous sale, London, Sotheby's 8 December 1979, lot 30 (GBP 3,,200 to Dobiaschofsky); Anoymous Sale, Berne, Dobiaschofsky, 5 May 1977, lot 343, where bought by the present owner.
Sotheby's London, 17 April 1996 (630**) GBP 16,100 · US$ · 24,412

INTERIOR OF THE PAINTERS STUDIO oil on panel, 39.5 x 57.5cm.
PROV.: Galerie Leegenhoek, Paris, bought there by the current owner of the painting.
Étude Tajan Paris, 25 June 1996 (25**) FRF 320,000 · US$ · 61,792

HERONS AND WATERFOWLS NEAR A RIVER WITH FISH AND REPTILES IN THE FOREGROUND oil on copper, 19.5 x 29cm. indistinctly sll 'IVK..'
Sotheby's Amsterdam, 6 May 1996 (7**) NLG 25,960 · US$ · 15,137

BUTTERFLIES AND BEETLES oil on panel, 10 5/8 x 14 3/8in. (27 x 36.6cm) sdlr 'J : V. Kessel. fecit anno. 1656'
PROV.: With Richard Green (*annual exhibition of old masters*, 1976, no. 18, illustrated in colour); A version is in the Rijksdienst Beeldende Kunst, The Netherlands (see their illustrated *summary catalogue*, 1992, p.158, no. 1306).
Christie's London, 7 July 1995 (13**) GBP 166,500 · US$ · 265,593

KESSEL Jan III van (Antwerp 1641-1680 Amsterdam) Dutch (Flemish)
THE ELEMENTS OF AIR AND FIRE: VULCAN AT WORK IN HIS FORGE WITH AEOLUS AND A PUTTO IN FLIGHT BEYOND, EXOTIC BIRDS AND POULTRY IN THE FOREGROUND, A LANDSCAPE IN THE DISTANCE oil on canvas, 53.7 x 84.4cm.
PROV.: also Abraham Willemsens (119) co-painter.
Christie's Amsterdam, 13 November 1995 (119**) NLG 29,900 · US$ · 18,844

FLOWERS, BUTTERFLIES, CATERPILLARS, BEETLES AND OTHER INSECTS oil on copper, 5 3/8 x 7 5/8in. (13.7 x 19.4cm.)
Sotheby's New York, 16 May 1996 (29**) US$ 74,000 · US$ · 74,000

KESSEL AND ATTR. TO PIETER VAN AVONT (1600-1652) Jan I van (1626-1679) Flemish
A PERSONIFICATION AND ALLEGORY OF SIGHT: A COLLECTOR'S CABINET oil on

silvered copper, 24¼ x 32 3/8in. ((61.6 x 82.3cm.)
        Christie's London, 19 April 1996 (135**) GBP 67,500   US$ 102,350

KETEL Cornelis (Gouda 1548-1616 Amsterdam) Dutch
PORTRAIT OF ADRIAEN CROMBOUTS, BURGOMASTER OF AMSTERDAM, BORN IN 1517
oil on oak panel, 41 x 32cm. sur mono 'CK'
PROV.: Anonymous Sale, Paris Hotel Drouot, 4 May 1953 (Cornelis Ketel 36,000FF).
        Étude Tajan Paris, 12 December 1995 (49**) FRF 35,000   US$ 7,050

KETTLE Tilly (1734-1786) British
PORTRAIT OF JOHN GRAHAM, AS A BOY, FULL-LENGTH, IN INDIAN DRESS HOLDING
A GARLAND OF FLOWERS AROUND THE NECK OF A GREYHOUND AT HIS SIDE, IN A
LANDSCAPE oil on canvas, 60 x 39¼in. (152.5 x 99.8cm.) slr 'Kettle pinxit' (ca 1775)
PROV.: By inheritance through Mary (d.1858), widow of the sitter's brother, George Edward
Graham-Foster-Piggott to Commander R.D. Graham, R.N., of Stawell House, Bridgewater,
Somerset; Christie's, 9 April 1937, lot 38 (440gns. to Frost and Reed); with Thomas Agnew and
Sons, by 1944.
EXH.: Cardiff, National Museum of Wales, on loan, 1992-96.
LIT.: L.G. Graeme, *Or and Sable: A Book of the Graemes and Grahams*, Edinburgh, 1903, p. 600.
        Christie's London, 18 April 1996 (23**) GBP 276,500   US$ 419,257

KEVER Jacob Simon Hendrik (Amsterdam 1854-1922 Laren (N.-Holland)) Dutch
A MOTHER AND CHILDREN FEEDING A GOAT IN A BACKYARD oil on canvas, 48.5 x 60
cm s 'Kever'
        Christie's Amsterdam, 25 April 1996 (27*) NLG 8,625   US$ 5,125

KEYSER Thomas de (Amsterdam 1596-1667 Amsterdam) Dutch
PORTRAIT OF A GENTLEMAN; PORTRAIT OF A LADY oil on panel (a pair), each: 9¼ x 7in.
(23.5 x 17.5cm.) the former inscr. and dur 'An°.1626/ AET: 59'; the letter ul 'An°.1628/ AET: 61'
PROV.: Acquired by the family of the present owner during the last century.
        Sotheby's London, 5 July 1995 (295**) GBP 24,150   US$ 38,523

KHNOPFF Fernand (Grembergen-Iez-Termonde 1858-1921 Brussels) Belgian
A FOSSET. UN CREPUSCULE oil on canvas, 14 3/4 x 26¼in. (37.5 x 66.7cm.) s mono on the
reverse
PROV.: The Artist's studio sale; Galerie Georges Giroux, Brussels, 27 Nov. 1922, lot 19; Gaffe
Collection, Brussels; Georges Willems-Giroux, Brussels; Galerie Georges Giroux; sale, Brussels, 18-
19 Oct. 1957, lot 15.
LIT.: R. L. Delevoy, C. de Croes and G. Ollinger-Zinque, *Fernand Khnopf: Catalogue de l'Oeuvre*,
Brussels, 1987, pp. 220-221 and 430, no. 165 (illus. p. 221).
        Christie's London, 15 March 1996 (44**) GBP 28,750   US$ 43,907

LA VENUE DE L'AUBE A FOSSET oil on canvas, 12 5/8 x15 3/4in. (32 x 40cm.) s 'Fernand
Khnopff' (ca 1882)
PROV.: Jules Dujardin, Brussels; Madame Giroux, Brussels.
EXH.: Brussels, Palais des Beaux-Arts, *Fernand Khnopff et ses raports avec la Seccession
Viennoise*, 2 Oct.-6 Dec. 1987, no. 20; Tokyo, Bunkamura Museum, Himeji, Municipal Museum of
Art, Nagoya, City Art Museum and Yamanashi, Museum of Art, *Fernand Khnopff*; 8 June-11 Nov.
1990, p. 71, no. 3 (illustrated in colour).
LIT.: R. L. Delevoy, et alia, *Fernand Khnopff; Catalogue de l'Oeuvre*, Brussels, 1987, pp. 411-2, no.
48 bis (illus.); M. Draguet, *Khnopff ou l'ambigu poétique*, Brussels, 1995 no. 29 (illus. in colour p.
33).
        Christie's London, 17 November 1995 (100***) GBP 45,500   US$ 71,172

KIEFER Anselm (1945 b.) German
PALETTE AND SNAKE photograph on treated lead in Artist's frame, 51¼ x 67in. (130 x 170cm.)

(1977-88)
PROV.: Marian Goodman Gallery, New York.
      Christie's London, 26 October 1995 (117**) GBP 31,050   US$ 49,006

DIE SEFIROTH emulsion, acrylic, shellac, lead and straw, steel wire and staples on canvas, 74 3/4 x
102 3/4in. (189.9 x 260.7cm.) (1985-1986)
PROV.: Gift of the artist; Sotheby's London, Whitechapel Art Gallery Foundation Auction, 1 July
1987, lot 781; Private collection, Columbus.
EXH.: Amsterdam, Stedelijk Museum, *Anselm Kiefer*, Dec. 1986-Feb, 1987, p. 91, no. 35
(illustrated).
LIT.: A. Hicks, 'Twilight of the Gods?', *Art & Auction*, Nov. 1990, p. 226 (illustrated).
      Christie's New York, 14 November 1995 (50**) US$ 299,500   US$ 299,500

DEIN ASCHENES HAAR, SULAMITH oil and straw on canvas, 51 1/4 x 67in. (130 x 170cm.)
titled (1981)
PROV.: Acquired directly from the Artist by the present owner in 1982.
EXH.: Munich, Kunstverein, *Zeitgenössische Kunst aus Münchner Privatbesitz*, July-August 1987.
      Christie's London, 30 November 1995 (44**) GBP 210,500   US$ 329,266

KIMPE Reimond (1885-1870) Dutch
VIEW OF VEERE HARBOUR oil on canvas, 87 x 93cm. sdll '37 R KIMPE'
PROV.: Acquired from the artist by the father of the present owner in 1938.
      Sotheby's Amsterdam, 7 December 1995 (10**) NLG 12,390   US$ 7,678

KIPPENBERGER Martin (Dortmund 1953 b.-) German
KISS ME! acrylic, plastic foam, lasagnasheets, cardboard on canvas, 180 x 120cm. monogrammed
and d lr 'K 83'; titled uc
      Wiener Kunst Auktionen, 26 March 1996 (327**) ATS 130,000   US$ 12,505

KIRCHNER Albert Emil (Leipzig 1813-1885 Munich) German
HEGAULANDSCHAFT MIT DER RUINE HOHENTWIEL oil on canvas, 55 x 90cm. sdlr
AKirchner 'Muenchen 1878'
EXH.: Akademische Kunstausstellung, Berlin, 1880; *Kunstausstellung*, Hannover, 1882.
LIT.: Boetticher, *Malerwerke des 19. Jahrhunderts*, I/2, p. 684, No. 36.
      Lempertz Cologne, 15 November 1995 (1805**) DEM 30,000   US$ 21,174

LIEGENDE FRAU pencil-drawing, 27.6 x 33.4cm.
      Hauswedell & Nolte Cologne, 1 December 1995 (352*) DEM 17,500   US$ 12,142

KIRCHNER Ernst Ludwig (Aschaffenburg 1880-1938 Frauenkirch) German
DAME MIT STIEFELN UND HUT charcoaldrawing, 101 x 71cm. sdll 'EL Kirchner 8' (1908)
      Hauswedell & Nolte Cologne, 5/06 June 1996 (348*) DEM 44,000   US$ 28,588

ZWEI MÄDCHEN AM BERGBACH black chalk and watercolours on smooth white cardboard,
50.1 x 38.2cm. stamped and numbered ll 'A Da/Bf 17' on the reverse (1921)
LIT.: This work is recorded in the *Ernst Ludwig Kirchner archives*, Henze and Ketterer,
Wichtrach/Bern.
      Lempertz Cologne, 1 June 1996 (770**) DEM 60,000   US$ 38,984

DAVOS-PLATZ AM BAHNHOF oil on canvas, 35 3/4 x 47¼in. (90.7 x 120cm.) incised letter 'K',
the Nachlass stamp numbered DA/Ab9 on the reverse (1931)
PROV.: The Artist's Estate; Roman Norbert Ketterer, Campione, Italy, 1969.
EXH.: Bremen, Kunsthalle, *Meisterwerke des Deutschen Expressionismus,* Mar.-Nov. 1960, no. 50.
This exhibition later travelled to Hannover, Kunstverein; The Hague, Gemeentemuseum; Cologne,
Wallraf-Richartz-Museum and Zurich, Kunsthaus, May-June 1961; Campione, Italy, Roman Norbert
Ketterer, *Moderne Kunst*, VI, 1969, no. 54 (illustrated in colour).

LIT.: D.E. Gordon, *Ernst Ludwig-Kirchner*, Cambridge, Massachusetts, 1968, no. 957, (illustrated p. 405).

Christie's London, 11 October 1995 (201**) GBP 89,500	US$	141,256

ZWEI WEIBLICHE AKTE UNTER BÄUMEN oil on canvas, 35½ x 27½in. (90 x 70cm.) (1912)
PROV.: Gerd Rosen, Buchhandlung und Galerie, Berlin (aquired by the father of the present owner circa 1948).
EXH.: Stuttgart, Stuttgarter Kunstkabinett, *Auktion 8*, 1950, no. 1473, illustrated in the catalogue.
LIT.: Donald E. Gordon, *Ernst Ludwig Kirchner*, Cambridge, Massachusetts, 1968, p. 302, no. 255, illustrated.

Sotheby's London, 24 June 1996 (41**) GBP 287,500	US$	443,331

KIRKEBY Per (1938 b.-l) Danish
NO. 1 oil on canvas, 94½ x 79in. (240 x 201cm.) sd and titled 'Per Kirkeby 1981' on the reverse
PROV.: Galerie Michael Werner, Cologne; Nigel Greenwood, London.
EXH.: London, Nigel Greenwood, *Per Kirkeby,* Dec. 1982.

Christie's London, 26 October 1995 (126**) GBP 13,800	US$	21,780

KISLING Moïse (Cracov 1891-1953 Sanary, Var) French (Polish)
PORTRAIT DE JEUNE GARCON oil on canvas, 15 3/4 x 10½in. (40 x 26cm.) sul 'Kisling' (1924)

Christie's Tel Aviv, 12 October 1995 (37**) US$ 43,700	US$	43,700

MIMOSAS oil on canvas, 40 x 30in. (101.6 x 76.2cm.) s and dedicated ll '
PROV.: Frederic R. Mann, Philadelphia, from whom acquired by the present owner.
EXH.: Philadelphia, Museum of Art, 1967 (on loan).
LIT.: H. Troyat and J. Kisling, *Kisling, 1891-1953*, Turin, 1982, vol. II, no. 104 (illustrated p. 216).

Christie's Tel Aviv, 12 October 1995 (39***) US$ 156,500	US$	156,500

TULIPES oil on canvas, 21½ x 15½in. (54.5 x 38.9cm.) sll 'Kisling' (ca. 1949)
PROV.: Crane Kallman Gallery, London.

Christie's Tel Aviv, 12 October 1995 (53**) US$ 107,000	US$	107,000

VASE WITH TULIPES oil on canvas, 16½ x 15in. (42 x 38cm.) sll 'Kisling' (1929)
PROV.: Collection Libermann, Paris.
LIT.: This painting will be reproduced in vol. III of the *catalogue raisonné of Moïse Kisling*, currently being prepared by Mr. Jean Kisling.

Étude Tajan Paris, 13 December 1995 (53**) FRF 265,000	US$	53,378

LES PAVOTS oil on canvas, 28 3/4 x 23 5/8in. (73 x 60cm.) sll 'Kisling' (1939)
PROV.: Collection Thenes, Paris.
LIT.: J.Kisling, *Kisling*, vol.III, Landshut, 1995, no.169 (ill. no.260) and no.174 (ill. p.261).

Christie's Tel Aviv, 14 April 1996 (16**) US$ 85,000	US$	85,000

LES ORCHIDÉES oil on canvas, 16¼ x 13in. (41.3 x 33cm.) sll 'Kisling'
PROV.: Wally Findlay Galleries, New York.

Sotheby's New York, 2 May 1996 (378**) US$ 63,000	US$	63,000

JEUNE FILLE ASSISE AU NATTES oil on canvas, 25 x 18 1/8in. (63.7 x 46.2) sll 'Kisling' (1930)
PROV.: Ernest Rouvier, Marseille.
EXH.: J. Kessel and J. Kisling *Kisling,* vol. I, Turin, 1971, no. 124 (illustrated p. 171).

Christie's London, 26 June 1996 (180**) GBP 64,200	US$	98,998

PAYSAGE DE PROVENCE oil on canvas, 18 1/8 x 21 5/8in. (55 x 46cm.) slr 'Kisling' (1918)
PROV.: Purchased by the grandfather of the present owner in Paris, ca 1918 and thence by descent to the present owner.
LIT.: H. Troyat and J. Kisling, *Kisling 1891-1953*, vol..I, Turin, 1982, no. 32 (illustrated p. 263).

Christie's London, 29 November 1995 (128**) GBP 20,000   US$ 31,284

NU oil on canvas, 28 3/4 x 21¼in. (73 x 54cm.) sd and inscr. 'Kisling Paris 1938'
PROV.: Léon Faïn, Paris; Galerie Tamenaga, Paris.
LIT.: J. Kessel, *Kisling 1891-1953*, vol. I., Turin, no. 75 (illustrated p. 339).
Christie's London, 29 November 1995 (154**) GBP 105,000   US$ 164,242

PORTRAIT DE FEMME oil on canvas, 19 3/4 x 15in. (50 x 38cm.) ur 'Kisling' (1946)
Christie's New York, 8 November 1995 (177**) US$ 90,500   US$ 90,500

VASE DE LIS oil on canvas, 13 x 8 1/4in. (33.1 x 22.1cm.) ll 'Kisling' (1938)
Christie's New York, 8 November 1995 (198**) US$ 74,000   US$ 74,000

LE PORT DE SAINT-MANDRIER oil on canvas, 21 3/4 x 18 1/4in. (55.3 x 46.4cm.) ll 'Kisling
St.Mandrier 1937' (1937)
PROV.: Anon. sale, Parke-Bernet Galleries, Inc., New York, Feb. 4, 1970, lot 70 (acquired by the
present owner).
Christie's New York, 8 November 1995 (231**) US$ 39,100   US$ 39,100

KITAJ Ronald (Cleveland 1932 b.-l) American
GOLEM oil on canvas laid down on board, 59¼ x 20 3/4in. (150.5 x 53cm.) (1980-81)
PROV.: Galerie Beyeler, Basel; Marlborough Fine Art, London; James Goodman Gallery, New
York.
EXH.: Basel, Galerie Beyeler, *Portraits et Figures*, February-April 1982, no. 51 (illustrated in colour
in the catalogue p. 68); London, Marlborough Fine Art, *R.B. Kitaj*, November-December 1985, no. 6
(illustrated in the catalogue p. 45, titled The Kabbalist).
Christie's London, 30 November 1995 (50**) GBP 56,500   US$ 88,378

KLEE Paul (Muenchenbuchsee 1879-1940 Locarno) German
NEGRIDE SCHÖNHEIT (PRAECISION) ink- and pencil-drawing on paper laid down on cardboard,
44 x 33cm. sdlr and titled on the cardboard (1927)
EXH.: Berlin, *Paul Klee als Zeichner*, Bauhaus-Archiv, 1985, cat. no. 70.
Hauswedell & Nolte Cologne, 1 December 1995 (360**) DEM 56,000   US$ 38,854

NEUES AUF ALTEM BADEN (NUOVO SU BASE VECCHIA) mixed technique on paper laid
down on board, 23 x 32cm. (29 x 35.5cm) slr 'Klee' titled lr 'Neues auf altem Baden' and dll '1931 M
1' (1931)
LIT.: P. Klee, *Teoria della forma e della figurazione*, under the auspices of Jurg Spiller, ed.
Feltrinelli, Milan 1959, p.38.
Fineart Milan, 19 March 1996 (53**) ITL 483,000,000   US$ 309,021

KLEINE ERINNERUNG AN NYMPHENBURG gouache and watercolour on paper, mounted in
card with blue gouache borders, sheet: 5 3/4 x 4 7/8in. (14.6 x 12.4cm.); mount: 8 x 6 1/8in. (20.3 x
15.6cm.) sll 'Klee' also titled, numbered and d '1921/94' on the mount
PROV.: Hans Goltz, Munich, 1931; Hebleck Dewees, Berlin, 1932-35; Galerie Ferdinand Möller;
Nierendorf Gallery, New York; Acquired from the above.
EXH.: Mew York, Museum of Modern Art, *Paul Klee*, 1941, no. 17; The Arts Club of Chicago, *Paul
Klee, Memorial Exhibition*, 1941, no. 17.
Sotheby's New York, 2 May 1996 (208**) US$ 200,500   US$ 200,500

MINIATÜRE OBEN UND UNTEN SCHWARZ GEFASST watercolour on paper mounted on the
artist's mount, 9 x 6 7/8in. 23 x 17.4cm. sdll Klee 1917 64 on the mount (1917)
PROV.: Galerie der Sturm (Herwarth Walden), Berlin (from 1917); Sale: Munich, Galerie Wolfgang
Ketterer, 5th June 1972, lot 812; Galerie Tarica, Paris (purchased by the present owner in the early
1970s).
EXH.: Berlin, Galerie Der Sturm, *Gösta Adrian-Nilsson, Paul Klee, Gabriele Münter. Gemälde,*

Aquarelle, Zeichnungen, 1917, no. 20.
      Sotheby's London, 24 June 1996 (44**) GBP 155,500   US$ 239,784

GESCHWISTER (BROTHER AND SISTER) oil on canvas, 27 3/4 x 17 3/4in. 70.7 x 45.2cm. sdlr
'Klee'; 1930 E. 8 on the stretcher
PROV.: Galerie Alfred Flechtheim, Berlin (1931-32); Roland Penrose, London; Mayor Gallery,
London; G. David Thompson, Pittsburgh; Mrs Helene S. Thompson, Pittsburgh (acquired from the
above. Sale: Sotheby's, New York, 18th May 1983, lot 43); Galerie Jan Krugier, Geneva (puchased
by the present owner in 1985).
EXH.: Berlin, Galerie Alfred Flechtheim, *Paul Klee, Neue Bilder und Aquarelle*,1931, no 9,
illustrated in the catalogue; Berlin, Nationalgalerie, (1932,on loan) London, The Mayor Gallery, *Paul
Klee*, 1935,no. 29London, The National Gallery, *Paul Klee*, 1879-1940, 1945, no. 135; Pittsburgh,
Carnegie Institute, Sarah Scaife Gallery of the Museum of Art, *Celebration*, 1974-75, no. 62,
illustrated in the catalogue (titled *Brother and Sister*); Geneva, Galerie Jan Krugier, *Dix ans
d'activite'*, 1983, no.64, illustrated in the catalogue; Venice, Ca' Pesaro and Milan, Palazzo Reale,
Paul Klee nelle collezioni private, 1986, no. 112, illustrated in colour in the catalogue.
LIT.: Jean Lurçat, 'Paul Klee' in *Omnibus*, no. 2, Berlin, 1932, p. 54, illustrated; *Cahiers d 'art*, Paris,
1934, no. 5-8, p. 180, illustrated; Edited by Jurg Spiller, *The Thinking Eye; Paul Klee Notebooks,*
1961, vol. I, p. 118, illustrated .
      Sotheby's London, 24 June 1996 (52**) GBP 2,861,500   US$ 4,412,490

PARK MIT DEM KÚHLEN HALBMOND oil and tempera on extensively incised and sculpted
plaster on gauze laid down on panel, in the Artist's original frame, 15 3/8 x 20½in. (39 x 52in.)
(including the frame) 14¼ x 19¼in. (36 x 49in. (36 x 49cm.) (excluding frame) sd and titled '1926
Park mit dem Kühlen Halbmond Klee'
PROV.: Private European Collector, by whom purchased directly from the Artist in the late 1920's.
      Christie's London, 25 June 1996 (17**) GBP 551,500   US$ 850,424

VERSIEGELTE DAME watercolour and pen and ink on Ingres laid paper laid down on the Artist's
mount with a thin band od brown watercolour on the mount just below the subject, 19¼ x 13 5/8in.
(48.5 x 34.7)(image), 23 5/8 x 18½in. (60 x 47cm.) (mount) sd numbered and titled 'Klee VIII 1930
P.2. Versiegelte Dame'
PROV.: Purchased directly from the Artist by the father of the present owner shortly after it was
painted.
EXH.: Berne, Kunstmuseum, *Ausstellung Paul Klee*, 1956, no. 592.; Munich Museum Villa Stuck,
Paul Klee Gemälde, Aquarelle, Zeichnungen, Druckgraphik, Feb.- April 1983, no. 52 (illustrated in
colour).
LIT.: This work is recorded in the *Artist's Werkkatalog* as no. 1930, P 2 (62).
      Christie's London, 25 June 1996 (18**) GBP 331,500   US$ 511,180

BERG UND LUFT SYNTHETISCH watercolour on paper laid down on the artist's original mount, 9
x 11¼in. (23 x 28.5cm.)image, 13 x 15 1/8in. (33 x 38.8cm.)mount sd numbered and titled 'Klee III
1930 X6 Berg und Luft synthetisch'
PROV.: Galerie Art Moderne, Basle, where purchased by the present owner in 1958.
EXH.: Martigny, Foundation Pierre Gianadda, *Paul Klee*, 24 May- 3 Nov. 1985, no. 38.
LIT.: This work is recorded in the *Artist's Werkkatalog* as no. III 1930 X6.
      Christie's London, 26 June 1996 (252**) GBP 95,000   US$ 146,492

SCENE UNTER MÄDCHEN oil transfer and watercolour on thick paper applied to the artist's
original mount, 15 3/8 x 9 3/8in. (39 x 23.7cm.) (subject), 19½ x 9 3/8in. (49.5 x 32cm.) (mount) sll
'Klee' d and titled lower edge '1923 148 scene unter Mädchen' inscr. 'S Cl.'
PROV.: Purchased directly from the artist by a swiss collector; anon. sale, Christie's London, 5 Dec.
1986, lot no. 246 (GBP187,000) where bought by the present owner.
LIT.: this work is recorded as follows in the *Artist's Werkverzeichnis*: 1923. 148 *Scene unter
Mädchen, Ölfarbezeichnung und Aquarell, französisch Inges MBM, leicht tonig.*
      Christie's London, 28 November 1995 (32**) GBP 287,500   US$ 449,711

MONDSCHEIN gouache and watercolour on linen, 7¼ x 9½in. (18.5 x 24.3cm.)(image) 12 x 13in. (30.5 x 33cm.) (mount) (1919)
PROV.: The Artist's Estate; Lily Klee, Bern (1940); Klee-Gesellschaft, Bern (1946); Jan Heyligers, Netherlands (1950); Galerie des Deux Rives, Cannes (1957).
Christie's London, 28 November 1995 (39**) GBP 232,500   US$ 363,679

FRUCHTBARES GEREGELT watercolor on paper suspended in the artist's mount, Image size:7 3/4 x 10 1/4in. (19.8 x 26cm.), Mount size(sight): 10 1/2 x 10 5/8in. (26.6 x 27cm.) ll 'Klee' and on the mount 'Fruchtbares geregelt 1933 L.8.' (1933)
PROV.: Lily Klee, Bern (1940-1946); Klee-Gesellschaft, Bern (1946-1950); Buchholz Gallery (Curt Valentin), New York (acquired by the late owner, 1950).
EXH.: Liège, Association pour le progrès intellectual et artisque de la Wallonie, *Paul Klee, peintures et dessins*, April, 1949, no. 24 (titled *Mesures fertiles*).
LIT.: *Oeuvre-Katalog Klee*, 1933, no. 28 (L.8).
Christie's New York, 8 November 1995 (246**) US$ 107,000   US$ 107,000

RECHTS UNFREUNDLICH brush and black ink on paper mounted by the artist on paper, Image size: 8 1/4 x 14in. (21 x 49.8cm.). Mount size: 13 7/8 x 19 5/8in. (35.3 x 49.8cm.) indistinctly ur and on the mount'1940 K4 Rechts unfreundlich' (March 1940)
PROV.: Lily Klee, Bern (1940-1946); Klee-Gesellschaft, Bern (1946-1951); Galerie Rosengart, Lucerne (1949-1951); A. Didie Graeffe, Gainesville, Florida (1951).
LIT.: *Oeuvre-Katalog Klee*, 1940, no. 284 (K4); *Florida Review*, fall, 1957 (illustrated on the cover); ed. S.Frey and J.Helfenstein, *Paul Klee, Verzeichnis der Werke des Jahres 1940*, Bern, 1991, p. 175 (illustrated);ed. M.Kuhn, *Gewagte Symbiosen, Bild und Bildtitel im Spätwerk Klee*, p. 96.
Christie's New York, 8 November 1995 (285**) US$ 55,200   US$ 55,200

KLEIN Johann Adam (1792-1875) German
ITALIAN COUNTRYFOLK RESTING ON THE WAY TO MARKET oil on canvas, 11 3/4 x 15 3/4in. (30 x 40cm.) sd 'J. Klein 1868'
Christie's London, 15 March 1996 (165**) GBP 10,120   US$ 15,455

KLEIN Yves (Nice 1928-1962 Paris) French
IKB 270 pigment and synthetic resin on canvas laid down on panel, 21 3/4 x 18in. (55.3 x 46cm.) sd '58' on the overlap impressed with the Artist's thumbprint and dedicated 'à Elyette, Monochrome, Dec '59' on the reverse
PROV.: a gift from the artist to Elyette Hélies-Astruc; private collection, Paris.
LIT.: This work is recorded in the *Yves Klein Archives* under no. IKB 270 and will be included in the new edition of the *catalogue Raisonné* of the Artist's work being prepared under the supervision of Rotraut Moquay-Klein.
Christie's London, 23 May 1996 (75***) GBP 109,300   US$ 165,506

IKB 272 pigment and synthetic resin on canvas laid down on panel, 30½ x 22in. (77.5 x 56cm.) (1957)
PROV.: Galleria Apollinaire, Milan; Acquired from the above by the father of the present owner in 1957.
EXH.: Milan, Galleria Apollinaire, *Proposta Monocroma Epoca Blu*, January 1957.
Christie's London, 27 June 1996 (54**) GBP 254,500   US$ 392,444

F3 charred cardboard laid down on panel, 51½ x 38 3/16in. (146 x 97cm.) (1961)
PROV.: Alexandre Iolas, Paris/New York.
EXH.: Krefeld, Museum Haus Lange, *Yves Klein: Monochrome und Feuer*, January-February 1961; Hanover, Kunstverein; Bern, Kunsthalle, *Yves Klein*, June-August 1971 (illustrated p. 55 next to a photograph of the artist creating the work).
LIT.: Paul Wember, *Yves Klein*, Cologne 1969, p. 123, no. F3 (illustrated).
Christie's London, 27 June 1996 (56**) GBP 188,500   US$ 290,671

IKB 271 pigment and synthetic resin on linen mounted on panel, 19 3/4 x 19 3/4in. (50 x 50cm.) dedicated 'à Bertini avec l'amitié de Yves Klein, 1960' on the overlap
PROV.: Galleria Apollinaire, Milan; Gianni Bertini, Milan; Galerie Bleu, Stockholm; Acquired from th eabove by the present owner in the 1970s.
EXH.: Milan, Galleria Apollinaire, *Proposta Monocroma Epoca Blu*, January 1957.
Christie's London, 27 June 1996 (59**) GBP 146,700 US$ 226,214

IKB pigment in synthetic resin on wood, 19 5/8 x 1 x 1in. (50 x 2.5 x 2.5cm.) s; s with the star and d '56'
PROV.: Galerie Beaubourg, Paris.
Sotheby's London, 27 June 1996 (192**) GBP 17,250 US$ 26,600

KLEINSCHMIDT Paul (1883-1949) German
WEISSE LILIEN MIT BAUMKUCHEN oil on canvas, 92.5 x 73cm. (ca. 1935)
Hauswedell & Nolte Cologne, 5/06 June 1996 (366**) DEM 64,000 US$ 41,583

KLEINT Boris (Masmünster 1903 b.-) German
POLARNACHT oil on canvas, 82 x 62cm. sll 'Kleint'; titled on the reverse
Hauswedell & Nolte Cologne, 5/06 June 1996 (369**) DEM 12,000 US$ 7,797

KLEYN Lodewijk Johannes (Loosduinen 1817-1897 The Hague) Dutch
SKATERS ON A FROZEN CANAL BEFORE WINDMILLS oil on panel, 13 ¼ x 20 5/8in. (33.6 x 52.4cm.) sll
Phillips London, 11June 1996 (14**) GBP 8,500 US$ 13,107

SUMMER: A WOODED RIVER LANDSCAPE WITH ANGLERS IN A ROWING BOAT AND SAILING BOATS BEYOND oil on panel, 30.5 x 38 cm s LJ Kleyn f'
Christie's Amsterdam, 25 April 1996 (139*) NLG 29,900 US$ 17,767

KLIMT Gustav (Baumgarten (Vienna) 1862-1918 Vienna) Austrian
KOFPSTUDIE FUR DIE LINKE FIGUR DES DECKENBILDES 'DER TANZ' pencil heightened with white chalk on paper, 44.5 x 25.4cm. (1885)
PROV.: With Franziska Klimt; Private collection, Vienna.
LIT.: Alice Strobl, *Gustav Klimt, Die Zeichnungen 1878-1903*, Verlag Welz, Salzburg 1980, Band I, no. 132 (illustrated); Emil Pircher, *Gustav Klimt, Ein Künstler aus Wien*, Verlag Wallishauser, Wien-Leipzig 1942, (illustrated no. 51, with title 'Die schöne Wienerin').
Dorotheum Vienna, 21 May 1996 (4**) ATS 250,000 US$ 24,006

AUG RUHEBEIT SITZENDE FRAU, DIE HÄNDE AUFGESTÜTZT red and lead pencils on paper, 21 x 13 7/8in. (53.4 x 45.5cm.) slr 'GUSTAV KLIMT' (1908)
PROV.: Michael Tollemache, London; Simon Sainsbury, London; James Kirkman, London; Alice Kaplan, New York (acquired from the above in 1978).
EXH.: Vienna, Galerie Ariadne, *Lagerkatalog Sommer-Herbst*, summer-fall, 1972, no. 109 (illus.).
LIT.: A. Strobl, *Gustav Klimt:: Die Zeichnungen 1904-1912*, Salzburg, 1982, vol. II, p. 154, no. 1697 (illus. p. 155).
Christie's New York, 7 November 1995 (36**) US$ 222,500 US$ 222,500

KLINE Franz (Wilke Barre (Penn.) 1910-1962 New York) American
UNTITLED brush and black ink on paper mounted on paper, 22½ x 17 7/8in. (57.1 x 45.1cm.) slc 'KLINE' (1947)
PROV.: Marlborough-Gerson Gallery, New York; Robert Miller Gallery, New York; Private collection, New York; Solomon & Co., New York.
EXH.: New York, Whitney Museum of American Art; Dallas Museum of Fine Arts; San Fransisco Museum of Art; Chicago, Museum of Contemporary Art, *Frans Kline 1910-1962*, October. 1968-May 1969, no.28.
Christie's New York, 22 February 1996 (17**) US$ 25,300 US$ 25,300

RED LANDSCAPE (PENNSYLVANIA) oil and brush and black ink on paper mounted on board, 23
3/4 x 3 3/4in. (60.2 x 90.8cm.)
PROV.: Acquired directly from the artist.; Anne Rowe Kline Snyder, Bethlehem. By descent to
present owner.

Christie's New York, 15 November 1995 (154**) US$ 43,700	US$	43,700

UNTITLED brush and black ink on paper, 13¼ x 10½in. (34 x27cm.) numbered 'ZD 460' on the
reverse (1951)
PROV.: Estate of the artist.; Private collection New York.

Christie's New York, 15 November 1995 (158**) US$ 20,700	US$	20,700

SWANEE oil on canvas, 35 x 47in. (89 x 119.3cm.) sd 'FRANZ KLINE' on the reverse (ca. 1958-59)
PROV.: Gift of the artist; Mary Grand, New York; Prudence Grand, New York; Acquired by the
present owner in 1963.
EXH.: Barcelona, Fundació Antoni Tàpies; London, Whitechapel
Art Gallery; Madrid, Museo Nacional Centro de Arte Reina Sofia, and Saarbrücken, Saadand
Museum, *Franz Kline: Art and the Structure of Identity*, Mar. 1994-Feb. 1995, p.114, no. 50
(illustrated).

Christie's New York, 7 May 1996 (9**) US$ 965,000	US$	965,000

SABRO oil on canvas, 78 3/4 x 47½in. (202 x 120.5cm.) (1956)
PROV.: Sidney Janis Gallery, New York; Galleria dell'Ariete, Milan; Noah Goldowsky, New York;
Mary McFadden, New York; James Goodman Gallery, New York; Sarah Campbell Blaffer
Foundation, Texas; Galerie Beyeler, Basel.
EXH.: New York, Whitney Museum of American Art, *Annual Exhibition of Painting, Sculpture,
Watercolors and Drawings*, Nov. 1957-Jan. 1958, no. 104; Arts Club of Chicago, *Franz Kline*, Dec.
1961-Jan. 1962, no. 3; Amarillo Art Center, *Abstract Expressionists*, 1977, no. 11; Basel, Galerie
Beyeler, *Exploring Abstraction*, July-Sept. 1989, no. 9 (illustrated); Barcelona, Fundació Antoni
Tàpies; London ,Whitechapel Art Gallery; Madrid, Museo Nacional Centro de Arte Reina Sofia, and
Saarbrucken, Saarland Museum, *Franz Kline: Art and Structure of Identity*, Mar. 1994 - Feb. 1995,
p.97, no. 36 (illustrated).

Christie's New York, 7 May 1996 (16**) US$ 662,500	US$	662,500

KLINKENBERG Johannes Christiaan Karel (The Hague 1852-1924 The Hague) Dutch
A VIEW IN DORDTRECHT, WITH THE MERWEDE KADE oil on panel, 38 x 26cm. s
'Klinkenberg'

Christie's Amsterdam, 25 April 1996 (186**) NLG 20,700	US$	12,300

WINTER: A VIEW OF THE OUDE WAAL, AMSTERDAM WITH THE ST. NICOLAASKERK
BEYOND, AT SUNSET oil on canvas, 81 x 131cm. slr 'Klinkenberg'

Christie's Amsterdam, 26 October 1995 (280**) NLG 74,750	US$	47,131

KLOMBECK Johan Bernard (Kleve 1815-1893 Kleve) Dutch
A SHEPHERD WITH HIS FLOCK ON A WOODED TRACK oil on panel, 23 3/8 x 35 5/8in. (59.5
x 90.5cm.) s inscr. indistinctly on an old label on the reverse and sealed
PROV.: see also Eugene Verboeckhoven (18) co-painter.

Phillips London, 14 November 1995 (18**) GBP 10,000	US$	15,642

A WOODED MOUNTAINOUS RIVER LANDSCAPE WITH FIGURES CONVERSING oil on
panel, 13 x 16cm. sd 'J B Klombeck 1844'

Christie's Amsterdam, 25 April 1996 (160*) NLG 25,300	US$	15,034

A WOODED RIVER LANDSCAPE WITH SKATERS ON A FROZEN RIVER oil on a panel,
unframed, 15.5 x 19cm. sdlr J.B.K.ft 1851'

Christie's Amsterdam, 26 October 1995 (180**) NLG 19,550	US$	12,327

TRAVELLERS IN STORMY WEATHER oil on panel, 39.5 x 54cm. sdlr 'J.B. Klombeck ft 1847'
Christie's Amsterdam, 26 October 1995 (292**) NLG 40,250 — US$ 25,378

A HERDSMAN AND CATTLE BY A POND IN THE FOREST oil on panel, 59 x 86cm. Signed by
both artists and dated 'JB Klombeck 1870/ Eugène Verboeckhoven
PROV.: Also Eugène Joseph Verboeckhoven (293) co-painter.
EXH.: Kleve, Museum Haus Koekkoek, *Johann Bernhard Klombeck. Ein Maler der Klever
Romantik*, 10 Oct.-5 Dec.1993.
LIT.: A. Nollert and G. de Werd, *Johann Bernhard Klombeck. Ein Landschaftsmaler der Klever
Romantik*, Kleve 1993, p. 57 (col.illus.).
Christie's Amsterdam, 26 October 1995 (293**) NLG 57,500 — US$ 36,255

KLUYVER Pieter Lodewijk Francisco (Amsterdam 1816-1,900 Amsterdam) Dutch
A WINTER WOODED LANDSCAPE oil on canvas, 31 x 39in. (88.8 x 99cm.) s 'Kluyver'
Christie's South Kensington, 13 June 1996 (40**) GBP 6,670 — US$ 10,285

AN EXTENSIVE WOODED LANDSCAPE WITH A SHEPHERD AND FLOCK ON A SANDY
PATH oil on panel, 40 x 60cm. s 'Kluyver'
Christie's Amsterdam, 25 April 1996 (159*) NLG 9,200 — US$ 5,467

KNELLER Sir Godfrey, Bt. (Lübeck 1646-1723 London) British (German)
PORTRAIT OF ELIZABETH HERVEY, COUNTESS OF BRISTOL (1676-1723) oil on canvas, 49
x 38½in. (124.5 x 98cm.) inscr.lr 'Elizabeth 2nd Wife/ of John Earl of Bristol'
Sotheby's London, 11-12 June 1996 (444**) GBP 38,900 — US$ 59,985

KNIBBERGEN François (The Hague 1597-1665) Dutch
FIGURES IN A BOAT MOORED BY A RUINED TOWER WITH ANIMALS NEARBY oil on
panel, 40.5 x 33cm. indistinctly s on the boat
PROV.: Q. Wesendonck, Berlin ca. 1905, as Salomon van Ruysdael; C. Hoogendijk, Amsterdam,
1910; Private collection, Amsterdam, 1976.
Sotheby's Amsterdam, 6 May 1996 (14**) NLG 11,800 — US$ 6,880

KNIGHT Dame Laura, D.B.E., R.A. (1877-1970) British
BOYS BATHING, NEWLYN KAY oil on canvas, 27 x 36in. (68.5 x 91.4cm.) sd 'Laura Knight'
1910
PROV.: Richard Green, London.
Christie's London, 20 June 1996 (10**) GBP 58,700 — US$ 90,517

CIRCUS PONIES oil on canvas, 15 3/4 x 20in. (40 x 50.8cm.) slr 'Laura Knight'
Christie's London, 21 November 1995 (212**) GBP 8,050 — US$ 12,592

KNIGHT Daniel Ridgway (1839-1924) American
PICKING WILD FLOWERS oil on canvas, 32 3/4 x 26½in. (83.2 x 67.3cm.) s and inscr. 'Ridgway
Knight/Paris'
PROV.: With O'Brian's, Chicago.
Christie's New York, 14 February 1996 (94**) US$ 55,200 — US$ 55,200

POISSY, LA SORTIE D'ÉCOLE oil on canvas, 48 x 55cm. slr 'Ridgeway Knight'
Étude Tajan Paris, 27 October 1995 (3**) FRF 42,000 — US$ 8,495

KNIGHT Louis Aston (Paris 1873-1948) American (French)
LA RISLE AT YOUPILLIERES, NORMANDY oil on canvas, 21 3/4 x 18¼in. (81.2 x 63cm.) s and
inscr. lr 'Ashton Knights Paris'
Christie's East, 21 May 1996 (77**) US$ 9,775 — US$ 9,775

KNIP Joseph August (Tilburg 1777-1847 Berlicum) Dutch
PEASANTS RESTING ON AN WOODED OUTCROP ABOVE A RIVER, WITH A MULETEER
FORDING THE WATER, IN AN ITALIANATE LANDSCAPE oil on canvas, 59.6 x 73.6cm. sdll
'I.A. Knip/1819'
        Christie's Amsterdam, 7 May 1996 (124**) NLG 12,650   US$ 7,376

PAESANTS RESTING ON A WOODED OUTCROP ABOVE A RIVER, WITH A MULETEER
FORDING THE WATER, IN AN ITALIANATE LANDSCAPE oil on canvas, 59.6 x 73.6cm. sdll
I.A.Knip/1819 (1819)
        Christie's Amsterdam, 13 November 1995 (160**) NLG 19,550   US$ 12,321

KNOEBEL Imi (Wolf) (1940 b.-) German
UNTITLED acryl on thick paper, 202 x 172cm. sdll mono 'IK 85'
        Hauswedell & Nolte Cologne, 6 June 1996 (261**) DEM 26,000   US$ 16,893

FIGURBILD acrylic on wood, 67 x 98¼in. (170 x 249.5cm.) (1988)
PROV.: Marc Richards Gallery, Santa Monica.
        Christie's New York, 15 November 1995 (264**) US$ 20,700   US$ 20,700

39A, 39B, 39C, 39D oil on wood (four attached panel), 66 3/4 x 98in. (169.5 x 249cm.) sd ini. '86'
PROV.: Prof Dr Peter Littmann, Metzingen.
        Christie's London, 23 May 1996 (160**) GBP 11,500   US$ 17,414

KOCH Ludwig (1866-1934) Austrian
DES KAISERS (FRANZ JOSEF) AUSFAHRT oil on canvas, 74 x 100.5cm. sdll 'LUDWIG KOCH.
1933'
        Wiener Kunst Auktionen, 26 September 1995 (221**) ATS 120,000   US$ 11,664

KOCH Pyke (Piet Frans Christiaan) (Beek (Ubbergen) 1901-1991 The Hague) Dutch
LEEUW IN INTERIEUR II - LION IN INTERIOR II oil on panel, 60.5 x 45cm. sd 'Pyke Koch '72',
and inscr. 'Tweede exemplaar geschilderd ca. 1930' on the reverse (Executed *circa* 1930)
PROV.: C. Wertheim, Hilversum; Mr. M. Tieleman, Amsterdam thence by descent.
EXH.: Paris, Institute Néerlandais, *Pyke Koch*, 14 October - 28 November 1982, nr. 3A.
LIT.: Carel Blotkamp, *Pyke Koch*, Utrecht 1972, no.5 p.66-67; p.156 (ill.) Exh.Cat. *Pyke Koch*,
Museum Boymans-van Beuningen, Rotterdam 1995, p. 211, no. 21 (ill.).
        Christie's Amsterdam, 5 June 1996 (277***) NLG 138,000   US$ 80,631

A Still-Life with Lemons

HET ONGEVAL - THE ACCIDENT oil on canvas, 36 x 46cm. slr With initials 'PK' (executed *circa* 1955-1958)
EXH.: Laussanne, Musée des Beaux Arts, *Pyke Koch*, 1995.
Christie's Amsterdam, 5 June 1996 (278**) NLG 92,000   US$ 53,754

A STILL-LIFE WITH LEMONS oil on canvas, 23 x 41cm. slr with ini. 'P' (ca. 1944)
LIT.: Exh.Cat. *Pyke Koch*, Museum Boymans-van Beuningen, Rotterdam 1955, p.219, no.46 (ill.).
Christie's Amsterdam, 6 December 1995 (184**) NLG 195,500   US$ 121,143

KOCHERSCHEIDT Kurt, {called} Kappa (Klagenfurt 1943-1992 Wels) Austrian
UNTITLED oil on canvas, 180 x 160cm. sdlr 'KAPPA 82'
LIT.: *Kocherscheildt. Bilder*, Morat Institut, Freiburg i. Breisgau 1986, (illustrated no. 30).
Wiener Kunst Auktionen, 26 March 1996 (457**) ATS 250,000   US$ 24,048

KOCHERSCHEIDT Kurt, {called} Kappa (Klagenfurt 1943-1992 Wels) Austrian
ANTIKES MIRAMARE resin, crayon on canvas, 121 x 131cm. (two parts) sd and titled 'Kocherscheidt 1968' on the reverse
Wiener Kunst Auktionen, 27 September 1995 (538**) ATS 100,000   US$ 9,720

KOEKKOEK B.C. (Middelburg 1803-1862 Kleve) Dutch
A RIVER LANDSCAPE WITH FIGURES RESTING ON A BANK BY A FARM pen and brush and black and brown ink and grey wash on paper, 14.5 x 18.5 cm s 'B:C:Koekkoek.'
Christie's Amsterdam, 25 April 1996 (62*) NLG 10,350   US$ 6,150

A COASTAL LANDSCAPE: A SUMMERDAY BREEZE oil on panel, 28 x 39cm. sd (with initials) 'B.C.K.f. 1833'
PROV.: Anon. sale, Kunstauktionshaus Schloß Ahlden, Aller, 22 April 1978,; lot no. 750(illus.no.100).
Christie's Amsterdam, 26 October 1995 (322**) NLG 126,500   US$ 79,760

A WOODED MOUNTAIN PATH WITH CATTLE AND A VILLAGE BEYOND oil on panel, 8 1/8 x 10¼in. (20.6 x 26cm.) sd 'B.C. Koekkoek/1848'
PROV.: General Henry Hopkinson, C.S.I. and thence by descent to Lord Colyton; Mrs. R.G.G. Copeland.
Gorissen, *B.C. Koekkoek 1802-1862*, Düsseldorf, 1962, no. 48/21 (illustrated).
Christie's London, 14 June 1996 (1**) GBP 54,300   US$ 83,732

FIGURES WITH A SLED BEFORE A VILLAGE IN WINTER oil on board, 9½ x 12 5/8in. (24 x 32cm.) s
Phillips London, 11th June 1996 (103 (a pair)) GBP 6,500   US$ 10,023

KOEKKOEK Hendrik Barend (Amsterdam 1849-1909 before London) Dutch
FIGURES IN A WOODED LANDSCAPE oil on canvas, 44½ x 56¼in. (113 x 143cm.) slc 'H.B. Koekkoek'
Christie's East, 20 May 1996 (112**) US$ 19,550   US$ 19,550

KOEKKOEK Hermanus (Jnr) (Amsterdam 1836-1909 The Hague) Dutch
FISHING SMACKS OFF THE COAST IN A STIFF BREEZE oil on canvas, 33.5 x 56cm. sd 'H. Koekkoek Jun. 1857'
Christie's Amsterdam, 25 April 1996 (252*) NLG 19,550   US$ 11,617

KOEKKOEK Hermanus Snr (Middelburg 1815-1882 Haarlem) Dutch
A VIEW ON AN ESTUARY WITH FIGURES UNLOADING VESSELS ON A JETTY oil on canvas, 14 3/4 x 23 3/8in. (37.5 x 59.3cm.) slc
Phillips London, 14 November 1995 (11**) GBP 10,000   US$ 15,642

VESSELS OFF A COASTLINE IN A STIFF BREEZE oil on canvas, 18 ¼ x 30 1/8in. (49 x 76.5cm.) slr

        Phillips London, 14 November 1995 (25**) GBP 51,000   US$ 79,775

FIGURES BY A BOAT ON A LAKE oil on canvas, 15¼ x 22½in. (38.7 x 56.5cm.) sd 'H. Koekkoek 1863'
PROV.: Mrs Mary Whitelock; with Frost and Reed, 1968.

        Christie's London, 15 March 1996 (3**) GBP 35,600   US$ 54,368

SHIPPING VESSELS IN A CALM oil on canvas, 21 5/8 x 29½in. (54.9 x 74.9cm.) sd 'H. Koekkoek/1857'

        Christie's London, 17 November 1995 (1**) GBP 24,150   US$ 37,776

KOEKKOEK Johannes Hermanus (Amsterdam 1778-1851 Amsterdam) Dutch
VARIOUS SHIPPING OFF THE COAST oil on panel, 29 x 39 cm s 'JH Koekkoek'

        Christie's Amsterdam, 25 April 1996 (134*) NLG 18,400   US$ 10,934

DUTCH SAILING-VESSELS IN A RIVER ESTUARY oil on panel, 21.5 x 30cm. s 'H(?) Koekkoek'

        Christie's Amsterdam, 26 October 1995 (182*) NLG 19,550   US$ 12,327

DUTCH FISHING PINKS TACKING OFF THE COAST IN A STIFF BREEZE oil on panel, 22 x 28cm. s 'J:H:koekkoek'

        Christie's Amsterdam, 26 October 1995 (183*) NLG 25,300   US$ 15,952

KOEKKOEK Johannes Hermanus Barend (1840-1912) Dutch
A VIEW OF ROTERDAM WITH FIGURES IN A ROWING-BOAT AND OTHER SHIPPING ON THE MAAS oil on canvas, 60 x 92cm sdll 'Joh. H.B. Koekkoek.1896'; s and inscr. with title and authencitated by the artist on a label on the stretcher

        Christie's Amsterdam, 26 October 1995 (330**) NLG 27,600   US$ 17,402

KOEKKOEK Marinus Adrianus (Middelburg 1807-1868 Amsterdam) Dutch
FIGURES ON A PATH IN A WOODED LANDSCAPE oil on canvas, 18½ x 25in. (47 x 63.5cm.) sdlc 'M.A. Koekkoek./1860.'

        Christie's New York, 14 February 1996 (78**) US$ 55,200   US$ 55,200

BRINGING HOME THE FLOCK oil on canvas, 80 x 102cm. sd 'MA Koekkoek 1867/Eg Verboeckhoven'

        Christie's Amsterdam, 25 April 1996 (230**) NLG 63,250   US$ 37,584

AN EXTENSIVE WOODED LANDSCAPE WITH PEASANTS, CATTLE AND SHEEP NEAR A BARN oil on canvas, 67.5 x 85cm. s 'M.A. Koekkoek'

        Christie's Amsterdam, 25 April 1996 (231**) NLG 19,550   US$ 11,617

A ROCKY RIVER LANDSCAPE WITH A MOORED SAILING-VESSEL AND TRAVELLERS ON A COUNTRY ROAD oil on panel, 21 x 29cm. sd 'M.A. Koekkoek 1850'
PROV.: Kunsthandel P.A. Scheen, The Hague, June 1957.

        Christie's Amsterdam, 26 October 1995 (317**) NLG 25,300   US$ 15,952

A WOODED LANDSCAPE WITH A TRAVELLER AND A DOG ON A SANDY FOREST LANE, A VILLAGE IN THE DISTANCE oil on panel, 15.5 x 21cm. slr 'M.A.K. f'

        Christie's Amsterdam, 26 October 1995 (319*) NLG 10,350   US$ 6,526

KOEKKOEK Willem (Amsterdam 1839-1895 Nieuwer-Amstel) Dutch
A VIEW OF A SQUARE IN A DUTCH TOWN WITH FIGURES BESIDE A WELL oil on canvas, 29 7/8 x 41 7/8in. (76 x 106.5cm.) sdlr (1875)

Phillips London, 14 November 1995 (26**) GBP 106,000	US$	165,806

A DUTCH TOWN WITH FIGURES BY A CANAL oil on canvas, 21½ x 27½in. (54.5 x 70cm.) s
'W. Koekkoek'

Christie's London, 17 November 1995 (6**) GBP 40,000	US$	62,568

STRASSE IN EIN HOLLÄNDISCHEN KLEINSTADT oil on canvas, 89 x 126cm. sll 'W.
Koekkoek'
PROV.: Gal. Heseler, München; private collection München.

Lempertz Cologne, 18 May 1996 (1587**) DEM 70,000	US$	45,635

A VIEW IN A VILLAGE, IN SUMMER oil on canvas, 55 x 70cm. s 'W. Koekkoek'

Christie's Amsterdam, 25 April 1996 (251**) NLG 48,300	US$	28,700

A VIEW IN ENKHUIZEN, IN WINTER oil on canvas, 55 x 69.5cm. sll 'W. Koekkoek' s again, d
'Utrecht 1878' inscr with title and with the artist's seal on a label on the stretcher

Christie's Amsterdam, 26 October 1995 (302**) NLG 80,500	US$	50,57

KOHLHOFF Wilhelm (Berlin 1893 b.-) German
AT THE RACES oil on canvas, 15 3/4 x 19 3/4in. (40 x 50cm.) s

Phillips London, 26 June 1995 (6**) GBP 5,500	US$	8,776

KOKOSCHKA Oskar (Pöchlarn 1886-1980 Montreux) Austrian
MÄDCHENAKT pencil-drawing and watercolour, 39.8 x 18.8cm. sdlr 'Oskar Kokoschka 6'
LIT.: Ernst Rathenau, *Oskar Kokoschka*, Berlin 1935, plate 7.

Hauswedell & Nolte Cologne, 1 December 1995 (366**) DEM 72,000	US$	49,955

NACH LINKS SCHREITENDES, NACKTES MÄDCHEN pencil-drawing and watercolour, 43 x
21cm. slr with monogram (ca. 1907)
PROV.: Collection Hevesi, Vienna (according to a label on the reverse).
LIT.: Ernst Rathenau, *Oskar Kokoschka*, Berlin 1935, plate 7.

Hauswedell & Nolte Cologne, 1 December 1995 (367**) DEM 175,000	US$	121,418

STANDING NUDE BOY charcoal and watercolour on buff paper, 16 15/16 x 12 3/8in. (43 x
31.5cm.) sll with initials 'OK' (ca. *1913*)
PROV.: Collection of Mrs. H. Williams, London; Private collection, London.
EXH.: 1981-82, Goethe Institutes of London,; Dublin, Sheffield and Glasgow, no. 35..
LIT.: Rathenau II, no. 25 (ill.).; This drawing will be included in the first volume of the forthcoming
Catalogue raisonné, of Kokoscka`s drawings from 1897 to 1916, currently being prepared by Alfred
Weidinger and Alice Strobl.

Phillips London, 26 June 1995 (4**) GBP 34,000	US$	54,252

KOLLER-PINELL Broncia (Sanok 1863-1934 Vienna) Polish (Austrian)
IM ATELIER oil on cardboard, 66x 63.5cm.
LIT.: S. Baumgartner, *Werkverzeichnis*, Salzburg, 1989 vol I, pl. 284.

Dorotheum Vienna, 6 December 1995 (498**) ATS 120,000	US$	11,834

KOLLWITZ Käthe (Köningsberg 1867-1945 Moritzburg) German
STUDYPAPER WITH STANDING FIGURE pencil-drawing, 35.9 x 31.5cm. slr 'Kathe Kollwitz'
(1896/97)

Hauswedell & Nolte Cologne, 1 December 1995 (376*) DEM 40,000	US$	27,753

SCHWANGERE, INS WASSER GEHEND charcoal on paper, 20 x 16½in. (50.8 x 41.9cm.) slr
'Kahte Kollwitz' (1909)
PROV.: Erich Cohn, New York.
LIT.: Herbert Bittner, *Käthe Kollwitz, Drawings*, New York 1959, no. 43 (illustrated pl. 43); Otto

Nagel, *Käthe Kollwitz, Die Handzeichnungen*, Stuttgart 1980, no. 512 (illustrated p. 287).

Sotheby's New York, 2 May 1996 (224**) US$ 33,350	US$	33,350

KONCHALOVSKY Piotr Petrovich (1876-1956) Russian
BULLFIGHT IN ARLES oil on canvas, 24 13/16 x 29 15/16in. (63 x 76cm.) sll inscr. and dated on
the reverse in cyrillic (1908)
PROV.: Acquired from the artist in 1923; Parke-Bernet, New York, 17 January 1945. Acquired by
the father of the present owner; Private collection.

Phillips London, 26 June 1995 (5**) GBP 10,000	US$	15,957

KONINCK Jacob (Amsterdam 1615 c.-after 1690 Copenhagen) Dutch
VUE D'UNE VILLE AU BORD D'UN ESTUAIRE oil on oakpanel, 63.5 x 80.5cm.
LIT.: W. Sumowski, *Gemälde der Rembrandt Schüler*, Landau 1983, vol. V, no. 2214a, p. 3254
(illustrated).

Étude Tajan Paris, 12 December 1995 (11**) FRF 55,000	US$	11,078

KONINCK Salomon (Amsterdam 1609-1656 Amsterdam) Dutch
LE CABINET DU PHILOSOPHE oil on oak panel, 18.5 x 23cm. (possibly around 1646)
LIT.: W. Sumowski, *Gemälde der Rembrandt Schüler*, Landau, 1983 no. 2117a, illustrated p. 3259.

Étude Tajan Paris, 12 December 1995 (36**) FRF 60,000	US$	12,086

KOOL Willem Gillisz. (1608/9-1666 Haarlem) Dutch
VIEW OF SCHEVENINGEN WITH FISH-MERCHANT AND A HORSEMAN oil on canvas, 36.5
x 71cm.

Dorotheum Vienna, 11 June 1996 (196*) ATS 110,000	US$	10,210

KOONING Willem de (Rotterdam 1904 b.-l) American (Dutch)
UNTITLED oil on newsprint mounted on canvas, 29¼ x 23¼in. (74.3 x 59.1cm.) sll 'de Kooning'
(1977)

Christie's New York, 22 February 1996 (19**) US$ 47150	US$	47,150

EAST HAMPTON IV oil on paper mounted on canvas, 41¼ x 30¼in. (104.8 x 76.8cm.) slr 'de
Kooning' (1976)
PROV.: Collection d'Art/Galerie, Amsterdam.

Christie's New York, 14 November 1995 (35**) US$ 288,500	US$	288,500

UNTITLED Charcoal and Graphite on paper, 11 x 8 3/8in. (28 x 21.3cm.) sddedl edge '1980 Happy
Birthday Linda with Love Bill de Kooning' (1980)
PROV.: Linda Hyman Fine Arts, New York.; Salander-O`Reilly Galleries, Beverly Hills.
EXH.: Beverly Hills, Salander-O`Reilly Galleries, *Willem de Kooning; An Exhibition of important
Paitings and works on; Paper*, Jan.-Feb. 1991, no. 34.

Christie's New York, 15 November 1995 (156**) US$ 13,800	US$	13,800

MAILBOX oil, enamel and charcoal on paper mounted on panel, 23¼ x 30in. (59.1 x 76.2cm.) sll 'de
Kooning' (1948)
PROV.: Charles Egan Gallery, New York; Governor and Mrs. Nelson Rockefeller, New York;
Marlborough-Gerson Galleries, New York; A Midwestern collector (acquired in 1970); By descent
to the present owner.
EXH.: New York, Charles Egan Gallery, *Willem de Kooning*, Apr.-May 1948;
New York, Whitney Museum of American Art, *Annual Exhibition of Contemporary American
Painting*, Nov. 1948-Jan. 1949, no. 34; Venice, *XX VII Esposizione Biennale Intemazionale d 'Arte*,
June-Oct. 1950, no. 338.; Northampton, Smith College Museum of Art and Cambridge,
Massachusetts Institute of Technology, The Hayden Gallery, *Willem de Kooning*, Apr.-June 1965,
no. 13 (illustrated); Amsterdam, Stedelijk Museum; London, The Tate Gallery and New York, The
Museum of Modern Art, *Willem de Kooning*, Sept. 1968-Apr. 1969, p. 63, no. 33 (illustrated);
New York, The Museum of Modern Art, *Twentieth Century Artfrom the Nelson Aldrich Rockefeller*

Collection, May-Sept.1969, p. 97 (illustrated);
Ithaca, Cornell University, Herbert F. Johnson Museum and New York, Whitney Museum of
Amencan Art, *Abstract Expressionism: The Formative Years*, Mar.-May 1978, no. 15; Pittsburgh,
Carnegie Institute, Museum of Art, *Willem de Kooning: Pittsburgh Intemational Series*, Oct. 1979-
Jan. 1980, p. 39 no. 8 (illustrated); New York, Whitney Museum of American Art, *Willem de
Kooning Drawings-Paintings-Sculpture*, Dec. 1983-Feb. 1984, p. 168, no. 172 (illustrated); Modern
Art Museum of Fort Worth, *Masterworks from Fort Worth Collections*, Apr.-June 1992, p. 34, no. 8
(illustrated); Berlin, Martin-Gropius-Bau and London, Royal Academy of Arts, *American Art in the
20th Century: Painting and Sculpture 1913-1993*, May-Dec. 1993, no. 95 (illustrated); Washington,
D.C., National Gallery of Art; New York, The Metropolitan Museum of Art and London, The Tate
Gallery, *Willem de Kooning Paintings*, Mar. 1994-May 1995, p. 111, no. 12 (illustrated).
LIT.: W. de Kooning, 'What Abstract Art Means To Me,' *The Museum of Modern Art/Bulletin*, vol.
XVIII, no. 3, Spring 1951, p. 5 (illustrated); T. Hess, *Willem de Kooning*, New York 1959, no. 75
(illustrated but incorrectly dated 1947); H. Rosenberg, *de Kooning*, New York 1973, no. 63
(illustrated); P. Larson, *de Kooning Drawings/Sculpture*, New York 1974, no. 9 (illustrated); H.
Gaugh, *De Kooning*, New York 1983, pp. 28-29, no. 22 (illustrated); W. Seitz, *Abstract
Expressionist Painting in America*, Cambridge and London 1983, no. 22 (illustrated); ed. D. Miller,
The Nelson A. Rockefeller Collection: Masterpieces of Modern Art, New York 1981, p. 170
(illustrated); *Willem de Kooning*, Kodansha Ltd., Publishers, Tokyo 1993, no. 12 (illustrated).
        Christie's New York, 7 May 1996 (10***) US$ 3,742,500   US$ 3,742,500

WOMAN-TORSO oil and graphite on paper mounted on canvas, 48 3/4 x 36¼in. (123.8 x 92.1cm.)
slr 'de Kooning' (ca. 1965-66)
PROV.: Allan Stone Galleries, Inc., New York; Andrew Crispo Gallery, New York.
EXH.: Amsterdam, Stedelijk Museum; London, The Tate Gallery; New York, The Museum of
Modern Art; Art Institute of Chicago and The Los Angeles County Museum of Art, *Willem De
Kooning*, Sept. 1968-Sept. 1969, no. 85. (illustrated).
LIT.: D. Sylvester, R. Schiff and M. Prather, *Willem De Kooning Paintings*, Washington, D.C. 1994,
p. 47, no. 13 (illustrated).
        Christie's New York, 7 May 1996 (24**) US$ 107,000   US$ 107,000

UNTITLED (TWO WOMEN) watercolour on vellum, 14 1/8 x 22 1/8in. (35.8 x 56.2cm.) slr and
dedicated 'Happy Birthday Love Bill'
PROV.: Solomon & Co., New York.
        Christie's New York, 22 February 1996 (28**) US$ 11,500   US$ 115,00

KOSSOFF Leon (1926 b.) British
HEAD OF CHAIM NO. 1 oil on board, 31½ x 25¼in. (80 x 64cm.)
PROV.: Bernard Jacobson Gallery, London, where purchased by the present owner circa 1988.
        Christie's London, 22 May 1996 (52**) GBP 34,500   US$ 52,241

KOUNELLIS Jannis (1936 b.l) Greek
UNTITLED oil on paper, 69 x 100cm. sd '1960' on the reverse
PROV.: Collection Giulio Einaudi, Perno.
        Finearte Milan, 12 December 1995 (225*) ITL 20,527,000   US$ 12,878

UNTITLED (CQS) india ink on paper, 11 5/8 x 18½in. (29.5 x 47cm.) sd '60' sd 'Roma 1959' on the
reverse
PROV.: Stein Gladstone, New York.
EXH.: Frankfurt, Frankfurter Kunstverein Steinernes Haus, *Vom Zeichen - Aspekte der Zeichnung
1960-1985*, November 1985-January 1986; Leverkusen Städtisches Museum, Zum Mythos der
Ursprunglichheit, 1984.
        Christie's London, 23 May 1996 (99**) GBP 14,950   US$ 22,638

KREPP Friedrich (active in Vienna ca. 1852-1862-) Austrian
EMPRESS ELISABETH 'SISI' oil on canvas, 143.6 x 109.3cm. slr 'Krepp'
    Wiener Kunst Auktionen, 26 March 1996 (34***) ATS 350,000   US$ 33,667

KREUZER Vinzenz (Gratz 1809-1888) Austrian
STILL-LIFE WITH RAISINS, APPLES, CHESTNUT AND PRUNES oil on copper, 21 x 27.5cm.
PROV.: Anon. Sale, paris, Drouot Montaigne, 6 december 1989 (maître Laurence Calmels) no. 27,
illustrated in colour.
    Étude Tajan Paris, 12 December 1995 (115**) FRF 115,000   US$ 23,164

FLOWERS IN A DECORATIVE VASE oil on canvas, 72 x 58.5cm. sd 'Vinzenz Kreuzer 1886'
    Dorotheum Vienna, 20 December 1995 (459**) ATS 200,000   US$ 19,723

KREUZINGER Josef (Vienna 1757-1829) Austrian
A PORTRAIT OF ARCHDUKE CHARLES (1771-1847), WEARING THE INSIGNIA OF THE
ORDER OF THE GOLDEN FLEECE AND THE STAR AND SASH OF THE ORDER OF MARIA
THERESA oil on canvas, 41 3/4 x 32 3/4in. (106.5 x 83cm.)
PROV.: Presented by the Archduke Charles in 1801 to William Wickham, P.C. (1761-1840); Thence
by descent.
    Sotheby's London, 6 December 1995 (45**) GBP 43,300   US$ 66,636

KRIKHAAR Herman (Hermannus Theodorus Willebrodrus) (Almelo 1930 b.) Dutch
STILLEVEN (GROTESQUE) oil on canvas, 130 x 162cm. sll with initials 'H Kr'
    Christie's Amsterdam, 6 December 1995 (341**) NLG 10925   US$ 6,770

KROLL Abraham Leon, N.A. (1884-1974) American
WEST SHORE TERMINAL oil on canvas, 36 x 48in. (91.5 x 122cm.) sdlr 'Leon Kroll 1913'
PROV.: Bernard Dannenberg Galleries, Inc., New York; Mr and Mrs. Frank Sinatra.
EXH.: Fitchburg, Massachusetts, Fitchburg Art Museum, *Leon Kroll - One Man Exhibition of
Paintings and Drawings*, 3 December 1958 - 30 Jan 1959, no. 11; New York, Dannenberg Galleries
Inc., *The Rediscovered Years - Leon Kroll*, 10-28 November 1970, no. 28, p. 10 (illustrated).
LIT.: F. Bowers and N. Hale (ed.), *Leon Kroll, a Spoken Memoir*, Charlottesville, 1983, no. 54
(illustrated).
    Christie's New York, 1 December 1995 (69**) US$ 123,500   US$ 123,500

KROUTHÉN Johan Fredrik (1858-1932) Swedish
KOR VID STRANDKANT oil on canvas, 72 x 104cm. sdll 'Johan Krouthén 1913'
    Bukowskis Stockholm, 29 November-1 December 1995 (76**) SEK 68,000   US$ 10,287

KRUSEMAN Frederik-Marinus (Haarlem 1817-1882 Elsene (Brussels)) Dutch
SKATERS ON A FROZEN RIVER BEFORE A WINDMILL oil on panel, 18 7/8 x 25 1/8in.(48 x
64cm.) sd (1853)
PROV.: With Williams & Son, 1951.
LIT.: This painting will be included in the forthcoming *catalogue raissoné* on the artist by Drs.
M.A.C. van Heteren and Dr. J.M.M. de Meere.
    Phillips London, 11 June 1996 (12**) GBP 35,000   US$ 53,971

FIGURES IN A FROZEN WINTER LANDSCAPE oil on canvas, 31 x 43½in. (78.8 x 110.5cm.)
sdlr 'FMKruseman. fc/1866.'
    Christie's New York, 2 November 1995 (83**) US$ 200,500   US$ 200,500

A FROZEN WINTER LANDSCAPE WITH SKATERS ON A POND oil on canvas, 20 x 27½in.
(50.8 x 69.8cm.) sdll 'FMKruseman fc./1875' sd inscr. 'FMKruseman./Bruxelles 1875./ Je sousigné
déclare avoir peint /le tableau ci-contre' on the reverse
PROV.: With Richard Green, London.
    Christie's New York, 22 May 1996 (110**) US$ 90,500   US$ 90,500

A WOODED WINTER LANDSCAPE WITH SPORTSMEN BY A MANSION oil on panel, 28.5 x
38cm. sd 'F.M. Kruseman 18(?)
      Christie's Amsterdam, 26 October 1995 (283*) NLG 16,,100   US$ 10,151

WINTER: FIGURES ON A SNOWY PATH AND SEVERAL SKATERS ON A FROZEN
WATERWAY oil on panel, 60 x 81.5 s 'F.M. Kruseman'
      Christie's Amsterdam, 26 October 1995 (294**) NLG 29,900   US$ 18,852

KRUSEMAN Jan Adam Jansz. (Haarlem 1804-1862 Haarlem) Dutch
AN ENCOUNTER ON A FROZEN RIVER oil on panel, 25½ x 33½in. (65 x85cm.) sll
      Sotheby's London, 13 March 1996 (4**) GBP 9,775   US$ 14,928

WINTERLANDSCAPE oil on panel, 28.5 x 38.5cm. sd 'A. Kruseman fc 1854'
      Dorotheum Vienna, 17 April 1996 (489**) ATS 220,000   US$ 20,787

KRUYS Cornelis (attr. to) (1645 active from-1702 d. before Haarlem) Dutch
A STILL-LIFE OF A PEONY, A SALVER, LEMONS ON A PLATE, A DISH OF OLIVES,
BREAD, WALNUTS, A KNIFE, A GLASS AND A TANKARD, ALL UPON A TABLE DRAPED
WITH A WHITE CLOTH oil on panel, 17 3/4 x 24 3/4in. (45.5 x 63cm.)
PROV.: With Galerie Arnot, Vienna, 1927, as by Pieter Claesz.; Baron Joseph von Roher, Cologne;
Thence by descent until sold in Sotheby's London, 19 April 1989, lot 166, when purchased by the
present owner.
      Sotheby's London, 6 December 1995 (127**) GBP 15,525   US$ 23,892

KUBIN Alfred (Leitmeritz 1877-1959) Austrian
OPFER DES SATAN ink-drawing, with brown wash, 18 x 17.6cm. (1901)
      Hauswedell & Nolte Cologne, 1 December 1995 (392*) DEM 20,000   US$ 13,76

DIE REISE Pen, ink, watercolour spluttered on paper, 25.4 x 18.3cm. (ca. 1903)
PROV.: Private collection, Vienna.
      Dorotheum Vienna, 21 May 1996 (15**) ATS 220,000   US$ 21,125

KUEHNE Max (1880-1968) American
BROOKLYN BRIDGE IN SNOW oil on canvas, 26¼ x 32¼in. (66.6 x 81.1cm.) slr 'Kuehne' (ca
1912)
PROV.: Hirschl & Adler Galleries Inc., New York.
EXH.: New York, Hirschl & Adler Galleries Inc., *The Early Paintings of Max Kuehne*, 24 Oct.-11
November 1972, no. 4 (illustrated).
      Christie's New York, 1 December 1995 (64**) US$ 40,250   US$ 40,250

KUHN Walt (1880-1949) American
SEATED WOMAN watercolour on paper, 21½ x 13¼in. (54.6 x 33.6cm.) (sheet) sdlr 'Walter Kuhn
'29'
PROV.: Mrs. Bliss Parkinson; Gift to the Museum of Modern Art, New York, from the above, 1965.
      Christie's East, 21 May 1996 (229**) US$ 15,525   US$ 15,525

PEACHES oil on canvas, 25 x 30in. (63.5 x 76.2cm.) sdll 'Walt Kuhn 1941'
PROV.: Estate of the artist; Kennedy Galleries Inc., New York.
EXH.: New York, Kennedy Galleries Inc., *Walt Kuhn: Paintings*, Oct.-Nov. 1967.
      Christie's New York, 23 May 1996 (157**) US$ 23,000   US$ 23,000

KUHNERT Wilhelm (Oppeln 1865-1926 Flims) German
LÖWE UND LÖWIN oil on canvas, 35½ x 48½in. (90.2 x 123.2cm.) s 'W. Kuhnert'
      Christie's London, 11 October 1995 (82**) GBP 78,500   US$ 123,895

THE FLEEING LION oil on panel, 15 7/8 x 30 3/4in. (40.2 x 78.1cm.) slr 'Wilh. Kuhnert' and s and
inscr. 'Wilhelm Kuhnert/Berklin/Löwe Auf der Flucht' on the reverse
PROV.: With the Fine Art Society, London.
      Christie's New York, 28 November 1995 (165**) US$ 184,000   US$ 184,000

KUPKA Frank (Frantisek) (Opocno (Bohemia) 1871-1957 Puteaux) French (Bohemian)
GEOMÉTRIQUE gouache on board, 13 3/8 x 14 3/4in. (34 x 37.5cm.) slr 'Kupka' (ca. 1930)
PROV.: with The Graham Gallery, New York; Private collection, London.
      Phillips London, 24 June 1996 (11**) GBP 8,000   US$ 12,336

KUWASSEG Charles Euphrasie (1838-1904) French
FISHERFOLK ON A BEACH, ETRETAT oil on canvas, 34 7/8 x 52½in. (88 x 133.3cm.) sd 'C.
Kuwasseg/père/1863'
      Christie's London, 14 June 1996 (12**) GBP 19550   US$ 30,146

A RIVERSIDE TOWN oil on canvas, 22¼ x 18¼in. (56.5 x 46.5cm.) sd and inscr. 'C. Kussaweg.
Fils, 1875'
PROV.: With MacConal-Mason and Son, London.
      Christie's South Kensington, 14 March 1996 (38**) GBP 7,475   US$ 11,416

LE VIEUX PONT ROMAIN DE ST. MARTIN, ITALY oil on canvas, 23 x 39½in. (58.4 x
100.4cm.) s 'C. Kuwasseg.' s inscr. 'C. Kuwasseg/Vieux Pont Romain de St. Martin, Italie' on the
reverse
      Christie's New York, 2 November 1995 (58**) US$ 18,400   US$ 18,400

LAC DE GARDE, ITALY AND VUE DE GENES, ITALY oil on canvas, 18 x 29½in. (45.7 x
74.9cm.) sdll 'C.Kuwasegg.fils/1884'
      Christie's East, 30 October 1995 (257*) US$ 14,950   US$ 14,950

KYLBERG Carl (1878-1952) Swedish
MORGON oil on canvas laid down on board, 84 x
100cm. sll 'C. Kylberg'
      Bukowskis Stockholm, 24-25 April 1996
(63**) SEK 640,000   US$ 96,959

INFÖR OÄNDLIGHETEN oil on canvas, 110 x
89.5cm. sll 'Carl Kylberg' (1951)
EXH.: Paris, 1955.
LIT.: Brita Knyphausen, *Carl Kylberg*, cat. no. 256
(illustrated no. 227); (illustrated in colour in the
Paris catalogue).
      Bukowskis Stockholm, 26-27 October
1995 (57**) SEK 1,000,000   US$ 146,451

Inför Oändligheten

DEN FLYGANDE HOLLÄNDAREN oil on canvas, 93 x 111cm. sll 'CK. Utförd' (1946-50)
EXH.: Liljevalch, Konsthall 1954, *Minnesulställningen*, no. 183; Nordiska Konstförbundet svenska
Sektionen, no. 56; Köpenhamn, Konstföreningen, 1956, no. 56; Odense, Fyns stifts konstförening,
1957; Hägerstensåsen, Riksförbundet för Bildande Konst, no. 107 (illustrated in colour on the cover
of the catalogue); Malmö, Konsthall, 1977, no. 107 (illustrated in colour on the cover of the
catalogue); Malmö, Konsthall, 1978-79; Kalmar, Konstmuseum, 1987; Skaraborg, Länsmuseum,
1988; Sala, Aguélimuseet, 1990; Uppland, Konstmuseum, 1991; Östergötland, Länsmuseum, 1992;
Liljevalch, Konsthall 1992, *Strindberg - Kylberg - Book.*

LIT.: Brita Knyphausen, *Carl Kylberg*, catalogue no. 313 (illustrated p. 148).
  Bukowskis Stockholm, 24-25 April 1996 (64**) SEK 760,000   US$ 115,139

MELLAN MAKTERNA oil on canvas, 90 x 115cm. indistinctly sll 'C. Kylerg'; s 'Carl Kylberg' on
the reverse (1931-40)
LIT.: Brita Knyphausen, *Carl Kylberg*, catalogue no. 313 (illustrated p. 148).
  Bukowskis Stockholm, 24-25 April 1996 (66**) SEK 490,000   US$ 74,235

LAANEN Jasper van der (1592-1626) Flemish
A WOODED RIVER LANDSCAPE WITH TRAVELLERS ON A TRACK, A FARMSTEAD
BEYOND oil on panel, 9¾ x 13¾in. 925 x 35cm.)
Christie's South Kensington, 18 April 1996 (170**) GBP 8,625 US$ 13,078

LAANEN Jasper van der (1592-1626) Flemish (Together with Hans Jordaens III)
JOSEPH SOLD INTO SLAVERY oil on canvas, 79.8 x 184.3cm.
Christie's Amsterdam, 13 November 1995 (135**) NLG 32,200 US$ 20,294

LABISSE Félix (Douai 1905-1982) French
LE BAPTEME DU FEU oil on canvas, ,100 x 80cm. sll 'Labisse' and s again and inscr. with title on
the reverse
PROV.: André Janssen, Antwerp.
EXH.: Knokke, Casino communal, *Exposition rétrospective F. Labisse, 2 July-11 September 1960;
Brussels, Societé Auxiliare,* Des expositions du palais des Beaux-arts,1972, no.224; Munich, Haus
der Kunst, *Der Surrealismus*, 11 March-7 May 1972; Paris, Palais du Louvre, *Le Surrealisme*, 9
June-25 September 1972, no. 224.
Christie's Amsterdam, 5 June 1996 (178**) NLG 19,550 US$ 11,423

L'AFFAIRE DE LONGPRÉ oil on canvas, 75 x 102cm. slr 'Labisse' and sd 1970 and inscr. with title
on the reverse
PROV.: Jean Krebs, Brussels.
EXH.: Rotterdam, Museum Boymans-Van Beuningen, *Felix Labisse*, 1972, no. 68.
Christie's Amsterdam, 5 June 1996 (181*) NLG 11,500 US$ 6,719

LE CONSEIL DE SANG oil on canvas, 97 x 130cm. slr 'Labisse' and s again and inscr. with title and
dated 1973 on the reverse and s again on the stretcher
Christie's Amsterdam, 5 June 1996 (183**) NLG 19,550 US$ 11,423

LABITTE Eugène Léon (1835 b.-) French
GUIDING THE GAGGLE oil on canvas, 31 x 43½in. (78.8 x 110.5cm.) sll 'E.LABITTE'
Christie's New York, 22 May 1996 (176**) US$ 18,400 US$ 18,400

LACH Andreas (Eisgrub 1817-1882 Vienna) Austrian
STILL-LIFE WITH GRAPES AND APPLES oil on canvas, 47.5 x 38.5cm. sd 'A. Lach 1834'
Dorotheum Vienna, 17 April 1996 (401**) ATS 180,000 US$ 17,008

**LACROIX Charles François Grenier de, {called} Lacroix de M (Paris, Avignon or Marseille b.
1720-1782 Paris/Berlin) French**
PECHEURS AU CLAIR DE LUNE oil on canvas, 76.5 x 126cm. sdlr 'De Lacroix /..?'
PROV.: Collection of a great amateur/collector from south France.
Étude Tajan Paris, 25 June 1996 (65**) FRF 105,000 US$ 20,275

PECHEURS PRES D'UN RIVAGE MÉDITERRANÉAN AVEC UN VAISSEAU oil on canvas, 95
x 135cm. sdll 'de Lacroix 1771'
PROV.: Collection Thierry Le Luron, before 1987; His Sale, Paris Hotel Drouot 16 June 1987, no.
47.
Étude Tajan Paris, 12 December 1995 (104**) FRF 350,000 US$ 70,499

LADELL Edward (1821-1886) British
GRAPES, HAZELNUTS, A PEACH, RASPBERRIES, A WINE FLUTE, A FLAGON WITH A
METAL COVER AND A TAZZA HOLDING FRUITS ON A WOODEN LEDGE oil on canvas, 18
x 14in. (45.7 x 35.6cm.) s mono. 'EL'
PROV.: With Richard Green, London.
Christie's London, 6 November 1995 (238**) GBP 24,150 US$ 37,776

A STILL LIFE OF GRAPES, PEACHES AND A BUTTERFLY ON A LEDGE oil on canvas, 14 x 12in. (35.6 x 30.5cm.)
PROV.: The Cooling Galleries, London.
Christie's East, 13 February 1996 (38**) US$ 7,475   US$ 7,475

A GILT JUG, A FLUTED WINE GLASS, A TAZZA OF FRUIT WITH A PEACH, GRAPES AND RASPBERRIES ON A TABLE oil on canvas, 19¾ x 16in. (50.2 x 40.7cm.) slr with monogram
PROV.: With Frost & Reed, Ltd., London.
Christie's New York, 2 November 1995 (206**) US$ 23,000   US$ 23,000

BLACK GRAPES ON A CARVED IVORY BOX, PEACHES, WHITECURRANTS AND HAZELNUTS WITH A 'HOCH GLASS' ON A MARBLE LEDGE oil on canvas, 18½ x 15½in. 947 x 39.3cm.) s mono
Christie's London, 7 June 1996 (676**) GBP 45,500   US$ 70,162

LAFARGE John (1835-1910) American
PARADISE VALLEY oil on canvas, 33 1/8 x 42½in. (84.1 x 107.9cm.) (ca. 1866-68)
PROV.: The artist; Doll and Richards Gallery, Boston, Massachusetts; Alice Sturgis Hooper, Boston, Massachusetts; By descent to the present owner.
EXH.: New York, National Academy of Design, *Catalogue of the Fifty-First Annual Exhibition*, Spring 1876, no. 188; Boston, Massachusetts, Doll and Richards Gallery, August 1876; Boston, Massachusetts, Museum of Fine Arts, *Fourteenth Catalogue, Works of Art Exhibited*, 1817, no. 178; Paris, France, Universal Exposition, *Catalogue Officiel public par le Commissariat général*, September 1878, no. 73; New York, Society of American Artists, *Retrospective Exhibition of the Society of American Artists*, December 5-25, 1892, no. 203N; Berlin, Germany, Berlin International Exposition, *Grosse Berliner Kunst-Ausstellung*, May 1-September 29, 1895, no. 961; Paris, France, Bing Gallery, Summer 1896 New York, Century Association, *Exhibition Records of the Century Association*, March 7, 1896; Boston, Massachusetts, Copley Society, Copley Hall, *Illustrated Catalogue: A Loan Collection of Pictures by Old Masters and Other Painters*, 1903, no. 6; New York, American Fine Arts Society, *Comparative Exhibition of Native and Foreign Art*, November 15-December 11, 1904, no. 94; Boston, Massachusetts, Museum of Fine Arts, *La Farge Memorial Exhibition*, January 1-31, 1911; Newport, Rhode Island, Newport Art Association, *Opening of the Howard Gardiner Cushing Memorial: Retrospective Exhibition of Newport Artists*, August 1-15, 1920, no. 21; New York, Wildenstein and Co., *Loan Exhibition of Paintings by John La Farge and His Descendants*, March 1931, no. 3; New York, Metropolitan Museum of Art, *An Exhibition of the Work of John La Farge*, March 23-April 26, 1936, no. 18, illus.; Newport, Rhode Island, Newport Art Association, *Retrospective Exhibition of the Work of Artists Identfied with Newport*, July 25-August 15, 1936, no. 72; New York, Whitney Museum of Amencan Art, *A Century of American Landscape Painting 1800- 1900*, January 19-February 25, 1938, no. 40; Springfield, Massachusetts, Springfield Museum of Fine Arts, MA: *A Century of American Painting and Sculpture, 1862-1932*, March 8-28, 1938, no. 36; New York, Museum of Modern Art, *Art in Our Time*, 1939, no. 42, illus.; Pittsburgh, Pennsylvania, Carnegie Institute, *Survey of American Painting*, October 24-December 15, 1940, no. 135; New York, Knoedler and Co., *Loan Exhibition in Honor of Royal Cortissoz and his 50 Years of Criticism in the New York Herald Tribune*, December 1-20, 1941, no. 26, illus.; Boston, Massachusetts, Museum of Fine *Arts, John La Farge*, February 24-April 24, 1988 and travelling.
LIT.: 'The Fine Arts. Exhibition of the National Academy,' *The New York Times*, April 8, 1876, p. 6; 'The Arts: Representative Pictures at the Academy,' *Appleton's Journal*, vol. 15, April 15, 1876, pp. 509-10; 'Fine Arts: The National Academy Exhibition II,' *The Nation*, vol. 22, April 20, 1876, p. 268; 'The National Academy of Design,' *ArtJournal*, vol. 2, |une 1876, p. 190; 'Art,' *Atlantic Monthly*, vol. 37, June 1876, p. 760; H. James, 'Art,' *Atlantic Monthly*, vol. 38, August 1876, p. 250-52; 'Art Notes,' *Independent*, vol. 28, September 28, 1876, p. 8; 'Local Affairs,' *Newport Journal, September 30, 1876, p. 2; 'Notes,'* Art Journal, vol. 3, September 1877, p. 255 'America at the Paris Exposition,' *Chicago Tribune*, March 24, 1878, p. 11; 'Local Affairs,' *Newport Daily News*, June 4, 1878, p. 2; W.J. Stillman, 'The Paris Exposition IX: American Painting,' *The Nation*, vol. 27, October 3, 1878, p. 211; R. Sturgis, 'The Paris Exhibition XV: The United States Fine Art Exhibit,' *The Nation*, vol. 27, November 28, 1878. p. 331; L. Gonse, ea., 'Exposition Universelle de 1878, Les Beaux- Arts et les

Arts Décoratifs,' *Gazette des Beaux-Arts*, 1879, p. 210; C.E. Clement and L. Hutton, *Artists of the Nineteenth Century and Their Works*, Houghton, Osgood and Company, Boston, Massachusetts, 1879, p. 30; 'Art Notes from Paris,' *Boston Evening Transcript*, April 17, 1879, p. 3; R.C. McCormick, 'Our Success at Paris in 1878,' *North American Review*, vol. 129, July 1879, p. 3; *Reports of the United States Commissioners to the Paris Universal Exposition*, 1878 Government Printing Office, Washington, DC, 188O, p. 112; G.P. Lathrop, 'John La Farge,' *Scribner's Monthly*, vol. 21, February 1881, pp. 510-11; 'Art and Artists,' *Boston Evening Transcript*, April 16, 1884, p. 6; A.B. Dodd, 'John La Farge,' *ArtJournal*, vol. 1, September 1885, p. 262; J.D. Champlin Jr. and C.C. Perkins, *Cyclopedia of Painters and Paintings*, Charles Scribner's Sons, New York, 1887, vol. 3, p. 4; *Appleton's Cyclopaedia of American Biography*, D. Appleton and Company, New York, 1887, vol. 3, p. 586; C. Waern, 'John La Farge, Artist and Writer,' *Portfolio*, vol. 26, April 1896, p. 27; R. Sturgis, 'Considerations of Painting,' *Architectural Record*, vol. 6, October-December 1896, pp. 222-23, illus.; 'The Fine Arts: Loan Exhibition of One Hundred Masterpieces_The American Pictures,' *Boston Weekly Transcript*, March 19, 1897, p. 7; S. Hartmann, *A History of American Art*, L.C. Page and Company, Boston, Massachusetts, 1902, p. 184; R.Johnson and J.H. Brown, eds., *The Twentieth CenturyBiographical Dictionary of Notable Americans*, Biographical Society, Boston, Massachusetts, 1904, vol. 4, n.p. R. Cortissoz, 'John La Farge,' *Outlook*, vol. 84, October 27, 1906, pp. 481-82; E. Knauffl, 'American Painting To-Day,' American Review of Reviews, vol. 36, December 1907, p. 690'Memorial Exhibition of La Farge Paintings,' *Boston Daily Advertiser* December 28, 1910, p. 5; 'The Fine Arts: La Farge's Work,' *Boston Evening Transcript*, December 28, 1910, p. 19; R. Cortissoz, *John La Farge: A Memoir and a Study*, Houghton Mifflin and Company, New York, 1911, pp.122, 127-31, 156, illus.; S.B. Lothrop, 'La Farge Memorial Exhibition,' *Museum of Fine Arts Bulletin*, Boston, Massachusetts, vol. 9, February 1911, p. 8; 'John La Farge: Editorial,' *Art World*, vol. 2, June 1917, p. 209; D.M. Armstrong and M. Armstrong, ea., *Day Before Yesterday*, Charles Scribner's Sons, New York, 192O, pp. 267-68, 303-04; A. Johnson and D. Malone, eds., *Dictionary of American Biography*, Charles Scribner's Sons, New York, 1928-1936, vol. 10, p. 533; G.P. du Bois, 'The Case of John La Farge,' *Arts Magazine*, vol. 17,January 1931, p. 268, illus.; 'The La Farge Exhibition,' *Stained Glass (Providence Journal Bulletin)*, vol. 26, March 1931, p. 83; 'Wildenstein Exhibit Shows La Farge Art For 3 Generations,' *New York Herald Tribune*, March 10, 1931, p. 21; 'The La Farges: Wildenstein Galleries,' *Art News*, vol. 29, March 14, 1931, p. 10; G.P. du Bois, 'John La Farge and His Descendants,' *Arts Magazine*, vol. 17, April 1931, p. 516; J.W. Lane, 'A Family of Painters,' *Commonwealth*, vol. 13, April 1, 1931, p. 598; E.H. Browne, 'Wizard of the Window,' *Columbia* 14, March 1935, p. 19; E.L. Cary, 'John La Farge: A Reminiscent Note,' *New York Times*, March 22, 1936, sec. 11, p. 8; R. Cortissoz, 'From the La Farge Exhibition Opening at the Metropolitan Museum of Art,' *New York Herald Tribune*, March 23, 1936, p. 10, illus.; A.H. Sayre, 'The Complete Work of John La Farge at the Metropolitan,' *Art News*, vol. 34, March 1936, p. 6; E.A. Jewell, 'In the Realm of Art: Comment on New Shows,' *New York Times*, March 29, 1936, sec. 9, p. 8; J.L. Allen, 'Exhibition of the Work of John La Farge,' *Bulletin of the Metropolitan Museum of Art*, vol. 31, April 1936, p. 76; SJ., 'Notes on the La Farge Exhibit,' *America*, vol. 54, May 2, 1936, p.83; W. Preston, *American Biographies*, Harper and Brothers, New York, 1940, p. 587; F. Watson, 'The Land of the Free,' *Magazine of Art*, vol. 33, November 194O, p. 612; 'Carnegie Institute Presents Great Survey of American Painting,' *Art Digest*, vol. 15, November 1, 1940, p. 6, illus.; H. Saint-Gaudens, *The American Artist and His Times*, Dodd, Mead & Company, New York, 1941, p. 153; W.F. Paris, *The Hall of American Artists*, New York University, New York, 1944, p. 56; R.B. Katz, 'John La Farge, Art Critic,' *Art Bulletin*, vol. 33, June 1951, pp. 108-09; R. Berkelman, 'John La Farge, Leading American Decorator,' *South Atlantic Quarterly*, vol. 56, January 1956, p. 40; J.T. Flexner, *Nineteenth Century American Painting*, G.P. Putnam's Sons, New York, 1970, pp. 148-58; RJ. Boyle, *American Impressionism*, New York Graphic Society, Boston, Massachusetts, 1974, p. 76, illus. H. Adams, 'Letter to the Editor,' *Art Bulletin*, vol. 56, December 1974, p. 332; H.B. Weinberg, *The Decorative Work of John La Farge*, Garland Press, New York, 1977, pp. 35, 37, illus.; J.L. Yarnall, 'John La Farge's New England Pasture Land,' *Newport History*, vol. 55, Summer 1982, pp. 79-89, illus.; J.L. Yarnall, 'John La Farge's The Last Valley,' *Newport History*, vol. 55, Fall 1982, p. 131, illus.; H. Adams, 'The Mind of John La Farge, *John La Farge*, Abbeville Press, New York, 1987, p. 29; K.A. Foster, 'John La Farge and the Amencan Watercolor Movement: Art for the 'Decorative Age','John La Farge, Abbeville, New York, 1987, p. 133; J.L. Yarnall, 'Nature and Art in the Painting of John La Farge,'John La

307

Farge, Abbeville Press, New York, 1987, pp. 89-92, illus.; H. Adams, 'John la Farge, the Inventive Maverick,' *Smithsonian*, vol. 18,July 1987, pp. 49, 51, illus.; K.F. Johnson, 'John La Farge,' *Antiques and The Arts Weekly*, September 18, 1987, p. 1, illus.; G.P. Weisberg, 'On the Art and Exhibition of John La Farge,' *Arts Magazine*, vol. 61, October 1987, p. 34; H. Adams, 'John La Farge: America's Genteel Old Master,' *Carnegie Magazine*, vol. 58, November-December 1987, p. 49, illus. ; 'La Farge Expert Speaks at Channing,' Neveport This Week, March 3, 1988, p. 7 W.H. Gerdts, *Art Across America: Two Centuries of Regional Painting 1710-1920*, Abbeville Press, New York, 1990, pp. 91-92, illus.; J.L. Yarnall, John La Farge: Watercolors and Drawings, Hudson River Museum, New York, 1990, p. 26; J.L. Yarnall,John La Farge in Paradise: The Painter and His Muse, William Vaneka Fine Arts, Newport, Rhode Island, 1995, pp. 8, 97, 102-11, 128, 144, 201, 205, illustrated.
UNPUBLISHED MANUSCRIPTS: H.A. La Farge, 'Catalogue Raisonné of the Works of John La Farge' (New Haven, Connecticut: Card File, La Farge Family Papers, Yale University, c. 1934-74), p. 44, oils B. La Farge, 'Paradise Valley' (New Canaan, Connecticut: Ms., Henry A. La Farge Papers, July 1938), p. 2; MJ. File O.S.F., 'An Evaluation of the Aesthetic Principles of John La Farge as Expressed in His Work in Glass' (Washington, D.C.: Ph.D. dies., Catholic University, October, 1945), p. 17; R.B. Katz, 'John La Farge as Painter and Critic' Cambridge, Massachusetts: Ph.D. dies., Harvard University, 1951), illus. fig. 12; E.H. Carell, 'John La Farge: Renaissance Spirit in America' (Austin, Texas: M.A. thesis, University of Texas, May, 1972), pp. 29-31; SJ. Clarke, 'A Chapter in East Meets West' (M.A. thesis, Summer 1973), p. 10; S. Hobbs, 'John La Farge and the Genteel Tradition in American Art' (Ithaca, New York: Ph.D. dies., Cornell University, 1974), pp. 16-17, p. 219, illus.; L.H. Wren, 'The Animated Prism: A Study of John La Farge as Author, Critic, and Aesthetician' (Minneapolis, Minnesota: Ph.D. dies., University of Minnesota, 1978), pp. 53-4, illus. plate 16; PJ. Lefor, 'John La Farge and Japan: An Instance of Oriental Influence in American Art' (Evanston, Illinois: Ph.D. dies., Northwestern University, June, 1978), pp. 6566, 69-72, 100, illus. plate 18; H. Adams, 'John La Farge, 1830-1870: From Amateur to Artist' (New Haven, Connecticut: Ph.D. dies., Yale University, 1980), vol. 1, pp. 287-304; vol. 2, illus. fig. 158 J.L. Yarnall, 'The Role of Landscape in the Art of John La Farge' (Chicago: Ph.D. dies., University of Chicago, 1981), pp. 180, 191, 201-30, illus. fig. 104; K.A. Foster, 'Makers of the Amencan Watercolor Movement: 1860-1890' (New Haven, Connecticut: Ph.D. dies., Yale University, 1982), p. 307.
ARCHIVAL MATERIALS: Vose Gallery Papers, Doll and Richards Gallery, 'List of Pictures by Mr. John La Farge sold by Doll & Richards, Inc. Boston' noting sale on September 7, 1876 to Alice Sturgis Hooper for $3,000; La Farge Family Papers, Yale University Library, entries in account books dating between June 5, 1895 and March 27, 1896 for insurance on picture while in Europe for exhibits; letters in letterpress books on same topic dating between November 25, 1896 and Mary 6, 1896; three individual letters discussing execution of picture, (1) La Farge to Russell Sturgis, December 1, 1904, (2) Russell Sturgis to La Farge, June 16, 1905, (3) La Farge to Grace Edith Barnes, July 25, 1905; Prints and Drawings Department, Museum of Fine Arts, Boston, Loan Card No. 1688.10 (1910) (also numbered 678.17, 225.25, 266.31, and 296.36), noting deposits and loans to the museum. This oilpainting will be included in the forthcoming publication by Yale University Press of the late *Henry La Farge catalogue raisonné* completed by James L. Yarnall and Mary A. La Farge.

Christie's New York, 23 May 1996 (18**) US$ 2,202,500   US$ 2,202,500

LAFRESNAYE Roger Noël François de (Mans (Sarthe) 1885-1925 Grasse (Alpes-Maritimes)) French
NU DEBOUT DEVANT LA CHEMINÉE oil on canvas, 30¼ x 23¼in. (77 x 59cm.) (c1910-11)
PROV.: Paul Chadourne, Paris.
EXH.: Paris, Galerie Barbazanges, *Exposition Rétrospective des Oeuvres de Roger de La Fresnaye*, Dec.1926, no.26; Paris, Petit Palais, *Les Maîtres de l'Art Independent 1895-1937*, June-Oct. 1937, no.24; Paris, Musée National d'Art Moderne, *Roger de la Fresnaye*, July-Oct. 1950, no.32; Sao Paulo, Musée d'Art Moderne, *IIème Biennale de Sao Paulo*, 1953-54, no.70.; Paris, Galerie de l'Institut, *Roger de La Fresnaye*, Nov.-Dec., 1962, no. 7.
LIT.: G. Seligmann, *Roger de la Fresnaye*, with a *catalogue raisonné*, Neuchâtel, 1969, no.69 (illustrated p.134).

Christie's London, 26 June 1996 (276**) GBP 21,850   US$ 33,693

FLEURS ET FEUILLAGE oil on canvas, 59 x 73cm. (ca. 1911)
PROV.: Galerie L. Feigen, New York; Private Collection.
LIT.: Germain Seligman, *Roger de La Fresnaye,Catalogue raisonné*, Editions Ides et Calendes,
Neuchâtel, 1969, illustrated p. 162, no. 155.
      Étude Tajan Paris, 28 March 1996 (36*) FRF 120,000   US$ 23,720

LAGOOR Johan (1645 - 1671 active) Dutch
A WOODED RIVER LANDSCAPE oil on canvas, 65 x 81cm. slr 'Lagoor'
PROV.: The 3rd Lord Northwick, Northwick Park, by 1864, and by descent to Captain E.G. Spencer-
Churchill, Northwick Park; sold, London, Christie's, 29 October 1965, lot 29.
EXH.: London, Royal Academy, *Dutch Art 1450-1900*, 1929, no. 502b, with companion; London,
Royal Academy, *Dutch Pictures 1450-1750*, 1952-53, no. 290.
LIT.: *Catalogue of the Pictures, Works of Art, etc. at Northwick Park*, 1864, no. 195, as by Verboom;
T. Borenius, *A Catalogue of the collection of pictures at Northwick Park*, 1921, no. 197; M.D.H., in
U. Thieme, F. Becker, *Allgemeine Lexicon der Bildenden Künstler*, vol. XXII, 1928, p. 219; M.
Schneider and W.G. Constable, *A Commemorative Catalogue of the Exhibition of Dutch Art 1450-
1900*, 1930, p. 70; G.S. Keyes, 'Jan Lagoor', in *Tableau*, 1979, no. 3, p. 36, no. 21 (illustrated).
      Sotheby's Amsterdam, 14 November 1995 (21**) NLG 41,300   US$ 26,029

LAGRENÉE Louis Jean François {called} Lagrenée L'Ainé (Paris 1725-1805 Paris) French
MOTHERS AND CHILDREN IN CLASSICAL INTERIORS oil on canvas (a pair), 9¾ x 14¼in.
(24.8 x 36.2cm.) s 'Lagrenée' (1777)
EXH.: (possibly) Salon 1777, no. 6, as 'deux petits tableaux de femmes et d'enfants'.
LIT.: M. Snadoz, *Les Lagrenée,* Paris, 1983, p. 251, nos. 296-7.
      Christie's London, 8 December 1995 (306**) GBP 13,800   US$ 21,237

A YOUNG LADY HOLDING A MUSIC SCORE / A YOUNG LADY CARESSING A PIGEON oil
on canvas (a pair of ovals), each: 81.3 x 65.2cm.) (before 1755)
PROV.: Collection Lalive de July, bought from the Artist at 840gns.; Sale Lalive, Paris, 1770 lot 119.
EXH.: Paris, Salon 1755, no. 126.
LIT.: M. Sadoz, *Les Lagrenée, I, Louis Lagrenée*, Paris 1983, pp. 86 and 166.
      Christie's Monaco, 14 June 1996 (38**) FRF 245,700   US$ 47,444

LAHAYE Reinier de (The Hague 1640-1695 Antwerp) Dutch
INTERIOR WCENE WITH A LADY STANDING PLAYING THE CITTERN oil on panel, 11¾ x
9½in. (30.3 x 24.1cm.) sll 'R DLe Haye'
PROV.: With Ger. Douwes, Amsterdam, by 1924; Anonymous sale, London, Christie's, 2 augustus
1946, lot 158, when sold with the certificate of Dr. Gustav Gluck, bought by Koetser; Hutchinson,
Knocklofty, County Tipperary, Ireland, according to a wax seal on the reverse.
LIT.: W. Bernt, *The Netherlandish Painters of the 17th Century*, 1969, vol. I, no. 482 (illustrated).
      Sotheby's London, 5 July 1995 (154**) GBP 8,050   US$ 12,841

LAHYRE Laurent (attr.) (1606-1656) French
LANDSCAPE WITH A WATERFALL, A HERDSMAN WITH COWS, SHEEP AND A GOAT oil
on panel, 41¼ x 31¼in. (104.8 x 79.4cm.) inscr. lr 'De Marne' (ca. 1653)
      Sotheby's New York, 16 May 1996 (44**) US$ 11,500   US$ 11,500

LAIRESSE Gérard de (Liège 1640-1711 Amsterdam) Flemish
VENUS AND CUPID AT THE FORGE OF VULCAN oil on canvas, 48 x 75 7/8in. (1670-80)
      Christie's London, 19 April 1996 (251**) GBP 36,700   US$ 55,648

LAISSEMENT Henri Adolphe (l-1921 d.) French
A GOOD HAND oil on panel, 21 x 25¾in. (53.3 x 65.4cm.) slr 'H. Laissement'
EXH.: Cincinnati, Taft Museum, *Cavaliers and Cardinals*, June 25-August 16, 1992 (this exhibition
later travelled to Washingtin, D.C., Corcoran Gallery of Art, September 19-November 15, 1992, and
Elmira, New York, Arnot Art Museum, November 21, 1992-January 17, 1993).

LIT.: E.M. Zafran, *Cavaliers and Cardinals*, Cincinnati, 1994, pp. 56-57 (illustrated).
    Christie's New York, 2 November 1995 (166**) US$ 17,250 — US$ 17,250

LALLEMAND Jean Baptiste (Dijon 1710-1803 Paris) French
LE REPOS DES BERGERS PRES DE LA RIVIERE oil on canvas, 116 x 113.5cm. slr indistinctly 'Lall.. P.. du Roi'
    Étude Tajan Paris, 28 June 1996 (123***) FRF 90,000 — US$ 17,379

LALLEMENT Georges (1575-1636) French
A STANDING MALE FIGURE IN ORIENTAL DRESS pen and brown ink and wash, silhouetted and laid down, 34.1 x 15.7cm. (between 1616-27)
PROV.: Jacques Petit-Hory.
EXH.: Norwich, Castle Museum, *The Northern Eye*, 1987, as *Jacques Bellange*.
    Sotheby's London, 3 July 1995 (115**) GBP 14,375 — US$ 22,930

LAM Wifredo (Sagua la Grande 1902-1982 Paris) Cuban
SENZA TITOLO oil on canvas, 50 x 70cm. sdll 'W. Lam 1965' (1965)
    Finearte Milan, 19 March 1996 (44**) ITL 32,200,000 — US$ 20,601

UNTITLED pastel on paper, 28¾ x 22 7/8in. (73.2 x 58.2cm.) sdlr 'W Lam 1959'
PROV.: Galerie Solomon, Paris.
    Sotheby's London, 21 March 1996 (24**) GBP 6,900 — US$ 10,538

COMPOSITION oil on canvas, 19¾ x 27½in. (50 x 70cm.) sd 'Wifredo Lam 1973'
PROV.: Renée Lachowsky, Brussels.
    Christie's London, 26 October 1995 (13**) GBP 18,975 — US$ 29,948

TOTEM oil on canvas, 50 x 40cm. sd and ini. lr (1967)
    Finearte Milan, 26 October 1995 (172**) ITL 23,000,000 — US$ 14,330

LAMB, R.H.A., R.U.A. Charles Vincent (1893-1964) Irish
A FISHERMAN WITH POLLAN oil on canvas, 24 x 20in. (61 x 51cm.) slr 'Lamb'; sd and inscr. 'A Fisherman with Pollan by C. Lamb 1926' on the backboard
EXH.: Dublin, Royal Hibernian Academy, 1926, no. 49.
LIT.: K. McConkey, *A Free Spirit Irish Art, 1860-1960*, London, 1990, pl. 45.
    Christie's London, 9 May 1996 (67**) GBP 18,975 — US$ 28,733

LAMBERT George (Kent 1700-1765) British
A WOODED RIVER LANDSCAPE, WITH FIGURES ON A PATH AND OTHERS CROSSING A BRIDGE IN THE FOREGROUND, A RUINED CASTLE VISIBLE BEYOND oil on canvas, 43 x 51in. (109.2 x 129.5cm.) sd, lc 'G. Lambert/1755'
PROV.: Painted for John Russell, 4th Duke of Bedford and by descent to the 12th Duke of Bedford; Christie's 19 January 1951, lot 30 (ll0gns. to the present owner).
LIT.: G. Scharf, *A Descriptive and Historical Catalogue Collection of Pictures at Woburn Abbey*, 1890, no. 383; E. Einberg, *George Lambert, Catalogue for the Exhibition*, Kenwood, Iveagh Bequest, 1970, under no. 28.
    Christie's London, 10 November 1995 (35**) GBP 13,800 — US$ 21,586

LAMBINET Émile Charles (1815-1877) French
APPLE PICKERS oil on canvas, 18¼ x 29in. (46.3 x 73.7cm.) sdlr 'Emile Lambinet 67.'
PROV.: with Watson Art Galleries, Montreal; with Imperial Galleries, Montreal.
    Christie's East, 13 February 1996 (92**) US$ 8,970 — US$ 8,970

LAMEN Christoffel Jacobsz. van der (1606/15-1651) Flemish
ELEGANT COMPANY oil on panel, 45 x 63cm.
    Dorotheum Vienna, 6 March 1996 (128**) ATS 140,000 — US$ 13,467

LAMPI Johann Battista II (1775-1837) Italian
PORTRAIT OF DR. JOHN ROGERSON, HALF LENGHT, IN A BLUE COAT oil on canvas, 25
7/8 x 22in. (70.2 x 55.9cm.) sdll 'Lampi filius [?]/pinxit 1797'
    Christie's London, 10 November 1995 (19**) GBP 10,925   US$ 17,089

LANCE George (1802-1864) British
FRUIT AND FLOWERS ON A STONE LEDGE oil on canvas, 29 x 41¼in. (73.7 x 104.8cm.) sdlr
'G Lance./1829'
PROV.: The Duke of Bedford; With The Wilton Gallery, London.
    Christie's New York, 2 November 1995 (205**) US$ 46,000   US$ 46,000

LANCIANO Polidoro da, {called} Polidoro Veneziano (1515 <circa>-1565) Italian
THE HOLY FAMILY WITH SAINTS ROCH AND ANTHONY ABBOT oil on canvas, 33¼ x 47in.
(84.7 x 119.5cm.)
PROV.: Possibly Gustav Rochertz, Berlin, 1920 (according to a photograph in the Witt Library,
Wilde Bequest).
    Sotheby's London, 5 July 1995 (121**) GBP 27,600   US$ 44,026

THE MADONNA AND CHILD WITH TOBIAS AND THE ANGEL oil on panel, 21 5/8 x 33½in.
(54.2 x 85.6cm.); with an added strip of approximately ½in. along the bottom edge
PROV.: Possibly Thomas Pitt, Wimpole street; (†) Christie's, London, May 25, 1833, lot 124 as
Giorgone (unsold); Captain E.G. Spencer-Churchill, M.C., Northwick Park; (†) Christie's, London,
May 28, 1965, lot 18 as *Bonifazio dei Pitati* [sic.], where purchased by the present owner.
LIT.: *Arundel Club Portfolio*, 1912, No. 7; B. Berenson, *Italian Pictures of the Renaissance:
Venetian School*, 1957, I, p.43 as *Bonifazio de'Pitati*. J. Pope-Hennessy, *Learning to Look*, 1991, p.
314.
    Christie's New York, 10 January 1996 (100**) US$ 51,750   US$ 51,750

SACRA CONVERSAZIONE oil on canvas, 90 x 111cm.
    Finearte Rome, 21 May 1996 (58**) ITL 25,300,000   US$ 16,249

LANCRET Nicolas (1690-1743) French
UM NÄCHTLICHES FEUER TANZENDE GESELLSCHAFT oil on linen, 77 x 109cm. sdll
'Lancret 1726'
PROV.: Private collection, Berlin.
    Lempertz Cologne, 15 November 1995 (1304**) DEM 210,000   US$ 148,221

LANDELLE Charles Zacharie (1812-1908) French
AN ORIENTAL BEAUTY oil on canvas, 24¼ x 20in. (61.5 x 50.8cm.) s 'Ch. Landelle'
    Christie's London, 15 March 1996 (123**) GBP 13,800   US$ 21,075

LANDSEER Sir Edwin Henry, R.A. (1802-1873) British
A POINTER GUARDING HIS KENNEL oil on board, 11½ x 95/8in. (29.3 x 24.5cm.)
PROV.: Sir John Fowler; Christie's, 6 May 1899, lot 67 (42gns. to Sampson); with W. Boswell &
Son, Norwich.
    Christie's London, 6 November 1995 (229**) GBP 8,970   US$ 14,031

NO HUNTING TILL THE WEATHER BREAKS oil on canvas, 27½ x 36½in. (69.9 x 92.7cm.)
PROV.: Bought from the artist by Henry William Eaton, later 1st Baron Cheyselesmore; sale,
Christie's, 7 May 1892, lot 46 (700gns.); With Leger Galleries (by 1953); H. A Sutch; Mrs. M.
Galvao; sale, Christie's, 13 February 1976, lot 60 (£1,700 to Cross); E. J. H. Cross; Ian Posgate.
EXH.: London, British Institution, 1865, no. 189; London, Royal Academy, *The Works of the Late
Sir Edwin Landseer, R.A.*, Winter 1974, no. 397; London, Grosvenor Gallery, *Works of Art
Illustrative of and Connected with Sport*, Winter 1890, no. 6; Philadelphia, Museum of Art, *Sir
Edwin Landseer*, October 25, 1981-January 3, 1982; this exhibition later traveled to London, Tate
Gallery, February 10-April 12, 1982, no. 152.

LIT.: *Art Journal*, 1865, p. 74; *The Times*, February 6, 1865, p. 5e; *Athenaeum*, no. 1946, February 11, 1865, p. 203; C.S. Mann, *Landseer Prints, 1874-1877*, London, 3, p. 18, 4, p. 126; A. Graves, *Catalogue of the Works of the Late Sir Edwin Landseer R.A.*, London, 1876, p. 33, no. 415.

Christie's New York, 28 November 1995 (48**) US$ 134,500	US$	134,500

THE DEER PASS '*I AM MONARCH OF ALL I SURVEY, MY RIGHT THERE IS NONE DARE DISPUTE*' oil on canvas, 39 x 84in. (99.1 x 213.4cm.)
PROV.: Commissioned by Captain Sir William Peel, R.N., V.C.; By descent to the Rt. Hon. Sir Frederick Peel by 1876; The Hon. George Peel; sale, Christie's, October 5, 1945, lot 121 (546 gns. to Leggatt); The 15th Lord Lovat, DSO, MC, TD, JP, DL, Thence by descent.
EXH.: London, British Institution 1852, no. 58.
LIT.: *Art Journal*, 1852, p. 70. 'the Late Sir Edwin Landseer', 1874; *Illustrated London News*, 21 February 1852, p. 147; *Athenaeum*, no. 1269, February 21, 1852, p. 231; A. Graves, *Catalogue of the Works of the late Sir Edwin Landseer*, R.A., London, 1876, p. 30, no. 378; J. A. Manson, *Sir Edwin Landseer, R.A.*, London, 1902, p. 147.

Christie's New York, 28 November 1995 (81**) US$ 398,500	US$	398,500

LANFRANCO Giovanni, {called} Giovanni di Stefano (Terenzo (near Parma) 1582-1647 Rome) Italian
THE HOLY FAMILY WITH THE INFANT SAINT JOHN THE BAPTIST oil on copper, 16½ x 12 3/8in. (42 x 31.5cm.) (1606-7)

Christie's London, 8 December 1995 (99**) GBP 32,200	US$	49,554

LANGEVELD Franciscus Arnoldus (Frans) (Amsterdam 1877-1939 Laren (N.-Holland)) Dutch
A HORSE-DRAWN CARRIAGE ON A SNOWY BRIDGE, AMSTERDAM oil on canvas, 51 x 65.5cm slr 'frans langeveld'

Christie's Amsterdam, 26 October 1995 (168*) NLG 14,950	US$	9,426

LANGHAMMER Artur (Lützen 1854-1901 Dachau) Austrian
MÄDCHEN IN WEIßEM KLEID oil on canvas, 116.5 x 79.3cm. (ca. 1900)
PROV.: Collection Arthur Roessler.

Wiener Kunst Auktionen, 26 March 1996 (139**) ATS 220,000	US$	21162

LANSKOY André (Moscow 1902-1976 Paris) French (Russian)
LE SENS DIRECT ET OPPOSÉ oil on canvas, 73 x 100cm. sll 'Lanskoy', inscr. with title and dated on the reverse '57' and numbered on the stretcher 'no. 5669' (1957)
PROV.: Galerie Louise Carré and Co., Paris.

Christie's Amsterdam, 5 June 1996 (323**) NLG 32,200	US$	18,814

CAMOUFLAGE oil on canvas, 65 x 50cm. sal 'Lanskoy' and inscr. with title on the reverse.

Christie's Amsterdam, 6 December 1995 (303**) NLG 33,350	US$	20,666

LES TERRES BLEUES oil on canvas, 38¼ x 57½in. (97 x 146cm.) sur 'Lanskoy' d titled on the reverse (1960)
PROV.: Galerie Europe, according to an old label on the reverse.

Étude Tajan Paris, 13 December 1995 (71**) FRF 180,000	US$	36,257

ÉTEIGNEZ LES LUMIERES oil on canvas, 57½ x 38¼in. (146 x 97cm.) sdll 'Lanskoy '64'
PROV.: Galerie Rambert, Paris; Aquired from the above by the present owner in 1988.
LIT.: This work will be included in the forthcoming *André Lanskoy catalogue raisonné* being prepared by André Schoeller.

Christie's London, 19 March 1996 (9**) GBP 18,400	US$	28,100

UNTITLED oil on canvas, 39½ x 28¾in. (100.5 x 73cm.) sdlr 'LANSKOY, Nov.'63'
LIT.: This work will be included in the forthcoming *André Lanskoy Catalogue Raisonné* being

prepared by André Schoeller.
Christie's London, 19 March 1996 (13**) GBP 14,950   US$ 22,831

COMPOSITION oil on canvas, 823 5/8 x 28¾in. (60 x 72.5cm.) slr 'Lanskoy' (1960)
PROV.: Galerie Pittiglio, Paris.
Sotheby's London, 21 March 1996 (14**) GBP 10,350   US$ 15,806

FINALE oil on canvas, 57½ x 38¼in. (145.5 x 97.2cm.) sd titled '60' on the reverse
PROV.: Fabian Carlsson, Gothenburg; acquired from the above by the present owner.
LIT.: To be included in the forthcoming *André Lanskoy Catalogue Raisonné* being prepared by
André Schoeller.
Christie's London, 23 May 1996 (42**) GBP 19,550   US$ 29,603

LAQUY Willem (Cologne 1738-1798 Cleve) German
KITCHENMAID WASHING THE DISHES FROM A BARREL oil on canvas, 53.5 x 44cm. sdmr
'Laquy pinx.1778'
Dorotheum Vienna, 6 March 1996 (172**) ATS 150,000   US$ 14,429

LARGILLIERE Nicolas de (Paris 1656-1746 Paris) French
PORTRAIT OF CATHERINE GUIMONT DU COUDRAY oil on canvas, 44½ x 33in. (113 x
83.8cm.)
PROV.: Legoupy, Paris 1922; Newhouse Galleries, New York, there acquired by the present owner
in 1957.
EXH.: Possibly Salon of 1704.
Sotheby's New York, 16 May 1996 (115**) US$ 134,500   US$ 134,500

PORTRAIT DU MARQUIS D'HAVRINCOURT oil on canvas, 82.5 x 65cm.
PROV.: Collection Comtesse of Northbrook, London before 1949; Galerie Wildenstein & Co, 1949;
Anonymous sale, New York, Sotheby's, 14 January 1988, lot 194 (illustrated in colour).
Étude Tajan Paris, 25 June 1996 (50**) FRF 120,000   US$ 23,172

LARKIN William (active ca. 1610/20-) British
PORTRAIT OF A LADY oil on panel, 40 x 36in. (101.6 x 91.4cm.)
PROV.: Coe Foundation (Sale: Parke-Bernet, Inc., New York, 19 November 1961, lot 20, as Anglo-
Flemish School); there purchased by Maurice H. Rosenblatt, from whom acquired by Lewis J.
Ruskin, Scottsdale, Arizona; Thence by descent to the present owner.
EXH.: Phoenix, Arizona, Phoenix Art Museum (on loan).
LIT.: Sir Roy Strong, *The English Icon*, 1969, p. 333, cat. no. 360, (illustrated) (as *Larkin*, and a
companion to another portrait of a lady, datable circa 1615).
Sotheby's New York, 16 May 1996 (19**) US$ 40,250   US$ 40,250

LARSSON Carl (Stockholm 1853-1919 Falun) Swedish
ANN-STINA watercolour and pastelcrayon on paper, 65 x 54.5cm. s mono. and dlr 'Sundborn 1905'
LIT.: Görel Cavalli-Björkman, *Carl Larsson Porträttmålaren*, 1992, p. ,100 (illustrated p. 101).
Bukowskis Stockholm, 29 November-1 December 1995 (82**) SEK 205,000   US$ 31,012

KARIN OCH ESBJÖRN oil on canvas, 94 x 122cm. sdlr 'C.L. Till Suzanne 1909'
EXH.: Liljevalch, Liljevalchs Konsthall, *Minnesutställningen*, 1920 and 1953; Lund, Lunds
Konsthall 1970-71; Göteborg, Göteborgs Konstmuseum, 1971; Helsingfors, Blaafverveket, Modum,
Sommaren med Carl Larsson, 1989; Danmark, Århus Konstmuseum 1989-90; National museum,
Carl Larsson, 1992; Göteborg, Göteborgs Konstmuseum, *Carl Larsson*, 1993; Tokyo, *Carl Larsson*,
1994.
LIT.: *Konst i Svenska hem*, vol. II:I, p. 209; H. & S. Alfons, *Carl Larsson - skildrad av honom själv*
(illustrated in colour p. 122); Langewiesche-Königstein, *Carl Larsson värld* (illustrated in colour p.
127).
Bukowskis Stockholm, 29 November-1 December 1995 (86**) SEK 1,525,000   US$ 230,699

313

TRÄDGÅRDSMÄSTAREN oil on canvas, 62 x 47cm. s 'C.L.' (1883)
EXH.: Nationalmuseum, *Opponenter av år 1885*, 1945; Liljevalch, Liljevalchs Konsthall,
Minnesutställningen, 1953; Helsingfors, Amos Andersons Konstmuseum, *Carl Larsson*, 1981;
Norway, Blaafarveverket, Modum, *Sommaren med Carl Larsson*, 1989; National museum, *Carl
Larsson*, 1992; Göteborg, Göteborgs Konstmuseum, *Carl Larsson*, 1993; Tokyo, *Carl Larsson*,
1994.

Bukowskis Stockholm, 29 November-1 December 1995 (88**) SEK 600,000	US$	90,767

LASH Lee American
42ND STREET, NEW YORK oil on canvas, 25 x 29¾in. (63.5 x 75.5cm.)
PROV.: Acquired directly from the artist by the previous owner.

Christie's East, 21 May 1996 (174**) US$ 17,250	US$	17,250

LASKE Oskar (Czernowitz 1874-1951 Vienna) Austrian
AUS DEM WURSTELPRATER gouache on paper, 53.8 x 36.6cm. sdlr 'O.Laske 1943'

Wiener Kunst Auktionen, 26 March 1996 (225**) ATS 250,000	US$	24,048

REINECKE FUCHS. GERICHT gouache on paper, 43 x 54cm. sdlr 'O. Laske 1932' twice; titled ll

Wiener Kunst Auktionen, 26 September 1995 (254**) ATS 90,000	US$	8,748

LASSNIG Maria (Kappel, Kärnten 1919 b.) German
TRAURIGE TRAUBEN oil on canvas, 24 x 41cm. sdlr '1982 M. Lassnig'; sd and titled 'M. Lassnig
1982' on the reverse on the frame

Wiener Kunst Auktionen, 26 March 1996 (433**) ATS 120,000	US$	11,543

ANTROPOMORPHE LANDSCHAFT oil on three-ply wood, 35 x 49.5cm. sdlr 'Lassnig 1995'
PROV.: Galerie Heide Hildebrand, Klagenfurt.
LIT.: Wieland Schmied, catalogue from Galerie Klewan, *Maria Lassnig, Bilder, Zeichnungen,
Aquarell, Grafik. 1946-1986*, Munich, 2 June-8 August 1992 (illustrated).

Wiener Kunst Auktionen, 27 September 1995 (440**) ATS 100,000	US$	9,720

DER NABEL DER WELT mixed technique on paper, 60 x 85.5cm. sdlr 'M. Lassnig 52'

Wiener Kunst Auktionen, 27 September 1995 (443**) ATS 100,000	US$	9,720

LASTMAN Pieter (1583-1633) Dutch
THE SACRIFICE OF MANOAH oil on panel, 72 x 53cm. sdll 'P.Lastman 1624'
EXH.: Amsterdam, Rembrandthuis, *Pieter Lastman, the man who taught Rembrandt*, 1991, cat. 18,
pp. 120-121.

Sotheby's Amsterdam, 14 November 1995 (67**) NLG 318,600	US$	200,794

LATOIX Gaspard (1890-1910, active) American
INDIAN ON HORSEBACK IN A DESERT LANDSCAPE oil on canvas, 32 x 23½in. (81.5 x
60cm.) sll 'Latoix'

Christie's New York, 13 March 1996 (86**) US$ 20,700	US$	20,700

LATOUCHE Gaston (1854-1913) French
LE TELEPHONE oil on panel, 30½ x 22in. (77.5 x 56cm.) s 'Gaston la Touche
PROV.: The Artist's studio sale; with Galerie Georges Petit, Paris, 1919, no. 37.
EXH.: Japan, Yomiuri Shimbun, *Women of Fashion: French and American Images of Leisure, 1880-
1920*, 1994, no. 70 (illus. in colour p. 82); The Hague, Boussod, Valadon et Cie, May 1913, no. 18;
Paris, Société Nationale des Beaux-Arts, 1914, no. 725; To be included in Roy Brindley and Selina
Evans' *forthcoming catalogue raisonné on Latouche*.

Christie's London, 17 November 1995 (34**) GBP 8,625	US$	1,3491

LAUGE Achille (1861-1944) French
LES MEULES A CAILHAU oil on canvas, 19¾ x 28¾in. (50 x 73cm.) sdll 'A.Laugé '29'
    Phillips London, 24 June 1996 (51**) GBP 7,000   US$ 10,794

LAURENCIN Marie (Paris 1885-1956 Paris) French
JEUNE FILLE A LA GUITARE oil on canvas, 21 5/8 x 18 1/8in. (55 x 46cm.) sur 'Marie Laurencin'
PROV.: Anon. sale, Parke-Bernet galleries, New York 1951, lot 33.
LIT.: This painting will be included in the fortcoming supplement *catalogue raisonné Marie Laurencin*.
    Christie's New York, 1 May 1996 (347**) US$ 123,500   US$ 123,500

LES DEUX FILLES oil on canvas, 18 x 15in. (46 x 38cm.) sur 'Marie Laurencin' (ca. 1950)
LIT.: This painting will be included in the forthcong supplement to the *Laurencin catalogue raisonné*.
    Christie's New York, 1 May 1996 (360**) US$ 129,000   US$ 129,000

ANEMONES IN A BLUE VASE oil on canvas, 49 x 64.5cm. sdll 'Marie Laurencin 1933'
EXH.: Daniel Marchesseau, *Marie Laurencin 1883-1956, catalogue raisonnéde l'oeuvre peint*, éditions du Musée Marie Laurencin, Japan, 1986, p. 247, no. 564.
    Étude Tajan Paris, 27 October 1995 (28**) FRF 275,000   US$ 55,625

JEUNE FILLE BLONDE EN ROUGE oil on canvas, 16 x 13in. (40.5 x 33cm.) sdur 'Marie Laurencin 1938'
LIT.: To be included in the forthcoming supplement to the *Laurencin catalogue Raisonné*.
    Christie's London, 29 November 1995 (205**) GBP 19,000   US$ 29,720

TETE DE JEUNE FILLE watercolour over pencil on paper, 13 7/8 x 10 3/8in. (35.3 x 26.4cm.) lr 'Marie Laurencin'
    Christie's New York, 8 November 1995 (225**) US$ 17,250   US$ 17,250

LAURENS Nicolas Auguste (1829-1908) French
A NUDE oil on canvas, 164 x 106cm. s 'N.A. Laurens'
    Christie's Amsterdam, 25 April 1996 (164*) NLG 9,200   US$ 5,467

LAURENT L. unknown
A FISHERMAN'S FAMILY oil on canvas, 25½ x 36¼in. (64.6 x 92.1cm.) slr 'L. Laurent'
    Christie's East, 20 May 1996 (42*) US$ 11,500   US$ 11,500

LAURI Filippo (Rome 1623-1694) Italian
DIANA AND ACTAEON oil on canvas, 29¼ x 38 3/8in. (74.3 x 97.5cm.) s 'Philipp Laura. f.'
LIT.: L. Salerno, *Pittori di paesaggio del seicento a Roma*, 1976, II, pp. 684 and 688, fig. 116.3.
    Christie's New York, 10 January 1996 (96**) US$ 13,800   US$ 13,800

LANDSCAPE WITH VENUS AND ADONIS oil on canvas, 98 x 130cm. s
    Finearte Rome, 21 May 1996 (101**) ITL 41,400,000   US$ 26,590

LAVAGNA Francesco (Napels, active 18th century, 2nd half-) Italian
STILL-LIFES OF FRUIT, FLOWERS AND PORCELAIN oil on canvas (a pair), each: 17½ x 31in. (44.6 x 78.7cm.)
    Sotheby's London, 17 April 1996 (87**) GBP 17,250   US$ 26,156

LAVERY Sir John, R.A., R.S.A., R.H.A. (Belfast 1856-1941) Irish
TANGIER, WHITE CITY oil on canvas, 24 x 32in. (61 x 81.4cm.) sd inscr.'Tangier - The White City J. Lavery 93', with an inscription on the reverse 'John Lavery The White City Tangier by John Lavery 75 Chelsea Gardens SW'
PROV.: Leicester Galleries, London.

EXH.: Ghent, 1902 (not traced); Berlin, Schulte Gallery, *John Lavery*, 1904 (not traced); London, Goupil Gallery, *John Lavery*, August 1908, no.51.
LIT.: W. Shaw-Sparrow, *John Lavery and his Work*, London, 1912, pp.3, 184, 189; K. McConkey, *Sir John Lavery,* Edinburgh, 1993, p.92, pl.2.

Christie's London, 21 November 1995 (131**) GBP 69,700	US$	109,025

THE WINTER SUN, HYDE PARK CORNER oil on panel, 25 x 30in. (63.5 x 76.2cm.) sll 'J Lavery' sd inscr. 'The Winter Sun Hyde Park Corner By Sir John Lavery R.A., LL.D. 1925' on the reverse
PROV.: Fine Art Society, London, Dec. 1973; Oscar and Peter Johnson, London.

Christie's London, 21 November 1995 (133**) GBP 31,050	US$	48,569

MARIA CARMI oil on canvas, 30 x 25in. (76.2 x 63.5cm.) sll 'J. Lavery'; sd and inscr. 'Maria Carmi by John Lavery 5 Cromwell Place London W14' on the reverse

Christie's London, 9 May 1996 (72**) GBP 16,675	US$	25,250

A WET DAY, CONCARNEAU oil on canvas, 11¼ x 13¼in. (28.5 x 33.7cm.) sll 'J. Lavery'; s and inscr. ' A wet day Concarneau J. Lavery 5 Cromwell Place London SW' on the stretcher (1904)
EXH.: London, Leicester Galleries, *Cabinet Pictures by John Lavery*, Nov. 1904, no. 29 as 'A Grey Day at Concarneau'.
LIT.: W. Shaw-Sparrow, *John Lavery and his Work*, London, 1911, p. 185; K. McConkey, *Sir John Lavery*, Edinburgh, 1993, p. 90, pl 101.

Christie's London, 9 May 1996 (75**) GBP 37,800	US$	57,238

SIDI-BU-SAID, TUNIS oil on canvas, 15 x 21½in. (38 x 54.6cm.) sll 'J Lavery'; sd and inscr. 'Sidi-bu-Said Tunis by John Lavery 1919' on the reverse

Christie's London, 9 May 1996 (125**) GBP 20,700	US$	31,345

THE AMBULANCE TRAIN oil on canvas-board, 25 x 30in. (63.5 x 76.2cm.) sdll and inscr. 'Dover J. Lavery 1918; sd and inscr. 'The Ambulence [sic.] Train 1917 by John Lavery' on the reverse
PROV.: The Hon. Mrs. Holt, the Artist's granddaughter.

Christie's London, 9 May 1996 (127**) GBP 21,850	US$	33,086

LA DAME AUX PERLES oil on canvas, in. 58¼ x 38¼in.(148 x 97.3cm.) slr 'J. Lavery'; sd and inscr. 'The Baroness von Hoelrigl (sic) La Dame aux Perles replica painted by John Lavery 1925' on the reverse
LIT.: K. McConkey, *Sir John Lavery, R.A. 1856-1941*, Ulster Museum exhibition catalogue, Belfast, 1984, p. 58.

Christie's London, 9 May 1996 (128**) GBP 84,000	US$	127,196

PORTRAIT OF A LADY SEATED ON A SOFA oil on canvas, 73 47in. (185.5 x 119.4cm.) sll 'J. Lavery' (ca 1900)
PROV.: The Hon. Mrs. Holt, the Artist's granddaughter.

Christie's London, 9 May 1996 (129**) GBP 17,250	US$	26,121

POTRAIT OF PHYLLIS IN A WHITE DRESS oil on canvas, 30½ x 25½in. (77.5 x 64.8cm.) sll 'J. Lavery'; s and inscr. 'Phyllis John Lavery 5 Cromwell Place London SW' on the reverse
PROV.: Barbizon House, London; Ian MacNicol, Glasgow; Anon. sale, Christie's, 4 Nov. 1966, lot 46 (55gns. to Brall); Anon. sale, Christie's, 13 Nov. 1986, lot 83, where purchased by the present owner.
EXH.: London, Goupil Gallery, *John Lavery*, June -July 1908, no. 53.

Christie's London, 9 May 1996 (130**) GBP 34,500	US$	52,241

LAVILLÉON Emmanuel Victor Auguste Marie de (1858-1944) French
LANDSCAPE oil on canvas, 92 x 61cm. sll 'La Villeon' numb '3358' on the reverse

Étude Tajan Paris, 1 February 1996 (120**) FRF 70,000	US$	14,325

LAWRENCE Sir Thomas, P.R.A. (1769-1830) British
JOHN PHILIP KEMBLE (1757-1823) AS ROLLA IN SHERIDAN'S 'PIZARRO' oil on canvas, 132 x 88in. (335.3 x 223.5cm.) (1799-1800)
PROV.: Sir Robert Peel, 2nd Bart., London, by whom acquired from the artist circa 1827; Peel Heirlooms (Sale: Robinson and Fisher, May 10-11, 1900, lot 214); Blakeslee (Sale: New York, April 23, 1915, lot 227); Mrs. E. W. Schields by whom given to the present owner in 1947.
EXH.: London, Royal Academy, 1800, no. 193; London, British Institution, 1806, no. 46; London, British Institution, 1844, no. 144; Kansas City, Missouri, Nelson-Rockhill Gallery (now Nelson-Atkins Museum of Art), from 1947.
LIT.: J. Farington, *The Diary of Joseph Farington*, 1978-84, under February 11, 1800 and February 24, 1803; D. E. Willams, *The Life and Correspondence of Sir Thomas Lawrence, Kt.*, 1831, Vol. I, p. 207; R. S. Gower, *Sir Thomas Lawrence*, 1900, p. 140; W.Armstrong, *Lawrence*, 1912, p. 143; K. Garlick, 'A Catalogue of the Paintings, Drawings and Pastels of Sir Thomas Lawrence,' *The Walpole Society*, XXXIX, 1964, p. 116; K. Garlick, *Sir Thomas Lawrence*, 1989, p. 216, no. 451C (where it is located incorrectly).
    Sotheby's New York, 11 January 1996 (104**) US$ 162,000   US$ 162,000

STUDY FROM NATURE, THE SOURCE OF THE MANIFOLD AT ILAM PARK oil on paper laid on canvas, 17½ x 27in. (44.5 x 68.6cm.) (ca 1790)
PROV.: William Russell; Christie's, 23 February 1861, lot 161 or 162, as 'Sir Thomas Lawrence, P.R.A., A small woody Landscape, with figures by Stothard, R.A.' or 'The Companion' (each bought in at GBP2.15s.; William Russell; Christie's, 6 December 1884, lot 81, with the companion (8gns. to Buttery); Thomas Agnew & Sons; Christie's, 18 June 1920, lot 83, with the companion (6gns. to Maitland); Colonel M.H. Grant, by 1925.
EXH.: London, Burlington Fine Arts Club, *English Paintings and Drawings c. 1780-1830*, 1933, no. 11; Bristol, City Art Gallery, *Sir Thomas Lawrence*, 1951, no. 32; London, The Arts Council of Great Britain, *Early English Landscapes from Colonel Grant's Collection*, 1952-3, no. 32; Arthur Tooth, November-December 1953, no. 14; London, Royal Academy, *Sir Thomas Lawrence, P.R.A., 1769-1830*, 1961, no. 32; Oxford, Ashmolean Museum, on loan, 1992-96.
LIT.: Col. M.H. Grant, *The Old English Landscape Painters*, Leigh-on-sea, 1925, II, p. 202, pl. 121; K. Garlick, *Sir Thomas Lawrence*, London, 1954, p. 64, pl. 20; Anon., review of the exhibition, *The Times*, 28 October 1961, p.4 'The two early landscapes which so uniquely illustrate a capacity for landscape painting, otherwise confined to the backgrounds of the portraits'; K. Garlick, *A catalogue of the paintings, drawings and pastels of Sir Thomas Lawrence,* The Walpole Society, 39, 1964, p. 209; K. Garlick, *Sir Thomas Lawrence, A complete Catalogue of the oil paintings*, Oxford, 1989, no. 890, pl. 7b; K. Garlick, *Two Lawrence Landscapes*, The Ashmolean, 1993, pp. 15-20, fig. 2.
    Christie's London, 18 April 1996 (25**) GBP 188,500   US$ 285,823

STUDY FROM NATURE: A VIEW OF DOVEDALE LOOKING TOWARDS THORPE CLOUD oil on paper laid on canvas, 17½ x 27in. (44.5 x 68.6cm.) (ca 1790)
PROV.: William Russell; Christie's, 23 February 1861, lot 161 or 162, as 'Sir T. Lawrence, P.R.A., A small woody Landscape, with figures by Stothard, R.A.' or 'The Companion' (each bought in at GBP2.15s.); William Russell; Christie's, 6 December 1884, lot 8, with the companion (8gns. to Buttery); Thomas Agnew and Sons; Christie's, 18 June 1920, lot 83, with the companion (6gns. to Maitland); Colonel M.H. Grant, by 1925.
EXH.: London, Burlington Fine Arts Club, *English Paintings and Drawings c. 1780-1830*, 1933, no. 19; Bristol, City Art Gallery, *Sir Thomas Lawrence*, 1951, no. 33; London, The Arts Council of Great Britain, *Early English Landscapes from Colonel Grant's Collection*, 1952-3, no. 33. Arthur Tooth, November-December 1953, no. 13; London, Royal Academy, *Sir Thomas Lawrence, P.R.A., 1769-1830*, 1961, no. 34; Oxford, Ashmolean Museum, on loan, 1992-96.
LIT.: Col. M.H. Grant, *The Old English Landscape Painters*, Leigh-on-sea, 1925, II, p. 202, pl. 121; K. Garlick, *Sir Thomas Lawrence*, London, 1954, p. 64, pl. 21; Anon., review of the exhibition, *The Times*, 28 October 1961, p. 4 'the two early landscapes which so uniquely illustrate a capacity for landscape painting, otherwise confined to the backgrounds of the portraits'; K. Garlick, 'A Catalogue of the paintings, drawings and pastels of Sir Thomas Lawrence', *The Walpole Society*, 39, 1964, p.209; K. Garlick, *Sir Thomas Lawrence, A complete catalogue of the oil paintings*, Oxford, 1989,

no.890, pl. 7a; K. Garlick, *The Lawrence Landscapes*, The Ashmolean, 1993, pp. 15-20, fig. 1.

Christie's London, 18 April 1996 (26**) GBP 265,500 — US$ 402,578

PORTRAIT OF FREDERIC LOCK OF NORBURY PARK, SURREY, BUST-LENGTH, IN A
BLACK COAT WITH A WHITE STOCK black, white and red chalk and stump on paper laid on
canvas, 23½ x 18¾in. (59.7 x 49.6cm.)
PROV.: By descent from the sitter to The Lord Wallscourt and thence to The Hon. Mrs. Leycester
Storr, and by descent to the present owner.
EXH.: Paris, *Exposition des pastellistes anglais du XVIII siècle*, 1911, no.82.

Christie's London, 30 November 1995 (5***) GBP 71,900 — US$ 112,467

LAWSON Ernest (1873-1939) American
THE EXCURSION BOAT oil on canvas, 25½ x 30½in. (64.7 x 77.5cm.) sll 'E. Lawson'
PROV.: Private Collection; Kennedy Galleries, New York; Mr. and Mrs. Frank Sinatra.

Christie's New York, 1 December 1995 (71**) US$ 156,500 — US$ 156,500

LOW TIDE oil on board laid down on panel-unframed, 8 x 9in. (20 x 24cm.) slc 'E.Lawson'

Christie's East, 28 November 1995 (186*) US$ 8,050 — US$ 8,050

OCEAN SHACK, KEY WEST, FLORIDA oil on canvas, 12¼ x 16in. (31 x 41cm.) slr 'Lawson'
PROV.: Berry-Hill Galleries, New York'.
LIT.: H. and S. Berry-Hill, *Ernest Lawson, American Impressionists*, Leigh-on-Sea, england 1968,
no. 128 (illustrated and illustrated on the cover).

Christie's New York, 23 May 1996 (90**) US$ 23,000 — US$ 23,000

WOODED LANDSCAPE WITH POND oil on canvas, 24¼ x 30in. (61½ x 76cm.) sll 'E Lawson'

Christie's New York, 23 May 1996 (92**) US$ 85,000 — US$ 85,000

SEGOVIA, SPAIN oil on canvas, 20 x 24½in. (50.8 x 62.2cm.) sll 'E Lawson'
PROV.: Dr. and Mrs. T.E. Hanley; ACA Galleries, New York; Bernard Danenberg Galleries Inc.,
New York.
EXH.: Hanley Gallery of Modern Art, no. 72.
LIT.: H. and S. Berry-Hill, *Ernest Lawson, American Impressionists*, Leigh-on-Sea, England 1968,
no. 48.

Christie's New York, 23 May 1996 (93**) US$ 145,500 — US$ 145,500

LAZZELL Blanche (1878-1956) American
STILL LIFE WITH JUG AND ORANGES oil on canvas, 18¼ x 16in. (46.3 x 40.6cm.) sdll 'Blanche
Lazzell 1918'

Christie's New York, 13 September 1995 (108**) US$ 9,200 — US$ 9,200

LE BAELLIEUR Cornelis (Antwerp 1607-1671 Antwerp) Flemish
THE WEDDING AT CANA oil on copper, 56 x 73cm.

Étude Tajan Paris, 26 March 1996 (1*) FRF 67,000 — US$ 13,496

LE KERMADEC Eugène Nestor (1879-1970) french
BACCHANTES -2EME VERSION oil on canvas, 39 3/8 x 28¾in. (,100 x 73cm.) sll 'E de
Kermadec' inscr. with title on the stretcher d '1953' on a gallery label on the reverse
PROV.: Galerie Louise Leiris, Paris, 1953; The Mayor Gallery, London.

Phillips London, 26 June 1995 (89**) GBP 4,200 — US$ 6,702

LEADER Benjamin Williams, R.A. (1831-1923) British
THE HAYFIELD oil on artist's board, 131/4 x 171/2in. (33.7 x 44.5cm.) sd 'B.W. Leader 1866' and s
inscr. 'The Hayfield/B.W. Leader' on the reverse
PROV.: John Blagburn; Christie's, 5 April 1884, lot 189 (63 gns. toMendoza); H.L.W. Lawson,
1902; The Rt. Hon. Viscountess Burnham; With Cooling Galleries, London.

EXH.: London, *West Ham Free Picture Exhibitions,* Easter 1902.
        Christie's London, 6 November 1995 (150**) GBP 12,075   US$ 18,888

A FINISHED STUDY FOR 'BY MEAD AND STREAM' oil on canvas, 36 x 60½in. (91.5 x 153.7cm.) sdll 'B.W.Leader./1893.'
PROV.: With Arthur Tooth, London; With Polak Gallery, London; Harrods, 1967.
LIT.: Connoiseur, March 1967.
        Christie's New York, 2 November 1995 (219A**) US$ 29,900   US$ 29,900

A RELIC OF THE PAST oil on canvas, 36¼ x 57¾in. (92 x 146.6cm.) sd 'B.W. Leader 1897' and s inscr. 'Relic of the .. B.W. Leader' on the reverse
PROV.: Sold by the Artist to Thos. Agnew & Sons for GBP,500 in December 1897; With Leggatt Bros., London, 1898; Joel Sale, Knight, Frank & Rurley, London 7-12 December, 1931; F.J. Lawes; Christie's 11 December 1942, lot 101 (65 gns. to Thompson).
LIT.: F.W. *Lewis Benjamin Williams Leader, R.A., 1831-1923,* 1971, p. 46, no. 406.
        Christie's London, 29 March 1996 (124**) GBP 24,150   US$ 36,881

LEAR Edward (1812-1888) British
THE ACROPOLIS, ATHENS pencil, pen and brown ink and watercolour heightende with white on grey paper, 12 x 19in. (30.5 x 48.3cm.) d inscr. and numbered 'Athens/5.6.9.June. /1848/9'
PROV.: With Agnew's, London.
        Christie's London, 2 April 1996 (85**) GBP 21,850   US$ 33,131

LEBASQUE Henri (Champigné, Main-et-Loire 1865-1937 Le Cannet, Alpes-Maritimes) French
PAYSAGE AU PRINTEMPS oil on canvas, 38 1/8 x 51 1/8in. (97 x 130cm.) sll with ini. 'L.' (ca. 1913)
PROV.: Manor Circle Gallery, New York; Maxwell Galleries Ltd., San Francisco (acquired by Richard Smart, 1969).
        Christie's New York, 1 May 1996 (160**) US$ 99,300   US$ 99,300

ROUTE DE CAMPAGNE, PONT ET CABRIOLET oil on canvas, 19¾ x 24in. (50 x 61cm.) slr 'Lebasque' (1895)
        Étude Tajan Paris, 10 June 1996 (9**) FRF 90,000   US$ 17,379

MAISONS SUR LE PORT A L'ILE D'YEU oil on canvas, 46 x 55cm. slr
        Étude Tajan Paris, 17 June 1996 (56*) FRF 92,000   US$ 17,765

RUE ANIMÉE A MONTEVRAIN oil on canvas, 25¾ x 21½in. (65.4 x 54.6cm.) sll 'H. Lebasque' (ca. 1900)
LIT.: This work will be included in the forthcoming *catalogue raisonné* by Denise Bazetoux.
        Sotheby's New York, 2 May 1996 (183**) US$ 118,000   US$ 118,000

AUTOMNE oil on canvas, 28 x 28in. (71.1 x 71.1cm.) sdll 'Lebasque 1900'
PROV.: M. Henri Vian, Paris (sold: Paris, Galerie Georges Petit, November 27, 1919, lot 23).
EXH.: Paris, Galerie Georges Petit, *Henri Lebasque*, 1907, no. 23.
LIT.: This work will be included in the forthcoming *catalogue raisonné* by Denise Bazetoux.
        Sotheby's New York, 2 May 1996 (184**) US$ 145,500   US$ 145,500

FILLETTE DEVANT UN VASE POSE SUR LA TABLE oil on board, 16 x 13in. (40.5 x 33cm.) slr with initials (ca. *1904*)
LIT.: This work will be included in the forthcoming *catalogue raisonné* on this artist currently being prepared by Madame Bazetoux.
        Phillips London, 26 June 1995 (9**) GBP 7,000   US$ 11,170

LES ENFANTS DANS UN VERGER EN FLEURS oil on canvas, 30½ x 42¼in. (77.5 x 107.5cm.)
slr 'Lebasque' (1914)
PROV.: Galerie Georges Petit, Paris; anon. sale, Hotel Drouot, Paris 14dec. 1981; Galerie Paul
Pétridès, Paris, by whom bought at the above sale.
LIT.: To be included in the *Lebasque catalogue raisonné* currently being prepared by Denise
Bazetoux.
      Christie's London, 26 June 1996 (148**) GBP 42,200   US$ 65,073

BORDS DE LA MARNE oil on canvas, 25¼ x 31½in. (64 x 80cm.) slr 'H. Lebasque'
PROV.: Purchased by the present owner's stephfather in the 1940's.
LIT.: To be included in the *Lebasque catalogue raisonné* currently being prepared by Denise
Bazetoux.
      Christie's London, 26 June 1996 (158**) GBP 71,900   US$ 110,871

LA MARNE A LAGNY oil on canvas, 21½ x 28 7/8in. (54.5 x 73.4cm.) slr 'H Lebasque'
      Christie's South Kensington, 27 November 1995 (22**) GBP 10,125   US$ 15,838

NATURE MORTE AU PANIER DE FRUITS oil on cardboard, 25 3/8 x 29½in. (64.5 x 75cm.) sll
'Lebasque'
EXH.: Paris, Musée Gallièra, *Exposition Célébrités et Révélations de la Peinture Contemporaine*,
March 1953; Nice, Musée de Nice, *Exposition Henri Lebasque*, no. 68.
      Christie's London, 29 November 1995 (191**) GBP 16,000   US$ 25,027

PAYSAGE A LA VASQUE FLEURIE oil on canvas laid down board, 19¾ x 16 1/8in. (50.4 x
41cm.) slr 'Lebasque' (ca. 1914)
      Christie's East, 7 November 1995 (62**) US$ 11,500   US$ 11,500

FILLETTE DEVANT UN VASE oil on board, 16 x 13in. (40.5 x 33cm.) lr 'H.L.' (ca 1904)
      Christie's New York, 8 November 1995 (159**) US$ 29,900   US$ 29,900

JEUNE FILLE A LA FENETRE EN FACE DE L'ILE D'YEU oil on canvas, 21 5/8 x 18 1/8sin. (55
x 46cm.) sll 'Lebasque'
PROV.: M. Lepelletier, Vosges.
LIT.: P. Vitry, *Henri Lebasque*, Paris, 1928, p. 115.
      Christie's New York, 8 November 1995 (176**) US$ 26,450   US$ 26,450

LEBOURG Albert Charles (Montfort-sur-Risle 1849-1928 Rouen) French
AVENUE A MAISONS-LAFITTE 1895 oil on canvas, 18 x 25 3/8in. (46 x 64.5cm.) sd 'Maisons
Lafitte 1895'
PROV.: Athur Tooth & Sons Ltd. London.
LIT.: To be included in the *Lebourg Catalogue raisonné* being prepared Wildenstein Institute.
      Sotheby's London, 20 March 1996 (23**) GBP 16,100   US$ 24,588

LE PORT DE ROUEN oil on canvas, 18 1/8 x 24in. (46 x 61cm.) sll 'alebourg'
      Phillips London, 27 November 1995 (15**) GBP 4,000   US$ 6,257

LEBRET Frans (Dordrecht 1820-1909 Dordrecht) Dutch
CATTLEHERD IN A LANDSCAPE oil on panel, 42 x 56cm. s
      A. Mak B.V. Dordrecht, 21 June 1996 (205*) NLG 10,000   US$ 5,843

SHEEP IN A BARN oil on canvas, 105 x 40cm. s 'Fr Lebret ft'
      Christie's Amsterdam, 26 October 1995 (164*) NLG 14,950   US$ 9,426

LEBRUN Charles (Paris 1619-1690 Paris) French
STUDY FOR TWO FIGURES: A MAN SUPPORTING A WOMAN red chalk heightened with
white chalk on buff paper, 30.2 x 29.5cm. (ca. 1649)

PROV.: Eugène David (L.839).
        Sotheby's London, 3 July 1995 (124**) GBP 8,625   US$ 13,758

LEBRUN Christopher (1951 b.)
RED HORSE (IPHIGENIA) oil on canvas-unframed, 105 x 86in. (266.6 x 218.5cm.) sd and titled
'CHRISTOPHER LEBRUN 30.3.87-26.5.87 'RED HORSE (IPHIGENIA)" on the reverse
PROV.: Ingrid Raab Gallery, Berlin; Private collection, San Fransisco.
        Christie's New York, 22 February 1996 (116**) US$ 16,675   US$ 16,675

LECK Bart Anthony van der (Utrecht 1876-1958 Blaricum) Dutch
COMPOSITIE NO. 1 oil on canvas, 46.5 x 56cm. sd inscr. on the reverse 'BvdLeck'18 no.1'
PROV.: Mrs. H. Kröller-Müller, The Hague, from 1918 until 1928.
EXH.: The Hague, Museum Kröller-Müller, Lange Voorhout, *Tentoonstelling van werken door Bart
van der Leck*, 20 July - 15 September 1927, no. 38 Otterlo, Kröller-Müller Museum, *Bart van der
Leck*, 10 September - 27 November 1994, no.80 (ill. in colour p. 58).
LIT.: Catalogue, *Verzameling van Mevrouw H. Kröller-Müller deel II: Verzameling op 1 januari
1921*, The Hague, 1928, p. 149; W.C. Feltkamp, *B.A. van der Leck, leven en werken*, Leiden 1956, p.
95, no. 80; C. Hilhorst, 'Bart van der Leck' in C. Blotkamp a.o., *De beginjaren de stijl* 1917-
1922, Utrecht 1982, p.179, p.; 174 (ill. in colour) English edition, *De Stijl:The formative years* 1917-
1922, Cambridge/London, 1986, p.174.
        Christie's Amsterdam, 5 June 1996 (254**) NLG 276,000   US$ 161,262

Compositie No. 1

DRIE PAPAVERS; THREE POPPIES oil
on canvas, 37 x 45cm. sdur with initials
'BvdL '21'
PROV.: Mrs. Smith-Van Stolk, Rotterdam.
EXH.: Rotterdam, Rotterdamsche
Kunstkring, *Tentoonstelling van werk van
B. van der Leck,* 24 Sept.-16 Nov. 1927, no.
42; Otterlo, Kröller-Müller Museum, *Bart
van der Leck,* 10 Sept. - 27 Nov. 1994,
no.101, p.79 (illustrated in colour).
LIT.: W.C. Feltkamp, *B.A. van der Leck,
leven en werken*, Leiden 1956, p. 95, no.
101, wrongly described as *drie Orchideeën.*
        Christie's Amsterdam, 5 June
1996 (255**) NLG 115,000   US$ 67,193

DESIGN FOR A TAPESTRY pencil and watercolour on paper, 45 x 33.5cm. with atelier stamp an
numbered 'no. 369' pencil and watercolour on paper.
PROV.: Estate of the artist.
        Christie's Amsterdam, 5 June 1996 (256**) NLG 13,800   US$ 8,063

LEE Doris Emrick (1905 b.) American
PROSPECTOR'S HOME NEAR PHANTOM GULCH oil on canvas, 27 x 22in. (68.5 x 56.3cm.) slr
'Doris Lee'; s and inscr. 'Prospector's Home' on the stretcher
PROV.: Associated American Artists, New York; Virginia Museum of Fine Arts, Richmond.
        Christie's East, 28 November 1995 (38**) US$ 8,625   US$ 8,625

LEE Frederick Richard, R.A. (1798-1879) British
A VIEW OF GARIBALDI'S VILLA AT CAPRERA, SARDINIA oil on canvas, 30 x 50¼in. (76.2 x
127.6cm.) sdlr 'F.R. Lee, R.A./1869' and inscr.'No 2/General Garibaldi's Residence at Caprera/from
sketches taken on the island/F.R. Lee R.A.' on an old label on the reverse
EXH.: London, Royal Academy, 1869, no. 199, as *Garibaldi's recidence at Caprera*, from sketches
taken on the island.
        Christie's London, 10 November 1995 (42**) GBP 16,100   US$ 25,184

LEE Man Fong (1913-1988) Chinese
THE MOUNTAINPEAK WU-I IN THE TJO SAN LING MOUNTAINS, SOUTH CHINA oil on
board, 61 x 91cm. sdll 27th November 1956 and inscr. with title in chinese
Sotheby's Amsterdam, 23 April 1996 (17**) NLG 68,440   US$ 40,668

A COCKEREL AND A HEN oil on board, 99 x 47cm. s in Chinese and stamped with the artist's
name in Chinese and d '1950'
PROV.: The collection of Mr. Tan Tek Peng, Jakarta. The Artist was commissioned to make the
painting for a room in his house in Jakarta.
Sotheby's Amsterdam, 23 April 1996 (65**) NLG 165,200   US$ 98,164

A COUPLE OF RABBITS oil on board, 99 x 47cm. s in Chinese and stamped with the artist's name
in Chinese and d '1950'
PROV.: The collection of Mr. Tan Tek Peng, Jakarta. The Artist was commissioned to make the
painting for a room in his house in Jakarta.
Sotheby's Amsterdam, 23 April 1996 (66**) NLG 129,800   US$ 77,129

LEEMANS Johannes (The Hague 1633 c.-1688) Dutch
STILL-LIFE WITH BIRDS AND HUNTING PARAPHERNALIA oil on canvas, 43¾ x 52½in. (111
x 133.5cm.) sdlc '1679'
PROV.: Madame Ganna Walska, Santa Barbara.
Sotheby's London, 5 July 1995 (248**) GBP 23,000   US$ 36,688

STILL LIFE WITH BIRD HUNTING INSTRUMENTS oil on canvas, 40 x 39 1/8in. (101.6 x
99.4cm.) s on the bottom of the net container *J. Leemans.*
PROV.: Leger Galleries, London, 1959; Schaeffer Galleries, New York, from whom acquired by the
present owner (Acc. no. 64.30).
EXH.: Los Angeles, University Galleries, University of Southern California; Seattle, Seattle Art
Museum; Honolulu Academy of Art; Santa Barbara, Santa Barbara Museum Art, *Reality and
Deception*, 1974-75, cat. no. 41 (by Donald J. Brewer and Alfred Frankenstein); Bellevue,
Washington, Bellevue Art Museum, *European and American Paintings from the Seattle Art Museum
Collection*, November 1975.
LIT.: 'Notable Works of Art now on the Market,' *The Burlington Magazine*, December 1959,
Supplement, illus. plate XIV; Peter C. Sutton, *A Guide to Dutch Art in America*, 1986, pp. 285, 340.
Sotheby's New York, 11 January 1996 (27**) US$ 37,375   US$ 37,375

LEEN Willem van (Dordrecht 1753-1825 Delfshaven) Dutch
PEACHES, PLUMS AND GRAPES IN A VASE WITH A POMEGRANATE, NASTURTIUMS
AND A SNAIL ON A LEDGE oil on panel, 16 ¼ x 12 1/8cm.) s 'van Leen. f.'
PROV.: With Antiques and Old Masters, Ltd., London.
Christie's London, 19 April 1996 (137**) GBP 16,100   US$ 24,412

LEES Derwent (1885-1931) British
COAST AT COLLIOURE oil on panel, 10 x 14in. (25.3 x 35.5cm.) sd 'Lees 1911' s 'Lees' on the
back
PROV.: F.B.C. Bravington.
EXH.: London, Redfern Gallery, Derwent Lees, May 1934, no. 10.
Christie's London, 20 June 1996 (38**) GBP 10,925   US$ 16,847

LEFAUCONNIER Henri Victor Gabriel (1881-1946) French
VILLAGE DANS LA MONTAGNE pencil and oil on canvas, 56.5 x 47.5 cm. (executed *circa* 1912)
Christie's Amsterdam, 5 June 1996 (245b*) NLG 13,800   US$ 8,063

LÉGER Fernand (Argenan 1881-1955 Gif-sur-Yvette) French
STILL-LIFE oil on canvassed cardboard, 33 x 41cm. sdlr 'F.Léger 30'
Finearte Milan, 12 December 1995 (302**) ITL 82,800,000   US$ 51,945

LA BICYCLETTE pen and ink on paper, 11½ x 17¾in. (29.5 x 45in.) sd mono 'Fl 44'
    Étude Tajan Paris, 13 December 1995 (34*) FRF 190,000   US$ 38,271

L'INSECTE DANS LA FLEUR (INSECT ON THE FLOWER) oil on canvas, 28¾ x 36¼in. (73 x 92cm.) sdlr 'F.LEGER 49' (1949)
PROV.: Former collection Mazurel.
    Étude Tajan Paris, 13 December 1995 (65**) FRF 770,000   US$ 155,098

LES AMOUREUX gouache on paper, 24½ x 19¾in. (62.2 x 50.2cm.) slr with ini.
PROV.: Estate of the artist.
EXH.: Paris, Grand Palais, *Comment peindre la Joconde*, 1977 (and travelling in Japan in 1987); Paris, Galerie Felix Vercel, *Centénaire de Fernand Léger*, 1981.
    Sotheby's New York, 2 May 1996 (323**) US$ 134,500   US$ 134,500

LA COUVERTURE DANS LE PAYSAGE oil on canvas, 19¾ x 25¾in. (50.2 x 65.4cm.) sdlr '49 F.LEGER'
    Sotheby's New York, 2 May 1996 (324**) US$ 118,000   US$ 118,000

LA POUPÉE BLEUE oil on canvasboard, 23 5/8 x 19 5/8in. (60 x 50cm.) sdlr 'F.LEGER 43' sd titled on the reverse
PROV.: Bergruen & Cie., Paris; Sale, Christie's London 1December 1980, lot 35 (purchased by the present owner at GBP16,000).
    Sotheby's London, 20 March 1996 (64**) GBP 128,000   US$ 195,480

LES TROIS FIGURES oil on canvas, 25 5/8 x 21¼in. (65 x 54cm.) sd 'F Léger 21' s titled and inscr. on the reverse '1er état'
PROV.: Galerie Louise Leiris, Paris; Galerie Beyeler, Basel; Svensk-Franska Konstgalleriet, Stockholm; Ragnar Sandberg, Stockholm; Hokin Gallery, Palm Beach .
EXH.: Stockholm, Liljevalchs Konsthall, *Fran Cezanne till Picasso*, 1954, no. 70; Copenhagen, Charlottenborg, *Efterarsudstillingen*, 1959, no. 6; Stockholm, Moderna Museet, *Fernand Léger*, 1964, no. 17b; Geneva, Galerie Bonnier, *H. Laurens, F. Léger*, 1974, no. 16.
LIT.: Georges Bauquier, *Fernand Léger, Catalogue raisonné, 1920-1924*, Paris, 1992, p. 150, no. 287, illustrated.
    Sotheby's London, 24 June 1996 (54**) GBP 1,101,500   US$ 1,698,535

COMPOSITION AVEC FIGURE oil on canvas, 25½ x 36¼in. (65 x 92cm.) sdlr 'F.LÉGER 30'; annotated 'definitif' and d on the reverse
PROV.: Galerie Louise Leiris, Paris; Galerie Beyeler, Basel; Purchased by the family of the present owner from the above in 1970.
EXH.: Basel, Galerie Beyeler, *Fernand Léger*, 1964, no. 29, illustrated in the catalogue; Stockholm, Moderna Museet, *Fernand Léger 1881-1955*, 1964, no. 40; Vienna, Museum des 20. Jahrhunderts, *Fernand Léger*, 1968, no. 28; Basel, Galerie Beyeler, *Fernand Léger*, 1969, no. 23, illustrated in colour in the catalogue; Düsseldorf, Städtische Kunsthalle, *Fernand Léger, 1969-70*, no. 59 (illustrated in colour in the catalogue).
LIT.: *XXe Siècle, Hommage à Fernand Léger*, Paris, 1971, p. 40 (illustrated in colour); Georges Bauquier, *Fernand Léger, Catalogue raisonné'1929-1931*, Paris, 1995, p. 218, no. 736 (illustrated).
    Sotheby's London, 24 June 1996 (58**) GBP 221,500   US$ 341,557

L'AVIATEUR oil on canvas, 19¾ x 25½in. (50.2 x 64.8cm.) sdlr 'F. LEGER' sd and titled L'aviateur 2e état' on the reverse (1920)
PROV.: Galerie Simon, Paris, 1930 (6070); Ethel King Russell, Newport, Rhode Island; Mrs John S. N. Russel, Newport, Rhode Island; Anon. sale; Sotheby Parke-Bernet, New York, 27 April 1972, lot 93 (illustrated in colour, $96,000);Marlborough Fine Arts, London, where purchased by the present owner in 1974.
EXH.: New York, Museum of Modern Art, *Fernand Leger*, Sept.-Oct. 1935; New York, Sidney Janis Gallery, Early Leger, 1951; London, Marlborough Fine Art, *Selected European Masters of the 19th*

and 20th Century, June-Sept.1973, no. 38 (illustrated in colour p. 77).
LIT.: *The Bulletin of the Museum of Modern Art*, New York, vol. I, no. 3, October 1935; G. Bauquier, *Fernand Leger Catalogue Raisonné, L'Oeuvre Peint 1920-1924*, vol. II, Paris, 1992, no. 205 (illustrated in colour p. 27 and erroneously described as l er état).

Christie's London, 25 June 1996 (27**) GBP 1,079,500   US$ 1,664,611

LA GRANDE PARADE gouache on paper, 26 x 31 7/8in. (66 x 81cm.) sd ini. 'F.L. 51'
PROV.: Private collection, Paris, purchased by the present owner before 1961.
EXH.: Requested for Leger: Five Themes and Variations held the Solomon Guggenheim Museum, New York, in 1962.
LIT.: L. Carré, 'La Vie dans l'Oeuvre de Léger' in *Cahiers d'Art*, no. 2, 1954, p. 143 (illustrated); to be included in the *catalogue raisonné of Léger's gouaches* currently being prepared by Georges Bauquier.

Christie's London, 25 June 1996 (52**) GBP 309,500   US$ 477,255

COMPOSITION CIRCULAIRE oil on canvas, 25½ x 36¼in. (64.8 x 92cm.) sdlr '49F. LEGER' and sd and titled on the reverse 'Composition Cirulaire, F. LEGER 49' (1949)
PROV.: Galerie Louise Leiris, Paris (13398); Anon. Sale, Sotheby's, London, 12 april 1972, lot 41 (GBP12,000; illustrated in colour).

Christie's London, 28 November 1995 (29**) GBP 111,500   US$ 174,410

NATURE MORTE (LE COMPAS) oil on canvas, 36 1/8 x 25¼in. (92 x 65.2cm.) sdlr 'F.LéGER 26' sd titled on the reverse 'NATURE-MORTE'
PROV.: Galerie Simon (Daniel-Henry Kahnweiler), Paris; Galerie Louise Leiris, Paris; G.F. Reber, Lausanne; Galerie Koller, Zurich; Anon. sale; Sotheby's, New York, Nov. 14, 1984, lot 61(illustrated in color); Sidney Janis Gallery.
EXH.: New York, Sidney Janis Gallery, *Exhibition of Paintings by Fernand Léger*, Dec., 1984-Jan., 1985, no. 20A.
LIT.: W. George, 'Fernand Leger,' *L'amour de l'art*, Paris, Aug., 1926, p. 263 (illustrated); W. George, *Fernand Léger*, Paris, 1929, p. 19 (illustrated); G. Bauquier, *Fernand Léger, Catalogue raisonné*, Paris, 1993, vol. III (1925-1928), p. 116, no. 459 (illustrated in color, p. 117).

Christie's New York, 30 April 1996 (45**) US$ 365,500   US$ 365,500

DAVID TRIOMPHANT gouache, pen, black ink and pencil on paper, image size: 4½ x 7in (11.4 x 17.8cm.); sheet size: 5½ x 8½in. (14 x 21.5cm.) stamped with ini. ll 'F.L.' (1935-1936)
PROV.: Alex Maguay, Paris.

Christie's East, 30 April 1996 (150*) US$ 8,050   US$ 8,050

LES TROIS FEMMES ET L'ENFANT oil on canvas, 36 1/4 x 28¾in. (92.1 x 75.5cm.) sdlr 'F. LEGER 52'; sd and titled 'F. LEGER 52 Les 3 femmes et l'enfant' on the reverse
PROV.: Theodore Schempp & co., New York; Acquired from the above by the late owner on April 30, 1954.

Christie's New York, 7 November 1995 (56**) US$ 882,500   US$ 882,500

L'ÉTÉ oil on canvas, 14 1/4 x 56 1/2in. (36.2 x 143.5cm.) lr 'F.LEGER 29' (1929)
PROV.: Galerie Louise Leiris, Paris; Léonce Rosenberg, Paris; Curt Valentin Gallery, inc., New York (acquired by the late owner, 1952).

Christie's New York, 8 November 1995 (206**) US$ 96,000   US$ 96,000

NATURE MORTE AUX FRUITS oil on canvas, 18 1/8 x 13in. (46 x 33cm.) lr 'F.LÉGER. 39' again on the reverse 'F.Léger. 39 nature morte aux fruits' (1939)
PROV.: Sam Tarica, Paris; Theodore Schemmp & Co., NewYork (acquired by the late owner, 1953).

Christie's New York, 8 November 1995 (250**) US$ 145,500   US$ 145,500

LA DANSEUSE ROUGE oil on canvas, 36 1/2 x 28¾in, (92.7 x 73cm.) lr 'F.LéGER. 30' again on
the reverse 'F.LéGER. 30 LA DANSEUSE ROUGE' (1930)
PROV.: Marumo, Guerin & Cie., Paris; Paul Rosenberg & Co., New York (acquired by the present
owner, 1963).
EXH.: Brussels, Palais des Beaux-Arts, *D'art français contemporain*, date unknown; New York,
World's Fair, French Pavillion, *Contemporary French Art*, 1939, no number (illustrated). The
exhibition traveled to New York, Riverside Drive Museum; Philadelphia, Museum of Art, Dec., 1939
and Mexico City; Kansas City, William Rockhill Nelson Gallery of Art, *French School of Painting in
1939*, Sept.-Oct., 1945, no. 34 (illustrated). The exhibition traveled to Denver, Art Museum, Nov.-
Dec., 1945; Omaha, Joslyn Memorial Museum, Dec., 1945-Jan., 1946; Minneapolis, Institute of Art,
Jan.-Feb., 1946; Milwaukee, Art Institute, March-April, 1946 and Pittsburgh, Carnegie Art Institute,
May, 1946; Palm Beach, Society of Four Arts, *The School of Paris*, Jan.-Feb., 1948, no. 25.

Christie's New York, 8 November 1995 (259**) US$ 343,500	US$	343,500

ETUDE POUR 'LES TROIS SOEURS' gouache, watercolour, pen, brush and India ink on paper
mounted at the edges on board, 18½ x 15in. (47 x 38cm.) sdlr with initials 'FL 51' (1951)
PROV.: Theodore Schempp & Co., New York (acquired by the late owner, 1952).

Christie's New York, 8 November 1995 (316**) US$ 233,500	US$	233,500

LEHMDEN Anton (Neutra 1929 b.-) Czech
VOGELFLUCH ÜBER RUINEN oil on panel, 44.5 x 44.5cm. sd 'Lehmden 1984-85'

Dorotheum Vienna, 8 November 1995 (705**) ATS 160,000	US$	16,050

LEICKERT Charles Henri Joseph (Brussels 1816-1907 Mainz) Belgian
A FROZEN WINTER LANDSCAPE WITH FIGURES SKATING BY A WINDMILL oil on
canvas, 30¾ x 22½in. (78.2 x 57cm.) s 'Ch Leickert ft'
PROV.: Knébel family, La Sarraz, and thence by descent to the present owner.

Christie's London, 14 June 1996 (10**) GBP 11,500	US$	17,733

FIGURES IN A FROZEN WINTER LANDSCAPE oil on panel, 8 1/8 x 17 3/8in. (20.6 x 44.2cm.)
slr 'Ch leickert'

Christie's New York, 2 November 1995 (85**) US$ 12,650	US$	12,650

SUMMERLANDSCAPE WITH FISHINGBOATS AND PEOPLE oil on canvas, 39 x 57cm. slr 'Ch
Leickert fec. 96' (1896)

A. Mak B.V. Dordrecht, 21 June 1996 (208*) NLG 12,146	US$	7,097

A RIVER LANDSCAPE WITH SHIPPING, FIGURES IN A ROWING-BOAT AND PAESANTS
ON A SANDY TRACK, DELFT IN THE DISTANCE oil on panel, 27.5 x 43.5cm.) sd 'Ch. Leickert
f 54'

Christie's Amsterdam, 25 April 1996 (150*) NLG 23,000	US$	13,667

A WINTER LANDSCAPE WITH SKATERS ON A FROZEN WATERWAY AND WINDMILLS
AND A CHURCHSPIRE BEYOND oil on panel, 28.5 x 42.5cm. s 'Charles Leickert f

Christie's Amsterdam, 25 April 1996 (161*) NLG 28,750	US$	17,084

A WINTER LANDSCAPE WITH SKATERS ON A FROZEN RIVER AND PEASANT ON A
SNOWY PATH ALONG A WINDMILL, AT SUNSET oil on canvas, 65 x 110cm. sd 'Ch. Leickert f
69'

Christie's Amsterdam, 25 April 1996 (250**) NLG 149,500	US$	88,835

A VIEW OF DELFT, WITH THE OUDE KERK, ON A SUMMERDAY oil on canvas, 64.5 x
101cm. s 'Ch. Leickert f68.'

Christie's Amsterdam, 25 April 1996 (257**) NLG 109,250	US$	64,918

A WINTER LANDSCAPE WITH SKATERS ON A FROZEN RIVER BY A FORTIFIED TOWER
oil on panel, 25 x 31cm. slr 'Ch Leickert'
    Christie's Amsterdam, 26 October 1995 (224*) NLG 19,550   US$ 12,327

SUMMER: A VIEW IN A TOWN WITH A MOORED HAY-BARGE AND OTHER SHIPPING
ALONG A QUAY oil on canvas, 27 x 36cm. slr 'Ch. Leickert f 59'
    Christie's Amsterdam, 26 October 1995 (229**) NLG 40,250   US$ 25,378

A WINTER LANDSCAPE WITH SEVERAL SKATERS AND A *KOEK AND ZOPIE* ON A
FROZEN WATERWAY ALONG A WINDMILL oil on canvas, 62 x 101cm. sdlr 'Ch. Leickertf81'
    Christie's Amsterdam, 26 October 1995 (308**) NLG 48,300   US$ 30,454

A TOWN ALONG A RIVER WITH A HAY-BARGE AND FIGURES IN A ROWINGBOAT
CONVERSING oil on canvas, 60 x 92.5cm. sdlr 'Ch. Leickertf92'
    Christie's Amsterdam, 26 October 1995 (309**) NLG 46,000   US$ 29,004

A WINTER LANDSCAPE WITH SKATERS ON A FROZEN RIVER ALONG A VILLAGE,
ACHURCH-SPIRE IN THE DISTANCE oil on panel, 23.5 x 32.5cm. sll 'Ch.Leickert'
    Christie's Amsterdam, 26 October 1995 (314**) NLG 23,000   US$ 14,502

TOWNSFOLK CONVERSING IN STREET oil on panel, 16 x 13.5cm. slr 'Ch.Leickert'
    Christie's Amsterdam, 26 October 1995 (315*) NLG 16,100   US$ 10,151

A VIEW IN OVERSCHIE, WITH ROTTERDAM AND THE ST. LAURENSKERK IN THE
DISTANCE oil on panel, 30.5 x 41cm. sdlr 'Ch.L.f 62'
PROV.: Kunsthandel P.A. Scheen, The Hague; Anon.sale, Christie's Laren, 24 March 1980, lot 403.
LIT.: Pieter A. Scheen, *Lexicon Nederlandse Beeldende Kunstenaars*, The Hague 1969, Vol. I,
illus.no. 160.
    Christie's Amsterdam, 26 October 1995 (321**) NLG 59,800   US$ 37,705

LEIGH William Robinson, N.A. (1866-1955) American
VIEW OF THE GRAND CANYON OF THE YELLOWSTONE oil on canvas, 32 x 22in. (83.8 x
55.8cm.) sdlr 'W.R. Leigh N.Y. 1913'
    Christie's New York, 13 September 1995 (95**) US$ 48,300   US$ 48,300

LEIGHTON Edmund Blair (1853-1922) British
MY FAIR LADY oil on canvas, 67¼ x 43 5/8in. (170.8 x 110.8cm.) sdll 'E. BLAIR LEIGHTON.
1914.'
    Christie's New York, 2 November 1995 (223**) US$ 43,700   US$ 43,700

LEIGHTON Frederic, Lord, P.R.A. (1830-1896) British
A DANCING GIRL WITH CYMBALS IN A WHITE ROBE oil on canvas, arched top, 87 x 47in.
(221 x 119cm.) (ca 1869)
PROV.: Commissioned by The Hon. Percy Wyndham, 44 Belgrave Square, London; The Hon. Lady
Lowther, Lowther Castle, Cumbria; J.B. Godfrey; Sotheby's Belgravia, 9 July 1974, lot 47 (bt.
Wengraff).
LIT.: M. D. Conway, *Travels in South Kensington,* 1882, p.l64; Leonee and Richard Ormond, *Lord
Leighton,* 1975, p.174, no.420; Charlotte Gere, *Nineteenth-Century Decoration*, 1989, pp.l8 and 23,
repr. pl.l8; Richard Ormond, 'Leighton and Mural Painting', *Apollo*, February 1996, p.55.
    Christie's London, 7 June 1996 (569**) GBP 87,300   US$ 134,618

A DANCING GIRL WITH CYMBALS IN A GREEN ROBE oil on canvas, arched top, 87 x 50in.
(221 x 128cm.) (ca 1869)
PROV.: Commissioned by The Hon. Percy Wyndham, 44 Belgrave Square, London; The Hon. Lady
Lowther, Lowther Castle, Cumbria; J.B. Godfrey; Sotheby's Belgravia, 9 July 1974, lot 47 (bt.
Wengraff).

LIT.: M. D. Conway, *Travels in South Kensington*, 1882, p.164; Leonee and Richard Ormond, *Lord Leighton*, 1975, p.174, no.420; Charlotte Gere, *Nineteenth-Century Decoration*, 1989, pp.18 and 23, repr. pl.18; Richard Ormond, 'Leighton and Mural Painting', *Apollo*, February 1996, p.55.

   Christie's London, 7 June 1996 (570**) GBP 100,500   US$ 154,973

A DANCING ATHLETE WITH AN OLIVE BRANCH oil on canvas, arched top, 87 x 50¾in. (221 x 128.9cm.) (ca 1869)
PROV.: Commissioned by The Hon. Percy Wyndham, 44 Belgrave Square, London; The Hon. Lady Lowther, Lowther Castle, Cumbria; J.B. Godfrey; Sotheby's Belgravia, 9 July 1974, lot 47 (bt. Wengraff).
LIT.: M. D. Conway, *Travels in South Kensington*, 1882, p.164; Leonee and Richard Ormond, *Lord Leighton*, 1975, p.174, no.420; Charlotte Gere, *Nineteenth-Century Decoration*, 1989, pp.18 and 23, repr. pl.18; Richard Ormond, 'Leighton and Mural Painting', *Apollo*, February 1996, p.55.

   Christie's London, 7 June 1996 (571***) GBP 58,700   US$ 90,517

LELIENBERGH Cornelis (1626-1676 after) Dutch
A DEAD HARE AND A HUNTING HORN HANGING FROM A HOOK AND A PARTRIDGE HANGING FROM A STRING, WITH DEAD SONGBIRDS, A SHOT GUN AND A HUNTING BAG ON A DRAPED LEDGE, DEAD SONGBIRDS IN A NICHE NEARBY oil on canvas, 78.9 x 65cm. indstinctly sslc 'C Lelienb f Ao 1664'

   Christie's Amsterdam, 7 May 1996 (111**) NLG 69,000   US$ 40,233

LELY Pieter Faes, {called} Sir Peter (1618-1680) British (Dutch)
PORTRAIT OF HENRIETTA BOYLE, COUNTESS OF ROCHESTER (1646-1687), THREE-QUARTER-LENGTH, SEATED, IN A YELLOW DRESS AND A BLUE WRAP, HOLDING A VASE OF ROSES, BY A DRAPED CURTAIN, A LANDSCAPE BEYOND oil on canvas, 49½ x 38¾in. (125.6 x 98.5cm.) inscr. 'Countess of Rochester'
PROV.: Presumably Edward Hyde, 1st Earl of Clarendon and by descent through Kathenne, Duchess of Queensberry to Charles, 13th Earl of Home, Douglas Castle, Lanarkshire; Christie's; 20 June 1919, lot 134 (330 gns. to Artherton[?]).
EXH.: London, South Kensington, *National Portrait Exhibition*, 1866, no. 927, lent by the Earl of Home.
LIT.: R.B. Beckett, Lely, London, 1951, p. 51, no. 441.

   Christie's London, 18 April 1996 (4**) GBP 36,700   US$ 55,648

LEMAIRE Jean (Dammartin (Seine-et-Marne) 1597-1659 Gaillou (Eure)) French
MOISE ENTERRANT L'EGYPTIEN oil on canvas, 122.5 x 155cm.
PROV.: Anonymous sale, London, The Green Rooms, 1711, lot 39; Collection Charles, first Count of Halifax; His sale, London, 7 March 1739, lot 84; Collection Sir Robert Sutton, 1746; Collection Judith, Countess of Sutherland, widow of Sir Robert Sutton, 1749; Her sale, London, Longford, 22 March 1754, lot 31 (incorrect measurements); Collection Gerard Vandergucht, before 1777; His sale, Christie's, London, 8 March 1777, lot 37; Anonymous sale, Christie's, London, 14 May 1791, lot 47; Collection Noël Desenfans, 1797; Collection Waller, first Viscount of Oxford.

   Étude Tajan Paris, 12 December 1995 (93**) FRF 190,000   US$ 38,271

LEMETTAY Pierre-Charles (Fécamp 1726-1759 Paris) French
VENUS DISARMING CUPID oil on canvas, 93.5 x 80cm. (ca. 1746)

   Christie's Monaco, 14 June 1996 (37**) FFr 222,300   US$ 42,926

LEMOYNE François (1688-1737) French
STUDY OTHE LEGS AND DRAPERY OF A SEATED FIGURE black chalk heightened with white chalk on buff paper, 20.7 x 22.8cm.
PROV.: Jacques Petit-Hory.

   Sotheby's London, 3 July 1995 (230**) GBP 6,900   US$ 11,007

LEMPICKA Tamara de (Warsaw 1907 (1898?)-1980 Cuervernaca) Polish
LE VOILE VERT oil on canvas, 18¾ x 13in. (46 x 33cm.) (1924-1925)
      Christie's New York, 8 November 1995 (239**) US$ 107,000   US$ 107,000

LEONE Andrea de (1610-1685) Italian
A TRUPETEER ONHORSEBACK WITH HIS TURKISH ASSISTANT LOOKING DOWN ON A
BATTLEFIELD oil on canvas, 73 x 88cm. sd mono 'ADL' 16(4?)8
      Christie's Rome, 4 June 1996 (551**) ITL 38,000,000   US$ 24,643

LÉPINE Stanislas Victor Edouard (1835-1892) French
MONTMARTRE, VUE SUR SAINT-DENIS oil on canvas, 8 x 13in. (20.3 x 33cm.) sll 'S Lépine'
(ca. 1874-76)
PROV.: Gérard Collection, Paris; Diéterle Collection, Paris; Sale: Hôtel Rameau, Versailles, 18 June
1974, no. 106.
LIT.: Robert Schmit, *Stanislaus Lépine 1835-1892*, Paris, 1993, no. 266 (illustrated p. 116).
      Sotheby's Arcade Auctions New York, 20 July 1995 (265*) US$ 21,850   US$ 21,850

LEPOITTEVIN louis (1847-1909) french
SHEPHERDESS WITH HER FLOCK IN AN EXTENSIVE RIVER LANDSCAPE oil on canvas,
62½ x 98 7/8in. (158 x 251cm.) sll
      Phillips London, 12th March 1996 (33**) GBP 5,800   US$ 8,858

LEROY Eugène (1910-)
RECLINING NUDE oil on canvas, 63 x 122cm. sdlr 'E. Leroy '61'
      Christie's Amsterdam, 5 June 1996 (310**) NLG 21,850   US$ 12,767

LE SIDANER Henri Eugène Auguste (Ile-Maurice 1862-1939 Versailles) French
PIGNON GRIS oil on canvas, 26 x 32¼in. (66 x 82cm.) (1914)
PROV.: Galerie Georges Petit, Paris; Anon. sale, Hôtel Drouot, Paris, 4 Dec. 1918; Kaplan Gallery,
London (acquired by Richard Smart, 1969).
EXH.: Paris, Galerie Georges Petit, *Exposition de la Société Nouvelle*, 1914, no. 41; London, Kaplan
Gallery, *A Selection of Impressionist and Post-Impressionist Paintings, Watercolours, Pastels and
Drawings*, 1966. no. 46 (illustrated).
LIT.: P. Pool, *Impresionism*, London 1967, no. 206 (illustrated p. 264); Y. Farinaux-Le Sidaner, *Le
Sidaner, l'oeuvre peint et gravé*, Paris 1989, no. 325 (illustrated p. 138).
      Christie's New York, 1 May 1996 (155**) US$ 68,500   US$ 68,500

LA MAISON A L'AUTOMNE oil on canvas, 36 3/8 x 29in. (92.4 x 73.6cm.) slr 'Le Sidaner'
(Gerberoy, 1924)
PROV.: B. Scaioli; Lady Lyle; sale, Christie's. London, 20 Paril 1951, lot 42.
EXH.: Paris, Galerie Georges Petit, *Le Sidaner*, Nov. 1927, no. 34.
LIT.: C. Mauclair, *Henri Le Sidaner, Oeuvres récentes*, Paris 1928, p. 132 (illustrated); Y. Farinux-
Le Sidaner, *Le Sidaner, l'oeuvre peint et gravé*, Milan 1989, no. 540 (illustrated, p. 207).
      Christie's New York, 1 May 1996 (164**) US$ 156,500   US$ 156,500

LE PONT LEVANT. VOLENDAM oil on panel, 10½ x 13¾in. (26.5 x 35cm.) sll 'Sidaner' (1902)
LIT.: Yann Farinaux, *Le Sidaner, l'oeuvre peint et gravé*, Editions André Sauret, 1989, cat.no.889
(ill.).
      Christie's South Kensington, 18 March 1996 (32**) GBP 8,050   US$ 12,294

LE CANAL NEIGE oil on canvas, 32 x 23¾in. (81.3 x 60.3cm.) (1901)
PROV.: Sale: New York, Christie's, November 14, 1984, lot 555; Acquired by the present owner at
the above sale.
LIT.: Yann Farinaux, *Le Sidaner, L'Oeuvre Peint et Gravé*. Paris, 1989, no. 101, illustrated p. 74.
      Sotheby's New York, 2 May 1996 (186**) US$ 68,500   US$ 68,500

LE BASSIN DU REFUGE oil on canvas, 28¾ x 36¼in. (73 x 92cm.) slr 'LeSidaner' (1924)
PROV.: Galerie Georges Petit, Paris.
EXH.: Brussels, Galerie du Studio, *Henri Martin - Henri Le Sidaner*, 1924, no. 24 Paris, Galerie
Georges Petit, *Le Sidaner*, 1925, no. 25.
LIT.: Yann Farinaux-Le Sidaner, *Le Sidaner, L'oeuvre peint et gravé*, Milan, 1989, p. 202, no. 527,
illustrated.

Sotheby's London, 20 March 1996 (34**) GBP 36,700	US$	56,048

MAISON AU BORD DE L'EAU oil on canvas, 18 1/8 x 15in. (46 x 38cm.) slr 'Le Sidaner'

Christie's London, 26 June 1996 (127**) GBP 34,500	US$	53200

LE MATIN, VENISE oil on canvas, 21 5/8 x 25¾in. (55 x 65.5cm.) ll 'Le Sidaner' (1918)
PROV.: Galerie Georges Petit, Paris; Anon. sale, Christie's, London, June 28, 1988, lot 165.

Christie's New York, 8 November 1995 (163**) US$ 92,700	US$	92,700

LESREL Adolphe Alexandre (1839-1890) French
THE RECITAL oil on panel, 21 5/8 x 26in. (54.9 x 66.1cm.) sdll 'A. A. Lesrel 1902'
PROV.: With MacConnal Mason & Son, Ltd., London.

Christie's New York, 2 November 1995 (132**) US$ 18,400	US$	18,400

LEVANON Mordechai (1901-1968)
SAFED oil on canvas, 28¾ x 36¼in. (73 x 92cm.) sdll 'Levanon 58'

Christie's Tel Aviv, 14 April 1996 (54**) US$ 18,400	US$	18,400

LÉVEQUE Auguste (Maurice François Giuslain) (Nivelles 1864-1921 Brussels) Belgian
LES ALLEGORIES DES ARTS oil on canvas, 87½ x 74¾in. (222 x 190cm.) sdll '1907'

Sotheby's London, 13 March 1996 (46**) GBP 25,300	US$	38,638

LEVINE Jack (1915 b.-l) American
KRONOS oil on canvas, 24 x 21in. (61 x 53.3cm.) sll 'JLevine'; inscr. ul with title (1983)
PROV.: The Artist; Kennedy Galleries, New York; Midtown Payson Galleries, New York.
EXH.: Ogunquit, Maine, The Museum of Art of Ogunquit, *The Art of Jack Levine*, Aug.-Sept. 1992;
New York, Midtown Payson Galleries, *Jack Levine An OVerview, 1930-1990*, Oct.-Nov. 1990.
LIT.: M.W. Brown, *Jack Levine*, New York 1989, p. 137 (illustrated).

Christie's East, 28 November 1995 (53**) US$ 14,950	US$	14,950

LEVY Rudolf (Stettin 1875-1944 Konzentrationslager) German
STILLEBEN MIT KARAFFE UBD SKULPTUR oil on canvas, 24 x 19¾in. (61 x 50cm.) sdlr 'R
Levy 1911'
LIT.: S. Thesing, *Rudolf Levy, Leben und Werk*, Neurenberg, 1990, no. 273.

Christie's Tel Aviv, 12 October 1995 (48**) US$ 11,500	US$	11,500

LEWIS Edmund Darch (1835-1910) American
SOUTH AMERICAN LANDSCAPE oil on canvas, 30 171 x 50in. (77.5 x 127cm.) slr 'Edmund
Darch Lewis'

Christie's East, 28 November 1995 (60*) US$ 19,550	US$	19,550

LEWIS John Frederick, R.A., P.O.W.S. (1805-1876) British
SHEIK EL BELLED: KOM OMBO pencil and watercolour heightened with white and gum arabic
on buff paper, 14 x 19¾in. (35.5 x 49.2cm.) sd lr 'J F Lewis/Kom Ombo/1850.'
PROV.: The Artist's sale; Christie's London, 4 May 1877, lot 132 (31gns. unsold); Mrs J.S. Kennedy;
Christie's, 22 Feb. 1958, lot 64 (5gns. unsold); with Agnew's; with The Fine Art Society, 1968.
LIT.: J.M. Lewis, *John Frederick Lewis, R.A.*, 1978, p.84, no.421.

Christie's London, 2 April 1996 (102**) GBP 14,950	US$	22,669

THE RABBIT WARREN, A SCENE IN AMPTHILL PARK, NEAR HOUGHTON RUIN, BEDFORDSHIRE oil on canvas, 30½ x 39¾in. (77.5 x 101cm.) sldr 'J.F. Lewis, 1825'
PROV.: Probably commissioned by Henry Fox, 3rd Lord Holland (1773-1840); R.G. Waldron, by whom sold, Sotheby's 5th November 1952, lot 107, Bt. Agnew, for GBP70t.
EXH.: British Institution, 1825, no. 385.
LIT.: Major General Michael Lewis, *John Frederick Lewis*, 1978, p.59, no. 32, illustrated, fig. 9.

Sotheby's London, 12 July 1995 (90**) GBP 53,200	US$	84,862

THE CARAVAN-AN ARAB ENCAMPMENT AT EDFOU watercolour over pencil heightened with white, 7 x 18in. (17.5 x 45.5cm.)
PROV.: Probably the artist's sale, Christie's, 5 May 1877, lot 277, bt. Nosida for 21 gns; R. Mackenzie, 1888; John Graham; W.G. Driver, his sale, Christie's, 16 October 1981, lot 93.
EXH.: Nottingham Castle, 1888, no. 47.

Sotheby's London, 17 April 1996 (719**) GBP 45,500	US$	68,992

LEWIS Max (Hamburg 1863-1930 Vienna) German
VALLEY VIEW oil on canvas, 33 x 30in. (84 x 76cm.) sll 'M. Lewis'

Christie's New York, 13 March 1996 (67**) US$ 40,250	US$	40,250

LEYDEN Lucas van (attributed to) (1494-1533) Dutch
LOTH AND HIS DAUGHTERS oil on panel, 30 x 41.5cm.
PROV.: With collection Goudstikker, Amsterdam.
EXH.: Fabri Editori, 1966 *Luca di Leida (Lucas van Leyden)*, p. 167, nos. III and IV. (illustrated).

Dorotheum Vienna, 6 March 1996 (18**) ATS 160,000	US$	15,391

LHERMITTE Léon Augustin (Mont Saint-Père (Aisne) 1844-1925 Paris) French
FIGURE SEATED BEFORE OUT-BUILDINGS SAINT-SERVAN pastel, 11¼ x 17¼in. (28.7 x 44cm.) slr 'L. Lhermitte'
PROV.: Sold Boussod, Valadon & Cie., 16592; Gille; Williams & Son, London (13248, 3565).
EXH.: *Exposition des Pastellistes*, 1894, no.?.
LIT.: Monique Le Pelley Fonteny, *Leon Augustin Lhermitte: Catalogue Raisonné*, Editions; Cèrcle d'Art, Paris, 1991, no.; 343, p. 222 as 'Les Barraques;du Bassin de Saint-Servan ou Le Bassin de Saint Servant' (illus.).

Phillips London, 11 June 1996 (62**) GBP 5,000	US$	7,710

FIGURES IN A KITCHEN INTERIOR charcoal on paper, 17¾ x 23½in. (45.1 x 59.7cm.) sdll 'L. Lhermitte-1895-'
PROV.: With Boussod, Valadon et Cie, 17591; Collection Gillé.
EXH.: Exposition des Aquarellistes, 1896, no. 105.
LIT.: G.G., *Le Matin*, January 21, 1896; Goeffroy G., *Le Journal*, January 25, 1896; G.G., *Le Pays*, February 3, 1896; H. Dac, *Le Monde*, February 5, 1896; A. Guyon-Verax, *Journal des Artistes*, February 16, 1896; A. de Mandre, *Paris-Mode*, March 1, 1896; M. Le Pelley Fonteney, *Léon Augustin Lhermitte*, Paris, 1991,; p. 477; no. 893 (illustrated).

Christie's New York, 22 May 1996 (170**) US$ 19,550	US$	19,550

GLEANERS AT SUNSET oil on canvas, 27 3/8 x 43½in. (69.5 x 110.5cm.) sdlr L. Lhermitte 1889'
PROV.: Sold Boussod, Valadon & Cie., 21146; Maclean, London; S. Holland; Sale Christie`s, London, 25, 26 and 29; June, 1908,; no. 402; Boussod, Valadon & Cie.; Kraushaar Gallery, New York, 190; Sotheby`s New York, Sale of Prince; Ruspoli, 26 October , 1955, no.73 in the catalogue.; Baltimore Private Collection; Sotheby`s, New York, Heastand sale; 11 December, 1956, no.58 in the; catalogue.; Sale Sotheby`s, New York, 6 April 1960, no. 80; Sale Sotheby`s, New York, 21 March,1963, no.74; London, Private Collection.
LIT.: Monique Le Pelley Fonteny, *Leon Augustin L'hermitte: Catalogue Raisonné*, Editions Cèrcle d'Art, Paris, 1991, no. 148, p. 134, as 'Glaneuses Le Soir' (illus.).

Phillips London, 11 June 1996 (66***) GBP 32,000	US$	49,345

LHOTE André (Bordeaux 1885-1962 Paris) French
VIEW OF THE OLD PORT OF BORDEAUX oil on canvas, 23¼ x 28¼in. (59 x 72cm.) slr 'A. LHote'

        Étude Tajan Paris, 13 December 1995 (49**) FRF 100,000   US$ 20,143

CAFE AU BORD DU LAC oil on canvas, 32 x 45¾in (81 x 116cm.) sdll 'A Lhote. 33'
        Christie's London, 29 November 1995 (226**) GBP 34,000   US$ 53,183

PORTRAIT DE FEMME EN BLEU oil on canvas, 31 7/8 x 19¼in. (81 x 49cm.) slr 'A.Lhote'
        Christie's London, 29 November 1995 (248**) GBP 20,000   US$ 31,284

L'ARCHITECTURE oil on paper laid down on canvas, 32 5/8 x 46 1/4in. (82 x 117.5cm.) ul 'A. LHOTE.' (1929)
PROV.: Mme André Lhote, Paris; Anon. sale, Christie's, New York, May 12, 1988, lot 297.
        Christie's New York, 8 November 1995 (242**) US$ 34,500   US$ 34,500

LIBERI Pietro (Padova 1614-1687) Italian
VENUS, AMOR, FLORA WITH A ROSE-LEAF SOWING GENIUS oil on canvas, 134 x 155cm. framed
        Dorotheum Vienna, 17 October 1995 (30**) ATS 250,000   US$ 25,076

VENUS DISARMING CUPID oil on canvas, 117 x 100cm. '20' on an old label on the reverse
        Christie's Rome, 21 November 1995 (249**) ITL 66,000,000   US$ 41,431

LIE Jonas (1880-1940) American
ON THE COAST OF NEW ENGLAND oil on canvas, 33¾ x 36in. (85.7 x 91.4cm.) slr 'Jonas Lie'
        Christie's New York, 23 May 1996 (120**) US$ 63,000   US$ 63,000

LIEBERMANN Max (Berlin 1847-1935 Berlin) German
STRANDWÄCHTER oil on cardboard, 45 x 38cm. sdlr 'M Liebermann 2' (1902)
PROV.: Collection Eduard Fuchs, Berlin.
        Hauswedell & Nolte Cologne, 1 December 1995 (420**) DEM 38,000   US$ 26,365

ALLEE IN SAKROW MIT ZWEI REITERN oil on canvas, 23¾ x 29½in. (60.3 x 75cm.) slr 'M. Liebermann' (prob. 1923)
PROV.: Heinrich Stahl, Berlin.
EXH.: Hamburg, Kunstverein, *Max Liebermann*, Nov.-Dec. 1926, no. 47; New York, Schönemann Galleries, *Max Liebermann*, March-April 1940; New York, French & Co., *Max Liebermann*, Jan.-Feb. 1948, no. 11.
        Christie's London, 11 October 1995 (127**) GBP 122,500   US$ 193,340

SCHAFHIRTIN pastel on paper, laid down on board, 29¼ x 25¾in. (74.2 x 65.5cm.) slr 'Max Liebermann' (1887)
PROV.: Paul Cassirer, Berlin, 1916; Aby S. Warburg, Hamburg, the grandfather of the present owner, by whom bought from the above in June 1916 for 8,000 Mark; Prof. T. Plaut, Hull, and thence by descent to the present owner.
EXH.: London, New Burlington Gallery, *Modern German Art*, July 1938, no. 159.
        Christie's London, 11 October 1995 (128**) GBP 155,500   US$ 245,423

WANNSEEGARTEN DER FAMILIE ARNHOLD oil on canvas, 27¾ x 34¾in. (70.3 x 88.3cm.) sdlr 'M. Liebermann 1911'
PROV.: Geheimrat Eduard Arnhold, Berlin (1849-1925), by whom bought directly from the Artist and thence by descent to the present owner.
        Christie's London, 11 October 1995 (132**) GBP 507,500   US$ 800,979

SELBSTBILDNIS oil on canvas, 35½ x 27½in. (90 x 70cm.) (1911-12)
PROV.: Kunsthalle, Bremen, by whom aquired from the Artist in Spring 1912, exchanged with the
Artist in 1920; Galerie Aktuaryus, Zurich (1945); Paul Cassirer, Berlin (11607) from whom
purchased by the father of Dr Charlotte Rhonheimer.
EXH.: Bremen, Kunsthalle, *Ausstellung des Deutschen Kunstlerbundes*, Feb.-March 1912, no. 136
(illustrated); Zurich, *Ausstellung von Werken aus dem Besitz von Mitgliedern der Vereinigung
Zurcher Kunstfreunde*, Sept.-Oct. 1927, no. 169; Zurich, Galerie Aktuaryus, *Max Liebermann*, 1945,
no. 27 (illustrated).
LIT.: G. Pauli, 'Die Ausstellung des deutschen Kunstlerbundes in Bremen' in *Kunst und Künstler*, no.
X, 1912, vol. 8, I May 1912, pp. 411-414 (illustrated p. 411); G. Pauli, 'Max Liebermann' in *Kunst
für alle*, no. XXVIII, 1913, vol. 10 (illustrated p. 217); C. Steiner, 'Die Neuerwerbungen in der
Bremer Kunsthalle' in *Der Cicerone*, no. V, Nov. 1913, vol. 22 (illustrated p. 792); *Katalog der
Gemälde und Bildhauerwerke in der Kunsthalle zu Bremen,* Bremen, 1913, no. 340 (illustrated p.
64); K. Scheffler, *'Deutsche Museen Moderner Kunst III;* Die Bremer Kunsthalle' in *Kunst und
Künstler*, no. XI, vol. 2, 1913, pp. 85, 101; L.E. Hanke, *Max Liebermann. Sein Leben und seine
Werke*, Berlin, 1914, p. 54; H.W. Singer, *Neuer Bildniskatalog*, vol. 3, Leipzig, 1937, possibly no.
20708; *Galerie und Sammler, Monatschrift der Galerie Aktuaryus*, no. XIII, Zurich, 1945 (illustrated
p. 97).

Christie's London, 29 November 1995 (211**) GBP 30,000	US$	46,926

WEG IM TIERGARTEN MIT SPAZIERGÄNGERN oil on linen, 39 x 59cm sdll 'M. Liebermann
21' (1921)
PROV.: Ullstein collection, Berlin.

Lempertz Cologne, 29 November 1995 (265**) DEM 350,000	US$	247,036

LICHTENSTEIN Roy (1923 b.) American
MODERN PAINTING WITH YELLOW INTERWEAVE oil on canvas, 56 x 47 7/8 in. (142.2 x
121.6cm.) sd 'rf Lichtenstein '67' on the reverse
PROV.: Leo Castelli Gallery, New York; Bert Stern, New York; Richard Gray Gallery, Chicago.
EXH.: Cincinatti, The Contemporary Arts Center, *Roy Lichtenstein Exhibitions of Painting and
Sculpture*, Dec. 1967, n.n. (illustrated).
LIT.: D. Walsman, *Roy Lichtenstein*, London 1971, no. 148 (illustrated).

Christie's New York, 14 November 1995 (44**) US$ 255,500	US$	255,500

CRAIG!! graphite and coloured pencils on paper, 5 7/8 x 6in. (15 x 15.2cm.) initialated 'rfl' le (1964)
PROV.: Acquired directly from the artist; Private collection, Londom\n.
EXH.: L'Isle sur sorgue, Association Art et Culture de Campredon, *The artists decide to play*, June-
Oct. 1991, p. 77 (illustrated).

Christie's New York, 15 November 1995 (203**) US$ 57,500	US$	57,500

IMPERFECT PAINTING oil and magna on shaped canvas-unframed, 83 x 79in. (210.8 x 200.6cm.)
sd 'rf Lichtenstein '86' on the reverse
PROV.: Leo Castelli Gallery, New York; Blum Helman Gallery, New York.
EXH.: Los Angeles, Blum Helman Gallery, *Jasper Johns, Ellsworth Kelly, Roy Lichtenstein, Robert
Rauschenberg, Frank Stella: New Work*, Dec. 1986-Jan. 1987; New York, Leo Castelli Gallery, *Roy
Lichtenstein*, March 1987.

Christie's New York, 15 November 1995 (334**) US$ 101,500	US$	101,500

MODERN PAINTING WITH STEPS oil and magna on canvas, 48 x 60in. (122.9 x 152.4cm.) sd
'Roy Lichtenstein '67' on the reverse
PROV.: Leo Castelli Gallery, New York.
EXH.: Boston, Institute of Contemporary Art, *Roy Lichtenstein: The Modern Works 1965-1970*,
Nov.-Dec. 1978 (illustrated).

Christie's New York, 7 May 1996 (12**) US$ 299,500	US$	299,500

STILL-LIFE WITH LAMP oil and magna on canvas, 54 x 74in. (137.2 x 188cm.) sd 'rf Lichtenstein 1976' on the reverse
PROV.: Leo Castelli Gallery, New York; Richard Gray Gallery, Chicago.
EXH.: Chicago, Richard Gray Gallery, *New Paintings and Drawings*, Jan.-Mar. 1977.
LIT.: J. Cowart, *Roy Lichtenstein: 1970-1980*, St. Louis 1981, p. 107 (illustrated); L. Alloway, *Roy Lichtenstein*, New York 1983, p. 84, no. 85 (illustrated).
Christie's New York, 7 May 1996 (27**) US$ 332,500   US$ 332,500

LIEVENS Jan (Leiden 1607-1674 Amsterdam) Dutch
A RIVERLANDSCAPE WITH A TRAVELLER ASLEEP BENEATH A TREE oil on panel, 18 1/8 x 26¼in. (46 x 66.7cm.) s ini. 'IL' (ca 1640)
PROV.: with Edward Speelman, London, circa 1960; with J.R. Bier, Haarlem (*Tentoonstelling van Hollandse 17e eeuwse Meesters*, 1962, no. 15, illustrated); with J. Dik, Vévey, 1970; with Bruno Meissner, Zurich, 1979.
EXH.: Brunswick, Herzog Anton Ulrich-Museum, *Jan Lievens, ein Maler im Schatten Rembrandts*, 5 Sept.-11 Nov. 1979, pp. 23 and 128, no. 44, Illustrated.
LIT.: C. Brown, Jan Lievens at Brunswick, *The Burlington Magazine,* CXXI, no. 920, Nov. 1979, p. 745; P. Eikemeier, Rezension der Lievens-Austellung, Braunschweig 1979, *Pantheon*, XXXVIII, 1980, p. 7; J. Michalkowa, 'Nie tylko W cieniu Rembrandta O Brunszwickiej Wystawie Jana Lievensa', *Biuletyn Historii Sztuki*, XLII. 1980. p. 208; W. Sumowski, Zur Jan Lievens-Ausstellung in Braunschweig, *Kunstchronik,* XXXIII, 1980, pp. 12 and 24, fig. 8; W. Sumowski, *Gemälde der Rembrandt-Schuler*, III, Landau/Pfalz, 1983, pp. 1814 and 1945, pl. 1306.
Christie's London, 7 July 1995 (41**) GBP 34,500   US$ 55,033

A YOUNG MAN TUNING A VIOLIN oil on canvas, 36½ x29in. (92.7 x73.7cm.) (around 1623)
Christie's London, 7 July 1995 (58**) GBP 100,500   US$ 160,313

LIGOZZI Jacopo (Verona 1547 c.-1632 after) Italian
THE MOCKING OF CHRIST oil on panel, 41 3/8 x 32 7/8in. (105.2 x 83.5cm.) (Ligozzi's Florentine period)
Christie's London, 8 December 1995 (61**) GBP 16,100   US$ 24,777

SAINT LOUIS OF FRANCE (LOUIS IX) oil on canvas, 54 x 39¼in. (137.2 x 99.7cm.)
Sotheby's New York, 16 May 1996 (58**) US$ 101,500   US$ 101,500

AN ALLEGORY OF THE REDEMPTION: THE VIRGIN WATCHING OVER THE DEAD CHRIST WITH SIN AND DEATH CHAINED TO THE CROSS oil on panel, 19 x 12½in. (48 x 32in.) (ca. 1587)
PROV.: Probably commissioned by Francesco I de' Medici (1541-87).
EXH.: Nottingham, 1968, no 15, as by Ligozzi.
LIT.: Richter, 1901,no. 33, as Allessandro Turchi; Vertova, 1968, p. 27, as Ligozzi; L. Coniegliello, *Jacopo Ligozzi - Le vedute del Sacro Monte della Verna i dipinti di Poppi e Bibbiena*, Exhibition catalogue, Poppi, 1982, pp. 25, 26 & 42, note 85, 139, fig. 11.
Sotheby's London, 6 December 1995 (27**) GBP 56,500   US$ 86,950

LILJEFORS Bruno (1860-1939) Swedish
SMYGANDE KATT oil on canvas, 47 x 96cm. sdlr 'Bruno Liljefors -92'
Bukowskis Stockholm, 29 November-1 December 1995 (92**) SEK 620,000   US$ 93,792

BOFINKAR I BLÅSIPPSBACKE oil on canvas, 33 x 23cm. sdll 'Bruno Liljefors 85'
Bukowskis Stockholm, 29-31 May 1996 (101**) SEK 650,000   US$ 95,597

JÄGARE OCH LYFTANDE RAPPHÖNS oil on canvas, 65 x 100cm. sdll 'Bruno Liljefors 1924'
Bukowskis Stockholm, 29-31 May 1996 (102**) SEK 290,000   US$ 42,651

LILLONI Umberto (Milan 1898-1980 Milan) Italian
TORRENTE A FERIOLO oil on canvas laid down on cardboard, 47 x 64.5cm. s 'Lilloni'
PROV.: Galleria Annunciata, Milano (under nr. 1461); Galleria Cairola, Milano.
EXH.: Societa' di Belle Arti di Verona, *49ma Esposizione Nazionale d'Arte*, Sala II, no. 26.
Finearte Milan, 12 December 1995 (161**) ITL 17,250,000   US$ 10,822

VEDUTA DI STOCCOLMA oil on canvas, 38 x 50cm s 'Stoccolma Lilloni' (1949)
Finearte Rome, 14 November 1995 (194**) ITL 18,400,000   US$ 11,551

A FERIOLO oil on canvas, 41.5 x 65cm. slr 'Lillono'; titled, d and the declaration of authenticity of
signature by Maria Luigia Lilloni on the reverse (1945)
Finearte Milan, 18 June 1996 (136*) ITL 17,825,000   US$ 11,560

RITRATTO A BELLAGO oil on canvas, 96.5 x 114cm. sdll 'Lilloni 1939' (1939)
EXH.: Milan, Galleria del Sagittario, *I chiaristi*, Oct.-Nov. 1970.
Finearte Milan, 26 October 1995 (182**) ITL 16,675,000   US$ 10,389

LINARD Jacques (Paris 1600-1645) French
STILL-LIFE OF A MELON, PEACHES, GRAPES AND FIGS IN A BASKET RESTING ON A
LEDGE oil on canvas, 20¼ x 24in. (51.4 x 61cm.) slc 'I LINARD' dlr '1636'
Sotheby's New York, 11 January 1996 (144**) US$ 134,500   US$ 134,500

LINDH Bror (1877-1941) Swedish
HÖSTDAG I VÄRMLAND oil on canvas, 133 x 156cm. s 'Bror Lindh'
EXH.: Rackstamuséet, Sweden.
Bukowskis Stockholm, 29-31 May 1996 (118**) SEK 98,000   US$ 14,413

LINDNER Richard (1901-1978) American (German)
THE BROTHERS oil on canvas mounted on masonite, 39¼ x 25 1/8in. (99.6 x 64cm.) sdll 'Lindner
1958'
PROV.: Betty Parsons Gallery, New York.
EXH.: Leverkusen, Städtisches Museum Schloss Morsbroich; Hannover, Kestner-Gesellschaft;
Berkeley, University of California, University Art Museum, and Minneapolis, Walker Art Center,
Richard Lindner, Oct. 1968-Aug. 1969, no. 43; Chicago, Museum of Contemporary Art, *Richard
Lindner:A Retrospective Exhibition*, May-July 1977, p. 11 (illustrated).
LIT.: D. Ashton, *Richard Linder*, New York 1968, no. 68 (illustrated); this painting will be included
in the forthcoming *catalogue raisonné Lindner*, currently being prepared by Anouk Papdiamandis
and edited by Werner Spies.
Christie's New York, 15 November 1995 (141**) US$ 46,000   US$ 46,000

LINDSTRÖM Fritz (1874-1962) Swedish
DÄR HEMMA oil on canvas, 71 x 120cm. sd 'F.L. -06.'
Bukowskis Stockholm, 29-31 May 1996 (119**) SEK 120,000   US$ 17,649

LINGELBACH Johannes (Frankfurt 1622-1674 Amsterdam) Dutch (German)
PEASANTS MERRY-MAKING IN THE COURTYARD OF A TAVERN oil on canvas, 18¼ x
15in. (46.4 x 38.1cm)
PROV.: The Duquesa Vinda de Rivas (acc. to an inscription on the stretcher).
Christie's London, 7 July 1995 (139**) GBP 8625   US$ 13,758

LINNELL John the Elder (1792-1882) British
FINE EVENING AFTER THE RAIN oil on panel, 18 x 27½in. (46 x 70cm.) sd J.Linnell 1820'
PROV.: Painted for Mr Tomkinson in exchange for a piano valued at 42 guineas With Gooden and
Fox, London; With Spink & Son, London; With Frost and Reed, London.
EXH.: London, Royal Academy, *Burlington International Fine Arts Fair*, 1979 (as 'Dolwyddelan
Valley with a Shepherd, Sheep and Cattle on a Path').

LIT.: David Linnell, Blake, Palmer, *Linnell and Co.: The Life of John Linnell*, 1994, pp.39, 357 (no.40b).

| | Christie's London, 6 November 1995 (154**) GBP 9,775 | US$ | 15,290 |

PORTRAIT OF JOSEPH MALLORD WILLIAM TURNER (1775-1851), HALF-LENGTH, IN A BROWN JACKET, IN A LANDSCAPE oil on canvas, 18 x 15in. (45.7 x 38.1cm.) (1838-39)
PROV.: David Thomas White, 1850, by whom sold to Mr. Birch, 1851; Mr. Pennell, 1851; Walter Thornbury; William Sharp; Christie's, 9 July 1881, lot 73 (82gns. to Agnews, on behalf of Sir Chades Tennant, Bt.); By descent to the present owner.
EXH.: Manchester, *Royal Jubilee Exhibition*, 1887; on loan to the National Portrait Gallery, London, 1975-1995.
LIT.: W. Thornbury, *The Life of J.M W. Turner, R.A.*, revised ea., 1877, pp. 389-91; A.T. Story, *Life of John Linnell*, 1892, II, p. 251; L. Cust, 'The Portraits of J.M.W. Turner R.A.', *The Magazine of Art*, 1895, p.247; C. Monkhouse, 'Some Portraits of J.M.W. Turner', *Scribner's Magazine*, XX, 1896, p. 94; National Portrait Gallery, *Complete Illustrated Catalogue*, 1981, p.578, no. L157; R.J.B. Walker, The Portraits of J.M. W. Turner: A Check-List', *Turner Studies*, III no. 1, Summer 1983, p.27, no. 27, repro.
D. Linnell, Blake, Palmer, *Linnell and Co.:The Life of John Linnell*, 1994, pp. 154, 174-5, 381, no. 248.

| | Christie's London, 10 November 1995 (27**) GBP 18,400 | US$ | 28,781 |

HAY AND HASTE oil on canvas, 27½ x 38¼in. (70 x 97cm.) sdlr 'J. Linnell/75'
PROV.: The Linnell family; Probably, the Executors of the Estate of the late David Price, Christie's 2nd April 1892, lot 84, bt. Agnews for 600 gns.
EXH.: Leger Galleries, October 1970.
LIT.: Listed on the *Artist's sketchbook* under 1874 and 1875; Alfred T. Story, *Life of John Linnell*, 1892, vol. II, p. 282.

| | Sotheby's London, 12 July 1995 (108**) GBP 11,500 | US$ | 18,344 |

THE WORLD OF KENT oil on canvas, 25¼ x 36in. (64.5 x 91.5cm.) sd 'J. Linnell 1853'
PROV.: Bought from the Artist by Ernest Gambart for 230gns.
EXH.: London, British Institution, 1853, no. 145.
LIT.: David Linell, Blake, Palmer, *Linell and Co.:The Life of John Linnel*, 1994, pp. 258, 364 (no. 170), 406 (no. 87).

| | Christie's London, 29 March 1996 (170**) GBP 14,950 | US$ | 22,831 |

LINNIG Egidius (Antwerp 1821-1860 Antwerp) Belgian
VARIOUS SHIPPING ON THE SCHELDT ESTUARY, ANTWERP IN THE DISTANCE oil on panel, 34 x 49.5cm. sd 'Egidi.Linnig 1853 f'

| | Christie's Amsterdam, 25 April 1996 (226**) NLG 19,550 | US$ | 11,617 |

LINNQVIST Hilding (1891-1984) Swedish
MÅLARENS ATTRIBUT oil on canvas, 93 x 65cm. slr 'HL (linked)' (1952)
EXH.: Liljevalch, Konsthall, *Hilding Linnqvist*, 1951, no. 298.
LIT.: F. Holmér, *Hilding Linnqvist*, pp. 165-166, (illustrated p. 166).

| | Bukowskis Stockholm, 24-25 April 1996 (80**) SEK 58,000 | US$ | 8,787 |

TORGBILD, CHINON oil on panel, 24 x 31.5cm. sdll 'Hilding Linnqvist 1921'
EXH.: Liljevalch, Liljevalchs Konsthall, *Hilding Linnqvist retrospektiv*, 1957.
LIT.: Folke Holmér, *Hilding Linnqvist*, p. 85ff; Bo Lagercrantz, *Hilding Linnqvist*, p. 48ff.

| | Bukowskis Stockholm, 26-27 October 1995 (68**) SEK 70,000 | US$ | 10,252 |

LINT Giacomo van (1723-1790) Italian
VEDUTA DEL FORO CON SANTA FRANCESCA ROMANA oil on canvas, 74.5 x 135cm.

| | Finearte Rome, 21 May 1996 (84**) ITL 80,500,000 | US$ | 51,702 |

LINT Hendrik Frans van, {called} Studio (Antwerp 1684-1763 Rome) Flemish
WOODED ARCADIAN LANDSCAPE WITH A SATYR AND AND NYMPHS NEAR A
CASCADE oil on canvas, 19¼ x 25½in. (49 x 64.9in.) sdll 'HF.van lint. de°. Studio./Ft. Roma.1736'
PROV.: With Richard Green, London.
LIT.: A. Busiri Vici, *Peter, Hendrik e Giacomo van Lint*, 1987, p. 225, no. 270 (illustrated).
    Sotheby's London, 5 July 1995 (79**) GBP 28,750   US$ 45,861

VEDUTA DEL TEMPIO DELLA SIBILLA A TIVOLI oil on canvas, 47 x 72cm. slc 'HF van Lint-
do studio'
LIT.: M. Roethlisberger, *Im licht von Claude Lorrain*, Haus der Kunst, Monaco, 12 March-29 May
1983, no.123; A. Busiri Vici, *Peter, Hendrik e Giacomo van Lint*, ed. Ugo Bozzi, Rome 1987,
no.101, pag. 105; illustrated no.34, pag. 92.
    Finearte Milan, 11 June 1996 (51**) ITL 138,000,000   US$ 89,494

ROME: A VIEW OF THE CASTEL SANT'ANGELO AND THE VATICAN BEYOND oil on
canvas, 18½ x 29in. (47 x 73.5cm.) sdll 'Lint F. Ro 1721'
PROV.: With Hazlitt, Gooden and Fox, London; Anonymous sale, Christie's London, 20 October
1961, lot 147.
LIT.: A. Busiri Vici, *Peter, Hendrik, and Giacomo van Lint*, 1987, p. 79, no. 64, (illustrated).
    Sotheby's London, 17 April 1996 (191**) GBP 36,700   US$ 55,648

CAPRICCIO WITH THE ERUPTION OF THE VESUVIO AND A PROCESSION OF PENITENTS
/ A RIVER LANDSCAPE WITH CHRIST AND TEH APOSTLES oil on copper (a pair), each: 22.7
x 33.5cm. sd 'HF Van Lint F. /1727'
    Christie's Rome, 21 November 1995 (257**) ITL 70,000,000   US$ 43,942

VIEW OF THE ENTRANCE OF THE PORT OF NAPLES WITH 'LE MASCHIO ANGIOINO'
AND 'THE VOMERO' oil on canvas, 48 x 73cm. sdll inscr. 'HF . van lint / Roma / 1743'
PROV.: Galerie Sestieri, Rome, 1987.
LIT.: A. Busiri Vici, *Peter, Hendrick e Giacomo van Lint, tre pittori di Anversa del'600 e 7,000
lavorano a Roma*, Rome 1987, p. 153, no. 174 (illustrated).
    Étude Tajan Paris, 25 June 1996 (14**) FRF 480,000   US$ 92,687

LANDSCAPE WITH BATHERS oil on canvas, 21 x 35.5cm s 'Studio fecit'
    Finearte Milan, 25 November 1995 (140**) ITL 43,700,000   US$ 27,433

LINT Peter van (1609-1690) Dutch
SUFFER THE LITTLE CHILDREN TO COME UNTO ME, AND FORGIVE THEM NOT oil on
canvas, unframed, 48 x 68½in. (122 x 174cm.)
    Christie's South Kensington, 18 april 1996 (16*) GBP 5,750   US$ 8,719

LIPPI Filippino (Italy c. 1457-1504) Italian
THE PIETA oil on panel, 6¼ x 3½in. (15.8 x 8.9cm.)
PROV.: Henry Harris; his sale, Sotheby's, London, Oct. 24-5 (2nd day), 1950, lot 192 as *Florentine
School* late 15th Century (GBP 10 to the present owner).
LIT.: J. Pope-Hennessy, *Learning to Look*, 1991, p. 313.
    Christie's New York, 10 January 1996 (93**) US$ 17,250   US$ 17,250

LISS Johann (1570-1629)
CHRIST IN THE GARDEN oil on copper, 11 1/8 x 8¼in. (28.2 x 21cm.) sd 'Ioanes. liss : F./ A:
D:i(6)2.:' and on the reverse 'Johann Liss'
PROV.: A. Berlan, Trieste, before 1823; with Ugo Jandalo, Rome; Professor Hans Purrmann, Zurich.
EXH.: Berlin, Akademie der Kunst, *Gemälde alter Meister aus Berliner Besitz*, 1925, p. 39, no. 224;
Berlin, Orangerie des Schlosses Charlottenburg, *Deutsche Maler und Zeichner des 17 Jahrhunderts*,
1966, p. 55, no. 50, fig. 48 (catalogue by R. Klessmann); Augsburg, Rathaus, *Johann Liss*, 2 Aug.-2
Nov. 1975, pp. 133-4, no. A41, fig.41(catalogue by R. Klessmann).

LIT.: A. Morassi, Un dipinto sconosciuto di Giovanni Lys, *L'Arte*, XXVI, 1923, pp. 115ff.,fig. 1; G.J. Hoogewerff, Verslag van verrichte studien en belangrijke voorvallen op kunstwetenschappelijk gebied, in *Mededeelingen van het Nederlandsch Historisch Instituut te Rome*, IV, 1924, pp. XLIVff., pl. 2; N. Pevsner and O. Grautoff, Barockmalerei in den romantischen Ländern, in *Handbuch der Kunstwissenschaft*, Wildpark-Potsdam1928, pp. 156-7 fig. 124; R.A. Peltzer, *Allgemeines Lexikon der Bildenden Kunstler* [Thieme Becker], XX111, Leipzig, 1929, p. 286; G. Fiocco, *Venetian Painting of the Seicento and Settecento*, Florence and New York, 1929, pp. 20 and 78; K. Steinbart *Johann Liss, der Maler aus Holstein,* Berlin, 1940, pp. 124-5 and 163, pl. 49; V. Bloch, Lissiana, in *Festschrift: Aan Max J. Friedländer*, The Hague, 1942 (German edition); *Oud Holland*, LXI, 1946; K. Steinbart, *Johann Liss Vienna*, 1946, pp. 40 and 62, figs. 48-9. V. Bloch, Liss and His 'Fall of Phaeton', *The Burlington Magazine*, XCII, no. 571, Oct. 1950, p. 281; R. Wittkower, *Art and Architecture in Italy 1600 to 1750*, Harmondsworth, 1958, p. 67; K. Steinbart, Das Werk des Johann Liss in alter und neuer Sicht, in *Saggi e memorie de storia dell' arte* 11, 1958-59, p. 199; V. Block, *Current and Forthcoming Exhibitions, German Painters and Draughtsmen of the Seventeenth Century*, in Berlin, The Burlington Magazine, CV111, no. 763, Oct. 1966, p. 546; C. Donzelli and G.M. Pilo, *I pittori del Seicento Veneto*, Florence, 1967, p. 242; C. Tumpel, Ikonographische Beiträge zu Rembrandt, in *Jahrbuch der Hamburger Kunstsammlungen*, X111, 1968, p. 99, no. 13.

Christie's London, 7 July 1995 (106**) GBP 518,500	US$	827,086

LISSE Dirk van der (Breda 1600c.-1669 The Hague?) Dutch
NYMPHS DRYING THEMSELVES AFTER BATHING oil on panel, 11¼ x 9in. (28.5 x 23cm.) slr with monogram 'DVL'
PROV.: Walther Bernt, Munich.

Sotheby's London, 5 July 1995 (155**) GBP 7,475	US$	11,924

LODI Carlo (with Antonio Rossi, 1700-1753)) (1701-1765) Italian
FIDING OF MOSES AND MOSES DRIVING THE BANDITS FROM THE WELL OF THE DAUGHTERS OF JETHRO tempera on canvas (a pair), each: 70½ x 135in. (179.1 x 342.9cm.)

Sotheby's New York, 16 May 1996 (65**) US$ 76,750	US$	76,750

LOHSE Richard Paul (Zurcich 1902-) German
VARIAZIONE C acrylic on canvas, 48 x 48cm. sd and titled on the reverse (1952-1972)

Finearte Milan, 19 March 1996 (35**) ITL 34,500,000	US$	22,073

LOIR Luigi (1845-1916) French
A STREET NEAR LES INVALIDES, PARIS oil on canvas, 24 x 35¾in. (61 x 90.8cm.) slr 'Loir Luigi'

Christie's New York, 14 February 1996 (128**) US$ 63,000	US$	63,000

LOIR Nicolas (Paris 1624-1679) French
THE VIRGIN AND CHILD WITH ST JOHN THE BAPTIST IN A LANDSCAPE oil on canvas, 24.5 x 31cm.

Christie's Monaco, 14 June 1996 (18**) FRF 54990	US$	10,618

LOISEAU Gustave (Paris 1865-1935 Paris) French
LE QUATORZE JUILLET, RUE CLIGNANCOURT oil on canvas, 25 1/8 x 20 7/8in. (64 x 53cm.) slr 'G. Loiseau'
LIT.: Didier Imbert Fine Art will include this painting in their forthcoming *catalogue raisonné*.

Christie's New York, 1 May 1996 (165**) US$ 112,500	US$	112,500

LE PORT DE FÉCAMP oil on canvas, 18 x 21½in. (46 x 55cm.) sdlr 'G. Loiseau 1924'

Étude Tajan Paris, 10 June 1996 (25**) FRF 220,000	US$	42,482

LE PORT DE FÉCAMP oil on canvas, 19 5/8 x 24in. (50 x 61cm.) sdll 'G Loiseau. 1924' d on the reverse and inscr. with title on the stretcher and on a label on the stretcher
PROV.: Galerie Durand-Ruel, Paris; Private collection London.

LIT.: This work will be included in the forthcoming *catalogue raisonné* on this artist currently being prepared by Monsieur Didier Imbert.

Phillips London, 26 June 1995 (8**) GBP 17,000	US$	27,126

LES MEULES oil on canvas, 21 1/4 x 31 7/8in. (54 x 81cm.) inscr. with title on the stretcher
PROV.: Galerie Durand-Ruel, Paris; O'Hana Gallery, London; Private collection London.
LIT.: This work will be included in the forthcoming *catalogue raisonné* on this artist currently being prepared by Monsieur Didier Imbert.

Phillips London, 26 June 1995 (24**) GBP 17,000	US$	27,126

LE VILLAGE ENNEIGÉ oil on canvas, 23 7/8 x 28 7/8in. (60.5 x 73.5cm. sdlr 'G. Loiseau 21 mars 99'
PROV.: Galerie Durand-Ruel, Paris; O'Hana Gallery, London; Private collection London.
LIT.: This work will be included in the forthcoming *catalogue raisonné* on this artist currently being prepared by Monsieur Didier Imbert.

Phillips London, 26 June 1995 (30**) GBP 25,000	US$	39,891

LE PONT DE L'ARCHÉVECHE oil on canvas, 21¼ x 25 3/8in. (54 x 64.5cm.) slr indistinctly
PROV.: Jacques O'Hana Ltd., London, 1950; Private collection, London.

Phillips London, 27 November 1995 (5**) GBP 9,000	US$	14,078

LA PLAINE DE NEUBOURG-LA MOISSON oil on canvas, 23¾ x 36 3/8in. (60.5 x 92.5cm.) s 'G.Loiseau', inscr. with title on a label on the reverse, also inscr. with title and d '1928' on the stretcher
PROV.: Galerie Durand-Ruel, Paris; O'Hana Gallery, London; Private collection, London.

Phillips London, 27 November 1995 (6**) GBP 12,000	US$	18,771

L'ENTRÉE DU VILLAGE oil on canvas, 46 x 55cm. sdlr 'G. Loiseau 1904'
LIT.: will be included in the forthcoming *catalogue raisonné Gustave Loiseau*, currently being prepared by M. Didier Imbert.

Étude Tajan Paris, 27 October 1995 (20**) FRF 120,000	US$	24,273

ROUTE DU VILLAGE oil on canvas, 19 5/8 x 24 1/8in. (50 x 61.3cm.) ll 'G Loiseau'
PROV.: Anon. sale, Sotheby's, New York, Feb. 18, 1988, lot 14 (acquired by the present owner).

Christie's New York, 8 November 1995 (165**) US$ 29,900	US$	29,900

LONGA Louis Anselme (1809-1869) French
FIGURES BEFORE A NORTH AFRICAN TOWN oil on canvas, 48 3/8 x 70¼in. (123 x 178.5cm.) sll 'Longa' (1845)

Phillips London, 11 June 1996 (67**) GBP 6,000	US$	9,252

LONGE Robert de {called} Il Fiammingo (1646-1709) Flemish
THE GODS ON THE OLYMPIC MOUNTAIN oil on canvas, 165 x 274cm.

Christie's Rome, 4 June 1996 (549**) ITL 10,000,000	US$	6,485

LONGHI Alessandro (Venice 1733-1813) Italian
PORTRAIT OF A CHILD, SAID TO BE MARIE LOUISE OF PARMA, IN ELEGANT DRESS WITH HER BIRD oil on canvas, 38 x 28½in. (96.5 x 72.4cm.)
PROV.: NewhouseGgalleries, New York, there acquired by the present owner in the 1950's.

Sotheby's New York, 16 May 1996 (76**) US$ 107,000	US$	107,000

LONGHI Pietro (Venice 1702-1785) Italian
PORTAIT OF A LADY WITH A ROSE oil on canvas, 73 x 61cm

Finearte Milan, 25 November 1995 (117**) ITL 32,200,000	US$	20,213

LOOSE Basile de (Zele (Dendermonde) 1809-1885 Brussels) Belgian
A FARMYARD SCENE oil on canvas, 30¼ x 36¼in. (77 x 92cm.) slr
      Sotheby's London, 13 March 1996 (8**) GBP 6,900   US$ 10,538

LOOTEN Jan (1618 ca-1681) Dutch
A MOUNTAINEOUS LANDSCAPE WITH TRAVELLERS AND CAVALRYMEN ON A ROAD,
AN EXTENSIVE VALLEY BEYOND oil on canvas, 139 x 218cm. sdll 'JL:fecit 1642'
      Christie's Amsterdam, 13 November 1995 (120**) NLG 39,100   US$ 24,642

LOOY Jacobus van der (1855-1930) Dutch
HET BLOEMVISIOEN OOSTINDISCHE KERS oil on canvas, 104 x 135cm. signed twice 'Jac v
Looy'
PROV.: The artist's estate; His Sale, Paul Brandt/verkooplokaal Notarishuis, Haarlem, 25 Jan. 1949,
lot no. 128.
EXH.: Haarlem, Het Huis van Looy (1930-1949).
LIT.: Jacobus van Looy, *De Wonderbaarlijke avonturen van Zededeus(deelI:43ste avond),* Haarlem
1901, p. 137; *Schilderijen en teekenwerk van Jacobus van Looy in het 'Huys van Looy' te Haarlem,*
1934(?), p.9; R. Bionda, Carel Blotkamp ed., *De Schilders van Tachtig,* Zwolle 1991, p.223.
      Christie's Amsterdam, 26 October 1995 (179**) NLG 43,700   US$ 27,554

LOPES, GREGORIO Gregorio (active 1518-before 1550-)
THE ASCENSION OF THE VIRGIN - A FRAGMENT oil on panel, 116.5 x 104.8cm.
EXH.: Stuttgart, Württembergisches Staatsgalerie, on loan inv. no. LS205.
      Christie's Amsterdam, 13 November 1995 (69*) NLG 46,000   US$ 28,991

LOTH Johann Carl (attr.) (Munich 1632-1698 Venice) German
GIUSEPPE SPIEGA I SOGNI oil on canvas, 140 x 156cm.
      Finearte Rome, 18 October 1995 (372**) ITL 43,700,000   US$ 27,227

LOUIS Morris (1912-1962) American
NUMBER 36 acrylic on canvas -unframed-, 84 x 38¼in. (213.2 x 97cm.) (1962)
PROV.: André Emmerich Gallery, New York; Mr. and Mrs. Phillip Stern, Washington, D.C.
EXH.: Washington, D.C., Washington Gallery of Modern Art, *Morris Louis,* March-April 1967, no.
14.
LIT.: D. Upright, *Morris Louis:The Complete Paintings, A Catalogue Raisonné,* New York 1985, p.
179, no. 518 (illustrated).
      Christie's New York, 14 November 1995 (12**) US$ 178,500   US$ 178,500

2-09 acrylic on canvas, 83 x 22in. (210.8 x 55.8cm.) (1961-62)
PROV.: André Emmerich Gallery, New York; The Marcia Simon Weisman Collection, Los Angeles.
EXH.: Los Angeles, Museum of Contemporary Art, *The Marcia Simon Weisman Collection,* Feb.-
May 1992. Los Angeles, Museum of Contemporary Art; Houston, *The Menil Collection;* New York,
The Solomon R. Guggenheim Museum and The Philadelphia Museum of Art, *Rolywholyover: A
Circus,* Sept. 1993-Jan. 1995.
LIT.: D. Upright, *Morris Louis: The Complete Paintings,* New York 1985, p. 182, no. 545
(illustrated).
      Christie's New York, 7 May 1996 (17**) US$ 96,000   US$ 96,000

LOWRY Laurence Stephen, R.A. (Manchester 1887-1976) British
FYLDE FARM oil on panel, 13 x 18½in. (33 x 47cm.) sdll 'L.S. Lowry 1943'
PROV.: Dr F.H. Kroch.
EXH.: London, Lefevre Gallery, *Paintings by L.S. Lowry,* Feb.-March 1945, no. 23; Liverpool,
Walker Art Gallery, *L.S. Lowry,* April-June 1973, no. 44.
      Christie's London, 20 June 1996 (120**) GBP 14,375   US$ 22,167

SAILING SHIPS oil on board, 6 x 8in. (15 x 21.5cm.) sdlr 'L.S. Lowry 1956'
PROV.: Helen Kapp, thence by descent to Edmund Kapp, from whom purchased by the present owner.
EXH.: London, Royal Academy, 1958, no. 126; London, Royal Academy, *L.S. Lowry*, Sept.-Nov. 1976, no. 217.

Christie's London, 20 June 1996 (122**) GBP 20,700   US$ 31,920

A MAN WALKING oil on board, 13 7½in. (33 x 19cm.) sdll 'L.S. Lowry 1961'
PROV.: Lefèvre Gallery, London.

Christie's London, 21 March 1996 (143**) GBP 23,000   US$ 35,125

AT THE PIT HEAD oil on panel, 17½ x 12½in. (44.5 x 31.8cm.) slr 'L.S. Lowry' (1920)
PROV.: Anon sale; Christie's, 1 March 1974, lot 32, where purchased by the present owner.

Christie's London, 21 March 1996 (156**) GBP 23,000   US$ 35,125

THE ARGUMENT oil on board, 7¼ x 5½in. (18.5 x 14cm.) sdlr 'L.S. Lowry 1962'
PROV.: Given by the Artist to Susanna Sutton (née Faulds).

Christie's London, 21 March 1996 (160**) GBP 29,900   US$ 45,663

STREET SCENE IN SNOW oil on panel, 14¼ x 24¼in. (36.2 x 31.6cm.) sdll 'L.S. Lowry 1941'
PROV.: Professor and Mrs. H.B. Maitland; Mrs. D.L. Dickey.
EXH.: Salford, Festival of Britain, City Museum and Art Gallery, *Retropective Exhibition of L. S. Lowry*, July-August 1951, no.53; Manchester, City Art Gallery, *Retrospective Exhibition of L.S. Lowry*, June-July 1959, no.35; Sheffield, Graves Art Gallery, *Works of L.S. Lowry*, Sept.-Oct. 1962, no.31; Sunderland, Arts Council of Great Britain, Art Gallery, *L.S. Lowry*, August-Sept. 1966, no.36: this exhibition travelled to Manchester, Whitworth Art Gallery, Sept.-Oct. 1966; Bristol, City Art Gallery, Oct.-Nov. 1966; and London, Tate Gallery, Nov. 1966-Jan. 1967; Sheffield, City Art Gallery, British Paiting 1900-1960, Nov.-Dec. 1975, no.97; Edinburgh, Scottish Arts Council, Arts Council Gallery, *L.S. Lowry*, Dec. 1977-Jan. 1978, no.25: this exhibition travelled to Hawick, Wilton Lodge Museum, Jan.-Feb. 1978; Aberdeen, Art Gallery, Feb.-March 1978; Dundee, Museum and Art Gallery, March-April 1978; Inverness, Museum and Art Gallery, April-May 1978; and Perth, Museum and Art Gallery, May-June 1978; Salford Art Gallery, *L.S. Lowry Centenary Exhibition*, Oct.-Nov. 1987, no.0, fig.13; and on loan; London, Barbican Art Gallery, L.S. Lowry, August-Oct. 1988, no.99 (ex-catalogue) Manchester, City Art Gallery (on loan).
LIT.: M. Levy, *The Paintings of L.S. Lowry*, London, 1975, pl.21.

Christie's London, 21 November 1995 (239**) GBP 104,900   US$ 164,086

POLITICAL MEETING, ASHTON-UNDER-LYNE oil on canvas, 12 x24in. (30.5 x 61cm.) sdll 'L.S. Lowry 1953'
PROV.: The Hon. the Lord Rhodes of Saddleworth, K.G., D.F.C.,P.C.,D.L., by whom purchased direct from, the Artist, and thence by descent.
EXH.: Accrimgton, Howarth Art Gallery, *Paintings and Drawings by by L.S. Lowry, R.A.*, 1971, no. 63; Salford, City Art Gallery, *Works by L.S. Lowry*, Nov.-Dec. 1993, no. 55: this exhibition travelled to Stalybridge, Astley Cheetham Art Gallery, May-June 1994.

Christie's London, 21 November 1995 (243**) GBP 122,500   US$ 191,616

LUCE Maximilien (Paris 1858-1941) French
A FLOODED LANDSCAPE, ROLLEBOISE oil on canvas, 27.5 x 41cm. sdll 'Luce 1925'

Christie's Amsterdam, 5 June 1996 (222*) NLG 7,475   US$ 4,368

UN JARDIN AU GRÉSILLON, POISSY oil on canvas, 21 1/4 x 25½in. (54 x 64.8cm.) sdll 'Luce 94'; sd again and titled on the stretcher 'MAXIMILIEN LUCE 1894 UN JARDIN AU GRESILLON'
PROV.: Jules de Paquit, Paris.
EXH.: Paris, Galerie des Néo-Impressionistes, *Tableaux de M. Luce et Aquarelles de Paul Signac*, Nov.-Dec. 1894, no. 11; Brussels, *La Libre Esthètique*, 1895, no. 386; Paris, Galerie Bernheim-Jeune, *50 ans de peinture, M. Luce*, June 1929, no. 59.

LIT.: P. Cazeau, *M. Luce*, Paris 1982, p. 80 (illustrated); J. Bouin-Luce and D. Bazetoux, *Maximilien Luce, Catalogue de l'oeuvre peint*, Paris 1986, vol. II, no. 104 (illustrated p. 32).

Christie's New York, 1 May 1996 (127**) US$ 233,500	US$	233,500

USINE AU CLAIR DE LUNE oil on canvas, 22 x 18 1/8in. (55.9 x 46cm.) sdlr 'Luce 98' (1898)
PROV.: Sale: London, Christie's, 25 February 1981, lot 28; Sale: Versailles, Martin et Debesnois, 1 June 1980, no. 64.
LIT.: Jean Bouin-Luce and Denise Bazetoux, *Mazimilien Luce, Catalogue Raisonné de l'Oeuvre Peint*, vol. II, Paris, 1986, no. 1067 (illustrated p. 266).

Sotheby's New York, 2 May 1996 (133**) US$ 151,000	US$	151,000

FEMME ASSISE oil on canvas, 18½ x 21¾in. (47 x 55.2cm.)
PROV.: Schweitzer Gallery, New York.
LIT.: Jean Bouin-Luce and Denise Bazetoux, *Maximilien Luce, Catalogue raisonné de l'oeuvre Peint*, vol II, Paris, 1986, no. 87, illustrated p. 28.

Sotheby's New York, 2 May 1996 (162**) US$ 46,000	US$	46,000

LE PARK-DELFSHAVEN oil on canvas, 46 x 64.5cm. sdll 'Luce 1907-1908'
PROV.: Private collection.
EXH.: Probably: Paris, Galerie Bernheim, 19 April-1 May 1909, no. 24.
LIT.: Philippe Cazeau, *Maximilien Luce*, La Bibliothèque des Arts, Lausanne - Paris, 1982, p. 154; *Maximilien Luce, catalogue de l'oeuvre peint*, Éditions JBL, 1986, p. 169, no. 1500.

Étude Tajan Paris, 27 October 1995 (23**) FRF 130,000	US$	26,296

LUCEBERT Lubertus Jacobus Swaanswijk, {called} (Amsterdam 1924-1994) Dutch

FIGURES oil on canvas, 75 x 110cm. sdlr 'Lucebert 73.VI.24'

Christie's Amsterdam, 5 June 1996 (360**) NLG 19,550	US$	11,423

BIG BOY WITH ORANGE COLOURED HAIR oil on canvas, 131 x 90cm. sdlr 'Lucebert 64', and inscr. with title and numbered 64/26 on the reverse
PROV.: Marlborough Gallery, London, no. 31226.1.

Christie's Amsterdam, 5 June 1996 (361**) NLG 13,800	US$	8,063

A SELF PORTRAIT oil on canvas, 50 x 72cm. sll 'Lucebert' (executed *ca.* 1976)

Christie's Amsterdam, 6 December 1995 (267**) NLG 25,300	US$	15,677

DE WATERMAN, DE WATERVROUW oil on canvas, 90 x 120cm. sdr 'Lucebert 68' inscr. with title on the reverse
PROV.: Galerie Christel, Helsinki.

Christie's Amsterdam, 6 December 1995 (279**) NLG 17,250	US$	10,689

AN ABSTRACT COMPOSITION pen and black ink, black crayon and gouache on paper, 44 x 60cm. slr 'Lucebert'

Christie's Amsterdam, 6 December 1995 (287*) NLG 12,650	US$	7,839

TWO FIGURES oil and mixed media on canvas, 40 x 30cm. sdll 'Lucebert `68'

Christie's Amsterdam, 6 December 1995 (320) NLG 10,925	US$	6,770

HET NARRENPAK acrylics on canvas, 90 x 130cm. sdlr centre 'Lucebert`79' and d again on the reverse and inscr. with title on the stretcher
PROV.: Galerie Springer, Berlin.

Christie's Amsterdam, 6 December 1995 (338**) NLG 29,900	US$	18,528

A FIGURE oil on canvas, ,150 x 100cm. sdlr 'Lucebert 61'

Christie's Amsterdam, 6 December 1995 (350**) NLG 46,000	US$	28,504

341

LUKE John, R.U.A. (1906-1975) Irish
THE LOCKS AT EDENDERRY tempera on board, 10½ x 14½in. (26.6 x 36.8cm.) sdll 'J. Luke 1944'; sd and inscr. "Edenderry' painted by John Luke, 1944', extensively with colour and method notes on a label attached to the reverse
PROV.: John Magee, Belfast; J.C. Sheridan, thence by descent.
EXH.: Belfast, Arts Council of Northern Ireland, *John Luke,* 1978, no. 44.
LIT.: J. Hewitt, *John Luke (1906-1975),* Belfast, 1978, p. 51, p. 52 (illustrated).
Christie's London, 9 May 1996 (139**) GBP 95,000 US$ 143,852

LUKS George Benjamin (1867-1933) American
LOWER AUSABLE LAKE, ADIRONDACK MOUNTAINS watercolour on paper, 14 x 20in. (35.5 x 50.8cm.) slc 'George Luks'; inscr. 'Lower Ausable Lake, Adirondack Mts' on the reverse
Christie's East, 21 May 1996 (71**) US$ 7,475 US$ 7,475

LUNDENS Gerrit (1622-1677 after) Dutch
BOORS PLAYING 'LE MAIN CHAUD' AND ANOTHER GAME IN TAVERNS oil on canvas (a pair), 40 x 31.5cm. slr 'g Lundens F 1671' and ssl
PROV.: Collection Lind, Stockholm.
EXH.: Stockholm, Nationalmuseet, since 1886.
Christie's Amsterdam, 7 May 1996 (65*) NLG 23,000 US$ 13,411

LUNDQUIST Evert (Född 1904 b.-l) Swedish
STÅENDE KVINNA oil on canvas, 116 x 106cm. sdll 'Evert Lundquist 1939'; s on the reverse
Bukowskis Stockholm, 26-27 October 1995 (70**) SEK 100,000 US$ 14,645

FRÅN SACRÉ-COEUR oil on canvas, 116 x 89cm. slr 'Lundquist' (1933)
EXH.: Stockholm, Moderna Museet, *evert Lundquist-utställningen,* 1974.
LIT.: Eugen Wretholm, *Evert Luindquist,* (illustrated p. 57), Moderna Museet catalogue, 1974 (illustrated p. 33).
Bukowskis Stockholm, 26-27 October 1995 (71**) SEK 95,000 US$ 13,913

BADAREN oil on canvas, 105 x 120cm. s' Evert Lundquist' on the reverse
Bukowskis Stockholm, 24-25 April 1996 (86**) SEK 165,000 US$ 24,997

LUNY Thomas (1759-1837) British
FIGURES DRAWING IN A ROWING BOAT BEFORE ST MICHAEL`S MOUNT oil on canvas, 17¾ x 24 1/4in. (45 x 61.5cm.)
Phillips London, 10 October 1995 (41*) GBP 4,500 US$ 7,102

TEIGNMOUTH HARBOUR, DEVON oil on canvas, 19½ x 26½in. (49 x 67cm.) sdll 'Luny 1827'
Sotheby's London, 12 July 1995 (5***) GBP 5,750 US$ 9,172

THE BATTLE OF TRAFALGAR oil on canvas, 33¾ x 50¾in. (85.5 x 129cm.) sdll 'Luny 1831'
PROV.: Phillips London, 20 June 1977, lot 33.
Sotheby's London, 17 April 1996 (706**) GBP 57,600 US$ 87,339

LÜPERTZ Markus (1941 b.-l) German
DIE ZUKUNFTSTRÄUME DER ENTLAUBTEN oil on canvas, 27½ x 39 1/8in. (70 x 99.5cm.) s titled on the reverse (1982)
PROV.: Galerie Michael Werner, Cologne.
Sotheby's London, 21 March 1996 (88**) GBP 9,775 US$ 14,928

SCHNECKE (DITYRAMBISCH) distemper on canvas, 51 x 62¾in. (129.5 x 159.5cm.) s ini. 'ML' (1972)
PROV.: Acquired directly from the artist by the present owner in 1972.
EXH.: Baden-Baden, Kunsthalle, *Markus Lüpertz: Bilder, Gouachen und Zeichnungen 1967-1973,*

August-September 1973; Hamburg, Kunsthalle, *Markus Lüpertz*, 1977 (illustrated in the catalogue p. 68).

        Christie's London, 26 October 1995 (118**) GBP 63,100   US$ 99,590

TOSKANISCHER SOMMER II oil on canvas, ,250 x 200cm. slr 'ML' (linked) sd; titled 'Markus Lüpertz Toskanischer Sommer II' on reverse (1991)

        Lempertz Cologne, 28 November 1995 (780**) DEM 90,000   US$ 63,523

LUTTICHUYS Simon (London 1610-1661) Dutch
STILL-LIFE OF AN ORANGE AND NUTS ON A METALL PLATE, A TANKARD, A SILVER GILT COVERED CUP, AN OVERTURNED ROEMER AND OTHER GLASSES, ALL ON A DRAPED LEDGE oil on canvas, 27¼ x 22½in. (69.2 x 57.2cm.)
PROV.: Sale: Christie's London, 1 December 1978, lot 69; Schickman Gallery, from whom purchased by the present owner.

        Sotheby's New York, 11 January 1996 (188**) US$ 29,900   US$ 29,900

LYNCH Albert (1851 b.) Peruvian
IN THE STUDIO oil on canvas, 51 x 35in. (129 x 89cm.) slr 'Albert Lynch'

        Christie's New York, 14 February 1996 (133**) US$ 43,700   US$ 43,700

LYNN John (fl. 1826-1845) British
A ROYAL VISIT TO THE ISLE OF WIGHT oil on canvas, 18½ x 27½in. (47 x 70cm.) sdll '1845'

        Phillips London, 18 June 1996 (33**) GBP 4,800   US$ 7,402

MAATEN Jacob Jan van der (1820-1879) Dutch
FIGURES ON A COUNTRY LANE WITH A GARDEN PARTY IN A PARK oil on canvas, 32 5/8
x 45 5/8in. (83 x 116cm.) sd '1859'
        Phillips London, 14 November 1995 (3**) GBP 8,000   US$ 12,514

FAGGOT-GATHERERS ON A PATH ALONG A SHIP-CANAL oil on canvas, 60 x 91 sdlr 'J.J. vd
Maaten ft 1856'
        Christie's Amsterdam, 26 October 1995 (25**) NLG 20,700   US$ 13,052

ON A HOT SUMMER DAY oil on canvas, 76 x 104cm. sd 'J.J. vd Maaten ft 1856'
        Christie's Amsterdam, 26 October 1995 (26*) NLG 17,250   US$ 10,876

MACCARI Mino (Siena 1898-1989 Rome) Italian
CARNEVALE oil on board, 60 x 110cm. slr 'Maccari'; inscr. 'da me dipinto circa il 1959, Min
Maccari' on the reverse (1959)
        Finearte Milan, 18 June 1996 (221**) ITL 32,200,000   US$ 20,882

BALLERINE oil on board, 60 x 110cm. sdll 'Maccari 962'; inscr. 'da me dipinto al Cinquale nel
1962, Mino Maccari' on the reverse (1962)
        Finearte Milan, 18 June 1996 (256**) ITL 32,200,000   US$ 20,882

MACKE August (Meschede (Westfalia) 1887-1914 Perthes-les-Hurlus) German
UNTER DEN LAUBEN IN THUN watercolour on paper, 36.6 x 49cm. (1913)
LIT.: Vriessen, *Verzeichnis der Aquarelle*, nr. 304 unter dem Titel *Ein Spaziergängenmotiv.*
        Lempertz Cologne, 29 November 1995 (273***) DEM 700,000   US$ 49,4071

MACKINTOSH Charles Rennie (1868-1928) Scottish
WINTER ROSE watercolour, 10¼ x 10in. (26 x 25.5cm.) sdlr 'C.R. MACKINTOSH/ 1916', inscr.
'Winter Rose-/C.R. Mackintosh/2 Hans Studios/43A Glebe Place Chelsea SW3' on the reverse
        Sotheby's London, 29 August 1995 (983**) GBP 36,700   US$ 59,404

MACLISE Daniel, R.A. (Cork 1806-1870) British
OTHELLO AND DESDEMONA oil on panel, 25½ x 30½in. (64.8 x 77.5cm.) sd 'D. Maclise/1859'
PROV.: Sir Charles Tennant and thence by descent.
EXH.: London, Guildhall, 1904, no. 71.
        Christie's London, 6 November 1995 (130**) GBP 19550   US$ 30,580

MACMONNIES LOW Mary Fairchild (America 1858-1946) American
GARDEN IN GIVERNY oil on canvas, 29¾ x 55½in. (75.6 x 141cm.) sll 'Mary MacMonnies'
        Christie's New York, 13 September 1995 (58**) US$ c   US$ 11,500

MACWHIRTER John (Scotland 1839-1911) Scottish
DARK LOCH CORNISK oil on canvas, 48 x 74in. (119.4 x 188cm.) slr 'MacW'
EXH.: London, The Royal Academy, 1899, no. 19; Edinburgh, The Royal Scottish Academy, 1900,
no. 351; London, The Fine Arts Society, Spring 1988, exh. cat. no.84.
        Christie's New York, 2 November 1995 (211**) US$ 13,800   US$ 13,800

MADELINE Paul (1863-1920) French
VALLÉE DE LA CREUSE oil on canvas, 54 x 65cm. sll 'P. Madeline'
        Étude Tajan Paris, 28 March 1996 (3*) FRF 48,000   US$ 9,488

MAES Dirck (Haarlem 1659-1717) Dutch
FUN ON THE ICE IN FRONT OF A CITY oil on canvas, 37 x 33cm. framed s mono on the large
sledge 'M'
        Dorotheum Vienna, 17 October 1995 (151**) ATS 220,000   US$ 22,067

WOODED LANDSCAPE WITH RESTING HORSEMEN oil on canvas, 51 x 73cm.
PROV.: Private collection, Vienna.
          Dorotheum Vienna, 17 October 1995 (304**) ATS 90,000   US$ 9,028

A HUNTING PARTY PICNICKING IN A WOODED LANDSCAPE oil on canvas, 23 1/8 x 27
3/8in. (58.8 x 69.5cm.) s 'D. Maas'
          Christie's London, 19 April 1996 (110**) GBP 16,100   US$ 24,412

A STAG HUNT IN A ROCKY LANDSCAPE oil on canvas, 39 7/8 x 58 5/8in. (101.3 x 148.9cm.)
PROV.: With Müllenmeister (acc. to a label on the reverse).
          Christie's London, 7 July 1995 (277**) GBP 10580   US$ 16,877

MAES Nicolaes (Dordrecht 1634-1693 Amsterdam) Dutch
PORTRAIT OF A YOUNG SPORTSMAN IN CLASSICAL DRESS AND A LADY IN A
LANDSCAPE: A PAIR OF PAINTINGS both oil on canvas, each: 22¼ x 17½in. (56.5 x 44.5cm.)
both signed ll
PROV.: G.T.A.M. Baron van Brienen van de Grootelindt, the Hague (Sale: Paris, May 8, 1865, lots
60-61); J. Dollfus, Paris (Sale: Paris, May 20, 1912, lots 58-59); Frost and Reed, New York.
LIT.: C. Hofstede de Groot, *A Catalogue Raisonné of the Works of the Most Eminent Dutch Painters
of the Seventeenth Century*, vol. VI, 1916, pp. 572, 591, cat. nos. 414, 526.
          Sotheby's New York, 11 January 1996 (67**) US$ 48,875   US$ 48,875

PORTRAIT OF A GENTLEMAN, HALF-LENGHT, WEARING A RED MANTLE oil on canvas,
42½ x 34½in. (108.2 x 88cm.) sd or bears signature 'MAES 1677'
          Sotheby's London, 6 December 1995 (168**) GBP 14,375   US$ 22,122

A PORTARIT OF A LADY, STANDING THREE-QUATER LENGHT BY A FOUNTAIN, IN A
LANDSCAPE SETTING oil on canvas, 26½ x 21¼in. (67 x 54cm.) (late 1670's)
PROV.: Anonymous sale, Amsterdam, Christie's, 30 October 1978, lot 403 (dfl. 14,000);
Anonymous sale, london, Christie's, 24 October 1986, lot 230.
          Sotheby's London, 6 December 1995 (241**) GBP 43,300   US$ 66,636

MAESTOSI F (Italy) Italian
SALA DELL'LLIAD, PITTI PALACE, FLORENCE oil on canvas, 31¾ x 39½in. (80.7 x 100.3cm.)
sll 'F Maestosie
          Christie's New York, 2 November 1995 (234**) US$ 14,950   US$ 14,950

MAGGIOTTO Domenico (attr.) (1713-1794) Italian
WOMEN BATHING IN A FOREST POOL AND SHEPHERDESSES TEASING A SLEEPING
SHEPHERD oil on canvas (a pair), each: 17¼ x 13¾in. (43.8 x 34.9cm.)
          Sotheby's New York, 16 May 1996 (64**) US$ 26,450   US$ 26,450

MAGNASCO Alessandro {called} Il Lissandrino (Genua 1667-1749) Italian
INTERIOR OF A PRISON WITH JOSEPH INTERPRETING DREAMS oil on canvas, 52¾ x
69¾in. (134 x 177cm.)
PROV.: Comte André Parfait de Bizemont, Orléans; Marquis de Ganay; with A. Ward-Jackson,
London, 1979.
EXH.: On loan, Leeds Castle, Kent, 1980-1995.
LIT.: A. de Bortoli, 'Aggiunte al Magnasco milanese', in *Arte Cristana*, 1990, p. 276, no. 739,
reproduced fig. 11, as painted entirely by Magnasco.
          Sotheby's London, 5 July 1995 (57**) GBP 111,500   US$ 177,859

MAGNASCO Alessandro {called} Il Lissandrino (attr.) (Genua 1667-1749) Italian
DANCERS AND MUSICIANS IN A GUARDROOM oil on canvas, 23½ x 46½in. (59.7 x
118.1cm.)
          Sotheby's New York, 16 May 1996 (139**) US$ 16,100   US$ 16,100

MAGNELLI Alberto (Florence 1888-1971 Paris) Italian
OMBRES VALLONEES, OR VAGUES MESUREES oil on canvas, 92 x 73cm sd 'Magnelli 63', s
on the reverse: 'Magnelli 'Ombres vallonées' Bellevue 1964'
PROV.: Galleria 'Il Collezionista', Roma.
EXH.: Roma, *Magnelli*, galleria 'Il Collezionista', 1970, cat.no.30.
LIT.: A.Maissonnier, *Alberto Magnelli l`oeuvre peint*, XX siècle, Parigi, 1975, no.859; D.Frasnay,
Peintres et Sculpteurs, leur monde, edit. Draeger, Parigi, 1969, p.46 (illustrated in colour);
N.Ponente, *Alberto Magnelli*, edit. 'Il Collezionista', Roma, 1973, ill. 196.
Finearte Rome, 14 November 1995 (220**) ITL 109,250,000   US$ 68,581

AUTOUR DE MOI oil on canvas, 24 x 29in. (61 x 73.7cm.) sdlr '38; sd and titled 'Paris 1938' on the
reverse
PROV.: Galerie Loeb, Paris; Acquired from the above by the present owner.
EXH.: Strasbourg, Maison d'Art Alsacienne, *Lardere, Magnelli, Severini, Signori*, March-April
1952, no. 3; Turin, Palazzo Belle Arti, Parco del Valentino, *Pittori d'Oggi*, Francia-Italia, Sept.-Oct.
1952; Forte dei Marmi, *Magnelli*, July-Aug. 1989, no. 7 (illustrated in colour in the catalogue).
LIT.: Anne Maisonnier, *Magnelli: L'Oeuvre Peint, Catalogue Raisonné*, p. 119, no. 494 (illustrated).
Christie's London, 23 May 1996 (12**) GBP 36,700   US$ 55,572

MAGRITTE René (Lessines 1898-1967 Brussels) Belgian
LA RECHERCHE DE L'ABSOLU gouache on paper, 14 1/8 x 10 5/8in. (36 x 27cm.) sll 'Magritte';
titled on the reverse 'La Recherche de l'Absolu' (ca. 1963)
PROV.: Renée Lachowsky, Brussels (acquired by the present owner in the 1960s).
LIT.: ed. D. Sylvester, *René Magritte, Catalogue Raisonné*, London 1994, vol. IV (*Gouaches,
Watercolours and Papier-Collés 1918-1967*), no. 1540 (illustrated p. 260).
Christie's New York, 1 May 1996 (372**) US$ 277,500   US$ 277,500

LE CICERONE oil on canvas, 21¼ x 25½in. (54 x 65cm.) sll 'Magritte' d titled '1947' on the reverse
PROV.: Collection Doctor Wiringer, Bruxelles; Claudio Bruni Sakralschik, New York; Galerie
Couleurs du Temps, Genève.
EXH.: Bruxelles, Dietrich, *René Magritte*, 24 January - February 1948, reproduced; New York, Hugo
Gallery, *René Magritte*, 1948, reproduced; Hollywood, Copley, *René Magritte*, 1950, reproduced;
Dusseldorf, Kunstmuseum, *Surrealisten*, 30 June -25 August 1957, reproduced in colour p. 5;
Charleroi, Palais des Beaux Arts, *Le Prix de l'Association Belge des Critiques d'art*, 5-20 April 1958,
reproduced; Liége, Musée d'art Wallon, *Les Artistes du Hainaut*, 23 January-21 February 1960,
reproduced in colour; Liege, Musée des Beaux Arts, *René Magritte*, 14 October-10 November 1960,
no. 41, reproduced; Belgique, Charleroi, *XXXVe Salon*, 1961; Hamburg and Rome, Kunsthaus und
Kunstverein, *René Magritte und der Surrealismus in Belgium*, 23 January -28 March 1982, no. 182,
reproduced; Bruxelles, Musée des Beaux Arts de Belgique, *René Magritte et le Surréalisme en
Belgique*, 24 September -5 December 1982, no. 167, reproduced; Lausanne, Fondation de
l'Hermitage, *René Magritte*, 19 June-18 October 1987, no. 76, reproduced in colour p. 196; Munich,
Kunsthalle, *Der Hypo-Kulturstiftung René Magritte, 13 November 1987 -14 February 1988, no. 68,
reproduced; Tokyo, Musée national d'art Moderne*, René Magritte, 21 MaY-10 July 1988, no. 69;
Basle and Paris, Galerie Isy Brachot, *René Magritte*, 13-19 June 1989, reproduced page 30; Tokyo,
Tokyo Art Expo, 29 Mars-2 April 1990; New York, The Pace Gallery, *René Magritte Paintings,
Drawings and Sculptures*, 11 May -30 June 1990, no. 6, reproduced.
LIT.: Harry Torczyner, *René Magritte, Signes et Images*, Editions Draeger, Le Soleil Noir, Paris
1977, no. 287, reproduced p. 152; Jacques Meuris, *Magritte*, Editions Casterman, Paris, no. 192,
reproduced p. 128; Jacques Meuris, *René Magritte*, Editions Taschen, reproduced p. 59.
Étude Tajan Paris, 10 June 1996 (57**) FRF 1,800,000   US$ 347,578

LA RECHERCHE DE L'ABSOLU gouache on paper, 17 7/8 x 13 7/8in. (45.5 x 35.2cm.) sd titled
1948'
PROV.: William Copley, New York and Los Angeles; Felix Landau Gallery, Los Angeles; Alan
Auslander Gallery, New York; Acquired from the above by the Benjamin family in 1965.
EXH.: New Haven, Yale University Art Gallery, *The Helen W. and Robert M. Benjamin Collection*,

1967, no. 104.
LIT.: David Sylvester (ed.), Sarah Whitfield and Michael Raeburn, *René Magritte, Catalogue Raisonné: Gouaches, Temperas, Watercolours and Papiers Collés, 1918-1967*, vol. 4, London, 1994, no. 1284, illustrated p.ll6.

Sotheby's New York, 2 May 1996 (260**) US$ 178,500	US$	178,500

LA RECHERCHE DE L'ABSOLU gouache on paper, 13 7/8 x 10 5/8in. (35.2 x 27cm.) sll 'Magritte' titled on the reverse (1960)
PROV.: Alexandre Iolas (acquired directly from the artist); Robert Elkon Gallery, New York; Acquired from the above by the Benjamin family in 1963.
EXH.: Paris, Galerie Rive-Droit, *René Magritte*, 1960, no. 18.
LIT.: David Sylvester (ed.), Sarah Whitfield and Michael Raeburn, *René Magritte, Catalogue Raisonné: Gouache, Temperas, Watercolours and Papers Collés, 1918-1967*, vol. 4, London, 1994, no. 1479, illustrated p. 226.

Sotheby's New York, 2 May 1996 (262**) US$ 129,000	US$	129,000

MAGRITTE René (Lessines 1898-1967 Brussels) Belgian
CECI CONTINUE DE NE PAS ETRE UNE PIPE pen and ink, 7½ x 10 5/8in. (19 x 27cm.) sdll 'Magritte 1952'
PROV.: Purchased by the parents of the present owner in the 1960s.
EXH.: *La Carte d'après Nature*, no. 8, Brussels January 1955, illustrated; Patrick Waldberg, *René Magritte*, Brussels, 1965, illustrated on the inside of the back cover; Louis Scutenaire, 'Now the painter is moved by a pipe ..', in *Surrealist Transformation*, no. 2, London, October 1968, p. 18, illustrated; Maurice Henry, *Antologia grafica del Surrealismo*, Milano, 1972, p. 151, illustrated; André Blavier, *Ceci n'est pas une Pipe, Contribution furtive à l'étude d 'un tableau de René Magritte*, Brussels, 1973, p. 24, illustrated.

Sotheby's London, 20 March 1996 (60**) GBP 28,750	US$	43,907

L'APPEL DE CIMES oil on canvas, 25 5/8 x 21¼in. (65 x 54cm.) sul 'Magritte' sd titled '1943' on the reverse
PROV.: Leon J. Stynen, Antwerp; Lieber, Antwerp; Christian Dotremont, Brussels; (1966); Renée Lachowsky, Brussels; Thomas Ammann, Zurich.
EXH.: Knokke, Casino Communal, *XVe festival beige d 'été; L'Oeuvre de René Magritte*, 1962, no. 70a; Lausanne, Fondation de l'Hermitage, *René Magritte*, 1987, no. 49, illustrated in colour in the catalogue.
LIT.: Marcel Marien, *Magritte*, Brussels, 1943, pl. 8, illustrated in colour ;
René Magritte, *La Destination: lettres à Marcel Marien (1937-1962)*, Brussels, 1977, letters and postcards, nos. 46-48, 1943, discussed; Patrick Waldberg, *René Magritte*, Brussels, 1965, p. 189, illustrated ; Uwe Schneede, *René Magritte. Leben und Werk*, Cologne, 1973, p. 75, discussed; p. 76, no. 42, illustrated; Bernard Noel, *Magritte*, Paris, 1976, p. 60, discussed ; Renée Riese Hubert, 'The other wordly landscapes of E. A. Poe and René Magritte', in *Sub-Stance*, Madison, Wisconsin, 1978, no. 21, p. 7; David Sylvester and Sarah Whitfield, *René Magritte, Catalogue raisonné, volume II: Oil Paintings and Objects, 1931-1948*, edited by David Sylvester, London, 1993, p. 308, no. 519, illustrated.

Sotheby's London, 24 June 1996 (55**) GBP 837,500	US$	1,291,442

LE BANQUET gouache on paper, 13¾ x 21in. (35 x 53.5cm.) slr 'Magritte' s titled on the reverse (ca. 1964)
PROV.: Renée Lachowsky and Lou Cosyn, Brussels; Purchased by the family of the present owner in the late 1960s.
LIT.: Sarah Whitfield and Michael Raeburn, *René Magritte, Catalogue raisonné, volume IV: Gouaches, Temperas, Watercolours and Papiers Collés*, edited by David Sylvester, London, 1994, p. 276, no. 1568, illustrated.

Sotheby's London, 24 June 1996 (56**) GBP 243,500	US$	375,482

LA FORET JOYEUSE gouache on paper, 18¼ x 14½in. (46.3 x 37cm.) slr 'Magritte' ds and titled 'Magritte 1948'
PROV.: Alexander Iolas, Paris, 1948.
EXH.: New York, Hugo Gallery, Magritte, May 1948.
LIT.: D. Sylvester, *René Magritte, catalogue raisonné, Gouaches, Temperas, Watercolours and Papiers Collés, 1918-1967*, vol. IV, 1994, p. 327, app. 144.
Christie's London, 25 June 1996 (39**) GBP 166,500

US$ 256,746

L'EMPIRE DES LUMIERES oil on canvas, 39 3/8 x 31½in. (,100 x 80cm.) s 'Magritte' sd and titled 'L'Empire des Lumières, Magritte 1938'
PROV.: Purchased directly from the Artist by the present owner in 1962.
EXH.: Edinburgh, Royal Scottish Academy, *The Belgian Contribution to Surrealism*, 1971, no. 52; Kongens Lyngby, Sophienholm, *The Belgian Contribution to Surrealism*, 1971, no. 52; Bordeaux, Centre d'Arts Plastiques Contemporains de Bordeaux, Magritte, 1977; Brussels, Palais des Beaux-Arts, *Retrospective Magritte*, 1978, no. 144. This exhibition later travelled to Paris, Centre national d'art et de culture Georges Pompidou, 1979; Humblebaek, Louisiana Museum, *René Magritte*, 1983, no. 76; Hovikodden, Kunstentret, *René Magritte: Paintings and Photographs*, 1984, no. 67; Tokyo, Musée d'art de Mitsukoshi, *Retrospective Magritte,* Nov. 1994 -Jan. 1995. This exhibition later travelled to Hyogo, Musée d'art Moderne de Hyogo,Jan-April 1995 and Fukuoka, Musée des Arts de Fukuoka, April-May 1995.
LIT.: *Letter from Harry Torczyner to the Artist*, 6 October 1958; S. Gablik, *Magritte*, London, 1970, p. 123; H. Michaux, *En Reuniant de Peintrues Inconnues*, Montpellier, 1972, p. 33; D. Sylvester, *René Magritte, Catalogue raisonné, Oil Paintings, Objects and Bronzes 1949-1967*, vol. III, London, 1993, no. 954 (illustrated p. 368).
Christie's London, 25 June 1996 (40**) GBP 2,531,500

US$ 3,903,624

LE CHEMIN DE DAMAS oil on canvas, 19½ x 28¾in. (50.2 x 73.2cm.) sul 'Magritte' titled 'Le Chemin de Damas' on the reverse (1966)
PROV.: Alexander Iolas, Paris, 1967;Anon. sale, Sotheby's, London, 5 December 1973, lot 95 (GBP35,000); Davlyn Gallery, New York, by whom acquired at the above sale and from whom purchased by the present owner.
EXH.: New York, Geneva, Milan and Paris, Galerie Iolas, *Magritte, les images en soi,* 1967; New York, Davlyn Gallery, 1974, no. 19.
LIT.: *Letter from Magritte to Bosmans*, 31 May 1966, in Magritte Bosmans, pp. 452-3; *letter from Magritte to Bosmans*, 17 July 1966, in Magritte Bosmans, p. 457; Louis Scutenaire, [untitled text], in *Paris Iolas*, 1967; S. *Gablik, Magritte*, London, 1970, no. 135 (illustrated p. 159); D. Sylvester, *René Magritte, Catalogue raisonné, Oil Paintings, Objects and Bronzes, 1949-1967, vol.* 111, London, 1994, no. 1042 (illustrated p. 431).
Christie's London, 25 June 1996 (44**) GBP 221,500

US$ 341,557

LA BONNE AVENTURE oil on canvas, 25½ x 23 1/8in. (64.7 x 54.4cm.) sur 'Magritte (1937)
PROV.: London Gallery, London, 1938; Roland Penrose, London, by whom bought from the above before the exhibition opening in April 1938; Hanover Gallery, London, by whom bought from the above circa 1960. Galleria La Medusa. Rome,1965.
EXH.: Brussels, Palais des Beaux-Arts, *Trois Peintres Surréalistes,* Dec. 1937, no. 20; London, London Gallery, *René Magritte: surrealist paintings and objects*, April-May 1938, no. 37 (as Good Fortune); London, Hanover Gallery, *René Magritte,* May- July 1964, no. 15; Turin, Notizie, *Magritte: opere scelte del 1925 al 1962*, March-April 1965 (illustrated); L'Aquila, Castello Spagnolo, 'Ommagio a Magritte' in *Alternative Attuali 2*, Aug.-Sept. 1965 (illustrated).
LIT.: *Letter from Magritte to EdwardJames*, 22 Sept. 1937; Newton, 'The self-sufficient idea: Magritte and Surrealism' in *'The Sunday Times*, London 10 April 1938, p. 15; letter from Magritte to Edward James, 16 Oct. 1939; D. Sylvester, *René Magritte, Catalogue raisonné, Oil Paintings, Objects and Bronzes, 1931-1948*, vol. II, London, 1993, no. 446 (illustrated p. 252).
Christie's London, 25 June 1996 (45**) GBP 221,500

US$ 341,557

348

LA LECTRICE SOUMISE oil on canvas, 36 1/8 x 28 7/8in. (92 x 73.5cm.) sdul 'magritte' and titled
on the reverse ' LA LECTRICE AGITéE' (1928)
PROV.: Galerie Le Centaure, Brussels; E. L. T. Mesens, Brussels; Enrico Baj, Milan.
EXH.: Aquila, Castello Spagnolo, Alternative attuali 2, Aug.-Sept. 1965 (unnumbered catalogue);
Brussels, Palais des Beaux-Arts, *Rétrospective Magritte*, Oct.- Dec. 1978, no. 69.; This exhibition
later travelled to Paris, Musée d'Art Moderne, Centre Georges Pompidou, Jan.- April 1979.
LIT.: *Letter from Magritte to Nougé* (April-May 1928) in Lettres Surréalistes, no. 146; L. Scutenaire,
René Magritte, Brussels, 1947 (illustrated); A. Robbe-Grillel and R. Magritte, La Belle Captive,
Brussels, 1975, p. 91 (illustrated); D. Sylvester, *René Magritte, Catalogue raisonné, Oil Paintings,
Objects and Bronzes 1916-1930*, Vol. I, London, 1992, no. 230 (illustrated p. 281).
    Christie's London, 28 November 1995 (41**) GBP 243,500   US$ 380,885

LE MAITRE DU PLAISIR oil on canvas, 25½ x 31½in. (65 x 80cm.) stl 'Magritte' sd titled on the
stretcher 'Magritte 1926- 'LE MAITRE DU PLAISIR''
PROV.: P.G. van Hecke, Brussels (1926); E.L.T. Mesens, Brussels (acquired from the above in
1933); Galerie Andre-François Petit, Paris (acquired from the above in 1960); Galerie Jacques
Tronche, Paris; Gino Lizzola, Milan; Anon. sale; Sotheby Parke Bernet Inc., New York, Nov. 14,
1984, lot 65 (illustrated in color); acquired from the above by the present owner.
EXH.: Brussels, Galerie Le Centaure, *Magritte*, April-May, 1927, no. 6; New York, Julien Levy
Gallery, *René Magritte*, Jan., 1938, no. 2; Paris, Galerie André-François Petit, *Hans Bellmer,
Salvador Dali, Max Ernst, René Magritte, Francis Picabia, Yves Tanguy*, Nov.-Dec., 1963
(illustrated in color); Arnhem, Gemeentemuseum, *Belgische Surrealisten*, July-Sept., 1964, no. 27;
Turin, Galleria Notizie, *Magritte: Opere Scelte del 1925 al 1962*, March-April, 1965 (illustrated).
The exhibition traveled to Rome, Galleria La Medusa, June, 1965; L'Aquila, Castello Spagnolo,
Alternative Attuali/2, Aug.-Sept., 1965, p. 7, no. 7 (illustrated); London, Marlborough Fine Art, Ltd.,
Magritte, Oct.-Nov., 1973, p. 57, no. 7 (illustrated); Darmstadt, Kunsthalle, *Realismus und Realität*,
May-July, 1975, p. 23, no. 15 (illustrated in color); New York, Marlborough Gallery, Inc., *Masters of
the 19th and 20th Centuries*, May-June, 1983, no. 29 (illustrated in color); Munich, Kunsthalle der
Hypo-Kulturstiftung, *René Magritte*, Nov., 1987-Feb., 1988, no. 28 (illustrated); Tokyo, Musée
Prefectural de Yamaguchi, *René Magritte*, April-May, 1988, p. 48, no. 15 (illustrated). The
exhibition traveled to Tokyo, Musée National d'Art Moderne, May-June, 1988; Madrid, Fundación
Juan March, *Magritte*, Jan.-April, 1989, p. 16, no. 5 (illustrated in color).
LIT.: P. Waldberg, *René Magritte*, Brussels, 1965, p. 81 (illustrated); H.H. Lerfeldt, *CRAS*, Sept.,
1973, p. 86; A. Robbe-Grillet and R. Magritte, *La belle captive*, Brussels,1975, p. 123 (illustrated);
M.M. Gedo, 'Meditations and Madness: The Art of René Magritte,' *In the Mind's Eye: Dada and
Surrealism*, Chicago, 1984, p. 80 (illustrated, fig. 18); D. Sylvester, S. Whitfield and M. Raeburn,
René Magritte, Catalague raisonné, London, 1993, vol. I *(Oil Paintings, 1916-1930),* pp. 172-173,
no. 85 (illustrated, p. 172).
    Christie's New York, 30 April 1996 (53**) US$ 222,500   US$ 222,500

L'ART DE LA CONVERSATION oil on canvas, 18¼ x 15in. (46.4 x 38cm.) stl 'Magritte' titled on
the reverse 'L'Art de la Conversation' (ca 1963)
PROV.: Galerie Malingue, Paris.
LIT.: D. Sylvester, S. Whitfield and M. Raeburn, *René Magritte, Catalague raisonné*, London, 1993,
vol. I *(Oil Paintings, 1916-1930)*, pp. 172-173, no. 983 (illustrated).
    Christie's New York, 30 April 1996 (56**) US$ 255,500   US$ 255,500

LA FOLIE ALMAYER gouache over pencil on paper laid down on paper laid down on panel, 13 7/8
x 10 1/2in. (35 x 26.5cm.) ll 'Magritte'
PROV.: Stephan Hahn, New York.
    Christie's New York, 8 November 1995 (265**) US$ 206,000   US$ 206,000

MAHLKNECHT Edmund (1820-1903) Austrian
BEGEGNUNGEN AUF DER ALM oil on canvas, 42.5 x 53cm. sd 'E. Mahlknecht 1855'
    Dorotheum Vienna, 6 November 1995 (14**) ATS 100,000   US$ 10,031

349

MAHRINGER Anton (Neuhausen/Württemberg 1902-1974 St Georgen im Gailtal) Austrian
SCHULHAUS AM ABEND oil on board, 47.5 x 61cm. sd mono. 'A.M.60'
      Dorotheum Vienna, 6 December 1995 (613**) ATS 160,000   US$ 15,778

MAHU Cornelis (Antwerp 1613-1689) Flemish
SHIP IN A ROUGH SEA, IN FRONT OF A ROCKY COAST oil on panel, 35 x 52.5cm. sr 'CM Hy'
      Dorotheum Vienna, 11 June 1996 (226**) ATS 150,000   US$ 13,923

A ROEMER ON A SILVER-GILT STAND, AN OVERTURNED PEWTER JUG, A GLASS, A PIE
ON PEWTER PLATES, AND NUTS ON A PARTLY DRAPED TABLE oil on panel, 23¼ x 34¾in.
(59 x 88.2cm.)
LIT.: N.R.A. Vroom, *a modest message,* Schiedam, 1980, II p. 94, no. 468.
      Christie's London, 19 April 1996 (138**) GBP 14,950   US$ 22,669

MAKS Kees (Cornelis Johannes) (Amsterdam 1876-1967 Amsterdam) Dutch
HOGESCHOOLRIJDER oil on canvas, ,100 x 93cm. sll 'C.J. Maks' and inscr. on a label on the
stretcher 'De heer Ernst Schuhmacher in de hooge school'
      Christie's Amsterdam, 5 June 1996 (268**) NLG 13,800   US$ 8,063

DE FRATELLINI IN HET CIRCUS MEDRANO TE PARIJS oil on canvas, ,200 x 274cm. sll 'C.J.
Maks' s again and inscr. with title on a label on the reverse (executed *circa 1920)
EXH.: The Hague, Koninklijke kunstzaal kleykamp, 1925; Amsterdam, Stedelijk Museum, *De Drie
Fraternelli*, 5-21 August 1927, no.4; Amsterdam, Stedelijk Museum, *Kees Maks*, March 1929;
Amsterdam, *de onafhankelijken*, March-April 1953; `s-Hertogenbosch, Noord Brabants Museum,
Kees Maks, 1876-1967, 17 March-7 May 1978, no. 14; The Hague, Pulchri Studio, *Kees Maks*, 1
July-19 August 1979, no. 8.
LIT.: Hans Redeker and Adriaan Venema , *Kees Maks* 1876-1967, Amsterdam 1976, p.58(ill.);
3Kunstbeeld, no. 1 (October 1976) p. 36 (ill.).
      Christie's Amsterdam, 5 June 1996 (269**) NLG 32,200   US$ 18,814

AMSTERDAMSE HARTJES oil on canvas, 78.5 x 102.5cm. slr 'C.J.Maks', s again and inscr. with
title on a label on the stretcher (ca. 1912)
EXH.: Amsterdam, Arti et Amicitiae, *Eigen bezit*, 5 June-5 July 1971.
      Christie's Amsterdam, 6 December 1995 (41*) NLG 13,800   US$ 8,551

HOGESCHOOLRIJDER oil on canvas, 84 x 110cm.
PROV.: Galerie Siau, Amsterdam.
      Christie's Amsterdam, 6 December 1995 (61*) NLG 18,400   US$ 11,402

A YOUNG WOMAN IN EVENING DRESS WITH A FAN oil on canvas, 191 x 118cm. sll
'C.J.Maks' (ca. 1933)
EXH.: Breda, de Beyerd, *Kees Maks 1876-1967*, 9 November-26 December 1979.
LIT.: Hans Redeker en Adriaan Venema, *C.J.Maks*, Amsterdam 1976, p.75 (ill.).
      Christie's Amsterdam, 6 December 1995 (175**) NLG 17,250   US$ 10,689

RECLINING NUDE ON A BLUE CLOTH oil on canvas, ,100 x 181cm. slr 'C.J.Maks' (ca.1933)
PROV.: Mrs C. Maks-Boas, Amsterdam.
LIT.: Hans Redeker en Adriaan Venema, *C.J.Maks*, Amsterdam 1976, p.71 (ill.).
      Christie's Amsterdam, 6 December 1995 (179**) NLG 17,250   US$ 10,689

AVANT LE DINER oil on canvas, 174 x 143cm.
PROV.: Mrs. C. Maks-Boas, Amsterdam; Galerie Siau, Amsterdam; Collection R. Zegers, Kerkdriel;
kunsthandel Rueb, Amsterdam.
EXH.: Amsterdam, Rijksmuseum Vincent van Gogh, *Kees Maks*, 1976.
LIT.: Hans Redeker en Adriaan Venema, *Kees Maks 1876-1967*, Amsterdam 1976, p. 26.
      Sotheby's Amsterdam, 7 December 1995 (192**) NLG 47,200   US$ 29,248

MALER ZU SCHWAZ Hans (Ulm ca. 1485-after 1529 Schwaz) German
A PORTRAIT OF A YOUNG WOMAN AGED NINETEEN oil on lime panel, 13½ x 9½in. (34 x
24cm.) inscr. along the top 'IM ALTER/19 JAR' bears date on the frame '1512'
PROV.: Baron Heinrich Thyssen-Bornemisza, by 1930.
EXH.: Munich 1930, no. 206; plate 10; Paris 1970, no. 8, plate 2; Dusseldorf 1970-1, no. 30;
Lausanne etc., 1986-7, no. 12.
LIT.: R. Heinemann 1937, vol. l, no. 253, vol. ll, plate 26; R. Heinemann, *Sammlung* 1958, no. 253;
H. von Mackowitz, *Der Maler Hans von Schwaz*, 1960, pp. 63-4, reproduced plate XVII, fig. 49, as
by Konrad Faber von Creuznach.
       Sotheby's London, 6 December 1995 (62**) GBP 43,300   US$ 66,636

MALGO Simon (c. 1745-1793)
LAKE GENEVA FROM THE SLOPES OF COLOGNY LOOKING TOWARDS EAUX-VIVES,
WITH AN ARTIST SKETCHING SEATED ON A BENCH WITH HIS COMPANIONS oil on
canvas, 22¾ x 32in. (58.4 x 81.3cm.)
PROV.: Dame Una Pope-Hennessy, and by descent.
LIT.: The catalogue of the exhibition, *Maegtige Schweiz: Inspirationer fra Schweiz*, Copenhagen,
Thorvaldsens Museum, March 15-April 30, 1973, p.114, under no.101; D. Buyssens, *Peintures et
Pastels de l'Ancienne École Genevoise: XVII - debut XIX Siecle*, Musée d'art et d'histoire, catalogue
des peintures et pastels, 1988, p.112, under no.204 as possibly with the collaboration of Jens Juel (the
staffage); J. Pope-Hennessy, *Learning to Look*, 1991, pp. 11, 314, pl. 32.
       Christie's New York, 10 January 1996 (101**) US$ 178,500   US$ 178,500

MALIAVIN Filipp Andreevich (1869-1940) Russian
BABA oil on canvas mounted on board, 49¾ x 37¾in. (126.5 x 95.5cm.) slr 'Ph. Maliavine'
       Christie's New York, 18 April 1996 (30**) US$ 28,750   US$ 28,750

MALINCONINCO Andrea (1624 / 1635-1698) Italian
SUSANNAH AND THE ELDERS oil on canvas, 127 x 198cm.
       Christie's Rome, 21 November 1995 (236**) ITL 28,000,000   US$ 17,577

MALO Vincent (Cambrai 1600-1668 Gheel) French
PEASANTS IN TAVERN INTERIOR oil on panel, 39.5 x 48.5cm
PROV.: New York, collezione privata.
EXH.: Galleria Caretto, *31a Mostra Maestri Fiamminghi ed Olandesi del XVI-XVII secolo*, Torino,
November-December 1990, no.53.
       Finearte Milan, 25 November 1995 (19**) ITL 28,750,000   US$ 18,048

MANARESI Ugo (1851-1917) Italian
HARBOUR SCENES oil on panel (a pair), a) 7 7/8 x 12 3/8in. (20 x 31.4cm.); b) 7½ x 12½in. (19.1
x 31.8cm.) each sd '81'
       Sotheby's Arcade Auctions New York, 20 July 1995 (537*) US$ 18,400   US$ 18,400

MANCADAN Jacob Sibrandi (Minnertsga 1602-1680 Leeuwarden) Dutch
CINCINNATUS CALLED FROM THE PLOUGH oil on panel, 37.8 x 50.5cm.
       Christie's Amsterdam, 7 May 1996 (86*) NLG 17,250   US$ 10,058

MANCINI Francesco (Sant'Angelo in Vado 1679-1758) Italian
FLORA oil on canvas, 61.5 x 48cm.
       Dorotheum Vienna, 6 March 1996 (48**) ATS 110,000   US$ 10,581

MANDELLI Pompilio (Luzzara 1912 b.-) italian
PAESAGGIO, 1962 oil on canvas, 110 x 74.5cm sd 'Mandelli 1962'
PROV.: Galleria San Luca, Bologna.
EXH.: Venezia, *XXXI Biennale Internazionale d`Arte*, 1962, no.79.
       Finearte Rome, 14 November 1995 (98) ITL 10,120,000   US$ 6,353

MANÉ-KATZ (1894-1962) French (Russian)
PARIS, LES CHAMPS ELYSÉES oil on canvas, 65 x 91.5cm. slr 'Mané Katz'
EXH.: Paris, 1951, *Mané Katz*, Galerie Charpentier.
       Étude Tajan Paris, 1 February 1996 (139) FRF 45,000   US$ 9,209

FEMME A SA TIOLETTE oil on canvas, 29 5/8 x 24 5/8in. (75.2 x 62.5cm.) sur 'Mané-Katz'
PROV.: Jean Tiroche Gallery, Jaffa, from whom purchased by the present owner in 1963.
       Christie's Tel Aviv, 12 October 1995 (7**) US$ 18,400   US$ 18,400

DEUX GARCONS AVEC UN ANE oil on canvas, 47½ x 23½in. (121 x 60cm.) slr 'Mané-Katz'
PROV.: Dr. and Mrs. Max Stern, Montreal.
       Christie's Tel Aviv, 12 October 1995 (45**) US$ 27,600   US$ 27,600

LA CHARETTE DE FLEURS oil on canvas, 36 x 28¾in. (91.4 x 73cm.) slr 'Mané-Katz' (1950-1959)
PROV.: O'Hana Gallery, London; Oscar Ghez, Geneva.
       Christie's Tel Aviv, 14 April 1996 (11**) US$ 29,900   US$ 29,900

L'ORCHESTRE oil on canvas, 28¾ x 23 5/8in. (73 x 60cm.) sul 'Mané-Katz'
       Christie's Tel Aviv, 14 April 1996 (55**) US$ 27,600   US$ 27,600

LES TROIS CAVALIER oil on canvas, 23 5/8 x 28 5/8in. (60 x 72.7cm.) slr 'Mané-Katz'
       Christie's East, 30 April 1996 (83**) US$ 17,250   US$ 17,250

HASSIDES oil on canvas, 8 5/85 x 13¾in. (22 x 35cm.) sll 'Mané-Katz'; s again on the reverse
       Christie's East, 30 April 1996 (132*) US$ 8,050   US$ 8,050

MUSICIAN oil on canvas, 18 x 12in. (45.8 x 30.5cm.) sul 'Mané Katz'
PROV.: Contemporary Art Master Gallery, New York.
       Christie's East, 7 November 1995 (162**) US$ 14,950   US$ 14,950

JEUNE HOMME AVEC AGNEAU oil on canvas, 32 x 15¾in. (81.2 x 40cm.) sur 'Mané-Katz' (1950-1959)
LIT.: R.S. Ariés, *Mané-Katz, The Complete Works*, London, 1972, vol. II, no. 313 (ill. p. 104).
       Christie's East, 7 November 1995 (165**) US$ 18,400   US$ 18,400

MANESSIER Alfred (1911 b.) French
HOMMAGE AU DAINT POETE JEAN DE LA CROIX oil on canvas, 74½ x 58¾in. (189 x 149.5cm.) sdll Manessier '58'; s and titled on the reverse
PROV.: Charles Laughton, Hollywood; Galeire de France, Paris.
LIT.: J.P. Hopkin, *Manessier*, London 1972, p. 185, no. 73 (illustrated in colour).
       Sotheby's London, 27 June 1996 (151**) GBP 17,250   US$ 26,600

MANET Edouard (Paris 1832-1883 Paris) French
ETUDE D'ARBRES oil on canvas, 21 1/8 x 11 3/8in. (53.6 x 28.4cm.) slr with ini. 'E.M.' (1859)
PROV.: Estate of the artist; sale, Hôtel Drouot, Paris, 4-5 February 1884, lot 68; M. de la Narde, Paris; A.M.L. Devillez, Brussels; M. Leten, Ghent.
EXH.: Ghent, Musée des Beaux-Arts, *La Peinture dans les Collections Gantoises*, March-May 1953, no. 106.
LIT.: E. Moreau-Nelaton, *Manet, raconté par lui-même*, Paris 1926, vol. II, no. 24; P. Jamot and G. Wildenstein, *Manet*, Paris 1932, vol. II, no. 76 (illustrated p. 219, pl. 466); A. Tabarant, *Manet et ses oeuvres*, Paris 1947, p. 27. no. 25; S. Orienti, *The Complete Paintings of Manet*, New York 1967, no. 18; M. Bodelson, 'Early Impressionist Sales, 1874-1894', *The Burlington Magazine*, June 1968, no. 68 (illustrated p. 344); D. Rouart and D. Wildenstein, *Edouard Manet, Catalogue raisonné*, Lausanne and Paris 1975, vol. I, no. 24 (illustrated p. 43).
       Christie's New York, 1 May 1996 (106**) US$ 266,500   US$ 266,500

MARINE oil on canvas, 15 1/8 x 18½in. (38.5 x 47cm.) sll 'Manet' (1869)
PROV.: Emmanuel Chabrier, Paris (Vente: Hotel Drouot, March 26th 1896, no. 13); Ernest
Chausson (Vente: Paris Hotel Drouot, June 5th, 1936, no. 32).
EXH.: Paris, Galerie Bernheim-Jeune, *Manet*, 1928.
LIT.: Georges Wildenstein and Paul Jamot, *Manet*, Paris, 1932, no. 165, illustrated; Adolphe
Tabarant, *Manet et ses Oeuvres*, Paris, 1947, p. 218, no. 208, illustrated; Denis Rouart and Sandra
Orienti, *Tout l'Oeuvre peint d 'Edouard Manet*, Paris, 1970, p. 102, no. 179, illustrated; Denis Rouart
and Daniel Wildenstein, *Edouard Manet, Catalogue raisonné*, Paris and Lausanne, 1975, vol. I, p.
138, no. 149, illustrated.

Sotheby's London, 24 June 1996 (5**) GBP 188,500	US$	290,671

FEMME EN PROMENADE TENANT UNE OMBRELLE OUVERTE pastel on canvas, 23 5/8 x
19¾in. (60 x 50cm.) (1880)
PROV.: Atelier Manet, Sale, Th. Duret, Paris, 4-5 Feb. 1884, (no lot number).
LIT.: Th. Duret, *Histoire d'Edouard Manet et de son Oeuvre*, Paris, 1902, pastel no. 59; E. Moreau-
Nelaton, *Manet catalogue manuscrit,* Paris, 1926, no. 404; P. Jamot, G. Wildenstein and M.L.
Bataille, *Manet*, Paris, 1932, no. 437; A. Tabarant, *Manet et ses Oeuvres,* Paris, 1947, P.398, no. 494;
D. Rouart and S. Onenti, *Tout l'Oeuvre peint d'Edouard Manet*, Paris, 1970, no. 338.

Christie's London, 26 June 1996 (112**) GBP 98,300	US$	151,581

JEUNE FILLE EN DESHABILLE pastel on canvas, 22 1/8 x 13 7/8in. (56.2 x 35.2cm.) sbl 'Manet'
Stamped with initials 'E.M.' (1882)
PROV.: Mme. Edouard Manet, Paris; Galerie Durand-Ruel, Paris; Leon Koella Leenhoff, Paris; Mrs.
Thomas Scott, Philadelphia (acquired from the above on Dec. 10, 1883); By descent to the late
owners.
EXH.: Paris, Ecole Nationale des Beaux-Arts, *Edouard Manet*, Jan.,1884, no. 125; Philadelphia,
Pennsylvania Academy of Arts, *Loan Exhibition of Paintings and Drawings by Representative
Modern Masters*, April-May, 1920, no. 128; Philadelphia, Museum of Art, *Edouard Manet*, Nov.-
Dec., 1966, pp.190-191, no. 181 (illustrated, p. 190; detail illustrated, p. 191). The exhibition
traveled to Chicago, The Art Institute, Jan.-Feb., 1967.
LIT.: T. Duret, *Histoire d'Edouard Manet et de son oeuvre*, Paris, 1902, p.290, no. 41; E. Moreau-
Nelaton,*Manet raconte par lui-meme*, Paris, 1926, vol. II, p.130, no. 125 (illustrated, fig. 352); A.
Tabarant, *Manet: Histoire catalographique*, Paris, 1931, p.504, no. 79; P. Jamot and G.
Wildenstein,Manet, Paris, 1932, vol. I, p.182, no. 523; A. Tabarant, *Manet et ses oeuvres*, Paris,
1947, p.448, no. 534; A. Staley, 'Further Acquaintance with Manet at the Philadelphia Museum of
Art,' *The Connoisseur*, Dec., 1966, p.270 (illustrated); S. Orienti, *The Complete Paintings of Manet*,
New York, 1967, p.118, no. 388 (illustrated); D. Rouart and D. Wildenstein, *Edouard Manet,
Catalogue raisonné*, Lausanne, 1975, vol. Il, p.34, no. 88 (illustrated, p.35).

Christie's New York, 30 April 1996 (3**) US$ 827,500	US$	827,500

MANETTI Domenico (Siena 1609-1663) Italian
THE ENCHANTMENT OF SAINT CATHERINA OF SIENA oil on canvas, 176 x 120cm.

Finearte Rome, 21 May 1996 (150**) ITL 17,250,000	US$	11,079

MANETTI Rutilio (Siena 1571-1639) Italian
THE MADONNA AND CHILD WITH THE INFANT SAINT JOHN THE BAPTIST AND SAINT
CATHERINE OF SIENA oil on canvas, 39¾ x 29 5/8in. (101 x 75.3cm.)
PROV.: Possibly the Chigi family (the frame is of a type associated with the Chigi collection); with
P. & D. Colnaghi & Co. Ltd., London, *Paintings by Old Masters*, Oct. 21-Nov. 7, 1969, no. 8, pl. VI
as Francesco Vanni, from whom purchased by the present owner.
LIT.: A. Bagnoli in the catalogue of the exhibition *L'Arte a Siena sotto i Medici*, Siena, Palazzo
Pubblico, May 3-Sep. 15, 1980, p. 176; P. Di Mambro, in L. Bianchi-D. Giunta, *Iconografia di S.
Caterina da Siena. 1, L'immagine*, 1988, no. 435, pp. 428-29; J. Pope-Hennessy, *Learning to Look*,
1991, p.315.

Christie's New York, 10 January 1996 (95**) US$ 48,300	US$	48,00

LOTH AND THE CHILD oil on paper, 198 x 253
EXH.: Siena, Palazzo Pubblico, *Rutlio Manetti*, 15 June-15 Oct. 1978, catalogue Centro Di, 1978, no.
81, p. 142.
LIT.: M. Gregori, 'Su due quadri caravaggeschi a Burghley House', in *Festschrift Ulrich Middeldorf*,
Berlin 1968, p. 420, note 25; A. Bagnoli, 'Aggiornamento do Rutilio Manetti', in *Prospettiva*, 13,
1978, p. 35.

Finearte Milan, 12 March 1996 (69*) ITL 17,825,000	US$	11,404

MANGLARD Adrien (Lyon 1695-1760 Rome) French
LE REPOS DU PECHEUR oil on canvas, 58 x 70cm.

Étude Tajan Paris, 28 June 1996 (104**) FRF 65,000	US$	125,51

MANGOLD Robert (1937 b.-) American
RED ECLIPSE/GREEN ECLIPSE (STUDY) acrylic and black crayon on two attached shaped
canvases, 20½ x 54in. (110.5 x 137.2cm.) sd and titled 'R Mangold 1987 'Red Eclipse/Green Eclipse
(Study)" on the reverse
PROV.: Paula Cooper Gallery, New York; Private collection, Geneva.

Christie's New York, 22 February 1996 (93**) US$ 36,800	US$	36,800

FOUR COLOR FRAME PAINTING 6 acrylic and graphite on four attached panels, 19 x 14in. (48.2
x 35.6cm.) sd titled 'R. Mangold FOUR COLOR FRAME PAINTING 6 1984' on the reverse
PROV.: Acquired directly from the artist.

Christie's New York, 15 November 1995 (252**) US$ 25,300	US$	25,300

IRREGULAR RED-ORANGE AREA WITH A DRAWN ELLIPSE acrylic and black crayon on
shaped canvas, 92¼ x 67¾in. (234.2 x 172cm.) sd and titled 'R. Mangold 1986 Irregular Red Orange-
Area with a drawn Ellipse' on the reverse
PROV.: Donald Young Gallery, Chicago; Joseph McHugh, Chicago; Mr. and Mrs. Paul T. Soffel,
Dallas.
EXH.: Chicago, Donald Young Gallery, *Robert Mangold: New Paintings*, Nov. 1986-Jan. 1987;
Maastricht, Bonnefanten Museum, *Robert Mangold: Recent Works*, Oct. 1989-Jan. 1990, p. 35
(illustrated).

Christie's New York, 15 November 1995 (350**) US$ 57,500	US$	57,500

MANGUIN Henri Charles (Paris 1874-1949 Saint-Tropez) French
NATURE MORTE A LA PASTEQUE oil on canvas, 28¾ x 25 3/8in. (73 x 60cm.) slr 'manguin'
(1903)
PROV.: Ambroise Vollard, Paris, by whom purchased from the Artist on 24 March 1906; anon sale,
Maître Blache, Versailles, 3 June 1981, lot 123, where purchased by the present owners.

Christie's London, 26 June 1996 (176**) GBP 36,700	US$	56,592

JEANNE DORMANT DANS UN FAUTEUIL oil on canvas, 21¾ x 18 1/8in (55 x 46cm.) slr
'Manguin' (1917)
PROV.: Mme, Henri Manguin, Saint-Tropez, 1949.
LIT.: L. and C. Manguin, *Henri Manguin*, 1980, no. 545 (illustrated p. 201).

Christie's London, 26 June 1996 (333**) GBP 10,350	US$	15,960

MANRAY (Philadelphia 1890-1976 Paris) American
STILL-LIFE WITH A RED TEA KETTLE oil on canvas, 12 x 10in. (30.5 x 25.4cm.) sd '1913'
PROV.: The Daniel Gallery, New York (acquired from the artist in 1914); Florence Cane, New York
(acquired from the above in 1914); Melville Cane, New York (son of the above); Terry Dintenfass
Gallery, New York; Acquired from the above by the present owner.
EXH.: New York, The Daniel Gallery, *Group Exhihition*, 1914 (sold for $30) Pasadena, Pasadena
Art Institute, *Retrospective Exhibition 1913-1944. Paintings, Drawings and Photographs by Man
Ray*, 1944 (?).
LIT.: This work will be included in the *Catalogue raisonné of the Paintings of Man Ray* being

compiled by Timothy Baum, Francis Naumann and Andrew Strauss.
　　　Sotheby's New York, 2 May 1996 (194**) US$ 26,450　　　　　　US$　　　26,450

ETUDE POUR 'RETOUR A LA RAISON' oil on board, 14 ½ x 10in. (36.9 x 25.3cm.) lr 'Man Ray
38-21' (1938)
PROV.: Acquired from the artist by the late owner, 1957.
　　　Christie's New York, 8 November 1995 (270**) US$ 36,800　　　　US$　　　36,800

MANZONI Piero (Soncino (Cremona) 1933-1963 Milan) Italian
ACHROME sewn canvas, 19 5/8 x 13¾in. (50 x 35 cm.) (1959)
PROV.: Notizie, Arte Contemporanea, Turin; Collection Bosi, Turin; Claude Berri, Paris.
EXH.: Paris, Musée d'art Moderne de la Ville de Paris; Herning, Kunstmuseum; Madrid, Fundacion
La Caixa, *Piero Manzoni*, March-December 1991, no. 55 (illustrated in the catalogue p. 125).
LIT.: Germano Celant, *Piero Manzoni: Catalogo Generale*, Milan 1989, p. 189, no. 5tcq
(illustrated); Freddy Battino and Luca Palazzoli, *Piero Manzoni:Catalogue Raisonné*, Milan 1991, p.
349, no. 630BM (illustrated).
　　　Christie's London, 23 May 1996 (77**) GBP 38,900　　　　　　US$　　　58,904

ACHROME kaolin on canvas, 39¼ x 27½in. (99.7 x 69.8cm.) (1958)
PROV.: Piero Fedeli, Milan; Gallena Blu, Milan; Galerie Karsten Greve, Cologne; Claude Berri,
Paris.
EXH.: Paris, Galerie Karsten Greve, *Piero Manzoni*, 1992 (illustrated in colour in the catalogue p.
33).
LIT.: Exhibition Catalogue: London, The Tate Gallery, *Piero Manzoni: Paintings, Reliefs & Objects*,
March-May 1974, p. 26, pl. 11, (illustrated); Germano Celant, *Piero Manzoni: Catalogo Generale*,
Milan 1989, p. 110, no. 13cq (illustrated); Freddy Battino and Luca Palazzoli, *Piero Manzoni:
Catalogue Raisonné*, Milan 1991, p. 313, no. 508 BM (illustrated).
　　　Christie's London, 27 June 1996 (53**) GBP 84,000　　　　　　US$　　　129,530

MANZU Giacomo (1908-1991) Italian
RELIGIOSO INGINOCCHIATO watercolour and gouache on paper, 19 5/8 x 14¾in. (50.5 x
37.5cm.) sdur 'Manzù 1952', s again ll 'Manzù'
PROV.: Alan Frumkin Gallery, New York.
EXH.: Minneapolis, Institute of Arts, 1963 (on loan).
　　　Christie's New York, 1 May 1996 (289*) US$ 8,625　　　　　　US$　　　8,625

NUDE oil on canvas, 31 x 40cm. sll 'Manzu' (1958-59)
LIT.: Inge Schnabel-Manzu, *Manzu Pittore*, Bergamo 1988, p. 217, illustrated.
　　　Sotheby's Milan, 28 May 1996 (163**) ITL 10350,000　　　　　US$　　　6,647

MARA Antonio, {called} lo Scarpetta (1680-1750 ca.) Italian
TROMPE L'OEIL STILL-LIFE WITH PAINTINGS, APRINT, A PAINTER'S PALETTE,
SCULPTURE AND OTHER OBJECTS oil on canvas, 30¼ x 55in. (76.5 x 139.6cm.)
PROV.: Rudolph Berliner, ca. 1910.
　　　Sotheby's London, 5 July 1995 (287**) GBP 10,350　　　　　　US$　　　16,510

TROMPE L'OEIL STILL-LIFE WITH PAINTINGS, PRINTS, A CLOCK, WRITING MATERIALS
AND OTHER OBJECTS oil on canvas (a pair), each: 27½ x 36¼in. (70 x 91.7cm.)
PROV.: Rudolph Berliner, ca. 1910.
　　　Sotheby's London, 5 July 1995 (288**) GBP 17,250　　　　　　US$　　　27,516

TROMPE L'OEIL STILL-LIFES WITH PAINTINGS AND A PRINT TACKED WOODEN
BOARDS IN FRONT OF WHICH ARE TABLES WITH A VIOLIN, LUTE, BOOKS, A SHEET
OF MUSIC AND OTHER OBJECTS oil on canvas laid down on panel (a pair), each 21¼ x 30in. (54
x 76.2cm.)
　　　Sotheby's New York, 11 January 1996 (164**) US$ 42,550　　　　US$　　　425,50

A TROMPE L'OEIL, WITH CARDS, ENGRAVINGS AND A PORTRAIT OF A SPANIEL oil on canvas, 23¾ x 29¼in. (60.3 x 75.6cm.)
PROV.: With Count Palmieri, Geneva.
EXH.: New York, National Academy of Design, *Italian Still life Paintings from three Centuries*, 1983, no. 29.
LIT.: L. Saferno, *La Nature Morte Italiana*, 1984, p. 413, pl. A67.
Christie's London, 28 March 1996 (127**) GBP 5,175   US$ 7,903

MARA Pol (1920 b.) Belgian
AND THE KITCHEN BECAME A WOMAN oil and coloured crayons on canvas, 162 x 130cm. sd and inscr. with title on the reverse 'Pol mara 75'
Christie's Amsterdam, 6 December 1995 (378*) NLG 10,350   US$ 6,413

MARASCO Antonio (Nicastro 1896-1975 Florence) Italian
PRESSI DI CALENZANO oil on canvas, 80 x 110cm. slr 'Marasco' sd titled '1961' on the reverse
EXH.: Roma, Quadriennale Nazionale d'Arte di Roma, 1961- 62, n. 347 (illustrated); Cosenza, Galleria La Bussola, *Antonio Marasco*, 1972, n. 9; Rende, Museo Civico, *Marasco*, 30 March - 30 April 1994, cat. p. 29, n. 55 (illustrated).
LIT.: Tonino Sicoli, 'Antonio Marasco Futurista', in *La Provincia di Catanzaro*, a. V111, no. 1, Catanzaro 1989, p. 275 (illustrated).
Christie's Milan, 20 November 1995 (145**) ITL 23,570,000   US$ 14,796

MARATTA Carlo (1625-1713) Italian
RITRATT DI ECCLESIASTICO oil on canvas, 66.5 x 48cm.
Finearte Rome, 22 November 1995 (120**) ITL 41,400,000   US$ 25,989

MARC Franz (München 1880-1916 Verdun) German
IM WALD tempera and pencil on paper, 13 x 6.3cm (1913)
PROV.: Acquired by the present owner in 1976 at Saleno. 214, Hauswedell & Nolte, lot 1006.
Hauswedell & Nolte Cologne, 5/06 June 1996 (499***) DEM 120,000   US$ 77,968

MARCH Y MARCO Vincente (1859-1914) Spanish
LE LAVANDAIE oil on canvas, 18 x 25 7/8in. (45.7 x 65.7cm.) s inscr. 'V. Maechi Roma'
Christie's London, 14 June 1996 (124**) GBP 23,000   US$ 35,466

MARCHAND André (1907 b.-l) French
ENVOL DES GRANDS FLAMANTS (DELTA DU RHONE) oil on canvas, 130 x 98cm. slr 'André Marchand' s titled on the reverse
Étude Tajan Paris, 28 March 1996 (84*) FRF 30,000   US$ 5,930

MARCHESI Giuseppe, {called} il Sansone (Bologna 1699-1771) Italian
HERCULES AND OMPHALE oil on canvas, 106 x 78in. (269 x 198cm.)
LIT.: Richter, 1901, no. 42.
Sotheby's London, 6 December 1995 (32**) GBP 45,500   US$ 70,022

MARCOLA Marco (1740-1793) Italy
A JEWISH WEDDING AND A CIRCUMCISION oil on canvas (a pair), each: 16½ x 31 7/8cm. (41.9 x 81cm.)
Sotheby's New York, 11 January 1996 (146**) US$ 90,500   US$ 90,500

MARCOUSSIS Louis (Markous) (1883-1941) French (Polish)
NATURE MORTE AUX FRUITS, BOUGEOIR ET COUTEAU gouache on card, 10 x 12¼in. (25.5 x 31.3cm.) slr 'Marcoussis'
Christie's South Kensington, 24 June 1996 (80**) GBP 9,775   US$ 15,073

MARÉES Hans von (1837-1887) German
DIE UNSCHULD oil on panel, 65 x 47cm. sll 'Giovanni di Marées'
PROV.: Gal. Fritz Gurlitt, Berlin (1884/85); Slg. Dresdner Galerie, Berlin; Gal. P. Cassirer, Berlin
(1900); Slg. Julius Heymann, Frankfurt/Main (bis 1940); Städtische Galerie, Frankfurt/Main (inv.-no.
1001); Christie`s, London, February 1963, lot 154; Private collection Switzerland.
EXH.: Städt. Museum Elberfeld, 1904, *Ausstellung von Werken von Hans von Marées und solcher
seiner Freunde*, No. 12; Kunstverein, Frankfurt am Main, December 1909, *Hans von Marées*, No.
27; Kunstverein, Frankfurt am Main, 1913, *Frankfurter Kunstschätze*, No. 24 (ill.).
LIT.: J. Meier-Graefe, *Hans von Marées*, Bd. II, Muenchen 1909, p. 514, no. 811; A. Volkmann,
Vom Sehen und Gestalten, 1912, p. 29; *Verlorene Werke der Malerei*, 1965, p. 118; U. Gerlach-
Laxner, *Hans von Marées*, München 1980, p. 210, WVZ-no. 213 (ill.).
Lempertz Cologne, 18 May 1996 (1599*) DEM 38,000	US$	24,773

MARIA Nicola de (Foglianise 1954 b.-) Italian
TESTA DONNA acrylics on canvas-unframed, 40 x 30cm. s and inscr. with title on the stretcher; sd
'1985' and inscr. with title again on the reverse
Christie's Amsterdam, 5 June 1996 (313**) NLG 34,500	US$	20,158

REGNO DEI FIORI watercolour and collage on paper, 49.5 x 72cm. slr 'De Maria' titled ll
Finearte Milan, 19 March 1996 (23*) ITL 13,800,000	US$	8,829

MARIANI Pompeo (1857-1927) Italian
A VIEW OF THE PORT OF GENOA AT DAWN oil on canvas, 20½ x 52in. (52 x 131cm.) sdll
'Genoa 1880'
Sotheby's London, 13 March 1996 (136**) GBP 46,600	US$	71,167

IL MOTIVO FAVORITO oil on board unframed, 29½ x 19¼in. (75 x 49cm.) s 'P. Mariani'
PROV.: The Bernasconi Collection.
Christie's London, 14 June 1996 (139**) GBP 14,950	US$	3053

SIGNORA A SAN SIRO bodycolour on paper laid down on canvas, 33 x 17in. 983.7 x 43.2cm.) s 'P.
Mariani'
PROV.: The Bernasconi collection.
Christie's London, 15 March 1996 (179**) GBP 11,500	US$	17,563

PRIMAVERA oil on panel, 22 x 28¼in. (56 x 71.8cm.) s inscr. 'P. Mariani Z'
PROV.: The Bernasconi Collection.
Christie's London, 15 March 1996 (180**) GBP 13,225	US$	20,197

MARIESCHI Michele (Venice 1796-1743 Venice) Italian
CAPRICCIO OF A RIVERLANDSCAPE WITH HOUSES oil on canvas, 58 x 93cm. (framed)
PROV.: Edwin S. Bayer collection, United States; Wildenstein New York; Henry E. e Lily Stehli
Bonner collection, New York; sold at Parke-Bernet, New York, 30 November; 1950, no. 9/10;
$3400; Christie's, London, 11 December 1984, no.63 GBP 45,000; Private collection Antwerp.
LIT.: Antonio Morassi in the memorial volume;of Ulrich Middeldorf, Berlin 1968: *Appunti su;
Michele Marieschi, Alter Ego del Canaletto*, p. 501; riproduzioni 7, 8 *opera caratteristica, sicara,
mirabili di Michele Marieschi*. (a typical, admirable; work of Marieschi); Egidio Martini;. 1981, p.
537, ripr.229: *opera autografa*.; Ralph Toledano, *Michele Marieschi*, no. c43, 2; *Opera autografa*,
(one`s own work).
Dorotheum Vienna, 17 October 1995 (50**) ATS 820,000	US$	82,251

CAPRICCIO OF A LANDSCAPE WITH HOUSES oil on canvas, 58 x 93cm. (framed)
Dorotheum Vienna, 17 October 1995 (51**) ATS 820,000	US$	82,251

THE PIAZZA SAN MARCO, VENICE, FROM THE TORRE DELL'OROLOGIO oil on canvas, 22
5/8 x 33 5/8 in. (57.5 x 85.4cm.) (1737-39)
Christie's London, 7 July 1995 (101**) GBP 139,000   US$ 221,726

MARILHAT Prosper-Georges-Antoine (1811-1847) French
ARABS AND CAMELS AT REST oil on canvas, 32 1/8 x 25½in. (81.6 x 64.8cm.) sd 'P. Marilhat
1847'
Christie's London, 14 June 1996 (100**) GBP 34,500   US$ 532,00

MARINI Marino (Pistoia 1901-1980 Viareggio) Italian
COMPOZSIZIONE CON UOMO E CAVALLI watercolour, gouache, coloured chalks and brush
and India ink on paper, 19½ x 13 5/8in. (49.5 x 34.6cm.) slc 'MARINO'
Christie's New York, 1 May 1996 (357**) US$ 17,250   US$ 17,250

CAVALLO E GIOCOLIERE (ACROBATA CON CAVALLO ROSSO) oil on canvas, 59 x 47¼in.
(150 x 120cm.) slr with ini. 'MM'; s twice and numbered on the reverse 'MARINO 23' (1958)
PROV.: Dominion Gallery, Montreal (acquired by the present owner, 1964).
LIT.: H. Read, P. Waldberg and G. di San Lazzaro, *Marino Marini, Complete Works*, New York
1970, no. 264 (illustrated, p. 433); E. Steingräber and L. Papi, *Marino Marini, Paintings*,
Johannesburg 1989, no. 376 (illustrated, p. 196).
Christie's New York, 1 May 1996 (363**) US$ 195,000   US$ 195,000

LA RISURREZIONE oil on paper laid down on canvas, 43¼ 33½in. (109.8 x 85.1cm.) slr
'MARINO' (1954)
PROV.: Drs. Fritz and Peter Nathan, Zurich (acquired from the artist); ACquired from the above by
Mr. Nathan Cummings in 1963.
EXH.: Zurich, Kunsthaus, *Marino Marini*, Jan.-Feb. 1962.
LIT.: H. Read, P. Waldberg and G. di San Lazzaro, *Marino Marini: Complete Works*, New york
1970, p. 421, no. 198 (illustrated in colour p. 199).
Christie's New York, 30 April 1996 (18**) US$ 486,500   US$ 486,500

ARCHITETTURA IN GRIGIO ink and tempera on board, 95 x 72cm. sld 'Marino' and dll '1956'
(1956)
EXH.: Turin, Galleria Gissi, *Maestri Italiani*.
LIT.: H. Read-P. Waldberg-G. Di San Lazzaro, *Marino Marini*, Silvana Editoriale, Milano, 1970,
no.230, p.431.
Finearte Milan, 19 March 1996 (45**) ITL 64,400,000   US$ 41,203

CAVALLE E CAVALIERE tempera, pen, brush and Indian ink on paper laid down on board, 33 x
23 5/8in. (83.8 x 60cm.) lower center 'MARINO 1955' (1955)
PROV.: Main Street Book Store Inc., Chicago (acquired by the late owner, 1957).
Christie's New York, 8 November 1995 (276**) US$ 63,000   US$ 63,000

MARIS Jacob (Jacobus Hendricus) (The Hague 1837-1899 Karlsbad) Dutch
ON THE BEACH oil on canvas, 25 1/8 x 21½in. (63.8 x 54.6cm.) slr 'J.Maris'
PROV.: The Dowager the Honorable Louise van Alphon-Horny; sale, Christie's, July 16, 1909, no.
23; M. Knoedler & Co., New York (until March 6, 1911); Meyer H. Lehman (by 1911); Mrs. Harriet
Lehman Weil and Mrs. Bertha Lehman Rosenheim; Mrs. Elsie Rosenheim Weil and Dr. Henry
Lehman Weil; George L. Weil, Washington, D.C. (by 1952).
Christie's New York, 2 November 1995 (78**) US$ 23,000   US$ 23,000

PICKING FLOWERS oil on canvas laid down on panel, 13.5 x 18cm. sll 'J.Maris'
Christie's Amsterdam, 26 October 1995 (4**) NLG 32,200   US$ 20,303

MARIS Simon (The Hague 1873-1935 Amsterdam) Dutch
A MOTHER AND CHILD ON A DUNE TOP oil on canvas, 82 x 66cm. slr 'Simon Maris'
EXH.: Amsterdam, Arti et Amicitiae, *Maris Tentoonstelling*, Sept.-Oct. 1942, no. 19; Amsterdam,
De Moderne Boekhandel, 1943/44.
       Christie's Amsterdam, 26 October 1995 (5*) NLG 20,700   US$ 13,052

MARIS Willem (The Hague 1844-1910 The Hague) Dutch
DRINKING CATTLE oil on canvas, 74 x 55cm. sll 'Willem Maris'
PROV.: L.J. Krüger Art Gallery, The Hague.
       A. Mak B.V. Dordrecht, 21 June 1996 (224*) NLG 24,000   US$ 14,023

MARKO Karoly, Snr (1791-1860) Hungarian
DIANA AND APOLLO IN A WOODED LANDSCAPE oil on canvas, 8¾ s=x 12in. (20 x 30cm.) s
and indistinctly dll
       Sotheby's London, 13 March 1996 (95**) GBP 9,200   US$ 14,050

MARLOW William R.A. (Southwark 1740-1813 Twickenham) British
VIEW OF THE RIVER RHONE, NEAR THE TOUR D'HERF AND THE CASTLE OF
MONTFAUCON 63.5 x 91.5cm., 63.5 x 91.5cm.
PROV.: Collection lady Lavinia Mynors, Triago Castle, Wales.
       Étude Tajan Paris, 26 March 1996 (148*) FRF 40,000   US$ 7,907

MARNEFFE François de (Brussels 1793-1877) Belgium
SKATINGSCENE oil on panel, 46 x 67cm. s with monogram, indisinctly d 'FDM, XII, 1824 (?)'
       Dorotheum Vienna, 13 September 1995 (525**) ATS 110,000   US$ 10,692

MARONIEZ Georges (1865 b.-) French
LA RECOLTE DES POMMES DE TERRE oil on canvas, 23¾ x 32in. (60.3 x 81.3cm.) sll
'G.Maroniez'
       Christie's New York, 22 May 1996 (178**) US$ 28,750   US$ 28,750

MARQUET Albert (Bordeaux 1875-1947 Paris) French
SAMOIS, LES VILLAS oil on canvas, 25 5/8 x 31 7/8in. (64 x 81cm.) sll 'Marquet' (1917)
PROV.: Galerie Druet, Paris (acquired from the artist, 1917); Galerie Schmit, Paris.
EXH.: Venice, *XV Esposizione Internazionale d'Arte*, 1926, no. 60.
LIT.: The Wildenstein Institute will include this painting in their forthcoming *Marquet catalogue
raisonné*.
       Christie's New York, 1 May 1996 (211***) US$ 272,000   US$ 272,000

LE PONT DE CHENNEVIERES, MARNE oil on canvas, 25 5/8 x 31 7/8in. (65 x 81cm.) sll
'Marquet' (1915)
PROV.: Galerie Druet, Paris; Galerie Schmit, Paris.
LIT.: The Wildenstein Institute will include this painting in their fortcoming *Marquet catalogue
raisonné*.
       Christie's New York, 1 May 1996 (340**) US$ 255,500   US$ 255,500

LE BASSIN D'ARCACHON oil on canvas, 13 x 16in. (33 x 41cm.) sll 'marquet' (ca. 1924-25)
PROV.: Will be included in the forthcoming *Albert Marquet catalogue raisonné*, currently being
prepared by J.-Cl. Martinet at the Wildenstein Institute.
       Étude Tajan Paris, 10 June 1996 (40**) FRF 250,000   US$ 48,275

EAU BLEUE, ALGER oil on canvas, 13 3/8 x 16½in. (34 x 41.9cm.) sll 'Marquet' (1942)
PROV.: Madame Marquet, Paris; Walter Guillaume, Paris; Jean Lacaze.
LIT.: This work will be included in the forthcoming *Marquet catalogue raisonné* by the Wildenstein
Institute.
       Sotheby's New York, 2 May 1996 (187**) US$ 76,750   US$ 76,750

VUE DE VENISE oil on canvas, 19¾ x 24in. (50.2 x 61cm.) sll 'Marquet' (1936)
PROV.: Galerie E. Druet, Paris.
EXH.: Paris, Galerie Robert Schmit, *25e exposition des Maîtres Français du XIXe et du XXe Siècles*, 1987; Lausanne, Fondation de Hermitage, *Albert Marquet (1875-1947)*, 1988, no. 87.
LIT.: This work will be included in the forthcoming *Marquet catalogue raisonné* by the Wildenstein Institute.

Sotheby's New York, 2 May 1996 (189**) US$ 255,500	US$	255,500

PARIS, QUAI DES GRANDS-AUGUSTINS, VERS NOTRE DAME oil on canvas, 24 1/8 x 19 7/8in. (61.3 x 50.5cm.) slr 'marquet' (1946)
PROV.: Madame Marquet (the artist's wife).
EXH.: Lyons, Galerie Saint-Georges, *Albert Marquet*, 1961, no. IX; Paris, Galerie Schmit, Exposition *Marquet*, 1967, no. 100, illustrated in the catalogue; To be included in the *Marquet Catalogue raisonné* being prepared by the Wildenstein Institute.

Sotheby's London, 24 June 1996 (69**) GBP 117,000	US$	180,416

PARIS, LE PONT NEUF, TRAVAUX oil on canvas, 23¾ x 28¾in. (60 x 73cm.) sll 'Marquet' (1906)
PROV.: Galerie Druet, Paris; Purchased by the grandfather of the present owner before 1968.
LIT.: To be included in the forthcoming *Marquet catalogue raisonné* currently being prepared by Jean Claude Martinet and the Wildenstein Institute.

Christie's London, 25 June 1996 (13**) GBP 161,000	US$	248,265

AU JARDIN PUBLIC oil on canvas, 10 5/8 x 16 1/8in. (27 x 41cm.) sll 'Marquet' (ca 1904)
PROV.: Hessele, Paris; Anon sale Maitre Blache, Versailles, 3 June 1981, lot 162, where purchased by the present owners.
LIT.: To be included in the forthcoming *Albert Marquet catalogue raisonné* currently being prepared by the Wildenstein Institute. Recorde under Wildenstein Institute no. 93.03.01/4616/2507.

Christie's London, 26 June 1996 (160**) GBP 56,500	US$	87,124

LE PORT DES SABLES D'OLONNE oil on canvas, 23¾ x 28 7/8in. (60.5 x 73.5cm.) slr 'marquet'
PROV.: Galerie Druet, Paris (9930); Crane Kalman Gallery, London; G.R. Kennerly, London, by whom purchased from the above in 1959.
LIT.: To be included in the forthcoming *Albert Marquet catalogue raisonné* currently being prepared by the Wildenstein Institute. Recorde under Wildenstein Institute no. 96.05.06/4686/1309.

Christie's London, 26 June 1996 (166***) GBP 172,000	US$	265,227

VEDUTA DI VENEZIA, L'ISOLA DI SAN GIORGIO oil on board, 33 x41cm. slr 'Marquet' (1936)
PROV.: Venice, Collection B. Balbi; Crema, Paolo Stamezzi; Paris, The Paris American Art Co.
EXH.: Milan, Societa' per Belle Arti ed esposizione Permanente, *Marquet Albert P.*

Finearte Milan, 26 October 1995 (192**) ITL 57,500,000	US$	35,826

VUE D'ALGER oil on board, 5¼ x 8 5/8in. (13 x 22cm.) sll 'Marquet' (1945)

Christie's East, 7 November 1995 (202a**) US$ 10,350	US$	10,350

LA PASSERELLE A SAINTE-ADRESSE oil on paper laid down on canvas, 19¾ x 24in. (50 x 61cm.) lr 'Marquet' (1905)
PROV.: Dr. A.M.Boulard, Créteil; Galerie Schmit, Paris.
EXH.: Zurich, Kunsthaus, *Albert Marquet*, June-Aug. 1948, no. 24. The exhibition traveled to Bordeaux, Musée de Peinture, May-June, 1948 and Paris, Musée National d'Art Moderne, Oct.-Dec., 1948. Venice, *La XXV Biennale*, June-Oct., 1950, no.34; Paris, Musée National d'Art Moderne, *Le fauvisme*, June-Sept. 1951, no. 83; New York, Widenstein & Co., Inc., *Marquet, A Loan Exhibitin of Marquet Sponsored by Count Jean Vyau de Legarde*, Jan.-Feb., 1953, no. 19;Vevey, Musée Jenisch, *Marquet*, June-Sept.,1953, no. 13 (illustrated); Paris, Maison de la Pensée Français, *Marquet*, Oct.-Dec., 1953, no.61; Paris, Galerie Charpentier, *Les Fauves*, March, 1962, no. 80; Bordeaux, Galerie des Beaux-Arts, *Albert Marquet*, May-Sept., 1975, no. 22 (illustrated). The exhibition traveled to Paris, Orangerie des Tuileries, Oct., 1975-Jan., 1976. Paris, Galerie Schmit, *Maîtres Français, XIX-*

XX siècles, May-July, 1986, no. 13 (illustrated in colour).
LIT.: F. Fosca, *Albert Marquet*, Paris, 1925, pl. 23 (illustrated); F. Daulte, 'Marquet et Dufy devant les mêmes sujets', *Connaissance des Arts*, Nov., 1957, p.89; J.E.Muller, *Le Fauvisme*, Paris, 1967, no. 98 (illustrated); M.Giry, *Fauvism, Origin and Development*, New York, 1982, p. 175 (illustrated, pl. 84).

Christie's New York, 8 November 1995 (168**) US$ 574,500   US$ 574,500

LE TOIT ROUGE, LE PYLA oil on canvas, 19 5/8 x 24in. (49.8 x 61cm.) ll 'Marquet' and on the reverse 'Le toit rouge Le Pyla 35' (1935)
PROV.: Mme. Marcelle Marquet; Galerie de l'Elysée (Alex Maguy), Paris (acquired by the family of the present owner, 1974).
EXH.: New York, Wildenstein & Co., *Albert Marquet, A Loan Exhibition for the Benifit of the Hospitality Committee of the United Nations*, Oct.-Dec., 1971, no. 49 (illustrated).

Christie's New York, 8 November 1995 (232**) US$ 217,000   US$ 217,000

LA SEINE GRISE, VIEUX PORT oil on panel, 13 x 16 1/4in. (33 x 41.2cm.) lr 'Marquet' (1927)
PROV.: Bernheim-Jeune & Cie, Paris (acquired by the family of the present owner, 1928).
EXH.: Buenos Aires, Jaques Helft, *L'école de Paris*, Sept., 1951, no.36.

Christie's New York, 8 November 1995 (254**) US$ 48,300   US$ 48,300

MARSEUS VAN SCHRIECK Otto, {called} Snuffelaer (Nymegen 1619-1678 Amsterdam) Dutch
NOCTURNAL LANDSCAPE WITH A THISTLE, MUSHROOMS, MOTHS AND A FROG oil on canvas, 23¼ x 18 5/8in. (59.1 x 47.3cm.) sdlr 'O. Marseus f/1671'
PROV.: Galerie Abraham Fontanel, Montpellier, from whom purchased by; J.J. De Bousssairolles, Montpellier, om February 10, 1805, for 240 frs.; Comte de Saporta, domaine du Moulin Blanc, près d'Aix-en-Provence.
LIT.: *l'Etat des Tableaux dressé par J.J. de Boussairolles à la fin de sa vie*, under no. 19; Alain Chevalier, *La collection de tableaux de Jacques-Joseph de Boussairolles 1741-1814, Mémoire de matrîse dactylographié*, Sorbonne-Paris IV, 1984, no.61.

Sotheby's New York, 11 January 1996 (72**) US$ 79,500   US$ 79,500

NATURES MORTES DE SOUS-BOIS AUX CHAMPIGNON oil on canvas (a pair), each: 32.5 x 41cm.

Étude Tajan Paris, 12 December 1995 (26**) FRF 45,000   US$ 9,064

MARSH Reginald (1898-1954) American
GIRL WALKING ON CITY STREETS; SUITS AND VOATS: A DOUBLE-SIDED PAINTING tempera on board, 23¾ x 19 7/8in. (60.4 x 50.5cm.) sdlr 'Reginald Marsh 1952'

Christie's New York, 13 March 1996 (132**) US$ 19,550   US$ 19,550

CENTRAL PARK LANE oil on gessoed masonite, 18 x 22in. (45.8 x 55.9cm.) slr 'Reginald Marsh'

Christie's East, 28 November 1995 (33**) US$ 28,750   US$ 28,750

MARSHALL Benjamin (1768-1835) British
PRIAM, A BAY RACEHORSE WITH SAM DAY JUN. UP, HELD BY WILLIAM CHIFNEY, WITH A GROOM, ON EPSOM RACECOURSE oil on canvas, 27¾ x 36in. (70.5 x 91.5cm.) sdll 'PRIAM /B. Marshall pt./1830
PROV.: Cecil Brown; Christie's, 21 February 1930, lot 106 (1200gns. to Knoedler); with Richard Green, 1973; Jack Dick, Greenwich, Connecticut from whom bought by the family of the present owner.
EXH.: on loan to The National Horseracing Museum, Newmarket, 1984-95.
LIT.: T.H. Taunton, *Portraits of Celebrated Racehorses*, III, pp. 65-70. A*pollo*, October 1973, p.302 (illus.); A. Noakes, *Ben Marshall*, 1978, p. 53, no. 195.

Christie's London, 30 November 1995 (67**) GBP 89,500   US$ 139,997

MARTENS Willem Johann (Amsterdam 1839-1895 Schöneberg (near Berlin)) Dutch
LA BELLA ADDORMENTATA (BLUMENKENNER) oil on panel, 18 1/8 x 14¼in. (46 x 36.2cm.)
s inscr. 'W.J. Martens. f Roma'
EXH.: Berlin, *Internationale Kunstausstellung*, 1891.
LIT.: *Universum VI*, 1890 (illustrated); *Moderne Kunst IV*, 1890 (illustrated); F. von Boetticher,
Malerwerke der Neunzehnten Jahrhunderts, Hofheim am Taunus, 1974, vol I, ii, p. 982, no. 11.

Christie's London, 14 June 1996 (14**) GBP 13,,800	US$	21,280

MARTIN Agnes (Maklin 1912 b.-) Canadian
UNTITLED 2 acrylic and graphite on linen, 72 x 72in. (182.8 x 182.8cm.) sd 'A. Martin 1988' on the
reverse
PROV.: The Pace Gallery, New York.
EXH.: New York, Salander O'Reilly Galleries, *Barnard Collects: The Educated Eye*, Sept.-Oct. 1989,
no. 79 (illustrated); New York, Whitney Museum of American Art; Milwaukee, Art Museum;
Miami, Center for the Arts; Houston, Contemporary Arts Museum, and Madrid, Museo Nacional
Centro de Arte Reina Sofia, Nov. 1992-Feb. 1994, *Agnes Martin*, p. 89 (illustrated).

Christie's New York, 14 November 1995 (24**) US$ 222,500	US$	222,500

MARTIN Elias (1739-1818) British?
PORTRAIT OF A FAMILY oil on canvas, 63 x 77cm. s E Martin' on the reverse (1768-1780)

Bukowskis Stockholm, 29 November-1 December 1995 (107**) SEK 75,000	US$	11,346

MARTIN Henri Jean Guillaume (1860-1943) French
PEUPLIERS AU BORD DU VERT oil on canvas, 29 5/8 x 27 3/8in. (75 x 69.5cm.) sll 'Henri
Martin' (ca. 1930)
PROV.: Galleria d'Arte Sacerdoti, Milan; Hirschl & Adler Galleries Inc., New York (acquired by
Richard Smart, 1973).

Christie's New York, 1 May 1996 (154**) US$ 70,700	US$	70,700

LE PONT A LA BASTIDE DU VERT oil on canvas, 26½ x 36in. (67.5 x 91.5cm.) slr 'Henri Martin'
PROV.: Private collection , Montpellier.

Étude Tajan Paris, 13 December 1995 (42**) FRF 380,000	US$	76,542

FEMME ASSISE SUR LE PORT; DEUX FEMMES SUR LE PORT oil on canvas (a pair), each:
24¼ x 11 3/8in. (61.6 x 28.9cm.)
PROV.: Estate of Mrs. Ted Bates.

Sotheby's New York, 2 May 1996 (170**) US$ 96,000	US$	96,000

LA TERRASSE oil on canvas, 29½ x 36¾in. (74.9 x 93.3cm.) s
PROV.: Hammer Galleries, New York.

Sotheby's New York, 2 May 1996 (174**) US$ 112,500	US$	112,500

MAISON A LA CAMPAGNE oil on canvas, 23 5/8 x 31 7/8in. (60 x 81cm.) lr 'Henri Martin' (ca
1910)
PROV.: Anon. sale, Sotheby Parke Bernet Inc., New York, May 21, 1982, lot 316 (acquired by the
present owner).

Christie's New York, 8 November 1995 (161**) US$ 29,900	US$	29,900

PRUNIERS EN FLEURS oil on canvas, 25¾ x 31 7/8in. (65.3 x 81cm.) ll 'Henri Martin' (1940)
PROV.: Wally Findlay Galleries, New York.

Christie's New York, 8 November 1995 (170**) US$ 29,900	US$	29,900

MARTIN-KAVEL François (19th/20th century-) French
VANITAS oil on canvas, 51 x 38in. (129.5 x 96.5cm.) slr 'Martin Kavel'

Phillips London, 11th June 1996 (52**) GBP 7,600	US$	11,719

MARTINEZ Gonzalo Bilbao Y (1860-1938) Spanish
A YOUNG GIRL READING UNDER A SUNLITE TREE oil on canvas, 33 x 14in. (83.8 x 36.9cm.)
slr 'G. Bilbao'
    Christie's East, 13 February 1996 (126**) US$ 6,,900   US$ 6,900

MARTINI Alberto (Oderzo 1866-1954 Milan) Italian
LA GROTTA DELLA SIRENÉ pastel on cardboard-paper, 88 x 58cm. sdlr 'Alberto Martini 1921'
LIT.: S. Orlandini, *Dopo settant'anni torna alla luce 'La grotta delle siRené' di Al. Martini della serie 'Fantasie del mare'* in 'Arte' no. 220, July-August 1991, ed. G. Mondadori, Milano, p. 34.
    Finearte Milan, 12 December 1995 (299**) ITL 24,150,000   US$ 15,151

MARUSSIG Piero (Trieste 1879-1937 Pavia) Italian
STILL-LIFE WITH APPLES oil on canvas, 39 x 50cm. s 'P. Marussig' s titled on the reverse
LIT.: Will be included in the *Catalogazione delle opere di P.Marussig*, currently being prepared by
C. Gian Ferrari.
    Finearte Milan, 12 December 1995 (159*) ITL 11,500,000   US$ 7,215

COLAZIONE SULL'ERBA oil on canvas, 50 x 65cm. slr 'Marussig'
    Finearte Milan, 19 March 1996 (33**) ITL 36,800,000   US$ 23,544

LEZIONE DI MANDOLINO oil on cardboard, 60.5 x 48.5cm. sur 'P. Marussig' (ca. 1920)
PROV.: Galleria del Milione, Milan; Galleria Rotta, Genua; Galleria Barbaroux, Milan; Diacron,
Diffusion Arte Contemporanea, Milan.
EXH.: Genua, Galleria Genova, *Piero Marussig*, 1941, p. 46 (illustrated).
    Sotheby's Milan, 28 May 1996 (189**) ITL 32,200,000   US$ 20,681

MASSON André (Balagny 1896-1987 Paris) French
LE VAINQUEUR DE MÉDUSE oil on canvas, 73 x 60cm. slr; titled and d on the reverse (1972-1973)
PROV.: Galerie Louise Leiris (arch. no. 15411, photo no. 58163); Private collection, Switzerland.
EXH.: New York, Blue Moon Gallery and Lerner Gallery, *André Masson*, November 1973
(illustrated p. 54 in the catalogue under no. 52).
    Étude Tajan Paris, 17 June 1996 (182*) FRF 70,000   US$ 13,517

NATURE MORTE DEVANT LA MER oil on canvas, 28¾ x 24 in. (73 x 61cm.) s 'André Masson'
    Christie's London, 26 June 1996 (215**) GBP 69,700   US$ 107,479

FIGURE DANS UN SOUTERRAIN oil on canvas, 31 7/8 x 21½in. (81 x 54.5cm.) s on the reverse
'André Masson' (1924)
    Christie's London, 26 June 1996 (231**) GBP 67,500   US$ 104,086

MANDOLE ET VERRES oil on canvas, 21 5/8 x 15 1/8in. (55 x 38.4cm.) lr 'André Masson' (1923)
PROV.: Galerie Simon, Paris; Galerie Louise Leiris, Paris; The Mayor Gallery Limited, London;
Michel Warren, New York (acquired by the late owner, 1961).
    Christie's New York, 8 November 1995 (204**) US$ 43,700   US$ 43,700

L'ABATTOIR oil on canvas, 38 5/8 x 51 3/8in. (98 x 103.5cm.) ll 'André Masson.' (1930)
PROV.: Paul Rosenberg & Co., New York (acquired by the present owner, 1964).
EXH.: New York, Paul Rosenberg & Co., *Paintings by André Masson*, Feb., 1953, no. 2; Paris,
Musée National d'Art Moderne, *Rétrospective de André Masson*, March-May, 1965, no. 21.
    Christie's New York, 8 November 1995 (260**) US$ 68,500   US$ 68,500

LE FAUCHEUR oil on canvas, 41 3/8 x 31 5/8in. (105 x 80.4cm.) (1930)
PROV.: Paul Rosenberg & Co., New York (acquired by the present owner, 1964).
EXH.: New York, Paul Rosenberg & Co., *The Paintings of André Masson*, Feb., 1953, no.3.
    Christie's New York, 8 November 1995 (290**) US$ 70,700   US$ 70,700

MASSYS Cornelis (Antwerp before 1508-after 1549) Flemish
CHRIST AND THE WOMAN AF SAMARIA, WITH THE APOSTLES SETTING OUT ON
THEIR TRAVELS BEYOND, IN A LANDSCAPE oil on panel, 30.9 x 55.9cm.
Christie's Amsterdam, 13 November 1995 (93*) NLG 48,300   US$ 30,441

WEITE LANDSCHAFT MIT EINER STADT oil on panel, diameter 32.5cm (ae tondo) s on the
reverse 'Lucas van Uden'
PROV.: Rheinische Privatsammlung.
Lempertz Cologne, 18 May 1996 (1094**) DEM 25,000   US$ 16,298

MASSYS Jan (circle of) (Antwerp 1509-1575) Flemish
LOT AND HIS DAUGHTER oil on panel (tondo), dm 14.5cm
Dorotheum Vienna, 11 June 1996 (284**) ATS 110,000   US$ 10,210

MAST Herman van der (Brielle 1550 c.-1610 Delft) Dutch
PORTRAIT OF A GENTLEMAN, AGED 33, STANDING THREE QUARTER LENGTH
WEARING A BLACK COSTUME WITH LACE COLLAR AND CUFFS; AND POTRAIT OF A
LADY AGED 24, STANDING THREE QUARTER LENGTH, WEARING A VELVET DRESS
WITH LACE COLLAR AND CUFFS, *VLIEGER*, AND BONNET, A GOLD CHAIN AROUND
HER WAIST oil on panel, 89 x 73.5cm. The first signed; dated al 'H. Mast 1589'; inscr. with the age
of the sitter ar 'HM 1587'; inscr. with the age of the sitter al 'Aeta Suae 24'
PROV.: probably in possession of the Della Faille family (see the following lot) and thence by
descent.
EXH.: Amsterdam, Rijksmuseum, 1899-1995, on loan.
LIT.: B.W.F. van Riemsdijk, *Twee aantekeningen uit Van Mander`s Schildersboek*, in Oud Holland,
XVII, 1899, p. 124; A.B. De Vries, *Het Noord-Nederlandsch portret in de tweede helft van de 16e;
eeuw*, 1934, p. 102, figs. 59 and 60; G.J. Hoogewerff, *De Noord-Nederlandsche Schilderkunst*, IV,
1941/42, pp. 613/14, fig. 292; P.J.J. van Thiel, *Alle Schilderijen van het Rijksmuseum te Amsterdam*,
1976, pp. 370/371, no. C616/617, with ill.
Christie's Amsterdam, 13 November 1995 (131**) NLG 69,000   US$ 43,486

MASTENBROEK Johan Hendrik van (Rotterdam 1875-1945 Rotterdam) Dutch
THE HARBOUR OF ROTTERDAM oil on canvas, 35 x 52cm. sd 'J.H. van Mastenbroek 1900'
A. Mak B.V. Dordrecht, 12 December 1995 (180**) NLG 11,000   US$ 6,816

ROTTERDAM HARBOUR oil on canvas, 41¾ x 81¾in. (106 x 207.5cm.) sd 'J.H. van Mastenbroek
96'
Christie's London, 14 June 1996 (11**) GBP 47,700   US$ 73,554

ON THE SCHELDT oil on canvas, 10 ¼ x 17 ¼in. (26 x 44cm.) slr
PROV.: Harry Wallis & son, London.
Phillips London, 14 November 1995 (12**) GBP 4,500   US$ 7,039

HET GROOTHOOFD, DORDTRECHT oil on canvas, 27 7/8 x 51½in. (71 x 131cm.) sd 'J.H. van
Mastenbroek. 1917'
Christie's London, 17 November 1995 (4**) GBP 13,225   US$ 20,687

A VIEW OF THE AMSTERDAMSE POORT, HAARLEM pen and brush and brown ink and
watercolour heightened with white on paper, 34 x 24 cm sd 'JH v Mastenbroek 96'
Christie's Amsterdam, 25 April 1996 (67*) NLG 6,900   US$ 4,100

MASTER HARTFORD (act. 16th Century) Italian
STILL-LIFE WITH POMEGRANATE / STILL-LIFE WITH BUTTERFLY (A PAIR) oil on canvas,
60 x 78cm
PROV.: Frascatie, collection Parisi; Algranti, asta del castello di Vigoleno, 16 May 1987, lotto
no.942.

EXH.: *Mostra di dipinti dal XIV al XVIII secolo*, Finarte, Milano, 20 April-10 May 1972, no.9, pag.22-25.
LIT.: F. Zeri, *Sull`esecuzione di 'nature morte' nella bottega del Cavalier d`Arpino e sulla presenza ivi del giovane Caravaggio*, in 'Diari di lavore 2', Torino 1976, ill.97, p.98; A.Cottino, *Maestro di Hartford*, in 'La natura morte in Italia', II, Milano 1989, p.691, ill.821-822, p.694.

Finearte Milan, 25 November 1995 (108**) ITL 94,3000,000	US$	591,965

MASTER MONTE OLIVETO (act. Asciano ca. 1305-early 1330s) Italian
THE CRUCIFIXION tempera on panel, gold ground, 17 x 12¾in. (43.5 x 32cm.) (ca. 1305)
LIT.: J.H. Stubblebine, *Duccio di Buoninsegna and his School*, 1979, vol. I, pp. 94, 188, vol. II, figs. 211, 470.

Sotheby's London, 5 July 1995 (67**) GBP 155,500	US$	248,046

MASTER NATIVITA JOHNSON (probably Florence act. 2nd half of the 15th Century-) Italian
MADONNA COL BAMBINO E SAN GIOVANNINO oil on panel, 109 x 66cm
PROV.: London, collection Dowdswell and Dowdswell; Paterson (New Jersey), collection Catholina Lambert, Bella Vista Castle; Asta American Art Association, New York, Februar 1916, lotto 252, as Giovanni Santi; Roma, collection Livingston Phelps; Asta American Art Galleries, New York, 20-21 Februar 1924, lotto 203, as Giovanni Santi; Parigi, collection Edouard Brandus; New York, collection Walter P. Chrisler (fino al 1989).
LIT.: E.Fahy, *Some Followers of Domenico Ghirlandaio*, 1968, PHD Dissertation from Harvard University, New York 1976, p.173.

Finearte Milan, 25 November 1995 (143**) ITL 253,000,000	US$	158,820

MASTER OF ASTORGA | (active 1st half of 16th Century-) Spanish
SAINT JOHN THE BAPTIST oil on panel, 42 x 32½in. (81.3 x 82.5cm.)

Christie's South Kensington, 18 april 1996 (9**) GBP 9,200	US$	13,950

MASTER OF INCISA SCAPACCINO (act. Ligurie-Piedmont around 1420 -) Italian
ENTHRONED VIRGIN BREASTFEEDING THE CHILD JESUS, SURROUNDED BY TWO ANGELS, THREE FEMALE AND THREE MALE SAINTS oil on panel, on gold ground, 47.5 x 25.7cm.
LIT.: M. Boskovits, 'Il Maestro di Incisa Scapaccino e alcuni problemi di pittura tardogotica in italia', in: *Paragone*, November 1991, no. 501, pp. 35-53, fig. 14a.

Étude Tajan Paris, 25 June 1996 (3**) FRF 200,000	US$	38,620

MASTER OF LOURINHA (active first half of the 16th Century-)
SAINT JEROME IN THE WILDERNESS oil on panel, 27¼ x 39in. (69.2 x 99.1cm.)
PROV.: Church of Ildefonsus (!), Oporto, Portugal in the 17th century; Mr. Hamburger, by 1910; Mr. Calabresi; Mr. Leitao, Lisbon, by whom sold in 1928 to Almeido Prado, by descent to the present owner.

Sotheby's New York, 16 May 1996 (12**) US$ 35,650	US$	35,650

MASTER OF SAN MINIATO (Florence 1478 ca - 1500 ca active) Italian
MADONNA WITH THE CHILD, OVER HER HEAD THE CRUCIFIXION SCENE WITH ST. FRANCIS OF ASSISI AND ST. GEROLAMO tempera on panel, 106.5 x 64.5cm. inscr. on the mount 'SANTA MARIA SANCTA DEI GENITRIX SANCTA VIRGO VIRGINUM CONSOLATRIX AFFLICTORUM' and 'ORA PRO NOBIS' on the base

Christie's Rome, 4 June 1996 (573**) ITL 68,000,000	US$	44,099

THE MADONNA AND CHILD tempera on panel, 10 7/8 x 10 1/8in. (37.8 x 25.8cm)
PROV.: with Van Diemen, Berlin, (as Pesellino).
LIT.: S. Castri, 'l Maestro di San Miniato', in *Il Maestro di San Miniato,*ed. G. Dalli Regoli, Pisa, 1988, p. 220, fig. 142.

Christie's London, 7 July 1995 (110**) GBP 34,500	US$	55,033

MASTER OF SAN TORPE (act. Pisa in the 14th Century) Italian
SAINT JOHN THE EVANGELIST tempera on panel, 21½ x 14½in. (54.5 x 37cm.)
EXH.: Nottingham, 1958, no. 2 plate III, as Sienese School of the 14th Century; Nottingham, 1981,
no. 32, plate I, as circle of Simone Martini.
LIT.: Richter, 1901, no. 29, as early Sienese School; Nicholson, 1968, p. 163, 'strictly Simonesque';
Cornforth, 1968, pp. 404-405, fig.5 as Sienese School; Vertova, 1968, p. 23ff., reproduced fig 8, as
by a Pisan follower of Simone Martini; Calvocoressi, 1976, pp. 144-145, illustrated fig, 7, as Sienese
School; Nottingham, University Art Gallary, *Locko Park and the Drury-Lowes*, exhibition catalogue
appendix, 1982, p. 38, no. 2, incorrectly recordiing Vertovas' views in giving the pictures
unreservedly to the master of San Torpé.
<table>
<tr><td>Sotheby's London, 6 December 1995 (13**) GBP 51,000</td><td>US$</td><td>78,486</td></tr>
</table>

MASTER OF THE (FEMALE) HALF LENGTHS (Bruges or Antwerp, active 1500 - 1530 c. active) Flemish
THE ADORATION OF THE HERDSMEN oil on panel, 56 x 41cm.
PROV.: Private collection, Madrid, ca. 1970; Private collection, Italy.
<table>
<tr><td>Dorotheum Vienna, 6 March 1996 (118**) ATS 450,000</td><td>US$</td><td>43,286</td></tr>
</table>

THE ADORATION OF THE HERDSMEN oil on panel, 65 x 65cm.
PROV.: Galerie David Koetser, Zürich; sold as work from the master of the (female) half lenghts
with ones own hands, on 3 September 1968 (for DEM 45,000); Private collection, Vienna.
<table>
<tr><td>Dorotheum Vienna, 11 June 1996 (216**) ATS 400,000</td><td>US$</td><td>37,128</td></tr>
</table>

THE MAGDALEN PAINTING oil on panel, 31 x 23.8cm.
<table>
<tr><td>Christie's Amsterdam, 13 November 1995 (124**) NLG 92,000</td><td>US$</td><td>57,982</td></tr>
</table>

MASTER OF THE (FEMALE) HALF LENGTHS (ATTR.) (Bruges or Antwerp, active 1500 - 1530 c. active) Flemish
SAINT JHERONYMUS IN A LANDSCAPE oil on panel, 48.5 x 40.5cm.
PROV.: Anonymous sale, Paris , Palais Galliera, 26 March 1974, no. 9 (illustrated), sold at 36,000
FRF, as 'Antwerp School'.
<table>
<tr><td>Étude Tajan Paris, 25 June 1996 (19**) FRF 125,000</td><td>US$</td><td>24,137</td></tr>
</table>

VIRGIN AND CHILD oil on panel, 41 x 29cm.
PROV.: Anonymous sale, Paris, Galerie Georges Petit, 27 May 1932, no. 26 (illustrated); Collection
Prof L. Justin Besançon.
<table>
<tr><td>Étude Tajan Paris, 25 June 1996 (20**) FRF 520,000</td><td>US$</td><td>100,411</td></tr>
</table>

MASTER OF THE BENTINCK-THYSSEN MADONNA (active in Bruges and Antwerp, early 16th century -) Flemish
THE VIRGIN AND CHILD oil on panel, 37¼ x 25¼in. (95 x 63.9cm.)
PROV.: Bacci Collection, Paris; Chillingworth Collection, sold Lucerne, Fischer, 5 September 1922,
lot 4; With J. Bohler, Zurich; With D. Heineman, Munich, 1926-9; Baron Heinrich Thyssen-
Bornemisza, by 1930.
EXH.: Munich 1930, no. 165; Dusseldorf 1970-1, no. 59; Lausanne etc., 1986-7, no. 4.
LIT.: Advertised in *International Studio*, August 1929, vol. XCII, p. 20; M.J. Friedlander, *Die
Altniederländische Malerei, 1934, vol. Xl, p. 137, no. 191a, as by Isenbrandt;* Heinemann, 1937, vol.
I, p. 77, no. 208, vol. II, plate 82; M.J. Friedländer, *Early Netherlandish Painting,* 1974, vol. XI, p.
89, no. 191a, reproduced plate 141, as by Isenbrandt; R. Andree, *Kunstmuseum Dusseldorf - Malerei,*
1976, no. 2.
<table>
<tr><td>Sotheby's London, 6 December 1995 (69**) GBP 106,000</td><td>US$</td><td>163,127</td></tr>
</table>

MASTER OF THE FEMALE HALF LENGTHS (active Antwerp between 1520-1540 16th Century) Flemish
THE MAGDALENE WRITING IN AN INTERIOR oil on panel, 16 x 11in. (41 x 28.5cm.)
PROV.: Cardinal Fesch Collection, (his 1841 catalogue no. 262, his 1844 catalogue no. 1362, as

Mabuse); Zay-Kolowrat Sale, Vienna, Dorotheum, 28 March - 2 April 1918, lot 1221; Mme de la L. de L., née Bagassière, Paris, her sale, Lucerne, 27July 1926, lot 31;

Max von Goldschmidt-Rothschild Collection, Frankfurt; With J. Bohler, Zurich, 1926; Anonymous sale (Hackenbroch?), Brussels, 8 December 1929; Baron Heinrich Thyssen-Bornemisza, by 1930. EXH.: Munich 1930, no. 218; Paris 1970, no. 11; Dusseldorf 1970-1, no. 33; Lausanne etc., 1986-7, no. 6.

LIT.: M.J. Friedländer, *Die Altniederländische Malerei*, vol. XII, 1935, p. 174, no. 94; R. Heinemann 1937, vol. I, no. 272; M.J. Friedländer, *Early Netherlandish Painting*, 1975, vol. Xll, p. 99, no. 94, reproduced pl. 43.

Sotheby's London, 6 December 1995 (70**) GBP 73,000	US$	112,342

MASTER OF THE FIESOLE EPIPHANY Philippo di Guiliano Matteo (?) (act. ca. 1500-)
MADONNA AND SAINT JOHN THE BAPTIST ADORING THE CHRIST CHILD shaped top, tempera om panel; in its original frame, 49½ x 27½in. (125.7 x 69.9cm.)
PROV.: Giorgio Augusto Wallis, Florence (Sale: J. M. Heberle, Berlin May 24, 1895, lot 114, as Umbrian School); Richard von Kaufmann (Sale: P. Cassirer, Berlin, December 4, 1917, lot 22 as Florentine Master, circa 1490); Sittenfield (Sale: Parke-Bernet Galleries, New York, December 2, 1938, lot 53 a, as Lorenzo de Credi); Sale: Christie's New York, April 4, 1990, lot 166 (as Bartolomeo di Giovanni) where acquired by M. Roy Gisher Fine Arts, Inc., New York from whom acquired in 1990 by the present collector.
EXH.: *Gemälde des XIV-XVI. Jahrhunderts aus der Sammlung von Richard von Kaufmann*, 1901, cat. no. 93 (as Florentine Master, circa 1500); G. de Francovich, 'Nouvi aspetti della personalita di Bartolomeo de Giovanni, ' *Bolletino d'Arte*, July 1926, p. 88 (as by Bartolomeo de Giovanni); E. Fahy, *Some Followers of Domenico Ghirlandajo*, 1976, pp. 45, 160-61, cat. no. 80 (as by Bartolomeo di Giovanni); 'The Restorer's Art,' *Journal of Art*, III, no. 1, October 1990 (Supplement), illustrated. in colour p. 21.

Sotheby's New York, 11 January 1996 (60**) US$ 79,500	US$	79,500

MASTER OF THE GLORYFICATION OF THE VIRGIN (Act. in Cologne, second half of the 15th century) German
THE VIRGIN AND CHILD oil on pine panel, 27 x 21¼in. (69 x 54cm.) (between 1470-1480)
PROV.: Walter Schnackenberg, Munich, in 1927; With J. Hinrichsen and P. Lindpaintner, Berlin, 1928; Baron Heinrich Thyssen-Bornemisza, by 1930.
EXH.: Munich 1930, no. 216; Paris 1970, no. 10, plate 1; Düsseldorf 1970-1, no. 32; Lausanne etc., 1986-7, no. 10.
LIT.: Advertised in the *Burlington Magazine*, vol. CCXCVII, December 1927, reproduced plate 6; Catalogue of the exhibition, *Gotischer Bildteppiche, Plastiken und Tafelbilder in der Kunsthandlung J. Hinrichsen und P. Lindpaintner*, Berlin, 1928, no. 47; R. Heinemann 1937, vol. I, no. 270; A. Stange, Deutsche Malerei der Gotik, vol. V, 1952, p. l9, reproduced fig. 26; A. Stange, *Kritisches Verzeichnis der deutschen Tafelbilder vorDurer*, 1967, vol. I, p.57, no. 146; A. Stange, *Deutsche malerei der Gotik*, 1969, vol. V, p. l9, reproduced fig. 26.

Sotheby's London, 6 December 1995 (65**) GBP 47,700	US$	73,407

MASTER OF THE LILLE ADORATION (act. Flanders, probably Antwerp act. ca. 1530) Flemish
SAINT JEROME oil on panel, 24¼ x 19¼in. (62 x 48.5cm.)

Sotheby's London, 17 April 1996 (123**) GBP 18,400	US$	27,900

MASTER OF THE PARROT (antwerp first three decades of the 16th Century-) flemish
MARIA WITH CHILD IN FRONT OF A GREEN CURTAIN oil on panel, 73.5 x 54cm.(framed)

Dorotheum Vienna, 17 October 1995 (93**) ATS 280,000	US$	28,086

MASTER OF THE PRODIGAL SON (16th Century) (1530-1560) Flemish
THE HOLY FAMILY, A LANDSCAPE BEYOND oil on panel, 82.7 x 72.3cm
PROV.: Elink Schuurman Duuring; Sale, Mark Dordrecht, 22 November 1938, lot 7, as P.C. van Aelst.

LIT.: G. Marlier, *Pierre Coeck d'Alost*, 1966, p. 240, no. 12.
         Christie's Amsterdam, 13 November 1995 (162**) NLG 46,000   US$ 28,991

MASTER OF THE STRACHE-ALTARS (Oberfranken (?) active in Bamberg in the late 15th century-) German
DIE KREUZIGUNG CHRISTI oil on panel, 84 x 62cm.
PROV.: Slg. Stenlein, München; 526. Lempertz-Auktion, Köln, 7-2-1972; Private Collection, Köln.
LIT.: Thieme-Becker, Bd. XXXVII, p. 318 f.; A. Stange *Malerei der Gotik*, Bd. IX, München/Berlin 1958, p. 107 col. ill. 224.
         Lempertz Cologne, 15 November 1995 (1316a**) DEM 250,000   US$ 176,454

MASTER OF THE VIRGO INTER VIRGINES (AND HIS STUDIO (ATTR.)) (1460 c.-1490 c.) Flemish (Dutch)
THE DEPOSITION tempera on panel, 20 x 20in. (50.8 x 50.8cm.) (1457)
         Sotheby's New York, 6 October 1996 (26*) US$ 27,600   US$ 27,600

MASTER OF VERRUCHIO (act. in Rimini act. first half of the 14th century) Italian
MADONNA AND CHILD oil on panel, 22 x 20¾in. (56 x 52.3cm.)
PROV.: Calvello Collection, Palermo; Anonymous sale, Rome, Galleria Innocenti, 19-23 February 1907, as Duccio.
EXH.: Rimini, Museo della Cittá, *Il Trecencento riminese*, 20 August 1995 - 7 January 1996, no. 35, (with the location wrongly given as London private collection).
         Sotheby's London, 17 April 1996 (78**) GBP 54,300   US$ 82,335

MATHIEU Georges (Boulogne sur Mer 1921 b.) French
COMPOSITION acrylic on paper, 57 x 76cm. slr 'Mathieu'
         Finearte Milan, 12 December 1995 (308**) ITL 13,800,000   US$ 8,657

GRADLON oil on canvas, 38 3/8 x 77in. (97.5 x 195.5cm.) sdlr 'Mathieu 64'
PROV.: Gimpel Fils Gallery, London; Galerie Arditti, Paris.
EXH.: London, Gimpel Fils, *Mathieu*, November 1964, no. 16 (illustrated in the catalogue).
LIT.: François Mathey, *Mathieu*, Paris 1969, p. 190 (illustrated in colour).
         Christie's London, 19 March 1996 (5**) GBP 14,375   US$ 21,953

MAREGES oil on canvas, ,100 x 60cm. sdll 'Mathieu 65' (1965)
         Finearte Milan, 26 October 1995 (149*) ITL 27,025,000   US$ 16,838

AYMAR COMPTE DE POITIERS VOULAIT DÉPOSSEDER EUDES oil on canvas, 180 x 60cm. sdlr 'Mathieu 60' (1960)
         Finearte Milan, 26 October 1995 (180**) ITL 29,900,000   US$ 18,629

MEE oil on canvas, 50.5 x 74cm. sll 'Mathieu' titled on the reverse (1969)
PROV.: Galleria del Millione, Milano; Galleria d'Arte Prisma, Cuneo.
         Sotheby's Milan, 28 May 1996 (145**) ITL 18,400,000   US$ 11,818

MATISSE Henri (Cateau-Cambrésis-Nord 1869-1954 Nice) French
ODALISQUE charcoal on paper laid down on paper, 12½ x 18¾in. (31.8 x 47.7cm.) slr 'Henri Matisse' (Nice, 1923)
PROV.: Galerie Renou et Colle, Paris (acquired by the family of the present owner, 1935).
EXH.: London, Leicester Gallery, 1933.
LIT.: W. George, *Dessins d'Henri Matisse*, Paris 1925, pl. 46 (illustrated).
         Christie's New York, 1 May 1996 (181**) US$ 211,500   US$ 211,500

Lydia (Etude pour 'Portrait au Manteau bleu')

LES CITRONS AU PLAT D'ÉTAIN oil on canvas, 21 5/8 x 26in. (55 x 66cm.) slr 'Henri Matisse'
(Noce, 1926)
      Christie's New York, 30 April 1996 (26**) US$ 4,072,500   US$ 4,072,500

FEMME ALLONGÉE (DECLINING NUDE) pencil on paper, 10 x 11¾in. (25.5 x 30cm.) sdlr
'Henri Matisse 30' (1930)
      Étude Tajan Paris, 13 December 1995 (59*) FRF 55,000   US$ 11,078

FEMME ASSISE DANS L'ATELIER DEVANT DES DESSINS India ink on paper, 18 1/8 x 22½in.
(46 x 57.2cm.) slr 'H Matisse'
PROV.: Acquired in Paris in the late 1970s by the present owners.
      Sotheby's New York, 2 May 1996 (312**) US$ 134,500   US$ 134,00

NATURE MORTE oil on canvas, 18 1/8 x 21¾in. (46 x 55cm.) slr 'Matisse' (1896)
PROV.: Desjardins Collection.
EXH.: Paris, Galerie Charpentier, *Le Pain et le vin*, 1954, n.n.; Paris Galerie Charpentier, *Cent
Tableaux de Collections Privées, de Bonnard à de Staël*, 1960, no. 71.
      Sotheby's London, 24 June 1996 (16**) GBP 243,500   US$ 375,482

FENETRE OUVERTE: ETRETAT oil on canvas, 28½ x 23 5/8in. 72.5 x 60cm. slr Henry-Matisse
PROV.: Bernheim-Jeune, Paris (acquired from the artist on 6th October 1920);
Paul Rosenberg, Paris and New York (acquired from the above on 8th November 1920);

Sale: London, Christie's, 29th June 1976, lot 264 (purchased by the present owner).
EXH.: Paris, Galerie Georges Petit, *Henri Matisse*, 1931, no. 80, illustrated in the catalogue; New York, Museum of Modern Art, *Henri Matisse, His Art and His Public*, 1951.
LIT.: Raymond Escholier, *Henri Matisse*, Paris, 1937, p. 27, illustrated in colour ;
Gaston Diehl, *Henri Matisse*, Paris, 1954, no. 88, illustrated (incorrect measurements); Alfred Barr, *Matisse, His Art and His Public*, New York, 1951, p. 209;
Guy-Patrice and Michel Dauberville, *Matisse*, Paris, 1995, vol. I, p. 230, no. 80, catalogued; p. 227, illustrated; vol. II, p. 908, no. 413, illustrated (incorrect measurements).

Sotheby's London, 24 June 1996 (48**) GBP 1,101,500	US$	1,698,535

PORTRAIT DE ROSABIANCA SKIRA charcoal on paper, 20 x 15½in. 51 x 39.5cm. sd 48; dedicated *en hommage à Rosabianca Skira*
PROV.: Albert and Rosabianca Skira, Geneva (a gift from the artist. See note to lot 47).
EXH.: Saint-Paul-de-Vence, Fondation Maeght, *A la Rencontre de Matisse, 1969, no. 83;* Geneva, Musée Rath et Cabinet des Estampes Genève, *Art du XXe siècle - Collections Genevoises*, 1973, no. 12.

Sotheby's London, 24 June 1996 (49*) GBP 243,500	US$	375,482

NU ALLONGÉ pen and indian ink on paper, 17¼ x 22in. 44 x 56cm. sd 1935 (1938)
PROV.: M. Kelekian, Paris; Acquired from the above in 1938 and thence by descent to the present owner.
EXH.: London, The Leicester Galleries, *Henri Matisse*, 1936, no. 38.
LIT.: *Cahiers d 'art*, no. 3-5, Paris, 1936, p. 89, illustrated; Isaac Grünwald, *Henri Matisse*, Stockholm, 1944, p. 109, illustrated; Alexandre Romm, *Matisse*, London, 1947, p. 35, illustrated; Gaston Diehl, Henri Matisse, Paris, 1954, p. 42, illustrated; Agnes Humbert, Matisse, dessins, Paris, 1956, pl. 19, illustrated; Raymond Escholier, *Matisse, ce vivant*, Paris, 1956, p. 143, illustrated; Jean Guichard-Meili, *Henri Matisse, son oeuvre et son univers*, Paris, 1967, p. 222, illustrated; Alfred Barr, *Matisse, His Art and His Public*, London, 1975; p. 250, illustrated; *Line drawings and prints, 50 works by Henri Matisse*, Dover Art Library, London and New York, 1979, p. 21, illustrated.

Sotheby's London, 24 June 1996 (50*) GBP 441,500	US$	680,802

NU ALLONGE Pen and indian ink on paper, 17¼ x 22in. 44 x 56cm. sdlr 1935
PROV.: M. Kelekian, Paris; Acquired from the above in 1938.

Sotheby's London, 24 June 1996 (50*) GBP 441,500	US$	680,802

LE SILENCE HABITE DES MAISONS brush and indian ink on J. Whatman paper laid down on board, 24¼ x 19¼in. (61.5 x 48.5cm.) sdlr 'H. Matisse juin 47'
PROV.: Buchholz Gallery (Curt Valentin), New York, by whom acquired directly from the Artist; Billy Baldwin, New York; Woodson Taulbee, New York; Anon. sale Sotheby's, New York 15 May 1985, lot 238 ($160,000).
EXH.: New York, Buchholx Gallery (Curt Valentin), *Contemporary Drawings*, 1950 no. 60 (illustrated on the cover).

Christie's London, 25 June 1996 (30**) GBP 463,500	US$	714,726

FEMME AU COLLIER pen and ink on paper, 20½ x 15¾in. (52.1 x 40cm.) sdll 'H. Matisse 8/43' (August 1943)
PROV.: Gerald Cramer, Geneva; Leicester Galleries, London; Acquired from the above by the previous owner in the early 1960's.

Christie's London, 26 June 1996 (246**) GBP 34,500	US$	53,200

NATURE MORTE AUX POMMES charcoal on paper, 14½ x 18 7/8in. (37 x 48cm.) sdlr 'juillet 44, H. Matisse' (Vence, July 1944)
PROV.: Heinz Berggruen, Paris by whom bought from the family of the Artist.

Christie's London, 26 June 1996 (249**) GBP 56,500	US$	87,124

NU DE DOS pen and black ink on paper, 10¼ x 7 7/8in. (26 x 20cm.) slr 'Henri Matisse'
PROV.: Wanda de Guébriant has kindly confirmed the authenticity of this work.
       Christie's South Kensington, 27 November 1995 (18*) GBP 8,437   US$ 13,197

CHERBOURG, LE BASSIN oil on board laid down on board, 13 x 16 1/8in (33 x 41cm.) sll 'Henri Matisse' (1918)
PROV.: Bernheim-Jeune, Paris (21295); Galerie Tanner, Zurich, from whom purchased by Hans Mettler in June 1919 for SF4,062; Hans Mettler, St. Gallen; his sale, Christie's, London, 2 July 1979, lot 20 (GBP20,000).
EXH.: Paris, Bernheim-Jeune, *Henri Matisse*, May 1919, no.20; Basle, Kunsthalle, *Henri Matisse*, Aug.-Sept. 1931, no.14; Lucerne, Musée des Beaux-Arts, *Henri Matisse*, 1949, no.59; London, Arts Council of Great Britain, *Henri Matisse, 1968*, no.78 (illustrated).
LIT.: *L'Amour de l'Art*, VIII, July 1927 (illustrated p.231); G. Diehl, *Matisse*, Paris, 1954, p.74.
       Christie's London, 29 November 1995 (124**) GBP 85,000   US$ 132,958

LYDIA (ETUDE POUR *PORTRAIT AU MANTEAU BLUE*) charcoal on paper, 26 3/8 x 18 5/8in. (67 x 47.2cm.) sdll ' Henri Matisse 19 XI 35'
PROV.: Frank Perls, California (circa 1974); Richard Gray Gallery, Chicago; acquired from the above by the present owner.
EXH.: San Francisco, J.B. Gallery, *Homage to Frank Perls*, Sept.-Oct. 1975, no. 18. The exhibition traveled to Los Angeles, Margo Leavin Gallery, Nov.-Dec. 1975.
       Christie's New York, 30 April 1996 (49**) US$ 772,500   US$ 772,500

LES TULIPES oil on canvas, 39 3/8 x 28¾in (,100 x 73cm.) sll 'Henry Matisse' (1914)
PROV.: Galerie Bernheim-Jeune, Paris (acquired from the artist on April 4,1914); F. Gurlitt, Paris (acquired from the above on June 5,1914); Galerien Thannhauser, Berlin Galerien Matthiesen, Berlin; Karl Bett, Bedin.
EXH.: Berlin, Galerien Thannhauser, *Henri Matisse*, Feb.-March, 1930, no. 24; Basel, Kunsthalle, *Henri Matisse*, Aug.-Sept., 1931, no. 43; New York, Marlborough Gallery, Inc., *Masters of the 19th and 20th Centuries*, Nov.-Dec., 1986, no. 31 (illustrated in color); Kyoto, Musée National d'art Moderne, *Fauvism and Modern Japanese Painting*, Jan.-Feb., 1993, p.138, no. 91 (illustrated in color, p. 139). The exhibition traveled to Tokyo, Musée National d'art Moderne, Feb.-March, 1993.
LIT.: 'D'après les oeuvres recentes d'Henri Matisse,' *Les Soirées de Paris, May 15,1914, vol.24, p.253 (illustrated); J. Flam,*Matisse, The Man and His Art, 1869-1918, New York, 1986, p.384, no. 381 (illustrated); G.-P. and M. Dauberville, *Henri Matisse chez Bernheim-Jeune*, Paris, 1995, vol. I, p.533, no. 141 (illustrated).
       Christie's New York, 30 April 1996 (52**) US$ 1,762,500   US$ 1,762,500

LES DEUX FEMMES oil on canvas, 28 7/8 x 23½in. (73.5 x 59.7cm.) sdlr 'Henri Matisse 38'
PROV.: Galerie Paul Rosenberg, New York; Acquired from the above by the family of the present owner circa 1946.
EXH.: Paris, Galerie Paul Rosenberg, *Oeuvres recentes de Henri Matisse*, Oct.-Nov., 1938; Pittsburgh, Carnegie Institute (on loan, 1939); Brussels, Palais des Beaux-Arts, *Exposition Picasso-Matisse*, May, 1946. The exhibition traveled to Amsterdam, Stedelijk Museum, 1946.; Chicago, The Art Institute, *Chicago Collectors*, Sept.-Oct.,1963 (incorrectly dated 1939); Chicago, The Art Institute (on loan, 1975-1995).
LIT.: *Cahiers d'art*, 'Expositions et nouvelles acquisitions des musées,' vol. 14, nos. 1-4, 1939, p. 76 (illustrated); J. Cassou, *Paintings and Drawings of Matisse*, Paris, 1939, p. 24 (illustrated in colour); G. Diehl, Henri Matisse, Paris, 1954, p. 119 (illustrated); M. Luzi and M. Carra, *L'opera di Matisse dalla rovilta 'fauve' all'intimismo*, 1904-1928, Milan, 1971, p. 106, no. 483; L. Delectorskaya, *with apparent ease, Henri Matisse*, Paris,1988, p. 32 (illustrated in colour, p. 263; unfinished versions illustrated, p. 262).
       Christie's New York, 7 November 1995 (48**) US$ 6,382,500   US$ 6,382,500

POISSONS CHINOIS gouache and paper cut and pasted and charcoal on paper mounted on canvas, 75 7/8 x 35 7/8in. (192.2 x 91cm.) sdlr 'HENRI MATISSE 51'

PROV.: Mme Henri Matisse, Paris (1954); Pierre Matisse, New York (1958); P.N. Matisse, Beverly Hills (1965); Acquired from the above by Victoria H. Sperry in 1965.
EXH.: Bern, Kunsthalle, *Henri Matisse, les grandes gouaches decoupées,1950-1954*,July-Sept., 1959, no. 4 (illustrated); Amsterdam, Stedelijk Museum, *Henri Matisse, les grandes gouaches decoupées*, April-June, 1960, no. 5; Paris, Musée des Arts Décoratifs , *Henri Matisse, les grandes gouaches decoupées*, March-May, 1961, p. 47, no. 11; New York, Museum of Modern Art, *The Last Works of Henri Matisse, Large Cut Gouaches*, Oct.-Dec., 1961, p. 45, no. 6 (illustrated in color, pl. K). The exhibition traveled to Chicago, The Art Institute, Jan.-Feb., 1962 and San Francisco, Museum of Art, March-April, 1962; Cleveland, Museum of Art, *Fifty Years of Modern Art, 1916-1966*,June-July, 1966, no. 113 (illustrated); Washington, D.C., National Gallery of Art, *Henri Matisse Paper Cut-Outs*, Sept.-Oct., 1977, p. 71, no. 127 (illustrated in color, pl. XV). The exhibition traveled to Detroit, Institute of Arts, Nov., 1977-Jan., 1978 and St. Louis, Art Museum, Jan.-March, 1978; Pasadena, Norton Simon Museum, *Dreaming in Color: The Art of Henri Matisse*, Nov., 1989-April, 1990 Pasadena, Norton Simon Museum, *Impossible Realities: Marcel Duchamp and the Surrealist Tradition*, July, 1991- March, 1992; New York, Museum of Modern Art, *Henri Matisse: A Retrospective*, Sept., 1992-Jan., 1993, p. 450, no. 392 (illustrated in color).
LIT.: M. Luzi, 'Temoignage: Henri Matisse,' *XXe Siècle*, 1952, pp. 55-57; G. Duthuit and P. Reverdy, 'Last Works by Matisse 1950-1954,' *Verve, nos. 35-36*, summer, 1958 (illustrated in color, p. 31); J. Lassaigne, *Matisse*, Geneva, 1959, p. 122 (illustrated, p. 120); H. Matisse, *Écrits et propos sur l'art*, Paris, 1972, p. 247; T. Reff, 'Matisse: Meditations on a Statuette and Goldfish,' *Arts Magazine*, no. 52, 1976, pp. 109-115; J. Elderfield, *The Cut-Outs of Henri Matisse*, New York,1978, p. 46, no. 26 (illustrated in colour, pl. 26); P. Schneider, Matisse, London, 1984, p. 694; A. Liberman, *The Artist In His Studio*, New York, 1988, p. 49, no. 4 (illustrated in colour, pp. 44-45 and 52-53).

Christie's New York, 7 November 1995 (50***) US$ 6,382,500	US$	6,382,500

NUE AU PEIGNOIR oil on canvas, 25½ x 18in. (65 x 46cm.) sdlr 'Henri.Matisse 33'
PROV.: Galerie Paul Rosenberg, New York (acquired from the artist in 1934); Acquired from the above by the family of the present owner ca. 1946.
EXH.: Brussels, Palais Des Beaux-Arts, *Exposition Picasso-Matisse*, May 1946. The exhibition traveled to Amsterdam, Stedelijk Museum, 1946; Chicago, The Art Institute, *Treasures of Chicago Collectors*, April-May 1961; Chicago, The Art Institute (on loan, 1975-1995).
LIT.: A.H. Barr, Jr., *Matisse, His Art and his Public*, London, 1975, p. 468 (illustrated).

Christie's New York, 7 November 1995 (53**) US$ 1,542,500	US$	1,542,500

FEMME NUE ASSISE charcoal on paper, 18 7/8 x 12in. (48 x 30.5cm.) lr 'H.Matisse, avril 1947' (April 1947)
PROV.: Galerie Maeght, Paris.
LIT.: ed. Galerie Maeght, *Derrière le Miroir*, no. 46, May, 1952 (illustated).

Christie's New York, 8 November 1995 (253*) US$ 255,500	US$	255,500

MATSYS Quentin (attributed) (1466-1530) Flemish
MARIA WITH CHILD oil on panel, 56 x 42.5cm.

Dorotheum Vienna, 6 March 1996 (111**) ATS 130,000	US$	12,505

MATSYS Quentin (studio of) (Louvain 1465-6-1530 Antwerp) Flemish
THE PRESENTATION IN THE TEMPLE oil on panel, 26¼ x 20¾in. (66.5 x 52.8cm.) (between 1509-13)
PROV.: Weber Collection, Brussels, until 1926; Baron Heinrich Thyssen-Bornemisza, by 1930.
EXH.: Munich 1930, no. 212; Paris 1970, no. 9; Düsseldorf 1970-1, no. 31; Lausanne etc., 1986-7, no. 3.
LIT.: R. Heinemann 1937, vol. I, no. 259, vol. II, plate 87; M.J. Friedlander, *Die Altniederländische Malerei*, 1934, vol. VII, p. 115, no. 9, plate XV; M.J. Friedländer, *Early Netherlandish Painting*, 1968, vol. Vll, p.61, no. 9, plate 14.

Sotheby's London, 6 December 1995 (67**) GBP 27,600	US$	42,475

MATTA Roberto Matta Echaurren {called} (Chiloé 1911 b.) Chilean (French)
LE SACRIFICE pastel on paper, 51¼ x 51¼in. (130 x 130cm.) (1972)
LIT.: To be included in the forthcoming *Matta Catalogue Raisonné* being prepared by Mme. G.
Ferrari-Matta.   US$ 18,441
      Sotheby's London, 21 March 1996 (33**) GBP 12,075

UNTITLED oil on canvas, 60 x 73cm. slr 'R. Matta'
      Bukowskis Stockholm, 24-25 April 1996 (174**) SEK 105,000   US$ 15,907

MATTEIS Paolo de (1662-1728) Italian
ADORATION OF THE MAGI oil on canvas, 127.5 x 102cm.
      Christie's Rome, 4 June 1996 (578**) ITL 19,000,000   US$ 2,322

MATTIOLI Carlo (Modena 1911 b.-) Italian
LANDSCAPE oil on canvas, 24 x 24cm. titled sd on the reverse (1970)
      Finearte Milan, 18 June 1996 (73*) ITL 17,825,000   US$ 11,560

MAUFRA Maxime Emile Louis (1861-1918) French
NUIT D'ORAGE, MORGAT oil on canvas, 54 x 65cm. sdlr 'Maufra 1901'
PROV.: Durand-Ruel, Paris, no. 3824; Galerie Durand-Ruel, New york, no.2751; Sir H.S. Howe,
New York (December 29, 1902).
LIT.: To be included in the forthcoming *catalogue raisonné* on the artist's work, being prepared by
Caroline Durand-Ruel Godfroy.
      Christie's Amsterdam, 5 June 1996 (230**) NLG 14,950   US$ 8,735

LA SALLE A MANGER APRES LE DEJEUNER oil on canvas, 36¼ x 28¾in. (92.1 x 73cm.) sdlr
'Maufra 1914'
PROV.: Galerie Durand-Ruel, Paris.
      Sotheby's New York, 2 May 1996 (164**) US$ 40,250   US$ 40,250

AU BORD DE L'ÉTANG A ROSPORDEN, FINISTERE oil on canvas, 23 7/8 x 23¾in. (60 x
73cm.) sdll 'Maufra 1911'
PROV.: Durand-Ruel, Paris (9756-13249, ph. 7127), by whom bought directly from the Artist on 19
October 1911; Arthur Tooth and Sons Ltd., London (4199), by whom purchased from the above on
14 January 1956.
      Christie's London, 29 November 1995 (116**) GBP 22,000   US$ 34,413

MAURER Alfred Henry (1868-1932) American
FAUVIST LANDSCAPE oil on board, 18 x 21¾in. (45.7 x 55cm.) sll with estate stamp ;A.H.
Maurer' (ca. 1923-27)
PROV.: Ione and Hudson Walker; The University Gallery, University of Minnesota, Minneapolis;
Babcock Galleries, New York; Sale: New York, Christie's, May 23, 1990, Lot 227.
      Christie's New York, 13 September 1995 (104**) US$ 11,500   US$ 11,500

FLOWERS oil and watercolour on gessoed panel, 21½ x 18in. (54.6 x 45.7cm.)
PROV.: E. Weyhe, New York.
EXH.: Hartford, Connecticut, Wadsworth Atheneum, on temporary loan, n.d.
      Christie's New York, 13 September 1995 (107**) US$ 17,250   US$ 17,250

MAUVE Anton (Zaandam 1838-1888 Arnhem) Dutch
A SHEPHERD AND FLOCK AT DUSK oil on canvas, 51 x 71 cm s 'A. Mauve f'
PROV.: Anon. sale, New York Sotheby's Parke Bernett, 14 January 1977, lot 53.
      Christie's Amsterdam, 25 April 1996 (102*) NLG 9,200   US$ 5,467

MAYER Auguste Etienne François (Brest 1805-1890 Brest) French
ON THE BOSPHORUS oil on canvas, 14¾ x 20in. (37.5 x 50.8) s 'A. Mayer'
      Christie's London, 17 November 1995 (177**) GBP 10925   US$ 17,089

MAYEUR DE MERPRES Adrien-Jean le (1880-1958) Dutch (?)
A NORTH AFRICAN SCENE oil on board, 22 x 26.5cm. slr (ca. 1920)
      Sotheby's Amsterdam, 23 April 1996 (16**) NLG 14,160   US$ 8,414

BALINESE WOMEN WEAVING oil on canvas, 76 x 90cm. sll
PROV.: Acquired directly from the Artist by the present owner.
      Sotheby's Amsterdam, 23 April 1996 (40**) NLG 295,000   US$ 175,293

BALINESE WOMEN WEAVING black chalk, watercolour and pastel, 47 x 63cm. sll 'Le Mayeur'
      Sotheby's Amsterdam, 23 April 1996 (93**) NLG 42,480   US$ 25,242

MAZZOLA (Girolamo) Francesco Maria {called} Parmigianino (Parma 1503-1540) Italian
THE MADONNA AND CHILD oil on panel, 13 3/8 x 17 5/8in. (34 x 44.8cm.) (around 1529)
PROV.: Bought by the dealer William Kent from the dealer Arnaldi in Florence in 1758 for Sir
Nathaniel Curzon, 5th Bt. later 1st Baron Scarsdale (1726-1804) and by descent at Kedleston.
LIT.: C. Gould, 'A Parmigianino Madonna and Child and his uncommissioned Paintings', in:*Apollo*,
CXXXV, 361, 1992, pp. 151-6.; C. Gould, *Parmigianino*, New York, London, Paris, 1994, PP. 96-7,
p. 186.
      Christie's London, 7 July 1995 (118***) GBP 881,500   US$ 1,406,125

MAZZOLA Girolamo Bedoli (Viadana 1500 c.-1569 Parma) Italian
THE VIRGIN WITH THE CHILD, ST. JOHN AND ST. CECILIA AND ST. GIROLAMO oil on
panel, 71 x 55cm.
      Christie's Rome, 21 November 1995 (219**) ITL 26,000,000   US$ 16,321

MAZZONI Sebastiano (Florence 1611 c.-1678 Venice) Italian
LOT AND HIS DAUGHTERS oil on canvas, 49 x 60½in. (124.5 x 154cm.) (mid 1660's)
PROV.: Albert Landsberg (d.1965), Villa Malcontenta, Venice; Thence by descent to the present
owner.
      Sotheby's London, 6 December 1995 (197**) GBP 80,700   US$ 124,192

MCPHAIL Rodger (1953 b.-|) British
GREY PARTRIDGE IN WINTER watercolour heightened with white, 18.5 x 23in. (47 x 58.4cm.) s
'R.McPhail'
      Christie's London, 14 May 1996 (144***) GBP 16,100   US$ 24,379

MCTAGGART Sir William, R.S.A., R.W.S. (1895-1910) Scottish
A HIGHLAND BURN oil on canvas, 32 x 43in. (81 x 90cm.) sd 'W McTaggart/ 1877'
PROV.: Purchased in 1877 at the Royal Scottish Academy exhibition by Mr. James Donald of
Glasgow; who sold the painting 25 November 1909 to bt. Mr R.H. Brechin of Glasgow.
EXH.: Edinburgh, Royal Scottish Academy, 1877; London, Whitechapel Art Gallery, 1912; Royal
Glasgow Institute, 1915 (as Guddling for Trout).
LIT.: *Scottish Art Review*, 1888; *Art Journal*, 1888, p.l34: 'A Highland Burn is a lovely sequestered
spot, where, under the spreading branches (of which, by-the-bye, every single leaf is a study), the
warbling waters have drawn the feet of the little people.'; James L. Caw, *William McTaggart, A
Biography and Appreciation*, James Maclehose & Sons, Glasgow 1917, pp.64, 71, 99, 239.
      Sotheby's London, 29 August 1995 (868**) GBP 58,700   US$ 95,015

MEADOWS James Edwin (1828-1888) British
SAILING BOATS OFF THE COAST; A ROWING-BOAT APPROACHING A FISHINH VESSEL.
oil on canvas (a pair), 23 x 46cm. / 55.5 x 79cm. both sd 'J.E. Meadows 1864'
      Christie's Amsterdam, 26 October 1995 (81**) NLG 11,500   US$ 7,251

MEADOWS William (1870-1895) British
A VIEW OF SANTA MARIA DELLLA SALUTE AND A VIEW OF THE DOGES PALACE AND
THE PIAZZA SAN MARCO oil on canvas, 8 x 16in. (20.4 x 40.8cm.) sll 'W Meadows'
    Christie's East, 13 February 1996 (217**) US$ 6,,900   US$ 6,900

MEEGEREN Han (Henricus Antonius) van (Deventer 1889-1947 Amsterdam) Dutch
THE LAST SUPPER oil on canvas (painted over a Hondius painting), 172 x 243cm. (after 1939)
PROV.: Collection Beuningen, Amsterdam until 1954; in the family until 1979; Collection
Sciclounoff, Geneve since 1979.
LIT.: R. Huyghe, *Tout l'oeuvre peint de Vermeer*, Paris, 1968, pp.l00-102;
Lord Kilbracken, 'Van Meegeren ou la vie d'un faussaire', *Mercure de France*, Paris, 1969; J. Russel,
'La farce de van Meegeren', *l'Oeil*, Paris, January 1950, n°14, pp.5-11; J. Decoen, *Vermeer-Van
Meegeren, deux authentiques Vermeer*, Rotterdam, 1951; P. Levantal, 'L'affaire Vermeer rebondit',
Connaissance des Arts, Paris, November 1971, n° 237, pp. 90 and following.
    Étude Tajan Paris, 12 December 1995 (120**) FRF 350,000   US$ 70,499

BEHIND BARS: A SELFPORTRAIT black and coloured chalks on paper, 46 x 22 cm s 'H van
Meegeren'
PROV.: P. Wilthagen, Rotterdam.
    Christie's Amsterdam, 7 February 1996 (365) NLG 13,800   US$ 8,404

MEER Barend van der (1659-1696 ca) Dutch
A PEELED LEMON AND SWEETMEATS ON A SILVER PLATE, TANGERINES, GRAPES, AN
OPEN WATCH, A WINE GLASS, A DECANTER, A STANDING CUP AND COVER AND A
CHINESE VASE ON A TABLE DRAPED WITH A CARPET oil on canvas, 35¼ x 28 7/8in. (89.5
x 73.3cm.) sd 'B v der Meer / 1686'
    Christie's London, 8 December 1995 (207**) GBP 26,450   US$ 40,705

MEIREN Jan-Baptist van der (1664-1708) Flemish
SCENE DE PORT DE LA MÉDITERRANÉE ORIENTALE oil on oakpanel, 26 x 33cm. sll 'J van
der Meiren'
    Étude Tajan Paris, 12 December 1995 (30**) FRF 45,000   US$ 9,064

HARBOR SCENE WITH ELEGANT FIGURES AND MERCHANTS oil on canvas, 15¼ x 16¼in.
(38.7 x 41.3cm.)
    Sotheby's New York, 2 April 1996 (117**) US$ 17,825   US$ 17,825

MELENDEZ Luis (Luis Egidio Melendez de Rivera Durazo (.) (1716-1780) Spanish
APPLES IN A BASKET, A JAR AND CONDIMENT BOXES ON A TABLE oil on canvas, 19 3/8
x 14¼in. (49.2 x 36.2cm.) s ini.'M' (between 1660-70)
    Christie's London, 8 December 1995 (57**) GBP 155,500   US$ 239,304

MELLIN Charles (Nancy 1597 (?)-1649 Rome) |
THE TRIUMPH OF GALATEA oil on canvas, 47½ x 48½in. (121 x 123.5cm.)
PROV.: Anonymous sale, Vienna, Dorotheum, 13 September 1952, lot 77, as by Lanfranco.
    Sotheby's London, 5 July 1995 (63**) GBP 43,300   US$ 69,070

MENJAUD Alexandre (Paris 1773-1832) French
JOSEPH INTERPRETING THE DREAMS OF THE PHARAO oil on canvas, 81 x 109.5cm.
    Étude Tajan Paris, 26 March 1996 (98*) FRF 35,000   US$ 6,918

MENZEL Adolf Friedrich Erdmann von (Breslau 1815-1905 Berlin) German
VOLTAIRE BEIM ANKLEIDEN Gouache on paper, tightened on cardboard, 24.5 x 18.5cm. sdll
'Menzel 1856'
PROV.: Private collection, Berlin.
LIT.: Hugo von Tschudi, *Adolf von Menzel*, München 1905, p. 246 col. ill., no. 344.

		US$	

Lempertz Cologne, 15 November 1995 (1835**) DEM 190,000 — US$ 134,105

MENZIO Francesco (Tempio Pausania 1899-1979 Turin) Italian
FANCIULLA SEDUTA tempera on stretched paper, ,100 x 71cm. s on the reverse
Finearte Milan, 12 December 1995 (134*) ITL 9,200,000 — US$ 5,772

MERLICEK Elisabeth (Vienna 1911-1988 Vienna) Austrian
ABENDSONNE oil on canvas, 92.5 x 110.5cm. slr 'E. MERLICEK'; inscr. and titled 'E. MERLICEK WIEN..' on the reverse
Wiener Kunst Auktionen, 27 September 1995 (423**) ATS 100,000 — US$ 9,720

MERZ Mario (Milan 1925 b.-I) Italian
PROGRESSIONE DI FIBONACCI mixed media and collage on cardboard, 70 x 100cm. sd on the reverse (1975)
Finearte Milan, 12 December 1995 (242*) ITL 36,225,000 — US$ 22,726

UNTITLED acrylic, snail shells, nails, plaster, spray paint and neon tube on burlap, 79 7/8 x 197in. (203 x 500cm.)
PROV.: Galerie Isy Brachot, Brussels.
Christie's London, 23 May 1996 (114**) GBP 31,050 — US$ 47,017

UNTITLED (WALLPIECE) mixed media on metal, ,300 x ,200 x 3.5cm. (1983)
LIT.: Peter Wibel/Christa Steinle, *Identität: Differenz, Eine Topographie der Moderne*, steirischer herbst '92, Böhlau-Verlag, p. 241.
Dorotheum Vienna, 8 November 1995 (787**) ATS 500,000 — US$ 50,157

MESDAG Hendrik Willem (Groningen 1831-1915 The Hague) Dutch
BOMSCHUITEN AT SEA pencil and watercolour on paper, 13 x 19 cm s 'HW Mesdag'
Christie's Amsterdam, 25 April 1996 (68*) NLG 2,875 — US$ 1,708

SHIPPING IN A CALM pen and black ink and watercolour heightened with white on paper, 27 x 41.5 cm s 'HW Mesdag'
Christie's Amsterdam, 25 April 1996 (70*) NLG 13,800 — US$ 8,200

THE BEACH AT SCHEVENINGEN, AT SUNSET oil on canvas, 63 x 98.5cm. sd 'H W Mesdag 1896'
PROV.: Herbert W. Pfehler, Zürich; Private Collection San Francisco, U.S.A.
Christie's Amsterdam, 25 April 1996 (194**) NLG 126,500 — US$ 75,168

MESSENSEE Jürgen (Vienna 1936 b.-) Austrian
SITZENDE FRAU oil on canvas, 146 x 161cm. sdul 'J. Messensee 69'
EXH.: Vienna, Galerie im Griechenbeisl, 1969.
Wiener Kunst Auktionen, 27 September 1995 (530**) ATS 200,000 — US$ 19,441

METCALF Willard Leroy (1858-1925) American
HILLSIDE PASTURE oil on canvas, 29 x 33in. (73.6 x 83.9cm.) sdll 'W.L. Metcalf. 24'
PROV.: Estate of the artist; B. F. Jones; Milch Galleries, New York;Vixeboxse Gallery, Cleveland, Ohio.
EXH.: Washington, D.C., Corcoran Gallery of Art, *Willard Metcalf Recent Paintings*, January 3-February 1, 1925; New York, Milch Galleries, *Willard Metcalf*, February 16-March 6, I925, no. 10; Pittsburgh, Pennsylvania, Carnegie Institute, *Willard Metcalf Retrospective,* January 8-February 21, 1926.
LIT.: E.de Veer and R.J. Boyle, *The Life and Art of Willard L. Metcalf*, New York, 1987, p. 152, no. 189, ilius., as *Hillside Pasture (No.2)*.
Christie's New York, 13 September 1995 (68**) US$ 43,700 — US$ 43,700

METZINGER Jean (Nantes 1883-1956 Paris) French
TETE DE JEUNE FEMME oil on cradled panel, 13 3/8 x 9¼in. (34 x 23.5cm.) sll 'Metzinger' (ca. 1918-20)
PROV.: Collcetion of the artist; Edgardo Acosta, Beverly Hills; Acquired from the above by the present owner.
EXH.: Paris, Musée d'Art Moderne; Rome, Galleria Nazionale d'Arte Moderna, *Les Cubistes*, 1973-74, no. 82.

Sotheby's New York, 2 May 1996 (215**) US$ 43,700	US$	43,700

VIOLON ET FLUTE oil on canvas, 31 7/8 x 23¾in. (81 x 60.3cm.) lr 'Metzinger' (1916-1917)
PROV.: Galerie Kleinmann & Cie., Paris; Galerie Art Vivant, Paris (acquired by the late owner, 1958).
EXH.: Chicago, The Art Institute, *Treasures of Chicago Collectors*, April-May, 1961, no number.

Christie's New York, 8 November 1995 (179**) US$ 90,500	US$	90,500

MEULEN Adam Frans van der (Brussels 1632-1690 Paris) Flemish
KING LOUIS XIV OF FRANCE CROSSING THE RHINE NEAR LOBITH ON 12 JUNE 1672 oil on canvas, 26 x 32½in. (66 x 82.5cm.) (1672)
PROV.: Lord carrington, Millaton Bridge, Devonshire;Carrington Heirlooms Sale, Christie's, 9 may 1930, lot 41 (54gns. to Forrester); The Marquess of Lincolnshire, K.G.; Christie's 14 Dec. 1934, lot 150 (withdrawn) and by descent.
LIT.: engraved by Simonneau.

Christie's London, 8 December 1995 (90**) GBP 21850	US$	33,626

LOUIS XIV DEVANT LA VILLE D'ARRAS oil on leather laid down on panel (oval), 22 x 36cm sll 'AF. MEULEN'
PROV.: Anonymous sale, Paris, Hôtel George V, 22 June 1990, no. 104 (illustrated in colour).

Étude Tajan Paris, 12 December 1995 (81**) FRF 95,000	US$	19,135

MEULEN Adam Frans van der (and studio) (Brussels 1632-1690 Paris) Flemish
A YOUNG PAGE KEEPING THE LEASHES OF A PRANCING HORSE / A CAVALRY OFFICER SEEN FROM THE BACK ON A PRANCING HORSE oil on canvas (a pair), 48.5 x 39cm / 48 x 39.3cm. (ca. 1677)

Christie's Monaco, 14 June 1996 (19**) FRF 527,700	US$	101,898

MEULEN Steven van der (1543 - 1563 c. fl.-)
PORTRAIT OF A GENTLEMAN, HALF-LENGTH, WEARING A FUR CAPE, NECKLACE AND GOLD THREAD-EMBROIDERED CAP oil on panel, 18 x 15¼in. (46 x 38.5cm.)
PROV.: William Beckford; his sale Fonthill Abbey, 2nd October 1822, lot 11 (withdrawn from sale), as a portrait of the Protector, Duke of Somerset, attributed to Holbein. (This picture was a companion to another portrait attributed to Holbein of François, Dauphin de Viennois); thence by descent to Susanna Euphemia, Duchess of Hamilton (Beckford's daughter); 12th Duke of Hamilton; Christie's, Hamilton Place, 17th June 1882, lot8; E.F.White; Alice Woodhams Gregg of Temple Grafton Court; thence by descent to the present owner.

Phillips London, 18 June 1996 (21**) GBP 8,000	US$	12,336

MEULEN TER François Pieter (1843-1927) Dutch
THE YOUNG SHEPHERD oil on canvas, 92 x 78 cm s 'ter Meulen'

Christie's Amsterdam, 7 February 1996 (295*) NLG 11,500	US$	7,004

MEULENER Pieter (1602-1654) Antwerp
ELEGANT COMPANY NEAR THE GATE OF A COUNTRY AMNSION, CATTLE WATERING IN THE FOREGROUND oil on panel, 33.8 x 45.4cm. indistinctly sdlc 'P(strengthened)Pmeulener 1645 (?)'
PROV.: J.W. Frederiks, Scheveningen, 1942.

Christie's Amsterdam, 7 May 1996 (92**) NLG 16,100	US$	9,388

MICHALLON Achille Etna (Paris 1796-1822 Paris) French
SHEPHERDS CONTEMPLATING THE RUINES OF AN OLD TOMB oil on canvas, 81 x 100cm.
sdll 'MICHALLON / 1816'
PROV.: Acquired by the current owner in the 1960's.
EXH.: Salon 1817, no. 577; Paris, Musée du Louvre, *Achille Etna Michallon (1796-1822)* 1994, no.
43, illustarted in the catalogue p. 68, no. 23.
LIT.: P. Conisbee, 'Tombs in 18th and early 19th Century Landscape Paintings', *Neoclassicismo, Atti
del Convegno internazionale*, London, 1971, pp. 22-30.

Étude Tajan Paris, 12 December 1995 (111**) FRF 470,000	US$	94,670

MICHAU Théobald (Tournai 1676-1765 Antwerp) Flemish
PEASANTS HARVESTING IN A WOODED RIVER LANDSCAPE oil on panel, 18 x 25in. (45.5 x
63.5cm.)
PROV.: Anonymous sale, Cologne, Lempertz, 5-7 May 1960, lot 65; Anonymous sale, London,
Christie's 1 December 1978, lot 25, where bought by the present owner.

Sotheby's London, 17 April 1996 (660**) GBP 17,825	US$	27,028

MICHIELI Andrea dei, {called} Andrea Vicentino (Venice 1539-1614 Venice) Italian
PORTRAIT OF SEBASTIANO VENIERO, VENECIAN ADMIRAL AND HERO OF THE SEA
BATTLE NEAR LEPANTO, 1571 oil on canvas (in 16th century renaissance frame), 118 x 95cm.
(between 1571-1577)

Dorotheum Vienna, 11 June 1996 (37**) ATS 180,000	US$	16,708

MIEL Jan (Beveren-Waes 1599 c.-1663 Turin) Flemish
ELEGANT HUNTSMEN RESTING ALONG A ROAD WITH A OLD WOMAN AND BOY
HAWKING THEIR WARES oil on lead, 6 x 10¼in. (15.2 x 26cm.)
PROV.: probably the Duc de Choiseul-Praslin, Paris (his Sale: Paris, Feburary 18, 1793, lot 121, as
'Jean Miel, deux petits tableaux de la première finette,' measuring 6 by 9 pouces) there sold for Ffl
499 to Guerins.

Sotheby's New York, 11 January 1996 (30**) US$ 24,150	US$	24,150

MIEREVELT Michiel Jansz. van (Delft 1567-1641 Delft) Dutch
PORTRAIT OF A BEARDED MAN oil on panel, 27¼ x 21¾in. (69.2 x 55.2cm.) sdcl 'M.
Miereved/Aetatis 80 Ao 1629'
PROV.: Bachhoven, Basel, 1840 (according to Bernt); Thos. Agnew & Sons, Ltd., London; Charles
R Paravicini; Sale: Christie's London, 22 April 1977, lot 67 (GBP3,800).

Sotheby's New York, 11 January 1996 (98**) US$ 54,625	US$	54,625

PORTRAIT OF JOHAN CAMERLIN (1567-1640), AGED 59, STANDING THREE QUARTER
LENGTH BY A TEBLE, WEARING BLACK COSTUME WITH LACE COLLAR AND CUFFS,
HIS LEFT HAND RESTING ON A BOOK; AND PORTRAIT OF HIS WIFE CATHARINA
CAMERLIN, *NEE* WIELANT (1592-1633), AGED 59, STANDING THREE QUARTER LENGTH
BY A TABLE, WEARING A BLACK DRESS WITH *MOLENKRAAG*, CUFFS AND A BONNET
both oil on panel, 110.5 x 84cm. and 109.5 x 82cm. The first s, inscr. with the age of the sitter; d
centre l 'AE(linked)tatis.59./Ao.1626./M.Miereveld.(in red); the second s, inscr. with the age of the
sitter; d centre r AE(linked)tatis.59./AO.1631./M.Miereveld.(in red)
PROV.: by descent to the sitter`s daughter Elisabeth della Faille; by descent to her son Johan della
Faille (1628-1713); his son Johan Bernhard della; Faille (1672-1729); his son Abraham Nicolaas
della Faille (1716-1793); his daughter Maria Catharina Tellegen, née della Faille (1740-1823) and to
her daughter Catharina Elisa Odulpha de Neree, née Tellegen; thence by eventual descent to the
present vendor`s estate.
EXH.: Amsterdam, Rijksmuseum, 1899-1905, on loan.
LIT.: *Catalogus der Schilderijen in het Rijksmuseum Amsterdam*, 1903, no. 1594; E.J. Wolleswinkel,
Het belang van kwartierstaatsonderzoek voor de identificatie van gepotretteerden', in *Leids
Kunsthistorisch Jaarboek*, VIII, 1989, pp. 94/95, figs. 1 and 2.

Christie's Amsterdam, 13 November 1995 (132**) NLG 207,000	US$	130,459

PORTRAIT OF MAURITS OF ORANGE, HALF LENGTH, WEARING ARMOUR, LACE
COLLAR AND ORANGE SASH oil on panel, unframed, 59 x 70 cm
      Christie's Amsterdam, 7 February 1996 (59*) NLG 12,650   US$ 7,704

MIERIS Frans the Elder van (Leyden 1635-1681 Leyden) Dutch
A WOMAN WRITING A LETTER BY CANDLELIGHT- *(en brunaille)* oil on panel, 18.5 x 14.8cm
sbl 'F. van Mieris'
PROV.: François Tronchin (1704-1798), Geneva (recorded as no. 42 in his manuscript inventory
drawn up in 1761; see below); sold to the Empress Catherina the Great of Russia for the Hermitage,
Saint Petersburg, in 1770 (see below) sold by the Hermitage in 1929 (according to V.F. Levinson
Lessing, see below) with D. Katz, Dieren, 1938; F.J. ten Bos, Almelo; Sale, Paul Brandt Amsterdam,
24 June 1959, lot 14, fig. VII (Dfl 6,000 to Ortman).
LIT.: E.Minich, *Catalogue of the Paintings of the Hermitage*,1774, no.720; *Catalogue of the
Paintings of the Hermitage*, 1863/1909, no.920; R. Gower, *The Figure Painters of Holland*, 1880,
p.114; A.Somof, *Catalogue of the Paintings of the Hermitage*, 1901, p.234, no.920, as the pendant to
a picture of a musician playing a guitar, present whereabouts unknown (Naumann, no. D.97); A. von
Wurzbach, *Niederländisches Künstler-Lexicon*, II, 1910, P.166; C. Hofstede de Groot, *A Catalogue
Raisonné etc.*, X, 1928, p.42, no.159, as the pendant to his no.182 and incorrectly as offered in the
Van der Marck sale in 1773 ; see below); M.N. Benisovich, *Les Collections de tableaux du
Conseiller François Tronchin et le Musée de l'Ermitage*, in `Geneva`, January 1953, p.43, no.42
(following the manuscript inventury of 1761; see above); E.Bénézit, *Dictionnaire critique et
documentaire des peintres etc.*, VI, 1953, p.117; V.F.Levinson-Lessing, *Collection de tableaux de
François de Tronchin. Histoire des collections de l'Ermitage*, in Reports of the Hermitage Museum,
XXXI, 1970, p.12, no.80; R. Loche a.o., *De Genève à l'Ermitage*, exhibition catalogue Geneva 1974,
pp.81/82, no.161, with ill. O. Naumann, *Frans van Mieris the Elder*, I, 1981, pp.76,79 and 111 and
II, p.96, no.83, fig.83, where dated 1670; E.J. Sluijter, *Leidse Fijnschilders*, 1988, pp.135/37, note 2.
      Christie's Amsterdam, 13 November 1995 (148**) NLG 80,500   US$ 50,734

MIERIS Willem van (Leyden 1662-1747 Leyden) Dutch
FLORA oil on panel, 7¼ x 6¼in. (18.8 x 16cm.)
PROV.: Hendrik Sorgh, his sale, Amsterdam, 28 March 1720, lot 50, with pendant, 50 florins; Pieter
van Copello, his sale, Amsterdam, Cok, 6 May 1767, lot 45, with pendant, 19 florins; W. van de
Lely, Burgemeester of Delft, his deceased sale, Amsterdam, van der Schley, 14 ff., December 1772,
lot 14, with pendant' J.E. Fiseau, her deceased sale, Amsterdam, van der Schley etc., 30-31 August
1997, lot 133, with pendant, 70 florins; Anonymous sale, Amsterdam, 21 September 1904, lot 100,
280 florins.
LIT.: C. Hofstede de Groot, *A Catalogue Raisonné..*, vol. X, 1928, p. 123, no. 71.
      Sotheby's London, 5 July 1995 (96**) GBP 12,650   US$ 20,179

PORTRAIT OF A GENTLEMAN, THREE QUARTER LENGHT, IN A BROWN ROBE, IN A
LIBRARY oil on panel, 9¼ x 6 5/8in. (23.5 x 16.9cm) sdll 'W. van./ Mieris./ fe-1696'
      Christie's London, 7 July 1995 (226**) GBP 24,150   US$ 38,523

MIGNARD Pierre (Circle of) (Troyes 1612-1695 Paris) French
DIANA AND ENDYMION oil on canvas, 37 x 47¼in. (94 x 120cm.)
PROV.: Estate of Walter Langer.
      Sotheby's Arcade Auctions New York, 17 January 1996 (90*) US$ 13,800   US$ 13,800

MIGNECO Giuseppe (Messina 1908 b.-l) Italian
PESCATORE CON PESCE oil on canvas, 45 x 35cm. sll 'Migneco' (1908)
LIT.: N.C. Luciani, *Migneca, Catalogo Generale*, vol. III, ed. Bonaparte, Milan, 1993, p. 310
(illustrated no. 2128).
      Finearte Milan, 18 June 1996 (202**) ITL 14,375,000   US$ 9,322

TERZO GRADO oilon canvas, 60 x 50cm. sdlr 'Migneco 60' (1960)
PROV.: Galleria Pace, Milan, no. 366.
      Finearte Milan, 18 June 1996 (216**) ITL 18,400,000   US$ 11,933

BASKET WITH LEMONS oil on hardboard, 40 x 30cm. slr 'Migneco' (1960)
EXH.: Turin, Galleria Gissi, *Collettiva di maestri contemporanei*, Dec. 1984.
      Finearte Milan, 26 October 1995 (135*) ITL 14,490,000   US$ 9,028

MILANI Aureliano (Bologna 1675-1749 Rome) Italian
TEH WORSHIP OF THE GOLDEN CALF oil on panel, 15 x 22in. (38.1 x 55.9cm.)
PROV.: Sir Henry H. Howarth, 45 Lexham Gardens, London; His (deceased) sale. London,
Christie's, 14th December 1923, lot 128, as Poussin, 14 gns to T. Borenius, presumably for Henry
George Charles, 6th Earl of Harewood (1882-1947); His wife, HRH Princess Mary, The Princess
Royal (1897-1965); Her (deceased) sale, London, Christie's, 25th March 1977, lot 11, as Aureliano
Milani.
EXH.: London, Kenwood, *Cabinet Pictures David Teniers*, 1972, no. 37, as attributed to Poussin; On
loan, Firle Place, Lewes 1983-90.
LIT.: G. Zanotti, *Storia dell'Accademia Clementina*, 1739, vol. II, p. 162; T. Borenius, *Catalogue of
the Pictures and Drawings at Harewood House*, 1936, p. 54, no. 96; D.C. Miller, 'Israelites
worshipping the Golden Calf', in *The Burlington Magazine*, vol. XCVI, June 1974, pp. 331-332, fig.
56; G. Sestieri, *Repertorio della Pittura Romana della Fine del Seicento e del Settecento*, 1994, vol.
III, reproduced plate 773.
      Sotheby's London, 5 July 1995 (56**) GBP 29,900   US$ 47,695

MILANI Aureliano (attr.) (Bologna 1675-1749 Rome) Italian
THE FLAGELLATION OF CHRIST oil on canvas, 41¾ x 30in. (106 x 76cm.)
LIT.: Richter, 1901, no. 85.
      Sotheby's London, 6 December 1995 (31**) GBP 9,200   US$ 14,158

MILLER Richard Edward (1875-1943) American
WOMAN WITH PARASOL oil on canvas, 29 x 24in. (73.6 x 60.9cm.)
      Christie's New York, 23 May 1996 (80**) US$ 244,500   US$ 244,500

SEWING oil on canvas, 36 x 28½in. (91.5 x 72.4cm.) slr 'Miller'
EXH.: Worcester, Worcester Art Museum.
      Christie's New York, 23 May 1996 (85**) US$ 387,500   US$ 387,500

THE GARDEN ROOM, GIVERNY oil on canvas, 48 x 36in. (116.8 x 91.5cm.) sul 'R.E. Miller (ca.
1910-11)
      Christie's New York, 30 November 1995 (54***) US$ 690,000   US$ 690,000

MILLET Jean François (Gruchy, near Cherbourg 1814-1875 Barbizon) French
THE HORSE oil on canvas, 65 ½ x 77 ½in. (166.4 x 196.9cm.)
PROV.: Mlle. Lian Ernout; with Wildenstein and Company, London (1969); The Art Institute of
Chicago (purchased).
EXH.: London, Wildenstein Gallery, *J.F. Millet*, 1969, no. 1; Tokyo, Gallery Seibu, *J.F. Millet et ses
amis-peintres de Barbizon,* 1971, no. 1 (Exhibition traveled to the Kyoto Municipal Museum and the
Fukuoka Cultural Centre); Buenos Aires, Gallery Wildenstein,J.F. Millet, 1971, no. 31; New York,
Wildenstein and Company, *A Selection of Paintings and Drawings by J.F. Millet*, 1976, no. 3.
LIT.: C. Amyot, *Document manuscript et pièces diverges se rapportant à J.F. Millet, archives of the
Musée Thomas Henry*, Cherbourg; A. Sensier, *La Vie et l'oeuvre de J.F. Millet*, Paris, 1881, p. 75; F.
Jacque, *La Livre d'or de J.F. Millet par un ancien ami*, Paris. p. 19; J. Cartwright, *Jean-François
Millet: His Life and Letters,* London and New York, 1896, p. 65; E. Moreau-Nelaton, *Millet raconte
par lui-meme,* Paris, 1921, vol. 1, p. 44; T. Crombie, 'London Galleries: Paysans et Paysages', *Apollo,*
November, 1969, vol. 90, no. 93, p. 433; J. Bouret, *L'Ecole de Barbizon et le paysage francais au
XIX siècle*, Neuchatel, 1972, p. 155 (illustrated); Art Institute of Chicago, *Annual Report 1975-76,*

Chicago, 1976 (illustrated on cover and inside cover); L. Lepoittevin, *Jean-Francois Millet, II, L'Ambiguité de l'Image*, Paris, 1973, pp. 44, 56, 90 (illustrated, fig. 36, p. 48); 'Major Museum Acquisitions', *The Connoisseur*, March, 1977 (illustrated, fig. 5).
    Christie's New York, 2 November 1995 (38**) US$ 442,500   US$ 442,500

A SLEEPING NYMPH WATCHED BY A SATYR oil on canvas, 15 x 11 7/8in. (38.1 x 30.3cm.) unframed slr. 'J.F. Millet' (ca.1846-47)
PROV.: Possibly Constant Troyon; sale, Hôtel Drouot, Paris, Januari 22-February 1, 1866, as *Baigneuse couchée*, with probably mistaken dimensions of 48 x 31cm; W.A. Coats, Dalskairth, Scotland; sale, Christie's, London, June 10, 1927, no. 75 (bt. Harcourt).
    Christie's New York, 2 November 1995 (39**) US$ 57,500   US$ 57,500

THE GLEANERS black crayon on paper, 9½ x 16 1/8in. (24.2 x 40.9cm.) slr 'J.F.M.'
PROV.: Private collection.
    Christie's New York, 22 May 1996 (156**) US$ 167,500   US$ 167,500

LA CARDEUSE (WOMAN CARDING WOOL) oil on canvas, 35½ x 29½in. (90.2 x 74.9cm.) slr 'J.F. Millet'
PROV.: With Arthur Stevens and Ennemond Blanc, 1863; Paran Stevens, New York, purchased in Paris, 1866; by descent to Mrs. Paran Stevens; by descent to Mrs. John L. Melcher (daughter of Paran Stevens); by descent to John S. Melcher (son of above), 1908; With Knoedler & Co.; sold to Meyer H. Lehman, New York; by descent to Mrs. Hamet Lehman Weil and Mrs. Bertha Lehman Rosenheim; by descent to Mrs. Elsie Rosenheim Weil and Dr. Henry Lehman Weil; by descent to Dr. George L. Weil, Washington D.C., 1952;
Thence by descent.
EXH.: Paris, *Salon*, 1863, no.1326; Brussels, summer 1863 (exhibition organized by dealer Arthur Stevens?); Paris, Grand Palais, *Jean-François Millet*, 1975, no.163 (exhibition also London, Hayward Gallery, 1976); Kobe, Hyogo Prefectural Museum of Modern Art, *Millet, Corot and the School of Barbizon*, 1980, no. T.12 (exhibition also Tokyo, Seibu Museum; Sapporo, Hokkaido Museum of Modern Art; Hiroshima Prefectural Museum; Kitakyushu Municipal Museum).
LIT.: Extensively commented upon in *Salon* reviews in 1863, including notices by Jules Castagnary, Ernest Chesneau, Théophile Gautier, Paul de Saint-Victor, Paul Mantz, Th. Thoré, and A. Viollet-le-Duc.; A. Sensier and P. Mantz, *La Vie et l'oeuvre de J.-F. Millet*, Paris 1881, pp. 221, 236, 240; W. Morris Hunt, *Talks on Art*, Boston, 1884, pp. 90-91; E. Durand-Gréville, 'La Peinture aux États-Unis,' *Gazette des Beaux-Arts*, July, 1887, p. 74; D.C. Thomson, *The Barbizon School of Painters*, London and New York, 1890, p. 235; J. Cartwright, *Jean-François Millet, his Life and Letters*, London 1896, pp. 237-38, 244; E. Staley, *Jean-François Millet*, London 1903, p. 67; E. Moreau-Nelaton, *Millet raconté par lui-même*, Paris, 1921, vol. 11, pp. 74, 120, 122, 124-135, fig. 183; A. Tabarant, *La vie artistique au temps de Baudelaire*, Paris 1942, p. 306 A. Reverdy, *L'École de Barbizon, l'évolution du prix des tableaux de 1850 à 1960*, Paris,1973, p. 22; A. Fermigier, *Jean-François Millet*, Geneva 1977, pp. 104, 111 (illustrated in colour, p. 102, with full-scale detail of head of *La Cardeuse*, p. 101).
    Christie's New York, 22 May 1996 (157***) US$ 3,412,500   US$ 3,412,500

MIRALLES Francisco (1848-1901) Spanish
THE BOATING PARTY oil on canvas, 28¾ x 36in. (73 x 91.5cm.) sll 'F. Miralles'
    Christie's New York, 22 May 1996 (224**) US$ 43,700   US$ 43,700

IN THE MARKET oil on canvas, 24 x 19¾in. (61 x 50.2cm.) s 'Miralles.'
    Christie's London, 15 March 1996 (147**) GBP 38,900   US$ 59,407

MIRO Joan (Barcelona 1893-1983) Spanish
PEINTURE oil on masonite, 21½ x 42½in. (54.6 x 108cm.) sd on the reverse 'Miró. 1950'
PROV.: Richard Feigen Gallery, New York (acquired by Otto Preminger, 1967).
LIT.: J. Dupin, *Joan Miró, Life and Work*, New York, 1962, no. 766 (illustrated p. 558).
    Christie's New York, 1 May 1996 (229**) US$ 316,000   US$ 316,000

LES JASMINS EMBAUMENT DE LEUR PARFUM DORÉ LA ROBE DE LA JEUNE FILLE oil on canvas, 39½ x 32¼in. (100.4 x 81.8cm.) scr 'Miró' sd titled on the reverse 'Miró 1952 Les jasmine embaument de leur parfum doré la robe de la jeune fille'
PROV.: Pierre Matisse Gallery, New York (1952); Mr. Allen Hofrichter, New York; Stephan Hahn, New York; Acquired from the above by Mr. Joseph H. Hazen on April 21, 1959.
EXH.: New York, Pierre Matisse Gallery, *Miró: Recent Paintings*, Nov.-Dec., 1953, no. 17 (illustrated); Cambridge, Massachusetts, Fogg Art Museum, *Paintings from the Collection of Joseph H. Hazen*, Oct.-Dec., 1966, no. 82 New York, Acquavella Galleries, Inc.,Joan Miró, Oct.-Nov., 1972, no. 55 (illustrated in colour).
LIT.: J. Dupin, *Joan Miró: His Life and Work*, New York, 1962, p. 560, no. 791 (illustrated).
Christie's New York, 30 April 1996 (15**) US$ 827,500 | US$ | 827,500

SANS TITRE gouache on black paper, 42½ x 29in. (108 x 73.6cm.) slr 'Miró' d on the reverse '25/III/70' (25 March 1970)
PROV.: Robert Haas, Paris; sale, Sotheby's New York, 15 November 1984, lot 203.
EXH.: New York, Pierre Matisse Gallery; Kervorkian, New York.;
Christie's New York, 1 May 1996 (237**) US$ 134,500 | US$ | 134,500

COMPOSITION black wash and coloured crayons on paper, 25 5/8 x 20½in. (65 x 52cm.) slr 'Miró'
PROV.: Galerie Maeght, Barcelona.
EXH.: Paris, Musée Nationale d'Art Moderne, Dessins de Miró, 1978, no. 242.
Christie's London, 10 November 1995 (249**) GBP 36,000 | US$ | 56,312

PERSONNAGES ET OISEAU DEVANT LE SOLEIL oil on burlap laid down on panel, 7 5/8 x 10 7/8in. (19.4 x 27.6cm.) scr 'miro' (1939)
PROV.: Pierre Matisse Gallery, New York; Lydia Winston Malbin, New York (1948; sold: Sotheby's New York, May 16, 1990, the Lydia Winston Malbin Collection, lot 68); Perls Galleries, New York (acquired at the above sale).
EXH.: New York, Pierre Matisse Gallery, *Joan Miró*, 1948, no. 10; Bloomfield Hills, Museum of Cranbrook Academy of Art, *20th Century Paintings from Private Collections*, 1948, no. 14 (incorrectly dated); Bloomfield Hills, Michigan, Museum of Cranbrook Academy of Art, *Mr. and Mrs. Harry Lewis Winston Collection*, 1951, no. 46; Ann Arbor, Michigan, *20th Century Paintings and Sculpture from the Collection of Mr. and Mrs. Harry Lewis Winston*, 1955, no. 46; Detroit Institute of Arts (and travelling), *Collecting Modern Art: Paintings, Sculpture and Drawings from the Collection of Mr. and Mrs. Harry Lewis Winston*, 1957-58, no. 74 (incorrectly dated); Detroit Institute of Arts, *Selections from the Lydia and Harry Lewis Winston Collections (Dr. and Mrs. Barnett Malbin)*, 1972-73, n.n.; Detroit Institute of Arts, *Cobra and Contrasts: the Lydia and Harry Lewis Winston Collection (Dr. and Mrs. Barnett Malbin)*, 1974, no. 127.
LIT.: Jacques Dupin, *Joan Miró: Life and Work*, New York, 1962, no. 531 (illustrated p. 541).
Sotheby's New York, 2 May 1996 (298**) US$ 360,000 | US$ | 360,000

ENFANT, CERF VOLANTE, ETOILE oil and pastel on canvas, 10¼ x 19¼in. (26 x 48.9cm.) sll 'Miró'; sd '1945' on the reverse
PROV.: Perls Galleries, New York.
LIT.: Jacques Dupin, *Joan Miró: His Life and Work*, New York, 1962, no. 674 (illustrated p. 551).
Sotheby's New York, 2 May 1996 (306**) US$ 145,500 | US$ | 145,500

PERSONNAGE DEVANT LE SOLEIL gouache, pastel and India ink on paper, 18 7/8 x 25¼in. (47.9 x 64.1cm.) sll 'Miró'; sd and titled 'Barcelone 18-12-1942' on the verso
Sotheby's New York, 2 May 1996 (308**) US$ 107,000 | US$ | 107,000

TROIS FEMMES oil and sand on board, 41¾ x 29½in. 106 x 75cm. sd 18-2-35 on the reverse
PROV.: Mr and Mrs Donald Winston, Los Angeles; Perls Galleries, New York; Alexander Calder, New York; Galerie Maeght, Paris; Acquavella Galleries, New York.
EXH.: Los Angeles, Los Angeles County Museum of Art, *Joan Miró*, 1959, no. ,100 ;Minneapolis Art Institute, 1960 (on loan); Saint-Paul, Fondation Maeght, Miro, 1968, no. 28, illustrated in the catalogue; Barcelona, Antiguo Hospital de la Santa Cruz, *Miró, 75 Aniversario Retrospectivo*, 1968-

69, no. 34, (illustrated in colour in the catalogue); Munich, Haus der Kunst, *Joan Miró*, 1969, no. 44; New York, Acquavella Galleries Inc., *XIX XX Century Master Paintings*, 1981, no. 17, illustrated in colour in the catalogue; Houston, The Museum of Fine Arts, *Miró in America*, 1982, pl. 16, i(llustrated in colour in the catalogue).
LIT.: Jacques Dupin, *Joan Miró, Life and Work*, London, 1962, p. 532, no. 406, illustrated; James Johnson Sweeney, *Joan Miró*, Barcelona, 1970, pl. 82, illustrated in colour; pl. 5, illustrated in a colour photograph of the 1968-69 exhibition in Barcelona; Michel Chilo, *Miró, l'artiste et l'oeuvre*, Paris, 1971, no. 50, illustrated.

Sotheby's London, 24 June 1996 (45**) GBP 2,421,500	US$	3,734,002

TETE D'HOMME oil on canvas, 10 5/8 x 8 5/8in. 27 x 22cm. sd 2-31; titled on the reverse (1931)
PROV.: Galerie Maeght, Paris; Albert Skira, Geneva (acquired from the above in the 1950's. See note to lot 47); Acquired from the above by the present owner.

Sotheby's London, 24 June 1996 (51**) GBP 199,500	US$	307,633

LE CHEVAL DE CIRQUE oil on canvas, 51 1/8 x 37 3/8in. (130 x 95cm.) sdlc 'Miró 1927' sd again on the reverse
PROV.: Riccardo Jucker, Milan; Galleria d'Arte del Naviglio, Milan; Anon. sale; Christie's, London, Dec. 6, 1977, lot 44 (GBP 55,000) (illustrated in colour); Adriana Pizzoli, New York; Pierre Matisse Gallery, New York (1984); Acquavella Gallery, New York.
EXH.: Basel, Kunsthalle, *Phantastiche Kunst des XX. Jahrhunderts*, August-October, 1952, p. 23, no. 139; Milan, Galleria d'Arte del Naviglio, *Miró*, May, 1963; Zürich, Kunsthaus, *Joan Miró: A Retrospective*, November., 1986-February., 1987, p. 114, no. 47 (illustrated in colour, p. 115). The exhibition traveled to Dusseldorf, Städtische Kunsthalle, February.-April, 1987, and New York, Solomon R.Guggenheim Museum, May-August, 1987.
LIT.: J. Dupin, *Joan Miró, Life and Work*, London, 1962, p. 517, no. 209 (illustrated).

Christie's New York, 30 April 1996 (48**) US$ 3,852,500	US$	3,852,500

LES AMOUREUX oil on panel, 16 x 12¾in. (41 x 23.6cm.) sd titled on the reverse 'Joan Miró 9-32 'Les Amoureux" (Montroig, summer 1932)
PROV.: Eigil Hjorth (circa 1038); by descent to the present owner.
EXH.: Paris, Galerie Pierre Colle, *Miró*, December 1932.
LIT.: J. Dupin, *Joan Miró, Life and Work*, London, 1962, p. 526, no. 329 (illustrated).

Christie's New York, 30 April 1996 (54**) US$ 992,500	US$	992,500

FIGURES DEVANT UN VOLCAN tempera on masonite, 15¾ x 11¾in. (40 x 29.8cm.) slc 'Miró' sd titled 'Joan Miró Figures devant un volcan 9/10-14/10/35' on the reverse
PROV.: Pierre Matisse Gallery, New York; Theodore Schempp & Co., New York; Acquired from the above by the late owner on May 24, 1944.
EXH.: Chicago, The Arts Club,Joan Miró: Works from Chicago Collections, February-March, 1961, no. 21 (illustrated); New York, Museum of Modem Art, *Joan Miró*, October 1993-January 1994, p. 407, no. 130 (illustrated; in colour, p. 210).
LIT.: C. Greenberg, *Joan Miró*, New York, 1948, p. 130 (illustrated, p. 74, pl. XXXIV); J. Dupin, *Joan Miró: His Life and Work*, New York, 1962, p. 533, no. 420 (illustrated and incorrectly dated December 9-14, 1935; illustrated again, p. 323);Y. Bonnefoy, *Miró*, Paris, 1964, p. 5; S. Stich,*Joan Miró: The Development of a Sign Language*, St. Louis, 1980, pp. 40-41.

Christie's New York, 7 November 1995 (44**) US$ 2,202,500	US$	2,202,500

TETE oil on canvas, 36 ¼ x 25¾in. (53.3 x 92cm.) on the reverse 'Miro 31/XII/73 Tête' (December 31, 1973)

Christie's New York, 8 November 1995 (266**) US$ 261,000	US$	261,000

MISERICORDIA Maestro della (Giovanni Gaddi?) (active in Florence 1325-1375-) Italian
CRUCIFIXION tempera on board, 72.5 x 44cm.

Finearte Milan, 11 June 1996 (57**) ITL 172,500,000	US$	111,868

MITCHELL Joan (1926-1993) American
VERA CRUZ oil on canvas, 92¾ x 78¾in. (235.5 x 200cm.) slr 'Joan Mitchell' (ca. 1960-62)
PROV.: Xavier Fourcade, Inc., New York; Private collection, San Francisco.
EXH.: Bern, Klipstein and Kornfield, *Joan Mitchell*, Oct. 1962, no. 12;
New York, Xavier Fourcade, Inc., *Joan Mitchell: The Sixties*, April-May 1985, n.n. (illustrated).
LIT.: M. Waldberg, *Joan Mitchell*, Paris 1992, p. 90 (illustrated).
Christie's New York, 14 November 1995 (10**) US$ 288,500 | US$ | 288,500

CHAMPS oil on canvas, 77 x 44¾in. (195.6 x 113.6cm.) slr 'Joan Mitchell' (1990)
PROV.: Galerie Jean Fournier, Paris.
EXH.: Paris, Galerie Jean Fournier, *Joan Mitchell Champs*, May-July 1990; Paris, Musée Jeu de
Paume, *Les Dernières Années*, June-Sept. 1994, p. 143.
Christie's New York, 15 November 1995 (151**) US$ 103,700 | US$ | 103,700

UNTITLED oil on canvas, 17 x 25in. (43.2 x 63.5cm.) slr 'J. Mitchell' (ca. 1957)
Christie's New York, 15 November 1995 (168**) US$ 40,250 | US$ | 40,250

TO THE HARBORMASTER oil on canvas, 76 x 118in. (193 x 299.7cm.) slr 'J. Mitchell' inscr.
'From a poem by Frank O'Hara' on the stretcher (1957)
PROV.: Donald Rugoff, New York; Xavier Fourcade, Inc., New York.
EXH.: Pittsburgh, Camegie Institute, Museum of Art, *1958 Pittsburgh International Exhibition of
Paintings and Sculpture*, Dec. 1958-Feb. 1959, no. 301; New York, Xavier Fourcade, Inc., *Joan
Mitchell_The Fifties,Important Paintings*, Mar.-Apr. 1980 (illustrated on the announcement card);
Boston, Museum of Fine Arts, *A Private Vision: Contemporary Art from the Graham Gund
Collection*, Feb.-Apr. 1982, p. 69 (illustrated); Washington, D.C., Corcoran Gallery of Art; Buffalo,
Albright-Knox Art Gallery and Ithaca, Cornell University, Herbert F. Johnson Museum, *Joan
Mitchell: A Retrospective*, Feb. 1988-Apr. 1989, pp. 47-48 (illustrated).
LIT.: B. Rose, *The American Artist Speaks*, New York 1982. C. Flobic, 'Joan Mitchell,' *Ninety*, Paris
1983, vol. 10. p. 7 (illustrated); M. Sawin, 'A Stretch of the Seine: Joan Mitchell's Paintings,' *Arts
Magazine*, March 1988, p. 30 (illustrated); To be included in the forthcoming monograph being
prepared by Klaus Kertess entitled *Joan Mitchell: Paintings*, to be published in 1997.
Christie's New York, 7 May 1996 (21**) US$ 464,500 | US$ | 464,500

MITTERTREINER Johannes Jacobus (1851-1890)
TOWNSFOLK STROLLING DOWN A STREET ON A SUMMER DAY oil on panel, 25.5 x 21cm.
slr 'J. Mittertreiner ft.'
Christie's Amsterdam, 26 October 1995 (201*) NLG 12,650 | US$ | 7,976

MODERSOHN Otto (Soest 1865-1943) German
CYCLAMES oil on board, 58 x 40cm. sdll 'O. Modersohn'
Christie's Amsterdam, 5 June 1996 (245a**) NLG 23,000 | US$ | 13,439

LANDSCHAFT MIT ZIEGE oil on canvas, 50 x 70cm. sdlr 'O Modersohn / 42' (1942)
Hauswedell & Nolte Cologne, 5/06 June 1996 (577**) DEM 46,000 | US$ | 29,888

MOORLANDSCHAFT MIT KANAL AM ABEND oil on cardboard, 67.8 x 82.7cm. slr 'Otto
Modersohn' sd 'Otto Modersohn 10. Mai 1921'
Lempertz Cologne, 1 June 1996 (892**) DEM 42,000 | US$ | 27,289

MODIGLIANI Amedeo (Livorno 1884-1920 Paris) Italian
NU ACCROUPI charcoal on thin buff paper, 16¾ x 10½in. (42.5 x 26.7cm.) (1910)
PROV.: Hunt and Mariska Diederich (acquired from the artist); Sydney G. Biddle; by descent.
EXH.: New York, Perls Galleries, Modigliani, The Sydney G. Biddle Collection, 1956; Verona,
Galleria Cello Scudo; Torino, Palazzo Reale, *Modigliani, dipinti e disegni. Incontri italiani 1900-
1920*, 1984-85, no. 16; Tokyo, The National Museum of Modern Art; Nagoya, Aichi Prefectural Art
Gallery, *Modigliani*, 1985, no. 24;.

LIT.: Ambrogio Ceroni, *Amedeo Modigliani, Dessins et Sculptures*, Milan, 1965, no. 78 p. 31, illustrated pl. 78; J. Lanthemann, *Modigliani Catalogue Raisonné, Barcelona, 1970, no. 523, illustrated p. 294; Therese Castineau - Barrielle,* La vie et l'oeuvre de Amedeo Modigliani, Paris, 1987, illustrated p. 61; Christian Parisot, *Modigliani Catalogue Raisonné, Dessins, Aquarelles*, vol. 1, Livorno, 1990, no. 36/10, illustrated p. 241; Osvaldo Patani, *Amedeo Modigliani, Catalogo Generale, Sculpture e Disegni, 1909-1914*, Milano, 1992, no. 67, illustrated p. 95.

Sotheby's New York, 2 May 1996 (192**) US$ 68,500	US$	68,500

HOMME ASSIS (APPUYE SUR UNE CANNE) oil on canvas, 49 5/8 x 29½in. (126 x 75cm.) sur 'Modigliani' (1918)
PROV.: Roger Dutilleul, Paris; Anon. sale, Paris, circa 1940-45, to J. Livengood, Paris, and thence by descent to the present owners.
EXH.: Venice, XVII Exposizione Biennale Internazionale d'Arte, Mostra Individuale di Amedeo Modigliani, 1930, no. 16 (titled 'Rittratto del dott. X').
LIT.: A. Ceroni, *Amedeo Modigliani*, Milan, 1958, no. 113 (illustrated, wrong size given); A. Ceroni and F. Cachin, *Tout l'oeuvre peint de Modigliani*, Paris, 1972, no. 252 (illustrated p. 101, wrong size given); O. Patani, *Amedeo Modigliani*, Milan, 1991, no. 265 (illustrated p. 268, wrong size given); C. Parisot, *Modigliani Catalogue Raisonné*, Livorno, 1991, no. 31/1918 (illustrated p. 215, wrong size given).

Christie's London, 25 June 1996 (15**) GBP 2,092,500	US$	3,226,677

PORTRAIT DU SCULPTEUR OSCAR MIESTCHANINOFF oil on canvas, 31 7/8 x 23 5/8in. (81 x 60cm.) sul 'Modigliani' dlr '1916'
PROV.: César de Hauke, Paris; Jacques Sarlie, New York; sale, Sotheby & Co., London, 12 Oct. 1960, lot 44 (illustrated in colour) (GBP38,000); Acquired at the above sale by the late owner.
EXH.: Cleveland, Museum of Art, *Modigliani: Paintings, Drawings, Sculpture*, Jan.-March, 1951, no. 51 (illustrated, p. 32);The exhibition traveled to New York, The Museum of Modern Art, April-June, 1951; Paris, Galerie Max Kaganovitch, *Oeuvres Choisies du XXe Siècle*, May-June, 1962, no. 46; Edinburgh, Royal Scottish Academy, *Modigliani*, Aug.-Sept., 1963, no. 19 (illustrated, pl. 12); The exhibition traveled to London, The Tate Gallery, Sept.-Nov., 1963; Paris, Centre Georges Pompidou, *Paris - Moscou - 1900-1930*, May-Nov., 1979, no. 164; Paris, Musee d'art Modeme de la Ville de Paris, *Amedeo Modigliani 1884-1920*, March-June, 1981, no. 40 (illustrated in colour, p. 125); Düsseldorf, Kunstsammlung Nordrhein-Westfalen, *Austellung Amedeo Modigliani*, Jan.-April, 1991, p. 223, no. 44 (illustrated); The exhibition traveled to Zurich, Kunsthaus, April-July, 1991. Lausanne, Fondation de L'Hemmitage, *Modigliani, Utrillo, Soutine, les peintres de Zborowski et leurs amis*, June-Oct., 1994, p. 163, no. 5 (illustrated in color).
LIT.: M. Raynal, *Modigliani*, New York, 1951, pl. 3 (illustrated in color); J. T. Soby, *Modigliani*, New York, 1954, p. 36 (illustrated); A. Pfannstiel, *Modigliani et son oeuvre*, Paris, 1956, p. 89, no. 110; B. Borchert, *Modigliani*, London, 1960, p. 8 (illustrated in colour, p. 9); Sotheby's 217th Season 1960-1961, London, 1961 (illustrated in colour, p. 193); J. Russell, *Modigliani*, London, 1963, (illustrated, pl. 12); A. Ceroni, *Amedeo Modigliani: dessins et sculptures*, Milan, 1965, p. 43, no. 181 (illustrated); J. Lanthemann, *Modigliani 1884- 1920, Catalogue Raisonné*, Barcelona, 1970, p. 115, no. 115 (illustrated, p. 189); L. Piccioni, *I dipinti di Modigliani*, Milan, 1970, p. 95, no. 153 (illustrated); A. Ceroni, Tout *l'oeuvre peint de Modigliani*, Paris, 1972, no. 153 (illustrated, p. 95); J. T. Soby, *Modigliani*, New York, 1972, p. 32; C. Roy, *Modigliani*, New York, 1985, p. 94 (illustrated); T. Castieau-Barrielle, *La vie et l'oeuvre de Amedeo Modigliani*, Paris, 1987, p. 114 (illustrated); W. Schmalenbach, *Amedeo Modigliani, Paintings, Sculptures drawings*, Munich, 1990, p. 223, no. 42 (illustrated in colour); O. Patani, *Amedeo Modigliani, Catalogo generale, dipinti*, Milan, 1991, p. 169, no. 156 (illustrated); C. Parisot, *Modigliani, Catalogue raisonné, peintures, dessins, aquarelles*, Livorno, 1991, vol. II, p. 296, no. 22/1916 (illustrated in colour, p. 122).

Christie's New York, 7 November 1995 (2***) US$ 9,352,500	US$	9,352,500

FEMME ASSISE blue coloured pencil and pencil on brown paper, 14 x 8¾in. (35.5 x 22.3cm.) s 'Modigliani' (1914)
PROV.: P. Brune, Paris by whom received from the Artist, and thence by descent to the present

owner.
LIT.: To be included in the forthcoming *Volume III of the catalogue raisonné de l'Oeuvre Complète d'Amadeo Modigliani* currently being prepared by Christian Parisot.
Christie's London, 26 June 1996 (315**) GBP 29,900   US$ 46,106

FEMME ASSISE DEVANT UNE CHEMINEE (BEATRICE HASTINGS) oil on canvas, 31¾ x 25 3/8in. (80.5 x 64.5cm.) stl 'Modigliani' (1915)
PROV.: Georges Chéron, Paris; Perls Galleries, New York; acquired from the above by the present owner in 1972.
EXH.: New York, Acquavella Galleries, *Amedeo Modigliani*, Oct.-Nov., 1971, no. 11 (illustrated in color).
LIT.: A. Ceroni, *I dipinti di Modigliani*, Milan, 1970, P. 90, no. 58 (illustrated); J. Lanthemann, Modigliani, 1884-1920, *Catalogue raisonné, sa vie, son oeuvre complet, son art*, Barcelona, 1970, p. ll2, no. 77 (illustrated, p. 179); O. Patani, *Amedeo Modigliani, catalogo generale dipinti*, Milan,1991, p. 91, no. 63 (illustrated in colour).
Christie's New York, 7 November 1995 (33**) US$ 1,487,500   US$ 1,487,500

CARIATIDE BLEU II bleu wax crayon over pencil on paper laid down on paper, 21 7/8 x 17 5/8in. (55.6 x 44.8cm.) (1913-1914)
PROV.: Hunt and Mariska Diederich, Paris (acquired from the artist); Sydney G. Biddle, New York; Anon. sale, Sotheby's, New York, May 10, 1989, lot 132; Galerie Schmit, Paris.
EXH.: New York, Perls Galleries, *Modigliani, The Sydney G. Biddle Collection*, Oct.-Nov., 1956, no. 8 (illustrated); New York, Perls Galleries, *The Nudes of Modigliani, For the benefit of the Dance Collection of the New York Public Library*, Oct.-Nov., 1966, no. 19 (illustrated); Washington, D.C., The National Gallery of Art, *Modigliani: An Anniversary Exhibition*, Dec., 1983-March, 1984, no number.
LIT.: M. Rotlisberger, 'Les Canatides de Modigliani, Notice Critique,' *Critica d'Arte*, March-April, 1960, vol. 38, p. 110, no. 33; A. Ceroni, *Amedeo Modigliani, dessins et sculptures*, Milan, 1965, no. 113 (illustrated); J. Lanthemann, *Modigliani, Catalogue raisonné, sa vie, son ocurre complet, son art*, Barcelona, 1970, no. 541 (illustrated, p. 298); C. Pansot, *Modigliani, Catalogue raisonné, dessins, aquarelles*, Paris, 1990, vol. 1, no. 13/13 (illustrated, p. 256); O. Patani, *Amedeo Modigliani, Catalogo generale sculture e disegni, 1909-1914*, Milan, 1992, no. 135 (illustrated in color, p. 137).
Christie's New York, 8 November 1995 (178**) US$ 255,500   US$ 255,500

MOELLER Louis Charles (1855-1930) American
MEMORIES oil on canvas, 24 x 18in. (61 x 45.7cm.) slr 'Louis Moeller NA'
Christie's New York, 13 September 1995 (35*) US$ 8,625   US$ 8,625

THE INTERESTING NOVEL oil on canvas, 10 x 8in. (25.4 x 20.3cm.) slr 'Louis Moeller'
Christie's East, 21 May 1996 (18**) US$ 6,,900   US$ 6,900

INTERESTED oil on canvas, 10 x 8in. (25.5 x 20.5cm.) slr 'Louis Moeller'
Christie's East, 21 May 1996 (45**) US$ 8,625   US$ 8,625

MOERMAN Albert Edouard (Ghent 1808-1856 Ghent) Belgian
AN EXTENSIVE WINTER LANDSCAPE WITH FIGURES ON A FROZEN RIVER AND A HUNTSMAN AND HORSE AND CART ON A PATH oil on panel, 21 5/8 x 31in. (55 x 78.8cm.) sll
Phillips London, 14 November 1995 (2**) GBP 16,000   US$ 25,027

MOESMAN Joop (1901-1988) Dutch
HET GEBIT oil on canvas, 54 x 73cm. sdlr 'Joop Moesman 1931'
LIT.: Her de Vries, Jak van der Meulen, Laurens Vancrevel, *Moesman*, Utrecht 1971, p. 44, no. 5 (illustrated).
Sotheby's Amsterdam, 7 December 1995 (174**) NLG 70,800   US$ 43,872

MOIA Federico, {or} Moja (Milan 1802-1885 Dolo near Venice) Italian
LE DÉPART DE LA PROCESSION A L'INTÉRIRUR DE L'ÉGLISE SAINT ETIENNE DU
MONT oil on canvas, 118 x 89cm. sdlr 'J. Moja 83 A'
      Étude Tajan Paris, 25 June 1996 (17**) FRF 70,000   US$ 13,517

MOILLON Louise (Paris 1609/10-1696 Paris) French
STILL-LIFE OF PEACHES IN A BLUE AND WHITE BOWL RESTING ON A TABLE WITH
GRAPES AND PLUMS oil on panel, 18 7/8 x 25¼in. (47.9 x 64.1cm.) (after the 1640's)
      Sotheby's New York, 16 May 1996 (85**) US$ 63,000   US$ 63,000

MOINE François Le (and studio) (1688-1737) French
HERCULES AND OMPHALE oil on canvas, 45¼ x 43¼in. (114.9 x 109.9cm.) (ca. 1724)
      Sotheby's New York, 16 May 1996 (248**) US$ 36,800   US$ 36,800

MOKADY Moshe (1902-1975) Israelian
HAIFA VIEW oil on canvas, 25 4/5 x 21 4/5in. (65 x 54cm.) slr 'Mokady' and s again in Hebrew
(1920s)
PROV.: The Artist's Estate.
EXH.: Cairo, Roger Bréval Gallery, 1926; Paris, Salon d'Automne, 1928; Paris, Gallerie Alice
Manteau, 1928.
LIT.: A. Pascal-Lévis, 'Au Salon del'Automne' in *Les Artistes d'aujourd'hui*, Jan. 1928 (illustrated).
      Christie's Tel Aviv, 12 October 1995 (73**) US$ 74,000   US$ 74,000

WOMAN oil on canvas, 36½ x 29in. (92.5 x 73.4cm.) slr 'Mokady'
      Christie's Tel Aviv, 14 April 1996 (39**) US$ 17,250   US$ 17,250

STILL LIFE WITH BOTTLES AND LANTERNS oil on canvas, 24¾ x 19in. (63 x 48cm.) slc
'Mokady' (1920's)
      Christie's Tel Aviv, 14 April 1996 (51**) US$ 26,450   US$ 26,450

HAIFA VIEW oil on canvas, 25¾ x 19¾in. (65.2 x 50.2cm.) sll 'Mokady', s again in Hebrew, s again
and inscr. '10 rue L'acretelle Paris XV' (on the reverse) (ca. 1926)
PROV.: Private Collection, Paris, and thence by descent to the present owner.
EXH.: Paris, Salon d'Automne, 1927.
LIT.: A.Pascal-Levis, 'Au Salon d'Automne' in *Les Artistes d'aujourd'hui*, 1 Jan. 1928 (ill.); *Moshe
Mokady, Retrospective Exhibition 1920-1970*, The Museum of Art, Ein Harod, April-May 1972. Ill.
in a photograph of the artist in his studio, showing the painting above the artist's head.; G. Tadmor,
Moshe Mokady, Jerusalem 1984, no.13 (ill.): erroneously described as a lost painting by the artist.
      Christie's Tel Aviv, 14 April 1996 (67***) US$ 55,200   US$ 55,200

MOLA Pier Francesco (Coldriero (Como) 1612-1666 Rome) Italian
ST. MADELENE ASLEEP oil on canvas, 122.5 x 93.5cm.
      Christie's Rome, 21 November 1995 (241**) ITL 28,000,000   US$ 17,577

RECTO: BACCHANALIA WITH FIGURES DRINKING BEFORE A STATUE OF PRIAPUS
VERSO A SKETCH recto: pen and brown ink with wash verso: light brown ink, 33.5 x 23.6cm.
watermark 'D L' (inverted) 'P'
      Phillips London, 5 July 1995 (123*) GBP 4,000   US$ 6,381

MOLANUS Mattheus (l-1645 d.) Dutch
A ROCKY RIVER LANDSCAPE WITH A TRAVELLER AND BEGGARS STANDING BY A
RUINED ARCH, CALSSICAL RUINS ON A HILLTOP BEYOND oil on copper laid down on
panel, 14.2 x 19.7cm.
EXH.: Cologne, *6. Westdeutsche Kunstmesse*, 7-16 March 1975, where acquired by the father of the
present owner.
      Christie's Amsterdam, 7 May 1996 (105**) NLG 36,800   US$ 21,458

VILLAGE AND FIGURES BY A RIVER oil on panel, 16 x 20in. (40.6 x 50.8cm.)
Sotheby's New York, 16 May 1996 (235**) US$ 24,150   US$ 24,150

MOLENAER Bartholomeus (Haarlem -1650 d.) Dutch
A VILLAGESCHOOL oil on panel, 38 x 55cm.
PROV.: Artdealer Charles A. Jackson, Manchester 1950 as Adriaen Brouwer.
EXH.: Southport, Atkinson Art Gallery, *Festival Exhibition of Local Art Treasures*, 1951, as Adriaen Brouwer.
Dorotheum Vienna, 6 March 1996 (2**) ATS 100,000   US$ 9,619

A grinning Boy in a fur Hat holding a Dog, and a Girl with a Cat, and a Boy gesturing

MOLENAER Jan Miense (Haarlem 1610-1668 Haarlem) Dutch
A GRINNING BOY IN A FUR HAT HOLDING A DOG, AND A GIRL WITH A CAT, AND A BOY GESTURING oil on canvas, 32¼ x 27in. (82 x 68.5cm.) s mono 'M' (ca. 1629)
Sotheby's London, 5 July 1995 (145**) GBP 28,750   US$ 45,861

A BOY AND A GIRL, BOTH DRESSED IN GREEN WITH LACE COLLARS, HE WEARING A HAT, SHE WEARING A BONNET AND HOLDING A RATTLE, IN A PAINTED CIRCLE - A FRAGMENT oil on canvas, 55.3 x 55.8cm.
EXH.: Stuttgard, Wuerttembergische Staatsgalerie, on loan, inv.no. LS211, as Judith Leyster.
Christie's Amsterdam, 13 November 1995 (65**) NLG 13,800   US$ 8,697

PEASANTS CAROUSING IN A TAVERN oil on panel, 52 x 67.5cm. sll 'JMolenaer'
PROV.: Anonymous sale, Amstedam, Muller, 26 November 1901, lot 409; Anon. sale, Amsterdam, Muller, 28 November 1916, lot 57; A.H. Kleiweg de Zwaan, Doorn, 1953.
Sotheby's Amsterdam, 14 November 1995 (19**) NLG 53,100   US$ 33,466

MOLENAER Klaes {or} Nicolaes (Haarlem 1630 before-1676 Haarlem) Dutch
WOODED LANDSCAPE WITH HOUSES, WITH WASHERWOMAN AND ANGLERS oil on panel, 40 x 55cm. slr 'K. Molenaer'
Dorotheum Vienna, 6 March 1996 (80**) ATS 450,000   US$ 43,286

PEASANTS RESTING BY A TORRENT, A FARM NEARBY oil on panel, 25.4 x 40.6cm. slr 'KMolenaer'
Christie's Amsterdam, 7 May 1996 (100*) NLG 10925   US$ 6,370

WINTERLANDSCAPE WITH SKATING FIGURES oil on canvas, 33.5 x 46.5cm.
PROV.: Private collection, West Falen; Sale, Lempertz Cologne, 24 November 1976, lot 508
Dorotheum Vienna, 11 June 1996 (249**) ATS 100,000   US$ 9,282
VENING RIVERLANDSCAPE WITH WINDMILLS AND BOATS oil on panel, 41.5 x 53cm. slr 'k. Molenaer'
EXH.: Kassel, Exhibition in the City Picture Gallery, 1669-1979.
Dorotheum Vienna, 11 June 1996 (261**) ATS 380,000   US$ 35,271

A VILLAGE KERMESSE oil on panel, 27¼ x 37¼in. (69 x 94.4cm.) sdcl '.k.Molenaer / 1665'
Sotheby's London, 6 December 1995 (229**) GBP 32,200   US$ 49,554

A VILLAGE WINTER SCENE WITH FIGURES SKATING IN THE BACKGROUND oil on
panel, 17¾ x 25¼in. (45 x 64cm.)
    Sotheby's London, 6 December 1995 (248**) GBP 10,925   US$ 16,813

PEASANTS AND TRAVELLERS ON THE BEACH NEAR SCHEVENINGEN ON A CLOUDY
DAY oil on panel, 58 x 73.5cm. s (strengthened) ll 'K.Molenaer'
PROV.: Anon. Sale, Christie`s London, 10 December 1993, lot 227, with col. ill..
    Christie's Amsterdam, 13 November 1995 (82*) NLG 17,250   US$ 10,872

A LANDSCAPE WITH TOWNSFOLK IN HORSE-DRAWN SLEDGES BY A FROZEN RIVER,
FARMS BEYOND oil on panel, 31.1 x 34.6 cm
    Christie's Amsterdam, 7 February 1996 (101*) NLG 23,000   US$ 14,007

MOLL Carl (Vienna 1861-1945 Vienna) Austrian
HEILIGENSTÄTTER PFARRKIRCHE IM HERBST oil on panel, 34 x 36cm. slr with monogram
PROV.: Private collection, Vienna.
    Dorotheum Vienna, 6 November 1995 (48**) ATS 450,000   US$ 45,141

DÖBLING oil on canvas, 60 x 60cm. slr with monogram
PROV.: With collection Salzer.
EXH.: Vienna, Künstlerhaus Vienna 1921/3450, *Ausstellung anläßlich des 60. Geburtstages Carl
Molls.*
    Dorotheum Vienna, 21 May 1996 (45**) ATS 900,000   US$ 86,422

VALLE MARTE, RAPALLO oil on canvas, 66 x 60cm. sll with monogram; inscr. 'Carl Moll, Valle
marte Rapallo' on an old label on the reverse (1931)
PROV.: Private collection, Germany.
LIT.: *Carl Moll, Seine Freunde-Sein Leben-Sein Werk*, Edition Galerie Welz Salzburg, 1985, p. 73
(illustrated no. 95).
    Dorotheum Vienna, 21 May 1996 (86**) ATS 450,000   US$ 43,211

MOTIV AUS ITALIEN (RAPALLO) oil on canvas, 70 x 60cm. s with monogram lr 'C M'; inscr.
'Rapallo' on the reverse
    Wiener Kunst Auktionen, 26 March 1996 (203**) ATS 200,000   US$ 19,238

BLICK AUF DEN DONAUKANAL MIT DER ASPERNBRÜCKE oil on canvas, 60 x 72cm. sll 'C.
Moll'
    Wiener Kunst Auktionen, 26 September 1995 (229**) ATS 850,000   US$ 82,623

PREINBACH IM WINTER oil on canvas, 80 x 80cm. s 'C. Moll' s titled 'C. Moll Preinbach im
Winter' (ca. 1903)
    Dorotheum Vienna, 6 December 1995 (432***) ATS 1,700,000   US$ 167,643

MOLLICA Achille (19th century) Italian
THE BIRD CATCHER`S CHILDREN oil on canvas, 30¼ x 19 7/8in. (76.7 x 50.5cm.) sd inscr.
'Napoli' (1882)
    Phillips London, 12th March 1996 (46**) GBP 6,000   US$ 9,163

MOLNAR Jozsef (Zsambek 1821-1899 Budapest) Hungarian
RENDEZVOUS oil on canvas, 112 x 96cm. sd 'J. Molnar P 1885'
    Dorotheum Vienna, 6 November 1995 (70**) ATS 120,000   US$ 12,038

MOLYN Pieter the Elder (London 1595-1661 Haarlem) Dutch
PEASANTS RESTING BY A TRACK IN THE DUNES, WITH TRAVELLERS APPROACHING
FROM A WOODED OUTCROP NEAR A FARM oil on panel, 40.3 x 62.5cm. (including wooden
strips of 0.5cm. added at all sides) sdll 'PM'(linked)'olijn fec/1640'

PROV.: W. leath; Sale, Shropham Hall, Norfolk, March 1831, as Jan van; Goyen, where acquired by Thomas Preston, Wymondham, Norfolk; (according to a label on the reverse); Anon. Sale, Mak van Waay Amsterdam, 17 December 1968, lot 152, with ill.; Anon. Sale, Paul Brandt Amsterdam, 14 November 1972, lot 10, with col.ill.; R. Schöpke, Frauenfeld; Sale, Sotheby`s London, 11 December 1985, lot 154, with ill. (sold GBP5.720).
EXH.: Chur, Buendner Kunstmuseum, *Sammlung R.&E. Schöpke - Flämische; und Niederländische Malerei des 17. Jahrhundert*, 5 September - 14; November 1976, with ill.

Christie's Amsterdam, 13 November 1995 (81*) NLG 16,100	US$	10,147

MOMMERS Hendrik (Haarlem 1623 c.-1693 Amsterdam) Dutch
A SHEPHERD, A SHEPHERDESS AND A BEGGAR WITH SHEEP AND GOATS oil on canvas, 2¾ x 22¼in. (68 x 56.5cm.) s 'HMOMMERS'

Christie's London, 8 December 1995 (224**) GBP 10,580	US$	16,282

MOMPER Joos the Younger de (Antwerp 1564-1635 Antwerp) Flemish
MOUNTAIN LANDSCAPE WITH WATERMILL NEAR A RIVER oil on panel, 35 x 49cm.

Dorotheum Vienna, 6 March 1996 (134**) ATS 250,000	US$	24,048

MOUNTAINLANDSCAPE WITH PAULUS' CONVERSION oil on panel, 46 x 74.5cm. Painted in co-operation with Hans Jordaens (Antwerp 1595-1643)
PROV.: Sale, Lempertz, Cologne, 5 November 1925, illustration X; Ph. van Limburg Stirum, Anregem, Belgium, 1954; Dr. Hans Wetzlar, Amsterdam; Sale, Sotheby's Mak van Way, Amsterdam, 9 June 1977, lot 57, no. 17.
EXH.: Laren, Singer Museum, *A Selection from the Collection of Dr. H.A. Wetzlar*, 1968/69, no. 17.
LIT.: Dr. Klaus Ertz, *Josse de Momper der Jüngere*, 1986, p. 518, illustration no. 180, dated ca. 1630.

Dorotheum Vienna, 6 March 1996 (153**) ATS 700,000	US$	67,334

THE COVERSATION OF SAINT PAUL oil on panel, 45.8 x 74.6cm.
PROV.: also Hans Jordaens III (121) co-painter. Baumeister; Sale, Lempertz Cologne, 29 November 1909, lot 130, with ill.; Wedever; Sale Lempertz Cologne, 25 November 1925, fig. X; Ph. van Limburg Stirum, Anregem, Belgium, 1954; Dr Hans Wetzlar, Amsterdam (†); Sale, Sotheby Mak van waay; Amsterdam, 9 june 1977, lot 57, with ill.
EXH.: Laren Singer museum, *A Selection from the Collection of Dr H.A. Wetzlar,*; 14 December 1968-26 January 1969, no. 17.
LIT.: K Ertz, *Josse de Momper de Juengere*, 1986, p. 518, no. 180, where dated to circa 1630.

Christie's Amsterdam, 13 November 1995 (121**) NLG 48,300	US$	30,441

WEITE FLUSSLANDSCHAFT MIT REITERSTAFFAGE OIL ON PANEL, 61 x 114cm.
PROV.: Private collection, Köln.

Lempertz Cologne, 18 May 1996 (1103**) DEM 60,000	US$	39,116

LA CONVERSION DE SAINT PAUL SUR LE CHEMIN DE DAMAS oil on canvas, 92 x 152cm.

Étude Tajan Paris, 25 June 1996 (39**) FRF 110,000	US$	21,241

LANDSCAPE WITH HARVESTERS oil on oak panel, 32¼ x 56in. (82 x 144cm.) (second half of the 1620's)
PROV.: Nottingham, 1968, no. 20, plate XIV, as Joos de Momper; Sheffield, Graves Art Gallery, on loan, 1992 - 1994.
EXH.: Richter, 1901, no. 160, as manner of Adriaen van der Venne; Nicolson, 1968, p. 163, 'one of the finestJoos de Mompers in existence.'; Cornforth, 1969, p. 1604, reproduced fig. 7, as Joos de Momper; Calvocoressi, 1976, p. 143, reproduced fig. 4, as by Joos de Momper; K Ertz, *Joose de Momper der Jungere*, 1986, pp. 229-30, 554, no. 325, reproduced p. 228, fig. 248, as with figures by Jan Brueghel the Younger.

Sotheby's London, 6 December 1995 (36**) GBP 793,500	US$	1,221,145

MOMPER Philippe de II (Antwerp 1610/1615-1675 Amsterdam) Flemish
BLICK AUF ROM MIT DE ENGELSBURG oil on panel, 48 x 75cm.
    Lempertz Cologne, 18 May 1996 (1105*) DEM 40,000   US$ 2,6077

MOMPO Manuel H. (1927-1992) Spanish
STREET ORGANISTS oil on canvas, 71 x 99cm. sdll 'H. MOMPO 1959'
PROV.: Gallery of Mortimer Brandt, New York; acquired from the above by the present owner.
    Sotheby's Madrid, 23 November 1995 (92**) ESP 1880,000   US$ 15,454

MONALDI Paolo (Rome 1725 c.-1779 after) Italian
SOSTA CON RISTORO oil on canvas, 27 x 32cm s 'P.M.'
    Finearte Milan, 25 November 1995 (136**) ITL 71,300,000   US$ 44,758

MONAMY Peter (Jersey 1670 or 1689-1748/49 Westminster, London) British
AN ENGLISH CUTTER-RIGGED YACHT IN TWO POSITIONS, TRADITIONALLY
BELIEVED TO BE THE ROYAL YACHT MARY II, THOUGHT TO BE OFF THE ISLE OF
SHEPPEY oil on canvas, 28 3/8 x 36in. (72 x 91.5cm.) sll indistinctly
PROV.: with Frank Sabin, London, 1956.
    Phillips London, 18 June 1996 (30**) GBP 16,000   US$ 24,672

MONCHABLON Jean Ferdinand (1855-1904) French
A SUMMER LANDSCAPE oil on canvas, 19¼ x 31¾in. (48.9 x 80.6cm.) slr 'JAN-
MONCHABLON'
PROV.: Private Collection, Switzerland.
    Christie's New York, 22 May 1996 (180**) US$ 19,550   US$ 19,550

MONDO Domenico (1723-1806 d. Naples) Italian
HAGAR AND THE ANGEL oil on canvas, 96 x 124.5cm. s mono 'D.M.'
    Christie's Rome, 21 November 1995 (237**) ITL 22,000,000   US$ 13,810

MONDRIAAN Piet (Pieter Cornelis) (Amersfoort 1872-1944 New York) Dutch
AN EVENING LANDSCAPE conté crayon on papercard, unframed, 21 x 24.5cm. s with initials lr
'P.M.' and d and inscr. ll with 'Herinnering aan een muziekavond 13 Dec. '06'
PROV.: Given by the artist to his friend the pianist Mien Philippona on the occasion of a musical
evening on 13 December 1906, thence by descent.
EXH.: Amsterdam Gemeentearchief Amsterdam, *Mondriaan aan de Amstel*, 1892-1912, 18
february-15 May 1994.
    Christie's Amsterdam, 5 June 1996 (258*) NLG 20,700   US$ 12,095

CHRYSANTHEMUM gouache and watercolour on paper, 12½ x 9in. (31.8 x 22.9cm.) (ca. 1920-24)
PROV.: Gerrit Rietveld (acquired from the artist); L & R Entwistle, London; Private collection,
Seatle; Private collection, New York.
EXH.: Princeton, New Jersey, Art Museum, 1993.
LIT.: Robert P. Welsh, *Piet Mondrian 1872-1944*, Gallery Pieter B. Van Voorst van Beest, The
Hague, 1988, no. 7 (illustrated).
    Sotheby's New York, 2 May 1996 (202**) US$ 107,000   US$ 107,000

BATEAU DANS UN FLEUVE oil on canvas laid down on board, 33 x 43cm.
PROV.: Kunsthandel Scherpel, Amsterdam.
    Sotheby's Amsterdam, 7 December 1995 (155**) NLG 18,880   US$ 11,699

Eglise de Zoutelande

ÉGLISE DE ZOUTELANDE oil on canvas, 35 x 24in. (88.9 x 61cm.) sdll ini. 'PM 1910'
PROV.: MJ. Heijbroek, Hilversum, Holland (acquired from the Artist circa 1911); sale, Parke-Bernet Galleries, Inc.; New York, March 21, 1962, lot 94 (illustrated in color); Richard L. Feigen &: Co., New York; acquired from the above by Phyllis Lambert in 1962.
EXH.: Amsterdam, Stedelijk Museum, *Sint Lucas: 20ste Jaarlijksche Tentoonstelling*, April-June, 1910, no. 480; Brussels, Musée Moderne, Kunstkring/Cercle d'art, *Doe Stil Voort: IVe Salon*, June-Aug., 1910, no. 70; Paris, Salon des Independants, April-June, 1911, no. 4343; Amsterdam, Stedelijk Museum, *PM:Piet Mondrian Herdenkings-tentoonstelling*, Nov.-Dec., 1946, p. 47, no. 42; The Hague, Gemeentemuseum, *Mondrian*, Feb.-April, 1955, no. 58 (illustrated); Berlin, Charlottenburg, *Holländische Kunst der Gegenwart*, June-July, 1955, no. 45. The exhibition traveled to Linz, Neue Galerie, Aug.-Sept., 1955; Rechlinghausen, Städtische Kunsthalle, Sept.-Oct., 1955, and Stuttgart, Wurttembergische Kunstverein, Oct.-Nov., 1955; Santa Barbara, Museum of Art, *Piet Mondrian*, 1872- 1944,1965, no. 35 (illustrated). The exhibition traveled to Dallas, Museum of Fine Arts, 1965, and Washington, D.C., Gallery of Modern Art, May-June, 1965; Toronto, Art Gallery of Ontario, *Piet Mondrian 1872-1944*, Feb.-March, 1966, p. 116, no. 57 (illustrated). The exhibition traveled to Philadelphia, Museum of Art, April-May, 1966, and The Hague, Gemeentemuseum, June-Aug., 1966; New York, Solomon R. Guggenheim Museum, *Piet Mondrian, Centennial Exhibition*, Oct.-Dec., 1971, p. 124, no. 41 (illustrated in colour). The exhibition traveled to Bern, Kunstmuseum, Feb.-April, 1972; New York, The Museum of Modern Art, *'The Wild Beasts': Fauvism and its Affinities*, March-June, 1976. The exhibition traveled to San Francisco, Museum of Art, June-Aug., 1976, and Fort Worth, Kimbell Art Museum, Sept. -Oct., 1976; Toronto, Art Gallery of Ontario, *The Mystic North: Symbolist Landscape Painting in Northern Europe and North America,1890-1940*, Jan.-March, 1984, p. 154, no. 101 (illustrated); The exhibition traveled to Cincinnati, Art Museum, March-May, 1984.
LIT.: W. Steenhoff, *Naar Aanleiding van de Lucas, Tentoonstelling, de Ploeg*, 1909-1910, pp. 366-367 (illustrated); J. Bradley, 'Piet Mondrian, 1872-1944, Great Dutch Painter of Our Time,' *Knickerbocker Weekly-Free Netherlands*,New York, Feb. 14, 1944, vol. 3, no. 51 (illustrated); M. Seuphor, *Piet Mondrian, Life and Work*, New York, 1956, p. 422, no. 321 (illustrated, p. 235; illustrated again, p. 378, no. 247, pl. 24); F. Elgar, *Mondrian*, New York, 1968, p. 38, no. 29 (illustrated in colour); L.J.F. Wijsenbeek, *Piet Mondrian*, New York, 1968, p. 57, no. 52 (illustrated, p. 56); C. Blok, *Piet Mondrian*, Amsterdam, 1974, p. 31 (illustrated); M.G. Ottolenghi, *L'opera completa di Mondrian*, Milan, 1974, p. 102, no. 235 (illustrated and again in colour, pl. XX); H.L.C. Jaffe, *Piet Mondrian*, New York, 1985, p. 74; C. Versteeg, *Mondrian*, The Hague, 1988, p. 58 (illustrated in color).

Christie's New York, 30 April 1996 (43**) US$ 1,872,500	US$	1,872,500

MONET Claude Oscar (Paris 1840-1926 Giverny) French
LE HAMEAU DE CHANTEMESLE AU PIED DU ROCHER oil on canvas, 23½ x 31½in. (59.7 x 80cm.) slr 'Claude Monet' (1880)
PROV.: Galerie Durand-Ruel, Paris; L. Bernard, Paris; sale, Hôtel Drouot, Paris, 111 May 1901, lot 45 (illustrated); Anon. sale, Galerie Georges Petit, Paris, 23 June 1924, lot 18 (illustrated); Arthur Tooth & Sons Ltd., London (acquired by the late owner).
LIT.: D. Wildenstein, *Claude Monet, Biographie et catalogue raisonné*, Geneva 1974, vol. I (1840-1881), no. 588 (illustrated p. 367).

Christie's New York, 1 May 1996 (113**) US$ 673,500	US$	673,500

LA SEINE PRES DE VERNON (EFFET DU MATIN) oil on canvas, 19½ x 32in. (49.5 x 81.3cm.)
sll 'Claude Monet' (ca. 1894)
PROV.: Galerie Bernheim-Jeune and Galerie Durand-Ruel, Paris (circa 1920); Galerie Bernheim-
Jeune, Paris (1938); Jean Gautier, Paris; sale, Hôtel Drouot, Paris, May 16, 1939, lot 222 (illustrated);
Anon. sale, Palais Galliéra, Paris, Nov. 30, 1970, lot 98; Trosby Galleries, Palm Beach (acquired by
the family of the present owner, 1971).
EXH.: Paris, Galerie Bernheim-Jeune, *Claude Monet*, Jan.-Feb., 1921, no. 29; West Palm Beach, The
Norton Gallery, *Claude Monet, An Impression*, March, 1993.
LIT.: D. Wildenstein, *Claude Monet, Biographie et catalogue raisonné*, Lausanne 1979, vol. III
(Peintures: 1887-1898), no. 1381 (illustrated, p. 179).

Christie's New York, 1 May 1996 (140**) US$ 574,500	US$	574,500

LA ROUTE DE LA ROCHE-GUYON oil on canvas, 24 x 32in. (60 x 81cm.) sll 'Claude Monet'
(1880)
PROV.: Former collection Narcisse Coqueret, who bought this work directly from the artist, March
1880; Private Collection, Geneve.
LIT.: Daniel Wildenstein, *Claude Monet, biographie et catalogue raisonné, Tome 1: 1840-1881*,
Lausanne et Paris, 1974, pp. 364, 365, n° 583.

Étude Tajan Paris, 10 June 1996 (11**) FRF 2,300,000	US$	444,127

LES GLACONS SUR LA SEINE A PORT VILLEZ (ICE ON THE SEINE IN PORT VILLEZ) oil
on canvas, 28¾ x 36¼in. (73 x 92cm.) sdll 'Claude Monet 1893'
PROV.: Purchased from Monet by Durand-Ruel in 1924; Charpentier Gallery, Paris, May 21, 1951,
number 54; Private collection.
LIT.: *Archives L. Venturi*, 1939, vol. 1, p. 462, 463, certificates 109-110 and 111; Daniel
Wildenstein, *Claude Monet, biographie et catalogue raisonné*, Lausanne-Paris, Bibliothèque des
Arts, 1979, described on page 162 under the number 1341 and reproduced on page 163.

Étude Tajan Paris, 13 December 1995 (37***) FRF 4,800,000	US$	966,845

LA ROUTE DE GIVERNY oil on canvas, 23 3/8 x 37 7/8in. (60 x 96.2cm.) sdlr 'Claude Monet, 85'
PROV.: Galerie Durand-Ruel, Paris (acquired from Monet in December 1885); Sale: H. M. Johnson,
New York, Chickering Hall, February 28, 1893, no. 44; Durand-Ruel and Boussod-Valadon et Cie,
Paris (acquired from the above sale); Nils B. Hersloff, Rochester, New York, 1916; Sale: Sotheby's,
Tokyo, October 3, 1969, lot 366.
EXH.: New York, Durand-Ruel Galleries, *Monet*, 1995, no. 39; Boston, St. Botolph Club, *Monet*,
1895, no. 14.
LIT.: Daniel Wildenstein, *Claude Moent: Biographie et Catalogue Raisonné*, vol. II, Lausanne/Paris,
1979, no. 970 (illustrated p. 155).

Sotheby's New York, 2 May 1996 (121**) US$ 607,500	US$	607,500

GLACONS, ENVIRONS DE BENNECOURT oil on canvas, 16 x 21¼in. (40.5 x 54cm.) sd 'Claude
Monet 93'
PROV.: Eugene Blot, Paris; Acquired by the father of the present owner in Paris circa 1920.
EXH.: Paris, Fête de l'Humanité, *Aux Sources de la peinture moderne, l'Impressionnisme*, 1974, no.
16 (catalogued with the incorrect title and measurements).
LIT.: 'Les objets de qualité se placent d'eux mêmes' in *Connaissance des Arts,* Paris, May 1961, pp.
68-73 illustrated; Daniel Wildenstein, *Claude Monet, Biographie et catalogue raisonné,* Tome V:
supplément aux peintures, dessins et pastels, Lausanne, 1991, p. 19, no. 2043-1338 bis, illustrated.

Sotheby's London, 24 June 1996 (22**) GBP 375,500	US$	579,029

LONDRES, BATEAUX SUR LA TAMISE pastel on paper, 12 x 18 1/8in. (30.5 x 46cm.) s stamped
'Claude Monet' (1901)
PROV.: Michel Monet, Giverny; M. et Mme. T. Bennahum, circa 1960; Anon. sale, Galliera, Paris,
27 Nov. 1974, lot 27; Wildenstein, Paris; Jean-Claude Bellier, Paris.
EXH.: New York, Ch.E. Slatkin Galleries, *Claude Monet and the Giverny Artists*, March-April 1960,

no. 5.
LIT.: D. Wildenstein, *Claude Monet catalogue raisonné*, Vol. V, Lausanne, 1991, p. 175, no. P104
(illustrated).
        Christie's London, 26 June 1996 (109**) GBP 56,500   US$ 87,124

BATEAUX DE PECHE AU LARGE DE POURVILLE oil on canvas, 21½ x 25 7/8in. (54.6 x
65.7cm.) sll 'Claude Monet' (1882)
PROV.: Galerie Durand-Ruel, Paris (Oct., 1882); Galerie Georges Petit, Paris (acquired from the
above in Sept., 1883); M. Goldschmidt & Co., Frankfurt; Alfred Wolf, Stuttgart; sale, Sotheby 8:
Co., London, April 24, 1963, lot 7 (illustrated in colour); M. Pearson (acquired at the above sale);
Hector Brame, Paris; Paul Mellon, Upperville, Virginia; sale, Christie's, New York, Nov. 15, 1983,
lot 15 (illustrated in color); Acquired at the above sale by the late owner.
EXH.: Buenos Aires, Museo Nacional de Bellas Artes, *De Manet a nuestros dias, exposicon de
pintura francesa*, July, 1949; Richmond, Virginia Museum of Fine Arts, *Exhibition of French
Paintings*, April, 1967-June, 1968.
LIT.: D. Wildenstein, *Claude Monet, Biographie et catalogue raisonné*, Lausanne, 1979, vol.II
(1882-1886, *Peintures*), p.62, no.714 (illustrated, p.63); D.Wildenstein, *Claude Monet, Catalogue
raisonné*, Lausanne, 1991, vol.V (*Supplément aux peintures, dessins, pastels, index*), p.39, no.714.
        Christie's New York, 30 April 1996 (5**) US$ 464,500   US$ 464,500

LE PALAIS CONTARINI oil on canvas, 28¾ x 36¼in. (73 x 93cm.) sdll 'Claude Monet 1908'
PROV.: Galerie Bernheim-Jeune and Galerie Durand-Ruel, Paris; (acquired from the artist in May,
1912); Galerie Durand-Ruel, Paris (acquired from Galerie Bernheim-Jeune in June, 1912); Adolph
Lewisohn, New York (acquired from the above in Jan., 1917);
Mr. and Mrs. Samuel A. Lewisohn, New York; By descent to the present owner.
EXH.: Paris, Galerie Bernheim-Jeune, *Claude Monet, 'Venice, '* May-June, 1912, no. 27 (illustrated);
Paris, Galerie Durand-Ruel, *Claude Monet*, March, 1914, no. 5; Chicago, Auditorium Hotel,
Tableaux Durand-Ruel, Feb., 1915; Boston, Brooks Reed Gallery, March and Oct.-Nov., 1915; St.
Louis, Noonan-Kocian Gallery, Nov., 1915; Cleveland, Feb., 1916; New York, Metropolitan
Museum of Art, *Impressionist and Post-lmpressionist Paintings*, May-Sept., 1921, p. 18, no. 78; New
York, Wildenstein & Co., Inc., *Claude Monet*, April-May, 1945, p. 58, no. 77; New York,
Metropolitan Museum of Art, *The Lewisohn Collection*, Nov.-Dec., 1951, p. 29, no. 55 (illustrated)
Cambodge, Massachusetts, Fogg Art Museum, July, 1957 June, 1979 (on periodic loan); St. Louis,
City Art Museum, *Claude Monet*, Sept.-Oct., 1957, no. 88 (illustrated). The exhibition traveled to
Minneapolis, Institute of Arts, Nov.-Dec., 1957; Cambridge, Massachusetts, Fogg Art Museum,
Impressionist and Post-lmpressionist Paintings, June-July, 1959; New York, The Museum of
Modern Art, *Claude Monet, Seasons and Moments*, March-May, 1960, pp. 42-43, no. 94 (illustrated).
The exhibition traveled to Los Angeles, County Museum of Art, June-Aug., 1960; Boston, Museum
of FineArts,June, 1979-Dec., 1995 (on periodic loan); New York, William Beadleston, Inc. *Claude
Monet*; Oct.-Nov., 1982, no. 19.
LIT.: A. Alexandre, 'La vie artistique, Claude Monet et Venise,' *Le Figaro*, Paris, May 29, 1912, p. 4;
G. Geffroy, 'La Venise de Claude Monet,' *La Depeche*, Paris, May 30, 1912, p. 1; H. Genet, 'Beaux-
Arts et Curiosite, Les 'Venice' de Claude Monet,' *L'Opinion*, Paris, June 1, 1912, p. 698); A. Michel,
'Promenades aux Salons VI, ' *Journal des Debats*; Paris,June 5, 1912, p. 1 'Art et Curiosité, Venise
vue par Claude Monet,'Les Temps, Paris, June 11, 1912, p. 4; H. Gheon, 'A travers les expositions,
Claude Monet,' *Art Décoratif (Supplement), Paris, June 20, 1912, p. 4; G. Geffroy, 'Claude Monet,'*
L'Art et les Artistes, Paris, Nov., 1920, pp. 78-79 (illustrated); R. Koechlin, 'Claude Monet,' *Art et
Décoration, Paris, Feb., 1927, p. 46 (illustrated) S. Bourgeois,* The Adolph Lewisohn Collection of
ModernFrench Paintings and Sculptures, New York, 1928, pp. 78-79 (illustrated); M. Malingue,
Claude Monet, Monaco, 1943, p. 140, no. 140 (illustrated); O. Reutersward, *Monet en
konstnarshistorik*, Stockholm, 1948, pp. 255-258 (illustrated, p. 257); A. Barbier, 'Monet, c'est le
peintre,' *Arts*, Paris, July 31-Aug. 6, 1952, p. 10; R. Jullian, 'Les Impressionnistes Français et l'Italie,'
Publications de l'Institut francais de Florence, Florence, 1968, lere série, NII-11, p. 19; G.
Seiberling, *Monet's Series*, NewYork, 1981, p. 381, no. 19; R. Gordon and A. Forge, *Monet*, New
York, 1983, p. 189 (illustrated in color); D. Wildenstein, *Claude Monet, Biographie et catalogue
raisonné*, Lausanne, 1985, vol. IV (1899-1926, Peintures), p. 244, no. 1766 (illustrated, p. 245), p.

385, letter no. 2012a, and p. 430, document nos. 240, 241 and 265; P. Piguet, *Monet et Venise*, Paris, 1986, p. 95 (illustrated).

Christie's New York, 30 April 1996 (29**) US$ 4,237,500	US$	4,237,500

CHARING CROSS BRIDGE A LA HAUTEUR DU PARLEMENT oil on canvas, 25½ x 31¾in. (64.8 x 80.6cm.) sdlr 'Claude Monet 99'
PROV.: Galerie Durand-Ruel, Paris (acquired from the artist in Nov., 1901); Paul Cassirer, Berlin (acquired from the above in 1903); Anon. sale; Hotel Drouot, Paris, April 26, 1926, lot 72 (illustrated); L.G. Picard, Paris (1930).
LIT.: 'Revue des ventes,' *LeJournal des Arts*, Paris, April 28,1926, p. 2 (illustrated); Curiosa, 'Revue des ventes d'avril, lundi 26 avril Hotel Drouot,' *Le Figaro artistique*, Paris, June 3, 1926, p. 540; L. Venturi, *Archives de l'Impressionnisme*, Paris, 1939, vol. 1,pp. 382-383; D. Wildenstein, *Claude Monet, Biographie et catalogue raisonné*, Lausanne, 1979, vol. IV (1899-1926, Peintures), p. 162, no.1531 (illustrated, p. 163), p. 359, letter nos. 1646 and 1647, and p. 427, document nos. 155, 161, and 163.

Christie's New York, 30 April 1996 (36**) US$,3962,500	US$	3,962,500

LE MONT KOLSAAS, EFFET DE SOLEIL oil on canvas, 25½ x 39¼in. (65 x 100cm.) sdll 'Claude Monet 95'
PROV.: Galerie Durand-Ruel, Paris (acquired from the artist in April, 1900); Jean d'Alayer, Paris (circa 1952); Anon. sale; Galerie Charpentier, Paris, June l3, l 958, lot 107 (illustrated, pl. XXV); E.J. van Wisselingh & Co., Amsterdam; M. Knoedler & Co., Inc., New York (Sept., 1961); Acquired from the above by the late owners in Jan., 1962.
EXH.: Paris, Galerie Durand-Ruel, *Tableaux de Claude Monet*, May, 1895, no. 32
Stockholm, Konstutsalloingen, *Exposition Generale des Beaux-Arts*, May-Oct., 1897, p. 177, no. 1679; Paris, Galerie Durand-Ruel, *Oeuvres recentes de Claude Monet*, Nov.-Dec., 1900, no. 21; Paris, Galerie Bernheim Jeune, *Oeuvres de Monet de 1894 à 1905*, March, 1906 Berlin, Galerien Thannhauser, *Claude Monet, Gedächtnisausstellung*, Feb.-March, 1928, no. 47; Paris, Wildenstein & Cie., *Monet*, June-July, 1952, p. 57, no. 68 (illustrated); London, Marlborough Fine Art, Ltd., *Claude Monet*, June-July, 1954, p. 41, no. 44; Stavanger, Norway, Rogaland Kunstmuseum, *Monet i Norge*, July-Sept., 1995 (illustrated, p. 91 and on the front and back covers). The exhibition traveled to Paris, Musée Rodin, Oct.-Dec., 1995, and Copenhagen, Ordrupgaard, Jan.-April, 1996.
LIT.: L. Venturi, *Les Archives de l'lmpressionnisme*, Paris, 1939, vol. 1, p. 376; O. Reutersward, 'Monet ach hens malen. Minnen och intryck av Prins Eugen,' *Ord och Bild*, Dec., 1947, p. 454; O. Reutersward, *Monet Konstnarshistorik*, Stockholm, 1948, pp. 214, 216, 217, 230 and 234; K. Hellandsjo, *Monet i Norge -1895*, Hovikodden, 1974, p. 5; D. Wildenstein, *Claude Monet, Biographie et catalogue raisonné*, Geneva, 1979, vol. III *(1887-1898, Peintures)*, p. 188, no. 1409 (illustrated, p. 189).

Christie's New York, 30 April 1996 (38**) US$ 1,267,500	US$	1,267,500

LA GORGE DE VARENGEVILLE oil on canvas, 25½ x 31 7/8in. (65 x 81cm.) sdlr 'Claude Monet 82'
PROV.: Galerie Durand-Ruel, Paris (acquired from the artist in April, 1882); Paul Berard, Paris; sale, Galerie Georges Petit, Paris, May 8, 1905, lot 8 (illustrated; titled La Cabane du douanier à Varengeville) Galerie Durand-Ruel, Paris (acquired at the above sale); Robert Treat Paine, Jr., Boston (circa 1911); André Meyer, New York; Wildenstein & Cie, Paris; George Ansley, London (circa 1954); Arthur Tooth & Sons, Ltd., London (circa l 965); Galerie Schmit, Paris.
EXH.: Paris, Galerie Durand-Ruel, *Exposition des oeuvres de Claude Monet, March, 1883, no. 33; Paris, Galerie Georges Petit,* Claude Monet à Auguste Rodin, June-July, 1889, no. 60; Paris, Calerie Durand-Ruel, *Paysages par Claude Monet* May-June, 1908, no. 15; New York, Durand-Ruel Galleries, *Claude Monet*, Feb., 1911, no. 13; Boston, Museum of Fine Arts, *Monet*, Aug., 1911, no. 37; Boston, Museum of Fine Arts, *Claude Monet Memorial Exhibition*, Jan., 1927, no. 75; Paris, Musée Rodin, *Claude Monet - Auguste Rodin, Centenaire de l'exposition*, Nov., 1989-Jan., 1990, p. 83, no. 60 (illustrated).
LIT.: G. Grappe, *Claude Monet*, Paris, 1909, p. 56; M. de Fels, *La vie de Claude Monet*, Paris, 1929, p. 235; O. Reutersward, *Monet*, Stockholm, 1948, p. 284; M. Rostand, *Quelques amateurs de*

l'epoque impressionniste, Paris, 1955, p. 278; L. Degand and D. Rouart, *Claude Monet*, Geneva, 1958, p. 75; D. Wildenstein, *Claude Monet*, Milan, 1971, p. 78 (illustrated); L. R. Bartolatto , *L 'opera completa di Claude Monet*, Milan,1972, no. 241 (illustrated, p. 104); D. Wildenstein, *Claude Monet, Biographie et catalogue raisonné*, Lausanne, 1979, vol. 11 (1882-1886, Peintures), p. 69, no. 730 (illustrated); V. Spate, *Claude Monet, la couleur du temps*, Paris, 1993, pp. 153-159.

Christie's New York, 7 November 1995 (18**) US$ 1,487,500	US$	1,487,500

NYMPHEAS oil on canvas, 39 3/8 x 32in. (,100 x 81.3cm.) slr 'Claude Monet'
PROV.: Galerie Durand-Ruel and Galerie Bernheim-Jeune, Paris (acquired from the artist in Dec., 1920); Galerie Bernheim-Jeune, Paris; Henri Canonne, Paris (acquired from the above in July, 1923) Private collection, Switzerland.
EXH.: Paris, Galerie Bernheim-Jeune, *Claude Monet*, Jan.-Feb., 1921, no. 42; Paris, Galerie Paul Rosenberg, *Claude Monet*, oeuvres de 1891 à 1919, April, 1936, no. 28 (illustrated).
LIT.: A. Alexandre, *Claude Monet*, Paris, 1921, no. 47 (illustrated in color, p. 118); A. Alexandre, *La Collection Canonne*, Paris, 1930, pp. 45-46; L. Venturi, *Les archives de l'impressionnisme*, Paris, 1939, vol. 1, p. 457; D. Rouart, J.D. Rey and R. Maillard, *Monet Nymphéas ou les miroirs du temps*, Paris, 1972, p. 165 (illustrated); D.Wildenstein, *Claude Monet, Biographie et catalogue raisonné*, Lausanne, 1979, vol. IV (1899-1926, Peintures), p. 230, no 1735 (illustrated, p. 231).

Christie's New York, 7 November 1995 (21**) US$ 5,062,500	US$	5,062,500

CHARING CROSS BRIDGE oil on canvas, 25 5/8 x 31 7/8in. (65 x 81cm.) sdlr 'Claude Monet 1903'
PROV.: Galerie Georges Bernheim, Paris; B.J. van Gelder, Paris, sale, Hotel Drouot, Paris, March 20, 1950, lot 125 (illustrated, pl. X); Etienne Bignou, Paris; Wildenstein & Cie., Paris; Georges Marci, Geneva.
EXH.: Paris, Galerie Georges Bernheim, *Tableaux de maîtres modernes*, 1916, no. 51; Tokyo, National Museum of Western Art, Monet, Oct.-Nov., 1982, no. 47; The exhibition traveled to Kyoto, National Museum of Modern Art, Dec., 1982 -Jan., 1983.
LIT.: D. Wildenstein, *Claude Monet, Biographie et catalogue raisonné*, Lausanne, 1985, vol. IV (*1899-1926, Peintures*), p. 160, no. 1528 (illustrated, p. 161).

Christie's New York, 7 November 1995 (27**) US$ 3,522,500	US$	3,522,500

MONNOYER Jean-Baptiste (Lille 1634-1699 London) French
STILL LIFE OF GRAPES, PEACHES, MELONS AND OTHER FRUIT CASCADING OVER A LEDGE WITH MONKEYS AND A CARVED STONE URN oil on canvas, 39 3/8 x 47¼in. (,100 x 120cm.)

Sotheby's New York, 11 January 1996 (79**) US$ 90,500	US$	90,500

PEONIES, IRISES, NARCISSI, SNOWDROPS AND OTHER FLOWERS IN A GLASS VASE ON A LEDGE oil on canvas, 25 x 30in. (63.5 x 76.3cm.)
PROV.: C.Hollingdale, Christie's 10 July 1925, lot 77, as Jean Baptiste.

Christie's South Kensington, 19 October 1995 (392**) GBP 7,875	US$	12,429

FLOWERS IN A STONE VASE oil on canvas, 90 x 75cm.

Libert & Castor Paris, 23 February 1996 (80**) FRF 80,000	US$	16,371

MONNOYER Jean-Baptiste (circle of) (Lille 1634-1699 London) French
A FLOWER STILL-LIFE WITH ROSAE, CAMPANULAE, VETCH, LARKSPUR, LIONSMOUTH AND OTHER FLOWERS IN DECORATIVE VASE oil on canvas, 47 x 36.5cm.

Dorotheum Vienna, 11 June 1996 (179**) ATS 280,000	US$	25,989

MONSTED Peder (Grenaa 1859-1941) Danish
CHILDREN WITH A SLEDGE IN A WINTER LANDSCAPE oil on canvas, 31½ x 47in. (80 x 119.5cm.) sd 'P. Monsted. 1914'

Christie's London, 15 March 1996 (61**) GBP 31,050	US$	47,419

A MOONLIT RIVER LANDSCAPE oil on canvas, 32 1/8 x 46½in. (81.6 x 118cm.) sd 'P. Monsted 1903'

Christie's London, 17 November 1995 (109**) GBP 12,075	US$	18,888

MONTÉZIN Pierre Eugène (Paris 1874-1946 Moëllan (Finistère)) French
LA FENAISON (THE HARVEST) oil on canvas, 61 x 73cm. sll 'Montezin'

Étude Tajan Paris, 1 February 1996 (118**) FRF 60,000	US$	12,278

PERSONNAGES DANS LA PRAIRIE oil on canvas, 36¼ x 28¾in. (92 x 73cm.) slr 'Montezin'

Christie's London, 26 June 1996 (157**) GBP 29,900	US$	46,106

PROMENADE SOUS LA PLUIE oil on canvas, 19¾ x 21¾in. (50 x 55cm.) slr 'montezin'
PROV.: Marcel Cayla, 15 Decembre 1951.

Christie's South Kensington, 27 November 1995 (87**) GBP 7,312	US$	11,438

L'AUTOMNE AU BORD DU LOING oil on canvas, 23 5/8 x 31 7/8in. (60 x 81cm.) lr 'Montezin'
again on the reverse 'Montezin L'automne au bord du Loin 2'

Christie's New York, 8 November 1995 (158**) US$ 10,350	US$	10,350

MONTFORT Octavianus (17th Century, active Piedmont, late-)
STILL-LIFE OF FRUIT AND FLOWERS IN A COPPER VESSEL watercolour on vellum, 39 x 54cm.

Sotheby's London, 3 July 1995 (215**) GBP 9,200	US$	14,675

STILL-LIFE OF FRUIT AND FLOWERS, WITH THREE FISH AND A LOBSTER IN A COPPER DISH watercolour on vellum, 39.4 x 52.2cm.

Sotheby's London, 3 July 1995 (216**) GBP 10,350	US$	16,510

MONTICELLI Adolphe Joseph Thomas (Marseille 1824-1886 Marseille) French
RENDEZ-VOUS SOUS LA VASQUE FLEURIE oil on panel, 18½ x 25¼in. (47 x 64.2cm.) s 'Monticelli'
LIT.: S. Stammégna, Catalogue des Oeuvres de Monticelli, Vol. II p. 149, no. 843 (illustrated).

Christie's London, 15 March 1996 (36**) GBP 25,300	US$	38,638

FETE D'APRES-MIDI oil on panel, 19¼ x 30½in. (49 x 77.2cm.) s 'Monticelli'
PROV.: M. Massoni; sale Hotel Drouot, Paris, 22June 1911, lot 28.

Christie's London, 15 March 1996 (37**) GBP 25,300	US$	38,638

MOORE Albert Joseph, A.R.W.S. (1841-1893) British
COMPANIONS oil on canvas, 17x9¼in.(43x23.5cm.) s with anthemion and signed and inscribed 'Albert Moore Esq/1 Holland House' on an old label on the reverse (1883)
PROV.: Leggatt Bros: Christie's, 25 March 1955, lot 138 (14 gns. to Dent).
EXH.: London, Dowdeswell Gallenes, 160 New Bond Street, 1883; London, Grafton Galleries, *Albert Moore Memorial Exhibition,* 1894.
LIT.: *Art Journal,* 1894, p.89; Alfred Lys Baldry, *Albert Moore,* 1894, pp. 54 (repr.), 59, 82, 104; Photgravure published by Dowdeswell's, 1883.

Christie's London, 6 November 1995 (124**) GBP 98,300	US$	153,762

ELLEN TERRY AS PORTIA oil on canvas, 11½ x 91/8in. (29.2 x 23.2cm.) s with anthemion 'A. Moore esq/1 Holland Lane'
PROV.: With John Gibson, Glasgow.
EXH.: Probably London, McClean's Gallery, 1885; Nwecastle upon Tyne, Laing Art Gallery, *Albert Moore and his Contemporaries,* 1972, no 137 (as 'A Girl's Head').
LIT.: Probably A.L. Baldry, *Albert Moore: His life and Works,* 1894, pp. 59, 105.

Christie's London, 7 June 1996 (573**) GBP 25,300	US$	39,013

MOORE Harry Humphrey (1844-1926) British (?)
LEAVING THE ALHAMBRA oil on canvas, 24¾ x 14½in.(63 x 37cm.) sdll 'H. Humphrey
Moore/87' (1887)

Christie's New York, 2 November 1995 (265**) US$ 63,000	US$	63,000

MOORE Henry, O.M., C.H. (Castleford, Yorkshire 1898-1986) British
RECLINING FIGURE watercolour pen and ink, black crayon and chalk on paper, 13 1/8 x 22in.
(33.3 x 55.9cm.) sdlr 'Moore 42'
PROV.: Curt Valentin, New York; Kleeman Galleries; Joseph Kelleher, Princeton, NewJersey; M.
Knoedler & Co., New York; Acquired from the by the benjamin family above in 1963.
EXH.: New Haven, Yale University Art Gallery, *The Helen and Robert M. Benjamin Collection*,
1967, no. 114.

Sotheby's New York, 2 May 1996 (276**) US$ 48,875	US$	48,875

STANDING FIGURES pastel, coloured crayon, gouache, watercolour and pen and ink on paper,
19¾ x 15in. (50.2 x 38.1cm.) sdll 'Moore '50'; titled on the verso
PROV.: Buchholz Gallery (Curt Valentin), New York; Frank Perls Gallery, Beverly Hills.

Sotheby's New York, 2 May 1996 (346***) US$ 123,500	US$	123,500

EWE AND LAMB black ballpoint pen and pencil on paper, 8 1/8 x 9 7/8in. 920.6 x 25cm.) s 'Moore'
on the back
PROV.: Waddington Galleries, London, from whom purchased by the present owner.
LIT.: this work is recorded in the *Henry Moore Foundation Archive* under the no. HMS3335.

Christie's London, 26 June 1996 (304**) GBP 13,225	US$	20,393

IDEAS FOR METAL SCULPTURE watercolour, coloured crayons, pencil, pen and black ink on
paper, 10 x 16¾in. (25.4 x 42.5cm.) sdlr 'Moore 39'
PROV.: Benjamin Watson, New York.
EXH.: London, Tate Gallery, *Henry Moore*, Festival of Britain, May-July 1951, no. 102.
LIT.: D. Sylvester (ed.), *Henry Moore, vol.I, Sculpture and Drawings 1921-1948*, London 1957, p.
210 (illustrated p. 210).

Christie's London, 29 November 1995 (245**) GBP 30,000	US$	46,926

STUDIES FOR STRINGED FIGURES white wax crayon and colored pencils over pencil on paper,
10 ½ x 7 1/8in. (26.7 x 18cm.) ll 'Moore 38' (1938)
PROV.: The Zwemmer Gallery, London (acquired by the late owner, 1958).
EXH.: Chicago, The School of Social Service Administration Building, *Chicago's Hommage to
Henry Moore*, Dec., 1967, no. 71.

Christie's New York, 8 November 1995 (221**) US$ 19,550	US$	19,550

EBB TIDE, SQUALL COMING ON oil on canvas, 15¾ x 25¾in. (40 x 65.4cm.) sd 'H.Moore 1867'
and s inscr. 'Ebb Tide squall/Henry Moore' on an old label on the reverse
PROV.: Sir R.P. Cooper, and by descent to the present owner.
EXH.: London, Royal Academy, 1868, no.170.

Christie's London, 6 November 1995 (165**) GBP 13,225	US$	20,687

MORAN Edward Percy(the third) (1862-1935) American
ON THE BEACH, EASTHAMPTON oil on canvas, 14½ x 20in. (37 x 51.2cm.) s 'Percy Moran; and
with the artist's device; sd 'July 1916' and inscr. with title on the reverse
PROV.: Livingstone Galleries, New York.

Christie's East, 21 May 1996 (97**) US$ 14,950	US$	14,950

MORAN Henry Marcus (1877-1960) American
THE EMPIRE STATE BUILDING oil on canvas, 30 x 22in. (76.2 x 55.2cm.) s and inscr. lr 'H
Marcus Moran/copyright/applied for 11-10-33'

Christie's East, 21 May 1996 (172**) US$ 8,625	US$	8,625

MORAN Thomas, N.A. (1837-1926) American
ON THE BERRY TRAIL-GRAND CANYON ARIZONA oil on canvas, 20 x 30in. (50.8 x 76.3cm.)
sdlr with ini. conjoined 'T Moran 1903'; sd and inscr. with title on the reverse prior to lining
PROV.: The Milch Galleries, New York; Louis Ettlinger Esq., New York.
LIT.: T. Wilkins, *Thomas Moran: Artist of the Mountains*, Norman 1966, p. 220.

Christie's New York, 30 November 1995 (38**) US$ 332,500	US$	332,500

STORMY COAST watercolour and gouache on paper in an arch, 6½ x 4 1/8in. (16.5 x 10.5cm.) slr
inscr. on the mat 'With Compliments of TMoran.'

Christie's New York, 13 September 1995 (31*) US$ 3,450	US$	3,450

MORANDI Giorgio (Bologna 1890-1964 Bologna) Italian
NATURA MORTA oil on canvas, 39 x 53cm. sdlr 'Morandi 929' (1929)
PROV.: Collection A. Osio, Rome, Collection S. Solari, Rome.
EXH.: Roma, Palazzo dele Esposizioni, *VII Quadriennale d'Arte Nazionale. Antologia della pittura e
scultura italiane*, November 1955 - April 1956, no. 70.
LIT.: G. Castelfranco and M. Valsecchi, *Pittura e scultura italiane dal 1910 al 1930*, Roma 1956, ill.
XLI; L. Vitali, *Morandi, Catalogo Generale*, ed. Electa, Milan 1977, vol I, no. 138.

Finearte Milan, 12 December 1995 (301**) ITL 1,656,000,000	US$	1,038,896

NATURA MORTA oil on canvas, 37.5 x 45cm. sul 'Morandi' (ca 1928)
EXH.: Napels, *La natura morta in Italia*, Palazzo Reale, Oct.-Nov.,1964, no.337 bis; Zurich, *La
natura morta in Italia*, Kunsthaus, Dec. 1964-Feb. 1965, no.194; Rotterdam, *La natura morta
italiana*, Boymans-van Beuningen Museum, March-April 1965, no.194; Firenze, *Arte Moderna in
Italia 1915/1935*, Palazzo Strozzi, Feb.-May, 1967, no.1214, cat. pag.228.
LIT.: L. Vitali, *Morandi catalogo generale*, vol.I, ed. Electa, Milan, 1977, no.133.

Finearte Rome, 12 June 1996 (218**) ITL 828,000,000	US$	542,951

NATURA MORTE pencil on paper, 14.5 x 20cm. slc 'Morandi'

Finearte Milan, 18 June 1996 (33*) ITL 14,950,000	US$	9,695

NATURA MORTA oil on canvas, 35 x 40cm. slc 'Morandi' (1958)
PROV.: Milan, Galleria del Milione; Milan, *collection A. Mazzotta*.
LIT.: L. Vitali, Morandi, *Catalogo Generale*, ed. Electa, Milan 1977, vol.II, no.1101.

Finearte Milan, 19 March 1996 (50**) ITL 431,250,000	US$	275,912

NATURA MORTE oil on canvas, 15¼ x 18¼in. (38.7 x 46.4cm.) slr 'Morandi' (1946)
PROV.: Emilio Jesi, Milan Galleria d'Arte del Naviglio, Milan; Hannah Troy, New York Miriam
Redein, New York Acquired from the above by the Benjamin family in 1964.
EXH.: Florence, Palazzo Strozzi, *Arte Italiana Contemporanea in Germania*, no. 146 New Haven,
Yale University Art Gallery, *The Helen and Robert M. Benjamin Collection*, 1967, no. 117 New
York, Galleria Odyssia, *Klee - Morandi*, 1969.
LIT.: Francesco Arcangeli, 12 *opere di Giorgio Morandi*, Milan, 1950, no. 3; Lamberto Vitali,
Giorgio Morandi - Pittore, Milan, 1964, no. 166, illustrated; Lamberto Vitali, *Morandi (1948/1961),
Catalogo Generale, vol. 1*, Milan, 1977, no. 533, illustrated.

Sotheby's New York, 2 May 1996 (258**) US$ 343,500	US$	343,500

NATURA MORTE oil on canvas, 15¾ x 18in. (40 x 45.7cm.) s 'Morandi' (1952)
PROV.: EmilioJessi, Milan; Hannah Troy, New York; Curt Valentin (Buchholz Gallery), New York;
Mr. and Mrs. Charles Gorham, New York; Staempfli Gallery, New York; Acquired from the above
by the Benjamin family in 1963.
EXH.: New York, Galleria Odyssia, *Seven Decades 1895-1965, Cross Currents in Modern Art*,
1966, no. 248 New Haven, Yale University Art Gallery, *The Helen and Robert M. Benjamin
Collection*, 1969, no. 118 New York, Galleria Odyssia, *Klee - Morandi*, 1967 San Francisco,
Museum of Modern Art; New York, Solomon R. Guggenheim Museum; Des Moines, Des Moines
Art Center, *Giorgio Morandi*, 1981 - 1982, no. 43.

LIT.: Lamberto Vitali, *Morandi (1948/1964), Catalogo Generale*, vol. II, Milan, 1977, no. 830, illustrated.

Sotheby's New York, 2 May 1996 (259**) US$ 530,500	US$	530,500

NATURA MORTE oil on canvas, 25 x 28cm. slr 'Morandi' (1959)
PROV.: Galleria del Milione, Milan; Collection G. Mattioli, Milan.
EXH.: Turin, Galleria Civica d'Arte Moderna, *Capolavori d'arte moderna nelle collezioni private*, 1959, no. 42, fig. 14.
LIT.: Jiri Siblik, *Giorgio Morandi*, Prague 1965, no. 59 (illustrated); Lamberto Vitali, *Gorgio Morandi Catalogo Generale*, Milan 1977, vol. II, no. 1133 (illustrated).

Sotheby's Milan, 28 May 1996 (231**) ITL 351,600,000	US$	225,819

NATURA MORTE oil on canvas, 12¼ x 14in. (31 x 35cm.) slc 'Morandi' (1959)
PROV.: Galleria del Milione, Milan; Albert Loeb end Jan Krugier Gallery, New York (1967); H.C. Goldsmith, New York; A. Polkes, New York; Roberts and Tunnard Gallery, London; L. Molina, Pavia; Marlborough Gallery, Inc., New York.
EXH.: Geneva, Galerie Krugier et Cie., *Giorgio Morandi Suites*, Nov., 1963, no. 32; Karlsruhe, Badischer Kunstverein, *Giorgio Morandi, Gemälde, Aquarelle, Zeichnungen, Radierungen*, June-July, 1964, no. 13 (illustrated, pl. 2); Hannover, Kestner-Gesellschaft, *Giorgio Morandi*, Nov.-Dec., 1964, no. 8 (illustrated); New York, Albert Loeb and Jan Krugier Gallery, *Homage to Silence or Metaphysica*, May-June, 1967, no. 29 (illustrated); San Francisco, Museum of Modern Art, *Giorgio Morandi*, Sept.-Nov., 1981, p. 172, no. 55 (illustrated, p. 123). The exhibition traveled to New York, Solomon R. Guggenheim Museum, Nov., 1981-Jan., 1982, and Des Moines, Art Center, Feb.-March, 1982; San Antonio, Museum of Art, *Private Treasures: Public View*, Feb.-March, 1985, no. 161.
LIT.: L. Vitali, *Morandi, Gatalogo Generale*, Milan, 1977, vol. II (1948-1964), no. 1144 (illustrated).

Christie's New York, 30 April 1996 (58**) US$ 211,500	US$	211,500

NATURA MORTA oil on canvas, 13 7/8 x 19 3/8in. (35 x 49cm.) slc 'Morandi' (ca. 1952)
PROV.: World House Galleries, New York; Mr. and Mrs. Harold FRanklin, New York (1960); Walter L. Randel, New York (1962); E.V. Thaw & Co., New York.
EXH.: New York, World House Galleries, *Giorgio Morandi: Oils, Watercolors, Drawings, etchings*, Dec.1960-Jan.1961, no. 22.

Christie's New York, 7 November 1995 (38**) US$ 464,500	US$	464,500

NATURA MORTA oil on canvas, 13 7/8 x 17 7/8in. (35 x 45.5cm.) slc 'Morandi' (ca. 1948)
PROV.: Robert T. Markson, Beverly Farms, Massachusetts; E.V. Thaw & Co., New York.
EXH.: New York, The Solomon R. Guggenheim Museum, *Giorgio Morandi*, Nov. 1981-Jan. 1982, pp. 108 and 170, no. 35 (illustrated. The exhibition traveled to Des Moines, Art Center, Feb.-March, 1982.

Christie's New York, 7 November 1995 (39**) US$ 266,500	US$	266,500

CORTILE DI VIA FONDAZZA oil on canvas, 10 x 8in. (25.4 x 20.3cm.) lr 'Morandi' (1956)
PROV.: Galleria del Milione, Milan; Galleria dell'Obelisco, Rome; World House Gallerias, New York; H.S.Tesoriere, New York; Herman C.goldsmith, New York (acquired by the present owner, 1964).
EXH.: New York, World House Galleries, *Giorgio Morandi: Retrospective*, Nov.-Dec., 1957, no. 31 (illustrated).
LIT.: L.Vitali, *Morandi Catalogo Generale*, Milan, 1977, vol. II (1948/1964), no. 1015 (illustrated).

Christie's New York, 8 November 1995 (293**) US$ 123,500	US$	123,500

MORBELLI Angelo (1853-1919) Italian
FRAGILINA oil on canvas, 50½ x 36¼cm. (128.2 x 92cm.) sd 'Morbelli 1899'
EXH.: Milan, Regia Accademia di Belle Arti di Brera, *Quarta Espozione Triennale di Milano*, 1900, p. 58, no. 474.
LIT.: Lucini, E*mporium*, Oct. 1900, vol. XII, p. 327, no. 70; Lucini, *Emporium,* Nov. 1900, vol II,

pp. 341-341, no. 71; To be included in Professor Giovanni Anzani's forthcoming *catalogue raisonné on Morbelli.*

Christie's London, 15 March 1996 (185**) GBP 661,500 — US$ 1,010,232

MOREAU Adrien (1843-1906) French
AFTER THE WEDDING oil on canvas, 24 x 32in. (61 x 81.3cm.) sdlr 'Adrien-Moreau. 1882.'

Christie's New York, 2 November 1995 (143**) US$ 23,000 — US$ 23,000

MOREAU Gustave (Paris 1826-1898 Paris) French
PERSIPHAE watercolour on paper, 11 x 7 1/8in. (28 x 18cm.) sdll. 'Gustave Moreau 1867'; inscr. as titled lc and inscr.' à Maxime du Camp/souvenir ../Gustave Moreau' lr (ca. 1860)
PROV.: Given by the artist to Maxime du Camp.

Christie's New York, 2 November 1995 (51**) US$ 266,500 — US$ 266,500

MOREELSE Paulus (Utrecht 1571-1638 Utrecht) Dutch
PORTRAIT OF A LADY, HALF LENGTH, WEARING A BLACK SILK DRESS, LACE COLLAR, A BLACK BOW AND PEARLS WITH A RING HANGING FROM ASTRING AROUND HER NECK oil on panel, 66.8 x 55.6cm sdur 'PM/1625'
PROV.: (Possibly) J. Bleuland; Sale H. van Ommeren Utrecht, 6 May 1839, lot 234, as a portrait Maria van Reigersbergen; dfl. 76,- to Cornelis Hulstein; Ph. j. van Zuylen van Neyenvelt van Hinderstein (1785-1864), Utrecht; given in 1858 to his second cousin Louise Cornets de Groot, thence by descent to the present owners.
EXH.: Amsterdam, Maatschappij Arti et Amicitiae, *tentoonstelling van schilderijen van Oude Meesters*, 1872, no. 171; Utrecht, Gebouw voor Kunsten en Wetenschappen, *Tentoonstelling van Oude Schilderkunst, 1894, no. 144; Amsterdam, Frederiks Muller,* Exposition de Maîtres Hollandais du XVIIe Siècle, 1906, no. 88, together with the so-called pendant; Utrecht, Centraal Museum, *Tentoonstelling van werken van Paulus Moreelse*, 1938, no. 24.
LIT.: Ch. Boissevain 'Iets over de tentoonstelling in Arti' in *De Gids*, X, June 1872, p. 535; *'Een Vrouwenportret, Eigen Haard'* 1895, pp. 72/73, with ill.; E.W. Moes, *Iconographia Batava*, II, 1905, p. 270; A. von Würzbach, *Niederländische Künstler-Lexicon*, II, 1910, p. 187, together with the so-called pendant; C.H. de Jonge, *Paulus Moreelse - Portret- en Genreschilder te Utrecht 1571-1638*, 1938, pp. 29 and 90, no. 82, fig. 59.

Christie's Amsterdam, 13 November 1995 (157**) NLG 270,250 — US$ 170,322

MOREL Casparus Johannes (Amsterdam 1798-1861 Amsterdam) Dutch
SHIPPING IN THE ROADS OF A HARBOUR oil on panel, 36 x 50 cm sd 'S.I. Moret f 1827'

Christie's Amsterdam, 25 April 1996 (6*) NLG 9,775 — US$ 5,808

MOREL Jan Baptiste (Antwerp 1662-1732 Brussels) Flemish
STILL-LIFES OF FLOWERS IN VASES oil on canvas (a pair), each: 63¾ x 46½in. (162 x 118cm.)

Sotheby's London, 18 October 1995 (73**) GBP 23,000 — US$ 36,301

MOREL-FATIO Antoine-Léon (1810-1871) French
THE GOLDEN HORN WITH THE SULEYMANIYE AND THE FATIH MOSQUES, CONSTANTINOPLE oil on canvas, 18¼ x 48½in. (46.3 x 123.2cm.) s 'Morel-Fatio'

Christie's London, 17 November 1995 (130**) GBP 166,500 — US$ 260,441

ALGER HARBOUR oil on canvas, 18¼ x 48½in (46.3 x 123.2cm.) s 'Morel-Fatio'

Christie's London, 17 November 1995 (133**) GBP 36,700 — US$ 57,407

MORELLET François (Cholet 1926 b.-l) French
SEULE DROITE TRAVERSANT 2 CARRES DANS 2 PLANS DIFFERENT oil on canvas mounted on woord into two parts, each: 15¾ x 15¾ x¾in. (40 x 40 x 2cm.); overall: 31½ x 15¾ x¾in. (80 x 40 x 2cm.) sd '1978', titled, numbered '78046' (coté gauche) on the reverse
PROV.: Galerie Nordenhake, Stockholm.

Sotheby's London, 21 March 1996 (62**) GBP 6,900 — US$ 10,538

MORENI Mattia (1920 b.-l) Italian
MOULIN ROUGE oil on canvas, 162 x 130cm sd '1963 Moreni'. sd and titled on the reverse
PROV.: Galleria San Luca, Bologna.

Finearte Rome, 14 November 1995 (209**) ITL 33,350,000   US$ 20,935

COMPOSIZIONE N.30 (GRADO) oil on canvas, 120 x 103cm sd 'Moreni 1951'. s and titled on the reverse
PROV.: Galleria San Luca, Bologna; Galleria del Milione, Milano, no.6416.
EXH.: Lissone, *VII Premio Nazionale di Pittura*, s.d.

Finearte Rome, 14 November 1995 (218**) ITL 258,75,000   US$ 16,243

CESPUGLIO SUL MARE oil on canvas, 65 x 108cm. sdlr '1953 Moreni' sd and titled on the reverse (1953)
EXH.: *VI Mostra nazionale di pittura 'Golfo di La Spezia*, no.111.

Finearte Milan, 19 March 1996 (84**) ITL 29,900,000   US$ 19,130

MORET Henri (Cherbourg 1856-1913 Paris) French
LA PLAGE D'EGMOND, HOLLANDE oil on canvas, 23 7/8 x 32in. (60.3 x 81.3cm.) sdll 'Henry Moret 1900'; titled on the reverse 'La plage d'Egmond Hollande'
PROV.: Galerie Durand-Ruel, Paris; David Findlay Galleries, New York (acquired by the present pwner, ca. 1986).

Christie's New York, 1 May 1996 (185**) US$ 25,300   US$ 25,300

MER CALME A L'ILE DE GROIX oil on canvas, 16 x 25½in. (54 x 65cm.) sdlr 'H. Moret 96'
PROV.: Durand-Ruel, Archives no. 3974.

Étude Tajan Paris, 10 June 1996 (10**) FRF 270,000   US$ 52,137

AUX CHAMPS oil on canvas, 13¾ x 25½in. (35 x 62cm.) sdlr 'Henry Moret 1893'
EXH.: Japan, Osaka Tokyo-Niigata, *Terres d'inspiration des peintres de Pont-Aven, Nabis et Symbolistes*, 2 april - 14 April 1987, Les Éditions de Grénelle, p. 67, Paris, 1987.

Étude Tajan Paris, 13 December 1995 (25**) FRF 460,000   US$ 92,656

LE LAVOIR A DOELAN oil on canvas, 29 x 23¾cm. (73.5 x 60.5cm.) s 'Henry Moret'

Christie's London, 26 June 1996 (156**) GBP 20,700   US$ 31,920

LA COTE BRETONNE oil on canvas, 21¼ x 25 5/8in. (54 x 65cm.) slr 'Henri Moret'
PROV.: Jules Destrée, Co-owner of Durand-Ruel, Paris, and thence by descent to the present owner.

Christie's London, 29 November 1995 (117**) GBP 16,000   US$ 25,027

LES FALAISES ROSES, LA COTE DE L'ENFER, FINISTERE oil on canvas, 28¾ x 36 3/8in. (73 x 92.5cm.) sdlr '.Henry Moret. 97'; titled on the stretcher 'La Côte de l'Enfer-Finistere' (1897)
PROV.: Galeries Paul Durand-Ruel, Paris (1897); Galerie des Granges, Geneva.
EXH.: Paris, Galeries Durand-Ruel, *Henry Moret - 'La mer,'* May, 1898, no. 29.

Christie's New York, 8 November 1995 (122**) US$ 26,450   US$ 26,450

MORGAN Frederick, R.O.I. (1856-1927) British
THE GLEANERS oil on canvas, 29¾ x 19¾in. (75.5 x 50.1cm.) sdll 'Fred Morgan/1880'
EXH.: London, Royal Academy, 1880, no. 603.

Christie's New York, 22 May 1996 (270**) US$ 36,800   US$ 36,800

MORGENSTERN Christian Ernst Bernhard (1805-1867) German
VORGEBIRGSLANDSCHAFT MIT JÄGERN oil on canvas, 89 x 118.5cm. sd 'Chr. Morgenstern/1851/München'

Christie's Amsterdam, 25 April 1996 (269**) NLG 40,250   US$ 23,917

MORISOT Berthe Marie Pauline (Bourges 1841-1895 Paris) French
DAME A L'OMBRELLE oil on canvas, 36¼ x 28½in. (92 x 72.5cm.) (1881)
PROV.: Henri Rouart, Paris; Ernest Rouart, Paris; M. Knoedler & Co., Inc., London (1936); Carroll
Carstairs Gallery, New York (1937); T P. Wood, Toronto.
EXH.: Brussels, Palais des Beaux-Arts, *Berthe Morisot*, 1904, no. 19; Paris, Galerie Durand-Ruel,
Berthe Morisot (Madame Eugène Manet) 1841-1895, March, 1896, no. 24; Paris, Galerie Durand-
Ruel, Exposition Berthe Morisot, April-May, 1902, no. 6; Paris, Galerie Marcel Bernheim, *Réunion
d'oeuvres par Berthe Morisot)*, June-July, 1922, no. 2; Paris, Galerie Bernheim Jeune, Exposition
d'oeuvres de Berthe Morisot, May, 1929, no. 2; London, M. Knoedler & Co., Inc., Berthe Morisot,
May-June, 1936, no. 5 (illustrated); Montreal, Museum of Fine Arts, *Canada Collects European
Painting 1860-1960*, Jan.-Feb., 1960, p. 47, no. 103 (illustrated, p. 38).
LIT.: D. Rouart, *Berthe Morisot*, Paris, 1948, no. 30 (illustrated); M.L. Bataille and G. Wildenstein,
Berthe Morisot, Catalogue des peintures, pastels et aquarelles, Paris, 1961, p. 30, no. 104
(illustrated, fig. 137).
Christie's New York, 7 November 1995 (17**) US$ 794,500   US$ 794,500

JULIE EN ROSE AU BORD DU LAC (RECTO); JULIE DE DOS (VERSO) pastel on blue paper,
Image size: 20½ x 17½in. (52.1 x 44.4cm.); Sheet size(irregular): 24¾ x 18¾in. (62.8 x 47.6cm.)
stamped with signature lr on the recto 'Berthe Morisot' (Lugt 1826)); stamped with signature on the
verso 'Berthe Morisot' (1886)
PROV.: Sam Salz, Inc., New York; Gustave M. Berne, Great Neck, New York; Anon. sale, Sotheby
Parke Bernet Inc., New York, Oct. 23, 1980, lot 308 (acquired by the family of the present owner).
LIT.: M.-L. Bataille and G. Wildenstein, *Berthe Morisot, Catalogue des peintures, pastels et
aquarelles*, Paris, 1961, nos. 512a and 512b (illustrated, figs. 506 and 509).
Christie's New York, 8 November 1995 (119**) US$ 63,000   US$ 63,000

MORLAND George (London 1763-1804 London) British
RURAL AMUSEMENT; RUSTIC EMPLOYMENT oil on circular copper (a pair), 12¼in. (31.1cm.)
diameter
LIT.: G. Dawe, The Life of George Morland, London, 1904, the prints reproduced opposite pages 64
and 68 with transposed[?] titles; G.C. Williamson, *George Morland, His Life and Works*, London,
1907, the pont of Rustic Employment illustrated opposite p.112; J.T. Herbert Bailey, in An Extra
Number of *the Connoisseur*, 'George Morland', London, 1906, the prints reproduced as the
frontispiece and final illustration (p.124). J.R. Smith, as ovals, 1788; Reworked with altered
costumes and coloured, published by Ackermann's, 1814.
Christie's London, 10 November 1995 (33**) GBP 11,500   US$ 17,988

MORLEY Harry, A.R.A. (Leicester 1881-1943) British
THE MARRIAGE FEAST AT CANA oil on canvas, 48 x 61½in. (122 x 156cm.) sll 'Harry Morley'
PROV.: The Artist's Family.
EXH.: London, Royal Academy, *Summer Exhibition*, 1933, no.680; Liverpool, Walker Art Gallery,
1933, on loan from Salford Art Gallery; Bradford, Corporation Art Gallery, Cartwright Memorial
Hall, Loan no.783.
Christie's South Kensington, 26 October 1995 (71***) GBP 8,437   US$ 13,316

MORLEY Malcolm (1931 b.) American
NATIONAL OPEN acrylic on canvas-unframed, 50 x 60in. (127 x 152.4cm.) (1968)
PROV.: Kornblee Gallery, New York.
Christie's New York, 14 November 1995 (32**) US$ 173,000   US$ 173,000

SUNDAY IN ANTIGUA watercolour on paper, 22 x 30in. (55.8 x 76.2cm.) slr 'Malcolm Morley' s
again d titled 'Malcolm Morley Sunday in ANTIGA 86' on the reverse (1986)
PROV.: Acquired directly from the artist.
EXH.: Maastricht, Bonnefanten Museum; Basel Kunsthalle; Liverpool, Tate Gallery; Southampton,
The Parrish Art Museum, *Malcolm Morley Watercolours*, March 1991-Feb. 1992, no. 43 (ill.).
Christie's New York, 15 November 1995 (225**) US$ 17,250   US$ 17,250

403

MORLOTTI Ennio (Lecco 1910-1992 Milan) Italian
NUDE oil on canvas, 80 x 90cm. slr 'Morlotti'; sd on the reverse (1967)
    Finearte Milan, 18 June 1996 (182*) ITL 23,000,000 — US$ 14,916

ROSE oil on canvas, 55 x 70cm. sdlr 'Morlotti 56' and signed on the reverse (1956)
    Finearte Milan, 19 March 1996 (62**) ITL 59,800,000 — US$ 38,260

IMBERSAGO oil on canvas, 50 x 70cm. (1959)
EXH.: Turin, *Pittori d'oggi, Francia Italia*, 1959, no.54.
    Finearte Milan, 26 October 1995 (159**) ITL 70,150,000 — US$ 43,707

COLLINA AD IMBERSAGO oil on canvas, 60 x 72cm. sll 'Morlotti' sd on the reverse (1959)
EXH.: Turin, Galleria Gissi, E. Morlotti, *documenti di un decennio*, May 1965, no.16 of the catalogue.
    Finearte Milan, 26 October 1995 (190**) ITL 109,250,000 — US$ 68,069

ROCCE oil on canvas, 30 x 40cm. slc 'Morlotti' (1982)
LIT.: This work is recorded at 'Archivio Ennio Morlotti' under supervision of Galleria Ruggerini e Zonca, Milano.
    Sotheby's Milan, 28 May 1996 (168**) ITL 23,000,000 — US$ 14,772

AUTUNNO oil on canvas, 65.5 x 85.5cm. sd titled 'Merate 1959' on the reverse
PROV.: Galleria del Milione, Milano.
LIT.: This work is recorded at the 'Archivio Ennio Morlotti' under supervision of Galleria Ruggerini e Zonca, Milano.
    Sotheby's Milan, 28 May 1996 (171**) ITL 75,880,000 — US$ 48,735

MORONE Domenico (Verona 1442-1517) Italian
MERCURIUS DEFENDS THE CITY AGAINST AN INVASION tempera on board, diameter 30.5cm.
    Finearte Milan, 11 June 1996 (43**) ITL 74,750,000 — US$ 48,476

MORONI Giovanni Battista (attr.) (Albino, Bergamo 1528/30-1578 Bergamo) Italian
PORTRAIT OF BARTOLOMEO CAPPELLO, IN A BLACK BIRETTA AND WHITE SURPLICE, HOLDING A DOCUMENT INSCRIBED WITH HIS NAME oil on canvas, 35 x 29in. (88.5 x 73.5cm.) d inscr. 'ANNO DNI Mo.Do. XLVI DIE XX. APRILIS AGAMENON PASQUALETUS CONSENSIT. BART. CAPPELLUS.'
PROV.: Manchester, *Art Treasures*, 1857, no. 196, as by Moroni of Bartolomeo Cappello; Nottingham, 1968, no. 14, plate X, as Moroni; Nottingham, 1982, no. 60, as *Veronese School*, 16th Century; Sheffield, Graves Art Gallery, on loan, 1992 - 1994.
EXH.: Waagen, 1857, pp. 498-499, as *Moretto*; Richter, 1901, no. 55, reproduced, as Polidoro da Lanziano; A. Venturi, *Storia dell'Arte Italiana*, vol. IX, part IV, 1929, p. 277, as *Moroni*; Nicolson, 1968, p. 163, as *Veronese School*; Vertova, 1968, p. 27, as *Moroni*; Smart, 1968, p. 206, as *Moroni*; Calvocoressi, 1976, p. 143, as *Moroni*; D. Cugini, *Moroni pittore*, 1978, p. 302, no. 55, as *Moroni*.
    Sotheby's London, 6 December 1995 (24**) GBP 34,500 — US$ 53,093

MORTELMANS Frans (Antwerp 1865-1936 Antwerp) Belgian
PINK ROSES ON A MOSSY BANK oil on copper, 19 171 x 31 171in. (49.5 x 80cm.) slr 'F. Mortelmans'
    Christie's East, 30 October 1995 (134*) US$ 12,650 — US$ 12,650

A BUNCH OF ROSES IN A WOODED LANDSCAPE oil on canvas, 24¼ x 34in. (61.6 x 86.3cm.) sll 'F.Mortelmans'
    Christie's East, 30 October 1995 (148*) US$ 8,050 — US$ 8,050

MORTENSEN Richard (Copenhagen 1910 b.-l) Danish
CYRNOS oil on canvas, ,100 x 81cm. sd mono. 'R.M.dec 58' and inscr. with title on the stretcher
PROV.: Galerie Denise Renée, Paris.
Christie's Amsterdam, 6 December 1995 (262**) NLG 40,250 · US$ · 24,941

MOSER Koloman (1868-1918) Austrian
ROSA TULPEN IN GRUNER VASE oil on canvas, 80 x 88cm. slr with monogram 'KM'
LIT.: *Koloman Moser*, Hochschule für angewandte Kunst, Museum für angewandte Kunst, Vienna, 1979, p. 280, no. 118.
Dorotheum Vienna, 21 May 1996 (25**) ATS 500,000 · US$ · 48,012

GERANIEN oil on canvas, 50 x 50cm. sd mono. 'K.M. 1909'
PROV.: Family of the Artist.
Dorotheum Vienna, 6 December 1995 (434**) ATS 170,000 · US$ · 16,764

MOSS Marlow (1890-1958) British
COMPOSITION YELLOW BLUE BLACK RED & WHITE oil on canvas, 92 x 46cm. sdll 'Marlow Moss 1956-57'
PROV.: W.F.Nijhoff, Lausanne.
EXH.: Amsterdam, Stedelijk Museum, *Marlow Moss*, 1962, cat. no. 301, no.46; Arnhem, Gemeentemuseum, *Marlow Moss*, 1995.
Christie's Amsterdam, 5 June 1996 (366**) NLG 23,000 · US$ · 13,439

MOTHERWELL Robert Burns (Aberdeen, Washington 1915-1991 Provincetown) American
UNTITLED (OPEN) acrylic and charcoal on canvas, 54 x 60in. (137.2 x 152.4cm.) ini. and dur 'RM 71'
PROV.: Knoedler & Company, New York.
Christie's New York, 22 February 1996 (29**) US$ 63,000 · US$ · 63,000

BESIDE THE SEA, 21 oil on paper, 29 x 22¾in. (73.7 x 57.8cm.) slc 'Motherwell' and sdur ini. 'RM 62' and numb. '21' lr
PROV.: Sidney Janis Gallery, New York.
LIT.: H.H. Arnason, *Robert Motherwell*, New York 1982, p. 147, no. 177 (illustrated).
Christie's New York, 15 November 1995 (195**) US$ 36,800 · US$ · 36,800

LAKEROL COLLAGE paper collage on paper, 35 7/8 x 17 7/8in. (91 x 45.4cm.) d and ini. lr 'RM 73'
PROV.: Douglas Drake Gallery, New York.
Christie's New York, 8 May 1996 (263**) US$ 34,500 · US$ · 34,500

MOTTE Jean-François de la (1635-1685) French
TROMPE-L'OEUIL: VANITAS oil on canvas, 63 x 48cm.
Étude Tajan Paris, 26 March 1996 (75*) FRF 52,000 · US$ · 10,279

MOUCHERON Frédérick de (Emden 1633-1686 Amsterdam) Dutch
HUGHE WOODED LANDSCAPE WITH HORSEMEN AT SUNSET oil on canvas, 110 x 145cm. slr 'F. de Moucheron'
Dorotheum Vienna, 6 March 1996 (105**) ATS 300,000 · US$ · 28,857

MOWBRAY Henry Siddons (1858-1928) American
REPOSE-A GAME OF CHESS oil on canvas, 11 7/8 x 13 7/8in. (30.3 x 35.2cm.) slr 'H. Siddons Mowbray'
Christie's New York, 13 March 1996 (46**) US$ 43,700 · US$ · 43,700

MUELLER Otto (Liebau/Schlesien 1874-1930 Breslau) German
ZWEI SITZENDE AKTE coloured crayon and watercolour on paper, 52 x 69cm. slr 'Otto Mueller'

EXH.: Munich, *Homage à Günther Franke*, Villa Stuck 1983, cat. no. 135 (illustrated p. 93).
Hauswedell & Nolte Cologne, 1 December 1995 (481**) DEM 40,000   US$ 27,753

SECHS MADCHENAKTE AM STRAND watercolour and ink pen over pencildrawing, 24.3 x
31.4cm. slr 'Otto Mueller' (ca. 1913)
Hauswedell & Nolte Cologne, 5-6 June 1996 (588**) DEM 32,000   US$ 20,791

MÜHL Otto (Grodnau 1925 b.-) Austrian
UNTITLED oil on canvas, 138.5 x 180cm. s with mono. and dlr 'M. 17.1.84'
Wiener Kunst Auktionen, 26 March 1996 (472**) ATS 170,000   US$ 16,352

MULIER Pieter II, {called} Cavaliere Tempesta (Haarlem 1637-1701 Milan) Dutch
GOATS IN AN ITALIANATE LANDSCAPE WITH A FARM BEYOND oil on canvas, 120 x
171cm.
Sotheby's Amsterdam, 14 November 1995 (50**) NLG 27,140   US$ 17,105

MULIER Pieter the Elder (Haarlem 1615-1670 Haarlem) Dutch
BOATS ON ROUGH SEA oil on panel, 54.5 x 88.5cm. sl 'J.P.'
PROV.: From the collection Friedrich von Amerling (as Simon de Vlieger); Sale Dorotheum, 3 May
1916, catalogue no. 50, illustration 13 (as Simon de Vlieger); Private collection, Vienna.
Dorotheum Vienna, 6 March 1996 (102**) ATS 250,000   US$ 24,048

FISHERMAN IN A SMALSCHIP DRAWING IN THEIR NETS, WITH A THREEMASTER AND
OTHER SHIPPING BEYOND, IN A STIFF BREEZE oil on panel, 51.9 x 96.5cm. slr on a piece of
driftwood 'PM'
Christie's Amsterdam, 7 May 1996 (13**) NLG 14,950   US$ 8,717

MARINE oil on panel, 50.5 x 68.5cm. s mono on the drift-wood
Lempertz Cologne, 18 May 1996 (1106*) DEM 22,000   US$ 14,343

MÜLLER Jacques (Emden -1673 Utrecht) German
ORIENTAL FIGURES AMONG ROMAN RUINS oil on canvas, 49¼ x 64in. (125 x 163cm.) slr 'J.
Muller.f.'
Sotheby's London, 6 December 1995 (121**) GBP 8,050   US$ 12,388

MULLER Karl (Darmstadt 1818-1893 Neuenahr) German
CHRIST AT EMMAUS oil on canvas laid down on panel, 43 x 61in. (109.2 x 154.9cm.) sdll 'Carl
Muller/Dusseldorf 1856'
PROV.: Miss Nina Lea.
Christie's East, 13 February 1996 (1**) US$ 6,,900   US$ 6,900

MULLEY Oskar (Klagenfurt 1891-1949 Garmisch) Austrian
EINSAMER BERGHOF oil on canvas, 80 x 120cm. s 'Mulley'
Dorotheum Vienna, 24 April 1996 (518**) ATS 280,000   US$ 26,456

AM BERGHANG oil on canvas, 75 x 100cm. inscr. and sll 'MULLEY KUFSTEIN'; inscr. and titled
'AM BERGHANG MULLEY' on the reverse
PROV.: Kunstverlag Wolfrum, Vienna,.
Wiener Kunst Auktionen, 26 September 1995 (176**) ATS 110,000   US$ 10,692
MUNAKATA Shiko (Aomori Prefecture 1903-1975) Japanese
GODDES ink and colours on paper, framed and glazed, 25 3/8 x 12 7/8in. (64.6 x 32.7cm.) sll
'Munakata haisha' sealed 'Nanpo no in'
Christie's New York, 31 October 1995 (466**) US$ 19,550   US$ 19,550

MUNCH Edvard (Lyten 1863-1944 Ekely) Norwegian
FRÜHJAHR ÅSGÅRSTRAND oil on canvas, 31½ x 23 5/8in. (80 x 60cm.) sdll ' E. Munch 1905'

PROV.: Given by the Artist to Toralf Tidemand, Oslo and thence by descent to the present owner.
EXH.: Hamburg, Galerie Commeter, Jan. 1906, no. 101.
LIT.: Schiefler's correspondence with Edvard Munch, *Hamburger Geschichte* (Briefwechsel 1902-1914), Hamburg, 1987, no. 101 (illustrated p. 506).

Christie's London, 28 November 1995 (37**) GBP 298,500	US$	466,917

MUNKACSY Michel Lieb {called} Mihaly or Michael (Munkacs 1844-1909 Endenich, near Bonn) Hungarian
BRINGING IN THE NIGHT ROVERS oil on panel, 46½ x 67in. (118.1 x 170.2cm.) sdll 'M de Munkacsy/1881'
PROV.: Henry C.Gibson Collection, until 1892.

Christie's New York, 14 February 1996 (127**) US$ 31,050	US$	31,050

PHARISÄER oil on canvas, 45 x 34in. (114.3 x 86.2cm.) s 'M.Munkacsy' (ca 1880)
PROV.: Possibly with Charles Sedelmeyer, Paris.
LIT.: F. Walter Ilges, *M. von Munkacsy*, Bielefield and Leipzig, 1899, p. 5 no. 4 (illustrated).

Christie's London, 14 June 1996 (31**) GBP 25,300	US$	39,013

IN ERWARTUNG oil on panel, 81 x 63cm. s 'M. de Munkacy'
PROV.: Galerie Sedelmayer, Paris.

Dorotheum Vienna, 17 April 1996 (474**) ATS 200,000	US$	18,897

A RECLINING NUDE WOMAN HALF-LENGTH oil on panel, 32 x 25in. (81.3 x 63.5cm.) sll 'M.de Munkacsy'
PROV.: Galerie Sedelmeyer, Paris.

Christie's East, 30 October 1995 (13*) US$ 7,475	US$	74,75

MUNNINGS Sir Alfred, P.R.A., R.W.S. (1878-1959) British
STUDY FOR A START AT NEWMARKET oil on panel, 18 x 22in. (46 x 56cm.) s 'A.J. Munnings' (ca 1937)
PROV.: L. Morris, by whom purchased at the 1938 exhibition; St. James's Galleries, London.
EXH.: London, Leicester Galleries, *Paintings by A.J. Munnings, R.A.* 1928, April-May 1938, no. 65.

Christie's London, 20 June 1996 (53***) GBP 106,000	US$	163,454

OFF TO THE MEET oil on canvas, 33½ x 38½in. (85 x 97.5cm.) sll 'A. Munnings'

Christie's New York, 28 November 1995 (202A**) US$ 167,500	US$	167,500

GARDEN SCENE oil on canvas, 20 x 24in. (50.8 x 61cm.) slr 'A.J. Munnings'
PROV.: Baron Cassel van Doorn; Sale, Parke Bernet, New York, 6 December 1958, lot 105.

Christie's New York, 28 November 1995 (203**) US$ 299,500	US$	2995,00

NED OSBORNE ON GREY TICK oil on canvas, 18¼ x 21in. (46.5 x 53.3cm.) s 'A.J. Munnings' (1913)
LIT.: A.J. Munnings, *An Artist's Life*, Suffolk, 1950, p. 278.

Christie's London, 20 June 1996 (55**) GBP 67,500	US$	104,086

A HUNTING MORN oil on canvas, 16½ x 22½in. (42 x 57.2cm.) sll 'A.J. Munnings', inscr. on the stretcher 'A Hunting Morn' (ca 1902)

Christie's London, 21 March 1996 (102**) GBP 47,700	US$	72,847

HAYMAKING ON THE STOUR oil on canvas, 20 x 24in. (50.8 x 61cm.) slr 'A J Munnings' (ca 1920-25)
PROV.: Ian MacNicoll, Glasgow; Christie's, 16 Dec. 1949, lot 115 (35gns. to Athorpe); Arthur Ackermann & Son Ltd., London.

Christie's London, 21 March 1996 (107**) GBP 67,500	US$	103,085

SHRIMP AND THE WHITE PONY oil on canvas, 25 x 30¼in. (63.5 x 77cm.) sdlr 'A.J. Munnings 1909'
PROV.: Stanley Howes, thence to his widow, by whom given to the Norwich Arts Trust on 2 Dec. 1970.

Christie's London, 21 November 1995 (208**) GBP 205,000	US$	320,663

THE BELVOIR KENNELS oil on canvas, 20 x 24in. (50.8 x 61cm.) sll 'A.J. Munnings'
EXH.: London, Alpine Club Gallery, *Pictures of the Belvoir Hunt and Other Scenes of English Country Life by AJ. Munnings, R.A.*, April 1921, no.13; Norwich, Castle Museum, *Loan Collection of Pictures by A.J. Munnings, R.A.*, August-Sept. 1928, no.76.
LIT.: L. Lindsay (intro.), *AJ. Munnings, R.A. Pictures of Horses and English Life*, London, 1927, p.51 (illustrated); Sir AJ. Munnings, *The Second Burst*, London, 1951, p.71.

Christie's London, 21 November 1995 (209**) GBP 102,700	US$	160,644

MUNSCH Jozef (1832-1896 Munich) German
DIE WERBER oil on canvas, 40 x 57¾in. (101.5 x 146.5cm.) s & inscr. 'Jos Munsch. München'

Christie's London, 11 October 1995 (69**) GBP 12,650	US$	19,965

MÜNTER Gabriele (Berlin 1877-1962 Murnau) German
SCHNEEGIPFEL BEI SONNENUNTERGANG oil on canvasboard, 13 x 16in. (33 x 40.5cm.) slr 'Münter' (1924)
PROV.: Dalzell Hatfield Galleries, Los Angeles (Sept. 1963).
EXH.: Berlin, *Große Kunstausstellung, Novembergruppe*, 1926, no. 2056.

Christie's London, 29 November 1995 (214**) GBP 30,000	US$	46,926

MUNTHE Gerard Arij Ludwig 'Morgenstjerne' (Dusseldorf 1875-1927) Dutch (German)
BEACHING THE *BOMSCHUITEN* oil on canvas laid down on board, 55.5 x 78 cm sd 'G. Morgenstjerne Munthe 1909'

Christie's Amsterdam, 25 April 1996 (79*) NLG 16,100	US$	9,567

THE ROSKAMBRUG IN KATWIJK AAN DE RIJN, IN WINTER oil on canvas, 71 x 101 sdll 'G. Morgenstjerne Munthe 7

Christie's Amsterdam, 26 October 1995 (44*) NLG 10,350	US$	6,526

MURA Francesco de (1696-1782) Italian
THE HOLY FAMILY WITH ST. GIOVANNINO oil on canvas, 77 x 64,5cm.

Finearte Rome, 24 October 1995 (511**) ITL 34,500,000	US$	21,495

MURANT Emmanuel (Amsterdam 1622-1700 c. Leeuwarden) Dutch
VILLAGE WITH A CHURCH NEAR A RIVER AND FISHERMEN oil on panel, 48 x 64.5cm. s with monogram
PROV.: Private collection, Austria.

Dorotheum Vienna, 11 June 1996 (272**) ATS 120,000	US$	11,138

MURILLO Bartolomé Esteban (Seville 1618-1682 Sevilla) Spanish
CHRIST THE MAN OF SORROWS oil on canvas, 17¾ x 15 3/8in. (45 x 39cm.) (ca 1670)
PROV.: Mr. Frere, H.M. Consul at Madrid; J.P. Miles, Leigh Court, Bristol, by 1857.
EXH.: Manchester, *Art Treasures of the United Kingdom*, 1857, no. 801, as Luis de Morales.

Christie's London, 8 December 1995 (54**) GBP 43,300	US$	66,636

MURRAY Elizabeth (1940 b.-) American
TRY oil on shaped canvas, 55¾ x 54¼in. (139.1 x 137.8cm.) sd titled ''Try' Elizabeth Murray Aug-September 1979' on the reverse
PROV.: Paula Cooper Gallery, New York.

Christie's New York, 22 February 1996 (124**) US$ 11,500	US$	11,500

TWIST OF FATE oil on shaped canvas, 55¾ x 54¼in. (139.1 x 137.8cm.) sd and titled ;"Twist of Fate ' Dec.1979 Elizabeth Murray' on the reverse
PROV.: Paula Cooper Gallery, New York.

Christie's New York, 22 February 1996 (125**) US$ 11,500	US$	11,500

MUSIC Antonio Zoran (Gorizia 1909 b.) Italian
CANALE DELLA GIUDECCE oil on canvas, 25½ x 31¾in. (65 x 81cm.) sdlr 'Music 80' (1980)
PROV.: Bought directly from the artist by the current owner.

Étude Tajan Paris, 13 December 1995 (80**) FRF 120,000	US$	24,171

MOTIVA DALMATA oil on canvas, 22 x 26cm. sdll 'Music 66'; sd and titled on the reverse

Finearte Milan, 18 June 1996 (205**) ITL 23575,000	US$	15,289

CENSIMENTO APPENNINICO oil on canvas, 50 x 60cm. sdlr 'Music 69' sd and titled on the reverse (1969)

Finearte Milan, 19 March 1996 (38**) ITL 33,350,000	US$	21,337

PAYSAGE DALMATE oil on canvas, 18 x 25¾in. (45.7 x 65.4cm.) sdlc 'Music 1953'; sd and titled '1953'
PROV.: Collection of the artist; Galerie de France, Paris; Acquired from the above by the father of the present owner.

Sotheby's New York, 2 May 1996 (320**) US$ 96,000	US$	96,000

CAVALLINI oil on canvas, 46 x 60cm. sdlc 'Music 1953'
PROV.: La Boetie Gallery, New York; Collection Hélène Rubinstein.

Finearte Milan, 26 October 1995 (198**) ITL 138,000,000	US$	85,981

MOTIVO DALMATA oil on canvas, 60 x 74cm. sdlc 'Music / 951'; sd '1952' and titled on the reverse
LIT.: *Harper's Bazaar*, June 1963 (illustrated).

Sotheby's Milan, 28 May 1996 (218**) ITL 238,600,000	US$	153,243

PAESAGGIO oil on canvas, 25 1/8 x 36 1/8in. (64 x 92cm.) sdlc 'Music 1955'; sd and titled on the reverse 'Music 1955 Paesaggio' (1955)
PROV.: Acquired from the artist by the present owner *circa* 1970.

Christie's New York, 8 November 1995 (295**) US$ 48,300	US$	48,300

MUSIN François Etienne (Oostende 1820-1888 Sint-Joost-ten-Node) Belgian
FISHING BOATS OFF A CITY, THOUGHT TO BE ROTTERDAM oil on canvas, 46 x 70 7/8in. (117 x 180cm.) slr

Phillips London, 11th June 1996 (10**) GBP 12,000	US$	18,504

VESSELS IN A CALM BEFORE A TOWN oil on panel, 8 7/8 x 19¾in. (22.5 x 50.2cm. s

Phillips London, 12th March 1996 (5**) GBP 4,200	US$	6,414

MUSSCHER Michel van (Rotterdam 1645-1705 Amsterdam) Dutch
LA COUTURIERE ENDORMIE oil on oak panel, 32 x 25cm.
PROV.: Sale 8 Feb. 1892, no. 180, according to an old label on the reverse of the panel: 'Centre de rassemblement artistique de Baden Baden, no. 691'; Sale 23 Oct. 1952, no. 6

Étude Tajan Paris, 12 December 1995 (40**) FRF 40,000	US$	8,057

SEATED WOMAN IN AN INTERIOR FEDDING HER PET PARROT oil on panel, 16 x 14in. (40.6 x 35.6cm.) s on the reverse
PROV.: A.C Moltke, Christiansholm, Denmark; Rasmussen, Copenhagen, 7 November 1969; The Leger Galleries, Ltd. London, from whom purchased by the present owner.

Sotheby's New York, 16 May 1996 (35**) US$ 40,250	US$	40,250

MUTTONI Pietro {called} della Vecchia (Venice 1603-1678 Venice) Italian
PONTIUS PILATE DISPUTING WITH THE PHARISEES oil on canvas, 31½ x 44¾in. (80 x
113.7cm.)
        Christie's London, 19 April 1996 (201**) GBP 32,200   US$ 48,825

MY Hieronymous van der (LeYden 1687-1761 Leyden) Dutch
PORTAIT OF THE COMPOSER ANTON WILHELM SOLNITZ (CA. 1708-1758) oil on panel, 7½
x 6in. (19 x 15cm.) sdcl 'H. vand/Mij.f/1743 (?5).
        Sotheby's London, 5 July 1995 (118**) GBP 12,650   US$ 20,179

MYN Herman van der (Amsterdam 1684-1741 London) Dutch
ELEGANT COMPANY IN AN INTERIOR oil on canvas, 20¾ x 25¼in. (53 x 64cm.) inscr. with
ini. lc 'LA'
        Sotheby's London, 5 July 1995 (282**) GBP 11,500   US$ 18,344

MYTENS Jan (The Hague 1614 c.-1670 The Hague) Dutch
PORTRAIT OF HENRIETTE CATHARINE VAN NASSAU ORANGE (1673-1708), STANDING
SMALL HALF-LENGHT BY A FOUNTAIN, WEARING A YELLOW SILK DRESS AND
PEARLS, A SPANIEL DRINKING FROM A BOWL, A LANDSCAPE BEYOND oil on panel, 43 x
32.1cm. sll 'JAMijtens F:'
PROV.: Mrs. van der Steen van Ommeren-Van Beek, Amsterdam; anon sale, Paul Brandt,
Amsterdam, 11 May 1971, lot 31; with A.H. Bies, Eindhoven, 1973, from whom purchased by the
mother of the present owners.
        Christie's Amsterdam, 7 May 1996 (58*) NLG 19,550   US$ 11,399

PORTRAIT OF A LADY, SAID TO BE FRANCES STEWART, DUCHESS OF RICHMOND AND
LENNOX, AS DIANA THREE-QUARTER LENGHT, WEARING A LAVENDER AND WHITE
SATIN GOWN, BESIDE A DOG IN A LANDSCAPE oil on canvas, 41¼ x 32¼in. (104.8 x
81.9cm.)
PROV.: Lt. Col. G.B. Croft-Lyons, F.S.A.
        Sotheby's New York, 16 May 1996 (77**) US$ 26,450   US$ 26,450

PORTRAIT OF A LADY OF THE VAN RYSWYCK VAN DE SANDE FAMILY IN THE GUISE
OF DIANA oil on canvas, 43½ x 35¼in. (110.5 x 89.5cm.) sll 'Mytens F.'; inscr. with two coats of
arms ur
PROV.: Hermert(?) Collection, The Hague (according to an old lable on the reverse of the stretcher).
        Sotheby's New York, 6 October 1996 (183*) US$ 16,100   US$ 16,100

MYTENS Martin II van (Stockholm 1695-1770 Vienna) Dutch
PORTRAIT OF A YOUNG BOY oil on canvas, 20½ x 17¼in. (52 x 44cm.)
        Sotheby's London, 5 July 1995 (115**) GBP 9,200   US$ 14,675

EMPRESS MARIA THERESIA oil on canvas, 228.7 x 146.1cm.
        Wiener Kunst Auktionen, 26 March 1996 (29**) ATS 640,000   US$ 61,562

NAIVEU Mathijs (Leyden 1647-1721 Amsterdam) Dutch
SELF-PORTRAIT OF THE ARTIST AT A WINDOW HOLDING A PALETTE AND BRUSHES
oil on panel, 11¼ x 10 3/8in. (28.6 x 26.4cm.) s lower middle *M.Naiveu* and d lower middle *Anno 1679*
PROV.: The Norton Galleries, New York, From Whom purchased by the present owner in November 1962.
EXH.: The Cleveland Museum of Art, *Dutch Art & Life in the 17th Century*, July 10-September 2, 1973.

Sotheby's New York, 11 January 1996 (68**) US$ 57,500	US$	57,500

A YOUNG GIRL AT A WINDOW WITH A BASKET OF FRUIT AN A PLATE OF OYSTERS oil on canvas, 15¾ x 13¼in. (40 x 33.5cm.)

Sotheby's London, 18 October 1995 (23**) GBP 4,370	US$	6,897

NAKKEN Willem Carel (The Hague 1835-1926 Rijswijk) Dutch
A PEASANT-GIRL WITH CATTLE, CHICKENS AND GOATS IN FRONT OF A MEDIEVAL GATEWAY, IN SUMMER oil on canvas, 43.5 x 56cm. s 'W.C. Nakken.f.'

Christie's Amsterdam, 25 April 1996 (155*) NLG 19,550	US$	11,617

NANNINGA Jaap (Jacob) (Winschoten 1904-1962 The Hague) Dutch
UNTITLED oil on canvas, 70 x 80cm. sdlr 'J. Nanninga'60'
PROV.: Galerie Espace Amsterdam.
LIT.: Erik slagter, *Nanninga schilder*, Amsterdam 1987, no. 366.

Christie's Amsterdam, 5 June 1996 (288**) NLG 28,750	US$	16,798

A COMPOSITION gouache and crayon on paper, 46.5 x 55cm. sdlr 'Nanninga 61'
LIT.: Erik slagter, *Nanninga schilder*, Amsterdam 1987, no. 402.

Christie's Amsterdam, 5 June 1996 (289*) NLG 17,250	US$	10,079

NASH John, R.A. (1893-1977) British
THE SLUICE GATE oil on canvas, 24 x 26in. (61 x 66cm.) s 'John Nash' (1930)
PROV.: Mrs. C.F. Bennion.
EXH.: London, Royal Academy, *John Nash*, Sept.-Oct. 1967, no. 36.

Christie's London, 20 June 1996 (2**) GBP 11,500	US$	17,733

NASMYTH Alexander, H.R.S.A., R.B.A. (1758-1840) Scottish
THE SISTERS OF GLEN COE: AN EXTENSIVE VIEW OF GLEN COE, WITH DROVERS ON A BRIDGE oil on canvas, 27½ x 35½in. (70 x 90cm.) sd (twice) mono. and inscr. 'Edin. /1827'
PROV.: W.L. Peacock; Christie's 6 February 1925, lot 119, one of two (6½gns. to Sampson).

Christie's London, 18 April 1996 (38**) GBP 14,950	US$	22,669

NATKIN Robert (1930 b.) American
NAPOLIAN'S TRYST acrylic on canvas, 76 x 86in. (193 x 218.4cm.) sll 'Natkin'; sd and titled 'Natkin 'Napolian's TRYST' 1970' on the stretcher

Christie's East, 7 May 1996 (91*) US$ 14,950	US$	14,950

NATTIER Jean Marc (Paris 1685-1766 Paris) French
PORTRAIT OF A LADY LEANING ON A BALUSTRADE oil on canvas, 31 x 24¾in. (78.7 x 62.9cm.) sdcl '1754'
PROV.: Wildenstein & Co., New York; Mrs. William B. Weaver, Greenwich, Cinnecticut.
LIT.: The present work will be included in the forthcoming *catalogue raisonné of the works of Jean Marc Nattier*, to be published by the Wildenstein Institute.

Sotheby's New York, 11 January 1996 (233**) US$ 51,750	US$	51,750

NAUMAN Bruce (Fort Wayne, Indiana, USA 1941 b.) American
WELCOME SHAKING HANDS watercolour, graphite and gouache on two attached sheets of paper,

76½ x 85in. (194.3 x 216cm.) sdlr 'B.Nauman 85'
PROV.: Leo Castelli Gallery, New York; Anthony d'Offay Gallery, London; Private collection, Paris.
LIT.: C.van Bruggen, D.Koepplin and F.Mayer, *Bruce Nauman Drawings 1965-86*, Basel 1986,
p.30,no.483 (ill.).

Christie's New York, 8 May 1996 (346**) US$ 85,000	US$	85,000

NAY Ernst Wilhelm (Berlin 1902-1968 Cologne) German
TANZ oil on canvas, 47¼ x 54 7/8in. (120 x 139cm.) sdlr 'Nay 51' sd titled on the reverse
PROV.: Galerie Gunther Franke, Munich.
EXH.: Munich, Galerie Gunther Franke, *Ernst Wilhelm Nay*, 1951, no. 9.
LIT.: L. Grote, *Deutsche Kunst im 20. Jahrhundert*, Munich 1953, no. 63, illustrated; Aurel Scheibler
& Siegfried Gohr, *Ernst Wilhelm Nay Werkverzeichnis der Ölgemälde, Band I: 1922-1951*, Cologne
1990, p. 340, no. 643, illustrated in colour.

Sotheby's London, 21 March 1996 (42**) GBP 65,300	US$	99,725

IRISCH BLAU oil on canvas, 78¾ x 63in. (200 x 160cm.) sd 'Nay 64' sd titled '1964' on the reverse
PROV.: Galerie Gunther Franke, Munich.
EXH.: Munich, Haus der Kunst, *Grosse Kunstausstellung*, 1965, p. 61, no. 254, illustrated; Mexico
City, Museo de Arte Moderno, *Ernst Wilhelm Nay*, 1976, no. 21.
LIT.: In *'Die Kunst und das schone Heim'*, Munich 1965, vol. 63/11, p. 19, no. 2, illustrated; Aurel
Scheiber & Siegfried Gohr, *Ernst Wilhelm Nay, Werkverzeichnis der Ölgemälde, Band II: 1952-
1968*, Cologne, 1990, p. 275, no. 1126, illustrated in colour.

Sotheby's London, 21 March 1996 (44**) GBP 117,000	US$	178,681

UNTITLED watercolour on vellum, 59 x 41cm. sdlr 'Nay 58' (1958)

Lempertz Cologne, 28 November 1995 (807**) DEM 40,000	US$	8,233

NEEFFS Pieter the Elder (Antwerp 1578-1656-1661 Antwerp) Flemish
THE INTERIOR OF A GOTHIC CHURCH oil on copper, 72 x 88.5cm. sdlr 'Pieter Neeffs 33'
(1633)

Dorotheum Vienna, 6 March 1996 (17**) ATS 130,000	US$	12,505

SCENE D'INTÉRIEUR D'ÉGLISE GOTHIQUE oil on oak panel, 25.5 x 41cm.

Étude Tajan Paris, 12 December 1995 (38**) FRF 47,000	US$	9,467

NEEFFS Pieter the Younger (Antwerp 1620-1675, after Antwerp) Flemish
WORSHIPPERS IN THE AISLE OF ANTWERP CATHEDRAL oil on canvas, 50.7 x 66.5cm sll
'DE JONGE/NEEFS'
PROV.: Comte Cavens; Sale, Galerie le Roy Brussels, 1922, lot 138, as *Isaack van Nickelen*; Jules
and Jean Lalière, Namur, no. 25, as *Pieter Neefs I*.

Christie's Amsterdam, 13 November 1995 (149**) NLG 34,500	US$	21,743

NEER Aert van der (Amsterdam 1603/4-1677 Amsterdam) Dutch
A WOODED RIVER LANDSCAPE WITH A WOMAN AND CHILD BY A COTTAGE AND
SPORTSMEN ON A PATH BY A FOOTHBRIDGE oil on oak panel, 13¼ x 20in. (34 x 51cm.) sdlr
'A.V. NEER. 1635.'
PROV.: Martin B. Asscher, London, 1941; Anonymous sale, ('The Property of a Gentleman'),
London, Christie's, 28 November 1975, lot 72.
EXH.: On loan, York City Art Gallery, March 1980-September 1986; On loan, Doncaster Museum
and Art Gallery, 1990-1993.
LIT.: Anon., 'Some Unpublished Seventeenth Century Dutch Paintings', *The Burlington Magazine*,
vol. LXXXI, December 1942, pp. 306-7 (illustrated pl. IIB); F. Bachmann, *Aert van der Neer*, 1982,
pp. 21-2, (ilustrated pl. 3).

Sotheby's London, 5 July 1995 (45**) GBP 89,500	US$	142,766

MOONLIT RIVER LANDSCAPE oil on panel, 7 x 9½in. (17.8 x 24.1cm.) slr 'A VN'
PROV.: Charles Carstairs, Esq. London and New York; Charles S. Towers, Huntington, New York
(Sale: Parke-Bernet Galleries, New York, 12 January 1955; lot 18 (illustrated); there purchased by
present owner).
Sotheby's New York, 16 May 1996 (167A**) US$ 36,800	US$	36,800

A MARSHY LANDSCAPE WITH FIGURES GATHERING REEDS oil on oak panel (an oval),
15½ x 20¾in. (39.2 x 52.7cm.) slr 'V.Neer' (ca. 1640)
EXH.: London, Johnny van Haeften, catalogue III, 1894, no. 23.
LIT.: This picture will be included in Wolfgang Schulz's forthcoming *catalogue raisonné of van der
Neer's paintings.*
Sotheby's London, 6 December 1995 (40**) GBP 32,200	US$	49,554

A MOONLIT RIVER LANDSCAPE oil on panel, 41 x 53cm. bears monogram lr 'AVDN'
Sotheby's Amsterdam, 6 May 1996 (48*) NLG 19,470	US$	11,353

A MOONLIT VILLAGE RIVER LANDSCAPE WITH BOATS oil on canvas, 26¾ x 38¼in. (68 x
97.4cm.)
PROV.: Major E.H. Griffith; Herbert Giradet, Kettwig, by 1970.
EXH.: London, Royal Academy, *Winter Exhibition*, 1910, no. 98; Solingen, *Niederländischen
Landschaften un Seestücken des 17. Jahrhunders aus westdeutschem Privatbesitz*, 1965-66, no. 32
(illustrated); Cologne & Rotterdam, *Sammlung Herbert Giradet,Holländische und Flämische
Meister*, Jan.-June 1970, no. 35 (illustrated, as s with monogram lr 'AV DN').
LIT.: C. Hofstede de Groot, *A Catalogue Raisonné..*, 1918, vol VII, no. 230, p. 416.
Sotheby's London, 5 July 1995 (257**) GBP 41,100	US$	65,561

NEGRI Pietro (Venice 1635/40 c.-1679 c. Venice) Italian
MERCURY AND ARGUS oil on canvas, 52 x 66¼in. (132 x 168cm.)
Sotheby's London, 18 October 1995 (69**) GBP 17,250	US$	27,225

NELSON Joan (1958 b.) American
UNTITLED oil and encaustic on panel-unframed, 14 7/8 x 14 7/8in. (37.8 x 37.8cm.) sd and
numbered 'Joan Nelson 1988 224' on the reverse
PROV.: Michael Kohn Gallery, Los Angeles.
Christie's New York, 15 November 1995 (368**) US$ 19,550	US$	19,550

NESCH Rolf (Oberesslingen 1893-1975 Oslo) German
PORT D`AMI green verdigris copperplate, ,100 x 117cm.
PROV.: Von der Heydt-Museum, Wuppertal (on loan).
EXH.: Hamburg/Bremen/Düsseldorf/Stuttgart 1958/1959, *Rolf Nesch* Cat. no. 234; Berlin; 1956
Akademie der Kuenste, *Rolf Nesch*, Cat. no. 22.
Lempertz Cologne, 29 November 1995 (366*) DEM 55,000	US$	38,820

NEVELSON Louise (1900-1988) American
FORGOTTEN CITY wall relief-wood, painted black, 31½ x 18½ x 1¾in. (80 x 47 x 4.5cm.) (1985)
PROV.: The Pace Gallery, New York.
Christie's New York, 22 February 1996 (27**) US$ 19,550	US$	19,550

FLOATING CLOUD VIII wall relief-wood, painted white, 30½ x 60 x 7½in. (77.4 x 152.3 x 19cm.)
PROV.: The Pace Gallery, New York.
Christie's New York, 22 February 1996 (35**) US$ 27,600	US$	27,600

DAWN'S LANDSCAPE XXXVI wall relief-wood, painted white, 47¼ x 39¼ x 6in. (120 x 99.7 x
15.2cm.) (1976)
PROV.: The Pace Gallery, New York.
Christie's New York, 22 February 1996 (41**) US$ 48,300	US$	48,300

DAWN'S LANDSCAPE XXXVI wall relief-wood painted white, 47¼ x 39¼ x 6in. (120 x 99.7 x 15.2cm.) (1976)
PROV.: The Pace Gallery, New York.

Christie's New York, 22 February 1996 (41**) US$ 48,300	US$	48,300

NEWMAN Barnett (New York 1905-1970 New York) American
THE WORD II oil on canvas-unframed, 90½ x 70½in. (230.5 x 179cm.) sdlr 'Barnett Newman 1954'
PROV.: Acquired directly from the artist in 1966; S.I. Newhouse, New York; Gagosian Gallery, New York.
EXH.: New York, Museum of Modern Art, *Barnett Newman*, Oct. 1971-Jan. 1972, p. 82 (illustrated); Bonn, Kunst und Ausstellungshalle der BRD, *Territorium Artis*, 1992, pp. 232-233 (illustrated); Berlin, Martin-Gropius-Bau, and London, Royal Academy of Arts, *American Art in the 20th Century: Painting and Sculpture 1913-1993*, May-Dec. 1993, no. 111 (illustrated); Hamburg Kunsthalle, *Kline, Newman, Rauschenberg, Still*, Dec. 1994-Jan. 1995.
LIT.: H. Rosenberg, *Barnett Newman*, New York 1978, no. 4 (illustrated).

Christie's New York, 14 November 1995 (37***) US$ 3,027,500	US$	3,027,500

NEYN Pieter de (Leyden 1597-1639) Dutch
FLUSSLANDSCHAFT MIT EINER FÄHRE oil on panel, 75 x 116cm.

Lempertz Cologne, 18 May 1996 (1110a*) DEM 14,500	US$	9,453

NEYTS Gillis (Ghent 1623-1687 Antwerp) Flemish
WOODED RIVERLANDSCAPE WITH A FARMERSHAUS AND SHEPHERDS oil on panel, 24 x 35cm. sll 'g. nyts. f'

Dorotheum Vienna, 6 March 1996 (16**) ATS 130,000	US$	12,505

AN EXTENSIVE LANDSCAPE WITH FIGURES SHOOTING BY A MARSH, A RUINED CASTLE BEYOND oil on panel, 14½ x 23½in. (36.8 x 59.7cm.) inscr. 'R. Savery'
PROV.: Felix Ziethen, Munich; Sale: Hugo Helbing, Munich, 22 September 1934, lot 58 (as Roelant Savery); The Brod Gallery, London.

Sotheby's New York, 16 May 1996 (134**) US$ 17,250	US$	17,250

NICHOLSON Ben, O.M. (Denham, Buckinghamshire 1894-1982) British
DECEMBER 31-49 (STILL-LIFE - WINTER) oil on canvas mounted on board, 32¾ x 28¼in. (83.2 x 71.8cm.) sd on the overlap '31 December 1949'
PROV.: Acquired from the artist; Durlacher Bros., New York; Sale: New York, Parke-Bernet Galleries, November 18, 1964, lot 110; Acquired by the Benjamin family from the above.
EXH.: New Haven, Yale University Art Gallery, *The Helen and Robert M. Benjamin Collection*, 1967, no. 130; Buffalo, Albright-Knox Art Gallery; Washington, D.C., Hirshhorn Museum and Sculpture Garden; New York, Brooklyn Museum, *Ben Nicholson: Fifty Years of His Art*, 1978-79, no. 49.
LIT.: J.P. Hodin, *Ben Nicholson: The Meaning of His Art*, London, 1957, pl.31, illustrated.

Sotheby's New York, 2 May 1996 (270**) US$ 118,000	US$	118,000

JAN 64 (BLACK PRINCE) oil on carved board, mounted in the artist's frame, 32¾ x 27¼in. (83.2 x 69.2cm.) (1964)
PROV.: Andre Emmerich Gallery, New York; Acquired from the above by the Benjamin family in 1964.
EXH.: New Haven, Yale University Art Gallery, *The Helen W. and Robert M.Benjamin Collection*, 1967,no. 131; Lincoln, Massachussetts, De Cordova Museum, *The British Are Coming!*, 1975, no. 45.
LIT.: *Exhibition catalogue*, Emmerich Gallery and Marlborough-Gerson, *Ben Nicholson 1955-65*, New York, 1965, no. 74 (not included in the exhibition).

Sotheby's New York, 2 May 1996 (273**) US$ 96,000	US$	96,000

NOV 1960 (ANNE) oil on carved board, 34½ x 20in. (87.6 x 50.8cm.) s titled on the reverse (1960)
PROV.: André Emmerich Gallery, New York; Acquired from the above by the Bejamin family in 1962.
EXH.: Buffalo, Albright-Knox Art Gallery, 1962 New Haven, Yale University Art Gallery, *The Helen and Robert M. Benjamin Collection*, 1967, no. 131.

Sotheby's New York, 2 May 1996 (274**) US$ 79,500	US$	79,500

4 FORMS pencil and wax crayon on paper, 15½ x 14½in. (39.4 x 36.8cm.) sd '1972' on the reverse
PROV.: André Emmerich Gallery, New York; Acquired from the above by the Benjamin family in 1974.
EXH.: New York, André Emmerich Gallery, *Ben Nicholson, Works on Paper (An exhibition in honour of the artist's 80th birthday)*, 1974.

Sotheby's New York, 2 May 1996 (278**) US$ 9,775	US$	9,775

PROJECT 1945-46 gouache, watercolour and pencil on card laid down on the Artist's prepared backboard in the Artist's original frame, 9 x 12in. (23 x 30.5cm.) sd titled and inscr. 'Ben Nicholson project 1945-46'
PROV.: The Artist, by whom exhibited at the British Council exhibition in 1947-48; Rachel Adler Gallery, New York.
EXH.: London, British Council, *Modern British Paintings for Europe 1947-1948*.

Christie's London, 26 June 1996 (268**) GBP 18,400	US$	28,373

ROSEVEOR oil and pencil on cut masonite in the artist's frame, 13 1/2 x 16in. (34.3 x 40.7cm.) on the reverse 'Ben Nicholson June 56 (Roseveor)' (1956)
PROV.: Gimpels Fils Ltd., London (acquired by the late owner, 1958).

Christie's New York, 8 November 1995 (220**) US$ 81,700	US$	81,700

NIEULANDT Willem, the Younger (1584-1635) Dutch /Flemish
THE CASTEL SANT'ANGELO AND THE PONTE SANT'ANGELO, ROME, SEEN FROM ACROSS THE TIBER, WITH SAINT PETER'S AND THE VATICAN BEYOND, ELEGANT TRAVELLERS DISEMBARKING FROM A BARGE IN THE FOREGROUND oil on panel, 46.8 x 72.1cm. dll '1611'
PROV.: Anon. Sale, Lepke Berlin, 21 March 1934, lot 672, as *Paul Bril* with P. de Boer, Amsterdam, ca. 1935.

Christie's Amsterdam, 7 May 1996 (38**) NLG 46,000	US$	26,822

ROME, THE FORUM oil on panel, 26 x 37¾in. (66 x 96cm.)

Sotheby's London, 6 December 1995 (123**) GBP 10,925	US$	1,6813

NIGRO Mario (Pistoia 1917-1992 Pistoia) Italian
DALLO 'SPAZIO TOTALE' oil on canvas, 73 x 50cm. sd titled on the reverse (1953-54)

Finearte Milan, 12 December 1995 (307**) ITL 16,675,000	US$	10,461

PROGETTO PER PANNELLO tempera on paper, 44 x 27cm. sdlr 'M. Nigro 50' (1950)
EXH.: Milan, Padiglione d'Arte Contemporanea, *Omaggio a Mario Nigro*, 25 March/25 April 1994.

Finearte Milan, 26 October 1995 (171**) ITL 12,650,000	US$	7,882

NIKEL Lea (1918 b.-)
COMPOSITION acrylic and collage on canvas, 63.8 x 79.8cm. (162 x 202.2cm.) sdlc 'Lea Nikel 89'; sd again on the reverse
EXH.: Tel Aviv, Givon Gallery, *Lea Nikel*, 1990 (illustrated in colour).

Christie's Tel Aviv, 12 October 1995 (104**) US$ 13,800	US$	13,800

NITSCH Hermann (1938 b.) Austrian
AKTIONSRELIKT blood, anilinecolours on wool on molino, 166 x 237cm. (ca. 1980)

Wiener Kunst Auktionen, 26 March 1996 (401**) ATS 200,000	US$	19,238

GROßES BLUTBILD blood, chalk, material, paper and plaster on canvas, 140 x 116cm. inscr. '..und sogleich floß Blut und Wasser heraus.' (1964)
EXH.: Turin, Galerie LP 220.
       Wiener Kunst Auktionen, 27 September 1995 (473**) ATS 180,000   US$ 17,497

SCHÜTTBILD dispersion and washed crayon on jute, 105 x 80cm. sd 'hermann nitsch 1962' on the reverse
       Wiener Kunst Auktionen, 29 November 1995 (877**) ATS 130,000   US$ 13,041

NOBLE John Sargent, R.B.A. (1848-1896) British
OTTER HUNTING oil on canvas, 36 x 56½in. (91.5 x 43.5cm.) s
PROV.: see also Walter H. W. Foster (51) co-painter.
       Phillips London, 10 October 1995 (51*) GBP 6,000   US$ 9,470

,
NOGARI Giuseppe (Venice 1699-1763 Venice) Italian
A PEASANT WOMAN HOLDING A BOWL OF SOUP oil on canvas, 22 x 15¾in. (56 x 40cm.)
       Sotheby's London, 5 July 1995 (213**) GBP 6,900   US$ 11,007

A YOUNG LADY PLAYING ON A MANDOLINE oil on canvas, 80 x 40.5cm.
PROV.: R. Pallucchini, *La pittura veneziana del Settecento*, 1994, 1, fig. 910.
       Dorotheum Vienna, 6 March 1996 (53**) ATS 250,000   US$ 24,048

PORTRAIT OF A GENTLEMAN oil on canvas, 60 x 46.5cm
       Finearte Milan, 25 November 1995 (70**) ITL 23,000,000   US$ 14,438

NOLAND Kenneth (Asheville, N. Carolina 1924 b.) American
SILENT ADIOS acrylic on canvas, 17 x 40 1/8in. (43 x 102cm.) sd and titled on the reverse '1970'
       Christie's London, 19 March 1996 (61**) GBP 8,050   US$ 12,294

COURSE magna on canvas, 69 x 64in. (175.2 x 162.5cm.) titled 'Course' on the reverse (1959)
PROV.: Galleria dell'Ariete, Milan.
EXH.: New York, French & Co., *Kenneth Noland*, Oct. 1959, no. 24; Milan, Galleria dell'Ariete, *Kenneth Noland*, Nov. 1960, no. 2.
       Christie's New York, 14 November 1995 (21**) US$ 200,500   US$ 200,500

WARM ABOVE acrylic on canvas, 25½ x 166½in. (64.8 x 422.8cm.) sd and titled 'WARM ABOVE Kenneth Noland 1968' on the reverse
PROV.: André Emmerich Gallery, New York.
       Christie's New York, 22 February 1996 (42**) US$ 12,650   US$ 12,650

ETERNAL SCHOLAR acrylic on canvas-unframed, 64½ x 156in. (163.9 x 396.2cm.) (1969)
PROV.: Wadington Galleries, London.
       Christie's East, 7 May 1996 (78**) US$ 17,250   US$ 17,250

REGAL GREY acrylic on canvas, 61 3/8 x 114¼in. (155.9 x 290.2cm.) sd and titled 'REGAL GREY Kenneth Noland 1970' on the reverse
PROV.: Kasmin Limited, London.
EXH.: New York, The Solomon R. Guggenheim Museum, *Kenneth Noland: A Retrospective*, April-June 1977, p. 141, no. 102 (illustrated).
       Christie's East, 7 May 1996 (82**) US$ 17,250   US$ 17,250

NOLDE Emil Hansen, {called} (Nolde 1867-1956 Seebüll) German
BERGSEE watercolour on paper, 34.7 x 47.5cm. slr 'Nolde'
       Hauswedell & Nolte Cologne, 1 December 1995 (497**) DEM 98,000   US$ 67,994

ROTE, VIOLETTE UND GELBE BLÜTEN watercolour on paper, 22.8 x 27.2cm. slr 'Nolde' (ca. 1935)

Hauswedell & Nolte Cologne, 1 December 1995 (498**) DEM 110,000	US$	76,320

JUNGE MARABUS watercolour on paper, 46.9 x 35cm. slr (before 1928)
PROV.: Salman Schocken, Berlin.
EXH.: Berlin, Galerie Ferdinand Möller, *Emil Nolde. Aquarell-Ausstellung*, 1928, catalogue no. 34 (illustrated in colour).

Hauswedell & Nolte Cologne, 5/06 June 1996 (615**) DEM 110,000	US$	71,470

ZWEI FRAUEN watercolour on paper, 22.2 x 15.3cm. slc 'Nolde'

Hauswedell & Nolte Cologne, 5/06 June 1996 (616**) DEM 110,000	US$	71,470

ROTE BLÜTEN VOR BERGLANDSCHAFT watercolour on simili-Japon, 35.5 x 47.1cm. sll 'Nolde' (1951-51)

Lempertz Cologne, 1 June 1996 (908***) DEM 110,000	US$	71,470

FRAU, KOPF STÜTZEND (SCHIEFLER-MOSEL 12) lithograph with extensive hand-colouring in watercolour, framed, 19 1/8 x 15¾in. (48.5 x 40cm.) s in pencil, inscr. in various other hands at the bottom sheet edge (1907)
EXH.: Chicago, Museum of Contemporary Art, *Art in a Turbulent Era*, March-April, 1978.

Christie's New York, 1 May 1996 (302**) US$ 39,100	US$	39,100

MEER UND ABENDWOLKEN oil on canvas, 26¼ x 34¾in. (66.6 x 88.3cm.) slr 'Emil Nolde', signed again and titled on the stretcher 'Emil Nolde, Meer und Abendwolken' (1936)
PROV.: Purchased by the present owner's father in 1956.
LIT.: *The Artist's Handlist*, 1930, recorded as *1936 Meer u. Abendwolken*; M. Urban, *Emil Nolde Catalogue Raisonné of the Oil Paintings*, vol. II, *1915-51*, London, 1990, no. 1163 (illus. p. 452).

Meer und Abendwolken

Christie's London, 11 October 1995 (139**) GBP 837,500	US$	1,321,812

SOMMERNACHMITTAG oil on canvas, 28½ x 34½in. (72.5 x 87.5cm.) sdll 'Emil Nolde 1903'
PROV.: Niels Bonnichsen,Stemmild, Denmark; Nolde's Nephew, to Whom given by the Artist; Emil Bonnichsen, Bylderup, Bov, Denmark, brother of the above, thence by descent to the present owners.
EXH.: Lübeck, Kunstverein, *Kunstausstellung in der Katharinenkirche*, 1904, no.36; Tønder.

Christie's London, 11 October 1995 (141**) GBP 309,500	US$	488,479

BLUMENGARTEN oil on camvas, 25¾ x 32 5/8in. (65.4 x 82.4cm.) sdlr 'Emil Nolde 8' sd & titled on the strecher (1908)
PROV.: Frau E. Lüyken, Hamburg (circa 1911-12); Schwartz, Icking, Munich; Anon. sale, Stuttgarter Kunstkabinett, Stuttgart, Nov. 1958, no. 766 (illustated in colour); H. Knecht, Stuttgart; Private collection, Hamburg.
EXH.: Hamburg, Galerie Commeter, *Nolde*, April 1911; Hamburg, Galerie Rudolf Hoffmann, *Nolde*, Oct.-Nov. 1946.
LIT.: *The Artist's Handlist*, 1910; a: no. 163; b: no. 165; c:no. 188; *The Artist's Handlist*, 1930 (as 1908 Blumengarten, junge und ältere Frau); W. Hoffmann, *Malerei im 20. Jahrhundert*, Munich, 1965 (illustated p. 57); M. Urban, *Emil Nolde Catalogue Raisonné of the Oil Paintings,* vol. I, 1895-1914, London, 1987, no. 271 (as 1908 Blumengarten (junge und ältere Frau)) (illustrated p. 244).

Christie's London, 11 October 1995 (144**) GBP 705,500	US$	1,113,479

JUNGE JÜDIN oil on canvas, 18 1/8 x 14¼in. (46.3 x 36.2cm.) slr 'Nolde' (1918)
PROV.: Wilhelm R. Valentiner, Berlin (before 1930); The Detroit Institute of Arts, Detroit (on loan from the above); Brigitta Valentiner-Bertoia, Barto, Pennsylvania; Gallerie Wilhelm Grosshennig, Düsseldorf (1966-67); Friedrich Flick, Düsseldorf.
EXH.: Dresden, Künstlervereinigung, *Sommerausstellung,* 1919, no. 96.
LIT.: M. Heiden, 'Neue Deutsche Kunst im Detroit Museum of Art' in *Museum der Gegenwart,* vol. 2, no. 1, Berlin, 1931, pp. 13-22; *Weltkunst,* vol. 36, no. 17, Munich, 1966 (illustated p. 768); M. Urban, *Emil Nolde, Catalogue Raisonné of the Oil Paintings,* vol. II, 1915-1951, London, 1990, no. 818 (illustrated p. 183).

Christie's London, 11 October 1995 (156**) GBP 397,500	US$	627,367

ROTER UN BLAUER MOHN watercolour on japan paper, 14 x 18½in. (35.6 x 47cm.) sll 'Nolde'
PROV.: Galerie Wilhelm Grosshennig, Düsseldorf; Acquired form the above by the present owner in the 1950s.

Sotheby's New York, 2 May 1996 (230**) US$ 156,500	US$	156,500

NOMÉ François Didier, {called} Monsú Desiderio (I) (with Cornelio Brusco (act. first half 18th century) (Metz 1593-ca. 1640 active Naples) Italian (French)
THE CONVERSION OF ST. PAUL oil on canvas, 76 x 101cm.
LIT.: M.R. Nappi *François De Nomé e Didier Barra, l'enigma Monsu Desiderio,* Rome, 1991 A, pp. 51-52 (illustrated).

Christie's Rome, 4 June 1996 (568**) ITL 56,000,000	US$	36,316

NONNOTTE Donat (1708-1785)
PORTRAIT OF A YOUNG NOBLEWOMAN, SEATED SMALL HALF-LENGTH, WEARING A RICHLY ORNATED PINK SILK DRESS, LACE CHEMISE AND CAP, HER PET DOG ON A TABLE BESIDE HER oil on canvas, 73 x 59cm. sll with initials 'D L'

Christie's Amsterdam, 13 November 1995 (21**) NLG 21,850	US$	13,771

PORTRAIT DU DOCTEUR DAVIEL, OCULISTE DU ROI oil on canvas, 98 x 79cm.
PROV.: Sale Mr P.M., Paris Galerie Georges Petit 28 May 1909, no. 5 (illustrated); Anonymous Sale, Paris Hotel Drouot, 5 December 1955, no. 19.

Étude Tajan Paris, 12 December 1995 (58**) FRF 70,000	US$	14,100

NOOMS Reinier, {called} Zeeman (1623 c.-1667 before) Dutch
A CALM: A *WIJDSCHIP* RUNNING, WITH FISHERMEN DRAWING IN NETS NEARBY; A STORM: A *TJALK* TACKING, A PINK, WITH ITS MAST LOWERED, IN THE FOREGROUND. both oil on canvas laid down on panel, 16.3 x 24.8cm. the first slr 'R Zeeman', the second with signature ll 'R Zeeman'
PROV.: With Enneking, Amsterdam, 1956.
EXH.: Delft, Prinsenhof, *VIIIe Oude Kunst en Antiekbeurs,* 10 August - 2 September 1956.

Christie's Amsterdam, 13 November 1995 (99*) NLG 27,600	US$	17,395

NOORDT Pieter van (active 1626-1648 in Leyden) Dutch
A STILL-LIFE OF FISH ARRANGED ON A TABLE WITH GAME oil on canvas, 102 x 152cm.

Sotheby's Amsterdam, 6 May 1996 (58*) NLG 14,160	US$	8,257

NOORT Adam van (1562-1641) Flemish
MADONNA AND CHILD oil on panel, 31¼ x 22 3/8in. (79.4 x 56.8cm.)
PROV.: Goudstikker, Amsterdam (acc. to an old label on the reverse); purchased by the grandparents of the present owners prior to 1929.

Sotheby's New York, 11 January 1996 (191**) US$ 23,000	US$	23,000

NORDENBERG Bengt (1822-1902) Swedish
NATTVARDSGÅNG oil on canvas, 83 x 120cm. sdll 'B. Nordenberg 1866'
EXH.: Düsseldorf, Verein Düsseldorfer Künstler zu gegenseitiger Unterstützung & Hilfe, Comission

für aus värtige Ausstellungen.

| | Bukowskis Stockholm, 29 November-1 December 1995 (112**) SEK 120,000 | US$ | 18,153 |

I SAKRISTIAN oil on canvas, 82 x 120cm. sd 'B. Nordenberg 1864'

| | Bukowskis Stockholm, 29 November-1 December 1995 (113**) SEK 85,000 | US$ | 12,859 |

NORMANN Adelsteen (1848-1918) Norwegian
A NORWEGIAN FJORD oil on canvas, 44½ x 69½in. (113.1 x 176.5cm.) slr 'A. Normann'

| | Christie's New York, 2 November 1995 (57**) US$ 27,600 | US$ | 27600 |

,
A NORWEGIAN FJORD oil on canvas, 35 x47in. (88.9 x 119.4cm.) sll 'A.Normann'
PROV.: Vicars Brothers, London.

| | Christie's East, 30 October 1995 (88*) US$ 12,650 | US$ | 12,650 |

NOTER David Emil Josef de (1825-1875 Alger) Belgian
A WOMAN IN AN INTERIOR WITH A VASE OF FLOWERS oil on canvas, 32 x 26½in (81.3 x 67.3cm.) slr 'David de Noter'

| | Christie's New York, 2 November 1995 (87**) US$ 18,400 | US$ | 18,400 |

NOTTE Emilio (Ceglie Messapico 1891-1982 Napoli) Italian
RITRATTO DI SALVATORE QUASIMODO oil on panel, 60 x 40cm sd 'E.Notte 1939'

| | Finearte Rome, 14 November 1995 (213 bis**) ITL 23,000,000 | US$ | 14,438 |

NOURSE Elizabeth (1859-1938) American
CAPPUCHIN MONK oil on canvas, 39 x 29in. (99 x 73.6cm.) slr 'E. Nourse'
PROV.: Cincinnati Art Galleries, Cincinnati, Ohio.

| | Christie's New York, 13 September 1995 (36**) US$ 17,250 | US$ | 17,250 |

NOVELLI Gastone (Vienna 1925-1968 Milan) Italian
LA MOTAGNA DEGLI ADEPTI mixed media on canvas, 135 x 135cm. slr; sd '62' and titled on the reverse
PROV.: Marlborough Gallery, Rome; Galleria Levi, Milan.
EXH.: Termoli, Castello Svevo, *Premio Termoli*.
LIT.: Zeno Birolli, *Novelli*, Milan 1976, p. 225, no. 1962.56 (309)(illustrated).

| | Sotheby's Milan, 28 May 1996 (229**) ITL 119,950,000 | US$ | 77,039 |

NOVELLI Pietro, {called} Monrealese (1603-1648) Italian
CHRIST IN THE HOUSE OF MARY AND MARTHA oil on canvas, 50 x 70in. (127 x 177.8cm.)
PROV.: J.W. Brett, 1833; E. Dwight, 1837, by whonm given to an institution by whom owned until the early 1990s.
EXH.: Boston, Boston Athenaeum, 1837, no. 9 (as by 4ft. 1 in.); Boston, Boston Athenaeum, 1837, no. 116 (as by Caravaggio).
LIT.: Robert F. Perkins and William J. Gavin, *Boston Athenaeum Art Exhibition Index, 1827-1874*, 1980, p. 30, p. 285.

| | Sotheby's New York, 11 January 1996 (174**) US$ 46,000 | US$ | 46,000 |

HERCULES AND ONPHALE oil on canvas, 78 x 95cm.

| | Finearte Rome, 21 May 1996 (112**) ITL 28,750,000 | US$ | 18,465 |

SAN GIACOMO MAGGIORE oil on canvas, 127 x 100.5cm

| | Finearte Milan, 25 November 1995 (104**) ITL 92,000,000 | US$ | 57,753 |

NOYES George (1864-1954) American
THE ARTIST'S HOME, CHESTNUT STREET oil on canvas, 25 x 30in. (63.5 x 76.2cm.) slc 'G L Noyes'

| | Christie's New York, 23 May 1996 (130**) US$ 34,500 | US$ | 34,500 |

NUVOLONE Guiseppe (Milano 1619-1703 Milano) Italian
THE SAMARITAN IN THE WELL oil on canvas, 119 x 162cm
      Finearte Milan, 25 November 1995 (74) ITL 23,000,000   US$ 14,438

NUYEN Wijnandus Johannes Josephus (The Hague 1813-1839 The Hague) Dutch
A ROCKY COASTAL SCENE WITH SAILORS RESTING pencil, pen and black and brown ink,
watercolour heightened with white on paper, 27 x 34cm. sdlr 'WJJ Nuyen 37'
EXH.: The Hague, Haags GemeenteMuseum, *Wijnand Nuyen, Romantische werken*, 1977, cat.no.
96a(illus.)p.110.
LIT.: J. Knoef, *Van Romantiek tot Realisme*, The Hague, 1947, pp.54-74.
      Christie's Amsterdam, 26 October 1995 (277**) NLG 29,900   US$ 18,852

NUZZI Mario, {called} Mario de' Fiori (Penna 1603-1673 Rome) Italian
CARNATIONS, ROSES, TULIPS AND OTHER FLOWERS IN AN URN ON A LEDGE; AND
TULIPS, ROSES, CARNATIONS AND NARCISSI IN A SCULPTED URN ON A LEDGE oil on
canvas, 37 x 24in. (94 x 60.9cm.) a pair (2)
      Christie's South Kensington, 18 april 1996 (261**) GBP 9,775   US$ 14,822

NYOMAN LEMPAD I Gusti (1865-1978) Indonesian
A FIGHT pen and black ink, bodycolour and goldpaint, 27 x 26cm.
      Sotheby's Amsterdam, 23 April 1996 (100**) NLG 14,160   US$ 8,414

OBERHUBER Oswald (Meran 1931 b.-) Austrian
UNTITLED sealing-wax on board, 85 x 84cm. (ca. 1952)
      Dorotheum Vienna, 21 May 1996 (191**) ATS 180,000   US$ 17,284

OCHTERVELT Jacob (Rotterdam 1634-1682 Amsterdam) Dutch
A MAN HOLDING A GIANT 'ROEMER' AND A WOMAN EMPTYING A BOWL ON A
BALCONY oil on canvas, 32.7 x 27.4cm. slc 'Ochtervelt'
PROV.: G. van der Pot, Rotterdam; Sale, Van Nymegen etc. Rotterdam, 6 June 1808, lot 94;
Viscount Harcourt, London; Hawk; Sale, American Art Association New York, 4 February 1931, lot
19; with J. Weitzner, New York, 1933; with L. Koetser, London, 1959 (autumn exhibition 2-30
November 1959, no. 7); with D. Katz, Dieren, 1962 (exhibition *Oude Hollandse en Vlaamse
Meesters*, 22 November 1962-15 January 1963, no.41); Anon. Sale, Galliéra Paris, 10 June 1964, lot
20; with I. Bier, Haarlem, 1967; Duyvendijk, Scheveningen, 1968; with P. de Boer, Amsterdam,
1970 (exhibition catalogue *Fine Old Master Paintings*, 16 March-1 June 1970, no. 45); with K.
Meissner, Zurich, 1979.
LIT.: S. Donahue Kuretzky, *The Paintings of Jacob Ochterveldt*, 1979, pp. 90/91, no. 89, fig. 73, as
to be dated to ca. 1675.
      Christie's Amsterdam, 7 May 1996 (57**) NLG 18,400   US$ 10,729

MUSICIANS PLAYING IN A ROTUNDA oil on canvas, 38 x 29½in. (96 x 75cm.) (ca. 1674)
PROV.: Nicolaas Doekscheer, his deceased sale, Rotterdam, van der Schley *et al*, 9 September 1789,
lot 50; Dr. Benedict, Berlin, 1924; J. Porges, Paris, 1925; Sold, Lucerne, Galerie Fischer, 24 August
1926, lot 616; With Galerie van Diemen, Berlin, circa 1929;
Baron Heinrich Thyssen-Bornemisza, by 1930.
EXH.: London, Forbes and Patterson, 1902, no. 8; Munich 1930, no. 244; Munich 1931; Paris 1970,
no. 31, plate 12; Düsseldorf 1970-71, no. 35; Lausanne etc., 1986-87, no. 34.
LIT.: *Cicerone*, vol. 19, 1 November 1927, reproduced on cover; *Art News*, vol.26, 14 April 1928,
p.14; E. Plietzsch, 'Jacob Ochtervelt', in *Pantheon*, vol.20, December 1937, p.368; R. Heinemann
1937, vol. I, no. 311; E. Plietzsch, *Holländische und Fflämische Maler des XVII Jahrhunderts*, 1960,
p.65, reproduced fig. 1; S.D. Kuretsky, *The Paintings of Jacob Ochtervelt (1634-1682)*, 1979, p.89,
no. 84.
      Sotheby's London, 6 December 1995 (108**) GBP 47,700   US$ 73,407

A STANDARD BEARER, SMALL HALF-LENGTH, SOLDIERS BEYOND oil on panel, 7½ x 6
3/8in. (19 x 16.2cm.) sd 'J. Ochtervelt. f./ 1665'
PROV.: E.A. Laetham, 1868, and by descent; Sotheby's 10 July 1974, lot 5 (as Ary de Vois); with
Herbert Bier, London.
EXH.: Leeds, City Art Gallery, *National Loan Exhibition*, 1868, no. 632.
LIT.: S.D. Kuretsky, *The Paintings of Jacob Ochtervelt*, Montclair, New Jersey, 1979, pp. 20, 57, 63-
4, no. 25, fig. 60.
      Christie's London, 7 July 1995 (63**) GBP 45,500   US$ 72,579

OCONOR Roderic, R.H.A. (Roscommon 1860-1940 Neuil-sur-Layon (Maine-et-Loire)) Irish
LE BARRAGE A MONTIGNY oil on canvas, 21¼ x 25½in. (54 x 64.8cm.) s and inscr. 'Barrage
Montigny Roderic O'Conor No.4' on the stretcher; stamped with a studio stamp on the reverse (1902)
PROV.: Roland, Browse & Delbanco, London.
LIT.: J. Benington, *Roderic O'Conor,* Dublin, 1992, no. 99.
      Christie's London, 9 May 1996 (40**) GBP 84,000   US$ 127,196

A QUIET READ oil on board, 29½ x 20 3/4in. (75 x 52.8cm.) (ca 1915)
PROV.: Crane Kalman, London, where purchased by the present owner's family.
      Christie's London, 9 May 1996 (89**) GBP 17,250   US$ 26,121

ODAZZI Giovanni (1663-1731) Italian
THE ANNUNCIATION oil on canvas, 38 4/4 x 29¼in. (98.4 x 73.7cm.) (1685-90)
PROV.: with the Heim Gallery, London (Paintings & Sculptures of the Italian Baroque, 20 May - 21

Sept. 1973, no. 17, illustrated).
LIT.: J. Urrea Fernandez, *La Pintura Italiana del Siglo XVIII en Espana*, Valladolid, 1977, p. 288;
M. Trimarchi, *Giovanni Odazzi Pittore Romano*, Rome, 1979, pp. 39-40, no. 22, fig. 26; G. Sestien,
Repertorio della Pittura Romana della Fine del Seicento e del Settecento, Turin, 1994, I, p. 138, and
III, pl. 826.

Christie's London, 8 December 1995 (100**) GBP 24,150	US$	37,165

OEHLEN Albert (1954 b.) German?
ALS GOTT DEN ROCK ERFAND, MUß ER GEIL GEWESEN SEIN 'ROCKMUSIK 3' acrylic on
canvas, 200 x 200cm. sdlr '84 A. Oehlen'

Wiener Kunst Auktionen, 27 September 1995 (569**) ATS 280,000	US$	27,217

OEPTS Wim (Willem Anthonie) (Amsterdam 1904-1988) Dutch
WEG IN 'T ZUIDEN oil on canvas, 33 x 41cm. sdlr 'Oepts 63'
PROV.: Kunsthandel M.L. de Boer, Amsterdam, no. 6619.

Christie's Amsterdam, 5 June 1996 (304**) NLG 11,500	US$	6,719

A HOUSE IN SOUTHERN FRANCE oil on canvas, 55 x 45cm. sdlr 'Oepts 63'

Christie's Amsterdam, 6 December 1995 (258**) NLG 18,400	US$	11,402

A LANDSCAPE oil on canvas, 38 x 46cm. sdlr 'Oepts 71'; inscr. with title on a label on the reverse
PROV.: Kunsthandel M.L. de Boer, no. 9544, Amsterdam.

Christie's Amsterdam, 6 December 1995 (260**) NLG 16,100	US$	9,976

COASTAL SCENE oil on canvas, 38 x 46.5cm. sdlr 'Oepts '69'

Sotheby's Amsterdam, 7 December 1995 (190**) NLG 18,880	US$	11,699

OGUISS Takanori (1901-1986) Japanese
VIEILLES ECURIES, SAINT DENIS: A DOUBLE SIDED PAINTING oil on canvas, not indicated
slr 'Oguiss' incised with the signature on the reverse (ca. 1937)
PROV.: Private Collection, Arizona.
EXH.: Genva, Musée Rath, 1937, no. 42.

Sotheby's New York, 2 May 1996 (356**) US$ 76,750	US$	76,750

PARIS, A SQUARE oil on canvas, 65 x 81cm. sll 'Oguiss'

Étude Tajan Paris, 27 October 1995 (32**) FRF 430,000	US$	86,978

O'KEEFFE Georgia (Sun Prairie, Wisconsin 1887-1986) American
GREEN LEAVES oil on canvas, 21½ x 17½in. (54.6 x 44.4cm.) s 'Georgie O'Keeffe' and inscr. with
artist's device on the reverse (1921)
PROV.: The Downtown Gallery, New York; Dr. Charles Henry, Georgia; Sale: New York,
Sotheby's, May 28, 1987, lot 320.
EXH.: New York, Anderson Galleries, *Fifty-one Recent Pictures*, March 1924.
LIT.: V. Barker, 'Notes on the Exhibition', *The Arts*, vol. V, no. 4, 1924, p. 223.

Christie's New York, 23 May 1996 (160**) US$ 178,500	US$	178,500

MY AUTUMN oil on canvas, 40 x 30in. (101.6 x 76.2cm.) s with the artist's star and s ini. OK'
PROV.: The artist; Doris Bry, New York.
EXH.: New York, *An American Place, Georgia O'Keeffe: 27 New Paintings, New Mexico, New York,
Lake George, Etc.*, 1930, no. 23 as *Yellow and Red Leaves*; New York, Whitney Museum of
Amencan Art, *Second Biennial Exhibition of Contemporary American Painting*, 1934, no. 14 as *This
Autumn*; New York, Museum of Modern Art, *Georgia O'Keeffe Retrospective Exhibition*, May-
August, 1946, no. 35 as *This Autumn*.
LIT.: This painting will be included in the forthcoming *catalogue raisonné* of the artist's work, a joint
project of the National Gallery of Art, Washington, D.C. and the Georgia O'Keeffe Foundation.

Christie's New York, 30 November 1995 (46**) US$ 937,500	US$	937,500

OLDENBURG Claes (Stockholm 1929 b.) American (Swedish)
BACON AND EGG enamel on plaster and muslin over wire, 42½ x 35 x 6½in. (108 x 88.8 x
16.5cm.) ini. and dll; ini. and d 'C.O. 1961 'C.O. 1961' on the reverse
PROV.: Sidney Janis Gallery, New York; Leon Kraushaar, New York; Karl Ströher, Darmstadt.
EXH.: New York, Ray Gun Manufacturing Company, *The Store*, Dec. 1961-Jan. 1962, no. 30.;
Berlin, Neue Nationalgalerie; Düsseldorf, Stadtisches Kunsthalle; Bern, Kunsthalle, *Sammlung 1968
Karl Ströher*, March-Oct. 1969, p. 90 (illustrated); Cologne, Museen der Stadt, *Westkunst:
Contemporary Art since 1939*, May-Aug. 1981, p. 453, no. 648 (illustrated).
LIT.: D. Herzka, *Pop Art One*, New York 1965, no. 12 (illustrated); J. Rublowsky, *Pop Art*, New
York 1965, p. 187 (illustrated); K. K. Schmidt, *Karl Ströher: Sammler und Sammlung*, Stuttgart
1982, p. 175, no. 416 (illustrated).

Christie's New York, 14 November 1995 (43**) US$ 288,500	US$	288,500

OLINSKY Ivan (1878-1962) American
LA FETE, SAN MARCO oil on canvas, 22¼ x 29in. (57 x 74cm.) sll 'Ivan G. Olinsky'
PROV.: The artist; Mrs. Leonore Miller, New York (the artist's daughter); Arvest Galleries, Boston.
EXH.: Boston, Arvest Galleries, *Ivan G. Olinsky N.A. (1878-1962)*, Oct.-Nov. 1985, no. 8.

Christie's New York, 23 May 1996 (122**) US$ 40,250	US$	40,250

OLITSKI Jules (1922 b.) American (Russian)
RADICAL CORRESPONDENCE-9 acrylic on canvas, 52 x 117in. (132.1 x 297.2cm.) sd and tilted
'Jules Olitski '82, Radical Corecpondence-9'
PROV.: André Emmerich Gallery, New York.

Christie's East, 14 November 1995 (185**) US$ 10,350	US$	10,350

GREEN FLIP OUT acrylic on canvas, 31 x 92in. (78.8 x 233.6cm.) s and titled 'Jules Olitski Green
Flip Out' on the reverse (1983)
PROV.: Andre Emmerich Gallery, New York; Kasmin Limited, London.

Christie's East, 7 May 1996 (79**) US$ 14,950	US$	14,950

OLSON Axel (1899-1986) Swedish
KVINNA VID KAMIN oil on canvas, 48 x 42cm. sdlr 'Axel Olson Berlin 1922'

Bukowskis Stockholm, 26-27 October 1995 (90**) SEK 78,000	US$	11,423

OLSON Erik (1901-1986) Swedish
TYNGLDLYFTAREN oil on canvas laid down on board, 47 x 43cm. sdll 'Erik O 1924'
PROV.: The family of the Artist.

Bukowskis Stockholm, 26-27 October 1995 (94**) SEK 120,000	US$	17,574

OLSON Olle (Hagalund) (1904-1972) Swedish
VÅR I HAGGALUND oil on canvas, 71 x 91cm. slr 'OLLE OLSSON \ HAGALUND'

Bukowskis Stockholm, 24-25 April 1996 (100**) SEK 230,000	US$	34,845

DEN RÖDA PUMPEN oil on canvas, 50 x 61cm. sll 'Olle Olsson Hagalund' (1960s)
EXH.: Liljevalch, Liljevalchs Konsthall, *Minnesutställningen 1973*.

Bukowskis Stockholm, 26-27 October 1995 (98a**) SEK 195,000	US$	28,558

PÅ LYXNORMA oil on canvas, 73 x 105cm. slr 'Olle Olsson-Hagalund'

Bukowskis Stockholm, 24-25 April 1996 (102**) SEK 420,000	US$	63,630

ONTANI Luigi (Vergato 1943 b.-l) Italian
PRESTANTIN mixed media on cardboard, 243 x 151cm. sd 'Capri 1986' and titled on the reverse

Sotheby's Milan, 28 May 1996 (224**) ITL 18,400,000	US$	11,818

OOST Jacob van (Brughes 1601-1671 Brughes) Flemish
PORTRAIT OF A COUPLE IN PASTORAL DRESS, POSSIBLY AS VENUS AND ADONIS:

THE RETURN OF A HUNTER WITH HIS BOUNTY oil on canvas, 65½ x 92½in. (166.4 x 235cm.)
PROV.: Julia A. Berwind, The Elms, Newport, Rhode Island (Sale: Parke-Bernet Galleries, Inc., New York (sold at The Elms), June 27, 28, 1962, lot 536 (as by Frans Snyders and Adriaen Hanneman), where purchased by; Schaeffer Galleries, Inc., New York, From whom acquired by the present owner in 1965 (Acc. no. 65.39).
LIT.: *Apollo*, January, 1965, p. XlIX; S.A.M. *Engagement Book*, Oct. 13-19, illus. *Trafalgar Galleries*, XII, 1985, London, p. 69, illus. fig. 4 (comparing the Seattle work to a painting in their catalogue).

Sotheby's New York, 11 January 1996 (28**) US$ 211,500	US$	211,500

OOSTEN Isaack van (Antwerp 1613-1661) Flemish
VILLAGE LANDSCAPE WITH DROVERS AND CATTLE / VILLAGE LANDSCAPE WITH A RESTING SHEPHERD SALUTING A RIDER AND A HUNTSMAN oil on panel (a pair), each: 12½ x 8¼in. (32 x 21cm.) sll 'J.V.O.; slr 'J.V.O.'

Sotheby's London, 5 July 1995 (193**) GBP 12,075	US$	19,261

LE RETOUR DES PAYSANS; LE REPOS DES CHASSEURS oil on oakpanel (a pair), each: 24 x 35cm. slr 'J v oosten fecit'

Étude Tajan Paris, 12 December 1995 (69**) FRF 350,000	US$	70,499

FLEMISH LANDSCAPE WITH VILLAGE AND DEER oil on copper, 17 x 22cm.

Dorotheum Vienna, 17 October 1995 (152**) ATS 200,000	US$	20,061

OOSTEN Isaack van (attr.) (Antwerp 1613-1661) Flemish
AUTUMN OR THE WINEVINTAGE / SUMMER OR THE HARVEST oil on copper (a pair), each: 27 x 33cm.

Étude Tajan Paris, 18 December 1995 (106**) FRF 150,000	US$	30,214

OPALKA Roman
'65/1-OO : DETAIL - 3029180 - 3047372 acrylic on canvas, 77½ x 53in. (196.9 x 134.7cm.) s and titled on the reverse
PROV.: Daniel Varenne, Geneva.

Christie's London, 27 June 1996 (65**) GBP 40,000	US$	61,681

OPPI Ubaldo (Bologna 1889-1942 Vicenza) Italian
GRUPPO DI TRE FEMMINE gouache on cardboard, 78 x 58cm. sll 'Ubaldi Oppi'

Finearte Milan, 26 October 1995 (216**) ITL 23,000,000	US$	14,330

OPPO Cipriano Efisio (Roma 1891-1962) Italian
CAMPAGNA DI MONTEPULCIANO oil on panel, 40.5 x 32.5cm sd 'Oppo' (1926)
EXH.: Venezia, *XXII Esposizione Biennale Internazionale d`Arte*, 1940, n.233.
LIT.: M.Corsi 'Artisti Contemporanei: Cipriano Efisio Oppo', in *Emporium* n.417, p. 145, September 1929.

Finearte Rome, 14 November 1995 (125**) ITL 11,500,000	US$	7,219

ORD Joseph Biays (1805-1865) American
STILL-LIFE WITH VASE, FRUIT AND NUTS oil on canvas, 18 x 24in. (45.7 x 61cm.) sdur 'J.B. Ord. 1843'; sd indistinctly on the reverse
PROV.: Mrs. Hortense A. Statts, Manchester, Vermont.

Christie's New York, 30 November 1995 (8**) US$ 79,500	US$	79,500

The Assumption of the Virgin

ORIOLI Pietro Francesco degli (Siena 1458-1496 Siena) Italian
THE ASSUMPTION OF THE VIRGIN tempera on panel (arched top), 56¾ x 18in. (144.2 x 45.7cm.)
PROV.: Sir W.W. Burrell, Bt.; (+) Christie's, London, June 12, 1897, lot 10 as *Ambrogio Bergognone* (28gns. to C. Butler); Charles Butler, Warren Wood, Hatfield; (†) Chnstie's, London, May 25-6 (1st day), 1911, lot 4 as *Ambrogio Bergognone* (310gns. to Carfax); Sir Edgar Speyer, Bt., New York, by 1927 as unknown artist, and by descent to Mrs Eleanore Speyer; sale, ParkeBernet, New York, Nov. 12, 1952, lot 15 as *Matteo di Giovanni* ($900); with P. & D. Colnaghi & Co. Ltd., London and New York as *Giacomo Pacchiarotto*.
LIT.: B. Berenson, *Italian Pictures of the Renaissance:Central Italian and North Italian Schools*, I, 1932, p. 309 as Giacomo Pacchiarotto; F. Zeri, 'Studies in Italian Paintings: A Predella by Giacomo Pacchiarotto', *Journal of the Walters Art Gallery*, XXVIIXXVI11, 1964-5, pp. 79-86; G. Coor, 'Notes on Six parts of Two Dismembered Sienese Altarpieces', *Gazette des Beaux-Arts*, LXV, 1965, pp.l29-36, figs. 3-4; L. Vertova, 'On Pacchiarotto's Dismembered Assumption', *Gazette des Beaux-Arts*, LXIX, 1967, pp. 159-63; F.R. Shapley, *Paintings from The Samuel H. Kress Collection: Italian Paintings Fifteenth to Sixteenth Century*, 1969, pp.111-2 as *Giacomo Pacchiarotto*; F. Zeri, *Italian paintings in the Walters Art Gallery*, I, 1976, p. 139 as *Giacomo Pacchiarotto*; P. Torriti, *La Pinacoteca Nazionale di Siena*, 1978, p. 88. A. Angelini, 'Pietro Orioli e il momento Urbinate' della pittura Senese del Quattrocento', in *Prospettiva*, XXX, 1982, p. 36; L.B. Kanter in the catalogue of the exhibition, *Painting in Renaissance Siena, 1420-1500*, Metropolitan Museum of Art, New York, Dec. 20, 1988-Mar. 19, 1989, p. 339, no. 1; J. Pope-Hennessy, *Learning to Look*, 1991, p. 318.
Christie's New York, 10 January 1996 (102**) US$ 107,000   US$ 107,000

ORPEN Sir William, R.A., R.W.S., R.H.A. (1878-1931) Irish
MYSELF AND CUPID oil on canvas, 40¼ x 34in. (102.3 x 86.4cm.) slr 'Orpen' (1910)
PROV.: Lady Orpen, thence by descent until 1974; Private Collection, New York.
EXH.: London, N.E.A.C., Summer, 1911, no.164; London, Royal Academy, *Winter Exhibition*, Jan.-March 1933, no.35, as 'Portrait of the Painter'; London, Fine Art Society, Dec. 1974, no.24; Dublin, National Gallery of Ireland, *William Orpen A Centenary Exhibition*, Nov.-Dec. 1978, no.73.
LIT.: P.G. Konody & S. Dark, *Sir William Orpen, Artist and Man,* London, 1932, p.269 as 'Portrait of the Artist (mirror in the background)'; T. Mullaly, *The Daily Telegraph*, 'Fascination of the Self' 7 Dec. 1974 (illus.); B. Arnold, *Orpen, Mirror to an Age*, London, 1981, pp.217, 216 & 268 (illus.).
Christie's London, 9 May 1996 (100**) GBP 150,000   US$ 227,135

PORTRAIT OF MARY, LADY GERARD IN A GREEN DRESS oil on canvas, 39 x 26½in. (99 x 67cm.) sdlr 'Orpen 1904'
PROV.: The Gerard Family; Blakesweire Manor, Hertfordshire, circa 1955.
LIT.: P.G. Konody & S. Darks, *Sir William Orpen, Artist and Man*, London, 1932, p. 266; B. Arnold, *Orpen Mirror to an Age*, London, 1981, pp. 116-118.

Christie's London, 9 May 1996 (106**) GBP 13,800	US$	20,896

ORSI Lelio (Reggio Emilia ca. 1511-1587 Novellara) Italian
THE DESCENT INTO LIMBO oil on panel, 26½ x 21 3/4in. (68.5 x 55cm.)
PROV.: Sold, London, Fosters, 28 June 1889, lot 60, as 'Lelio da Novellara, The Ascension, panel', bought Girling, where acquired by Sir John Charles Robinson, according to his unpublished accounts, preserved in the Ashmolean Museum, Oxford, as follows: '523 Lelio Orsi da Novellara the Ascension, July 1889 sale at Fosters GBP23-10-0'; His sale, Berlin, Lepke, 31 March 1914, lot 9, as Lelio Orsi, *Christus in der Vorhölle*, where
purchased by the grandfather of the present owner.
LIT.: A. Venturi, *Storia dell'Arte Italiana*, 1933, vol. IX, pp. 641-642, fig. 387; R. Salvini & A.M. Chiodi, *Lelio Orsi*, exhibition catalogue, 1950, p. xix; F. Arcangeli, 'Mostra di Lelio Orsi' in *Paragone*, 1950, vol. 7, p. 50; R. Salvini, 'Su Lelio Orsi e La Mostra di Reggio Emilia' in *Bollettino d 'Arte*, January-March 1951, C. Volpe, 'Una Copia da Correggio di Lelio Orsi', in *Arte Antica e Moderna*, 1958, 2, p. 179; V. Romani, *Lelio Orsi*, 1984, p. 72, note 122; E. Monducci & M. Pirondini, *Lelio Orsi*, exhibition catalogue, 1987, p. 237, no. 203 (as whereabouts unknown), reproduced.

Sotheby's London, 5 July 1995 (69**) GBP 397,500	US$	634,072

ORTEGA Martin Rico Y (1833-1908) Sanish
THE LAGUNA, VENICE oil on canvas, 16¾ x 28 3/4in. (42.5 x 73cm.) slc 'RICO'

Christie's New York, 10 January 1996 (137**) US$ 27,600	US$	27,600

ORTIZ Nicolás Martínez (1907-1990) Spanish
JOTA VASCA oil on cartonboard, 92 x 73cm. sd '61'
PROV.: Collection Nelson, Madrid; Acquired from the above by the present owner in 1985.
LIT.: M. Logroño, *Nicolás Martínez Ortiz*, Panorama de la Pintura Contemporánea, no. 8, Madrid, Ibérico Europeo de Ediciones, 1973, (illustrated).

Sotheby's Madrid, 23 November 1995 (77**) ESP 1,204,375	US$	9,900

OS Jan van (Middelharnis 1744-1808 The Hague) Dutch
SHIPPING OFF DORDRECHT IN CHOPPY SEAS oil on panel, 9 5/8 x 13½in. (24.5 x 34.3cm.)

Christie's South Kensington, 18 april 1996 (274**) GBP 5,520	US$	8,370

HOLLYHOCKS POPPIES AND AN ANEMON AND OTHER FLOWERS WITH WHITECURRANTS IN A TERRACOTTA POT, WITH APRICOTS, GRAPES LEMONS, POMEGRANATES, A PLUM AND COCKSCOMB ON A MARBLE LEDGE oil on panel, 19 5/8 x 15 3/8in. (49.9 x 39cm) s 'J. Van Os, fecit' (on the ledge)
EXH.: Similar works by Van Os, depicting a vase of flowers with fruit on a straighter ledge viewed from below in a landscape are in the Warrington Art Gallery and the Virginia Museum.

Christie's London, 7 July 1995 (19**) GBP 172,000	US$	274,366

OSBORNE Walter Frederick, R.H.A. (1859-1903) British
LA RUE DE L'APPORT, DINAN oil on canvas, 17¾ x 13¼in. (45.1 x 33.7cm.) sdll 'Walter Osborne 1883', s twice 'F.W. Osborne' on the stretcher
EXH.: Dublin, Royal Hibernian Academy, 1884, no. 220.
LIT.: J. Sheehy, Walter Osborne, Cork, 1974, no. 77.

Christie's London, 9 May 1996 (69**) GBP 28,750	US$	43,534

OSSLUND Helmer (1866-1938) Swedish
HÖSTDAG I NORDINGRÅ oil on canvas, 98 x 130cm. sll 'Helmer Osslund'
    Bukowskis Stockholm, 29 November-1 December 1995 (116**) SEK 350,000   US$ 52,947

HÖSTSTÄMNING, ÅNGERMANLAND oil on cardboard, 68 x 74cm. s 'Osslund'
EXH.: Rome, *Esposizione Internationale D'Arte,* 1911.
    Bukowskis Stockholm, 29-31 May 1996 (135**) SEK 265,000   US$ 38,974

A peasant Family in an Interior

OSTADE Adriaen Jansz. van (Haarlem 1610-1685 Haarlem) Dutch
FARMER IN A BARN oil on panel, 24 x 21.5cm. sdlc 'A. Ostade .643. (1643)
    Dorotheum Vienna, 6 March 1996 (98**) ATS 280,000   US$ 26,933

A BOOR GREETING AN OLD WOMAN SEATED BY A TABLE IN A BARN, OTHER BOORS
SMOKING NEARBY oil on panel, 36.2 x 46.4cm. indistinctly sdll 'Avostade 1636'
PROV.: With F. Drey, London, 1950 (inv.no. 5340); with P. de Boer, Amsterdam, 1961 (summer
exhibition, no. 56, with ill.).
    Christie's Amsterdam, 7 May 1996 (54***) NLG 103,500   US$ 60,350

PEASANTS DRINKING AND SMOKING IN AN INTERIOR oil on panel, 9¼ x 8in. (23.5 x
20.3cm.) sdll '16.'
PROV.: Erlanger.
EXH.: Paris, Galerie Charpentier, *Le Pain et le Vin*, 1954, no. 161.
    Sotheby's New York, 11 January 1996 (243**) US$ 31,050   US$ 31,050

PEASANTS MERRY-MAKING IN A BARN oil on panel, 16¼ x 13 3/8in. (41.3 x 34cm.) sdll 'AV
ostaden' 1632'
PROV.: With Delahante; purchased from the above by Sir Abraham Hume and by descent to John
William Spencer, 2nd Earl Brownlow (d. 1867), Belton House, Grantham, and by inheritance to The
Lord Brownlow, 7th Baron, and the Trustees of the Brownlow Chattels Settlement; Christie's, 6 April
1984, lot 80 (GBP14,000).

EXH.: London, British Institution, 1824, no. 106.
LIT.: Sir A. Hume, *A Descriptive Catalogue of a Collection of Picture* 1824, no. 119; C. Hofstede de Groot, *A Catalogue Raisonné*, etc., III London, 1912, p. 313, no. 559.

| | Christie's London, 19 April 1996 (166**) GBP 32,200 | US$ | 48,825 |

A PEASANT FAMILY IN AN INTERIOR oil on oak panel, 16 x 18in. (41 x 46.5cm.) sll '.ostade f.' (ca. 1665)
PROV.: Ecuyer de Julienne, his sale, Paris, Remy *et al*, 30 March-22 May 1767, lot 157 (with so-called pendant by Pieter van Laer); Empress Catherine II of Russia; With van Diemen, Berlin, 1933; With Markgraf & Co., Berlin, from whom purchesed in 1933 by Baron Heinrich Thyssen-Bornemisza for 10,,000 Reichmarks.
EXH.: Paris 1970, no. 32, plate 11; Düsseldorf 1970-1, no. 36; Bielefeld 1973, no. 19; Lausanne etc., 1986-7, no. 27.
LIT.: A. Somov, *Catalogue de la Galerie de Tableaux, 2.ème Partie*, (Catalogue of paintings in the Hermitage, Saint Petersburg), 1901, p. 270, no. 946; C. Hofstede de Groot, *A Catalogue Raisonné..*, vol. III, 1910, p. 285, no. 471, as painted *about 1665*; R. Heinemann 1937, vol. I, no. 314, vol. II, plate 132; Bielefeld 1973, no. 19.

| | Sotheby's London, 6 December 1995 (117**) GBP 111,500 | US$ | 171,591 |

OSTADE Isaac Jansz. van (Haarlem 1621-1649 Haarlem) Dutch
A WINTER LANDSCAPE WITH WOODGATHERERS PUSHING A SLEDGE ON THE ICE, A FARMER LEADING HIS HORSE-DRAWN SLEDGE UP A RAMP TOWARDS A BARN, ONLOOKERS ON A BRIDGE BEYOND, A WOMAN SELLING APPLES FROM A SLEDGE NEARBY oil on panel, 37.1 x 33.9cm. sll 'IsackvanOstade'
PROV.: M. Wasserman, Paris; with F. Kleinberger, Paris; A. de Ridder, Schönberg; Sale, Georges Petit, Paris, 8 June 1924, lot 50, with illustration; with J. Goudstikker, Amsterdam, 1932.
EXH.: Amsterdam, Kunsthandel J. Goudstikker,*Tenstoonstelling van Hollandsche Winterlandschappen uit 17e eeuw*, 6-29 February 1932, no. 69, with illustration.; Delft, Stedelijk Museum het Prinsenhof, *Kersttentoonstelling Nederlandse Meesters uit particulier bezit*, 21 December 1952-1 February 1953, no. 56.
LIT.: C. Hofstede de Groot, *A Catalogue Raisonné etc*. III, 1910, p. 554, no. 287; W. Bode, *Die Gemäldegalerie des Hernn A. de Ridder in seiner Villa Schönberg bei Cronberg in Taunus*, 1910, p. 34, with illustration and 1913, pl. 45.

| | Christie's Amsterdam, 7 May 1996 (60**) NLG 230,000 | US$ | 134,111 |

AN ELEGANT COUPLE WATCHING A FISHMONGER LOADING A HORSEDRAWN WAGGON ON THE BEACH oil on panel, 66.7 x 93.2cm. indistinctly sdlr 'Isack.Van Ostade/1649'
PROV.: Schneider, Paris; Sale, Paris, 6 April 1876, lot 27; Earl of Dudley (Ukp); Sale, christie's 25 June 1892, lot 18 (sold GBP 1,000); with Kleinberger, Paris, 1911; A. Krupp von Bohlen und Halbach, Essen (Ukp); Sale, Christie's New York, 13 January 1987, lot 132, with colour ill.
LIT.: C. Hofstede de Groot, *A Catalogue Raisonné etc.*, III, 1910, p. 493, no. 120 and p. 579.

| | Christie's Amsterdam, 7 May 1996 (138**) NLG 92,000 | US$ | 53,644 |

INTERIOR ON SCENE oil on panel, 26 x 26cm
PROV.: Amsterdam, collection Goudstikker; Amsterdam, collection Dr. Wetzlar; Amsterdam, sale Lanz Muller, 13-19/3/1951, lotto no.71; Londra, sale Sotheby`s, 15/7/1990, lotto no.32.
EXH.: Galleria Caretto, *32a Mostra Maestri Fiamminghi ed Olandesi del XVI-XVII secolo*, Torino, November-December 1991, no.40.

| | Finearte Milan, 25 November 1995 (32*) ITL 23,000,000 | US$ | 14,438 |

OUDRY Jacques Charles (Paris 1720-1778 Lausanne) French
A STILL-LIFE OF A RABBIT, AND A SILVER COFFEE POT, A BLUE AND WHITE PORCELAIN CUP AND SAUCER, BREAD AND CHEESE ALL ON STONE LEDGE oil on canvas, 40½ x 30in. (103 x 76.2cm.) sdll. 'J.C. Oudry./1761'
PROV.: H. Opperman, *J.B. Oudry*, vol. II, 1977, p. 1171, fig. 396.

| | Sotheby's London, 17 April 1996 (88**) GBP 9,200 | US$ | 13,950 |

OUDRY Jean Baptiste (Paris 1686-1755 Paris (Beauvais?)) French
'RENDEZ-VOUS AU CARREFOUR DU PUITS DE ROI, FORET DE COMPIEGNE' OR 'LE
BOTTE DU ROI' pen and point of the brush and black ink and grey wash over black chalk,
heightened with white on faded blue paper, 31.2 x 55.2cm. s 'JB Oudry' (1730's)
PROV.: Deveaux Collection, sale, Paris, Hotel Drouot, 27-28 November 1907, cat.88, illus.; de
Dioncourt; Comte de l'Aigle.
EXH.: Paris , Musée des Arts décoratifs, *La Vénerie française*, 1923, cat.l80.
LIT.: Jean Loquin, *Catalogue Raisonné de l'Oeuvre de Jean-Baptiste Oudry Peintre du Roi (1686-1755)*, Paris 1912, cat.649; Jean Vergnet-Ruiz, *Oudry*, no.II, p.l75, no.28; Hal N. Opperman, *Jean-Baptiste Oudry,* Chicago 1972, vol. II, p.730, cat.D588; Hal Opperman and Pierre Rosenberg, *J-B. Oudry*, exh. cat., Paris, Galeries Nationales du Grand Palais, 1982-83, p.l38, under cat.60.
Sotheby's London, 3 July 1995 (173**) GBP 100,500   US$ 160,313

A ROYAL STAG-HUNT pen and point of the brush and black ink and grey wash over black chalk,
heightened with white on faded blue paper, 32.4 x 52.8cm. sd 'J.B.Oudry/1733'
PROV.: Deveaux Collection, sale, Paris, Hotel Drouot, 27-28 November 1907, cat.89, illus.; de
Dioncourt; Comte de l'Aigle.
EXH.: Paris, Musée des Arts Décoratifs, *La Vénerie française*, 1923, cat. 181.
LIT.: Jean Loquin, *Catalogue Raisonné de l'Oeuvre de Jean-Baptiste Oudry Peintre du Roi (1686-1755)*, Paris 1912, cat.655; Jean Vergnet-Ruiz, *Oudry*, no.II, p.l75, no.29; Hal N. Opperman, *Jean-Baptiste Oudry,* Chicago 1972, vol. II, p.730, cat.D582.
Sotheby's London, 3 July 1995 (174**) GBP 73,000   US$ 116,446

OVENS Jürgen (Tönning 1623-1678 Friedrichstadt) German
PORTRAIT OF A CLERC, HALF-LENGHT HOLDING A BOOK oil on panel, 16 x 12in. (41.5 x
31cm.)
PROV.: Frederick, 4th Marquess of Bristol.
LIT.: Farrer, 1913, no. 157; *Inventory*, 1952, p. 30, as *Jurrien Ovens*; *The Antique Collector*, 1961, p.
220.
Sotheby's London, 11-12 June 1996 (493**) GBP 11,500   US$ 17,733

OWEN William, R.A. (1769-1825) British
CHILD READING ON A TERRACE WITH A LANDSCAPE BEYOND oil on canvas, 35 x 26
3/4in. (88.9 x 67.9cm.)
PROV.: J.J. Gillespie Fine Art Galleries, Pittsburgh, Pa (from an old printed label on the reverse).
Sotheby's Arcade Auctions New York, 20 July 1995 (70*) US$ 11,500   US$ 11,500

OYENS David (Amsterdam 1842-1902 Brussel) Dutch
INTERIEUR oil on canvas, 40 x 48 cm s 'David Oyens and inscr. with title on a label on the stretcher
PROV.: Kunsthandel Huinck & Scherjon, Amsterdam, inv. no.1129; Kunsthandel Wed. Oldenzeel,
Rotterdam.
Christie's Amsterdam, 25 April 1996 (111*) NLG 8,050   US$ 4,783

PAEP Thomas de (1628 c. Malines-1670) Flemish
A BUNCH OF GRAPES HANGING FROM A NAIL IN A STONE WALL oil on canvas laid down
on board, 70 x 55.1cm. sll 'T D Paep'
    Christie's Amsterdam, 7 May 1996 (43**) NLG 18,400   US$ 10,729

PAGGI Giovanni Battista (1554 -1627) Italian
ESTHER BEFORE AHASVEROS oil on canvas, 51½ x 42in. (130.8 x 106.7cm.) sd '1575'
    Sotheby's New York, 11 January 1996 (111**) US$ 34,500   US$ 34,500

PALADINO Mimmo (1948 b. Paduli) Italian
COMPOSIZIONE mixed technique and collage on canvas-three-triptich, 70 x 105cm. sd on the
reverse (1981)
    Finearte Milan, 18 June 1996 (225**) ITL 55200,000   US$ 35,798

LA BALENA IMMALATA oil and mixed media on canvas (tryptich), each: 78¾ x 39 3/8in (,200 x
100cm.) overall 78¾ x 118in. (,200 x 300cm.) (1981)
PROV.: Tjerk Wiegersma Fine Art, Paris.
EXH.: Paris, Gallerie Bellier, *Polyptyques et Paravents, Un Siècle de Création, 1890-1990*, Paris
(illustrated in the catalogue p. 98-99).
    Christie's London, 23 May 1996 (142**) GBP 36,700   US$ 55,572

PORTA D' OCCIDENTE oil on panel in Artist's frame, 97 x 73¼in. (246.4 x 186cm.) sd and titled
on the reverse (1988)
PROV.: Galerie Templon, Paris.
EXH.: Paris, Galerie Templon, *Mimmo Paladino*, March-April 1989 (illus. in the catalogue, p. 1).
    Christie's London, 26 October 1995 (128**) GBP 28,750   US$ 45,376

VESPERO oil on canvas, 118 x 128in. (,300 x 325cm.) slr with ini; sd 1984 and titled on the reverse
PROV.: Waddington Galleries, London; Marshall Frankel, Chicago.
EXH.: London, Waddington Galleries, *Mimmo Paladino*, October 1984, no. 34 (illustrated in colour
in the catalogue p. 53); Washington, Hirshhorn Museum and Sculpture Garden; Akron, Akron Art
Museum, *A New Romanticism: Sixteen Artists from Italy*, October 1985-April 1986, no. 40
(illustrated in colour in the catalogue p. 85); Chicago, Museum of Contemporary Art, *The Marshall
Frankel Collection*, February-April 1988, no. 77 (illustrated in colour in the catalogue p. 20).
    Christie's London, 27 June 1996 (76**) GBP 41,100
        US$ 63,377

VIA DELLA CROCE oil on driftwood on panel, 14 x 10 x 2¼in. (35.6 x 25.4 x 5.7cm.) sd 'paladino
1985' on the reverse
PROV.: Sperone Westwater Fischer, New York.
    Christie's New York, 15 November 1995 (309**) US$ 19,550   US$ 19,550

PALAGI Pelagio (1775 Bologna-1860 Turin) Italian
THE DEATH OF CAESAR oil on canvas, 38 x 70cm.
    Finearte Rome, 24 October 1995 (306**) ITL 22,425,000   US$ 13,972

PALAMEDES Palamedes I (1607 London?-1638 Delft) Dutch
A CAVALRY BATTLE oil on panel, 19.5 x 26cm. indistinctly slr
    Sotheby's Amsterdam, 6 May 1996 (45*) NLG 11,800   US$ 6,880

PALAZUELO Pablo (1916 b. -) Spanish
COMPOSICION oil on canvas, 101.5 x 122cm. sdlr 'PALAZUELO '53'
PROV.: Estate of G. David Thompson, Pittsburgh; Acquired from the above by the present owner in
1966.
EXH.: Pittsburgh, Carnegie Institute of Art, *Alcoa Collection of Contemporary Art: An Exhibition of
Works Acquired from the G. David Thompson Collection*, 1967, cat. no. 40 (illustrated); This

exhibtion later travelled to several University's in the USA; Pittsburgh, University Art Gallery, *Pittsburgh collects 2: Alcoa Collection of Contemporary Art*, 1971, p. 29 of the catalogue (illustrated); Dublin, Municipal Gallery of Art; Swansea, Glynn Vivian Art Gallery; Sheffield, Graves Art gallery; Birmingham, City Museum and Art Gallery; Worms, Städisches Kulturinstitut; Oslo, Henie Onstad Gallery; Birmingham, City Museum and Art Gallery; London, Institute of Contemporary Art; Lausanne, Musée Cantonale des Beaux-Arts; Vienna, Wiener Secession; Milan, Centro Culturale San Fedele; Tel Aviv, Municipal Museum of Art; Athens, Doxiades Design School, *Alcoa Collection of Contemporary Art*, 1972-75, cat. no. 30. p. 33 (illustrated).

Sotheby's Madrid, 23 November 1995 (109***) ESP 5,405,000 — US$ 44,429

PALING Johannes Jacobus (1844 Amsterdam-1892 Laren (N.-Holland)) Dutch
MOTHERHOOD oil on canvas, 78.5 x 60.5 cm s 'Joh.J. Paling'

Christie's Amsterdam, 25 April 1996 (26*) NLG 9,775 — US$ 5,808

PALMA Antonio (1510 <circa> Serinalta-1575 Venice) Italian
VIRGIN AND CHILD WITH SAINTS JOHN THE BAPTIST AND JEROME oil on canvas, 26 3/8 x 40¼in. (67 x 102.2cm.)

Sotheby's New York, 16 May 1996 (194**) US$ 10,925 — US$ 10,925

PALMA Jacopo Negretti (Nigreti), {called} Palma Giovane (1544 Venice-1628 Venice) Italian
LA PISCINE PROBATICA oil on canvas, 80 x 137cm

Finearte Milan, 25 November 1995 (81) ITL 17,250,000 — US$ 10,829

THE ADORATION OF THE SHEPHERDS pen and brown ink and wash over black chalk heightened with white, 19.4 x 19.9cm. (ca. 1626)
PROV.: Dr. Rudolf, his Sale, Sotheby's London, 4 July 1977, lot 30; P & D. Colnaghi & Co. Ltd., *Ols Master Paintings and Drawings*, 1979, cat 58.

Sotheby's London, 3 July 1995 (122**) GBP 4,600 — US$ 7,338

THE ADORATION OF THE SHEPHERDS pen and brown ink with grey wash over traces of black chalk laid down, 18.9 x 13.7cm.

Phillips London, 6 December 1995 (176**) GBP 6,800 — US$ 10,465

PALMER Samuel, R.W.S. (1805 Walworth, London-1881 Reigate, Surrey) British
ILLUSTRATION TO MILTON'S 'LYCIDAS' watercolour heightened with bodycolour, 15½ x 23in. (39.4 x 58.4cm.) signed indistinctly and inscribed on the reverse of the backing card 'This is a 6 sheet London Board/I advise that it should never be thinned/by removing paper from the back/Stoutness increases permanence and lustre/S. Palmer' and further inscribed on an old label attached to the backboard 'No: 1/Lycidas/'Together both, ere the high lawns appeared/Under the opening eyelids of the morn,/We drove afield, and both together heard,/What time the grey fly winds her sultry horn.'/Samuel Palmer./Furze Hill, Red Hill.' (ca 1864)
PROV.: George Gurney by 1879 until 1891; John Edward Giles, Palmer's cousin, circa 1891.
EXH.: London, Royal Society of Painters in Watercolours, 1873, no. 112; London, Grosvenor Gallery, *Winter Exhibition*, 1879, no.l,074 lent by George Gurney; London, Fine Art Society, 1881, no.90; London, Royal Academy, *Winter 1891*, no.l39 lent by George Gurney.
LIT.: *The Shorter Poems of John Milton with Twelve Illustrations by Samuel Palmer, Painter and Etcher*, 1889, p.xx, repr. facing p.2; *Samuel Palmer: A Vision Recaptured: The Complete Etchings and the Paintings for Milton and for Virgil*, 1978, p.65 no.XVI (a) as untraced; R. Lister, *Catalogue Raisonné of the Works of Samuel Palmer*, 1988, pp.218-9, no. M8, repr. and listed as untraced since 1891.

Christie's London, 11 July 1995 (50***) GBP 89,500 — US$ 142,766

PALMERUCCIO Guiduccio di (active ca. 1325 -) Italian
THE EVANGELIST SAINT JOHN / MADONNA ENTHRONED WITH CHILD / SAINT CATHERINA OF ALEXANDRIA tempera on panel (tryptich), 160 x 140cm.
PROV.: Rome, collection Nevin; Rome, Galleria Sangiorgi, 22-27 April 1907, no. 225; Florence,

collection of countess Serristori.
LIT.: M. Salmi, 'Nuove opere di Guio Palmerucci', in *La Diana*, anno V, fasc. IV, 1931, pp. 267-269;
B. Berenson, *Italian Pictures of the Renaissance. Central Italian and North Italian Schools*, Phaidon,
London 1968, vol. I, p. 312, vol. II, fig. 102; E. Neri Lusanna, 'Percorso di Guiduccio Palmerucci', in
Paragone, 325, March 1977, p. 28, illustration no. 30; F. todini, *La pittura umbra dal Duecento al
primo Cinquecento*, ed. Longanesi, Milan 1989, part I, p.,221 and part II, p. 169, fig. 354.

Finearte Milan, 3 April 1996 (129**) ITL 368,000,000	US$	235,144

PALMEZZANO Marco di Antonio (1459 c. Forli-1539 Forli) Italian
CHRIST CARRYING THE CROSS oil on panel, 22 1/8 x 19¾in. (65.2 x 49.3cm.) s inscr. 'Marchus
palmezanus / pictor foroliviensis / faciebat' (1520's)

Christie's London, 19 April 1996 (241**) GBP 100,500	US$	152,388

CRISTO PORTACROCE oil on board, 70 x 57cm. s 'Marcus Palmezzanus faciebat' on the cross

Finearte Rome, 22 November 1995 (107**) ITL 82,800,000	US$	51,977

THE MYSTIC MARRIAGE OF SAINT CATHERINE WITH THE ARCHANGEL RAPHAEL
AND TOBIAS, SAINTS AUGUSTINE AND PHILIP BENIZZI oil on panel, 101¾ x 71 5/8in.
(258.4 x 182.2cm.) signed and dated 'Marhcus palmezeinus / pictor forlivensis Faciebat
Mccccxxxvii' and inscribed on a tablet 'D[omi]na lucia ol[im] Vxor Magistri /
Jovanis Calzolarij Splendido(?) viri De / Cesena fecit fieri / An[n]o d[omi]ni XXXvii' and on a book
'Ave Regina Celorvm / mater Regis Angelor[vm] / Sancta Maria flos Virginv[m] / Vel Rosa vel
lilivm fvn / de preces Ad. filiv pro.salvte.fidelivm / Gavde virgo Ma / ter Christi qve per / avrem
Concepisti chabrielle nvntio'
PROV.: Painted for the church of San Agostino, Cesena, from where probably alienated in or after
the1790s; Alexander Baring, 1st Lord Ashburton (1774-1848), or his son William, 2nd Lord
Ashburton (1799-1864), at The Grange, Hampshire or Bath House, London; By inheritance to the
latter's widow, Louisa, Lady Ashburton (1827-1903); Her grandson, Lord Spencer Compton (1893-
1915), and subsequently by inheritance through elder brother, William, 6th Marquess of
Northampton.
LIT.: B.Berenson, *Italian Pictures of the Renaissance - Central Italian and North Italian Schools*,
London, 1968, I, p. 312.

Christie's London, 7 July 1995 (115**) GBP 221,500	US$	353,326

PANINI Francesco (1745 -1812) Italian
INTERIOR OF THE BASILICA DI SAN PIETRO oil on canvas, 75 x 100cm.

Christie's Rome, 21 November 1995 (214**) ITL 15,000,000	US$	9,416

PANINI Giovanni Paolo (1691/92 Piacenza-1765 Rome) Italian
BATHERS BY ROMAN RUINS AND A GARDEN LOGGIA WITH STROLLERS CAUGHT IN
HIDDEN WATER JETS oil on canvas (a pair), each: 28¾ x 23¾in. (73 x 60.3cm.) (ca. 1715)

Sotheby's New York, 11 January 1996 (117**) US$ 145,500	US$	145,500

A CAPRICCIO WITH THE PANTHEON, ARCH OF JANUS, THE FARNESE HERCULES AND
THE STATUE OF MARCUS AURELIUS oil on canvas, 37¾ x 52in. (95.9 x 132.1cm.) sdlr 'I. Paul
Pan./Romae 1737'
LIT.: F. Arisi 'Panini, Il genio del Barocco', in: *Libertà* (a Piazenza Newspaper). 17 June 1991, p. 8
(illustrated).

Sotheby's New York, 11 January 1996 (134**) US$ 222,500	US$	222,500

CAPRICCIO OF OVERGROWN ROMAN RUINS WITH FIGURES oil on canvas, 46½ x 35¾in.
(118.1 x 90.8cm.) (1720-25)

Sotheby's New York, 16 May 1996 (68**) US$ 90,500	US$	90,500

A CAPRICCIO OF CLASSICAL RUINS WITH FIGURES oil on canvas, 23½ x 53¾in. (59.7 x 136.7cm.)
    Christie's South Kensington, 18 april 1996 (136**) GBP 6,900   US$ 10,462

A CAPRICCIO OF CLASSICAL RUINS WITH THE MAISON CARREE AT NIMES, THE TEMPLE OF THE SYBIL AT TIVOLI, THE PONT DU GARD NEAR NIMES AND THE BORGHESE VASE oil on canvas, 29¼ x 39¼in. (74.3 x 99.7cm.) sd 'I.P. PANINI / ROMÆ (linked) / 1739'
PROV.: Charles Castairs, Paris; His sister, Mrs. Maria Castairs Brooks; Sotheby Parke-Bernet, New York, 20 May 1971, lot 65 (with the pendant, $40,000); with Leger Galleries, London (*Old Master Exhibition*, 3-27 May 1972).
LIT.: F. Arisi, *Gian Paolo Panini e i fasti della Roma del'700*, Rome, 1986, p. 279, illustrated, and under no. 278, and p. 426, under no.392.
    Christie's London, 7 July 1995 (102**) GBP 243,500   US$ 388,419

PANINI Giovanni Paolo (Studio of) (1691/92 Piacenza-1765 Rome) Italian
A CAPRICCIO OF CLASSICAL RUINS WITH SOLDIERS AT A POOL oil on canvas, 40¾ x 64½in. (103.5 x 163.7cm.)
    Christie's South Kensington, 6 November 1995 (467**) GBP 12,937   US$ 20,236

PANN Abel (1883 -1963)
LE SACRIFICE D'ABRAHAM pastel on paper, 18½ x 23½in. (47 x 60cm.) slr and titled 'Etude pour le sacrifice d'Abraham, Abel Pann'
    Christie's Tel Aviv, 14 April 1996 (52A**) US$ 10,925   US$ 10,925

PAOLETTI Antonio Ermolao (1834 |-1912) Italian
THE YOUNG MUSICIAN oil on panel, 9 x 13½in. (22.8 x 34.3cm.) s and inscr. 'Antonio Paoletti di Giovni / Venezia'
    Christie's South Kensington, 14 March 1996 (176**) GBP 9,420   US$ 14,386

THE THREE GRACES oil on canvas, 26 x 42in. (66 x 106.7cm.) s inscr. lr 'Antonio Paoletti fu Giovni/Venezia'
PROV.: With Richard Green, London.
    Christie's New York, 22 May 1996 (255**) US$ 68,000   US$ 68,000

PAPE Abraham de (1620 c. -1666) Dutch
A KITCHEN INTERIOR WITH AN ELDERY MAN CARESSING A KITCHEN MAID oil on panel, 49 x 38cm. slr on the table 'A.DE PAPE'
PROV.: Anonymous sale, London, Sotheby's, 21 March 1973, lot 5, bought de Wit for GBP 3,500.
    Sotheby's Amsterdam, 6 May 1996 (1***) NLG 37,760   US$ 22,017

PAPE Frank Cheyne (1878 -1972) British
THE LEGEND OF SIEGFRIED pencil and watercolour heightened with bodycolour and varnished, in an embossed copper 'Arts and Crafts' frame (5 pieces), 36½ x 34in.) 93 86.5cm.) sd. 'F.C Papé 4'
    Christie's London, 6 November 1995 (112**) GBP 28,750   US$ 44,971

PARENTINO Bernardo (1437 c. -1531) Italian
CRUCIFIXION WITH SOLDIERS GAMBLING AT THE FOOT OF THE CROSS oil on panel transfered to canvas and later remounted on panel, 12½ x 8 7/8in. (31.8 xc 22.5cm.)
PROV.: Possibly Beltrami, Cremona ('una tavoletta con figure alte appena un piede, ma d'una espressione tenerissima,' see Selvatico in literature below).
LIT.: Possibly Pietro Selvatico, ed. of Vasari-Milanesi, Vol. V, 1849, pp. 187-88; Possibly E. Tietze-Conrat, *Mantegna; paintings drawings, engravings: complete edition*, 1955, p. 192.
    Sotheby's New York, 11 January 1996 (42**) US$ 57,500   US$ 57,500

PARKER Henry H. (1858 -1930) British
THE LLEDR VALLEY oil on canvas, 24 x 36in.(61 x 91.5cm.) slr 'Henry H. Parker'
      Phillips London, 23 April 1996 (126*) GBP 9,000   US$ 13,647

A SURREY CORNFIELD oil on canvas, 20 x 30in. (50.8 x 76.2cm.) s 'Henry H.Parker', sinscr. 'A
Surrey Cornfield/Henry H.Parker'
      Christie's South Kensington, 7 March 1996 (49**) GBP 8,200   US$ 12,523

PARKER Lawton S. (1868-1954) American
FIELD OF POPPIES oil on canvas, 24 x 19¾in. (61 x 50.3cm.) slr 'Lawton Parker'
      Christie's New York, 13 September 1995 (70**) US$ 59,700   US$ 59,700

PARRISH Maxfield (1870-1966) American
VILLA CICOGNA AT BISUSCHUI-THE LOWER TERRACE oil on paper, 27¾ x 17¾in. (70.5 x
45cm.) sll with ini. 'MP'
PROV.: Far Gallery, New York; Vose Galleries, Boston; Mr. and Mrs. William Piedmonte,
California; La Galleria, San Mateo, California.
EXH.: Windsor, Vermont, The Oaks, Maxfield Parrish Museum, Aug.-Dec. 1978.
LIT.: E. Wharton, *Italian Villas and Their Gardens*, New York, 1904, pp. 214-218.
      Christie's New York, 13 March 1996 (65**) US$ 55,200   US$ 55,200

OLD KING COLE oil on canvas, 44 x 132in. (111.7 x 335.2cm.) inscr. lr 'Painted for the Mask and
Wig Club of the University of Pennsylvania By F. Maxfield Parrish 1895'
EXH.: Chadds Ford, Pennsylvania, Brandywine River Museum, *Maxfield Parrish: Master of the
Make-Believe*, June-September 1974, no. 2; Southhampton, New York, Parrish Art Museum, *The
Dream World of Maxfield Parrish*, June-July 1975; Philadelphia, Pennsylvania, Philadelphia
Museum of Art, *Philadelphia: Three Centuries of American Art*, April-October 1976, no. 383.
LIT.: J.B. Carrington, 'The Work of Maxfield Parrish,' *The Book* Buyer, vol. 16, April 1898, p. 221;
H. Henderson, 'The Artistic Home of the Mask and Wig Club,' *House and Garden*, April 1904, pp.
168-174; H. St. Gaudens, "Maxfield Parrish,' *The Critic*, vol. 46, June 1905, pp. 512-513;
C. Brinton, 'A Master of the Make-Believe,' *Century Magazine*, vol. 84, July 1913, p. 349; The Art
Guide to Philadelphia, Philadelphia, Pennsylvania, 1925, p. 63; C. Ludwig, *Maxfield Parrish*, New
York, 1973, pp. 14, 15153, pl. 43; A. B. Percy, in *Philadelphia: Three Centuries of American Art*,
Philadelphia, Pennsylvania, 1976, pp. 449-450; A. Gilbert, *Maxfield Parrish: The Masterworks*,
Berkeley, California, 1992, pp. 16, 115-117, 119; L. Cutler, J. Goffman, and the American
Illustrators Gallery, *Maxfield Parrish*, New York, 1993, p. 97.
      Christie's New York, 23 May 1996 (169**) US$ 662,500   US$ 662,500

PARSONS Beatrice (1870 -1955)
THE ANNUNCIATION. 'HAIL, THOU ART HIGHLY FAVOURED' oil on canvas, unframed, 45 x
72in. (,114 x 183cm.) sdll '1897-9'
EXH.: London, Royal Academy, 1899, no.879.
      Phillips London, 18 June 1996 (87**) GBP 9,000   US$ 13,878

PASCIN Jules (Pincas) (1885-1930) American (Bulgarian)
FEMME ASSISE oil on canvas, 35 x 28in. (89 x 71cm.) slr 'Pascin' (1925-1926)
LIT.: This painting will be included in a forthcoming volume of the *Pascin catalogue raisonné*.
      Christie's New York, 1 May 1996 (171**) US$ 85,000   US$ 85,000

LE MODELE ETENDU oil on canvas, 32 x 25¾in. (81.3 x 65.3cm.) sul 'Pascin'
PROV.: Anon. sale, Paris, 20 November 1966; Lucy Krogh, Paris; Acquavella Galleries, Caracas,
from whom purchased by the present owner in 1974.
      Christie's Tel Aviv, 12 October 1995 (58**) US$ 66,300   US$ 66,300

COLETTE ASSISE oil on canvas, 36 x 28¾in. (91.4 x 73cm.) slr 'Pascin' (1927)
PROV.: Perls Galleries, New York.

EXH.: Philadelphia, Museum of Art, 1965 (on loan).
LIT.: Y.Hemin, Krohg, K.Perls, A.Rambert, *Pascin, catalogue raisonné peintures, aquarelles, pastels, dessins*, Paris, 1984, vol.I, no.,600 (ill. p.306).

Christie's Tel Aviv, 14 April 1996 (30**) US$ 107,000	US$	107,000

VILLAGE CUBAIN oil on canvas, 23¼ x 24in. (59.1 x 61cm.) (1917-18)
PROV.: Perls Galleries, New York.
LIT.: Yves Hemin, Guy Krohg, Klaus Perls and Abel Rambert, *Pascin: Catalogue raisonné, Peintures, Aquarelles, Pastels, Dessins*, vol. I, Paris 1984, no. 272 (illustrated p. 146).

Sotheby's New York, 2 May 1996 (351**) US$ 28,750	US$	28,750

LE NU DE LYSIS oil on canvas, 35 7/16 x 26 5/8in. (90 x 67.6cm.) slr 'Pascin' (1925)
PROV.: Mrs. A. Taliano, St. Catharines, Canada; Perls Galleries, New York.
EXH.: New York, Perls Galleries, *Jules Pascin: 1885-1930*, 1952, no. 10 (as *Nu de Dos*).
LIT.: Yves Hemin, Guy Krohg, Klaus Perls and Abel Rambert, *Pascin: Catalogue raisonné, Peintures, Aquarelles, Pastels, Dessins*, vol. 1, Paris, 1984, no. 520, illustrated p. 277.

Sotheby's New York, 2 May 1996 (384**) US$ 54,625	US$	54,625

HAMMAM-LIFE, TUNISIE oil on and gouache on black paper laid down on canvas, 93½ x 118¾in. (237.5 x 301.6cm.) titled inscr. 'Vue Prise de la Gare' (1924)
PROV.: Valentine Gallery, New York; Mr. and Mrs. E. Powis Jones, New York (1931); Vassar College Art Gallery, Poughkeepsie, NY (gifted from the above, 1954); Sale: Christie's New York, May 14, 1980, lot 43; Perls Galleries, New York.
LIT.: J. Delteil, 'On the Death of Pascin' from *Creative Art*, June 1931, vol. 8, no. 6 (illustrated p. 429 (incorrectly identified as a tapestry)); Yves Hemin, Guy Krohg, Klaus Perls and Abel Rambert, *Pascin: Catalogue raisonné, Peintures, Aquarelles, Pastels, Dessins*, vol. 1, Paris 1984, pl. XVI (illustrated p. 200).

Sotheby's New York, 2 May 1996 (393**) US$ 60,250	US$	60,250

PEINTRE ET MODELE AUTOUR D'UNE TABLE oil on canvas, 26½ x 21½in. (67.5 x 54.5cm.) slr 'Pascin' (ca. 1911-13)
PROV.: Leopold Hermann, Budapest; Sale Sotheby's, London 4th July 1974, lot 274.

Sotheby's London, 20 March 1996 (232**) GBP 13,225	US$	20,197

LA DAME AU TURBAN oil on canvas, 16 1/8 x 13in. (41 x 33cm.) slr with atelier stamp (1907)
PROV.: Anon. sale, Sotheby's Tel Aviv, 30 May 1989 lot 14 ($38,000).

Christie's London, 26 June 1996 (322**) GBP 18,400	US$	28,373

PERSONNAGES oil and pen and ink on board, 23 5/8 x 29in. (60 x 74cm.)

Christie's South Kensington, 27 November 1995 (67**) GBP 13,500	US$	21,117

HERMINE A LA BLOUSE BLEUE oil on canvas, 21¾ x 18 1/4in. (55.2 x 46.3cm.) lr (1912)
PROV.: Galerie de l'Elysée (Alex Maguy), Paris; Isadore Cummings; Mr. and Mrs. Robert B. Mayer, Larchmont, New York.

Christie's New York, 8 November 1995 (175**) US$ 25,300	US$	25,300

PASINELLI Lorenzo (1629 Bologna-1700) Italian
REBECCA AND ELIEZER oil on canvas, 49¾ x 67½in. (126.2 x 171.5cm.) (ca. 1665)

Sotheby's London, 5 July 1995 (120**) GBP 13,800	US$	22,013

PASINI Alberto (1826 Parma-1899 Turin) Italian
LA SENTINELLA oil on canvas, 17½ x 10½in. (44.5 x 26.5cm.) sd 'A. Pasini 1877'
PROV.: Turin, Esposizione Nazionale di Belle Arti, 1880, no. 607.
LIT.: Catalogue of the exhibition, *Esposizione Nazionale*, Turin, 1880; Chirtani, *L'Illustrazione Italiana*, 'L'Esposizione di Torino', 1880, no. 354, p.23; G. Mongeri, *La Perseveranza*, 'L'Arte Moderna all'Esposizione Nazionale di Torino, Pittura di geriere', Milan, 24 July 1880, no. 7457; E.

Seletti, *Memori storiche*, 'La città di Busseto, capitale un tempo della Stato Pallavicino', Milan, 1883, p. 298; A. de Gubernatis, *Dizionario degli artisti italiani viventi, Pittori, Scultori, Architetti*, Florence, 1889; G. Carotti, *Emporium*, 'Artisti contemporanei Alberto Pasini in memorium', Bergamo, Dec. 1899, p. 499, fig. 4; U. Fleres, *Nuova Antologia*, 'Alberto Pasini', 1900, vol. I; A. Pariset, *Dizionario biografico de Parmigiani illustri benemeriti nelle scienze, nelle lettere e nelle arti o per altra guisa notevoli*, Parma, 1905; A. Coma, *Dizionario della storia dell'arte italiana*, Pisa, 1930; D. Soresina, *Enciclopedia diocesana fidentina, I Personaggi Fidenza*, 1961; V. Botten Cardoso, *Pasini*, Genova, 1991, p. 340, no. 702 (illustrated).

Christie's London, 15 March 1996 (85**) GBP 18,400	US$	28,100

THE MOSQUE OF MAHOMOUDIE oil on canvas, 13 x 15¾in. (33 x 40cm.) sd "A Pasini 1868 Constantinopel'
PROV.: Mr. Joseph Gerli, New York; Miss Agatha Gerli, New York.

Christie's London, 15 March 1996 (135**) GBP 28,750	US$	43,907

PASSAROTI Bartolomeo (1529 -1592) Italian
FIGURE STUDY pen and brown ink, 32.7 x 23cm.

Étude Tajan Paris, 24 November 1995 (116*) FRF 42,000	US$	8,595

PASSAROTTI Bartolomeo (attr.) (1529 Bologna-1592 Bologna) Italian
THE HOLY FAMILY WITH INFANT SAINT JOHN THE BAPTIST oil on metal, 13½ x 10in. (35.5 x 26cm.)
PROV.: Frederick, 1st Marquess of Bristol.
LIT.: 1st Marquess, 1837, in her dressing room, *The Virgin and Child and St John, Joseph* behind; Farrer, 1913, no. 4, where said to be signed on the back 'Zuccari..(?) 1524'.

Sotheby's London, 11-12 June 1996 (468**) GBP 17,250	US$	26,600

PATCH Thomas (1725 Devonshire-1782 Florence) British
A VIEW OF THE ARNO WITH THE PONTE SANTA TRINITA oil on canvas, 35¼ x 48¼in.(89.5 x 122.5cm.) (ca 1745)
PROV.: Captain Bertram Currie, Dingley Hall, Market Harborough; Christie's, 27 March 1953, lot 60 (400gns. to Agnew); with Thomas Agnew & Sons, London.
EXH.: Florence, Forte de Belvedere, *Firenze e La Sua Immagine*, 29 June-30 Sept. 1994, no. 100.
LIT.: see FJ.B. Watson, *Walpole Society*, 28, l 940, *Thomas Patch: Notes on his Life*, together with a Catalogue of his known Works, p. 38, for discussion of similar works; E. Waterhouse, *The Dictionary of British 18th Century Painters in Oils and Crayons*, London, 1981, p.268, illus.

Christie's London, 18 April 1996 (35**) GBP 177,500	US$	269,143

PATENIR Joachim (1480 c. Dinant/Bavignes-1524 Antwerp) Flemish
SAINT JEROME IN A LANDSCAPE oil on panel, 38 x 49.5cm.

Christie's Amsterdam, 13 November 1995 (90*) NLG 16,100	US$	10,147

PAULUCCI Enrico (1901 b. Genua-) Italian
VALLE DI S. MARIA, TETTI oil on canvas, 46 x 55cm. sdlr 'Paullucci 47'
EXH.: *IV Premio Bergamo*.

Finearte Milan, 18 June 1996 (76*) ITL 16100,000	US$	10,441

PAUSER Sergius (1896 Vienna-1970) Austrian
STRAUSS MIT MARGUERITEN oil on canvas, 29 x 23 5/8in.(73.5 x 60cm.) s
PROV.: Private collection London; Private collection, Sweden.

Phillips London, 26 June 1995 (138) GBP 8,000	US$	12,765

PAVESI P. (19th century) Italian
THE PERFORMING MONKEY watercolour over traces of pencil, 25¾ x 19¼in. (65.4 x 48.9cm.) sll 'P. Pavesi'

Sotheby's Arcade Auctions New York, 20 July 1995 (557*) US$ 13,800	US$	13,800

PAVY Philippe (late 19th Century) French
AN ARAB STREET MARKET oil on panel, 15 x 21in. (38 x 53.5cm.) sd 'Ph. Pavy/1887' on the
reverse
    Christie's London, 15 March 1996 (74**) GBP 13,800   US$ 21,075

PAYNE Edgar Alwin (1882 -1947) American
VENETIAN BOATS oil on canvas laid down on board, 12¾ x 12¾in. (32.4 x 32.4cm.) slr 'Edgar
Payne'
PROV.: Petersen Galleries, Beverly Hills, California.
    Christie's New York, 13 September 1995 (54*) US$ 6,900   US$ 6,900

LAKE IN THE HIGH SIERRA oil on canvas, 49½ x 59in. (125.8 x 149.8cm.) sll 'Edgar Payne'
    Christie's New York, 13 March 1996 (80**) US$ 96,000   US$ 96,000

FRENCH TUNA BOATS oil on canvas, 28 x 33¼in. (71.1 x 84.4cm.) sll 'Edgar Payne'; inscr. with
title on the reverse
    Christie's New York, 23 May 1996 (114**) US$ 40,250   US$ 40,250

PEAKE Robert (attributed to) (ca. 1551 -1619) English
A PORTAIT OF A LADY, STANDING THREE-QUARTER LENGHT, IN THE CHARATER OF
A NYMPH OF DIANA, WEARING A GREEN AND SCARLET-TRIMMED DRESS WITH LACE
AND JEWEL-ENCRUSTED SLEEVES AND BODICE, A PEARL NECKLACE AND
EARRINGS, WITH FLOWERS IN HER HAIR, AND A LANDSCAPE BEYOND oil on canvas, 34
x 25¾in. (86.5 x 65.5cm.)
PROV.: With Sidney Sabin, 1958, as by *Marcus Gheeraerts de Younger*.
    Phillips London, 12 December 1995 (32**) GBP 85,000   US$ 130,809

PEALE Mary Jane (1826 America-1902) American
STILL LIFE WITH APPLES, GRAPES, FIGS AND PLUMS oil on canvas, 17 x 26¼in. (43 x
67cm.) sdlr 'MJ Peale 1887'
PROV.: Craig and Evans Fine Art dealers, Philadelphia, Pennsylvania; C.L.W. French, Boston,
Massachusetts.
EXH.: Boston, Massachusetts, Museum of Fine Arts, n.d.
    Christie's New York, 13 September 1995 (15**) US$ 23,000   US$ 23,000

PEALE Rembrandt (1778 Bucks (Pennsylvania)-1860 Philadelphia) American
PORTAIT OF GEORGE WASHINGTON (AFTER GILBERT STUART) oil on canvas, 19¾ x
15½in. (50.2 x 39.4cm.)
EXH.: Philadelphia, Pennsylvania, Independence Hall of Philadelphia, 1922; Philadelphia,
Pennsylvania, Pennsylvania Academy of Fine Art, April 1923, no. 221; Newark, New Jersey,
Newark Galleries, Inc., November 1930.
    Christie's New York, 13 September 1995 (3**) US$ 11,500   US$ 11,500

GEAORGE AND MARTHA WASHINGTON oil on canvas laid down on panel (a pair), each: 36 x
29¼in. (91.4 x 74.3cm.) sll 'Rembrandt Peale'
PROV.: The artist's studio, before 1860; Purchased from the above by Charles J. Coggill, New York;
Mrs. S. Edward Nash (née Isabel Coggill), New York; Stephen P. Nash, New York, her son; By
descent in the family to the present owner.
EXH.: New York, Sanitary Fair, before 1860; New York, Colonial Dames, *Washington Bicentennial
Exhibition*, February-March 1932; New York, Museum of the City of New York, 1946-1955, on
loan.
    Christie's New York, 23 May 1996 (4**) US$ 233,500   US$ 233,500

PEARLSTEIN Philip (1924 b. -) American
RECLINING NUDE ON PINK AND PURPLE DRAPES oil on canvas, 48 x 60in. (122 x 154.6cm.)
slr 'PEARLSTEIN' (1968)

PROV.: Allan Frumkin Gallery, Chicago.
EXH.: New York, National Academy of Design, *146th Annual Exhibition*, Feb.-Mar. 1971; Chicago, The Art Intitute of Chicago, *Selections from the Collection of Dr.Eugene Solow*, May-Aug. 1988, no.19.
LIT.: R.Bowman, *Philip Pearlstein: The Complete Paintings*, New York 1983, p.329, no.,313 (ill.).

Christie's New York, 8 May 1996 (328**) US$ 32,200	US$	32,200

PEARSALL Henry W. (fl 1824 -1861) British
ON THE AVON, NEAR BREDON, WORCESTERSHIRE oil on canvas, 14 x 18in. (35.5 x 46cm.) sd (1854)
PROV.: sometime with Frost and Reed.
EXH.: Royal Academy 1854, no. 1074.

Phillips London, 23 April 1996 (128*) GBP 13,000	US$	19,712

PECHSTEIN Hermann Max (1881 Zwickau-1955 Berlin) German
FRANK oil on canvas, 57.5 x 51cm. s with monogram (1916)

Hauswedell & Nolte Cologne, 1 December 1995 (519**) DEM 60,000	US$	41,629

HERBST, BAUME UND DUNEN oil on canvas, 27½ x 32¾in. (70 x 83cm.) sd 'M. Pechstein 1912'
PROV.: B.C. Holland, Chicago; Purchased by the present owner circa 1984.
EXH.: Chicago, The Arts Club of Chicago, *75th Anniversary Exhibition*, 1992, n.n.

Sotheby's London, 24 June 1996 (40**) GBP 243,500	US$	375,482

FISCHFANG AUF HOHER SEE water colour on powerfull pencil drawing with Chamoicoloured drawingpaper, 25 x 34cm. framed under glass sdlr monogram 'HMP (linked) 1920. (1920)

Lempertz Cologne, 29 November 1995 (384**) DEM 35,000	US$	24,704

PEDERSEN Carl-Henning (1913 b.) Danish
TUSCANIAN SUITE NO. 20 oil on canvas, 55 x 40.5cm. sd and titled 'Siena CHP80' on the reverse
PROV.: Lovenzelli Art, Milan.

Christie's Amsterdam, 5 June 1996 (355*) NLG 17,250	US$	10,079

LA DAME ET LICORNE I oil on canvas, 124 x 104cm. sd and inscr. with title on the reverse 'Carl-Henning Pedersen, Molemnes 1986'
PROV.: Galerie Ariel, Paris, no. 10461.

Christie's Amsterdam, 6 December 1995 (333**) NLG 29,900	US$	18,528

UNTITLED water colour on paper, 41.5 x 29.5cm. s with initials and dlr '45'

Sotheby's Amsterdam, 7 December 1995 (216**) NLG 10,620	US$	6,581

PEDRINI Domenico (1728 Bologna-1800) Italian
LA BENEDIZIONE DI GIACOBBE / LA CACCIATA DI AGAR oil on canvas (a pair), 140 x 96cm.

Finearte Rome, 21 May 1996 (118**) ITL 77050,000	US$	49,486

PEDRINI Giovanni, {called} Giampietrino (attr.) (16th Century, first half Milan, active-) Italian
SAINT CATHERINE oil on canvas, 23 x 17¾in. (58.5 x 45.5cm.)

Sotheby's London, 6 December 1995 (161**) GBP 17,250	US$	26,547

PEETERS Bonaventura the Elder (1614 Antwerp-1652 Hoboken) Flemish
A SHIPWRECK oil on panel, 25½ x 32¾in. (64.5 x 83.5cm.) bears ini. lr 'B.P'

Sotheby's London, 5 July 1995 (179**) GBP 7,475	US$	11,924

A WIJDSCHIP SAILING CLOSE-HAULED OFF A QUAY WITH A THREE-MASTER AT ANCHOR, OTHER SHIPPING NEARBY, IN A STIFF BREEZE oil on canvas, 72.5 x 91.5cm. sdll

'BP/1652'
        Christie's Amsterdam, 7 May 1996 (6**) NLG 27,600   US$ 16,093

A MERCHANTMAN FOUNDERING OFF A ROCKY COAST IN A GALE oil on panel, 41 x 69.2cm.
PROV.: Georg Adam Manger (according to a label on the reverse); Katherina Gugenham (according to an annotation on the label).
        Christie's Amsterdam, 7 May 1996 (97*) NLG 10,350   US$ 6,035

MERCHANTMEN ENTERING A LEVANTINE HARBOUR, IN A STORM, A GALLEY FOUNDERING IN THE FOREGROUND, ONLOOKERS ON A JETTY NEARBY oil on canvas, 60.3 x 83.4cm. scl on a piece of driftwood 'B Peeters'
        Christie's Amsterdam, 13 November 1995 (35a) NLG 20,700   US$ 13,046

EINE SCHIFFSWERFT IN EINEM FLÄMISCHEN HAFEN oil on panel, 48 x 80cm. sdlr 'B. Peeters fec. 1636'
PROV.: Slg. Sir Charles Bannerman, Bt., Aberdeenshire/Scotland.
        Lempertz Cologne, 15 November 1995 (1352**) DEM 19,000   US$ 13,411

A BRAZILIAN HARBOUR SCENE WITH DUTCH SHIPPING IN CHOPPY SEAS oil on canvas, 22½ x 33½in. (57 x 85cm.)
        Sotheby's London, 17 April 1996 (173**) GBP 25,300   US$ 38,362

PEETERS Clara (1589 Antwerp (?)-1655) Flemish
A STILL-LIFE OF ROSES, LILIES, AN IRIS AND OTHER FLOWERS IN A CERAMIC VASE TOGETHER WITH A POT WITH CARNATIONS AND A BUTTERFLY ON A LEDGE oil on oak panel, 25¾ x 19¾in. (65.7 x 50.2cm.) sdll 'CLARA P.A° 1612'
PROV.: Possibly Emil Glückstadt, Copenhagen, his deceased sale, Copenhagen, Winkel and Magnussen, fourth day's safe, 5 June 1924, lot 23, to V. Hansen; Mrs. Agnethe Jacobsen, Copenhagen, by 1960.
EXH.: Copenhagen, *Kunstforeningens udstilling af Hollandske og flamske stilloen fra 1600 - Tallet*, 1965, no. 67.
LIT.: P. Gammelbo, *Dutch Still-life painting from the 16th to 18th Centuries in Danish collections*, 1960, p. 30, no. 28, reproduced p. 31; A.S. Harris and L. Nochlin, *Women Artists 1550 -1950*, 1978, p. 132; M-L. Hairs, *The Flemish Flower Painters of the XVIIth Century*, 1985, p. 352; P.H. Decoteau, *Clara Peeters 1594 - c. 1640 and the Development of Still-life painting in Northern Europe*, 1992, p. 179, no. 8 *et passim*, reproduced p. 22, fig. 8.
        Sotheby's London, 6 December 1995 (60**) GBP 155,500   US$ 239,304

A STILL-LIFE OF FISH, OYSTERS AND CRAYFISH WITH A CAT oil on panel, 34 x 48cm. sll 'CLARA P'
PROV.: H..B.. Collction, Leipzig, by whom sold, Berlin, Lepke, 27 February 1928, lot 118.
LIT.: P. Hibbs Decoteau, *Clara Peeters*, 1992, pp. 39-41, 194, reproduced p. 39, fig. 26.
        Sotheby's Amsterdam, 6 May 1996 (9**) NLG 135,700   US$ 79,125

PEETERS Gillis I (1612 Antwerp-1653) Flemish
PAYSAGE DE RIVIERE AVEC LE BAPTEME DU CHRIST oil on oakpanel, 37 x 57cm. sll 'G Peeters'
PROV.: Collection M.I.F. Parsons, London, after 1932; Anonymous sale, Paris, Hôtel Drouot, 17 November 1958 (Maître Rheims), no. 89bis.
        Étude Tajan Paris, 12 December 1995 (12**) FRF 80,000   US$ 16,114

PEINADO Joaquín (1898 -1975) Spanish
BODEGON CON JARRA, COPAS Y ALCACHOFA oil on canvas, 38 x 61cm. sdlr 'Peinado '58'
PROV.: Private collection, France.
        Sotheby's Madrid, 23 November 1995 (85**) ESP 1292,500   US$ 10,624

PEPLOE Samuel John, R.S.A. (1871-1935) Scottish
BARRA oil on panel, 10 x 12in. (25.5 x 30.5cm.) oil study of a mother and child on the reverse
        Sotheby's London, 29 August 1995 (1001**) GBP 23,000   US$ 37,229

PERCY Sidney Richard Williams (1821-1886) British
A WELSH LANDSCAPE oil on canvas, sdll 'S R Percy. 71' 24 x 38in. (61 x 96.5cm.)
PROV.: With J. J. Gillespie Company, Pittsburgh.
        Christie's New York, 14 February 1996 (65**) US$ 112,500   US$ 112,500

CATTLE AND FIGURES BY A LOCH oil on canvas, 23¾ x 38¼in. (60 x 97cm.) sdlr '1871'
PROV.: Property of the family since the 1930s and thence by descent.
        Phillips London, 12 December 1995 (58**) GBP 23,000   US$ 35,396

SHEEP AND DROVERS, MORNING AND EVENING oil on canvas (a pair), each: 9 x 14½in.
(22.9 x 36.8cm.) each sd, the first '73', the second '64'
PROV.: The Cooling Galleries, London.
        Sotheby's Arcade Auctions New York, 17 January 1996 (266*) US$ 8,625   US$ 8,625

NEAR KESWICK, CUMBERLAND oil on canvas, 24 x 38in. (61 x 96.5cm.) sdll 'S R Percy'
        Christie's New York, 2 November 1995 (208**) US$ 23,000   US$ 23,000

CADER IDRIS, NORTH WALES oil on canvas, 24 x 38in. (61 x 96.5cm.) sdll 'SRPercy. 1844'
        Christie's New York, 2 November 1995 (210**) US$ 57,500   US$ 57,500

NEAR DOLGELLY, NORTH WALES oil on canvas, 44 x 72in. (111.8 x 182.9cm.) sdlr 'S R Percy.
1860'
        Christie's New York, 2 November 1995 (213**) US$ 36,800   US$ 36,800

CATTLE IN A HIGHLAND LANDSCAPE oil on canvas, 24 x 38in. (61 x 96.5cm.) sdll
'SRPercy/1870'
        Christie's New York, 22 May 1996 (278**) US$ 81,700   US$ 81,700

CATTLE AND SHEEP WATERING IN A LAKE LANDSCAPE WITH FIGURES CONVERSING
ON A PATH oil on canvas, 24 x 38½in. (61 x 97.8cm.) sd 'S.R.Percy 1862'
        Christie's South Kensington, 7 March 1996 (96**) GBP 9,500   US$ 14,508

PÉREZ Alonzo (1893-1914 active) Spanish
THE BOUQUET oil on panel, 24 1/8 x 39 3/8in. (61.3 x 100cm.) sll 'Alonzo-Perez'
        Christie's New York, 2 November 1995 (152**) US$ 18,400   US$ 18,400

PÉREZ Bartolomé (1634-1693) Spanish
A TULIP, PEONIES, ROSES, MORNING GLORY AND OTHER FLOWERS IN A SCULTED
URN ON A PEDESTAL oil on glass, 13½ x 11¼in. (34.3 x 28.6cm.) s 'Bme P'
PROV.: The Comtesse Edouard de St.Maurès (early 19th century)(?) inscription on the back).
        Christie's London, 8 December 1995 (53**) GBP 25,300   US$ 38,935

PERILLI Achille (1927 b. Rome) Italian
POCHI SEGNI oil on canvas, 50 x 70cm sd 'Achille Perilli `57 Pochi segni' (1957)
        Finearte Rome, 14 November 1995 (144*) ITL 13,225,000   US$ 8,302

PERMEKE Constant (Antwerp 1886-1952 Ostende) Belgian
LA ROULOTTE oil on canvas, 75 x 60cm. slr 'Permeke' (Executed *circa* 1923)
PROV.: Galerie Georges Giroux, Brussels.
EXH.: Brussels, Palais des Beaux Arts, *Retrospective Permeke,* 1947.
        Christie's Amsterdam, 5 June 1996 (218A**) NLG 74,750   US$ 43,675

A STANDING NUDE Charcoal on paper, 122 x 87cm. sll 'Permeke'
    Christie's Amsterdam, 5 June 1996 (221*) NLG 29,900   US$ 17,470

LA BAIGNADE oil on canvas, 75 x 60cm. sll 'Permeke' (ca. 1917)
PROV.: Alex Finck, Brussels; Elie Burthoul, Brussels; Galerie Georges Giroux, Brussels.
EXH.: Ostend, Provinciaal Museum voor Moderne kunst, *Constant Permeke*, December 1986-March
1987, without cat.numbers.
    Christie's Amsterdam, 6 December 1995 (196**) NLG 28,750   US$ 17,815

A MAN oil on canvas, 60 x 65cm. slr 'Permeke'
    Christie's Amsterdam, 6 December 1995 (247**) NLG 18,400   US$ 11,402

PERRAULT Léon Jean Basile (1832-1908) French
L'HOTESSE oil on canvas, 44¼ x 34¼in. (112.3 x 87cm.) sd 'L. Perrault/1873'
    Christie's London, 17 November 1995 (36**) GBP 18,400   US$ 28,781

A YOUNG PEASANT GIRL, SLEEPING oil on canvas, 37¼ x 61in. (94.7 x 155cm.) sdll 'L.
Perrault 74'
    Christie's New York, 2 November 1995 (97**) US$ 55,200   US$ 55,200

PETHER Henry (1828 - 1865 fl.) British
THE NEW HOUSES OF PARLIAMENT, SHOWING THE CONSTRUCTION OF THE
VICTORIA TOWER AND WESTMINSTER BRIDGE, BY MOONLIGHT oil on canvas, 24 x 36in.
(61 x 91.5cm.) slr indistinctly
    Phillips London, 18 June 1996 (43**) GBP 11,000   US$ 16,962

PETERSON Jane (Mrs Bernard Phillipp) (1876-1965) American
LADY WITH A PARASOL gouache on paper, 24 x 18in. (61 x 45.7cm.) slr 'Jane Peterson'; inscr.
'Summer. Painted at Gloucester, Mass, Girl with Parasol and my dog Dodo' on the reverse
EXH.: New York, H.V. Allison Galleries, *Jane Peterson (1876-1965) and Hayley Lever (1876-
1958)*, April 1990, no. 3 (illustrated on cover).
    Christie's New York, 23 May 1996 (127**) US$ 27,600   US$ 27,600

PETITJEAN Edmond Marie (1844-1925) French
FISHING BOATS MOORED ALONG A COAST oil on canvas, 18 x 25½in. (45.7 x 64.8cm.)
PROV.: Borghi & Co., Inc., New York (as 'Marine').
    Sotheby's Arcade Auctions New York, 20 July 1995 (269*) US$ 10,350   US$ 10,350

PETITJEAN Hippolyte (1854 -1929) French
LES BAIGNEUSES oil on canvas, 25¾ x 31¾in. (65.4 x 81cm.) sll 'Hipp Petitjean'
    Christie's New York, 1 May 1996 (186**) US$ 28,750   US$ 28,750

FEMME NUE DEBOUT gouache and watercolour on paper laid down at the edges on board, 12½ x
6in. (31.7 x 15.2cm.) stamped lr 'Atelier Hipp. Petitjean' (Lugt 2022c)
PROV.: Barry-Lardy et Cie, Paris.
    Christie's East, 7 November 1995 (16*) US$ 7,475   US$ 7,475

PETTENKOFEN August Xaver Karl Ritter von (Vienna 1822-1889 Vienna) Austrian
KAUERNDES MÄDCHEN oil on board, 65 x 51cm. sll 'Pettenkofen'
    Dorotheum Vienna, 6 November 1995 (73**) ATS 200,000   US$ 20,063

A MARKET SQUARE oil on panel, 3 x 6¼in (7.7 x 15.8cm.) s with ini. 'A.P.'
    Christie's South Kensington, 12 October 1995 (93*) GBP 8,775   US$ 13,849

MARKTPLATZ IN SZOLNOK watercolour on paper laid down on cartonboard, 24.4 x 30.3cm. sll
'pettenkofen; inscr. 'A. v. Pettenkofen' on the reverse
      Wiener Kunst Auktionen, 29 November 1995 (557**) ATS 110,000   US$ 11,035

PEVSNER Antoine (Orel 1884-1962 Paris) French (Russian)
ABSTRACT COMPOSITION oil on canvas laid down on board, in the Artist's original frame, 17½ x
17½ (44.5 x 44.5cm.) sd twice 'Pevsner 15' (1915)
PROV.: Darmstadt, Hessisches Landesmuseum, 1993-1996 (on loan).
LIT.: F. Schrenk, Informationen aus dem Hessischen Landesmuseum in Darmstadt, Darmstadt, Feb.
1993, p. 13 (illustrated).
      Christie's London, 26 June 1996 (254**) GBP 58,700   US$ 90,517

PFEILER Maximilian (18th Century, 1st quarter, active Rome) German
STILL-LIFE OF FIGS, WINE, GLASSES AND BISCOTTI, PEACHES, MORNING GLORY,
GRAPES AND MELON, ALL IN A LANDSCAPE oil on canvas, 31 1/8 x 26¾in. (79 x 67.9cm.) sll
on stone 'M. Pfeiller'
      Sotheby's New York, 11 January 1996 (82**) US$ 20,700   US$ 20,700

PLUMS, PEARS, PEACHES, FIGS ON A PLATE, PINK ROSES,GRAPES,MORNING GLORY,
PETUNIAS AND ALIZZARD ON A ROCKY BANK oil on canvas, 40¾ x 62¾in. (103.5 x 159.4)
      Christie's London, 7 July 1995 (2**) GBP 20,700   US$ 33,020

PHILIPS Charles (1708-1747) British
LADIES AND MAIDS OF HONOUR IN GREENWICH PARK: A GROUP PORTRAIT OF
JULIANA, DUCHESS OF LEEDS, LADY CHARLOTTE HAMILTON, LADY ISABELLA
TUFTON, AND HENRIETTA, COUNTESS OF POMFRET, ALL WEARING RIDING HABITS,
TWO SEATED IN A CHAISE, AND TWO STANDING, WITH A GROOM AND HORSES, IN
FRONT OF THE OBSERVATORY oil on canvas, 36 x 45in. (91.4 x 114.3cm.) d inscr. 'May 16
1730'
PROV.: Captain Bertram Currie, Dingley Hall, Market Harborough; Christie's 27 March 1953, lot 62
(200gns. to Cutberth).
      Christie's London, 18 April 1996 (10**) GBP 20,700   US$ 31,387

PIAZZETTA Giambattista (Giovanni Battista) (Venice 1683-1754 Venice) Italian
STUDY OF A GIRL RESTING HER HEAD ON HER HAND Black chalk heightened with white on
faded blue paper, 40.6 x 31.2cm. watermark star above an eagle within a shield
      Phillips London, 6 December 1995 (181***) GBP 21,000   US$ 32,318

PICABIA Francis (François Marie Martinez-) (Paris 1879-1953 Paris) French/Cuban
LES DEUX PEUPLIERS, EFFET DE SOLEIL, BORDS DE L'YONNE oil on canvas, 21 5/8 x 25
5/8in. (55 x 65cm.) sdlr 'Picabia 1906'; sd again and titled on the stretcher 'F. Picabia, Les deux
peupliers, effet de Soleil, bords de l'Yonne 1906'
PROV.: Anon. sale, Hôtel Drouot, Paris, 8 March 1909, lot 53 (illustrated).
      Christie's New York, 1 May 1996 (187**) US$ 77,300   US$ 77,300

CANAL DE ST. MAMMES oil on canvas, 24 x 28 7/8in. (61 x 73.3cm.) sd 'Picabia 7' (1907)
      Sotheby's New York, 2 May 1996 (185**) US$ 63,000   US$ 63,000

UNCANA gouache, watercolour and black crayon over pencil, 42x 30in. (,107 x 76cm.) slr 'Francis
Picabia'; titled ll (1929)
PROV.: Sale, Sotheby's, London, 1 April 1981, lot 252 (purchased by the present owner).
      Sotheby's London, 20 March 1996 (52***) GBP 89,500   US$ 136,683

VUE DE SAINT-TROPEZ oil on canvas, 21 2/8 x 25 5/8in. (54 x 65cm.) sd 'Picabia 1904'
PROV.: Paul Poiret, Paris; his sale Hôtel Drouot, Paris, 18 November 1925, lot 45, where bought by
Mme. M Pouillot, Paris and thence to present owner.

Christie's London, 26 June 1996 (107**) GBP 47,700   US$ 73,554

L'HOMME DEBOUT gouache and watercolour on cardboard, 39 3/8 x 29½in. (,100 x 75cm.) sll
'Francis Picabia' (c1926)
PROV.: Galleria d'Arte, Falsetti, Prado; Kent Fine Art, New York; Galerie Neuendorf, Frankfurt.
EXH.: Nimes, *F. Picabia*, Summer 1986; Edinburgh, Royal Scottish Academy, *Picabia 1879-1953*,
30 July-4 Sept. 1988, no.25; Paris, Didier Imbert Fine Art, *Picabia*, 27 April-13 July 1990, no.22;
Antwerp, Gallery Ronny van de Velde, *Picabia*, 28 Feb.-25 April 1993; Mallorca, Fondacio Pilar e
Joan Miró, *Picabia,* 5 Oct.-3 Dec. 1995; Barcelona, Fundacio Antoni Tápies, *Picabia*, 19 Dec. 1995-
3 March 1996.
LIT.: M.L. Borras, *Picabia*, London, 1985, no. 438 (illustrated no. 597, p. 316).
Christie's London, 26 June 1996 (208**) GBP 69,700   US$ 107,479

LA FEMME DE L'AMOUR watercolour pencil and charcoal on paper, 41 3/8 x 29½in. (,105 x
75cm.) s inscr. 'Francis Picabia / la femme de l'amour' s inscr. again on the backboard
EXH.: Paris, Theophile Briant, *Picabia,* Oct. 1928 (10631).
Christie's London, 26 June 1996 (217**) GBP 38,900   US$ 59,985

LOTRULI -VISAGE DE OLGA oil on paper laid down on canvas, 36 1/8 x 25 5/8in. (92 x 65cm.) s
titled 'Francis Picabia / Lotruli' (1929)
Christie's London, 26 June 1996 (221**) GBP 71,900   US$ 110,871

WASHERWOMEN (LAVANDIERES) oil on canvas, 92 x 73cm. slr 'Picabia' (1935)
PROV.: Bought by the current owner at Galerie Romanet in Algier, around 1940-42.
EXH.: Chicago, Arts Club, January 1936, no. 5.
LIT.: Maria Lluisa Borrás, *Picabia*, Editions Albin Michel, Paris 1985, p 527, illustrated p. 402, no.
814.
Étude Tajan Paris, 28 March 1996 (49**) FRF 120,000   US$ 23,720

COUPLE AU PROFIL DE MARCEL DUCHAMP oil on board, 20½ x 24 7/8in. (52 x 63cm.) slc
'FRANCIS PICABIA' (betweeen 1924 and 1927)
PROV.: Simone Collinet, Paris; Enrico Baj, Milan, purchased from the above in Feb. 1958.
EXH.: Leverkusen, Städtisches Museum Schloss Morsbroich, *Picabia*, Feb.-April 1967, no. 44. This
exhibition later travelled to Eindhoven, Stedelijk van Abbe-Museum, April-June 1967; Paris Centre
National de l'Art et de Culture Georges Pompidou, *Francis Picabia*, Jan-March 1976, no. 166
(illustrated).
LIT.: J.H. Martin & H. Seckel. *Francis Picabia* ed. Musée National d'Art Moderne, Paris, 1976, no.
166, p. 189 (illustrated p.136).
Christie's London, 29 November 1995 (167**) GBP 55,000   US$ 86,032

PORTRAIT DE FEMME oil on board, 18 x 15in. (45.7 x 38cm.) sll 'Francis Picabia' (1942-1943)
Christie's East, 7 November 1995 (1646**) US$ 17,250   US$ 17,250

PICART Jean-Michel (1600 c. -1682) Flemish
ROSES AND CARNATIONS IN A *FAÇON-DE-VENISE* VASE ON A STONE LEDGE oil on a
panel, 42.2 x 32.6cm
Christie's Amsterdam, 13 November 1995 (155**) NLG 25,300   US$ 15,945

PICASSO Pablo Ruiz (Malaga 1881-1973 Mougins) Spanish
BOUTEILLE DE BASS ET GUITARE pastel on paper, 18¼ x 24¼in. (46.4 x 66.6cm.) sd on the
reverse 'Picasso 1912'
PROV.: Galerie Kahnweiler, Paris; Galerie Simon, Paris; Dr. G. F. Reber, Lausanne; Douglas
Cooper, Paris (acquired from the above, 1940); Anon. sale, Sotheby's, London, 24 April 1968, lot
137; Stieiregen (acquired at the above sale); Anon. sale, Christie's, New York, 15 May 1986, lot 130;
Stanley J. Seeger, New York.
LIT.: C. Zervos, *Pablo Picasso*, Paris, 1942, vol. 2** *(Oeuvres de 1912 à 1917)*, no. 375 (illustrated,

443

p. 182); F. Russoli and F. Minervino, *L'opera completa di Picasso Cubista*, Milan, 1972, no. 548 (illustrated, p. 113); P. Daix, *Pablo Picasso: The Cubist Years 1907-1916*, Boston 1979, p. 287 (cited under no. 511); J. Palau i Fabre, *Picasso Cubism (1907-1917)*, New York, 1990, no. 812 (illustrated, p. 286).

Christie's New York, 1 May 1996 (191**) US$ 96,000   US$ 96,000

L'INDEPENDANT (NATURE MORTE A L'ÉVENTAIL) oil on canvas, 24 x 19¾in. (61 x 50cm.) slr 'Picasso' s inscr. on the reverse 'Picasso Ceret à Vollard' (1911)
PROV.: Ambroise Vollard, Paris; Paul Guillaume, Paris; Mr. and Mrs. Henry Clifford, Radnor, Pennsylvania; Galene Rosengart, Lucerne; Acquired from the above by the late owner.
EXH.: Philadelphia, Museum of Art, *Masterpieces of Philadelphia Priuate Collections*, summer, 1947, p. 74, no. 56; New York, Sidney Janis Gallery, *Cubism 1910-1912*, Jan.-Feb., 1956, no. 31 (illustrated); Philadelphia, Museum of Art, *Picasso: A Loan Exhibition of His Paintings, Drawings, Sculpture, Ceramics, Prints and Illustrated Books*, Jan.-Feb., 1958, p. 17, no. 57a (illustrated); Philadelphia, Museum of Art (on loan, 1965); Dallas, Museum of Fine Arts, *Picasso, Two Concurrent Retrospective Exhibitions*, Feb.-March, 1967, p. 94, no. 19 (illustrated p.29); Philadelphia,

L'Indépendant (Nature Morte à l'Eventail)

Museum of Art (summer loan, 1970); Basel, Kunstmuseum, *Picasso, aus dem Museum of Modem Art, New York und Schweizer Sammlungen*, June-Sept., 1976, p. 48, no. 21 (illustrated in colour, p. 49); New York, The Museum of Modern Art, *Pablo Picasso, A Retrospective*, May-Sept., 1980 (illustrated, p. 144).
LIT.: W. George, *La grande peinture contemporaire de la collection Paul Guillaume*, Paris, 1,930 (illustrated, pl. 129); C. Zervos, *Pablo Picasso*, Paris, 1942, vol. II* (*oeuvres de 1906-1912*), p. 131, no. 264 (illustrated)
G. Habasque, *Cubisme*, Geneva, 1959, p. 50 (illustrated in colour); J. Leymarie, *Picasso, Métamorphoses et Unité,* Geneva, 1971, p. 36 (illustrated in colour); F. Russoli and F. Minervino, *L'opera completa di Picasso cubista*, Milan, 1972, p. 108, no. 412 (illustrated); J.-L. Daval, *Journal de l'art modeme 1884-1914*, Geneva, 1973, p. 242 (illustrated in colour); R. Rosenblum, *Picasso and the Typography of Cubism* London, 1973, p. 74, no. 126 (illustrated); M. Gasser, 'Bilder aus einer Privatsammlung', *Du*, Dec., 1974, p. 26, no. 406 (illustrated); J. Palau i Fabre, *Picasso en Cataluna*, Barcelona, 1975, no. 230 (illustrated); P. Daix and J. Rosselet, *Picasso, The Cubist Years, 1907-1916*, London, 1979, p. 267, no. 412 (illustrated); W. Rubin, *Picasso and Braque, Pioneering Cubism*, New York, 1989, p. 197 (illustrated in colour); J. Palau i Fabre, *Picasso, Cubism (1907-1917)*, New York, 1990, p. 215, no. 595 (illustrated in colour, p. 216).

Christie's New York, 7 November 1995 (4**) US$ 7,042,500   US$ 7,042,500

LA PLAGE, JUAN-LES-PINS oil on canvas, 15 x 18in. (38.1 x 45.7cm.) sdlr 'Picasso 37' d on the reverse 'J. Les Pins 13-Aout 37. II'
PROV.: Pierre Loeb, Paris; E.V. Thaw & Co. and Stephen Hahn, New York.

Christie's New York, 1 May 1996 (344**) US$ 464,500   US$ 464,500

BUSTE D'HOMME ASSIS oil on cardboard laid down on panel, 37 7/8 x 25½in. (96.3 x 64.8cm.) sd and numbered ul 'Picasso 12.3.69 III' (12 March 1969)
PROV.: Galerie Louise Leiris, Paris; Daniel Varenne, Geneva.
LIT.: C. Zervos, *Pablo Picasso*, Paris 1976, vol. 31 (*Oeuvres de 1969*), no. 94 (illustrated pl. 29).

Christie's New York, 1 May 1996 (388**) US$ 233,500   US$ 233,500

TETE D'HOMME (DOUBLE FACE) / STUDY IN INK (VERSO) gouache and ink on paper, 17½ x 13in. (44 x 33cm.) sdll 'Picasso 12 septembre 39' s '2 septembre 39, inscr. Royan' on the reverse (1939)
PROV.: Galerie Jeanne Bucher, Paris; *Collection Gildas Fardel*, Paris.
      Étude Tajan Paris, 10 June 1996 (56**) FRF 900,000   US$ 173,789

GUÉRIDO AVEC GUITARE gouache on paper, 10½ x 8¼in. (27 x 21cm.) sdlr 'Picasso 27.2.1926'
PROV.: Hotel Drouot, Paris (Maître Bellier) 27 February 1926.
LIT.: Christian Zervos, *Pablo Picasso*, Editions 'Cahiers d'Art', Paris vol. IV, *Oeuvres de ,920 à 1922*, no. 81, p. 194 (illustrated p. 26).
      Étude Tajan Paris, 13 December 1995 (46**) FRF 550,000   US$ 110,784

FEMME ASSISE oil on canvas, 46 x 38cm. sdul 'Picasso 31.3.53' (1953)
LIT.: Christian Zervos, *Pablo Picasso, Oeuvres de 1946 á 1953*, vol.15, ed. Cahiers d'Art, Parijs 1965, no.253, p.143.
      Finearte Milan, 19 March 1996 (66**) ITL 920,000,000   US$ 588,612

EL TIO PEPE DON JOSE india ink on paper laid down on card, 10¾ x 8 3/8in. (27.3 x 21.3cm.) s inscr. 'Picasso El tio Pepe Don José à 40 años' (1905)
PROV.: Estate of Edward Bernays.
EXH.: Washington, National Gallery of Art, *Picasso The Saltimbanques*, 1980, no. 42; Cambridge, Fogg Art Museum; Art Institute of Chicago; Philadelphia Museum of Art, *Master Drawings by Picasso*, 1981, no. 6; Barcelona, Museo Picasso; Bern, Kunstmuseum, *Picasso 1905-1906*, 1992, no. 52; Nassau County Museum of Art, *Long Island Collections*, 1993.
LIT.: Christian Zervos, *Pablo Picasso, oeuvres de 1903 à 1906, supplément*, vol. 22, Paris, 1965, no. 217, illustrated pl. 78; Pierre Daix and Georges Boudaille, *Picasso 1900-1906*, Neuchatel 1966, no. XII.29, illustrated pp. 78 & 265; Josep Palau i Fabre, *Picasso the Early Years 1881-1907*, New York, 1981, no. 1106, illustrated p. 413.
      Sotheby's New York, 2 May 1996 (191***) US$ 68,500   US$ 68,500

LA VERRE TAILLE SUR FOND BLEU oil on canvas, 7½ x 10 5/8in. (19.1 x 27cm.) sll 'Picasso' (1922)
PROV.: Galerie Louise Leiris, Paris; Perls Galleries, New York.
LIT.: Christian Zervos, *Pablo Picasso: Supplement aux Années 1920-1922*, vol. 30, Paris 1975, no. 289 (illustrated p. 99).
      Sotheby's New York, 2 May 1996 (205**) US$ 162,000   US$ 162,000

BAIGNEUS (LA PLAGE A DINARD) oil on canvas, 16¼ x 8½in. (41.3 x 21.6cm.) sdll 'Picasso 28'
PROV.: G. David Thompson, Pittsburgh; Richard Feigen Gallery, New York; Acquired from the above by the Benjamin family in 1964.
EXH.: Zurich, Kunsthaus and Dusseldorf, Kunstmuseum, *G. David Thompson Collection*, 1960-61, no. 174; New Haven, Yale University Art Gallery, *The Helen and Robert M. Benjamin Collection*, 1967, no. 144.
LIT.: Christian Zervos, 'Picasso à Dinard' in *Cahiers d'Art*, 1929, vol. I, illustrated p. 13; Christian Zervos, *Pablo Picasso; Oeuvres de 1926 à 1932*, vol. 7, Paris, 1955, no. 233, illustrated p. 92.
      Sotheby's New York, 2 May 1996 (266**) US$ 426,000   US$ 426,000

MODELE DANS L'ATELIER oil on canvas, 15 x 18in. (38 x 46cm.) sur 'Picasso' d '24.3.65. VI' on the reverse
PROV.: Galerie Louise Leiris, Paris; Galerie Beyeler, Basel.
EXH.: Galerie Beyeler, Basel, *Picasso: Werke von 1932-1965*, 1967, no. 59, illustrated in the catalogue.
LIT.: Christian Zervos, *Pablo Picasso, oeuvres de 1965 à 1967*, Paris, 1972, vol. 25, pl. 37, no. 63, illustrated.
      Sotheby's London, 20 March 1996 (67**) GBP 153,300   US$ 234,117

JEUNE FILLE ESPAGNOLE DEVANT LA MER oil on board, 20¾ x 13 3/8in. (52.5 x 34cm.) sll
'Picasso' (1901)
PROV.: M. Labbe (purchased in 1905); Mlle. Labbe (daughter of the above); M. Guerin, Versailles
(purchased from the above); Purchased from the above by the present owner.
        Sotheby's London, 24 June 1996 (35**) GBP 496,500   US$ 765,613

FEMME ASSISE oil on board, 9 x 5 7/8in. 23 x 15cm. sd 5.12.39; sd on the reverse
PROV.: Heinz Berggruen, Paris.
LIT.: Christian Zervos, *Pablo Picasso, oeuvres de 1937 à 1939*, 1958, vol. 9, pl. 174, no. 372,
illustrated (incorrectly catalogued as oil on canvas).
        Sotheby's London, 24 June 1996 (46**) GBP 936,500   US$ 1,444,102

NU DEBOUT LES BRAS CROISES brush and ink on paper, 42½ x 28 3/8in. 108 x 72cm. sd
25.12.23 (1923)
PROV.: Albert Skira, Geneva (a gift from the artist); Acquired from the above by the present owner.
EXH.: Lausanne, Palais de Beaulieu, *Chefs-d'oeuvre des collections suisses, de Manet à Picasso*,
1964, no. 240, illustrated in the catalogue; Geneva, Musée de l'Athénée, *De Cézanne à Picasso*,
1967; Geneva, Musée Rath, *Art du XXème siècle collections genevoises*, 1973.
LIT.: Christian Zervos, *Pablo Picasso, oeuvres de 1923 à 1925,* Paris, 1952, vol. 5, pl. 68, no. 138,
illustrated; Alan Wofsy, *The Picasso Project: Picasso's Paintings, Watercolours, Drawings and
Sculpture, Neoclassicism II, 1922-1924*, San Francisco, 1996, p. 182, no. 23-232, illustrated.
        Sotheby's London, 24 June 1996 (47*) GBP 205,000   US$ 316,114

TETE DE FEMME DE PROFIL oil on canvas, 13 x 9½in. (33 x 24cm.) inscr. 'Juan-les-Pins' d '24'
on the stretcher
PROV.: Estate of the artist; Marina Picasso, Geneva; Galerie Jan Krugier, Geneva.
EXH.: New York, Jan Krugier Fine Art, *Pablo Picasso, Petits Formats*, 1989, no. 11.
LIT.: David Douglas Duncan, *Picasso's Picassos*, London, 1961, p. 210, illustrated Alan Wofsy, *The
Picasso Project: Picasso's Paintings, Watercolours, Drawings and Sculpture, Neoclassicism II*,
1922-1924, San Francisco, 1996, p. 223, no. 24-122, illustrated.
        Sotheby's London, 24 June 1996 (57**) GBP 177,500   US$ 273,709

FEMME ASSISE DE PROFIL DANS UN FAUTEUIL BLUE oil on canvas, 45 5/8 x 35in. (,116 x
89cm.) sdur 'Picasso' sd '23.4.60' on the reverse
PROV.: Galerie Louise Leiris, Paris; Galleria Toninelli, Milan.
        Sotheby's London, 24 June 1996 (70**) GBP 441,500   US$ 680,802

IRIS JAUNES oil on canvas, 19¾ x 16 3/8in. (50 x 41cm.) sll 'Picasso' (spring 1901)
PROV.: Mr. and Mrs. Mark Oliver, London; Alex Reid & Lefevre, London; Captain S. W. Sykes,
Cambridge (1935); sale, Sotheby's; London, 22 June 1966, lot 13 (GBP 15,900 to Ellis); T. Arnold
and Fannie Askin, New York.
EXH.: Paris, Galerie Vollard, *Exposition de tableaux de F. Iturrino et de P. R. Picasso*, June-July
1901, no. 6; London, Alex Reid & Lefevre, *Thirty Years of Pablo Picasso*, June, 1931, no. 37;
Cambridge, Fitzwilliam Museum, 1939-1966 (on extended loan).
LIT.: C. Zervos, *Pablo Picasso*, Paris, 1932, vol. I (*oeuvres de 1895 à 1906*), no. 58 (illustrated pl.
28); A. Cirici-Pellier, *Picasso avant Picasso*, Geneva, 1950, p. 204, no. 43 (illustrated); P. Daix, G.
Boudaille and J. Rosselet, *Picasso: The Blue and Rose Periods, A Catalogue Raisonné of the
Paintings, 1900-1906*, Neuchatel, 1966, no. V.25 (illustrated p. 169); J. Palau i Fabre, *Picasso, The
Early Years, 1881-1907*, New York, 1980, no. 626 (illustrated p. 243).
        Christie's London, 25 June 1996 (7**) GBP 551,500   US$ 850,424

FEMME NUE black ink on paper, 42¾ x 28 3/8in. (108.5 x 72cm.) slr 'Picasso' (1923)
PROV.: Private Collection, Switzerland'.
EXH.: Lausanne, Palais de Beaulieu, *Chefs d'Oeuvre des Collections Suisses*, 1 May- 25 Oct. p. 68.
LIT.: C. Zervos, *Pablo Picasso, Oeuvres de 1923 à 1925*, vol. 5, no. 137 (illustrated p. 68).
        Christie's London, 25 June 1996 (14**) GBP 265,500   US$ 409,406

VERRE, BOUTEILLE, POISSON oil and ripolin on canvas, 25 5/8 x 32¼in. (65 x 81.5cm.) sd 'Picasso 22'
PROV.: D.-H. Kahnweiler (Galerie Simon), Paris; Galerien Flechtheim Berlin/Düsseldorf (13493/12293, as *Wein und Fisch*), from whom purchased by the previous owner circa 1925.
EXH.: Hamburg, Kunstverein (on loan).
LIT.: G. Stein *Picasso*, London, 1943 no. 39 (provenance given as Galerie Simon); C. Zervos, *Pablo Picasso, Oeuvres de 1920 à 1922* vol 4. Paris, 1951, no. 401 (illustrated p. 168).
Christie's London, 25 June 1996 (29**) GBP 881,500   US$ 1,359,291

TETE D'HOMME DE PROFIL oil on canvas, 25 5/8 x 21¼in. (65 x 54cm.) sur 'Picasso' d '9.3.63.II' on the reverse
PROV.: Galerie Louise Leiris, Paris (014063); Marlborough Gerson Gallery, New York (N41855); Marlborough Galleria d'Arte, Rome (RD0331); Galleria d'Arte l'Appodo, Bari.
LIT.: C. Zervos, *Pablo Picasso, Oeuvres de 1962 et 1963*, vol. 23, Paris, 1972, no. 173 (illustrated p. 86).
Christie's London, 25 June 1996 (58**) GBP 276,500   US$ 426,369

TETE D'HOMME A LA PIPE oil on canvas, 36¼ x 28 5/8in. (92 x 73cm.) sur 'Picasso' d and numbered '3.6.65.II' (on the reverse)
PROV.: Galerie Louise Leiris, Paris (014124), by whom purchased directly from the Artist.
LIT.: C. Zervos, *Pablo Picasso, Oeuvres de 1962 à 1963*, vol. 25, Paris, 1972, no. 151 (illustrated p. 84).
Christie's London, 25 June 1996 (60**) GBP 304,000   US$ 468,774

LES COMMUNIANTS oil on canvas, 13¾ x 9½in. (35 x 24.1cm.) sdur 'Picasso 19'
PROV.: Jacques Doucet, Paris; J. Hartford Bryce.
EXH.: New York, Jacques Seligmann & Co., *20 years in evolution of Picasso 1903-1923*, Nov. 1,937 no. 13 (illustrated).
LIT.: C. Zervos, *Pablo Picasso, Oeuvres de 1917 à 1919*, vol. III, 1949, no. 286 (illustrated pl. 10).
Christie's London, 26 June 1996 (272**) GBP 150,000   US$ 231,303

SCENE DE TAUROMACHIE gouache, brush and black ink on paper, 14 7/8 x 21¼in. 938 x 54cm.) s 'Picasso 25.3.59'
Christie's London, 26 June 1996 (297**) GBP 71,900   US$ 110,871

TETE DE FEMME ink and coloured crayon on cardboard laid down on canvas, 28.5 x 22cm. d 'jeudi 16.9.71. VI'
LIT.: Christian Zervos *Pablo Picasso*, éditions cahiers d'Art, Paris vol. 33, illustrated p. 69, no. 190.
Étude Tajan Paris, 28 March 1996 (57***) FRF 90,000   US$ 17,790

L'AVENUE FROCHOT, VUE DE L'ATELIER oil on canvas, 9 3/8 x 7½in. (24 x 19cm.) s on the reverse 'Picasso' (1911)
PROV.: Galerie Kahnweiler, Paris; Alfred Flechtheim, Düsseldorf, by whom purchased from the above in early 1912; Hermann Lange, Krefeld.
EXH.: Cologne, Städtische Austellungshalle, *Sonderbund Internationale Kunstausstellung*, May-Sept. 1912, no. 224 (lent by Flechtheim); Munich, Modern Galerie Heinrich Thannhauser, *Ausstellung Pablo Picasso*, Feb. 1913, no. 63 (lent by Flechtheim).
LIT.: C. Zervos, *Pablo Picasso, Oeuvres de 1906-1912*, vol. 2*, Paris, 1951, no. 268 (illustrated p. 133); F. Russoli, *L' Opera Completa di Picasso* Cubista, Milan, 1 972, no. 428 (illustrated p . 1 9); P. Daix andJ. Rosselet, *Picasso: the Cubist Years 1907-1916*, London, 1979, no. 443 (illustrated p. 274); M. Theresa Ocana, *Picasso Landscapes 1890-1912*, Barcelona, 1994, p. 317 (illustrated p. 316).
Christie's London, 28 November 1995 (24**) GBP 188,500   US$ 294,854

LES DEUX FENETRES gouache on paper, 24 x 23in. (61 x 58.5cm.) sll 'Picasso' (1923)
PROV.: Galerie Flechtheim, Berlin and Düsseldorf (14166); Hermann Lange Krefeld; on loan,

Munich, Bayerische Staatsgemälde Sammlungen, Munich (L.176).
      Christie's London, 28 November 1995 (26**) GBP 117,000   US$ 183,013

GUITARE SUR UNE TABLE oil on canvas, 39 x 38in. (99 x 97.5cm.) sll 'Picasso' (1921)
PROV.: Pierre Loeb, Paris, by whom acquired directly from the Artist; Saidenberg Gallery, New
York (1947); Lydia and Harry Winston, New York, by whom acquired from the above in 1953.
EXH.: Ann Arbor, 1955, no. 54 (illustrated on the cover of the catalogue); Detroit, 1957-1958, pp.
18, 70, no. 84 (illustrated); Detroit, Detroit Institute of Arts, *The Varied Works of Picasso*,
Detroit, 1972-1973; New York, 1973-1974, pp. 160, 161, no. 82 (illustrated).
LIT.: C. Zervos, *Pablo Picasso, vol. IV, Oeuvres de 1920 à 1922*, Paris, 1942, p. 128 (illustrated pl.
334); p. 100 (verso illustrated pl. 282); L. Degand and J. Arp, 'La Collection Harry and Lydia
Winston au Musée de Detroit, ' *Aujourd'hui*, Paris, 1957 (illustrated p. 30); J.C. Taylor, 'Harry Lewis
Winston: Futurist and Other Twentieth Century Art,' in *Great Private Collections*, New York, 1963
(illustrated p. 303); G. Baro, 'Collector: Lydia Winston,' *Art in America*, vol. 55, no. 5, September-
October 1967, p. 72; G. Baro, 'Futurism Preserved: Lydia Winston Malbin,' *The Collector in
America*, New York, 1971, p. 183; G. Baro, 'A Lifelong Education of the Senses,' in: *Living with Art*,
New York, 1988 (illustrated p. 140).
      Christie's London, 28 November 1995 (28**) GBP 1,013,500   US$ 1,585,328

DEUX FEMMES NUES ASSISES pencil on paper, 14½ x 21in. (36.9 x 53cm.) slr 'Picasso' dated
and numbered ul '1 juillet 66 I'
PROV.: Galerie Louise Leiris, Paris (no. 62982); Galeria Theo, Madrid (44); Evelyn Airnis Gallery,
Toronto.
EXH.: Basel, Galerie Beyeler, *Picasso*, April-July 1981, no. l02; Basel, Galerie Beyeler, *Nudes-nus-
nackte*, June-Aug. 1984, no. 76; Basel, Galerie Beyeler, *Picasso-der Maler und seine Mode*, July-
Oct.1986, no. 84.
LIT.: C. Zervos, *Pablo Picasso, Oeuvres de 1965 à 1967*, vol.25, Paris, 1972, no. 216 (illustrated p.
110).
      Christie's London, 29 November 1995 (233***) GBP 54,000   US$ 84,467

BUSTE DE FEMME oil on canvas, 25½ x 21¼in. (65 x 54cm.) dated and numbered on the reverse
'2.4.76.II'
LIT.: C. Zervos*, Pablo Picasso, Oeuvres de 1965 à 1967*, vol. 25, Paris, 1972, no. 321 (illustrated p.
139).
      Christie's London, 29 November 1995 (242**) GBP 138,000   US$ 215,861

TETE D'HOMME oil on canvas, 24 x 19 5/8in. (61 x 49.8cm.) d on the reverse '10.12.64.V' (1964)
PROV.: Estate of the Artist, Paris; Claude Picasso, Paris.
LIT.: C. Zervos, *Pablo Picasso*, Paris, 1971, vol. XXIV (*Oeuvres de 1964)*, no. 314 (illustrated, pl.
124); C.-P. Warncke, *Pablo Picasso, 1881-1973*, vol. II (*Les Oeuvres de 1937 à 1973*) Cologne,
1992, p. 621, no. 8 (illustrated in colour, p. 620).
      Christie's New York, 30 April 1996 (63**) US$ 409,500   US$ 409,500

GARÇON A LA COLLERETTE gouche on board, 30 1/8 x 25¾in. (76.6 x 65.5cm.) sll 'Picasso'
(1905)
PROV.: Haldsdurk Collection, Berlin; Oscar Huldschinsky, Berlin; Mrs. A. Furstenberg, Amsterdam;
Wildenstein & Co. Inc., New York; André Meyer, New York; sale, Sotheby Parke Bernet Inc., New
York, Oct. 22, 1980, lot 32 (illustrated in color).
EXH.: Amsterdam, Stedelijk Museum (on loan, 1945-1949); Washington, D.C., National Gallery of
Art, *Exhibition of the Collection of Mr. and Mrs. André Meyer*, June-July, 1962, p. 30 (illustrated).
LIT.: C. Zervos, *Pablo Picasso*, Paris, 1957, vol. I (*oeuvres de 1895 à 1906)*, p. XLVII, no. 273
illustrated pl. 120); P. Daix, G. Boudaille and J. Rosselet, *Picasso 1900-1906*, 1966, p. 279, no.
X111.18 (illustrated); A. Moravia and P. Lecaldano, *Picasso blu e rosa*, 1968, p. 104, no. 214
illustrated); J. Palau i Fabre, *Picasso, The Early Years 1881-1907*, Barcelona, 1985, p. 548, no. 1173
illustrated, p. 429).
      Christie's New York, 7 November 1995 (30**) US$ 12,102,500   US$ 12,102,500

TETE oil and sand on canvas laid down on canvas, 21 1/8 x 12 5/8in. (53.7 x 32.1cm.) sll 'Picasso' (1928)
PROV.: Valentine Gallery, New York; Claire Zeisler, Chicago; Richard Gray Gallery, Chicago.
EXH.: Chicago, The Art Institute, *Picasso in Chicago: Paintings, Drawings and Prints from Chicago Collections*, February - March 1968, p. 33, no. 32 (illustrated in the exhibition catalogue); Chicago, Museum of Contemporary Art, *In the Mind's Eye, Dada and Surrealism*, December 1984-January 1985, p. 208 (illustrated in the exhibition catalogue).
LIT.: C. Zervos, *Pablo Picasso*, Paris, 1955, vol. VII (*oeuvres de 1926 à 1932*), no. 121 (illustrated, pl. 52).
Christie's New York, 7 November 1995 (43**)
US$ 486,500   US$ 486,500

Le Miroir

LE MIROIR oil on canvas, 51¼ x 38 1/8in. (130.2 x 96.8cm.) sll 'Picasso' d on the stretcher '12 Mars XXXII'
PROV.: Galerie Louise Leiris, Paris (acquired from the artist in 1958); The Gustav Stern Foundation, Inc., New York.
EXH.: Paris, Galerie Georges Petit, *Picasso*, June-July, 1932, no. 217; Zurich, Kunsthaus, *Picasso*, Sept.-Oct., 1932; New York, Museum of Modern Art, *Picasso: Forty Years of His Art*, Nov., 1939-Jan., 1940, p. 155, no. 245 (illustrated); The exhibition traveled to Chicago, The Art Institute, Feb.-March, 1940; St. Louis, City Art Museum, March-April,1940; Boston, Museum of Fine Arts, April-May, 1940 and San Francisco, Museum of Art, June-July, 1940; Sao Paulo, Museo de Arte Moderno, *Exposicaio Picasso, Bienalle*, Dec., 1953-Feb., 1954, p. 31, no. 26 (illustrated, pl. 26); Paris, Musée des Arts Decoratifs, *Picasso, Peintures 1900-1955*,June-Oct., 1955, no. 72 (illustrated); London, Tate Gallery, *Picasso*, 1960, no. 127 (illustrated); New York, Museum of Modern Art, *Pablo Picasso: A Retrospective*, May-Sept., 1980, p. 293 (illustrated).
LIT.: *Cahiers d'art*, 1932, vol. VII, nos. 3-5, p. 148 (illustrated); A.H. Barr, Jr., *Picasso: Fifty Years of His Art*, New York, 1946, p. 175 (illustrated); C. Zervos, *Pablo Picasso*, Paris, 1952, vol. VII (oeuvres de 1926 à 1932), no. 378 (illustrated, pl. 166); F. Elgar, *Picasso: A Study of His Work*, Paris, 1955, p. 215 (illustrated); J. Camon-Aznar, *Picasso y el Cubismo*, Madrid, 1956, p. 501, fig. 373 (illustrated); P. Daix, *Picasso*, Paris, 1964, p. 146 (illustrated in color, p. 148); J. Berger, *The Success and Failure of Picasso*, London, 1965, p. 108, no. 61 (illustrated); A. Fermigier, *Repertoire de l'oeuvre*, Paris, 1967, p. 193 (illustrated in colour); W. Rubin, *Picasso in the Collection of the Museum of Modern Art*, New York, 1971, pp. 140 and 141 (illustrated, p. 226); ed. G. Golding, 'Picasso and Surrealism,' *Picasso in Retrospect*, New York, 1973, pp. 110-,112 (illustrated, pl. 182); T. Hilton, *Picasso*, New York, 1975, p. 220, no. 164; L. Nochlin, 'Picasso's Color: Schemes and Gambits,' *Art in America*-Special Issue on Picasso, Dec., 1980, p. 179 (illustrated in colour, p. 119, fig. 18); 'Picasso, The Fantastic Period, 1931-1945,' *Picasso Series*, vol. V, 1981, no. 17 (illustrated); *The Sciences*, vol. 23, no. 5, Sept.-Oct., 1983 (illustrated on the cover); C.P. Warocke, *Pablo Picasso 1881-1973*, Cologne, 1992, vol. I, p. 352 (illustrated in colour); C. Geelhaar, *Picasso, Wegbereiter und Förderer seines Aufstiegs 1899-1939*, Zürich, 1993, p. 193, no. 211 (illustrated); J. Freeman, *Picasso and the Weeping Women, The Years of Marie-Thérèse Walter and Dora Maar*, Los Angeles,1995, p. 147, fig. 109 (illustrated in colour, p. 149).
Christie's New York, 7 November 1995 (45**) US$ 20,022,500   US$ 20,022,500

FEMME COUCHEE oil on canvas, 38 1/8 x 51¼in. (97 x 130cm.) sll 'Picasso' (21/8/1941)
PROV.: Kootz Gallery, New York; Himan Brown, New York (acquired from the above in 1947); The Metropolitan Museum of Art, New York (gift from the above in 1977).
EXH.: Worcester, Art Museum, *Picasso-His Later Works 1938-1961*,Jan.-Feb., 1962, p. 11, no. 5 (illustrated, p. 10); Toronto, The Art Gallery, *Picasso and Man*, Jan.-Feb., 1964, p. 132, no. 232

(illustrated); New York, Acquavella Galleries, *Picasso, A Loan Exhibition for the Benefit of Cancer Care*, Inc., April-May, 1975 (illustrated); Brookville, New York, Hillwood Art Center, *Madame in Her Boudoir 1870-1940*, Oct.-Nov., 1981; Roslyn Harbor, New York, The Nassau County Museum of Art, *The Avant Garde of France: The 1940s and 1950s*, June-Sept., 1994, p. 5 (illustrated).
LIT.: C. Zervos, *Pablo Picasso*, Paris, 1960, vol. XI (*oeuvres de 1940 et 1941*), no. 285 (illustrated, pl. 113).

Christie's New York, 7 November 1995 (51**) US$ 574,500	US$	574,500

NATURE MORTE, FRUITS ET POT oil on canvas, 18 1/8 x 21¾in. (46 x 55.3cm.) sdll 'Picasso 13.2.38.'
PROV.: Sam Salz, New York.
EXH.: Paris, Galerie Paul Rosenberg, 1938.
LIT.: *Cahier d`Art*,'La dernière exposition de Picasso', vol. 14, nos.1-4, 1939, p. 87(illustrated); C. Zervos, *Pablo Picasso*, Paris, 1960, vol.IX (*oeuvres de 1937 à 1939*), no. 105 (illustrated, pl. 50).

Christie's New York, 7 November 1995 (54**) US$ 288,500	US$	288,500

TETE DE FEMME AU CORSAGE RAYE (PORTRAIT DE FRANCOISE) charcoal on paper, 26 x 20in. (66 x 51cm.) dal. '7.9.50.'
PROV.: Estate of the Artist (No. 5346); Heinz Berggruen, Paris; Waddington Galleries, London; Jeffrey Cohen, Londen.

Christie's New York, 7 November 1995 (57**) US$ 272,000	US$	272,000

LE DEJEUNER SUR L'HERBE coloured wax crayons, brush and black ink on panel, 14 x 18in. (35.5 x 45.7cm.) dal. '11.8.59' and dedicated 'Picasso 19.10.69. Pour mon ami Norman Granz'
PROV.: Norman Granz, Geneva (gift from the Artist on October 19, (1969).
LIT.: D. Cooper, *Pablo Picasso, Les Déjeuners*, Paris, 1962, pl. 10 (illustrated in colour); C. Zervos, *Pablo Picasso*, Paris, 1968, vol. XIX (oeuvres de 1959 à 1961), no. 39 (illustrated, pl. 9).

Christie's New York, 7 November 1995 (59**) US$ 409,500	US$	409,500

L'INDEPENDANT (NATURE MORTE A L'EVENTAIL) oil on canvas, 24 x 19¾in. (61 x 50cm.) slr 'Picasso'; s and inscr. on the reverse 'Picasso Ceret à Vollard' (1911)
PROV.: Ambroise Vol1ard, Paris; Paul Guillaume, Paris; Mr. and Mrs. Henry Clifford, Radnor, Pennsylvania; Galerie Rosengart, Lucerne; Acquired from the above by the late owner.
EXH.: Philadelphia, Museum of Art, *Masterpieces of Philadelphia Private Collections*, summer, 1947, p. 74, no. 56; New York, Sidney Janis Gallery, *Cubism 1910-1912*, Jan.- Feb., 1956, no. 31 (illustrated); Philadelphia, Museum of Art, *Picasso: A Loan Exhibition of H's Paintings, Drawings, Sculpture, Ceramics, Prints and Illustrated Books*, Jan.-Feb., 1958, p. 17, no. 57a (illustrated); Philadelphia, Museum of Art (on loan, 1965); Dallas, Museum of Fine Arts, *Picasso, Two Concurrent Retrospective Exhibitions*, Feb. -March, 1967, p. 94, no. 19 (illustrated, p. 29). Philadelphia, Museum of Art (summer loan, 1970); Basel, Kunstmuseum, *Picasso, aus dem Museum of Modern Art, New York und Schweizer Sammlungen*, June-Sept., 1976 p. 48, no. 21 (illustrated in color, p. 49); New York, The Museum of Modern Art, *Pablo Picasso, A Retrospective*, May-Sept., 1980 (illustrated, p. 144).
LIT.: W. George, *La grande peinture contemporaine de la collection Paul Guillaume*, Paris, 1930 (illustrated, pl. 129); C. Zervos, *Pablo Picasso*, Paris, 1942, vol. 11* (*oeuvres de 1906-1912*), p. 131, no. 264 (illustrated); G. Habasque, *Cubisme*, Geneva, 1959, p. 50 (illustrated in colour); J. Leymane, *Picasso, Métamorphoses et Unité*, Geneva, 1971 p. 36 (illustrated in colour); F. Russoli and F. Minervino, *L'opera completa di Picasso cubista*, Milan, 1972, p. 108, no. 412 (illustrated); J.-L. Daval,Journal de l'art moderne 1884-1914, Geneva 1973, p. 242 (illustrated in colour); R. Rosenblum, *Picasso and the Typography of Cubism*, London, 1973, p. 74, no. 126 (illustrated); M. Gasser, 'Bilder aus einer Privatsammlung', *Du*, Dec. 1974, p. 26, no. 406 (illustrated); J. Palau i Fabre, *Picasso en Cataluna*, Barcelona, 1975, no. 230 (illustrated); P. Daix and J. Rosselet, *Picasso, The Cubist Years, 1907- 1916*, London, 1979, p. 267, no. 412 (illustrated); W. Rubin, *Picasso and Braque, Pioneering Cubism*, New York, 1989, p. 197 (illustrated in colour); J. Palau i Fabre, *Picasso, Cubism (1907-1917)*, New York 1990, p. 215, no. 595 (illustrated in colour, p. 216).

Christie's New York, 8 November 1995 (4**) US$ 7,042,500	US$	7,042,500

PORTRAIT DE JANE THYLDA black chalk with traces of pink pencil on paper laid down on board, 12 x 9 3/8in. (30.4 x 23.8cm.) ul 'Picasso' ll 'JANE THYLDA' with collector's stamp of Gustav Engelbrecht (Lugt 1148) lr
PROV.: Gustav Engelbrecht, Hamburg.
EXH.: Philadelphia, Museum of Art, 1967 (on loan).

Christie's New York, 8 November 1995 (157**) US$ 107,000	US$	107,000

VERRE, JOURNAL ET BOUTEILLE DE BASS oil on panel mounted on board, 9 1/2 x 7 1/4in. (24 x 18.4cm.) ul 'Picasso' (1914)
PROV.: Bignou Gallery, New York; Theodore Schempp & Co., New York (acquired by the late owner, 1944).
EXH.: Chicago, The Arts Club, *An Exhibition of Cubism*, Oct.-Nov., 1955, no. 22; Chicago, Art Institute, *Picasso in Chicago*, Feb.-March, 1968, no. 24; New York, Saidenberg Gallery Inc., *Hommage to Picasso for his 90th birthday, Exhibition for the benefit of the American Cancer Society*, Oct., 1971, no. 23 (illustrated).
LIT.: C.Zervos, *Pablo Picasso*, Paris, 1975, vol. 29 (*Supplément aux années 1914-1919*), no. 17 (illustrated, pl.8).

Christie's New York, 8 November 1995 (182**) US$ 305,000	US$	305,000

PIPE ET VERRE oil and sand on canvas, 10 5/8 x 8 5/8in. (27 x 22cm.) ur 'Picasso 18' (1918)
PROV.: Galerie L'Effort Moderne (Léonce Rosenberg), Paris; Paul Rosenberg & Co., New York (acquired by the present owner, 1963).
EXH.: New York, Paul Rosenberg & Co., *Picasso, an American Tribute: The Twenties*, April-May, 1962, no. 4 (illustrated).
LIT.: C. Zervos, *Pablo Picasso*, Paris, 1949, vol. 3 (*Oeuvres de 1917 à 1919*), no. (illustrated, pl. 51).

Christie's New York, 8 November 1995 (189**) US$ 283,000	US$	283,000

LA PIQUE oil on canvas, 15 x 18¾in. (38.1 x 46.3cm.) ll 'Picasso' on the reverse '8.3.60.III' (March 8 1960)
PROV.: Galerie Louise Leiris, Paris; Saidenberg Gallery Inc., New York (1961); Mr. and Mrs. Taft B.Schreiber (acquired from the above); sale, Sotheby Parke-Bernet Inc., Manalapan, Florida, March 20, 1979, lot 211.
EXH.: Los Angeles, University of California, Art Galleries, *'Bonne Fête' Monsieur Picasso from Southern California Collectors*, Oct.-Nov.,1961, no. 45; Worcester, Art Museum, *Picasso: His Later Works, 1938 to 1961*, Jan.-Feb., 1962, no. 112 (illustrated).
LIT.: C. Zervos, *Pablo Picasso*, Paris, 1968, vol. 19 (*Oeuvres de 1959 à 1961*), no. 211 (illustrated, pl. 59).

Christie's New York, 8 November 1995 (237**) US$ 129,000	US$	129,000

PIENE Otto (1928 b.) German
STERNBILD 2 oil on canvas, 78¾ x 59in. (,200 x 150cm.) sd titled '89/90' on the reverse and on the stretcher
PROV.: Galerie Schoeller, Dusseldorf.

Christie's London, 23 May 1996 (139**) GBP 10,350	US$	15,672

PIERI Stefano (1542 -1629) Italian
THE HOLY FAMILY WITH THE INFANT SAINT JOHN THE BAPTIST oil on canvas, 39 7/8 x 31¾in. (101.3 x 80.7cm.) s mono 'SP'
PROV.: Mrs. Eva Bogner Regis, Sussex (according to an old label on the reverse).

Christie's London, 19 April 1996 (197**) GBP 25,300	US$	38,362

PIERNEEF Jacob Hendrik (1886-1957) South African
KAMEELDORING-BOME oil on canvas, 51 x 69cm. sll 'Pierneef' inscr. with the title on the stretcher.

Christie's Amsterdam, 26 October 1995 (84*) NLG 12,650	US$	7,976

PIETERS Evert (Amsterdam 1856-1932 Laren (N.-Holland)) Dutch
A YOUNG GIRL PEELING FRUIT oil on panel, 16¼ x 12½in. (41.3 x 31.8cm.) sdll 'E.
Pieters./1912'
        Christie's New York, 14 February 1996 (72**) US$ 18,400   US$ 18,400

A SHELL FISHER oil on canvas, 121 x 90cm. sll 'E. Pieters'
        Christie's Amsterdam, 26 October 1995 (42*) NLG 12,650   US$ 7,976

PIGNONI Simone (Florence 1614-1698 Florence) Italian
LABAN SEARCHING FOR THE HOUSEHOLD IDOLS oil on canvas, added canvas on four sides,
overall: 37¼ x 53in. (170.8 x 134.6cm.); without additions: 56¾ x 42in. (144.1 x 106.7cm.)
        Sotheby's New York, 16 May 1996 (51**) US$ 25,300   US$ 25,300

PILLEMENT Jean (Jean Baptiste) (1728 Lyon-1808 Lyon) French
A RIVER LANDSCAPE WITH DROVERS, CATTLE AND GOATS CROSSING A BRIDGE oil
on canvas, 28½ x 39½in. (72 x 100.5cm.) sdll 'J Pillement 1789'
PROV.: With A. Seligmann, 1925; With Messrs. M. Knoedler & Co. Inc., 1959; With Maurice
Segoura, 1979.
EXH.: Paris, A. Seligmann, May-June 1925; On loan, City of London Club, 1980-1995.
LIT.: *Apollo*, December 1959, vol. LXX, no. 418, p. 202.
        Sotheby's London, 5 July 1995 (53**) GBP 67,500   US$ 107,673

LANDSCAPE WITH SHEPHERDS NEAR A SMALL LAKE AND THE RUINS OF A VILLAGE
ON A HILL oil on canvas, 66.5 x 96cm. sd 'J Pillement/1785'
        Christie's Monaco, 14 June 1996 (36**) FFr 234,000   US$ 45,185

PINACCI Guiseppe (Sienna 1642-1718) Italian
CAVALRY BATTLE oil on canvas, 28½ x 52¾in. (72.5 x 134cm.)
        Sotheby's London, 5 July 1995 (127**) GBP 12,650   US$ 20,179

PINCHON Robert Antoine (1886-1943) French
LA SEINE AUX ENVIRONS DE ROUEN oil on canvas, 60 x 81cm. slr
        Étude Tajan Paris, 17 June 1996 (61**) FRF 73,000   US$ 14,096

PINGRET Henri Edouard Théophile (St Quentin 1788-1875) French
PORTRET OF AN ALCHEMIST, PROBABLY J.F. BÖTTGER oil on canvas, 46 x 38cm. sd 'Ed
Pingret 1832'
EXH.: Salon de 1833 (as *a german alchemist*).
        Étude Tajan Paris, 26 March 1996 (88***) FRF 40,000   US$ 7,907

PINTORICCHIO Bernardino di Betto, {called} (attr.) (1454 -1513 Siena) Italian
MADONNA AND CHILD gold ground and tempera on panel, 18¼ x 14½in. (46.4 x 36.8cm.)
PROV.: Collection of the late Count and Countess Guy de Boisrouvray.
        Sotheby's New York, 16 May 1996 (3**) US$ 48,875   US$ 48,875

PIOLA Domenico (Genua 1627-1703 Genua) Italian
AMORE CACCIATORE oil on canvas, 192 x 124cm.
        Finearte Rome, 18 October 1995 (397**) ITL 55,200,000   US$ 34,393

PIPER John, C.H. (Epsom, Surrey 1903-1992) British
TRYFAN FROM LLYN BOCHLWYD watercolour, bodycolour, pen, brush, black ink and coloured
crayon, 21 x 27in. (53.3 x 68.5cm.) sll 'John Piper', s again 'John Piper' s inscr. on the reverse 'Tryfan
from Llyn Bochlwyd water-colour by John Piper' (1949)
EXH.: Florida, Palm Beach Society of Four Artists, *Contemporary British Painting*, Jan. 1956, no.30
as Tryfan Mountain: this exhibition travelled to Florida, University of Miami, Lowe Gallery, Feb.-
March 1956; Havana, Patronato de Bellas Artes Y Museos Nacionales, March-April 1956; Alabama,

Birmingham Museum of Art, May-June 1956; and New York, E & A Silberman Galleries, Oct.-Nov.
1956; London, Marlborough Fine Art, *John Piper Retrospective Exhibition*, March-April 1964, no.84
(illustrated).

Christie's London, 21 November 1995 (53**) GBP 10,925	US$	17,089

PIRANDELLO Fausto (Rome 1899-1975) Italian
LA CARRIOLA oil on panel, 75 x 53cm (1943/ 44)
EXH.: Roma, *25 Artisti del Secolo*, Galleria del Secolo, November-December 1944.
LIT.: *Oeuvre catalogue* in the archives F.Pirandello in Galleria Gianferrari, Milano.

Finearte Rome, 14 November 1995 (214**) ITL 37950,000	US$	23,823

NATURA MORTA A TEORIA DIFFUSA oil on canvas, 50 x 70cm. s, s titled onthe reverse
(1960's)
EXH.: Imola, *XII Nazionale d'Arte Figurative*, 1970.
LIT.: This work is recorded at Dott.ssa Claudia Gianferrari, Milano and will be included in the
Fausto Pirandello catalogue raisonné.

Sotheby's Milan, 28 May 1996 (162**) ITL 29,900,000	US$	19,204

OGGETTI E UOVO oil on masonite, 70.5 x 50cm. s
EXH.: Venioce, *XVII Biennale Internazionale d'Arte*, 1956; Palm Beach, Florida, Norton Gallery of
Art, *Special Summer Exhibition*, 1968.

Sotheby's Milan, 28 May 1996 (180**) ITL 29,900,000	US$	19,204

SEATED WOMAN oil and graphite on board, 28 x 20in. (71.2 x 50.8cm.) slr 'PIRANDELLO'
PROV.: Catherine Viviano Gallery, New York.

Christie's East, 7 May 1996 (80**) US$ 13,800	US$	13,800

PISIS Filippo de (Ferrara 1896-1956 Milan) Italian
IL CAPPOTTO SULLA SEDIA oil on cardboard, 45 x 54cm. slr 'de Pisis 31' on the reverse the inscr
of the author is indistinctly (1931)
LIT.: G. Briganti, D*e Pisis, Catalogo Generale*, part I, p.277, no.1931-61.

Finearte Rome, 12 June 1996 (217**) ITL 69,000,000	US$	45,246

VASO CON FIORI oil on canvas, 70 x 50cm. sll 'de Pisis'; dlr 'Milano 48'

Finearte Milan, 18 June 1996 (255**) ITL 74,750,000	US$	48,476

VASO CON GAROFANO oil on masonite, 31 x 24cm. slr 'Pisis' on the left inscr. 'V.F.'

Finearte Milan, 19 March 1996 (30**) ITL 13,225,000	US$	8,461

OMAGGIO A TIEPOLO oil on canvas, 60 x 53.5cm. sdlr 'De Pisis 41' (1941)

Finearte Milan, 19 March 1996 (37**) ITL 62,100,000	US$	39,731

PARIGI, PONT DES ARTS oil on carton, 45.5 x 36cm. sdlr 'De Pisis 26' (1926)
PROV.: Milan, Galleria Annunciata; Milan, collection Jesi.
EXH.: Paris, Galerie au Sacre du Printemps, *De Pisis*, 23 April-7 May 1926, no.25 of the catalogue
with the presentation of G. De Chirico; Milan, Galleria Annunciata, Vicenza *Omaggio a De Pisis,* 7
March- 3 April 1964; Palazzo Chiericati, *L'Arte moderna nel collezionisme vicento*, 4-26 Sept. 1971,
no. 64.
LIT.: G. Briganti, *De Pisis, gli anni di Parigi*, Milan 1987, illustrated p.80; G. Briganti, *De Pisis,
Catalogo generale*, ed. Electa, Milan 1991, vol.I, no. 1936 24, p.98.

Finearte Milan, 19 March 1996 (47**) ITL 81,650,000	US$	52,239

NATURA MORTA oil on board, 50 x 69cm. sdlr 'Pisis 41' (1941)

Finearte Milan, 19 March 1996 (67**) ITL 46,000,000	US$	29,431

NATURA MORTA CON MELOGRANI oil on panel, 50 x 70cm. sd 'Pisis 30'
PROV.: Galleria Varese, Varese; Vitorio Barabaroux, Milano.

Christie's Milan, 20 November 1995 (154**) ITL 55,389,000	US$	34,770

DUCCIO oil on canvas, 65 x 60cm. sd titled 'Duccio Pisis 41'
PROV.: Galleria La Vetrina, Roma.
EXH.: Verona, *Filippo de Pisis*, 1969, no. 204 (illustrated).

Christie's Milan, 20 November 1995 (195**) ITL 41,247,000	US$	25,893

VASCO CON FIORI oil on canvas-board, 22 x 18½in. (55.8 x 47cm.) slr 'de Pisis'

Christie's South Kensington, 27 November 1995 (137**) GBP 10,125	US$	15,838

NATURA MORTE CON FRUTTA oil on canvas laid down on board, 34.6 x 44cm. slr 'Pisis' (1949)
PROV.: Galleria Annunciata, Milan; Galleria La Casa dell'Arte, Sasso Marconi.

Sotheby's Milan, 28 May 1996 (193**) ITL 31,050,000	US$	19,942

PISSARRO Camille (Saint-Thomas 1830-1903 Paris) French
LA SEIN EPRISE DU PONT-NEUF (HIVER) oil on canvas, 21¼ x 25½in. (54 x 65cm.) sdll 'C.
Pissarro. 1902'
PROV.: Galerie Durand-Ruel, Paris; Stern, New York; sale, Parke-Bernet Galleries Inc., New York,
9 Dec. 1959, lot 66; Mr. and Mrs. Werner E. Josten, New York (acquired at the above sale).
EXH.: New York, Wildenstein & Co. Inc., *Camille Pissarro*, March-May 1965, no. 82 (illustrated);
Princeton, New Jersey, University Art Museum, 1976 (on loan).
LIT.: L. R. Pissarro and L. Ventun, *Camille Pissarro, son art-son oeuvre*, Paris 1939, vol. I, p. 250,
no. 1,221 (illustrated, vol. II, pl. 240); J. Rewald, *The History of Impressionism*, New York, 1973, p.
569 (illustrated).

Christie's New York, 1 May 1996 (137**) US$ 464,500	US$	464,500

LA PRAIRIE DE MORET oil on canvas, 21 x 25¼in. (53.3 x 64cm.) sdlr C. Pissarro 1901'
PROV.: Miss Lithauer; The Lefevre Gallery (Alex Reid & Lefevre), London; Mrs Chester-Beatty,
London (purchased from the above in 1946 for GBP1900); Sir Alfred Chester-Beatty, Dublin (sale:
Sotheby's, London, 28th June 1967, lot 7); Purchased at the above sale by the present owner.
EXH.: Paris, Galerie Bernheim-Jeune, *Camille Pissarro*, 1908, no. 20.
LIT.: Ludovic-Rodo Pissarro and Lionello Venturi, *Camille Pissarro, son art - son oeuvre*; Paris
1939, no. 1188 (illustrated), catalogued with the incorrect measurements.

Sotheby's London, 24 June 1996 (61**) GBP 238,000	US$	367,001

TEMPS DE PLUIE, APRES-MIDI, ERAGNY oil on canvas, 18 x 21¾in. (46 x 55cm.) sd 'C.
Pissarro 99' (1899)
PROV.: Galerie Thannhauser, Berlin; The Mayor Gallery, London; Purchased by the father of the
present owner in 1981.
LIT.: L.R. Pissarro and L. Venturi, *Camille Pissarro, son art - son oeuvre*, Paris, 1939, no. 1092
(illustrated pl. 218).

Christie's London, 25 June 1996 (11**) GBP 188,500	US$	29,0671

PRINTEMPS A ERAGNY oil on canvas, 25¾ x32 1/8in. (65.4 x 81.5cm.) sdll 'C. Pissarro, 1900'
PROV.: Paul Rosenberg, Paris; Galerie Druet, Paris (9927); Lefèvre Gallery, London; Lord Astor of
Hever.
LIT.: L.-R. Pissarro & L. Venturi, *Pissarro, Son Art - Son Oeuvre*, Paris, 1939, no. 1138, (illustrated
pl. 226).

Christie's London, 28 November 1995 (5**) GBP 848,500	US$	1,327,233

LA CARRIERE A L'HERMITAGE, PONTOISE oil on canvas, 21 7/8 x 18 1/8in. (55.7 x 46cm.) sd
'C. Pissarro 1878'
PROV.: Lucien Pissarro, the Artist's son, London.
EXH.: London, Tate Gallery, *Pissarro*, June-Oct. 1931, no. 4; This exhibition later travelled to
Birmingham; Birmingham Museum, Oct.-Nov. 1931; Nottingham, Castle Museum, Nov.-Dec. 1931;
Stockport, War Memorial Buildings, Jan. 1932 (no. 8) and Sheffield, Mappin Art Gallery, March,

1932 (no. 8).
LIT.: L. R. Pissarro & L. Venturi,Camille Pissarro, *Son Art - Son Oeuvre*, Paris, 1939, no. 438 (illustrated pl. 88).

Christie's London, 28 November 1995 (6**) GBP 122,500 US$ 191,616

VUE DE STAMFORD BROOK COMMON oil on canvas, 21¼ x 25 5/8in. (54 x 65.1cm.) sdlr 'C. Pissarro. 1897'
PROV.: Paul Rosenberg Paris; Wildenstein & Co., New York; Mrs. Greer Marechal, New York (by whom acquired from the above on 11 April 1978).

Christie's London, 28 November 1995 (13**) GBP 430,500 US$ 673,393

POMMIER A ERAGNY oil on canvas, 18 3/8 x 22in. (46.7 x 56cm.) sdll 'C.Pissarro 1884'
PROV.: O Sochaczewer, Amsterdam; Galerie de l'Elysée (Alex Maguy), Paris; Mr. and Mrs. Roy Titus, New York (acquired from the above on Sept.7, 1974).
EXH.: Lyon, Galerie Alfred Poyet, *C.Pissarro*, May, 1929, no.9; New York, Wildenstein & Co., Inc., *C.Pissarro*, March-May, 1965,no.47 (ill.); Tel Aviv, Museum, *Masters of Modern Art*, May-Sept., 1982, no.124.
LIT.: L.R.Pissarro and L.Venturi, *Camille Pissarro, son art-son oeuvre*, Paris, 1939, vol.I. p.171, no.,635 (ill., vol.II, pl.131).

Christie's New York, 30 April 1996 (28**) US$ 574,500 US$ 574,500

JEUNE PAYSANNE A SA TOILETTE gouache on linen, 13 1/8 x 9 7/8in. (33.3 x 25cm.) sdlr 'C. Pissarro. 1888'
PROV.: A. Dureau, Paris; Arthur B. Davies, New York; Mrs. Charles M. Liebman, New York; sale, Parke-Bernet Galleries, Inc., New York, Dec. 7, 1955, lot 59 (illustrated); acquired by Lola and Siegfried Kramarsky from the above sale.
EXH.: Paris, Galerie Boussod et Valadon, *Camille Pissarro*, Feb.,1890, no. 25; Paris, Galerie Durand-Ruel, *L'oeuvre de Camille Pissarro*, April, l904, p. 23, no. 16; San Francisco, Palace of the Legion of Honor, *19th Century French Drawings*, March-April, 1947, p. 53, no. 84 (illustrated).
LIT.: L.R. Pissarro and L. Venturi, *Camille Pissarro, son art-son oeuvre*, Paris, 1939, vol. I, p. 278, no. 1421 (illustrated, vol. II, pl. 276); J. Pissarro, *Camille Pissarro*, New York, 1993, p. 218 (illustrated in colour).

Christie's New York, 7 November 1995 (11**) US$ 195,000 US$ 195,000

ENTRÉE D'UN VILLAGE oil on canvas, 13 x 16 1/8in. (33 x 41cm.) sll 'C. Pissarro' (ca 1863)
PROV.: Mme. Rouf, Paris.
EXH.: Jerusalem, The Israel Museum, *Camille Pissarro: Impressionist Innovator*, Oct. 1994-Jan. 1995, p. 83 no. 22 (illustrated in colour); The exhibition later travelled to New York, The Jewish Museum, Feb.-July 1995.
LIT.: L.R. Pissarro and L. Venturi, *Camille Pissarro, son art-son oeuvre*, Paris, 1939, vol. II, p. 81, no. 32 (illustrated, vol. II, pl. 6); R. Shikes and P. Harper, *Pissarro, His Life and Work, London, 1980, p. 65 (illustrated in colour); J. Pissarro,* Camille Pissarro, New York, 1993, p. 43, no. 33 (illustrated in colour).

Christie's New York, 7 November 1995 (16**) US$ 387,500 US$ 387,500

EFFET DE NEIGE E MONTFOUCAULT oil on canvas, 15 x 18in. (38 x 46cm.) sdlr 'C. Pissaro 1891'
PROV.: Georges Lecomte, Paris; Arthur Tooth & Sons, Ltd., London (1964); Richard J. Robertson, Darien, Connecticut (acquired from the above in Oct., 1964).
EXH.: Paris, Musée de l'Orangerie, *Exposition Camille Pissarro*, Feb.-March, 1930, no. 80bis; Paris, Galerie Durand-Ruel, Exposition Camille Pissarro, June-Sept., 1956, no. 73.
LIT.: G. Lecomte, *Camille Pissarro*, Paris, 1922 (illustrated, facing p. 66); L.R. Pissarro and L. Venturi, *Camille Pissarro, son art - son oeuvre*, Paris, 1939, vol. 1, p. 188, no. 761 (illustrated, vol. II, pl. 158).

Christie's New York, 7 November 1995 (20**) US$ 750,500 US$ 750,500

UN CLOS A VARENGEVILLE oil on canvas, 18½ x 22in. (47 x 55.9cm.) sdll 'C. Pissarro. 99'
(1899)
PROV.: The Lefevre Gallery (Alex. Reid & Lefevre, Ltd.), London.
LIT.: L. R. Pissarro and L. Venturi, *Camelle Pissarro, son art - son oeuvre*, Paris, 1939, vol. I, no.
1083 (illustrated, vol. II, pl. 217).
Christie's New York, 8 November 1995 (131**) US$ 222,500

	US$	222,500

PISSARRO Lucien (Paris 1863-1944 Hewood (Somerset)) British (French)
A FOGGY MORNING, MORTLAKE oil on canvas, 18¼ x 21¾in. (46.4 x 55.3cm.) sd mono ' LP
1907' s inscr. 'Lucien Pissarro The Brook Hammersmith' on the stretcher
PROV.: S.L. Bensusan, by whom purchased at the 1913 exhibition; Mrs. M. Hodson; Christie's, 21
May 1965, lot 181 (280gns. to F.C.B. Bravington); Private Collection.
EXH.: London, N.E.A.C., *Summer Exhibition*, May-June 1907, no.1; London, Hampshire House,
Hammersmith Social Club, June 1907 (not numbered); London, Fine Arts Palace Shepherd's Bush,
Coronation Exhibition, Dec. 1911, no.2; Southport, Atkinson Art Gallery, *Spring Exhibition*,
Jan.1912, no.37, as *Misty Morning*, Acton; London, Carfax & Co., *Lucien Pissarro*, May 1913, no.6;
London, Fine Art Society, *Camden Town Group Remembered*; Nov.-Dec. 1976, no.6; London,
Anthony d'Offay, *Lucien Pissarro 1863-1944*,July-August 1983, no.13.
LIT.: A. Thorold, *A Catalogue of the Oil Paintings of Lucien Pissarro*, London, 1983, no.9, p.83
(illustrated).
Christie's London, 21 November 1995 (148**) GBP 32,200

	US$	50,368

RYE, SUNSET oil on canvas, 21¼ x 25½in. (54 x64.8cm.) sdll mono. 'LP 1913' d and inscr. on the
stretcher 'Rye from the Harbour Sunset'
PROV.: G. Blackwell, to whom given by the artist.
EXH.: London, N.E.A.C., *Summer Exhibition*, June-July 1913, no.4 as *Rye from the Sands*; London,
N.E.A.C., *Winter Exhibition*, Nov.-Dec. 1913, no.13 as *Rye from the Harbour*; Birkenhead, Arts
Exhibitions Bureau, Williamson Art Gallery, *Travelling Exhibition of Oils, Watercolours and
Drawings by Lucien Pissarro*, July-August 1935, no.13: this exhibition travelled to Belfast, City
Museum and Art Gallery, May-June 1936; Rochdale, Corporation Art Gallery, June-July 1936; and
Gateshead, Shipley Art Gallery, August 1936, no.12.
LIT.: L. Pissarro, Sketchbook 52, *Pissarro Family Archive*, The Ashmolean Museum, Oxford; J.B.
Manson, Mr. Geoffrey Blackwell's Collection of Modern Pictures, *The Studio*, LXI, 15 May 1914,
p.0, p.6 (illustrated); A. Thorold, *A Catalogue of the Oil Paintings of Lucien Pissarro,* London, 1983,
no.2, p.1 (illustrated).
Christie's London, 21 November 1995 (149**) GBP 16,100

	US$	25,184

PITTONI Giovanni Battista (1687-1767) Italian
A) CLEMENZA OF SCIPIONE B) SALOMONE AND THE QUEEN OF SABA oil on paper laid
down on canvas, 41 x 54cm.
Finearte Rome, 18 October 1995 (398**) ITL 54,050,000

	US$	33,676

PLA Y RUBIO Alberto (1867 b.) Spanish
THE HAYWAGON oil on canvas, 29 x 24¾in. (73.7 x 62.9cm.) slr 'Pla Rubio'
Christie's New York, 2 November 1995 (244**) US$ 10,350

	US$	10,350

PLANKH Victor (Troppau 1904-1941 Athens) Austrian
KNIENDER AKT MIT WEIßEM TUCH oil on canvas, 118 x 94cm. sdlr 'V. Plankh 30'
EXH.: Hagen,Der Künstlerbund, *Die verlorene Moderne*; Vienna, 1900-1938 Schloß Halbturn,
Wechselausstellung der Österreichischen Galerie Wien 1993, p. 178; Passau, Museum Moderne
Kunst *Stiftung Wörlen*.
Dorotheum Vienna, 21 May 1996 (49**) ATS 160,000

	US$	15,364

PLEISSNER Ogden Minton (1905-1983) American
THE WIND RIVER watercolour on paper, 8 5/8 x 13 5/8in. (22 x 34.6cm.)(sight) slr 'Pleissner' (ca.
1940)

PROV.: Goodspeed's Book Shop, Inc., Boston, Massachusetts.
Christie's New York, 13 September 1995 (101*) US$ 12,650   US$ 12,650

ALONG THE NORTH FORK watercolour on paper, 15¾ x 22¾in. (40 x 57.7cm.) slr inscr. with title on the reverse 'Pleissner'
Christie's New York, 13 September 1995 (102*) US$ 17,250   US$ 17,250

PO Giacomo del (Rome 1652-1726 Naples) Italian
ALLEGORIES OF VICTORIE AND FAME oil on canvas, 21¼ x 16 1/8in. (53.9 x 41cm.)
PROV.: Lady Tierney; Dame Una Pope-Hennessy, and by descent.
LIT.: J. Pope-Hennessy, *Learning to look*, 1991, p. 314.
Christie's New York, 10 January 1996 (98**) US$ 32,200   US$ 32,200

ST. JOHN THE EVANGELIST oil on canvas (an oval), 102 x 75.5cm. (1705 (?))
Christie's Rome, 21 November 1995 (233*) ITL 19,000,000   US$ 11,927

POEL Egbert Lievensz. van der (Delft 1621-1664 Rotterdam) Dutch
BURNING FARMHOUSES WITH VILLAGERS oil on panel, 10 x 13in. (25.4 x 33cm.) sll 'EL van der Poel'
Sotheby's New York, 11 January 1996 (83**) US$ 11,500   US$ 11,500

AN ARTIST AT WORK IN HIS STUDIO oil on panel, 28.3 x 22.4cm. sll 'Ev(linked)an der Poel'; inscr. centre l on a box 'SAND'
PROV.: (probably) A.J. Bösch; Sale, 1885; L. Lilienfeld, Vienna; Sale, Sotheby`s New York, 17 May 1972, lot 27.
LIT.: A. von Wurzbach, *Niederländisches Künstler-Lexikon, II, 1910, p.336, as a 'Hauptwerk. ungewönlich geistreich'*; G. Glueck, Niederländische Gemälde aus der Sammlung des Herrn Dr Leon; Lilienfeld in Wien, 1917, pp. 40/41 and 66, no. 57, with ill.; A. Goldschmitt, 'Egbert van der Poel und Adriaen van der Poel', in *Oud Holland*, XL, 1992, ill. p. 60 and opposite p. 61.
Christie's Amsterdam, 13 November 1995 (133**) NLG 23,000   US$ 14,495

POELENBURGH Cornelis van (Utrecht 1586/1595-1667 Utrecht) Dutch
A CAMPAGNE LANDSCAPE WITH PEASANT WOMEN CARRYING BASKETS OF WASHING, AND OTHER FIGURES NEAR ROMAN RUINS oil on panel, 8 x 10¼in. (20.3 x 26cm.)
Sotheby's London, 5 July 1995 (156**) GBP 6,900   US$ 11,007

THE JUDGEMENT OF PARIS oil on panel, 12½ x 10¼in. (31.9 x 25.8cm.) sll 'C.P.'
PROV.: The Campou Family, Provence, according to a seal on the reverse; A. Deprez, 1918.
Sotheby's London, 5 July 1995 (160**) GBP 20,700   US$ 33,020

CHRIST ON THE CROSS, WITH SAINT MARY MAGDALENA, SAINT JOHN AND THE VIRGIN MARY oil on panel, with arched top, 13 x 10in. (33 x 25.4cm.) slc 'C.P.'
PROV.: Anonymous sale, Berlin, Lepke, 24 February 1914, lot 96; Büx sale, Berlin, Lepke, 25-28 February 1919, lot 168; Anonymous sale, Amsterdam, Christie's, 14 November 1991, lot 181.
Sotheby's London, 5 July 1995 (161**) GBP 18,400   US$ 29,351

DIANA AND HER ATTENDANTS oil on copper, 13 x 17in. (33 x 43.2cm.) s ini 'C.P.'
Sotheby's New York, 11 January 1996 (96**) US$ 60,250   US$ 60,250

NYMPHS AND SATYRS IN A LANDSCAPE oil on copper, 14¼ x 19in. (36.2 x 48.3cm.) sll ini. 'C.P.'
PROV.: Adalbart B. Mangold (Sale: Sotheby's London 21 March 1973 lot 38 (illustrated).
Sotheby's New York, 16 May 1996 (167**) US$ 17,250   US$ 17,250

POLIAKOFF Serge (Moscow 1900-1969 Paris) French (Russian)

COMPOSITION ROUGE ET VERTE gouache, 60.5 x 45cm. slr 'Serge Poliakoff' (ca. 1962)

       Hauswedell & Nolte Cologne, 2 December 1995 (220**) DEM 25,000   US$ 17,345

COMPOSITION JAUNE FOND ROUGE oil on canvas, 19¾ x 24in. (50 x 61cm.) sll with ini. 'SP', s again on the reverse

       Christie's Tel Aviv, 14 April 1996 (87**) US$ 33,350   US$ 33,350

COMPOSITION oil on canvas, 31¾ x 39¼in. (80.6 x 99.8cm.) sll 'Serge Poliakoff' (1955)

PROV.: Galerie Blanche, Stockholm.

LIT.: To be included in the forthcoming *Serge Poliakoff Catalogue Raisonné* being prepared by Alexis Poliakoff, the Artist's son.

       Christie's London, 19 March 1996 (18**) GBP 60,900   US$ 93,005

COMPOSITION oil on canvas, 32 x 23 5/8in. (81.2 x 60cm.) sll 'Serge Poliakoff' and sd '1950, 1950-54'

LIT.: To be included in the forthcoming *Serge Poliakoff Catalogue Raisonné* being prepared by Alexis Poliakoff, the Artist's son.

       Christie's London, 19 March 1996 (24**) GBP 82,900   US$ 126,604

COMPOSITION oil on canvas, 51 5/8 x 38¼in. (,131 x 97cm.) s 'Serge Poliakoff' (ca 1957)

PROV.: Galerie Bing, Paris; Galerie Levi, Milan; Galerie Prazan-Fitoussi, Paris.

EXH.: Basel, Kunsthalle Basel, *Robert Jacobson - Serge Poliakoff*, January - March 1958, no. 49; Paris, Galerie Prazan-Fitoussi, *10 Oeuvres Majeures de l'Art Abstrait des années 50,* October - Decemeber 1989, no. 8 (illustrated in colour in the catalogue).

LIT.: To be included in the forthcoming *Serge Poliakoff Catalogue Raisonné* being prepared by Alexis Poliakoff, the Artist's son.

       Christie's London, 11 October 1995 (12**) GBP 97,200   US$ 153,409

COMPOSITION ROUGE ET BLANCHE gouache on paper, 25 x 19in. (63.5 x 48.3cm.) slr 'Serge Poliakoff' (1967-68)

PROV.: Galerie de France, Paris; Fuji T.V. Gallery, Tokyo.

EXH.: Paris, Galerie de France, *Poliakoff Gouaches: 1944-1969*, 1977, no. 56, illustrated on the exhibition poster; Tokyo, Fuji T.V. Gallery, *Serge Poliakoff* 1978, no. 38, illustrated.

LIT.: To be included in the forthcoming *Serge Poliakoff Catalogue Raisonné*, being prepared by Alexis Poliakoff, Paris.

       Sotheby's London, 21 March 1996 (36**) GBP 7,475   US$ 11,416

COMPOSITION - BLEU, ROUGE ET LIE DE VIN oil on canvas, 25 3/8 x 32in. (64.5 x 81cm.) s 'Serge Poliakoff' (1965)

PROV.: Galerie im Erker, St.Gallen; Basel Galerie d'art Moderne.

EXH.: St. Gallen, Galerie im Erker, *Serge Poliakoff*, April-June1965, no. 42; Luzern, Galerie Raber, *Serge Poliakoff*, August 1965, no. 34; Locarno, Galleria Flaviana, *Serge Poliakoff*, October 1965, no. 29 (illustrated in the catalogue). Basel, Galerie d'art Moderne, *Serge Poliakoff*, 1966, no. 33.

LIT.: To be included in the forthcoming *Serge Poliakoff Catalogue Raisonné* being prepared by Alexis Poliakoff, the artist's son.

       Christie's London, 23 May 1996 (34**) GBP 41,100   US$ 62,235

COMPOSITION oil on canvas, 28½ x 35½in. (72.5 x 90cm.) s 'Serge Poliakoff' (1966)

PROV.: Galerie de Poche, Paris.

LIT.: To be included in the forthcoming *Serge Poliakoff Catalogue Raisonné* being prepared by Alexis Poliakoff, the artist's son.

       Christie's London, 26 October 1995 (49**) GBP 29,900   US$ 47,191

COMPOSITION oil on canvas, 32 x 25¼in. (81.3 x 64cm.) sll (ca 1957)
PROV.: Galerie Berggruen, Paris.
    Christie's London, 27 June 1996 (11**) GBP 65,300   US$ 100,694

COMPOSITION - ROUGE, JAUNE, BLANC, BLEU AUX TRAITS oil on canvas, 51 ¼ x 35 3/8in.
(,130 x90cm.) slr and d 1952 on the reverse (1952)
PROV.: Prof. Hugo Krayenbühl, Zurich.
EXH.: Liège, A.P.I.A.W., *Serge Poliakoff*; February-March 1953, no. 8; Brussels, Palais des Beaux-
Arts, *Serge Poliakoff*; April-May 1953, no. 7; Veruiers, Musée Communal d'Art de Veruiers, *Serge
Poliakoff*, 1953, no. 8; San Francisco, San Francisco Museum of Modern Art, Art From France,
November 1956; Basel, Kunsthalle, *Serge Poliakoff*, January-March 1958, no. 31; Hamburg,
Kunstverein, *Serge Poliakoff*, April-May 1958, no. 20 (illustrated in the catalogue); Copenhagen,
Statens Museum for Kunst, *Serge Poliakoff*, May-June 1958, no. 27 (illustrated in the catalogue);
Bern, Kunsthalle, *Serge Poliakoff*; April-May 1960, no. 45; St. Gallen, Galerie im Erker, *Serge
Poliakoff*, 1962, no. 2.; Paris, Musée National d'Art Moderne, *Serge Poliakoff*; September-November
1970, no. 27 (illustrated in colour in the catalogue p. 6).
LIT.: In: *Cimaise*, no. 4, Michel Ragon, Paris, March 1956, p. 14 (illustrated); Dora Vallier, *Serge
Poliakoff,* Paris 1959, p. 56, no. 24 (illustrated); Jean Cassou, *Serge Poliakoff*, Amriswil 1963, no. 6
(illustrated in colour); *Exhibition Catalogue: Serge Poliakoff Retrospective 1938-1963*, London,
Whitechapel Gallery, *SergePoliakoff Retrospective 1938-1963*, 1963 (illustrated in the catalogue pl.
V); Exhibition Catalogue: Locarno, Galleria Flaviana*, Serge Poliakoff*, 1965 (illustrated in colour);
Giuseppe Marchiori, Serge Poliakoff, Paris 1976, p. 49 (illustrated pp. 48-49); To be included in the
forthcoming *Serge Poliakoff Catalogue Raisonné* being prepared by Alexis Poliakoff, the artist's son.
    Christie's London, 27 June 1996 (22**) GBP 199,500   US$ 307,633

COMPOSITION oil on canvas, 35 1/8 x 45 7/8in. (89.1 x 116.5cm.) slr (1958)
PROV.: Galerie Knoedler, New York.
EXH.: Paris, Galerie Knoedler, *Poliakoff 1959* (illustrated in colour in the catalogue pp. 12 and 13);
Stockholm, Svensk Franska Konstgallenet, *Serge Poliakoff,* January 1960; Stockholm, Moderna
Museet, *The Museum of Our Wishes*, December 1963-February 1964, no. 140 (illustrated in the
catalogue p. 65); Paris, Musée Nationale d'Art Moderne, *Serge Poliakoff*, September-November
1970, no. 50 (illustrated in the catalogue).
LIT.: Dora Vallier, *Serge Poliakoff*, Paris 1959, pl. IX (illustrated in colour).
To be included in the forthcoming Serge *Poliakoff Catalogue Raisonné* being prepared by Alexis
Poliakoff, the artist's son.
    Christie's London, 27 June 1996 (33**) GBP 84,000   US$ 129,530

COMPOSITION oil on canvas, 32 x 25¾in. (81.3 x 65.4cm.) slr (ca 1962-63)
PROV.: Svensk-Franska Konstgalleriet, Stockholm.
    Christie's London, 27 June 1996 (37**) GBP 65,300   US$ 100,694

COMPOSITION ROUGE oil on sand on canvas, 36¼ x 28¾in. (92 x 73cm.) sll 'Serge Poliakoff'
(1961)
PROV.: Madeleine Evraert, Brussels; Lefebre Gallery, New York.
    Sotheby's London, 27 June 1996 (143**) GBP 36,700   US$ 56,592

COMPOSITION - JAUNE , BLEUE ET ROUGE oil on canvas, 35¼ x 46in. (89.5 x 117cm.) sd
'III.'54', d on the reverse '1954'
PROV.: Galerie Luca Scacchi, Milan.
LIT.: To be included in the forthcoming *Serge Poliakoff Catalogue Raisonné* being prepared by
Alexis Poliakoff, the Artist's son.
    Christie's London, 30 November 1995 (5**) GBP 194,000   US$ 303,457

COMPOSITION - JAUNE ET ROUGE oil on canvas, 40 x 32¼in. (101.5 x 82cm.) s 'Poliakoff' and
s on the reverse 'Poliakoff' (ca 1955-56)
PROV.: Galerie Jeanne Bucher, Paris; acquired from the above by the present owner in the 1960's.

459

LIT.: To be included in the forthcoming *Serge Poliakoff Catalogue Raisonné* being prepared by
Alexis Poliakoff, the Artist's son.
       Christie's London, 30 November 1995 (8**) GBP 76,300   US$ 119,349

POLKE Sigmar (Oels 1941 b.) German
UNTITLED watercolour and goldpigment on paper, 109.5 x 70cm. sd (1982)
       Hauswedell & Nolte Cologne, 2 December 1995 (225**) DEM 13,000   US$ 9,020

OHNE TITEL goache und ink drawing, 99 x 70cm. sdlr 'S. Polke 1982'
       Hauswedell & Nolte Cologne, 6 June 1996 (346**) DEM 15,000   US$ 9,746

UNTITLED acrylic on canvas, 71 x 59in. (,180 x 150cm.) s on the reverse (1985)
PROV.: Galerie Bama, Paris.
LIT.: In: 'Galeries Magazine', no. 6, Paris October 1995, p. 47 (illustrated).
       Christie's London, 19 March 1996 (72***) GBP 91,700   US$ 140,043

COMPOSITION dispersion and wax on fabric, 27½ x 35½in.(70 x 90cm.) s'Sigmar Polke' and sd '85'
on the overlap
PROV.: Luhring Augustine Gallery, New York.
       Christie's London, 23 May 1996 (155**) GBP 17,250   US$ 26,121

LIEBESPAAR dispersion on canvas, 59 x 51 1/8in. (,150 x 130cm.) sd 'Sigmar Polke 1988' on the
reverse
PROV.: Acquired directly from the Artist by the present owner.
       Christie's London, 26 October 1995 (114a**) GBP 80,700   US$ 127,367

CHINE-BILD dispersion on silk, 35½ x 28in. (90 x 71cm.) s on the reverse (1968)
PROV.: Galerie Thomas Borgmann, Cologne; Wolfgang May, Essen (acquired in the early 1970s).
EXH.: Tübingen, Kunsthalle; Dusseldorf, Städtische Kunsthalle; Eindhoven, Stedelijk van Abbe-
Museum, *Bilder, Tücher: Werkauswahl. 1962-1971*, April-July 1976, no. 110 (illustrated in the
catalogue p. 64).
       Christie's London, 27 June 1996 (71**) GBP 95,000   US$ 146,492

THE REVENGE OF THE KANAKS lacquer and dispersion
on Nigersunan fabric, 88½ x 118 7/8in. (224.8 x 302cm.) sd
'88 on the stretcher; sd '88 on the reverse
PROV.: Galerie Michael Werner, Cologne/New York.
LIT.: In: 'Parkett', no. 26, Bice Curier, *Interview with Sigmar
Polke*, Zurich, October 1990, p. 13 (illustrated).
       Christie's London, 27 June 1996 (73**) GBP
210,500   US$ 324,595

SPIEGELEIER AUF BÚGELEISEN BRATEN NACH
PROF. CORCHON acrylic, lacquer and ink on vellum, 100 x
70cm. sdlr titled 'S. Polke 79 Spiegeleier auf Buegeleisen
braten nach Prof. Corchon'
       Lempertz Cologne, 28 November 1995 (852**)
DEM 52,000   US$ 367,02

UNTITLED gouache on paper, 69 x 99cm. sdlr 'S.Polke 82'
       Lempertz Cologne, 31 May 1996 (395**) DEM

*Spiegeleier auf Bügeleisen braten
nach Prof. Corchon*
28,000   US$ 18,254

POLLOCK Jackson (Cody, Wyoming 1912-1956 Springs, Long Island) American
SOMETHING OF THE PAST oil on canvas, 56 x 38in. (142.3 x 96.5cm.) sdlc 'J. Pollock 46' (1946)
PROV.: Art of This Century, New York; Peggy Guggenheim, Venice; Michel Tapie, Paris. Felix

Landau Gallery, Los Angeles; Mr. and Mrs. Harry W. Anderson, Atherton; Harold Diamond, New York; A Midwestern collector (acquired in 1970); By descent to the present owner.
EXH.: New York, *Art of This Century, Jackson Pollock*, Jan.-Feb. 1947, no. 6; Ithaca, Cornell University, Herbert F. Johnson Museum of Art and New York, Whitney Museum of American Art, *Abstract Expressionism: The Formative Years*, Mar.-May 1978, no. 66; East Hampton, Guild Hall Museum and New York University, Grey Art Gallery and Study Center, *Krasner and Pollock: A Working Relationship*, Aug.-Dec. 1981; Modern Art Museum of Fort Worth, *Masterworks from Fort Worth Collections*, Apr.-June 1992, p. 37, no. 11 (illustrated).
LIT.: *Tiger's Eye*, Mar. 1948, vol. I, no. 3, p. 106 (illustrated); F. Bayl, 'Jackson Pollock,' *Die Kunst und das Schore Hein 9*, June 1961, p. 331, no. 3 (illustrated); *New International Illustrated Encyclopedia of Art*, New York 1967, vol. I (illustrated on frontispiece and titled *Composition*); I. Tomassoni, *Pollock*, New York 1968, no. 36 (illustrated and titled *Composition 1946*); F.V. O'Connor and E.V. Thaw, *Jackson Pollock: A Catalogue Raisonné of Paintings, Drawings and Other Works*, New Haven and London 1978, vol. I, p. 153, no. 160 (illustrated).

Christie's New York, 7 May 1996 (22**) US$ 2,422,500	US$	2,422,500

PONCE Antonio (Valladolid 1608-1662 after Madrid (?)) Spanish
A STILL-LIFE WITH A BASKET OF FRUIT ON A STONE PLINTH oil on canvas, 23½ x 36¼in. (60 x 92cm.)

Sotheby's London, 5 July 1995 (129**) GBP 20,700	US$	33,020

PONSAN Edouard-Bernard-Debat (1847-1913) French
WASHDAY oil on canvas, 26 x 36in. (66 x 91.4cm.) sdll 'E Debat-Ponsan 1910'

Sotheby's Arcade Auctions New York, 20 July 1995 (403*) US$ 10,350	US$	10,350

POORTER Willem de (Haarlem 1608-1648 after) Dutch
ESTHER BEFORE AHASVERUS oil on canvas, 37.5 x 49.5cm.

Sotheby's Amsterdam, 14 November 1995 (74**) NLG 14,160	US$	8,924

PORPORA Paolo (atr.) (act. in Naples 1617-1673) Italian
STILL-LIFE WITH RAISINS, MELONS AND FIGS oil on canvas, 148 x 99cm.

Libert & Castor Paris, 23 February 1996 (77*) FRF 330,000	US$	67,530

PORTAELS Jan François (1818 -1895) Belgian
AN ORIENTAL BEAUTY oil on panel, 54 x 43.5cm. sll 'J.Portaels'

Christie's Amsterdam, 26 October 1995 (59*) NLG 31,050	US$	19,578

PORTIELJE Edouard Antoine (Antwerp 1861-1949 Antwerp) Belgian
THE LETTER oil on canvas, 18 1/8 x 15in. (46.6 x 38.1cm.) slr 'Edward Portielje.'

Christie's New York, 14 February 1996 (79**) US$ 10,350	US$	10,350

PORTIELJE Jan Frederik Pieter (Amsterdam 1829-1908 Antwerp) Dutch
AN ORIENTAL BEAUTY oil on panel, 23¼ x 19in. (59 x 48.3cm.) s inscr. 'Portielje/Anvers'

Christie's London, 17 November 1995 (120**) GBP 10,580	US$	16,549

POSSENTI Antonio (Lucca 1933 b.) Italian
QUATTRO PITTORI A GIVERNY oil on panel, 100 x 100cm s 'Possenti' s and titled on the reverse (1989)
LIT.: A.Possenti, *Sogni di legno*, 1990, (illustrated in colour).

Finearte Rome, 14 November 1995 (139**) ITL 16,100,000	US$	10,107

POT Hendrick Gerritz. (Haarlem 1585 c.-1657 Amsterdam) Dutch
PORTRAITS OF JACOB VAN DER MERCKT AND HIS WIFE PETRONELLA WITSEN oil on oak panel (a pair), each: 16½ x 13in. (41.8 x 32cm.) (ca. 1635)
PROV.: Jacob and Petronella van der Merckt, Amsterdam, until 1676; Burgemeester Bors van Waveren, Amsterdam, who married about 1660 one of the three daughters of the sitters, born about

1630 and also named Petronella; Their daughter Jacoba Bors van Waveren (1666-1754), who married Abraham Ortt (1650-1691); Their daughterJacoba Elisabeth Ortt, who married G. Bors van Waveren, Amsterdam; Van Eys, Amsterdam; M. van Hoven van der Voort, great-great-great-granddaughter of the sitters; Her nephew and nieces Bock; Jonkheer P.H.A. Martini Buys, Rotterdam, by circa 1905; Sale, Amsterdam, 15 April 1947, lot 559; R.Th. Bijleveld, Velp, by 1952. EXH.: Rotterdam Museum for History and Art, to whom lent by Jonkheer Martini Buys in about 1905; Amsterdam, Rijksmuseum, *Drie Eeuwen Portret in Nederland*, 1952, nos. 128 and 129; Arnhem, Gemeentemuseum, *17e Eeuwse Meesters uit Gelders Bezit*, 1953, nos. 52 & 53; On loan to Southampton Art Gallery, 1980-1995. LIT.: A. Bredius and P. Haverkorn van Rijsewijk, 'Hendrik Gerritsz. Pot', in *Oud Holland*, V, 1887, p.173, nos. Xlll and XIV; E.W. Moes, *Iconographia Batava*, II, 1905, nos. 4969-1 and 9168-1; E. de Jongh, *Portretten van echt en trouw*, exhibition catalogue, Haarlem, 1986, p. 32, reproduced p. 33, figs. 20 a & b, as whereabouts unknown; P. ten Doesschate-Chu, *in Im Lichte Hollands*, exhibition catalogue, Basel, 1987, p. 202, under catalogue no. 75, note 7, as whereabouts unknown.

| | Sotheby's London, 5 July 1995 (48**) GBP 166,500 | US$ | 265,593 |

POTHAST Bernard (1882-1966) British
BY THE WINDOW oil on canvas, slr 'BPothast' 25¼ x 30in. (64.2 x 76.3cm.)

| | Christie's New York, 2 November 1995 (89**) US$ 13,800 | US$ | 13,800 |

POTTER Mary (1900-1981) British
THE FISH oil on canvas, 14 x 17in. (35.5 x 43.2cm.) (1930)
PROV.: The Artist, thence by descent.
LIT.: Newton and Welshpool, Oriel 31 Davies Memorial Gallery and 31 High Street, *Mary Potter: 1900-1981 Selective Retrospective*, Sept.-Nov. 1989, nov. 1989, no. 5 This exhibition later travelled to Kendal, Abbot Hall Art Gallery; Bath Victoria Art Gallery; Norwich, Castle Museum and Lincoln, Usher Gallery (Nov. 1989-May 1990).

| | Christie's London, 22 May 1996 (1**) GBP 10,925 | US$ | 16,543 |

POTTER Paulus (Enkhuysen 1625-1654 Amsterdam) Dutch
A DISTINGUISHED HORSEMAN BEING WELCOMED BY A FARMER WITH A GLASS OF WINE IN A MEADOWLANDSCAPE WITH COWS oil on panel, 29 x 40cm. sdll 'Paulus Potter F 1650'
PROV.: Earl of Kilmore, 1882; Charles Yerkes, before 1898 (famous collection); Sedelmayer, Paris, 1898; Dr. J. Hooykaas, no. 132; S. del Monte, Brussels (famous collection); Sale Sotheby's, 24 June 1959.

| | Dorotheum Vienna, 6 March 1996 (5**) ATS 250,000 | US$ | 24,048 |

CATTLE STANDING ON A RIVERBANK oil on panel, 18½ x 24¾in. (47 x 62.9cm.) sdlc 'paulus potter f 1643'
PROV.: Probably Sir Francis Cook (died 1901); Sir Frederick Cook, his son, Doughty House, Richmond, Surrey, by 1912, thence by descent to his son; Sir Herbert Cook, Bt., in the Long Gallery at Doughty House, by 1932; The Cook Collection (Sale: Sotheby's, London, 25 June, 1958, lot 106, illus.) there purchased for GBP400; by Cromwell; Sale: Christie's, London, March 29, 1974, lot 88.
EXH.: Sheffield, Graves Art Gallery, *Exhibition of Dutch Masterpieces*, March-April 1956, no. 38.
LIT.: C. Hofstede de Groot, *A Catalogue Raisonné.*, vol. IV, 1912, p. 624, cat.no. 83 (as painted circa 1645); Sir Herbert Cook (ed.), *Catalogue of the Paintings at Doughty House, Richmond and elsewhere in the Collection of Sir Frederick Cook, Bt.*, vol. II, 1915, (entries by J.O. Kronig), p. 18, cat. no. 225, illus.; M. W. Brockwell (ed.), *Abridged Catalogue of the Pictures at Doughty House, Richmond, Surrey in the Collection of Sir Herbert Cook*, Bart, 1932, p. 29, cat. no. 225.

| | Sotheby's New York, 16 May 1996 (82**) US$ 90,500 | US$ | 90,500 |

A LANDSCAPE WITH A MILKMAID AND HER CATTLE oil on oak panel, 19¾ x 14¾in. (50 x 37.5cm.) sdlr 'Paulus Potter f. 1648'
PROV.: King Stanislaus of Poland; Moritz Potocky Collection, Paris; Baron Heinrich Thyssen-Bornemisza, by 1930.

EXH.: Munich 1930, no. 260, plate 66; Bern 1960, no. 20; Lausanne etc., 1986-7, no. 39.
LIT.: R. Heinemann 1937, vol. I, no. 333, vol. II, plate 143;.

Sotheby's London, 6 December 1995 (106**) GBP 243,500	US$	374,731

CATTLE IN A FIELD WITH TRAVELLERS IN A WAGON ON A TRACK BEYOND AND A
CHURCH TOWER IN THE DISTANCE A RAINSTORM APPROACHING oil on panel, 14¾ x
22in. (37.5 x 56cm.) sdll 'Paulus Potter. F:1652'
PROV.: Louis-Cesar-Renaud de Choiseul, Duc de Choiseul-Praslin, Paris (1735-1791); sale, Paillet,
Paris; 18 Feb. 1793, lot 70 (28,200 francs to Le Brun Jr.); Robit Collection, Paris; sale, Paillet, Paris,
11 May 1801 (= 1st day), lot 94 (29,700 francs). Chades-Ferdinand d'Artois, Duc de Berry, Paris
(1778-1820); His widow, Caroline-Ferdinande-Louise de Bourbon, Duchesse de Berry (1798-after
1833); sale, Paris, 4-6 April 1837 (37,000 francs to Demidoff); Prince Anatole Demidoff, San
Donato, Florence; sale, Paris, 18 April 1868, lot 10 (112,000 francs to Mundler for J. Rothschild);
Baron James de Rothschild, Paris (1792-1868); His son, Baron Mayer Alphonse de Rothschild
(1827-1905); His daughter, Charlotte de Rothschild, Baroness Maurice Ephrussi (1864-1934).
EXH.: Mauritshuis, The Hague, *The Pleasures of Paulus Potter's Countryside*, 8 Nov. 1994-5 Feb.
1995, pp. 138-40 (no. 26, illustrated in colour p. 139 and on the cover of the catalogue)
LIT.: J. Smith, *A Catalogue Raisonné*, etc., V, London, 1834, pp. 137-8, no. 44; IX, London, 1842,
pp. 626-7, no. 24 'This capital production is painted throughout with the most elaborate care.'; C.
Blanc, Le trésor de la curiosité tiré des catalogues de vente, Paris, 1857-8, II, pp. 161, 193 and 424;
C. Hofstede de Groot, *A Catalogue Raisonné, etc.*, IV, London, 1912, p. 607, no. 45; A.L. Walsh,
Paulus Potter: his works and their meaning (unpublished dissertation), Columbia University, 1985,
pp. 243, 245 and 381, fig. B79.

Christie's London, 7 July 1995 (39**) GBP 661,500	US$	1,055,192

POTTHAST Edward Henry (1857-1927) American
BEACH SCENE coloured pencil and watercolour on paper, 4¾ x 5¾in. (12.2 x 14.6cm.) slr 'E.
Potthast'
PROV.: Hirschl & Adler Galleries, Inc., New York; Meredith Long & Company, Houston, Texas;
Sale: New York, Christie's, May 29, 1987, lot 166.
EXH.: New York, Hirschl & Adler Galleries, Inc., *Exhibition of Paintings and Drawings by Edward
Henry Potthast*, September 1968.

Christie's New York, 13 September 1995 (65*) US$ 8,050	US$	8,050

ALONG THE MYSTIC RIVER oil on canvas, 16 x 20in. (40.6 x 50.7cm.) sll 'E Potthast'
PROV.: Grand Central Art Galleries, New York.

Christie's New York, 23 May 1996 (117**) US$ 68,500	US$	68,500

POTUYL Hendrik (ca. 1615) Dutch
A PEASANT WOMAN PEELING TURNIPS IN A BARN WITH A PILE OF KITCHEN
UTENSILS IN THE FOREGROUND, A BOY STANDING NEARBY oil on panel, 67.6 x 115.7cm.
indistinctly sll 'VP..'
PROV.: Anon. Sale, Christie's, 29 January 1842.

Christie's Amsterdam, 7 May 1996 (5**) NLG 14,950	US$	8,717

POURBUS Frans the Elder (attr.) (Brughes 1540 c.-1581 Antwerp) Flemish
PORTRAIT OF KING PHILIPS II OF SPAIN oil on canvas, 119 x 85cm.
LIT.: Collection of a noble family; Sale 19th Century in France, as Juan Pantajo de la Cruz, ale cat.
nr. 190.

Dorotheum Vienna, 6 March 1996 (180180) ATS 180,000	US$	17,314

POURBUS Pieter (Gouda 1523-1584 Brughes) Flemish
PORTRAITS OF A GENTLEMAN OF VEERE AND OF HIS WIFE oil on panel (a pair), each: 27 x
20¼in. (68.5 x 51.3cm.) the former inscr. and dul and r 'ANO DNI 1563/AETATIS SUE 41'; the
latter inscr. and dul and r 'ANO DNI 1563/ AETATIS SUE 45'
PROV.: Anonymous sale, Vienna, Dorotheum, 13 November 1956, lot 106.

LIT.: Paul Huvenne, *Pierre Pourbus Peintre brugeois 1524-1584*, exhibition catalogue, Bruges, Memling Museum, 1984, p. 43, as by Pourbus, present whereabouts unknown.

      Sotheby's London, 5 July 1995 (296**) GBP 21,850   US$ 34,854

POYNTER Sir Edward (James) John, Bt, P.R.A., R.W.S. (1836-1919) British
'BEWARE, TRUST HER NOT, SHE IS FOOLING THEE' pencil and watercolour with gum arabic, 20¾ x 14½in. (52.7 x 36.8cm.) sd mono '1865' s inscr. '.. No. 2 Bloomsbury/Edward j. Poynter' on the reverse
PROV.: With Charles Nicholls & Son., Manchester.

      Christie's London, 7 June 1996 (559**) GBP 10,925   US$ 16,847

PRACHENSKY Markus (Innsbruck 1932 b.) Austrian
ETRURIA ORIZONTALE 6 acrylic on canvas, 130 x 175cm. sdlr 'PRACHENSKY 84'; sd and titled on the reverse

      Wiener Kunst Auktionen, 26 March 1996 (454**) ATS 130,000   US$ 12,505

UNTITLED oil on canvas, 87 x 67cm. sll 'PRACHENSKY' (1954/55)

      Wiener Kunst Auktionen, 27 September 1995 (445**) ATS 140,000   US$ 13,608

ALM IM WINTER tempera on paper, 61 x 86cm. sd 'Prachensky 44'

      Dorotheum Vienna, 6 December 1995 (527**) ATS 250,000   US$ 24,653

PRATELLA Attilio (Lugo 1856-1932 (1949?) Naples) Italian
BRINGING IN THE NETS oil on canvas, 17 1/8 x 25in. (43.5 x 63.5cm.) s

      Phillips London, 11th June 1996 (71**) GBP 6,200   US$ 9,561

FIGURES ON A BEACH, NAPLES oil on canvas, 20½ x 41in. (52.1 x 104.2cm.) slr 'Pratella .A.'

      Christie's New York, 2 November 1995 (236**) US$ 51,750   US$ 51,750

PREDIS Ambrogio de (ca. 1455 -after 1520) Italian
PORTRAIT OF FILIPPO BEROALDO oil on panel, 14¾ x 11in. (37.5 x 27.9cm.) inscribed with name of sitter at top
PROV.: Dr. Albert Figdor, Vienna; Goudstikker, Amsterdam.
EXH.: Amsterdam, *International Exhibition of Old Master Paintings at the Rijksmuseum*, 1936, cat. no. 126 (as by *Ambrogio de Predis*).

      Sotheby's New York, 11 January 1996 (57**) US$ 96,000   US$ 96,000

PRENDERGAST Maurice Brazil (Saint-Jean, Terre-Neuve 1859-1924 New York) American
CENTRAL PARK, NEW YORK CITY, 4TH JULY watercolour and pencil on paper, 14 1/8 x 20 7/8in. (35.9 x 53cm.) slr 'Prendergast' inscr. 'CENTRAL PARK, NEW YORK CITY, 4TH JULY' on the reverse (ca. 1900-03)
PROV.: The artist; Charles Prendergast; Mrs. Charles Prendergast, Westport, Connecticut; Babcock Galleries, New York.
EXH.: New York, Whitney Museum of American Art, *The Friends Collect: Recent Acquisitions of the Friends of the Whitney Museum of American Art*, May-June 1964, no. 118; New York, Andrew Crispo Gallery, *Ten Americans: Avery, Burchfield, Demuth, Dove, Homer, Hopper, Marin, Prendergast, Sargent, Wyeth*, May-June, 1974, no. 122; New York, American Federation of Arts, *American Master Drawings and Watercolours: A History of Works on Paper from Colonial Times to the Present*, Nov. 1976-Jan. 1977; New York, Hirschl & Adler Galleries, *The Artist in the Park*, April-May, 1980, no. 83; New York, Museum of the City of New York, *Calvert Vaux: Architect and Planner*, April-Aug. 1989.
LIT.: T.E. Stebbins, Jr., *American Master Drawings and Watercolors*, New York, 1976, p. 249, illus. as Central Park; L. Bantal, *The Alice M. Kaplan Collection*, Jamestown, Rhode Island, 1980, p. 189, illus.; C. Clark, N.M. Mathews, and G. Owen, *Maurice Brazil Prendergast and Charles Prendergast: A Catalogue Raisonné*, Williamstown, Massachusetts, l990, p. 412, no. 793.

      Christie's New York, 30 November 1995 (58**) US$ 442,500   US$ 442,500

PRENTICE Levi Wells (1851-1935) American
BASKET OF RASPBERRIES oil on canvas, 6 x 8in. (15.2 x 20.3cm.) slr 'L.W. Prentice.'
    Christie's New York, 13 September 1995 (39**) US$ 6,900   US$ 6,900

STILL-LIFE WITH PORCELAIN AND STRAWBERRIES oil on canvas, 10 x 14 1/8in (25.4 x 35.8cm.) slr 'L.W. Prentice'
    Christie's New York, 23 May 1996 (51**) US$ 48,300   US$ 48,300

BASKET OF PLUMS oil on canvas, 12 x 18in. (30.5 x 45.7cm.) slr 'L.W. Prentice' s again on the reverse
    Christie's New York, 23 May 1996 (57**) US$ 36,800   US$ 36,800

PRETI Mattia {called} Cavaliere Calabrese (1613 Taverna-1699 Malta) Italian
THE SACRIFICE OF ISAAC oil on canvas, 52¼ x 38¼in. (132.7 x 97.2cm.) (ca. 1635)
    Sotheby's New York, 16 May 1996 (23**) US$ 90,500   US$ 90,500

PORTRAIT OF AN ANATOMIST oil on canvas, 100 x 80.5cm
    Finearte Milan, 25 November 1995 (77**) ITL 26,450,000   US$ 16,604

PRIAMO DELLA QUERCIA (documented in Lucca, Siena and Volterra (1426-1467)-) Italian
MADONNA AND CHILD tempera on panel, 18¾ x 13¼in. (47.5 x 34cm.) (ca. 1450)
PROV.: Probably acquired in the late 1890's by the great-grandmother of the present owner.
    Sotheby's London, 6 December 1995 (10**) GBP 32,200   US$ 49,554

PRIKKER Johan Thorn (1868-1932)
ROODE KOOL - RED CABBAGE pastel and gouache on paper, 45.5 x 58cm. s with ini, d and indistinctly inscr. lr 'ThP03'
PROV.: Dr. W.J.H. Leuring, The Hague, thence by descent.
EXH.: Utrecht, Vereeniging voor de kunst, *Tentoonstelling van werken door Johan Thorn Prikker*, 5 October - 2 November 1919; The Hague, Pulchri Studio, *Tentoonstelling van werken door Johan Thorn; Prikker*, 5 - 26 September 1928, no. 42; Utrecht, Vereeniging voor de kunst, *Herdenkingstentoonstelling Johan Thorn Prikker*, 27 November - 18 december 1932, no. 32; The Hague, Gemeente Museum, *Nieuwe beweging Nederlandse schilderkunst rond* 1910, October - December 1955, no. 9 in cat, no.77 in exhibition; Enschede, Rijksmuseum Twenthe, *Nieuwe beweging Nederlandse schilderkunst rond* 1910, 3 - 25 March 1956, no. 9 Amsterdam, Stedelijk Museum, *Johan Thorn Prikker*, 6 September - 10 October 1968, no. 29 (ill. in cat.); Mechelen Stedelijk Museum, *Fauvisme in de Europese kunst*, August-November 1969.
LIT.: A. B. Loosjes-Terpstra, *Moderne kunst in Nederland 1900- 1914*, Utrecht 1959 (1987 reprint), p/ 15; Plasschaert, *J. Thorn Prikker*, Kölnischer Kunstverein 1920, no. 38-41.
    Christie's Amsterdam, 6 December 1995 (210**) NLG 51,750   US$ 32,067

PRINCETEAU René (1843 -1914) French
CAVALIERS SUR LA PLAGE DE DIEPPE oil on canvas, slr
    Étude Tajan Paris, 17 June 1996 (28**) FRF 220,000   US$ 42,482

PRITCHETT Edward (1828-1864 fl.) British
THE MOLO, VENICE FROM THE DOGANA oil on board, 123¾ x 17¾in. (34.8 x 45.1cm.) numbered 'Yo/371' on the reverse
    Christie's South Kensington, 9 November 1995 (228*) GBP 9,000   US$ 14,078

THE ENTRANCE TO THE GRAND CANAL, VENICE FROM THE WEST oil on canvas, 26¼ x 35½in. (67 x 90.2cm.) s 'E.Pritchett'
    Christie's South Kensington, 14 February 1996 (288**) GBP 12,375   US$ 19,012

PROCACCINI Giulio Cesare (Bologna 1574-1625 Milan) Italian
THE HOLY FAMILY WITH THE INFANT SAINT JOHN oil on panel, 38¼ x 35¾in. (97.2 x
65.4cm.) (1618-20)
        Sotheby's New York, 11 January 1996 (113**) US$ 167,500   US$ 167,500

PROCTER Dod, A.R.A. (1892-1972) British
GIRL IN A CHAIR oil on canvas, 35½ x 50¼in. (89.5 x 127.5cm.) slc 'Dod Procter' s nummbered
and inscr. on the stretcher 'Dod Procter 32 Elsworthy Rd NW3/no.2 'Girl in a Chair'' (ca 1934)
PROV.: The Artist's Estate JohnJames, the model's brother Belgrave Gallery, London; Lefevre
Gallery, London.
EXH.: London, Royal Academy, 1935, no.7; London, Fine Art Society, *Dod and Ernest Procter,*
1973, no. 11 Newcastle, Laing Art Gallery, *Dod Procter*, July-August 1990, no.39, p.21 (illustrated):
this exhibition travelled to Liverpool, Walker Art Gallery; and Penzance, Newlyn Art Gallery.
LIT.: *Royal Academy Illustrated*, London, 1935, p.81; L. Wortley, *British Impressionism A Garden
of Bright Images*, London, 1988, p.9 (illustrated).
        Christie's London, 21 November 1995 (98**) GBP 25,300   US$ 39,575

YOUNG ROMAN oil on canvas, 31 x 22½in. (78.8 x 57cm.) s inscr. 'Dod Young Roman'
PROV.: Brook Street Art Gallery, London.
EXH.: London, Royal Academy, 1929, no. 413; Pittsburgh, Carnegie Institute (not traced).
LIT.: *Royal Academy Illustrated*, London, 1929, p.84.
        Christie's London, 20 June 1996 (11**) GBP 9,200   US$ 14,187

PROSALENTIS Emilios (1859-1926) Greek
MOONLIGHT SCENE WITH FIGURES oil on canvas, 16 x 17¼in. (40.7 x 70cm.) sll in Greek
'E.Prosalentis'
        Christie's East, 13 February 1996 (24**) US$ 10,350   US$ 10,350

PRUD'HON Pierre Paul (Cluny 1758-1823 Paris) French
A SEATED FEMALE NUDE black and white chalk on blue paper, 20½ x 12¼in. (52 x 31.1cm.)
PROV.: Sophie Duprat, a gift from the artist; Cambray; Gaston Le Breton; Paris, Galerie Georges
Petit, 6-8 Dec. 1921, lot 132 (sold for FRF 16,000) (illustrated).
LIT.: J. Guiffrey, *L'Oeuvre de Pierre-Paul Prud'hon, Archives de l'art français*, 1924, no. 1137.
        Christie's New York, 22 May 1996 (25**) US$ 189,500   US$ 189,500

PSEUDO PIER FRANCESCO FIORENTINO (Florence 1444/45-doc. until 1497) Italian
MADONNA AND CHILD WITH THE INFANT SAINT JOHN THE BAPTIST oil on panel, with
an arched top, 28 x 14in. (71.1 x 35.5cm.)
PROV.: Anon. sale, Rome, Christie's, 26 Nov. 1986, lot 50, where bought by the present owner.
        Sotheby's London, 5 July 1995 (230**) GBP 65,300   US$ 104,163

MADONNA WITH CHILD tempera on board, 141 x 70cm.
        Finearte Rome, 18 October 1995 (392**) ITL 109,250,000   US$ 68,069

PUIGAUDEAU Ferdinand Loyen du (1864-1930) French
VILLAGE DE BRETAGNE-CONVERSATION SUR LA PLACE oil on canvas, 54 x 65cm. (21¼ x
25¾in.) slr 'F du Puigaudeau'
        Phillips London, 24 June 1996 (6**) GBP 6,000   US$ 9,252

PULLICINO Alberto (1719-before 1765) French
VUE DE LA VALETTE oil on canvas, 58 x 126cm.
        Étude Tajan Paris, 26 March 1996 (135**) FRF 140,000   US$ 27,673

PUPINI Biagio, {called} dalle Lame (1511 - 1575 active) Italian
RECTO: VENUS AND CUPID IN VULCAN`S FORGE VERSO: STUDY FOR A HOLY FAMILY
Recto: pen and brown ink with brown and grey wash heightened with white (partly oxidised), over

black chalk and stylus indications; on blue paper prepared with a light brown wash Verso: black
chalk, 40.7 x 27.2cm.

        Phillips London, 6 December 1995 (166**) GBP 8,000   US$ 12,311

PURRMANN Hans (Speyer 1880-1966 Basle) German
STILLLEBEN MIT TÜRKENBAND oil on panel, 75 x 63cm. slr 'H Purrmann'; sd on the reverse
(1942)

        Hauswedell & Nolte Cologne, 1 December 1995 (553**) DEM 104,000   US$ 72,157

GRAUES HAUS AN SUDITALIENISCHEM HAFEN, PORTO D'ISCHIA oil on canvas, 52 x
62cm. sll 'H. Purrmann' (1957)
PROV.: Georg Meistermann.
EXH.: Essen, *8 Ausstellng des Deutschen Künstlerbundes*, 1958, catalogue no. 150 (illustrated).

        Hauswedell & Nolte Cologne, 5/06 June 1996 (693**) DEM 180,000   US$ 116,951

FLOWERS IN A BIEDERMEIER VASE oil on canvas, 28¾ x 23 5/8in. (73 x 60cm.) slr
'H.Purrmann, sand inscr. 'Herrn u. Frau H.P. Stierer in Freundschaft Zugeeignet. Hans Purrmann.
Monfagnola 27.IV.54'
EXH.: 1950 (3-25 June), Kaiserslautern, Pfalzgalerie, *Hans Purrmann*, no.69, as executed in 1946.

        Phillips London, 27 November 1995 (24**) GBP 27,000   US$ 42,234

KLEINER AKT oil on wood, 19.5 x 16cm. framed slr 'Purrmann' on an old label on the reverse with
pencil 'Kl. Akt 1918 (2583a) and stamp 'Keutz & Meiners' (1918)

        Lempertz Cologne, 29 November 1995 (418**) DEM 31,000   US$ 21,880

PUTZ Leo (Merano 1869-1940) German
PORTRAIT FRAU LILLI MOLL oil on linen, 204 x 150cm. framed slr 'Leo Putz' on the reverse are
two labels on wich the artist has written 'Frau Moll gemalt von Leo Putz 1913' and 'Neubekum
Westfalen Frau Moll' (1913)

        Lempertz Cologne, 29 November 1995 (427**) DEM 70,000   US$ 49,407

PYNAS Jan Symonsz. (Haarlem 1583/85-1631 Amsterdam) Dutch
THE MAGDALEN KNEELING AT THE FOOT OF THE CROSS oil on panel, 81.6 x 59cm.
indistinctly s (strengthened) and d (strengthened) lr 'J Py.s f. 1610'

        Christie's Amsterdam, 7 May 1996 (33**) NLG 25,300   US$ 14,752

QUAST Pieter Jansz. (Amsterdam 1605/1606-1647 Amsterdam) Dutch
BOORS DRINKING AT TABLE IN AN INN oil on panel, 21.5 x 20.5cm. slr 'PQ'(linked)
      Christie's Amsterdam, 7 May 1996 (2) NLG 12,650   US$ 7,376

PEASANTS IN A TAVERN oil on panel, 13 x 11 1/8in. (33 x 28.3cm.) s mono. 'PQ' (around 1637)
PROV.: Anon. sale, Sotheby's New York, 17 May 1972, lot 83; George S. Abrams, Newton,
Massachusetts; with S. Nijstad, The Hague, 1978; with Robert Noortman, London and Maastricht,
1987; with David Koetser, Zurich.
EXH.: The Hague, Mauritshuis, *A Collector's Choice*, 1982, no. 69 (illustrated).
      Christie's London, 7 July 1995 (53**) GBP 32,200   US$ 51,364

RAAPHORST Cornelis (Nieuwkoop 1875-1954 Wassenaar) Dutch
KITTENS AT PLAY IN FRONT OF A DELFT-BLUE TILED FIREPLACE oil on canvas, 60 x 80cm. sll 'C Raaphorst'
      Christie's Amsterdam, 18 June 1996 (286*) NLG 14,950   US$ 8,735

THE YOUNG STUDENTS oil on canvas, 61 x 81cm sll 'C.Raaphorst'
      Christie's Amsterdam, 7 September 1995 (158*) NLG 10,925   US$ 6,668

RAEBURN Sir Henry, R.A., P.R.S.A. (Stockbridge, near Edinburgh 1756-1823 Edinburgh) Scottish
DOUBLE PORTRAIT OF WILLIAM THOROLD WOOD AND CHARLES THOROLD WOOD, FULL-LENGHT, IN YELLOW SMOCKS, BESIDE A TREE oil on panel, 50½ x 40in. (128.4 x 101.6cm.) inscr. lr 'William Thorold Wood/Charles Thorold Wood
PROV.: A.M. Lever; Christie's, 16 Jan. 1925, lot 157 (95gns. to Nicholson); with The Erich Gallery, New York, 1925; A.L. Nicholson, New York, by 1935; Anon. sale Parke-Bernet, 15-16 February 1944.
      Christie's London, 10 November 1995 (30**) GBP 8,625   US$ 13,491

PORTRAIT OF THE AGED LADY HOLLAND oil on canvas,124 x 100cm.
PROV.: Anonymous Sale, Paris 23 November 1927, no 41, illustrated (195,000 FRF); Anonymous Sale, Paris, 2 April 1936, no 11, illustrated; Collection Gaboriaud; His sale, Paris, Galerie Charpentier, 17 May 1950, no 11, illustrated; Anonymous Sale, Paris, 12-13 November 1952 (Maître Rheims), no 76, illustrated.
EXH.: *The Twelfth Hundred of Paintings by Old Masters*, Galerie Sedelmeyer, 1913, no 87, illustrated.
      Étude Tajan Paris, 12 December 1995 (59**) FRF 60,000   US$ 12,086

RAFFAELI Jean François (1850-1924) French
AN ELEGANT LADY FEEDING A GOAT ON A COASTAL PATH oil on canvas, 9 3/4 x 12 3/4in. (24.8 x 32.5cm.) s 'J.F. Raffaeli f'
      Christie's London, 14 June 1996 (56**) GBP 6,900   US$ 10,640

RAFFAELLINO DEL GARBO (Florence c. 1470-1524 Florence) Italian
MADONNA WITH CHILD AND STS. JOHN, MAGDALENA AND CATHERINE oil on panel, diameter 96cm. (tondo)
      Finearte Rome, 21 May 1996 (72**) ITL 46,000,000   US$ 29,544

RAFFALT Ignaz (Weisskirchen (Styria) 1800-1857 Hainbach, near Vienna) Austrian
ABENDDÄMMERUNG ÜBER EINER LANDSCHAFT MIT FIGÜRLICHER STAFFAGE oil on panel, 48 x 62cm. sd 'Raffalt 1850'
      Dorotheum Vienna, 6 November 1995 (121**) ATS 140,000   US$ 14,044

DER ENTENJÄGER oil on panel, 53.5 x 73cm. sdll 'Raffalt.: (1)851'
EXH.: Neuer Österreichischer Kunstverrein, 1951.
      Wiener Kunst Auktionen, 26 March 1996 (60**) ATS 230,000   US$ 22,124

RAHOULT Charles Diodore (1819-1874) French
ALLEGORY OF SUMMER: THE GODDESS CERES SURROUNDED BY PUTTI; A PICNIC NEAR THE WATERFALL oil on canvas, 25¼ x 51¼in. (64.2 x 130.2cm.); 61 x 52½in. (,155 x 133.4cm.)
      Christie's New York, 10 January 1996 (89**) US$ 23,000   US$ 23,000

RAIBOLINI Giacomo, {called} Francia (Bologna 1486 c.-1557 Bologna) Italian
THE MADONNA AND CHILD, A SHEPHERD IN AN EXTENSIVE RIVER LANDSCAPE BEYOND oil on panel, 22 x 16 5/8in. (55.9 x 42.2cm.)
      Christie's London, 19 April 1996 (242**) GBP 21,850   US$ 33,131

MADONNA WITH THE CHILD AND TWO SAINTS oil on panel, 74 x 56cm
     Finearte Milan, 25 November 1995 (133**) ITL 69,000,000   US$ 43,315

RAINER Arnulf (Baden, near Vienna 1929 b.) Austrian
UNTITLED oil, charcoal and pencil on photograph laid down on board, 28½ x 20in. (72.4 x
50.8cm.) sd ini. A.R. 83' and sd and ded. 'für Wolfgang Taube zur Erinnerung an seinen Besuch' on
the reverse
PROV.: Acquired directly from the Artist by the present owner in 1983.
     Christie's London, 19 March 1996 (79**) GBP 13,225   US$ 20,197

SCHWARZE SCHLANGEN (MEDUSA) oil and oilcrayon over an oil painting (Medusa, 1911 by
Joseph Jost Vienna 1888b.) on three-ply board, 50 x 83cm. slr 'ARainer'; sd 'A, Rainer 1987' and
titled 'Schwarze Schlangen' on the reverse
EXH.: Rome, Palazzo Braschi, *Austriaci a Roma*, April-May 1996.
     Dorotheum Vienna, 21 May 1996 (282***) ATS 300,000   US$ 28,807

KOPF oil charcoal and pastel on paper laid down on canvas, 24 3/8 x 18 ¼in. (62 x 46.4cm.) sd titled
'62/69'
PROV.: Galerie Heike Curtze, Düsseldorf.
     Christie's London, 23 May 1996 (57**) GBP 23,000   US$ 34,827

RECTO: RANDZEICHNUNG; VERSO: ZENTRALZEICHNUNG crayon on paper, 44 x 60cm. sdlr
'TRR 52'
PROV.: Collection Gerhard Rühm.
LIT.: Otto Breicha, Wieland Schmied, *TRRR 1951/52. Arnulf Rainer. Siebzehn frühe Arbeiten aus
der Sammlung Gerhard Rühm*, Galerie Klewan, Munich 1994, cat. no. 6 (illustrated).
     Wiener Kunst Auktionen, 26 March 1996 (334**) ATS 230,000   US$ 22,124

SCHWARZE ÜBERMALUNG plastic on wool,138 x 70cm. sdlr 'A. Rainer 57'; sd 'A. Rainer 1957'
on the reverse
EXH.: Baden-Baden, Staatliche Kunsthalle, *Arnulf Rainer Retrospektive*, Feb.-April 1981, cat. no.
88.
LIT.: Exhibition catalogue, *Arnulf Rainer*, Kunstverein Hamburg 1971, cat. no. 16 (illustrated no.
19).
     Wiener Kunst Auktionen, 26 March 1996 (391**) ATS 1,300,000   US$ 125,048

KOPFPROFIL waxcrayon on paper, 44.3 x 31.2cm. sd and titled lr 'A. Rainer 66'
     Wiener Kunst Auktionen, 26 March 1996 (421**) ATS 150,000   US$ 14,429

LINKE KURVE oil on board, 36 3/4 x 31½in. (93.3 x 80cm.) sd twice '56 and '59 and titled on the
reverse
PROV.: Acquired directly from the artist by the present owner.
     Christie's London, 27 June 1996 (57**) GBP 56,500   US$ 87,124

VERTIKALGESTALTUNG ink on paper, 70 x 100cm. sdlr 'TRR 52'
     Wiener Kunst Auktionen, 27 September 1995 (442**) ATS 600,000   US$ 58,322

VERTIKALGESTALTUNG oil and crayon on cardboard primed wiith chalk, 71.5 x 103cm. sdlr
'TRR 52'
PROV.: Collection Gerhard Rühm.
LIT.: Exhibition catalogue, *TRRR 1951/52*; *Arnulf Rainer. Siebzehn frühe Arbeiten aus der
Sammlung Gerhard Rühm*, Galerien Klewan, Munich 1994, no. 12 (illustrated); Exhibition catalogue,
Arnulf Rainer. Frühe Werke. 1949-1959, Galerie Thoman, Innsbruck 1995, no. 8 (illustrated).
     Wiener Kunst Auktionen, 27 September 1995 (448**) ATS 700,000   US$ 68,042

68ER oilcrayon and graphic pencil on cardboard, 62.5 x 44cm. sd 'A.Rainer 68'
        Dorotheum Vienna, 8 November 1995 (745**) ATS 200,000 — US$ 20,063

RAMENGHI Bartolomeo I (circle of) (Bagnacavallo 1484-1542 Bologna) Italian
ST. JOHN THE BAPTIST oil on panel, 67.5 x 43cm.
PROV.: Sale Christie's London, 15 November 1946, lot123 as *Albertinelli*; German collector; Collection Bernheim.
        Dorotheum Vienna, 11 June 1996 (4**) ATS 200,000 — US$ 18,564

RAMOS Mel (1935 b.) American
I STILL GET A THRILL WHEN I SEE BILL oil on canvas, 80 x 70in. (203.2 x 177.8cm.) s 'MEL RAMOS' on the reverse (1976)
PROV.: Louis K. Meisel Gallery, New York; private Collection, San Francisco.
EXH.: The Oakland Museum, *Ramos' Paintings 1959-1977,* Sept.-Nov. 1977, p. 18, no. 46 (illustrated); Waltham, Brandeis University, The Rose Art Museum, *Mel Ramos: a twenty year survey,* April-May 1980, p. 27, no. 53 (illustrated).
        Christie's New York, 22 February 1996 (62**) US$ 28,750 — US$ 28,750

THE PHANTOM oil on canvas, 30 3/8 x 18 5/8in. (79.7 x 47.3cm.) s and titled "THE PHANTOM' BY MEL RAMOS' on the reverse (1963-1964)
PROV.: Leo Castelli Gallery, New York; Charles Cowles, New York.
        Christie's New York, 8 May 1996 (306**) US$ 43,700 — US$ 43,700

RAMOS MARTINEZ Alfredo (1872-1946) Mexican
REINA XOCHTL gouache on newspaper, 20 11/16 x 15 9/16in. (52.5 x 39.5cm. sll 'Ramos Martinez'
PROV.: Acquired from the artist in 1940 by the father of the present owner.
        Phillips London, 26 June 1995 (16**) GBP 5,200 — US$ 8,297

RAMSAY Allan (Edinburgh 1713-1784 London) Scottish
PORTRAIT OF ANNE WARBURTON, SISTER OF SIR PETER WARBURTON AND WIFE OF THOMAS SLOUGHTER, HALF-LENGTH, WEARING A ROSE AND WHITE TRIMMED SILK DRESS oil on canvas, a painted oval, 30 x 25in. (76.5 x 63.5cm.)
        Phillips London, 18 June 1996 (26**) GBP 6,000 — US$ 9,252

RAMSAY Allan (and studio) (Edinburgh 1713-1784 London) Scottish
THE STATE CORANATION PORTRAITS OF GEORGE III; AND QUEEN CHARLOTTE, BOTH FULL-LENGHT, WEARING ROBES oil on canvas (a pair), each: 96 x 63in. (,244 x 160cm.)
PROV.: Painted for George Hervey, 2nd Earl of Bristol (1721-1775); On loan to the Ministry of Works in the 1950's.
LIT.: Seguier, 1819, nos. 1 & 2; Farrer, *St James's Square*, 1913, nos,311 and,305 respectively; *The Antique Collector*, 1961, pp. 218-219, illustrated p. 219; Oliver Millar, *Pictures in the Royal Collection - The later Georgian Pictures*, 1969, vol.I, p. 942.
        Sotheby's London, 11-12 June 1996 (448**) GBP 117,000 — US$ 180,416

RAMSEY Milne (1847-1915) American
STILL-LIFE WITH PEACHES AND WINE oil on canvas, 19½ x 16in. (49.6 x 40.7cm.) sd 'Milne Ramsey 12.76'
PROV.: Chapellier Galleries, New York; Mr. and Mrs. Frank Sinatra.
        Christie's New York, 1 December 1995 (76**) US$ 11,500 — US$ 11,500

RANFT Richard (1862-1931) Swiss
LES LAVANDIERES oil on canvas, 23½ x 32in. (59.7 x 81.3cm.) slr 'Richard Ranft'
        Christie's New York, 22 May 1996 (179**) US$ 11,500 — US$ 11,500

RAPHAEL Raffaello Santi {or} Sanzio, {called} (studio of) (Urbino 1483-1520 Rome) Italian
THE MADONNA DELL'IMPANNATA oil on panel, 59½ x 48in. (151.1 x 121.9cm.)
PROV.: Possibly Palazzo Altoviti, Rome, where acquired in 1843 for $50,000 (according to
tradition) by Hiram Powers, Rome, on behalf of his patron Col. John Smith Preston, Columbia, South
Carolina; by descent to Mrs. Mary Putnam, Texas; Victor Corse Thorne, Philadelphia.
LIT.: P. Farina, *The Original and Authentic Madonna dell'Impannata by Raffaello Sanzio*, 1929 (as
by Raphael); O. Fischel, 'Raffaelo Santi,' *Allgemeines Lexikon der Bildenden Kunstler*, Thieme-
Becker, eds., vol. XXIX, 1935, p. 441; P. Farina, 'La Madonna dell'Impannata di Raffaelo scoperta in
America,' *Arte cristiana*, 25, no. 3, March 1937, pp. 54-67 (as by Raphael); A. Porcella, 'La vera
'Madonna dell'Impannat' di Raffaello,' *L'illustrazione Vaticana*, 8, no. 5, 1937, pp. 209-,212 (as by
Raphael); P. Sanpaolesi, 'Due esami radiografici di dipinti', *Bolletino d'arte*, 31, May 1938, pp. 495-
,505 (with the Pitti panel as by Raphael); L. Serra, *Raffaello*, 1941, pp. 118-,120 (as not able to judge
from photographs); L. Dussler, *Raffael: Kritisches Verzeichnis der Gemälde, Wandbilder und
Bildteppiche*, 1966, p. 27 (as a period replica); L. Dussler, *Raphael: A Critical Catalogue of his
Pictures, Wall-Paintings and Tapestries*, 1971, pp. 38-39 (as a period replica); D.A. Brown, *Raphael
and America*, 1983, p. 102, note,140 (as a period replica).
Sotheby's New York, 11 January 1996 (179**) US$ 63,000 | US$ | 63,000

RAPHAEL Joseph (1872-1950) American
HILLY LANDSCAPE WITH HOUSES oil on canvas, 31½ x 39½in. (80 x 100.5cm.) sll 'Joe
Raphael'
Christie's New York, 30 November 1995 (72**) US$ 23,000 | US$ | 23,000

RAPOUS Michele Antonio (Turin/Piemonte 1730 after-1788 after) Italian
STILL-LIFE oil on canvas, 90 x 91cm
Finearte Milan, 25 November 1995 (65**) ITL 32,200,000 | US$ | 20,213

RAU Emil (Dresden 1858 b.) German
TYROLEAN COUPLE oil on canvas, 47 x 38in. (119.4 x 96.5cm.) slr 'E.RAU'
PROV.: Joseph Fijalkowski, 1949; Thence by descent to the present owner. | US$ | 13,800
Christie's New York, 14 February 1996 (80**) US$ 13,800

RAULIN Alexandre French
FIGURES ON THE RIVA DEGLI SCHIAVONE, VENICE oil on canvas, 14 x 20in. (35.6 x
50.8cm.) sdll 'A.Raulin 1843'
Christie's South Kensington, 14 March 1996 (165**) GBP 5,750 | US$ | 8,781

RAUPP Karl (Darmstadt 1837-1918 Munich) German
ERHOFFTE HEIMKEHR oil on canvas, 63 x 101cm. s and indistinctly d 'K. Raupp München'
Dorotheum Vienna, 6 November 1995 (108**) ATS 160,000 | US$ | 16,050

RAUSCHENBERG Robert (Port Arthur, Texas 1925 b.) American
GLIDER oil and silkscreen inks on canvas, 96 x 65in. (243.8 x 152.4cm.) sd 'GLIDER
RAUSCHENBERG 1962' on the reverse
PROV.: Ileana Sonnabend, New York; Galerie Beyeler, Basel.
EXH.: Paris, Galerie Ileana Sonnabend, *Seconde Exposition: Oeuvres 1962-1963*, Feb.-March 1963;
Venice, *XXXII Biennale Internazionale d'Arte*, 1964, p. 279, no. 74; Amsterdam, Stedelijk Museum;
Cologne, Kölnischer Kunstverein and Musée d'Art Moderne de la Ville de Paris, *Robert
Rauschenberg*, Feb.-July 1968, p.,106 (illustrated); Berlin, Staatliche Kunsthalle; Kunsthalle
Düsseldorf; Frankfurt, Städelsches Kunstinstitut; Humlebaek, Louisiana Museum of Modern Art;
Munich, Stadtische Galerie im Lenbachhaus; London, The Tate Gallery, *Robert Rauschenberg-
Werke 1950- 1980*, March 1980-June 1981, p. 311, no. 28 (illustrated); Basel, Galerie Beyeler,
Rauschenberg, March-May 1984, no. 7 (illustrated); Basel, Galerie Beyeler, *Landschaften und
Horizonte*, Oct.-Dec. 1987, no. 35 (illustrated); Paris, Galerie Enrico Navarra, *Oeuvres Choisies*,
Sept.-Oct. 1989; New York, Lang & O'Hara Gallery, and London, Runkel-Hue-Williams Ltd, *Robert
Rauschenberg Paintings 1962-1980*, Feb.-June 1990, pp. 4-5 (illustrated); New York, Whitney

Museum of American Art, *Robert Rauschenberg: The Silkscreen Paintings, 1962-1964*, Dec. 1990-March 1991, no. 14 (illustrated).
Christie's New York, 14 November 1995 (46**) US$ 827,500

US$ 827,500

PLUME (SPREAD) solvent transfer, crushed tin cans and graphite on fabric collage mounted on panel, 42 x 36in. (106.8 x 91.5cm.) sd and titled "PLUME (SPREAD)' RAUSCHENBERG 77' on the reverse
PROV.: The Marcia Simon Weisman Collection, Los Angeles.
Christie's New York, 8 May 1996 (354**) US$ 40,250

US$ 40,250

UNTITLED (EGYPTIAN SERIES) solvent transfer on gauze and paper mounted on panel, 69 x 40½in. (170.2 x 102.8cm.) sdll 'RAUSCHENBERG 74'
Christie's New York, 22 February 1996 (79**) US$ 19,550

US$ 19,550

RAVEL Eduard John E. (1847-1920)
Swiss
PORTRAIT OF A SEATED LADY HOLDING A PAIR OF SPECTACLES pastel on paper, 38 3/4 x 28in. (98.5 x 71.1cm.) sdlr 'EDOUARD RAVEL./1889'
Christie's New York, 14 February 1996 (99**) US$ 17,250

US$ 17,250

Glider

RAVENSWAAY Jan van (Hilversum 1789-1869 Hilversum) Dutch
IDYLLIC LANDCAPE WITH PEOPLE AND A TOWN BEYOND oil on canvas,110 x 93cm. sd (indistinctibly) 'Jan van Ravenswaay .'
Dorotheum Vienna, 17 April 1996 (423**) ATS 200,000

US$ 18,897

RAVESTEYN Jan Anthonisz (The Hague 1572 c.-1657 The Hague) Dutch
ALEXANDER VAN DER CAPELLEN, HEER VAN DE BOEDELHOF AND MERVELT; EMILIA VAN ZUYLEN VAN NYEVELT oil on panel (a pair), each: 64 x 54cm. both inscr. on the reverse, the first with the legend: 'ALEXANDER VANDER CAPELLEN/HEER VAN DEN BOEDELHOFF/AARTSBERGEN & ERVELT/ ob.Ao 1656/Beschreven IN DE RIDDERSCHAP/der graefschap/Zutphen/Rigter der Stad Doesburg'; and the second: '.ZUYLEN VAN./TOT AARTSBERGEN/1626 trouwd/VAN DER CAPELLEN/TOT DEN BOEDELHOFF'
PROV.: Alexander van der Capellen, 's-Heeraartsbergen, thence by descent.
LIT.: E.W. Moes, *Iconografia Batava*, 1898, vol. I, no. 1470; E.W. Moes, *Iconografia Batava*, 1905, vol. II, no. 9411.
Sotheby's Amsterdam, 14 November 1995 (20**) NLG 70,800

US$ 44,621

BILDNIS EINES OFFIZIERS oil on panel,109 x 78cm. indistinctly ar
Lempertz Cologne, 18 May 1996 (1128*) DEM 25,000

US$ 16,298

PORTRAIT OF AN ELEGANT LADY HOLDING A FAN oil on panel, 48 x 35¼in. (121.9 x 89.5cm.) s and inscr. ur 'Anno. 1631/JVR.(in ligature)f.'

PROV.: Sale: A. Mak, Amsterdam, 18-20 November 1924, lot 54 (illustrated); Lewis J. Ruskin,
Scottdale, Arizona, thence by descent to the present owner.
EXH.: Phoenix, The Phoenix Art Museum, on loan.

Sotheby's New York, 6 October 1996 (122*) US$ 31,050	US$	31,050

RAVILIOUS Eric (1903-1942) British
THE CEMENT PIT pencil, watercolour and bodycolour, 17 3/4 x 22in. (45 x 56cm.) sdlr 'Eric
Ravilious June 34'
PROV.: Zwemmer Gallery, London.

Christie's London, 21 March 1996 (1**) GBP 17,250	US$	26,344

RAYNER Louise J. (1832-1924) British
WINDSOR pencil and watercolour heightened with bodycolour, 9 x 14in. (22.8 x 35.6cm.) s 'Louise
Rayner'

Christie's London, 6 November 1995 (20**) GBP 8,970	US$	14,031

REAM Morston C. (1859-1910) American
STILL-LIFE WITH GRAPES, PEACH, PLUM, LADY APPLE AND WINE GLASS oil on canvas,
12 x 10in. (30.5 x 25.4cm.) slr 'M.C. Ream'

Christie's East, 28 November 1995 (81***) US$ 11,500	US$	11,500

RECCO (Naples -1654 Naples) Italian
FLOWERS IN A GLASS VASE oil on panel, (oval) 40.5 x 30.5cm. (framed)

Dorotheum Vienna, 17 October 1995 (12**) ATS 120,000	US$	12,037

NATURA MORTA DI PESCI oil on canvas,121 x 170cm.

Finearte Rome, 22 November 1995 (94**) ITL 47,150,000	US$	29,598

RECCO Giacomo (Naples 1603-1654 Naples) Italian
BOUQUET IN A GLASS VASE oil on panel, 40 x 31cm. (framed)

Dorotheum Vienna, 17 October 1995 (13**) ATS 120,000	US$	12,037

RECCO Giuseppe (Naples 1634-1695 Alicante (?)) Italian
THE PUNISHMENT OF KING ADONIBEZEC oil on canvas,148 x,200 s 'G Recco' (ca. 1694)

Christie's Rome, 21 November 1995 (230**) ITL 50,000,000	US$	31,387

VASO DI ANEMONI E TULIPANI oil on canvas, 61 x 50cm. ini. 'G.R.' on the plate of stone

Finearte Rome, 22 November 1995 (156**) ITL 48,300,000	US$	30,320

RECCO Nicola Maria (Naples, active 18th Century-) Italian
STILL-LIFES OF FISH AND CRUSTACEANS oil on canvas (a pair), each:36 x 48½in. (91.5 x
123.5cm.) sll 'Nic.M./Recco P'; slr 'Nic; MRecco'

Sotheby's London, 5 July 1995 (110**) GBP 23,000	US$	36,688

REDFIELD Edward Willis, N.A. (1869-1965) American
OFF MANAN oil on canvas, 21½ x 25in. (54.7 x 63.5cm.) slr'E.W. Redfield'; s and inscr. with title
on the stretcher

Christie's New York, 13 September 1995 (67**) US$ 25,300	US$	25,300

CENTRE BRIGDE FARM oil on canvas, 32 x 38in. (81.3 x 96.5cm.) sdlr 'E.W. Redfield. 1914'
PROV.: R.H. Love Gallenes, Inc., Chicago, Illinois.
EXH.: Columbus, Georgia, The Columbus Museum of Art, *Masterworks of American Impressionism
from the Pfeil Collection*, 1992, pp. 215-217, no. 64 (This exhibition travelled extensively).

Christie's New York, 30 November 1995 (70**) US$ 85,000	US$	85,000

REDON Odilon (Bordeaux 1840-1916 Paris) French
LA MORT D'OPHELIE oil on canvas, 11 3/4 x 15 3/4in. (30 x 40cm.) slr 'Odilonn Redon'
PROV.: Collection Piot, Paris (ca 1923-ca 1971).
EXH.: Paris, Galerie Druet, *Exposition d'Oeuvres d'Odilon Redon (1840-1916), Peintures, pastels, aquarelles, dessins, eaux-fortes, art décoratif,* 11 June 1923, no. 53.
LIT.: A. Wildenstein, *Odilon Redon, Catalogue Raisonné de l'oeuvre peint et dessiné,* vol. II, Paris 1994, no.,906 (illustrated p. 80).
        Christie's London, 26 June 1996 (139**) GBP 84,000   US$ 129,530

BOUQUET DE FLEURS DANS UNE VASE BLUE pastel on paper laid down on canvas, 22 x 17 3/4in. (55.9 x 45cm.) sll 'ODILON REDON'
PROV.: Samuel and Saidye Bronfman, Montreal.
EXH.: Montreal, Museum of Fine Arts, *Canada Collects European Painting, 1860-1960,* Jan-Feb., p.64, no.,180 (illustrated, p. 58.).
        Christie's New York, 7 November 1995 (29**) US$ 607,500   US$ 607,500

REDOUTÉ Pierre Joseph (Saint-Hubert (near Liege) 1759-1840 Paris) French
AN ELABORATE STILL-LIFE OF FLOWERS IN A GLASS VASE RESTING ON AN ALABASTER PEDESTAL, WITH A BIRD NEST AND A MELOM BELOW oil on canvas, 39 x 31½in. (99.1 x 80cm.) sd 'P.J. Redouté pinxit an 4. (1796)
EXH.: Paris, Salon 1796, no. 391.
LIT.: C. Léger, *Redouté et son temps*, 1945, p. 147; Peter Mitchell, *European Flower Painters,* 1973, p. 210; Mitchell and Fabrice Faré, *La Vie Silencieuse en France, La Nature Morte au XVIIIe Siècle*, 1976, p. 316, no.,506 (illustrated).   US$
        Sotheby's New York, 16 May 1996 (126**) US$ 1,487,500   1,487,500

RED ANEMONES IN A GLASS JAR, PINK ROSES, NARCISSI, CONVULVULUS, HAREBELLS AND DAISIES IN A BASKET, WITH CHERRIES, A BIRD'S NEST, A SNAIL AND OTHER FLOWERS ON A LEDGE oil on canvas, 24¼ x 20in. (61.6 x 50.8cm.) sd 'P.J. Redouté Fecit 1793'
        Christie's London, 19 April 1996 (233**) GBP 89,500   US$ 135,709

REED David (1946 b.-) American
,234 acrylic on canvas-unframed, 25 x 100in. (63.5 x 254cm.) sd and titled 'DAVID REED '234' 1986' on the overlap
PROV.: Max Protetch Gallery, New York.
        Christie's New York, 22 February 1996 (158**) US$ 12,650   US$ 12,650

REEKERS Hendrik (Haarlem 1815-1854 Haarlem) Dutch
A STILL-LIFE WITH FRUIT IN A BOWL oil on panel, 42.5 x 36cm Slr 'H. Reekers'
        Christie's Amsterdam, 26 October 1995 (195*) NLG 16,100   US$ 10,151

REGGIANINI Vittorio (Modena 1858 b.-) Italian
A DECLARATION OF LOVE oil on canvas, 29 3/4 x 40 1/8in. (75.5 x 102cm.) s
EXH.: Associazione Nationale degli Artisti, Piazza Pitti, Florence.
        Phillips London, 11 June 1996 (78**) GBP 15,000   US$ 23,130

REGNAULT Jean Baptiste, baron (Paris 1754-1829 Paris) French
HEAD OF A WOMAN IN THE GUISE OF A BACCHANTE: AN UNFINISHED PORTRAIT oil on canvas, s or inscr. 'Regnault'
        Sotheby's New York, 16 May 1996 (97**) US$ 11,500   US$ 11,500

REGO Paula (Lissabon 1935 b.-) Portuguese
UNTITLED watercolour and acrylic on paper, 27 x 39 3/4in. (68.5 x 101cm.) sd 'Paula Rego 1984'
        Christie's London, 22 May 1996 (124**) GBP 14,950   US$ 22,63?

REGOYOS Darío de (1857-1913) Spanish
PAISAJE NOCTURNO NEVADO oil on canvas, 89 x 120cm. sdlr '86 Haarlem Holanda / D. de
Regoyos'
PROV.: Privat collection, Madrid.
EXH.: Madrid, Real Academia de Bellas Artes de San Fernando, *Tesoros de las Coleciones
Particulares Madrileñas: Pinturas Españoelas del Romanticismo al Modernismo*, 1991, cat. no. 34,
p.,136 (illustrated in colour).
LIT.: Rodrigo Soranio, *Darío de Regoyos (Historia de una Rebeldía)*, Madrid, 1921, p. 145; Juan
San Nicolás, catálogo de la exposicíon *Regoyos y El País Vasco*, San Sebastian, Sala Garibai, 1994,
p. 26 (illustrated).
Sotheby's Madrid, 23 November 1995 (74**) ESP 12,715,000   US$ 104,517

REID Robert Payton, A.R.S.A. (1859-1945) Scottish
MARGUERITES oil on canvas, 30 x 20in. (76 x 51cm.) slr 'R.PATON REID'
Sotheby's London, 29 August 1995 (834**) GBP 23,000   US$ 37,229

REID Stephen (Aberdeen 1873 b.) Scottish
TEH APPEAL FOR MERCY oil on canvas, 48½ x 72½in. (123.3 x 181.6cm.) sd 'Stephen Reid/36'
and s inscr. 'Witch! /Stephen Reid/,117 Abbey Road' and 'No.1 Witch!/Stephen Reid/108a King
Henry's
Road/N.W.3' on old labels on the reverse
PROV.: H. De Casseres; Christie's, 28 March 1956, lot 44 (16 gns. to Campo).
Christie's London, 6 November 1995 (134**) GBP 20,700   US$ 32,379

REIGNIER Jean-Marie (Lyon 1815-1886 Lyon) French
STILL-LIFE WITH FLOWERS IN A VASE, OTHER FLOWERS AND A WHITE COCKATOO
ON A STONE LEDGE oil on canvas, 39 x 30in. (99.1 x 76.2cm.)
PROV.: Frost & Reed, Ltd. London and Bristol, by 1965.
LIT.: *The Connoisseur*, 1963, only illustrated; S.H. Pavière, *Floral Art: Great masters of Flower
Painting*, 1965 (colour illustration pl. 25).
Sotheby's New York, 16 May 1996 (147**) US$ 82,250   US$ 82,250

REINHARDT Ad (Buffalo 1913-1967 New York) American
UNTITLED oil on masonite in artist's frame, 56 x 21½in. (142.2 x 54.6cm.) sdll 'Reinhardt '47'
PROV.: Betty Parsons Gallery, New York.
Christie's New York, 8 May 1996 (257**) US$ 74,000   US$ 74,000

ABSTRACT 1 oil on canvas, 32 x 39 7/8in. (81.2 x 101.5cm.) sdlr 'Reinhardt 48'
PROV.: Alex Turney, New York; Ira Spierman Inc. New York.
EXH.: Washington D.C., Corcoran Gallery of Art, *Ad Reinhardt: Seventeen Works*, Sept.-Dec. 1984,
no. 6 (illustrated).
LIT.: L. Lippard, *Ad Reinhardt*, New York 1981, p. 48, no. 32 (illustrated).
Christie's New York, 7 May 1996 (3**) US$ 107,000   US$ 107,000

REITER Johann Baptist (Urfahr (near Linz) 1813-1890 Vienna) Austrian
DIE RIBISELKÖNIGIN oil on canvas, 80 x 58cm. s 'Joh. Bap. Reiter'
Dorotheum Vienna, 6 November 1995 (67**) ATS 200,000   US$ 20,063

REMBRANDT or Rembrandt Harmensz van Rijn (Leyden 1606-1669 Amsterdam) Dutch
CUPID BLOWING A SOAP BUBBLE oil on canvas, 29½ x 36½in. (75 x 92.6cm.) sdlr
Rembrandt/f. 1634'
PROV.: Private Russian Collection, Berlin, in 1923 (according to Valentiner); Private Collection,
Holland, (according to the 1930 exhibition catalogue); With Goudstikker, Amsterdam 1930, bears his
label on the stretcher; Baron Heinrich Thyssen-Bornemisza, Castle Rohoncz, by 1930.
EXH.: Amsterdam, Goudstikker, April-May 1930, no. 48; Munich 1930, no. 269, plate 47; Paris
1970, no. 35, plate 6; Düsseldorf 1970-71, no. 41; Lausanne etc., 1986-7, no. 25.

LIT.: W.R. Walentiner, *Rembrandt. Wiedergefundene Gemälde, Klassiker der Kunst*, 2nd ed., 1923, p. XXI, p. 35, no. 40; A. Bredius, *Rembrandt Gemälde*, 1935, pp. 19-20, reproduced plate 470, wrongly as on panel; R. Heinemann 1937, vol. I, no. 345, vol. II, plate 125; W. Sumowski, 'Nachträge zum Rembrandtjahr 1956', in *Wissenschaftliche Zeitschrift der Humboldt-Universität zu Berlin, Gesellschafts-und sprachwissenschaftliche Reihe*, vol. VII, 1957-8, p. 231, as by a Rembrandt pupil, perhaps Ferdinand Bol; H.F. Wijman, 'Rembrandt en Hendrickje Uylenburgh te Amsterdam', in *Amstelodamum Maandblad.*, no. 43, 1956, pp. 94-103, as by Rembrandt, possibly a portrait of Hendrick Uylenburgh's son Gerrit; K Bauch, *Rembrandt Gemälde*, 1966, p. 10, no. 157, as possibly partly by a Rembrandt pupil, perhaps Govaert Flinck; P. Lecaldano, G. Martin, The Complete Paintings of Rembrandt, 1969, p. 131, reproduced, as not by Rembrandt; A. Bredius, ed. H. Gerson, Rembrandt. *The Complete Edition of the Paintings*, 1969, p. 592, no. 470, reproduced p. 380, as by Govaert Flinck; J. Bruyn, B. Haak, S.H. Levie, P.J.J. van Thiel, E. van de Wetering (Stichting / Foundation Rembrandt Research Project), *A Corpus of Rembrandt Paintings*, vol. II, 1986, pp. 479-486, no. A91, reproduced, with details and X-ray, as by Rembrandt; P. Huys Janssen, in *Rembrandt's Academy*, exhibition catalogue, 1992, pp. 158-161, under no.16, as by Rembrand*t*, influencing Flinck's *Sleeping Cupid* of 1655.

Sotheby's London, 6 December 1995 (118***) GBP 3,851,500	US$	5,927,208

THE SENSE OF TOUCH: THE STONE OPERATION oil on panel, 8½ x 7in. (21.6 x 17.7cm.) (between 1610-1620)
PROV.: An English private collection (according to W.R. Valentiner, see below). Acquired shortly before 1939 by Dr. C.J.K. van Aalst; thence by descent (on consignment with Cramer 1968 - 1979).
EXH.: Leyden, Stedelijk Museum de Lakenhal, *Rembrandt als Leermeester*, 1956, no. 3.; Stockholm, Nationalmuseum, Rembrandt och hans Tid, 1992-3, no. 47 (entry for nos. 46-8 by Dr. Christopher Brown, who has kindly made available his English text).
LIT.: V. Bloch, 'Zum frühen Rembrandt', *Oud Holland*, L, 1933, pp. 97-102 (publishing The Sense of Hearing); A. Bredius, *Rembrandt Gemälde*, Vienna, 1935 (Dutch and English editions published in 1,935 and 1,937 respectively), no. 42 (for The Sense of Hearing); *Dutch & Flemish Masters in the collection of Dr. C.J.K. van Aalst, Huis-te-Hoevelaken*, privately printed, ed. J.W. von Moltke, 1939, pl. 330; O. Benesch, 'An Early Group Portrait Drawing by Rembrandt', *The Art Quarterly*, III, 1940, pp. 3-4 (including an editorial note by W.R. Valentiner); reprinted in O. Benesch, *Collected Writings, I, Rembrandt*, ed. Eva Benesch, London, 1970, pp. 134ff. and p.137 for The Sense of Hearing; H. Kauffmann, 'Die Fünfsinne in der niederländischen Malerei der 17 Jahrhunderts', *Kunstgeschichtliche Studien*, 1944, pp. 145-6 (for The Sense of Hearing); G. Knuttel, *Rembrandt, de Meester in zijn werk*, Amsterdam, 1956, p. 240; J. Rosenberg, 'Die Rembrandt Ausstellung in Holland', *Kunstchronik*, IX, 1956, pp. 345-54; J. Rosenberg, *Rembrandt Life and Work*, London, 1964, 2nd ed., p. 371; K. Bauch, *Der frühe Rembrandt und seine Zeit. Studien zur geschichtlichen Bedeutung seines Frühstils*, Berlin, 1960, p. 48; O. Benesch, 'Caravaggism in the drawings of Rembrandt', *extrait des Actes du XVIIème Congrès International d'Histoire de l'Art*. The Hague, 1955, pp. 385ff.; reprinted in Benesch, *Collected Writings* etc., pp. 177-178; K. Bauch, Rembrandt Gemälde, Berlin, 1966, p. 48; A. Bredius, *Rembrandt. The Complete edition of the Paintings*, (revised by H. Gerson), London, 1969, no.,421 A; The Rembrandt Research Project, J. Bruyn et al., *A Corpus of Rembrandt Paintings*, The Hague, Boston, London, 1982, no. B2; G. Schwartz, *Rembrandt, his Life, his Paintings*, Harmondsworth, 1985, p. 34.; C. Tumpel, *Rembrandt*, Amsterdam, 1986, no. A 28.

Christie's London, 7 July 1995 (57**) GBP 386,500	US$	616,526

HEAD OF CHRIST oil on panel, 24 x 19in. (61 x 48.3cm.)
PROV.: With E. Plietzsch, Berlin, 1920; Van Diemen & Co., Berlin by 1922; Lord Melchett Court, Romney, Hampshire; Duveen Brothers, New York, at least by 1935, Harry John, Milwaukee by 1966; Sale: Sotheby's New York, January 11, 1990, lot 45 (withdrawn).
EXH.: Milwaukee, Wisconsin,Wisconsin Collects; Washington, D.C., Phillips Memorial Gallery, *The Functions of Color in Painting*, February 16- March 23, I941, cat. no. 50 (as by Rembrandt); Chicago, Art Institute, *Rembrandt after Three Hundred Years. An Exhibition on Rembrandt and his followers*, October 25- December 7, 1969; travelling on to Minneapolis and Detroit, cat. no. 18 (as by Rembrandt).

LIT.: C. Hofstede de Groot, *Die holländische Kritik derjetzigen Rembrandtforschung*, 1922, p. 41 (as by Rembrandt); K. Bauch, *Rembrandt Gemälde*, 1966, cat. no.,228 (as by Rembrandt, circa 1660-61); H. Gerson, *Rembrandt Paintings*, 1968, pp. 432-33, cat. no. 378, illus. (not seen by the author); A. Bredius, *Rembrandt: The Complete Edition of the Paintings*, ed. by H. Gerson, 1969, p. 614, cat. no. 627, illus. p.,528 (not seen by Gerson); G. Schwartz, *Rembrandt: his life, his paintings*, 1985, p.,380 (as not by Rembrandt); C. Tumpel, *Rembrandt: Mythos und Methode*, 1986, p. 422, cat. no. A21 (as circle of Rembrandt, circa 1655-60); C. Tumpel, *Rembrandt*, 1993, p. 425, no. A21 (as *Rembrandt Circle*, circa 1655/60); W. Liedtke, *Rembrandt/ Not Rembrandt*, 1995, (exhibition catalogue), pp. 122, 123, note 1, under cat. no. 35 (as *Circle of Rembrandt*, circa 1650, relating it to the Metropolitan Museum painting); H. von Sonnenburg, *Rembrandt/ Not Rembrandt*, 1995, companion exhibition catalogue to the preceding, p.l20, under cat. no. 25, illus., fig.,156 (noting that the Metropolitan Museum picture as a *Dordrecht Follower of Rembrandt*, circa 1660).

Sotheby's New York, 11 January 1996 (261**) US$ 74,000   US$ 74,000

Potrait of the Artist as a young Man wearing a black Beret and steel Gorget

REMBRANDT or Rembrandt Harmensz van Rijn (Leyden 1606-1669 Amsterdam) (studio of) Dutch
PORTRAIT OF THE ARTIST AS A YOUNG MAN WEARING A BLACK BERET AND STEEL
GORGET oil on panel, 17 x 13½in. (43.2 x 34.3cm.)
PROV.: P. Locquet (Sale: Amsterdam, September 22, 1783, lot 325, as by Rembrandt, 'Hoog 17,
/breed 13 duim. Paneel. Een Manshooft verbeeldende een Borststuk, hy vertoont zich in 't Harnas en
heeft een Muts op het Hooft, als gelykende naar een fixe penseelstreek [17 high by 13 inches wide.
Panel. A man's head bust-length, he is wearing armor and as a cap on his head. it is strong with firm
brushwork]' there purchased for,350 guilders by Yver Armand-Francois-Louis de Mestral de Saint-
Saphorin (1738-1805) probably purchased during his term as Danish envoy in The Hague [1780 -
1788](Sale: Vienna, May 19, 1806, lot 11), there unsold; Bernard de Mestral de Saint-Saphorin; Sale:
Christie's, London, April 11, 1986, lot 6, there purchased by the present owner.
LIT.: T. von Frimmel, *Studien und Skizzen zur Gemäldekunde*, 2, 1916, pp. 89-93; J. Bruyn, B. Haak,
S.H. Levie, PJJ. van Thiel and E. van der Wetering, *a Corpus of Rembrandt Paintings* vol. I, 1625-
1631, 1982, p. 235, under no. 6.2 and 239-40, under cat. no. A2, copy no. 5, and illus., fig. 7 (as
unseen by the committee, and a copy of the picture in the Moa Museum, Japan).
    Sotheby's New York, 16 May 1996 (28**) US$ 68,500   US$ 68,500

REMINGTON Frederic Sackrider, A.N.A. (1861-1909) American
FIVE-FLOOT HURDLE BAREBACK ink wash and gouache on paper, 15 5/8 x 20 1/8in. (39.7 x
51.2cm.) slr 'Frederic Remington' and inscr. 'West Point Riding Hall'
PROV.: Coe Kerr Gallery, New York.
    Christie's New York, 23 May 1996 (106**) US$ 31,050   US$ 31,050

REMPS Andrea Domenico (Venice 1620 c. - 1622 active) Italian
A TROMPE-L'OEUIL OF A PRINT OF A SHEPHERD BY SIMONE CANTARINI, A SCORE,
PAMPHLETS, AND LETTERS AFFIXED TO A PARTITION oil on canvas, 29 1/8 x 24in. (74 x
61cm.)
PROV.: Fracis Hawcroft (Former Keeper of the Whitworth Gallery), and by bequest to the present
owner.
    Christie's London, 8 December 1995 (350**) GBP 12,075   US$ 18,583

REMPS Andrea {or} Domenico (attributed) (Venice 1620 c. - 1622 active) Italian
TROMPE L'OEIL FROM A LANDSCAPE PAINTING ATTACHED ON A PANEL oil on canvas,
71.5 x 86.5cm. titled 'Venetia'
    Dorotheum Vienna, 6 March 1996 (58**) ATS 120,000   US$ 11,543

RENI Guido (Bologna 1575-1642 Bologna) Italian
THE CHRIST CHILD ASLEEP UPON THE CROSS oil on canvas, 9½ x 12¼in. (24 x 31cm.)
inventory number ll. '17.' (first half of the 1620's)
PROV.: The Counts of Cordoba, Spain, their wax seal affixed to the stretcher (according to Pepper
below); Thomas Watson Jackson, Oxford, sold London, Christie's, 14 May 1915, lot 44, as Reni,
with companion, 6½ gns. to Buttery; Anonymous sale, London, Christie's, 8 December 1989, lot 125.
LIT.: D.S. Pepper, *Guido Reni*, 1988, pp. 330-1, no. 17, plate 11.
    Sotheby's London, 6 December 1995 (155**) GBP 23,000   US$ 35,396

RENOIR Pierre-Auguste (Limoges 1841-1919 Cagnes-sur-Mer) French
ETUDES: TETES DE FEMMES, NUS, PAYSAGES ET PECHES oil on canvas, 16 1/8 x 13in. (41
x 33cm.) slr 'Renoir' (1895-1896)
PROV.: Wolfgang Kurger, Berlin.
LIT.: M. Fitzgerald, 'Picasso: In the Beaux Quartiers', in *Art in America*, December 1992, p. 90
(illustrated in colour); M. Fitzgerald, *Making Modernism: Picasso and the Creation of the Market for
Twentieth Century Art*, New York 1995, fig. 38 (illustrated p. 105).
    Christie's New York, 1 May 1996 (119**) US$ 310,500   US$ 310,500

AU BORD DE LA RIVIERE oil on canvas, 18 3/8 x 22 1/8in. (46.7 x 56.2cm.)
LIT.: ed. Bernheim-Jeune, *L'atelier de Renoir*, Paris 1931, no.,181 (illustrated pl. 58).
Christie's New York, 1 May 1996 (132**) US$ 178,500   US$ 178,500

MADAME LE BRUN ET SA FILLE oil on canvas, 8 3/8 x 6 7/8in. (21.3 x 17.4cm.) sll 'Renoir'
PROV.: Galerie Fiquet, Paris; Estate of George Lurcy, New York; sale, Parke-Bernet Galleries Inc.,
New York, 7 November 1957, lot 20 (illustrated; acquired by the late owner).
Christie's New York, 1 May 1996 (147**) US$ 420,500   US$ 420,500

LA MODISTE crayon Comté on paper, 12 x 6in. (30.5 x 15.5cm.) slr 'Renoir'
LIT.: This painting Will included and reproduced in the *Pierre Auguste Renoir catalogue raisonné*
currently being prepared by Dauberville at Editions Bernheim-Jeune.
Étude Tajan Paris, 13 December 1995 (22*) FRF 150,000   US$ 30,214

PAYSANNE DEBOUT DANS UN PAYSAGE oil on canvas, 14½ x 8 3/4in. (36.8 x 22.2cm.) sul
'renoir' (1884)
PROV.: Ambroise Vollard, Paris; Private collection, Paris; Hans Cohn.
LIT.: Ambroise Vollard, *Tableaux, Pastels et Dessins de Pierre-Auguste Renoir*, vol. II, Paris, 1918
(illustrated); François Daulte, *Auguste Renoir, Catalogue Raisonné de l'Oeuvre Peint, Figures, 1860-
1890*, vol. I, Lausanne 1971, no.,468 (illustrated).
Sotheby's New York, 2 May 1996 (115**) US$ 228,000   US$ 228,000

LA BAIE D'ALGER oil on canvas, 20 x 25½in. (51 x 65cm.) sd 'Renoir 81'
PROV.: Durand-Ruel, Paris.
EXH.: Paris, Galerie Durand-Ruel, *Exposition de tableaux de Monet, Pissarro, Renoir et Sisley*,
1899, no. 82; Paris, Galerie Durand-Ruel, *Tableaux, pastels, dessins par Renoir*, 1920, no. 38; Paris,
Galerie Durand-Ruel, *Paysages par Monet, Pissarro, Renoir et Sisley*, 1933, no. 27; Paris, Galerie
Charpentier, *Chefs-d 'Oeuvres de Collections Françaises*, 1962, no. 67, illustrated in the catalogue.
LIT.: Elda Fezzi, *L 'Opera completa di Renoir, nel periodo Impressionista 1869-1883*, Milan, 1972,
p. 109, no. 463, illustrated.
Sotheby's London, 24 June 1996 (11**) GBP 551,500   US$ 850,424

TETTE DE FEMME oil on canvas, 12¼ x 10in. (31 x 25.5cm.) sul 'Renoir' (ca 1887)
PROV.: Ambroise Vollard, Paris; Martin Fabiani, Paris; Leonard Benatov, Paris.
LIT.: Ambroise Vollard, *Tableaux, Pastels et Dessins de Pierre-Auguste Renoir*, Paris, 1918, no. 47,
i l lustrated; François Daulte, *Auguste Renoir, Catalogue raisonne: Figures (1860-1890)*, Lausanne,
1971, no. 516, illustrated .
Sotheby's London, 24 June 1996 (15**) GBP 386,500   US$ 595,991

BUSTE DE FEMME, CORSAGE JAUNE pastel on paper, 23 5/8 x 18 7.8in. (60 x 48cm.) slr
'Renoir' (ca. 1883)
PROV.: Paul Durand-Ruel, Paris (acquired from the artist on 3 February 1892 for his private
collection);Joseph and Georges Durand-Ruel, Paris; Durand-Ruel, Paris (acquired from the above on
6 November 1924) Hugo Perls, Berlin (acquired from the above on 15 October 1928); Acquired by
the family of the present owner prior to 1930.
EXH.: Paris, Galerie Durand-Ruel, *Aquarelles, pastels, dessins par Renoir*, 1921, no. 36.
LIT.: To be included in volume VI (*Les pastels, aquarelles et dessins*) of the *Renoir Catalogue
raisonné* being prepared by Francois Daulte.
Sotheby's London, 24 June 1996 (19**) GBP 1211,500   US$ 186,815 7

PORTRAIT DE CLAUDE MONET pencil on paper, 20 x 15 3/4in. (51.5 x 40cm.) sll 'Renoir' (ca.
1885-90)
PROV.: Claude Monet, Giverny; Michel Monet, Giverny; Thence by descent to the present owner.
LIT.: Ambroise Vollard, *Tableaux, Pastels et Dessins de Pierre-Auguste Renoir*, Paris, 1918, pl. 78,
no.,309 (illustrated).
Sotheby's London, 24 June 1996 (27**) GBP 111,500   US$ 171,935

DANSEUSE ESPAGNOLE DANS UNE ROBE ROUGE oil on canvas, 16 1/8 x 12 3/4in. (41 x 32.5cm.) slr 'Renoir' (ca.1896)
PROV.: Dr. Georges Viau, Paris (vente: Paris, Galerie Durand-Ruel, 2e vente Viau, 21st- 22nd March 1907, lot 71); Bernheim-Jeune, Paris (purchased at the above sale) Paul Graupe, Berlin (sale: Berlin, Deutsche und Französische Gemälde, Paul Graupe, 13th November 1930, lot 27); O'Hana Gallery, London (purchased at the above sale) Maurice Gutman, New York; Purchased by the present owner in 1958 .
EXH.: London, O'Hana Gallery, *Exhibition of French Masters of the 19th and 20th Centuries* 1957, no. 31.
LIT.: To be included in volume II (*Les Figures, 1893-1905*) of the *Renoir Catalogue raisonné* being prepared by Francois Daulte.
Sotheby's London, 24 June 1996 (30**) GBP 331,500   US$ 511,180

LA FAMILLE oil on canvas, 63 3/8 x 51 5/8in. (,161 x 130cm.) s (stamped) 'Renoir' (1896)
PROV.: Ambroise Vollard, Paris and thence by descent to Eduard Jonas, Paris; Walter Chrysler, New York; sale Sotheby's London, 1 July 1959, lot 25 (GBP 11,000) to O'Hana Gallery); O'Hana Gallery, London; Anon sale, Christie's London, 27 November 1989, lot 15 (GBP2,200,000).
LIT.: To be included in Volume II of the *Renoir Catalogue Raisonné, Figures 1891-1905* currently being prepared by François Daulte.
Christie's London, 25 June 1996 (12**) GBP 397,500   US$ 612,953

VASE DE ROSES oil on canvas, 16 3/4 x 15 3/4in. (42.5 x 40cm.) s stamped 'Renoir'
LIT.: Bernheim-Jeune (ed.), *L'Atelier de Renoir*, vol. II, Paris 1931, p. 467 (illustrated pl. 150).
Christie's London, 26 June 1996 (120**) GBP 172,000   US$ 265,227

YOUNG LADY 'EN PROFIL' oil on canvas, 25 x 14.5cm. slr 'Renoir'
LIT.: Ambroise Vollard, *Tableaux, pastels et dessins de Pierre-Auguste Renoir*, II, Paris, 1918, p. 24.
Étude Tajan Paris, 27 October 1995 (19**) FRF 350,000   US$ 70,796

JEUNE FILLE BLONDE oil on canvas, 18¼ x 22in. (46.5 x 55.8cm.) sll 'Renoir' (ca 1886)
PROV.: Bernheim-Jeune, Paris; Jos. Hessel, Paris (1374c); Galerie Tanner, Zurich; R. Biedermann-Mantel, Winterthur; Dr. Arthur Wilhelm, Basle; Galerie Dr. Raeber, Basle (61233).
EXH.: Schaffhausen, Museum zu Allerheiligen, *Die Welt des Impressionismus,* June-Sept. 1963, no.,105 (illustrated).
LIT.: F. Daulte*, Auguste Renoir: Catalogue Raisonné de l'Oeuvre Peint, Vol. 1, Figures, 1860-1890*, Lausanne, 1971, no.,503 (illustrated).
Christie's London, 28 November 1995 (4**) GBP 749,500   US$ 1,172,376

LE PRINTEMPS (LES QUATRE SAISONS) pastel on paper, 17¼ x 11in. (44 x 28cm.) sll 'Renoir'
PROV.: Georges Charpentier, Paris; sale, Hotel Drouot, Paris, 11 April 1907, lot 69 (illustrated); Galerie Bernheim-Jeune, Paris; Gaston Bernheim, Paris and thence by descent to the present owner.
LIT.: François Daulte will include this pastel in vol. VI (*Pastels,Aquarelles et Dessins)* of this forthcoming *Pierre-Auguste Renoir catalogue raisonné.*
Christie's London, 28 November 1995 (10**) GBP 210,500   US$ 329,266

PAYSAGE EN NORMANDIE oil on canvas, 16½ x 22in. (41.8 x 56cm.) (1895)
PROV.: A. Vollard, Paris; Arthur Tooth & Sons, London, 1945; Dr. F. Nathan, Zurich; Galerie Dr. Raeber, Basle (55,059).
LIT.: A. Vollard, *Tableaux Pastels et Dessins de Pierre Auguste Renoir*, vol. 1, Paris, 1918, no.,457 (illustrated p. 115); G. Rivière, *Rernoir et ses Amis*, Paris, 1921, (illustrated p. 95).
Christie's London, 28 November 1995 (12**) GBP 122,500   US$ 191,616

PAYSAGE DE LA ROCHE-GUYON oil on canvas, 18 x 22in, (45.7 x 55.9cm.) stamped sign.lr ; 'Renoir' (1887)
PROV.: The Artist's Studio; Prince Kojiro Matsukata, Tokyo; Wildenstein & Co., New York; Benjamin and Minna Reeves, New York (by whom acquired from the above on 9 April 1954).

EXH.: New York, Wildenstein & Co., *Renoir: an exhibition to benefit the American Association of Museums 1969* (loaned by Benjamin and Minna Reeves).
LIT.: Bernheim-Jeune (ed.), *L'Atelier de Renoir*, vol. 1, Paris, 1931, no. 14 (illustrated pl. 9).
Christie's London, 28 November 1995 (14**) GBP 331,500   US$ 518,536

NU ASSIS SUR UN DRAP BLANC-GABRIELLE oil on canvas, 8 3/4 x 7 7/8in. (22 x 20cm.) sul 'renoir' (ca 1909-10)
PROV.: Ambroise Vollard, Paris.
LIT.: A. Vollard, *Tableaux, Pastels et Dessins de Pierre-Auguste Renoir*, vol.II, Paris 1918 (illustrated p. 96).
Christie's London, 29 November 1995 (132**) GBP 28,000   US$ 43,798

PORTRAIT DE GABRIELLE black chalk and pencil on paper, 24¼ x 18 7/8in. (62 x 48cm.) slr 'Renoir'
PROV.: bought by the grandfather of the present owner in Paris, circa 1950, and thence by descent to the present owner.
Christie's London, 29 November 1995 (133**) GBP 50,000   US$ 78,211

JEUNE FEMME, VUE DE FACE, DANS UNE ROBE NOIR A COL BLANC pastel on paper laid down on board, 18½ x 15 1/8in. (47 x 38.5) sur 'Renoir' (between 1878-1879)
LIT.: To be included in the forthcoming vol. VI of the *Renoir catalogue raisonné, Renoir, Pastels, Aquarelles et dessins*, currently being prepared by François Daulte.
Christie's London, 29 November 1995 (139**) GBP 98,000   US$ 153,293

LE PONT D'ARGENTEUIL oil on canvas, 21 3/8 x 25 7/8in. (54.3 x 65.8cm.) slr 'Renoir' (1882)
PROV.: Galerie Durand-Ruel, Paris; G.F. Reber, Lausanne; Marie Harriman Gallenes, New York; Mr. and Mrs. Robert E. Eisner, New York; William Beadleston, Inc., New York; Mr. and Mrs. Daniel C. Searle, Chicago.
EXH.: Paris, Galerie Durand-Ruel, *Oeuvres importantes de Monet, Pissarro, Renoir, Sisley*, Jan., 1925, no. 25 (illustrated); San Francisco, California Palace of the Legion of Honor, *French Paintings from the Fifteenth Century to the Present Day*, June-July, 1934 no. 144; New York, Wildenstein & Co., Inc., *From Paris to the Sea down the River Seine*, Jan.-Feb., 1943, no. 31 (illustrated); New York, Wildenstein & Co., Inc., *Renoir, For the Benefit of the Citizens Committee for the Children of New York City*, April-May, 1958, no. 51 (illustrated); Maastricht, Noortman and Brod, *Impressionists*-An; Exhibition of French Impressionist Paintings, April-May, 1983, no. 28 (illustrated). The exhibition traveled to London, Noortman, June-July, 1983; Los Angeles, County Museum of Art, *A Day in the Country, Impressionism and the French Landscape*, June-Sept., 1984, p. 153, no. 45 (illustrated in color). The exhibition traveled to Chicago, The Art Institute, Oct., 1984-Jan., 1985, and Paris, Galeries Nationale d'Exposition du Grand Palais, Feb.-April, 1985.
LIT.: A. Vollard, *La vie et l'oeuvre de Pierre-Auguste Renoir*, Paris, 1919, p. 80 (illustrated); A. Vollard, *Auguste Renoir*, Paris, 1920, p. 64 (illustrated); J. Meier-Graefe, *Renoir*, Leipzig, 1929, p. 205, no. 199; (illustrated and incorrectly dated 1888) M. Drucker, *Renoir*, Paris, 1944 (illustrated, pl. 95 and incorrectly dated 1888).
Christie's New York, 30 April 1996 (4**) US$ 1,982,500   US$ 1,982,500

FEMME ASSISE pastel on paper, 25 5/8 x 19½in. (65.2 x 49.5cm.) slr 'Renoir' (1879)
PROV.: Galerie Barbanzanges, Paris; Percy-Moore Turner, London; Mrs. Jacques Balsan; Mr. and Mrs. George N.Richard, New York.
EXH.: New York, Wildenstein & Co., Inc., *A Loan Exhibition for the benefit of the American Association of Museums in Commemoration of the Fiftieth Anniversary of Renoir's Death*, March-May, 1969, no.33 (ill.); New York, Metropolitan Museum of Art, June, 1981-March, 1987 (on loan).
Christie's New York, 30 April 1996 (6**) US$ 420,500   US$ 420,500

DEUX BAIGNEUSES oil on canvas, 13 x 16 1/8in. (33 x 41cm.) sll 'Renoir' (1896)
PROV.: Henry Bernstein, Paris: sale, Hôtel Drouot, Paris, June 10, 1911, lot 22; Etienne Druet, Paris;

Galerie Georges Petit, Paris; Charles Pacquement, Paris: sale, Galerie Georges Petit, Paris, Dec.12, 1932, lot 51; Alfred Savoir, Paris.
EXH.: Venice, 'Mostra Retrospettiva di A.R.', *XXI Esposizione Biennale Internationale d'Arte*, summer, 1938, p.245, no.12; Geneva, Musée de l'Athenée, *De l'Impressionnisme à l'Ecole de Paris*, 1960, no.74 (ill.); Lausanne, Palais de Beaulieu, *Chefs-d'oeuvre des collections Suisses de Manet à Picasso*, May-Oct., 1967, no.66 (ill.); Paris, Musée de l'Orangerie, *Chefs-d'oeuvre des collections Suisses de Manet à Picasso*, May-Oct., 1967, no.67 (ill.).
LIT.: J.Mauny, 'The Charles Pacquement Collection', *The Arts*, New York, Jan., 1928, p.9 (ill.); P.du Colombier, 'Le centenaire de Renoir', *Beaux Arts*, Paris, 1941, p.6, no.7 (ill.).
Christie's New York, 30 April 1996 (30**) US$ 1,432,500   US$ 1,432,500

LEONTINE LISANT oil on canvas, 21¼ x 25½in. (54 x 65cm.) slr 'Renoir' (1909)
PROV.: Galerie Bernheim-Jeune, Paris; Galerie Durand-Ruel, Paris (Dec. 26, 1919); Durand-Ruel Galleries, New York 3 July 1920); H.D. Hughes, New York 23 July 1920); Durand-Ruel Galleries, New York (30 Dec. 1926).2,532,500.
EXH.: New York, Durand-Ruel Galleries, *Exhibition of Paintings by Modern French Masters*, April, 1920, no. 9; New York, Durand-Ruel Galleries, *Loan Exhibition of Portraits by Renoir*, March-April, 1939, no. 19; Los Angeles, County Museum of Art, *The Development of Impressionism*, Jan.-Feb., 1940, no. 63 (illustrated); New York, Duveen Gallery, *Renoir*, Nov.-Dec., 1941, p. 106, no. 84 (illustrated).
LIT.: Durand-Ruel, *Selection of Paintings from the Durand-Ruel Galleries*, New York, 1948, no. 3 (illustrated); P. Fosca, *Renoir*, Paris, 1961, p.,155 (illustrated); François Daulte will include this painting in the forthcoming volume III (*Figures, 1906-1919*) of his *Renoir catalogue raisonné*.
Christie's New York, 30 April 1996 (39**) US$ 2,532,500   US$ 2,532,500

PORTAIT DE NINI LOPEZ (PROFIL BLOND) oil on canvas, 10¼ x 8 5/8in. (26 x 22cm.) str 'Renoir' (1876)
PROV.: Paul Berard, Paris; sale, Galerie Georges Petit, Paris, May 8, 1905, lot 25 (illustrated); Galerie Durand-Ruel, Paris (acquired at the above sale); G. Camentron, Paris (acquired from the above on June 2, 1905); Galerie Schmit, Paris.
EXH.: Paris, Galerie Schmit, *Pour mon plaisir XIXe-XXe siècles*, May-July, 1982, no. 81 (illustrated in color).
LIT.: M. Berard, *Renoir à Wargemont*, Paris, 1938, n.p. (illustrated); F. Daulte, *Auguste Renoir, Catalogue raisonné de l'oeuvre peint*, Lausanne, 1971, vol. I (*figures, 1860-1890*), no.,222 (illustrated); E. Fezzi and J. Henrv, Tout l'oeuvre peint de Renoir, periode impressionniste, 1869-1883, Paris, 1985, p. 100, no.,256 (illustrated).
Christie's New York, 7 November 1995 (12**) US$ 992,500   US$ 992,500

FEMME NUE DE DOS pastel on paper laid down on japan paper, 23 5/8 x 18 1/8in. (60 x 46.1cm.) str 'Renoir' (ca 1879)
PROV.: Emile Bergerat, Paris; Galerie Durand-Ruel, Paris (acquired from the above on Feb. 12, 1901); Adrien Hebrard, Paris (acquired from the above on Feb. 3, 1906); Prince de Wagram, Paris; Galerie Durand-Ruel, Paris (acquired from the above on May 15, 1908); P. Estevez, Paris (acquired from the above on May 24, 1913); Victor Helin, Chateauroux; Galerie Schmit, Paris.
EXH.: Tokyo, Isetan Museum of Art, *Renoir*, Sept.-Nov., 1979, no. 87 (illustrated in colour). The exhibition traveled to Kyoto, Municipal Museum, Nov.-Dec., 1979; Paris, Galerie Schmit, *25 Ans d'Exposition, maîtres Français XlXe-XXe siècles*, May-July, 1990, no. 56 (illustrated).
LIT.: François Daulte will include this pastel in the forthcoming *vol. VI (pastels, aquarelles et dessins) of his Renoir catalogue raisonné*.
Christie's New York, 7 November 1995 (19**) US$ 607,500   US$ 607,500

NATURE MORTE AUX POMMES oil on canvas, 8 x 16 1/8in. (20.3 x 41cm.) sul 'Renoir'
PROV.: Galerie Bernheim-Jeune, Paris (acquired by the familie of the present owner).
Christie's New York, 8 November 1995 (110**) US$ 123,500   US$ 123,500

JEUNE FILE AVEC UN BOUQUET pen brown ink on paper laid down on paper, 7 1/8 x 4½in. (18 x 11.5cm.) slr 'Renoir' (1879)
PROV.: Edmond Renoir, Paris; John Rewald, New York; sale, Sotheby & Co., London, July 7, 1960, lot 100; Frank Perls Gallery, Beverly Hills; Mr. and Mrs. Billy Wilder, Los Angeles; sale, Christie's, New York, Nov. 13, 1989, lot 1.
EXH.: Los Angeles, Municipal Art Gallery, *The collection of Mr. and Mrs. John Rewald*, March-April, 1959, no. 113; Santa Barbara, University of California, The Art Gallery, *Selections from the Collection of Mr. and Mrs. Billy Wilder*, Oct.-Nov., 1966, no. 49.
LIT.: J. Rewald, *Renoir Drawings*, New York, 1946, p. 15 (illustrated, p. 7); P. Viladas, 'A Life in Pictures,' *House & Garden*, April, 1989, pp.,155 and,158 (illustrated in colour).

Christie's New York, 8 November 1995 (118**) US$ 36,800	US$	36,800

BAIGNEUSE (NU AU LINGE) oil on canvas, 13 x 8¼in. (33 x 21cm.) stamped with signature bl 'Renoir' (Lugt 2137b) (1892)

Christie's New York, 8 November 1995 (120**) US$ 195,000	US$	195,000

NATURE MORTE AUX FRUITS oil on canvas, 7 7/8 x 11in. (20 x 28cm.) stamped with signature lr 'Renoir'. (Lugt 2137b)
PROV.: Claude Renoir, Paris.
LIT.: F. Dois and M. Ramonato, *Renoir à Essoyes*, 1992, p. 9 (illustrated in colour).

Christie's New York, 8 November 1995 (124**) US$ 134,500	US$	134,500

RESNICK Milton (1932 b.) American
UNTITLED oil on canvas, 52½ x 152in. (133.4 x 386.1cm.) sdll 'RESNICK', s again and d 'RESNICK 1960' on the reverse
PROV.: Acquired directly from the artist.

Christie's New York, 22 February 1996 (34**) US$ 46,000	US$	46,000

STORAGE oil on canvas, 78 x 72in. (198.1 x 182.9cm.) sdlr 'RESNICK '58', titled 'STORAGE' on the overlap, sd and titled again 'STORAGE' RESNICK 1958' on the stretcher
PROV.: Acquired directly from the artist.

Christie's New York, 8 May 1996 (247**) US$ 16,100	US$	16,100

RESTOUT Jean the Younger (Rouen 1692-1768 Paris) French
HECTOR TAKING LEAVE OF ANDROMACHE oil on canvas, 50½ x 76¼in. (128.3 x 193.7cm.) sdlr 'JRestout 1728'
PROV.: Charles-Alexandre de Calonne (1734-1802), [His Sale: Paris, 21-30 April 1788, lot 153, purchased back by Lebrun for,600 livres (with Restout's Continence oy Scipio lot 154)]; Calonne's second sale, London, 23 March 1795, lot 43 [with Restout's Continence de Scipio, lot 44]; Baroness Reitzes, Palais Reitzes, Vienna, from whom purchased by the present owner.
EXH.: Paris, Galéries Nationales du Grand Palais; Philadelphia Museum of Art; Fort Worth, Kimbell Art Museum, *The Loves of the Gods: Mythological Painting from Watteau to David*, October 15, 1991-August 2, 1992, pp. 318-325, cat. no. 34, pp. 318-325, illus. in color p.,319 (catalogue entry by Colin B. Bailey).
LIT.: L. Poinsinet de Sivry et al., *Le Nécrologe des hommes célebres de France* 17 vols. Paris 1767-82; B. Gaston,'Notes et documents. 'L'exposition des chefs-d'oeuvre des musées de province: Ecole Française, XVIIe et XVIIIe siècles', *Bulletin de la Société de l'Histoire de l'Art Français, 1931, pp. 189-217; P. Rosenberg and A. Schnapper,* Jean Restout (1692-1768), Musée des Beaux Arts, Rouen, exhibition catalogue, 1970, p. 209; P. Rosenberg, 'Le Concours de peinture de 1727,' *Revue de l'Art*, vol. 37 (1977), pp. 29-42; P. Rosenberg and A. Schnapper, 'Paintings by Restout on Mythological and Historical Themes: Acquisition by the National Gallery of Canada of Venus Presenting Arms to Aeneas,' *National Gallery of Canada Annual Bulletin*, 6, 1982-83, pp. 42-54.

Sotheby's New York, 11 January 1996 (152**) US$ 222,500	US$	222,500

REYNOLDS Sir Joshua, P.R.A. (Plympton (Devonshire) 1723-1792 London) British
PORTRAIT OF MRS. RICHARD PENNANT, NÉE ANNE SUSANNA WARBURTON, HALF

LENTH, IN A WHITE DRESS WITH A PINK SHAWL LINED WITH FUR oil on canvas, 29¼ x 24¼in. (74 x 65.1cm.)
LIT.: A. Graves and W. Cronin, *A history of the works of Sir Joshua Reynolds*, IV, London, 1901, p. 1384.

Christie's London, 10 November 1995 (22**) GBP 16,100	US$	25,184

PORTRAIT OF LADY ANNE BUTLER, LATER LADY ORMONDE AND HER CHILD oil on canvas, 30¼ x 25¼in. (76.8 x 64.1cm.)
PROV.: Duke of Westminster, London, by 1871; Sir William Agnew, London, by 1891; with A.B. Soully, London, 1934.
EXH.: London, Royal Academy of Arts, *Exhibition of Works by the Old Masters*, 1871, p. 6, no. 41 (lent by the Duke of Westminster); London, Grosvenor Gallery, *Exhibition of the Works of Sir Joshua Reynolds*, December 31, 1883-March 29, 1884, no. 48 (lent by the Duke of Westminster); London, Royal Academy of Arts, *Exhibition of Works by the Old Masters*, 1891, p. 12, no. 37 (lent by Agnew); London, Thos. Agnew & Sons, 1895.
LIT.: A. Graves and W.V. Cronin, *A History of the Works of Sir Joshua Reynolds, P.R.A.*, 1899, Vol. I, p. 138.

Sotheby's New York, 11 January 1996 (213**) US$ 37,375	US$	37,375

PORTRAIT OF SIR GERARD NAPIER, 6TH BT. (1739-1765), THREE-QUARTER-LENGHT, IN THE UNIFORM OF THE DORSETSHIRE MILITIA, IN A LANDSCAPE oil on canvas, 50 x 40in. (,127 x 101.6cm.) (1762)
PROV.: The sitter's widow and by descent to Gerard Phelips, Montacute House, Somerset: Christie's 29 November 1929, lot 46 (620gns. to A. de Cassares).
EXH.: On loan to Aberdeen Art Gallery, 1948-1996.
LIT.: A. Graves and V.W. Cronin, A *History of the Works of Sir Joshua Reynolds, P.R.A.*, London 1899, II p. 687; E.K. Waterhouse, *Reynolds*, London, 1941, pp. 51 adn 94.

Christie's London, 18 April 1996 (15**) GBP 65,300	US$	99,014

RHO Manlio (Como 1901-1957 Como) Italian
COMPOSIZIONE oil on canvas, 34 x 23.5cm. slr 'M. RHO' (1930)

Finearte Milan, 19 March 1996 (81**) ITL 23,000,000	US$	14,715

RIBARZ Rudolf (Vienna 1848-1904 Vienna) Austrian
AUFZIEHENDES GEWITTER, MOTIV AUS HOLLAND oil on panel, 26.6 x 35cm. slr 'Ribarz' titled and inscr. on the reverse

Wiener Kunst Auktionen, 26 September 1995 (131**) ATS 140,000	US$	13,608

KIRCHTURM IN DER CHAMPAGNE oil on panel, 55.3 x 45.3cm. slr 'Ribarz'; titled on a label on the reverse
EXH.: Berlin, *Große Berliner Kunstaustellung*, 1894, no. 2053.

Wiener Kunst Auktionen, 26 September 1995 (139**) ATS 550,000	US$	53,462

RIBERA Jusepe de (José), {called} Lo Spagnoletto (Jàtiva (Valencia) 1591-1652 Naples) Spanish
SAINT JUDE THADDEUS oil on canvas, 25½ x 19in. (65 x 49.5cm.) (1616)
PROV.: By descent in the Imperiali-Francavilla family, Naples and later Rome.
EXH.: Naples, Castel Sant'Elmo, *Ribera*, 1992, no. 1.7b.
LIT.: N. Spinoza, *Jusepe de Ribera*, catalogue of the Naples exhibition, 1992, pp. 124-5, no. 1.7a (illustrated in colour); A.E. Pérez Sanchez, N. Spinoza, *Jusepe de Ribera*, exhibition catalogue, New York, 1992, p. 66, under no. 7, p. 259.

Sotheby's London, 5 July 1995 (72**) GBP 56,500	US$	90,126

SAINT PHILIP oil on canvas, 25½ x 19½in. (65 x 49.4cm.) (1616)
PROV.: By descent in the Imperiali-Francavilla family, Naples and later Rome.
EXH.: Naples, Castel Sant'Elmo, *Ribera*, 1992, no. 1.7a.

LIT.: N. Spinoza, *Jusepe de Ribera*, catalogue of the Naples exhibition, 1992, pp. 125, no. 1.7a (illustrated in colour); A.E. Pérez Sanchez, N. Spinoza, *Jusepe de Ribera*, exhibition catalogue, New York, 1992, p. 66, under no. 7, p. 259.

Sotheby's London, 5 July 1995 (73**) GBP 43,300   US$ 69,070

RIBERA Jusepe de (José), {called} Lo Spagnoletto (and studio) (Jàtiva (Valencia) 1591-1652 Naples) Spanish
SAINT ATHONY ABBOT oil on canvas, 30½ x 25½in. (77.5 x 64.8cm.)

Sotheby's New York, 16 May 1996 (53**) US$ 28,750   US$ 28,750

RICCHI Pietro (attr.) (Lucca 1605-1675 Udine) Italian
DIANA AND HER HANDMAIDENS SHOOTING BOWS AND ARROWS AT WINGED AMORES IN A LANDSCAPE oil on canvas, 51 x 74in. (129.5 x 188cm.)

Sotheby's New York, 16 May 1996 (176**) US$ 123,500   US$ 123,500

RICCI Arturo (Florence 1854-1919) Italian
THE ARTIST'S STUDIO oil on canvas, 41¼ x 31in. (104.8 x 78.8cm.) slr inscr. 'Arturo Ricci/Firenze'

Christie's New York, 2 November 1995 (141**) US$ 25,300   US$ 25,300

THE ART CLASS oil on canvas, 27 x 36in. (68.6 x 91.5cm.) sll 'Arturo. Ricci'

Christie's New York, 2 November 1995 (153**) US$ 25,300   US$ 25,300

RICCI Marco (Belluno 1676-1730 Venice) Italian
CONCERTINO oil on canvas, 49.5 x 63cm.
LIT.: A. Scarpa Sonino, *Marco Ricci*, ed. Berenice, Milan, 1991, no. 56, p.,127 (illustrated no. 72).

Finearte Milan, 3 April 1996 (85**) ITL 34,500,000   US$ 22,045

MOUNTANEOUS LANDSCAPE WITH PEOPLE / RURAL HOUSE WITH ANTIQUE ELEMENTS AND A LARGE CHURCH IN THE BACKGROUND tempera on paper (a pair), each: 30 x 45cm.
PROV.: Collection Canessa, Rome, until 1963.
EXH.: Venice, Bassano del Grappa, *Marco Ricci*, 1963, nos. 87-88.
LIT.: G. M. Pilo in the Venetian catalogue, *Marco Ricci*, 1963, nos. 87-88, pp. 112-114; A. Scarpa Sonino, *Marco Ricci*, Milan 1991, nos. T65-T66, p. 253, fig. 182-,148 (considered to have been executed on parchment).

Christie's Rome, 4 June 1996 (574**) ITL 45,000,000   US$ 29,183

LANDSCAPE WITH PEOPLE GETTING WATER FROM A CLASSICAL FOUNTAIN, RUINS AND A VILLAGE BEYOND oil on canvas, 59 x 96cm.

Christie's Rome, 4 June 1996 (585**) ITL 28,000,000   US$ 18,158

RICCI Sebastiano (Cividal di Belluno 1659-1734 Venice) Italian
PAN oil on canvas, 39¼ x 34¼in. (,100 x 88cm.) (ca. 1725)

Sotheby's London, 5 July 1995 (75**) GBP 32,200   US$ 51,364

SAINT HELENA DISCOVERING THE CROSS oil on canvas, 39¼ x 19½in. (99.7 x 49.5cm.)
PROV.: Possibly Cavalieri L. and B. Spiridon, Rome.
EXH.: Possibly Florence, Palazzo Pitti, *Mostra della Pittura Italiana del seicento e del settecento*, 1922, cat. no.,837 (no dimensions are given in the catalogue, and in the second, extensively revised edition, the work is only attributed to Ricci).
LIT.: Possibly Thieme/Becker, 'Sebastiano Ricci,' *Kunstler-Lexikon*, 1934, p. 254. Possibly Jeffery Daniels, *Sebastiano Ricci*, p. 153, under catalogue 529b.

Sotheby's New York, 11 January 1996 (244**) US$ 36,800   US$ 36,800

RICCIARDELLI Gabriele (1740s to 1780s, active from the-) Italian
A PEASANT FAMILY AND THEIR FLOCK RESTING BESIDE A SPHINX AND CLASSICAL
COLLUMNS ON THE BANKS OF A RIVER, A CAPRICCIO WITH THE TOMB OF CEACILIA
METELLA BEYOND oil on canvas, laid down on masonite, 38 3/4 x 52¼in. (98.4 x 132.7cm.) sd
'GABRIELLE RICCIARDELLI/P/MDCCLVII' (1757)
PROV.: Sale: Christie's London, 28 March 1969, lot 17.

Sotheby's New York, 16 May 1996 (213**) US$ 28,750	US$	28,750

RICHET Léon (Solesmes (Sarthe) 1847-1907 Fontainebleau (Seine-et-Marne)) French
PAYSAGE oil on canvas, 32 x 39½in. (81.3 x 100.3cm.) slr 'Léon Richet'

Christie's New York, 22 May 1996 (148**) US$ 12,650	US$	12,650

RICHTER Edouard Frederic Wilhelm (1844-1913) French
IN THE HAREM oil on canvas, 45 3/ x 29in. (116.3 x 73.6cm.) sd 'E Richter - Paris. 1883'

Christie's London, 15 March 1996 (125**) GBP 20,700	US$	31,613

RICHTER Gerhard (Gerd) (Waltersdorf (Oberlausitz) 1932 b.-l) German
UNTITLED oil on panel, 40 x 60cm. sd and titled on the reverse (1980)

Hauswedell & Nolte Cologne, 2 December 1995 (233**) DEM 59,000	US$	40,935

UNTITLED watercolour and graphite on paper, 12½ x 9 3/4in. (31.8 x 23.8cm.) sdlr 'Richter
11.10.90'
PROV.: Galerie Daniel Fusban, Munich.

Christie's New York, 15 November 1995 (259***) US$ 31,050	US$	31,050

UNTITLED oil on canvas, 39½ x 38 3/4in. (100.3 x 98.4cm.) sd numbered ',255 Richter 70' on the
reverse (1970)
PROV.: H. Quaedflieg, Germany.
LIT.: J. Harten, *Gerhard Richter Paintings*, Cologne 1986, p. 115, no. 255/1 (illustrated); B.
Buchloh, P. Gidal and B. Pelzer, *Gerhard Richter Catalogue Raisonné, 1962-1993*, Ostfildern-Ruit
1993, no. 255-1 (illustrated).

Christie's New York, 15 November 1995 (262**) US$ 68,500	US$	68,500

ÄPFELS (sic) oil on canvas, 16½ x 23in. (42 x 60cm.) sd 'Richter 1984'
PROV.: Galerie Fred Jahn, Munich.
EXH.: Munich, Galerie Fred Jahn, *Gerhard Richter: 9 Paintings 1982-1987*, Jan. 1988 (illustrated on
the cover of the announcement card).
LIT.: J. Harten, *Gerhard Richter Paintings*, Cologne 1986, p. 310, no. 560/2 (illustrated); B.
Buchloh, P. Gidal and B. Pelzer, *Gerhard Richter Catalogue Raisonné, 1962-1993*, Ostfildern-Ruit
1993, no. 560/2 (illustrated).

Christie's New York, 7 May 1996 (36**) US$ 354,500	US$	354,500

ABSTRAKTES BILD oil on canvas, 19 3/4 x 27 ½in. (50 x 70cm.) sd 'Gerhardt Richter 1981'
numbered '475-2' on the reverse
PROV.: Acquired directly from the artist by the present owner in 1982.
EXH.: Bielefeld, Kunsthalle Bielefeld; Mannheim, Mannheimer Kunstverein, *Gerhard Richter:
Abstrakte Bilder 1976 bis 1981*, January-May 1982.
LIT.: Jurgen Harten, *Gerhard Richter: Bilder / Paintings 1962-1985*, Cologne 1986, p. 247, no. 475-
2 (illustrated); *Gerhard Richter, Werkubersicht / Catalogue Raisonné: 1962-1993*, Ostfildern-Ruit
1993, no. 475-2 (illustrated in colour).

Christie's London, 19 March 1996 (71**) GBP 43,300	US$	66,127

UNTITLED watercolour on paper, 9½ x 13 3/8in. (24 x 34cm.) sdll 'Richter 13.okt.90'
PROV.: Galerie Fred Jahn, Munich.

Sotheby's London, 21 March 1996 (70**) GBP 9,775	US$	14,928

LANDSCHAFT 2 acrylic, watercolour and pastel on paper, 12 5/8 x 9¼in. (32 x 23.6cm.) sd 'Richter 19.2.84'
      Christie's London, 23 May 1996 (157**) GBP 23,000   US$ 34,827

BLECH oil on canvas, 20 x 26.8cm. sd and numbered 'Richter 88, 681/1-30' on the reverse
LIT.: Daniel Buchholz, Gregorio Magnani (ed.), *International Index of Multiples*, Spiral/Wacoal Center, Tokyo, Cologne 1993, p. 162; *Richter, Graphiken and Multiples*, 1994, p. 142, no. 55 (illustrated).
      Wiener Kunst Auktionen, 26 March 1996 (317**) ATS 100,000   US$ 9,619

HECKE oil on canvas, 78 3/4 x 67in. (,200 x 170cm.) sd 1982 and numbered,504 on the reverse
PROV.: Galerie Thomas Borgmann, Cologne.
LIT.: Jürgen Harten, *Gerhard Richter: Bilder/Paintings 1962-1985*, Cologne 1986, p. 266, no.,504 (work in progress illustrated); *Gerhard Richter: Werkübersicht/Catalogue Raisonné 1962-1993*, Ostfildern-Ruit 1993, no.,504 (illustrated in colour).
      Christie's London, 27 June 1996 (72**) GBP 161,000   US$ 248,265

ABSTRAKTES BILD oil on canvas, 16 1/8 x 20in. (41 x 51cm.) sd '1991' on the reverse
PROV.: Marian Goodman Gallery, New York.
LIT.: *Gerhard Richter Catalogue Raisonné: 1962-1993*, Ostfildern-Ruit 1993, p. 192, no. 752-1, illustrated.
      Sotheby's London, 27 June 1996 (263**) GBP 12,075   US$ 18,620

REGENBOGEN oil on canvas, 19 3/4 x 21 3/4in. (50.2 x 55.2cm.) sd and numbered '261/33 Richter 1970' on the reverse
PROV.: Galerie Schmela, Düsseldorf.
LIT.: K. Honnef, *Gerhard Richter*, Recklinghausen 1976, no. 31 (illustrated); J. Harten, *Gerhard Richter Paintings*, Cologne 1986, p.,116 no. 261/3 (illustrated); B,. Buchloh, P. Gidal and B. Pelzer, *Gerhard Richter Catalogue Raisonné, 1962-1993*, Ostfildern-Ruit 1993, no. 261/3 (illustrated).
      Christie's New York, 14 November 1995 (48**) US$ 145,500   US$ 145,500

RICHTER Giovanni (Johan Anton) (Stockholm 1665-1745 Venice) Swedish
THE BACINO DI SAN MARCO, VENICE oil on canvas, 44½ x 63 5/8in. (,113 x 161.6cm.) (after 1717)
EXH.: Padua, Palazzo della Ragione, *Luca Carlevarijs e la veduta veneziana del settecento*, 25 September-26 December 1994, no. 70 (catalogue entry by Dario Succi).
      Sotheby's New York, 16 May 1996 (73**) US$ 167,500   US$ 167,500

RICO Y ORTEGA Martin (Madrid 1833-1908 Venice) Spanish
THE LAGUNA, VENICE oil on canvas, 16 3/4 x 28 3/4in. (42.5 x 73cm.) slc 'RICO'
      Christie's New York, 14 February 1996 (137**) US$ 27,600   US$ 27,600

RIDOLFO Michele di, del Ghirlandaio (attr.) (1503-1577) Italian
THE VIRGIN AND CHILD AND ST. JOHN oil on panel, 66 x 51cm.
      Christie's Rome, 21 November 1995 (187**) ITL 30,000,000   US$ 18,832

RIEGEN Nicolaas (Amsterdam 1827-1889 Amsterdam) Dutch
A DUTCH *SCHOENER* AND OTHER SHIPPING IN A STIFF BREEZE oil on canvas,116 x 180cm.) sd 'N. Riegen.1861 Amsterdam'
      Christie's Amsterdam, 25 April 1996 (149*) NLG 19,550   US$ 11,617

A FISHINGBOAT AND OTHER BOATING IN A RIVER ESTUARY oil on canvas, 44 x 68cm. sll 'N. Riegen'
      Christie's Amsterdam, 26 October 1995 (189*) NLG 16,100   US$ 10,151

RIEPP Johann Balthasar (Kempten 1703-1764 Vils, Tirol) Austrian
HERACLID, THE WEEPING PHILOSOPHER oil on canvas, 100.5 x 81cm.
      Dorotheum Vienna, 11 June 1996 (71**) ATS 80,000   US$ 7,426

RIETSCHOOF Jan Claes (Hoorn 1652-1719) Dutch
A DUTCH FLAGSHIP AND OTHER SHIPPING IN CHOPPY SEAS oil on canvas, 40 x 51¼in.
(,102 x 130.5cm.)
PROV.: Acquired by the family of the present owner in the early 19th Century.
      Sotheby's London, 5 July 1995 (181**) GBP 12,650   US$ 20,179

A *WIJDSCHIP* GOING ABOUT ITS APPROACHES A DUTCH THREE-MASTER, OTHER
SHIPPING BEYOND oil on, 76.4 x 103.9cm. sll with monogram 'WvW'
PROV.: Anon. Sale, Christie`s London, 13 March 1987, lot 57, as *follower of Aernout Smit*, with ill.
(sold GBP2600); Anon. Sale, in these rooms, 7 May 1992, lot 148, where acquired by the present
owner.
      Christie's Amsterdam, 13 November 1995 (222) NLG 27,600   US$ 17,395

DUTCH SHIPPING IN CHOPPY SEAS oil on canvas, 61 x 83.6cm.
      Sotheby's Amsterdam, 14 November 1995 (41**) NLG 23,600   US$ 14,874

RIGOLOT Albert Gabriel (Paris 1862-1932 Paris) French
AUTUMNAL RIVER LANDSCAPE oil on canvas, 31 3/4 x 45½in. (80.6 x 115.5cm.) sll 'A.
Rigolot'
      Christie's New York, 22 May 1996 (185**) US$ 14,950   US$ 14,950

LE BORD DE LA RIVIERE oil on canvas, 38¼ x 63½in. (97.2 x 161.3cm.) sll 'ARigolot'
      Christie's New York, 2 November 1995 (125**) US$ 13,800   US$ 13,800

RING Hermann tom (Münster 1521-) German
PORTRAIT OF A WOMAN, AGED 28, SMALL HALF-LENGTH, WEARING A BLACK DRESS,
LACE COLLAR WITH CAP oil on panel, 30.7 x 25.5cm. inscr. and d al and r
'ANoDNI.1565./AE(linked)TATIS.SVE.28'
      Christie's Amsterdam, 13 November 1995 (125**) NLG 34,500   US$ 21,743

RINGEL Franz (Graz 1940 b.) Austrian
DIE AUSSENWELT DER FERNSEHSPRECHERIN mixed media on paper laid down on board,150
x 130cm. sdur 'Ringel 69'; sd and titled 'Ringel 1969' on the reverse
      Wiener Kunst Auktionen, 26 March 1996 (412**) ATS 220,000   US$ 21,162

DER TÄTER mixed media 8 carboard parts laid down on canvas,195 x 130cm. sdar 2x 'F Ringel 67'
and 'Ringel 67' titled and s twice on the reverse
LIT.: *Ausstellungskatalog*, Museum des 20. Jahrhunderts; Vienna, 27 August-6 October 1974, ill.
p.9; *M.J.M. Ringel, Monographie*, Verlag Falter-Deuticke, Vienna 1991, ill. no. 6.
      Wiener Kunst Auktionen, 27 September 1995 (541**) ATS 400,000   US$ 38,881

SPANIER oil on canvas,200 x 170cm. sdll 'M.J.M. Ringel 81'
      Wiener Kunst Auktionen, 27 September 1995 (557**) ATS 220,000   US$ 21,385

RINK Paul (Paulus Philippus) (Veghel 1861-1903 Edam) Dutch
IRIS oil on canvas,152 x,108 cm sd 'Paul Rink, 1892' and s and inscr again with title on the reverse
EXH.: The Hague, *Pictura*, 1904, cat. no. 53 (?).
      Christie's Amsterdam, 25 April 1996 (46**) NLG 41,400   US$ 24,600

RIOPELLE Jean Paul (Montreal 1923 b.) Canadian
AU LARGE oil on canvas, 19 5/8 x 25½in. (50 x 65cm.) sd 'Riopelle 57' and s titled on the reverse
LIT.: This work is registered under no. 1957. 76H and will be included in the forthcoming *Jean*

Riopelle Catalogue Raisonné being prepared by Iseult Riopelle, the Artist's daughter.

Christie's London, 19 March 1996 (41**) GBP 20,700	US$	31,613

UNTITLED oil on canvas, 35 x 45 5/8in. (89 x 116cm.) sd '58'
PROV.: Françoise Riopelle, Canada; Dr John Hackey, Senneville. Ken Son, Toronto; Acquired from
the above by the present owner in 1960.
LIT.: This work is registered under no. 1958.102H and will be included in the forthcoming *Jean-Paul Riopelle Catalogue Raisonné* being prepared by Yseult Riopelle, the Artist's daughter.

Christie's London, 23 May 1996 (30**) GBP 52,100	US$	78,892

PEINTURE BLANCHE, ROUGE ET NOIRE oil on canvas, 38 1/8 x 51 1/ (97 x 130cm.) s 'Riopelle'
(1965)
PROV.: Gimpel Fils, London.
LIT.: This work is registered under no. 1962.040H and will be included in the forthcoming *Jean-Paul Riopelle Catalogue Raisonné* being prepared by Yseult Riopelle, the Artist's daughter.

Christie's London, 23 May 1996 (47**) GBP 32,200	US$	48,758

UNTITLED oil on canvas, 31 7/8 x 39¼in. (81 x 100cm.) s 'Jean Riopelle' (ca 1958)
PROV.: Jacques Dubourg, Paris; M.V. Archibald, Chantilly.
LIT.: To be included in the forthcoming *Jean Paul Riopelle Catalogue Raisonné* being prepared by
Yseult Riopelle, the artist's daughter.

Christie's London, 26 October 1995 (29**) GBP 28,750	US$	45,376

FLECHES oil on canvas, 21¼ x 25 5/8in. (54 x 65cm.) sdlr 1950, sd and titled 1950 on the stretcher
PROV.: Georges Duthuit, Paris.
EXH.: Hanover, Kestner Gesellschaft, *Jean-Paul Riopelle*, September-October 1958, no. 7.

Christie's London, 27 June 1996 (9**) GBP 91,700	US$	141,403

D'UNE CHASSE oil on canvas, 39½ x 25½in. (,100 x 65cm.) slr (1973)
PROV.: Pierre Matisse Gallery, New York.

Christie's London, 27 June 1996 (50**) GBP 34,500	US$	53,200

UNTITLED oil on canvas, 15 x 21 7/8in. (38 x 55.5cm.) sd '60'

Sotheby's London, 27 June 1996 (170**) GBP 14,375	US$	22,167

VILLANELLE oil on canvas, 54 x 64.7cm sdlr 'riopelle 57' (1957)

Lempertz Cologne, 28 November 1995 (879**) DEM 70,000	US$	49,407

RIPPL-RONAI József (Kapsovar 1861-1927/30 Kapsovar) Hungarian
FEMMES A RIGA oil on canvas, 23¼ x 28½in. (59.1 x 72.4cm.) sdlr 'Ronaî 1904'
LIT.: This work will be included in the forthcoming *catalogue raisonné* by Maria Csernitzky and the
Hungarian National Gallery, Budapest.

Sotheby's New York, 2 May 1996 (157**) US$ 35,650	US$	35,650

RITSEMA Coba (Jacoba Johanna) (Haarlem 1876-1961 Amsterdam) Dutch
A STILL LIFE WITH FRUIT ON A DISH oil on canvas, 54.5 x 64 cm s 'Coba R' s on the reverse

Christie's Amsterdam, 25 April 1996 (32*) NLG 8,625	US$	5,125

RIVERS Larry (New York 1923 b.-) American
THE QUEEN OF SPADES oil on canvas, 32 x 24in. (81 x 61cm.) sd and titled "The Queen of
Spades' I 1964 Rivers' on the reverse
PROV.: Acquired directly from the artist; Private collection, Houston.
EXH.: London, Edward Totah Gallery, *Larry Rivers: Paintings and Drawings*, March-April 1983,
no.5 (illustrated); Modern Museum Art of Fort Worth, *100th Anniversary Exhibition: Masterworks
from Fort Worth Collections*, April-June 1992, p.56, no.30 (illustrated).

Christie's New York, 22 February 1996 (74**) US$ 74,000	US$	74,000

DRUGSTORE oil on canvas, 84 x 65½in. (213.4 x 166.4cm.) sd titled 'DRUG STORE Rivers 59' on the reverse (1959)
PROV.: Marlborough-Gerson Gallery, New York; Barry Benedak, Baltimore; James Corcoran Gallery, Santa Monica.
EXH.: Waltham, Brandeis University, Rose Art Museum; The Pasadena Art Museum; New York, The Jewish Museum; Detroit Institute of Arts, and The Minneapolis Institute of Arts, *Larry Rivers*, April 1965-Feb. 1966, p. 68, no. 32 (illustrated).
LIT.: S. Hunter, *Larry Rivers*, Barcelona 1989, p. 69, no. 12 (illustrated).

Christie's New York, 14 November 1995 (8**) US$ 112,500	US$	112,500

LAST CIVIL WAR VETERAN oil pn panel, 13¼ x 10in. (33.7 x 25.4cm.) sd and titled "LAST CIVAL WAR VETERAN' Rivers 1959-60' on the reverse
PROV.: Gimpel Fils Gallery, Ltd., London.

Christie's New York, 8 May 1996 (309**) US$ 63,000	US$	63,000

RIZZI Felice {called Brusasorzi} (ca. 1540-1605) Italian
LOT AND HIS DAUGHTERS oil on slate, arched top, 23½ x 11in. (59.7 x 27.9cm.)
EXH.: Béziers, Musée des Beaux-Arts, *Collections privées de Béziers et sa région*, July-September 1967, 1969, p. 32, cat. no. 16 (as German School?).

Sotheby's New York, 16 May 1996 (22**) US$ 17,250	US$	17,250

ROBBE Henri (Hendrick) Alexander (Kortrijk 1807-1899 Brussels) Belgian
ROSES IN A VASE ON A DRAPED TABLE WITH PEARLS AND A SHELL oil on canvas, 32 x 25 3/4in. (81.2 x 65.5cm.) s 'H. Robbe'

Christie's London, 17 November 1995 (56**) GBP 18,975	US$	29,681

ROBBE Louis Marie Dominique Romain (Brussels 1806-1887 Brussels) Belgian
SHEEP AND GOATLS IN A MEADOW oil on canvas, 54 x 72cm. s 'Robbe'

Christie's Amsterdam, 25 April 1996 (224A*) NLG 13,800	US$	8,200

ROBERT Hubert (Paris 1733-1808 Paris) French
LANDSCAPE WITH A WATERFALL, A CASTLE AND FIGURES BY THE SIDE OF A STREAM oil on canvas, 49 1/16 x 76 3/4in. (124.6 x 194.9cm.) sd 'H. ROBERT/1794'

Sotheby's New York, 11 January 1996 (141**) US$ 200,500	US$	200,500

WASHING WOMEN UNDERNEATH A BRIDGE, A VESTAL TEMPLE NEARBY oil on canvas,108 x 142.5cm.

Étude Tajan Paris, 12 December 1995 (107**) FRF 1200,000	US$	241,711

LES PYRAMIDES / LES DESSINATEURS oil on canvas (a pair), each: 47 x 119cm.
PROV.: Former collection Camille Groult; Anonymous sale, Paris, Hotel Drouot, 26 March 1953, no. 115-116; Anonymous sale, Paris Drouot Montaigne, 12 December 1989, no. 25 (illustrated in colour).

Étude Tajan Paris, 12 December 1995 (110**) FRF 420,000	US$	84,599

VIEW OF THE CHATEAU DE FRANCIERES, NEAR COMPIEGNE, HOME OF THE MARQUIS DE TRACY oil on canvas, 17 3/4 x 21 3/4in. (45.1 x 55.2cm.)
PROV.: Tracy family, by descent in the family (acc. to an old onscription on the reverse of the frame); Général Beaumont Hennocque; Général de Larminat; Cailleux, paris, from whom acquired in July 1969 by Mr. Brewster.

Sotheby's New York, 16 May 1996 (155**) US$ 35,650	US$	35,650

LES LAVANDIERES DANS UN PARC oil on canvas, 47 x 57cm. sdlr 'H. Robert 1795'
PROV.: Private French Collection since the 1920's.

Étude Tajan Paris, 25 June 1996 (59**) FRF 440,000	US$	84,963

UN TEMPLE ANTIQUE ET UN PONT EN RUINE AVEC DES LAVANDIERES oil on canvas, 39.5 x 60.5cm.
PROV.: Anonymous Sale, Paris Galerie Charpentier, 6 December 1952, no. 19; Collection Prof. L. Justin Besançon.
        Étude Tajan Paris, 25 June 1996 (66**) FRF 350,000   US$ 67,585

ROBERT Hubert (Paris 1733-1808 Paris) French
L'ESCALIER oil on canvas, 15 3/4 x 33¼in. (40.2 x 84.3cm.) sdll 'H.Robert/ 1763'
PROV.: Trouart Collection, sold 22-27 February 1779, lot 71; With G. Wildenstein, Paris, 1928; With Birtschansky, Munich, 1930; Baron Heinrich Thyssen-Bornemisza, by 1937.
EXH.: Munich 1930, no. 275, plate 128a; Paris 1970, no. 48, plate 20; Düsseldorf Kunstmuseum, 1970-1, no. 42; Biefeld, Kunsthalle, *Landschaften aus vier Jahrhunderten aus dem Kunstmuseum Dusseldorf*, 1973, no. 27; Lausanne etc., 1986-7, no. 51; Brussels, Palais des Beaux-Arts, *La Collection Bentinck-Thyssen*, 1987, no. 51; Rome, Villa Medici, *Fragonard e Robert a Roma*, 1991, no. 127.
LIT.: P. de Nolhac, *Hubert Robert*, 1910, p. 103; *Pantheon*, January 1917; R. Heinemann 1937, vol. I, no. 352, vol. II, plate 273.
        Sotheby's London, 6 December 1995 (77**) GBP 117,000   US$ 180,055

THE PARK OF A COUNTRY VILLA WITH FIGURES PROMENADING NEAR A CASCADE OF WATER Oil on canvas, 19 3/4 x 25 3/4in. (49.7 x 65.7cm.) (mid 1780's)
LIT.: This painting will be included in the forthcoming *catalogue raisonné*, currently being prepared by The Wildenstein Institute.
        Sotheby's London, 6 December 1995 (200**) GBP 43,300   US$ 66,636

ROBERTS David, R.A., H.R.S.A. (Edinburgh 1796-1864 London) Scottish
JERUSALEM FROM THE ROAD LEADING TO BETHANY pencil and watercolour heightened with white on buffpaper, 12 3/4 x 18 3/in. (32.4 x 47.6cm.) sd inscr. 'David Roberts. Jerusalem from the Mount of Olives./April 8th.1839.' and with further indistinct inscription 'Jerusalem/From the road leading/ to Bethany./Bought at the sale of Mr/James Hopgood's Collection/at Christie's. March 27 18.' (on a label attached to the backing)
PROV.: Francis, 1st Earl of Ellesmere; Christie's London, 2 Apr. 1870, lot 5 (43gns. to Hopgood); Sir James Hopgood; Christie's London, 27 Mar. 1897, lot118 as 'Jerusalem from the Mount of Olives', 14 x 19in. (19 gns. to Agnews); Anon. sale, Christie's London, 27 May 1918, with 'Fragments of the Great Colossus at the Memnonium', lot 28 (21gns. to Sampson); R. Brocklebank; W. Lawson Peacock; Christie's London, 6 Feb. 1925, lot 37 (10½gns. to Brocklebank); Sir Edmund Brocklebank and thence by descent.
LIT.: N. Ran, ed., *David Roberts, R.A.: The Holy Land*, 1987, 2nd. ed. 1989, pp. I43-5, III-69.
        Christie's London, 2 April 1996 (89**) GBP 80,700   US$ 122,365

THE GATE OF METWALEY, CAIRO pencil and watercolour heightened with white, 13½ x 19 3/4in. (34.2 x 24.7cm.) sd inscr. 'David Roberts. R.A./ Cairo Dec 28th(?) /1838'
PROV.: Anon. sale, Sotheby's London, 22 March 1979, lot122 as 'The Principal Mosque at Bulak'. (GBP2,800 to Danny); Anon. sale, Christie's London, 29 March 1983, lot163 (GBP5500); with Mathaf Gallery.
EXH.: London, Barbican Art Gallery, *David Roberts*, 1986, no.,138 (illustrated).
        Christie's London, 2 April 1996 (99***) GBP 47,700   US$ 72,328

TEMPLE OF KOM OMBO, UPPER EGYPT pencil and watercolour heightened with bodycolour on grey paper, 12 7/8 x 19¼in. (32.8 x 48.8cm.) sd and inscr. 'David Roberts RA/Koum/Ombo/Nov 21st 1838.'
LIT.: K. Sim, *David Roberts R.A. 1796-1864*, 1984, pp. 133, 143.
        Christie's London, 11 July 1995 (107**) GBP 29,900   US$ 47,695

MORNING, RUINS OF KOM-OMBO oil on canvas, 22 x 51in. (55.9 x 129.5cm.) sd 'David Roberts R.A. 1853' inscr. 'Morning/Ruins of Kom-Ombo' on the reverse

PROV.: Painted for Ernest Gambart for GBP125.
EXH.: London, Barbican Art Gallery, *David Roberts*, 1986-7, ex cat.
      Christie's London, 29 March 1996 (223**) GBP 43,300   US$ 66,127

ROBERTS Edwin Thomas (London 1840-1917) British
A SUMMER EXPEDITION oil on canvas, 36 x 28in. (91.4 x 71.1cm.) s 'Edwin Roberts'
      Christie's South Kensington, 7 March 1996 (187**) GBP 6,800   US$ 10,385

ROBERTS William, R.A. (London 1895-1980) British
PUNTING ON THE CHERWELL oil on canvas, 19 x 15in. (48 x 38cm.) sul 'Roberts' (1939)
PROV.: Sotheby's 10 Nov. 1981, lot 116, where purchased by the present owner.
EXH.: London, Hamet Gallery, *William Roberts, R.A.*, 1973, no. 4; London, Parkin Gallery, *William Roberts R.A.* 1976, no.7; London Macleam Gallery, *William Roberts, R.A., 1895-1980,* Sept.-Oct. 1980, no. 17 (illustrated).
      Christie's London, 21 March 1996 (17**) GBP 12,650   US$ 19,319

ROBERTSON Anna Mary ('Grandma' Moses) (1860-1961) American
BUILDING THE FENCE oil on board, 16 x 19in. (40.7 x 48.3cm.) slr 'Moses' (6 March 1950)
PROV.: American-British Art Center, Nwe York; Ala Story.
LIT.: O. Kallir, *Grandma Moses*, New York 1973, p. 307, no.,903 (illustrated).
      Christie's New York, 23 May 1996 (178**) US$ 29,900   US$ 29,900

THE HOME OF BROTHER JOE'S oil on masonite, 15 3/ x 19 7/8in. (40 x 50.6cm.) slr 'Moses' (prob. 13 Oct. 1943)
PROV.: The American British Art Centre, Inc., New York; Mr. and Mrs. Frank Sinatra.
LIT.: O. Kallir *Grandma Moses*, New York, 1973, no. 292, p. 292.
      Christie's New York, 1 December 1995 (74**) US$ 40,250   US$ 40,250

ROBINSON Theodore (Irasburg 1852-1896) American
GIRL WITH PUPPIES oil on canvas, 20 3/4 x 11 5/8in. (52.7 x 29.5cm.) sdll 'T. Robinson 1881'
LIT.: This painting will be included in the forthcoming *catalogue raisonné T. Robinson* being prepared by I. Spanierman and S. Johnston.
      Christie's New York, 23 May 1996 (74**) US$ 63,000   US$ 63,000

ROBUSTI Domenico, {called} Domenico Tintoretto (Venice 1560-1635 Venice) Italian
APOLLO AND MINERVA oil on canvas, 22½ x 49in. (57 x 124cm.) (1590's)
PROV.: Count Telecki, Siebenburgen, Hungary; With Paul Cassirer, Berlin; Baron Heinrich Thyssen-Bornemisza, by 1930.
EXH.: Munich 1930, no. 319, plate 96, as *Jacopo Tintoretto*; Paris 1970, no. 12, plate 4, as *Jacopo Tintoretto*; Düsseldorf 1970-1, no. 50, as *Jacopo Tintoretto*; Lausanne etc., 1986-7, no. 15, as *Jacopo Tintoretto*.
LIT.: E. von der Bercken, 'Einige unbekannte Werke Jacopo Tintorettos', in *Pantheon*, 1929, vol. IV, p. 452, as *Jacopo Tintoretto*; B. Berenson, *Italian Pictures of the Renaissance*, 1932, p. 559, as *Jacopo Tintoretto*; R. Heinemann 1937, vol. I, no. 416, vol. II, plate 219, as *Jacopo Tintoretto*; E. von der Bercken, *Die Gemälde des Jacopo Tintoretto, 1942, p. 114, no. 177, plate 10, as Jacopo Tintoretto; R. Pallucchini,* La giovinezza del Tintoretto, 1950, p. 151, as 'difficilmente assegnabile a Jacopo Tintoretto'; B. Berenson, *Italian Pictures of the Renaissance; Venetian School*, 1957, vol. I, p. 174, as *Jacopo Tintoretto*; G. de Vecchi & C. Bernari, *L'opera completa del Tintoretto*, 1970, pp. 134, 136, no. E2, reproduced, as *not byJacopo Tintoretto*; R. Pallucchini & P. Rossi, *Tintoretto. Le opere sacre e profane*, 1982, vol. l, p. 246, no. A 55, as *Domenico Tintoretto*.
      Sotheby's London, 6 December 1995 (81**) GBP 23,000   US$ 35,396

PORTRAIT OF AN VENETIAN ADMIRAL oil on canvas (in original frame),116 x 98cm.
PROV.: Private collection.
EXH.: ed. G.M. Pilo, 'Postilla a Jacopo tintoretto ritratti giovanili', in *Arte Documenti*, 5, 1995, pp. 128-Bi; Catalogue from the Picture-Gallery from the Arthistoric Museum, illustration nos. 64 and 67;

Catalogue fro the exhibition *Jacopo Tintoretto, Porträts*, Venice and Vienna, 1994, pp. 110,111 and
1144,145 (illustrated in colour).
        Dorotheum Vienna, 6 March 1996 (45**) ATS 600,000   US\$ 57,715

ROCCA Michele (Parmigiano the Younger) (Parma 1670-1751 Venice) Italian
THE PENITENT MAGDALEN oil on canvas, 82 3/4 x 66in. (,210 x 167.5cm.) slr 'Michele
Rocca/Parmeno/Pinx'
        Sotheby's London, 17 April 1996 (121**) GBP 16,100   US\$ 24,412

ROCCA Michele (Parmigiano the Younger) circle of (Parma 1670-1751 Venice) Italian
THE INFANCY OF BACCHUS oil on canvas laid down on panel, 12¼ x 16 3/4in. (31.2 x 42.5cm.)
        Christie's South Kensington, 22 February 1996 (98**) GBP 44,750   US\$ 68,751

ROCKWELL Norman Perceval (New York 1894-1978) American
PUMPKIN CARVING oil on acetate, 14½ x 12in. (36.9 x 30.5cm.)(sight) sill 'Norman Rockwell';
inscr. on the mat 'My Best to Dr. Walter Sturdy sincerely Norman Rockwell'
PROV.: The artist; Dr. Walter Sturdy by descent in the family to the present owner.
        Christie's New York, 13 September 1995 (123**) US\$ 9,200   US\$ 9,200

GUIDING INFLUENCE oil on canvas, 38 x 28¼in. (96.5 x 71.6cm.) slr 'Norman Rockwell' (1931)
PROV.: George Washington Bicentennial Committee; Sears, Roebuck & Co., Chicago; Mrs. Claude
Parker, Los Angeles.
EXH.: Washington D.C., Smithsonian Institution, National Museum of American History, *George
Washington: A Figure Upon the Stage*, Feb. 1982-Feb. 1983, p. 44 (illustrated).
LIT.: Sears, Roebuck & Co., Chicago, 1932, spring catalogue (illustrated on the cover); L.N. Mofat,
Norman Rockwell, A Definitive Catalogue, Vol. I, p. 412, no. A,419 (illustrated as 'Washington's
Bicentennial Birthday').
        Christie's New York, 30 November 1995 (79**) US\$ 607,500   US\$ 607,500

THE APPLE PEELER, (HAIR SPLITTER EVANS) oil on canvas, 34 x 18in. (86.5 46cm.) slr
'Norman Rockwell' (1927)
PROV.: Dr. and Mrs. Leslie Greenbaum, Rancho Mirage, California.
LIT.: L.N. Moffatt, *Norman Rockwell: A Definitive Catalogue*, Stockbridge, Massachusetts, 1986,
vol. I, p. 364, no. A250, illus.; Reproduced: *Saturday Evening Post* (January 8, 1927) p. 185.
        Christie's New York, 13 September 1995 (126**) US\$ 55,200   US\$ 55,200

RODIN Auguste (René François Auguste) (Paris 1840-1917 Meudon) French
FEMME NUE DEBOUT watercolor over pencil on paper laid down on board, 12 5/8 x 9 3/8in. (32 x
23.8cm.) lr 'la nuit appaisant les plots'
        Christie's New York, 8 November 1995 (143**) US\$ 28,750   US\$ 28,750

LE TEMPS white gouache over pencil on tracing paper mounted on gray paper, 5 3/8 x 5 3/8in. (13.6
x 13.6cm) with collector's stamp of Marcel Louis Guérin on the mount (Lugt 1872b) (1885-1890)
PROV.: Marcel Louis Guérin, Paris.
EXH.: Washington, D.C., National Gallery of Art,*The Drawings of Rodin*, Nov., 1971-jan., 1972, no.
58 (illustrated). The exhibition traveled to New York, The Solomon R. Guggenheim Museum,
March-May, 1972.
        Christie's New York, 8 November 1995 (146**) US\$ 8,625   US\$ 8,625

RODRIGUEZ Manuel Garcia y (1863-1925) Spanish
STILL-LIFE OF ROSES AND CARNATIONS oil on canvas, 42 3/4 x 27in. (108.6 x 68.6cm.) sd
'Sevilla 1921'
        Sotheby's Arcade Auctions New York, 17 January 1996 (578*) US\$ 8,625   US\$ 8,625

ROELOFS Willem (Amsterdam 1822-1897 Berchem near Antwerp) Dutch
COTTAGES BY A CANAL oil on canvas laid down on panel, 11 3/4 x 17½in. (29.8 x 44.5cm.) s

'W. Roelofs'
PROV.: Verduyn van Vliet; with Larensche Kunsthandel, Amsterdam, 1908.
    Christie's London, 15 March 1996 (5**) GBP 8,625   US$ 13,172

WATERING COWS oil on canvas, 70 x 102cm. s 'W. Roelofs'
    Christie's Amsterdam, 25 April 1996 (195**) NLG 115,000   US$ 68,334

A WOODED POLDER LANDSCAPE WITH A PEASANTWOMAN AND A BOY NEAR A
FARMHOUSE oil on canvas, 41 x 64cm. sd 'W. Roelofs 55'
PROV.: Collection H.P. Dekker, Amsterdam; Anon. sale, Mak van Waay Amsterdam, November
1956, cat.no.,358 Collection B. de Geus van den Heuvel, Nieuwersluis; His sale,; Sotheby's Mak van
Waay Amsterdam 26/27 April 1976, cat.no.315; anon. sale, Sotheby's Amsterdam, 15 April 1985.
EXH.: Laren, singermuseum, 1957, cat.no. 223; Amsterdam, Stedelijk Museum, *Van Romantiek tot
Amsterdamse School*,; 1958, cat.no.C.15; Amsterdam, Museum Willet Holthuizen, year unknown.
    Christie's Amsterdam, 26 October 1995 (306**) NLG 27,600   US$ 17,402

ROERICH Nikolai (1874-1947) Russian
A MOUNTAIN LANDSCAPE oil on board, 24½ x 29½in. (62.2 x 75cm.) sll with mono.; inscr. in
Russian 'Finlandia' and in Finnish 'Suomi' on the reverse
    Christie's New York, 18 April 1996 (15**) US$ 10,925   US$ 10,925

ROESEN Severin (1846-1870 (1871\1872)) American
FLORAL STILL-LIFE WITH NEST OF EGGS oil on canvas, 30 x 24in. (76.2 x 61cm.)
    Christie's New York, 13 March 1996 (6**) US$ 96,000   US$ 96,000

RÖHL Karl Peter (1890-1975) German
SCHWARZ-BLAU (GROSSES QUADRET) gouache over pencil, 20½ x 15 1/8in. (52 x 38.5cm.) sd
'1922'
PROV.: Galerie Gmurzynska, Cologne.
    Sotheby's London, 20 March 1996 (270**) GBP 4,025   US$ 6,147

ROHLFS Christian (Nierendorf (Holstein) 1849-1938 Hagen) German
NARZISSEN UND TULPEN tempera on canvas, 61 x 45.5cm. slr with mono. (ca. 1927)
    Hauswedell & Nolte Cologne, 5-6 June 1996 (708**) DEM 80,000   US$ 51,978

PAAR tempera and watercolour over charcoal drawing on heavy japanese paper, 53.5 x 39cm. sd
mono 'CR 26'
    Lempertz Cologne, 1 June 1996 (954**) DEM 27,000   US$ 17,543

RÖLING Gerard Victor Alphons ('s-Hertogenbosch 1904-1981) Dutch
VOORBEREIDING TOT HET FEEST oil on canvas, 80 x 93.5cm. sdll 'G.V.A. Röling 1943'
EXH.: Amsterdam, Huinck & Scherjon, *Röling*, 20 March-17 april 1948, no. 33.
    Christie's Amsterdam, 5 June 1996 (279**) NLG 57,500   US$ 33,596

ROMAKO A Anton (1832-1889) Austrian
PIFFERARI VOR EINEN ALTAR oil on canvas, 18¼ x 14¼in. (46.4 x 36.3cm.) s & inscr.'A.
Romako/Roma'
PROV.: Anon. sale, Christie's, 17 October 1958, lot127 (85 gns).
    Christie's London, 11 October 1995 (31**) GBP 11,500   US$ 18,150

ROMANELLI Giovanni Francesco (Raffaellino) (Viterbo 1610-1662 Viterbo) Italian
HAGAR AND ISMAEL IN THE DESERT oil on canvas, 20 1/8 x 26 7/8in. (51 x 68.5cm.) (ca
1637)
PROV.: Anon. [R. Godwin-Austen, Shalford House, Guildford, Surrey] Sale ('Pictures from a house
in the country, where they have been since their purchase from the Orleans Gallery'), Chnstie's, 27
May 1882, lot 104, as N. Poussin (20gns. to Denison); Christopher Beckett Denison, 41 Upper

Grosvenor Street, London; Christie's, 20 June 1885 (=8th day), lot 1056, as *N. Poussin* (3gns.); H.D. Molesworth; with Colnaghi, London.

Christie's London, 8 December 1995 (94**) GBP 58,700	US$	90,335

ANGELICA AND MEDORO oil on canvas (a tondo), diameter 27in. (68.6cm.)
PROV.: L.N. Stafford and Co. (Sotheby Parke-Bernet, New York, 6 June 1980, lot 16); Barbara Piasecka Johnson, Princeton, New Jersey.

Sotheby's New York, 11 January 1996 (108**) US$ 63,000	US$	63,000

ROMITI Sergio (Bologna 1928 b.-l) Italian
SUL CIELO oil on canvas, 70 x 65cm. sdll 'Romiti 60' (1960)
EXH.: Venice, *XXX Biennale Internazionale d'arte*, 1960.

Finearte Milan, 26 October 1995 (155*) ITL 23,000,000	US$	14,330

ROMNEY George (Dalton in Furness (Lancashire) 1734-1802 Kendal, Westmorland) British
PORTRAIT OF WILLIAM HAYLEY (1745-1820) oil on canvas, 29½ x 24in. (74.9 x 61cm.) (1777-79)

Sotheby's New York, 16 May 1996 (193**) US$ 9,200	US$	9,200

RONNER-KNIP Henriëtte (Amsterdam 1821-1909 Brussel) Belgian (Dutch)
THE PIANO LESSON oil on canvas, 17½ x 26in. (44.4 x 66cm.) s 'Henriette Ronner'

Christie's London, 14 June 1996 (15**) GBP 62,000	US$	95,605

AFTERNOON TEA oil on panel, 9 3/8 x 12 5/8in. (23.8 x 32.5cm.) s 'Henrietee Ronner'
PROV.: With Galerie Georges Giroux, Brussels, no. 2946; with J.B. Bennet & Sons, Glasgow;J.B.Bennet & Sons; Christie's, 5 June 1930, lot102 (40 gns. to Mitchell).

Christie's London, 14 June 1996 (16**) GBP 18,400	US$	28,373

THE ARTIST CAT oil on artist's pallet, 10 x 14 3/4in. (25.4 x 37.5cm.) slr 'Henrietta Ronner'

Christie's South Kensington, 14 March 1996 (1**) GBP 10,120	US$	15,455

HIDE AND SEEK oil on panel, 12 7/8 x 17 3/4in. (32.8 x 45cm.) s ' Henriette Ronner'

Christie's London, 15 March 1996 (10**) GBP 32,200	US$	49,175

CURIOSITY oil on panel, 12 5/8 x 17 3/4in. (32 x 45.2cm.) s 'Henriette Ronner'

Christie's London, 17 November 1995 (94**) GBP 20,700	US$	32,379

A SPANIEL AND PUPPIES IN A BASKET, TWO GREYHOUNDS BY A GATEWAY oil on panel, 47 x 36 cm sd 'Henriëtte. Knip. 1846'

Christie's Amsterdam, 25 April 1996 (114*) NLG 9,200	US$	5,467

A DANGEROUS GAME oil on canvas, 85 x 50cm. sd 'Henriette Ronner 5 april 1880'

Christie's Amsterdam, 25 April 1996 (157*) NLG 17,250	US$	10,250

ROOS Jan {called} Giovanni Rosa (Antwerp 1591-1638 Genua) Flemish
A HORSE, CATTLE AND SHEEP NEAR A CLASSICAL TOMB WITH A SHEPHERD BOY AND A SHEPHERDESS NEARBY, IN AN ITALIANATE LANDSCAPE oil on canvas, 81.7 x 106.5cm.

Christie's Amsterdam, 7 May 1996 (27**) NLG 10,350	US$	6,035

ROOS Johann Melchior (Heidelberg 1663-1731 Brunswick) German
MOUNTAINOUS LANDSCAPE WITH CATTLE AND GOATS RESTING NEAR A WATERFALL oil on canvas, 37 x 51 3/4in. (94 x 131.5cm.)

Sotheby's London, 5 July 1995 (172**) GBP 6,900	US$	11,007

ROOS Philipp Peter, {called} Rosa da Tivoli (Frankfurt am Main 1655/57-1706 Rome) German
SHEPHERD WITH HERD oil on canvas, 56.3 x 70.8cm
      Finearte Milan, 25 November 1995 (120*) ITL 10,350,000   US$ 6,497

PEASANTS AND CATTLE IN EXTENSIVE LANDSCAPES oil on canvas (a pair), 38 5/8 x 50in.
(98 x 127cm.) one indistinctively signed 'ROSA' (on the plinth)
      Christie's London, 7 July 1995 (385**) GBP 14,950   US$ 23,848

ROOSENBOOM Albert (1845-1875) Belgian
TO SERVE AND PROTECT oil on canvas, 27 x 21cm. s 'A Roosenboom'
      Christie's Amsterdam, 25 April 1996 (216*) NLG 11,500   US$ 6,833

ROOSENBOOM Margaretha (The Hague 1843-1896 Voorburg) Dutch
A STILL LIFE WITH TULIPS AND VIOLETS IN A VASE, ROSES, A FAN, A GLOVE AND A
JEWEL-BOX ON A DRAPED TABLE oil on panel, unframed, 42.5 x 54.5cm. slr (strengthened)
'Marg. Roosenboom'
      Christie's Amsterdam, 26 October 1995 (198**) NLG 17,250   US$ 10,876

ROOSENBOOM Nicolaas Johannes (Schellingwoude (Ransdorp) 1805-1880 Assen) Dutch
AN EXTENSIVE WINTER LANDSCAPE WITH A MOORED BOAT AND SKATERS ON A
FROZEN RIVER oil on canvas, 31 5/8 x 41½in. (80.2 x 105.5cm.) slr; inscr. 'Bruxelles'
      Phillips London, 14 November 1995 (1**) GBP 7,500   US$ 11,732

SKATERS ON A FROZEN WATERWAY NEAR A RUIN, A TOWN IN THE DISTANCE oil on
canvas, 61 x 79 cm s 'N.J. Roosenboom'
      Christie's Amsterdam, 25 April 1996 (15) NLG 8,625   US$ 5,125

ROOSKENS Anton (Joseph Anton) (Horst 1906-1976) Dutch
FIGURES oil on canvas, 65 x 81cm. sdar 'Rooskens 68' sd again and inscr. with title and numbered 8
on the reverse
      Christie's Amsterdam, 5 June 1996 (300**) NLG 19,550   US$ 11,423

FIGURES AND A BIRD oil on canvas, 50 x 40cm. sdlr 'Rooskens 74', and inscribed with 'no. 613'
on the reverse (1974)
      Christie's Amsterdam, 5 June 1996 (321*) NLG 19,550   US$ 11,423

DUTCH LANDSCAPE oil on canvas, 65 x 81cm. sdlr 'Rooskens 72', and inscr. with title and
numbered 'no. 472' on the reverse
      Christie's Amsterdam, 5 June 1996 (352**) NLG 23,000   US$ 13,439

COMPOSITION WITH WHITE LINES oil on canvas, 76 x 94cm. sur 'Rooskens' (ca. 1951)
PROV.: Benjamin Bernstein, Philadelphia.
EXH.: Frankfurt, Zimmer Gallery, 1953, no.5.
      Christie's Amsterdam, 5 June 1996 (359**) NLG 29,900   US$ 17,470

FLYING BIRDS oil on canvas, 81 x 65cm. sdlr 'Rooskens 73' inscr. with title and numbered on the
reverse 'no. 485'
      Christie's Amsterdam, 6 December 1995 (285**) NLG 11,500   US$ 7,126

UNTITLED oil on canvas, 65 x 85cm. sdlr 'Rooskens 66' and s again and numbered on the reverse
'no. 9'
EXH.: Helsinki, Didrichsenin Taidemuseo Didrichsens Konstmuseum, *Cobra*, 25 Septemebr - 21
October 1979, no. 34.
      Christie's Amsterdam, 6 December 1995 (325**) NLG 14,950   US$ 9,264

LANGSLAPER oil on canvas, 76 x 90cm. sdlr 'Rooskens 69' and inscr. with title and d and
numbered on the reverse 'CK.F No 313'
<blockquote>Christie's Amsterdam, 6 December 1995 (339**) NLG 34,500   US$ 21,378</blockquote>

ROOTIUS Jan Albertsz (attr.) (Hoorn 1624-1666 Hoorn) Dutch
FLOWERS ON A MARBLE LEDGE oil on canvas, 52 x 46.5cm. s indistinctly 'J.A.oo.'
<blockquote>Étude Tajan Paris, 28 June 1996 (49**) FRF 75,000   US$ 14,482</blockquote>

ROPS Felicien Joseph Victor (Namur 1833-1898 Essonnes) Belgian
LA FEMME AU MASQUE oil on paper laid down on board, 11 x 9in. (28 x 13cm.) (ca 1888)
PROV.: Georges Viau, Paris; Mme O. Sainsère, Paris.
<blockquote>Christie's London, 14 June 1996 (37**) GBP 27,600   US$ 42,560</blockquote>

L'AGONIE DU MORS ET VITA watercolour and charcoal, 6¼ x 11½in. (16 x 29cm.)
PROV.: Sotheby's London, 1 March 1982, lot 160.
<blockquote>Sotheby's London, 17 April 1996 (821**) GBP 15,525   US$ 23,541</blockquote>

ROSA Francesco de, {called} Pacecco de Rosa (Naples 1600-1654) Italian Naples
LANDSCAPE WITH A SHEPHERD AND HIS FLOCK OF SHEEP oil on canvas, 49¼ x 58¼in.
(,125 x 148cm.)
<blockquote>Sotheby's London, 6 December 1995 (189**) GBP 7,475   US$ 11,504</blockquote>

ROSA Salvator (Arnella or Napels 1615-1673 Rome) Italian
JUDAH GIVING THAMAR HIS SIGNET RING oil on canvas, 26 1/8 x 19 3/4in. (66.4 x 50.2cm.)
(1660's)
PROV.: The Earl of Jersey; Christie's, 15 july 1949, lot165 (12gns. to Cevat)Anon. Sale,
Christie's,330 March 1979, lot 20 (GBP4,800).
<blockquote>Christie's London, 8 December 1995 (95**) GBP 14,950   US$ 23,007</blockquote>

SHEPHERDESSES AND MONKS IN ITALIANATE LANDSCAPES oil on canvas, 95.2 x 135cm.
/ 95.4 x 139.7cm.
<blockquote>Christie's Amsterdam, 13 November 1995 (36** (1)) NLG 17,250   US$ 10,872</blockquote>

AN ITALIANATE RIVER WITH FIGURES ON A BANK; AND A ROCKY ITALIANATE
LANDSCAPE WITH FIGURES IN A BOAT ON A STREAM oil on canvas, 19 x 25½in. (48.2 x
64.8cm.) (a pair)
<blockquote>Christie's South Kensington, 18 april 1996 (120*) GBP 5,750   US$ 8,719</blockquote>

A CAVALRY ENGAGEMENT ON A BRIDGE oil on canvas, 35 3/4 x 63in. (90.8 x 160cm.)
<blockquote>Christie's South Kensington, 18 april 1996 (188**) GBP 5,520   US$ 8,370</blockquote>

TWO SCENES OF WITCHCRAFT oil on canvas (a pair of tondos), each: 52.5cm. (diameter) (1640-
1649)
PROV.: Collection Busiri, Rome, until 1963.
EXH.: Rome, 1956, *Il Seicento europeo*, no. 254a-b.
LIT.: L. Salerno, catalogue Rome 1956, *Il Seicento europeo*; L. Salerno, *L'Opera completa di
Salvator Rosa*, Milan 1975, no. 75, p. 90.
<blockquote>Christie's Rome, 4 June 1996 (587**) ITL 40,000,000   US$ 25,940</blockquote>

ROCKY LANDSCAPE WITH 'SANTA MARIA EGIZIACA' oil on canvas, 65 x 49cm. inscr.
'SALVE SALVATOR SILVESTRIS RURIS AMATOR' on the reverse
PROV.: Loghlack Brisoc Collection; Collection Busiri-Vici, Rome, Until 1966.
LIT.: L. Salerno, 'Due opere tarde di Salvator Rosa' in: *Arte in Europa. Scritti di Storia dell'Arte in
onore di Edoardo Arslan*, Milan, 1966, I, p. 721, pl.,467 (illustrated); L. Salerno, *L'Opera completa
di Salvator Rosa*, Milan 1975, no. 250, p.,104 (illstrated).
<blockquote>Christie's Rome, 4 June 1996 (592**) ITL 40,000,000   US$ 25,940</blockquote>

ROSA Salvator (circle of) (Arnella or Napels 1615-1673 Rome) Italian
A CAVALRY BATTLE OUTSIDE A FORTIFIED TOWN oil on canvas, 45 x 72 3/8in. (114.3 x 183.7cm.)
      Christie's South Kensington, 7 December 1995 (163***) GBP 31,500   US$ 48,476

ROSAI Ottone (Florence 1895-1957 Ivrea) Italian
LA DOMENICA oil on board, 50 x 70cm. slr 'O. Rosai' (1956)
LIT.: Luigi Cavallo, *Ottone Rosai*, ed. Galleria II Castello, Milan, 1973, no. 338, (illustrated in colour CXLII).
      Finearte Milan, 18 June 1996 (260**) ITL 24,725,000   US$ 16,034

PAESAGGIO CON CASE oil on canvas, 65 x 50cm. slr 'O. Rosai' (ca 1956)
      Finearte Milan, 19 March 1996 (32**) ITL 27,600,000   US$ 17,658

STRASA CON CASE E CIPRESSO oil on canvas, 70 x 56cm. sdll 'Rosai 33' (1933)
      Finearte Milan, 19 March 1996 (60**) ITL 94,300,000   US$ 60,333

MUSICANTE oil on canvas, 41 x 51cm. slr 'O. Rosai 41.' (1941)
      Finearte Rome, 2 April 1996 (204**) ITL 51,750,000   US$ 33,067

INTERNO DI CAFFÉ oil on canvas, 26.5 x 31.5cm. slr 'O. Rosai' (1920-22)
      Christie's Milan, 20 November 1995 (155**) ITL 64,817,000   US$ 40,689

VASE WITH FLOWERS oil on board, 37 x 50cm. sdlr 'O. Rosai 45' (1945)
      Finearte Milan, 26 October 1995 (161**) ITL 20,700,000   US$ 12,897

DUE OMINI AL TAVOLO oil on canvas, 60 x 73cm. sd 'O. Rosai 40'
PROV.: Galleria Santacroce, Firenze.
      Sotheby's Milan, 28 May 1996 (159**) ITL 32,200,000   US$ 20,681

ROSATI Giulio (Rome 1858-1917 Rome) Italian
ARAB WARRIORS pencil, watercolour and bodycolour on paper, 29 x 20½in. (73.5 x 52cm.) sd 'G. Rosati/1896'
      Christie's London, 15 March 1996 (108**) GBP 20,700   US$ 31,613

ROSE Guy (San Gabriel (California) 1867-1925 Pasadena) American
NOTRE DAME DE GRACE, HONFLEUR oil on canvas, 24 x 28 3/4in. (66 x 73cm.) slr 'Guy Rose' titled on the reverse
      Christie's New York, 23 May 1996 (67**) US$ 156,500   US$ 156,500

THE DISTANT TOWN oil on canvas, 24 x 29in. (61 x 73.6cm.) slr 'Guy Rose' titled on the reverse
      Christie's New York, 23 May 1996 (68**) US$ 134,500   US$ 134,500

VIEW IN THE SAN GABRIEL MOUNTAINS oil on canvas, 29¼ x 25 1/8in. (74.2 x 63.8cm.) slr 'Guy Rose'
      Christie's New York, 23 May 1996 (112***) US$ 233,500   US$ 233,500

ROSENQUIST James (Grand Forks (North Dakota) 1933 b.) American
UNTITLED acrylic on canvas mounted on panel, unframed, 60 x 60in. (152.4 x 152.4cm.) sd 'James Rosenquist 1990' on the overlap
PROV.: Acquired directly from the artist.
      Christie's New York, 8 May 1996 (445**) US$ 55,200   US$ 55,200

THE KABUKI BLUSHES oil on canvas, 67½ x 72in. (717.5 x 182.8cm.) (1984)
PROV.: Leo Castelli Gallery, New York.
EXH.: Moscow, Central Hall of Artists, *Rosenquist 1961-1991*, Feb.-March 1991, p. 72 (illustrated);

Valencia, Centro Julio Gonzalez, *James Rosenquist*, May-Aug. 1991, p. 151, no. 54 (illustrated).
LIT.: J. Goldman, *James Rosenquist*, Denver 1985, p.,182 (illustrated).
Christie's New York, 14 November 1995 (52**) US$ 156,500   US$ 156,500

EXIT oil on canvas, 30 1/8 x 33in. (76.5 x 83.8cm.) sd titled 'JAMES ROSENQUIST 1961 EXIT'
PROV.: Green Gallery, New York.; Private collection, Pittsburgh.
Christie's New York, 15 November 1995 (223**) US$ 55,200   US$ 55,200

FEMALES AND FLOWERS oil on canvas, 66 x 78in. (167.7 x 198.2cm.) (1984)
PROV.: Richard L. Feigen & Co., Inc., New York; Alfred Taubman, Bloomfield Hills.
EXH.: Denver Art Museum; Houston, Contemporary Arts Museum; Des Moines Art Center; Buffalo, Albnght-Knox Art Gallery, New York, Whitney Museum of American Art and Washington, D.C., Smithsonian Institution, National Museum of American Art, *James Rosenquist Retrospective*, May 1985-Jan. 1987.
Christie's New York, 7 May 1996 (46**) US$ 96,000   US$ 96,000

ROSLIN Alexandre (Malmö 1718-1793 Paris) Swedish
PORTRAIT OF JEAN ERIC REHN oil on canvas, 63 x 54cm. sdll 'Roslin 1756'
Bukowskis Stockholm, 29 November-1 December 1995 (125**) SEK 500,000   US$ 75,639

ROSSELLI Cosimo di Lorenzo (Florence 1439-1507 Florence) Italian
THE MADONNA AND CHILD ENTHRONED BETWEEN SAINTS GEORGE AND FRANCIS OF ASSISI tempera and gold on panel, 44 x 64in. (111.8 x 162.6cm.)
Sotheby's New York, 11 January 1996 (46**) US$ 123,500   US$ 123,500

ROSSELLI Matteo (Florence 1578-1650 Florence) Italian
REBECCA AND ELIEZER oil on canvas, 63¼ x 52¼in. (161x 132.5cm.)
Sotheby's London, 5 July 1995 (74**) GBP 45,500   US$ 72,579

ROSSETTI Dante Gabriel (Gabriel Charles Dante) (London 1828-1882 Birmingham) British
MRS. WILLIAM MORRIS pen and ink, 9 x 6 3/4in. slr mono. 'DGR/1873' (ca. 1872-74)
PROV.: Probably given by the artist to ellen Eps (later married to Edmond Gosse); Sir Edmond Gosse and Lady Gosse; thence by descent to the present owner.
LIT.: Joseph Pennell, *Modern Illustration*, 1895 reproduced facing p. 27; Virginia Surtees, *The Paintings and Drawings of Dante Gabriel Rossetti - A Catalogue Raisonné*, Clarendon Press, Oxford, 1971, Vol. I, p. no. 396.
Sotheby's London, 10 July 1995 (106**) GBP 32,200   US$ 51,364

ROSSI Antonio (with Carlo Lodi (1701-1765)) (1700-1753) Italian
FIDING OF MOSES AND MOSES DRIVING THE BANDITS FROM THE WELL OF THE DAUGHTERS OF JETHRO tempera on canvas (a pair), each: 70½ x 135in. (179.1 x 342.9cm.)
Sotheby's New York, 16 May 1996 (65**) US$ 76,750   US$ 76,750

ROSSI Francesco de', {called} Cecchino Salviati (Florence 1510-1563 Rome) Italian
PORTRAIT OF A MAN WEARING A BLACK HAT (A CLERIC?) oil on panel, 11¼ x 8 7/8in. (28.6 x 22.5cm.)
PROV.: Algranti, London, from whom acquired by the present collector.
Sotheby's New York, 11 January 1996 (58**) US$ 145,500   US$ 145,500

A PROCESSION CROSSING THE BRIDGE NEAR THE CASTEL SANT'ANGELO pen and brown ink with wash over black chalk, heightened with white; lunette shaped, 9.5 x 20.2cm. inscr. 'Salviatti'
PROV.: John Thane (Lugt 1544); William Esdaile (Lugt 2617); E B West, his sale, November 1820; Sotheby's, London, 6th July 1967, lot 18 (sold for GBP 350; illustrated).
LIT.: J. Bean, *15th and 16th Century Drawings in the Metropolitan Museum of Art*, New York, 1986, cat. no. 234, p. 233; L. Mortari, *Francesco Salviati*, Rome, 1992, cat. and pl. no. 2 of drawings

section, p. 169.

> Phillips London, 17 April 1996 (110**) GBP 9,200   US$ 13,950

ROSSI Giovanni Battista (active 1749-1782-) Italian
THE SACRIFICE OF NOAH oil on canvas, 31 3/4 x 49¼in. (80.6 x 125.1cm.)

> Sotheby's New York, 6 October 1996 (126**) US$ 31,050   US$ 31,050

ROSSI Luigi (Castagnola 1853-1923 Tesserete) Italian
LA POLENTA oil on canvas, 14 3/4 x 21½in. (37.5 x 55cm.) slr

> Sotheby's London, 13 March 1996 (133**) GBP 13,800   US$ 21,075

DOLCI PENSIERI oil on canvas, 10½ x 13 3/4in. (26.5 x 35cm.) sll
EXH.: Daverio, Antichità Silbernagl, *Luigi Rossi*, no. XXIV.

> Sotheby's London, 13 March 1996 (134**) GBP 9,775   US$ 14,928

ROTARI Pietro Antonio (Verona 1707-1762 Saint Petersburg) Italian
PORTRAITS OF A BOY AND A GIRL oil on canvas (a pair), each: 17 x 13in. (43.2 x 33cm.) (1st half of the 1750's)
PROV.: R. Rusch, Dresden; H.M. Gutman, Berlin (Sale: Graupe, Berlin 12-14 April 1934 lot 37 & 38; Sale Christie's New York, 6 June 1984 lot151 (as a pair); Roberto Polo.

> Sotheby's New York, 11 January 1996 (132**) US$ 134,500   US$ 134,500

PORTRAIT OF A RUSSIAN LADY WITH A FAN pastel on paper laid down on canvas, 17 3/4 x 13½in. (45.1 x 34.3cm.)

> Sotheby's New York, 16 May 1996 (177**) US$ 33,350   US$ 33,350

A YOUNG GIRL oil on canvas, 17 3/4 x 14in. (45 x 35.4cm.) (probably 1762)
PROV.: Reputedly Graf Solms; Acquired by the uncle of the present owner in June 1948 through the good offices of the Staatsgalerie, Stuttgart.

> Sotheby's London, 17 April 1996 (185**) GBP 41,100   US$ 62,320

EINE JUNGE FRAU IN EINEM PELZGEFÜTTERTEN MANTEL oil on canvas, 50 x 38cm.

> Lempertz Cologne, 18 May 1996 (1134**) DEM 25,000   US$ 16,298

ROTELLA Mimmo (Catanzaro (Calabria) 1918 b.) Italian
UNTITLED collage, 53 x 58cm. sll stamped 'Rotella' (ca 1960)
PROV.: Collection Giampiero Giani, Torino.

> Finearte Milan, 12 December 1995 (276**) ITL 11,500,000   US$ 7,215

MACCHIE collage on canvas,141 x 176cm. slr 'Rotella' (1955)
LIT.: T. Trini, *Rotella*, ed. Prearo, Milan 1974.

> Finearte Milan, 26 October 1995 (166**) ITL 29,900,000   US$ 18,629

ROTHKO Mark (Dvinsk 1903-1970 New York) American (Russian)
NO. 16 oil on canvas, 67½ x 54in. (,171 x 137cm.) sd 'Mark Rothko 1949' on the reverse
PROV.: Betty Parsons Gallery, New York; Marlborough Galleria d'Arte, Rome; Julian Levy, Connecticut.
EXH.: New York, Museum of Modern Art; London, Whitechapel Art Gallery; Amsterdam, Stedelijk Museum; Palais des Beaux-Arts de Bruxelles; Kunsthalle Basel; Rome, Galleria Nazionale d'Arte Moderna, and Musée d'Art Moderne de la Ville de Paris, *Mark Rothko*, Jan. 1961-Jan. 1963, no. 9 (illustrated); Ridgefield, Larry Aldrich Museum, *Brandeis University Creative Arts Awards, 1957-1966: Tenth Anniversary Exhibition*, April-June 1966, no. 65.; Berlin, Martin-Gropius-Bau, *Der unverbrauchte Blick*, Jan.-April 1987, n.n. (illustrated).
LIT.: *Prospect Retrospect Europa 1946-1976*, Düsseldorf 1976, p. 66; D. Piper, *The Mitchell Beazley Library of Art-vol 3: New Horizons*, London 1981, p.,218 (illustrated).

> Christie's New York, 14 November 1995 (5**) US$ 310,500   US$ 310,500

UNTITLED oil on paper mounted on canvas-unframed, 38 7/8 x 25in. (98.8 x 63.5cm.) (1968)
PROV.: Marlborough-Gerson Gallery, New York; Galerie Beyeler, Basel; Hubert de Givenchy, Paris.

Christie's New York, 14 November 1995 (20**) US$ 266,500	US$	266,500

ROTTENHAMMER Johann (Hans) the Elder (Munich 1564-1625 Augsburg) German
MINERVA, FORTUNE AND ABUNDANCE oil on copper, 12¼ x 9in.(31.5 x 23cm.)

Sotheby's London, 17 April 1996 (122**) GBP 49,900	US$	75,663

ROUAULT Georges (Paris 1871-1958 Paris) French
FLEURS DE CONVENTION oil on paper laid down on canvas, 22 x 15 3/4in. (55.8 x 40cm.) slr 'G.Rouault' titled on the crossbrace (1947)
PROV.: Otto M. Gerson, New York; Acquired from the above by Mr. Joseph H. Hazen on Feb. 18, 1953.
EXH.: Jerusalem, Israel Museum, *Paintings from the Collection of Joseph H. Hazen*, summer, 1966, no. 37 (illustrated). The exhibition traveled to Cambridge, Massachusetts, Fogg Art Museum, Oct.-Dec., 1966; Los Angeles, University of California, The Art Galleries, Jan.-Feb., 1967; Berkeley, University of California, Art Museum, Feb.-March, 1967; Houston, Museum of Fine Arts, April-May, 1967, and Honolulu, Academy of Arts, June-Aug., 1967.
LIT.: M. Brion, *Georges Rouault*, Paris, 1953, no. 35 (illustrated) B. Dorival and I. Rouault, *Rouault, L'oeuvre Peint*, Monte-Carlo, 1988, vol. II, p. 219, no. 2,267 (illustrated).

Christie's New York, 30 April 1996 (14**) US$ 244,500	US$	244,500

PAYSAGE LÉGENDAIRE oil on paper laid down on canvas, 29 x 21½in. (73.7 x 54.6cm.) slr 'G. Rouault' (1938)
PROV.: J. K. Thannhauser, New York (acquired by the present owner, 1958).
EXH.: San Francisco, Museum of Art, *Art in the 20th Century, Commemorating the Tenth Anniversary of the Signing of the United Nations Charter*, June-July, 1955.
LIT.: B. Dorival and I. Rouault, *Rouault, L'oeuvre peint*, Monte- Carlo, 1988, vol. II (1929-1956), p. 119, no. 1738 (illustrated).

Christie's New York, 1 May 1996 (223**) US$ 244,500	US$	244,500

NU DEBOUT (STANDING NAKED FIGURE) oil on paper laid down on canvas, 15 x 7in. (38 x 17.5cm.) suc 'G. Rouault' (ca. 1910)
PROV.: Former collection Josef Muller, Paris.
EXH.: Zurich, Kunsthaus, *Rouault*, 1948, no. 42 of the catalogue.
LIT.: B. Dorival & I. Rouault, *Rouault, l'oeuvre peint*, éditions André Sauret, Monte carlo, 1988, p. 149, no. 498.

Étude Tajan Paris, 10 June 1996 (23**) FRF 130,000	US$	25,103

DANSEUSE ROUSSE oil and gouache on thick paper laid down on canvas, 18 5/8 x 13in. (37.3 x 33cm.) studio stamp on the reverse
PROV.: The Artist's Estate.

Christie's London, 25 June 1996 (54**) GBP 111,500	US$	171,935

LA PARADE oil and gouache on tracing paper, 21 5/8 x 19 5/8in. (64 x 50cm.) studio stamo on the reverse (ca 1931-39)

Christie's London, 28 November 1995 (46**) GBP 188,500	US$	294,854

FILLE (FEMME AUX CHEVEUX ROUX) watercolour, gouache and pastel on paper mounted at the edges on board, 27½ x 19 3/4in. (70 x 50cm.) sduc 'G. Rouault 1908' (1908)
PROV.: René Peltier, Paris; sale, Hôtel Drouot, Paris, Oct. 29, 1927, lot 59 (illustrated); M. van Leer (acquired at the above sale); Dikran G. Kélékian, New York; Mr. and Mrs. Lee A. Ault, New Canaan, Connecticut; M. Knoedler & Co., Inc., New York (acquired from the above Dec., 1951); Galerie Max Kaganovitch, Paris (acquired from the above, Feb., 1955); Acquired from the above by the late owner.

EXH.: Boston, The Institute of Modern Art, *Georges Rouault, Retrospective Loan Exhibition*, Oct.-Dec., 1940, p. 29, no. 61 (illustrated); The exhibition traveled to Washington, D.C., The Phillips Memorial Gallery, Dec., 1940-Jan., 1941, and San Francisco, Museum of Art, Feb.-March, 1941; New York, Mane Harriman Gallery, *Georges Rouoult, A Selection from the Traveling Loan Exhibition*, Apnl-May, 1941, no. 30 (illustrated); Chicago, The Art Institute, *Twenty-first International Exhibition of Watercolours*, May-Aug., 1942, no. 18; New York, Valentine Gallery, *The Lee Ault Collection, Modern Paintings*, April, 1944, no.48 (illustrated); New York, The Museum of Modem Art, *Georges Rouault, Paintings and Prints*, April-June, 1945, p. 115, no. 22 (illustrated, p. 50); New York, The Museum of Modern Art, *Paintings from New York Private Collections*, summer, 1946; Cleveland, Museum of Art, *Works of Georges Rouault, Retrospective Exhibition*, Jan.- March, 1953, p. 28; The exhibition traveled to New York, The Museum of Modern Art, March-May 1953 and Los Angeles, County Museum, July-Aug., 1953.
LIT.: 'Revue d'lnformation artistique', *Beaux-Arts*, 1927, p. 306; R. Frost and A. Crane, *Contemporary Art*, New York, 1942, p. 97 (illustrated); E. A. Jewell, *Georges Rouault*, New York, 1945, p. 16 (illustrated); J. T. Soby, *Georges Rouault*, New York, 1947, pp. 12 and 16, no. 22 (illustrated, p. 54); B. Dorival and I. Rouault, *Rouault, L'oeuvre peint*, Monte-Carlo, 1988, vol. I, no.,178 (illustrated, p. 64).
Christie's New York, 8 November 1995 (5**) US$ 354,500

| | US$ | 354,500 |

JUGES oil on board laid down on canvas, 7 3/8 x 6 5/8in. (18.8 x 16.8cm.) lr 'G Rouault' (1937)
PROV.: Ambroise Vollard, Paris; Wally Findlay Galleries, New York (acquired by the present owner, 1965).
LIT.: B.Dorival and I.Rouault, *Rouault, L'oeuvre peint*, Monte-Carlo, 1988, vol. II (1929-1956), no. 1932 (illustrated, p. 161).
Christie's New York, 8 November 1995 (230**) US$ 42,550

| | US$ | 42,550 |

PIERROT oil on board laid down on canvas, 13 1/4 x 10in.(33.6 x 25.4cm.) lr 'G Rouault' (1938)
PROV.: Galerie Hervé, Paris (acquired by Mrs. Sherburn m.Becker, 1964).
LIT.: B.Dorival and I.Rouault, *Rouault, L'oeuvre peint, Monte Carlo, 1988, vol. II (*1929-1956), no. 1985 (illustrated, p. 170).
Christie's New York, 8 November 1995 (234**) US$ 66,300

| | US$ | 66,300 |

ROUFFIO Paul (France 1855-1911) French
TRIO A CAPELLA oil on canvas, 47½ x 61½in. (120.7 x 156.2cm.) sll 'Paul Rouffio.'
Christie's New York, 2 November 1995 (177**) US$ 48,300

| | US$ | 48,300 |

ROUSSEAU Henri Emilien (1875-1933) French
ROTTERDAM, VUE DE HOLLANDE oil on canvas, 46 x 55cm. sd 'H. Rousseau 1902'
PROV.: Anon. Sale, Christie's Amsterdam, 16 November 1988, lot 96 (illustrated).
Christie's Amsterdam, 25 April 1996 (179*) NLG 13,800

| | US$ | 8,200 |

ROUSSEAU Théodore (Etienne Pierre Théodore) (Paris 1812-1867 Barbizon (Seine-et-Marne)) French
MONT SAINT MICHEL oil on paper, laid down on canvas, 7 3/4 x 13in. (19.7 x 33cm.) sll 'TH. Rousseau.'
PROV.: Possibly Durand-Ruel, Paris; Brightmeyer; M.A. Marmontel; sale, Hotel Drouot, Paris, March 28-29,; 1898, no. 104; With E.J. van Wisselingh, Amsterdam; With Hazlitt, Gooden & Fox, London.
EXH.: Paris, Cèrcle des Arts, Rue de Choiseul, June 1867, no. 36.
LIT.: *Notice des études peintes par Théodore Rousseau Exposées au Cèrcle des Arts*, Librairie de l`Academie des Bibliophiles, Paris, June; 1867, no. 36; A. Sensier, *Souvenirs sur Théodore Rousseau*, Paris, 1872, p. 35; C. Le Senne, *Introduction to catalogue for Marmontel sale*, p. 13; P. Dorbec, *Théodore Rousseau*, Paris, 1910, p. 38; This painting will be included in volume II of the forthcoming *catalogue raisonné on Rousseau* by Michel Schulman.
Christie's New York, 22 May 1996 (117**) US$ 59,700

| | US$ | 59,700 |

SOLEIL COUCHANT oil on canvas, 10 3/8 x 19 3/4in. (26.3 x 50.2cm.) slr 'TH. Rousseau'
PROV.: Wallbrown Collection, New York; sale 1886; S.D. Warren Collection; sale, Jan. 8, 1903, lot.
27, ($4,400; to Mrs. Macbeth); Private Collection, New York (Early 20th Century).
LIT.: This painting will be included in volume II of the *forthcoming catalogue raisonné on Rousseau*
by Michel Schulman.
Christie's New York, 22 May 1996 (122**) US$ 74,000   US$ 74,000

LES PRES-BOIS EN FRANCHE-COMTE. AU FOND, LES MONTAGNES DU DOUBS black
lead, pen and brown ink over brown washed paper, 5¼ x 8 1/8in. (13.3 x 20.7cm.) stamped ll 'TH.R'
PROV.: The Artist`s Studio; sale, Hotel Drouot, Paris, April 27-; May 2, 1868, no. 226; Alfred
Sensier, Paris; Rignault Collection; Georges Aubry Collection.
EXH.: Paris, Musée de l`Orangerie, *De Clouet à Matisse:Dessins Francais des Collections
Amèricaines*, 1958-59, no.,147 (lent by; Mr. and Mrs. John Reward).
LIT.: A. Terrasse, *L`Univers de Théodore Rousseau*, Paris, 1976; This painting will be included in
volume I of the forthcoming *catalogue raisonné on Rousseau* by Michel Schulman.
Christie's New York, 22 May 1996 (124**) US$ 10,925   US$ 10,925

WOODED RIVER LANDSCAPE pen and brown ink over washed paper, pen and brown ink framing
lines, 4½ x 5 1/8in. (11.4 x 13cm.) stamped ll 'TH.R'
LIT.: This drawing will be included in volume I of the forthcoming *catalogue raisonné on Rousseau*
by Michel Schulman as no. 228.
Christie's New York, 22 May 1996 (125**) US$ 7,820   US$ 7,820

PAYSAGE MONTAGNEUX DU CANTAL oil on paper laid down on board, 6 x 9½in. (15.3 x
24.1cm.) artist`s stamp lower right
PROV.: Collection Marquis de Brion; With the Hazlitt Gallery, 1959; Sir Anthony Blunt; Private
Collection.
EXH.: 1961, (November), London Hazzlit; Gallery, no. 16; 1982 (January), Norwich, University; of
East Anglia; 1982, (March), London Hazzlit Gallery, no. 15.
Phillips London, 12 March 1996 (34**) GBP 7,200   US$ 10,996

LE CHATEAU DES ROCHERS PRES VITRE oil on paper, laid down on canvas, 6 3/4 x 9 7/8in.
(17.2 x 25.1cm.) (painted 1831-1832 or 1835 during the artist`s visits to Normandy)
PROV.: Sir Anthony Blunt; With Kinnaird, 1960; W.J. Gaskin; Private Collection.
EXH.: 1956, London Hazzlit Gallery, no. 33; 1961 (November), London, Hazzlit Gallery, no. 19;
1982(January), Birmingham, Barber; Institute; 1982 (March), London, Hazzlit; Gallery, no. 5.
Phillips London, 12 March 1996 (35**) GBP 12,000   US$ 18,326

LANDSCAPE oil on canvas, 6 3/4 x 10 1/8in. (17.2 x 25.7cm.) slr 'TH. Rousseau'
PROV.: With Goupil, New York.
Christie's New York, 2 November 1995 (108**) US$ 17,250   US$ 17,250

**ROUSSEL Ker Xavier (Lorry-lès-Metz (Moselle) 1867-1944 L'Etang-la-Ville (Yvelines))
French**
L'ÉTÉ (SUMMER) oil 'a la colle' on paper laid down on canvas, 26 x 19 3/4in. (66 x 50cm.) slr
mono. 'K X R' (ca. 1925)
PROV.: Galerie Druet, Paris; De Hauke & Co., New York; Antoine Salomon, Paris; JPL Fine Arts,
London.
EXH.: Paris, Galerie Druet, *Sept artistes contemporains*, 10-21 February 1930, n° 75, reproduced;
Marseille, Musée Cantini, *Le peintre et sa palette*,
15 Oct.-5 Nov. 1973, no. 15 reproduced (exposition organised by Fondations Wildenstein);
Lausanne, Galerie Raymondin, *Bonnard-Vuillard-Roussel*, 13 March -25 April 1986.
LIT.: J.P. Monery, *Catalogue de l'exposition K.X. Roussel at the Annonciade*, Musée de Saint-
Tropez, 1993, reproduced p. 37.
Étude Tajan Paris, 13 December 1995 (29**) FRF 120,000   US$ 24,171

ROWLANDSON Thomas (London 1756-1827 London) British
THE OLD SWAN INN, WITH A VIEW OF PUTNEY BRIDGE BEYOND pen and ink and
watercolour, 10 x 17in. (25.4 x 43.2cm.)
PROV.: Sotheby's, New York, 1975.
Christie's London, 11 July 1995 (25**) GBP 11,500 — US$ 18,344

ROY Jean-Baptiste de {called} De Roy of Brussels (Brussels 1759-1839 Brussels) Belgian
A STILL-LIFE OF FLOWERS IN A VASE ON A LEDGE oil on canvas (oval), 53.5 x 48cm. sdlr
'JB DeRoy 1793'
Sotheby's Amsterdam, 6 May 1996 (43**) NLG 18,880 — US$ 11,009

ROY Marius (b.1833) French
AU QUARTIER, HUIT HEURES ET DEMIE oil on canvas, 59 x 79in. 9,150 x 200cm.) sd 'Marius
Roy 1883'
EXH.: Paris, Salon, 1883, no. 2127.
Christie's London, 15 March 1996 (42**) GBP 45,500 — US$ 69,487

ROYBET Ferdinand (Uzès (Gard) 1840-1920 Paris) French
LES PETITS PAGES oil on panel, 55 x 45.5cm. sll 'F. Roybet'
Étude Tajan Paris, 1 February 1996 (66*) FRF 43,000 — US$ 8,799

A STANDING CAVALIER HOLDING A YELLOW FLAG oil on panel, 32 x 25¼in. (81.2 x
64.2cm.) sul 'F.Roybet'
Christie's East, 13 February 1996 (140**) US$ 12,075 — US$ 12,075

RUBENS Sir Peter Paul (Pierre-Paul) (Siegen (Westphalia) 1577-1640 Antwerp) Flemish
STUDY OF A REARING HORSE oil on canvas, transferred from panel, 27½ x 18 3/4in. (69.9 x
47.6cm.)
Sotheby's New York, 11 January 1996 (66**) US$ 288,500 — US$ 288,500

**RUBENS Sir Peter Paul (Pierre-Paul) (& School) (Siegen (Westphalia) 1577-1640 Antwerp)
Flemish**
A PORTRAIT OF THE ARCHDUKE ALBERT OF AUSTRIA oil on oak panel, 39 3/4 x 29 3/4in.
(,101 x 75.4cm.) (ca. 1609-1614)
PROV.: Earl of Upper Ossory, Upper Ossory Park, Bedfordshire, by 1815 and until after 1830; Earl
of Strathmore, London; Earl of Harewood, London; With Spink, London; With Bottwieser, Berlin,
from whom bought by Baron Thyssen; Baron Heinrich Thyssen-Bornemisza, by 1930.
EXH.: London, The British Institution, 1815, lent by the Earl of Ossory; Munich 1930, no. 279;
Munich 1930; Graz, Grazer Künstlerhaus, *Rubens und sein Kreis*, 1954, no. 27; Cologne, Kunsthalle,
Weltkunst aus Privatbesit, 11 May - 4 April 1968, no. F. 23; Lausanne etc., 1986-7, no. 18.
LIT.: J. Smith, *A Catalogue Raisonné*, vol. II, 1830, p. 272, no. 917; L. Burchard, in G.
Gluck,Rubens, van Dyck und ihr Kreis, 1933, pp. 380-81; G. Gluck, in F. Thieme, U. Becker,
Allgemeines Lexikon der Bildenden Künstler, vol. XXIX, 1935, p. 141; R. Heinemann 1937, vol.I,
no. 358, vol. II, plate 104; G. Gluck, 'Rubens as Portrait Painter', *The Burlington Magazine*, vol.
LXXVI, 1940, pp. 177; H.G. Evers, *Peter Paul Rubens*, 1942, p. 491, note 79; M. De Maeyer,
Albrecht en Isabella en de Schilderkunst. Bijdrage, 1955, p. 111; R. Heinemann, *Sammlung* 1958,
no. 358; W. Prohaska, *Peter Paul Rubens 1577 - 1640, Ausstellung zur 400. Wiederkehr seines
Geburtstages*, exhibition catalogue, Vienna, Kunsthistorisches Museum, 1977, pp. 64-65; U. Peter,
'Zur Restaurierung des Rubens Gemaldes Erzherzog Albrecht von Osterreich', *Maltechnik-Restauro*,
vol. LXXXIV, 1978, pp. 178-181, reproduced; H. Althofer, 'Restaurierungszentrum' in Düsseldorfer
Museen, 1979, pp. 426-7, reproduced; H. Vlieghe, *Corpus Rubenianum, part XIX, Rubens Portraits*,
vol. II, 1987, p. 47, reproduced fig. 19; M.Jaffé, *Rubens*, 1990, p. 210, no. 327, reproduced.
Sotheby's London, 6 December 1995 (89**) GBP 111,500 — US$ 171,591

RUBENS Sir Peter Paul (Pierre-Paul) (circle of) (Siegen (Westphalia) 1577-1640 Antwerp) Flemish
STUDY OF A REARING HORSE oil on canvas, transferred from panel, 27½ x 18 3/4in. (69.9 x 47.6cm.)
PROV.: Sir Robert Walpole (1676-1745), Houghton Hall, by descent to his grandson from whom acquired along with his entire collection in 1772 by Catherine II of Russia, by descent until it became part of the State collection at the Hermitage and then sold on their behalf by Stroganoff, Leningrad (Sale: Lepke, Berlin, May 12-13, 1931, lot 83 as attributed to Anthonis van Dyck); where purchased by Ernest and Feodora Reinhardt, Berlin, Lugano and Riverdale, New York; from whom acquired by The Norton Galleries, New York; from whom acquired in December 1976 by the present owner.
EXH.: Cleveland, Cleveland Museum of Art, *Idea to Image*, entry by Mark M. Johnson, February-March 1980, pp. 68-72, illus., fig. 87.
LIT.: *Aedes Walpolianae*, 1752, p. 38 ('A Horse's Head, a fine Sketch by Vandyke'); F. Labensky, *Livret de la Galerie impériale de l'Hermitage de Saint-Petersbourg*, 1,838 (as by Rubens); John Smith, *Supplement to the Catalogue Raisonné*, 1842, part 9, p. 297, cat. no.,197 (as by Rubens); Baron B. de Koehne, *Ermitage Impérial: Catalogue de la Galerie des Tableaux*, 1863, cat. no. 637 (as by Van Dyck); G.F. Waagen, *Die Gemaldesammlung in der Kaiserlichen Ermitage zu St. Petersburg, nebst Bemerkungen uber andere dortige Kunstsammlungen*, 1864, p. 153 (as by Rubens); A. Somoff, *Ermitage Impérial: Catalogue de la Galerie des Tableaux- Deuxième Partie Ecoles Néerlandaises et Ecole Allemande*, 1901 [with editions published in 1897, 1908 and 1916], p. 87, cat. no.,637 (as by Rubens, and as on panel); Michael Jaffé, *Rubens and Italy*, 1977, p. 114R, note24 (as a fragment by Rubens, noting the relation of the present picture to a painting of the *Destruction of Pharoah's Army* in the Goldberg Collection, London, and the *Saint George Slaying the Dragon*, Prado, Madrid).
     Sotheby's New York, 11 January 1996 (66**) US$ 288,500

US$	288,500

RUBENS Sir Peter Paul (Pierre-Paul) (with Jan Brueghel the Younger 1601-1678) (Siegen (Westphalia) 1577-1640 Antwerp) Flemish
LANDSCAPE WITH PAN AND SYRINX oil on oakpanel, 23 x 37¼in. (58 x 94.5cm.)
PROV.: Graf Schonborn, Schloss Pommersfelden; Graf A.M. Schonborn, his sale, Paris, Drouot, 17-18 May 1867, lot 210, 7,000 francs; Salomon Goldschmidt, his (anonymous) sale, Paris, Georges Petit, 14-17 March 1898, lot 95, 9,200 francs to Max; Baron Rothschild, Vienna; Kunstsalon Franke, Leipzig, 1933; With Rosenberg & Stiebel, New York, circa 1960; Brian Jenks, Astbury Hall, Shropshire (according to Jaffé, see Literature); With Edward Speelman, London, 1979-80.
EXH.: On loan, London, National Gallery, 1980-1988; London, Agnew's, *Thirty-five Paintings from the Collection of the British Rail Pension Fund*, 8 November-14 December 1984, no. 3, reproduced in the catalogue; On loan, Leeds Castle, 1988-1995; Boston, Museum of Fine Art, Toledo, Museum of Art, *The Age of Rubens*, September 1993-April 1994, no. 17.
LIT.: G. Campori, *Riccolta di catal. ed. invent. ined.*, 1870, p.,191 (according to Sutton op. cit.); Possibly J. Denuce, 'Brieven en Documenten betreffend Jan Brueghel I en II', in *Bronnen voor de geschiedenis van de Vlaamsche kunst*, vol. III, 1934, p. 142; A. Pigler, *Barockthemen*, 1956, p. 191; M. Jaffé, 'Rubens and Raphael', in *Studies in Renaissance and Baroque Art presented to Anthony Blunt*, 1967, p. 100, reproduced fig. 3; M. Jaffé, *Rubens and Italy*, 1977, p. 23, note 50; K Ertz, *Jan Brueghel derAltere*, 1979, pp. 417, 420, 622-3, no. 384a, reproduced p. 419, fig.,504 (as by *Rubens and Jan Brueghel the Elder*, datable circa 1623); *The Burlington Magazine*, September 1980, p. 664, reproduced p. 646, fig. 63; K Ertz, *Jan Brueghel the Younger*, 1984, pp. 70, 81, 417-8, no. 256, reproduced p.,417 (as by *Rubens and Studio and Jan Brueghel the Younger*, datable to the late 1620s); M. Jaffé, *Rubens, Catalogo Completo*, 1989, p. 231, no. 442, reproduced, (as by *Rubens and Jan Brueghel the Elder*, painted circa 1617); P.C. Sutton, *The Age of Rubens*, catalogue of the Boston-Toledo exhibition, 1993, pp. 260-263, no. 17, reproduced in colour, (as by *Rubens and Jan Brueghel the Elder*).
     Sotheby's London, 5 July 1995 (42**) GBP 749,500

US$	1,195,565

RUBIN Reuven (1893-1974) Israelian (Roumanian)
ROAD TO JERUSALEM oil on canvas, 13 x 16 1/8in. (33 x 41cm.) sll 'Rubin', s again and titled on

the stretcher 'Rubin Road to Jerusalem'
PROV.: Acquired from the artist by Dr.Eugene A.Solow, 1964.
    Christie's New York, 1 May 1996 (326**) US$ 25,300   US$ 25,300

SPRINGTIME NEAR SAFED oil on canvas, 25½ x 36 7/8in. (64.8 x 92.7cm.) slc 'Rubin'; sd and
titled on the stretcher 'RUBIN SPRINGTIME NEAR SAFED 1966'
PROV.: Galerie Motte, Geneva (acquired by the present owner, ca. 1966).
EXH.: Geneva, Galerie Motte, *Rubin*, 1966.
    Christie's New York, 1 May 1996 (386**) US$ 92,700   US$ 92,700

CROWNING OF THE LAW oil on canvas, 36 x 29in. (91.5 x 73.6cm.) sul 'Rubin'; s in Hebrew, s
again, d and titled '1937' on the stretcher
PROV.: Frederic R. Mann, Philadelphia, from whom acquired by the present owner.
EXH.: Jerusalem, The Israel Museum, *Reuven Rubin Retrospectiove*, May 1966, no. 41. This
exhibition later travelled to Tel Aviv, Museum of Art; Philadelphia, Museum ofArt, 1967 (on loan).
LIT.: A. Werner, *Rubin*, Tel Aviv, 1958, p. 18 (illsutrated); S. Wilkinson, *Reuven Rubin*, New york,
1971, no. 36 (illustrated p. 65; incorrectly dated 1939); H. Gazmu *Reuven Rubin*, Tel Aviv, 1984,
p.,114 (illustrated).
    Christie's Tel Aviv, 12 October 1995 (12**) US$ 66,300   US$ 66,300

OLD OLIVE TREES IN SPRINGTIME oil on canvas, 40¼ x 30 1/8in. (102.2 x 76.5cm.) slr 'Rubin';
s again, titled and d on the reverse '1966/67'
PROV.: O'hana Gallery, London, from whom purchased by the family of the present owner in 1980.
    Christie's Tel Aviv, 12 October 1995 (65**) US$ 35,650   US$ 35,650

RABBI WITH TORAH oil on canvas, 10 3/4 x 14¼in. (27.2 x 36.2cm.) slr 'Rubin'
PROV.: Art Gallery Hadassa Klachkin, Tel Aviv, from whom bought by the father of the present
owner in the 1960's.
    Christie's Tel Aviv, 14 April 1996 (8**) US$ 19,550   US$ 19,550

POMEGRANATES NEAR OPEN WINDOW oil on canvas, 40 x 30in. (101.6 x 76.2cm.) slr 'Rubin',
s again in Hebrew, s again twice and titled on the reverse (ca. 1960)
    Christie's Tel Aviv, 14 April 1996 (24**) US$ 57,500   US$ 57,500

SAFED IN GALILEE oil on canvas, 38 1/8 x 62 5/8in. (97 x 159cm.) sdll 'Rubin 1939-1951', s again
in Hebrew, sd again and titled on titled stretcher
PROV.: Purchased directly from the Artist by the late owner in 1960.
EXH.: Tel-Aviv, Museum of Art, *Reuven Rubin-Retrospective Exhibition*, Spring, 1955.
    Christie's Tel Aviv, 14 April 1996 (34**) US$ 121,300   US$ 121,300

MOTHER AND CHILD oil on canvas, 32 x 25½in. (81.2 x 64.8cm.) sll 'Rubin', s again in Hebrew,
sd and titled '1939' (on the stretcher)
    Christie's Tel Aviv, 14 April 1996 (60**) US$ 36,800   US$ 36,800

RUGENDAS George Philipp I (Augsburg 1666-1742 Augsburg) German
THE LIBERATION OF VIENNA, AFTER THE BATTLE ON THE KAHLENBERG IN 1683 oil on
canvas,104 x 134cm.
LIT.: *Art & Business Sztuka Polskai Antyki*, 3/4, 1993, p. 91.
    Dorotheum Vienna, 17 October 1995 (189**) ATS 160,000   US$ 16,049

RUIJTEN Jan Michel (1813-1881) Belgian
A VIEW IN A STREET WITH NUMEROUS VILLAGERS oil on canvas, 47.5 x 60cm. sd 'Jan
ruijten fct 1867, Antwerpen'
    Christie's Amsterdam, 26 October 1995 (70**) NLG 20,700   US$ 13,052

RUISDAEL Jacob Isaaksz. van (Haarlem 1628/29-1682 Haarlem) Dutch
A BOSKY LANDSCAPE WITH PEASANTS SEATED OUTSIDE A THATCHED COTTAGE BY
A CORNFIELD oil on canvas, 22¼ x 27in. (56.8 x 68.2cm.) s with monogram lr
PROV.: William Wells, Redleaf, by 1824, his deceased sale, London, Christie's, 12-13 May 1848,
GBP,273 to Glendinning (but bought byJohn Smith, according to Hofstede de Groot);
John Smith, by whom sold in 1851 to George Fiedd, his {deceased) sale, London, Christie's, 10 July
1893, lot 33, GBPl,260 to Sedelmeyer; With Ch. Sedelmeyer, Paris, 1897/8, from whom bought by
Rodolphe Kann, Paris, until 1907, no. 76; Bought with the entire Kann collection in August 1907 by
Duveen Brothers, London; J. Pierpont Morgan, New York, by 1909; With Knoedler & Co., New
York, before 1946; With W.R. Drown, London.
EXH.: London, The British Institution, 1824, no. 97, lent by William Wells; Probably London,
Marlborough House, *exhibition of pictures from the collection of George Field* (according to
Waagen, see Literature); Manchester, *Art Treasures*, 1857, no. 852, lent by George Field; Possibly
London, Royal Academy, *Winter Exhibition*, 1885, no. 103; New York, Metropolitan Museum,
Hudson-Fulton Celebration, 1909, no. 108, reproduced in the catalogue, where dated 1650-60; On
loan, Doncaster Museum and Art Gallery, 1977-1993.
LIT.: J. Smith, *A Catalogue Raisonné*, vol. VI, 1835, p. 67, no. 213; Dr. G.F. Waagen, *Galleries and
Cabinets of Art in Great Britain*, vol. IV, 1857, p. 194, no. 2: *'This fine picture, the light clouds in
which remind us of Hobbema.'*; C. Sedelmeyer, *Catalogue of,300 Paintings by Old Masters*, 1898, p.
198, no. 177, reproduced p.199; E. Michel, 'La Galerie de M. Rudolphe Kann', in *Gazette des Beaux-
Arts*, vol. xxv, 1901, p. 394, reproduced p. 395; C. Sedelmeyer (ed.), *The Catalogue of the Rudolphe
Kann Collection*, 1907, vol. I, p. 77, no. 76, reproduced; C. Hofstede de Groot, *A Catalogue
Raisonné*, vol.IV, 1912, p. 44, no. 120; J. Rosenberg, *Jacob van Ruisdael*, 1928, p. 77, no. 88.

Sotheby's London, 5 July 1995 (46**) GBP 276,500	US$	441,059

A WATERFALL WITH BENTHEIM CASTLE BEYOND, TRAVELLERS ON A FOOTBRIDGE
NEARBY oil on canvas, 67.3 x 50.8cm. slr 'JvR(linked)uysDael'
PROV.: Prince Galitzin; M. Auguiot, Paris; Sale, Drouot, Paris, 1 March 1875, lot 26 (sold Ffr.
7650); M. Kann, Paris; with C. Sedelmeyer, Paris (exhibition catalogue,300 paintings, no. 187); R.
Wanamaker, Philadelphia, 1911; with E. Fischof, Paris; Sale, Galerie Georges Petit PAris, 14 June
1913, lot 62, with ill. (sold Ffr. 23,100); Baron M. von Nemes, München; Sale, Frederik Muller,
Amsterdam, 13 November 1928, lot 63 (sold Fl. 7,700 to Spanjaard); Anon. Sale, Frederik Muller,
Amsterdam, 28 November 1939, lot 980, with ill. (sold Fl. 6,000 to Kok).
LIT.: C. Hofstede de Groot, *A Catalogue Raisonné etc.*, IV, 1911, pp. 86/87, no. 284; J. Rosenberg,
Jacob van Ruisdael, 1928, p. 87, no. 240.

Christie's Amsterdam, 7 May 1996 (81**) NLG 460,000	US$	268,222

RIVER SCENE WITH A WATERFALL oil on canvas, unframed, 27 x 21in. (68.6 x 53.3cm.) s on
rock lr 'JR (in ligature) uisDael'
PROV.: Arhur George, Earl of Onslow, Richmond and West Clandon Place (Sale: Christie's,
London, July 22, 1893, lot 29, where the description of the painting is mistakenly reversed), there
purchased by; Conaghi, London; Paris, Charles Sedelmeyer by 1894; Karl von der Heydt, Berlin by
1894, until after 1904; Galerie van Diemen, Berlin by 1921; Forumato Arzemo, by July 1921;
Enrique Burgers; Alberto de Nunez; Galerie Saint Georges, from which acquired by the family of the
present owner on July 19, 1954.
EXH.: Düsseldorf, *Kunsthistorische Ausstellung Düsseldorf 1904: Meisterwerke westdeutscher
Malerei und andere Gemälde alter meister aus privatbesitz*, 1904, pp. 147-148, cat. no. 374.
LIT.: *Paintings by Old Masters*, Galerie Sedelmeyer, 1894, pp. 50-51, cat. no. 41, illus.; C. Hofstede
de Groot, *A Catalogue Raisonné.*, Vol. IV, 1912, p. 69, cat. no. 204; J. Rosenberg, *Jacob van
Ruisdael*, 1928, cat. no. 135.

Sotheby's New York, 11 January 1996 (41**) US$ 772,500	US$	772,500

A WOODED RIVER LANDSCAPE WITH A WATERFALL AND TRAVELLERS NEAR A
SMALL WOODEN BRIDGE oil on canvas, 24 5/8 x 19¼in. (62.5 x 48.9cm.) sll 'JRuisdael' (mid to
ate 1660's)
PROV.: Mrs. Brinton; Sale: Christie's London 9 July 1982, lot 69 (as *attr. to Ruidael*); The Edward

James Foundation, London; P. and D. Colnaghi, Ltd. London.

Sotheby's New York, 16 May 1996 (33**) US$ 332,500   US$ 332,500

HÚGELLANDSCHAFT MIT EINEM WASSERFALL oil on canvas, 70 x 56cm. sll 'Ruisdael'
PROV.: Slg. Baldus.

Lempertz Cologne, 18 May 1996 (1135**) DEM 280,000   US$ 182,541

A DUNE LANDSCAPE WITH A PEASANT AND HIS DOG ON A PATH IN THE
FOREGROUND AND A VIEW OF A VILLAGE BEYOND oil on oak panel, 27¼ x 35¼in. (69.3 x
91cm.) sdlr 'Ruisdael 1647'
PROV.: G. Wilbraham, Delamere House, Northwich, Cheshire, by 1835, presumably by descent at
Delamere to George Wilbraham, his sale, London, Christie's 18July 1930, lot 32, to Goudstikker;
With Goudstikker, Amsterdam, bears his number on the reverse: *2636*; his catalogue, 1930-1, no. 63;
Baron Heinrich Thyssen-Bornemisza, by 1930.
EXH.: London, British Institution, 1838, no.,135 (as painted when the artist was ten years old!);
Düsseldorf 1970-1, no. 45; Bielefeld, Kunsthalle, *Landschaften aus vier Jahrhunderten aus dem
Kunstmuseum Düsseldorf*, 1973, no. 8; The Hague, Mauritshuis, & Cambridge, Mass., The Fogg
Museum of Art, *Jacob van Ruisdael*, 1982, no. 5; Lausanne etc., 1986-7, no. 40.
LIT.: J. Smith, *A Catalogue Raisonné.*, vol. VI, 1835, p.43, no. 134; C. Hofstede de Groot, *A
Catalogue Raisonné.*, vol. VI, 1912. pp.280-1, no. 910; R. Heinemann 1937, vol. I, no.365, vol. II,
plate 156; R. Andree, *Kunstmuseum Düsseldorf - Malerei*, 1976, no. 7; S. Slive, H.R. Hoetink, *Jacob
van Ruisdael*, exhibition catalogue, 1982, pp. 36-7, no. 5, reproduced; E.J. Walford, *Jacob van
Ruisdael and the perception of Landscape*, 1991, p. 62.

Sotheby's London, 6 December 1995 (100**) GBP 419,500   US$ 645,583

A WOODLAND LANDSCAPE WITH A POND oil on canvas, 21 3/4 x 27½in. (55.6 x 69.9cm.) slr
'Ruisdael'
PROV.: With Galerie Heinemann, Munich, 1927; Baron Heinrich Thyssen-Bornemisza, by 1930.
EXH.: Norwich, Norwich museum, *Loan Collection of Pictures illustrating the Evolution of painting
from the seventeenth century to the present day*, 24 October-21 November 1925, no. 3; Munich 1930,
no. 286; Lausanne etc., 1986-87, no. 42.
LIT.: J. Rosenberg, *Jacob van Ruisdael*, 1928, p. 93, no. 348; R. Heinemann 1937, vol. I, no. 369.

Sotheby's London, 6 December 1995 (102**) GBP 78,500   US$ 120,806

A WOODED LANDSCAPE WITH TRAVELLERS ON A TRACK BY A POOL oil on inset panel,
8 3/8 x 11 7/8in. (21.3 x 30.2cm.) s mono. 'JVR' (around 1650)
PROV.: Possibly Jacques Ignatius de Roore (1668-1747), painter and picture dealer, The Hague;
sale, Verheyden, 4 Sept. 1747; Van Helsteuter (=van Eyl Sleyter?) Amsterdam; sale, Paris, 25 Jan.
1802 (1,330 francs); Earl Spring, Christie's, 29 Nov. 1974, lot 53 (7,000 gns).
LIT.: J. Smith, *A Catalogue Raisonné, etc.*, VI, London 1835, p. 31, no. 89; C. Hofstede de Groot, *A
Catalogue Raisonné*, etc., IV, London, 1912, p. 168, no. 532.

Christie's London, 7 July 1995 (45**) GBP 78,500   US$ 125,219

RUISDAEL Jacob Isaaksz. van (attr.) (Haarlem 1628/29-1682 Amsterdam) Dutch
A WOODLAND LANDSCAPE WITH A CLOISTER oil on canvas, 29 3/4 x 37¼in. (76 x 95cm.) s
with monogram lr
PROV.: With Galerie Sankt Lucas, Vienna, November 1928, as formerly in an Imperial collection,
and with attribution endorsed by Hofstede de Groot; Baron Heinrich Thyssen-Bornemisza, by 1930.
EXH.: Munich 1930, no. 285; Paris 1970, no. 38, plate 14; Lausanne etc.; Düsseldorf 1970-71, no.
45; On loan, Basel, Kunstmuseum, 16 January 1974, no. 4; Lausanne etc., 1986-87, no. 41.
LIT.: R. Heinemann 1937, vol. I, no. 368, as Ruisdael.

Sotheby's London, 6 December 1995 (101**) GBP 67,500   US$ 103,878

RUIZ Juan (18th Century, 2nd quarter)
A PANORAMIC VIEW OF NAPLES SEEN FROM THE BAY, WITH THE MOLO GRANDE IN
THE CENTRE; A PANORAMIC VIEW OF NAPLES SEEN FROM MERGELLINA, WITH

PIZZOFALCONE AND THE CASTEL DELL' OVO TO THE RIGHT, AND VESUVIUS
BEYOND both oil on canvas, each: 13 3/4 x 40 3/4in. (35 x 104cm.)
PROV.: The Counts Sandizell, Schloß Sandizell; Thence by descent.
 Sotheby's London, 5 July 1995 (81**) GBP 69,700   US$ 111,182

RUOPPOLO Giovan Battista (Napels 1626-1693 Napels) Italian
A) NATURA MORTA CON MELE, PESCHE E FICHI B) NATURA MORTA CON UVA, CEDRI
E ANGURIA (A PAIR) oil on canvas, 75 x 101cm. slr secondly 'G.B. Ruo.'
 Finearte Rome, 22 November 1995 (160**) ITL 138,000,000   US$ 86,629

RUOPPOLO Giovan Battista (attr.) (Napels 1626-1693 Napels) Italian
A STILL-LIFE OF PEACHES, PEARS, GRAPES, CHERRIES AND A RIPE MELON / A STILL-
LIFE OF PEACHES, GRAPES AND THE OPENED HALVES OF A WATER MELON oil on
canvas (a pair), each: 82 x 73.2cm. (before 1688)
 Sotheby's London, 5 July 1995 (135**) GBP 34,500   US$ 55,033

RUOPPOLO Giuseppe (1631-1710 c.) Italian
STILL-LIFE WITH WATERMELONS, GRAPES AND FLOWERS WITH A WOODED
LANDSCAPE SURROUNDING oil on canvas, 98 x 130cm.
 Bukowskis Stockholm, 29 November-1 December 1995 (239**) SEK 160,000   US$ 24,204

RUSCHA Ed (1937 b.) American
IN THE YEAR OF OUR LORD 1984 oil on canvas, 54 x 60in. (137.2 x 152.4cm.) sd and titled 'IN
THE YEAR OF OUR LORD 1984 Edward Ruscha 1978' on the reverse.
PROV.: Acquired directly from the artist.
EXH.: San Francisco Museum of Modern Art; New York, Whitney Museum of American Art;
Vancouver Art Gallery; The San Antonio Museum of Art, and Los Angeles County Museum of Art,
The Works of Ed Ruscha, March 1982-May 1983, p.139, no.48 (illustrated).
 Christie's New York, 22 February 1996 (77**) US$ 17,250   US$ 17,250

METROPOLITAIN oil on paper mounted on cardboard in artist`s frame, 8 x 9in. (22.2 x 18.5cm.) sll
'RUSCHA' dlr 'PARIS 1961'
PROV.: Acquired directly from the artist.
 Christie's New York, 15 November 1995 (243**) US$ 31,050   US$ 31,050

UNTITLED acrylic and oil on canvas-unframed, 60 1/8 x 60in. (152.7 x 152.4cm) sd 'Ed Ruscha
1987' on the reverse, sd and titled again 'RUSCHA 1987 'UNTITLED'' on the stretcher
PROV.: Acquired directly from the artist.
 Christie's New York, 8 May 1996 (337**) US$ 51,750   US$ 51,750

RUSKIN John, H.R.W.S. (London 1819-1900 Coniston, Lancashire) British
LUCERNE pencil and watercolour heightened with white, 5½ x 8 5/8in. (14 x 21.8cm.) sd 'J.Ruskin/
1863'
PROV.: By descent from the Artist.
 Christie's London, 2 april 1996 (81**) GBP 43,300   US$ 65,656

RUSS Robert (Vienna 1847-1922 Vienna) Austrian
MOTIV AM GARDASEE oil on canvas,104 x 76cm. slr 'Robert Russ'
 Dorotheum Vienna, 6 November 1995 (49**) ATS 750,000   US$ 75,235

MOTIV AUS SIRMIONE AM GARDASEE oil on canvas,101 x 75cm. s 'Robert Russ'
 Dorotheum Vienna, 17 April 1996 (488**) ATS 500,000   US$ 47,243

ARCO AM GARDASEE oil on panel, 54 x 74cm. sll 'Robert Russ'; s and titled on a label on the
everse
 Wiener Kunst Auktionen, 26 September 1995 (140**) ATS 440,000   US$ 42,770

SOMMERMORGEN IN ITALIEN mixed technique on cardboard, 73 x 92cm. slr 'Robert Russ'
Wiener Kunst Auktionen, 26 September 1995 (145**) ATS 280,000   US$ 27,217

RUSSELL George (1867-1935)
THE SWING oil on canvas, 21 32in. (53.3 x 81.5cm.) slr with monogram
Christie's London, 9 May 1996 (22**) GBP 16,100   US$ 24,379

RUTHART Karl Andreas (Dantzig 1630 c.-1703 after Aquila) German
STUDIES OF TWO HUNTING DOGS, A GLOSSY IBIS, THREE BATS AND TWO
SWALLOWS oil on canvas, 6 3/4 x 17½in. (17.2 x 44.5cm.)
PROV.: the Marchesi Strozzi, Palazzo Strozzi, Florence.
Christie's London, 8 December 1995 (293**) GBP 17,250   US$ 26,547

RUYSCH Rachel (Amsterdam 1664-1750 Amsterdam) Dutch
TULIPS, ROSES, PEONIES, HUNEYSUCKLE, AURICULAE, CONVOLVULI, COCKSCOMB
AND OTHER FLOWERS IN A GLASS VASE ON A MARBLE LEDGE WITH BUTTERFLIES
AND INSECTS oil on canvas, 24½ x 21 in. (62.3 x 53.2cm.) sd 'RACHEL RUYS / 171.'
PROV.: Anon. Sale, Christie's London 23 March 1973, lot 94 (30,000gns. to Colnaghi).
Christie's London, 8 December 1995 (36**) GBP 342,500   US$ 527,085

RUYSDAEL Jacob Salomonsz. van (Haarlem 1630 c.-1681 Haarlem) Dutch
A WOODED RIVER LANDSCAPE oil on panel, 56 x 84cm.
Sotheby's Amsterdam, 6 May 1996 (41**) NLG 18,880   US$ 11,009

RUYSDAEL Salomon Jacobsz. van (Naarden 1600 after-1670 Haarlem) Dutch
LANDSCAPE WITH NUMEROUS BOATS ON RIVER NEAR A TOWER oil on panel, 16½ x
22in. (42 x 56cm.) sdll 'SVRuijsDAEL 1662'
PROV.: K.W. Bachstitz, The hague; D. Heinemann, Munich, 1930; Jules Porgès, Paris; Benjamin
Siegel, Detroit; Anonymous sale, New York, Sotheby's, 9 June 1983, lot 152, where purchased by
the present owner.
LIT.: W. Stechow, *Salomon van Ruysdael*, 1938, p. 131, no. 529; W. Stechow, *Salomon van
Ruysdael*, 1975, p.151, no. 529.
Sotheby's London, 5 July 1995 (15**) GBP 47,700   US$ 76,089

A *WIJDSCHIP* AND OTHER SMALL DUTCH VESSELS ON THE RIVER WAAL, WITH THE
TOWN OF GORINCHEM TO THE RIGHT oil on oak panel, 16½ x 14 3/4in. (42 x 37.3cm.) s with
monogram on the gunwale of the vessel ll 'SVR', and d on the leeboard of the same vessel '1659'
PROV.: Laurent-Richard, his sale, Paris, Durand-Ruel, 23-25 May 1978, lot108 (sold for FRF
4,950); Prince Paul Demidoff, San Sonato, near Florence, his sale on the premises, S. Donato near
Florence, Le Roy etc., 15 March-10 April 1880, lot 1106 (sold for 6,100 lire); Possibly J.F. Du Sart,
deceased, his sale, Brussels, Le Rot, 26-28 June 1884, lot 129; Comtesse de Labadye, Paris; with
François Kleinberger, Paris, 1903; Jonkheer Ch. van de Poll (deceased), Haarlem, by 1915;
Anonymous sale, Amsterdam, Sotheby Mak van Waay, 7 November 1978, lot 92.
EXH.: On loan, London, Geffrye Museum, 1981-1995.
LIT.: *Onze Kunst*, no. 28, 1,915 (illustrated p. 77); W. Stechow, *Salomon van Ruysdael*, revised ed.,
1975, p. 77, no. 57 (as signed in monogram, but with no mention of date).
Sotheby's London, 5 July 1995 (32**) GBP 1,541,000   US$ 2,458,127

CAVALRY ATTACKING INFANTRY oil on canvas, sdlr 'SRuysdael/1,650 (3?)
Sotheby's London, 5 July 1995 (203**) GBP 6,900   US$ 11,007

FISHERMEN IN A ROWING BOAT WITH A FERRY SETTING OUT FROM A LANDING
STAGE, ON A CLOUDY DAY ON SUMMER oil on panel, 62 x 89cm. sdll 'S.vR 1641'
PROV.: J.B. Foucart, Valenciennes (his stamp on the reverse); Sale, 12 October 1898, lot 98 (sold
FRF 1425); with C. Hoogendijk, Amsterdam (exhibited 1899, no. 21); His sale, Frederik Muller
Amsterdam, 14 May 1912, lot 73, with ill. (sold NLG 3,400); Madame Joseph Fievez (†); Sale,

Galerie Fievez Brussels, 30 April 1947, lot 83, where acquired by the present owner.
EXH.: Amsterdam, Rijksmuseum, 1907-1912, on loan from C. Hoogendijk, inv.no. 2082A.
LIT.: W. Stechow, *Salomon van Ruysdael*, 1975, p. 119, no. 332.

Christie's Amsterdam, 7 May 1996 (76**) NLG 207,000   US$ 120,700

A WOODED LANDSCAPE WITH A DROVER WATERING HIS HERD AND TRAVELLERS AT AN INN, A CHURCH IN THE DISTANCE oil on canvas, 33 3/8 x 39½in. (84.8 x 100.5cm.) s mono. 'S.VR'
PROV.: King Leopold II of the Belgians; (Probably) T.V. Golding, Studley Court, Southport; Christie's, 12 Dec. 1908, lot 60 (145gns. to the Sackville Gallery); with F. Kleinberger, Paris (catalogue, 1911, no. 66, illustrated, described as signed); Stefan von Auspitz, Vienna;with K.W. Bachstitz, The Hague (Bulletin, 19 illustrated); with Agnew's, by whom acquired from the above and sold to Lady Ludlow, Warren Towers, Newmarket,Cambridgeshire; Christie's, 18 Feb. 1944, lot112 (800gns. to Agnew's); with Agnew's, from whom acquired by the father of the present owners.
EXH.: Toledo, Ohio, 1912, no. 209.
LIT.: W. Stechow, *Salomon van Ruysdael*, Berlin, 1975, p.94, no. 174.

Christie's London, 8 December 1995 (19**) GBP 38,900   US$ 59,865

A RIVER LANDSCAPE WITH PEASANTS AND CATTLE ON A FERRY oil on canvas, 31½ x 43½in, (80 x 110.5cm.) sd 'SVRVYSDAEL/165.'
PROV.: Cardinal Fesch, Archbishop of Lyon, Rome (Catalogue, 1841, no. 222); sale, Rome, 17 March 1845 et. seq., lot207 (,195 scud); Private Collection, U.S.A., from ca. 1870; with Rosenberg and Stiebel, New York, 1972.
LIT.: W. Stechow, Salomon van Ruysdael, Berlin, 1938, p. 127, no. 373C, and p. 133, no. 411.

Christie's London, 8 December 1995 (22**) GBP 135,500   US$ 208,526

AFFORESTED DUNE-LANDSCAPE WITH FARMHOUSES oil on panel, 37 x 50cm.
PROV.: Sold at Dorotheum, Wien, 1959 (Ös 78.000.); Private collection USA.
EXH.: Kunsthandel Goudstikker; Rotterdam, 1927 (no. 58), Amsterdam 1927 (do.); no. 112; Galerie A.S. Drey München; Rosenberg & Striebel in New York, 1950;.
LIT.: Wolfgang Stechow, *Salomon van Ruysdael*,1938, p. 134, no.,550 *Hütte hinter Weiden*; Wolfgang Stechow, *Salomon van Ruysdael*, 1975, p. 155, no.,550 *Hütte hinter Weiden*.

Dorotheum Vienna, 17 October 1995 (117**) ATS 250,000   US$ 25,076

A RIVER LANDSCAPE WITH RIDERS AND A COACH ON THE TOWPATH, AND FISHERMEN UNLOADING THEIR CATCH oil on oak panel, 17 3/4 x 27in. (44.9 x 68.5cm.) sdll 'S.VR 1649'
PROV.: Bears an unidentified seal on the reverse.

Sotheby's London, 6 December 1995 (38A**) GBP 221,500   US$ 340,874

A *WIJDSCHIP* AND OTHERS SMALL DUTCH VESSELS ON AN ESTUARY oil on oak panel, 16¼ x 20 3/4in. (41.5 x 53cm.) slc ini. 'SR' (ca. 1650)
PROV.: M Lefèvre Bougon, Amiens his sale, Paris, Mannheim, *et al*, 1-2 April 1895, lot 50, (Très remarquable tableau de la plus parfaite conservation et d'un effet lumineux et charmant') 4,050 francs; Krupp von Bohlen und Hahlbach, Villa Hügel, Essen, by 1937, bears their inventory number *KH,157* on the reverse; Thence by descent to the present owner.
EXH.: Essen, Villa Hügel, 1953-4 (without catalogue); Essen, Villa Hügel, *Aus der Gemäldesammlung der Familie Krupp*, 30 April- 31 October 1965, no. 81.
LIT.: W. Stechow, *Salomon van Ruyrdael*, 2nd. ed., 1975, p. 115, no. 310, as datable ca. 1650.

Sotheby's London, 6 December 1995 (8**) GBP 716,500   US$ 110,264 7

A LANDSCAPE WITH TRAVELLERS BY A VILLAGE oil on panel, 20½ x 32 3/4in. (52 x 83.4cm.)

Sotheby's London, 6 December 1995 (136**) GBP 40,000   US$ 61,557

A RIVER LANDSCAPE WITH PEASANTS FERRYING CATTLE AND TUMBLEDOWN
BUILDINGS ON THE BANK BEYOND oil on oak panel, 10½ x 22½in. (27 x 57.5cm.) when it was
sold in 1986 this picture was described as signed and dated 1632
PROV.: Anonymous sale, London Sotheby's, 9 April 1986, lot 49.
Sotheby's London, 6 December 1995 (238**) GBP 36,700   US$ 56,479

A WOODED LANDSCAPE WITH CHILDREN PLAYING ON A PATH BY A COTTAGE AS
TRAVELLERS ON COACHES APPROACH oil on panel, 21 7/8 x 27in. (55.6 x 68.6cm.) sd
'SVRuysdael/1658' (SVR in monogram)
PROV.: Major Richard Rawnsley, Will Vale, Lincolnshire; Christie's, 16 April, 1937, lot152
(252gns. to Vicars); Anon. Sale, Christie's, 29 June 1951, lot128 (441gns. to Evelyn); J. Singer,
London, 1951; with Eugene Slatter, London (Dutch and Flemish Masters, 1952, no. 7); Anon. Sale
(as property of M.S.), Galerie Charpentier, Paris, 24 March 1953, lot 56; Anon. Sale, Sotheby's, 12
Dec. 1984, lot 64 (sold for GBP40,000).
EXH.: Boston, Museum of Fine Arts, *Prized Possessions: European Paintings from Private
Collections of Friends of the Museum of Fine Arts, Boston*, 17 June-16 Aug.1992, p. 204, no. 130,
and p. 41, pl. 40, illustrated in colour (catalogue by P.C. Sutton).
LIT.: llustrated London News, 26 April 1952; W. Stechow, *Salomon van Ruysdael*, Berlin, 1975, p.
106, no. 244a.
Christie's London, 7 July 1995 (42**) GBP 51,000   US$ 81,353

RYBACK Issachar Ber (1897-1935)
POULES AUX CHAMPS oil on canvas, 19¼ x 35 7/16in. (49 x 91cm.) slr 'I.Ryback', inscr. with
artist's address and titled 'Coq et poules' on the reverse
PROV.: a gift from the wife of the artist to the present owner's mother.
Phillips London, 24 June 1996 (19**) GBP 4,800   US$ 7,402

RYCKAERT David II (or I) (Antwerp 1586-1642 Antwerp) Flemish
SILVER-GILT COVERD CUPS, A TAZZA, A NAUTILUS CUP, AN OVER-TURNED DISH,
BEAKERS' PORCELAIN DISHES AND A VASE, AND A CUP ON A WOODEN BOX WITH
SHELLS, CORAL, COINS AND JEWELLERY ON A COVERED TABLE oil canvas, 40 3/8 x
53½in. (103.5 x 136cm.) sd 'DAVDT. RYCKAERTS./.1616'
Christie's London, 8 December 1995 (38A**) GBP 139,000   US$ 213,912

RYCKHALS Frans (attr.) (Middelburg 1600-1647) Dutch
INTERIOR OF A STABLE oil on panel, 42 x 55cm.
Étude Tajan Paris, 18 December 1995 (114**) FRF 38,000   US$ 7,654

RYCKX Lambrecht (active 16th century) Flemish
MARIA WITH CHILD IN A LANDSCAPE oil on panel, 53 x 45.5cm.
Dorotheum Vienna, 6 March 1996 (110**) ATS 110,000   US$ 10,581

RYMAN Robert (Nashville (Tennessee) 1930 b.-) American
UNTITLED casein and graphite on paper, 12 x 12in. (30.4 x 30.4cm.) sdlr 'R. Ryman 58' s again
'Robert Ryman ' on the panel (1958)
PROV.: Private collection New York.
Christie's New York, 15 November 1995 (254**) US$ 21,850   US$ 21,850

INITIAL oil on foamcore with wood blocks, 23 x 23in. (58.4 x 58.4cm.) sd and titled 'Ryman 89
'INITIAL" on the reverse
PROV.: The Pace Gallery, New York; Private collection, New York.
EXH.: New York, The Pace Gallery, *Robert Ryman: New Paintings*, April-May 1990, no. 8
(illustrated); London, Tate Gallery; Madrid, Museo Nacional Centro de Arte Reina Sofia; New York,
The Museum of Modern Art; San Francisco, Museum of Modern Art and Minneapolis, Walker Art
Center, *Robert Ryman*, Feb. 1993-Oct. 1994, pp. 200-201, no. 77 (illustrated).
Christie's New York, 15 November 1995 (338**) US$ 96,000   US$ 96,000

513

RYSBRACK Pieter Andreas (1690-1748) Flemish
A VIEW OF CHISWICK GARDENS, RICHMOND, FROM ACROSS THE NEW GARDENS
TOWARDS THE BAGNIO oil on canvas, 24 x 42in. (61 x 106.7cm) (1729-31)
PROV.: Presumably painted for Lord Burlington's eldest sister, Lady Elizabeth Boyle who married
Sir Henry Bedingfeld, 3rd Bt. and by descent in the Bedingfeld family at Oxburgh Hall, Norfolk until
1952.
LIT.: J. Harris, *The Artist and the Country House*, London, 1979, p.183, no. 187g.C.M. Sicca, 'Lord
Burlington at Chiswick: Architecture and Landscape', *Garden History*, 1982, X, no.1, p.55, illus.
fig.16; J. Harris, *The Palladian Revival: Lord Burlington, His Villa and Garden at Chiswick*, 1994,
p.221, no. 82 (discussed and illustrated, but recorded as 'present whereabouts unknown', and not
included in the accompanying exhibition).
Christie's London, 10 November 1995 (37**) GBP 51,000   US$ 79,775

RYSSELBERGHE Théo van (Ghent 1862-1926 Saint-Clair) Belgian
LA PLAGE DE MORGAT, BRETAGNE oil on canvas, 46 x 55cm. s (in monogram) dlr '1904' and
inscr. withe titleon the stretcher
PROV.: Hermes, Frankfurt am Main.
Christie's Amsterdam, 6 December 1995 (213**) NLG 43,700   US$ 27,079

FEMME NUE ASSISE oil on canvas, 39 3/8 x 25½in. (,100 x 65cm.) sur with monogram, dur '08'
(1908)
PROV.: Galerie Georges Giroux, Brussels (1917); De Maere, Belgium; Le Soly, Paris; Anon. sale,
Sotheby's, London, 3 December 1986, lot 220.
LIT.: Ronald Feltkamp will include this painting in his forthcoming *Van Rysselberghe catalogue
raisonné*.
Christie's New York, 1 May 1996 (179**) US$ 25,300   US$ 25,300

SAINT TROPEZ, VUE DE LA CHAPELLE ST. ANNE oil on canvas, 28 3/4 x 36¼in. (73 x 92cm.)
s mono. 'VR' (ca 1920)
Christie's London, 10 November 1995 (251**) GBP 43,000   US$ 67,261

FEMME NUE, BRAS ÉLÉVÉS oil on canvas, 25 x 18 7/8in. (63.5 x 48cm.) sll with mono. 'VR'
Christie's East, 7 November 1995 (25**) US$ 11,500   US$ 11,500

SABATINI Lorenzo (1530 c.-1576) Italian
THE HOY FAMILY WITH ST. JOHN oil on panel, ,100 x 71cm.
Christie's Rome, 4 June 1996 (572**) ITL 50,000,000   US$ 32,425

SABBATINI Andrea, {called Andrea da Salerno} (ca. 1480-1530) Italian
MADONNA AND CHILD IN A MANDORLA OF ANGELS APPEARING TO SAINT
SEBASTIAN AND ROCH IN A LANDSCAPE WITH ANCIENT RUINS tempera (and oil) on
panel, transferred to canvas, 70 x 47½in. (177.8 x 120.7cm.) slc ini. 'B.F.M.D. (X X) IIII.' (ca. 1524)
LIT.: M. Rotilli, *L'Arte del Cinquecento nel Regno di Napoli*, 1976, pp. 127-27, p. 103-,107
(illustrated).
Sotheby's New York, 16 May 1996 (10**) US$ 68,500   US$ 68,500

SABUROSUKE Okada (Saga Prefecture 1869-1939) Japanese
VIEW OF NICE watercolour on paper framed and glazed, 9 x 12in. (23 x 30.6cm.) slr 'Okada'
Christie's New York, 31 October 1995 (455**) US$ 16,100   US$ 16,100

**SACCHIS Giovanni Antonio de', {called} Pordenone (Pordenone 1483/84 c.-1539 Ferrara)
Italian**
BUST OF A BEARDED MAN, HALF-LENGHT oil on canvas, 45.3 x 38.7cm.
Finearte Milan, 12 March 1996 (68*) ITL 35,650,000   US$ 22,809

SADÉE Philip Lodewijk Jacob Frederik (The Hague 1837-1904 The Hague) Dutch
WAITING FOR FATHER oil on paper laid down on panel, 30 x 25cm. sll 'Ph Sadée'
Christie's Amsterdam, 7 September 1995 (228*) NLG 10,350   US$ 6,317

SADLER Walter Dendy (1854-1923) British
AFTER DINNER, REST AWHILE oil on canvas, 34 x 48in. (86.3 x 122cm.) s 'W. Dendy Sadler
PROV.: With William Rivett, Liverpool.
EXH.: London, Royal Academy 1904, no. 841.
LIT.: Henry Blackburn (ed.) *Royal Academy Notes*, 1904, p.32.
Christie's London, 29 March 1996 (92**) GBP 31,050   US$ 47,419

SAETTI Bruno (Bologna 1902-1984) Italian
NATURA MORTE CON CHITARRA oil on canvas, 80 x 100cm. sdlr 'Saetti 55'
PROV.: Roma, *Vll Quadriennale Nazionale d'Arte di Roma*, 1955-1956, cat., p. 20; Monaco di
Baviera, Grosse Hause Der Kunst Kunstausstellung, *Arte Italiana dal 1910 ad oggi*, 7 June-5
September 1957; Bologna, Galleria d'Arte Moderna *Bruno Saetti*; Madrid, Ateneo, Sala de Santa
Caterina, *Bruno Saetti*, 1958, cat.no. Vll (illustrated).
EXH.: In *Il Popolo*, Roma 24 February 1961 (illustrated).
Christie's Milan, 20 November 1995 (141**) ITL 42,426,000   US$ 26,633

SAFTLEVEN Cornelis (Gorinchem 1607-1681 Rotterdam) Dutch
ANIMALS WAITING FOR EMBARKMENT IN NOAH'S ARK oil on panel, 42.5 x 53.5cm. sd
'C.Saftleven 1663'
PROV.: Sale Frederik Muller, Amsterdam, 5 June 1914, lot 65 (dfl. 65); Dr. Ir. A.M. De Wild, 's-
Gravenhage; A. van Stolk, Rotterdam.
LIT.: W. Schulz, *Cornelis Saftleven*, 1978, p. 196, no. 536.
Dorotheum Vienna, 6 March 1996 (269**) ATS 80,000   US$ 7,695

SAFTLEVEN Cornelis (Gorinchem 1607-1681 Rotterdam) Dutch
A CAT PEEPING THROUGH A FENCE oil on panel, 11 x 13.5cm. s with ini. and dlr 'CS 1666'
PROV.: Anon. sale, Rotterdam, Vis. 25 June 1800, lot 75; A. Vermande, his widow's sale, Haarlem,
Engesmet, 21 September 1820, lot 2; Anon. sale, Rotterdam, Lamme, 5 November 1868, lot 70; Th.
Boeree, Bergen op Zoom; C.H. de Loches Rambonnet, Hilversum, thence by descent.
LIT.: W. Schultz, *Cornelis Saftleven*, 1978, p. 220, no. 619.
Sotheby's Amsterdam, 14 November 1995 (1***) NLG 413,000   US$ 260,28•

SAFTLEVEN Herman III (Rotterdam 1609-1685 Utrecht) Dutch
A RHENISH CAPRICCIO WITH SMALL VESSELS NEAR THE BANK OF A RIVER oil on oak
panel, 8¼ x 11in. (21 x 28in.) sdll mono. 'HS 1675'
PROV.: Anon. sale, Stockholm, Bukowskis, 15 March 1933, lot ,164 (as dated 1635); With S.
Nystad, The Hague, 1967, (as dated 1670); Anonymous sale, Amsterdam, Mak van Waay, 15-17
November 1976, lot 49 (as dated 1636); With Gebr. Douwes, Amsterdam, 1977; With Julie Kraus,
Paris, 1978.
EXH.: Delft, Antiekbeurs, 1977, catalogue p. 160, (as dated 1675).
LIT.: G.L.M. Daniels, in *Antiek*, March 1981, pp. 461-8, reproduced, (as dated 1675); W. Schulz,
Herman Saftleven, 1982, p. 177, no. 199.

Sotheby's London, 6 December 1995 (262**) GBP 11,500	US$	17,698

A RHENISH RIVER LANDSCAPE AT SUNSET oil on panel, 8¼ x 10¾in. (20.7 x 27.7cm.) sdll
mono. 'HSL 1675'
PROV.: J.B. van Lanken, Antwerp, 1835 (according to the label on the reverse); James Whatman,
Vg., his sale, London, Christie's, 20 February 1882, lot 38, to Colnaghi; Anonymous sale, London,
Christie's, 19 July 1973, lot 38, to Temmerman; Anonymous sale, Amsterdam, Christie's, 10
November 1992, lot 132.
EXH.: W. Schulz, *Herman Saftleven 1609-1685*, 1982, p. 177, no. 197.

Sotheby's London, 6 December 1995 (263**) GBP 27,600	US$	42,475

SAFTLEVEN Herman III (attributed to) (Rotterdam 1609-1685 Utrecht) Dutch
PEASANTS RETURING FROM MARKET ON A MOUNTAIN PATH, HARVESTERS AT
WORK IN A FIELD BEYOND, A TOWN AND A VALLEY IN THE DISTANCE. oil on canvas,
51.4 x 61.8cm. sdlr 'HS (linked) 1650(?)'

Christie's Amsterdam, 7 May 1996 (130**) NLG 28,750	US$	16,764

SAIN Edouard Alexandre (Cluny (Saone-et-Loire) 1830-1910 Paris) French
DRESSING UP THE DOLL oil on canvas, 19¾ x 24 1/8in. (50.2 x 61.3cm.) sll 'E. Sain'

Christie's New York, 2 November 1995 (70**) US$ 20,700	US$	20,700

SAINT-ANDRÉ Simon Renard de (Paris 1613/1614-1677) French
A VANITAS STILL-LIFE WITH A PALETTE AND BRUSHES, PIECES OF SCULPTURE,
CORAL AND AN OPEN BOOK AND OTHER OBJECTS oil on canvas, 21 x 24in. (53.2 x
61.4cm.)

Sotheby's London, 6 December 1995 (4**) GBP 20,700	US$	31,856

SAINT-PHALLE Niki de (1930 b.) American (French)
TIR AVEC L'AVION (SHOOTING WITH AN AEROPLANE) mixed media on canvas painted with
colours, 51 x 76¾in. (,130 x 195cm.) (1961)
PROV.: Galerie Beaubourg, Paris.

Étude Tajan Paris, 13 December 1995 (78**) FRF 135,000	US$	27,193

UNTITLED mixed media assemblage on board, 18½ x 15¾in. (47 x 40cm.) s 'N. de Saint Phalle,
Mai '61'
PROV.: a gift from the Artist to the present owner in 1961.

Christie's London, 19 March 1996 (14**) GBP 16,100	US$	24,588

SAITO Yoshishige (1904 b.) Japanese
WORK(RED) oil on wood panel, 54 3/16 x 47 5/8in. (137.7 x 121cm.) s 'Y. Saito'; roman script,
'Yoshishige'; Japanese script, d '64'
PROV.: Tokyo Gallery, Tokyo, Japan.

Christie's New York, 31 October 1995 (484**) US$ 101,500	US$	101,500

WORK (RED) oil on wood, 13 x 9¼in.(33 x 23.5cm.) s 'Y. Saito'; roman script, 'Yoshi'; Japanese
script, d '62'

PROV.: Tokyo Gallery, Tokyo, Japan.
LIT.: Tokyo Metropolitan Art Museum, Tochigi Prefectural Museum of Fine Arts, The Museum of Modern Art, Hyogo; Ohara Museum of Art, Fukui Prefectural Museum of Art, *Saito Yoshishige Exhibition* 1984, exhibition catalogue (Tokyo: above 5 museums, 1984), pl. 126.
Christie's New York, 31 October 1995 (486**) US$ 23,000 — US$ 23,000

SALA Emile Grau (1911-1975) Spanish
EL BAILE oil on canvas, ,100 x 81cm. sd '34'; sd 'Noviembre 1934' on the reverse
Sotheby's Madrid, 23 November 1995 (64**) ESP 4,935,000 — US$ 40,566

ESPAGNOLES DEVANT LE BALCON oil on canvas, 23 3/8 x 29in. (59.5 x 73.6cm.) slr 'Grau Sala'; sd and titled on the reverse 'Grau Sala 1963. Espagnoles devant le balcon'
Christie's East, 30 April 1996 (203**) US$ 23,000 — US$ 23,000

SALA Paolo (Milan 1859-1929 Milan) Italian
FIORI E MURANO oil on canvas, 27¾ x 37in. (70.5 x 94cm) s 'Paolo Sala'
Christie's London, 17 November 1995 (153**) GBP 8,280 — US$ 12,952

SALEH Raden Sarief Bastaman (Semarang 1814-1880 Buitenzorg (Dutch Indies)) Javan
A PORTRAIT OF A GIRL WITH HER DOG oil on canvas, 78.5 x 67.5cm. sdlr 'Raden Saleh/1856'
Sotheby's Amsterdam, 23 April 1996 (62***) NLG 106,200 — US$ 63,105

SALES Carl von (Koblenz 1791-1870 Fürstenfeld) German
PORTRÄT DER PRINZESSIN ELISABETH VON BAYERN, SPÄTERE KÖNIGIN VON PREUßEN oil on canvas, 72.5 x 60cm. sd 'C. v. Sales 1827'
Dorotheum Vienna, 6 November 1995 (30**) ATS 280,000 — US$ 28,088

PORTRÄT DES KÖNIG MAX JOSEF I VON BAYERN (POSTHUM ENTSTANDEN) oil on canvas, 68 x 55cm. sd 'C. v. Sales 1829'
Dorotheum Vienna, 6 November 1995 (31**) ATS 220,000 — US$ 22,069

SALIETTI Alberto (Ravenna 1892-1961 Chiavari) Italian
ARLECCHINO E BALLERINA tempera on board, ,147 x 140cm. slr 'Salietti'
Finearte Milan, 12 December 1995 (275**) ITL 13,800,000 — US$ 8,657

SALISBURY Frank Owen (London, active 1874-1962) British
THE SEN SISTERS oil on canvas (oval), 60in. (152.5cm.) (diameter) sll 'Frank O. Salisbury' (ca 1928)
PROV.: Given to the Metropolitan Museum of Art, New York, by the artist in 1954.
EXH.: Liverpool, Walker Art Gallery, *Fifty Sixth Autumn Exhibition of Modern Art*, 1928, no.4, p.13 (illustrated) London, Grafton Galleries, *Recent Paintings by Frank Owen Salisbury*, June 1929, no.78; Paris, *Salon de Societé des Artistes Français*, 1932, no.2159; London, Royal Institute Galleries, *Portraits and Pageants: An Exhibition of the Art of Frank Owen Salisbury*, May 1953, no.20; New York, Barnard College, *Feminine Elegance*, Nov.-Dec 1958; New York, Metropolitan Museum of Art, Costume Institute.
Dec. 1982-August 1983 (on loan).
LIT.: F.O. Salisbury, *Portrait and Pageant Kings, Presidents, and People*, London, 1953, p.2 (illustrated)
Christie's London, 21 November 1995 (228**) GBP 89,500 — US$ 139,997

SALLE David (1952 b.) American
SAILORS SET ON SHORE acrylic on canvas, 60 x 42in. (152.5 x 106.6cm.) s titled d "Sailors Set on Shore' David Salle 1991' on the reverse
PROV.: Gagosian Gallery, New York.
Christie's New York, 15 November 1995 (306**) US$ 34,500 — US$ 34,500

FALSE QUEEN felt hat, acrylic and oil on canvas, 96 x 72in. (,244 x ,183 sd and titled on the reverse '1992'
PROV.: Gagosian Gallery, New York; Galeria de Arte Soledad Lorenzo, Madrid.
LIT.: Richard Pandiscio, *David Salle*, New York 1994, p. 194, no. ,102 (illustrated in colour).
    Christie's London, 30 November 1995 (49**) GBP 51,000   US$ 79,775

SALUCCI Alessandro (Florence 1590-1657 after Rome) Italian
THE RAPE OF HELENA oil on canvas, 97 x 135cm.
    Christie's Rome, 21 November 1995 (256**) ITL 44,000,000   US$ 27,621

SALVI Giovan Battista Salvi, {called} Sassoferrato (Sassorerrato 1609-1685 Rome) Italian
MADONNA WITH CHILD AND ANGELS oil on canvas, 29½ x 23¾in. (74.9 x 60.3cm.) inscr. ll with the number '255'
    Sotheby's New York, 16 May 1996 (52**) US$ 101,500   US$ 101,500

THE MADONNA AND CHILD WITH THE INFANT SAINT JOHN THE BAPTIST AND SAINT ELIZABETH oil on canvas, (an oval), 19¾ x 14½in. (50.5 x 36.7cm.)
    Christie's South Kensington, 18 april 1996 (71**) GBP 8,970   US$ 13,601

SAINT BARBARA oil on canvas, 26¼ x 20in. (66.7 x 50.8cm.)
PROV.: Mrs. Newcomb, September 1862, no. 5, and by descent to Miss Newcomb; Dorothy Bryant (all according to labels on the reverse).
    Christie's London, 19 April 1996 (194**) GBP 41,100   US$ 62,320

SAMSON Jeanne (19th century) French
OVERHEARD! Oil on canvas, 31 7/8 x 22 5/8in. (81 x 57.5cm.) sll
    Phillips London, 14 November 1995 (54**) GBP 5,000   US$ 7,821

SANCHEZ BARBUDO Salvador (Sevilla 1857-1917 Rome) Spanish
PECHEURS DE SINIGAGLIA oil on canvas, 37 3/8 x 21 3/8in. (94.9 x 54.3cm.) slr and inscr. 'Barbudo/Sinigaglia'
    Christie's East, 13 February 1996 (118**) US$ 10,350   US$ 10,350

SANDBERG Ragnar (1902-1972) Swedish
MAN OCH MÅSAR oil on canvas, 86 x 86cm. sdlr 'R.S. / 39'
    Bukowskis Stockholm, 24-25 April 1996 (120**) SEK 500,000   US$ 75,750

RONEDE PAR oil on canvas, 29.5 x 33cm. slr 'R.S.'
    Bukowskis Stockholm, 24-25 April 1996 (122**) SEK 90,000   US$ 13,635

LILLA BOMMENS HAMN oil on canvas, 27 x 67cm. sdlr 'R.S. 1941'
    Bukowskis Stockholm, 26-27 October 1995 (115**) SEK 110,000   US$ 16,110

SANDBY Paul, R.A. (Nottingham 1725-1809 London) British
VIEW OF THE THAMES ESTUARY AT ESSEX oil on canvas, 25½ x 40½in. (64.8 x 102.9cm.) sdll 'P Sandby R.A./1807'
    Sotheby's New York, 11 January 1996 (131**) US$ 43,125   US$ 43,125

SANDE BAKHUYZ Hendricus van de (The Hague 1795-1860 The Hague) Dutch
A TREELINED RIVER LANDSCAPE with figures and cattle on a path, 29 x 37¼in. (73.6 x 94.6cm.) sdll 'de Sande Bakhuyzen fl/1826'
    Christie's New York, 22 May 1996 (108**) US$ 34,500   US$ 34,500

A WOODED LANDSCAPE WITH A HORSEMAN CONVERSING WITH A HERDSMAN AND CATTLE ON A SANDY TRACK, A COUNTRY HOUSE BEYOND oil on canvas, 82 x 108cm. s
d vd S Bakhuyzen'

Christie's Amsterdam, 26 October 1995 (230*) NLG 20,700	US$	13,052

SANO DI PIETRO (Siena 1406-1481 Siena) Italian
VIRGIN AND CHILD gold ground, tempera on panel, 17 x 12½in. (43.2 x 31.8cm.)
PROV.: Collection of the late Count and Countess Guy de Boisrouvray.

Sotheby's New York, 16 May 1996 (4**) US$ 63,000	US$	63,000

SANO DI PIETRO (STUDIO OF) | (Siena 1406-1481 Siena) Italian
THE MADONNA AND CHILD tempera on gold ground panel, shaped top, 21¼ x 15in. (54 x 38.1cm.)
PROV.: H. Harris, 1929.

Christie's London, 7 July 1995 (331**) GBP 65,300	US$	104,163

SANTACROCE Francesco di Gerolamo da (Venice 1516-1584) Italian
MADONNA COL BAMBINO oil on panel, 88 x 64cm

Finearte Milan, 25 November 1995 (110**) ITL 32200,000	US$	20,213

SANTOMASO Giuseppe (Venice 1907-1990) Italian
PAGINA DI DIARIO N 7 collage and mixed media on paper laid down on canvas, 58.5 x 62cm. slr 'Santomaso' s titled on the reverse
PROV.: Galleria Sianesi, Milano.
LIT.: This work is recorded at the 'Archivio Santomaso' under supervision of Galleria Blu, Milano.

Christie's Milan, 20 November 1995 (128**) ITL 11785,000	US$	7,398

SANTORO Rubens (Cosenza 1859-1942 Naples) Italian
GONDOLA ON A VENETIAN CANAL WITH ELEGANT FIGURES CROSSING A BRIDGE oil on canvas, 15 3/8 x 20¼in. (39 x 51.5cm.) slr

Phillips London, 11th June 1996 (80**) GBP 28,000	US$	43,177

GONDOLAS ON A CANAL VENICE oil on canvas, 19 5/8 x 14¾in. (50 x 37.5cm.) slr 'Rubens Santoro'

Phillips London, 14 November 1995 (90**) GBP 28,000	US$	43,798

A SUNLIT DOORWAY oil on panel, 9½ x 7¼in. ,924 x 18.5cm.) s 'Rubens Santoro'

Christie's London, 15 March 1996 (84**) GBP 80,700	US$	123,244

SCORGIO VENEZIANO WITH THE CAMPANILE OF SAN GENEMIA oil on canvas, 19¾ x 14¼in. (50 x 36.3cm.) s 'Rubens Santoro'
PROV.: With MacConnal-Mason & Son.

Christie's London, 15 March 1996 (161**) GBP 28,750	US$	43,907

SARGENT John Singer (Florence 1856-1925 London) American
PINE FOREST watercolour and gouache on paper laid down on board, 12 x 18in. (30.5 x 45.7cm.)
PROV.: Collection of Mrs. Hugo Pitman, niece of the artist; Rex Evans Gallery, Los Angeles, California.
EXH.: Los Angeles, California, Los Angeles County Museum of Art, *Eight American Masters of Watercolour*, April 23-June 16, 1968, no. 21.

Christie's New York, 13 September 1995 (59**) US$ 17,250	US$	17,250

SARTORIO Giulio Aristide (1860-1932) Italian
ISOLE DI ARICA oil on canvasboard, 21¼ x 24¾in. (54 x 62.9cm.) sd and titled 'MCMXXIV' (1924)

Sotheby's Arcade Auctions New York, 20 July 1995 (538*) US$ 12,075	US$	12,075

SARTORIUS Francis the Elder (London 1734-1804 London) British
THE MATCH BETWEEN THE HOUNDS OF THE HON. JOHN SMITH BARRY AND HOGO
MEYNELL AT NEWMARKET, 1762 oil on canvas, 25 x 40in. (63.5 x 10l.6cm.) inscr. lr 'The Bay
Gelding Small /c. with the Portraits of / Blue-cap and Wanton. / who beat two Hounds of Hugo
Meynell Esq. / Over the Beacon-Course / at New Market in/October 1762. For ,200 / each side'
PROV.: Hon. James Smith Barry, Marbury Hall, Cheshire and by descent to the vendor.
EXH.: London, Grosvenor Gallery, 1888.
Christie's London, 10 November 1995 (60**) GBP 51,000 US$ 79,775

SARTORIUS John Nost (London 1759-1828) British
THE RT. HON. CHARLES JAMES FOX'S SEAGULL BEATING THE PRINCE OF WALES'
ESCAPE AND LORD BARRYMORE'S HIGHLANDER IN THE OATLANDS STAKES, ASCOT
1790 oil on cavas, 28 x 36in. (71.1 x 91.4cm.) sdll 'Hbl. CJ. Fox's Seagul beating H.R.H.P. of
Wales's Escape / Ld. Barrymore's Highlander .. for the Oatland Stakes / of 100gs Each 15
July [?]. Paid 25gs Each .. in July 1789. / This sweepstake was Run June 8 1790 over Ascot Heath / J
N Sartorius pint.'
PROV.: Medmenham Abbey; Sotheby's, 24June 1942, lot 88 (sold 150gns.); with Arthur Ackermann
& Son, London; Mrs. E.M. Gordon, Biddlesden Park, Northamptonshire; Christie's, 18 April 1986,
lot 24 (sold GBP38,000).
Christie's London, 10 November 1995 (61**) GBP 29,900 US$ 46,770

SASSU Aligi (Milan 1912 b.) Italian
CAVALLI AL MARE mixed technique on paper laid down on masonite, 50 x 60cm. slr 'Sassu'
Finearte Milan, 18 June 1996 (248**) ITL 19,550,000 US$ 12,678

LA TERRA E VUOTA tempera on canvassed paper, 32 x 49cm. slr 'Sassu' sd and titled on the
reverse (1985)
Finearte Milan, 19 March 1996 (87**) ITL 14,375,000 US$ 9,197

I CAVALIERI tempera on cardboard, 29 x 20cm. (1932)
LIT.: R. Carrieri, *Gli uomini rossi di Aligi Sassu*, ed. Vangelista, Milan 1971, p.141.
Finearte Milan, 26 October 1995 (138*) ITL 13,800,000 US$ 8,598

ALICE oil on canvas, 50 x 59cm. s (1959-61)
Sotheby's Milan, 28 May 1996 (160**) ITL 28750,000 US$ 18,465

LISA E LAURA oil on canvas, 59 x 50cm. slr; sd '1983' and titled on the reverse
PROV.: Galleria d'Arte Appiani 32, Milan.
EXH.: Turin, Galleria d'Arte Davico, *Aligi Sassu*, October-November 1986.
Sotheby's Milan, 28 May 1996 (213**) ITL 28,750,000 US$ 18,465

SATO Key (Oita City 1906-1978) Japanese
GLACIS DE BRUME oil on canvas, 35 x 46in. (89 x 117cm.) sdll 'Key Sato 57', s and titled on the
reverse 'Key Sato, Glacis de Brume'
Christie's South Kensington, 18 March 1996 (47**) GBP 6,325 US$ 9,659

SAURA Antoni (Huesca 1930 b.) Spanish
CRUCIFIXION pencil and enamel paint on paper, 87 x 115cm. sdlr 'A.Sauna '69' (1969)
Christie's Amsterdam, 5 June 1996 (314**) NLG 36,800 US$ 21,502

UNTITLED acrylic, watercolour, crayon and pencil on paper, 26¾ x 38¾in. (68 x 98.5) sdul 'Saura
53'
Christie's London, 19 March 1996 (22**) GBP 8,050 US$ 12,294

BRIGITTE BARDOT oil on canvas, 51 x 38½in. (129.5 x 96.8cm.) sd and titled '63' on the stretcher
PROV.: Pierre Matisse Gallery, New York; Marlborough Gallery, New York.
      Christie's London, 19 March 1996 (34**) GBP 41,100   US$ 62,767

RETRATO IMAGINARIO DE VELASQUEZ oil on canvas, 11½ x 7¾in. (29.5 x 19.5cm.) s three
times (1954-55)
      Sotheby's London, 21 March 1996 (91**) GBP 5,175   US$ 7,903

UNTITLED acrylic, gouache, ink and crayon on paper, 24 5/8 x 35½in. (62.5 x 90.3cm.) sd 'Saura
61'
      Christie's London, 23 May 1996 (35**) GBP 10,925   US$ 16,543

SELF PORTRAIT oil on canvas, 23½ x 28 ¾in. (59.7 x 73cm.) sd 'Saura 60'
PROV.: Notizie, Arte Contemporanea, Turin.
      Christie's London, 23 May 1996 (39**) GBP 19,550   US$ 29,603

BALDOVINETTA oil on canvas, 51 1/8 x 38¼in. (,130 x 97.3cm.) sd 'Saura 63' sd titled on the
reverse
PROV.: Jason McCoy, New York; Pierre Matisse Gallery, New York.
EXH.: New York, Pierre Matisse Gallery, *Antonio Saura*, 1964; Lugano Museo d'Arte Moderna,
Antonio Saura, September-November 1994, no. 29 (illustrated in the catalogue p. 135).
      Christie's London, 23 May 1996 (66**) GBP 49,900   US$ 75,560

LUCRETIA oil on canvas, 63 7/8 x 51¼in. (,162 x 130cm.) sd on the stretcher '1959'
PROV.: Marlborough Gallery, London; Pierre Matisse Gallery, New York.
      Christie's London, 26 October 1995 (31**) GBP 43,300   US$ 68,340

THE THREE GRACES oil on canvas, each panel: 76¾ x 38in. (,195 x 96.5cm.); overall: 76¾ x ,114
7/8in. (,195 x 291.7cm.) i) sdul '59; ii) sdur '59; iii) sdul '59
PROV.: Pierre Matisse Gallery, New York.
EXH.: New York, Museum of Modern Art; Washington, Corcoran Gallery of Art; Columbus,
Columbus; Gallery of Fine Arts; St. Louis, Washington University; Coral Gables, Lowe Art Gallery;
San Antonio, Marion Koogler McNay Art Institute; Chicago, Art Institute of Chicago; New Orleans,
Isaac Delgado Museum of Art; Toronto, Art Gallery of Toronto; Manchester, Currier Gallery of Art,
New Spanish Painting and Sculpture, July 1960-January 1962 (illustrated in the catalogue p. 40);
Lugano, Museo d'Arte Moderna della Citta di Lugano, *Antonio Saura*, September-November 1994,
p. 131, no. 16 (illustrated in colour in the catalogue p. 40).
LIT.: Georges Boudaille, Antonio Saura, Paris 1968; In: 'Cimaise', no. 131-132, Paul Gauthier,
Saura, 1974; Alexandre Cinci Pellicer, Lectura de Antonio Saura, in 'Antonio Saura: Expositión
antalógica 1948-1980, Madrid/Barcelona 1980; Gerard de Cortanze, *Antonio Saura*, Paris 1994, pp.
112-,113 (illustrated in colour over two pages).
      Christie's London, 27 June 1996 (43**) GBP 254,500   US$ 392,444

PORTRAIT IMAGINAIRE DE PHILIPPE II oil on canvas, 51 1/8 x 38in. (,130 x 96.5cm.) sd '81';
sd '1981', titled, and numbered '2-81' on the reverse
PROV.: Galerie Stadler, Paris.
      Sotheby's London, 27 June 1996 (202**) GBP 32,200   US$ 49,653

CRUCIFIXION watercolour, ink and crayon on card, 74 x 104cm. sd '67'
PROV.: Galerie Stadler, Paris.
      Sotheby's Amsterdam, 7 December 1995 (213**) NLG 21,830   US$ 13,527

SAVERY Jacob I (Courtrai 1565 c.-1602/03 Amsterdam) Flemish
AN EXTENSIVE LANDSCAPE WITH A BULL HUNT oil on panel, 14¼ x 21½in. (36.2 x
54.6cm.)
      Christie's London, 8 December 1995 (4**) GBP 29,900   US$ 46,014

SAVERY Roelandt Jacobsz. (Courtrai 1576-1639 Utrecht) Flemish
LA CHASSE AU CERF oil on oakpanel, 51 x 77cm.
PROV.: Collection Heim-Gairac, Paris, 1953.
EXH.: Paris, Galerie Heim-Gairac, *Paysages Flamands de Henri met de Bles à Jan Brueghel*, April-
May 1953, no. 38; Gand, Musée des Beaux-Arts, *Roelandt Savery*, 1954, p. 27, no. 58 (illus).
LIT.: Y. Thierry, *La peinture Flamande au XVIIe siècle*, Paris-Brussels 1953, p. 36, no. 21 (illus.);
K.J. Müllenmeister, *Roelandt Savery die Gemälde*, Freren 1988, pp. 93, 228, no. 75 (illus.).

Étude Tajan Paris, 12 December 1995 (9**) FRF 600,000	US$	120,856

SAVERYS Albert (Deynze 1886-1964) Belgian
A SUMMER RIVER LANDSCAPE oil on board, 40 x 50cm. slr 'Saverijs'

Christie's Amsterdam, 6 December 1995 (239*) NLG 12,650	US$	7,839

SAVINIO Alberto (Andrea de Chirico) (Athene 1891-1952 Rome) Italian
COMPOSIZIONE CON STATUA E MANICHINO oil on canvas, 55 x 46cm. slr 'Savinio' (ca 1928)
EXH.: Milan, Galleria Medea, *44 opere di Alberto Savinio*, March/April 1970, no.19 of the catalogue
and presentation of F. Passoni.
LIT.: Maurizio Fagiolo Dell'Arco, *Alberto Savinio, guida all'opera*, in *Bolaffi, Catalogo nazionale
d'arte moderna*, Milan, 1980, p.218; Maurizio Fagiolo Dell'Arco, *Savinio*, ed. Fabbri, Milan 1989,
no.48, p.242, illustrated p.133.

Finearte Milan, 19 March 1996 (56**) ITL 402,500,000	US$	257,518

CROIX MARINE oil on canvas, 73 x 91cm. sdur 'Savinio 1929' titled on the stretcher
PROV.: Galleria Medea, Milano.
EXH.: Milano, Società per le Belle Arti e d'Esposizione Permanente, *Mostra di Pittori e Scultori che
recitano a soggetto*, March-May 1971; Milano, Galleria Medea, *44 opere di Alberto Savinio*, March-
April 1970, no. 39 (illustrated).
LIT.: Pia Vivarelli, *Savinio, Gli anni di Parigi*, dipinti 1927-1932, Milano 1990, pag ,232
(illustrated).

Christie's Milan, 20 November 1995 (173***) ITL 648,175,000	US$	40,6890

SAY Frederick Richard (1827-1860) British
PORTRAIT OF MRS SARAH FRANCES COOPER AND HER DAUGHTERS, SELINA
STANDING TO THE LEFT, AND CICELY FLORENCE, WITH HER HEAD ON HER
MOTHER'S LAP, AND THEIR DOG, IN THE GROUNDS OF MARKREE CASTLE, CO.SLIGO
oil on canvas, 77 7/8 x 55 7/8in. (,198 x 142cm.)
PROV.: Painted for Edward Joshua Cooper of Markree Castle, Co.Sligo thence by descent to the
present owner.

Phillips London, 18 June 1996 (90**) GBP 9,500	US$	14,649

SCANAVINO Emilio (Genua 1922-1986 Milan) Italian
GERMINAZIONE oil on canvas, 92 x 73cm. sd 'Scanavino 1959' sd titled on the reverse
LIT.: G. Ballo, *Scanavino*, ed. Cappelli, Bologna.

Finearte Milan, 12 December 1995 (230*) ITL 17,250,000	US$	10,822

SCHAALJE C.J. (active by 1709-after 1806) Dutch
STILL-LIFE OF ROSES, MORNING GLORY, VARIEGATED TULIPS, IRIS AND OTHER
FLOWERS IN A STONE VASE ON A LEDGE oil on panel, 17 x 13in. (43.2 x 33cm.) sdlr 'C
Schaalje f/1806'

Sotheby's New York, 11 January 1996 (170**) US$ 17,250	US$	17,250

SCHACHINGER Gabriel (1850-1912) German
A STILL-LIFE WITH ROSES, PEONIES, HOLY HOCKS, ASTERS AND OTHER FLOWERS IN
A BRASS KETTLE ON A STONE LEDGE oil on canvas, ,110 x 90cm. sd 'G. Schachinger
München 1902'

Christie's Amsterdam, 25 April 1996 (266**) NLG 51,750	US$	30,750

SCHÄFER Henry Thomas (1873-1915 fl.) British
CLASSICAL WOMAN BY A TEMPLE oil on canvas, 38¼ x 25in. (97 x 63.5cm.) sd sd on a label
on the stretcher (1889)
PROV.: Arthur Tooth & Sons.
            Phillips London, 23rd April 1996 (108*) GBP 5,500   US$ 8,340

SCHALCKEN Godfried Cornelisz. (Made (near Dordrecht) 1643-1706 The Hague) Dutch
A LADY AT HER TOILET BENEATH A CANOPY IN A WOODED LANDSCAPE oil on panel,
14½ x 11¼in. (37 x 28.8cm.) (ca. 1690)
PROV.: Henry Hirsch, 23 Park Lane London; His Sale Christie's 11 May 1934, lot 143, as G.
Schalcken, 73.10 gns. to C. Duits; *Art Market*, Stockholm, 1935, as by *Adriaen van der Werff*;
Monsieur Zatzenstein, according to an old label on the reverse of the frame.
            Sotheby's London, 17 April 1996 (32***) GBP 309,500   US$ 469,295

OLD WOMAN, BEARING BOOK AND SPECTACLES oil on canvas, 81.5 x 70cm. slr 'G.
Schalken'
PROV.: Ehemals Königliche Gemäldegalerie; Dresden, Inventarnummer 1722, n A 1771, Cat. 1908
n; 1788; erworben 1727 von der Kurfürstin von Sachsen auf der Ostermesse in Leipzig.
LIT.: Thierry Beherman, 1918; *Maeght Editeur*, Depot legal 4th trimester 1988.
            Dorotheum Vienna, 17 October 1995 (85**) ATS 280,000   US$ 28,086

SCHALL Jean Frédéric (attr.) (Strasbourg 1752-1825 Paris) French
LA SERVANTE OFFICIEUCE' OR ADMINISTERING A LOVE POTION oil on copper, 16 x
20½in. (40.6 x 52.1cm.)
PROV.: Paulo de Koeningsberg, Buenos Aires; Sale N.C. Naon, Buenos Aires, 1978, lot 32; Sale:
Christie's New York, 12 January 1994, lot ,145 where acquired by the present owner.
            Sotheby's New York, 11 January 1996 (220**) US$ 39,100   US$ 39,100

SCHEIBL Hubert (Gmunden 1952 b.) Austrian
UNTITLED oil on canvas, ,200 x 175cm. sd 'Hubert Scheibl 1985' on the reverse
            Wiener Kunst Auktionen, 26 March 1996 (465**) ATS 90,000   US$ 8,657

SCHELFHOUT Andreas (Andries) (The Hague 1787-1870 The Hague) Dutch
FIGURES BEFORE A COTTAGE IN AN EXTENSIVE WOODLANDSCAPE oil on panel, 14 x
17in. (35.5 x 43cm.) s
            Phillips London, 11th June 1996 (15**) GBP 8,000   US$ 12,336

HOLLÄNDISCHES WINTERLANDSCHAFT MIT EISLÄUFERN. oil on canvas, 47 x 64cm. slr
'A. Schelfhout'
            Lempertz Cologne, 15 November 1995 (1881**) DEM 16,500   US$ 11,646

FIGURES ON A FROZEN CANAL oil on panel, 8 x 11½in. (20.4 x 29.2cm.) sdll 'A. Schelfhout 67'
(1867)
PROV.: Mrs. E.M.Cook; with Richard Green Gallery, London.
EXH.: Sterling and Francine Clark Institute, *Jongkind and the Pre-Impressionist's*, Dec.1976-Feb.
1977, no. 103.
            Christie's New York, 22 May 1996 (106**) US$ 34,500   US$ 34,500

WINTER: FIGURES ON A FROZEN WATERWAY WITH ICED BOATS NEAR A BARN oil on
cardboard, 20 x 25 cm s 'A. Schelfhout'
            Christie's Amsterdam, 25 April 1996 (14*) NLG 25,300   US$ 15,034

A WINTER LANDSCAPE WITH FIGURES AND A SLEDGE ON A FROZEN DITCH BY A
FARM oil on panel, 24.5 x 28.5cm.) s 'A. Schelfhout f.'
            Christie's Amsterdam, 25 April 1996 (151**) NLG 46,000   US$ 27,334

A WINTER LANDSCAPE WITH PEASANTS BY A HORSE-DRAWN SLEDGE NEAR A
CASTLE oil on panel, 41.5 x 54cm. s 'A. Schelfhout f'
PROV.: W.H. Patterson, Fine Arts Ltd., London.
Christie's Amsterdam, 25 April 1996 (249**) NLG 69,000   US$ 41,001

AN EXTENSIVE RIVER LANDSCAPE WITH TRAVELLERS ON A SANDY PATH oil on panel,
11.5 X 15CM. s 'A. Schelfhout'
Christie's Amsterdam, 26 October 1995 (204**) NLG 17,250   US$ 10,876

A HILLY RIVER LANDSCAPE WITH FIGURES IN THE FOREGROUND, A TOWN BEYOND
oil on panel, 17 x 22.5cm. sdlr 'A.Schelfhout f.53'
Christie's Amsterdam, 26 October 1995 (205**) NLG 13,800   US$ 8,701

SOLDIERS TRAVELLING IN A WINTER LANDSCAPE oil on panel, 20.5 x 26.5 sdlr 'A.
Schelfhout'
Christie's Amsterdam, 26 October 1995 (206**) NLG 20,700   US$ 13,052

A WINTERLANDSCAPE WITH SKATERS PUSHING A SLEDGE ON A FROZEN
WATERWAY pencil, pen and brush and brown ink and watercolour heightened with white on paper,
16.5 x 21 cm s 'A.Schelfhout f'
Christie's Amsterdam, 7 February 1996 (25*) NLG 8,050   US$ 4,903

SCHELLINKS Willem (Amsterdam 1627 (?)-1678 Amsterdam) Dutch
SOUTH ITALIAN PORT SCENE WITH SHIPS UNLOADING IN A SMALL HARBOUR oil on
canvas, 16 x 19in. (40.6 x 48.3cm.)
Sotheby's New York, 11 January 1996 (275**) US$ 20,700   US$ 20,700

SCHENCK August Friedrich Albrecht (1828-1901) Danish
SHEEP IN FROM THE COLD oil on canvas, 59 x 99½in. (,150 x 252.7cm.) sdlr 'Schenck/68'
PROV.: Henry Gibson; Pennsylvabia Academy of Fine Arts, Philadelphia.
Christie's East, 13 February 1996 (61**) US$ 12,650   US$ 12,650

SCHENDEL Bernardus van (Weesp 1649-1709 Haarlem) Dutch
FAMILY CELEBRATING THE BIRTH OF A CHILD , 56 x 76cm. slr 'Brs. Schyndel'
PROV.: Unites States, private collection.
Dorotheum Vienna, 17 October 1995 (132**) ATS 250,000   US$ 25,076

SCHENDEL Gillis van, the younger (Abcoude ca. 1635-1678/79 Amsterdam) Dutch
BRAZILIAN LANDSCAPE WITH A MAN CARRYING A SPEAR, PORTERS AND A
COWHERD BY A RIVER, BATHERS IN THE DISTANCE oil on canvas, 26¾ x 24in. (67.9 x
61cm.) slr 'IVSchendel f' (ca. 1660-70)
Sotheby's New York, 16 May 1996 (84**) US$ 40,250   US$ 40,250

SCHENDEL Petrus van (Ter Heyde (Breda) 1806-1870 Brussels) Belgian (Dutch)
THE ORANGE SELLER oil on panel, 24½ x 19¼in. (62.2 x 49cm.) sd 'P. van Schendel fct/1834'
Christie's London, 15 March 1996 (5A**) GBP 17,250   US$ 26,344

A NIGHT MARKET oil on a panel, 62.5 x 49cm s(remnants)d 'P van Schendel fecit/1834'
Christie's Amsterdam, 26 October 1995 (192**) NLG 29,900   US$ 18,852

SCHERREWITZ Johan Frederik Cornelis (Amsterdam 1868-1951 Hilversum) Dutch
FISHERFOLK ON A BEACH oil on canvas, 14¼ x 20½in. (36.2 x 52cm.) slr 'JScherrewitz'
PROV.: With Watson Art Galleries, Montreal.
Christie's New York, 10 January 1996 (76**) US$ 10,350   US$ 10,350

ON THE BEACH AT SCHEVENINGEN oil on canvas, 16 x 23 5/8in. (40.7 x 60cm.) sll
    Phillips London, 12th March 1996 (8**) GBP 6,800   US$ 10,385

FISHERFOLK ON A BEACH oil on canvas, 14¼ x 20½in. (36.2 x 52cm.) slr 'JScherrewitz'
    Christie's New York, 14 February 1996 (76**) US$ 10,350   US$ 10,350

SCHEUERER Julius (München 1859-1913 Planegg) German
POULTRY AT THE EDGE OF THE WOOD oil on panel, 16 x 40cm. sll 'Jul. Scheuerer München'
    Dorotheum Vienna, 13 September 1995 (664**) ATS 140,000   US$ 13,608

SCHIAVONI Felice (Trieste 1803-1881 Venice) Italian
VENERE E CUPIDO oil on canvas, ,198 x 150cm. sdlr 'F.E. Schiavoni 1831 Venezia' (1831)
    Finearte Rome, 18 October 1995 (265**) ITL 10,4650,000   US$ 65,202

SCHIEDGES Petrus Paulus (The Hague 1813-1876 Amersfoort) Dutch
VARIOUS SHIPPING ON A RIVER oil on panel, unframed, 25 x 34 cm sd 'Schiedges '57'
    Christie's Amsterdam, 7 February 1996 (46*) NLG 10,925   US$ 6,653

SCHIELE Egon (Tulin 1890-1919 Vienna) Austrian
SITZENDES JUNGES MÄDCHEN, NACH LINKS GENEIGT, VON VORN GESEHEN pencil-
drawing on paper, 49.3 x 36cm. sdll 'EGON/SCHIELE/1911'
    Hauswedell & Nolte Cologne, 1 December 1995 (573**) DEM 150,000   US$ 104,073

HOCKENDER (SELBSTBILDNIS) watercolour and gouache over pencil on paper, 17¼ x 11¾in.
(43.8 x 29.8cm.) sdlr 'EGON SCHIELE 1912'
PROV.: Anon. sale , Dorotheum, Vienna, June 9, 1961, lot 311; Janine Wolkenberg, New York;
Galerie St.Etienne, New York; George Encil, Canada; Marlborough-Gerson Gallery, New York
(acquired by Dr.Eugene A.Solow, 1966).
EXH.: New York, Galerie St.Etienne, *Egon Schiele (1890-1918): Watercolours and Drawings from
American Collections*, 1965, no.35 (ill.); London, Marlborough Fine Art, *Bauhaus, Expressionisme,
Dada*, Jan., 1966 (not in the catalogue); Des Moines, Art Center, *Egon Schiele and the Human Form:
Drawings and Watercolours*, Sept.-Oct., 1971, no.25 (ill.). The exhibition traveled to Colombus,
Gallery of Fine Arts, Nov.-Dec., 1971, and Chicago, The Art Institute, Jan.-Feb., 1972.; Chicago,
The Art Institute, *Chicago Collects: Selections from the Collection of Dr.Eugene A.Solow*, May-
Aug., 1988, no.56 (ill. in colour on the cover).
LIT.: W.Hofmann, *Egon Schiele: 'Die Familie'*, Stuttgart, 1968, fig.6 (ill.); A.Comini, *Egon Schiele's
Portraits*, Berkeley, 1974, fig.,130 (ill.); E.Mitsch, *Egon Schiele, 1890-1918*, Salzburg, 1974, fig.42
(ill., p.80); J.Hobhouse, 'Nudes: The Vision of Egon Schiele and Pierre Bonnard', *Connoisseur*, June,
1984, p.102; J.Kallir, *Egon Schiele: The Complete Works*, New York, 1990, no. 1167 (ill., p.482).
    Christie's New York, 1 May 1996 (327***) US$ 827,500   US$ 827,500

BERG AM FLUß oil on paper laid down on cardboard, 12¼ x 17 5/8in. (31 x 44.8cm.) s 'S.10'
(1910)
PROV.: Dr Heinrich Rieger, Vienna; Alfred Spitzer, Vienna; Erich Wagner, London; Anon. sale,
Stuttgarter Kunstkabinett, Stuttgart, 29-30 May 1959, sale 33, lot 821; Galerie Maercklin, Stuttgart.
EXH.: Vienna, Sammlung Dr. Rieger, 1935; Vienna, Österreichische Galerie, Egon Schiele-
Gemalde, April-Sept. 1968, no. 22 (illustrated).
LIT.: O. Kallir, Egon Schiele, Oeuvre-Katalog der Gemälde, Vienna, 1966 no. ,120 (illustrated p.
240); R. Leopold, Egon Schiele-Paintings, Watercolours, Drawings Salzburg, 1973, no. ,163
(illustrated p. 556); G. Malafarina, L'Opera di Egon Schiele, Milan, 1982 no. 155J. Kallir, Egon
Schiele, the Complete Works New York 1990, no. ,187 (illustrated p. 298); E. Mitsch, Egon Schiele,
1890-1918, London 1993, p. 75 (illustrated fig.30).
    Christie's London, 11 October 1995 (184**) GBP 78,500   US$ 123,895

KAUERNDES MÄDCHEN MIT AUFGESTÜTZTEM BEIN, SICH STREICHELND pencil on
paper, 19 x 12½in. (48.3 x 31.8cm.) sdlr '1913'

PROV.: Sale: Wolfgang Ketterer, Munich,June 8-10, 1970, lot 1472; Sale: Dorotheum, Vienna, March 24, 1972, lot ,595 Jean Lenthal, Paris;
Acquired from the above by the present owner in December 1973.
EXH.: Vienna, Galerie 10, *Von Schiele his Leherb*, circa 1970; Munich, Haus der Kunst, *Egon Schiele*, 1975, no. 201; Zurich, Galerie M. Knoedler; New York, M. Knoedler & Co., *Gustav Klimt, Egon Schiele, James Ensor, Alfred Kubin: Künstler der Jahrhundertwende*, 1983, no. 14; Martigny, Fondation Pierre Gianadda, *Schiele*, 1995, no. 85.
LIT.: Jane Kallir, *Egon Schiele: The Complete Works*, New York 1990, no. 1349 (illustrated p. 505).

Sotheby's New York, 2 May 1996 (238**) US$ 118,000	US$	118,000

LESENDER AKT pencil on paper, 45.4 x 28.3cm. sdlr 'EGON/ SCHIELE/1914'

Wiener Kunst Auktionen, 26 September 1995 (177**) ATS 450,000	US$	43,742

SITZENDE FRAU DAS RECHTE BEIN ERGREIFEND gouache, watercolour and charcoal on paper, 17½ x 11½in. (45 x 29cm.) sdll 'Egon Schiele 1917'
PROV.: Acquired by the father of the present owner in the 1920's.
EXH.: 1994-95 (Nov.-June), Tulln (Austria), Egon Schiele Museum.
LIT.: Jane Kallir, *Egon Schiele: The Complete Works*, New York: Harry n. Abrams Inc., 1990, no.D2012, p.,538 (ill.).

Phillips London, 27 November 1995 (25**) GBP 70,000	US$	109,495

LIEGENDER AKT MIT BLONDEM HAAR (SITZENDER AKT, VERSO) watercolour and pencil on cream wove paper, 12 x 17 5/8in. (30.5 x 44.7cm.) sdur 'Egon Schiele 1912'
PROV.: Dr. Alfred Spitzer, Vienna; Galerie St. Etienne, New York; William H. Saunders, New York; Galerie St. Etienne, New York, from whom acquired by the present owner.
EXH.: New York, Galerie St. Etienne, Egon Schiele (1890-1918): Watercolours and Drawingsfrom American Collections, March-April 1965, no. 34 (illustrated in the catalogue); New York, Galerie St. Etienne, Egon Schiele (1890-1918): Watercolours and Drawings, Oct.-Dec. 1968, no._50 (illustrated in the catalogue).
LIT.: G. Malafarina, L'Opera di Egon Schiele, Milan, 1982, no. D49; J. Kallir, Egon Schiele, the Complete Works, New York, 1990, no. 1137 (illustrated p. 478).

Christie's London, 28 November 1995 (31**) GBP 199,500	US$	312,060

LIEGENDER HALBAKT MIT ROTEM HUT gouache, watercolour and black crayon with white heightening on tan paper, 12 3/8 x 17¾in. (31.5 x45.1) d and ini. 'S.10'
PROV.: Alfons Keller (?); Kornfeld and Klipstein, sale 157, 10 June 1976, lot 905.
EXH.: Bern, Gutenkunst and Klipstein, Egon Schiele: Bilder, Aquarelle, Zeichnungen, Graphik, Sept.-Oct. 1956, no. 11 (illustrated); St. Gallen, Kunstmuseum, Kunst aus Österreich, April-May 1957, no. 95.
LIT.: J. Kallir, Egon Schiele: The Complete Works, New York, 1990, no. ,547 (illus. p. 410).

Christie's London, 28 November 1995 (33**) GBP 397,500	US$	621,774

SELBST PORTRAIT IM LEDERWESTE MIT ABGEWINKELTEM ELLBOGEN gouache, black chalk and pencil on paper, 18 7/8 x 12¼in. (48 x 31cm.) sdlr 'EGON SCHIELE 1914'
PROV.: William H. Schab Gallery, New York; Alice M. Kaplan, New York (acquired from the above in 1967).
EXH.: New York, Galerie St. Etienne, *Arnold Schoenbergs Vienna*, Nov., 1984-Jan., 1985 (illustrated in color, pl. 16); New York, Museum of Modern Art, *Vienna 1900: Art, Architecture & Design*, July-Oct., 1986, p. ,176 (illustrated); Washington, D.C., National Gallery of Art, *Egon Schiele*, Feb.-May, 1994, p. 136, no. 47 (illustrated in color, p. 137, pl. 65).
LIT.: *Die Aktion*, vol. 5, nos. 11-12, March 13, 1915, p. ,130 (uncoloured version illustrated); A. Comini, *Egon Schiele's Portraits*, Berkeley, 1974, p. xxviii, no. 125a (illustrated, pl. 125a); C. Bantel, *The Alice M. Kaplan Collection*, New York, 1981, p. ,140 (illustrated, p. 141); J. Kallir, *Egon Schiele: The Complete Works*, New York,1990, p. 543, no. 1668 (illustrated, p. 542; and in colour, p 187, pl. 72); J. Kallir, *Egon Schiele*, New York, 1994, p. ,136 (illustrated in colour, p. 137, pl. 65).

Christie's New York, 7 November 1995 (37**) US$ 1,872,500	US$	1,872,500

SCHIFANO Mario (Homs (Lybia?) 1934 b.) Italian
PARTICOLARE DI PROPAGANDA mixed media oil technic on unite, ,140 x 180cm s on the
reverse 'Schifano' (1962)
PROV.: Galleria Rondanini, Roma.

Finearte Rome, 14 November 1995 (211**) ITL 27600,000	US$	17,326

PORTA acrylic and enamel on canvas, ,120 x 120cm. suc 'Schifano'

Sotheby's Milan, 28 May 1996 (98**) ITL 11500,000	US$	7,386

SCHIFFER Anton (Gsraz 1811-1876 Vienna) Austrian
EVENINGVIEW FROM THE MOUNTAINS ON THE GMUNDER LAKE BY TRAUNSTEIN oil
on paper, 44.5 x 59.7cm. s

Hauswedell & Nolte Cologne, 6 June 1996 (195*) DEM 21,000	US$	13,644

OUTSIDE THE PALACE GATES oil on board, 19½ x 25 1/8in. (49.5 x 63.8cm.) sd '1864'

Sotheby's Arcade Auctions New York, 17 January 1996 (533*) US$ 9,775	US$	9,775

SCHINDLER Emil Jakob (Vienna 1842-1892 Westerland, Sylt) Austrian
NACH DEM REGEN oil on panel, 36.5 x 70cm.

Dorotheum Vienna, 13 September 1995 (686**) ATS 110,000	US$	10,692

Eine Gotische Kathedrale hinter Bäumen

SCHINKEL Karl Friedrich (Neuruppin 1781-1841 Berlin) German
EINE GOTISCHE KATHEDRALE HINTER
BÄUMEN pencil, pen and grey ink and watercolour
on card laid down on paper, 9 5/8 x 8 7/8in. (24.3 x
22.5 cm.) (1814-15)
PROV.: property of the direct descendants of the
artist.

Christie's London, 11 October 1995 (1**) GBP 95,000	US$	149,937

EINE WEITE ITALIENSCHE LANDSCHAFT
(RECTO) ENTWURF FÜR EIN GOTISCHES
FENSTER (VERSO) watercolour on paper (recto)
pencil on paper (verso0, 7 x 11 1/8in. (17.8 x
28.2cm.) inscr.'Fenster der Ahnen
Gruft/no.3/Fenster auf der Nordseite' (1804)
PROV.: Property of direct descendants of the artist.

Christie's London, 11 October 1995 (17**) GBP 67,500	US$	106,534

SCHIÖLER Inge (1908-1971) Swedish
LANDSKAP SKANSTULL oil on canvas, 65 x 72cm. s 'Schiöler'
EXH.: Svensk Franska Konstgalleriet 1938, no. 66.

Bukowskis Stockholm, 24-25 April 1996 (131a**) SEK 160,000	US$	24,240

SOMMARÅNG, KOSTER oil on canvas, 74 x 83cm. sdll 'INGE SCHIÖLE/1966'

Bukowskis Stockholm, 24-25 April 1996 (131**) SEK 120,000	US$	18,180

UTSIKT ÖVER KOSTERSKÄR oil on canvas, 65 x 74cm. sdll 'Inge Schiöler 1960'

Bukowskis Stockholm, 26-27 October 1995 (122**) SEK 115,000	US$	16,842

STRANDPARTI I oil on canvas, 66 x 74cm. sdll 'Inge Schiöler 1967'

Bukowskis Stockholm, 26-27 October 1995 (123**) SEK 100,000	US$	14,645

SCHJERFBECK Helene (1862-1946) Finnish
DAFFODILS oil on canvas, 59.5 x 42cm. slr 'H.S.'
EXH.: Liljevalch, Liljevalchs Konsthall, *De drogo Paris*, 1988, cat. no. ,248 B.
        Bukowskis Stockholm, 29 November-1 December 1995 (20**) SEK 520,000   US$ 78,665

ROSES IN A VASE oil on canvas, 40 x 33cm. slr 'H.S.'
        Bukowskis Stockholm, 29 November-1 December 1995 (207**) SEK 570,000   US$ 86,228

LILLA RIKA I oil on canvas, 44.5 x 29.5cm. sul 'H Schjerfbeck.' (1885)
EXH.: Helsingfors, Ateneum, *Realismen*, 1962, no. 171; Helsingfors, Ateneum, *Helene Schjerfbeck*, no. 87.
LIT.: Athela, *Helene Schjerfbeck*, p. 357, no. 131.
        Bukowskis Stockholm, 29-31 May 1996 (242**) SEK 920,000   US$ 135,306

SCHLESINGER Felix (Hamburg 1833-1910) German
OVER THE FENCE oil on panel, 16 5/8 x 11 3/8in. (42.2 x 28.9cm.) slr 'F.Schlesinger.'
        Christie's New York, 10 January 1996 (83**) US$ 29,900   US$ 29,900

DIE HERZENFREUNDE oil on panel, 9½ x 7in. (24.2 x 17.8cm.) s 'F. Schlesinger'
        Christie's London, 11 October 1995 (68**) GBP 11,500   US$ 18,150

A YOUNG GRIL FEDDING HER RABBIT oil on panel, 7 x 5¾in. (17.8 x 14.7cm.) sur 'F. Schlesinger'
        Christie's East, 13 February 1996 (160**) US$ 18,400   US$ 18,400

OVER THE FENCE oil on panel, 16 5/8 x 11 3/8in. (42.2 x 28.9cm.) slr 'F.Schlesinger.'
        Christie's New York, 14 February 1996 (83**) US$ 29,900   US$ 29,900

FEEDING THE RABBITS oil on canvas, 14 x 16¾in. (36 x 42.7cm.) s 'F. Schlesinger'
        Christie's London, 17 November 1995 (21**) GBP 23,000   US$ 35,977

SCHLICHTER Rudolf (1890-1955) German
WALDBACH MIT BLUMEN AM UFER oil on painters cardboard, 83.7 x 67.5cm. sdlr 'R. Schlichter 1940'
PROV.: Stuttgarter Kunstkabinett, 35. Auktion, 20./21. Mai 1960, Cat. no. 583; Roman Norbert Ketterer.
        Lempertz Cologne, 29 November 1995 (442**) DEM 13,000   US$ 9,176

SCHMALIX Hubert (Graz 1952 b.-) Austrian
CYPRESS PARK-JESUS CHRIST I oil on canvas, ,176 x 134.5cm. sd 'Schmalix 91' on the reverse
        Dorotheum Vienna, 21 May 1996 (154**) ATS 280,000   US$ 26,887

SCHMALZIGAUG Jules (Antwerp 1882-1917 The Hague) Belgian
HET DYNAMISCHE VAN DE DANS oil on canvas, ,100 x 129.6cm. sdlr 'Schmalzigaug 1913', indinstinctly inscr. on the artist's label on the reverse
PROV.: R. and J. Van de Velde. Antwerp.
EXH.: Rome, Galleria Sprovieri, april-May 1914, no.2; Antwerp, Kunst van Heden, April-May 1923, no.186.
LIT.: P. Mertens, Jules Schmalzigaug 1882-1917, Brussels 1984, pp. 84-85 (ill. in colour pl.49).
        Christie's Amsterdam, 5 June 1996 (242**) NLG 172,500   US$ 100,789

SCHMIDT Martin Johann, {called} Kremser Schmidt (Grafenwörth bei Krems 1718-1801 Stein an der Donau) German
DAS ROSENWUNDER oil on canvas, 30 x 24cm.
LIT.: Rupert Feuchtmüller, *Der Kremser Schmidt*, 1989, p. 481-482.
        Dorotheum Vienna, 17 October 1995 (171**) ATS 160,000   US$ 16,049

SCHMIDT-ROTTLUFF Karl (Rottluff 1884-1976 Berlin) German
LEUCHTTURM oil on canvas, 24¾ x 29in. (65.5 x 79cm.) sdll 'S.Rottluff 13', signed again and
titled on the stretcher
PROV.: Martha and dr. Paul Rauert, Hochkamp b. Hamburg; purchased by the present owner's father
in the 1950s.
EXH.: Syndey, Museum of New South Wales, 1962. This exhibition later travelled to Brisbane,
Adelaide and Melbourne; New Orleans, New Orleans Museum of fine Art, New Orleans Collections,
Nov. 1971-Jan. 1972; New Orleans, New Orleans Museum of Fine Art, German and Austrian
Expressionism, Nov. 1975-Jan. 1976, no. 96 (illus p.90).
LIT.: W. Grohmann, Karl Schmidt-Rottluff, Stuttgart, 1956, p.,287 (with incorrect dimensions) G.
Wietek, Karl Schmidt-Rottluff in Hamburg und Schleswig-Holstein, Neumünster,1984, no.58
(illustrated p.186; with incorrect dimensions).

Christie's London, 11 October 1995 (143***) GBP 430,500	US$	679,451

SCHMUTZLER Leopold (1864-1941) Austrian
NUDE WITH A BUTTERFLY IN A COASTAL LANDSCAPE oil on board, 47 ¼ x 34in. (,120 x
86.3cm.) slr

Phillips London, 14 November 1995 (36**) GBP 6,000	US$	9,385

SCHOENFELD Johann Heinrich (Riss 1609-Augsburg 1683) German
CRUCIFIXION oil on canvas, ,137 x 89cm.

Finearte Milan, 11 June 1996 (38*) ITL 19550,000	US$	12,678

SCHOENMAKERS Johannes (Dordrecht 1755-1842) Dutch
A CANAL LANDSCAPE NEAR A VILLAGE oil on panel, 36 x 51.5cm. slr 'J. Schoenmakers'

Sotheby's Amsterdam, 6 May 1996 (36**) NLG 12,980	US$	7,569

SCHOEVAERDTS Mathijs (Mathieu) (Brussels, active 1665-after 1694, active) Flemish
A COASTAL LANDSCAPE WITH MERCHANTS GATHERED AROUND A FISHMONGER
BEFORE A FORTIFIED GATEWAY; AND TOWNSFOLK GATHERED ON A RIVER BANK
BY A VILLAGE, A BRIDGE BEYOND oil on canvas, 28.3 x 40.8cm.
PROV.: Anon. Sale, Christie's London, 22 July 1988, lot 92, with col. ill.

Christie's Amsterdam, 7 May 1996 (47**) NLG 40,250	US$	23,469

A COASTAL LANDSCAPE WITH MERCHANTS GATHERED AROUND A FISHMONGER
BEFORE A FORTIFIED GATEWAY; AND TOWNSFOLK GATHERED ON A RIVER BANK
BY A VILLAGE, A BRIDGE BEYOND oil on canvas, 28.3 x 40.8cm
PROV.: Anon. Sale, Christie`s London, 22 July 1988, lot 92, with col.ill.

Christie's Amsterdam, 13 November 1995 (150**) NLG 57,500	US$	36,239

SCHOOL German/Austian
CONSTANTINOPLE FROM THE SEA oil on canvas, 36 x 48in. (91.5 x 121.8cm.)

Christie's New York, 2 November 1995 (258**) US$ 28,750	US$	28,750

SCHOOL Piedmontese (second quarter of the 18th century-)
ELEGANT FIGURES SEATED IN THE PICTURE AND PORCELAIN CABINET OF A PALACE
oil on canvas, 20¼ x 32½in. (51.4 x 82.6cm.)

Sotheby's New York, 16 May 1996 (70***) US$ 162,000	US$	162,000

SCHOOL OF BRUGES, CIRCA 1500 Flemish
PORTRAIT OF A WOMAN, SMALL HALF LENGTH, WEARING A BLACK DRESS WITH
WHITE CHEMISE AND BONNET, HOLDING A BIBLE oil on panel, 31 x 21.6cm.

Christie's Amsterdam, 13 November 1995 (50**) NLG 32,200	US$	20,294

SCHOONHOVEN Johannes Jacobus (Jan) (Delft 1914-1994) Dutch
A RELIEF a white painted 'papier maché' relief, 50 x 22cm. sd on the reverse 'J.J. Schoonhoven

1963'
PROV.: A gift from the artist to the present owner.
    Christie's Amsterdam, 5 June 1996 (365**) NLG 43,700   US$ 25,533

T 75-,133 ink on paper, 65 x 50cm. sd '1975' and titled
    Sotheby's Amsterdam, 7 December 1995 (234**) NLG 11,800   US$ 7,312

SCHOONOVER Frank Earle (1877-1972) American
THE DEERSTALKER oil on canvas, 39¼ x 30in. (99.7 x 76.2cm.) sdlr 'FE Schoonover 19'
    Christie's New York, 23 May 1996 (175**) US$ 43,700   US$ 43,700

SCHOTEL Johannes Christiaan (Dordrecht 1787-1838 Dordrecht) Dutch
SAILERS IN A STORM oil on panel, 27 x 38.5cm. s 'I.C. Schotel f.'
    Bukowskis Stockholm, 29 November-1 December 1995 (208**) SEK 210,000   US$ 31,768

SCHOUBROECK Pieter (Hassheim 1570-1607 Frankenthal) Dutch
THE MIRACLE OF CHRIST IN A WOODEDLANDSCAPE oil on copper, 43.5 x 84cm. sdll 'O: SCHOUTEBROUCK, 16.'
PROV.: Private collection, Austria.
    Dorotheum Vienna, 6 March 1996 (140**) ATS 550,000   US$ 52905

SCHREYER Adolf (Frankfurt 1828-1899 Cronberg) German
ARAB HORSEMAN oil on canvas, 34 x 46¾in. (86.4 x 118.3cm.) sll 'Ad. Schreyer'
    Christie's New York, 10 January 1996 (45**) US$ 74,000   US$ 74,000

ARAB HORSEMEN oil on canvas, 34 x 46¾in. (86.4 x 118.3cm.) sll 'Ad. Schreyer'
    Christie's New York, 14 February 1996 (45**) US$ 74,000   US$ 74,000

ARAB HORSEMEN AT AN ENCAMPMENT oil on canvas, 27½ x 47¼in. (70 x 120cm.) s 'Ad. Schreyer'
    Christie's London, 14 June 1996 (76**) GBP 32,200   US$ 49,653

AN ARAB HORSEMAN oil on canvas, 32¼ x 25¾in. (82 x 65.5cm.) s 'Ad. schreyer'
    Christie's London, 17 November 1995 (129**) GBP 25,300   US$ 39,575

A REGAL PROCESSION oil on canvas, 33½ x 46¼in. (85.1 x 117.5cm.) slr 'Ad. Schreyer'
    Christie's New York, 2 November 1995 (255**) US$ 96,000   US$ 96,000

ARAB HORSEMEN CHARGING oil on canvas, 23½ x 38¼in. (59.7 x 97.2cm.) sll 'Ad. Schreyer'
    Christie's New York, 2 November 1995 (262**) US$ 36,800   US$ 36,800

SCHRODL Anton (1820-1906) Austrian
BRINGIN IN THE HARVEST oil on canvas, 30 x 58in. (76.2 x 147.3cm.) slr 'A. Schrodl'
    Christie's East, 13 February 1996 (57**) US$ 9,775   US$ 9,775

SCHROTZBERG Franz (Vienna 1811-1889 Graz) Austrian
EMPEROR FRANZ JOSEPH I oil on canvas, 144.3 x 111.5cm.
    Wiener Kunst Auktionen, 26 March 1996 (33**) ATS 250,000   US$ 24,048

SCHRYVER Louis Marie de (Paris 1862-1942 Paris) French
ON THE RUE DE RIVOLI oil on canvas, 28¾ x 36¼in. (73 x 92.1cm.) sd 'LOUIS DE SCHRYVER/.1892'
    Christie's New York, 14 February 1996 (129**) US$ 277,500   US$ 277,500

THE FLOWER SELLER oil on canvas, 20 x 24¼in. (50.9 x 61.6cm.) sdll 'DE SCHRYVER-Paris-/1886-88' s 'De Schryver' on the reverse
    Christie's New York, 14 February 1996 (131**) US$ 46,000   US$ 46,000

SCHULMAN David (Hilversum 1881-1966 Laren (N.-Holland)) Dutch
WINTER IN LAREN oil on canvas, 57 x 84cm slr 'D Schulman'
    Christie's Amsterdam, 18 June 1996 (411*) NLG 8,050   US$ 4,703

SCHULTZE Bernard (Schneidemühl (East Prussia) 1915 b.) German
GRÜNE UND ROTE MATERIE oil on canvas, collage on canvas, 47¼ x 47¼in. (,120 x 120cm.) sd '1956/57' sd titled 'Frankfurt/M Deutschland' on the reverse
PROV.: A gift from the Artist to the present owner.
    Sotheby's London, 21 March 1996 (38**) GBP 11,500   US$ 17,563

SCHULZ Karl Friedrich {called Jagdschulz} (1796-1866) German
RÜCKKEHR VON DER JAGD oil on canvas, 50.5 xc 67cm. sdll 'Carl Schulz 1834'; sd again cl 'Carl Schulz 1835'
    Christie's Amsterdam, 26 October 1995 (344**) NLG 32,200   US$ 20,303

SCHUMACHER Emil (Hagen 1912 b.) German
OHNE TITEL oil and sand on wrapping paper, 57 x 83cm. sdlr 'Schumacher 82'
    Hauswedell & Nolte Cologne, 6 June 1996 (390**) DEM 31,000   US$ 20,142

DESERTO oil on canvas, 67.5 x 45.5cm. slr 'Schumacher 62.' (1962)
PROV.: Firenze, galleria l'Indiano.
    Finearte Rome, 2 April 1996 (218**) ITL 48300,000   US$ 30,863

RED AND BLACK COMPOSITION mixed media on canvas, 19 5/8 x 27 ½in. (50 x 70cm.) sd '65'
PROV.: Redfern Gallery, London.
    Christie's London, 23 May 1996 (55**]) GBP 49,900   US$ 75,560

NERO oil on wood, 87¾ x 63¾in. (,223 x 162cm.) sdlr '62; titled on the reverse
PROV.: Galerie Alice Pauli, Lausanne; Galerie Sander, Darmstadt.
EXH.: Sao Paulo, VII Bienal de Sao Paulo, September-December 1963; Berlin, Galerie Georg Nothelfer, Das ist es: l5 Jahre Galerie G. Nothefer, September-October 1988 (illustrated in colour in the catalogue p. 47); Berlin, Galerie Georg Nothelfer, Die Wurde und der Mut-l'art moral, April-September 1991 (illustrated in colour in the catalogue p. 38); Frankfurt, Städelsches Kunstinstitut, Emil Schumacher, September 1992-January 1993; Cottbus, Brandenburgische Kunstsammlungen, Die Gouachen der 80er Jahre-Malerei auf Porzellan, June-August 1994.
LIT.: Werner Schmalenbach, Emil Schumacher, Cologne 1981, p. 54, no. 37 (illustrated).
    Christie's London, 27 June 1996 (41**) GBP 73,000   US$ 112,567

HEKU mixed media on canvas, 31½ x 23 5/8in. (80 x 60cm.) sdlr '59
PROV.: Galerie Rudolf Zwirner, Cologne.
    Christie's London, 27 June 1996 (46**) GBP 32,200   US$ 49,653

ZILP-ZALP oil on canvas, 19 5/8 x 15in. (50 x 38cm.) sd '57' s titled again on the stretcher
PROV.: Christian Rosset, Geneva; acquired directly from the above by the present owner in 1973.
    Sotheby's London, 27 June 1996 (132**) GBP 24,150   US$ 37,240

COMPOSITION tempera on canvas, 19¾ x 23 5/8in. (50 x 60cm.) sdlr 'Schumacher Roma 63'
PROV.: Galleria La Medusa, Rome; Galleria L'Isola, Rome; Galleria L'Indiano, Florence.
    Sotheby's London, 27 June 1996 (138**) GBP 35,600   US$ 54,896

SCHÜTZ Christian Georg the Elder (Flörsheim 1718-1791 Frankfurt) German
LANDSCAPE WITH CLASSICAL RUINS oil on panel, 28.5 x 39cm.
      Dorotheum Vienna, 17 October 1995 (180**) ATS 160,000   US$ 16,049

SCHÜTZ Christian Georg the Elder (Flörsheim 1718-1791 Frankfurt) German
VIEW OF A GERMAN VILLAGE ON THE RHINE BORDER oil on canvas, 115.5 x 144cm.
      Étude Tajan Paris, 26 March 1996 (21*) FRF 115,000   US$ 22,732

A RHENISH LANDSCAPE WITH FISHERMEN / A RHENISH LANDSCAPE WITH
TRAVELLERS oil on copper (a pair), each: 6¾ x 8¼in. (17.6 x 21.3cm.) the former slr 'SCHUZ' and
bears inscr. 'Schütz. p b 1718 gest. 1791'
      Sotheby's London, 6 December 1995 (228**) GBP 18,400   US$ 28,316

SCHÜTZ Franz (1751-1781 Switzerland)
TRAVELLERS CROSSING A BRIDGE BY A WATERFALL oil on canvas, 90.7 x 107.5cm. sd on
the bridge ll 'F.Schuetz fec.à.Frankfort 1775'
      Christie's Amsterdam, 13 November 1995 (92*) NLG 10,350   US$ 6,523

SCHÜZ II Christiaan Georg (1751-1823) GERMAN
FLUßLANDSCHAFT MIT FIGUREN oil on panel, 12 x 15 ½in. (30.5 x 39.5cm.) s 'Schüz.fe'
      Christie's London, 11 October 1995 (26**) GBP 9,200   US$ 14,520

SCHWARZ Mommie (1876-1942) Dutch
LANDARBEIDERS oil on canvas, 62 x 52cm. bears the signature lr
PROV.: Collection F. Kleinhof, Twello.
      Sotheby's Amsterdam, 7 December 1995 (207**) NLG 59,000   US$ 36,560

SCHWEICKHARDT Hendrik Willem (Hamm in der Mark 1746-1797 London) Dutch
(German)
`BOEREN BUIJTENVREUGT`: A WEDDING DANCE IN A VILLAGE oil on canvas, 74.8 x
101.8cm sdlr 'JW: Schweickhardt/1782'
PROV.: Commissioned by Cornelis van Heemskerck, The Hague, 1782 (dfl. 425); His Sale,
Rietmulder The Hague, 18 November 1783, lot 73 (sold dfl 221); Jacques Bergeon; Sale, Doorschot
The Hague, 4 November 1789, lot 31 (dfl 51,11); Anon. Sale, Van Marle & Bignell ,The Hague, 16
December 1969, lot 143, with ill.
EXH.: E. J. Sluijter, *Hendrik Willem Schweickhardt (1746-17,970* in Oud Holland, LXXXIX, 1975,
pp. 171-,172 and 190, fig. 42.
      Christie's Amsterdam, 13 November 1995 (147**) NLG 69,000   US$ 43,486

A PAIR OF 'GRISAILLES EN ROSES' DEPICTING PUTTI AT PLAY IN PARK LANDSCAPE oil
on canvas (a pair), each: 80.5 x 105.5cm. each: s 'H.W.Schweickhardt/1777'
      Sotheby's Amsterdam, 6 May 1996 (4**) NLG 37,760   US$ 22,017

SCHWING S. (19th century) German
A YOUNG GIRL BY A WOODED STREAM oil on canvas, 39¾ x 26¾in. (,101 x 67.9cm.) sdlr
'S.Schwing/1884'
      Christie's East, 13 February 1996 (159**) US$ 8,625   US$ 8,625

SCHWITTERS Kurt (1887-1948) German
COLLAGE (HARTWIG & VOGEL) collage on board, image: 6½ x 5¼in. (16.5 x 13cm.) mount: 11
3/8 x 8 7/8in. (29 x 22.5cm.) sdlr 'Kurt Schwitters 1926'
PROV.: Louis Marcoussis, Paris (acquired from the artist; by deacent to the present owner).
      Christie's New York, 1 May 1996 (202**) US$ 46,000   US$ 46,000

KORTINGBILD painted wood and metal assemblage on canvas, 28¾ x 23 5/8in. (73 x 60cm.) s with
the ini., titled and d '32'; s, titled and inscr. 'Leonard Körtling Gewidmet' on the reverse

PROV.: Ernst Schwitter, Lysaker, 1948; Marlborough Fine Art, London.
EXH.: Copenhagen, Kunstforeningen; Stockholm, Kunstnarshuset, *Kurt Merz Schwitters 1887-1948*, no. 102; London. Marlborough Fine Art, *Schwitters*, 1963, no. 167; Düsseldorf, Städtische Kunsthalle; Berlin, Akademie der Kunste; Stuttgart, Staatsgalerie; Basel, Kunsthalle, *Kurt Schwitters*, 1971, no. 194; London, Marlborough Fine Art; Zurich, Marlborough Fine Art, *Kurt Schwitters*, 1972-1973, no. 56; Madrid, Fundacion Juan March, *Kurt Schwitters*, 1982, no. 91.

Sotheby's New York, 2 May 1996 (212**) US$ 162,000 — US$ 162,000

KATHARINAHISSEN collage on paper laid down on the Artist's original mount, 5 3/8 x 4¾ (14 x 12cm.)collage, 11 x 9 5/8in (28 x 24.5cm.)mount s 'Schwitters' (1936)
PROV.: G. David Thompson, Pittsburgh;Galerie Beyeler, Basel;Marlborough Fine Art, London, (337), from whom purchased by the present owner on 24th October 1972.
EXH.: Zurich, Thompson collection, 1960. This exhibition later travelled to Dusseldorf and The Hague; London, Marlborough Fine Art, Kurt Schwitters, 1963; New York, Marlborough-Gerson, Kurt Schwitters, 1965; San Fransisco, San Fransisco Museum of Art, Kurt Schwitters Jan.-Feb. 1966; London, Marlborough Fine Art, Kurt Schwitters, 6-28 Oct.1972, no.59.

Christie's London, 26 June 1996 (259**) GBP 25,300 — US$ 39,013

GREEN ISLAND, YELLOW ISLAND oil and collage on paper, 5 x 3 7/8in. (12.7 x 9.8cm) s with ini. and dlr 'KS 47'
PROV.: G.David Thompson; Galerie Beyeler, Basle; Marlborough Fine Art, London.
EXH.: Zurich, Kunsthaus, *Thompson Collection*, 1960-61; London, Marlborough Fine Art, *Kurt Schwitters in Exile: The Late Work 1937-1948, October 1981, no.151; New York, Marlborough Gallery,* Kurt Schwitters, May-July 1985, no.58.

Christie's South Kensington, 27 November 1995 (226**) GBP 9,562 — US$ 14,957

COLLAGE WITH PLAYING CARD oil and collage on board, 10¾ x 8 ½in. (27.2 x 21.6cm.) ll 'K.Schwitters 1940 Collage with playing card' (1940)
PROV.: Gift from the artist to the present owner, *circa* 1945.
EXH.: London, The Modern Art Gallery Ltd., *Masterpieces by Great Masters, also Paintings and Sculpture by Kurt Schwitters*, Dec., 1944, no. 3a.

Christie's New York, 8 November 1995 (287**) US$ 36,800 — US$ 36,800

SCILTIAN Gregorio (Rostov on the Don 1900-1985) Italian (Armenian)
IL RISVEGLIO oil on canvas, 90 x 70.5cm. sll 'G. Sciltian op. CCC/XXXVI' (1970)
EXH.: Moscow, *Gregorio Sciltian*, Museo Puskin, Dec. 1983.
LIT.: R. Civello, *Sciltian Opera Omnia*, U. Hoepli, Milan, 1986, tav.353, no.176.

Finearte Rome, 12 June 1996 (200**) ITL 40,250,000 — US$ 26,393

LA LETTERA D'AMORE oil on board, 87 x 70cm. slc 'G. sciltian, op. XXI' (1949)
LIT.: G. Scilitan, *La realtà di Sciltian*, ed. Hoepli, Milan, 1968, no. 39 (illsutrated); R. Civello, *Sciltian, Opera omnia*, ed. Hoeplia, Milan, 1986, no. 190, (illustrated no. 79).

Finearte Milan, 18 June 1996 (227**) ITL 36,800,000 — US$ 23,865

INTRUMENTI MUSICALI oil on canvas, 70 x 80cm. sll 'Gregorio Sciltian' (1937)
EXH.: Milan, Galleria del Milione, 1942; Venice, *XXIII Biennale Internazionale d'arte*, 1942; Milan, Rotonda della Besana, *Antologica*, 1980; Ferrara, Palazzo dei Diamanti, *Sciltian*.
LIT.: Renato Civello, *Sciltian, opera omnia*, ed. Hoepli, Milan 1986, no.83.

Finearte Milan, 19 March 1996 (78**) ITL 48,300,000 — US$ 30,902

COSMO E MICROCOSMO oil on canvas, ,105 x 95cm. (1943)
EXH.: Paris, Galerie de l'Elysée, *Gregorio Sciltian*, 1949; Milan, Rotonda di Via Besana, *Gregorio Sciltan, Mostra Antologica dal 1916*, 1980, no. 29 (illustrated).
LIT.: Gregorio Sciltian, *La Realtà di Sciltian*, Milan 1968, no. ,102 (illustrated in colour); Alexander Watt, *Paris Commentary*, in *The Studio*, Vol. CXXXVIII, no. ,677 (illustrated).

Sotheby's Milan, 28 May 1996 (191**) ITL 80,400,000 — US$ 51,638

RAGAZZO CON CANESTRO DI FRUTTA oil on canvas, 86 x 70cm. sll (1925-26)
PROV.: Acquired directly from the artist at the end of the 30s.
Sotheby's Milan, 28 May 1996 (197**) ITL 33,350,000   US$ 21,419

SCOTT Samuel (London 1702/03-1772 Bath) British
WESTMINSTER FROM LAMBETH: WITH WESTMINSTER ABBEY, THE TOWER OF ST.
MARGARET'S, THE PALACE OF WESTMINSTER AND WESTMINSTER BRIDGE oil on
canvas, 30½ x 57in. (77.2 x 144.8cm.) sd 'S. Scott. 1748'
PROV.: Possibly Sir Lawrence Dundas; Probably Jemima, Marchioness Grey (1722-1797), and by
descent through her grandson Thomas Philip, 2nd Earl de Grey (and 5th Baron Lucas), to Nan, 8th
Baroness Lucas and 12th Baroness of Dingwell; Her younger daughter, The Hon. Mrs. Spencer
Loch; with Agnews, 1959.
LIT.: R. Kingzett, A Catalogue of the Works of Samuel Scott, Walpole Society, 48, 1982, pp. 59-60
(C), pl. 22a.
Christie's London, 18 April 1996 (34**) GBP 430,500   US$ 65,2767

SCULLY Sean (1946 b.) British
TWO ONE ONE oil on canvas, 90 x ,107 7/8in. (228.6 x 274.3cm.) sd and titled '1985'
PROV.: Juda Rowan Gallery, London.
Christie's London, 30 November 1995 (52**) GBP 51,000   US$ 79,775

HORIZONTAL-VERTICAL oil and acrylic on canvas, unframed, 84 x 84in. (213.2 x 213.2cm.) sd
and titled 'Sean Scully 1979 'HORIZONTAL-VERTICAL" on the reverse
PROV.: Acquired directly from the artist.
Christie's New York, 8 May 1996 (423**) US$ 36,800   US$ 36,800

SEAGO Edward (1910-1974) British
STRAND-ON-THE-GREEN, CHISWICK oil on board, 20 x 26in. (51 x 66cm.) sll 'Edward Seago'
Christie's London, 21 November 1995 (138**) GBP 8,625   US$ 13,491

SEEGER Hermann (Halberstadt 1857 b.-l) German
IN THE DUNES oil on canvas, 33½ x 42½in. (85 x 108cm.) s 'H.Seeger'
Christie's South Kensington, 12 October 1995 (154**) GBP 5,625   US$ 88,78

SEGUIN Armand (Bretagne 1869-1903 Chateauneuf-du-Faou) French
LA GARDIENNE D'OIES A PONT-AVEN oil on canvas, 47 x 23½in. (119.4 x 59.7cm.) sdll
'Armand Seguin/Pont Aven 1891'
PROV.: Roderic O'Conor Family.
Sotheby's New York, 2 May 1996 (137**) US$ 96,000   US$ 96,000

SEIGNAC Guillaume (Rennes (Ille-et-Villaine) 1870-1924) French
ODALISQUE oil on canvas, 18 x 21½in. (45.7 x 54.6cm.) sll 'G.SEIGNAC'
Christie's New York, 10 January 1996 (43**) US$ 21,850   US$ 21,850

ODALISQUE oil on canvas, 18 x 21½in. (45.7 x 54.6cm.) sll 'G.SEIGNAC'
Christie's New York, 14 February 1996 (43**) US$ 21,850   US$ 21,850

SEIGNAC Paul (Bordeaux (Gironde) 1826-1904 Paris) French
CHRISTMAS MORNING oil on panel, 21 x 26½in. (53.4 x 67.3cm.) slr 'Seignac'
Christie's New York, 2 November 1995 (172**) US$ 32,200   US$ 32,200

SEITER Daniel (1649-1705) Italian
DIANA AND ENDYMION oil on canvas, 96.5 x 133.3cm.
Christie's Rome, 21 November 1995 (240**) ITL 24,000,000   US$ 15,066

SEITZ Georg (Johann Georg) (Nuremberg 1810-1780 Vienna) German
AN ELEGANT STILL LIFE WITH PEONIES, TULIPS AND GRAPES ON A MARBLE LEDGE
AND A STILL LIFE WITH PEONIES, TULIPS, CHERRIES, BUTTERFLY AND A BIRD ON A
MARBLE LEDGE. oil on canvas, 27¾ x 22in. (70.5 x 55.9cm.) sdlr 'G Seitz/1849'
Christie's East, 30 October 1995 (137*) US$ 25,300   US$ 25,300

SELLAER Vincent (Malines 1500 before-1589 Malines) Flemish
VENUS WITH PUTTI oil on panel, 37½ x 46½in. (95.5 x 118cm.)
Sotheby's London, 17 April 1996 (17**) GBP 12,650   US$ 19,181

SENET PÉREZ Rafael (Spanish 1856-1927) Spanish
ALONG THE GRAND CANAL oil on canvas, 29½ x 17 5/8in. (75 x 44.8cm.) slr inscr. 'R.
Senet/Vevezia'
Christie's New York, 2 November 1995 (233**) US$ 16,100   US$ 16,100

SERRES Dominic, R.A. (Gascogne 1722-1793 London) British (French)
THE BATTLE OF QUIBERON BAY, 20 NOVEMBER 1759 oil on canvas, 60 x 95in. (152.5 x
241.5cm.) sdlr 'D. Serres: 1766'
PROV.: Concise Catalogue of oil paintings in the National Maritime Museum, Woodbridge, 1988, p.
359, no. BHC2266.
Christie's London, 10 November 1995 (50**) GBP 13,800   US$ 21,586

SERRES John Thomas (1759-1825) British
VIEWS OF THE BAYS OF NAPLES oil on canvas (a pair), 23¾ x 36¼in. (60.3 x 92.1cm.) sdll
'Giov,ni T. Serres 1815' and sdlr 'Giov.ni Tom. Serres 1810'
Christie's London, 10 November 1995 (53**) GBP 21,850   US$ 34,178

SÉRUSIER Paul (Louis Paul Henri) (Paris 1863-1927 Morlaix) French
LE FANEUR-HOMMAGE A VAN GOGH oil on canvas, 28¼ x 35¾in. (72 x 91cm.) slr 'P. Sérusier'
(1892)
PROV.: H. Boutaric, Paris; M. Delourme, Paris.
EXH.: According to Marcel Guicheteau this work is likely to have been exhibited at the chateau de
Saint-Germain in 1892.
LIT.: M. Guicheteau, Paul Sérusier, Paris, 1976, no. 61 (illustrated in colour p. 69).
Christie's London, 25 June 1996 (9**) GBP 177,500   US$ 273,709

JEUNE FILLE AUX FLEURS gouache, 84 x 63cm.
Étude Tajan Paris, 28 March 1996 (1) FRF 50,000   US$ 9,883

SEVERINI Gino (Cortona 1883-1966 Paris) Italian
DANSEUSE gouache on paper, 25 3/8 x 19in. (64.3 x 48.2cm.) slc 'G. Severini' (1957)
PROV.: Edgardo Acosta Gallery, los Angeles; Ansley Graham Gallery, Los Angeles; Stevens
Gallery , Beverly Hills; Anon. sale, Cristie's New York, 1 November 1978, lot 180.
Christie's New York, 1 May 1996 (356**) US$ 25,300   US$ 25,300

PAESAGGIO TOSCANO oil on canvas, 25½ x 19¾in. (65 x 50in.) (1912-13)
PROV.: N. Nobilio, Florence; Galleria Annunciata, Milan; Galerie Tarica, Paris.
EXH.: Rome, Ridotto del Teatro Costanzi, Galleria Giosi, Prima Esposizione di Pittura Futurista,
1913, no. 4?; Rotterdam, Rotterdamsche Kunstkring, Les peintres et les sculpteurs futuristes italiens,
1913, no. 33?; Florence, Galleria Gonnelli, Esposizione di Pittura Futurista di 'Lacerba', 1913-1914,
no. 3?; Florence, Palazzo Strozzi, XVII Mostra Internazionale d'Arte Premio del Fiorino, 1966, no. 1;
Turin, Galleria Civica d'Arte Moderna, I Pittori Italiani dell'Associazione Internazionale Arti
Plastiche, Unesco, 1968.
LIT.: Letter from the Artist to Ardengo Soffici, September 1913; Letter from the Artist to Giovanni
Papini, February 1914, Archivo della Fondazione Primo Conti, Fiesole; U. Apollonio, Il Futurismo,
Milan, 1970 (illustrated p. 213);D. Fonti, Gino Severini Catalogo Ragionato, Milan, 1988, no. ,108

(illustrated p. 129).

		US$	714,726
Christie's London, 25 June 1996 (16**) GBP 463,500			

BALCONE S ROCA DI PAPE oil on canvas, 45½ x 35in. (115.5 x 89cm.) slr 'G. Severini' (summer of 1928)
PROV.: Paul Rosenberg, Paris.
EXH.: Geneva, Galerie Moos, 21 Artistes du Novecento Italien, 1929; Milan, Palazzo della Permanente, Seconda Mostra del Novecento Italiano, 1929; Basle, Kunsthalle, Moderne Italiener, 1930, no. 270; Berne, Kunsthalle, Kunstler des neuen Italien, 1930, no. 202; Buenos Aires, Amigos des Arte, Mostra del Novecento Italiano1930, no. 151; Paris, Galerie Jacques Bonjean, Gino Severini, 1931, no. 9; Rome, Palazzo Venezia, Cino Severini, 1961, no. 99; Paris, Musee National d'art Moderne, Gino Severini, 1967, no. 59.
LIT.: Letter from the Artist to Leonce Rosenberg dated 10th September 1928; M. Jirmounsky, L'exposition italienne à Buenos Aires in 'Beaux Arts', April 1931; D. Fonti, Gino Severini, Gatalogo ragionato, Milan, 1988, no. ,346 (illustrated p. 374).

		US$	171,935
Christie's London, 25 June 1996 (37**) GBP 111,500			

NATURE MORTE AVEC COMPOTIER ET VERRE ink and gouache on paper, 6 7/8 x 10 5/8in. (17.5 x 27cm.) s 'G Severini' sd and titled 'Severini 1916 nature morte: Compotier et Verre' on the reverse
PROV.: Romana Severini Brunai, Rome, daughter of the Artist.

		US$	53,200
Christie's London, 26 June 1996 (211**) GBP 34,500			

DANSEUSE oil on canvas, 93 x 72cm. slr 'G. Severini' and signed on the reverse (1957-1958)

		US$	58,754
Finearte Milan, 26 October 1995 (185**) ITL 94300,000			

SEYMOUR James (London 1702 c.-1752 London) British
MR AMBROSE PHILLIPS'S TWO RACEHORSES IN A STABLE WITH A GROOM oil on canvas, 23 x 29in. (58.4 x 73.6cm.) s 'J S/1747'
PROV.: Fermor-Hesketh family, by whom sold Christie's, 15 July 1988, lot 14.

		US$	239,273
Sotheby's London, 12 July 1995 (131**) GBP 150,000			

SHAHN Ben (Kowno 1898-1969 New York) American (Lithuanian)
F. SCOTT FITZGERALD AND OTHER gouache on paper, 12 x 15¾in. (31 x 40.5cm.); (sight): 10 x 12½in. (25 x 32cm.)
PROV.: Blanche Bonestell, New York.

		US$	25,300
Christie's New York, 23 May 1996 (156**) US$ 25,300			

SHARP Dorothea (1874-1955) British
A SUNLIT GARDEN oil on canvas, 30 x 25in. (76.2 x 63.5cm.) s 'Dorothea Sharp'

		US$	24,827
Christie's London, 20 June 1996 (74**) GBP 16,100			

HILL FLOWERS oil on canvas, 25 x 30in. (63.5 x 76.2cm.)
PROV.: James Connell & Sons Ltd., London, where purchased by the present owner's family during the 1930's.

		US$	17,089
Christie's London, 21 November 1995 (13**) GBP 10,925			

SHAYER William J., Snr (Southampton 1788-1879 Shirley (near Southampton)) British
ISLE OF WIGHT WITH FIGURES AND HORSES oil on canvas, 22 x 30in. (56 x 76cm.) sd bears title on a lable on the stretcher (1854)

		US$	11,477
Phillips London, 23 January 1996 (83*) GBP 7,500			

SHAYER William Joseph (Southampton 1811-1860) British
THE HAY WAGON OUTSIDE THE INN oil on canvas, 18 x 24in. (45.7 x 61cm.) sdlr 'William Shayer/18.1'

		US$	6,900
Christie's East, 13 February 1996 (46**) US$ 6,900			

SHEETS Millard Owen (1907-1989) American
THE RIVER CANYON watercolour and gouache on paper, 41 x 28in. (56 x 71cm.) sdll 'Millard
Sheets 1937'
        Christie's East, 21 May 1996 (179**) US$ 16,100   US$ 16,100

SHINN Everett (Woodstwon (New Jersey) 1876-1953 New York) American
THE PARK IN WINTER pastel on Artist's board, 21½ x 27in. (54.6 x 68.5cm.) s 'Everett Shinn'
PROV.: Chapellier Galleries, New York; Mr. and Mrs. Frank Sinatra.
LIT.: Chapellier, *Americam Art Selections*, New York, 1975, vol. 5, n.p., (illustrated).
        Christie's New York, 1 December 1995 (67**) US$ 90,500   US$ 90,500

SICHEL Nathaniel (1843-1907) German
PORTRAIT OF AN ORIENTAL GIRL oil on canvas, 23¾ x 20 1/8in. (60.5 x 51cm.) sar 'N. Sichel'
        Phillips London, 11 June 1996 (30**) GBP 4,000   US$ 6,168

SICILIA José Maria (1954 b.) Spanish
FLEUR BLANC acrylic on canvas-unframed, ,112 x 112in. (,300 x 300cm.) sd and titled 'fluer Blanc
Sicilia Paris 87' on the reverse
PROV.: Blum Helman Gallery, New York.
        Christie's New York, 15 November 1995 (316**) US$ 19,550   US$ 19,550

FLEUR LIGNE NOIR acrylic on canvas, unframed, ,118 x 118in. (,300 x 300cm.) sd and titled
"Fleur Ligne Noir' Sicilia Paris 87' on the reverse
PROV.: BlumHelman Gallery, New York.
        Christie's New York, 8 May 1996 (403**) US$ 20,700   US$ 20,700

SICKERT Walter Richard, A.R.A. (Munich 1860-1942 Bathampton, Somerset) British
AUBERVILLE oil on canvas, 16 x 13in. (40.5 x 33cm.) sd inscr.'Sickert Auberville 1913'
        Christie's London, 20 June 1996 (33**) GBP 17,250   US$ 26,600

PONTE DELLA GUGLIE SUL CANNAREGIO oil on canvas, 14½ x 17½in. (38 x 45.7cm.) sll
'Sickert' (ca 1896)
PROV.: Ernest Hewit, thence by descent to the present owner.
EXH.: London, Fine Art Society, Sickert Loan Exhibition, May-June 1973, no. 28: this exhibition
travelled to Edinburgh; Nottingham, University Department of Fine Art, Queen of Marble and Mud;
The Nineteenth Century Anglo-American Vision of Venice: 1880-1910 Works by Whistler, Sickert
and Sargent, Feb.-March 1978, no.14; Venice, Museo Correr, Venezia Nell'Ottocento Immagini e
Mito, Dec. 1983-March 1984, no. 142; Manchester, City Art Gallery (on long-term loan).
LIT.: W. Baron, Sickert, London, 1973, no.90, p.54.
        Christie's London, 21 March 1996 (119**) GBP 23,000   US$ 35,125

SIGNAC Paul (Paris 1863-1935 Paris) French
QUIMPER pencil and watercolour on paper, 28 x 45.5cm. sd and inscr. with titl ll 'P. Signac 4 mai
27'
        Christie's Amsterdam, 5 June 1996 (214**) NLG 43,700   US$ 25,533

FECAMP, SOLEIL oil on canvas, 18 1/8 x 21¾in. (46 x 55.2cm.) slr 'P Signac' (1886)
PROV.: Galerie Goldschmidt, Frankfürt.
        Sotheby's New York, 2 May 1996 (134**) US$ 118,000   US$ 118,000

ETUDE POUR PLACE DE LICES A SAINT-TROPEZ oil on panel, 7 3/8 x 10 5/8in. (18.8 x 27cm.)
ini. lr 'PS' and s and titled on the reverse 'Paul Signac Place de Lices a S. Tropez' (1895)
PROV.: Germaine Teisset; Felix Fénéon, Paris; his Estate sale, Hôtel Drouot, Paris, 30 May, 1947,
lot 108; Anon. sale, Hôtel Drouot, Paris, March 23, 1953, lot 144; Anon. sale, Palais Galliéra, Paris,
Dec. 10, 1966, lot 81; Anon. sale, Sotheby's, London, 30 April, 1969, lot 48, GBP4,500, acquired by
the late owner.

LIT.: M. Ferretti-Bocquillon, Signac et Saint-Tropez, Saint-Tropez, 1992, Musée de la Annonciade, p. 61 (illustrated, fig. 3); To be included in the forthcoming *Paul Signac catalogue raisonné* currently being prepared by Françoise Cachin.

Christie's London, 29 November 1995 (123**) GBP 17,000	US$	265,92

SILLÉN Herman Af (1857-1908) Swedish
VY MOT SÖDER FRÅN KASTELLHOLMEN oil on canvas, 70 x 100cm. sdlr 'H. Af Sillén 1889'

Bukowskis Stockholm, 29 November-1 December 1995 (135**) SEK 165,000	US$	24,961

SILO Adam (attr.) (Amsterdam 1674-1766 Amsterdam) Dutch
SHIPS IN AN ESTUARY oil on canvas, 64 x 86cm. bears initials lr 'LB'

Sotheby's Amsterdam, 6 May 1996 (28**) NLG 22,420	US$	13,073

SILVA Francis Augustus (New York 1835-1886 New York) American
DUNES oil on canvas, 10½ x 30in. (26.6 x 76.2cm.) sdll 'FA Silva 1875'
PROV.: Berry-Hill Galleries Inc., New York.

Christie's New York, 23 May 1996 (40**) US$ 20,700	US$	20,700

LAKESIDE COTAGE gouache on paper laid down on board, 7 x 13½ (18 x 34cm.) slr 'Francis A. Silva'

Christie's East, 28 November 1995 (94*) US$ 8,050	US$	8,050

LAKESIDE, BRANCHPORT NEW YORK gouache on paper laid down on board, 6½ x 13½in. (16.5 x 34.5cm.) sdll 'F.A. Silva Branchport, NY 82'

Christie's East, 28 November 1995 (100*) US$ 9,200	US$	9,200

SIMA Josef (Jaromer (Eastern Bohemia) 1891-1971 Paris) French
UNTITLED oil on canvas, 36¼ x 28½in. (92 x 72.5cm.) sd lr 'J. Sima 1962'
PROV.: A gift from the Artist to the present owner.

Sotheby's London, 21 March 1996 (13**) GBP 12,650	US$	19,319

SIMON Yohanan (1905-1976) Israelian
NEGEV ROCKS oil on canvas, 2/8 3/8 x 39½in. (72 x 100.5cm.) s in Hebrew and dll '61'

Christie's Tel Aviv, 12 October 1995 (67**) US$ 9,200	US$	9,200

SIMON Yohanan (1905-1976) Israelian
LES TROIS VASES oil on canvas, 13¾ x 10½in. (34.9 x 26.7cm.) sll 'Yohanan Simon', slr in Hebrew, s again in English and Hebrew and titled on the stretcher

Christie's Tel Aviv, 14 April 1996 (20**) US$ 7,130	US$	7,130

SIMONETTI Ettore (19th Century-l) Italian
THE JEWEL BOX pencil and watercolour on paper, 29¾ x 21in. (75.5 x 53.3cm.) s inscr. 'Ettore Simonetti/Roma'

Christie's London, 14 June 1996 (80**) GBP 29,900	US$	46,106

SIMONI Gustavo (1846 b.-) Italian
ARABS PLAYING CHESS watercolour on paper, 26 x 19½in. (66 x 49.5cm.) sdll 'G. Simoni. 87.' (1887)

Christie's New York, 14 February 1996 (41**) US$ 10,925	US$	10,925

ARAB MUSICIANS pencil and watercolour heightened with gum arabic on paper, 24½ x 38¼in. (62 x 97cm.) s 'G. Simoni/Roma'

Christie's London, 15 March 1996 (70**) GBP 20,700	US$	31,613

SIMONINI Francesco Antonio (Parma 1686-1753 Venice) Italian
COSSACKS FORDING THE MOUTH OF A RIVER, A CASCADE NEARBY oil on canvas, 44 1/8
x 67 7/8in. (,112 x 172.5cm.)
        Christie's London, 8 December 1995 (85**) GBP 47,700   US$ 73,407

SINGER William Henry (1868-1943) Dutch
THE FROZEN RIVER oil on canvas, 97 x ,106 cm s 'WH Singer Jr' and inscribed with title on the
stretcher (1942)
LIT.: R.W.P. de Vries, W.H. *Singer, the man and the artist*, Bussum, p.64, illus. no.85.
        Christie's Amsterdam, 25 April 1996 (36*) NLG 16,100   US$ 9,567

SIRONI Mario (Sassari 1885-1961 Milan) Italian
IL CICLISTA mixed media on paper, 53 x 56cm. slr 'Sironi' (1918)
EXH.: Luzern, Kunstmuseum, 1960; Rotterdam Museum Boymans van Beuningen, *Mario Sironi en
8 hedendaagse Italiaanse schilders*, 1964.
LIT.: 'Inediti di Sironi', in *Domus*, December 1961.
        Finearte Milan, 12 December 1995 (289**) ITL 46,000,000   US$ 28,858

PAESAGGIO URBANO oil on canvas, 69 x 79cm. slr 'Sironi' sd on the reverse 'Mario Sironi nov
1932' (1932)
PROV.: Milan, Palazzo Reale, *Mario Sironi*, Feb/March 1973, no. 96 of the catalogue.
LIT.: Marco Valsecchi, *Mario Sironi*, ed. Editalia 1962, no.35.
        Finearte Milan, 19 March 1996 (75**) ITL 195500,000   US$ 125,080

COMPOSIZIONE CON FIGURE E CASA BIANCA oil on canvas, 49.5 x 59.5cm. slr 'Sironi' s
'Sironi W.N. 7'
PROV.: Galleria dell'Annunciata, Milano.
        Christie's Milan, 20 November 1995 (137**) ITL 41247,000   US$ 25,325

IL CAVALLO BIANCO oil on panel, 40 x 50cm. sll 'Sironi' (1928)
PROV.: Collection Gussoni, Milano; Galleria Edmondo Sacerdoti, Milano; Galleria Milano, Milano.
LIT.: Raffaele De Grada, *Mario Sironi*, Milano 1972, p. 112, tav. XX (illustrated).
        Christie's Milan, 20 November 1995 (152**) ITL 65996,000   US$ 41,429

FIGURA DI DONNA oil on panel, 50 x 30cm. slr 'Sironi' (ca. 1920)
        Christie's Milan, 20 November 1995 (157**) ITL 29462,000   US$ 18,495

COMPOSITION oil on canvas, 54 x 56cm. slr 'Sironi' (1940)
        Finearte Milan, 26 October 1995 (179**) ITL 63250,000   US$ 39,408

COMPOSIZIONE tempera and pencil on paper, 31 x 43cm. (1945-50)
PROV.: Eredità Sironi, no. ,689 dell'inventario.
        Sotheby's Milan, 28 May 1996 (88**) ITL 11,500,000   US$ 7,386

SISLEY Alfred (Paris 1839-1899 Moret-sur-Loing) British
THE WAVE; LADY'S COVE, LANGLAND BAY oil on canvas, 25½ x 31½in. (64.8 x 80cm.) sdll
'Sisley 97'
PROV.: Estate of the artist, Paris 1899; Jeanne Dietsch-Sisley, Paris (sale: Hôtel Drouot, Paris, 18
May 1909, no. 3); Mrs. Georges Lurcy; French & Co., New York.
EXH.: Paris, Champ de Mars, *Société Nationale des Beaux-Arts*, 1898, no. 1136; Paris, Galerie
Bernheim-Jeune, *L'Atelier de Sisley*, 1907, no. 20.
LIT.: François Daulte, *Alfred Sisley: Catalogue Raisonné de l'Oeuvre Peint*, Lausanne, 1959, no.
,877 (illustrated).
        Sotheby's New York, 2 May 1996 (126**) US$ 354,500   US$ 354,500

LE CANAL DU LOING oil on canvas, 14½ x 21¼ in. (37 x 54cm.) slr (1884)
PROV.: Gaston Alexandre Camentron, Paris; Durand-Ruel, Paris (purchased from the above on January 12th, 1899); Dr. Albert C. Barnes, Philadelphia (purchased from the above on first August,; 1913) The Lefevre Gallery (Alex Reid and Lefevre, London).
EXH.: Paris, Galerie Durand-Ruel, *Sisley*, 1902, no. 42; London, Grafton Gallery, *Paintings (by Boudin..Sisley*, 1905, no. 314.
LIT.: François Daulte, *Alfred Sisley, Catalogue raisonne de l'Oeuvre Peint*, 1959,; no. 531, illustrated.

Sotheby's London, 24 June 1996 (6**) GBP 397,500	US$	612,953

LES JARDINS SOUS LA NEIGE pastel on paper, 14½ x 17¾in. (37 x 45cm.) slr 'Sisley'
PROV.: Acquired by the father of the present owner before 1939, thence by descent.

Christie's London, 26 June 1996 (108**) GBP 76,300	US$	117,656

LE PONT DE MORTE AU SOLEIL oil on canvas, 25 5/8 x 31 7/8in. (65 x 81cm.) sdlr 'Sisley 92'
PROV.: Georges Feydeau, Paris; sale, Hotel Drouot, Paris, April 4, 1903, lot 43; Galerie Bernheim Jeune, Paris (acquired at the above sale); Galerie Barbazanges, Paris; Alex. Reid & Lefevre, London; D.W.T. Cargill, Lanark.
EXH.: Glasgow, Alex. Reid & Lefevre, *Important French Pictures*, 1929, no. 32; London, Royal Academy of Arts, *Exhibition of French Art,1200-1900*, Jan.-March 1932, p. 232, no. 506 (illus. pl. 69).
LIT.: F. Daulte, *Afred Sisley, Catalogue raisonné de l'oeuvre peint*, Lausanne, 1959, no. ,788 (illus.).

Christie's New York, 30 April 1996 (35**) US$ 1,212,500	US$	1,212,500

BORDS DU LOING oil on canvas, 15 x 21 5/8in. (38 x 55cm) sdll 'Sisley. 85' (1885)
PROV.: Galerie Durand-Ruel, Paris (1886); Dr. Albert Charpentier (acquired from the above on March 18, 1930); Charles Ribon, Bogotá.
EXH.: Paris, Galerie Durand-Ruel, *Tableaux de Sisley*, Feb.-March, 1930, no. 54.
LIT.: F. Daulte, *Alfred Sisley, Catalogue raisonné de l'oeuvre peint*, Lausanne, 1959, no. ,618 (illustrated).

Christie's New York, 7 November 1995 (8**) US$ 497,500	US$	497,500

EFFET DE NEIGE A ARGENTEUIL oil on canvas, 21¼ x 25 5/8in. (54 x 65cm.) sdll 'Sisley. 74'
PROV.: François Depeaux, Paris; sale, Galerie Georges Petit, Paris, May 31, 1906, lot 59 (illustrated); Maurice Barrett-Decap, Biarritz; sale, Hotel Drouot, Paris, Dec. 12, 1929, lot 13 (illustrated); Henri Canonne, Paris; Private collection, Geneva.
EXH.: London, Royal Academy of Arts, Exhibition of French Art 1200-1900, Jan.-March, 1931, no. 504; Paris, Galerie Paul Rosenberg, Exposition d'oeuvres importantes de grands maîtres du dix-neuvième siècle, May-June, 1931, no. 76.
LIT.: A. Alexandre, La Collection Canonne, Paris, 1930 (illustrated in color); F. Daulte, Afred Sisley, *Catalogue raisonné de l'oeuvre peint*, Lausanne, 1959, no. ,147 (illustrated).

Christie's New York, 7 November 1995 (13**) US$ 1,982,500	US$	1,982,500

L'ALLEE DES PEUPLIERS AU BORD DU LOING oil on canvas, 28½ x 35½in. (72.3 x 90.2cm.) sll 'Sisley.' (1892)
PROV.: Collection La Tour d'Ygest, Paris; Matthiesen Gallery Ltd., London; Samuel and Saidye Bronfman, Montreal.
LIT.: F. Daulte, *Alfred Sisley, Catalogue raisonné de l'oeuvre peint*, Lausanne, 1959, no. ,796 (illustrated).

Christie's New York, 7 November 1995 (24**) US$ 1,487,500	US$	1,487,500

LE PONT DE MORET oil on canvas, 13 x 16 1/8in. (33 x 41cm.) sll 'Sisley' (1892)
PROV.: Galerie georges Petit, Paris.
LIT.: F. Daulte, *Alfred Sisley, Catalogue raisonné de l'oeuvre peint*, Lausanne, 1959, no. ,793 illustrated).

Christie's New York, 7 November 1995 (26**) US$ 464,500	US$	464,500

SKREDSVIG Christian Eriksen (1854-1924) Norwegian
ST. HANS AFTEN E NORGE oil on canvas, en grisaille, 16 x 28¾in. (40.5 x 73cm.) sd 'Chr.
Skredsvig 1887'
PROV.: With A. Bargue Fils, Paris.
      Christie's London, 15 March 1996 (67**) GBP 8,625   US$ 13,172

SLEVOGT Max (Landshut 1868-1932 Neukastel) Austrian
GRÄSER UND SCHMETTERLINGE oil on canvas, 29¼ x 30¾in. (74.3 x 78.2cm.) slr 'Slevogt'
(1917)
PROV.: Carl Steinbart, NBerlin, and thence by descent to the present owner.
EXH.: Berlin, Preußische Akademie der Künste, Max Slevogt: Gemälde, Aquarelle, Pastelle,
Zeichnungen-zu seinem 60. Geburtstage, Oct.-Nov. 1928, no. 124; Düsseldorf, Stätisches
Kunstmuseum (on loan from the above for several years from March 1931).
      Christie's London, 11 October 1995 (133**) GBP 56,500   US$ 89,173

SLOAN John (Lock Haven (Pennsylvania) 1871-1951 Hanover (New Hampshire)) American
HUMORESQUE oil on canvas, 20 x 24in. (50.7 x 61cm.) sll 'John Sloan' inscr. with the title on the
reverse (ca. 1915)
PROV.: St. Ignatius Convent; M. R. Schweitzer Gallery, New York; Sale: New York, Plaza Auction
Gallery, 20 April 1961.
EXH.: New York, Mrs. Harry Payne Whitney's studio, *Exhibition of Paintings, Etchings, and
Drawings by John Sloan*, January-February, 1916, no. 1; New York, Hudson Guild, *Exhibition of
Paintings, Etchings and Drawings byJohn Sloan*, February-April, 1916, no. 1; Chicago, Illinois,
Carson, Pine, Scott, *George Bellows, William Glackens, Robert Henri, John Sloan*, January, 1918.
LIT.: Art News, January 5, 1918; Recorded John Sloan Consignment Book, John Sloan and Helen
Farr *Sloan Archives*, Delaware Art Museum R. Elzea,John *Sloan's Oil Paintings: A Catalogue
Raisonné*, Newark, Delaware, 1991, vol. 1, p. 167, no. 367, illus.;This work appears as JS,306 in the
artist's records.
      Christie's New York, 30 November 1995 (62**) US$ 46,000   US$ 46,000

SLOANE Eric (1910-1985) American
NOSTALGIC SUMMER oil on masonite, 24 x 42in. (61 x 106.7cm.) sll 'Eric Sloane'; s inscr. on the
reverse 'Cornwall Bridge, Conn.' (ca. 1958)
PROV.: Fischer Galleries, Washington, D.C.
      Christie's New York, 13 September 1995 (96**) US$ 24,150   US$ 24,150

HUNTING IN WINTER oil on masonite, 24 x 35¼in. (61 x 89.5cm.) sll 'Eric Sloane'
      Christie's New York, 13 September 1995 (98*) US$ 9,200   US$ 9,200

**SLUIJTERS Jan (Johannes Carolus Bernardus) ('s-Hertogenbosch 1881-1957 Amsterdam)
Dutch**
HYACINTHS oil on canvas, 58 x 47cm. Sal 'Jan Sluijters'
EXH.: Hoensbroek, Kasteel Hoensbroek, *Jan Sluijters*, 30 May-30 June 1958, no. 24; `s-
Hertogenbosch, Provinciaal Museum, *Jan Sluijters*, 6-27 July 1958, no. 24; Helmond, Gemeente
museum, *Jan Sluijters*, 30 July-10 August 1958, no. 24; Breda, Cultureel Centrum De Beyerd, *Jan
Sluijters*, 12-31 August 1958, no. 24; Tilburg, Paleis-raadhuis, *Jan Sluyters*, 5-28 September 1958,
no. 24; Laren Singer Memorial Foundation, *Jan Sluijters*, 17 December 1966-12 February 1967, no.
43.
      Christie's Amsterdam, 5 June 1996 (250**) NLG 48,300   US$ 28,221

A LADY WEARING A GREEN HAT coloured crayon and watercolour on paper, 25 x 28cm. sll (in
monogram)
      Christie's Amsterdam, 5 June 1996 (252*) NLG 20,700   US$ 12,095

A SAILING BOAT ON A LAKE oil on cardboard laid down on board, 12.5 x 28.5cm. slr (in monogram) (*ca.* 1911)
    Christie's Amsterdam, 5 June 1996 (262**) NLG 34,500   US$ 20,158

A REGATTA oil on cardboard, 25.5 x 72cm. sdll 'Jan Sluijters 11'
    Christie's Amsterdam, 5 June 1996 (263**) NLG 63,250   US$ 36,956

MULATTIN charcoal, coloured crayons and watercolour on paper, 76 x 55cm. (ca. 1920)
EXH.: 's Hertogenbosch, Noordbrabants Museum, *Jan Sluijters 1881-1957, aquarellen en tekeningen*, 8 June-25 August 1991, no. 124.
LIT.: Anita Hopmans, *Jan Sluijters, aquarellen en tekeningen*, Zwolle 1991, no. 124(ill.).
    Christie's Amsterdam, 6 December 1995 (169**) NLG 17,250   US$ 10,689

ALMOUT TA CHEME, TEN NOORDEN VAN CINTRA (PORTUGAL) oil on canvas, 58 x 71cm. sll 'Jan Sluijters', and inscr. with title on the stretcher
    Christie's Amsterdam, 6 December 1995 (180*) NLG 17,250   US$ 10,689

STILLEVEN MET VIOLEN EN VERGEET-MIJ-NIET oil on canvas, 32 x 49cm. slc 'Jan Sluijters' and inscr. with title and d on a label on the stretcher '1941'
PROV.: Kunsthandel G.J.Nieuwenhuizen Segaar, The Hague.
    Christie's Amsterdam, 6 December 1995 (200**) NLG 25,300   US$ 15,677

A FEMALE NUDE oil on canvas, 65 x 50cm.
PROV.: Estate of the artist.
    Christie's Amsterdam, 6 December 1995 (215**) NLG 40,250   US$ 24,941

A VILLAGE STREET IN LEENDE (NOORD-BRABANT) oil on canvas, 58 x 73cm. sdll 'Jan Sluijters 9'
    Christie's Amsterdam, 6 December 1995 (217**) NLG 34,500   US$ 21,378

SMEDLEY William Thomas (1858-1920) American
THE WHITE DRESS: PORTRAIT A YOUNG WOMAN IN A PARK oil on canvas, 50 x 26in. (,127 x 66cm.) sdll 'WT Smedley 1903'
    Christie's New York, 30 November 1995 (53**) US$ 16,100   US$ 16,100

SMEERDYK Anton (Antonie) ('s-Graveland 1885-1965 Roermond) Dutch
A SUNNY DAY ON THE BEACH oil on canvas, 96 x 157cm. sll 'Ant. Smeerdijk' (executed *ca.* 1912)
    Christie's Amsterdam, 6 December 1995 (231**) NLG 39,100   US$ 24,229

SMEETS Richard (1955 b.-) Dutch
A BEACH SCENE acrylics on canvas, ,180 x 200cm. sd on the reverse 'Richard Smeets 84'
    Christie's Amsterdam, 5 June 1996 (357**) NLG 6,900   US$ 4,032

SMET Gustave de (Ghent 1877-1943) Belgian
MOLEN AAN DE SCHELDE / A MILL ALONG THE BANKS OF THE RIVER SCHELDE oil on canvas, 89 x 114cm. sll 'Gustave de Smet' (executed in 1899)
LIT.: Peter Boyens, *Gust. De Smet*, Antwerpen, 1989, p. 301, no. 23(ill.).
    Christie's Amsterdam, 6 December 1995 (206) NLG 23,500   US$ 14,562

MEISJESPORTRET oil on card, 49 x 48cm. slr 'Gust. de Smet' (1919)
PROV.: Collection A. van Dijk, Antwerp; Collection Dr. W.L. Ladenius, Haarlem; Kunsthandel Bodes, The Hague; Collection R.J. Bruininga, Monster.
LIT.: Piet boyens, *Gust. de Smet*, Antwerp 1989; p. 356, no. ,513 (illustrated).
    Sotheby's Amsterdam, 7 December 1995 (206**) NLG 35,400   US$ 21,936

SMET Léon de (Ghent 1881-1966) Belgian
NATURE MORTE: VASE DE FLEURS ET GRAVURE SUR BOIS JAPONAISE oil on canvas,
30¼ x 25in. (76.8 x 63.5cm.) sd 'Léon de Smet 1917'
PROV.: Rutland Galleries, London; Galleries Maurice Steinberg, Chicago.
Sotheby's New York, 2 May 1996 (159**) US$ 79,500   US$ 79,500

BOUQUET DE FLEURS DANS UNE CRUCHE-BOUQUET MET BLOEMEN IN EEN KRUIK oil
on canvas, 31¼ x 25¾in. (79.5 x 65.5cm.) sll 'Leon de Smet'
Christie's London, 26 June 1996 (205**) GBP 14,950   US$ 23,053

LE CANAL-DE GRACHT oil on canvas, 29 7/8 x 35¼in. (76 x 89.5cm.) sll 'LEON DE SMET'
Christie's London, 26 June 1996 (226**) GBP 12,650   US$ 19,507

SMILLIE George Henry, N.A. (1840-1921) American
VERMONT MEADOWS oil on canvas, 15¼ x 24in. (38.7 x 61cm.) sdll 'Geo. H. Smillie Aug. '85'
PROV.: Sale: New York, Sotheby's, September 28, 1973, lot 41.
Christie's New York, 13 September 1995 (22**) US$ 10,350   US$ 10,350

SMIT Aernout (1641-1710 Amsterdam) Dutch
DUTCH MEN O'WAR, INCLUDING A FLAGSHIP FIRING A SALUTE, AN ARMED
MERCHANTSMAN (FLUTE), AND AN ENGLISH KETCH IN A SHORT CHOP oil on canvas,
39¼ x 56¾in. (99.8 x 144.5cm.)
Sotheby's London, 6 December 1995 (139**) GBP 21,850   US$ 33,626

SMITH Carlton Alfred (1853-1946) British
WHEN THE WORK IS DONE watercolour with touches of white heightening on whatman paper, 31
x 48in. (78.8 x 121.9cm.) sd 'Carlton A. Smith '95' and inscr. '72 Park Rd./Haverstock
Hill/N.W./When the work is done/Carlton a. Smith' on an old label on the reverse
PROV.: Mrs Garnett; Christie's, 6 July 1928, lot 36 (unsold at 38gns.).
EXH.: London, Royal Academy, 1895, no. 1001.
Christie's London, 6 November 1995 (32**) GBP 16,100   US$ 25,184

SMITH David (1906-1965) American
UNTITLED (STANDING WOMAN PROFILE) oil and enamel on canvas, 72 x 17½in. (182.9 x
44.4cm.) sdur 'David Smith 9/28/56'
PROV.: Estate of David Smith; M.Knoedler & Co., Inc., New York.
EXH.: Washington D.C., Hirshhorn Museum and Sculpture Garden; San Antonio, Museum of Art,
David Smith: Painter, Sculptor, Draftsman, Nov. 1982-June 1983, p.119, no.76 (ill.).
Christie's New York, 22 February 1996 (22**) US$ 41,400   US$ 41,400

SMITH George (London 1829-1901 London) British
LACE-MAKING oil on panel, 40.5 x 35 cm sd 'George Smith 1866'
Christie's Amsterdam, 25 April 1996 (117**) NLG 24,150   US$ 14,350

SMITH George of Chichester (1714-1776) British
EXTENSIVE LANDSCAPE WITH FISHERMEN AND SHEPHERDS BY A POND, A CASTLE
ON THE HILL BEYOND oil on canvas, 45¼ x 57½in. (114.9 x 146.1cm.) slr 'Geo Smith'
PROV.: Sale: Christie's, London, 4 February 1924, lot 126.
Sotheby's New York, 6 October 1996 (129*) US$ 90,500   US$ 905,00

SMITH Henry Pember (1854-1907) American
HOMESTEAD BY THE POND oil on canvas, 20 x 28in. (50.8 x 71.2cm.) slr 'Henry P Smith'
Christie's New York, 13 September 1995 (18*) US$ 3,680   US$ 3,680

VENICE oil on canvas, 40 x 30 1/8in. (101.6 x 76.5cm.) slr 'Henry P. Smith'
Christie's New York, 13 September 1995 (33*) US$ 9,200   US$ 9,200

SPRINGTIME IN VENICE oil on canvas, 28 x 20in. (71.1 x 50.8cm.) slr 'Henry P. Smith'
    Christie's East, 21 May 1996 (49**) US$ 10,350   US$ 10,350

SMITH Leon Polk (1906 b.) American
CORRESPONDENCE ORANGE-RED acrylic on canvas, 86 x 65¾in. (,216 x 167cm.) sd titled
'LEON POLK SMITH CORRESPONDENCE ORANGE-RED 1968'
    Christie's New York, 15 November 1995 (146**) US$ 11,500   US$ 11,500

NO. 7,809 acrylic on shaped canvas, diameter: 80 in. (203.2cm.) sd numb. LEON POLK SMITH NO
7,809 1978'
    Christie's New York, 22 February 1996 (46**) US$ 9,200   US$ 9,200

SMITH Sir Matthew (Halifax (Yorkshire) 1879-1959 London) British
FLOWERS WITH A LIGHT BLUE BACKGROUND oil on canvas, 24 x 20in. (60 x 50.8cm.)
PROV.: Arthur Tooth & Sons Ltd., London; Guy Tooth, private collection; Purchased by the present
owner from the Tooth family.
EXH.: Paris, Salle Balzac, Le Peinture Britannique Contemporaire, Oct. 1957, no. 82.
    Christie's London, 21 March 1996 (20**) GBP 21,850   US$ 33,369

SMYTHE Lionel Percy R.A. (1839-1918) British
THE GLEANERS oil on canvas, 30 x 50in. (76.2 x 127cm.) sdll "L. Smythe 1892'
EXH.: London, Royal Academy, 1892, no. ,136 as A Landscape.
LIT.: The Spectator, 7 May 1892.
    Christie's London, 21 November 1995 (104**) GBP 17,250   US$ 26,983

SNAYERS Pieter (Antwerp 1592-1666 after Brussels) Flemish
BANDITS ATTACKING A CARAVAN IN AN EXTENSIVE LANDSCAPE oil on panel, 21½ x
30in. (54.6 x 76.2cm.) sll mono. 'PS'
    Sotheby's New York, 16 May 1996 (141**) US$ 19,550   US$ 19,550

SNAYERS Pieter (attr.) (Antwerp 1592-1666 after Brussels) Flemish
SPANISH TROOPS RAISING THE SIEGE OF GROLLE oil on canvas, 49¼ x 66½in. (,125 x
169cm.) inscr. lr 'GROLLAS/ ANTE HOLLANDUM EXER/ CITV FVGAT/ LA ET VRBE
OBSIDIONE LIBERAT M/ 9BRIS MDXCVI'
PROV.: Anonymous sale Sotheby's London, 11 April 1990, lot 28, where purchased by the present
owner.
EXH.: Maastricht, London and Rome, Chaucer Fine Arts and Galleria Gasparrini, 1987, no. 14.
    Sotheby's London, 6 December 1995 (182**) GBP 34,500   US$ 53,093

SNELLINCK Andries (Antwerp 1587-1653) Flemish
RÉUNION GALANTE DANS LE PARC D'UN CHATEAU oil on copper, 67 x 93cm. slc
'ANDRIES SNELLINX'
    Étude Tajan Paris, 28 June 1996 (60**) FRF 60,000   US$ 11,586

SNICK Jozef van (1860-1945) Belgian
A CARPENTER AT WORK oil on panel, 26½ x 21in. (67 x 53cm.) sdll '1889'
    Sotheby's London, 13 March 1996 (14**) GBP 13,225   US$ 20,197

SNYDERS Frans (Antwerp 1579-1657) Flemish
STILL-LIFE GRAPES, PEAR, APRICOTS, REDCURRANTS AND CHERRIES IN A TAZZA, A
BLUE AND WHITE PORCELAIN BOWL WITH WILD STRAWBERRIES AND A PINK
CARNATION, AND AN OPEN WALNUT, ALL ON A TABLE oil on copper, 13½ x 19¾in. (34 x
50cm.)
    Sotheby's London, 5 July 1995 (62**) GBP 188,500   US$ 300,686

GRAPES, QUINCES, PEACHES, APRICOTS, AN APPLE, FIGS AND A MELON IN A BASKET, WITH TULIPS AND A ROSE IN A GLASS VASE, BUNCHES OF ASPARAGUS, LEMONS IN A WAN-LI DISH AND RADISHES ON A DRAPED TABLE oil on canvas, 82.3 x 101.7cm.
PROV.: with P. de Boer, Amsterdam, as Frans Snyders.
          Christie's Amsterdam, 7 May 1996 (51**) NLG 69,000   US$ 40,233

A VENDOR OF FRUITS AND 'EGETABLES oil on canvas, 65¼ x 95¼in. (165.7 x 241.9cm.) sd on the edge of the table at right *F Snyders fecit. 1627*
PROV.: Count Potocki, Lancut Castle, Poland; Fritz Frey, Bürgenstockhotels, Bürgenstock am Vierwaldstätter See, Switzerland.
LIT.: Edith Greindl, *Les Peintures Flamands de Nature Morte au XVIIe Siècle*, 1956, p. 52, 181; Fritz Frey, *Der Bürgenstock*, 1966, p. 48; Hella Robels, 'Frans Snyders' Entwicklung als Stillebenmaler', *Wallraf-Richartz-Jahrbuch*, 1969, p. 65; Edith Greindl, *Les Peintures Flamands de Nature Morte au XVIIe Siècle*, 1983, pp. 75, 375, no. 56 (illustrated p. 295, fig. 202); Hella Robels, *Frans Snyders*, pp. 202-203, no. 37 (illustrated).
          Sotheby's New York, 11 January 1996 (80**) US$ 1,542,500   US$ 1,542,500

A VENDOR OF WILD GAME oil on canvas, 67¾ x 95¼in. (172.1 x 241.9cm.)
PROV.: Count Potocki, Lancut Castle, Poland; Fritz Frey, Bürgenstockhotels, Bürgenstock am Vierwaldstätter See, Switzerland.
EXH.: Münster, Westfälisch Landes Museum für Kunst und Kulturgeschichte, *Stilleben in Europa*, 1979/80, travelling on to Baden-Baden, no. 197a.
LIT.: Edith Greindl, *Les Peintures Flamands de Nature Morte au XVIIe Siècle*, 1956, p. 52, ,181 (as signed and dated 1627); Fritz Frey, *Der Bürgenstock*, 1966, p. 55; Hella Robels, *Frans Snyders*, 1989, p. 203, no. 38 (illustrated); Edith Greindl, *Les Peintures Flamands de Nature Morte au XVIIe Siècle*, 1983, pp. 75, 375, no. 55.
          Sotheby's New York, 11 January 1996 (81**) US$ 442,500   US$ 442,500

STILL-LIFES WITH FRUIT AND VEGETABLES oil on panel (a pair), 26¾ x 13in. (67.9 x 33cm.)
          Sotheby's New York, 11 January 1996 (142**)
US$ 85,000   US$ 85,000

LE CUISINIER DANS LE GARDE-MANGER oil on canvas, 229.5 x 135.5cm.
          Étude Tajan Paris, 12 December 1995 (70**)
FRF 300,000   US$ 60,428

A Vendor of Fruit and Vegetables

SOEST Gérard (Soest (near Utrecht) (?) 1600-1681 London) British (Flemish)
PORTRAIT OF A BOY, FULL LENGHT, AS MARS, WITH A DOG IN A GARDEN oil on canvas, 49¼ x 36¼in. (125.7 x 93.3cm.)
          Christie's London, 18 April 1996 (2**) GBP 21,850   US$ 33,131

SOFFICI Ardengo (Rignano sull'Arno 1879-1964 Poggio a Caiano) Italian
CASE A POGGIO A CAIANO oil on paper, 68.5 x 50cm. sdll 'Soffici 47' (1947)
          Finearte Milan, 26 October 1995 (162**) ITL 40,250,000   US$ 25,078

SPIAGGIA oil on canvas laid down on board, 45.2 x 65cm. sd '27' (1927)
PROV.: Acquried directly from the artist.
LIT.: Giuseppe Raimondo-Luigi Cavallo, *Ardengo Soffici*, Florence 1967, p. CCCXXXII, no. ,295 (illustrated).
          Sotheby's Milan, 28 May 1996 (177**) ITL 75,880,000   US$ 48,735

SOHN Carl Ferdinand (1805-1867) German
DIE BEIDEN LEONOREN oil on canvas, 68½ x 52¼in. (,174 x 132.7cm.) sd 'Carl Sohn. 1834'
LIT.: Possibly in F. von Boetticher, malerwerke des 19 Jahrhunderts, Hofheim am Taunus, 1974, vol.

II, 2, p. 765, no. 8.
> Christie's London, 17 November 1995 (19**) GBP 58,700   US$ 91,819

SOLANA José Gutiérrez (1886-1945) Spanish
MASCARAS CON ESCOBAS Y CARETA NEGRA oil on canvas, 46 x 38cm. sdlr 'J. Solana'
> Sotheby's Madrid, 23 November 1995 (73***) ESP 13,285,000   US$ 109,203

MASCARAS CON ARCO DE GUIRNALDA, GUITARRA Y BOTA pastel, coloured crayon and
charcoal on paper, 39 x 32cm. sll 'J.Solana' (ca. 1928-1933)
> Sotheby's Madrid, 23 November 1995 (75**) ESP 4,112,500   US$ 33,805

SOLDATI Atanasio (Parma 1896-1953 Milan) Italian
PAESAGGIO CON CASE oil on canvas, 60 x 55cm. slr 'Soldati' (1941)
EXH.: *Dal Futurismo a oggi, pittori e scultori italiani*, March-Dec. 1959.
> Finearte Milan, 19 March 1996 (57**) ITL 48,300,000   US$ 30,902

COMPOSIZIONE oil on canvas, 36 x 52cm. sll 'Soldati' (1945)
PROV.: Milan, collection Ernesto Bestagini.
EXH.: Turin, Galleria Civica d'arte Moderna, *Atanasio Soldati*, Nov. 1969/Jan. 1970, no.134, p.42,
tav.95.
> Finearte Milan, 19 March 1996 (71**) ITL 64,400,000   US$ 41,203

COMPOSITION oil on canvas, 54 x 81cm. slr 'Soldati' (ca 1941)
> Finearte Milan, 26 October 1995 (167**) ITL 69,000,000   US$ 42,991

SOLE Giovanni Gioseffo dal (1654-1719) Italian
THE PENITENT MAGDALENE oil on canvas, 47¾ x 38¾in. (,121 x 98cm.)
> Sotheby's London, 5 July 1995 (104**) GBP 17,250   US$ 27,516

SOLIMENA Angelo (1629-1716) Italian
ST MADELEINE DOING PENITENCE oil on canvas, ,125 x 101cm. s mono 'A.S.'
> Christie's Rome, 21 November 1995 (183**) ITL 15000,000   US$ 9,416

SOLIMENA Francesco (Nocera 1657-1747 Barra) Italian
SAN FELICE DA CANTALICE oil on canvas, 19 7/8 x 23¾in. (50.5 x 60.5cm.) (1732)
PROV.: with Galerie Heim-Gairac, Paris, 1954 (advertised in The Burlington Magazine, XCVI, Feb.
1954, p. Xl); with the Hazlitt Gallery, London (Seventeenth and Eighteenth Century Oil Sketches,
May 1961, no. 19, pl. 7b); from whom purchased by the late owner's husband.
LIT.: F. Zeri, La Galleria Pallavicini in Roma. Catalogo dei dipinti, Florence, 1959, p. 248, under no.
462; B. Nicolson in Current and Forthcoming Exhibitions, The Burlington Magazine, CIII, no. 698,
May 1961, p. 195; N. Spinosa, Pittura napoletana del Settecento dal Barocco al Rococo, Naples,
1986, p. 118, no. 55, and p. 211, fig. 60.
> Christie's London, 8 December 1995 (92**) GBP 78,500   US$ 120,806

THE ARRIVAL OF TERTULLIUS AND PATRICIUS AT SUBIACO TO ENTRUST SAINT
BENEDICT WITH THEIR SONS MAURUS AND PLACIDUS oil on canvas, 26¾ x 60¼in. (67.9 x
153cm.)
PROV.: Purchased by the family of the present collector in the 1930's.
> Sotheby's New York, 11 January 1996 (181A**) US$ 37,950   US$ 37,950

SAINT JOHN oil on canvas, 18 x 13¾in. (45.7 x 34.9cm.) (ca. 1680)
> Sotheby's New York, 16 May 1996 (49**) US$ 23,000   US$ 23,000

THE ROYAL HUNT OF DIDO AND AENEAS oil on canvas, 29 x 30in. (73.7 x 76.8cm.) (ca 1739-
-0)
PROV.: Scholz-Forni Collection, Hamburg; Anon. Sale, Christie's, 9 duly 1982, lot 66; with

Matthiesen (The Settecento, 4 Nov.-20 Dec. 1987, pp. 157-9, no. 36, pl. 30).
EXH.: Wiesbaden, Italienische Malerei des 17. und 18. Jahrhunderts, I935, no.179; Naples, Mostra della pittura napoletana dei tre secoli, 1938.
LIT.: (Possibly) B. de Dominici, Vite.., 1742, IV, p. 451; W.R. Deusch, Weltkunst, Xl, no. 47, Nov. 1937, p. 2; Nagler, Künsterlexikon, XIX, p. 66.;U. Thieme and F. Becker, Allgemeines Lexicon der Bildenden Kunstler, XXXI, Leipzig, 1937, p. 246; A. von Schneider, Aus der Sammlung Scholz-Fomi, Hamburg, 1937, no. 19; M. Goering, Pantheon, XI11, no. 5, May 1940, p. 120.; F. Bologna, Francesco Solimena, Naples, 1958, pp. ,118 and 248, fig. 209, where dated immediately prior to 1740; D. Miller, The Gallery of Aeneid in the Palazzo Bonaccorsi at Macerata, Arte Antica e Moderna,1963, pp. ,153 and 258, 1964, p. 113. M. Levey, Solimena's 'Dido Receiving Aeneas and Cupid disguised as Ascanius', The Burlington Magazine, CXV, no. 843, June 1973, pp. 385-6, note 2; O. Ferran, Considerazione sulle vicende artistiche a Napoli durante il viceregno austriaco (1707-1734), Storia dell'Arte, 1979, no. 35, p. 17.; F. Bologna, Solimena al Palazzo Reale di Napoli per le nozze di Carlo di Borbone, Prospettiva, 16,p.65 no. 21; F. Haskell, Patrons and Painters: Art and Society in Baroque Italy, New Haven and London, 1980, pp. 224, note 4; N. Spinosa, Pittura napoletana del settecento dal Barocco al Rococo, Naples, 1986, p. 111, under no. 36.

Christie's London, 7 July 1995 (107**) GBP 43,300	US$	69,070

SOLIMENA Francesco a follower of (Nocera 1657-1747 Barra) Italian
DIANA DISCOVERING THE PREGNANCY OF CALLISTO oil on canvas, 140.6 x 176.5cm.

Christie's Amsterdam, 7 May 1996 (133**) NLG 86,250	US$	50,292

SOMMER Otto (19th Century, active-l) American
UNION DROVER WITH CATTLE FOR THE ARMY oil on canvas, 30 x 44in. (76.2 x 111.8cm.) sdl 'Otto Sommer N.Y. 1866'
PROV.: Mr. Victor D. Spark, New York.

Christie's New York, 13 March 1996 (34**) US$ 29,900	US$	29,900

SON Joris van (Antwerp 1623-1667 Antwerp) Flemish
A STILL-LIFE OF A GARLAND OF FRUIT AND FLOWRES oil on canvas, 27½ x 23¼in. (70 x 59cm.) sdlr 'J.VAN SON 1662.'

Sotheby's London, 6 December 1995 (184**) GBP 32,200	US$	49,554

SONDERBORG Kurt R. H. (1923 b.-) Danish/German
28-XII-60 tempera on vynil mounted on board, 43½ x 27¾in. (,110 x 70.5cm.) sd '61'
PROV.: Lefebre Galleriey, New York.
EXH.: Biennale de Sao Paolo, 1963.

Sotheby's London, 21 March 1996 (39**) GBP 9,775	US$	14,928

SOREAU Isaack (Hanau 1604 b. 1620-1638 active-l) Flemish
STILL LIFE OF A BASKET OF VEGETABLES AND FRUIT INCLUDING ASPARAGUS AND ARTICHOKES ON A WOODEN TABLE oil on copper, 24 1/8 x 25¾in. (61.3 x 65.4cm.)

Sotheby's New York, 11 January 1996 (73**) US$ 211,500	US$	211,500

SOROLLA Y BASTIDA Joaquín (Valencia 1863-1923 Cercedilla, prov. Madrid) Spanish
PORTRAIT OF THE ACTOR, RAMON PENA, HALF-LENGHT, WEARING A GREY SUIT oil on canvas, 28¾ x 21¼in. (73 x 54cm.) s inscr. 'A Pena/Sorolla'
LIT.: B de Pontorba, la Vida y la Obra de Joaquin Sorolla, Madrid 1970, p. 211, no. 2113.

Christie's London, 15 March 1996 (145**) GBP 29,900	US$	456,63

THE GEESE oil on canvas, 14 x 23in. (35.5 x 58.5cm.) sd 'J Sorolla/19.8'
PROV.: Purchased by George Keyes, Boston, from the artist and thence by descent to the presnet owner.
LIT.: A de Beruete y Moret, Sorolla y Bastida in Eight Essays on Joaquin Sorolla y Bastida, Neew York, Hispanic society of America, 1909, vol. I, pl. 112.

Christie's London, 15 March 1996 (146**) GBP 45,500	US$	69,48'

BOY IN THE BREAKERS, JAVEA oil on canvas, 23¼ x 35in. sdll 'J. Sorolla Bastida/1900'
PROV.: Mr. Fred Maxwell.
EXH.: Paris, Galerie Georges Petit, 1906; Berlin, Düsseldorf and Cologne, Gallery Schulte, 1907;
New York, Hispanic Society of America, *Joaquin Sorolla y Bastida at the Hispanic Society of America* February 4-March 8, 1909; Buffalo, Albright-Knox Museum, 1909; Boston, Copley Society, 1909.
LIT.: 'Sorolla y Bastida', New York, *Hispanic Society of America*, 1909, p. 349, no. 107; B.Pantorba, *La vida y la obra de Joaquin Sorolla*, Madrid, 1953, no.l422.

Christie's New York, 22 May 1996 (116**) US$ 321,500	US$	321,500

SOULACROIX Frédéric (Charles Joseph Fréderic) (Montpellier (Hérault) 1825-1879) French
AN ELEGANT LADY IN AN INTERIOR oil on canvas, 30¼ x 18 1/8in. (76.9 x 46cm.) sll
'F.Soulacroix'
PROV.: Florence Art Gallery, Florence.

Christie's New York, 14 February 1996 (101**) US$ 101,500	US$	101,500

THE RECITAL oil on canvas, 42½ x 71in. (,108 x 180.4cm.) sdlr 'F. Soulacroix/Florence'

Christie's New York, 2 November 1995 (139**) US$ 134,500	US$	134,500

A 'TETE A TETE' oil on canvas, 34¾ x 26¼in. (88.2 x 66.6cm.) sll 'F. Soulacroix'

Christie's New York, 22 May 1996 (235**) US$ 103,700	US$	103,700

SOULAGES Pierre (Rodez 1919 b.) French
UNTITLED OIL ON PAPER LAID DOWN ON CANVAS, 25 x 19¾in. (63.5 x 50cm.) slr
'Soulages' (ca. 1960)
PROV.: A gift from the Artist to the present owner.

Sotheby's London, 21 March 1996 (25**) GBP 18,400	US$	281,00

PEINTURE: 11 JUILLET 1958 oil on canvas, 63¾ x 51 1/8in. (,162 x 130cm.) (1958)
PROV.: Galerie de france, paris; M. Charles Laughton, Hollywood.
LIT.: Pierre Encrevé, *Soulages, L'Oeuvre Complet Peintures I: 1946-1959*, Paris 1994, p 264, no. ,332 illustrated in colour.

Sotheby's London, 21 March 1996 (45***) GBP 172,000	US$	262,676

PEINTURE, 14 AOUT 66 oil on canvas, 38 1/8 x 51 1/8in. (97 x 130cm.) sd and titled on the reverse
PROV.: Gimpel Fils Gallery, London;Galerie de France, Paris; Acquired from the above by the present owner in 1969.
EXH.: London, Gimpel Fils Gallery, Pierre Soulages, January-February 1967, no. 8 (illustrated in colour in the catalogue).
LIT.: Montreal, Musée d'art Contemporain; Québec, Musée de Québec, Soulages, July-October 1968, no. 28 (illustrated in colour in the catalogue); Paris, Musée National d'art Moderne, Retrospective Soulages March-May 1967, no. 75.

Christie's London, 26 October 1995 (47**) GBP 76,300	US$	120,423

PEINTURE, 27 MAI 1961 oil on canvas, 79¼ x 62¾in. (201.4 x 159.4cm.) slr; sd and titled '27 Mai 1961' on the reverse
PROV.: Kootz Gallery, New York; Edward J. Mathews, New York; Norman C. Stone, San Fransisco.
EXH.: New York, Kootz Gallery, *Soulages*, October-November 1961.
LIT.: Pierre Encrevé, *Soulages, L'Oeuvre Complet: Peintures, vol. II: 1959-1978*, Paris 1996, p. 80, no. ,457 (illustrated in colour).

Christie's London, 27 June 1996 (32**) GBP 144,500	US$	222,822

PEINTURE, 25 MAI 1958 oil on canvas, 23 5/8 x 31 7/8in. (60 x81cm.) slr; titled on the reverse
1958)
PROV.: Galerie de France, Paris; Howard Wise, Cleveland; Waddington Galleries, London; Mr and

Mrs C. Maggs, Eagle's Nest, Constantia Nek (South Africa).
EXH.: Cape Town, South African National Gallery, Frined's collection, February-March 1971, no. 74.
LIT.: Pierre Encrevé, Soulages, L'Oeuvre Complet: Peintures, vol. I: 1946-1959, Paris 1994, p. 260, no. ,328 (illustrated in colour).
Christie's London, 27 June 1996 (38**) GBP 111,500   US$ 171,935

PEINTURE, 17 JUIN 1958 oil on canvas, 35 x 45¾in. (89 x 116cm.) sd 'Soulages 58', d '17/6/58' on the reverse
PROV.: M. Ernest Duveen, London; Gimpel Fils Gallery, London; David E Bright, Beverly Hills.
EXH.: New York, Duveen Brothers, Exhibition of World Masters, 1958.
LIT.: Pierre Encrevé, Soulages, L'Oeuvre Complet: Pemture, vol. 1: 1946-1959, Paris 1994, p. 221, no. ,330 (illustrated in colour).
Christie's London, 30 November 1995 (6**) GBP 78,512   US$ 122,809

SOUTINE Chaim (Smilovichi, near Minsk 1894-1943 Paris) French (Lithuanian)
NATURE MORTE AU CHOU ROUGE oil on canvas laid down on board, 21 x 17 171in. (53.3 x 44.5cm.) slr 'Soutine' (ca. 1918)
PROV.: Max Moss, New York, from whom purchased by Mr. and Mrs. Ralph F. Colin in 1948.
EXH.: New York, M. Knoedler & Co., Inc., *The Colin Collection*, April-May 1960, no. 75 (illustrated); New York, Marlborough Gallery Inc., *Chaim Soutine 1893-1943*, Oct.-Nov. 1973, no. 10 (illustrated).
LIT.: P. Courthion, *Soutine, Peintre du déchirant*, Paris, 1972, pp. 84 and ,250 (illustrated p. 251H and in colour p. 85); M. Tuchman, 'Soutine distorted the pictures but not the people' in *Art News*, Oct. 1973, p. 85 (illsutrated); M. Tuchmann, E. Dunow and K. Perls, *Chaim Soutine, Catalogue Raisonné*, London, 1993, vol. I, no. 16 (illustrated in colour p. 366).
Christie's Tel Aviv, 12 October 1995 (21**) US$ 79,500   US$ 79,500

NATURE MORTE A LA SOUPIERE oil on canvas, 23¾ x 28 5/8in. (60.5 x 72.7cm.) slr 'C. Soutine' (ca. 1916)
PROV.: Lucien Lefebvre-Foinet, Paris; Valentine Gallery, New York, from whom purchased by Mr. and Mrs. Ralph F. Colin ca. 1950.
EXH.: New York, Valentine GaHery, *Twenty-three Paintings by Soutine*, March-April 1939, no 9; New York, Museum of Modem Art, Soutine, Nov.-Dec. 1950, pp. 46 and ,112 (illustrated p. 36). This exhibition
later travelled to Cleveland, Museum of Art, *Modigliani-Soutine Exhibition*, Jan.-March 1951; San Francisco, California Palace of the Legion of Honor, *Paintings by Chaim Soutine 1894-1943*, Aug.-Sept. 1951.
This exhibition later travelled to Palm Beach, Society of the Four Arts, no. 1; Venice, XXVI Biennale, *Soutine,* 1952, no. 1 (illustrated)
New York, M. Knoedler & Co., Inc., *The Colin Collection*, April-May 1960, no. 74 (illustrated); New York, Marlborough Gallery Inc., *Chaim Soutine 1894-1943*, Oct.-Nov. 1973, no. 8 (illustrated); Munster, Westfälisches Landesmuseum fur Kunst und Kulturgeschichte, *Chaim Soutine 1893-1943*, Dec. 1981-Feb. 1982, no. 2, pp. 34, 73, 77-78, and 24 (illustrated p. 72 and in colour p. 145). This exhibition later travelled to Tübingen, Kunsthalle; London, Hayward Gallery and Lucern, Kunstmuseum.
LIT.: M. Breuning, 'The Cataclysmic World of Chaim Soutine' in *The Art Digest*, Nov. 15 1950, p. 11; F. Arcangeli, 'Corot et Soutine à Venezia' in *Paragone*, Sept. 1952, pp. 61-62; J. Lassaigne, *Soutine*, Paris, 1954, no. 2 (illustrated in colour); E. Szittya, *Soutine et son temps*, Pans, 1955, p. 114; P. D'Ancona, *Some Aspects of Expressionism: Modigliani, Chagall, Soutine, Pascin*, Milan, 1957, p. 59 (illustrated in colour p. 51); M. Castaing and J. Leymarie, *Soutine*, Paris, 1963, p. 18; D. Sylvester, *Chaim Soutine*, 1893-1945, London, 1963, p. 6; A. Forge, *Soutine*, London, 1965, p. 11; R. Negri, 'Chaim Soutine' in *L'Arte Moderna*, vol. 10, no. 90, 1967, p. ,371 (illustrated); P. Courthion, *Soutine, Peintre du déchirant*, Paris, 1972, p. 30 (illustrated p. 117C and in colour p. 31); A. Wemer, *Jewish Chronicle Literary Supplement*, 1 Dec. 1972, p. v (illustrated); R. Cogniat, *Soutine*, Paris, 1973 (illustrated in colour on the back of the cover); J. Lassaigne, *Soutine,* Paris, 1973 (illustrated in

colour); A. Wemer, *American Artist*, Dec. 1973, p. 53 (illustrated); A. Wemer, *Chaim Soutine*, New York, 1977, no. 2 (illustrated in colour); Y. Friedrichs, 'Deutschland entdeckt Soutine' in *Du*, no. 2, 1982, p. 82 (illustrated); E.-G. Güse, 'Ekstatisches leiden' in *Die Weltkunst*, Jan 1982, p. 20 (illustrated); R. Cork, 'Pummelling the Pigment in the Pyrenees' in *The Evening Standard*, 29 July 1982; ed. Gallerie Bellman, *Soutine (1894-1943)*, New York, 1983, p. 9 (exhibition catalogue); M. Tuchman, E. Dunow and K. Perls, Chaim Soutine, Catalogue Raisonné, London, 1993, vol. I, no. 2 (illustrated in colour p. 352).

Christie's Tel Aviv, 12 October 1995 (46**) US$ 145,500   US$ 145,500

LE PAYSAN oil on canvas, 25¼ x 21/4in. (64 x 55.2cm.) (1919-1920)
PROV.: Léopold Zborowski, Paris; The Barnes Foundation, Merion, Pennsylvania, 1923; Bignou Gallery, Inc., New York, from whom purchased by Mr. and Mrs. Ralph Colin in 1945.
EXH.: Paris, Paul Guillaume, *Acquisitions of Dr. Albert C. Barnes*, Jan.-Feb. 1923. This exhibition later travelled to Philadelphia, Pennsylvania Academy of Fine Arts; New York, Bignou Gallery Inc., *Soutine*, March-April 1943, no. 10; New York, Bignou Gallery Inc., *Exhibition of Modern Paintings*, Jan. 1945, no. 16; Boston, Museum of Fine Arts, *Group Show*, March 1950; New York, The Metropolitan Museum of Art, *Summer Loan Show*, July-Aug. 1950; Cambridge, Massachusetts, Harvard University, Busch-Reisinger Museum, *Impressionism and Expressionism*, Feb.-March 1954, no. 44; Minneapolis, Walker Art Center, Expressionism, 1900-1955, Jan.-March 1956 (illustrated). This exhibition later travelled to Boston, The Institute of Contemporary Art; San Francisco, Museum of Art; Cinnati, Art Museum and Contemporary Arts Center; Baltimore, Museum of Art and Buffalo, Albright Art Gallery; New York, M. Knoedler & Co., Inc., *The Colin Collection*, April-May 1960, no. 76 (illustrated); New York, Brearley School, Feb.-March 1963; London, Tate Gallery, *Chaim Soutine*, Sept.-Nov. 1963, no. 9 (illustrated). This exhibition later travelled to Edinburgh, Arts Festival. New York, Marlborough Gallery Inc., *Chaim Soutine 1893-1943*, Oct.-Nov. 1973, no. 5 (illustrated); Munster, Westfälisches Landesmuseum fur Kunst und Kulturgeschiche, *Chaim Soutine 1893-1943*, Dec. 1981-Feb. 1982, no. 20 (illustrated in colour p. 163). This exhibition later travelled to Tübingen, Kunsthalle and London, Hayward Gallery.
LIT.: 'The Passing Shows: Chaim Soutine' in *Art News*, 1 April 1943, p. 23; J. Canaday, 'Matter of Seeing' in *New York Times*, 17 April 1960, Section 2, p. 11 (illustrated); M. Tuchman, 'Portraits de Soutine' in *Art de France*, no. 4, 1964, p. ,210 (illustrated); A. Forge, *Soutine*, London, 1965, p. 38, no. 7 (illustrated p. 48 and in colour p. 215D); P. Courthion, *Soutine, Peintre du déchirant*, Paris, 1972, p. 48 (illustrated and again in colour p. 214D); M. Tuchman, E. Dunow and K. Perls, *Chaim Soutine, Catalogue Raisonné*, London, 1933, vol. 11, no. 38 (illustrated p. 575).

Christie's Tel Aviv, 12 October 1995 (52**) US$ 195,000   US$ 195,000

NATURE MORTE AUX POIVRONS ET CAROTTES oil on canvas, 23 5/8 x 18 1/8in. (60 x 46cm.) sur 'C.Soutine' (ca. 1918)
PROV.: Raoul Pellequer, Paris; Galerie Percier, Paris (1926-1942). Madame Leray, Paris, from whom purchased from the above in 1942, thenceby descent to the present owner.
EXH.: Paris, Galerie André Weil, 1953; Paris, Galerie Charpentier, 1959, no.60.
LIT.: M.Tuchman, E.Dunow, K.Perls, *Chaïm Soutine (1893-1943)*, vol.I, London 1993, no.14 (ill. in colour p.364); P.Cabanne, *Arts*, June 1959, p.16; P.Courthion, *Soutine, Peintre du déchirant*, Lausanne, 1972, pl.D (ill. p.186).

Christie's Tel Aviv, 14 April 1996 (25**) US$ 90,500   US$ 90,500

LA ROUTE QUI MONTE oil on canvas, 25 5/8 x 18 3/8in. (65 x 48cm.) slr 'C. Soutine ' (1921)
PROV.: Georges Bernheim, Paris; Georges Halphen, La Chapelle en Geuval, France.
LIT.: P. Courthion, *Soutine, peintre du Déchirant*, Lausanne, 1972 (illus. p. 207/C).

Christie's London, 28 November 1995 (38**) GBP 133,500   US$ 208,822

LA FILLE EN ROSE oil on canvas, 34¼ x 24 7/8in. (87 x 63.5cm.) sll 'Soutine' (1925)
PROV.: Otto M. Gerson, New York; M. Knoedler & Co., Inc., New York; Otto M. Gerson, New York (1951); Acquired from the above by Mr. Joseph H. Hazen on Nov. 9, 1951.
EXH.: New York, Metropolitan Museum of Art, *Impressionist and Modern Paintings from Private Collections*,July-Sept., 1957 New York, Solomon R. Guggenheim Museum, *Van Gogh and*

Expressionism,July-Sept., 1964; Jerusalem, Israel Museum, Paintings from the collection of Joseph H. Hazen, summer, 1966, no.38 (illustrated); The exhibition traveled to Cambridge, Massachusetts, Fogg Art Museum, Oct.-Dec., 1966; Los Angeles, University of California, The Art Galleries,Jan.-Feb., 1967; Berkeley, University of California, Art Museum, Feb.-March, 1967; Houston, Museum of Fine Arts, April-May, 1967, and Honolulu, Academy of Arts,June-Aug., 1967; Los Angeles, County Museum of Art, *Chaim Soutine: 1893-1943*, Feb.-April, 1968, p.99, no. 45 (illustrated). The exhibition traveled to Jerusalem, Israel Museum, summer, 1968; New York, Perls Galleries, *Chaim Soutine*, Nov.-Dec., t 963, no.15 (illustrated in colour); New York, M. Knoedler & Co., Inc., *The Protean Century, 1870-1970*, Feb., 1970, no. 61 (illustrated); New York, Marlborough Gallery, *Chaim Soutine*, Oct.-Nov., 1973, p.61, no. 45 (illustrated).
LIT.: M. Tuchman, 'Portraits de Soutine,' *Art de France*, vol. IV, 1964, pp.206-,217 (illustrated, p.216); K.G. Kline, 'Form and Frenzy,' *Art News*, Dec., 1969, pp.50 and 58 (illustrated, p.50); P. Courthion, *Soutine, peintre du déchirant*, Paris, 1972, p.260c (illustrated); H. Kramer, 'Soutine Works Displayed in a Moving Exhibition,' *New York Times*, Oct. 13,1973, p.29; E. Genauer, 'Art & the Artist,' *New York Post* (Magazine), Oct. 20, 1973, p. l4 (illustrated); M. Tuchman, Chaim Soutine: 1893-1943, Stuttgart, 198l, p. 62; M. Tuchman, E. Dunow and K. Perls, *Chaim Soutine, Catalogue Raisonné*, Cologne, t993, vol. II, p.598, no. 58 (illustrated in colour, p.601).

Christie's New York, 30 April 1996 (8**) US$ 717,500	US$	717,500

SPADINI Armando (Poggio a Caiano 1883-1925 Rome) Italian
LA CASA ROSA DI BALLA oil on canvas, 64 x 92cm s 'Spadini' (1922)
LIT.: A. Venturi/E.Cecchi, *Andrea Spadini*, A.Mondadori Edit., Milano, 1927, ill.174.

Finearte Rome, 14 November 1995 (230**) ITL 92000,000	US$	57,753

SPAENDONCK Cornelis (with Gerard van Spaendonck, 1746-1822) (Tilburg 1756-1840 Paris) Dutch
STILL-LIFE WITH ROSES, PRIMULAS AND LARKSPUR IN A GLASS VAE ON A STONE LEDGE oil on panel, 11 x 8¾in. (27.9 x 22.2cm.) iscr. on the verso 'Je déclare que ces petits tableaux/faisant pendant ont été fait par mon frère/G van Spaendonck et terminé par moi/Corneille van Spaendonck'

Sotheby's New York, 16 May 1996 (119**) US$ 56,350	US$	56,350

SPAENDONCK Gerard van (Tilburg 1746-1822 Paris) Dutch
BOUQUET OF FLOWERS IN A VASE ON A LEDGE goache and watercolour, 21.5 x 16.5cm. slr 'G van Spaendonck'

Étude Tajan Paris, 24 November 1995 (158*) FRF 33,000	US$	6,753

SPAENDONCK Gerard van (with Cornelis van Spaendonck (1756-1840) (Tilburg 1746-1822 Paris) Dutch
STILL-LIFE WITH ROSES, PRIMULAS AND LARKSPUR IN A GLASS VAE ON A STONE LEDGE oil on panel, 11 x 8¾in. (27.9 x 22.2cm.) iscr. on the verso 'Je déclare que ces petits tableaux/faisant pendant ont été fait par mon frère/G van Spaendonck et terminé par moi/Corneille van Spaendonck'

Sotheby's New York, 16 May 1996 (119**) US$ 56,350	US$	56,350

SPALA Vaclav (Zlunice (East Bohemia) 1885-1946 Prague) Czech
FLOWERS IN A VASE oil on canvas, 82 x 66cm. (32¼ x 26in.) sll with ini. 'VS', d "22'
PROV.: Private collection, London.

Phillips London, 24 June 1996 (5**) GBP 8,000	US$	12,336

SPANGENBERG Louis (1824-1893) German
VESUVIUS FROM POMPEI oil on canvas, 26 x 37½in. (66 x 95.2cm.) sd 'L. Spangenberg 83'
EXH.: Dresden, Kunstausstellung, 1883, no. 66.

Christie's London, 17 November 1995 (159**) GBP 11,500	US$	17,988

SPEAR Ruskin, R.A. (1911-1990) British
'ERNIE' , 24 x 20in. (61 x 51cm.)
PROV.: Acquired direct from the artist.
       Christie's South Kensington, 21 September 1995 (101***) GBP 4,275   US$ 6,657

SPENCELAYH Charles (Rochester 1865-1958) British
THE POLITICAL ARGUMENT oil on panel, 10 x 12in. (25.5 x 30.5cm.) sll 'C. SPENCELAYH',
inscr. with title and the artist's address '19 Queen's Road, West Didsbury, Manchester' on a label on
the rverse
PROV.: Acquired directly from the artist and thence by descent.
LIT.: Aubrey Noakes, *Charles Spencelayh and his Paintings*, 1978, ill. p.l.36.
       Phillips London, 18 June 1996 (57**) GBP 35,000   US$ 53,971

DEPARTED SPIRITS oil on panel, 14 x 10in. (35.5 x 25.5cm.) slr 'C.SPENCELAYH', s again, inscr.
with title and the artist's address '19 Queen's Road, West Didsbury, Manchester' on a label on the
reverse
PROV.: Acquired directly from the artist and thence by descent.
EXH.: James Green's Bond Street Galleries, April 1957, no.110, 20gns.
LIT.: Aubrey Noakes, *Charles Spencelayh and his Paintings*, 1978, p.53.
       Phillips London, 18 June 1996 (58**) GBP 30,000   US$ 46,261

JUST ARRIVED oil on canvas, 16 x 12in. (30.5 x 40.5cm.) sll 'C SPENCELAYH'
       Sotheby's London, 29 August 1995 (773**) GBP 19,550   US$ 31,645

SPENCER Sir Stanley, R.A. (Cookham on Thames (Berkshire) 1891-1959 Cookham) British
FLOWERING ARTICHOKES oil on canvas-board, 14 x 18in. (35.5 x 45.7cm.) sdlr ini 'SS 36'
(1936)
PROV.: Wilma, Countess Cawdor, by whom purchased at the 1936 exhibition.
EXH.: London, Arthur Tooth & Son Ltd., Stanley Spencer, June-July 1936, no.6 as 'Globe
Artichokes'; Cookham, Stanley Spencer Gallery, Works by Sir Stanley Spencer, April 1962, no.8 as
'Globe Artichokes'; Leamingston Spa, Mason-Watts Fine Art, A Flower Show, Nov. 1987, no.27,
where purchased by the present owner.
LIT.: K. Bell, Stanley Spencer A Complete Catalogue of the Paintings, London, 1992, no.205, p.,269
(illustrated).
       Christie's London, 21 March 1996 (137**) GBP 11,500   US$ 17,563

THE CRUCIFIXION oil on canvas, 36 x 30¼in. (91.4 x 76.8cm.) (1934)
PROV.: John Hobday, Toronto, commissioned directly from the artist in 1934; Edwin Hewitt
Gallery, New York, 1954, where purchased by Toby Everard Spence, thence by descent.
EXH.: London, St. Paul's Cathedral, Exhibition of Modern British Religious Art, June-July 1993.
LIT.: S. Spencer, letter to John Hobday, Toronto, 2 Jan. 1936; S. Spencer, letter to Toby Everard
Spence, 27 March 1954; A. Causey, Stanley Spencer and the Art of his Time, Royal Academy
Exhibition Catalogue, London,1980, p.2; Dr. B. Kennedy, Burlington Magazine, Nov. 1981, 123,
no.4, pp.67-73, no.79 (illustrated); K. Pople, Stanley Spencer, London, 1991, p.4; K. Bell, Stanley
Spencer, A Complete Catalogue of the Paintings, London, 1992, no.1, p.2 (illustrated).
       Christie's London, 21 November 1995 (168**) GBP 463,500   US$ 725,012

COTTAGE GARDENS, LEONARD STANLEY oil on canvas, 20 x 30in. (50.8 x 76.2cm.) (ca 1939)
PROV.: with Arthur Tooth & Sons, London, 1940, Captain Sir R.A. Hornby, by whom purchased at
the 1942 exhibition.
EXH.: London, Leicester Galleries, Stanley Spencer, Nov. 1942, no.41, as Leonard Stanley
Cookham, Stanley Spencer Gallery, Loan Exhibition, 1962, no.l8; London, Royal Academy, Stanley
Spencer, R.A., Sept.-Dec. 1980, no.6, p.6 (illustrated).
LIT.: K. Bell, Stanley Spencer A Complete Catalogue of the Paintings, London, 1992, no.8, p.4
illustrated).
       Christie's London, 21 November 1995 (169**) GBP 31,050   US$ 48,569

CARRYING MATTRESSES oil on paper laid on board, 12 x16¾in. (30.5 x 42.5cm.) (ca 1920-21)
PROV.: Gifted by the Artist to Gerald and Nora Summers in the early 1930's, thence by descent to
the present owner.
LIT.: K. Bell, Stanley Spencer A Complete Catalogue of the Paintings, London, 1992, no. 43, p.8
(illustrated).
        Christie's London, 21 November 1995 (170**) GBP 25,300   US$ 39,575

SPERL Johann (Buch (near Nurenberg) 1840-1914 Aibling) German
VOR EINEM BAUERNHAUS SPIELENDE KINDER Oil on panel, 34.2 x 21.8cm. slr 'J. Sperl'
        Lempertz Cologne, 18 May 1996 (1644**) DEM 54,000   US$ 35,204

SPILIMBERGO Adriano (Buenos Aires 1908-1975 Milan) Argentinean
VENEZIA, PUNTA DELLA DOGANA, CHIESA DELLA SALUTE oil on canvas, 80 x 100cm.
(1950's)
LIT.: Thgis work is registrated in the 'archivio Spilimbergo', under supervision of Galleria Ponto
Rosso, Milano, under no. 1/3342.
        Sotheby's Milan, 28 May 1996 (138**) ITL 2,1850,000   US$ 14,033

DE ZEEDIJK pastel, Indian ink and watercolour on paper, 49 x 65cm. sdur 'L. Spilliaert 8'
PROV.: Acquired from the artist by the grandmother of the present owner, thence by descent.
        Christie's Amsterdam, 5 June 1996 (234a**) NLG 195,500   US$ 114,227

AMOR Brush and black ink on paper, unframed, 26.5 x 34.5cm sd and inscr. with title ll ' L Spilliaert
Aout 1902'
        Christie's Amsterdam, 5 June 1996 (218*) NLG 16,100   US$ 9,407

BAIGNEUSE pastel on cardboard, 86.5 x 70cm. sdur 'L.Spilliaert/1913
PROV.: G. van Geluwe, Brussels.
        Christie's Amsterdam, 6 December 1995 (185**) NLG 74,750   US$ 46,319

A FOREST AT SUNDOWN watercolour on paper, 40 x 60cm. sdlr 'L.Spilliaert 1930'
PROV.: Estate of the Artist.
        Christie's Amsterdam, 6 December 1995 (187**) NLG 74,750   US$ 46,319

A MAN IN A BLACK COAT pen and pencil and brush and black ink, unframed, 23 x 19cm. s with
ini. 'LSP' and slr 'L.Spilliaert' and inscr. ul 'pr. mettre à l'atelier avec les autres Leon Spilliaert'
        Christie's Amsterdam, 6 December 1995 (198*) NLG 10,350   US$ 6,413

FLEURS ARTIFICIELLES-KUNSTBLOEMEN pastel with brown and black wash on board, 27 3/8
x 35 1/8in. (69.6 x 89.1cm.) sd 'L. Spilliaert 1913' sd inscr. and numbered on the reverse 'II Fleurs
Artificielles Ostende 1913'
PROV.: Madeline Spilliaert, Ostend, the daughter of the Artist.
        Christie's London, 29 November 1995 (156**) GBP 16,000   US$ 25,027

L'APOCALYPSE watercolour on paper, 31 x 39cm. sdul 'Spiliaert 1926'
PROV.: Christian Fayt Art Gallery, Knokke Heist.
        Sotheby's Amsterdam, 7 December 1995 (163**) NLG 30,680   US$ 19,011

SPIRIDON Ignace (19th Century-l) Italian
TEMPTATION oil on canvas, 33 x 23½in. (83.8 x 59.7cm.) s 'ISpiridon'
        Christie's South Kensington, 12 October 1995 (190***) GBP 7,312   US$ 11,540

SPITZWEG Carl (Munich 1808-1885 Munich) German
DER EINSIEDLER oil on canvas, 21½ x 16in. (54.5 x 40.6cm.) s mono. (rhombus)
PROV.: Countess NOstitz Prince Hugo Salm zu Salm.
        Christie's London, 11 October 1995 (61**) GBP 133,500   US$ 210,70l

DAS QUARTETT oil on canvas, 15½ x 8¾in. (39.4 x 22.2cm.) s mono. (rhombus) (1860-65)
PROV.: with Galerie Gaspari, Munich.
LIT.: G. Roennefahrt, Carl Spitzweg, Munich, 1960 p.,256 no.1086 (illus.).
      Christie's London, 11 October 1995 (62**) GBP 67,500   US$ 106,534

AM NYMPHENBURGERPARK, MÜNCHEN oil on panel, 15¼ x 18½in. (38.7 x 47cm.) s mono.
(rhombus) (1870-75)
      Christie's London, 11 October 1995 (71**) GBP 56,500   US$ 89,173

WALDLICHTUNG MIT VIEH AN DER TRÄNKE oil on panel, 15 x 17.3cm.
PROV.: Suedeutsche Privatsammlung.
LIT.: Prof. Dr. S. Wichmann, will include this work in his catalogue raissonné: *Spitzweg paintings*.
      Lempertz Cologne, 18 May 1996 (1645**) DEM 50,000   US$ 32,597

SPOHLER Jacob Jan Coenraad (Amsterdam 1837-1923 Amsterdam) Dutch
A FROZEN RIVER LANDSCAPE WITH SKATERS AND A WINDMILL oil on panel, 21 x 31 cm
s 'JJ Spohler'
      Christie's Amsterdam, 25 April 1996 (18*) NLG 21,850   US$ 12,984

A WINTER LANDSCAPE WITH SKATERS AND A HORSE-PULLED SLEDGE ON A FROZEN
WATERWAY oil on panel, 21 x 15.5 cm s 'J.J.C.Spohler'
      Christie's Amsterdam, 7 February 1996 (174*) NLG 8,625   US$ 5,253

A WINTER LANDSCAPE WITH SKATERS ON A FROZEN RIVER, AND FIGURES PUSHING
A SLEDGE ON A SNOWY BANK oil on panel, 21.5 x 27.5 cm s 'JJC Spohler'
      Christie's Amsterdam, 7 February 1996 (186*) NLG 12,650   US$ 7,704

SPOHLER Jan Jacob (Nederhorst den Berg 1811-1879 Amsterdam) Dutch
ICE SKATERS IN A FROZEN LANDSCAPE oil on panel, 11½ x 16 1/8in. (29.1 x 41.2cm.) s 'J.J.
Spohler fe'
      Christie's London, 14 June 1996 (6**) GBP 9,775   US$ 15,073

SAILING VESSELS IN AN ESTUARY WITH FIGURES ON A BANK oil on canvas, 14¾ x 19in.
(37.5 x 48.2cm.) s 'J.J. Spohler f.'
      Christie's London, 17 November 1995 (3**) GBP 6,325   US$ 9,894

SKATERS ON A FROZEN WATERWAY ALONG WINDMILLS oil on panel, 24.5 x 31cm. s (and
indistinctly) d 'J.J. Spohler'
      Christie's Amsterdam, 18 June 1996 (264*) NLG 17,250   US$ 10,079

SKATERS IN A FROZEN LANDSCAPE oil on canvas, 19½ x 26¼in. (49.5 x 66.7cm.) sll
'J.J.Spohler.f'
      Christie's New York, 2 November 1995 (84**) US$ 29,900   US$ 29,900

A RIVER LANDSCAPE IN SUMMER WITH ANGLERS, WINDMILLS BEYOND AND A
TOWN IN THE DISTANCE oil on canvas, 61 x 83.5cm. s J.J. Spohler f'
      Christie's Amsterdam, 25 April 1996 (248**) NLG 55,200   US$ 32,801

A WINTER LANDSCAPE WITH SKATERS AND SLEDGERS ON A FROZEN RIVER oil on
panel, 24 x 30cm. sll 'J.J.Spohler'
      Christie's Amsterdam, 26 October 1995 (225*) NLG 17,250   US$ 10,876

A PEASANT COUPLE PUSHING A SLEDGE, A *KOEK AND ZOPIE* AND SEVERAL OTHER
SKATERS ON A FROZEN WATERWAY ALONG WIND-MILLS oil on canvas laid down on
apanel, 64.5 x 90cm. s 'J.J. Spohler f'
      Christie's Amsterdam, 26 October 1995 (310**) NLG 71,300   US$ 44,956

SPOHLER Johannes Franciscus (Rotterdam 1853-1894 Amsterdam) Dutch
FIGURES ON A STREET BEFORE A CANAL oil on panel, 7 7/8 x 6¼in. (20 x 16cm.) s
      Phillips London, 11th June 1996 (2 (a pair)**) GBP 12,000   US$ 18,504

SPRANGER Bartholomeus (Follower of) (Antwerp 1546-1611 Prague) Flemish
THE JUDGEMENT OF MIDAS oil on canvas, 60 x 98cm.
      Sotheby's Amsterdam, 6 May 1996 (49*) NLG 8,496   US$ 4,954

SPRINGER Cornelis (Amsterdam 1817-1891 Hilversum) Dutch
A DUTCH TOWN WITH FIGURES BY A CANAL oil on panel, 16¼ x 13½in. (41.5 x 34.5cm.) sd
mono 'CS 48' sd and authenticated 'De ondergetekende makelaar dat dit schilderijtje voorstellende/
(gezicht op de prinsengracht hoek bij heeregracht te Amsterdam) Door hem is vervaardigd in het jaar
1858./ Amsterdam Nov. 69' on an old label on the reverse'
      Christie's London, 15 March 1996 (1**) GBP 80,700   US$ 123,244

THE INTERIOR OF THE NIEUWE KERK, AMSTERDAM oil on panel, 32.5 x 25.5cm. sd 'C.
Springer. 57'
      Christie's Amsterdam, 25 April 1996 (258a**) NLG 63,250   US$ 37,584

THE OLD CONVENT, HASSELT oil on panel, 44 x 34.5cm. sd 'C. Springer 1863' sd again and
authenticated with the Artist's seal on the reverse
PROV.: Anon. Sale, Sotheby's London, 28 Nov 1979, lot 30 (GBP12,000).
LIT.: W. Laanstra, Cornelis Springer, Cornelis Springer, Utrecht 1984, p. 141, no. 63-13 (illustrated).
      Christie's Amsterdam, 25 April 1996 (247**) NLG 253,000   US$ 150,336

A VIEW IN A TOWN WITH TOWNSFOLK CONVERSING ON A SQUARE AT THE
ENTRANCE OF A CHURCH oil on panel, 49 x 38.5cm. s with monogram, s again and indistinctly d
'C.Springer 5(?)'
      Christie's Amsterdam, 26 October 1995 (203***) NLG 270,250   US$ 170,397

STACKHOUSE Robert (1942 b.) American
VIEWS INSIDE 'RUBY BIRTH' watercolour, charcoal abd graphite on paper mounted on linen-
unframed, 89½ x 143¾in. (227.3 x 365.1cm.) sd titled 'views inside 'ruby birth' 19th bienal de sao
paulo r. stackhouse 1.88' lower edge
PROV.: Dolan/Maxwell Gallery, New York.
      Christie's East, 7 May 1996 (177**) US$ 6,900   US$ 6,900

STAEL Nicolas de (Saint Petersburg 1914-1955 Antibes) French (Russian)
LA ROUTE D'UZES oil on canvas, 25 9/16 x 31 7/8in. (65 x 81cm.) sll (1954)
PROV.: Jacques Dubourg, Paris; Raymond Carré, Paris.
EXH.: Paris, Galerie Jacques Dubourg, Nicolas de Staël, June 1954; Paris, Galerie Jacques Dubourg,
Hommage a Nicolas de Staël, June 1957, no. 16.
LIT.: Françoise de Staël and Jacques Dubourg, Nicolas de Staël: Catalogue Raisonné des Peintures,
Paris 1968, no. ,772 (illustrated).
      Christie's London, 27 June 1996 (12**) GBP 315,000   US$ 485,736

ETUDE DE NU oil on canvas, 18 1/8 x 24in. (46 x 61cm.) (1953)
PROV.: Estate of Nicolas de Staël, Paris.
EXH.: Geneva, Galerie Motte, *Nicolas de Staël (1914-1955), Peintures et Dessins*, July-August
1967, no. 28.
LIT.: Jacques Dubourg and Françoise de Staël, *Nicolas de Staël: Catalogue Raisonné des Peintures*,
Paris 1968, p. 263, no. ,580 (illustrated).
      Christie's London, 27 June 1996 (16**) GBP 177,500   US$ 273,709

COMPOSITION ON BLUE GROUND collage on coloured paper, 23 x18½in. (58.5 x 47cm.) slr
'Nicolas' (1953)

PROV.: Dr. Peter Nathan, Zurich; Collection Walter Franz, Cologne.
EXH.: London, Gimpel Fils, *Nicolas de Staël*, June-July 1963, no. 23 (illustrated); Rotterdam,
Museum Boymans-van Beuningen; Zurich, Kunsthaus, Boston, Museum of Fine Arts; Chicago, Art
Institute of Chicago; New York, Solomon R. Guggenheim Museum, *De Staël*, May 1965-April 1966,
no. 78 (illustrated in colour in the catalogue).
LIT.: Eberhard Ruhmer, *Nicolas de Staël: Die Kunst und das Schöne Heim*, vol. 59, no. 1, Munich
1960, pp. 6-9 (illustrated p. 8).
Christie's London, 30 November 1995 (1**) GBP 26,450   US$ 41,373

CIEL ROUGE oil on canvas, 23 5/8 x 32in. (60 x 82cm.) (1954)
PROV.: Galerie Schmit, Paris; Collection Catherine Lecompte, Paris.
LIT.: Jacques Dubourg et François de Staël, *Nicolas de Staël, Catalogue Raisonné des Peintures*,
Paris, 1968, p. 304, no. ,719 (illustrated).
Christie's London, 30 November 1995 (4**) GBP 161,000   US$ 251,838

MARINE oil on canvas, 18 1/8 x 21 5/8in. (46 x 55cm.) s on the reverse (1954)
PROV.: Galerie Jeanne Bucher, Paris; Galerie Schmit, Paris; Collection Catherine Lecompte, Paris.
LIT.: Jacques Dubourg et François de Staël, *Nicolas de Staël, Catalogue Raisonné des Peintures*,
Paris, 1968, p. 358, no. ,950 (illustrated).
Christie's London, 30 November 1995 (9**) GBP 113,700   US$ 177,851

STAEL Pieter (1576-1622) Dutch
A ROCKY LANDSCAPE WITH ABRIDGE AND FIGURES oil on canvas, 31½ x 39½in. (79.8 x
100cm.)
Sotheby's London, 6 December 1995 (192**) GBP 9,200   US$ 14,158

STAMOS Theodoros (New York 1922 b.) American (Greek)
WAXAHACHIE oil on canvas, 61 x 49in. (,155 x 124.5cm.) sll 'Stamos' sd titled 'WAXAHACHIE
1960 STAMOS' on the reverse
PROV.: André Emmerich Gallery, New York; Private collection, Richmond.
Christie's New York, 15 November 1995 (133**) US$ 11,500   US$ 11,500

DOUBLE YELLOW SUNBOX oil and graphite on canvas, 48 x 72in. (121.9 x 182.9cm.) sll
'Stamos', s again, titled and d "DOUBLE YELLOW SUN BOX' 1966-7 STAMOS' on the overlap
PROV.: Acquired directly from the artist.
Christie's New York, 22 February 1996 (13**) US$ 12,650   US$ 12,650

UNTITLED NO.2 oil on canvas, 66 x 61in. (167.7 x 154.9cm.) sll 'Stamos' (1960)
PROV.: Louis K.Meisel Gallery, New York.
EXH.: New York University, The Grey Art Gallery, *Tracking the Marvelous*, April-May 1981, p.36
(ill.); Chicago, R.H.Love Modern, *Abstraction by American Masters Over 50*, Dec. 1986-Jan. 1987;
New York, ACA Galleries, *Stamos: An Overview*, Dec. 1991-Jan. 1992, p.31 (ill.).
Christie's New York, 8 May 1996 (245**) US$ 43,700   US$ 43,700

STANHOPE John Roddam Spencer (1829-1908) British
FLORA oil on panel, 50¾ x 20¾in. (128.7 x 52.7cm.) (ca 1894)
PROV.: Joseph Dixon; Christie's, 18 March 1911, lot 36, as 'The Birth of Venus' (36 gns. to Thorne);
with Mrs. Charlotte Frank, London.
LIT.: Nottingham, Djanogly Art Gallery, University of Nottingham, *Heaven on Earth*, 1994, no. 62.
Christie's London, 7 June 1996 (576***) GBP 73,000   US$ 112,567

ANDROMEDA oil on paper laid down on panel, 49½ x 20 1/8in. (125.7 x 51.3cm.)
PROV.: Joseph Dixon; Christie's, 18 March 1911, lot 36, as (21 gns. to Thorne); with Mrs. Charlotte
Frank, London.
LIT.: Nottingham, Djanogly Art Gallery, University of Nottingham, *Heaven on Earth*, 1994, no. 62.
Christie's London, 7 June 1996 (577**) GBP 62,000   US$ 95,605

ROBINS OF MODERN TIMES oil on canvas, 19 x 33¾in. (48.2 x 85.7cm.) s inscr. '..ins of Modern../4/J.R. Spencer Stanhope/50 Harley Street/Cavendish Square' (before 1860)
EXH.: Liverpool, Liverpool Academy, *Thirty-Sixth Exhibition*, 1860, no. 464, priced at 25 guineas.
Christie's London, 7 June 1996 (578**) GBP 221,500   US$ 341,557

STAUDACHER Hans (Sankt Urban, lake Ossiach 1923 b.) Austrian
UNTITLED oil on canvas, ,100 x 70cm. slr 'H. Staudacher' (1982)
Dorotheum Vienna, 21 May 1996 (150**) ATS 110,000   US$ 10,563

SO ODER SO oil, plastic, collage on cardboard, ,130 x 85cm. sd and titled 'H. Staudacher 1953-59' on the reverse
Wiener Kunst Auktionen, 26 March 1996 (338**) ATS 120,000   US$ 11,543

UNTITLRF oil, varnish and mixed technique on canvas laid down on three-ply wood, ,130 x 85cm. slc 'H. Staudacher'; sd 'H. Staudacher 1979' on the reverse
Wiener Kunst Auktionen, 27 September 1995 (452**) ATS 120,000   US$ 11,664

UNTITLED oil, varnish and mixed technique on three-ply wood, ,130 x 85cm. sduc '1958-9 H. Staudacher'; sd twice 'H. Staudacher 1958' on the reverse
Wiener Kunst Auktionen, 27 September 1995 (459**) ATS 140,000   US$ 13,608

STAVEREN Jan Adriaensz. van (Leyden 1625-1668 after Leyden) Dutch
A VIEW OF A FORTIFIED VILALGE BY A MOAT WITH PEASANTS RETURNING FROM MARKET IN A ROWIG BOAT IN THE FOREGROUND oil on panel, 35 x 47.5cm. sdlr 'JS(linked TAVEREN/1655'
Christie's Amsterdam, 7 May 1996 (103*) NLG 13,800   US$ 8,047

STEEN Jan Havicksz. (Leyden 1623/1626-1679 Leyden) Dutch
THE DISSOLUTE HOUSEHOLD OR THE EFFECT OF INTEMPERANCE: A DISORDERLEY FAMILY INTERIOR oil on canvas, 34 x 41in. (86 x 106cm.) bears s 'JSteen' (mid 1660's)
PROV.: Perhaps Richard Pickfatt, his sale, Rotterdam, 12 April 1736; Perhaps Jan Danser Nijman, his deceased sale, Amsterdam, van der Schley etc., 16-17 August 1797, lot 235, ,700 florins; Perhaps de Sereville, his sale, Paris, Paillet etc., 22-24January 1812, 6,853 francs; Duc d'Alberg, Ambassador of France at Turin, his sale, London, Christie's, 13-14 June 1817, lot 58, ,345 gns.; George Watson Taylor, his sale, London, Christie's, 13-14 June 1823, lot 52, ,220 gns; William Beckford, by 1833; H.AJ. Munro, his deceased sale, London, Christie's, 1 June 1878, lot 105, according to Hofstede de Groot, (correct title, support and dimensions, and also from the Beckford collection, but with divergent description) GBP1312.10s to Graves; Perhaps anonymous sale, Paris, 28January 1887, for 4,100 francs; Adolphe Schloss, Paris, by 1907, his sale, Paris, Charpentier, 25 May 1949, lot 57, for 2,800,000 Francs; Percy B. Meyer, Portman Square, London; With William Hallsborough Ltd., London, from whom acquired by George Spitz, on the advice of Walther Bernt, in June 1956, for 54,000 DM.
EXH.: Leiden, *Rembrandt*, 1906, no. 60; London, Royal Academy, *Winter Exhibition*, 1952, no. 546.
LIT.: J. Smith, *A Catalogue Raisonné*, vol. IV, 1833, pp. 2-3, no. 1; G.F. Waagen, *Kunstwerke und Kunstler in England*, voL II, 1838, p. 335; T. van Westrheene, *Jan Steen: Etude sur l 'art en Hollande*, 1856, p. 113, no. 62; C. Blanc, *Histoire de Peintres de toutes les Ecoles-Ecole Hollandaise*, 1861, vol. II, pp. 4, 16; A. Bredius, *De Leidsche Tentoonstelling in MCMVI..*, 1907, p. 49, reproduced plate XXII; C. Hofstede de Groot, *A Catalogue Raisonné..*, voL I, 1907, p. 40, no. ,110 (as a self-portrait of the artist with his wife); A. von Wurzbach, *Niederländisches Künstler-lexikon, 19l0, vol. II, p. 657;* l'Art et les Artistes, June 1910, p. 104; Nagler, *Kunstler-Lexikon*, 2nd ed., 1912, vol. XIX, p. 318; A. Bredius, *Jan Steen*, 1930, no. 16; Apollo, May 1950, reproduced p. 121; Britain and Holland, 1950, vol. 2, no. 3, reproduced on the cover and p. 70; Illustrated London News, Christmas 1950, reproduced; H. Shipp, *Dutch Painters*, 1955, repr. plate XVI; K. Braun, *Alle tot nu bekende schilderijen van Jan Steen*, 1980, no. 190; P.C. Sutton, in *Masters of Seventeenth-Century Dutch Genre Painting*, exhibition catalogue, 1984, p. 323, reproduced p. 322, fig. 1.
Sotheby's London, 5 July 1995 (9**) GBP 144,500   US$ 230,499

A TAVERN INTERIOR WITH BOORS AT A TABLE AND SERVING GIRL DRINKING oil on panel, 13 5/8 x 11in. (34.5 x 28cm.) s 'JSteen'
PROV.: Visscher Bodger (label on the reverse); with Colnaghi, London; Anon. Sale, Christie's London, 30 Nov. 1973, lot 125; with David Koetser, Zurich, 1975.
      Christie's London, 8 December 1995 (26**) GBP 34,500   US$ 53,093

A HURDY-GURDY PLAYER IN THE COURTYARD OF A COUNTY INN oil on canvas, 33½ x 25½in. (85 x 65cm.) slr 'JSteen' (ca. 1662-4)
PROV.: Cornelis Backer, his deceased sale, Amsterdam, Soeterwoude, near Leiden, 16 August 1775, lot 3, ,200 florins to W. Cooler; Wijnand Coole, his deceased sale, Rotterdam, Constant, 6 August 1782, lot 65; Thomas Theodoor Cremer, his deceased sale, Rotterdam, van Leen et al, 16-17 April, 1816, lot 108, ,700 florins; Anonymous sale, Amsterdam, Mak, 19 May 1919, lot 69; Jonas Lek, Brussels, his sale, Amsterdam, Fk. Muller, 31 March 1925, lot 89; Private collection, Holland, from which expropriated by the Germans, and purchased for the projected museum at Linz at a sale at Lange, Berlin, 1943; Released by the Austrian Government to the family of the former owners, by whom offered London, Christie's, 10 April 1981, lot 8, (estimate GBP70,000-100,000, unsold).
LIT.: J. Smith, *A Catalogue Raisonné..*, vol. IV, 1833, p. 34, no. 105; J. Westrheene, Jan Steen: Etudes sur l'Art en Hollande, 1856, no. 371; C. Hofstede de Groot, *A Catalogue Raisonné..*, vol. I, 1907, p. 112, no. 430; K Braun, Het komplete werk van Jan Steen, 1980, p. 109, no. 167, reproduced.
      Sotheby's London, 6 December 1995 (39**) GBP 155,500   US$ 239,304

THE ITINERANT QUACK DOCTOR oil on canvas, 42½ x 54½in. (107.9 x 138.7cm.) slr 'I STEEN' (ca. 1666-68)
PROV.: Count Esterhazy, Nordkirchen; Possibly the Duc d'Arenberg (according to Hofstede de Groot); With Dr. A. Pauli, Amsterdam, 1927; With Haberstock, Berlin, 1930; Baron Heinrich Thyssen-Bornemisza, by 1930.
EXH.: Düsseldorf, 1886, no. 318; London, Royal Academy, *Dutch Exhibition*, 1929, no. 257; Munich 1930, no. 306, plate 54; Bern 1960; Paris 1970, no. 40, plate 11; Düsseldorf 1970-1, no. 49; On loan to the Metropolitan Museum of Art, New York, 1982-1985; Lausanne etc., 1986-7, no. 33.
LIT.: C. Hofstede de Groot, A Catalogue Raisonné.., vol. I, 1907, p. 61, no. 184; R. Heinemann 1937, vol.I, no. 395, vol. II, plate 138; Braun, *Het complete werk van Jan Steen*, 1980, p. 124, no. 270, reproduced p. 125, and detail of signature reproduced p. 84.
      Sotheby's London, 6 December 1995 (97**) GBP 221,500   US$ 340,874

THE DUCK SELLER oil on canvas, 33 34/ x 26¾in. (85.8 x 68cm.) sll 'JSteen' (ca. 1666-68)
PROV.: Nicolaas Doekscheer, his deceased sale, Rotterdam, van der Schley *et al*, 9 September 1789, lot 45, ,385 florins to Fouquet; Jean-Jacques de Faesch, his deceased sale, Amsterdam, de Vries *et al*, 3-4 July 1833, lot 54, for ,810 florins to Chaplin, by whom brought to England; Edward W. Lake, his sale, London, Christie's, 11-12 July 1845, GBP,137 to Rutley; Fritz Gans, Frankfurt, by 1907; With Bachstitz, The Hague, circa 1930; Baron Heinrich Thyssen-Bornemisza, by 1930.
EXH.: Brighton, 1884, no. 177; Munich 1930, no. 305; Munich 1931; Bern 1960; Düsseldorf 1970-1, no. 48; On loan to the Metropolitan Museum of Art, New York, 1982-85; Lausanne etc., 1986-7, no. 32.
LIT.: J. Smith, *A Supplement to the Catalogue Raisonné..*, 1842, vol. IX, p. 504, no. 80 ('painted in a broad masterly manner'); J. Westrheene, *Jan Steen: Etudes sur l'Art en Hollande*, 1856, no. 396; C. Hofstede de Groot, *A Catalogue Raisonné..*, vol. I, 1907, p. 97, no. 364; R. Heinemann 1937, vol. I, no. 394, plate 139; R. Andree, *Kunstmuseum Dusseldorf-Malerei*, 1976, no. 19; K Braun, *Het complete werk van Jan Steen*, 1980, p. 124, no. 269, reproduced p.125.
      Sotheby's London, 6 December 1995 (104**) GBP 133,500   US$ 205,448

STEENBERGEN Albertus Alides (1814-1900) Dutch
A STILL LIFE WITH FUIT oil on canvas, 57 x 47cm. sdlr 'Alb. Steenbergen/1849'
      Christie's Amsterdam, 26 October 1995 (196**) NLG 21,850   US$ 13,777

STEENWYCK Hendrick the Younger van (Frankfurt-am-Main 1580 c.-1649 London) Dutch
GUARDS SLEEPING IN A VAULTED HALL oil on copper, 13¼ x 15¾in. (33.7 x 40 cm.) sd ini.
'H.V.S./1627'
EXH.: Stockholm, Nationalmuseum.
LIT.: A similar drawing, which is signed (?) and dated 16.5, is in the J. Paul Getty Museum, Malibu
(G.R.Goldner, European drawings. I. catalogue of the Collections. The J. Paul Getty Museum,
Verona, 1988, p. 222, no. 98).

Christie's London, 8 December 1995 (29**) GBP 34,500	US$	53,093

STEER Philip Wilson, O.M. (Birkenhead (Cheshire) 1860-1942 London) British
GIRL IN A LARGE HAT oil on canvas, 24 x 20in. (61 x 50.8cm.) sd 'Steer 92'
PROV.: Possibly George Moore; possibly Lady Cunard.
EXH.: Possibly, London, Goupil Gallery, *P. W. Steer*, 1894, no.42; possibly, Dublin, 1899 as
'Portrait of a Lady'; possibly, London, National Portrait Gallery, *British Painting since Whistler*,
1940, no.64 as 'A Coster Girl'.
LIT.: D.S. MacColl, *Philip Wilson Steer*, London, 1945, pp.68, 193; B. Laughton, *Philip Wilson
Steer 1860-1942*, Oxford, 1971, p.133, no.109.

Christie's London, 20 June 1996 (8**) GBP 16,675	US$	25,713

STEEWYCK Hendrik van (the younger) (1580-1649 London) Dutch
FIGURES IN A CHURCH INTERIOR oil on panel, 75.5 x 107.5cm.

Sotheby's Amsterdam, 14 November 1995 (35**) NLG 34,220	US$	21,567

STEFANO Francesco di {called il Pesellino} (Florence ca. 1422-1457 Florence) Italian
THE VIRGIN AND CHILD ENTHRONED tempera on panel, gold ground, unframed, 21 x 13½in.
(54 x 34.5cm.)
PROV.: Mrs. B. Marshall, 1967; Anonymous sale, London, Sotheby's, 6 December 1967, lot 83,
GBP25,500 to Weitzner; With The Hallsborough Gallery, London, 1973; Anonymous sale,
Sotheby's, London, 19 March 1975, lot 24.
EXH.: London, *Fanfare for Europe-the British Art Market*, exhibition sponsored by Sotheby's,
Christie's and the British Antique Dealers' Association, and held at Christie's, January 1973, no. 29;
Bath, Assembly Rooms,International Art Treasures Exhibition, August-September 1973, no. 1; On
loan, Bowes Museum, Barnard Castle, County Durham,1977-1995.

Sotheby's London, 5 July 1995 (50**) GBP 298,500	US$	476,152

STEINBERG Saul (Rimmical-Sarat, near Bucarest 1914 b.) American (Roumanian)
TWO EASTERN SUNSETS watercolour, graphite and rubber stamps on paper mounted, 29¾ x 19
7/8in. (75.6 x 50.6cm.) sdlc 'Steinberg 1973'
PROV.: Sidney Janis Gallery, New York; Private collection New York.
EXH.: New York, Whitney Museum of American Art; Washington D.C., Smithsonian Institution,
Hirshorn Museum and Sculpture Garden; London, Serpentine Gallery, and Saint-Paul de Vence,;
Fondation Maeght, *Saul Steinberg Retrospective*, April 1978-April 1979, p. ,146 (illustrated).

Christie's New York, 15 November 1995 (224**) US$ 29,900	US$	29,900

ALLEGORY 1 graphite , coloured crayons, coloured inks and rubber and embossed stamps on paper,
22 5/8 x 28¾in. (57.4 x 73cm.) sdlr twice '1970 SAUL STEINBERG' d titled on the reverse
'ALLEGORY '1
PROV.: Sidney Janis Gallery, New York; Galerie Maeght, New York; Margo Leavin Gallery, Los
Angeles; private Collection, Chicago.

Christie's New York, 22 February 1996 (60**) US$ 10,350	US$	10,350

STEINHARDT Jakob (Zerkov (now Poland) 1887-1968 Naharia) Israelian (German)
ON THE TERRACE oil on canvas, 23 5/8 x 31¾in. (60 x 80.5cm.) sdlr 'J. Steinhardt 1944'

Christie's Tel Aviv, 12 October 1995 (82**) US$ 6,325	US$	6,325

STELLA Frank (Malden (Mass.) 1936 b.) American
D. SCRAMBLE: ASCENDING GREEN VALUES/ASCENDING SPECTRUM acrylic on canvas-unframed, 69 x 69in. (175.2 x 175.2cm.) sd and titled 'D. SCRAMBLE: ASCENDING GREEN VALUES/ASCENDING SPECTRUM F. Stella '78' on the stretcher
PROV.: M. Knoedler & Co. Inc., New York.
        Christie's New York, 15 November 1995 (335**) US$ 145,500   US$ 145,500

SHARDS II acrylic and oilstick on aluminum, 40 x 45 x 6in. (101.6 x 114.3 x 15.2cm.) sd wall relief 'F. Stella '82' on the reverse
PROV.: M. Knoedler & Co., New York.
        Christie's New York, 22 February 1996 (102**) US$ 85,000   US$ 85,000

WAKE ISLAND RAIL acrylic, oilstick, metal foil, glitter and colored silkscreen inks on paper mounted on Tycore-unframed, 61 1/8 x 84½in. (155.2 x 214.6cm.) sd 'F. Stella '80' upper right
PROV.: Leo Castelli Gallery, New York; Shaindy Fenton, Fort Worth.
        Christie's New York, 22 February 1996 (105**) US$ 28,750   US$ 28,750

UNTITLED oil on canvas, 11 x 11in. (28 x 28cm.) sd '60' on the overlap
PROV.: Leo Castelli Gallery, New York; Seymour H. Knox, Buffalo, New York.
LIT.: Lawrence Rubin, Frank Stella Paintings: 1958-1965, New York 1986, no. 106.
        Christie's London, 23 May 1996 (73**) GBP 25,300   US$ 38,310

DELAWARE CROSSING alkyd on canvas, 12 x 12in. (30.5 x 30.5cm.) sd 'Stella 61' on the overlap
PROV.: Galerie Lawrence, Paris; Béatrice Monti, Milan; Adriano Buzzati, Italy; Galleria la Salita, Rome.
EXH.: Paris, Galerie Lawrence, Frank Stella, Nov. 1961.
LIT.: Lawrence Rubin, Frank Stella, Paintings 1958-1965, p. 144, no. 133.
        Christie's London, 30 November 1995 (30**) GBP 45,500   US$ 71,172

ABAJO metallic powder in polymer emulsion on canvas, 96 x 110in. (243.8 x 279.5cm.) (1964)
PROV.: Leo Castelli Gallery, New York; Walter Chrysler, Norfolk; M. Knoedler & Co., Inc., New York; Frank Stella, New York; Lawrence Rubin, New York.
EXH.: Sao Paulo, Museu de Arte Moderna, *VIII Bienal de Sao Paulo*, Sept.-Nov. 1965; Boston, Museum of Fine Arts, *A Private Vision: Contemporary Art from the Graham Gund Collection*, Feb.-Apr. 1982, p. 43 (illustrated); Cambridge, Harvard University, Fogg Art Museum, *Frank Stella: Selected Works*, Dec. 1983-Jan. 1984; Providence, Brown University, David Winton Bell Gallery and Southampton, Parrish Art Museum, *Definitive Statements: American Art 1964-1966*, March-June 1986, p. ,147 (illustrated).
LIT.: L. Rubin, *Frank Stella Paintings: 1958 to 1965*, New York 1986, pp. 224-225, no. 233 (illustrated).
        Christie's New York, 7 May 1996 (19**) US$ 827,500   US$ 827,500

STELLA Joseph (Muro Lucano (Italy) 1877-1946 New York) American
STILL LIFE WITH EGGPLANT crayon and pencil on paper laid down in board, 16 1/8 x 18 5/8in. (41 x 47.4cm.) slr 'Joseph Stella'
PROV.: Richard York Gallery, New York; Sale: New York, Christie's, March 14, 1991, lot 219.
        Christie's New York, 13 September 1995 (121**) US$ 8,050   US$ 8,050

STEN John (1879-1922) Swedish
TRE SOLBADANDE KVINNOR oil on canvas, ,129 x 162cm. slr 'John Sten'
        Bukowskis Stockholm, 24-25 April 1996 (134**) SEK 80,000   US$ 12,120

STERN Ignaz, {called} Stella (attr.) (Mariahilf 1680-1748 Rome) German
TWO AMORS, ONE SHOOTING HIS BOW AND ARROW oil on canvas, 32 x 25¾in. (81.3 x 65.4cm.)
        Sotheby's New York, 16 May 1996 (130**) US$ 18,400   US$ 18,400

STERN Ludovico (Rome 1709-1777) Italian
FLOWER STILL-LIFE IN A SCULPTED VASE oil on canvas, 73 x 62.5cm.
    Étude Tajan Paris, 25 June 1996 (10**) FRF 60,000   US$ 11,586

STERN Max (1872-1943) German
WÄSCHERINNEN AUF DER WIESE oil on linen, 60 x 50cm. sll 'Max Stern'
    Lempertz Cologne, 29 November 1995 (460*) DEM 12,000   US$ 8,470

STEVENS Alfred (Brussel 1823-1906 Paris) Belgian
MOTHER WITH HER CHILDREN ON A TERRACE oil on canvas, 26½ x 38½in. 967.3 x 97.8cm.)
sd 'A. Stevens/83'
    Christie's New York, 2 November 1995 (26**) US$ 200,500   US$ 200,500

IN THE COUNTRY oil on canvas, 30¾ x 22in. (78.1 x 55.9cm.) sll 'A.Stevens'
    Christie's New York, 22 May 1996 (99**) US$ 277,500   US$ 277,500

STILL Clyfford (Grandin, North Dakota 1904-1980) American
1955-D oil on canvas-unframed, ,116 5/8 x 111in. (296.2 x 281.9cm.) sd and titled 'Clyfford 1955-D
1955' on the reverse
PROV.: Marlborough-Gerson Gallery, New York; Ahmet Ertegun, New York; Private collection,
Connecticut.
EXH.: The Buffalo Fine Arts Academy, Albright Art Gallery, *Clyfford Still*, Nov.-Dec. 1959, no. 62
(illustrated); New York, Marlborough-Gerson Gallery, *Clyfford Still*, Oct.-Nov. 1969, pp. 54-55, no.
28 (illustrated); New York, Marisa del Re Gallery, *Masters of the Fifties: American Abstract
Painting from Pollock to Stella*, Oct.-Dec. 1985, p. 56 (illustrated); Fort Lauderdale, Museum of Art,
An American Renaissance: Painting and Sculpture since 1940, Jan.-March 1986, n.n. (illustrated);
Berlin, Martin-Gropius-Bau, *Der Unverbrauchte Blick*, Jan.-April 1987, n.n. (illustrated); Paris,
Musée National d'art Moderne, Centre Georges Pompidou, *Années 50*, June-Oct. 1988, n.n.
(illustrated).
LIT.: E.C. Goosen, 'Painting as Confrontation,' *Art International*, vol. IV/I 1960, p. 43 (illustrated);
D. Kuspit, 'Clyfford Still: The Ethics of Art,' *Artforum*, May 1977, p. 37.
    Christie's New York, 14 November 1995 (29**) US$ 684,500   US$ 684,500

STOFFE Jan Jacobsz. van der (Leyden 1611-1682) Dutch
A CAVALRY SKIRMISH oil on panel, 21¾ x 28¾in. (55.3 x 73cm.) sll 'JVD Stoffe.'
    Christie's London, 20 October 1995 (107**) GBP 6,900   US$ 10,890

STÖHRER Walter (1937 b.-l) German
UNTITLED oil on canvas, ,177 x 179cm. sd '1973'
    Hauswedell & Nolte Cologne, 6 June 1996 (422**) DEM 40,000   US$ 25,989

STOITZNER Josef (Vienna 1884-1951 Bramberg Pinzgau) Austrian
BLUHENDES WASSER oil on canvas, ,100 x 150cm. sll 'Josef / Stoitzner'
    Dorotheum Vienna, 21 May 1996 (88**) ATS 150,000   US$ 14,404

STOK Jacobus van der (Leyden 1794/95-1864 Amsterdam) Dutch
A FERRY-BOAT oil on panel, 30 x 38cm. s 'J. v.d. Stok'
PROV.: Anon. sale, Frederik Muller Amsterdam, June 1957, lot no. unknown.
    Christie's Amsterdam, 26 October 1995 (318*) NLG 14,950   US$ 9,426

STOOP Dirck (Utrecht 1610 c.-1686 Utrecht (?)) Dutch
A PAGE WATERING A GREY OUTSIDE A TAVERN, A MAID SERVING A TRAVELLLER
NEARBY oil on panel, 33.5 x 47.5cm. indistinctly slr 'D. Stoop'
    Christie's Amsterdam, 7 May 1996 (94*) NLG 18,800   US$ 10,962

STOOP Dirck (attr.) (Utrecht 1610 c.-1686 Utrecht (?)) Dutch
THE ARRIVAL OF CATHERINE DE BRAGANZA AT PORTSMOUTH, 25 MAY 1662 oil on
canvas, 26 x 46½in. (66.3 x 118.1cm.) indistinctly dll '168*'
    Sotheby's London, 17 April 1996 (681**) GBP 42,200   US$ 63,988

STORCK Abraham Jansz. (Amsterdam 1644-1708 Amsterdam) Dutch
A DUTCH HARBOUR WITH A BEZAN YACHT AND A GALJOOT MOORED AT A QUAY, A
BOEIER YACHT UNDER SAIL AND A MAN-O'-WAR ANCHORED BEYOND, WITH
FIGURES BATHING FROM A ROWING BOAT oil on canvas, 24¾ x 31¾in. (62.9 x 80.6cm.)
PROV.: Freiherr Hugo von Mecklenburg auf Pautlitz; his Sale: Lepke, Berlin, 3-4 June 1919, lot 69;
Sale; Christie's, London, 15 December 1978, lot 18 (as signed).
    Sotheby's New York, 16 May 1996 (80**) US$ 107,000   US$ 107,000

A CAPRICCIO OF BACINO DI SAN MARCO, VENICE, FROM THE PUNTA DI DOGONA
WITH A GALLEY, A MAN-O'-WAR, GONDOLAS AND OTHER SHIPPING oil on canvas, 32¾
43 7/8in. (83.2 x 111.4cm.)
PROV.: Mrs Frances Henderson, 24 Hyde Park Square, London; Christie's 15 November 1918, lot
,149 (60 gns. to Lark).
    Christie's London, 19 April 1996 (112**) GBP 32,200   US$ 48,825

A MEDITERRANEAN HARBOUR WITH TRAVELLERS EMBARKING, A DUTCH MAN-O'-
WAR BEYOND oil on canvas, 33½ x 21in. (84.5 x 68.5cm.) sd 'A: Storck/Fec. A. 167.' (on the
ruined entablature)
    Christie's London, 7 July 1995 (253**) GBP 24,150   US$ 38,523

**STORCK Abraham Jansz. (with Thomas Heeremans (1160-1697)) (Amsterdam 1644-1708
Amsterdam) Dutch**
AMSTERDAM, A VIEW IN WINTER ALONG THE FROZEN OUDE SCHANS, SEEN FROM
THE SCHEEPJESBRUG TOWARDS THE Y, WITH THE MONTALBAANSTOREN TO THE
LEFT oil on canvas, sdll 'FMANS 1682'
PROV.: Anonymous Sale London, Sotheby's 9 July 1975, lot 97, as by Heeremans (GBP 6000).
    Sotheby's London, 6 December 1995 (48**) GBP 34,500   US$ 53,093

STORCK Jacob Jansz. (Amsterdam 1641-1693 after Amsterdam) Dutch
MARINE HOLLANDAISE oil on canvas, 57 x 81.5cm.
PROV.: Sale Mme Ch.G., Paris, Hôtel Drouot, 11 June 1958 (Maître Lemée), no. 21 (illustrated pl.
II, attribué à Abraham Storck, 475,000 FFR).
    Étude Tajan Paris, 12 December 1995 (35**) FRF 160,000   US$ 32,228

STREECK Juriaen van (Amsterdam 1632 c.-1687 Amsterdam) Dutch
PEACHES AND GRAPES IN A WAN-LI DISH, WITH A GIANT 'ROEMER' AND APRICOTS
ON A DRAPED LEDGE oil on canvas, 55.8 x 51.8cm
    Christie's Amsterdam, 7 May 1996 (39**) NLG 34,500   US$ 20,117

FRUECHTESTILLEBEN oil on canvas, 83 x 69.5cm.
LIT.: W. Bernt, *Die Niederländischen Maler des 17.Jahrhunderts*, Bd. II Muenchen 1970, no. 1142.
    Lempertz Cologne, 18 May 1996 (1150**) DEM 30,000   US$ 19,558

STREVENS John (1793-1868) Flemish (?)
BODAS DE ORO oil on canvas, 76 x 101cm. s; s and titled on the reverse
    Sotheby's Madrid, 23 November 1995 (55*) ESP 1,175,000   US$ 9,658

STROIFFI Ermanno (Padova 1616-1693 Venezia) Italian
THE MEAL IN EMMAUS oil on canvas, ,134 x 193cm.
    Finearte Milan, 11 June 1996 (9*) ITL 23,000,000   US$ 14,916

STROZZI Bernardo {called} Cappuccino {and} Prete Genovese (Genoa 1581-1644 Venice) Italian
FLOWERS IN SILVER VASES WITH LEMONS AND AN ARTICHOKE ON A TABLE;AND FLOWERS IN CERAMIC VASES WIYH ORANGES, APPLES AND A BOWL OF PEACHES AND CHERRIES ON A TABLE oil on canvas (a pair), 40 x 58in. (101.6 x 147cm.) 37 3/8 x 57 1/8 (95 x 195.2cm.)
EXH.: Paris, Galerie Charpentier, 1965, as by Salini; Paris, Galerie Pardo, *Thème de l'âge classique*, 16 May-30June 1989, pp. 42-5 (catalogue by F. Moro).
LIT.: G. Maggi, *Antichitá viva*, 1962, pp. 9-13, fig. 42, as by Salini; L. Salerno, *Nuovi studi sulla natura morta italiana*, Rome, 1989, p. 56, fig. 42; J. Spike, *Naturalia*, Turin, 1992, pp. 64-5; L. Mortari, *Bernardo Strozzi*, Rome, 1995, pp. 175-6, no. 427, illustrated.

Christie's London, 19 April 1996 (231**) GBP 243,500	US$	369,219

STRUYCKEN Peter (The Hague 1939 b.) Dutch
STRUCTUUR XVI-67 celluloid paint on perspex, ,100 x 100cm. inscr. with title on the reverse a left (Executed in 1967)
EXH.: Sao Paulo, International Biennale, 1967, no. 36.

Christie's Amsterdam, 6 December 1995 (357**) NLG 11,500	US$	7,126

STRY Jacob van (Dordrecht 1756-1815) Dutch
BOATS ON THE MAAS BY DORDRECHT oil on panel, 57 x 73.5cm. slc 'J.V.Stry'
PROV.: With A. Whitcombe, Cheltenham.

Sotheby's Amsterdam, 14 November 1995 (62*) NLG 23,600	US$	14,874

STUCK Franz von (Tettenwies 1863-1928 Tetschen) German
HELENA oil on canvas, laid down on a panel in a contemporary frame designed and painted by the artist, 32¼ x 20½in. (82 x 52cm.) sd 'Franz/von/Stuck/1924' and inscr. on frame 'Tadelt nicht die Troer, und hellumschienten Achaeer,/die um ein solches Weib so lang ansehn!/Homer Ilias. '
LIT.: H. Voss, *Franz von Stuck Werkkatalog der Gemälde*, Munich, 1973, p. 310, no. 573/,130 (illus. p. 227).

Christie's London, 11 October 1995 (90**) GBP 84,000	US$	132,576

STUHLMÜLLER Karl (Munich 1858-1930 Munich) German
BAUERNMARKT IN MÜNCHEN oil on cardboard, 34.7 x 56.4cm. s and inscr. ll 'K. Stuhlmüller München'

Wiener Kunst Auktionen, 26 March 1996 (123**) ATS 160,000	US$	15,391

STURGESS John (fl.1875-1884-) British
A CRUSH AT A GATE oil on canvas, 20 x 32¼in. (51 x 82cm.) sdll 'J.Sturgess 81', s and inscr. with title on a label on the stretcher

Phillips London, 18 June 1996 (77**) GBP 8,000	US$	12,336

STUVEN Ernst (Hamburg 1657-1712 Rotterdam) Dutch (German)
A STILL-LIFE OF FRUIT AND CORN BENEATH OAK LEAVES oil on canvas, 34¾ x 29in. (88 x 74cm.) slr 'E. Stuven'
PROV.: With Trafalgar Galleries, London, 1968, as by Rachel Ruys; Anonymous sale, Christie's London, 26 November 1971, as by Mignon.

Sotheby's London, 6 December 1995 (170**) GBP 20,125	US$	30,971

STYKA Adam (Kielce (Poland) 1890-1970) French
DESERT BRIDE oil on canvas, 25½ x 21 3/8in. (64.8 x 54.3cm.) sll 'ADAM STYKA'

Christie's East, 13 February 1996 (210**) US$ 10,350	US$	10,350

SULTAN Donald (1951 b.) American
FLOWERS AND VASE JAN. 10 1986 oil, spackle and tar on vinyl tiles mounted on masonite (four panels), 96 x 96in. (243.8 x 243.8cm.) each initialated, titled and d 'Flowers and Vase Jan 10 1986 D.

S.' ll edge; each sd and titled 'FLOWERS AND VASE Jan 10 1986 SULTAN' on the reverse
PROV.: Blum Helman Gallery, New York.

Christie's New York, 15 November 1995 (360**) US$ 96,000 — US$ 96,000

SAILBOAT APRIL 7, 1984 tar, spackle and oil on vinyl tiles mounted on masonite, 96 x 96in.
(243.9 x 243.9) four panels-initialed, titled and d 'Sailboat April 7 1,984 D.S.' right edge of the upper
right right panel-each titled, numbered consecutively and dated 'Sailboat April 7 1984 204 (1-4)' on the
reverse
PROV.: Blum Helman Gallery, New York.

Christie's New York, 22 February 1996 (123**) US$ 44,850 — US$ 44,850

SURVAGE Léopold Sturvage, {called} (Moscow 1879-1968 Paris) French (Russian)
PAYSAGE CUBISTE (CUBIST LANDSCAPE) oil on canvas, 31½ x 39¼in. (80 x 100cm.) slr
'Survage' (ca. 1920)
LIT.: Will be included in the catalogue raisonné Léopold Survage, currently being prepared by Eric
Brosset.

Étude Tajan Paris, 13 December 1995 (67**) FRF 220,000 — US$ 44,314

NICE oil on canvas, 36¼ x 29in. (92.1 x 73.7cm.) sll 'L Survage' (ca. 1916)

Sotheby's New York, 2 May 1996 (213**) US$ 19,550 — US$ 19,550

SUTHERLAND Graham Vivian, O.M. (London 1903-1980) British
PALM TREE oil on canvas, 25½ x 21½in. (65 x 55cm.) sd 'Sutherland, 29.iv.57' d inscr. 'Palm Tree
29.iv.57' on the reverse
PROV.: Levevre gallery, London; Arthur Jeffress Gallery, London, where purchased by the present
owner's father.
EXH.: Munich, Haus der Kunst, *Graham Sutherland*, March-May 1967, no. 54; this exhibition
travelled to: The Hague, Gemeentemuseum; Berlin, Haus am Waldsee and Cologne, Wallraf-
Richartz Museum (June-Nov. 1967).

Christie's London, 22 May 1996 (24**) GBP 23,000 — US$ 34,827

SWAINE Francis (Monamy) (1740-1782) British
A SMACK-RIGGED YACHT, A KETCH-RIGGED YACHT AND ROWING BOATS, WITH A
MAN-O'-WAR BEYOND, IN A CALM oil on canvas, 55¼ x 50in. (,141 x 127cm.) sll 'F. Swaine'

Christie's London, 18 April 1996 (30**) GBP 19,550 — US$ 29,644

SWANEVELT Herman van (Woerden (near Utrecht) 1600-1655 Paris) Dutch
AN ITALIANATE LANDSCAPE WITH PEASANTS ON A ROCKY TRACK oil on panel, 18½ x
25½in. (47 x 64.8cm.)
PROV.: Sir Torquil Munro, Bart, Chritie's, 25 September 1942, lot 76, sold 33gns. (to Beer).

Christie's South Kensington, 6 November 1995 (135**) GBP 8,437 — US$ 13,197

ITALIANATE LANDSCAPE WITH TRAVELLERS ALONG A COUNTRY ROAD oil on canvas
laid down on panel, 20 x 26in. (50.8 x 66cm.) slr and d indistinctly 'HVS(in
ligature)WANEVELT.\A WOERDEN\ 16(50?)'

Sotheby's New York, 6 October 1996 (90*) US$ 14,950 — US$ 14,950

AN ANGEL SUCCOURING A PROPHET oil on canvas, 13½ x 11 1/8in. (34.3 28.2cm.) sd mono.
'HVS. 1649'

Christie's London, 7 July 1995 (294**) GBP 23,000 — US$ 36,688

SWEERTS Michiel (Brussels 1624-1664 Goa, India) Flemish
A YOUNG MAN IN A TURBAN HOLDING A ROEMER: THE FINGERNAIL TEST oil on
canvas, 29¼ x 23 5/8in. (74 x 60cm.) (1648-50)
PROV.: Dr. Bruno Kaiser, Bern, and by inheritance in 1940-1 to the father of the present owner.

Christie's London, 8 December 1995 (34**) GBP 221,500 — US$ 340,874

DOMESTIC SCENE WITH LUTE PLAYER AND TRIC-TRAC PLAYERS oil on canvas, 74 x 100cm. s with inscr. 'MS'
PROV.: Bologna, collection Hercolani.
LIT.: V. Bloch, *Michael Sweerts*, The Hague 1968, pag.23, 28, note 19 and 91, fig. 18; R.Kulzen, *Franzosische Anklange im Werk von Michael Sweerts*, in 'Essays in Northern European Art 15th-17th Century. Presented to Egbert Haverkamp-Begemann on his Sixtieth Birthday', Doornspijk (Davaco) 1983, pag. 128-129, fig. 2; L. Laureati, *I Bamboccianti*, Rome 1983, pag. 323, fig. 13.24-13.25, pag.327, fig. 13.27.
Finearte Milan, 11 June 1996 (54**) ITL 380,650,000   US$ 246,855

WOMAN GROOMING HER CHILD'S HAIR, WITH ANOTHERCHILD BY THE HEART, ALL IN A KITCHEN INTERIOR oil on canvas, 17¼ x 13in. (43.8 x 33cm.) (ca. 1650)
PROV.: An old, unidentified auction or catalogue label in French on the verse lists the painting as no. 10, *Ecole hollandaise*.
Sotheby's New York, 16 May 1996 (14**) US$ 173,000   US$ 173,000

SWOBODA Rudolph L. (1859-1914) Austrian
THE RAFAI MOSQUE, CAIRO oil on panel, 21¾ x 15in. (55.2 x 38cm.) sd 'Rudolf Swoboda. Cairo./1885'
PROV.: With The Cooling Galleries.
Christie's London, 15 March 1996 (115**) GBP 67,500   US$ 103,085

SYMONS George Gardner (1863-1930) American
EARLY SNOW oil on canvas, 25 x 30in. (63.8 x 76.3cm.) slr 'Gardner Symons'; inscr. with title on the stretcher
Christie's East, 28 November 1995 (191*) US$ 8,625   US$ 8,625

SYS Maurice (1880-1972) |
A BEND IN THE RIVER LEIE oil on canvas, 57 x 70cm. slr 'Maurice Sys' (*ca.* 1910)
Christie's Amsterdam, 6 December 1995 (249**) NLG 28,750   US$ 17,815

TAAFFE Philip (1955 b.)
GINOSTRA FLOWERS oil and paper collage on canvas, 61 x 83in. (155 x 211cm.) sd titled 'P.
Taafe 1993 Ginostra Flowers'
PROV.: Galerie Max Hetzler, Cologne.
EXH.: Cologne, Galerie Max Hetzler, *Philip Taaffe*, Oct. 1993.

Christie's New York, 7 May 1996 (34**) US$ 101,500	US$	101,500

TAMBURI Orfeo (Jesi 1906-1994 Paris) Italian
FINESTRE oil on canvas, 56 x 42cm s 'Tamburi'. on the reverse (ca.1959)
PROV.: Galleria Russo, Roma; Galleria Parametro, Roma.

Finearte Rome, 14 November 1995 (162) ITL 11,500,000	US$	7,219

RUDERI AL PALATINO oil on canvas, 50 x 60cm s 'Tamburi' (ca.1944-`45)

Finearte Rome, 14 November 1995 (201**) ITL 13,225,000	US$	8,302

TETTI DI PARIGI oil on canvas, 46 x 58cm. slr 'Tamburi' (1994)

Finearte Milan, 18 June 1996 (99*) ITL 14,375,000	US$	9,322

LONDRA, UN 'MEWS' oil on masonite, 34.5 x 32.5cm. slr 'Tamburi' (1967)

Sotheby's Milan, 28 May 1996 (10*) ITL 10,925,000	US$	7,017

TANCREDI Parmeggiani (Feltre 1927-1964 Rome) Italian
SENZA TITOLO oil on cardboard, 125 x 170cm (ca.1954)
PROV.: Galleria Schettini, Milano, no.48.
EXH.: Milano, *I Tancredi di Schettini*, Galleria Schettini, 1979, cat.no.28.

Finearte Rome, 14 November 1995 (210**) ITL 49,450,000	US$	31,042

IL GIOCO DELLA PALLA tempera on masonite, 100 x 150cm.
PROV.: Galleria La Steccata, Parma.
EXH.: Venice, *40 ima Mostra collettive Bevilacqua La Masa*.

Finearte Milan, 26 October 1995 (199**) ITL 69,000,000	US$	42,991

COMPOZIONE mixed media on paper laid down on canvas, 70.3 x 100.3cm. s
LIT.: This work is recorded in the 'Associazione Nazionale Galleria D'Arte Moderne' under no.
2979/96/M.

Sotheby's Milan, 28 May 1996 (147**) ITL 19,550,000	US$	12,556

PAPAVERI tempera and mixed media on chipboard, 110.5 x 119.5cm. slr

Sotheby's Milan, 28 May 1996 (207**) ITL 34,500,000	US$	22,158

TANGUY Yves (Paris 1900-1955 Woodbury (Connecticut)) American (French)
BAR AMERICAIN gouache, 21 x 14.4cm. sdlr 'Y.TANGUY.25'
LIT.: Patrick Waldberg, *Yves Tanguy*, Brussels 1977, p. 76; *Yves Tanguy*, Katharina Schmidt (ed.),
Munich 1982, p. 62.

Hauswedell & Nolte Cologne, 1 December 1995 (599**) DEM 60,000	US$	41,629

UNTITLED gouache and card laid down on canvas board, 6¾ x 10¾in. (17.1 x 27.3cm.) sd '44'
PROV.: Mr. and Mrs.Joseph R. Shapiro; Richard Feigen Gallery, New York and Chicago; Acquired
from the above by the Benjamin family in 1964.
EXH.: New Haven, Yale University Art Gallery, *The Helen W. and Robert M. Benjamin Collection*,
1967,no. 159; Tokyo, Isetan Museum of Art; travelling exhibition: Hiroshima, Yokohama,
Yamanashi, Asakihawa and Osaka, *Surrealism*, 1983, no. 78.
LIT.: Kay Sage Tanguy, Pierre Matisse (ed.), *Yves Tanguy: Un Recueil de ses Oeuvres*, New
York,1963, no.337, illustrated p. 154.

Sotheby's New York, 2 May 1996 (261**) US$ 57,500	US$	57,500

UN GRAND TABLEAU QUI REPRESENTE UN PAYSAGE oil on canvas, 45 7/8 x 33¾in. (116.5 x 90.8cm.) sdlr 'YVES TANGUY 27'
PROV.: Galerie Surréaliste, Paris (acquired from the artist in 1927); Mrs. William P. Mazer, New York.
EXH.: Paris, Galerie Surréaliste, *Yves Tanguy*, May-June, 1927, no. 17; Paris, Centre Georges Pompidou, Musée National d'art Moderne, *Yves Tanguy Rétrospective*, June-Sept., 1982, p. 144, no. 21 (illustrated in color). The exhibition traveled to Baden-Baden, Staatliche Kunsthalle, Oct., 1982-Jan., 1983; New York, The Solomon R. Guggenheim Museum, *Yves Tanguy, A Retrospective*, 1983, pp. 7-17, no. 30 (illustrated in colour on the cover).
LIT.: P. Matisse, *Yves Tanguy, Un Receuil de ses oeuvres*, Paris,1963, p. 58, no. 63 (illustrated, p. 59); P. Waldberg, *Yves Tanguy*, Brussels, 1977, p. 75 (illustrated).

Christie's New York, 7 November 1995 (41**) US$ 904,500	US$	904,500

LE PRODIGUE oil on canvas, 11 1/8 x 9in. (28.2 x 22.9cm.) lr 'YVES TANGUY 43' (1943)
PROV.: Brook Street Gallery, London; Hugh Chislom, Jr., Hillsboro, California (1963); Galerie Krugier, Geneva.
LIT.: P.Matisse, *Yves Tanguy, un recueil de ses oeuvres*, New York, 1963, no. 308 (illustrated, p.141); P.Waldberg, *Yves Tanguy*, Brussels, 1977, p. 206 (illustrated).

Christie's New York, 8 November 1995 (262**) US$ 129,000	US$	129,000

TAPIES Antoni (Barcelona 1923 b.) Spanish
DIAGONALE DE MOUSSE oil and mixed media on canvas, 32 x 39¼in. (81 x l00cm.) s on the reverse (1987)
PROV.: Adriana Schmidt Gallery, Stuttgart.
EXH.: London, Annely Juda Fine Art, *Antoni Tapies: Paintings, Sculpture, Drawings and Prints*, April-May 1988, no. 23 (illustrated in colour in the catalogue).
LIT.: To be included in the forthcoming *Antoni Tapies Catalogue Raisonné* (Vol. VI) being prepared by Anna Agusti, Barcelona.

Christie's London, 19 March 1996 (37**) GBP 29,900	US$	45,663

TRACES SUR NOIR acrylic, chalk and mixed media on paper laid down on canvas, 31½ x 23½in. (80 x 60cm.) slr 'Tapies' and sd 'Tapies 1986' on the reverse
PROV.: Galerie Beyeler, Basel.
EXH.: Basel, Galerie Beyeler, *Antoni Tapies*, June-September 1988, no. 65 (illustrated in colour in the catalogue).
LIT.: To be included in the forthcoming *Antoni Tapies Catalogue Raisonné* (Vol. VI) being prepared by Anna Agusti, Barcelona.

Christie's London, 19 March 1996 (43**) GBP 29,900	US$	45,663

BROWN AND TURQUISE mixed media on canvas, 31 5/8 x 26in. (80.5 x 66.cm.) s on the reverse (1967)
PROV.: Galerie Maeght, Paris; Galerie Buren, Stockholm; acquired from the above by the present owner in 1968.
EXH.: Paris, Galerie Maeght, *Tápies*, November 1967, no. 27; Vienna, Museum des 20. Jahrhunderts, Antoni Tápies, March-April 1968, no. 57.
LIT.: Joan Brossa, Joaquim Gomis, Joan Prats and Frances Vicens, *Antoni Tápies o l'Escarnidor de Diademes*, Barcelona 1967, pl. XCII (illustrated in colour); Georges Raillard, *Tápies*, Paris 1976, p. 84, pl. 94 (illustrated); Anna Agusti, *Tápies: The Complete Works*, vol. II, 1961-1968, Barcelona 1990, p. 358, no. 1671 (illustrated in colour).

Christie's London, 23 May 1996 (63**) GBP 87,300	US$	132,193

GEOMETRIC ON WHITE mixed media on canvas, 44 7/8 x 57½in. (114 x 146cm.) sd '1975' on the reverse
PROV.: Martha Jackson Gallery, New York.
EXH.: Boston, Nielsen Gallery, *Tápies*, September 1976, no. 13. Saskatoon, Mendel Art Gallery, *Antoni Tápies*, May-June 1977, no. 11 (illustrated in colour in the catalogue); New York, Martha

Jackson Gallery, *Antoni Tápies: Paintings, Works on Cardboard and Paper*, April-May 1978, no. 21 (illustrated in the catalogue).
LIT.: Anna Agusti, Tápies: *The Complete Works*, vol. III, 1969-1975, Barcelona 1992, P. 459, no. 2931(illustrated).

Christie's London, 23 May 1996 (80**) GBP 56,500	US$	85,554

CHAISE acrylic on canvas, 57½ x 44¾in. (146 x 113.5cm) s on the reverse (1982-83)
PROV.: Galerie Maeght-Lelong, Paris; Galerie Beyeler, Basel; The Elkon Gallery, New York.
EXH.: Paris, Galerie Maeght Lelong, *Tápies*, September 1983, no. 22 (illustrated in the catalogue p. 10); Basel, Galerie Beyeler, *Expressive Malerei nach Picasso*, October-December 1983 (illustrated in colour in the catalogue pl. 60); Basel, Galerie Beyeler, *Tápies*, June-September 1988, no. 26 (illustrated in colour in the catalogue); New York, The Elkon Gallery, *Antoni Tápies*, June-July 1988, p. 26; New York, The Elkon Gallery, *Antoni Tápies*, March-May 1989, p. 8.
LIT.: , Juan Perucho in: 'El Europeo', *Evocacion de Antoni Tápies*, June 1990, p. 67, no. 24; To be included in the forthcoming *Antoni Tápies Catalogue Raisonné* (Vol. V) being prepared by Anna Agusti, Barcelona.

Christie's London, 26 October 1995 (64**) GBP 68,600	US$	108,270

DOOR-WALL mixed media on canvas, 63¾ x 51¼in. (162 x 130cm.) s on the reverse (1970)
PROV.: Galerie Maeght, Paris.
EXH.: Zurich, Galerie Maeght, *Tàpies: Peintures, Objects*, March-April 1971, no. 10; Basel, Galerie Beyeler, Highlights, March-April 1972, no. 33 (illustrated in colour in the catalogue); Siegen, Städtische Galerie im Haus Seel, *Antoni Tàpies*, June-July 1972, no. 18 (illustrated in the catalogue p. 33); Basel, Galerie Beyeler, *Antoni Tàpies*, June-September 1988, no. 19.
LIT.: Anna Agusti, *Tápies:The Complete Works*, vol. III, 1969-1975, Barcelona 1992, p. 152, no. 2240 (illustrated).

Christie's London, 27 June 1996 (42**) GBP 89,500	US$	138,011

CHAISE BLANCHE CRAQUELEE mixed media on wood, 63¾ x 51¼in. (162 x 130.2cm.) s on the reverse (1988)
PROV.: Galerie Lelong, New York.
LIT.: In 'Architectaural Digest', Joan Chatfield-Taylor, Au Elkins Revival, *Classic Lines and Contemporary Art in San Fransisco*, New York, February 1996, pp. 144-151 (illustrated in colour p. 146).

Christie's London, 27 June 1996 (44**) GBP 144,500	US$	222,822

UNTITLED oil on wood, 25½ x 31 7/8in. (64.8 x 80.7cm.) s on the reverse (1985)
PROV.: Galerie Maeght, Paris.

Christie's London, 27 June 1996 (49**) GBP 47,700	US$	73,554

WINDING RELIEF. NO. XXI oil, sand, fabric and plaster on canvas, 25 3/8 x 39 1/8in. (64.5 x 99.5cm.) sd '1957' on the reverse
PROV.: Galerie Stadler, Paris; Galerie Grange, Lyon; Mme. Rossier, Lyon.
LIT.: Michel Tapié, *Antoni Tápies*, Barcelona 1959; no. 1, illustrated; Alexandre Cirici, *Tàpies Witness of Silence*, New York 1972, p. 182, no. 144, illustrated; *Antoni Tàpies, Mémoire, Autobiographie*, Paris 1981, p. 347, illustrated; Anna Agusti, *Tàpies: The Complete Works: 1943-1960*, vol. I, Barcelona 1988, p. 285 no. 575, illustrated.

Sotheby's London, 27 June 1996 (135**) GBP 36,700	US$	56,592

NEGRO CON GRIETAS mixed media on canvas, 51¼ x 63¾in. (130 x162cm.) sd '1962' on the reverse
PROV.: Galerie Stadler, Paris; Galerie im Erker, St. Gallen.
EXH.: St. Gallen, Galerie im Erker, Antoni Tàpies: Gemälde, June-July 1963, no. 6 (illustrated in the catalogue pl. V).
LIT.: Pere Gimferrer, *Tàpies i l'Esperit Català*, Barcelona 1974, p. 199 (illustrated pl. 216); Anna Agusti, *Tàpies: The Complete Works*, vol. II, 1961-1968, Barcelona 1990, p. 106, no. 1085

(illustrated); Josep Vallès Rovira, *Tàpies Empremta (Art-Vida)*, Barcelona 1983.
Christie's London, 30 November 1995 (23**) GBP 166,500   US$ 260,441

WIDE AND CENTRAL TRIANGLE mixed media on canvas, 35 x 45 5/8in. (89 x 116cm.) s on the reverse (1967)
PROV.: Galerie Maeght, Paris.
EXH.: Basl, Galerie Beyeler, *Dream of the Absolute*, June-Sept. 1994 (illustrated in colour in the catalogue).
LIT.: Anna Agusti, *Tàpies: The Complete Works*, vol.II, 1961-68, Barcelona, 1990, p. 386, no. 1759 (illustrated); Vera Linhartová, *Tàpies*, London 1972, pl. 56 (illustrated).
Christie's London, 30 November 1995 (25**) GBP 47,700   US$ 74,613

CRACKLED WHITE mixed media on canvas, 78¾ x 129 7/8in. (200 x 330cm.) s on the reverse of the left panel (1988)
PROV.: Galerie Lelong, Paris; Marisa del Re Gallery, New York.
EXH.: Lund, Lundskonsthall; Stockholm, Prins Eugens Waldermarsude, *Antoni Tàpies*, November 1993-April 1994 (illustrated in colour in the catalogue p.67).
LIT.: Ralph Hermanns, *Tápies*, Lunds 1993, p. 89 (illustrated in colour).
Christie's London, 30 November 1995 (43**) GBP 172,000   US$ 269,044

TAPPERT Georg (Berlin 1880-1957 Berlin) German
VARIETE oil on canvas; another oil on the reverse 'Akt auf Wiese mit Klatschmohn', 47½ x 43¼in. (120.7 x 109.9cm.) s 'Tappert' (1913)
PROV.: The Artist's Estate; Leonard Hutton Galleries, New York, From whom bought by the present owner.
EXH.: Berlin, Grosse Berliner Kunstaustellung, *Abt. Novembergruppe*, May-July 1928; Kassel, Kunstverein, *Georg Tappert Gedächtnis Ausstellung*, May-June 1959, no. 9; Berlin, Galerie Nierendorf, *Georg Tappert*, Oct. 1963-Jan. 1964, no. 25; New York, Leonard Hutton Galeries, *Georg Tappert Retrospective*, April-May 1964, no. 13 (titled Three Actresses); New York, Galerie Hutton Galeries, *Fauves and Expressionists*, April-June 1968, no. 112 (titled Three Actresses), p. 44 (illustrated); Hamburg, BAT-Haus, *Georg Tappert. Wiederentdeckung eines Expressionisten*, April-June 1977, no. 25 (illustrated); Berlin, Berlinische Galerie, *Georg Tappert. Ein Berliner Expressionist 1880-1957*, Nov. 1980-Jan. 1981, no. 15.
LIT.: G. Wietek, *Georg Tappert 1880-1957*, Munich, 1980, no. 144, (illustrated in colour p. 104 and in black and white p. 181).
Christie's London, 11 October 1995 (152**) GBP 89,500   US$ 141,256

TARBELL Edmund Charles (West Groton (Massachusetts) 1862-1938) American
MARY READING oil on canvas, 50¼ x 40¼in. (127.5 x 102.2cm.)
PROV.: Josephine Tarbell Ferrell, the artist's daughter; Mrs. Albert Cannon; Mrs. John Julius King; Edward Shein, Seekonk, Massachusetts.
EXH.: Boston, Massachusetts, Museum of Fine Arts, *Frank W. Benson and Edmund C. Tarbell Exhibition of Paintings, Drawings, and Prints*, November-December 1938, no. 162; New Castle, New Hampshire, *Edmund C. Tarbell Memorial Exhibition*, July-Aug., 1939, no. 3; Washington, D.C., *National Collection of Fine Arts*, Smithsonian Institution, 1955, on loan; Washington, D.C., National Gallery of Art and the Smithsonian Institution, *Smithsonian Institution Centennial Exhibition*, July-Aug. 1962.
LIT.: P.J. Pierce, *Edmund C. Tarbell and the Boston School of Painting, (1889-1980)*, Hingham, Massachusetts 1980, p. 205, p. 142 (illustrated).
Christie's New York, 30 November 1995 (31**) US$ 310,500   US$ 310,500

TAUNAY Nicolas Antoine (Paris 1755-1830 Paris) French
LE GÉNÉRAL BONAPARTE REÇOIT LE SABRE D'UN OFFICIER AUTRICHIEN oil on canvas, 38.5 x 60cm. sll 'Taunay' (ca. 1801)
Étude Tajan Paris, 12 December 1995 (57**) FRF 50,000   US$ 10,071

LE CHANTEUR DE COMPLAINTES oil on canvas, 33.2 x 41.5cm. s 'taunay'
PROV.: Sale Taunay, Hotel Drouot, Paris, 28 February 1831, lot 29 ;
Sale Taunay, Hotel Drouot, Paris, 6 March 1835, lot 23; Sale Baron Leonino, Galerie Charpentier,
Paris, 18-19 March 1937, lot 51 (15.,000 Frs.); Anonymous sale, Galerie Charpentier, Paris, 10 June
1954, lot 53; Anonymous Sale, Palais Galliera, Paris, 29 November 1965, lot 130 (20.,000 Frs.);
Anonymous Sale, Palais Galliera, Paris, 7 December 1967, lot 156 (22.,000 Frs.).
LIT.: The present painting will beincluded in the *catalogue raisonné* on the artist, currently being
prepared by Madame Lebrun-Jouve.
Christie's Monaco, 14 June 1996 (45**) FRF 56,160   US$ 10,844

TENIERS David II (Antwerp 1610-1690 Brussels) Flemish
A FAMILY CONCERT ON THE TERRACE OF A COUNTRY HOUSE: A SELF PORTRAIT OF
THE ARTIST AND HIS FAMILY oil on panel transferred to canvas, 16½ x 14in. (42 x 35.3cm.) slr
'D. TENIERS. F'
PROV.: Probably in the possession of the family of the artist until after 1719; In Paris in 1765,
according to an inscription on the reverse of the canvas; John Astley, his sale, London, Christie's, 2-3
May 1777, lot 44 (to 'Dyamouth'); John Trumball, his anonymous sale, London, Christie's, 18
February 1792 (not 1812 as stated by Smith), lot 72, 210 gns;
J.F. Tuffen, his sale, London, Christie's, 11 April 1818, lot 86, 165 gns. to 'Whyte'; Count
Lichnowsky, Kuchelna, Poland, 1906; With Paul Cassirer, Amsterdam, 1927; With D.A.
Hoogendijk, Amsterdam, 1936; E.J. van Wisselingh, Amsterdam; With Knoedler, New York; With
Newhouse Gallery, New York, 1969; Bob Smith collection, from whom on loan to the National
Gallery, Washington, 1971-2; With P. & D. Colnaghi, London, 1974; With Richard Green, London.
EXH.: Berlin, Kaiser Friedrich-Museums-Verein, 1906, no. 137; The Hague, Gemeentemuseum,
Nederlandsch Muziekleven 1600-1800, 1936, no. 588 (illustrated in the catalogue); On loan, National
Gallery, Washington, 1971-2; On loan Bowes Museum, Barnard Castle, 1977-1991; Brussels, Palais
des Beaux-Arts, *Bruegel, Une dynastie de peintres*, 18 September -18 November 1980, no. 203;
Antwerp, Koninklijk Musuem voor Schone Kunsten, *David Teniers the Younger*, 11 May-1
September 1991, no.39; On loan, York City Art Gallery, 1992-1995.
LIT.: J. Smith, *Catalogue Raisonné of the Works of the most eminent Dutch Flemish and French
Painters*, vol. III, 1831, p. 375, no. 440; N. de Pauw, 'Les trots peintres David Teniers et leurs
homonymes', in *Annales de l'Academie Royale d'Archéologie de Belgique*, vol. 50, 4th series, no. 10,
1897, pp. 336, 349; *L'Art Belge*, January 1937 (illustrated); R.D. Leppert, 'David Teniers the
Younger and the Image of Music', in *Jaarboek Koninklijk Museum voor Schone Kunsten Antwerpen*,
1978, p. 114 (illustrated fig. 35); M. Klinge, in *Bruegel, Une dynastie de peintres, catalogue of the
Brussels exhibition*, 1980, p. 269, reproduced in colour; M. Klinge, in *Adriaen Bronwer, David
Teniers the Younger*, exhibition catalogue, Noortman & Brod, 1982, p. 9, reproduced p. 10, plate 2;
M. Klinge, *David Teniers the Younger*, catalogue of the Antwerp exhibition, 1991, p. 39, reproduced
in colour p. 129, and a detail p. 130; M. Klinge, 'Das Berliner Familienbildnis von David Teniers
dem Jungeren', in *Die Malerei Antwerpens*, an international colloquium in Vienna 1993, published
Cologne 1994, pp. 104-113, plate 2.
Sotheby's London, 5 July 1995 (34***) GBP 441,500   US$ 704,259

PORTRAIT OF A LADY AS THE MAGDALENE oil on panel, 6½ x 4¾in. (16.6 x 12.3cm.)
PROV.: John Churchill, 1st Duke of Marlborough, (recorded by Vertue at Blenheim Palace by
1740); Thence by descent to George Charles, 8th Duke of Marlborough, His Sale, London, Christie's
26 July 1886, lot 170, 29 gns to Davis; Mrs Isabella Frances Weston, her sale, London, Christie's, 21
October 1949, lot 58, 65 gns, bought for HRH Princess Mary, the Princess Royal (1897-1965), Her
(deceased) sale, London, Christie's, 26 November 1976, lot 2.
EXH.: London, Kenwood, *Cabinet Pictures of David Teniers*, 1972, no. 30; On loan, London,
Kenwood, 1972-1976; On loan, Victoria and Albert Museum, London, 1977 - 1989; Brussels, Palais
es Beaux-Arts, *Bruegel Une dynastie de peintres*, 1980, no. 216h; On loan, Doncaster Museum and
rt Gallery, 1990 - 1993.
Sotheby's London, 5 July 1995 (35**) GBP 12,650   US$ 20,179

SCIPIONE AFRICANUS oil on panel, 6¾ x 9in. (17.2 x 23.3cm.)
PROV.: With Duits, London, 1934; Henry George Charles, 6th Earl of Harewood (1882-1947), His
wife, HRH Princess Mary, The Princess Royal (1897-1965), Her (deceased) sale, London, Christie's,
26 November 1976, lot 9.
EXH.: London, Kenwood, *Cabinet Pictures by David Teniers*, 1972, no. 21; On loan, London,
Kenwood, 1972-1976; On loan, London, Victoria and Albert Museum, 1977-1989; Brussels, Palais
des Beaux-Arts, *Bruegel Une dynastie de peintres*, 1980, no. 216c; On loan, Doncaster Museum and
Art Gallery 1990-1993.
LIT.: T. Borenius, *Catalogue of the Pictures..in the collection of the Earl of Harewood..*, 1936, p. 68,
no. XV or XVI.
        Sotheby's London, 5 July 1995 (36**) GBP 9,775   US$ 15,593

THE REST ON THE RETURN FROM EGYPT oil on panel, 6¾ x 9¼in. (17.3 x 23.3cm.)
PROV.: HRH Princess Mary, the Princes Royal (1897-1965), Her (deceased) sale, London,
Christie's, 26 November 1976, lot 7.
EXH.: London, Kenwood, *Cabinet Pictures by David Teniers*, 1972, no. 10; On loan, London,
Kenwood, 1972-1976; On loan, London, Victoria and Albert Museum, 1977-1989; Brussels, Palais
des Beaux-Arts, *Bruegel Une dynastie de peintres*, 1980, no. 216g; On loan, Doncaster Museum and
Art Gallery 1990-1993.
        Sotheby's London, 5 July 1995 (37**) GBP 19,550   US$ 31,185

PORTRAIT OF A YOUNG WOMAN oil on panel, 8¾ x 6½in. (22 x 16.8cm.)
PROV.: Sir James Carmichael, Bt.; Mrs Holbrooke, Bladon Castle, Burton-on-Trent, her sale,
London, Christie's, 17 February 1939, lot 146, 52 gns to Borenius, presumably for Lord Harewood;
Probably Henry George Charles, 6th Earl of Harewood (1882-1947); His wife , HRH Princess Mary,
The Princess Royal (1897-1965); Her (deceased) sale, London, Christie's, 26 November 1976, lot 3.
EXH.: London, Kenwood, *Cabinet Pictures of David Teniers*, 1972, no. 28; On loan London,
Kenwood, 1972-1976; On loan, Victoria and Albert Museum, London, 1977 - 1989; On loan,
Doncaster Museum and Art Gallery, 1990 - 1993.
        Sotheby's London, 5 July 1995 (40**) GBP 9,200   US$ 14,675

SAINT JOHN THE BAPTIST IN THE WILDERNISS oilon panel, 8¾ x 6½in. (22.1 x 16.9cm.)
inscr. '**Palma 6 broot/ 7 palma/ **' on the reverse
PROV.: John Churchill, 1st Duke of Marlborough, (recorde by Vertue at Blenheim Place by 1740);
Thence by descent to Georg Charles, 8th Duke of Marlborough; His sale, London, Christie's, 26 July
1886, lot 156, 5gns, to Murray; Henry George Charles, 6th Earl of Harewood (1882-1947); His wife ,
HRH Princess Mary, The Princess Royal (1897-1965); Her (deceased) sale, London, Christie's, 26
November 1976, lot 10.
EXH.: London, Kenwood, *Cabinet Pictures of David Teniers*, 1972, no. 25; On loan, London,
Kenwood, 1972-1976; On loan, Victoria and Albert Museum, London, 1977 - 1989; On loan,
Doncaster Museum and Art Gallery, 1990 - 1993.
LIT.: T. Borenius, *Catalogue of the Pictures...in the collection of the Earl of Harewood..*, 1936, p.
68, no. XIX.
        Sotheby's London, 5 July 1995 (41**) GBP 14,950   US$ 23,848

TWO STREET MUSICIANS oil on panel, 18.5 x 13.5cm.
PROV.: Sale London, Sotheby's, 30 Oct. 1946; Private collection, South America; Sale Vienna,
Dorotheum, 18 sept. 1979, lot 137 (illustrated in colour); Prof. Franz Stoss, Vienna.
        Dorotheum Vienna, 6 March 1996 (1**) ATS 180,000   US$ 17,314

PEASANT COUPLE WITH TWO COWS AND SHEEP IN A LANDSCAPE oil on panel, 12½ x
15in. (31.8 x 38.1cm.) slr 'D.TENIERS FEC.' (1660's)
PROV.: Van Diemen, Berlin (acc. to Bernt); Dowdeswell & Dowdeswell, London.
        Sotheby's New York, 11 January 1996 (92**) US$ 34,500   US$ 34,500

SAINT HIERONYMUS IN THE CAVE oil on canvas, 24.5 x 17.5cm.
      Dorotheum Vienna, 11 June 1996 (218**) ATS 150,000   US$ 13,923

A *SINGERIE*: MONKEYS PLAYING AT CARDS IN A TAVERN, WITH ANOTHER SEATED
ON A TABLE ABOVE TAKING A BUNCH OF GRAPES FROM A BASKET. oil on canvas, 27.5
x 38.7cm. s(?)lr 'D. Teniers.fec'
      Christie's Amsterdam, 13 November 1995 (63*) NLG 25,300   US$ 15,945

BOORS HALTING BY A GRAVE IN A GROTTO, A VILLAGE ON A HILLTOP AND A
LANDSCAPE BEYOND oil on panel, 29.1 x 41.8cm. sll 'DT.F'
      Christie's Amsterdam, 13 November 1995 (136**) NLG 74,750   US$ 47,110

A ALCHEMIST IN HIS STUDY oil on panel, 12 x 8¾in. (30.5 x 22.2cm.) slr 'D.TENIERS.FEC.'
      Christie's London, 20 October 1995 (89**) GBP 14,950   US$ 23,595

GAME OF SKITTLES oil on panel, 42 x 64cm inscr. 'D. Teniers fecit'
EXH.: Galleria Caretto, *32a Mostra Maestri Fiamminghi ed Olandesi del XVI-XVII secolo*, Torino,
November-December 1991, no.33.
      Finearte Milan, 25 November 1995 (61**) ITL 92,000,000   US$ 57,753

SAINT PAUL THE HERMIT VISITED BY SAINT ANTHONY ABBOT IN THE DESERT oil on
canvas, 83.8 x 118cm. slc 'D TENIERS f'
PROV.: Possibly Thomas Weld of Lulworth Castle, Dorset (1750-1810); Humphrey Joseph Weld
(1854-1928); Thence by descent; Anonymous sale, London, Christie's, 10 July 1992, lot 14.
      Sotheby's Amsterdam, 6 May 1996 (10**) NLG 141,600   US$ 82,566

TENIERS David III (Antwerp 1638-1685 Brussels) Flemish
PORTRAIT OF THE ARTIST'S WIFE, ANNA MARIA BONNARENS, SEATED BEFORE
CASTLE PERK, THE ARTIST'S RESIDENCE, NEAR BRUSSELS oil on canvas, 62½ x 63in.
(158.8 x 160cm.)
PROV.: Given to the present owner by Mrs. Price in 1964 (Acc. no. 64.61).
      Sotheby's New York, 11 January 1996 (11**) US$ 26,450   US$ 26,450

TENIERS David the Elder (Antwerp 1582-1649 Antwerp) Flemish
THE ADORATION OF THE MAGI oil on panel, 24¾ x 18¾in. (63 x 47.7cm.) sdll 'DAVID
TENIERS ANNO 16*9'
PROV.: Ferlov sale, New York, Anderson, 5 April 1921, lot 42.
LIT.: E. Duverger and H. Vlieghe, *David Teniers der Ältere*, 1971, p. 76, plate 45, where described
as signed and dated 1649.
      Sotheby's London, 5 July 1995 (153**) GBP 17,250   US$ 27,516

SAINT JEROME IN A FOREST BY A STREAM oil on copper, 14 1/8 x 17¼in. (35.9 x 43.8cm.)
      Sotheby's New York, 16 May 1996 (25**) US$ 37,375   US$ 37,375

TEN KATE Johan Mari (1831-1910) Dutch
FIGURES IN AN INTERIOR oil on canvas, 24½ x 38in. (62.2 x 96.5cm.) slr 'Jan Tenkate'
      Christie's New York, 14 February 1996 (75**) US$ 9,200   US$ 9,200

TENKATE Herman Frederik Dutch
CAVALIERS IN AN INTERIOR oil on panel, 17½ x 25½in. (44.4 x 64.8cm.) slr 'Herman ten Kate
ft'
      Christie's South Kensington, 13 June 1996 (161**) GBP 8,050   US$ 12413

TERWESTEN Matheus (The Hague 1670-1757 The Hague) Dutch
VENUS AND BACCHUS; VENUS AND PARIS oil on canvas (a pair), each: 39 x 48cm.
      Bukowskis Stockholm, 29 November-1 December 1995 (247**) SEK 160,000   US$ 24,204

THANGUE Henry Herbert La, R.A. (1859-1929) British
HARNESSING DONKEY oil on canvas, 35 x 32in. (88.8 x 81.3cm.) s 'H.H. La Thangue'
PROV.: J. Denham Christie, Newcastle-upon-Tyne; S. Marguerita.
EXH.: London, Royal Academy, 1930, no. 624; London Royal Academy, *Winter Exhibition*, Jan.-
March 1933, no. 213.
LIT.: *The Royal Academy Illustrated*, London, 1930, p.16.

Christie's London, 20 June 1996 (60**) GBP 73,000	US$	112,567

THAULOW Frits (Christiania 1847-1906 Volendam) Norwegian
LE PONT (AUDENARDE; EFFET DE NUIT) oil on canvas, 29 x 36¼in. (73.7 x 92.1cm.) slr 'Fritz
Thaulow.' (1902)
PROV.: Arthur Fouques-Duparc; sale, Galerie Georges Petit, Paris, May 8, 1919; D. Lorenzo
Pellerano; sale, Guerrico & Williams, October 1933, no. 13.
EXH.: Paris, Galerie Georges Petit, *Frits Thaulow*, January 5-31, 1917.

Christie's New York, 2 November 1995 (225**) US$ 32,200	US$	32,200

THELANDER P-G (Pär) (1936 b.) Swedish
GET-31 oil on canvas, 126 x 115cm. sll 'P.G. Thelander' (1992)
EXH.: Konstakademien 1994, no. 25 (illustrated no. 1 and in colour p. 34).

Bukowskis Stockholm, 24-25 April 1996 (140**) SEK 160,000	US$	24,240

THERRIEN Robert (1947 b.) American
UNTITLED oil on canvas mounted on panel-unframed, 96 x 63 3/4in. (244 x 160cm.) stamped with
ini. and d 'RT 85' on a metal plaque affixed to the reverse
PROV.: Leo Castelli Gallery, New York; Galerie Denise René; Hans Mayer, Düsseldorf.

Christie's New York, 15 November 1995 (354**) US$ 23,000	US$	23,000

THIEBAUD Wayne (1920 b.-) American
TOY COUNTER STUDY oil on canvas, 10 x 12in. (25.5 x 30.9cm.) sdlr 'Thiebaud 1962'; sd and
titled 'Thiebaud 1962 Toy Counter Study' on the stretcher
PROV.: Allan Stone Gallery, New York; Private Collection, Denver.

Christie's New York, 14 November 1995 (30**) US$ 90,500	US$	90,500

NINE CANDY APPLES oil on canvas, 14 x 16in (35.5 x 40.6cm.) sur 'Thiebaud' sd 'Thiebaud' on
the stretcher
PROV.: Pnvate collection, Fort Worth.
EXH.: Houston, Rice University, De Menil Institute for the Arts, *Wayne Thiebaud*, Jan.-Feb. 1975.
The Fort Worth Art Museum, *Wayne Thiebaud: Recent Work*, May-June 1981.

Christie's New York, 7 May 1996 (25**) US$ 244,500	US$	244,500

FREEWAY TRAFFIC oil on masonite, 16 x 20in. (40.6 x 50.8cm.) sdll 'Thiebaud 1983' inscr.
'FREEWAY 5 Freeway lanes' on the reverse
PROV.: Allan Stone Gallery, New York.
EXH.: San Francisco Museum of Modern Art; Newport Harbor Art Museum; Milwaukee Art
Museum; Columbus Museum of Art and Kansas City, The Nelson-Atkins Museum of Art, *Wayne
Thiebaud*, Sept.-Nov. 1985, no. 78 (illustrated). St. Paul, Minnesota Museum of Art, *American Art:
The Fifties Through the Seventies-Minnesota Museum of Art and Area Collections*, June-Sept. 1991.

Christie's New York, 7 May 1996 (41**) US$ 74,000	US$	74,000

THIELEN Jan Philips van (Mechelen 1618-1667 Boisschot (Mechelen)) Flemish
FLOWER STILL-LIFE oil on canvas, 54 x 41cm.

Dorotheum Vienna, 6 March 1996 (125**) ATS 250,000	US$	24,048

A GARLAND OF FLOWERS SURROUNDING A STATUE OF CERES oil on canvas, 54 1/8 x 40
5/8in. (137.5 x 103.3cm.)

Christie's London, 19 April 1996 (126**) GBP 23,000	US$	34,87

A TULIP, ROSES, A DAFFODIL, HYACINTS AND ORANGE BLOSSOM IN A GLASS VASE
ON TABLE WITH A DRAGONFLY AND A CABBAGE WHITE BUTTERFLY oil on panel, 19½
x13 5/8in. (49.5 x 37.7cm.)
    Christie's London, 8 December 1995 (39**) GBP 56,500   US$ 86,950

THIELER Fred (Königsberg 1916 b.-l) German
KOMPOSITION 0-4-57 oil on canvas, 70 x 100cm. sd titled on the reverse (1957)
PROV.: Collection Varick Steele, London.
    Hauswedell & Nolte Cologne, 6 June 1996 (438**) DEM 13,300   US$ 8,641

KOMPOSITION B-I-58 oil on canvas, 51½ x 35in. (130 x 89cm.) sd titled '1958' on the reverse
PROV.: Galerie Stangl, Munich.
EXH.: Venice, *XXIX Biennale Internazionale dell'Arte*, 1958, p. 261, no. 59.
LIT.: Andrea Firmenich & Jörn Merkert, *Fred Thieler, Monographie und Werkverzeichnis: Bilder
von 1942-1993* Cologne 1995, p. 300, no. 5/246.
    Sotheby's London, 21 March 1996 (40**) GBP 23,000   US$ 35,125

FR.6. KOMPOSITION mixed technique on muslin, 130 x 150cm. sdll 'F. Thieler 84' (1984)
EXH.: 1984 Freiburg, Galerie pro arte,; 1987 München, Galerie Gunzenhauser.
LIT.: Melchior Nr. 8/130 ill.; *Väter und Söhne des Aufbruchs zur Abstraktion*, Gal. Gunzenhauser,
München; 1990, ill. p. 101.
    Lempertz Cologne, 28 November 1995 (960**) DEM 48,000   US$ 33,879

**THIEME Anthony (Antonius Johannes) (Rotterdam 1888-1954 Greenwich (Connecticut))
American (Dutch)**
HOISTED SAILS oil on canvas, 25 x 30in. (63.5 x 76.2cm.) slr 'A. Thieme'; inscr. with title
    Christie's East, 28 November 1995 (194*) US$ 8,050   US$ 8,050

THOMA Hans (Bernau 1839-1924 Karlsruhe) German
SCHAFHERDE BEI OBERBURSEL oil on cardboard, 68 x 102cm. sdll mono 'HTh (linked) 96'
PROV.: Slg. Dina-Zimmermann, Berlin (1909); Hessische Privatsammlung.
LIT.: H. Thode, *'Thoma- Des Meisters Gemälde' in: Klassiker der Kunst, ill. 15,* Stuttgart/Leipzig
1909, p. 393 (ill.); Cat. *Hans Thoma in Frankfurt und im Taunus Dokumentation der
Museumgesellschaft Kronberg e. V., ill. 3)*, Kronberg 1983, ill. p. 60.
    Lempertz Cologne, 18 May 1996 (1647**) DEM 60,000   US$ 39,116

THOMPSON Bob (1937-1966) American
EUROPE oil on canvas, 40 5/8 x 49 7/8in. (103.2 x 126.7cm.) sd and titled 'B THOMPSON '58
'EUROPA"
PROV.: Vanderwoude Tannenbaum Gallery, New York.
    Christie's New York, 22 February 1996 (26**) US$ 14,950   US$ 14,950

PINK AND BLUE FIGURES oil on canvas, 30½ x 38½in. (77.5 x 97.8cm.) sd twice 'B
THOMPSON PARIS '62' on the reverse
PROV.: Vanderwoude Tannenbaum Gallery, New York.
    Christie's New York, 22 February 1996 (37**) US$ 16,100   US$ 16,100

JUDGEMENT OF PARIS (CRANACH) oil on canvas, 10 x 8in. (25 x 20.2cm.) sd and titled 'B
Thompson '63 N.Y. 'Judgement of Paris ' (Cranach)'
PROV.: Richard Gray Gallery, Chicago.
    Christie's East, 7 May 1996 (30*) US$ 12,650   US$ 12,650

THÖNY Wilhelm (Graz 1888-1949 New York) Austrian
STRAßE oil on canvas, 25 x 23.8cm. s 'W. Thöny' (ca. 1923)
    Dorotheum Vienna, 6 December 1995 (513**) ATS 280,000   US$ 27,612

THORBURN Archibald (1860-1935 Godalming) Scottish
A COVEY OF PARTRIDGE IN FLIGHT pencil and watercolour with touches of white heightening,
18 7/8 x 29½in. (48 x 74.9cm.) sd 'Archibald Thorburn. 1901'
    Christie's London, 14 May 1996 (146**) GBP 23,000   US$ 34,827

RUNNING BEFORE THE BEATERS pencil and watercolour heightened with bodycolour, 20½ x
28½in. (52.1 x 72.4cm.) sd 'Archibald Thorburn/1921'
PROV.: With Vicar Brothers, London.
    Christie's London, 14 May 1996 (158**) GBP 40,000   US$ 60,569

A GREY FALCON watercolour heightened with bodycolour, 15¼ x 10¾in. (39 x 27.5cm.) sd
'A.Thorburn/Nov.22'
    Sotheby's London, 29 August 1995 (682**) GBP 12,650   US$ 20,476

THULDEN Theodor van (attributed to) ('s-Hertogenbosch 1606-1669 's-Hertogenbosch) Dutch
THREE ALLEGORIC FIGURES oil on canvas, 99 x 113.5cm.
    Finearte Milan, 3 April 1996 (53**) ITL 74750,000   US$ 47,764

THE TRIUMPH OF NEPTUNE AND HIS WIFE AMPHITRITE oil on copper, 40 x 50cm.
    Dorotheum Vienna, 11 June 1996 (287**) ATS 200,000   US$ 18,564

TICHO Anna (1894-1980)
JERICHO watercolour, pencil, pen and ink on paper, 12½ x 15 5/8in. (32 x 39.8cm.) slr 'A.Ticho'
    Christie's Tel Aviv, 14 April 1996 (71**) US$ 11,500   US$ 11,500

The Madonna and Child in Glory with Angels

TIEPOLO Giovanni Battista (Venice 1696-1770 Madrid) Italian
CARICATURE OF A STANDING MAN WEARING A WIG AND A HEAVY CLOAK, SEEN FROM BEHIND pen and brown ink, brown and grey wash, 8 x 5¼in. (20.4 x 13.4cm.))
PROV.: Probably Lauro Bernardino Coriani de'Conti d'Algarotti; Probably Breadalbane family, Langton House, Berwickshire; Dowell's, Edinburgh, 25 March 1925 lot 1004; John Grant; Arthur Kay; Christie's, London, 9 April 1943, part of lot 243.; with F.A. Drey, 1 944.
    Christie's New York, 10 January 1996 (25**) US$ 11,500   US$ 11,500

THE MADONNA AND CHILD IN GLORY WITH ANGELS pen and black ink and grey wash over black chalk, 27.1 x 22.4cm. (ca. 1759)
    Sotheby's London, 3 July 1995 (195**) GBP 23,000   US$ 36,688

THE HEAD OF A YOUNG WOMAN SEEN ALMOST IN PROFILE, LOOKING TO THE RIGHT
red chalk heightened with white chalk on faded blue paper, 19.7 x 13.3cm. (ca. 1751-53)
PROV.: Bossi; Beyerlen (numbered in pen and brown ink on the verve: 24 Xrs N.3254); Duc de Talleyrand.
EXH.: Venice, San Giorgio Maggiore, Fondazione Giorgio Cini, *Disegni veneti di collezioni inglesi* (catalogue by Julien Stock), 1980, cat.76, illustrated.; Brussels, Palais des Beaux Arts, *Dessins Vénitiens du dix-huitième siècle*, 1983, cat. 18.
LIT.: J. Cailleux, *Tiepolo et Guardi dans les collections françaises*, Paris 1952, no.28; A. Morassi, *Dessins Vénitiens du Dix-huitième siècle de la collection du Duc de Talleyrand*, Milan 1958, no.28.
    Sotheby's London, 3 July 1995 (150**) GBP 38,900   US$ 62,05

THE HOLY FAMILY WITH ANGELS pen and brown ink and wash over black chalk, 27.7 x
19.6cm. (ca. 1762)
PROV.: Somasco Convent, S. Maria della Salute, Venice; Count Leopold Cicognara Antonio
Canova, his half-brother, Monsignor Giovanni Battista Sartori-Canova; Francesco Pesaro; purchased
from him in 1842 by Col. Edward Cheney, Badger Hall, Shropshire; by inheritance to his brother-in-
law, Col. Alfred Capel-Cure, Blake Hall, Ongar, Essex;
sale, Sotheby's London, 29 April 1885, in lot 1024; E. Parsons; Duc de Talleyrand.
EXH.: Venice, Fondazione Giorgio Cini, *Disegni Veneti di collezioni inglesi* (catalogue by Julien
Stock), 1980, cat.84; Brussels, Palais des Beaux Arts, *Dessins Vénitiens du dix-huitième siècle,* 1983,
cat.
LIT.: A. Morassi, *Dessins Vénitiens du Dix-Huitième siècle de la Collection du Duc de Talleyrand*,
Milan 1958, cat.7.

Sotheby's London, 3 July 1995 (167**) GBP 45,500   US$ 72,579

TIEPOLO Giovanni Domenico (Venice 1727-1804 Venice) Italian
THE TIEPOLO FAMILY oil on canvas, red ground, 25 x 36½in. (63.5 x 92.5cm.) inscr. on the dog's
collar 'B. T.'
PROV.: Possibly belonged to Giovanni Battista's wife, Cecilia Tiepolo; Edward Cheney, London,;
His (deceased) sale, London, Christie's, 29ff April 1885, lot 139, as *P. Longhi*, 31 Gns. to Davis;
Archibald Phillip, 5th Earl of Rosebery, Mentmore, Bedfordshire; By descent to Eva, Countess of
Rosebery, widow of the 6th Earl; By whom sold in these Rooms, 24 March 1976, lot 11.
EXH.: London, Whitechapel Art Gallery and Birmingham Museum and Art Gallery,Eighteenth
Century Venice, 1951, no. 57, reproduced pl. 5, as by Pietro Longhi, but 'the general handling is
markedly superior to the general run of his work'; Venice, *Mostra del Tiepolo*, 1951, no. 127 (as by
Giovanni Domenico Tiepolo); London, Royal Academy, *European Masters of the Eighteenth
Century*, 1954-55, no. 319, reproduced in the volume of reproductions, p. 15, (as by Giovanni
Domenico Tiepolo); On loan, Doncaster Museum, 1977-1993; Paris, Musée du Petit Palais, Le
portrait en Italie au siècle de Tiepolo, 1982, no. 49; London, Thos. Agnew & Son Ltd., *Thirty-five
paintings from the Collection of the British Rail Pension Fund*, November-December 1984, no. 32.
LIT.: Possibly G.F. Waagen, *Galleries and Cabinets of Art in Great Britain*, supplementary vol. IV,
1857, p. 171 (as by Pietro Longhi); J. Byam Shaw in *The Burlington Magazine*, vol. 93, 1951, pp.
61-62, reproduced p. 60 (as by Giovanni Domenico Tiepolo); F.J.B. Watson in The Burlington
Magazine, vol. 93, 1951, p. 204; F.J.B. Watson in *The Burlington Magazine*, vol. 94, 1952, p. 44,
note 10; T. Pignatti in *L'Arte*, 1951, vol. 2, no. 4 (as by Lorenzo Tiepolo); A. Morassi, *G.B. Tiepolo*,
1955, p. 13 (as by Lorenzo Tiepolo); Donzelli, *I Pittori Veneti del '700*, 1957, p. 314; J. Byam Shaw,
The Drawings of Domenico Tiepolo, 1962, p. 83 under no. 54, and p. 85, no. 56; M. Precerutti-
Garberi, 'Segnalazioni Tiepolesche', in *Commentari*, vol. XV, 1964, p. 10-12 (as by Giandomenico);
G. Piovene & A. Pallucchini, *L 'Opera completa di Giambattista Tiepolo*, 1968, reproduced p. 83
(mentioning the various attributions); M. Muraro in *Atti del Congresso Internazionale di Studi sul
Tiepolo*, 1970, p. 72, reproduced fig. 8 (as by Lorenzo Tiepolo); A. Rizzi in the catalogue of the
Giambattista Tiepolo exhibition, Udine 1971, pp. 183 andI 185, reproduced fig. 113 (mentions the
attributions to Lorenzo and Giovanni Domenico Tiepolo); G. Knox, *Giambattista and Domenico
Tiepolo, A Study and Catalogue Raisonné of the Chalk Drawings*, 1980, vol. I, pp. 235, 303, no.
P.104 (as by Domenico); M. Levey, *G.B. Tiepolo*, 1986, pp. 251-252, pl. 216 (as Domenico); F.C.
Thiem, 'Lorenzo Tiepolos Position innerhalb der Künstlerfamilie Tiepolo', in *Pantheon*, 1993, vol.
LI, pp. 141-142, reproduced plate 8, (as by Lorenzo Tiepolo).

Sotheby's London, 5 July 1995 (52**) GBP 606,500   US$ 967,459

TIFFANY Louis Comfort (1848-1933) American
ARABS AT MARKET oil on canvas laid down on board, 7 1/8 x 10in. (18.4 x 25.4cm.)
PROV.: By descent in the artist's family to the present owner.

Christie's New York, 13 September 1995 (30*) US$ 4,600   US$ 4,600

**TILBORGH Gillis the Younger van, and a follower of Lucas van Uden (Brussels 1625 ca.-1678
a. Brussels) Flemish**
PORTRAIT OF A PATRICIAN FAMILY WITH A PROSPECT OF THEIR CHATEAU AND

DEMESME BEYOND oil on canvas, 64½ x 88¼in. (164 x 224cm.)
PROV.: The counts Sandizell, Schloss Sandizell; Thence by descent.
        Sotheby's London, 5 July 1995 (195**) GBP 52,100   US$ 83,107

TILIUS Jan (attr.) (1660-1719) Dutch
A YOUNG MAN AT A GAMBLING TABLE ACROSS FROM ANOTHER PLAYING THE
FLUTE oil on panel, 11 x 10 1/8in. (27.9 x 25.7cm.)
        Sotheby's New York, 11 January 1996 (221**) US$ 13,800   US$ 13,800

TILLEMANS Peter (Antwerp 1684 c.-1734 Norton, near Bury St Edmunds) Flemish
A RHENISH LANDSCAPE WITH PEASANTS CONVERSING ON A TRACK, A HILLTOP
CASTLE BEYOND oil on canvas, 34¾ x 45¼in. (88.3 x 115cm.)
        Christie's South Kensington, 18 april 1996 (142**) GBP 6,670   US$ 10,114

HUNTING SCENE oil on canvas, 46 x 43in. (116.9 x 109.2cm.)
        Christie's New York, 28 November 1995 (2A**) US$ 20,700   US$ 20,700

TING Walasse (1929 b.)
GEISHA WITH PARROTS watercolour on paper, 177.5 x 96.5cm. stamped with signature (in
Chinese) upper left
        Christie's Amsterdam, 5 June 1996 (332*) NLG 13,800   US$ 8,063

THREE ELEGANT LADIES watercolour on Japan, 177 x 96cm. marked with the artist`s stamp,
upper centre
        Christie's Amsterdam, 6 December 1995 (400*) NLG 11,500   US$ 7,126

TISCHLER Victor (Vienna 1890-1951 Beaulieu-sur-Mèr) Austrian
STILL-LIFE WITH EXOTIC FLOWERS oil on canvas, 50.5 x 47cm. s 'V Tischler'
        Dorotheum Vienna, 6 December 1995 (548**) ATS 120,000   US$ 11,834

TISI Benvenuto, {called} Garofalo (Garofalo (near Ferrara) 1481-1559 Garofalo) Italian
MADONNA AND CHILD oil on panel, 42½ x 62¼in. (107 x 158.2cm.) (ca. 1525)
PROV.: Sale London, Christie's, 10 July 1987, lot 116.
LIT.: A.M. Fioravanti Baraldi, *Il Garofalo - Bevenuto Tisi*, 1993, p. 178, no. 109.
        Sotheby's London, 17 April 1996 (16**) GBP 20,700   US$ 31,387

THE HOLY FAMILY ON A PORCH, A ROCKY LANDSCAPE WITH A TOWN BEYOND oil on
panel, 12½ x 15 5/8in. (31.7 x 39.7cm.)
        Christie's London, 19 April 1996 (243**) GBP 38,900   US$ 58,984

TITIAN Tiziano Vecellio, {called} (Pieve di Cadore 1488/89-1576 Venice) Italian
RIPOSO NELLA FUGA IN EGITTO oil on canvas, 91 x 160cm
LIT.: W.Suida, *Forgotten splendor in Titian`s Treasures*, in 'Art in America', 1941; B.Berenson,
Pitture italiane del Rinascimento. La scuola veneta, Phaidon, London 1957, p.191; R.Pallucchini,
Tiziano, ed. Sansoni, Firenze 1969, vol.I, pp.9 & 32-33; F.Valcanover, *Tiziano*, ed. Rizzoli, Milano
1969, no.13, p.90, fig.13, p.91; H.E.Wethey, *Titian: the Religious Paintings*, ed. Phaidon, London
1969, p.125.
        Finearte Milan, 25 November 1995 (132***) ITL 828,000,000   US$ 519,774

TOBIASSE Théo (1927 b.) Israelian (French)
LE MARCHAND DES QUATRE SAISONS oil on canvas, 35 x 45 5/8in. (89 x 116cm.) sd and
titled lc 'Theo Tobiasse 60'
PROV.: Galerie de Paris, New York, from whom purchassed by the present owner in 1961.
        Christie's Tel Aviv, 12 October 1995 (32**) US$ 13,800   US$ 13,800

577

LA NUIT DE L'OISEAU oil on canvas, 35 x 45 5/8in. (89 x 116cm.) sdlr 'Theo Tobiasse 60'
PROV.: Galerie de Paris, New York, from whom purchased by the present owner in 1961.
    Christie's Tel Aviv, 12 October 1995 (69**) US$ 19,550   US$ 19,550

LA PETITE FILLE AU MOUTON oil on canvas, 28 x 23in. (71.1 x 58.4cm.) sul 'Theo Tobiasse',
titled and dur 'La petite fille au mouton' (1966)
PROV.: Galerie Ferero, Geneva.
    Christie's Tel Aviv, 14 April 1996 (77**) US$ 12,650   US$ 12,650

TOCQUÉ Louis (Paris 1696-1772 Paris) French
PORTRAIT OF PRINCE NIKITA AKIMFIEVITICH DEMIDOFF (1724-1787) oil on canvas, 87 x
56¾in. (220 x 142.5cm.)
PROV.: Commisioned by Nikita Demidoff in St'etersburg (1757-1759); By descent to Prince Anatoli
Demidoff, Prince of San Donato, Florence; By descent to Princess Abamelek-Lazarew, née
demidoff, of Villa Demodoff, Pratolino (Florence) by 1929; HRH Prince Paul of Yugoslavia by
1968.
EXH.: London, Royal Academy, *France in the Eighteenth Century, 1968, no. 662; On loan, Leeds
Castle, 1980-1995.*
LIT.: *Comte A. Doria,* Louis Tocqué, 1929, p. 104, no. 77, reproduced fig. 27; G.W. Lundberg,
Roslin, 1957, vol. II-III, p. 61, under no. 328.
    Sotheby's London, 5 July 1995 (58**) GBP 84,000   US$ 133,993

TOFFOLI Louis (1907 b.-l) French
LA SIESTE oil on canvas, 18 x 15in. (45.7 x 38.1cm.) slr 'Toffoli'
PROV.: Acquired from the artist by the family of the present owner.
    Christie's East, 7 November 1995 (251*) US$ 7,475   US$ 7,475

VENDEUR ARABE oil on canvas, 28¾ x 36¼in. (73 x 92cm.) slr 'Toffoli'
PROV.: Acquired from the artist by the family of the present owner.
    Christie's East, 7 November 1995 (258*) US$ 10,925   US$ 10,925

TOMKINS William, A.R.A. (London 1732 c.-1792 London) British
VIEW ON THE TAY AT DUNKELD oil on canvas, 35½ x 53¼in. (90 x 135.5cm.)
    Sotheby's London, 12 July 1995 (79**) GBP 33,350   US$ 53,198

TONGEREN Jan van (Oldebroek 1897-1991) Dutch
STILLEVEN MET BLOEMPOT oil on canvas, 65 x 60cm. sdlr 'J.v.Tongeren 1979' and s again and
inscr. with title on a label on the back
PROV.: Galerie Siau, Amsterdam.
LIT.: Exh.cat. *Jan van Tongeren, schilderijen tentoonstelling*, Amsterdam, Galerie Siau, 1982, p.6
(ill.).
    Christie's Amsterdam, 6 December 1995 (191*) NLG 11,500   US$ 7,126

TOORENVLIET Jacob (Jason) (Leyden 1635/36-1719 Leyden) Dutch
THE FIVE SENSES oil on panel (a set of five), each: 8¼ x 6¼in. (21.2 x 16.2cm.) each s
(reinforced) 'J. Toornvliet'
    Sotheby's London, 18 October 1995 (20**) GBP 36,700   US$ 57,923

AN ALCHEMIST WITH HIS APPRENTICE IN HIS STUDIO oil on copper, 69 x 46.5cm.
    Sotheby's Amsterdam, 6 May 1996 (63*) NLG 37,760   US$ 22,017

TOOROP Charley (Katwijk 1891-1955 Bergen) Dutch
JATURE MORTE oil on canvas, 59.5 x 50.5cm. sll 'C.Toorop, and s again and inscr. with title and d
'loumanach Juillet 1928' on the reverse
ROV.: Dr. D.Hannema, Rotterdam; C.J.H.Brinkman, Leiden.
XH.: Amsterdam, Kunsthandel Van Lier, *Carley Toorop en W.Demeter*, 1933; Brussel,

Kunsthandel Goudstikker, *Charley Toorop*, 1933, no.18 Leiden, Stedelijk Museum De Lakenhal, *Kunst van Vrienden*, 1967, no.25.
LIT.: Nico Bredero, *Charley Toorop*, Utrecht 1982, p.281, no.253 (ill.).
Christie's Amsterdam, 6 December 1995 (183**) NLG 20,700   US$ 12,827

STILLEVEN MET KLOMPEN oil on panel, 64 x 77cm. sll 'C.Toorop', and s again and inscr. with title and d on the reverse '1946-1947-1948-1949 Bergen'
PROV.: Mrs D. van Ravenstein-Hintzen, Amsterdam, thence by descent; On loan to the Museum Kröller-Müller, Otterlo from 1950-1995.
EXH.: The Hague, Haags Gemeentemuseum, *Charley Toorop*, 8 April-24 June 1951, no.110; Amsterdam, Stedelijk Museum, *Charley Toorop*, 2 July-30 September 1951, no.110; Eindhoven, Van Abbemuseum, *Charley Toorop*, 6 October-25 November 1951, no.110; Arnhem, Gemeentemuseum, *Vrouwen schilderen*, 25 September-20 November 1955, no.23; Groningen, Gronings Museum, *Charley Toorop en Suzanne Valadon*, 1955-56, no.9; 's Hertogenbosch, Noordbrabants Museum, *Charley Toorop*, 1961-1962, no.110; Amsterdam, Stedelijk Museum, *Charley Toorop*, 17 March-1 May 1983 Paris, Musée d'Art Moderne de la Ville de Paris, *La Beauté exacte Art Pays Bas XXe siecle*, 25 March-17 July 1994, no.217; Otterlo, Museum Kröller-Müller, *Charley Toorop, werken in de verzameling van het Kröller-Müller Musem,*(ill) 29 October 1995, no.34.
LIT.: A.M.Hammacher, *Charley Toorop, een beschouwing van haar leven en werk*, Rotterdam 1952, no.231; N.Brederoo, *Charley Toorop, Leven en werken*, Amsterdam 1982, cat.no.341 (ill.); Paris, Musée d'Art moderne de la Ville de Paris, *La Beauté exacte, Art Pays Bas XXe Siècle, De Van Gogh à Mondriaan*, 1994, p.336; Otterlo, Museum Kröller-Müller, *Charley Toorop, werken in de verzameling van het Kröller-Müller Museum*, p.92-93.
Christie's Amsterdam, 6 December 1995 (190**) NLG 69,000   US$ 42,756

LE MONTAGNARD oil on canvas, 70 x 58.8cm. sll with ini. 'C.T.', and s again and d and inscr. with title on the reverse 'Charley Toorop/1923/St Paul/Montagnard
PROV.: H.P.Bremmer, The Hague; Kunsthandel Nieuwenhuizen Segaar, The Hague; Tieman, Achel.
EXH.: Utrecht, Vereniging voor de kunst, 1926; Amsterdam, Stedelijk Museum, 1927, no.111; The Hague, Galerie Nova Spectra, *Herdenkingstentoonstelling bij het 75ste geboortejaar van Charley Toorop*, 1996;.
LIT.: J.G. van Gelder, *Concept oeuvre-catalogus van Charley Toorop, werken van 1914/42*, ongepubliceerd manuscript no.1923/2; A.M.Hammacher, *Charley Toorop*, Rotterdam 1952, no.73; N.J.Bredero, *Charley Toorop leven en werken*, Utrecht 1982, blz.230, no.53 (ill.).
Christie's Amsterdam, 6 December 1995 (204*) NLG 10,350   US$ 6,413

TOOROP Jan (Johannes Theodorus) (Poerworedjo (Java) 1858-1928 The Hague) Dutch
STIGMATA coloured crayons on paper, 34 x 20cm. s twice ll 'J Th Toorop' dlr '1922' and inscr. with title on the backing.
LIT.: To be included in the *catalogue raisonné* on the artist's work, being prepared by G.W.C. van Wezel.
Christie's Amsterdam, 6 December 1995 (24*) NLG 18,400   US$ 11,402

A PORTRAIT OF ADRIAAN (ARI) VOLKER crayons on paper, 42 x 34cm. sal 'J. Th. Toorop'
Christie's Amsterdam, 6 December 1995 (229**) NLG 23,000   US$ 14,252

HET AANZOEK coloured pencils heightened with white on paper, unframed, 21.5 x 13.5cm. sdll 'Jth Toorop 1898'
Christie's Amsterdam, 6 December 1995 (230**) NLG 28,750   US$ 17,815

TORMER Benno Friedrich (1804-1859) German
CHARITY oil on panel, 15¼ x 12¼in. (38.8 x 31.2cm.) sdll 'B. Törmer. Rom 1854'
PROV.: With Cooling Galleries, London.
Christie's New York, 14 February 1996 (6**) US$ 13,800   US$ 13,80

TORRE Giulio del (1856-1932) Italian
YOUNG SMOKERS oil on panel, 23.2 x 17.5cm. sdar 'G. del Torre Venezia. 1897'
PROV.: Christie`s, December 1902 (Lot.no. 24).
      Wiener Kunst Auktionen, 26 September 1995 (54**) ATS 200,000   US$ 19,441

TORRES GARCIA Joaquin (Montevideo 1874-1949 Montevideo) Uruguayan
COMPOSITION AU MASQUE oil on panel, 50 x 35.5cm. sll 'J. Torrès-Garcia' dlr '31' (1931)
LIT.: Will be included in the forthcoming *catalogue raisonné Torrès-Garcia*, currently being
prepared by Madame Cecilia de Torrès.
      Rémi Ader Paris, 27 February 1996 (99***) FRF 235,000   US$ 48,090

TORRI Flaminio (Bologna 1621-1661 Modena) Italian
A SYBIL oil on canvas, 35 3/8 x 29in. (89.9 x 73.7cm.)
      Christie's London, 8 December 1995 (345**) GBP 16,100   US$ 24,777

TORRIGLIA Giovanni Battista (Florence, active 1858-1937) Italian
AT THE SPINNING WHEEL oil on canvas, 29¼ x 43¾in. (74.5 x 111cm.) scl 'G.B.Torriglia'
      Christie's New York, 14 February 1996 (103**) US$ 90,500   US$ 90,500

LA FILATRICE oil on canvas, 17¼ x 23½in. (44 x 59.5cm.) s 'G.B. Torriglia'
PROV.: With Louis Pisani, Florence.
      Christie's London, 15 March 1996 (150**) GBP 29,900   US$ 45,663

TOSCANI Giovanni di Francsco (Florence 1370/1380 c.-1430 Florence) Italian
HEAD OF A SAINT, POSSIBLY SAINT JOSEPH tempera on panel, gold ground, a fragment, 7 x
6½in. (17.8 x 16.7cm.)
      Sotheby's London, 18 October 1995 (50**) GBP 29,900   US$ 47,191

TOSI Arturo (Busto Arsizio 1871-1956 Milan) Italian
LANDSCAPE WITH TREE oil on canvas, 40 x 33cm. slr 'A. Tosi'
PROV.: Galleria del Milione, Milan, no. 4826.
      Finearte Milan, 12 December 1995 (310*) ITL 10,925,000   US$ 6,854

VENEZIA, PUNTA DELLA DOGANA oil on canvas, 50 x 60cm. sld 'A. Tosi
      Finearte Milan, 19 March 1996 (39**) ITL 27,600,000   US$ 17,658

PAESAGGIO oil on canvas, 70 x 90cm. slr 'A. Tosi'
      Finearte Milan, 19 March 1996 (61**) ITL 37,950,000   US$ 24,280

NATURA MORTA oil on hardboard, 59 x 48cm. slr 'A. Tosi'
      Finearte Milan, 19 March 1996 (73**) ITL 27,600,000   US$ 17,658

NATURA MORTA, CILIEGIE E BUSTO oil on board, 50 x 60cm. sul 'A. Tosi' (1939)
EXH.: Venice, *XII Esposizione Biennale Internazionale d'Arte, 1940; Milan, Galleria d'Arte
Moderna,* Mostra di A. Tosi, April-May 1951; Venice, *XXVIII Espozione Biennale Internazionale
d'Arte,* 1956; Milan, Galleria Gian Ferrari, *Mostra celebrativa di A. Tosi,* 1968.
      Finearte Milan, 26 October 1995 (187**) ITL 27,600,000   US$ 17,196

**TOULOUSE-LAUTREC Henri Marie Raymond de Toulouse-Lautrec-Monfa (Albi 1864-1901
Château de Malromé (Gironde)) French**
NU ACADEMIQUE: BUSTE oil on canvas, 31¾ x 25½in. (80.6 x 64.8cm.) s and also stamped with
the monogram (ca. 1883)
PROV.: Raoul Tapié de Célyran; Maurice Exsteens, Paris; Galerie Klipstein & Kornfeld, Bern; E.J.
van Wisselingh & Co., Amsterdam; Hirschl & Adler Galleries, New York; Huntington Hartford,
New York; Sale: Parke-Bernet Galleries, New York, March 10, 1971, lot 35.
EXH.: Paris, Galerie Manzi-Joyant, *Toulouse-Lautrec*, 1914, no. 169; Basel, Kunsthalle, *Toulouse-*

Lautrec, 1947, no. 152; Brussels, Palais des Beaux-Arts, *Toulouse-Lautrec*, 1947, no. 7; Bern,
Galerie Klipstein & Kornfeld, *Choix d'une collection privée*, 1960, no. 69.
LIT.: Maurice Joyant, *Henri de Toulouse-Lautrec, 1864-1901, Peintre*, vol. 1, Paris, 1926, p.259; M.
G. Dortu, *Toulouse-Lautrec et son Oeuvre*, vol. 2, New York, 1971, no. 208 (illustrated p. 91).

Sotheby's New York, 2 May 1996 (108**) US$ 173,000	US$	173,000

A L'ÉLYSÉE-MONTMARTRE oil on canvas, 28 7/8
x 20in. (73.3 x 50.8) (1888)
PROV.: M. Leclanche, Paris; sale, Hôtel Drouot,
Paris, Nov. 6, 1924, lot 98 (titled Au Moulin Rouge);
M. Perls, Paris.
LIT.: G. Coquiot, *Lautrec ou quinze ans de moeurs
parisiennes 1885-1900*, Paris, 1921, p. 81
(illustrated; titled *Au Moulin Rouge*); M.Joyant,
Henri de Toulouse-Lautrec 1864-1901, Paris, 1926,
vol. I, p. 265; P. de Lapperent, *Toulouse-Lautrec*,
Paris, 1927, p. 33; M.G. Dortu, *Toulouse-Lautrec et
son oeuvre*, New York, 1971, vol. 11, p. 144, no.
P.311 (illustrated, p. 145); G. Caproni and G.M.
Sugana,*L'opera completa di Toulouse-Lautrec*,
Milan, 1977, p. 100, no. 206 (illustrated).

Christie's New York, 7 November 1995 (23**) US$ 1,212,500	US$	1,212,500

A l'Elysée-Monmartre

TOURNIER Nicolas (attr.) (Montbéliard 1590-1639 (?) Toulouse) French
A GUITARIST AND FLUTIST oil on canvas, 43¾ x 35in. (111.1 x 88.9cm.)

Sotheby's New York, 11 January 1996 (209**) US$ 18,975	US$	18,975

TOWNE Charles (Wigan 1763-1840 Liverpool) British
A HUNTER AND A GROOM IN A LANDSCAPE oil on canvas, 40½ x 50½in. (102.9 x 128.3cm.)
sdur 'CHAs TOWNE. Pinxit/1816'

Christie's New York, 28 November 1995 (8**) US$ 90,500	US$	90,500

TOZZI Mario (Fossombrone 1895-1979 Paris) Italian
NATURA MORTA oil on canvas, 39 x 44cm. sll 'Mario Tozzi' (1943)

Finearte Milan, 12 December 1995 (270**) ITL 23,000,000	US$	14,429

SGUARDO INTERROGATIVO oil on canvas, 55 x 46cm. sdll 'Mario Tozzi 971' (1971)
LIT.: M. Pasquali, *Catalogo ragionato generale dei dipinti di M.Tozzi*, ed. Mondadori, Milan, no.
71/74.

Finearte Milan, 12 December 1995 (305**) ITL 41,400,000	US$	25,972

TESTINA IN ROSSO oil on canvas, 35 x 27.5cm sd 'Mario Tozzi 1966'
LIT.: M.Pasquali, *Catalogo ragionato generale dei dipinti di Mario Tozzi*, G.Mondadori & Ass.,
Milano, 1988, vol.II, no.66/37 (inv. no.1267), (illustrated in colour).

Finearte Rome, 14 November 1995 (216**) ITL 29,900,000	US$	18,770

VOLTO DI DONNA oil on canvas, 46 x 31cm. sdll 'Mario Tozzi 967' (1967)

Finearte Milan, 18 June 1996 (203**) ITL 28,175,000	US$	18,272

FIGURA IN UN INTERNO oil on canvas, 46 x 38cm. slr 'Mario Tozzi' (ca. 1942)

Finearte Milan, 18 June 1996 (263**) ITL 28,750,000	US$	18,64

LA PALLA A SPICCHI oil on canvas, 55 x 46cm. sll 'Mario Tozzi' (1975)
EXH.: Sasso Marconi, La casa dell'arte, *Grandangolo 2*. Oct.-Dec. 1982, p. 34; Lucca, Galleria
Poleschi, *Ommagio a Mario Tozzi*, Feb. 1983.

Finearte Milan, 19 March 1996 (58**) ITL 46,000,000	US$	29,431

L'ATELIER oil on canvas, 143 x 114cm. sl in the centre 'M. Tozzi' (1927-1928)
EXH.: Milan, Palazzo della Permanente, 1929; Paris, Galerie Bernheim, 1929; Paris, Galerie Zak,
1929; Basel, Kusthalle, 1930; Berna, Kunsthalle, 1930; Brescia, Galleria del Cavalletto, 1968; Lucca,
Galleria Poleschi, 1983; Firenze, Galleria Palazzo Vecchio, 1984; Ferrara, Palazzo dei Diamanti,
1984; Bologna, Galleria Marescalchi, 1985.
LIT.: M. Pasquali, *Mario Tozzi*, G. Mondadori e Ass., Milan 1988, vol.I, p.229, no.28/1 (ill. in
colour).

Finearte Rome, 2 April 1996 (240**) ITL 235,750,000	US$	150,639

FIGURA oil on canvas, 65 x 54cm. sdlr 'Mario Tozzi 1968'
PROV.: Galleria La Collona, Firenze.
LIT.: M. Pasquali, *Mario Tozzi, Catalogo Generale Ragionato*, Milano, 1988 vol II, p. 194, no.
68/53.

Christie's Milan, 20 November 1995 (143**) ITL 54,211,000	US$	34,031

TESTINA oil on canvas, 36 x 27cm. sdlr 'Mario Tozzi 967' (1967)
PROV.: Galleria Nuovo Saggitario, Milano.
LIT.: Marilena Pasquali, *Catalogo Ragionato Generale dei Dipinti di Mario Tozzi*, Milano, 1988, vol
II, p. 163, no. 67/53 (illustrated).

Sotheby's Milan, 28 May 1996 (165**) ITL 27,600,000	US$	17,726

TREVISANI Francesco Cavaliere (Capo d'Istria 1656-1746 Rome) Italian
THE FLAGELLATION AND THE CROWNING WITH THORNS oil on canvas (a pair), 29½ x
38½in. (74.9 x 97.8cm.)
PROV.: Palazzo Colonna, Rome.
LIT.: *Cataloga dei quadri, e pitture esistenti nel Palazzo dell'Eccellentissima Casa Colonna in
Roma*, 1783, cat. no. 1151 (the pair as in 'Prima maniera di Francesco Trevisani'; Frank R.
DiFederico, *Francesco Trevisani*, 1977, pp. 79-80 (both as location unknown); E. Safarik, *Catalogo
Sommario della Galleria Colonna in Roma*, 1981, p. 138, under cat. no. 194 (incorrectly noting the
present *Flagellation* (known only through the early inventory) as a pendant to a much larger picture
of the *Mocking of Christ* still in the PalazzoColonna).

Sotheby's New York, 11 January 1996 (177**) US$ 46,000	US$	46,000

MASSACRE OF THE INNOCENTS oil on canvas, 21 x 14¾in. (53.3 x 37.5cm.) s on the reverse of
the stretcher 'trevisani-pi-in'

Sotheby's New York, 11 January 1996 (260**) US$ 44,850	US$	44,850

TROGER Paul (Zell 1698-1762 Vienna) Austrian
PIETA oil on copper, 40 x 25cm.

Étude Tajan Paris, 28 June 1996 (81*) FRF 40,000	US$	7,724

TROMBADORI Francesco (Siracusa 1886-1961 Rome) Italian
PIAZZA CAVALIERI DI MALTA oil on canvas, 52 x 62cm. slr 'F. Trombadori' (ca. 1958)

Christie's Milan, 20 November 1995 (191**) ITL 16,499,000	US$	10,357

TROMP Jan Zoetelief (Batavia (Dutch Indies) 1872-1947 Breteuil-sur-Iton (France)) Dutch
A FISHERMAN AND CHILDREN RETURNING HOME oil on canvas, 25.5 x 35.5cm. s 'J.
Zoetelief Tromp'

Christie's Amsterdam, 25 April 1996 (188**) NLG 21,850	US$	12,984

BEACH PLEASURE oil on canvas, 37.5 x 57cm. s 'J. Zoetelief Tromp'
    Christie's Amsterdam, 25 April 1996 (203**) NLG 57,500   US$ 34,167

TROPININ Vasilii Andreevich (Karpovka (Novgorod) 1776-1857 Moscow) Russian
DIE SPITZENKÖPPLERIN oil on canvas, 82 x 67cm. sdll 'W. Tropinin'
PROV.: Russian nobility.
    Lempertz Cologne, 18 May 1996 (1648**) DEM 32,000   US$ 20,862

TROTTER John (fl. 1756-1792-) British
PORTRAIT OF CAPTAIN JOHN ALSTON oil on canvas, 49 x 40in. (125.5 x 101.5cm.)
PROV.: By descent from the sitter.
    Sotheby's London, 12 July 1995 (64**) GBP 28,750   US$ 45,861

TROUILLEBERT Paul Désiré (Paris 1829-1900 Paris) French
FIGURE IN A PUNTING BOAT ON A LAKE oil on canvas, 20 x 24¾in, (50.7 x 61.8cm.) sll
    Phillips London, 11 June 1996 (65**) GBP 12,000   US$ 18,504

UNE RUELLE A BEAUNE oil on canvas, 16 x 11 1/8in. (40.6 x 28.3cm.) slr 'Trouillebert'
    Christie's New York, 22 May 1996 (146**) US$ 19,550   US$ 19,550

WASHERWOMAN ON THE BANKS OF A RIVER oil on canvas, 17 1/8 x 11½in. (43.5 x 29.3cm.)
indistincly slr 'T..ll..t'
    Christie's East, 13 February 1996 (87**) US$ 9,200   US$ 9,200

FIGURES ON A VILLAGE ROAD oil on canvas, 18 x 24in. (45.7 x 61cm.) sd 'Trouillebert 1878'
LIT.: To be included in Claude Marumo's forthcoming *catalogue raisonné on Trouillebert*.
    Christie's London, 17 November 1995 (83**) GBP 12,075   US$ 18,888

LANDING THE PUNT oil on canvas, 8¾ x 10¾in. (22.3 x 27.4cm.) sll 'Trouillebert'
    Christie's New York, 2 November 1995 (120**) US$ 18,400   US$ 18,400

TROYEN Rombout van (Amsterdam 1605 c.-1650 Amsterdam) Dutch
THE FIRE AT SODOM oil on canvas, 59.5 x 84.5cm. traces of signature lc
    Étude Tajan Paris, 28 June 1996 (37*) FRF 38,000   US$ 7,338

TROYON Constant (Sèvres 1810-1865 Paris) French
THE POND pastel on silk laid down on canvas, 25½ x 21¼in. (64.8 x 54cm.) sll 'TROYON'
LIT.: This painting was engraved by Marvy and reproduced in 'La Revue de l`artiste' from 1845
under the title 'Une Source'.
    Christie's New York, 22 May 1996 (133**) US$ 11,500   US$ 11,500

TRÜBNER Wilhelm (Heidelberg 1851-1917 Karlsruhe) German
AUSSICHTSPLATZ AM STARNBERGERSEE oil on canvas, 24¼ x 30in. (61.5 x 76.2cm.) s 'W.
Trübner' (prob. 1911)
    Christie's London, 11 October 1995 (92**) GBP 13,800   US$ 21,780

TSINGOS Thanos (1914-1965) Greek
FLOWERS IN A GARDEN oil on canvas, 73 x 92cm. (28¾ x 36¼in.) slr 'Tsingos'
PROV.: Private collection, London.
    Phillips London, 24 June 1996 (4***) GBP 5,500   US$ 84,81

TUCKER Allen (1866-1939) American
THE WHITE HOUSE oil on canvas, 25 1/8 x 35 1/8in. (61.3 x 89.3cm.) sll 'Allen Tucker'
PROV.: Private collection, New Jersey.
    Christie's New York, 23 May 1996 (137**) US$ 9,775   US$ 9,775

TUKE Henry Scott, R.A., R.W.S. (York 1858-1929) British
BASKING oil on canvas, 22 x 37¼in. (56 x 95cm.) sdll 'H.S. Tuke 1885'
EXH.: London, N.E.A.C., Marlborough Gallery, *First Exhibition*, 1886, no.28; Liverpool, Walker
Art Gallery, *16th Autumn Exhibition*, Sept.-Dec. 1886, no.150; Melbourne, Royal Art Society,
Summer Exhibition, 1890 (not traced); London, Arthur Ackermann & Sons, *The Pleasures of
Observation*, June 1990, no. l5 as A Hot Summer's Day.
LIT.: M. Tuke Sainsbury, *Henry Scott Tuke A Memoir*, London, 1933, pp.76-77; B.D. Price, *The
Registers of Henry Scott Tuke 1858-1929)* Falmouth, 1983, ref. R57.
Christie's London, 21 November 1995 (93**) GBP 43,300 — US$ 67,730

TUNNARD John, R.A. (1900-1971) British
ABSTRACTION 1936 oil on gesso-prepared board, 17½ x 24in. (44.5 x 61cm.) sd 'John Tunnard
1936'
PROV.: Julian Trevelyan, R.A., by whom acquired direct from the Artist.
EXH.: London, Arts Council of Great Britain, John Tunnard 1900-1971, March-April 1977, no. 10.
Christie's London, 22 May 1996 (2**) GBP 7,475 — US$ 11,319

TURCATO Giulio (Mantua 1912-1995 Roma) Italian
COMPOSIZIONE oil on canvas, 66 x 74cm. s 'Turcato' (1955)
Finearte Milan, 12 December 1995 (238*) ITL 18,400,000 — US$ 11,543

GRANDE RETICOLO oil on canvas, 120 x 220cm. slr 'Turcato' (ca 1968)
Finearte Rome, 12 June 1996 (203**) ITL 37,950,000 — US$ 24,885

TURNER George (1843-1910) British
THE TRENT NEAR ANCHOR CHURCH oil on canvas, 20 x 30in. (51 x 76cm.) sdll 'G.Turner
1875', s and inscr. with title on the reverse
Phillips London, 18 June 1996 (74**) GBP 8,500 — US$ 13,107

TURNER Joseph Mallord William, R.A. (London 1775-1851 London) British
A BRIDGE OVER A RIVER BY MOONLIGHT pencil and watercolour with scratching out, 8 1/8 x
12½in. (20.6 x 31.8cm.) (1794)
PROV.: J.E. Taylor; Christie's London, 8 July 1912, lot 106 (210gns. to Gooden and Fox); anon.
sale, Christie's London 20 July 1923, lot 76 (57gns. to Goldblatt).
Christie's London, 2 April 1996 (29**) GBP 35,600 — US$ 53,980

LONDON: AUTUMNAL MORNING watercolour with scratching out, 25¾ x 39in. (65.4 x 99.1cm.)
(ca. 1804)
PROV.: Probably painted for the engraver J. Burnet; G.R. Bumet, 1860; C.E. Flavell; Christie's
London, 26 Mar. 1860, lot 151 (unsold); Probably anon. sale, Foster's, 19 Nov. 1860, lot 111 as
'London from Battersea' (sold to White); Miss James; Christie's London, 22 Jun. 1891, lot 161 (ll0
gns. to Agnew's); C.F. Huth; Christie's London, 6 Jul. 1895, lot 60 (350gns. to Agnew's). W.
Permain; Chnstie's London, 18 May 1901, lot 73 (150gns. to Ischenhauser); R. Brocklebank;
Christie's London, 7 Jul. 1922, lot 33, illustrated (650gns. to Brocklebank); Sir Edmund Brocklebank
and thence by descent.
EXH.: London, Royal Academy, 1801, no.329; London, Cook's Gallery, 1824, no.91; London,
Guildhall, *Loan Exhibition*, 1899, no.97; London, 47 Victoria Street, *Franco-British Exhibition*,
1908, no.496.
LIT.: F. Wedmore, *Turner and Ruskin*, 1900, Vol. I, illustrated facing p.8.; C.F. Bell, *The Exhibited
Works of J.M.W. Tumer, R.*A., 1901, pp.41, 167; W. Armstrong, *Turner,* 1902, p.262, as 'London,
from the South'; AJ. Finberg, *The Life of J.M.W. Turner, R.A.*, 1939, 2nd ed. 1961, pp.464, 485; A.
Wilton*, The Life and Work of J.M.W. Turner*, 1979, p.331 no.278, illustrated; A. Wilton, *Turner in
his Time*, 1987, pp.85, 165; D. Hill, *Turner on the Thames*, 1993, p.22, pl.28, illustrated in colour.
Christie's London, 2 April 1996 (30**) GBP 76,300 — US$ 115,694

CHAMBERY, FRANCE watercolour, 10 x 11in. 25.4 x 27.9cm.) inscr. '641953 Courmayeur' (on two old labels attached to the backing) (1836)
PROV.: Frank h. Downes, Glasgow; Frank Downes, Glasgow; Prof. the Rev. William D. Maxwell, Glasgow and by descent.
        Christie's London, 2 April 1996 (63**) GBP 80,700   US$ 122,365

THE CONFLUENCE OF THE SEINE AND THE MARNE bodycolour on blue paper, 5¼ x 7¼in. (13.6 x 18.5cm.) inscr. and numb. in red on the reverse '8/Junction of Seine and Marne/at Charenton (ca 1832)
PROV.: Charles Heath; sold by Order of the Court of Chancery; Christie's, 22 May 1852, lot 57 (40gns., to Lambe); Robert Hanbury; Christie's, 13 May 1884, lot 132 (26gns., to Walford); C.E. Hughes and by descent to the present owner.
LIT.: A. Wilton, *The Life and Work of J.M.W. Turner*, London & Freiburg 1979, p. 416, no. 988, repr.
        Christie's London, 11 July 1995 (33**) GBP 17,250   US$ 27,516

LANDSCAPE WITH A RAINBOW oil on canvas, 36 x 54in. (91.5 x 137cm.) (after 1820)
        Phillips London, 12 December 1995 (46**) GBP 90,000   US$ 138,504

TUSQUETS Y MAIGNON Ramon (Raimondo) (Barcelona 1837-1904 Rome) Spanish
BOATS ON THE LAGOON IN VENICE oil on canvas, 80 x 39½in. (203 x 100cm.) s and inscr. lr 'Roma'
        Sotheby's London, 13 March 1996 (122**) GBP 14,375   US$ 21,953

TWACHTMAN John Henry (Cincinnati (Ohio) 1853-1902 Gloucester (Mass.)) American
WINTER LANDSCAPE, CINCINATTI oil on board, 10 1/8 x 14in. (25.7 x 35.6cm.) slr 'J.H. Twachtman'
LIT.: This painting will be included in the forthcoming *catalogue raisonné Twachtman* being prepared by Ira Spanierman and Lisa N. Peters.
        Christie's New York, 30 November 1995 (50**) US$ 23,000   US$ 23,000

TWOMBLY Cy (Lexington (Virginia) 1928 b.) American
UNTITLED (ROMA) oil-based house paint, coloured crayon, graphite and oil on canvas, 38 x 49 3/4in. (96.5 x 126.4cm.) sur 'Twombly' (1961)
PROV.: Galleria del Naviglio, Milan; Collection Marelli, Bergamo.
EXH.: Milan, Galleria del Naviglio, *Cy Twombly*, 1961; Brescia, Galleria d'Arte La Nuova Citta Arte Contemporanea, *Alla rinfusa*, 1982; Brescia, Galleria d'Arte La Nuova Citta Arte Contemporanea, *American Panorama*, 1991, n.n. (illustrated).
LIT.: R. Daolio, 'Aspetti dell'luformale in Italia', *Flash Art Edizione Raliana no. 115*, Milan 1983, p. 14 (illustrated); F. Gualdoni, 'Arse a Roma 1945-1980,' *Politi Editore*, Milan 1988, p. 96 (illustrated); AA.VV, 'La Pittura in Italia, il Novecento/2 1945-1990,' *Electa*, Milan 1993, vol. 2, p. 891 (illustrated); H. Bastian, *Cy Twombly: Catalogue Raisonné of the Paintings, Volume II, 1961-1965*, Munich 1993, p. 56, no. 10 (illustrated).
        Christie's New York, 14 November 1995 (36**) US$ 574,500   US$ 574,500

CAPTIVA oil, coloured chalks and graph paper collage on paper, 29½ x 41½in. (74.9 x 105.3cm.) sd and titled 'Cy Twombly Captiva 74' on the reverse
PROV.: Galerie Yvon Lambert, Paris.
EXH.: Paris, Galerie Yvon Lambert, *Cy twombly*, April-May 1974.
LIT.: Y. Lambert, *Cy Twombly, Catalogue Raisonné des Oeuvres sur Papier, Vol. VI 1973-1976*, Milan 1979, p. 121, no. 125 (illustrated).
        Christie's New York, 15 November 1995 (353**) US$ 36,800   US$ 36,800

UNTITLED oil and pastel on canvas laid down on board, 137 x 99cm. (1971)
PROV.: Ginevra, Galerie J. Benador.
        Finearte Rome, 2 April 1996 (227**) ITL 110,400,000   US$ 70,543

10 DAYS WAIT AT MUGDA oil, wax crayon and lead pencil on canvas, 39½ x 41in. (100 x
104.1cm.) sdlr and titled '1963' and numbered 43 on the reverse
PROV.: Galleria del Leone, Venice; Acquired from the above by the present owner in the 1960s.
        Christie's London, 27 June 1996 (58**) GBP 128,000   US$ 197,379

ROMA pen and black ink, graphite, coloured crayons and gouache on paper, 19 5/8 x 27 3/8in. (49.8
x 69.5cm.) sd and titled lr 'Cy Twombly 'roma' 1962'
PROV.: Scharf Fine Art, Inc., New York.
        Christie's New York, 8 May 1996 (345**) US$ 68,500   US$ 68,500

TYTGAT Edgar (Brussels 1879-1957 Brussels) Belgian
BOUQUET DE FLEURS oil on canvas, 63 x 47cm. sdlr Edgard Tytgat Nivelles 1927'; sd 'Nivelles
1927', numbered '112' and titled on the reverse
        Sotheby's Amsterdam, 7 December 1995 (183**) NLG 15,340   US$ 9,506

UBALDINI Domenico di Bartolomeo, {called} Domenico Puligo (1492 Florence-1527) Italian
MADONNA WITH THE CHILD oil on panel, 75 x 57cm.
        Christie's Rome, 21 November 1995 (220**) ITL 58,000,000   US$ 36,409

UBERTINI Francesco {called} Bacchiaca (attr.) (1494 Florence-1557 Florence) Italian
THE ROAD TO CAVALRY, CHRIST BEARING THE CROSS oil on panel, 18 3/4 x 22½in. (47.5
x 57.5cm.)
PROV.: Cardinal Rossi; John Watkins Brett, London, 1864; Drury-Lowe collection by 1901; Offered
in Sotheby's London, 24 mArch 1965, lot 60, bought in.
EXH.: Leeds, *National Exhibition of Works of Art*, 1868, no. 70, as by *Raphael*; London, 1884, no.
228, as Italian School, 15th century; London, Royal Academy, *Winter Exhibition*, 1893, no. 162, as
Italian School, 15th century; Nottingham, 1968, no. 11, cover plate, as by *Bacchiacca*.
LIT.: Richter, 1901, no. 44, reproduced, as by *Bacchiacc*a; A. Cameron Taylor, 'On Christ Carrying
the Cross', in *The Connoisseur*, 1903, p. 89; B. Berenson, *Florentine Painters of the Renaissance*,
1909, p. 109; R. Salvini, *'Francesco Ubertini'*, in *Thieme Becker*, XXXIII, 1939, p. 523, as not by
Bacchiacca; B. Berenson, *Italian Pictures of Renaissance: Florentine School*, 1963, vol. I, p. 20, as
by Bacchiacca; L. Nikolenko, *Francesco Ubertini called 'Il Bacchiacca'*, 1966, p. 13, p. 36, fig. 6, as
by Bacchiacca.
        Sotheby's London, 6 December 1995 (18**) GBP 17,250   US$ 26547

UDEN Lucas van (1595 Antwerp-1673 Antwerp) Flemish
STATELY AFFORESTED RIVERLANDSCAPE WITH TRAVELLERS oil on panel, 24 x61cm.
(framed)
        Dorotheum Vienna, 17 October 1995 (157**) ATS 160,000   US$ 16,049

UECKER Günther (1930 b. Wendorf (Mecklenburg)) German
STURZ laquer and nails on canvas, 78 3/4 x 63in. (200 x 160cm.) sd '86' twice on the reverse
PROV.: Galleria Martano, Turin; Galerie Hans Mayer, Dusseldorf.
EXH.: Lodz, Museum Sztuki W Lodzi, *Günther Uecker*, June 1989.
LIT.: Richard W. Gassen und Bernhard Holeczek, *Uecker*, Heidelberg 1987, p. 161 (illustrated in
colour).
        Christie's London, 23 May 1996 (141**) GBP 29,900   US$ 45,276

HOMMAGE A LOTHAR WOLLEH oil, painted nails and canvas over wood, 42 7/8 x 85 7/8in.
(109 x 218cm.) sd titled 'Uecker 90'
PROV.: Lothar Wolleh, Cologne.
        Sotheby's London, 27 June 1996 (212**) GBP 33,350   US$ 51,426

GEGENSTRÖMUNG oil and nails on canvas on board, 85 x 85cm. sd and titled on the reverse
'Uecker 65 Gegenströming'
        Lempertz Cologne, 31 May 1996 (489*) DEM 53,000   US$ 34,552

UGOLINO DI NERIO (1317 - 1327 active Siena) Italian
THE MADONNA AND CHILD ENTHRONED WITH SAINT PETER, AN UNKNOWN MALE
SAINT, AND FOUR ATTENDANT ANGELS; THE CRUCIFIXION ABOVE tempera on gold
ground panel, 23 x 9 5/8in. (58. x 24.6cm.)
PROV.: Possibly Church of Santa Eugenia, Siena; with Grassi, 1924 (according to a note on a
photograph at I Tatti); Mortimer L. Schiff; Christie's, London, June 24, 1938, lot 67 as *School of
Duccio* (300gns to Smith). Florence J. Gould; (†) Sotheby's, New York, April 25, 1985, lot 88 as
Follower of Duccio.
LIT.: R. Offner, *Italian Pictures of the New York Historical Society and Elsewhere*, Part II, Art in
America, VII 1919, p. 195 as by an *Ugolino-Lorenzetti follower*; R. van Marle, *The Development of
the Italian Schools of Painting*, II, 1924, p. 156, note 2 as *School of Segna di Bonaventura*; B.
Berenson, *Missing Pictures of the Sienese Trecento*, International Studio, XCVII, Oct. 1930, p. 31,
fig. 5 as *School of Duccio,* showing affinities to Ugolino; B. Berenson, *Quadri senza Casa - il
Trecento Senese I*, Dedalo, XI, Oct. 1930, pp. 263 and 267 illustrated, as *School of Duccio*; G. Coor,

Contributions to the Study of Ugolino di Nerio's Art, Art Bulletin, XXXVII, 1955, p. 159, as *Follower of the Badia a Isola Master and Ugolino*; B. Berenson, *Homeless Pictures of the Renaissance*, 1969, p. 22, pl. 12; M. Meiss, *Painting in Florence and Siena after the Black Death*, 1951, p. 149, note 69; J.H. Stubblebine, *Duccio di Buoninsegna and his School*, 1979, I, p. 189; II, fig. 472 as *Follower of Ugolino*; J. Pope-Hennessy, *Learning to Look*, 1991, p. 313.

Christie's New York, 10 January 1996 (99**) US$ 77,300	US$	77,300

UNTERBERGER Franz Richard (1838 Innsbruck-1902 Neuilly-sur-Seine) Belgian
THE MONASTERY GARDENS, AMALFI oil on canvas, 45 ¼ x 39 3/8in. (115 x 100cm.) s

phillips London, 14 November 1995 (22**) GBP 10,000	US$	15,642

URSELINCX Johannes (1598 c. Frankenthal-1664 Amsterdam) German
REBECCA AND ISAAK oil on panel, 93 x 145cm.

Dorotheum Vienna, 11 June 1996 (281**) ATS 180,000	US$	16,708

THE MEETING OF JACOB AND RACHEL oil on apenl, 39.5 x 63.5cm. sll 'J. vrselincx'

Sotheby's Amsterdam, 6 May 1996 (30**) NLG 15,930	US$	9,289

URY Lesser (1861 Birnbaum-1931 Berlin) German
RENDEZ-VOUS IN CAPRI oil on canvas, 15 x 11½in. (38.2 x 29.2cm.) s and inscr. lr 'L. Ury Capri'

Christie's Tel Aviv, 12 October 1995 (2**) US$ 21,850	US$	21,850

MOSES oil on canvas, 14 5/8 x 11.8in. (37.4 x 29.3cm.) sll 'L. Ury'
PROV.: Mrs. Alice King, Great Britain (brought to England in the 1930s) by whom given to the present owner in the early 1970s.

Christie's Tel Aviv, 12 October 1995 (10**) US$ 16,100	US$	16,100

LANDSCHAFT MIT BAUERNHOF pastel and charcoal on cardboard, 13 7/8 x 19 3/8in. (35.2 x 49.3cm.) sdlc 'L.Ury 92'
PROV.: Bought directly from the Artist by the grandfather of the present owner.

Christie's Tel Aviv, 14 April 1996 (10**) US$ 12,650	US$	12,650

CARRIAGES BY A RIVER, BERLIN oil on canvas, 10½ x 8 1/16in. (26.5 x 20.5cm.) s(indistinctly)dll '1888'
PROV.: Acquired from the artist by the father of the present owner.

Phillips London, 26 June 1995 (36**) GBP 10,000	US$	15,957

LANDSCHAFT MIT BÄUME oil on canvas, 34 5/8 x 26¼in. (88 x 66.5cm.) sdll 'L. Ury 93' (1893)

Christie's London, 29 November 1995 (210**) GBP 23,000	US$	35,977

DIE ORTSCHAFT oil on canvas, 12 3/8 x 16 1/8in. (31.4 x 41cm.) lr 'L Ulry' (1885-1890)

Christie's New York, 8 November 1995 (164**) US$ 23,000	US$	23,000

UTRECHT Adriaen van (1599 Antwerp-1653 Antwerp) Flemish
A PEACOCK AND A PEAHEN ON A PERCH, TURKEYS, A PHEASANT AND POULTRY BY A WELL oil on canvas, 63 7/8 x 79 3/4 in. (162.3 x 202.6) sdcr 'Adriaen van Utrecht / fecit ano 1652'

Christie's London, 7 July 1995 (4**) GBP 111,500	US$	177,859

UTRILLO Maurice (1883 Paris-1955 Dax) French
RUE DE PONTOISE oil on canvas, 15 x 18¼in. (38 x 46.3cm.) slr 'Maurice, Utrillo, V,' s and inscr. on the stretcher 'Maurice, Utrillo, V, Poissy (Seine-et-Oise)' (ca. 1940)
PROV.: H. Dietz, Amsterdam; William Brandt, Amsterdam; Walter Rosenblum, New York; Stephen Silagy Gallery, Beverly Hills (acquired by Richard Smart, 1968).
LIT.: P. Pétridès, *L'oeuvre complet de Maurice Utrillo*, Paris 1969, vol. III, no. 1617 (illus. p. 127).

Christie's New York, 1 May 1996 (161**) US$ 112,500	US$	112,500

PLACE DE VILLAGE oil on board laid down on cradled panel, 14 7/8 x 21 7/8in. (37.8 x 55.6cm.)
sll 'Maurice, Utrillo, V,' (ca. 1909)
PROV.: The Lefevre Gallery (Alex. Reid & Lefevre Ltd.), London; Estate of Norman K. Winston;
sale, Christie's, New York, 6 Nov. 1979, lot 37 (acquired by the previous owner; gift to the High
Museum of Art, 1981).
LIT.: P. Pétridès. *L'oeuvre complet de Maurice Utrillo*, Paris 1959, vol. I, no. 132 (illustrated p. 181).

Christie's New York, 1 May 1996 (177**) US$ 200,500	US$	200,500

LA CASERNE oil on board laid down on cradled panel, 10 5/8 x 13 3/4in. (27 x 35cm.) slr 'Maurice
Utrillo, V' (ca. 1940)
PROV.: Galerie de l'Elysée (Alex Maguy), Paris.

Christie's New York, 1 May 1996 (219**) US$ 123,500	US$	123,500

LE MAQUIS DE MONTMARTRE oil on paper laid down on canvas, 8 3/4 x 11½in. (22 x 29cm.)
slr 'Maurice Utrillo' inscr. 'Montmartre à sa bonne Lucie' d 'Juillet 1941'
LIT.: Paul Pétridès, *L'oeuvre complet de Maurice Utrillo*, III, Paul Pétridès éditeur, Paris 1969, pp.
270-271, no. 2114.

Étude Tajan Paris, 10 June 1996 (42**) FRF 370,000	US$	71,447

L'USINE DE VILLETANEUSE gouache on paper mounted at the edges on board, 10¼ x 13/4in. (26
x 35cm.) sdlr 'Maurice Utrillo, V, Juin 1923'
PROV.: Goddman Walker Fine Arts, Boston; R. Thrall, New Haven, Connecticut; Gallery Rabow,
San Fransisco, from whom purchased by Theodore M. Lilienthal ca. 1956.
EXH.: Chicago, The Art Institute, *14th International Exhibition of Watercolours, Pastels, Drawings
and Monotypes*, March-June 1935, no. 61.
LIT.: P. Pétrides, *L'oeuvre complet de Maurice Utrillo*, Paris, 1966, vol. IV, no. AG112 (illustrated p.
153).

Christie's Tel Aviv, 12 October 1995 (18**) US$ 20,700	US$	20,700

LA MOULIN DE LA GALETTE coloured wax crayons and pencil on paper laid down on board, 12
7/8 x 16 7/8in. (32.5 x 43cm.) slr 'Maurice, Utrillo, V' (ca. 1920)

Christie's Tel Aviv, 14 April 1996 (52**) US$ 16,100	US$	16,100

RUE DE BANLIEUE oil on board laid down on cradled panel, 23¼ x 31in. (59.1 x 78.7cm.) slr
'Maurice Utrillo' (ca. 1917)
PROV.: John P. Gerstley, New York.
LIT.: Paul Pétridès, *L'Oeuvre Complet de Maurice Utrillo*, vol. II, Paris 1969, no. 691 (illustrated p.
197).

Sotheby's New York, 2 May 1996 (352**) US$ 222,500	US$	222,500

RUE A SANNOIS oil on canvas, 19½ x 18in. (49.5 x 45.7cm.) slr 'Maurice Utrillo' (ca. 1918)
PROV.: Mme. Roques, Paris.
LIT.: Paul Pétridès. *l'Oeuvre Complet de Maurice Utrillo*, vol II, Paris, 1969, no. 1194, illustrated p.
493.

Sotheby's New York, 2 May 1996 (358**) US$ 96,000	US$	96,000

BOURG LA REINE oil on canvas, 15 x 18in. (38.1 x 45.7cm.) sd titled '1943'
PROV.: Dalzell-Hatfield Galleries, Los Angeles; Herman Goldsmith, New York.
LIT.: Paul Pétridès, *L'Oeuvre Complet de Maurice Utrillo,* vol. III, Paris, 1969, no. 2218, p. 298,
illustrated p. 299.

Sotheby's New York, 2 May 1996 (375**) US$ 98,750	US$	98,750

MONTMARTRE - MOULIN DE LA GALETTE oil on canvas, 9½ x 13in. (24.2 x 33cm.) s inscr.
(Maurice Utrillo V / Montmartre' (ca 1925)
PROV.: Galerie P. Pétridès, Paris; Galerie Beyeler, Basel.

Christie's London, 26 June 1996 (174**) GBP 45,500	US$	70,162

MAISONS A PUTEAUX oil on canvas, 23 3/4 x 31 3/4in. (60 x 80.5cm.) sll 'Maurice Utrillo' (ca 1913)
PROV.: Alex Reid & Lefevre, London; Cyril Franklin, London, and thence by descent.
LIT.: P. Pétridès, *L'Oeuvre Complet de Maurice Utrillo*, Vol. I, Paris 1959, no. 374 (illustrated p. 438).

Christie's London, 26 June 1996 (186**) GBP 172,000	US$	265,227

ÉGLISE DE SCEAUX-LES-CHARTREUX, SEINE-ET-OISE oil on canvas, 23 5/8 x 32in. (60 x 81cm.) sd 'MauricUtrillo, V, 1926' sd and titled again on the reverse (1926)
PROV.: Crane Kalman Gallery, London; G.R. Kennerley, London by whom purchased from the above.
EXH.: Paris, Galerie Serret-Fabiani, *Quelques Oeuvres Choisies du XXème Siècle*, Nov. 19.1, no. 32.

Christie's London, 26 June 1996 (199**) GBP 54,300	US$	83,732

LA FERME DEBRAY A MONTMARTRE gouache, 46 x 31cm. sdlr 'Maurice Utrillo 1933'

Étude Tajan Paris, 28 March 1996 (50**) FRF 120,000	US$	23,720

A PLACE DU TERTRE, SOUS LA NEIGE oil on canvas, 14 7/8 x 21½in. (38 x 55cm.) slr 'Maurice Utrillo V' (ca 1938)
EXH.: Monaco, Musée Océanographique, *Maurice Utrillo*, 11 April-21 May 1995.

Christie's London, 29 November 1995 (115**) GBP 75,000	US$	117,316

EGLISE DE CAMPAGNE oil on canvas, 21½ x 29in. (54.5 x 73.5cm.) slr 'Maurice Utrillo V.' (ca 1907)
PROV.: Leopold Zborowski, Paris, from whom purchased by the grandfather of the present owner.
EXH.: Paris, Galerie Charpentier, *Cent Tableaux par Utrillo*, 1959; Paris, Galerie Charpentier, *Chefs d'Oeuvres de Collections français*.
LIT.: P. Pétridès, *L'Oeuvre Complet de Maurice Utrillo*, vol.I, Paris, 1959, no. 65 (illustrated p. 115).

Christie's London, 29 November 1995 (126**) GBP 55,000	US$	86,032

L'EGLISE SAINT-GERMAIN-DES-PRES A PARIS oil on canvas, 15 x 21 3/4in. (38 x 55.3cm.) ll 'Maurice, Utrillo, V, 1925',and again on the reverse 'Maurice, Utrillo, V, 1925 Église Saint Germain-des-Prés, à Paris' (1925)
PROV.: Suzanne Valadon, Paris; Dr. O.Fischer, Berlin; Dr. Neuberger, Berlin and São Paulo; Galerie Paul Cassirer, Berlin; Leonard Hutton Galleries, New York; Anon. sale, Parke-Bernet Galeries, Inc., New York, Dec. 8, 1965, lot 50 (acquired by the present owner).
LIT.: P.Pétridès, *L'oeuvre complet de Maurice Utrillo*, Paris, 1973, vol. V (Supplément), no. 2722 (illustrated, p. 241).

Christie's New York, 8 November 1995 (200**) US$ 134,500	US$	134,500

LE LAPIN AGILE oil on board laid down on cradled panel, 16 1/4 x 23 1/4in. (41 x 59cm.) lr 'Maurice, Utrillo, V',and ll 'Montmartre'

Christie's New York, 8 November 1995 (210**) US$ 123,500	US$	123,500

UYL Jan Jansz the Elder den (1595 Amsterdam-1638 Amsterdam) Dutch
STILL-LIFE WITH A 'HANS IN THE CELLAR', A PEWTER PLATE AND BREAD, ALL RESTING ON A DRAPED TABLE oil on panel, 17 x 17 3/8in. (43.2 x 34cm.)

Sotheby's New York, 11 January 1996 (101**) US$ 140,000	US$	140,000

STILL-LIFE WITH A PEWTER FLAGON, A FILLED GLASS, A PEWTER PLATE WITH TWO ROLLS, A KNIFE, HALF OF A WALNUT AND A NAPKIN ON A CLOTH-COVERED TABLE; A BREAKFAST STILL LIFE oil on panel, 24½ x 20½in. (62.2 x 52.1cm.) s with the Artist's mark of an owl
PROV.: Sale: Berlin, P. Graupe, March 23, 1936, lot 13 (as by Pieter Claesz.); P. de Boer, Amsterdam; Stocker Collection since 1944; Verner Amell, London where acquired by the present collector in 1989.

EXH.: Amsterdam, P. de Boer Gallery, *Summer Exhibition*, 1936, no. 20 (as Den Uyl); Dordrecht, Dordrecht Museum, *Nederlands Stilleven uit vier eeuwen*, 1954, cat. no. 94; New York, Newhouse Galleries, Inc., *Old Master Paintings,* October 3-November 3, 1989, cat. no. 11, (illustrated).
LIT.: P. de Boer, *'Jan Jansz. den Uyl,'* Oud Holland, 1940, pp. 8, 14, no. 7 (illustrated) p. 11, fig. 7; N. R. A. Vroom, *De Schilders van het Monochrome Banketje*, 1945, no. 275, (illustrated); N. R. A. Vroom*, A Modest Message as Intimated by the 'Painters of the Monochrome Banketje'*, 1980, Vol. I, p. 217; Vol. 2, fig. 661.
      Sotheby's New York, 11 January 1996 (122**) US$ 442,500   US$ 442,500

Still-life with a pewter Flagon a filled Glass, a pewter Plate with
two Rolls, a Knife, half of a Walnut and a Napkin on a Cloth
covered Table, a Breakfast Still-life

UYTTENBROECK Moses van (1600 c. The Hague-1647 before The Hague (?)) Dutch
TWO NYMPHS BATHING oil on panel, 19½ x 15 3/4in. (49.8 x 39.8cm.) sdll with ini. 'M.v.W. / 1644'
PROV.: Anon. sale, 10 March 194?, lot 125, according to the remains of a label pasted to the reverse.
      Sotheby's London, 5 July 1995 (159**) GBP 13,800   US$ 22,013

VAARBERG Joannes Christoffel (Weesp 1825-1871 Amsterdam) Dutch
SOLDIERS BRAWLING IN A TAVERN oil on panel, 53.5 x 67 cm s 'JC Vaarberg f'
Christie's Amsterdam, 25 April 1996 (21*) NLG 12,650 — US$ 7,517

BRAVE STORIES oil on panel, 31 x 24 cm sd 'JC Vaarberg 60'
Christie's Amsterdam, 7 February 1996 (28*) NLG 8,625 — US$ 5,253

VACCARO Andrea (Naples 1598 c.-1670 Naples) Italian
THE JUDGEMENT OF SALOMON oil on canvas,,102 x 127cm.
Finearte Rome, 21 May 1996 (95**) ITL 28,750,000 — US$ 18,465

VADDER Lodewyk de (Brussels 1605-1665 Brussels) Flemish
BRABANTIAN FORREST-LANDSCAPE WITH FARMHOUSES AT A LAKE AND FARMERS
oil on canvas, 46 x 60cm. (framed)
PROV.: Ausländischer Privatbesitz.
Dorotheum Vienna, 17 October 1995 (150**) ATS 280,000 — US$ 28,086

VAES Walter (Antwerp 1882-1958) Belgian
GLADIOLI oil on canvas, 45 x 55cm. sdlr 'Walter Vaes 42'
Christie's Amsterdam, 6 December 1995 (193*) NLG 10,350 — US$ 6,413

THE SNOWY GARDEN AT 'CALVARIE-BERG' OF THE ST PAUL'S CATHEDRAL,
ANTWERP oil on canvas, 64 x 82cm. slr 'Walter Vaes'
EXH.: The Hague, Haags Gemeentemuseum, 1960, cat. no. 63; The Hague, Haags
Gemeentemuseum, 1969, cat. no. 15; St. Niklaas, Stedelijk Museum, 1988, cat. no. 69.
A. Mak B.V. Dordrecht, 12 December 1995 (299*) NLG 21,000 — US$ 13,013

A BREAKFAST STILL LIFE oil on canvas, 52 x 91.5cm. s 'Walter Vaes'
Christie's Amsterdam, 26 October 1995 (46) NLG 16,100 — US$ 10,151

VAIL Eugene Laurent (1857-1934) French/American
ON THE THAMES oil on canvas, 69¼ x 82½in. (175.9 x 209.5cm.) sdll 'Eug.Vail/Londres./1886'
PROV.: With Richard York Gallery, New York.
EXH.: Philadelphia, The Pennsylvania Academy of The Fine Arts, *The Paris Universal Exhibition of
1889: American Artists at the World's Fair*, September 15, 1989-July 30, 1990; Washington, The
National Portrait Gallery, *American Art at the 1893 World's Fair*, April 16-August 15, 1993.
Christie's New York, 14 February 1996 (141**) US$ 43,700 — US$ 43,700

VALADON Suzanne (Bessines-sur-Gartempe (Haute-Vienne) 1867-1938 Paris) French
MARIE COCA AVEC L'ABRI oil on canvas, 25¾ x 36 1/2in. (65.3 x 92.5cm.) ll 'Suzanne Valadon
1927' (1927)
LIT.: P.Pétridès, *L'oeuvre complet de Suzanne Valadon*, Paris, 1971, no. P,171 (illustrated).
Christie's New York, 8 November 1995 (192**) US$ 34,500 — US$ 34,500

VALCKENBORCH Frederick van (Antwerp 1566-1623 Nurenberg) Flemish
PHANTASY LANDSCAPE WITH HUNTERS AND CANOEISTS oil on canvas, 85 x 115cm.
LIT.: Catalogue from the Picture Gallery of the Arthistoric Museum, Vienna 1991, p. 126,
illustration no. 370.
Dorotheum Vienna, 6 March 1996 (141**) ATS 160,000 — US$ 15,391

NOCTURNAL CARNIVAL SCENE oil on canvas, 29 1/8 x 32 7/8in. (74 x 83.5cm.)
Sotheby's New York, 11 January 1996 (63**) US$ 13,800 — US$ 13,800

TROJAN WAR: AENEAS CARRIES HIS FATHER ANCHISES OUT OF BURNING TROY oil on
panel, 44.5 x 64cm.
Dorotheum Vienna, 17 October 1995 (136**) ATS 135,000 — US$ 13,541

VALCKENBORCH Lucas van (Louvain 1535-1597 Frankfurt) Flemish
A ROCKY LANDSCAPE, WITH AN IRON FOUNDRY TO THE LEFT, AND A BROAD RIVER
TO THE RIGHT oil on oak panel, 9½ x 17½in. (23.5 x 44cm.) (between 1580-1590)
PROV.: Gösta Stenman collection, Helsinki, 1925; Dr. Einar Perman, Stockholm, 1955; Professor
H.J. Hellema, Laren; With Pieter de Boer, Amsterdam, from whom acquired by the late owner.
EXH.: Helsingborg, September 1929; Amsterdam, Pieter de Boer, 1934, *De Helsche en de Flaweelen
Brueghel*, cat. no. 197, reproduced in the catalogue p. 29 (wrongly as by Maerten van
Valckenborch); Amsterdam, 1963, cat no. 43, reproduced in colour in the catalogue; Laren, Singer
Memorial Foundation, June 1963, *Modernen van Toen 1570-1630*, cat. no. 149, reproduced in the
catalogue fig. 53, and in colour; Amsterdam, 1972, cat no. 48.
LIT.: B.H. Hinze, 'Några Nederländska Landskapmålningar i Finländsk.Privatago', in *Tidshrift för
Kunstvetenskap* 10, 1925-6, p. 102f reproduced; R.E. Evrard, *Les artistes et les usines à fer*, 1955,
reproduced fig. 27; J.S. Stiennon, *Les Sites Mosans de Lucas I et Martin I van Valckenborch*, 1954,
no. 28; A. Wied, *Lucas und Marten van Valckenborch*, 1990, pp. 23, 29-30, 49, 162, no. 56,
reproduced.
        Sotheby's London, 6 December 1995 (44**) GBP 36,700   US$ 56,479

VALENCIENNES Piere Henri de (Toulouse 1750-1819 Paris) French
A CLASSIVAL LANDSCAPE WITH A FIGURE KNEELING BY THE EDGE OF A POND oil on
canvas, 27¾ x 38¼in. (70.5 x 97.2cm.) sdll 'P. valenciennes/1806'
PROV.: Roth Miles, ca. 1975, there purchased by the present collector.
        Sotheby's New York, 11 January 1996 (153**) US$ 112,500   US$ 112,500

**VALENTIN DE BOULOGNE Jean (Monsu 'Moise'), {called} Valentin (Coulommiers 1591-
1632 Rome) French**
THE CROWNING WITH THORNS oil on canvas, 57½ x 42¼in. (146.1 x 107.3) (before 1613)
PROV.: Aw. Rainoldi, Milan, by 1943; Private collection, Germany.
LIT.: R. Longhi, 'Ultima studi sul Caravaggio e la sue cerchia - Ultimissime sul Caravaggio '
Proporzioni I, 1943, p. 58 no. 80; R. Longhi, 'A propos de Valentin,' *La Revue des Arts*, March-April
1958, II, p. 61; R. Longhi, 'Terbrugghen e Valentin,' *Paragone*, 131, 1960, pp. 57-60, illus. pl. 44; A.
Brejon de Lavergnée and J. P. Cuzin, *I Caravaggisti Francesi*, 1973, p. 244; J. P. Cuzin 'Problèmes
du Caravagisme, Pour Valentin', *Revue de l'art*, 28, 1975, p. 57; B. Nicolson; *The International
Caravaggesque Movement*, 1979, p. 104; M. Mojana, *Valentin de Boulogne*, 1989, p. 52, pl.1 (as the
earliest known picture by the artist, datable to 1615/18); B. Nicolson and L. Vertova, *Caravaggism in
Europe*, 1989, I, p. 202.
        Sotheby's New York, 11 January 1996 (118**) US$ 882,500   US$ 882,500

SAINT HIERONYMUS oil on canvas,,132 x 152cm. (between 1623-1626)
PROV.: Gift of a private collectionneur at the Abby of Notre-Dame de Melleraye around 1850;
Galerie Heim, London 1968; Anonymous sale, Paris, Hotel Drouot, 1 April 1987 (Maîtres Millon-
Jutheau), n° 21, reproduced in colour (1,700,000 FF); Anonymous Sale, Paris, Hotel Drouot, 26 June
1989 (Maîtres Libert et Castor), n° 28, reproduced in colour.
EXH.: *Quarante peintures et sculptures des collections de la galerie*, London, Galerie Heim, 1966,
n° 10.
LIT.: *Valentin et les Caravagesques français*, Paris, Grand-Palais, 1974, pp.,138 et 252, illustrated p.
14, fig. 14; Ch. Wright, *Catalogue of the Master Paintings in the Collection of Mr and Mrs
J.W.Feather*, Surrey, 1974, pp.24 and 25; J.P.Cuzin, 'Pour Valentin', *Revue de l'Art*, no 28, 1975, p.
59; B. Nicolson, *The International Caravagesque Movement*, Oxford, 1970, p. 105; Ch. Wright, *The
french painters of the Seventeenth Century*, Boston, 1985, p. 268; M. Mojana, *Valentin de Boulogne*,
Milan, 1989, n° 30, illustrated p. 113.
        Étude Tajan Paris, 12 December 1995 (94**) FRF 1,300,000   US$ 261,854

VALKENBORCH Lucas, van (1535-1597)
A VIEW OF A CASTLE BY A LAKE WITH SHEPHERDS AND SHEEP IN A MEADOW AND
TRAVELLERS ON A PATH NEARBY - A FRAGMENT oil on panel unframed, 15 x 23.5cm
        Christie's Amsterdam, 13 November 1995 (48*) NLG 25,300   US$ 15,945

VALKENBURCH Dirk van (Amsterdam 1675-1727 (1721) Amsterdam) Dutch
A HOUND WITH GAME BIRDS AND A MUSKET IN THE GROUNDS OF A VILLA oil on
canvas, 39¾ x 49¾in. (,101 x 126.5cm.) s 'D. Valckenburg fecit'
PROV.: Ferdinand Bonaventura, Graf von Harrach (1637-1706), Vienna; Thence by descent.
EXH.: G. Waagen, *Die Vornehmsten Kunstdenkmäler in Wien*, 1866, vol. I, p. 323; A. Wurzbach,
Niederländisches Künstler-Lexicon, 1910, vol. p. 739; G. Heinz, *Katalog der Graf Harrach'schen
Gemäldegalerie*, 1960, p. 78, no. 22.

Sotheby's London, 5 July 1995 (13**) GBP 45,500	US$	72,579

VALLAYER-COSTER Anne (Paris 1744-1818 Paris) French
STILL-LIFE WITH A FRUIT BASKET, A GUN AND A HARE ON A LEDGE oil on canvas (an
oval), 66 x 54.5cm. slc 'vallayer Coster'
PROV.: Collection Baron Beurnonville; His Sale, Paris, Hotel Drouot, 9 May 1881 (maître Pillet)
no.,179 (400FF).
LIT.: M. Roland Michel, *Anne Vallayer Coster 1744-1818*, Paris 1970, p. 199, no.,296 (as lost).

Étude Tajan Paris, 12 December 1995 (112**) FRF 95,000	US$	19,135

STILL-LIFE WITH FLOWERS IN A BLUE PORCELAIN VASE oil on canvas (an oval), 25 5/8 x
21 5/8in. (65.1 x 54.9cm.) slr 'Melle Vallayer'
PROV.: Groult (Sale: Paris, 20 November 1941, lot 34, illus. pl. XVIII); Cezare Lanza, Genoa,
Galerie Cailleux, Paris.
EXH.: Paris, Galerie Cailleux, *Peinture de la Réalité au XVIIIe siècle*, 1945, cat. no. 36; Paris, Musée
de l'Orangerie, *La Nature morte de l'Antiquité à nos jours*, 1952, cat. no. 81; Rennes, Musée de
Rennes, *Nature morte anciennes et modernes*, 1953, cat. no. 22; Rotterdam, Museum Boymans,
Quatre siècles de nature morte en France, 1954, cat. no. 62, illus. pl. 34; London, Royal Academy,
European Masters of the 18th Century, 1954-1955, cat. no. 226; Zurich, Kunsthaus, *Schönheit des 18
Jahrhunderts*, 1955, no. 343; Paris, Galerie Cailleux, *Eloge de l'Ovale, Peintures et pastels du XVIIIe
siecle français*, November-December, 1975, cat. no. 41.
LIT.: M. Fare, *La nature morte en France*, 1961, vol. II, illus. no. 407; M. Roland Michel, *Anne
Vallayer-Coster*, 1970, p. 115, no. 28, illus. p. 126; M. and F. Fare, *La vie silencieuse en France, La
nature morte au XVIIIe siècle*, 1976, p. 233, no. 364, illustrated.

Sotheby's New York, 16 May 1996 (122**) US$ 112,500	US$	112,500

NATURE MORTE AUX INSTRUMENTS DE MUSIQUE MILITAIRE oil on canvas,,160 x 130cm.
sdll 'Melle Vallayer 1771'
PROV.: In the family of the present owner since the 18th century.
EXH.: Paris, *Salon de 1771*, no. 141.
LIT.: D. Diderot (ed. Jean Seznec), *Salons*, vol. IV (Salons de 1769, 1771, 1775, 1781), Oxford
1967; Bachaumont (ed. Jacques Laget), *2e Lettre*, Buc 1997, p. 27; Anonymous, *La muse errante au
Salon*, Paris 1771; Letters of M. Raphaël the Younger, *élève des écoles gratuites de Dessin, neveu de
feu M. Raphaël, peintre de l'académie de saint Luc, à un de ses amis, architecte à Rome; sur les
Peintures, Sculptures & Gravures qui sont exposées cette années au Louvre*, Paris, 7 september
1771; *Plaintes de Badigeon, marchand de couleurs, sure les critiques du Salon de 1771*, Paris 1771;
Mercure de France, Paris, October 1771, vol. I, p. 193; M. Roland Michel, *Anne Vallayer Coster*,
Paris 1970, p. 185, no. 259.

Étude Tajan Paris, 25 June 1996 (52***) FRF 1,900,000	US$	366,887

NATURE MORTE AUX INSTRUMENTS DE MUSIQUE MILITAIRE oil on canvas,,160 x 130cm.
sdll 'Melle Vallayer 1771'
PROV.: In the family of the current proprietors in Paris, probably since the 18th Century.
EXH.: Salon de 1771, n° 141.
LIT.: D. Diderot, *Salons* (ea. Jean Seznec), .IV, (Salons de 1769, 1771, 1775, 1781), Oxford, 1967;
Bachaumont, *2ième Lettre* (ed. Jacques Laget), Buc, 1995, p. 27; Anonyme, *La muse errante au
Salon*, Paris, 1771; *Lettres de M. Raphael Ie jeune, élève des écoles gratuites de Dessin, neveu de feu
M. Raphael, peintre de l'académie de saint Luc, à un de ses amis, architecte a Rome; sur les
Peintures, Sculptures & Gravures qui sont exposées au Louvre, Paris, 7 septembre 1771; L'Ombre*

de Raphael, ci-devant peintre de l'académie de Saint Luc, a son neveu raphael élève des Ecoles Gratuites de Dessin, en réponse à sa lettre sur les Peintures, Gravures et Sculptures exposées cette années au Louvre, Paris, 1771; *Plaintes de Badigeon, marchand de couleurs, sur les critiques du Salon de 1771*, Paris, 1771; *Mercure de France*, Paris, Oct. 1771, vol.I, p. 193; M. Roland Michel, *Anne Vallayer Coster*, Paris, 1970, p. 185, no. 259.

Étude Tajan Paris, 25 June 1996 (52***) FRF 1,900,000	US$	366,887

VALLET-BISSON Fréderique (France 1865-) French
SELF-PORTRAIT oil on canvas, 87¾ x 60½in. (222.9 x 153.7cm.) slr 'Fréderique Vallet'

Christie's New York, 2 November 1995 (174**) US$ 17,250	US$	17,250

VALLIN Jacques Antoine (Paris (?) 1760 c.-1831 after) French
TWO NYMPHS RUNNING TROUGH ROSEBUSHES AFTER STEALING THE BOW AND ARROWS OF SLEEPING CUPID, THREE AMORS IN PURSUIT oil on panel, 18¾ x 26½in. (47.6 x 67.3cm.) slr 'Vallin'
EXH.: Possibly Paris, Salon, 1806, no.,517 (as *un paysage représentant une chasse de diana*).
LIT.: Claude Gérard Marcus, 'Jacques Antoine Vallin', *Art et Curiosité* July-September 1980, p. 112, no. VIII p. 109, (illustrated fig. VIII).

Sotheby's New York, 16 May 1996 (113**) US$ 39,100	US$	39,100

A BACCHANTE PLAYING WITH THE TAMBOURINE: AN OIL SKETCH oil on canvas, 22 x 16½in. (55.9 x 41.9cm.)

Sotheby's New York, 6 October 1996 (173***) US$ 9,200	US$	9,200

VALLOTTON Félix Edouard (Lausanne 1865-1925 Paris) French (Swiss)
TORSE A L'ARMOIRE (FEMME NUE ROUSSE DEBOUT) oil on canvas, 38 3/8 x 30¾in. (97.5 x 78cm.) sdlr 'F.VALLOTTON. 13'
PROV.: Galerie Druet, Paris; Anon. sale, Sotheby's London, Dec. 4, 1968, lot 47; B.C.Holland, Inc., Chicago.
EXH.: Paris, Galerie Druet, *Exposition de peintures de Félix Vallotton*, 1914, no.7 (ill.); Chicago, The Art Institute, *Private Collects: Selections from the Collection of Dr.Eugene A.Solow*, May-Aug., 1988, no.60 (ill., p.9, fig.8).
LIT.: F.Vallotton, 'Livre de raison', in H.Hahnloser, *Félix Vallotton et ses amis*, Paris, 1936, p.305, no.967; D.E.Gordon, *Modern Art Exhibitions 1900-1916*, Munich, 1974, no.1724 (ill., p.303).

Christie's New York, 1 May 1996 (329**) US$ 85,000	US$	85,000

MONTBRETIAS ET CLÉMATIS oil on canvas, 23¾ x 18in. (60.5 x 46cm.) slr 'F. VALLOTTON' (1907)
PROV.: Galerie Dr. Raeber, Basle.
LIT.: Will be included in the forthcoming *catalogue raisonné de Felix Vallotton*, currently being prepared by Marina Ducrey.

Étude Tajan Paris, 10 June 1996 (17**) FRF 200,000	US$	38,620

WOMEN AT THEIR SEWING oil on canvas, 16½ x 24in. (42 x 61cm.) sdll 'F. Vallotton 1901'
PROV.: Former Collection of Henry-Jean Laroche.
LIT.: Will be included in the *catalogue raisonné of Felix Vallotton's work* currently being prepared by Marina Ducrey.

Étude Tajan Paris, 13 December 1995 (10***) FRF 760,000	US$	153,084

BOUQUET OF NASTURTIUMS oil on canvas, 32 x 21¼in. (81 x 54cm.) sdlr 'F. Vallotton 20' (1920)
PROV.: Former Collection of Henry-Jean Laroche.
LIT.: Will be included in the *catalogue raisonné of Felix Vallotton's work* currently being prepared by Marina Ducrey.

Étude Tajan Paris, 13 December 1995 (11**) FRF 250,000	US$	50,357

THE BASKET OF CHERRIES oil on canvas, 21¼ x 28¾in. (54 x 73cm.) sdlr 'F. Vallotton 21' (1921)
PROV.: Former Collection of Henry-Jean Laroche.
LIT.: Will be included in the *catalogue raisonné of Felix Vallotton's work* currently being prepared by Marina Ducrey.

Étude Tajan Paris, 13 December 1995 (12***) FRF 280,000	US$	56,399

PITCHER FLOWERS WITH BLUE TABLECLOTH gouache, 14 x 9¾in. (35.5 x 24.5cm.) sdlr 'F. Vallotton 24' (1924)
PROV.: Former Collection of Henry-Jean Laroche.
LIT.: Will be included in the *catalogue raisonné of Felix Vallotton's work* currently being prepared by Marina Ducrey.

Étude Tajan Paris, 13 December 1995 (13**) FRF 120,000	US$	24,171

BOUQUET OF TULIPS AND DAISIES oil on canvas, 21¾ x 15in. (55 x 38cm.) sdlr 'F. Vallotton 15' (1915)
PROV.: Former Collection of Henry-Jean Laroche.
LIT.: Will be included in the *catalogue raisonné of Felix Vallotton's work* currently being prepared by Marina Ducrey.

Étude Tajan Paris, 13 December 1995 (14**) FRF 160,000	US$	32,228

VALTAT Louis (Dieppe 1869-1952 Choisel, near Rambouillet) French
VASE DE FLEURS oil on canvas, 18 1/8 x 21¾in. (46 x 55.3cm.) sll 'L. Valtat' (ca. 1925))
PROV.: E. J. van Wisselingh & Co., Amsterdam; Anon. sale, Parke-Bernet Galleries, Inc., New York, 8 May 1957, lot,104 (illustrated); Gustave Ring, Washington D.C.; M. Knoedler & Co., New York (acquired from the above, 1958); Mrs. W. A. Green (acquired from the above, 1958); Hirschl & Adler Galleries Inc., New York (acquired by Richard Smart, 1973).
LIT.: Louis-André Valtat will include this painting forthcoming supplement to the Valtat *Catalogue raisonné*.

Christie's New York, 1 May 1996 (159**) US$ 66,300	US$	66,300

LE JARDIN DE L'ARTISTE A CHOISEL oil on canvas, 31¾ x 39½in. (80.5 x 103cm.) sll 'L. Valtat' (ca. 1918)
PROV.: David W. Hughes & Co., London.
LIT.: Louis Andé Valtat will include this painting in the forthoming second volume of the *Valtat catalogue raisonné*.

Christie's New York, 1 May 1996 (210**) US$ 55,200	US$	55,200

COQUELICOTS (POPPIES) oil on canvas, 18 x 21½in. (46 x 55cm.) slr ini 'LV' (1914)

Étude Tajan Paris, 10 June 1996 (15**) FRF 120,000	US$	23,172

AUTOPORTRAIT oil on canvas, 21¾ x 18in. (55.2 x 45.7cm.) stamped ini. 'L.V.' (1892)
PROV.: Hirschl & Adler Galleries, New York.
LIT.: Jean Valtat, *Louis Valtat: Catalogue de l'Oeuvre Peint, 1869-1952*, vol. I, Paris, 1977, no. 20 (illustrated p. 3).

Sotheby's New York, 2 May 1996 (160**) US$ 118,000	US$	118,000

NATURE MORTE A LA THÉIERE ET LA BOITE DE THÉ oil on canvas, 13¼ x 18¼in. (34 x 46.5cm.) slr 'L.Valtat'
LIT.: J.Valtat, *Louis Valtat, Catalogue de l'oeuvre peint 1869-1952*, vol.I, Paris 1977, no.1240 (ill. p.138).

Christie's South Kensington, 24 June 1996 (48**) GBP 9,775	US$	15,073

LA MER A AGAY oil on canvas, 31 7/8 x 39½in. (81 x 100.5cm.) slr 'L.Valtat' (ca 1917-18)
PROV.: Anon. sale, Christie's London, 27 June 1989, lot,360 (GBP 120,000).
EXH.: Montrouge, Centre Culturel et Artistique, *Louis Valtat*, May-June 1987, no. 6 (illustrated).

LIT.: To be included in the forthcoming *Valtat catalogue Raisonné* currently being prepared by Louis-André Valtat.

        Christie's London, 26 June 1996 (152**) GBP 27,600   US$ 42,560

BARQUES SUR LA LAC DU BOIS DE BOULOGNE oil on canvas, 10 5/8 x 13¾in. (27 x 35cm.) slr 'L. Valtat' (1936)
LIT.: Dr. J. Valtat, *Louis Valtat Catalogue de l' oeuvre peint 1869-1952*, vol.I., Neuchâtel, 1977, no.2,451 (illustrated p.273).

        Christie's London, 26 June 1996 (319**) GBP 12,650   US$ 19,507

VASE DE FLEURS oil on canvas laid down on masonite, 13,171 x 10 ¼in. (34.3 x 26cm.) slr ini. 'L.V.' (ca. 1925-1930)

        Christie's East, 7 November 1995 (31*) US$ 6,900   US$ 6,900

VASE DE MARGUERITES oil on canvas, 24 x 18in. (61 x 45.8cm.) slr 'L. Valtat' (ca. 1920)

        Christie's East, 7 November 1995 (201**) US$ 13,800   US$ 13,800

FLEURS ET FRUITS oil on canvas, 32 x 25 5/8in. (81.3 x 65.2cm.) ll 'L.Valtat' (1920)
PROV.: David B. Findlay Galleries, New York (acquired by Mrs. Sherburn M. Becker, 1963).
LIT.: Dr. J.Valtat, *Louis Valtat, Catalogue de l'oeuvre peint 1869-1952*, Paris, 1977, vol I, no. 1483 (illustrated, p.165).

        Christie's New York, 8 November 1995 (160**) US$ 55,200   US$ 55,200

VASE DE FLEURS ET FEUILLAGE D'AUTOMNE oil on canvas, 32 x 25 5/8in. (81.2 x 65cm.) lr 'L.Valtat' (1936)
LIT.: Dr. J.Valtat, *Louis Valtat, Catalogue de l'oeuvre peint 1869-1952*, vol. I, no. 2,438 (illustrated, p. 271).

        Christie's New York, 8 November 1995 (199**) US$ 79,500   US$ 79,500

VANDERBANK John (London 1694-1739 London) British
GROUP PORTRAIT OF JOHN CARTERET, 1ST EARL OF GRANVILLE, WITH HIS FAMILY IN AN INTERIOR oil on canvas, 108¼ x 151½in. (,275 x 385cm.)
PROV.: By descent trough Louisa, Viscountess Weymouth to Lord John Thynne; Christie's, 1st May 1911, lot 66, as Kneller (70gns. to Cohen).
LIT.: J. Kerslake, *Early Georgean Portraits*, I, London, 1977, p. 106.

        Christie's London, 10 November 1995 (10**) GBP 20,700   US$ 32,379

VANDERHAMEN Y LÉON Juan van der (circle of) (1596-1631) Spanish
FRUIT IN A WICKER BASKET ON A TABLE oil on canvas, 21½ x 30in. (54.6 x 76.2cm.)
EXH.: London, H. Terry-Engell Gallery, Nov.-Dec. 1964 (as Juan van der Hamen y Leon).
LIT.: Theodore Crombie, 'A Netherlands November', *Apollo* 1964, vol. 80, no. 33 (illustrated p. 410, no.1, as *Juan van der Hamen y Leon*).

        Sotheby's New York, 2 April 1996 (170**) US$ 47,150   US$ 47,150

VANGI Giuliano (Barberino di Mugello 1931 b.-) Italian
MALE FIGURE oil on canvas,,195 x 135cm. sdlr 'Vangi 92'

        Finearte Milan, 18 June 1996 (37*) ITL 13,800,000   US$ 8,949

VANITAS TEXTS Master of the (1650 c. active, Madrid?-l) Spanish
VANITAS STILL-LIFES oil on canvas (a pair), each: 19½ x 26in. (49.5 x 66cm.) the former inscr. uc 'VANA EST/PVLCHRITVD'; the letter inscr. lc 'VAS*LOS/CONTRITVR'

        Sotheby's London, 5 July 1995 (286**) GBP 28,750   US$ 45,861

VANLOO Amédée (Charles Amédée Philippe), de Prusse (Rivoli (near Turin) 1719-1795 Paris) French
LA SULTANE COMMANDANT DES OUVRAGES AUX ODALISQUES oil on canvas, 18 x

21¾in. (45.7 x 55.2cm.) (1772-75)
      Sotheby's New York, 11 January 1996 (232**) US$ 40,250   US$ 40,250

VANLOO Carle (Charles André) (Nice 1705-1765 Paris) French
STUDY OF A MALE NUDE oil on canvas, 39 x 28¾in. (99.1 x 73cm.) inscr.ur 'Du cabinet de M/Le
Baron de Castille' (1728-32)
PROV.: Possibly the son of Carle Vanloo (His sale: Paris, February 28, 1770, lot 2, 83 by 61 cm.);
Possibly Francois Boucher (His Sale: Paris, February, 1- March 9, 1771, lot 75bis, 82 by 61 cm.);
Possibly Sale: Paris, May 7 ff, 1771, lot 9; Possibly Louis-Michel Vanloo (inventory *après le décés*
April 22, 1771; His Sale: Paris, December 14ff., 1772, lot 73 for,269 livres 19 sous, 92 by 72 cm.);
Baron de Castille, acc. to an inscription on the painting.
      Sotheby's New York, 16 May 1996 (262**) US$ 24,150   US$ 24,150

VANLOO Jacob (Sluys 1614 c.-1670 Paris) French
PORTRAIT OF A CHILD IN A ROSE PINK DRESS WITH A PLUMED HAT, FONDLING A
PUPPY oil on canvas, 60 x 45½in. (,153 x 115.5in.)
EXH.: Birmingham, 1953, no. 104, as *Gerard de Lairesse*; Kingston-upon-Hull, Ferens Art gallery,.
Dutch Painting of the 17th Century, 1961, no. 57, as *Gerard de Lairesse*; Nottingham, 1982, plate II,
no. 38, as *Gerard de Lairesse*.
LIT.: Richter, 1901, no. 123, as *Gerard de Lairesse*.
      Sotheby's London, 6 December 1995 (38**) GBP 29,900   US$ 46,014

VANLOO Jean Baptiste (Aix-en-Provence 1684-1745 Aix-en-Provence) French
PORTRAIT OF LORD JOHN HERVEY (1696-1743) LORD PRIVY SEAL oil on canvas, 48 x
39in. (,122 x 99cm.)
PROV.: By descent.
LIT.: John Kerslake, *Early Georgian Portraits*, 1977, vol. I, p. 140.
      Sotheby's London, 11-12 June 1996 (447**) GBP 100,500   US$ 154,973

VANNINI Ottavio (Florence 1585-1643 Florence) Italian
A STUDY IF YOUNG ARCHITECT HOLDING A SCROLL AND A SEPARATE STUDY OF
ANOTHER HEAD red chalk, 29.9 x 26.4cm. bears old attribution in brown ink on the mount 'Di
Ottavio Vannini'
PROV.: H.S. Reitling (L.2274a on the mount), his sale, Sotheby's London, 9 December 1953, lot
114.
LIT.: C. Thiem, *Florentiner Zeichner des Frühbarock*, Munich 1977, p. 344, no.,112 (illustrated).
      Sotheby's London, 3 July 1995 (114*) GBP 27,600   US$ 44,026

VAROTARI Alessandro, {called} Padovanino (Padua 1588-1648 Venice) Italian
VENUS AT HER TOILET WITH TWO CUPIDS oil on canvas, 50¾ x 43¾in. (,129 x 111cm.) (after
1627)
      Sotheby's London, 17 April 1996 (82**) GBP 20,700   US$ 31,387

A SATYR TRYING TO TOUCH A SLEEPING NYMPH oil on canvas,,136 x 159cm.
      Christie's Rome, 4 June 1996 (534**) ITL 34,000,000   US$ 22,049

VASARELY Victor (Vasarhelyi) (Pécs 1908 b.) French (Hungarian)
KORSIN acrylic on canvas, 96 x 84cm. s 'Vasarely' sd titled '1971 (1984) nr. 3724'
      Hauswedell & Nolte Cologne, 6 June 1996 (453**) DEM 17,000   US$ 11,045

TRIDIUM-C tempera on canvas, 89 x 89in. (,226 x 226cm.) sd and titled 'Vasarely 'TRIM-C' 1968'
on the reverse
PROV.: Sidney Janis Gallery, New York.
      Christie's East, 14 November 1995 (66*) US$ 10,350   US$ 10,350

OND-III acrylic on canvas, 63 x 63in. (,160 x 160cm.) slc 'Vasarely'; sd and titled 'Vasarely-OND-III 1968' on the reverse

Christie's East, 14 November 1995 (68*) US$ 19,550	US$	19,550

ATTAM acrylic on canvas, 31 7/8 x 31 7/8in. (81 x 81cm.) sl edge 'Vasarely'; s twice, titled, d and numbered-'3.,106 VASARELY-'ATTAM' 1979 Vasarely' on the reverse

Christie's East, 14 November 1995 (83**) US$ 14,950	US$	14,950

MEANDRES E 1 mixed media, 42 x 69cm. slc 'Vasarely'; sd and titled on the reverse (1908)

Finearte Milan, 18 June 1996 (201*) ITL 23,575,000	US$	15,289

ILAVA oil on canvas, 76½ x 51 1/8in. (194.4 x 130cm.) slc 'Vasarely' sd titled '1956'
PROV.: Galerie Denise René, Paris.

Christie's London, 19 March 1996 (42**) GBP 21,850	US$	33,369

HAMOU oil on canvas, 40 1/8 x 40 1/8in. (,102 x 102cm.) slr 'Vasarely' sd and titled '1985' on the reverse

Christie's London, 19 March 1996 (62**) GBP 9,775	US$	14,928

2,221 TORONY N acryl on board,,120 x 79.5cm. slr on the back 'Vasarely', sd and titled on the reverse (1970)

Finearte Milan, 26 October 1995 (150*) ITL 12,075,000	US$	7,523

ORANDE 2 oil on canvas,,100 x 100cm. slc 'Vasarely'; s on the reverse (1984)

Bukowskis Stockholm, 26-27 October 1995 (163**) SEK 58,000	US$	8,774

APOTHIKERI oil on canvas, 51 1/8 x 38 1/8in. (,130 x 97cm.) s; sd '1953' and titled on the reverse
PROV.: Helios Art SA, Brussels; Galerie Art Latin, Stockholm.

Sotheby's London, 27 June 1996 (184**) GBP 27,600	US$	42,560

VASNETSOV Apollinari Mikhailovich (1856-1933) Russian
BOATS MOORED BEFORE A FORTIFIED TOWN oil on canvas, 30 7/8 x 38in. (78.5 x 96.5cm.) sdll (1913)

Phillips London, 14 November 1995 (47**) GBP 18,000	US$	28,156

VASSILIEFF Marie (1884-1958) french (?)
MON POUPÉE oil on canvas-board, 22 x 18in. (56 x 46cm.) sll 'Vassilieff'
PROV.: Galerie Charpentier, Paris, from whom purchased by the present owner.

Christie's South Kensington, 27 November 1995 (99**) GBP 7,875	US$	12,318

VEDOVA Emilio (Venice 1919 b.) Italian
PRESENZA 1959 oil on canvas,,120 x 120cm. sd '1959' and titled on the reverse
PROV.: Acquired directly from the artist by the family of the present owner.

Sotheby's Milan, 28 May 1996 (188**) ITL 170,800,000	US$	109,698

VEERENDAEL Nicolaas van (Antwerp 1640-1690 Antwerp) Flemish
A SWAG OF PINK AND WHITE ROSES, A PEONY, A PARROT TULIP, BLOSSOM, ISIANTHUS, A CARNATION, NARCISSI, LILY OF THE VALLEY AND OTHER FLOWERS, WITH A BUMBLE BEE AND A RED ADMIRAL, IN A CARTOUCHE - A FRAGMENT oil on canvas, 18 1/8 x 26 5/8in. (46 x 67.6 cm.)
EXH.: London, Royal Academy, *Works by the Old Masters*, Jan-March 1886, no. 99.

Christie's London, 19 April 1996 (117**) GBP 19,550	US$	29,644

VELAZQUEZ Eugenio Lucas (1817-1870) Spanish
AQUELARRE oil on panel, 11 x 8 7/8in. (28 x 22.6cm.) sdll 'E. Lucas'
LIT.: J. M. Arnaiz, *Eugenio Lucas, su vida y su obra*, Madrid, 1981, no. 167, pp. 378-,379

599

(illustrated).

Christie's New York, 22 May 1996 (114**) US$ 28,750 — US$ 28,750

VELDE Bram van (Zoeterwoude 1895-1981 Grimaux) Dutch
UNTITLED watercolour on paper, 24 x 18cm. slr 'Bram van V'
PROV.: Collection d'art, Amsterdam.

Christie's Amsterdam, 5 June 1996 (292*) NLG 13,800 — US$ 8,063

UNTITLED (LA CHAPELLE-SUR-CAROUGE) gouache on paper, 53½ x 59 1/16in. (,136 x 150cm.) (1976)
PROV.: Gallery Maeght, Paris; Gallery Lefebre, New York, Albert Levison, Los Angeles.
LIT.: Zurich, Galerie Maeght, *Bram van Velde*, October-December 1976, no. 37 (illustrated in colour in the catalogue); Barcelona, Galeria Maeght, *Bram van Velde, Retrospectiva 1908-1978*, October-November 1978, no. 34 (ilustrated in colour in the catalogue), Dordrecht, Dordrechts Museum, *Bram van Velde, Retrospectieve 1907-1978,* January-Febryary 1979, no. 37 (illustrated); New York, Gallery Lefebre, *Bram van Velde, 1895-1981*, February-March 1982 (illustrated in colour in the catalogue p. 5).
To be included in the forthcoming *Bram van Velde Catalogue Raisonné* being prepared by Rainer Michael Mason and Catherine Putman.

Christie's London, 27 June 1996 (31**) GBP 78,500 — US$ 121,049

PROJECT D'AFFICHE COLOGNE NO.2 gouache on annonay-velin, 66 x 54cm. (1966)

Lempertz Cologne, 31 May 1996 (501*) DEM 27,000 — US$ 17,602

VELDE Esaias van de (Amsterdam 1590/91 c.-1630 The Hague) Dutch
A WINTER LANDSCAPE oil on panel, 6¼ x 9½in. (16.2 x 24.2cm.) sdlr 'E.V.D.VELDE.1629'

Sotheby's London, 6 December 1995 (1**) GBP 54,300 — US$ 83,564

VELDE Geer van (Lisse 1898-1977 Paris) Dutch
A COMPOSITION WITH FRUIT ON A TABLE gouache on paper, 26 x 20cm. s with initials lr 'Gv.V'

Christie's Amsterdam, 5 June 1996 (291*) NLG 11,500 — US$ 6,719

A COMPOSITION oil on canvas, 64.5 x 60cm. sll with initials 'GvV' (executed *circa* 1950)
PROV.: Kunsthandel M.L.de Boer, Amsterdam, no. 18,441 .

Christie's Amsterdam, 5 June 1996 (293**) NLG 34,500 — US$ 20,158

A COMPOSITION oil on canvas, 73 x 60cm. s with initials lr 'GvV' and s again on the reverse 'G.van Velde'
PROV.: Galerie Louis Carré, Paris.

Christie's Amsterdam, 5 June 1996 (294**) NLG 48,300 — US$ 28,221

L'ÉTÉ DE FEMME, BLUE NUIT oil on canvas, 63 x 76cm. s with ini.lr 'GvV', and with inscr. of the title on the stretcher (ca. 1946)
PROV.: Galerie Maeght, Paris.

Christie's Amsterdam, 5 June 1996 (344**) NLG 40,250 — US$ 23,517

A SELF PORTRAIT oil on canvas, unframed, 92 x 73cm. s with initials lr 'G.v.V.' and s again 'Geer van Velde Paris' on the reverse

Christie's Amsterdam, 6 December 1995 (270**) NLG 29,900 — US$ 18,528

VELDE Henry van de (Antwerp 1863-1957 Oberageri or Zurich (Switzerland)) Belgian
FRAUENPORTRAIT oil on linen,,103 x 78.5cm. sll 'van de Velde' (1888)
EXH.: Antwerpen 1987/1988/Otterlo 1988, *Henry van de Velde* (1863 - 1957), Cat. no. 23 col. ill. p. 47.

Lempertz Cologne, 29 November 1995 (482**) DEM 36,000 — US$ 25,409

VELDE Willem the Elder van de (Leyden 1641 c.-1693 Greenwich) Dutch
TEH ENGLISH AND DUTCH FLEETS EXCHANGING SALUTES AT SEA WITH THE
'PRINCE' AND THE 'GOUDEN LEEUW' IN THE FOREGROUND oil on canvas, 62 7/8 x 84in.
(159.8 x 214cm.) sdlr 'W.v.velde : doude f. 1684'
PROV.: Perhaps painted for King James II of England (see below); L. Stokbroovan Hoog-en
Aartswoud; sale, C.S. Roos, Hoorn, 3 Sept. 1867, lot 208; George H. Story, New York (label on the
reverse); Lady Wolverton, Iwerne House, Iwerne Minster, Blandford, Dorset, grandmother of the late
owner.
LIT.: F. Fox, *Great Ships*, 1980, p. 4, detail illustrated on the cover. M.S. Robinson, *The Paintings of
the Willem van de Veldes*, Greenwich, 1990, II, pp. 961-3, no. 420, illustrated.

Christie's London, 8 December 1995 (13**) GBP 309,500	US$	476,300

VELDE Willem the Younger van de (Leyden 1633-1707 Greenwich, London) Dutch
AN INNSHORE SCENE IN A CALM, WITH A *WEYSCHUT* RAISING SAIL IN SHALLOWS
NEAR PILINGS, A *BOEIER* BEING ROWED AWAY FROM THE SHORE AND MEN-O'-WAR
AR ANCHOR OFFSHORE oil on canvas, 11¼ x 12¾in. (28.4 x 32.7cm.) s ini. on a plank 'WVV'
PROV.: William Hastings, his deceased sale, London, Christie's, 28 March 1840, lot 91,
GBP138.12s; where bought by Welbore Ellis, 2nd Earl of Normanton, Somerley, entry no.,118 in his
manuscript catalogue, as no. 44; His son, James Charles Welbore Ellis, 3rd Earl of Normanton, until
after 1884; Max von Grunelius, Frankfurt, bears his label on the reverse of the frame, with inventory
number: V, 285; His son, Ernst-Max von Grunelius.
EXH.: London, Royal Academy, 1884, no. 84 (The Calm, 11 by 13in., lent by the 3rd Earl of
Normanton).

Sotheby's London, 5 July 1995 (2**) GBP 80,700	US$	128,729

A BRITISH MAN-O'-WAR pencil and sepia, 47 x 103cm. d inscr. indistinctly '1696'

A. Mak B.V. Dordrecht, 3 October 1995 (86***) NLG 51,000	US$	32,156

AN ENGLISH GALIOT AT ANCHOR WITH FISHERMEN LAYING A NET oil on canvas, 15¼ x
22in. (39 x 56cm.) sdlr 'W.V.Velde J 1691'
PROV.: Private Collection, England; With Hoogendijk, The Hague, 1929-30; With Goudstikker,
Amsterdam, 1930-32, no. 32; Baron Heinrich Thyssen-Bornemisza, by 1937.
EXH.: Amsterdam, Rijksmuseum, Oude Kunst, 1929, no. 153, p. 44; Paris 1970, no. 42, plate 13;
Düsseldorf 1970-71, no. 57; Bielefeld, Kunsthalle, *Landschaften aus vier Jahrhunderten aus den
Kunstmuseum Düsseldorf*, 1973, no. 11; Lausanne etc., 1986-7, no. 46.
LIT.: R. Heinemann 1937, vol. I, no. 439; M. Russell, *Jan van de Capelle*, 1975, reproduced plate
57; M.S. Robinson, *A Catalogue of the Paintings of the Elder and Younger Willem van de Velde*,
1990, pp. 706-708, no. 95 (1), reproduced.

Sotheby's London, 6 December 1995 (115**) GBP 36,700	US$	56,479

VENARD Claude (1913 b.) French
POISSONS oil on canvas, 33½ x 63in. (85 x 160cm.) sdlr 'Venard '54'
PROV.: with Arthur Tooth & Sons Ltd., London.

Phillips London, 24 June 1996 (32**) GBP 4,200	US$	6,476

VENNE Adriaen Pietersz. van de (Delft 1589-1662 The Hague) Dutch
TWO PRINCESS OF NASSAU (MAURITS AND FREDERIK HENDRIK) oil on canvas (en
grissaille), 38¼ x 44¾in. (97.3 x 113.7cm.) (after 1621)
PROV.: Anonymous sale, London, Christie's 29 January 1971, lot 35, (as by John the Baan), where
bought by the present owner.

Sotheby's London, 17 April 1996 (657**) GBP 19,550	US$	29,644

VERBEECK Cornelis (Haarlem 1590 c.-1633 c. Haarlem) Dutch
A THREE-MASTER SETTING OUT FROM AN ESTUARY WITH ELEGANT RIDERS
WAVING GOODBYE ON THE SHORE, A TOWN IN THE DISTANCE oil on panel, 22.8 x
37.8cm. s in yellow on the blue flag on the stern 'CVB'

Christie's Amsterdam, 7 May 1996 (17**) NLG 138,000	US$	80,466

VERBOECKHOVEN Eugène Joseph (Warneton 1798-1881 Brussels) Belgian
A SHEEP, GOAT AND CHICKEN ON A HILLSIDE oil on panel, 7 x 9¾in. (17.8 x 24.8cm.) sdll
'Eugene Verboeckhoven ft. 1863'; sd and inscr. 'je soussigné declare/que le tableau ci contre/et
original/Eugene Verboeckoven/,Bruxelles/1863' on the reverse

Christie's East, 13 February 1996 (40**) US$ 9,775	US$	9,775

A SHEPHERD WITH HIS FLOCK ON A WOODED TRACK oil on panel, 23 3/8 x 35 5/8in. (59.5
x 90.5cm.) s inscr. indistinctly on an old label on the reverse and sealed
PROV.: see also Bernard klombeck (18) co-painter.

Phillips London, 14 November 1995 (18**) GBP 10,000	US$	15,642

THE SHEPHERDS AND HIS HERD CROSSING A BRIDGE IN A WINTER LANDSCAPE oil on
panel, 8¼ x 12¼in. (21 x 31.1cm.) sd '1865'
PROV.: Richard Green, Ltd., London.
LIT.: Norbert Hostyn and P. & V. Berko, *Eugène Verboeckhoven*, Brussels, 1984, p.,263
(illustrated).

Sotheby's Arcade Auctions New York, 17 January 1996 (514*) US$ 23,000	US$	23,000

A COW, SHEEP AND CHICKEN IN A MEADOW oil on panel, 23 x 29.5cm. sd
'Eugène/Verboeckhoven' sd again and authenticated on the reverse

Christie's Amsterdam, 25 April 1996 (228**) NLG 21,850	US$	12,984

A HERDSMAN AND CATTLE BY A POND IN THE FOREST oil on panel, 59 x 86cm. Signed by
both artists and dated 'JB Klombeck 1870/ Eugène Verboeckhoven
PROV.: Also Johann Bernard Klombeck (293) co-painter.
EXH.: Kleve, Museum Haus Koekkoek, *Johann Bernhard Klombeck. Ein Maler der Klever
Romantik*, 10 Oct.-5 Dec.1993.
LIT.: A. Nollert and G. de Werd, *Johann Bernhard Klombeck. Ein Landschaftsmaler der Klever
Romantik*, Kleve 1993, p. 57 (col.illus.).

Christie's Amsterdam, 26 October 1995 (293**) NLG 57,500	US$	36,255

**VERBOECKHOVEN & HENRY CAMPOTOSTO (D. 1910) Eugène Joseph (Warneton 1798-
1881 Brussels) Belgian**
A PASTORAL REFRESHMENT; AND THE YOUNG SHEPHERDESSES oil on panel (a pair),
24½ x 34¾in. (62.5 x 88cm.) sd 'Campotosto Henry/Eugene Verboeckhoven 1874/1875'

Christie's London, 15 March 1996 (6**) GBP 45,500	US$	69,487

VERBRUGGEN Gaspar Pieter the Elder (Antwerp 1635-1681 Antwerp) Flemish
STILL-LIFE WITH FRUIT, FLOWERS AND A STONE CARTOUCHE oil on canvas, 61 x 50¾in.
(154.9 x 128.9cm.) inscr. on the cartouche 'NIHIL STABILE'
PROV.: Recieved into collection of present owner in 1840.
EXH.: Possibly shown in 1811 at the Pennsylvania Academy of Fine Arts.

Sotheby's New York, 16 May 1996 (60**) US$ 29,900	US$	29,900

A STILL-LIFE OF A STONE URN DECORATED WITH GARLANDS OF FLOWERS oil on
canvas, 18¼ x 14¼in. (46.2 x 37cm.) sll 'gas.p. Verbruggen./f.'

Sotheby's London, 6 December 1995 (212**) GBP 9,200	US$	14,158

PARROT TULIPS, CARNATIONS, CHRYSANTHEUMS, HYACINTHS, ROSES,
HONEYSUCKLE AND OTHER FLOWERS IN A SCULPTED URN WITH RAMBLING ROSES,
NARCISSI AND OTHER FLOWERS IN A STONE NICHE oil on canvas, 41 1/8 x 33 5/8in. (,102 x
85.4cm.) sll 'gasper.ped:Ve.bruggen / f'

Christie's London, 7 July 1995 (1**) GBP 25,300	US$	40,357

VERBURGH Rutger (Rotterdam 1678-?) Dutch
LE CHARLATAN oil on oakpanel, 34 x 26.5cm. sll 'R: Verburgh. f'
    Étude Tajan Paris, 12 December 1995 (83**) FRF 110,000   US$ 22,157

VERDUSSEN Jan Peeter (Antwerp 1700-1763 Avignon) Flemish
CAMPEMENT MILITAIRES PRÉS DE NAMUR oil on canvas (a pair), each: 66.5 x 95cm. each: sll
'J.P.Verdussen'
    Étude Tajan Paris, 12 December 1995 (82**) FRF 170,000   US$ 34,242

HUNTSMEN WITH THEIR HORSES AND HOUNDS AT REST IN A WOODED LANDSCAPE
oil on canvas, 20½ x 24¾in. (52.1 x 62.9cm.)
    Sotheby's New York, 16 May 1996 (163*) US$ 7,475   US$ 7,475

VERELST Pieter (Dordrecht 1618 c.-1668 after) Dutch
AN ELDERLY LADY oil on panel, 73.5 x 59cm.
PROV.: Anonymous sale, London, Christie's, 2 April 1954, lot 124; C. Homburg, Amsterdam, 1963.
    Sotheby's Amsterdam, 14 November 1995 (107*) NLG 12,980   US$ 8,181

VERELST Simon Pietersz (The Hague 1644-1721 London) Dutch
STILL-LIFE OF ROSES, TULIPS, CARNATIONS, A SUNFLOWER AND OTHER FLOWERS IN
A GLASS VASE ON A STONE PLINTH WITH TWO BUTTERFLIES oil on canvas, 41¾ x 32¾in.
(,106 x 83cm.)
PROV.: With Pieter de Boer, Amsterdam 1935; London Art Market, 1937; With Rayner Mac
Cormal, London; With Grosvenor Galleries, Harrogate.
EXH.: Amsterdam, Pieter de Boer, *Bloemstukken van Oude Meesters*, 1935, no. 125.
LIT.: F. Lewis, *Simon Pietersz. Verelst*,. 1979, p. 43, no. 145.
    Sotheby's London, 5 July 1995 (245**) GBP 18,400   US$ 29,351

A STILL-LIFE OF TULIPS, CARNATIONS, ROSES, POPPIES, AN IRIS AND SUNFLOWERS
IN AN URN ON A STONE LEDGE oil on canvas, 46 x 36¾in. (,117 x 93.5cm.) bears signature lr
'S. Verelst Fecit'
    Sotheby's London, 17 April 1996 (159**) GBP 14,950   US$ 22,669

A STILL-LIFE OF ROSES, TULIPS, A POPPY AND A HOLLYHOCK IN A GILT VASE, WITH
A SNAIL, BUTTERFLIES AND A DRAGONFLY ON A STONE LEDGE oil on canvas, 28½ x
23½in. (72 x 59.5cm.)
PROV.: C. Manuel, London, June 1935; Sir William Churchman, BT. (1864-1947); thence by
descent.
    Sotheby's London, 6 December 1995 (159**) GBP 41,100   US$ 63,250

VERHAEGHT Tobias (Antwerp 1561-1631 Antwerp) Flemish
A HORSE-DRAWN WAGGON ON A ROAD WITH TRAVELLERS HALTING BY THE SWAN
INN, A TOWN BEYOND oil on panel, 47.8 cm x 65cm.
    Christie's Amsterdam, 13 November 1995 (46*) NLG 20,700   US$ 13,046

VERHAS Frans (Termonde 1832-1894 Schaerbeek) Belgian
A STANDING NUDE oil on panel, 34 5/8 x 23½in. (88 x 59.7cm.) slr 'Frans Verhas'
    Christie's New York, 2 November 1995 (104**) US$ 17,250   US$ 17,250

VERHEYEN Jan Hendrik (Utrecht 1778-1846 Utrecht) Dutch
A DUTCH TOWN oil on panel, 19 x 25¼in. (48.3 x 64.2cm.) s 'J.H. Verheen'
    Christie's South Kensington, 14 March 1996 (32**) GBP 6,670   US$ 10,186

VERLAT Charles (1824-1890) Belgian
UN CHEVAL ARAB, JERUSALEM oil on canvas, 47½ x 63½in. (120.5 x 161.2cm.) sd 'Charles
Verlat Jerusalem/1877'

PROV.: Anon. Sale, Eugène van Henck & Fils, Anvers, lot 47 (2800Bfr. to Madame Istas).
   Christie's London, 17 November 1995 (127**) GBP 56,500   US$ 88,378

VERMEER Barent (Haarlem 1659-before 1702 Haarlem) Dutch
STILL-LIFE WITH FRUIT AND A COCKATOO oil on canvas, 86.5 x 127cm. sll 'Bv'
PROV.: Leggatt Brothers, London; Private Collection, Italy.
   Dorotheum Vienna, 6 March 1996 (298**) ATS 380,000   US$ 36,553

VERNET Carle (Antoine Charles Horace) (Bordeaux 1758-1836 Paris) French
LE DÉPART DES CAVALIERS POUR UNE COURSE oil on canvas, 113.5 x 145.5cm.
   Étude Tajan Paris, 25 June 1996 (63**) FRF 460,000   US$ 88,825

VERNET Claude Joseph (Avignon 1714-1789 Paris) French
LES BAIGNEUSES oil on canvas, 26¼ x 32½in. (66.5 x 82.5cm.) sdll 'J. Vernet.f./1759'
PROV.: Monsieur de Poulhariez, Marseilles, commissioned with pendant from the artist in 1753
(deux tableaux reppresentent des marines ou il ait aussi un peu de paysage et des sujets gracieux
comme un lever et un coucher du soleil sans faire des tempêtes, et parmi les figurines, des femmes
des environs de Rome......) and paid for in 1759; d'Hericourt collection, sold together with pendant,
Paris, Remy, 29 December 1766, lots 73 and 74, for 2,399 and 3,531 livres respectively Etienne
Françios, Duc de Choiseul (1719-1785), no.,105 in his 1771 inventory, sold Paris, Boileau, 6 April
1772, lot 132, 5,950 francs; Louis François de Bourbon, Prince de Conti (1717-1776), his deceased
sale, Paris, Remy, 8 April to 6 June 1777, lot 734, 5,100 francs; With Dulac, Paris, his sale, Paris,
Paillet and Chariot, 30 November 1778, 5,001 francs; Tonnelier, his deceased sale, Paris, Foliot and
Gaubert, 28 November 1783, 4,701 francs; Anonymous undated sale, Paris, Paillet, late 18th century
(according to Ingersoll-Smouse, *op. cit.*); Robit Collection, sold Paris, Paillet and Delaroche, 11 May
1801, lot 159, 2,820 francs; With Bryant's Gallery, London, 1801-2; Acquired in the 1820's by the
great great grandfather of the present owner.
EXH.: W. Buchanan, *Memoirs of Paintings*, 1824, vol. II, p. 70; L. Lagrange, *Les Vernet. Joseph
Vernet et la peinture au XVIIIe siècle*, 1864, pp. 202, 211-13,,337 C142, and,364 R102; J. Belleudy,
J.-J. Balechou, Graveur du Roi, 1908, no. 47; F. Ingersoll-Smouse, *Joseph Vernet: peintre de marine*,
1926, vol. I, p.89, no. 696; P. Conisbee, *Claude-Joseph Vernet 1714-1789*, catalogue of the
exhibition, London, Kenwood House, 1976, under no. 69.
   Sotheby's London, 5 July 1995 (83**) GBP 155,500   US$ 248,046

MORNING FOG AND SUNSET IN ITALIAN PORTS oil on canvas (a pair), each: 32 x 54½in. (81
x 138cm.) sdlr 'J. Vernet Romae 1745'
PROV.: Probably Drake; Sale: Christie's, London, July 26, 1859, lots,482 and 471, purchased by Earl
of Drax, Plantigh Towers, Kent; (Sale: Christie's, London, February 19, 1910, lot 108), purchased by
Brunner; Thos. Agnew and Sons, Ltd., London; Sale: Sotheby's, New York,January 12, 1989, lot
157, illus., where purchased by the present collector.
LIT.: Florence Ingersoll-Smouse, *Joseph Vernet: Peintre de Marine*, 1926, vol I, p. 46, under *livre de
raisonné* numbers 123-126, illus. pl. XI, fig. 23, and pl. XIII, fig. 26.
   Sotheby's New York, 11 January 1996 (136**) US$ 497,500   US$ 497,500

A MEDITERRANEAN COASTAL SCENE WITH FISHERFOLK AT SUNSET oil on canvas, 22¼
31¼in. (56.5 x 79.4cm.) sd 'J Vernet f/ 1764'
PROV.: Commisioned by M. Godefroy le jeune; Lespinasse d' Artel; sale, Paris, 11 July 1803, lot
44.
EXH.: Paris, Salon, 1765, no. 73.
LIT.: L. Lagrange, *Les Vernet, Joseph Vernet et la Peinture au XVIIIème siècle*, Paris 1864, p. 342,
. 192; F. Ingersoll-Smouse, *Joseph Vernet Peintre de Marine 1714-1789*, Paris 1926, I, pp. 96-7,
. 787.
   Christie's London, 7 July 1995 (78**) GBP 221,500   US$ 353,326

VERNON Emile (British 19th/20th Century) British
A DARK HAIRED ROSE oil on canvas, 61 x 50.3cm. sll
    Phillips London, 14 November 1995 (55**) GBP 4,800   US$ 7,508

VERONESI Luigi (Milan 1908 b.) Italian
COMPOSIZIONE P2 - 1971 tempera on waxed canvas, 80 x 60cm. sdll 'L. Veronesi 71' sd, titled
and inscr,897 on the reverse
    Finearte Milan, 19 March 1996 (16*) ITL 13,225,000   US$ 8,461

VERROCCHI Agostino (1619 - 1636, doc. Rome) Italian
STILL-LIFE OF GRAPES IN A BASKET APPLES; ALL ON A LEDGE oil on canvas, 19¾ x
26¾in. (50.5 x 68cm.)
    Sotheby's London, 5 July 1995 (132**) GBP 8,625   US$ 13,758

VERSCHURING Hendrick (Gorinchem 1627-1690 Dordrecht) Dutch
TRAVELLERS IN A MOUNTAIN VILLAGE oil on panel, 41.5 x 49.2cm. indistinctly sdll 'H
Verschuring f 1670'
    Christie's Amsterdam, 7 May 1996 (1**) NLG 13,800   US$ 8,047

SOLDIERS DIVIDING BOOTY IN A GUARDROOM oil on canvas, 23½ x 28 7/8in. (59.7 x
73.4cm.) (1650's)
PROV.: V. Herzog, Vienna; with Bachstitz, Berlin; E. Glückstadt, Copenhagen; Karoline Moltke;
sale, Copenhagen, 19 March 1934, lot 171.
LIT.: C. Hofstede de Groot, *A Catalogue Raisonne, etc.*, V, London, 1913, p. 18, no. 37, as *Gerard
Ter Borch*; SJ. Gudlaugsson, *Gerard Ter Borch*, The Hague, 1960, II, p. 277, no. D13, as *Hendrik
Verschuring*.
    Christie's London, 8 December 1995 (222**) GBP 19,550   US$ 30,086

VERSCHUUR Wouter (Amsterdam 1812-1874 Vorden) Dutch
WATERING THE HORSES oil on canvas, 26 x 37¾in. (66.1 x 95.9cm.) sll 'WVersschuur'
    Christie's New York, 14 February 1996 (74**) US$ 145,500   US$ 145,500

ELEGANT FIGURES RIDING oil on canvas, 16 x 13¾in. 940.4 x 35cm.) sd 'W. Verschuur.S. 1845'
    Christie's London, 15 March 1996 (9**) GBP 9,430   US$ 14,401

HORSES IN A BARN oil on panel, 17½ x 26¼in. (44.5 x 67cm.) slr 'W. Verschuur.'
    Christie's New York, 2 November 1995 (81**) US$ 145,500   US$ 145,500

A HORSE, A DONKEY AND CHICKENS IN A LANDSCAPE oil on panel, 33 x 29cm. s 'W.
Verschuur'
    Christie's Amsterdam, 26 October 1995 (287**) NLG 18,400   US$ 11,602

VERSTEEGH Michiel (1756-1843)
IN THE GROCERY SHOP oil on panel, 41 x 35cm. s 'M Versteegh fecit'
PROV.: Collection Jhr. H.F. de Court, Dordrecht Kunsthandel P.A. Scheen, The Hague.
EXH.: Dordrecht, Blussé en van Braam, *Tentoonstelling van nog in leven zijnde Dordrechtse
meesters*, 1819, cat. no.,107 (as:Een kruidenierswinkel met stoffagie, bij onderscheide avondlichten);
Haarlem, *Tentoonstelling van nog in leven zijnde Nederlandsche meesters*, 1825, cat. no.,457 (as*:
een kruidenierswinkel, met twee vrouwen bij kaarslicht*); Enschede, Rijksmuseum Twenthe,
romantische school, year unknown cat.no.40(?).
LIT.: Pieter A. Scheen, *Lexicon Nederlandse Beeldende Kunstenaars*, The Hague 1970, vol. II, p. 50
(as: Kruidenierswinkel met twee vrouwen bij kaarslicht), illus.no. 46.
    Christie's Amsterdam, 26 October 1995 (193**) NLG 46,000   US$ 29,00

VERSTRAELEN Anthonie (Gorinchem 1593/94-1641 Amsterdam) Dutch
A WINTER LANDSCAPE WITH FIGURES SKATING AND WALKING ON A FROZEN RIVER

oil on panel, 9 x 13¼in. (22.9 x 33.7cm.) s 'AVS'
      Sotheby's New York, 16 May 1996 (87**) US$ 96,000   US$ 96,000

VERTANGEN Daniel (The Hague 1598 c.-1684 before The Hague) Dutch
TEH JUDGEMENT OF PARIS oil on canvas, 23½ x 30½in. (59.7 x 77.5cm.)
PROV.: Ambrose Heath Wilkons Martin, As a gift from his father by 1877, acccording to his label
on the reverse; Sale: Sotheby's, New York, 7 November 1984, lot,141 (illustrated).
      Sotheby's Arcade Auctions New York, 17 January 1996 (91*) US$ 10,925   US$ 10,925

VERTIN Petrus Gerardus (The Hague 1819-1893 The Hague) Dutch
THE VILLAGE SQUARE, WASSENAAR oil on canvas, 27¾ x 32¼in. (70.5 x 81.9cm.) sd P.G.
Vertin 1841'
PROV.: Anon. sale Christie's, 16 Nov. 1982, lot 251.
      Christie's London, 14 June 1996 (4**) GBP 20,700   US$ 31,920

TOWNSFOLK STROLLING IN A SNOWY STREET oil on panel, 24 x 18 cm sd 'PG Vertin f.85
(?)'
PROV.: Salon Artistique de M.M. Couveé, The Hague.
      Christie's Amsterdam, 25 April 1996 (10*) NLG 10,925   US$ 6,492

A VIEW IN A TOWN WITH NUMEROUS FIGURES IN A SNOWY STREET oil on panel, 24.5 x
20 cm s 'PG Vertin'
      Christie's Amsterdam, 7 February 1996 (17*) NLG 8,625   US$ 5,253

VERVEER Samuel Leonardus (Salomon Leonardus) (The Hague 1813-1876 The Hague) Dutch
A CAPRICCIO VIEUW OF A CROWDED MARKET IN THE JODENBREESTRAAT,
AMSTERDAM, WITH THE PORTUGUESE SYNAGOGE IN THE BACKGROUND DURING
THE FEAST Of TABERNACKLES oil on panel, 60.5 x 79cm. sdll 'S.L.Verveer.ft 53'
      Christie's Amsterdam, 26 October 1995 (202**) NLG 195,500   US$ 123,266

VERWEY Kees (Amsterdam 1900 -1995 Haarlem) Dutch
A SELF PORTRAIT oil on canvas, 60 x 50cm. sll 'Kees Verwey' dlr '84'
      Christie's Amsterdam, 5 June 1996 (62*) NLG 8,050   US$ 4,703

A STILL LIFE WITH A CLASSICAL SCULPTURE oil on canvas,,110 x 122cm. sul 'K.Verwey'
and dlr "30'
EXH.: Amsterdam, Stedelijk Museum, *De Onafhankelijken*, 18 February-12 March 1933, no.,267 (as
stilleven).
      Christie's Amsterdam, 6 December 1995 (177**) NLG 48,300   US$ 29,929

VERWILT François (Rotterdam 1620 c.-1691 Rotterdam) Dutch
THE PENITENT MAGDALEN, AND A HERMIT IN ROCKY LANDSCAPES oil on panel, 26 x
24.4cm. the first slr 'f.v.wilt' the second sll 'f.v.wilt'
      Christie's Amsterdam, 13 November 1995 (74*) NLG 8,050   US$ 5,073

VESPIGNANI Renzo (Rome 1924 b.-) Italian
PARCHEGGIO oil on panel, 70.5 x 101.5cm sd 'Vespignani 1959', titled and d on the reverse
      Finearte Rome, 14 November 1995 (195**) ITL 18,975,000   US$ 11,911

VESTER Willem (Heemstede 1824-1895 Haarlem) Dutch
AN EXTENSIVE WINTER LANDSCAPE WITH A HORSE AND CART ON A TRACK AND
SKATERS ON A FROZEN RIVER oil on canvas, 32½ x 9 5/8in. (82.7 x 126cm.) indistinctly signed
PROV.: Frost & Reed Ltd.
      Phillips London, 12th March 1996 (9**) GBP 8,000   US$ 12,217

VETTURALI Gaetano (Lucca 1701-1783 Lucca) Italian
SUSANNAH AND THE ELDERS oil on canvas, 72 x 139cm
      Finearte Milan, 25 November 1995 (134**) ITL 19,550,000   US$ 12,272

IL BAGNO DI BETSABEA oil on canvas, 72 x 137cm
      Finearte Milan, 25 November 1995 (135**) ITL 19,550,000   US$ 12,272

VEYRASSAT Jules Jacques (Paris 1828-1893 Paris) French
AT THE FARRIER'S oil on canvas, 78 x 61cm. slr 'J. Veyrassat'
      Dorotheum Vienna, 6 November 1995 (99**) ATS 160,000   US$ 16,050

VIANI Giovanni Maria (Bologna 1636-1700 Bologna) Italian
MYTHOLOGICAL SCENE oil on canvas,,144 x 226cm
      Finearte Milan, 25 November 1995 (79**) ITL 25,300,000   US$ 15,882

VIBERT Jean Georges (Paris 1840-1902 Paris) French
AN ELEGANT LADY BY THE SEA oil on panel, 11 3/8 x 8¾in. (29 x 22.5cm.) sd and inscr. 'J.G.
Vibert'/a Marie 15 Août 1890'
      Christie's New York, 14 February 1996 (107**) US$ 21,850   US$ 21,850

VICTORS Jan (Amsterdam 1620-1676 c. Dutch Indies) Dutch
PORTRAIT OF PROFESSOR FRANCISCUS BURMANUS (1628 -1679), SEATED THREE-
QUARTER-LENGTH, AT A TABLE BY A DRAPED BOOKCASE, WEARING BLACK DRESS
AND CUFFS; AND PORTRAIT OF MARIA BURMANUS *NÉE* HEYDANUS (1628-1706),
SEATED THREE-QUARTER-LENGTH AT A TABLE BY A CURTAIN, WEARING A BLACK
DRESS WITH LACE COLLAR, CUFFS AND BONNET.,,117 x 96cm. The first with signature al
'Jan Victors', the second s and indistinctly d ar 'Johannes.Victors.fc16.5', both with signatures and
inscriptions on the reverse of the relined canvases.
PROV.: By descent to Jonkheer Mr L. van den Berch van Heemstede, The Hague; His Sale,
Venduehuis der Notarissen The Hague, 1 November 1966, lot 114.
LIT.: E.W. Mose *Iconographia Batava*, I, 1836, p. 210, no. 1836 (the woman only) as portrait of
Sara Crucius and erroneously dated 1684 G.Isarlo, 'Rembrandt et son entourage', in *La Renaissance,*
XIX,1936,no.9, p. 3, the woman only; *Het Rapenburg*, III, p. 756; *Geschiedenis van het Geslacht
Wittert*, II, pp. 1053/55, figs. 11 and 12, as *portraits of Christoph van den Berch and Sara Crucius*;
F.G.L.O. van Kretschmar, 'Verkeerd benaamde portretten van Professor; Franciscus Burmanus en
zijn vrouw', in *Jaarboek van het Centraal Bureau voor Genealogie*, XXI, 1967, pp. 87/90, figs. 10
and 11; D. Miller, *Jan Victors*, dissertation Delaware, 1983, p. 284, nos. a 17 and; A 18, with ills.; W.
Sumowski, *Gemälde der Rembrandt-Schüler*, IV, 1989, p. 2617, under; no. 1814.
      Christie's Amsterdam, 13 November 1995 (17*) NLG 34,500   US$ 21,743

GENTLEMAN TAKING REFRESHMENTS OUTSIDE THE SWANN INN oil on canvas, 89 x,121
cm. inscr. d 'De Swaan 1711'
      Christie's Amsterdam, 7 February 1996 (107*) NLG 13,800   US$ 8,404

VIEIRA DA SILVA Maria Elena (Lisbon 1908-1992) French (Portuguese)
COMPOSITION watercolour on paper laid down on board, 9 7/8 x 6 3/8in. (25.2 16.2cm.) sd 'Vieira
da Silva 50'
PROV.: Galerie Jeanne Bucher, Paris.
LIT.: Guy Weelen and Jean François Jeager *Vieira da Silva: Catalogue Raisonné*, Geneva 1994, p.
177, no.,912 (illustrated).
      Christie's London, 19 March 1996 (2**) GBP 9,200   US$ 14,050

ORANGE tempera on canvas, 15 x 21¾in. (38 x 55.5cm.) sd 'Vieira da Sliva '62'
PROV.: M. Knoedler and Co. Gallery, New York.
EXH.: New York, Knoedler Gallery, *Vieira da Silva*, Oct.-Nov. 1963.
LIT.: Guy Weelen and François Jaeger, *Vieira da Silva: Catalogue Raisonné*, Geneva, 1994, p. 372,

no. 1844 (illustrated).
        Christie's London, 26 October 1995 (5**) GBP 29,900   US\$ 47,191

MANOIR EN SOLOGNE oil on canvas, 19 6/8 x 24in. (50 x 61cm.) sdlr '49
PROV.: Galerie Pierre, Paris; Collection Collinet, Paris.
EXH.: Basel, Kunsthalle, *Germaine Richier, Bissière, H. R. Schiess, Vieira da Silva, Raoul Ubac*,
June-July 1954, no.,105 (illustrated in the catalogue, titled *Saint-Sépulcre*); Hanover, Kestner-
Gesellschaft; Wuppertal, Kunst-und Museumsverein; Bremen, Kunstverein, *Vieira da Silva*, March-
June 1958, no. 32 (titled Saint-Sépulcre and dated incorrectly).
LIT.: In: 'Correio da Manha', Gilles Guilbert, *Vieira da Silva, una grande pintora portuguesa que
vive em Paris*, December 1954 (illustrated; titled *Composiçao*); Jacques Lassaigne and Guy Weelen,
Vieira da Silva, Barcelona/Paris 1978, p. 160, no. 182 (illustrated
in colour); Michel Butor, *Vieira da Silva*, Paris 1983, p. 30 (illustrated in colour); Claude Roy, *Vieira
da Silva*, Barcelona 1988, no. 18 (illustrated); Guy Weelen and Jean-François Jaeger, *Vieira da Silva:
Catalogue Raisonné 1926-1992*, Geneva 1994, p. 132, no. 673 (illustrated).
        Christie's London, 27 June 1996 (8**) GBP 87,300   US\$ 134,618

LA CAGE AUX OISEAUX oil on canvas, 25 5/8 x 31 7/8in. (65 x 81cm.) sdlr '48
PROV.: Galerie Jeanne Bucher, Paris.
EXH.: Stockholm, Galerie Blanche, *Vieira da Silva*, September-October 1950, no. 6.
LIT.: Guy Weelen and Jean-François Jaeger, *Vieira da Silva: Catalogue Raisonné 1926-1992*,
Geneva 1994, no.,586 (illustrated).
        Christie's London, 27 June 1996 (13**) GBP 78,500   US\$ 121,049

LE PRINTEMPS gouache on paper, 19¼ x 11¾in. (49 x 31cm.) sdlr 'Vieira da Silva 56'
PROV.: Albert Skira, Geneva (acquired directly from the artist in 1956); Acquired directly from the
above by the present owner.
EXH.: Geneva, Galerie du Perron, *Vieira da Silva*, 1956, no. 22, illustrated (catalogued with
incorrect title); London, The Hanover Gallery, 1957, no. 19, illustrated; Turin, Palazzo Belle Arti,
Pittori d'Oggi Francia-Italia, 1959, no. 182.
LIT.: Guy Wheelen & Francois Jaeger, *Vieira da Silva Catalogue Raisonné*, Geneva 1994, p. 272,
no. 1373, illustrated.
        Sotheby's London, 27 June 1996 (106**) GBP 12,075   US\$ 18,620

LES IRRESOLUTIONS RESOLUES XIV gouache and pencil on paper laid down on canvas, 27½ x
19½in. (70 x 49.5cm.) s twice d '69'
PROV.: Galerie Jeanne Bucher, Paris.
EXH.: Paris, Galerie Jeanne Bucher, *Vieira da Silva*, 1969, illustrated ;
Lisbon, Galeria Sao Mamede, *Vieira da Silva*, 1970, p. 75, no. 31, illustrated; Lisbon, Fundacao
Calouste Gulbenkian; Paris, Galeries Nationales du Grand Palais, *Vieira da Silva*, 1988.
LIT.: Guy Wheelen & Jean François Jeager, *Vieira da Silva Catalogue Raisonné*, Geneva 1994, p.
475, no. 2316, illustrated.
        Sotheby's London, 27 June 1996 (130**) GBP 17,250   US\$ 26,600

VIGÉE-LEBRUN Elisabeth (Marie Louise Elisabeth) (Paris 1755-1842 Paris) French
PORTRAIT OF A YOUNG BOY, THOUGHT TO BE THE DAUPHIN, LATER LOUIS XVII black
and red chalk and graphite, 15 x 9.5cm.
        Sotheby's London, 3 July 1995 (144**) GBP 13,225   US\$ 21,096

VIGNERON Piere Roch French
A YOUNG SPANISH CADET oil on canvas, 33¾ x 26¾in. (85.5 x 68cm.) sdll 'Vigneron / 1833'
        Christie's South Kensington, 14 March 1996 (236**) GBP 9,430   US\$ 14,401

VIGNON Claude (Tours 1593-1670 Paris) French
ECCE HOMO oil on canvas,,113 x 93.5cm.
        Étude Tajan Paris, 28 June 1996 (92**) FRF 60,000   US\$ 11,586

DEMOCRITUS AND HERACLES oil on canvas,,100 x 155cm.
LIT.: C. Pacht Bassani, 'Qualche inedito di Claude Vignon', in: *Richerche di Storia dell'Arte*, no. 7 1979, p. 96, fig. 13.
        Christie's Rome, 4 June 1996 (569**) ITL 20,000,000   US$ 12,970

DIOGENES LOOKING OUT FOR A HONOURABLE MAN oil on canvas,,100 x 155cm.
LIT.: C. Pacht Bassani, 'Qualche inedito di Claude Vignon', in: *Richerche di Storia dell'Arte*, no. 7 1979, p. 96, fig. 12.
        Christie's Rome, 4 June 1996 (570**) ITL 20,000,000   US$ 12,970

VIGNON Victor Alfred Paul (Villers-Cotterets 1847-1909 Meulan) French
PAYSAGE AVEC CHARRETTE oil on canvas, 18 1/8 x 15in. (46 x 38cm.) sll 'V. Vignon'; d '1886' on the stretcher
PROV.: David Findlay Galleries, New York (acquired by the present owner, 1979).
        Christie's East, 30 April 1996 (21**) US$ 10,350   US$ 10,350

VILLAGE oil on canvas, 18 1/8 x 21 7/8in. (46 x 55.5cm.) slr 'V. Vignon.'
PROV.: David Findlay Galleries, New York (acquired by the present owner, 1979).
        Christie's East, 30 April 1996 (24**) US$ 13,800   US$ 13,800

LE HAMEAU oil on canvas, 18 1/8 x 15in. (46 x 38cm.) skr 'V. Vignon.'
PROV.: David Findlay Galleries, New York (acquired by the present owner, 1979).
        Christie's East, 30 April 1996 (54***) US$ 11,500   US$ 11,500

VILLA Aleardo (1865-1906) Italian
PORTRAIT OF ELEONORA DUSE, SEATED THREE-QUARTER LENGTH oil on canvas, 55 1/8 x 33 5/8in. (,140 x 85.5cm.) sdlr 'AVilla' (linked) '92'
PROV.: Ruggero Leoncavallo; Gabriele D'Annunzio; Benito Mussolini as a gift from d'Annunzio; Albert Kohler.
        Phillips London, 14 November 1995 (88***) GBP 20,000   US$ 31,284

VILLEERS Jacob de (Leyden 1616-1667 Rotterdam) Dutch
MOUNTAINOUS LANDSCAPE WITH FIGURES oil on panel, 28½ x 39½in. (72.4 x 100.3cm.)
PROV.: Oscar Hellstrom, Sweden from whom acquired by the present owner in 1939 (Acc. no. 39.30).
EXH.: Indianapolis, John Herron Art Museum; San Diego, The Fine Arts Gallery, *The Young Rembrandt and His Times*, April 11-may 18, 1958, cat. no. 60 (attributed to Hercules Pietersz. Seghers); Tacoma, Washington, The broadway Gallery, *Old Master paintings*, 1958; Bellevue, Washington, Bellevue Art Museum, *European and American Paintings from the Seattle Art Museum Collection*, November 1975.
LIT.: W. Sumowski, *Gemälde der Rembrandt-Schüler*, 1983, Vol.IV, pp.2879, 2887, note 77 and illus., 2928.
        Sotheby's New York, 11 January 1996 (18**) US$ 11,500   US$ 11,500

WIDE WOODED LANDSCAPE WITH CASTLE, A VILLAGE BEYOND oil on panel, 67 x 88cm.
        Dorotheum Vienna, 11 June 1996 (253**) ATS 120,000   US$ 11,138

VILLON Jacques (Gaston Duchamp, {called}) (Damville (Eure) 1875-1963 Puteaux) French
EN PLEIN VOL oil on canvas, 29 x 36¼in. (73.7 x 92.1cm.) sdlr 'Jacques Villon 56'
PROV.: Galerie Louis Carré, Paris; Royal S. Marks, New York.
        Sotheby's New York, 2 May 1996 (402**) US$ 29,900   US$ 29,900

REFLEXION oil on canvas, 36 3/8 x 25¾in. (92.5 x 65.3cm.) sdll 'JACQUES VILLON 51' sd and titled on the reverse 'REFLEXIONS Jacques Villon 51'
PROV.: Galerie Louise Carré, Paris.
EXH.: Liège, Association pour le progrès intellectuel et artistique de la Wallonie, Villon, 1952, no.

36; Turin, Galleria Civica d'Arte Moderna, *Peintres d'aujourd'hui*, France-ltalie, 1953; Albi, Musée Toulouse-Lautrec, *Exposition Jacques Villon*,1955, no. 41; Pittsburgh, Carnegie Institute, *The 1955 Pittsburgh International Exhibition of Contemporary Painting*, 1955, no. 313, (illustrated pl.119); Salisbury, The Rhodes National Gallery, *Rembrandt to Picasso*, 1957, no. 160; Oslo, Kunstnernes Hus, *Jacques Villon*, 1959-60, no. 54; Bergen, Bergens Kunstforening, *Jacques Villon; Maleri*, 1960, no. 64; Stockholm, Moderne Museet, *Jacques Villon, Maleri och Grafik 1902-1959*, 1960, no. 64; Paris, Musée Galliéra, *10 ans de Biennale de Menton: Les Grands Prix*, 1960, no. 12; Paris, Galerie Charpentier; Gendt, *Tableaux de Jacques Villon*, 1961, no.78 (illustrated); Sao Paolo, Museo de Arte Moderna, *VI Bienal de Sao Paolo*, Sept-Dec. 1961, no. 26; Zurich, Kunsthaus, *Jacques Villon*, 1963, no. 57.
LIT.: P. Cabanne, 'Le Trio Duchamps', in *Connaisance des Arts*, 1975, no.,214 (illustrated p. 227).

Christie's London, 29 November 1995 (234**) GBP 12,000	US$	18,771

VINCKBOONS David (Malines/Mechelen 1576-1632 c. Amsterdam) Flemish
LE DÉPART POUR LA FOIRE oil on canvas, 57 x 104.5cm.
PROV.: Collection Paul Delaroff, 1914; His sale, Paris, Galerie Georges Petit, 23-24 April 1914 (Maître Lair Dubreuil), no. 19 (as *Brueghel and Peeter Snayers*)(,920 FF to Sortais); Sale collection M G.S., Paris, Hôtel Drouot, 10 June 1925, no. 11 (illustrated, as *Pieter Brueghel the Younger*).

Étude Tajan Paris, 12 December 1995 (8**) FRF 200,000	US$	40,285

WALDLANDSCHAFT MIT BIBLISCHER FIGURENSTAFFAGE oil on panel, 34.5 x 55.5cm.
PROV.: 609. Lempertz-auktion, Köln, 21-11-1985, Lot 231; Rheinische Privatsammlung.

Lempertz Cologne, 18 May 1996 (1170*) DEM 33,000	US$	21,514

VINCKBOONS David {studio of} (Malines/Mechelen 1576-1632 c. Amsterdam) Flemish
ELEGANT COMPANY FEASTING AND MAKING MUSIC IN A GARDEN oil on panel, 20¼ x 32¼in. (51.2 x 82.2cm.)

Sotheby's London, 5 July 1995 (283**) GBP 16,100	US$	25,682

VINEA Francesco (Forli 1845-1902 Florence) Italian
REVERLY oil on canvas, 19 5/8 x 23½in. (49.9 x 59.7cm.) sdlr 'F.Vinea/FIRENZE 1883'

Christie's New York, 14 February 1996 (109**) US$ 14,950	US$	14,950

A MERRYMENT oil on canvas laid down on masonite, 29 x 39in. (73.8 x 99cm.) slr 'Vines'

Christie's East, 13 February 1996 (187**) US$ 6,900	US$	6,900

VINOGRADOV Sergei Arsenevich (1869-1938) Russian
LANDSCAPE WITH ISBA oil on canvas, 27 x 21in. (68.5 x 53.4cm.) sdlr in cyrillic 'S. Vinogradov, 1896'

Christie's New York, 18 April 1996 (24**) US$ 9,200	US$	9,200

VITALE Filippo (Napels 1585 c.-1650) Italian
JACOB GIVING BLESSING TO ISAÄC oil on canvas, 96 x 125cm.
PROV.: Collection Majetti, Rome (until 1922).
LIT.: R. Longhi, 'G.B. Spinelli e i naturalisti napoletani del Seicento', in *Paragone*, 1969, n. 227, pp 42-52, (attributed Annella De Rosa); R. Causa, 'La pittura del Seicento a Napoli dal naturalismo al barocco', in AA. VV., *Storia di Napoli*, vol. V, Tome II, Cava de' Tirreni, 1972, p. 929; F. Bologna in AA.VV., *Battistello Caracciolo e il primo naturalismo a Napoli*, catalogue, Naples, 1991, pp. 78, 136-138,,178 note 241, fig. 95, p. 110.

Christie's Rome, 21 November 1995 (229**) ITL 60,000,000	US$	37,665

VITALI Candido (Bologna 1680-1753 Bologna) Italian
TROPHÉE DE CHASSE AUX OISEAUX; TROPHÉE DE CHASSE AU LIEVRE oil on canvas (a pair), each: 54.5 x 66cm.

Étude Tajan Paris, 25 June 1996 (32**) FRF 145,000	US$	27,999

VITRINGA Wigerus (Leeuwarden 1657-1721 Wirdum) Dutch
A CALM WITH GALLIOTS AT ANCHOR, A ROWING BOAT PUTTING OUT AND A MAN-
O'-WAR oil on canvas, 15½ x 19in. (39.3 x 48.3cm.) bears ini. lc 'WVV'
      Sotheby's London, 6 December 1995 (216**) GBP 10,350   US$ 15,928

VIVARINI Bartolomeo (ca. 1432-ca. 1499) Italian
THE MADONNA AND CHILD oil on canvas, transferred from panel, 24 x 18¼in. (61 x 46.4cm.)
sdlr or inscr. 'BARTHOLOMES VIVARINVS/ DE MVRIANO PINXIT 148(1?)
PROV.: Baron M. Lazzaroni, Rome; Newhouse Galleries, Inc. New York, 1936.
      Sotheby's New York, 16 May 1996 (191**) US$ 28,750   US$ 28,750

VIVIN Louis (1861-1936) French
L'OPERA A PARIS oil on canvas, 28¾ x 36¼in. (73 x 92cm.) sll 'L. VIVIN'
PROV.: Perls Galleries, New York; Mr. and Mrs. Peter A. Ruibel, New York Gift to the Phoenix Art
Museum, 1964).
EXH.: El Paso, Museum of Art, *French Paintings and Sculpture from the Phoenix Art Museum
Collection*, June-Sept. 19,665, no. 54 (illustrated).
      Christie's East, 7 November 1995 (61**) US$ 23,000   US$ 23,000

VLAMINCK Maurice de (Paris 1876-1958 Rueil-la-Gadelière (Eure-et-Loire)) French
LE CHAMPS DE BLÉS oil on canvas, 25 x 31 1/8in. (63.5 x 79cm.) sll 'Vlaminck'
PROV.: Dr. and Mrs. M. B. Sulzberger, San Franciso; sale, Parke-Bernet Galleries Inc., New York,
19 Jan,. 1950, lot 67 (illustrated); Maxwell Galleries Ltd., San Francisco (acquired by Richard Smart,
1972).
LIT.: The Wildenstein Institute will include this painting in the forthcoming *Vlaminck catalogue
raisonné*.
      Christie's New York, 1 May 1996 (162**) US$ 123,500   US$ 123,500

LE MOULIN oil on canvas, 23 5/8 x 31 7/8in. (60 x 81cm.) slr 'Vlamink'
LIT.: The Wildenstein Institute will include this painting in their forthcoming *catalogue raisonné M.
de Vlamink*.
      Christie's New York, 1 May 1996 (336**) US$ 101,500   US$ 101,500

LA TABLE DE CUISINE oil on canvas, 32 x 46in. (81.4 x 117cm.) sll 'Vlaminck' (ca. 1932)
PROV.: Dr. A. Roudinesco, Paris (acquired from the artist); Anon. sale, Parke-Bernet Galleries Inc.,
New York, 10 Oct. 1968, lot 52.
LIT.: R. Rey, *Maurice de Vlaminck*, Paris 1955, pl. 27 (illustrated); The Wildenstein Institute will
include this painting in their forthcoming *Vlaminck catalogue raisonné*.
      Christie's New York, 1 May 1996 (405**) US$ 79,500   US$ 79,500

LE TOIT ROUGE oil on canvas, 21¼ x 28/4in. (54 x 73cm.) slr 'Vlaminck' (ca. 1912)
PROV.: Hjalmar Gallberg, Stockholm.
EXH.: Stockholm, Liljevalchs Konsthall, *Fran Cézanne till Picasso-Fransk Konst i Svensk Ago*,
Sept. 1954 (possibly no. 388, *Paysage*).
      Christie's Tel Aviv, 12 October 1995 (51**) US$ 92,700   US$ 92,700

RUE EN HIVER gouache and watercolour on paper, sizes not indicated slr 'Vlaminck'
PROV.: James Vigeveno Galleries, Los Angeles.
      Sotheby's New York, 2 May 1996 (369**) US$ 43,125   US$ 43,125

PAYSAGE oil on canvas, 23 5/8 x 28¾in. (60 x 73cm.) s
LIT.: This work will be included in the forthcoming *catalogue raisonné* by the Wildenstein Institute.
      Sotheby's New York, 2 May 1996 (381**) US$ 101,500   US$ 101,500

LE TOURNANT oil on can vas, 21¼ x 25¼in. (54 x 64cm.) sll 'Vlaminck' (1930)
PROV.: Wildenstein & Co., New York; anon sale Christie's, London 1 Dec. 1970, lot 70 (GBP

10,500).
EXH.: On loan, Santa Barbara, Museum of Art.
       Christie's London, 26 June 1996 (182**) GBP 58,700   US$ 90,517

VASE DE FLEURS oil on canvas, 24 x 18¼in. (61 x 46.3cm.) sll 'Vlaminck'
       Christie's London, 26 June 1996 (236**) GBP 52,100   US$ 80,339

JEUNE FEMME DANS UN POTAGER oil on canvas, 32 x 39½in. (81 x 100cm.) sll 'Vlaminck'
PROV.: Georges Bernheim, Paris; Georges Luney, New York; his sale Parke Bernet, New York, 7
Nov. 1975 lot 62.
       Christie's London, 26 June 1996 (308**) GBP 80,700   US$ 124,441

LA MAISON FERMÉE oil on canvas, 21½ x 18½in. (54.5 x 47cm.) slr indistinctly (ca. 1922)
PROV.: Acquired in the 1920's by the grandfather of the present owner.
       Phillips London, 27 November 1995 (19**) GBP 11,000   US$ 17,206

LE MOULIN oil on canvas, 60 x 81cm. slr 'Vlaminck'
       Étude Tajan Paris, 27 October 1995 (29**) FRF 230,000   US$ 46,523

SCENE DE RUE oil on canvas, 50 x 65cm. sll 'Vlaminck'
LIT.: This painting will be included in the forthcoming *catalogue raisonné Maurice de Vlaminck*,
currently being prepared by the Wildenstein Institute.
       Étude Tajan Paris, 28 March 1996 (48**) FRF 220,000   US$ 43,487

SCENE DE PARIS oil on canvas, 32 x 29¼in. (81 x 100cm.) sll 'Vlaminck' (ca 1919)
PROV.: Galerie Pétridès, Paris.
       Christie's London, 29 November 1995 (125**) GBP 57,000   US$ 89,160

ROUTE DE VILLGE oil on canvas, 25¾ x 32in. (65.4 x 81.2cm.) slr 'Vlaminck'
PROV.: M. Lewin, by whom given to the Tel Aviv Museum of Art.
       Christie's London, 29 November 1995 (189**) GBP 40,000   US$ 62,568

MAISONS oil on canvas, 25 1/2 x 31 7/8in. (64.8 x 81cm.) ll 'Vlaminck'
PROV.: Galerie Paul Pétridès, Paris; David B.Findlay, Inc., New York (acquired by Mrs. Sherburn
M.Becker, 1959).
       Christie's New York, 8 November 1995 (201**) US$ 200,500   US$ 200,500

VASE DE FLEURS oil on canvas, 20¾ x 17¾in. (52.8 x 45.1cm.) lr 'Vlaminck'
PROV.: Etienne Bignou, Paris; George Lurcy; sale, Parke-Bernet Galleries, New York, Nov. 7, 1957,
lot 50; Clifford Michel, New York; M. Knoedler & Co., New York (acquired by Mrs. Sherburn
M.Becker, 1959).
       Christie's New York, 8 November 1995 (233**) US$ 66,300   US$ 66,300

LES VOILIERS oil on canvas, 28¾ x 36 1/4in. (73 x 92cm.) ll 'Vlaminck'
PROV.: M.Cetinet, Chatou; Galerie Drouant-David, Paris.
       Christie's New York, 8 November 1995 (256**) US$ 112,500   US$ 112,500

VLIEGER Simon Jacobsz. de (attr.) (Rotterdam 1600-1653 Weesp) Dutch
FISHING BOATS AND A DUTCH STATE YACHT IN CALM WATER oil on canvas, 53 x 69cm.
PROV.: Sale 1933 Dorotheum auction no. 418, catalogue no. 43 (illustrated as *Simon de Vlieger*
(ATS 2,500, todays course ATS 120,000) to the father of the present owner.
       Dorotheum Vienna, 6 March 1996 (271**) ATS 220,000   US$ 21,162

VLIET Don, van (Los Angeles 1941b.) American
LIGHT RUBBER MOUNTAINS IN THE DISTANCE STRETCHED oil on canvas,,162 x 130cm.
sd and titled 'Van Vliet 1987 Light Rubber Mountains In The Distance Stretched'

PROV.: Galerie Michael Werner, Köln (with labels on the reverse).
        Lempertz Cologne, 31 May 1996 (502**) DEM 16,000   US$ 10,431

VOERMAN Jan Snr (Kampen 1857-1941 Hattem) Dutch
COWS ALONG THE RIVER IJSSEL oil on panel, 31 x 52 cm s with ini. 'J.V.' and stamped on the
reverse 'nalatenschap Jan Voerman'
PROV.: Kunsthandel François Buffa et Fils, Amsterdam.
        Christie's Amsterdam, 25 April 1996 (80*) NLG 17,250   US$ 10,250

VOGEL Cornelis Johannes de (Dordrecht 1824-1879 Dordrecht) Dutch
A MYTHOLOGICAL SCENE oil on canvas, 72½ x 74in. (184.1 x 188cm.) sd on the reverse
'C.Vogel/1816'
        Christie's East, 13 February 1996 (2**) US$ 7,475   US$ 7,475

**VOGELAER Carel van, {called} Distelblom (Carlo dei Fiori) (Maastricht 1653-1695 Rome)
Dutch**
STILL LIFE OF FLOWERS IN A GLASS VASE: 'THE BLACK ROSE' oil on canvas, 24¾ x
19¼in. (62.9 x 48.9cm.)
        Sotheby's New York, 11 January 1996 (74**) US$ 46,000   US$ 46,000

A STILL-LIFE OF FLOWERS IN A VASE oil on canvas, 37 x 29¼in. (94 x 74cm.)
        Sotheby's London, 17 April 1996 (4**) GBP 16,100   US$ 24,412

VOGELER Heinrich (Bremen 1872-1942 Kasachstan) German
HAMBURGER HAFEN oil on canvas, 35.5 x 60.5cm. sdlr 'H VOGELER 28'
        Hauswedell & Nolte Cologne, 1 December 1995 (619**) DEM 16,500   US$ 11,448

VOIS Ary de (Utrecht 1632 c.-1680 Leyden) Dutch
FISHERMAN oil on panel, 21 x 16cm.
        Bukowskis Stockholm, 29-31 May 1996 (296**) SEK 62,000   US$ 9,118

VOLLERDT Johan Christian (Leipzig 1708-1769 Dresden) German
LANDSCAPES WITH FIGURES oil on panel (a set of four paintings), each: 9½ x 13½in. (24.1 x
34.3cm.) two panel inscr. (Hackert)
        Sotheby's New York, 16 May 1996 (67**) US$ 79,500   US$ 79,500

VOLLMAR Ludwig (Säckingen 1842-1884 Munich) German
SPIEL MIT KÄTZCHEN oil on canvas, 69 x 56cm. sll 'L. Vollmar München'
        Dorotheum Vienna, 6 November 1995 (71**) ATS 140,000   US$ 14,044

WINDING WOOL oil on canvas, 36 x 26in. (89 x 66cm.) s inscr. 'Ludwig Vollmar München'
        Christie's London, 15 March 1996 (13**) GBP 19,550   US$ 29,856

VOLLON Alexis (Paris 1865-1945) French
A VIEW OF THE PONT ALEXANDRE III WITH THE EIFFEL TOWER AND LES INVALIDES
IN THE DISTANCE oil on canvas, 25½ x 32in. (64.7 x 81.2cm.) slr 'Alexis Vollon'
        Christie's East, 20 May 1996 (266**) US$ 13,800   US$ 13,800

VOLLON Antoine (Lyon 1833-1900 Paris) French
STILL-LIFE WITH FRUIT, A BOWL AND A PORCELAIN DISH oil on canvas, 66 x 54cm. slr 'A
Vollon'
        A. Mak B.V. Dordrecht, 21 June 1996 (348*) NLG 11,000   US$ 6,427

VOLTZ Friedrich Johann (Nördlingen 1817-1886 Munich) German
CATTLE IN A FARMYARD ALONG A RIVER WITH A FISHERMAN BEYOND oil on panel,
13¾ x 25¼in. (35 x 64.2cm.) sdll 'Fr. Voltz 1881.'

Christie's New York, 2 November 1995 (60**) US$ 34,500   US$ 34,500

VONCK Jan (Jacobus) (1630 c.-1662 c.) Dutch
A SCARLET MACAW PERCHED IN A TREE WITH A MOORHEN AND DUCKS IN A
LANDSCAPE oil on canvas, 54½ x 32in. (138.5 x 81.3cm.)
    Christie's South Kensington, 7 December 1995 (268**) GBP 10,350   US$ 15,928

VOORDEN August Willem van (Rotterdam 1881-1921 Rotterdam) Dutch
MORGENSTEMMING oil on canvas,,101 x 51cm. sdlr 'August W. v. Voorden 1908' s inscr. with
the title on a label on the stretcher
PROV.: Kunsthandel D. Vaarties, Rotterdam.
    Christie's Amsterdam, 26 October 1995 (75*) NLG 11,500   US$ 7,251

VOORT Cornelis Pietersz van der (Antwerp (?) 1576-1624 Amsterdam) Dutch
PORTRAITS OF A GENTLEMAN AND HIS WIFE oil on canvas (a pair), each: 78¾ x 50in. (,200
x 127cm.) d inscr. 'Ætatis. fuæ. 26. / Anno. 1618' and d inscr. 'Ætatis. fuæ. 19. / Anno. 1618'
PROV.: With Leggatts, London, from whom acquired by the late owner in 1961, as by *Michiel van
Miereveldt.*
    Sotheby's London, 5 July 1995 (8**) GBP 56,500   US$ 90,126

VOS Cornelis de (Hulst, near Antwerp 1585-1651 Antwerp) Belgian
PORTRAIT OF A LADY IN ELEGANT DRESS oil on panel, 41¾ x 28¾in. (,106 x 73cm.) s mono.
'DV'
PROV.: Frederick James Lamb, Viscount Melbourne (died 1853), Melbourne House, London, where
acquired in 1855 (either by purchase or by descent) by Francis, Earl of Cowper, Panshanger,
Hertfordshire; Lady Desborough, Panshanger, Hertfordshire; Duits, Ltd, London, from whom
acquired by Maurice H. Goldblatt, Duits, Ltd., acting on behalf of Lewis J. Ruskin, Scottsdale,
Arizona; thence descent to the present owner.
LIT.: M.L. Boyle, *Portraits at Panshanger*, 1885, p. 373.
    Sotheby's New York, 16 May 1996 (18**) US$ 68,500   US$ 68,500

VOS Maerten I de (Antwerp 1532-1603 Antwerp) Flemish
THE TRIUMPH OF DAVID oil on panel, 20¼ x 30 3/8in. (51.5 x 77cm.) sdll 'F. MERTE/DE.
VOS/1576.'
PROV.: Anonymous Sale, Cologne 26 March 1971, no. 355.
LIT.: A. Zweite, *Marten de Vos als Maler*, Berlin 1981, no. 61, p. 290.
    Libert & Castor Paris, 29 November 1995 (46**) FFr 180,000   US$ 36,835

VOS Maerten I de (attr.) (Antwerp 1532-1603 Antwerp) Flemish
ADORATION OF THE MAGI oil on panel, 42¾ x 29¾in. (108.6 x 75.6cm.)
    Sotheby's New York, 6 October 1996 (125**) US$ 37,375   US$ 37,375

VOS Paul de (Hulst 1592-1678 Antwerp) Belgian
DOGS BRINGING DOWN A STAG oil on canvas (cooperation with Jan Wildens (1586-1653), 38¾
66 1/4in. (98.4 x 168.3cm.)
PROV.: Captain Fraser Mckenzie, Netley park, Gurnshall; Christie's 1 July 1927, lot 127, as Snyders
(32gns. to Leger); Anon. Sale, Christie's 18 April 1978, lot 97; Anon. Sale, Christie's 31 Oct. 1980,
lot 79.
    Christie's London, 8 December 1995 (208**) GBP 33,350   US$ 51,323

A HUNTING SCENE oil on linen,,136 x 158cm. framed
PROV.: Private collection, Belgium.
    Lempertz Cologne, 15 November 1995 (1430**) DEM 28,000   US$ 19,763

A COCKEREL ATTACKING A TURKEY COCK AND OTHER DOMESTIC FOWL IN A RIVER
LANDSCAPE oil on canvas, 47 7/8 x 72in. (121.7 x 182.8cm.) sll 'P D. VOS.F.'

PROV.: Anon. Sale, Bukowski's, Stockholm, 21 Feb. 1935, lot 29.
    Christie's London, 20 October 1995 (104**) GBP 17,250   US$ 27,225

VOS Simon de (Antwerp 1603-1676 Antwerp) Flemish
THE MASSACRE OF THE INNOCENTS; THE SEVEN ACTS OF MERCY oil on copper (a pair),
each: 21¼ x 27½in. (54 x 70cm.)
    Sotheby's London, 17 April 1996 (72**) GBP 21,850   US$ 33,131

CHRIST IN THE HOUSE OF MARTHA AND MARY oil on panel, 21¼ x 31½in. (54 x 80cm.)
    Christie's South Kensington, 18 april 1996 (18**) GBP 5,520   US$ 8,370

VOSMAER Jacob Woutersz. (Delft 1584-1641) Dutch
A STILL-LIFE OF FLOWERS IN A GLASS VASE PARTLY FRAMED WITHIN A MARBLE
NICHE oil on oak panel, 30¼ x 24¼in. (76.5 x 61.5cm.) sdll 'Jacob W. Vosmaer. 1619'
PROV.: With M. Knoedler & Co., London, New York or Paris, 1928; Anonymous sale, London,
Sotheby's, 8 April 1970, lot 73, GBP3,800 to Brod Gallery; With KJ. Müllenmeister, Solingen, 1971;
With Berry-Hill, New York, 1976; Anonymous sale, New York, Christie's, 12January 1978, lot 126;
Private collection, Rotterdam; Anonymous sale, Monaco, Christie's, l9 June 1988, lot 12; With Pieter
de Boer, Amsterdam, from whom acquired by the late owner.
LIT.: R. Warner, *Dutch and Flemish Fruit and Flower Paintings of the XVIIth and XVIIIth
Centuries*, 1928, p. 227, reproduced plate 108c; L. Bol, *'Goede Onbekenden'*, 1982, p. 89-90,
reproduced p. 90, fig. 8; B. Brenninkmeijer-de Rooy, *Boeketten de Gouden Eeuw*, exhibition
catalogue, 1992, p. 104, no. 27.
    Sotheby's London, 6 December 1995 (59**) GBP 155,500   US$ 239,304

VRANCX Sebastiaen (Antwerp 1573-1647 Antwerp) Flemish
FARMER WORKING IN THE PALACE GARDEN, ALLEGORY ON THE SPRING oil on panel,
26 x 37cm.
    Dorotheum Vienna, 6 March 1996 (94**) ATS 220,000   US$ 21,162

SOLDIERS ATTACKING A CONVOY ON A COUNTRY ROAD oil on panel, 50 x 65.3cm
PROV.: Mrs Westendorp; Sale, Frederik Muller Amsterdam, 8 July 1941, lot 1, as *Pieter Balten*;
Anon. Sale, Frederik Muller Amsterdam, 14 October 1941, lot 291, as *Pieter Balten*.
    Christie's Amsterdam, 13 November 1995 NLG 57,500   US$ 36,239

VRANX Sebastian (and Studio) (Antwerp 1573-1647) Flemish
CAVALRY ENGAGEMENT oil on panel, 19¾ x 33¾in. (50 x 85.5cm.)
    Sotheby's London, 18 October 1995 (40**) GBP 24,150   US$ 38,116

**VREDEMAN DE VRIES Paul & Frans Francken the Younger (1567-1630) (Antwerp 1566-
1630 c. Amsterdam) Dutch**
SALOME PRESENTING THE HEAD OF ST JOHN THE BAPTIST TO KING HEROD oil on
panel, 24¼ x 35¼in. (61.5 x 89.8cm.) (ca. 1610-1615)
LIT.: G. Glück, *Die Sammlung Tritsch*, pp. 19-41 (illustrated); U. Härting, *Frans Francken der
Jüngere*, 1989, p. 259, no. 98 (illustrated).
    Sotheby's London, 17 April 1996 (59**) GBP 28,750   US$ 43,594

VREEDENBURGH Cornelis (Woerden 1880-1946 Laren) Dutch
A VIEW OF THE KEIZERSGRACHT, AMSTERDAM oil on canvas, 40 x 60 cm sd and inscr. with
title 'C. Vreedenburgh, 1928'
    Christie's Amsterdam, 25 April 1996 (87*) NLG 18,400   US$ 10,934

A VIEW OF THE AMSTEL, AMSTERDAM oil on canvas, 81.5 x 128cm. sd 'C. Vreedenburgh
1927'
    Christie's Amsterdam, 25 April 1996 (206**) NLG 115,000   US$ 68,334

A RIVER-VESSEL ON THE IJ, AMSTERDAM WITH THE THE DOME OF THE RONDE
LUTHERSE KERK BEYOND oil on canvas, 82 x 127cm. sdlr 'C Vreedenburgh 1921'
Christie's Amsterdam, 26 October 1995 (177**) NLG 17,250   US$ 10,876

VREL Jacobus (1654 c. active, maybe in Delft) Dutch
A COBBLED STREET IN A TOWN WITH FIGURES oil on panel, 14¼ x 11in. (36.3 x 27.8cm.)
Sotheby's London, 5 July 1995 (6**) GBP 32,200   US$ 51,364

A DUTCH INTERIOR WITH A WOMAN SEATED BEFORE A FIREPLACE oil on panel, 25½ x
18¾in. (65 x 48cm.) (1650's)
PROV.: Duyvendijk, The Hague; with the Brod Gallery, London.
Sotheby's London, 5 July 1995 (7**) GBP 51,000   US$ 81,353

VRIES Dirck de (Friesland 1590 - 1609 active Venice) Dutch
A MASKED FEAST oil on canvas, 42½ x 63in. (107.8 x 160cm.)
PROV.: Count Karatsonyi de Karatsonyfalva et Beddra, his sale, Berlin, 24 February 1930, lot 32, as
Pozzoserrato.
LIT.: R.A. Peltzer, 'Lod. Toeput (Pozzoserrato) und die Landschaftsfresken der Villa Maser', in
Münchner Jahrbuch der bildenden Kunst, series x, 1933, p. 278, reproduced fig. 7; B.W. Meijer, 'A
proposito della Vanita della ricchezza e di Ludovico Pozzoserrato', in *Toeput a Treviso*, 1988, p. 118,
reproduced fig. 19, as by de Vries and whereabouts unknown.
Sotheby's London, 6 December 1995 (226**) GBP 16,100   US$ 24,777

**VRIES Roelof Jansz van (erroneously 'Jan Reynier') (Haarlem 1630/31-1681 after Amsterdam)
Dutch**
FARMERHOUSES AT A FOREST-ROAD oil on panel, 24 x 31cm. slc 'r. Vries'
Dorotheum Vienna, 6 March 1996 (133**) ATS 120,000   US$ 11,543

WOODED RIVERLANDSCAPE WITH A CASTLE AND A HORSEMAN oil on panel, 28 x
34.5cm. sll 'R. vries'
Dorotheum Vienna, 11 June 1996 (251**) ATS 75,000   US$ 6,961

FARMHOUSE ON THE RIVERSIDE WITH TRAVELLERS oil on canvas, 48 x 65cm. sll 'R. Vries,
f.'
LIT.: Vgl. Walther Bernt, *Die Niederländischen Maler*, Bd. ill. no. 265.
Dorotheum Vienna, 17 October 1995 (137**) ATS 200,000   US$ 20,061

A FORRESTLANDSCAPE WITH WANDERERS oil on panel, 63 x 49.5cm. (framed)
PROV.: United States, private collection.
Dorotheum Vienna, 17 October 1995 (140**) ATS 75,000   US$ 7,523

VROOM Cornelis Hendricksz. (Haarlem 1591 c.-1661 Haarlem) Dutch
RIVERLANDSCAPE WITH A FISHERMAN'S BOAT, A CITY BEYOND oil on panel, 21 x 28cm.
PROV.: Sale, Christie's, 19 March 1875.
Dorotheum Vienna, 11 June 1996 (246**) ATS 180,000   US$ 16,708

VUCHT Gerrit van (1610-1697 Schiedam) Dutch
A WOODEN BOX, BOOKS, A LUTE, A *FACON-DE-VENISE* WINEGLASS AND BOTTLES ON
A DRAPED LEDGE oil on panel, 34.5 x 27.3cm.
Christie's Amsterdam, 13 November 1995 (40*) NLG 23,000   US$ 14,495

VUCHT Jan van der (1603-1637) Dutch
A CHURCH INTERIOR WITH CHRIST DRIVING OUT THE MONEY-CHANGERS oil on panel,
16¾ x 21¼in. (42.5 x 54cm.) s 'I.v.vucht'
Christie's London, 8 December 1995 (236**) GBP 13,225   US$ 20,352

CHURCH INTERIORS WITH FIGURES oil on panel (a pair), each 7 3/8 x 8 7/8in. (18.7 x 22.5cm.)
one slr with monogram
PROV.: Mme. Karel Ooms-van Eersel, Antwerp (Sale: Antwerp, 15 May 1922, lot 813, as by W. van
der Vliet, only one picture mentioned in catalogue (the monogrammed painting of the present pair
with the red wax seal of the sale on the reverse).
Sotheby's New York, 11 January 1996 (159**) US$ 23,000 — US$ 23,000

THE INTERIOR OF A RENAISSANCE-STYLE CHURCH WITH AN ELEGANT COUPLE
STANDING NEAR THE ENTANCE, A BEGGAR SEATED NEARBY oil on panel, 42.5 x 52.8cm.
sll 'J.v.Vucht'
PROV.: Anon. Sale, Sotheby`s London, 24 March 1971, lot 3; Anon. sale, Sotheby`s London, 7
October 1981, lot 113.
Christie's Amsterdam, 13 November 1995 (29*) NLG 16,100 — US$ 10,147

VUILLARD Edouard (Cuiseaux (Saône-et-Loire) 1868-1940 La Baule) French
MONSIEUR ARTHUR FONTAINE DANS SON SALON oil on board laid down on board, 12 7/8 x
22¼in. (32.8 x 56.5cm.) sdll 'E Vuillard 1904'
PROV.: Arthur Fontaine, Paris; Jean-Arthur Fontaine, Paris; Arthur Tooth & Sons Ltd., London;
Anon. sale, Christie's, London, 25 March 1980, lot. 20 (acquired by Curtis E. Calder).
EXH.: London, Arthur Tooth & Sons Ltd., *Recent acquisitions*, Nov.-Dec. 1960, no. 21 (illustrated);
London, Arthur Tooth & Sons Ltd., *E. Vuillard, A Loan Exhibition in Aid of Dorton House School
for Blind Children, Sevenoaks*, April-May 1969, no. 9 (illustrated).
Christie's New York, 1 May 1996 (142**) US$ 107,000 — US$ 107,000

FEMME DANS L'ATELIER oil on board, 12¾ x 14 7/8in. (32.4 x 37.8cm.) sll 'E. Vuillard' (ca.
1915)
PROV.: A.M.G. Bernheim de Villers, Paris; Mrs. Bruce Kelham; Galerie Salis, Salzburg; Acquired
from the above by Mrs. Joanne Toor Cummings.
EXH.: Paris, Galerie Bernheim de Villers, *Vuillard*, Nov. 1909, no. 57; Paris, Musée des Arts
Decoratifs, *E. Vuillard*, May-July 1938, p. 24, no. 134; San Francisco, California Palace of the
Legion of Honor, *Edouard Vuillard, 1868-1940*, Nov. 1971, no. 446.
LIT.: This painting will be included in the forthcoming *catalogue raisonné* being prepared by
Antoine Salomon and Annette Leduc Beaulieu from the records and under the responsibility of
Antoine Salomon.
Christie's New York, 30 April 1996 (22**) US$ 118,000 — US$ 118,000

VASE DE FLEURS oil on board laid down on cradled panel, 18¾ x 23¾in. (47.5 x 60.3cm.) sur 'E.
Vuillard' (1906)
PROV.: Galerie Bernheim-Jeune, Paris; Emile Laffon, Paris (acquired from the above, 1907); Mme
Potel, Paris; Galerie Druet, Paris; Arthur Tooth & Sons Ltd., London; Lady Baillie-Witney, London
(acquired from the above); Marlborough Gallery, London (ca. 1953); A. & R. Ball, New York
(acquired by the late owner, 1956).
EXH.: London, Arthur Tooth & Sons Ltd., *Recent Acquisitions*, Nov.-Dec. 1947, no. 18; London,
Marlborough Gallery, *Paintings and Drawings by European Masters*, Nov.-Dec., 1953, no. 31;
London, Marlborough Gallery, *Roussel, Bonnard, Vuillard*, May-June, 1954, no. 69 (illustrated);
New York, Parke-Bernet Galleries Inc., *Art Treasures Exhibition*, June, 1955, no. 103.
LIT.: This painting will be included in the forthcoming *Vuillard catalogue raisonné* being prepared
by Antoine Salomon and Annette Leduc Beaulieu from the records and under the responsibility of
Antoine Salomon.
Christie's New York, 1 May 1996 (163**) US$ 134,500 — US$ 134,500

VUE DE LA FENETRE oil on board, 12 1/8 x 7 7/8in. (31 x 20cm.) slr stamp 'E. Vuillard' (1889-90)
PROV.: Paul Guillaume, Paris; James Vigeveno Galleries, Los Angeles (acquired from the above);
acquired by the family of the present owner in 1954.
LIT.: This painting will be included in the forthcoming *Vuillard catalogue raisonné* being prepared
by Antoine Salomon and Annette Leduc Beaulieu from the records and under the responsability of

Antoine Salomon.
      Christie's New York, 1 May 1996 (176**) US$ 79,500   US$ 79,500

PORTRAIT OF FELIX VALLOTON oil on cardboard, 10¼ x 8¾in. (26 x 22cm.) slr stamped (ca. 1897)
PROV.: Former collection Ker-Xavier Roussel; Paul Valloton; Madame Paul Valloton; Galerie Paul Valloton (12 March 1949).
EXH.: Basel, Kunsthalle, *Eduard Vuillard & Charles Hug*, 26 March- 1 May 1949, no. 23; Rochester, New York *Artist of La Revue Blanche*, 22 January-1 April 1984, no. 80 of the catalogue; Genève, Galerie Valloton, *Edouard Vuillard*, 22 June- 2 September 1989, no. 1 of the catalogue.
      Étude Tajan Paris, 10 June 1996 (8**) FRF 180,000   US$ 34,758

NU ASSIS mixed media, coloured crayons, gouache etc., 9 x 6¾in. (23 x 17.5cm.) slr ini. 'ev'
PROV.: Sale Natanson, no. 85; Galerie Bernheim Jeune, Paris; Private collection, Paris.
      Étude Tajan Paris, 13 December 1995 (47**) FRF 170,000   US$ 34,242

CHEVAL AU PATURAGE pastel on paper, 7 5/8 x 6¼in. (19.4 x 15.9cm.) stamped with signature (Lugt no. 2497a) (ca. 1890)
      Sotheby's New York, 2 May 1996 (131**) US$ 26,450   US$ 26,450

LA SALLE A MANGER oil on board laid on cradled panel, 9½ x 18½in. (24.1 x 47cm.) s (ca. 1900)
PROV.: Alexandre Natanson, Paris; Galerie Bernheim-Jeune, Paris; The Lefevre Gallery, London; Terence Rattigan, London (sold: Sotheby's, London, July 1, 1959, lot 127, at GBP2,400); The World House Gallery Corporation, New York; Sale: Sotheby's, London, December 5, 1962, lot,152 (at GBP2,000); Arthur Tooth and Sons, London .
EXH.: London, The Lefevre Gallery, *A Group of French Paintings of the XIX and XX Centuries*, 1954, no. 19 London, Arthur Tooth and Sons, *E. Vuillard Loan Exhibition*, 1969, no. 18.
LIT.: This work is to be included in the forthcoming *Edouard Vuillard catalogue raisonné* being prepared by Antoine Salomon and Annette Leduc Beaulieu from the records and under the responsibility of Antoine Salomon.
      Sotheby's New York, 2 May 1996 (150**) US$ 107,000   US$ 107,000

CHEZ MAXIME oil on paper laid down on board, 19½ x 19½in. (49.9 x 49.5cm.) s stamped (1905)
PROV.: Jacques Roussel, Paris; Galerie Motte, Geneva; Acquired from the above by the present owner on November 18, 1961.
EXH.: Lyon, Musée des Beaux-Arts; Barcelona, Caixa de Pensions; Nantes, Musée des Beaux-Arts, *Vuillard*, 1990-91, p. 27.
      Sotheby's New York, 2 May 1996 (151**) US$ 90,500   US$ 90,500

LES JOUEURS DE CARTES peinture a la colle on paper laid down on canvas, 17¼ x 30½in. (43.8 x 77.5cm.) s stamped
PROV.: Collection of the artist; Galerie de l'Art Moderne, Paris; Roland, Browse & Delbanco, London; Hirschl & Adler Galeries, New York; Oscar Kimelman Wallkitz, New York.
LIT.: This work will be included in the forthcoming *Edouard Vuillard catalogue raisonné* being prepared by Antoine Salomon and Annette Leduc Beaulieu from the records and under the responsibility of Antoine Salomon.
      Sotheby's New York, 2 May 1996 (155**) US$ 156,500   US$ 156,500

MARIE VUILLARD ÉCRIVANT oil on board, 14 3/8 x 11 3/8in. (36.5 x 29cm.) slr (stamped) 'E. Vuillard' (ca 1895)
PROV.: The Artist's Estate; Galerie Charpentier, Paris; E. J. Van Wisselingh & Co., Amsterdam (229), from whom purchased by the father of the present owner circa 1964.
EXH.: Paris, Galerie Charpentier, *Vuillard 1868-1940*; Milan, Palazzo Reale, Edouard Vuillard, 1959, no. 26 (illustrated). Zurich, Kunsthaus, *E. Vuillard*, 1964, no. 137; The Hague, Gemeente Museum (on loan from the present owner's father).

LIT.: J. Salomon, *Vuillard admiré par Jacques Salomon*, Paris, 1961 (illustrated p. 39); F. Russoli, *I Maestri del colore, Vuillard*, Milan, 1969 (illustrated in colour on the cover); F. Russoli, *Chefs d'oeuvres d'art, Grands Peintres, Vuillard*, Paris, l967 (illustrated in colour on the cover); J. Dugdale, *The Masters, Vuillard*, London, 1967 (colour plate IV).

Christie's London, 25 June 1996 (2**) GBP 287,500

US$ 443,331

MADAME HESSEL DANS SA CHAMBRE AU CHATEAU DES CLAYES oil on panel, 16 x 12½in. (41 x 32cm.) s 'E Vuillard' (ca 1930)
PROV.: Jos Hessel, Paris; Paul Rosenberg, Paris; Roger Bernheim, Paris; Private Collection, Paris.
EXH.: Paris, Galerie Schnit, 1991, no. 40 (illustrated in colour).

Christie's London, 25 June 1996 (3**) GBP 155,500

US$ 239,784

DAME A LA TOILETTE. LES MAINS SUR LES HANCHES thinned oil on board laid down on crandled panel, 23¾ x 21¾in. (60 x 55cm.) s stamped 'E. Vuillard' (ca 1902-03)
PROV.: Renou et Colle, circa 1950; purchased by the Grandfather of the present owner before 1968.
LIT.: To be included in the forthcoming *Vuillard catalogue raisonné* currently being prepared by Antoine Salomon and Annette Leduc Beailieu from the records.

Christie's London, 26 June 1996 (105**) GBP 36,700

US$ 56,592

L'ATELIER DE COUTURE (PREMIER PROJET) oil on canvas, 18½ x 45½in. (47 x 115cm.) (1892)
PROV.: Estate of the Artist, Paris; Wildenstein & Co., Inc., New York (circa 1949); Mrs. Charles Stachelberg (formerly Mrs. Walter Ross), New York (circa 1955); by descent to the present owner.
EXH.: Cleveland, Museum of Art, *Edouard Vuillard*, Jan.-March, 1954, p. 101. The exhibition traveled to New York, The Museum of Modern Art, April-June, 1954; New York, Wildenstein & Co., Inc., *Vuillard*, Oct.-Nov., 1964, no. 7 (illustrated); University Park, Pennsylvania, State University, *Edouard Vuillard, 1868-1940:Centennial Exhibition*, April-May,1968, no. 20 (illustrated); New York, Brooklyn Museum, *The Intimate Interiors of Edouard Vuillard*, May-July, 1990, no.,100 (illustrated in colour as the frontispiece).
LIT.: S. Preston,*Vuillard*, New York, 1985, p. 29 (illustrated); G. Groom, *Edouard Vuillard: Painter-Decorator, Patrons and Projects*, 1892-1912, New Haven, 1993, pp. 19-41(illustrated, p. 21); this painting will be included in the forthcoming *Vuillard catalogue raisonné* being prepared by Antoine Salomon and Anette Leduc Beaulieu from the records and under the responsability of Antoine Salomon.

Christie's New York, 30 April 1996 (40***) US$ 2,642,500

US$ 2,642,500

LA CHAMBRE VERTE peinture à la colle on board, 24 x 21 3/8in. (61 x 54.3cm.) sdlr 'E.Vuillard 5'
PROV.: Galerie Bernheim-Jeune, Paris (acquired from the artist on Dec. 13, 1905); Sonderbund, Cologne (acquired from the above on June 8,1912); Galerie Paul Cassirer, Berlin, M. Knoedler & Co., Inc., New York; Mr. and Mrs. Harold T. Marcus, New York (1948); Alex. Reid & Lefevre, London (1957); Mr. Claes Nordmark, Stockholm (acquired from the above in 1958).
EXH.: Paris, Galerie Bernheim-Jeune, *Vuillard*, Feb., 1911, no. 17; Cologne, Städtische Ausstellungshalle, *Sonderbund International Kunstausstellung*, May-Sept., 1912, no. 276; New York, Jacques Seligmann & Co., Inc., *Vuillard- His Dynamic Early Period* , Nov., 1948, no. 16; London, Alex. Reid & Lefevre, *Paintings by Twentieth Century French Masters*, March, 1958, p. 18, no. 17 (illustrated); Stockholm, National Museum,Fem Sekler Fransk Konst, Aug.-Nov., 1958, no. 169.
LIT.: 'Twentieth Century Artists Past and Present: Works from Exhibitions in London and Paris,' *The Illustrated London News*, March 1, 1958, p.,349 (illustrated); this painting will be included in the forthcoming *Vuillard catalogue raisonné* being prepared by antoine salomon and Anette Leduc Beaulieu from the records and under the responsability of Antoine Salomon.

Christie's New York, 30 April 1996 (42**) US$ 486,500

US$ 486,50(

LES CHARDONS pastel on tan paper laid down on board, 9¾ x 12½in. (24.8 x 31.9cm.) sll with ini. 'E.V.' (ca 1932-1938)
PROV.: F.A.R. Gallery, New York.

EXH.: Paris, Musée des Arts Decoratifs, exposition 1932 no. 9; Paris, Galerie Beaux-Arts, *pastels de Vuillard*, 1949; London, Wildenstein & o., Ltd., *pastels by Edouard Vuillard*, March 1950, no. 9; Geneva, Galerie Motte, *Edouard Vuillard*, May, 1950, no. 8.

Christie's East, 30 April 1996 (51**) US$ 10,925	US$	10,925

PORTRAIT DE MADAME VUILLARD oil on canvas, 18 1/8 x 15in. (46 x 38.1cm.) (ca 1905)
PROV.: Joan W. Payson, New York; sale, Sotheby Parke Bennet Inc., New York, Oct. 20, 1976, lot 16 (illustrated in color)($ 35,000).
EXH.: London, Wildenstein & Co., Ltd., *Edouard Vuillard*, June,1948, p. 11, no. 13; Edinburgh, Royal Scottish Academy, *Pierre Bonnard and Edouard Vuillard*, Aug.-Sept., 1948, p. 16, no. 66; Paris, Galerie Charpentier, Vuillard, 1948, no. 20; Paris, Galerie Hector Brame, *Hommage à Madame Vuillard*, Jan.-Feb., 1953, p. 29, no. 23; Milan, Palazzo Reale, *Edouard Vuillard*, Oct.-Nov., 1959, p. 31, no. 56 (illustrated); Albi, Musée Toulouse-Lautrec, *Hommage à E. Vuillard*, 1960, no. 35 (illustrated, pl. 3).
LIT.: J. Salomon, *Vuillard*, Paris, 1945, p.,105 (illustrated); A. Chastel, *Vuillard 1868-1940*, Paris, 1946 p. 31(illustrated); *Illustrated London News*, vol. 212, no. 5697, June 26, 1948, p. 717; J. Salomon, *Vuillard Admiré*, Paris, 1961, p. 95; 'Vuillard Admiré' *L'Oeil*, Nov., 1961, no. 83, p. 56; J. Salomon, *Vuillard*, Paris, 1968, p.,106 (illustrated in colour, p. 107).

Christie's New York, 7 November 1995 (28**) US$ 222,500	US$	222,500

FEMME DANS UN INTERIEUR peinture a la colle on paper laid down on canvas, 36 5/8 x 52in. (93 x 132cm.) s stamped 'E. Vuillard' (ca 1920)
PROV.: Marie Vuillard (sister of the Artist); The Joseph Rosen Foudation, New York; sale Sotheby Parke Bernet Inc., New York, May 1975, lot,115 (illustrated in colour)($ 23,000).
LIT.: This painting will be included in the forthcoming *Vuillard catalogue raisonné* being prepared by Antoine Salomon and Antoinette Leduc Beaulieu from the record and under the supervision of Antoine Salomon.N.

Christie's New York, 7 November 1995 (31**) US$ 145,500	US$	145,500

VASE D'ANEMONES SUR UNE TABLE oil on board laid down on cradled panel, 15½ x 18 5/8in. (39.4 x 47.4cm.) sbr ini 'E.V.' (ca. 1906)
PROV.: Jacques Blot, Paris; E.J. van Wisselingh & Co., Amsterdam; Estate of Edma Alma Porter, Toronto; sale, Christie's, London, 1 Dec. 1987, lot 152; Galerie Schmit, Paris.
EXH.: Montreal, Musée des Beaux-Arts, *La Canada collectionne: Peinture Européenne, Jan-Feb., 1960, no. 175; Paris, Galerie Schmit,* Maîtres Français, *XIX-XX siècles*, May-July 1988, no. 80 (illustrated in colour).

Christie's New York, 8 November 1995 (11**) US$ 233,500	US$	233,500

FLEURS ET FRUITS DANS LE PARC pastel on tan paper laid down on canvas, 36 5/8 x 36 5/8in. (96 x 96cm.) stamped with signature lr 'E Vuillard' (Lugt 2497a) (ca. 1932)
PROV.: Estate of the artist; Galerie de l'Elysée (Alex Maguy), Paris (acquired by the family of the present owner, 1967).

Christie's New York, 8 November 1995 (134**) US$ 32,200	US$	32,200

FEMME EN BLEU AUX PAVILLONS (ETUDES) peinture à la colle/ and charcoal on paper laid down on canvas, 18 x 17¾in. (45.7 x 45.1cm) ll 'E. Vuillard' (Lugt 2497a) (1910)
PROV.: Estate of the artist; Mr. Hallsborough, London; Anon. sale, Sotheby's, London, April 11, 1962, lot 17 (acquired by the late owner).

Christie's New York, 8 November 1995 (156**) US$ 46,000	US$	46,000

MADAME HESSEL COUSANT SOUS LA LAMPE oil on board laid down on panel, 15¾ x 14¾in. (40 x 40cm.) lr 'E.Vuillard' (ca 1905)
PROV.: Arthur Fontaine, Paris; sale, Hôtel Drouot, Paris, April 13, 1932, lot 76 (illustrated); Dr. Albert Charpentier, Paris (acquired from the above).

Christie's New York, 8 November 1995 (194**) US$ 195,000	US$	195,000

WAARDEN Jan van der (Haarlem 1811-1872 Haarlem) Dutch
A STILL-LIFE WITH GRAPES, PRUNES, PEACHES, PEARS, ROSES AND OTHER FLOWERS
ON A MARBLE LEDGE oil on canvas, 60 x 50cm. s ini 'V:D:W:'
> Christie's Amsterdam, 25 April 1996 (256**) NLG 25,300   US$ 15,034

WAAY Nicolaas van der (Amsterdam 1855-1936 Amsterdam) Dutch
IN DEN VROEGEN OCHTEND oil on canvas, 80 x 68cm. s 'N. v.d. Waay' s titled on a label on the
reverse
> Christie's Amsterdam, 25 April 1996 (192**) NLG 25,300   US$ 15,034

WAEL Cornelis de (attr.) (Antwerp 1592-1667 Rome) Flemish
SAINT JOHN PREACHING TO THE MULTITUDE oil on canvas, 74.5 x 94.5cm.
> Sotheby's Amsterdam, 6 May 1996 (57*) NLG 25,960   US$ 15,137

WAGNER Fritz (Munich 1896-1939 Munich) German
THE DISCUSSION oil on canvas, 31½ x 39½in. (80 x 100.3cm.) s and inscr. 'Fritz Wagner /
Müchen'
> Christie's Kensington, 14 March 1996 (184**) GBP 10,925   US$ 16,684

WAGNER Paul Hermann (1852 b.) German
AYE AYE CAPTAIN oil on canvas, 41 x 23¾in. (104.2 x 60.3cm.) s and inscr. up 'Paul Wagner
München'
> Christie's New York, 1 February 1996 (114**) US$ 27,600   US$ 27,600

WAINWRIGHT William John (England 1855-1931) British
A VASE OF SUMMER FLOWERS AND FRUIT ON A LEDGE IN A LANDSCAPE; AND A
VASE OF ASSORTED FLOWERS AND SONGBIRDS ON A LEDGE oil on canvas, 26 x 22in. (66
x 55.9cm.); 26¼ x 22 1/8in. (66.7 x 56.2cm.) one sll 'J Wainwright' and the other sdll 'John
Wainwright 1867' a pair
> Christie's New York, 2 November 1995 (202**) US$ 19,550   US$ 19,550

WAITE Edward Wilkins (1854-1924) British
THE FALL OF THE LEAF oil on canvas, 40 3/8 x 60½in. (102.6 153.7cm.) sd 'E.W. Waite 96'
EXH.: London, Royal Acadamy, 1900, no. 328.
LIT.: H. Blackburn (ed.), *Royal Academy Notes,* 1900, p.18.
> Christie's London, 6 November 1995 (140**) GBP 19,550   US$ 30,580

THE BROOK HE LOVED oil on canvas, 21½ x 17in. (54.6 x 43.2 cm.) sd 'Edward Waite 1892'
> Christie's London, 29 March 1996 (161**) GBP 21,850   US$ 33,369

WALDE Alfons (Oberndorf (near Kitzbühel) 1891-1958) Austrian
DORFSTRASSE, TYROL oil on canvas, 29½ x 47¼in. (75 x 120cm.) sdlr 'a walde', titled and dated
'Dorfstrasse, 1931' on two artist's labels on the reverse
PROV.: Bought by the present owner's parents in the 1930s.
> Christie's London, 11 October 1995 (129**) GBP 117,000   US$ 184,659

AURACHER KIRCHL oil on board, 23 5/8 x 16 5/8in. (60 x 42.2cm.) sll 'A. Walde' (ca 1930)
PROV.: Purchased by the present owner in Kitzbühel in the 1930's.
> Christie's London, 26 June 1996 (242**) GBP 69,700   US$ 107,479

DORFSTRAßE IM WINTER, KITZBÜHEL oil on board, 19¼ x 30 3/8in. (49 x 72.2cm.) s 'A. Walde'
d and inscr. 'Tirol 1932' on the Artist's label on the reverse (1932)
PROV.: Purchased by the present owner in Kitzbühel, circa 1932.
> Christie's London, 26 June 1996 (243**) GBP 62,000   US$ 95,60?

EROTIK oil on cardboard, 33 x 23.5cm. sur 'A Walde'; inscr. 'Alfons Walde Kitzbühel Tirol' on a label on the reverse
        Wiener Kunst Auktionen, 26 September 1995 (181**) ATS 300,000   US$ 29,161

NACH DER VESPER oil on cardboard, 70 x 75.6cm. slr 'a. Walde'; titled on a label on the reverse
        Wiener Kunst Auktionen, 26 September 1995 (202**) ATS 450,000   US$ 43,742

TIROLER BERGSOMMER oil on cardboard, 47.5 x 54.5cm. slr 'a. Walde'; titled, inscr. and d 'ALFONS WALDE Kitzbühel, Tirol, Austria 1955' on a label on the reverse
        Wiener Kunst Auktionen, 26 September 1995 (282**) ATS 1350,000   US$ 131,225

Tiroler Bergsommer

WALDMÜLLER Ferdinand Georg (Vienna 1793-1865 Hinterbrühl (near Mödling, Lower Austria)) Austrian
PORTRAIT OF LOUISE BARONESS HÄRDTL oil on canvas, 52.5 x 42.8cm. sdre 'Waldmüller 1853'
PROV.: A. Kende, 106. Kunstaution, 19 November 1930, no. 714.
LIT.: Bruno Grimschitz *Ferdinand Georg Waldmüller*, Verlag Galerie Welz, Salzburg 1957, p. 348, no. 777 (illustrated).
        Wiener Kunst Auktionen, 26 September 1995 (64**) ATS 220,000   US$ 21,385

WALTON Edward Arthur, R.S.A., P.R.S.W. (-) Scottish
PORTRAIT OF MISS BETTY MYLNE oil on canvas, 48¼ x 28in. (122.5 x 71cm.) slr 'E A Walton'
PROV.: James Mylne, Esq., 1923.
EXH.: Edingburgh, Royal Scottish Academy, 1900, no. 269; *Walton Exhibition*, 1923.
        Sotheby's London, 29 August 1995 (938***) GBP 41,100   US$ 66,526

WALTON Henry (Dickleborough (Norfolk) 1746-1813 London) British
PORTAIT OF THE REV. CHARLES TYRELL OF THURLOW, SUFFOLK oil on canvas, 29½ x 24½in. (75 x 61.5cm.)
PROV.: By descent on the Tyrell family, Gipping Hall; Commander W.W. Browne, R.N. The Rookery, Rougham; John Walter Harvey, sold by his estate at Sotheby's London, 15 march 1978, lot 60, bt. for GBP 21,000.
EXH.: Spinks.
LIT.: E. Farrer, *Portraits in Suffolk Houses, (West)*, 1908, p. 318, no. 10; *The Connoisseur* 1909, Vol. XXV, pp. ,143 and ,145 (illustrated); David Coombs, *Sport and the Countryside*, 1978, p. 66 (illustrated).
        Sotheby's London, 12 July 1995 (45A**) GBP 54,300   US$ 86,617

WARD Edward Matthew, R.A. (1816-1879) British
HIGHGATE FIELDS DURING THE GREAT FIRE OF LONDON IN 1666 oil on canvas, 48 3/8 x 76 5/8in. (,123 x 194.5cm.) s and inscr. lr 'E M Ward ARA. Painted in 1848 Retouched and altered in 1851'
PROV.: acquired by William Long of Grappenhall, ca. 1864 thence by descent.
EXH.: London Royal Academy, 1848, no.416.
LIT.: *Art Journal 1848*, p.173.
        Phillips London, 18 June 1996 (54***) GBP 29,800   US$ 45,952

WARD James, R.A. (London 1769-1859 London) British
THE FAIR SHOW oil on canvas, 28 x 36in. (71 x 91.5cm.) s with monogram, inscr. 'RA', d '1837'

PROV.: Alfred Woodiwiss; H.Sheridan, Exeter; sold Sotheby's, London, 13th March 1985, lot 110, GBP8000.
EXH.: Royal Academy, London, 1838, no.263; Newman Street Galleries, London, 1841.
LIT.: Julia Frankeau, *William Ward and James Ward, their lives and works*, 1904, p.138, no.263; C.Reginald Grundy, *James Wars R.A.*, 1909, p.43, no.296; E.J.Nygren, 'James Ward-Controversy in Paint', *Art Bulletin*, 1979, pp.457-9, (ill.p.459, fig.13).

Phillips London, 18 June 1996 (55**) GBP 9,000 — US\$ 13,878

WARDLE Arthur, R.I, R.B.C., P.S. (London 1864-1949) British
THE FLUTE OF PAN oil on canvas, 61 x 42¾in. (108.6 x 154.9cm.) s 'Arthur Wardle'
EXH.: London, Royal Academy, 1899, no. 682.
LIT.: Henry Blackburn (ed.), *Royal Academy Notes*, 1899, p. 131, repr.

Christie's London, 7 June 1996 (575**) GBP 76,300 — US\$ 117,656

WARHOL Andy (Pittsburgh 1930-1987) American
2 DOLLAR BILL serigraph on canvas, 6 x 10¼in. (15 x 26in.) (1962)

Étude Tajan Paris, 10 June 1996 (69**) FRF 65,000 — US\$ 12,551

BLACK FLOWERS synthetic polymer and silkscreen inks on canvas, 23¾ x 23¾in. (60.3 x 60.3cm.) sd twice ' ANDY WARHOL 1964' on the reverse
PROV.: Leo Castelli Gallery, New York; The J.L. Hudson Gallery, Detroit.

Christie's New York, 22 February 1996 (75**) US\$ 54,050 — US\$ 54,050

MULTICOLOUR MARYLIN synthetic polymer and silkscreen inks on canvas, 18 1/8 x 13¾in. (46 x 35cm.) sd '79/86' on the overlap
PROV.: Galerie Bischofsberger, Zurich.

Christie's London, 23 May 1996 (91**) GBP 48,800 — US\$ 73,895

SELF PORTRAIT WITH HANDS AROUND NECK synthetic polymer and slkscreen inks on canvas, 16 x 13in. (40.7 x 33cm.) stamped with the authentication of Warhol Committee (1975)
PROV.: Armand Castellani, Florida.

Christie's London, 23 May 1996 (95**) GBP 20,700 — US\$ 31,345

KNIVES acrylic and synthetic polymer silkscreened on canvas, 70 x 52 1/8in. (,178 x 132.5cm.) sd '82' on the overlap
PROV.: Galerie Beaubourg, Paris; Galeria Fernando Vjando, Madrid.

Sotheby's London, 27 June 1996 (239**) GBP 54,300 — US\$ 83,732

THE SCREAM synthetic polymer silkscreend on canvas, 52 x 38in. (132.1 x 96.5cm.) sd '84' on the overlap
PROV.: O.K. Harris, New York.

Sotheby's London, 27 June 1996 (247**) GBP 62,000 — US\$ 95,605

LENIN acrylic and synthetic polymer silkscreened on canvas, 22 x 16in. (56 x 40.5cm.) authenticated by Fred Hughes on the reverse (1986)
PROV.: Galerie Bernd Klüser, Munich; Cleto Polcina Arte Moderna, Rome.

Sotheby's London, 27 June 1996 (258***) GBP 52,100 — US\$ 80,339

TORSO SERIES synthetic polymer and silkscreen inks on canvas-unframed, two panels: each 14 x 11in. (35.5 x 28cm.) sd inscr. indistinctly '1978 Andy Warhol' on the overlap of the left panel; each stamped with the Andy Warhol Estate number A793.,104 and A793.,105 respectively

Christie's East, 7 May 1996 (142**) US\$ 19,550 — US\$ 19,550

RED AIRMAIL STAMPS rubber stamp and silkscreen ink on canvas, 20 1/8 x 16in. (51.1 x 40.6cm.) sd 'Andy Warhol 62' on the stretcher
PROV.: Martha Jackson Gallery, New York; Leon Mnuchin, New York.

EXH.: New York, Museum of Modern Art; Art Institute of Chicago; London, Hayward Gallery; Cologne, Museum Ludwig; Venice, Palazzo Grassi, and Paris, Musée National d'art Moderne, Centre Georges Pompidou, *Andy Warhol: A Retrospective*, Feb. 1989-Sept. 1990, p. 203, no. 192 (illustrated).
LIT.: R. Crone, *Andy Warhol*, New York and Washington, D.C. 1970, p. 239, no. 439 (illustrated).

Christie's New York, 14 November 1995 (45**) US$ 178,500	US$	178,500

BLACK ON BLACK RETROSPECTIVE synthetic polymer and silkscreen inks on canvas, 29¾ x 74in. (75.6 x 188cm.) sd and titled 'Andy Warhol 79 Black on black retrospective' on the reverse of the overlap
PROV.: Galerie Bruno Bischofberger, Zurich.

Christie's New York, 14 November 1995 (57**) US$ 184,000	US$	184,000

MAO synthetic polymer and silkscreen inks on canvas, unframed, 12 x 10in. (30.5 x 25.4cm.) sd 'Andy Warhol 73' on the overlap
PROV.: Leo Castelli Gallery, New York.

Christie's New York, 8 May 1996 (295***) US$ 43,700	US$	43,700

UNTITLED (BLUE/GREEN MARILYN-REVERSAL SERIES) synthetic polymer and silkscreen inks on canvas, 18 x 14in. (45.7 x 35.6cm.) stamped with signature 'Andy Warhol' on the overlap
PROV.: Waddington Galleries, London.

Christie's New York, 8 May 1996 (355**) US$ 46,000	US$	46,000

WASHINGTON Georges (Marseille 1827-1910 Paris) French
ARAB HORSEMEN AT A WADDI oil on canvas, 30 x 38½in. ,976 x 98cm.) s 'G Washington'

Christie's London, 15 March 1996 (100**) GBP 10,350	US$	15,806

A MOUNTED ARAB WARRIOR oil on canvas, 32 x 25½in. (81.3 x 64.5cm.) s 'G. Washington'

Christie's London, 15 March 1996 (107**) GBP 21,275	US$	32,491

WATENPHUL Max Peiffer (Weferlingen 1896-1976 Rome) German
VENEDIG, AM CANAL GRANDE oil on painters cardboard, 57 x 50cm. slr mono. 'MPW' (1947)

Lempertz Cologne, 29 November 1995 (394**) DEM 42,000	US$	29,644

WATERHOUSE John William, R.A. (Rome 1849-1917 London) British
BOREAS oil on canvas, 37 x 27in. (94 x 68.8cm.) sdll 'J.W. Waterhouse 1903'
PROV.: With N. Mitchell, London.
EXH.: London, Royal Academy, 1904, no.618.
LIT.: Henry Blackburn (ed.), *Academy Notes*, 1904, p.28; R.E.D. Sketchley, 'The Art of J.W. Waterhouse', *Art Journal*, Christmas Number, 1909, p.32 (list); Anthony Hobson, *The Art and Life of J.W. Waterhouse*, 1980, p.189, no.l47; Anthony Hobson, *J.W. Waterhouse*, 1989, p.89.

Christie's London, 29 March 1996 (81***) GBP 848,500	US$	129,581 6

THE ROSE BOWER oil on canvas, 16½ x 14¼in. 41.9 x 36.2cm.)
LIT.: Anthony Hobson, *John William Waterhouse*, 1989, p.89, pl.70.

Christie's London, 7 June 1996 (574**) GBP 10,350	US$	15,960

WATERLOW Sir Ernest Albert, R.A. (London 1850-1919 London) British
MAY oil on canvas, 50½ x 37½in. (128.2 x 94.6cm.) s 'E.A. Waterlow' (1891)
PROV.: Sir R.P. Cooper, and by descent to the present owner.
EXH.: London, Royal Academy, 1891, no.81; Dublin, Royal Hibernian Academy, 1892, no.113.
LIT.: Henry Blackburn (ed.), *Royal Academy Notes*, 1891, pp. 6, 34, repr.; *Royal Academy Pictures*, 1891, p.56, repr.; *Athenaeum*, 3314, 2 May 1891, p.572, and 3316, 16 May 1891, p.642; The Times, 1 May 1891, p.8; C. Collins Baker, 'Sir E.A. Waterlow, R.A., P.R.W.S.', *Art Journal,* Christmas Number, 1906, pp.4 (repr.), 11, 32.

Christie's London, 6 November 1995 (159**) GBP 25,300	US$	39,575

WATSON George Spencer, R.A. (London 1869-1934 London) British
THE FOUNTAIN oil on canvas, 30¼ x 25¼in. (76.8 x 64.2cm.) sd 'G.S. Watson/1900'
PROV.: W.H. Leaver, 1st Viscount Leverhulme (died 1925); Presented by him to the Lady Lever Art
Gallery, Port Sunlight, Wirral, Merseyside; Lady Lever Art Gallery Sale; Christie's, 6 June 1958, lot
,168 (40 gns. to The Fine Art Society).
LIT.: R.R. Tatlock, *English Painting of the XVIIIth-XXth Centuries: A Record of the Collections in
the Lady Lever Art Gallery*, Port Sunlight .., 1928, p.115, no. 2901.

Christie's London, 6 November 1995 (123**) GBP 20,700	US$	32,379

PORTRAIT OF A YOUNG WOMAN IN A STRAW HAT oil on canvas, 34½ x 27in. (87.5 x
68.5cm.) slr ini. 'G.S.W.'
EXH.: Bristol, Pelter Sands Art Gallery, *George Spencer Watson*, Oct. 1988, no.59, p.12 (ill.).

Christie's Kensington, 26 October 1995 (109**) GBP 8,437	US$	13,316

WATTEAU Antoine (Jean Antoine) (Valenciennes 1684-1721 Nogent-sur-Marne) French
A CHINESE MUSICIAN PLAYING A HURDY-GURDY WITH A COMPAGNION IN A
LANDSCAPE oil on canvas, 9 1/16 x 7¼in. (23 x 18.4cm.) (1714-16)
PROV.: Painted for the cabinet du Roi, Chateau de la Muette; possibly Bezançon de Wagner.
LIT.: E. Dacier and Vuaflart, *Jean de Julienne et les graveurs de Watteau*, 1922-29, no. D.233, for
the engraving after the painting; H. Adhémar and R. Huyghe, *Watteau, sa vie - son oeuvre*, 1950, pp.
94-98, p. 96, pp. 203/204.

Sotheby's New York, 11 January 1996 (151**) US$ 90,500	US$	90,500

WATTEAU Louis Joseph, {called} Watteau de Lille (Valenciennes 1737-1798 Lille) French
A VILLAGE FAIR WITH FEASTING BOORS, ELEGANT COUPLES AND A QUACK oil on
canvas, 67 x 89cm.
LIT.: comp. Exhibition catalogue *Watteau*, Washington, 1984; Paris 1984, Berlin 1985, p. 59, pl. 9.

Dorotheum Vienna, 11 June 1996 (173**) ATS 90,000	US$	8354

WATTS Frederick Waters (1800-1862) British
A HAMPSTEAD COTTAGE oil on canvas, 26½ x 32¾in. (67.4 x 83.2cm.)
PROV.: With Newhouse Galleries, New York.

Christie's New York, 14 February 1996 (63**) US$ 19,550	US$	19,550

WAYEN PIETERSZEN Abraham van der (Middelburg 1817-1880 Maria Hoorebeeke) Dutch
VILLAGERS ON A FROZEN RIVER IN WINTER oil on panel, 19½ x 26in. (49.6 x 66cm.) sd 'A
Pieterszen 1845'

Christie's London, 14 June 1996 (7**) GBP 21,850	US$	33,693

WEBB Edward Walter (1810-1851) British
BARNET FAIR oil on canvas, 25¾ x 35¾in. (65.5 x 91cm.) slr 'E W Webb/1849'
LIT.: Sally Mitchell, *The Dictionary of British Equestrian Artist*, 1985, p. ,450 (illustrated).

Sotheby's London, 12 July 1995 (139**) GBP 23,000	US$	36,688

WEBB James (1825 c.-1895 London) British
AMSTERDAM HARBOUR oil on canvas, 30¼ x 50 3/8in. (76.9 x 128cm.) sdll 'James Webb.
1881/Amsterdam'
PROV.: M.S. Nathan.

Christie's New York, 14 February 1996 (139**) US$ 29,900	US$	29,900

TEH RETURN OF THE FISHING FLEET oil on canvas, 30 x 50in, (76.3 x 127cm.) sd 'James Webb
77'
PROV.: Stanley Wilson; Christie's 8 June 1925, lot ,157 (21 gns. to Sampson).

Christie's London, 6 November 1995 (167**) GBP 10,350	US$	16,190

AMSTERDAM HARBOR oil on canvas, 30¼ x 50 3/8in. (76.9 x 128cm.) sdll 'James Webb. 1881/Amterdam'
PROV.: M.S.Nathan.
Christie's New York, 10 January 1996 (139**) US$ 29,900 — US$ 29,900

WEBER Rudolf (Vienna 1872-1949 Krems/Stein) Austrian
SEGELBOOTE IM HAFEN oil on canvas, 90.5 x 129cm. sd 'Rud. Weber 1899'
Dorotheum Vienna, 17 April 1996 (510**) ATS 120,000 — US$ 11,338

WECHELEN Jan van & Cornelis Dalem (ca. 1530/35-1573) (Antwerp 1530 c.-1570 c. after) Flemish
CHRIST ON THE ROAD TO CALVARY oil on panel, 11¼ x 19¾in. (28.6 x 50.2cm.) slr H VA/WECHLEN
PROV.: Probably Peeter Stevens, Antwerp (Sale: Antwerp, August 13, 1668, lot 33, 'Nostre Seigneur portant sa Crois hors la Ville de Ierusalem avec beaucoup de monde'; Sale: Sotheby's, London, March 24, 1971, lot 41, (where it is noted that the reverse of the panel bears a monogram and the date 1638) there acquired by Hollstein; Sale: Christie's New York, July 10, 1981, lot 76; Sale: Christie's, New York, January 18, 1983, lot 162, there purchased by the present collector.
EXH.: Saint Petersburg, Florida, Museum of Fine Arts, *Art and Life in Northern Europe, 1500-1800: the Gilbert Collection*, catalogue by Debra Miller, December 15, 1990-February 24, 1991, p. 45, cat. mo. 21, illus.
Sotheby's New York, 11 January 1996 (78**) US$ 57,500 — US$ 57,500

WEDIG Gottfried von (Godert de) (Cologne 1583-1641 Cologne) German
STILL-LIFE WITH A CAT STEALING FISH OFF A BLUE AND WHITE PLATE, A BURNING CANDLE, A BREAD ROLL AND OTHER OBJECTS ON A TABLE oil on panel, 16 5/8 x 21¼in. (42.2 x 54cm.)
Sotheby's New York, 11 January 1996 (218**) US$ 28,750 — US$ 28,750

WEEKS Edwin Lord (Boston 1849-1903 Paris) British (American)
UNE CARAVANE DU SOUDAN ENTRANT DANS UNE FONDAK A MAROC oil on canvas, 32½ x 39½in. (82.5 x 100.5cm.) s 'E.L. Weeks' (ca 1881-82)
PROV.: Sir John Aird, Bt.; sale, Christie's London 1935, lot ,103 (39gns. to Mitchell); with Arthur Tooth; with David Messum, 1981.
EXH.: Possibly Paris, *Salon 1882*, no. 2673.
LIT.: To be included in Dr. Ellen K. Morris forthcoming *catalogue raisonné on Weeks*.
Christie's London, 15 March 1996 (69**) GBP 227,000 — US$ 346,671

THE CHESS PLAYERS oil on canvas, 28¾ x 39½in. (73 x 100.5cm.) sd 'E.L. Weeks 1897'
PROV.: With Mathaf Gallery.
LIT.: To be included in Dr. Ellen Morris' forthcoming *catalogue raisonné on Weeks*.
Christie's London, 15 March 1996 (81**) GBP 26,450 — US$ 40,394

WEENIX Jan (Amsterdam 1642 (?)-1719 Amsterdam) Dutch
A STILL-LIFE OF FRUIT WITH AN ELK HOUND SCARING PIGEONS BENEATH A SCULPTED URN, AN ORNAMENTAL PARK AND GARDENS WITH A BOATING PARTY BEYOND oil on canvas, 80¼ x 98in. (,204 x 249cm.)
PROV.: James, 6th Baron Talbot de Malahide, Malahide Castle, Co. Dublin; his sale, London, Christie's, 29 October 1941, lot 428, as *J.B. Weenix*.
Sotheby's London, 5 July 1995 (29**) GBP 122,500 — US$ 195,406

A DEAD HARE ON A PLINTH BY A SCULPTED URN WITH A BASKET OF FRUIT, A DEAD PHEASANT, MALLARD, GROUSE, JAY AND CHAFFINCH, A DOG WATCHING A GOLDFINCH AND A BOY BEARING A BASKET OF FRUIT IN A PARK oil on canvas, 48 x 41/8in. (122x 163cm.) sd 'J.Weenix.f.1705'
PROV.: William, 12th Duke of Hamilton (1845-1895); His only child, Lady Mary Hamilton, who

married in 1906 James, Marquess of Graham (later 6th Duke of Montrose), Easton Park, Wickham Market; Christie's, 23 May 1919, lot ,158 (510gns. to Peacock); Acquired by the mother of the present owner before 1945.

Christie's London, 8 December 1995 (47**) GBP 331,500	US$	510,157

A DEAD HARE AND BIRDS BY A STONE MONUMENT, WITH A GUN AND OTHER HUNTING ACCOUTREMENTS, AND A SPANIEL BARKING AT A DOVE IN A GARDEN oil on canvas, 73 x 64in. (185.4 x 162.5cm.)
PROV.: Lord Haldon, Haldon House, Exeter; Christie's 28 Feb. 1891, lot 34 (1,050 gns to Agnews); Ascher Wertheimer, 8 Connaught Place, London; Christie's March 1923, lot ,114 (,640 gns. to Gooden and Fox).

Christie's London, 19 April 1996 (234**) GBP 265,500	US$	402,578

WEENIX Jan Baptist (Amsterdam 1621-1664 after Huis ter Mey, near Utrecht) Dutch
ITALIANATE LANDSCAPE WITH FIGURES TENDING TO THEIR FLOCK OF SHEEP AND GOATS oil on canvas, 34¼ x 49¼in. (87 x 125cm.) sdll '..1656'

Sotheby's London, 5 July 1995 (185**) GBP 21,850	US$	34,854

WEENIX Jan Baptist (attr.) (Amsterdam 1621-1664 after Huis ter Mey, near Utrecht) Dutch
TRAVELERS RESTING NEAR RUINS oil on canvas, 22¾ x 25¼in. (58 x 63.7cm.)
PROV.: With R.H. Ward, no. 33A; With Thos. Agnew & Sons, no. 6809; Anonymous Sale Sotheby's Amsterdam, 2 June 1986, lot 157.

Sotheby's London, 17 April 1996 (60**) GBP 23,000	US$	34,875

WEERTS Jean Joseph (Roubaix 1847-1927 Paris) French
PORTRAIT OF A LADY oil on canvas, 59½ x 42in. (151.1 x 106.7cm.) sll 'J.J. WEERTS.'

Christie's East, 13 February 1996 (134**) US$ 8,050	US$	8050

WEIGHT Carel, R.A. (London 1908 b.) British
COPS AND ROBBERS oil on canvas, 44½ x 57in. (,113 x 144.8cm.) sdur 'Carel Weight 1956'
EXH.: London, Royal Academy, 1956, no. 390.
LIT.: R.V. Weight, *Carel Weight A Haunted Imagination*, London, 1994, pp.61-62 (illustrated).

Christie's London, 20 June 1996 (95**) GBP 28,750	US$	44,333

THE MASTER STROKE DR TASBUSCH oil on board, 35 x 21¾in. (89 x 55.5cm.) sdlr 'Carel Weight 1954'
EXH.: Bournemouth, Russel-Cotes Art Gallery and Museum, *Carel Weight and Ruskin Spear*, July-Sept. 1965, no.8.
LIT.: R.V. Weight, *Carel Weight, A Haunted Imagination*, London, 1994, pp. 77, ,120 (illustrated), misdated to 1960.

Christie's London, 21 March 1996 (19**) GBP 17,250	US$	26,344

WEILAND Johannes (Vlaardingen 1856-1909 The Hague) Dutch
HOMEWORK oil on canvas, 82 x 68cm sdlr 'J.Weilandf05'
PROV.: Sale Jhr. F.E. Sandberg, Paul Brandt Amsterdam, 21 Feb. 1950, lot no. 305 (illus.); Anon.sale Mak van Waay, Amsterdam, 7 March 1961, lot no. 508.

Christie's Amsterdam, 26 October 1995 (23x) NLG 26,450	US$	16,677

WEILER Max (Absam (near Solbad Hall, Tyrol) 1910 b.) Austrian
MOHNBLUME IM STEINGARTEN (BLAUE PFLANZE) oil on canvas, 80 x 80.5cm. slr 'M G Weiler' (1956)
LIT.: Otto Breicha, *Max Weiler, Die innere Figur*, Verlag Galerie Welz, Salzburg 1989, p. ,106 (illustrated in colour).

Wiener Kunst Auktionen, 26 March 1996 (341**) ATS 650,000	US$	62,52

WIE EINE LANDSCHAFT, DIE GRAUE BERGE tempera on canvas, 96 x 196cm. sdlr 'Weiler 65'; inscr. d, titled and numbered 'Max Weiler 65. Die grauen Berge 165. WV 604' on the reverse
LIT.: Otto Breicha, *Max Weiler. Die innere Figur. ,171 Bildwerke seit 1933*, Verlag Galerie Welz, Salzburg 1989, p. ,216 (illustrated); Otto Breicha, *Max Weiler. 'Wie eine Landschaft'. Bilder von 1961-1967*, Österreichische Galerie. Belvedere, Vienna 3 May-30. July 1995, p. 28 (illustrated p. 100).

Wiener Kunst Auktionen, 27 September 1995 (455**) ATS 1,100,000	US$	106,924

DER HIMMEL ALS DIE SONNE UNTERGING tempera on canvas, ,105 x 99cm. sdlr 'Weiler 71'
EXH.: *Max Weiler. Himmelsluft und Wolkenart*, Österreichisches College, Europäisches Forum Alpbach, 16-19 August 1992 (illustrated p. 22).

Wiener Kunst Auktionen, 27 September 1995 (467**) ATS 450,000	US$	43,742

DIE SÜDWINDWOLKE oil on paper with ground, pencil, 66 x 109cm. sd 'Weiler 84'

Dorotheum Vienna, 8 November 1995 (849**) ATS 320,000	US$	32,100

WEIßENKIRCHNER Hans Adam (Laufen 1646-1695 Graz) German
ALLEGORICAL SCENE oil on canvas, ,130 x 166.5cm. (1684-85)
PROV.: Schloß Eggenberg, Graz.

Wiener Kunst Auktionen, 26 March 1996 (10**) ATS 180,000	US$	17,314

WEISSENBRUCH Jan (Johannes) (The Hague 1822-1880 The Hague) Dutch
PEASANTS CONVERSING OUTSIDE A TOWN, IN SUMMER oil on panel, 34 x 44.4cm. slr 'Jan Weissenbruch f.'

Christie's Amsterdam, 26 October 1995 (300**) NLG 85,100	US$	53,657

WENGLEIN Joseph (Munich 1845-1919 Bad Tölz) German
KÜHE AN SUMPFIGEM GEWÄSSER IN DER UMGEBUNG VON DACHAU oil on panel, 27 x 45cm. slr 'J. Wenglein'

Lempertz Cologne, 18 May 1996 (1658*) DEM 32,000	US$	20,862

WENGLER Johann Baptist (1815-1889) German
DER TANZ IM KELLER oil on canvas, 35¼ x 40¼in. (90 x 105cm.) sd 'J B Wengler/847'

Christie's London, 11 October 1995 (64**) GBP 14,950	US$	23,595

WERFF Adriaen van der (Kralingen, near Rotterdam 1659-1722 Rotterdam) Dutch
PORTRAIT OF A FAMILY BY A CLASSICAL FOUNTAIN IN A PARK SETTING oil on canvas, 30¼ x 23½in. (76.5 x 59.7cm.) sdlc 'A.V.WERFF F. 16**'
PROV.: Anonymous sale, London, Sotheby's 15 November 1961, lot 123.

Sotheby's London, 17 April 1996 (31**) GBP 12,650	US$	19,181

SUSANNAH oil on canvas, 19 1/8 x 15 5/8in. (48.6 39.7cm.)
PROV.: J. Doherty, Foxlydiate House, Redditch, Worcestershire, 1880.

Christie's London, 7 July 1995 (274**) GBP 9,775	US$	15,593

WERNER Carl Friedrich Heinrich (Weimar 1808-1894 Leipzig) German
DIE KLAGENMAUER, JERUSALEM watercolour, gouache and pencil on paper, 13¾ x 19¾in. (35 x 50cm.) sdlr 'C. Werner f. 1863'

Christie's Tel Aviv, 14 April 1996 (2**) US$ 21,850	US$	21,850

ON HE OUTSKIRTS OF CAIRO pen and brown ink and watercolour heightened with gum arabic on paper, 18¾ x 25 3/8in. (47.7 x 64.4cm.) sd 'C. Werner f. 1864'

Christie's London, 15 March 1996 (132**) GBP 16,100	US$	24,588

WERNER Joseph, {called} the Younger (Berne 1637 b.-1710 Berne) Swiss
PALLAS ATHENE gouache heightened and edged with gold on vellum, laid down, 5½ x 4¼in.

(14.4 x 10.8cm.) inscr. and d
'LA.PALLAS.DEL.SR./CAVALLEIRE.IOSEPHO./DI.VVERNER.PITTORE./
E.MIGNATORE./EXCELLENTISIMO./ 1664

        Sotheby's London, 6 December 1995 (120**) GBP 21,850   US$ 33,626

WERTMÜLLER Adolf Ulric (Stockholm 1751-1811 Wilmington, Delaware, USA) Swedish
ARIADNE ABANDONED AND CUPID ASLEEP oil on canvas (a pair), each: 12½ x 15¾in. (31.8
x 40cm.) sdlr 'A: Wertmüller S./à Paris 1788'
LIT.: M. Benisovich, 'Wertmüller et son livre de raison initulé *la Notte*', *Gazette des Beaux-Arts*,
July-August 1956. pp. 39, 51.

        Sotheby's New York, 16 May 1996 (110**) US$ 37,375   US$ 37,375

WESSELMAN Tom (Cincinnati (Ohio) 1931 b.) American
LITTLE GREAT AMERICAN NUDE 25 liquitex on board, 12¾ x 11¾in. (32.5 x 29.8cm.) sd '65'
on the reverse
PROV.: Green Gallery, New York.

        Christie's London, 23 May 1996 (90**) GBP 41,100   US$ 62,235

STUDY FOR BEDROOM PAINTING oil on canvas-unframed, 6 3/8 x 8¼in. (16.2 x 21cm.) sd
'Wesselman 69' on the overlap; sd titled and dedicated 'STUDY FOR BEDROOM PAINTING
Wesselman 1969' on the stretcher
PROV.: Acquired directly from the artist.

        Christie's East, 7 May 1996 (143**) US$ 6,325   US$ 6,325

STUDY FOR BLACK AND WHITE MOUTH oil on canvas, 12¼ x 16in. (31 x 40.6cm.) sd
'Wesselmann 67' sd titled again 'STUDY FOR BLACK AND WHITE MOUTH 1967 Wesselmann'
on the reverse
PROV.: Sidney Janis Gallery, New York.

        Christie's New York, 22 February 1996 (61**) US$ 19,550   US$ 19,550

STUDY FOR BEDROOM PAINTING *22* oil and graphite on canvas, 9 1/8 x 11in. (23.2 x 27.9cm.)
sd twice 'Wesselmann 69' on the overlap; titled and d 'Study for Bedroom Ptg 2 1969' on the stretcher
PROV.: Acquired directly from the artist.

        Christie's New York, 22 February 1996 (71**) US$ 23,000   US$ 23,000

STEEL DRAWING/MONICA NUDE WITH MATISSE (VARIATION 1) enamel on laser-cut steel,
51 x 86in. (129.4 x 218.4) sd 'WESSELMANN 87' on reverse
PROV.: Sidney Janis Gallery, New York.

        Christie's New York, 22 February 1996 (84*) US$ 27,600   US$ 27,600

BLONDE VIVIENNE (3-D) oil on cut-out aluminum, 78 x 78 x 10in.(198.1 x 198.1 x 25.4cm.
sd'WESSELMANN 88' on the reverse
PROV.: Sidney Janis Gallery, New York.
EXH.: New York, Sidney Janis Gallery, *Tom Wesselmann: New York*, Oct.-Nov. 1988, p1, no.1
(illustrated).

        Christie's New York, 22 February 1996 (88***) US$ 111,400   US$ 111,400

BEDROOM FACE WITH GREEN WALLPAPER oil on canvas, unframed, 55¼ x 60in. (133.4 x
152.4cm.) sd and titled twice 'Wesselmann 1984-86 'BEDROOM FACE WITH GREEN
WALLPAPER"
PROV.: Sidney Janis Gallery, New York.

        Christie's New York, 8 May 1996 (332**) US$ 51,750   US$ 51,750

WET Jacob the Younger (Haarlem 1640-1697 Amsterdam) Dutch
CHRIST PREACHING TO THE MULTITUDE oil on canvas, 94.4 x 157.6cm. sll 'J.d.Wet'

        Christie's Amsterdam, 13 November 1995 (73**) NLG 14,950   US$ 9,42.

WET Jacob Willemsz. de (the Elder) (Haarlem 1610-1671 (after 1675)) Dutch
THE TRIUMPH OF MORDECHAI oil on panel, 60.5 x 84cm. sll 'J.d.Wet'

Sotheby's Amsterdam, 14 November 1995 (4*) NLG 18,880	US$	11,899

WEYERMAN Jacob Campo {called Campovivo) (Breda 1677-1747 The Hague) Dutch
FLOWERS IN A VASE ON A TABLE oil on canvas, 54 x 41.5cm. slr 'Campovivo f'

Étude Tajan Paris, 12 December 1995 (48**) FRF 35,000	US$	7,050

WHEELWRIGHT Roland (1870-1955) Australian
JOAN OF ARC TAKEN PRISONER oil on canvas, 54½ x 90½in. (138.4 x 228.6cm.) sd 'R.
Wheelwright/1906' and s inscr. 'R. Wheelwright/ 18 Grosvenor Rd/Watford/ Herts' on the reverse
PROV.: Major R. Sodnal.
EXH.: London, Royal Academy, 1906, no. 364.
LIT.: *Royal Academy Pictures*, 1906, p. ,133 (illustrated); Henry Blackburn (ed.), *Academy Notes*,
1906, pp. 22, 87 (illustrated).

Christie's London, 29 March 1996 (114**) GBP 47,700	US$	72,847

WIEGERS Jan (Kommerzijl (Groningen 1893-1959 Amsterdam) Dutch
FARMHOUSES oil on canvas, 80 x 70cm. sdlr 'Jan Wiegers '29'
PROV.: J.C. Steenmeijer, Groningen; thence by descent.

Christie's Amsterdam, 5 June 1996 (274*) NLG 28,750	US$	16,798

VIEW OF A VILLAGE IN FRANCE oil on canvas, 62 x 71cm. sd '24'
PROV.: Collection F. Kleinhof, Twello.
LIT.: Adriaan Venema, *De Ploeg 1918-1930*, Baarn 1978, p. ,174 (illustrated).

Sotheby's Amsterdam, 7 December 1995 (156**) NLG 24,780	US$	15,355

WIEGHORST Olaf Carl (1899-1988) American
THE TRAIL HERD oil on canvas, 34 1/8 x 38 1/8in. (87 x 97.2cm.) slr 'O. Wieghorst'

Christie's New York, 13 September 1995 (94**) US$ 23,000	US$	23,000

WIEGMAN Matthieu (Mattheus Johannes Marie) (Zwolle 1886-1971 Bergen) Dutch
A VIEW IN A VILLAGE oil on vanvas, unframed, 46 x 56 cm s 'Matth. Wiegman'

Christie's Amsterdam, 7 February 1996 (517) NLG 8,050	US$	4,903

WIERINGEN Cornelis Claesz. van (Haarlem 1580 c.-1633 Haarlem) Dutch
A WOODED LANDSCAPE WITH TOBIAS AND THE ANGEL oil on panel, 25 7/8 x 36 1/8in.
(65.5 x91.7cm)
PROV.: August Schubert; anon. sale, Christie's 10 July 1981, lot.1, as 'D.D. van Santvoort'; with
Hoogsteder-Naumann ltd, New York.

Christie's London, 7 July 1995 (34**) GBP 65,300	US$	104,163

WIGGINS Guy Carleton (Brooklyn (N.Y.) 1883-1962) American
FIFTH AVENUE IN THE SNOW oil on canvas, 25 x 30in. (63.5 x 76.2cm.) slr 'Guy Wiggins NA.'
(late 1940's)
PROV.: Mr. and Mrs. Frank Sinatra.

Christie's New York, 1 December 1995 (61**) US$ 23,000	US$	23,000

THE FLAT IRON BUILDING IN WINTER oil on canvas, 16 1/8 x 12 1/8in. (41 x 30.7cm.) sll 'Guy
Wiggins'
PROV.: Mr. and Mrs. Frank Sinatra.

Christie's New York, 1 December 1995 (62**) US$ 46,000	US$	46,000

OLD TRINITY oil on canvas, 30¼ x 25in. (76.7 x 88.9cm.) slr 'Guy Wiggins'; sd '1930' on the
reverse
PROV.: Mr. and Mrs. Frank Sinatra.

Christie's New York, 1 December 1995 (63**) US$ 39,100	US$	39,100

OLD TRINITY IN WINTER oil on canvas, 24 x 20in. (61 x 50.8cm.) sll 'Guy Wiggins NA'
Christie's New York, 13 September 1995 (76**) US$ 21,850	US$	21,850

WILDENS Jan (Antwerp 1586-1653 Antwerp) Flemish
PAESAGGIO CON VIANDANTI oil on canvas, ,112 x 163cm.
Finearte Rome, 22 November 1995 (139*) ITL 17,825 ,000	US$	11,190

A WOODED LANDSCAPE WITH THE GOOD SAMARITAN oil on canvas, 36 x 49in. (91.5 x 124.5cm.)
Christie's London, 7 July 1995 (276**) GBP 8,050	US$	12,841

WILHELMSON Carl (Fiskebackskil 1866-1928 Göteborg) Swedish
MÄNNEN VID KYRKAN oil on canvas, ,111 x 136cm. slr 'C. Wilhelmson' (1907)
EXH.: Göteborg, 1908; Stockholm, 1908; Oslo, 1908; Berlin, 1910; Lund, 1911; Stockholm, 1912; Stockholm, 1929; Göteborgs Konstmuseum *Carl Wilhelmson västkustmålaren*, 1974.
LIT.: Axel L. Romdahl, *Carl Wilhelmson*, 1938, pp. 130, 131, ,216 (illustrated p. 131).
Bukowskis Stockholm, 29 November-1 December 1995 (159**) SEK 400,000	US$	60,511

TRE FLICKOR oil on canvas, ,105 x 122cm. s 'C. Wilhelmson' (1913)
EXH.: Göteborg, 1915; Malmö, Stockholm, Uppsala, 1916; Copenhagen, 1918; Stockholm, 1922.
LIT.: Axel L. Romdahl, *Carl Wilhelmson*, 1938, pp. 222, cat. no. 424.
Bukowskis Stockholm, 29 November-1 December 1995 (160**) SEK 390,000	US$	58,998

WILKIE Sir David (Cults, near Edinburgh 1785-1841 Gibraltar, near) British
THE ERRAND BOY oil on panel, 15 x 20in. (38 x 50.5cm.) (1817-18)
PROV.: Sir John Swinburne, Bt., 1818; Sir John Swinburne, Bt.; Christie's, 15 June 1861, lot ,123 (435gns. to Agnews); John Knowles, July 1861; John Knowles; Christie's, 8 April 1865, lot ,170 (1050gns. to Farrer, presumably Henry Farrer, the dealer); Charles Huth, 1865; Charles Huth; Christie's, 6 July 1895, lot ,119 (810gns. to Agnews, probably on behalf of Sir Charles Tennant, Bt.); Sir Charles Tennant, 1st Bt., by 1896, and by descent.
EXH.: London, Royal Academy, 1818, no. 110; London, British Institution, *Loan Exhibition*, 1842, no. 25; London, British Institution, *Loan Exhibition*, 1865, no. 152; London, Royal Academy, *Winter Exhibition*, 1906, no. 37; Edinburgh, *Scottish National Exhibition*, 1908, no. 85; Glasgow, *Scottish Exhibition of National History, Art, and Industry*, 1911, no. 168; New Haven, Yale Centre for British Art, and Raleigh, North Carolina Museum of Art, *Sir David Wilkie of Scotland*, 1987, no. 19; London, Richard L. Feigen & Co., *Sir David Wilkie*, 1994, no. 14.
LIT.: Anon., in *New Monthly Magazine*, IX, 1818, p.44; R. Hunt, in *Examiner*, 7 June 1818, p.365; Anon., in *Art-Union*, 1839, p.59; Anon., in *Art-Union*, 1842, p.159; Anon., in *Athenaeum*, 2 July 1842, p. 584; Anon., in *Blackwood's Edinburgh Magazine*, Lll, p. 584; A. Cunningham, *Life of Sir David Wilkie*, London, 1843, II, p.8; III p.525; Anon., in *Art Journal*, 1865, p.l92; W. Morgan Agnew, *Catalogue of .. the Collection of Sir Charles Tennant*, London, 1896 - neither paginated nor numbered; R. Sutherland Gower, *Sir David Wilkie*, London, 1902, pp.92, 129; W. Bayne, *Sir David Wilkie, R.A.*, 1906, p.79.
Christie's London, 10 November 1995 (34**) GBP 238,000	US$	372,282

WOODED LANDSCAPE WITH A WAYSIDE SHRINE oil on panel, 7 7/8 x 5 7/8in. (20 x 15cm.)
PROV.: Collection of the Lennox Library, New York; Thomas Agnew & Sons, London.
Phillips London, 18 June 1996 (38**) GBP 8,000	US$	12,336

WILLAERTS Adam (Antwerp 1577-1664 Utrecht) Flemish
VILLAGE AT THE RIVER WITH FERRY-BOAT AND A CROWD OF PEOPLE oil on canvas, 55 x 65.5cm. sll and indistinctly d 'A. W. f.'
Dorotheum Vienna, 6 March 1996 (14**) ATS 250,000	US$	24,048

A COASTAL LANDSCAPE WITH SAILORS IN A ROWING BOAT, A MERCHANTMAN AT ANCHOR BEYOND, VILLAGERS WAVING GOODBYE IN THE FOREGROUND oil on panel, 45.7 x 63.5cm. sdlc '1641/A. WILLARTS.F,'
PROV.: Mrs S.C. Warren, until 1897.

Christie's Amsterdam, 7 May 1996 (109*) NLG 21,850	US$	12,741

A TOWN QUAY WITH TRAVELLERS BRAWLING AND MERRYMAKING oil on panel, 23½ x 29 1/8in. (59.7 x 74cm.) indistinctly sd '1658'

Christie's Kensington, 18 april 1996 (283**) GBP 5,750	US$	8,719

WILLEMSENS Abraham (1627 active-1672) Dutch
THE ELEMENTS OF AIR AND FIRE: VULCAN AT WORK IN HIS FORGE WITH AEOLUS AND A PUTTO IN FLIGHT BEYOND, EXOTIC BIRDS AND POULTRY IN THE FOREGROUND, A LANDSCAPE IN THE DISTANCE oil on canvas, 53.7 x 84.4cm.
PROV.: also Jan van Kessel III (119) co-painter.

Christie's Amsterdam, 13 November 1995 (119**) NLG 29,900	US$	18,844

WILLINK Carel (Albert Carel) (Amsterdam 1900-1983) Dutch
WALL OF THE THERMAL MUSEUM IN ROME oil on canvas, ,100 x 75cm. sdal 'Willink 61'
EXH.: Amsterdam, Stedelijk Museum, *Carel Willink*, 22 September-23 October 1961; Brussels Galerie d'Art, *Carel Willink*, 12 March-22April 1967.
LIT.: H.L. Jaffé, *Willink*, Amsterdam 1979, no. 279 (ill.), p. ,158 (ill.) Walter Kramer, *Willink*, The Hague, Rotterdam 1973, no.,213 (p.,189 ill.).

Christie's Amsterdam, 5 June 1996 (283**) NLG 80,500	US$	47,035

WILSON Charles Edward (1870s-1936 c.) British
THE LITTLE WAIF pencil and watercolour, 10 x 7in. (25.4 x 17.8cm.) s 'C.E.Wilson' and inscribed 'A little Waif' under the mount

Christie's London, 6 November 1995 (21**) GBP 7,475	US$	11,692

WILSON Richard, R.A. (Penegoes (Montgomeryshire) 1714-1782 Llanberis (Denbigshire)) British
AN EXTENSIVE WELSH LANDSCAPE WITH COTTAGES NEAR A LAKE oil on canvas, 32 x 49in. 81.3 x 124.5cm.) (ca 1744-45)
PROV.: Colonel M.H. Grant; Anon. sale, Sotheby's, 14 June 1961, lot 89 (GBP4800).
EXH.: London, The Arts Council of Great Britain, *Early English Landscapes from Colonel Grant's Collection*, 1952-3, no. 16 (as by *Sir Nathaniel Dance- Holland, Bt., R.A.*, and as of *Lose Hill, Derbyshire*); London, Tate Gallery, Cardiff, National Museum of Wales, and New Haven, Yale Center for British Art, *Richard Wilson, The Landscape of Reaction*, 1982-3, no. 6, pl.1; Cardiff, National Museum of Wales, on loan, 1992-96.
LIT.: D. Solkin, in the introduction to the exhibition catalogue cited above, pp. 26-7.

Christie's London, 18 April 1996 (24**) GBP 210,500	US$	319,181

WINCK Christian Thomas (Eichstädt 1738-1797 Munich) German
SUSANNAH BEFORE THE JUDGES oil on copper, 42.5 x 30cm. sdll 'Christ: Winkh Pinxit, 1762' sll incised in paint 'Christ Winck, 1762'
PROV.: Stadtarzt Dr. Mader, Innsbruck (1913); Private Collection Innsbruck.
LIT.: Exhibition catalogue *Malerei und Plastik des 18. Jahrhundert*, München, 1913, no. 218; Thieme Becker *Künstlerlexicon*, 1947, p. 57.

Dorotheum Vienna, 17 October 1995 (206**) ATS 300,000	US$	30,092

THE JUDGEMENT OF SALOMON oil on copper, 42.5 x 30cm. (ca 1762)
PROV.: Stadtarzt Dr. Mader, Innsbruck (1913); Private Collection Innsbruck.
LIT.: Exhibition catalogue *Malerei und Plastik des 18. Jahrhundert*, München, 1913, no. 219; Thieme Becker *Künstlerlexicon*, 1947, p. 57.

Dorotheum Vienna, 17 October 1995 (207**) ATS 350,000	US$	35,107

WINCK Johan Amandus (1748 c.-1817) German
ZWEI STILLEBEN MIT FRUECHTEN, NAGETIEREN UND ERLEGTEM FLUGWILD oil on
copper, 19.6 x 26.2cm. 1st slr 'Joan Wink' 2nd sll 'Joan. Aman. Wink'
LIT.: (on the artist) Gerhard P. Woeckel, *Der Stillebenmaler Johann Amandus Winck*, in: *Kunst in
Hessen und am Mittelrhein*, Heft 3, Darmstadt 1963, p. 70ff.; Idem, *Neuentdeckte Stilleben des
Münchner Malers Johann Amandus Winck*, in: *Kunst in Hessen und am Mittelrhein*, Heft 13,
Darmstadt 1973, p. 63ff.

Lempertz Cologne, 18 May 1996 (1178**) DEM 68,000	US$	44,331

A RED AND WHITE TOY SPANIEL WITH AN APPLE IN A LANDSCAPE oil on canvas, 16¼ x
22¾in. (41.3 x 57.7cm.) sd Joan Amand Wink. pinxit/Monacho 1797.'
PROV.: With count Alarico Palmieri, Geneva.

Christie's London, 28 March 1996 (57**) GBP 10,925	US$	16,684

WINDTRAKEN P.W. (Dutch Master, late seventeenth century -) Dutch
WALDBODENSTILLEBEN MIT BLUMEN, EINER SCHLANGE UND EINEM FROSCH oil on
canvas, 85 x 66cm. sdlm 'P.W. Windtraken 1690' on the revers e labeled 'Nassauischen Kunstvereins,
Wiesbaden'
PROV.: Collection Fischer (Wiesbaden); Collection Baldus.

Lempertz Cologne, 18 May 1996 (1179**) DEM 76,000	US$	49,547

WINT Peter de (Stone 1784-1849 London) British
LINCOLN CATHEDRAL FROM THE RIVER WITHAM AT DUSK oil on canvas, 14 x 21 5/8in.
(35.6 x 54.9cm.) inscr.on the reverse of the frame reads 'Miss Bostock's Loan/Rotation No 60/
'Lincoln Cathedral from the River/evening'
PROV.: Helen Tatlock; Harriet Helen Tatlock; Muriel Grace Bostock.
EXH.: Lincoln, Usher Art Gallery, *Peter de Wint Exhibition*, 1937, no. 76, as 'Lincoln Cathedral
from Brayford, Sunrise'; Reading, Reading Art Gallery, 1966, no.82; London, Agnew's, *Loan
Exhibition of Paintings and Drawings by Peter de Wint*, 1966, no.40.

Christie's London, 30 November 1995 (167**) GBP 23,000	US$	35,977

WINTER Fritz (Altenbögge 1905-1976 Hersching) German
GLEICHGEWICHT waxcrayon and collge on paper, 19¾ x 27½in. (50 x 70cm.) (before 1956)
EXH.: Venice, *XXVIII Biennale di Venezia, Esposizione Internazionale d'Arte*, 1956, no. 90.

Sotheby's London, 27 June 1996 (109**) GBP 6,900	US$	10,640

LINEAR VOR GRAU oil on canvas, 45 3/8 x 57 7/8in. (115.3 x 146.5cm.) sdlr 'F Winter 54'; sd and
titled on the reverse
PROV.: Galerie Springer, Berlin.
EXH.: Palm Beach, Norton Gallery of Art, *Special Summer Exhibition*, 1968.
LIT.: Gabriele Lohberg, *Fritz Winter: Leben und Werk*, Munich 1986, no. 1664 (illustrated).

Sotheby's London, 27 June 1996 (141**) GBP 32,200	US$	49,653

KOMPOSITION ROT - GELB oil on canvas, 70 x 51cm. sdlr (monogram) 'FW 42' 'FRITZ
WINTER DIESSEN/AMMERSEE (unclear)KOMPOSITION 42 ROT GELB' reverse, with pencil on
label (1942)
EXH.: Kassel, Staatliche Kunstsammlungen, *Fritz Winter*, 1965, cat. no.; 109, ill. 10; Düsseldorf,
Kunstverein der Rheinlande und Westfalen, *Wanderausstellung; Zum 60. Geburtstag*, and
Mannheim, Kunsthalle, 1966.
LIT.: G. Lohberg no. 753 (illustrated)

Lempertz Cologne, 28 November 1995 (1005**) DEM 70,000	US$	49,407

**WINTERHALTER Franz Xaver (Menzenschroad (Black Forest) (Menzel-Schwand?) 1806-
1873 Frankfurt) German**
SOPHIA GEORGIANA ROBERTINA WELLESLEY AND LADY FEODOROWNA CECILIA
WELLESLEY, DAUGHTER OF THE 1ST EARL OF COWLEY oil on canvas (a pair), each: 21½ x

17in. (54.6 x 43.2cm.) the first sd '1863'; the second sd 'Paris 1864'
PROV.: Henry Richard Wellesley, Earl of Cowley; Sophia, 1st Viscountess of Bertie; By descent
from the above (sale, Sotheby's. London, 17 February 1971, lots 49 & 50); R.G. Rennie (acquired at
the above sale).
LIT.: Richard Ormond and Carol Blackett-Ord, *Franz Xaver Winterhalter and the Courts of Europe
1830-70*, London, 1987, nos. ,430 and 441, p. 236.

Sotheby's Arcade Auctions New York, 17 January 1996 (568*) US$ 10,350	US$	10,350

WISINGER Olga <née> Florian (Vienna 1844-1926 Grafenegg, Lower Austria) Austrian
GEDECKTE TAFEL IN SCHLOSS HOHENBURG (GROSSHERZOG VON LUXEMBURG) oil
on cardboard, 26 x 41cm. slr 'O. Wisinger Florian'; s and titled on a label on the reverse
PROV.: Prof. Stefan Loos (Cousin Adolf Loos).

Wiener Kunst Auktionen, 26 September 1995 (146**) ATS 600,000	US$	58,322

WISSING Willem (William) (Amsterdam 1656-1687 Burleigh) Dutch
PORTRAIT OF MADAM HENRIETTA DE KEROUALLE (C. 1650-1728) oil on canvas, 47½ x
39in. (,121 x 99cm.) inscr. lr 'Madam Henrietta de Kuerovalle/Sister to ye Dutchefs of
Portsmouth./Wife of Philip Earl of Pembroke/1674.'

Sotheby's London, 12 July 1995 (26**) GBP 23,000	US$	36,688

WIT Jacob de (Amsterdam 1695-1754 Amsterdam) Dutch
SPRING AND SUMMER, AUTUMN AND WINTER oil on panel (a pair), 39 1/8 x 34¼ in. (99.4 x
87cm.) / 39¾ x 34¼in. (,101 x 87cm.) one sdll 'J. de Wit F. 1746'
PROV.: J.M. Furstner, Jr., Amsterdam (Sale: C.F. Roos & Cie., Amsterdam, April l, 1890, lot 214);
Hamburger Bros. Gallery, Amsterdam; Sale: Hugo Helbing, Frankfurt am Main, December 9-10,
1930, lots ,433 and 434; C.F.D. Beker, Renkum (near Arnheim); Sale: Mak van Waay, Amsterdam,
April 7, 1970, lot ,314 Jacob Stodel Gallery, Amsterdam, 1970.
LIT.: A. Staring, *Jacob de Wit*, 1958, pp. 154, 194, illus. no. 102 (*Autumn and Winter*).

Sotheby's New York, 11 January 1996 (205**) US$ 28,750	US$	28,750

WITHOOS Matthias, {called} Calzetta Bianca (Amersfoort 1627-1703 Hoorn) Dutch
A VANITAS: A CELESTIAL GLOBE, A LANTERN, SKULLS, MANUSCRIPTS AND BOOKS
WITH HOLLYHOCKS AND THISTLES NEAR CLASSICAL RUINS oil on canvas, 71.8 x 53cm.
slr 'M. wthoos'

Christie's Amsterdam, 13 November 1995 (44*) NLG 13,800	US$	8,697

WITTE Emmanuel de (Alkmaar 1615/1617-1691/1692 Amsterdam) Dutch
DUTCH HARBOUR SCENE IN A CALM, WITH STATES YACHT IN THE FOREGROUND oil
on panel, 9½ x 13¼in. (24.2 x 33.6cm.)
PROV.: W.D. Lighthall, acc. to an old label on the reverse, as by Jan van Goyen.

Sotheby's London, 5 July 1995 (20**) GBP 36,700	US$	58,542

WITTE Jasper de (Anvers 1624-1681) Flemish
LA KERMESSE FLAMANDE oil on leather laid down on panel, 29 x 37cm. slc 'Jaspar de wit f'

Étude Tajan Paris, 12 December 1995 (79**) FRF 110,000	US$	22,157

WITTEL Gaspar van, {called} Vanvitelli (Amersfoort 1653-1736 Rome) Dutch
A VIEW OF ORTE pen and brown ink and watercolour with touches of of bodycolour, over
indications in black chalk, 28.1 x 42.3cm. s ini. 'G.V:W.'

Sotheby's London, 3 July 1995 (127**) GBP 24,150	US$	38,523

WOESTYNE Gustave van de (Ghent 1881-1947 Brussels-Uccle) Belgian
A HEAD OF A FARMER green pencil on prepared canvas, unframed, 32 x 29cm. sd and inscr. lr 'G.
van de Woestijne 1914, Abenyburgch'

Christie's Amsterdam, 6 December 1995 (205*) NLG 23,500	US$	14,562

WOLFLI Adolf (1864-1930) Swiss
TRIBAL WOMAN WITH A CLUB pencil and coloured pastels on paper, 19¾ x 14¾in. (50 x
37.5cm.) inscr. and d '1930' in pencil on the reverse
       Phillips London, 26 June 1995 (14**) GBP 6,800   US$ 10,850

WOLMARK Alfred (1877-1961) British
THE FLAT IRON BUILDING, NEW YORK oil on canvas, 36 x 22in. (91.5 x 55.8cm.) slr
'Wolmark' (ca 1919)
PROV.: Fine Art Society, London.
EXH.: Hull, Ferens Art Gallery, *Alfrred Wolmark*, March-April 1975, no.75; Bradford, Arts Council
of Great Bntain, *Cartwright Hai Cityscape 1910-1939 Urban Themes in American, German and
British Art*,July-August 1977, no.146: this exhibition travelled to Portsmouth, City Museum and Art
Gallery, August-Oct. 1977; Newcastle-upon-Tyne, Laing Art Gallery, Oct.-Dec. 1977; and London,
Royal Academy, Jan.-March 1978.
       Christie's London, 21 March 1996 (135**) GBP 9,200   US$ 14,050

WOLS Alfred Otto Wolfgang Schultz, {called} (Berlin 1913-1951 France) German
UNTITLED oil on canvas, 13¾ x 10 5/8in. (35 x 27cm.) s centre right edge (ca 1946)
PROV.: Galerie René Drouin, Paris; Samy Chalom , Paris; Sotheby's London, Contemporary Art
Auction, December 5 1985, lot 365; Galerie Thomas Borgmann, Cologne.
EXH.: Paris, Galerie Drouin, *Wols*, May-June 1947; Bern, Kunsthalle, *Tendances Actuelles III*,
January-March 1955, no. 135; Zurich, Kunsthaus; Düsseldorf, Kunstsammlung Nordrhein-
Westfalen, *Wols*, November 1989-February 1990, no. 210 (illustrated in colour catalogue p. 264).
       Christie's London, 27 June 1996 (7**) GBP 100,500   US$ 154,973

UNTITLED goache, watercolour, pencil and ink on gouache, 8 5/8 x 4¾in. (22 x 12cm.) slr 'WOLS'
(1947-49)
PROV.: René Rasmussen, Paris; Collection Fischer, Krefeld; Heinz Friederichs, Frankfurt.
EXH.: London, Goethe-Institute, *Wols, Drawings and Watercolours*, 1985, p. 87, no. 48, illustrated;
Bremen, Graphisches Kabinett; Kunsthandel Wolfgang Werner, *Wols, Zeichnungen und Aquarelle*,
1985, p. 87, no. 48, illustrated; Zurich, Kunsthaus Zurich, *Wols,Bilder, Aquarelle, Zeichnungen-
Photographien Druckgraphik*, 1989-90, no. 122, illustrated.
       Sotheby's London, 27 June 1996 (136**) GBP 27,600   US$ 42,560

WOLTER Hendrik Jan (1873-1952) Dutch
HAZY MORNING: ST. IVES oil on paper laid down on panel, 36 x 44cm. stamped slr 'H.J. Wolter'
       Christie's Amsterdam, 5 June 1996 (8**) NLG 10,350   US$ 6,047

THE HARBOUR OF POLPERRO, CORNWALL oil on canvas, 65.5 x 81cm. sdll 'H.J. Wolter'
LIT.: Klaas de Poel, *Hendrik Jan Wolter*, Zwolle 1992, p. 44 (ill. in colour).
       Christie's Amsterdam, 5 June 1996 (276**) NLG 18,400   US$ 10,751

A VIEW OF THE AMSTEL, AMSTERDAM, WITH AMSTEL HOTEL IN THE DISTANCE oil on
canvas, unframed, 60 x 72.5cm. sll 'H.J.Wolter' (ca. 1914-1920)
LIT.: Klaas de Poel, *Hendrik Jan Wolter, schilder van licht en kleur*, Zwolle 1992, p.60).
       Christie's Amsterdam, 6 December 1995 (173**) NLG 66,700   US$ 41,331

MISTY MORNING, AMSTERDAM oil on plywood, 35.5 x 44cm. sll 'H.J. Wolter'
PROV.: Watson Art Galleries, Montreal.
       Christie's Amsterdam, 26 October 1995 (74*) NLG 13,800   US$ 8,701

WOLVECAMP Theo Wilhelm (Hengelo 1925-1992 Amsterdam) Dutch
COMPOSITIE NO. 22 oil on canvas, ,115 x 120cm. sd and. titled on the reverse 'Wolvecamp 57'
EXH.: Helsinki, Didrichsenin Taidemuseo Didrichens Konstmuseum, *CoBrA*, 25 September - 21
October 1979, no.37.
       Christie's Amsterdam, 6 December 1995 (276**) NLG 18,400   US$ 11,402

WOOD Christopher (Knowsley, near Liverpool 1901-1930 Salisbury) British
THE THREE HAEDED MAN, LUNAR PARK BALLET oil on board, 16 x 10½in. (40.5 x 26.6cm.)
(1930)
PROV.: Mercury Gallery, London, July 1970; Lord Beaumont of Whitley; Crane Kalman Gallery,
London; Clifton Pugh, Australia.
LIT.: E. Newton, *Christopher Wood*, London, 1938, no. 3, p. 80 (illustrated).
Christie's London, 21 November 1995 (156**) GBP 8,050   US$ 12,592

WOOD Thomas Waterman (America 1823-1903) American
AT THE SPINNING WHEEL oil on canvas, 10¾ x 8 1/8in. (27.4 x 21.2cm.) sdlr 'T. W. Wood 1867'
PROV.: Ward & Sons, Inc. Agawam, Massachusetts.
Christie's New York, 13 September 1995 (34*) US$ 6,900   US$ 6,900

WOODVILLE Richard Caton (1856-1927) british
LE LENDEMAIN D'IÉNA ET D'AUERSTAEDT, 1806 oil on canvas, 36 x 60in. (91.4 x 152.3cm.)
sd 'R.Caton Woodville/1909'
Christie's London, 7 June 1996 (654**) GBP 33,350   US$ 51,426

WOOL Christopher (1955 b.) American (?)
UNTITLED (P42) alkyd and flashe on aluminium and steel, 72 x 48in. (,183 x 122cm.) sd titled
'WOOL '87 Untitled (P42)' on the reverse
PROV.: Luhring Augustine & Hodes Gallery, New York.; Galerie Jean Bernier, Athens.
EXH.: Boston, Museum of Fine Arts and the Institute of Contemporary Art, *The BiNational: Art of
the Late 80s*, Sept.-Nov. 1988.
Christie's New York, 15 November 1995 (280**) US$ 16,100   US$ 16,100

WOPFNER Joseph (Schwaz, Tirol 1843-1927 Munich) Austrian
AVE oil on canvas, 14 x 23½in. (35.5 x 59.7cm.) s inscr. "Ave.'Jos: Wopfner Munchen' (1880s)
Christie's London, 11 October 1995 (77**) GBP 13,800   US$ 21,780

WOUTERS Rik (Mechelen 1882-1916 Amsterdam) Belgian
NATURE MORTE AU CHAMPIGNONS ET FLEURS - STILLEVEN MET PADDESTOELEN EN
BLOEMEN watercolour with brush and black ink on paper, 20¼ x 29¾in. (51.5 x 75.5cm.) (ca
1910-12)
PROV.: Nel Wouters, Brussels; Robert Giron, Brussels.
LIT.: To be included in the forthcoming *volume III of the catalogue raisonné of the watercolours and
drawings of Rik Wouters* Currently being prepared by Olivier Bertrand.
Christie's London, 26 June 1996 (302**) GBP 5,750   US$ 8,867

WOUWERMAN Jan (Haarlem 1629-1666 Haarlem) Dutch
TRAVELLERS IN THE DUNES ON A PATH BY A LAKE, FARMS BEYOND oil on canvas, 68.7
x 99cm. slr 'PHW' (linked)
PROV.: Anon. Sale, Luzern, 31 August 1933, lot 513, with ill., as Philips Wouwerman; with
Malmedé, Cologne, 1933; Anon. Sale, Sotheby`s London, 28 October 1987, lot 80, with ill., as;
attributed to Jan Wouwerman.
Christie's Amsterdam, 13 November 1995 (76*) NLG 17,250   US$ 10,872

WOUWERMAN Philips (Haarlem 1619-1668 Haarlem) Dutch
A HILLY LANDSCAPE WITH PHEASANTS ON A PATH oil on panel, 10¾ x 13¼in. (27 x
33.5cm.) s mono. 'PH W'
PROV.: Boughton Knight, Downton Castle, Ludlow, Herefordshire, 1909; Presumebly by descent at
Downton to Major W.M.P. Kincaid-Lennox; with Waterman, Amsterdam 1991.
LIT.: C. Hostede de Groot, *A Catalogue Raisonné..*, vol .II, 1909, pp. 602-3, no. 1053.
Sotheby's London, 5 July 1995 (5**) GBP 40,000   US$ 63,806
RIDERS WATERING THEIR HORSES AT A RIVER oil on oak panel, 14¾ x 11in. (37.5 x 28cm.)
slr mono. 'P SL W'

PROV.: Probably acquired the last quarter of the 18th Century for Audley End House by Sir John Griffin, 4th Lord Howard de Walden, 1st Baron Braybrooke, (1719-1797); Thence by descent to the present owner.

Sotheby's London, 6 December 1995 (41**) GBP 54,300   US$ 83,564

HARVEST SCENE oil on panel, 12¾ x 15¾in. (32.5 x 40cm.) (1650's)
PROV.: Joachim Rendorp, Amsterdam, his (deceased) sale, Amsterdam, van der Schley, 9- 10 July 1794, lot 67, ,355 florins to Coclers; John Maitland, London, sold London, Christie's, 30July 1831, ,255 gns. to Woodburn; John Gott, Leeds, 1875, according to a label affixed to the reverse; Possibly Gott Heirlooms, Armley House, near Leeds, sold London, Christie's, 1 December 1894, lot 66 or 68; P.S. van Gelder, Geneva, sold Geneva, Moss, 7 October 1933, lot 165; With W. Paech, Amsterdam, before 1939.
EXH.: Leeds, Art Museum, 1875, no. 78.
LIT.: J. Smith, *A Catalogue Raisonné, Supplement*, vol. IX, 1842, p. 208, no. 206; C. Hofstede de Groot, *A Catalogue Raisonné*, 1909, voL II, p. 570, no. 956, and p. 571, no. 961.

Sotheby's London, 6 December 1995 (201**) GBP 34,500   US$ 53,093

WRIGHT Gilbert Scott (1880-1958) British
A COACH AND FOUR AND A HUNTING PARTY OUTSIDE THE BELL INN oil on canvas, 28 x 36in. (71 x 91.5cm.) slr 'Gilbert S Wright'

Phillips London, 12 December 1995 (63**) GBP 14,000   US$ 21,545

WRIGHT Joseph of Derby, A.R.A. (Derby 1734-1797 Derby) British
PORTRAIT OF MISS THEODORA FORTUNE oil on canvas (an oval), 39 x 34in. (99 x 86.5cm.) (ca. 1765-70)
PROV.: Mr. and Mrs. van Horn Wly and Mr. and Mrs. Alfred Zantzinger; By whom given to the Phoenix Art Museum.

Sotheby's London, 12 July 1995 (77**) GBP 29,700   US$ 47,376

WTTEWAEL Peter (1596-1660) Dutch
A JESTER HOLDING A FLUTE oil on panel, 56.8 x 36.3 cm sdul 'Peter W..Wael/ft 1653'

Christie's Amsterdam, 13 November 1995 (163**) NLG 40,250   US$ 25,367

WUERMER Carl (1900-1983) German
SUNNY WINTER'S DAY oil on canvas, 25 x 30in. (63.5 x 76.3cm.) slr 'Carl Wuermer'
PROV.: Grand Central Art Galleries Inc., New York.

Christie's East, 28 November 1995 (6**) US$ 8,625   US$ 8,625

WUNDERLICH Paul (Eberswalde, near Berlin 1927 b.-) German
PER ASPERA AD ASTRA oil on canvas, ,162 x 130cm. sll 'Paul Wunderlich' d lr '63' (1963)

Lempertz Cologne, 28 November 1995 (1011**) DEM 28,000   US$ 19,763

WYANT Alexander Helwig (Port Washington 1836-1892 New York) American
OPENING IN THE WOODS oil on canvas, 14 x 17in. (35.5 x 43.2cm.) slr 'A.H. Wyant'

Christie's New York, 13 September 1995 (19*) US$ 3,680   US$ 3,680

FOREST LANDSCAPE oil on canvas, 14 x 18in. (35.6 x 45.7cm.) scl 'A. H. Wyant N.Y.'

Christie's New York, 2 November 1995 (6*) US$ 8,050   US$ 8,050

WYCK Jan (Haarlem 1645-1700 Mortlake) Dutch
A GREY STALLION TETHERED TO A POST, A SPANIEL BY HIS SIDE oil on canvas, 31 x 35in. (78.5 x 89cm.) slr 'J Wyck'

Sotheby's London, 12 July 1995 (132**) GBP 47,700   US$ 76,089

KING WILLIAM III AND HIS TROOPS PREPARING FOR BATTLE oil on canvas, 60½ x 85in. (
LIT.: O. Millar, 'Jan Wyck and John Wootton at Anthony', The Natioanl Trust Yearbook 1975-76,

London, 1975, p. 38.

Christie's London, 18 April 1996 (5**) GBP 27,600   US$ 41,850

A CAVALRY BATTLE BELOW A FORTRESS oil on canvas, 38¼ x 49¼in. (98.5 x 125.2cm.) slr 'JWijck'

Christie's London, 18 April 1996 (6**) GBP 20,700   US$ 31,387

WYCK Thomas (Beverwijk, near Haarlem 1616 c.-1667 Haarlem) Dutch
AN ITALIANATE FRUIT AND VEGETABLE MARKET SCENE oil on canvas, 28¼ x 23½in. (72 x 59.5cm.) sll 'Twyck' (Tw in ligature)
PROV.: Anonymous sale in these Rooms, 11 december 1974, lot 74.
EXH.: On loan, Bowes Museum, Barnard Castle, Co. Durham, 1976-1984; On loan, York, Fairfax House, 1985-1992.

Sotheby's London, 5 July 1995 (43**) GBP 17,250   US$ 27,516

HARBOURSCENE WITH PEOPLE AND BOATS oil on canvas, 61 x 50.5cm. s (indistinctly) '..W..'

Christie's Rome, 4 June 1996 (580**) ITL 13,000,000   US$ 8,431

WYCKAERT Maurice (1923 b.)
PAYSAGE AVEC CRAVATE oil on canvas, ,100 x 81cm. sll; titled on the reverse
PROV.: Galerie Lens Fine Art, Antwerp.

Sotheby's Amsterdam, 7 December 1995 (274**) NLG 11,800   US$ 7,312

WYETH Andrew Newell (Chadd's Ford, Pennsylvania 1917 b.) American
WASHINGTON AND LAFAYETTE tempera on panel, 16½ x 12¼in. (41.9 x 31.1cm.) slr 'Andrew Wyeth'
PROV.: Acquired directly from the artis; By descent in the family to the present owner.
EXH.: *Woman's Day*, July 1955, p. 28 (illustrated).

Christie's New York, 13 March 1996 (64***) US$ 244,500   US$ 244,500

FRONT DOOR AT TEEL'S watercolour on paper, 28 x 20in. (71.1 x 50.8cm.) slr 'Andrew Wyeth' (1954)
PROV.: Mr. and Mrs. Lawrence Fleischman, Detroit, Michigan; Kennedy Galleries, Inc., New York; Coe Kerr Gallery, New York; Marcelle Fine Art, New York.
EXH.: Wichita, Kansas, Wichita Art Museum, *Andrew Wyeth - Wyeth's World: An Exhibition of Watercolors, Temperas and Drawings by Andrew Wyeth*, September-November 1967; Oklahoma City, Oklahoma, Oklahoma Museum of Art, Red Ridge, *The Wonder of Andrew Wyeth_Temperas, Watercolors, Drybrush, Drawings, 1939-1966*, December 1967; New York, Kennedy Galleries Inc., *1900-1960: American Masters*, March 1968; Kingsport, Tennessee, Kingsport Fine Arts Center, *Works by Andrew Wyeth*, December 1972.

Christie's New York, 23 May 1996 (168**) US$ 34,500   US$ 34,500

WYETH James (1946 b.) American
PUMPKIN POT watercolour and pencil paper, 29¾ x 22in. (76.2 x 55.8cm.) sll 'J Wyeth' (1978)
PROV.: Nicholas Wyeth, Inc., New York.

Christie's New York, 13 September 1995 (124**) US$ 25,300   US$ 25,300

WYETH Newell Convers (1882-1945) American
ALONG THE BRANDYWINE (HE NEVER CAUGHT A THING AND HE RUINED JON'S REPUTATION AS A FISHERMAN) oil on canvas, 47¼ x 38in. (,120 x 96.5cm.) sdll 'N.C. Wyeth 1913'
PROV.: The Wyeth Family, Chadds Fors, Pennsylvania; Newman Galleries, Philadelphia, Pennsylvania.
LIT.: J.L. Long, *War, or, What Happens When One Loves One's Enemy*, Indianapolis, Indiana 1913 (illustrated as frontispiece).

Christie's New York, 13 March 1996 (62**) US$ 52,900   US$ 52,900

WYLD William, R.W.S. (London 1806-1889 Paris) British
VIEW OF VENICE FROM THE LAGOON oil on panel, 11½ x 17in. (29 x 43cm.) slr 'W. Wyld'
PROV.: Eugene Feral (1870-1880); Thence by descent to Jules Feral; Thence by descent to the
present owner.

Sotheby's London, 12 July 1995 (111**) GBP 8,050	US$	12,841

WYLLIE Charles William (1853-1923) British
HEARTS OF OAK oil on canvas, 20 x 40¼in. (51 x 102cm.) slr 'Charles W.Wyllie'

Phillips London, 18 June 1996 (65**) GBP 6,000	US$	9252

WYLLIE William Lionel, R.A. (London 1851-1931 Hampstead) British
UNLOADING CARGO FROM A STEAMSHIP IN A DOCK AT SUNSET oil on canvas, 17 x 30in.
sdlr 'W. Wyllie 1900'

Phillips London, 10 October 1995 (113*) GBP 4,800	US$	7,576

WYNANTS Jan (Haarlem 1625/1630-1684 Amsterdam) Dutch
WOODED RIVERLANDSCAPE WITH A HORSEMAN oil on canvas, 49 x 59cm. sdll 'J. Wynants
1675'

Dorotheum Vienna, 6 March 1996 (83**) ATS 160,000	US$	15,391

A HAARLEM DUNELANDSCAPE oil on linen, 46.4 x 38cm. sdlr monogram 'J.W.'

Lempertz Cologne, 15 November 1995 (1437**) DEM 13,000	US$	9,176

LANDSCAPE WITH AN ASSAULTED HORSEMAN oil on canvas, 78 x 88cm. sd 'Jan Wynants
1663'
PROV.: Marquis de Choiseul de Stainville, sold 23 November 1789 for 1,702 florins; His sale to M.
Clos, Paris, for 2,420 florins ; His sale, 18 November 1812 to M. Fabre for 4,500 florins; Lord Ch.
Townshend, sold 11 April 1835, London, to M. Nieuwenhuys for GBP 194.50; baron A.G. Verstolk
se Soelen, The Hague; Collection Thomas Baring and James Lloyd & Humpherey St. John Mildmay,
London; H. Bingham Mildmay; His sale, 24 June 1893 for GBP 430.10; Swedish-French Art
Gallery, Stockholm; Private collection, Göteborg.
EXH.: London, Royal Academy, *Exhibition of the work of Old Masters*, 1876, no. 234.
LIT.: Hofstede de Groot, *a catalogue raisonné* vol. VIII, pp. 539-50, no. 297; Smith, *Catalogue
Raisonné*, vol. IV, p. 251, no. 81, vol. IX, p. 742, no. 17; Dr Waagen, Suppl. p. 154; Ch. Blanc,
Tresor, II, p. 295; W. Roberts, *Memoirs of Christie's*, II, p. 222.

Bukowskis Stockholm, 29 November-1 December 1995 (257**) SEK 355,000	US$	53,704

WYNTRACK Dirck (Drenthe (?) 1625 before-1678 The Hague) Dutch
A WOODED LANDSCAPE WITH GEESE BEFORE A LAKE oil on canvas, 22 x 28in. (55.9 x
71cm.)

Christie's London, 8 December 1995 (257**) GBP 7,475	US$	11,504

PAYSAGE MARÉCAGEUZ AVEC DES CANARDS oil on oakpanel, 55 x 46cm. sll 'D. Wyntrack'
PROV.: Sale M. Haro father, Paris, Hôtel Drouot, 2 April 1897 (Maître Duchesne), no. 87 (FFR
100).

Étude Tajan Paris, 12 December 1995 (25**) FRF 50,000	US$	10,071

WYTMANS Mattheus (Gorichem ca. 1650-ca. 1689 Utrecht) Dutch
PORTRAIT OF A LADY oil on canvas, 21¼ x 17¼in. (54.5 x 44.2cm.) an inscription on the reverse,
'Marie Smoni des van Nys' possibly refers to the sitter
PROV.: Mrs. van den Bergh, Gerrards Cross, Buckinghamshire.

Sotheby's London, 17 April 1996 (37**) GBP 6,900	US$	10,462

YEATS Jack Butler, R.H.A. (London 1871-1957 Dublin) Irish
THE BOAT BUILDER oil on panel, 14¼ x 9¼in. (36.2 x 23.5cm.) sll 'Jack B. Yeats' inscr. on the reverse 'The Boat Builder' (ca 1913)
PROV.: The Estate of the late Sir Peter Scott, C.B.E.
EXH.: Dublin, Mills Hall, *Pictures of life in the West of Ireland*, Feb.-March 1914, no. 36: this exhibition later travelled to London, Walker Art Gallery, June-July 1914, no. 19; Belfast, Art Society, 1914.
LIT.: H. Pyle, *A Catalogue Raisonné of the Oil Paintings of Jack Butler Yeats I*, London, 1992, no. 78, p.4.

Christie's London, 21 November 1995 (18**) GBP 95,000	US$	148,600

A WALK OVER oil on panel, 9 x 14in. (24 x 36cm.) sll 'Jack B. Yeats' (1914)
PROV.: Darrell Figgis, by whom purchased direct from the artist; Figgis sale, where purchased by Professor Thomas Bodkin, thence by descent.
EXH.: London, Walker Art Gallery, *Jack B. Yeats Pictures of Life in the West of Ireland*, June-July 1914, no.22; Dublin, Royal Hibernian Academy, 1914, no.411; London, Grafton Galleries, *Allied Artists 11th Salon*, July 1919; London, National Gallery, *British Painting since Whistler*, April 1940, no. 124; London, National Gallery, *Nicholon & Yeats*, Jan. 1942 (exh. catalogue); Dublin, National College of Art, *National Loan Exhibition*, June-July 1945, no.ll. (illustrated); Dublin, Municipal Gallery, *Bodkin Irish Collection*, June-July 1962, no. 83.
LIT.: H. Pyle, *Jack B. Yeats A Catalogue Raisonné of the Oil Paintings*, London, 1992, no. 93 (illustrated, III, p. 39).

Christie's London, 9 May 1996 (57*) GBP 205,000	US$	310,418

The Frontispiece

THE FRONTISPIECE oil on canvas, 14 x 21in. (35.5 x 53.4cm.) sll 'Jack B. Yeats'; inscr 'The Frontispiece' on the stretcher (1947)
PROV.: Purchased direct from the Artist by Leo Smith in June 1947.
LIT.: H. Pyle, *Jack B. Yeats, A Catalogue Raisonné of the Oil Paintings, II*, London, 1992, no. 847.

Christie's London, 9 May 1996 (58**) GBP 100,500	US$	152,180

THE FLASH CAPTAIN oil on panel, 9¼ x 14½in. (23.5 x 36.8cm.) slr 'Jack B.Yeats'; inscr. 'The Flash Captain' on the reverse (1945)
PROV.: Mr. Halligan, by whom purchased at Victor Waddington Galleries, Dublin, in 1945, thence to Miss F.C. Halligan, Drogheda; Sotheby's, Ireland, Slane Castle, 12 May 1981, lot 486.
EXH.: Drogheda, Art Gallery, *Loan Exhibition of Works by Irish Artists*, Sept.-Nov. 1948.
LIT.: H. Pyle, *Jack B. Yeats, A Catalogue Raisonné of the Oil Paintings, II*, London, 1993, no. 690 (illustrated, III, p. 380).

Christie's London, 9 May 1996 (59**) GBP 35,600	US$	53,907

THE FLAPPING MEETING oil on canvas, 14 x 18in. (35.5 x 45.8cm.) sll 'Jack B.Yeats' (1926)
PROV.: Captain Guy Gough, by whom purchased at the 1926 exhibition; Anon. sale: Sotheby's, 9 Dec. 1970, lot 99a; Victor Waddington, London; Purchased by the present owner's father in 1971, thence by descent.
EXH.: London, Arthur Tooth & Son, *Paintings of Irish Life by Jack Butler Yeats*, April 1926, no. 13.
LIT.: H. Pyle, *Jack B. Yeats A Catalogue Raisonné of the Oil Paintings, II*, London, 1992, no. 316 (ilustrated III, p. 134).
Christie's London, 9 May 1996 (146**) GBP 139,000   US$ 210,478

AUTUMN oil on canvas, 14 x 18in. (35.5 x 45.8cm.) sll 'Jack B. Yeats', inscr. 'Autumn' (sic) on the stretcher (1945)
PROV.: Sir John Rothenstein, by whom purchased at the 1946 exhibition.
EXH.: London, Wildenstein, *Oil Paintings by Jack Butler Yeats*, Feb.-March 1946, no. 14.
LIT.: H. Pyle, *Jack B. Yeats A Catalogue Raisonné of the Oil Paintings, II*, London, 1992, no. 715.
Christie's London, 9 May 1996 (147**) GBP 58,700   US$ 88,886

HIGH SPRING TIDE (ROSSES POINT, SLIGO) oil on canvas, 18 x 24in. (46 x 61cm.) slr 'Jack B Yeats'; inscr. 'High Spring Tide Rosses Point' on the edge of the stretcher (1924)
PROV.: T. O'Sullivan, Dublin, by whom purchased at Victor Wadington Galleries, Dublin in 1945.
EXH.: London, Gieves Art Gallery, *Jack Yeats Paintings of Irish Life*, Jan. 1924, no.28; Dublin, Engineers' Hall, *Pictures of Life in the West of Ireland*, March-April 1924, no.16; Dublin, Contemporary Picture Galleries, *Jack Yeats Paintings*, Oct.-Nov. 1940, no.10; Leeds, Temple Newsam House, *Jack Yeats Loan Exhibition*, June-August 1948, no.5; London, Arts Council of Great Britain, Tate Gallery, *Jack Yeats Loan Exhibition*, August-Sept. 1948, no 5; this exhibition travelled to Aberdeen, Art Gallery; and Edinburgh, Royal Scottish Academy.
LIT.: H. Pyle, *Jack B. Yeats A Catalogue Raisonné of the Oil Paintings, II*, London, 1992, no. 230.
Christie's London, 9 May 1996 (148**) GBP 67,500   US$ 102,211

YON Edmond Charles Joseph (Paris 1836-1897 Paris) French
AU BOR DE LA MER oil on canvas, 39½ x 59in. (100.4 x 151.1cm.) slr 'Edmond Yon.'
PROV.: With Kaplan Gallery, London.
Christie's New York, 22 May 1996 (100**) US$ 55,200   US$ 55,200

YUON Konstantin (1875-1958) Russian
VIEW OF THE TROITSE-SERGIEVA LAVRA oil on canvas, 24 x 20in. (61 x 51cm.) slr in cyrillic 'K. Yuon'
Christie's New York, 18 April 1996 (25**) US$ 25,300   US$ 25,300

ZAGANELLI Francesco di Bosio (Cotignola 1470 ca.-1532 Ravenna) Italian
MADONNA WITH CHILD AND THE INFANT SAINT JOHN oil on panel, 60 x 46cm.
PROV.: From the heritage from Dr. Dr. Walter Boveri, Zürich.

Dorotheum Vienna, 6 March 1996 (27**) ATS 500,000	US$	48,095

ZAIS Giuseppe (Forno de Canale, Agordo 1709-1784 Treviso) Italian
PEASANT FAMILY BY THE BANK OF A RIVER oil on canvas, 18 7/8 x 25in. (47.9 x 63.5cm.)

Sotheby's New York, 2 April 1996 (116*) US$ 23,000	US$	23,000

ZAMPIGHI Eugenio Eduardo (Modena 1859-1944 Maranello) Italian
ENTERTAINING THE BABY oil on canvas, 28 x 35½in. (43.2 x 102.2cm.) sll 'E Zampighi'

Christie's New York, 2 November 1995 (169**) US$ 18,400	US$	18,400

ZANCHI Antonio (Este, Padua 1631-1722 Venice) Italian
DEJANIRA RAPED BY THE CENTAURE NESSO oil on canvas, 197.5 x 303
PROV.: Private collection , Trento (ca. 1930); collection Gasparini; collection Foresti, Milan (ca. 1965).
LIT.: A. Riccoboni, 'Novità Zanchiane', in *Studi di storia dell'Arte in onore di Antonio Morassi*, 1971, pp. 261-263 (illustrated); P. Zampetti, 'Antonio Zanchi', in *I Pittori Bergamaschi. Il Seicento IV*, Bergamo 1987, no. 183, p. 590 (illustrated p. 627).

Finearte Milan, 3 April 1996 (105**) ITL 92,000,000	US$	58,786

A CLASSICAL PHILOSOPHER oil on canvas, 40¾ x 34¾in. (103 x 88cm.) (ca. 1660-65)

Sotheby's London, 5 July 1995 (90**) GBP 15,525	US$	24,765

ZANIN Francesco (19th Century) Italian
IL RIENTRO DELL BUCINTORO NEL GIORNO DELL'ASCENSIONE oil on canvas, 24 x 44¾in.
(61 x 113.5cm.) sd 'Zanin Fran. 1888'
PROV.: With Frost & Reed, London; with Findlay Galleries, Chicago.

Christie's London, 14 June 1996 (132**) GBP 12,650	US$	19,507

ZAO WOU-KI (Peking 1921 b.) French (Chinese)
PAYSAGE AUX AMOUREUX oil on canvas, 45¼ x 50in. (115 x 128cm.) slr (1950)
PROV.: Laury Aldrich Museum of Contemporary Art.
EXH.: Virginia Museum of Fine Art, *The Aldrich Collection*, 1 Jan.-1 May 1959.

Étude Tajan Paris, 10 June 1996 (61**) FRF 300,000	US$	57,930

TOWER BRIDGE oil on canvas, 15 x 18 1/8in. (38 x 46cm.) s; sd and titled 'XI.1952'

Sotheby's London, 27 June 1996 (155**) GBP 8,625	US$	13,300

Paysage aux Amoureux

VILLE BLANCHE oil on canvas, 18 x 25½in. (45.8 x 64.8cm.) sdlr 'Zao Wou-Ki 55', titled, sd again
ZAO WOU-KI 'ville blanche' 1955' on the stretcher

Christie's New York, 22 February 1996 (10**) US$ 10,350	US$	10,350

A TÉLÉPHÉRIQUE oil on canvas, 21¾ x 18in. (55.2 x 45.8cm.) slr 'Zao Wou-Ki' d titled 'Sep. 50
a Téléphérique' on the reverse s 'ZAO WOU-KI' on the stretcher (1950)
ROV.: Kleeman Gallery, New York.

Christie's New York, 15 November 1995 (131**) US$ 13,800	US$	13,800

ZARITSKY Joseph (Borispol (Ukraine) 1891-1985) Israelian
TEL AVIV watercolour and pencil on paper, 21¼ x 29 1/8in. (54 x 74cm.) slr in Hebrew
PROV.: Acquired directly from the artist by the present owner.
LIT.: M. Omer, *Zaritsky*, Tel Aviv, 1987, no. 81 (illustrated p. 89).
      Christie's Tel Aviv, 12 October 1995 (70**) US$ 14,950   US$ 14,950

YECHIAM watercolour and pencil on paper, 10 5/8 x 14 4/5in. (27.1 x 37.3cm.) sll 'Zaritsky'; s
again in Hebrew
PROV.: Acquired directly from the artist by the present owner.
LIT.: ed. Y. Yariv, *Zaritsky Watercolours*, Tel Aviv, 1992, no. 120 (illustrated).
      Christie's Tel Aviv, 12 October 1995 (72**) US$ 9,200   US$ 9,200

PORTRAIT OF MRS. AYALA ZACKS oil on canvas, 39 x 35½in. (99 x 90.2cm.) sll in Hebrew
(1968-1970)
LIT.: M.Omer, *Zaritsky*, Israël, 1987, pp.202-205. no.198 (ill. p.24).
      Christie's Tel Aviv, 14 April 1996 (83**) US$ 25,300   US$ 25,300

COMPOSITION oil on canvas, 47¼ x 79in. (120 x 205.5cm.) sll 'J.Zaritsky', s again in Hebrew
(1960's)
PROV.: Acquired directly by the present owner from the Artist in the 1970's.
      Christie's Tel Aviv, 14 April 1996 (84**) US$ 43,700   US$ 43,700

ZATZKA Hans (Vienna 1859-1945) Austrian
LOVE`S AWAKENING oil on canvas, 32¼ x 19 7/8in. (82 x 50.5cm.) s and s on the reverse
      Phillips London, 12th March 1996 (11 (a pair)** GBP 9,500   US$ 14,508

ZEE VAN DER Jan (1898-1988) Dutch
A LANDSCAPE oil on canvas, 60 x 80 cm sd 'J.v.d.Zee '57'
      Christie's Amsterdam, 7 February 1996 (612*) NLG 9,430   US$ 5,743

ZICK Januarius (Munich 1730-1797 Ehrenbreitstein) German
MARIA MIT KIND oil on panel, 24 x 18.5cm. sll 'Ja. Zick'
PROV.: Slg. M. and Th. Klopfer; Auktion Helbing, München, 24-11-1908, no. 480; Rheinische
private collection.
LIT.: O. Metzger, 'Neue Forschungen zum Werk von Januarius Zick, II. Zicks Gemäldenachlaß', in:
Walraf-Richartz-JB. 28, 1966, p. 303 (no. 40); J. Straßer, *Januarius Zick*, Weißenhorn 1994, p. 385,
WVZ-no. G200.
      Lempertz Cologne, 18 May 1996 (1182**) DEM 35,000   US$ 22,818

ZIEM Félix François Georges Philibert (Beaune 1821-1911 Paris) French
LE BASSIN DE VENISE oil on canvas, 21¾ x 33 5/8in. (55.2 x 85.4cm.) slr 'Ziem.
PROV.: The Cooling Galleries, Toronto.
      Christie's New York, 10 January 1996 (135**) US$ 28,750   US$ 28,750

VENETIAN GONDOLA BEFORE THE DOGE PALACE oil on canvas, 74 x 108cm. slr
PROV.: This work will be included in he *Felix Ziem catalogue raisonné* currently being prepared by
Madame Burdin-Hellebrandt.
      Étude Tajan Paris, 13 December 1995 (19**) FRF 240,000   US$ 48,342

THE BACINO, VENICE oil on panel, 27¼ x 38½in. (69.2 x 97.8cm.) s 'Ziem
PROV.: Howard Young; with Vose Galleries, Boston; Mr. Edward Donnely, Boston.
      Christie's London, 17 November 1995 (165**) GBP 16,100   US$ 25,18●

THE GRAND CANAL, VENICE oil on panel, 16¾ x 28¼in. (42.6 x 71.8cm.) sll 'Ziem.
      Christie's New York, 2 November 1995 (232**) US$ 36,800   US$ 36,80●

LEANDRE TOWERS AT CONSTANTINOPLE oil on panel, 23 x 28.5cm. slr 'Ziem' ; inscr. with title on a label on the frame.
    Christie's Amsterdam, 26 October 1995 (116**) NLG 18,400   US$ 11,602

ZIESENIS Johann Georg (Copenhagen 1716-1776 Hanover) Danish
BILDNISSE DES KURFÜRSTEN KARL THEODOR VON DER PFALZ UND SEINER GEMAHLIN ELISABETH AUGUSTE oil on linen, 85 x 70cm.
    Lempertz Cologne, 15 November 1995 (1440**) DEM 36,000   US$ 25,409

ZOCCHI Guglielmo (Florence 1874 b.) Italian
THE CENTER OF ATTENTION oil on canvas laid down on board, 27¾ x 43¾in. (70.5 x 111.1cm.) slr 'G. Zocchi.'
    Christie's New York, 14 February 1996 (18**) US$ 27,600   US$ 27,600

VANITY oil on canvas, 17 40¼in. (43.2 x 102.2cm.) slr 'G. Zocchi'
    Christie's New York, 2 November 1995 (179**) US$ 18,400   US$ 18,400

ZONARO Fausto (Padua 1854-1929 San Remo) Italian
SWEET ASIAN WATERS oil on canvas, 26½ x 18½in. (67.3 x 47cm.) s 'F. Zonaro'
    Sotheby's New York, 2 April 1996 (245A*) US$ 23,000   US$ 23,000

ELEGANT FIGURES STROLLING DOWN A MEDITERRANEAN QUAY oil on panel, 21.5 x 39.5cm. s 'F. Zonaro'
    Christie's Amsterdam, 25 April 1996 (238**) NLG 20,700   US$ 12,300

AN AFTERNOON IN A ROWBOAT WITH A VIEW OF ISTANBUL IN THE DISTANCE oil on canvas, 26 x 38in. (66 x 96.5cm.) slr 'F Zonaro'
    Christie's East, 30 October 1995 (249**) US$ 81,700   US$ 81,700

ZORACH Marguerite Thompson (Santa Rosa (California) 1887-1968 l) American
STILL-LIFE OF FLOWERS IN A WHITE PITCHER oil on canvas, 29 x 20 1/8in. (73.6 x 51.2cm.) slr 'Marguerite Zorach'
    Christie's New York, 13 September 1995 (122**) US$ 23,000   US$ 23,000

ZORACH William (Jurburg (Lithuania) 1887-1966) American (Lithuanian)
SEATED NUDE pencil on paper, 19 x 25in. (48.3 x 63.5cm.) sdlr 'William Zorach 1942'
PROV.: The Downtown Gallery, New York.
    Christie's New York, 13 September 1995 (110*) US$ 10,350   US$ 10,350

SPRINGTIME oil on canvas, 34½ x 28in. (87.6 x 71.1cm.)(sight) sdlr 'Wm Zorach 1912'
EXH.: Brooklyn, New York, *William Zorach, Paintings, Watercolours and Drawings, 1911-1922*, 26 Nov. 1968-19 January 1969, p. 24, no. 2 (illustrated).
    Christie's New York, 13 September 1995 (112**) US$ 57,500   US$ 57,500

ZORN Anders Leonard (Mora, Dalécarlie 1860-1920 Mora) Swedish
NAKEN PÅ STRAND oil on canvas, 73 x 53cm. sdll 'Zorn 1907'
LIT.: Gerda Boëthius p. 552.
    Bukowskis Stockholm, 29-31 May 1996 (170**) SEK 1,200,000   US$ 176,486

VID SPISEN oil on canvas, 97 x 73cm. sdlr 'Zorn 98'
EXH.: *Riksförbundet för bildande konst*, no. 59; Berlin, Bruno v. Paul Cassier, *Kunst und erlaganstalt*, no. 471.
LIT.: Gerda Boëthius, Stockholm 1949, p. 367, catalogued 1898, p. 548.
    Bukowskis Stockholm, 29-31 May 1996 (173**) SEK 1,250,000   US$ 183,840

Naken på Strand

NAKET I BARRSKOG oil on canvas, 52 x 34cm. slr
'Zorn' (1900)
    Bukowskis Stockholm, 29-31 May 1996
(179**) SEK 710,000   US$ 104,421

**ZUBER-BUHLER Fritz (Le Locle 1822-1896
Paris) Swiss**
A YOUNG BEAUTY WITH A PARAKEET oil on
canvas, 27½ x 22 1/8in. (68.7 x 56.2cm.) s 'ZUBER-
BUHLER'
PROV.: Anon. sale; Plaza Art Auction Galleries
Inc., New York, 23 Feb. 1935, lot 120, to Mr.
Abraham Hornstein, New York; Thence by descent
to Mrs Gertrude Hornstein; Thence by descent to the
present owner.
    Christie's New York, 2 November 1995
(67**) US$ 27,600   US$ 27,600

ZUCCARELLI Francesco, R.A. (Pitigliano (Tuscany) 1702-1788 Florence) Italian
ITALIANATE LANSCAPES WITH A HUNTSMAN RESTING BY A STREAM AND
PEASANTS DRIVING A COW oil on canvas (a pair), each: 17 x 25in. (43.2 x 63.5cm.)
PROV.: With Erich Galleries, New York; Sold toAmerican Art Association, Anderson Galleries Inc.,
18-19 April 1934, lots 114 and 114a; with Newhouse Galleries, New York.
    Sotheby's London, 5 July 1995 (80**) GBP 47,700   US$ 76,089

LANDSCAPE -1744 oil on canvas, 75 x 117cm. sdl 'Francesco Zuccarelli fecit 1744'
    Finearte Milan, 11 June 1996 (56**) ITL 287,500,000   US$ 186,446

AN ITALIANATE LANDSCAPE WITH WOMEN SPORTING WITH A DECOY BIRD oil on
canvas, 15½ x 22in. (39.4 x 55.9cm.)
    Sotheby's New York, 16 May 1996 (245**) US$ 33,350   US$ 33,350

FOREST LANDSCAPE WITH FIGURES oil on canvas, 49 x 81cm. (framed)
    Dorotheum Vienna, 17 October 1995 (48**) ATS 250,000   US$ 25,076

PASTORAL LANDSCAPE WITH FARM AND PYRAMID oil on canvas, 62 x 93cm.
PROV.: According to a label on the reverse: 'belonged to J. Mustritt of Wiss, probably bought by
Nurse (?) Eller Mossi (?) of Norwich about 1846'.
    Bukowskis Stockholm, 29-31 May 1996 (301**) SEK 125,000   US$ 18,384

LANDSCAPE WITH A RESTING MAN IN CLASSICAL CLOTHING AND A LADY ON
HORSEBACK oil on canvas, 49 x 64cm.
    Christie's Rome, 4 June 1996 (533**) ITL 34,000,000   US$ 22,049

ZUCCHI Jacopo del {called} del Zucca (Florence 1541 c.-1589/90 Rome or Florence) Italian
ALLEGORY OF THE LAST JUDGEMENT oil on copper, 15 x 11½in. (38.1 x 29.2cm.)
    Sotheby's New York, 11 January 1996 (210**) US$ 40,250   US$ 40,250

ZÜRCHER Frederik Willem (Nieuwer-Amstel 1835-1894 The Hague) Dutch
SMALL TALK oil on canvas, 50 x 65 cm s 'F.W. Zürcher'
    Christie's Amsterdam, 25 April 1996 (116) NLG 8,050   US$ 4,78

ZYLMANS Letty (b. 1902) Dutch
A DANCER oil on canvas, ,100 x 80cm. slr 'Zijlmans'
        Sotheby's Amsterdam, 23 April 1996 (88**) NLG 9,440   US$ 5,609